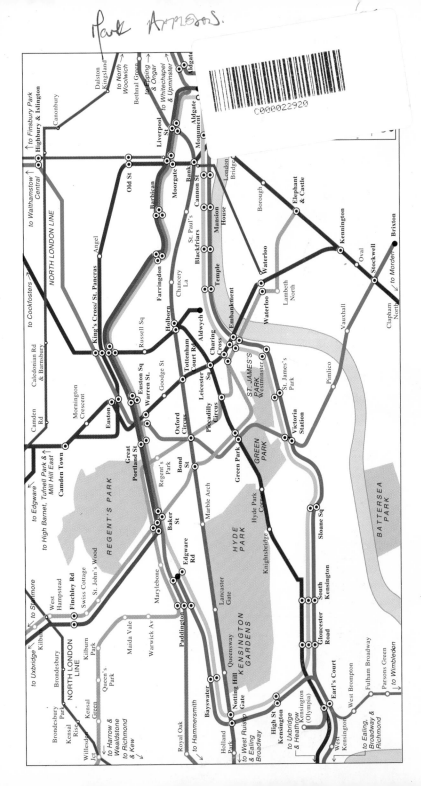

Park Approos.

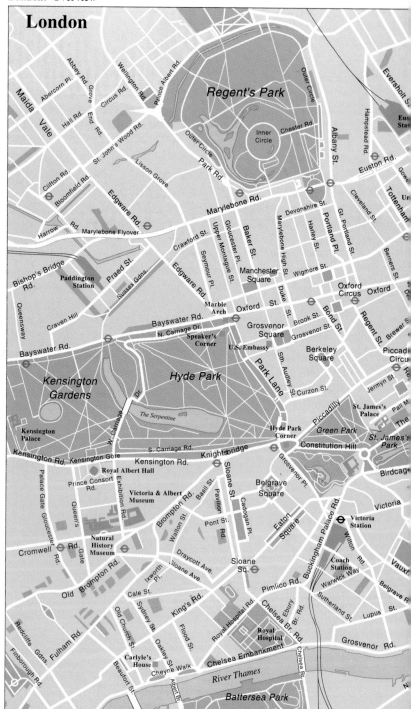

London

London: Westminster and Whitehall

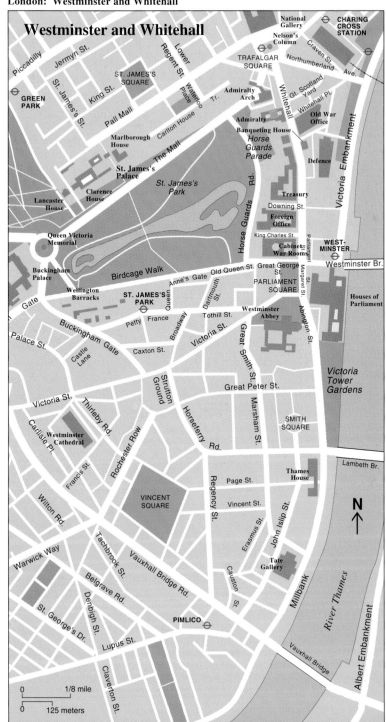

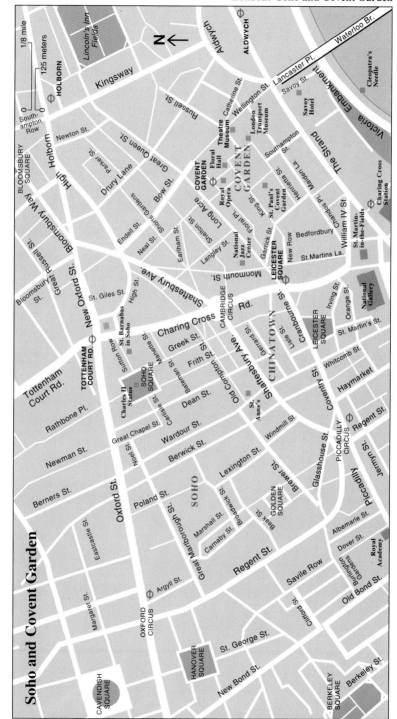

Soho and Covent Garden

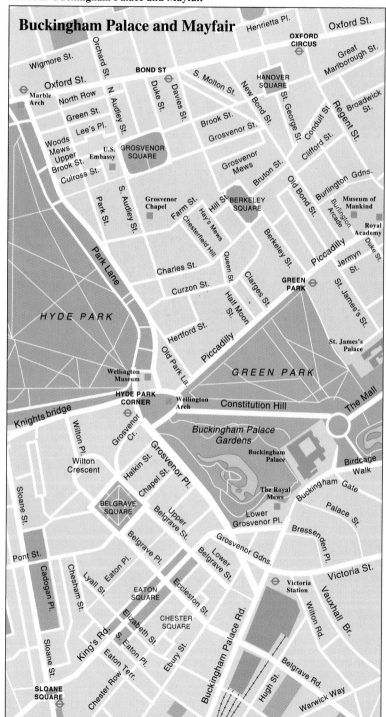

Kensington, Brompton, and Chelsea

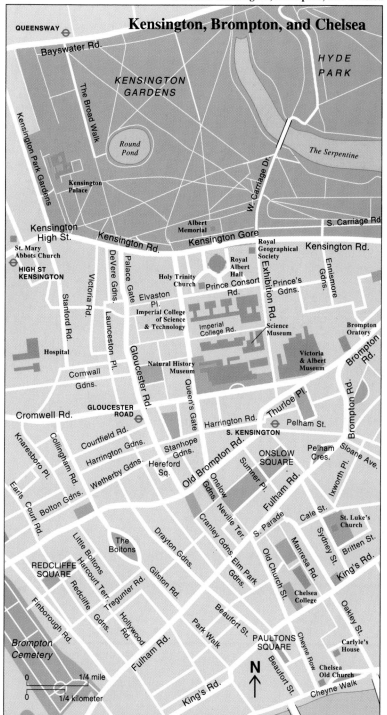

QUEENSWAY

Bayswater Rd.

KENSINGTON GARDENS

The Broad Walk

Kensington Park Gardens

Round Pond

HYDE PARK

The Serpentine

W. Carriage Dr.

Kensington Palace

S. Carriage Rd.

Kensington High St.

St. Mary Abbots Church

HIGH ST KENSINGTON

Albert Memorial

Kensington Rd.

Kensington Gore

Kensington Rd.

Royal Geographical Society

DeVere Gdns.

Palace Gate

Victoria Rd.

Stanford Rd.

Launceston Pl.

Holy Trinity Church

Prince Consort Rd.

Royal Albert Hall

Exhibition Rd.

Prince's Gdns.

Ennismore Gdns.

Elvaston Pl.

Imperial College of Science & Technology

Imperial College Rd.

Science Museum

Brompton Oratory

Hospital

Gloucester Rd.

Natural History Museum

Queen's Gate

Victoria & Albert Museum

Brompton Rd.

Cornwall Gdns.

Cromwell Rd.

GLOUCESTER ROAD

Harrington Rd.

Thurloe Pl.

Pelham St.

Brompton Rd.

Knaresboro Pl.

Collingham Rd.

Courtfield Rd.

Harrington Gdns.

Stanhope Gdns.

S. KENSINGTON

Pelham Cres.

Sloane Ave.

Ixworth Pl.

Earls Court Rd.

Bolton Gdns.

Wetherby Gdns.

Hereford Sq.

Old Brompton Rd.

Onslow Gdns.

ONSLOW SQUARE

Summer Pl.

Pelham St.

Fulham Rd.

Cale St.

St. Luke's Church

Sydney St.

Britten St.

Little Boltons

The Boltons

Harcourt Terr.

Drayton Gdns.

Cranley Gdns.

Neville Terr.

S. Parade

Elm Park Gdns.

Old Church St.

Manresa Rd.

King's Rd.

REDCLIFFE SQUARE

Redcliffe Gdns.

Tregunter Rd.

Gilston Rd.

Hollywood Rd.

Chelsea College

Oakley St.

Finborough Rd.

Beaufort St.

Park Walk

PAULTONS SQUARE

Cheyne Row

Carlyle's House

Brompton Cemetery

Fulham Rd.

King's Rd.

Beaufort St.

Chelsea Old Church

Cheyne Walk

N

0   1/4 mile

0   1/4 kilometer

London: City of London

The City

Leman St.
Commercial St.
ALDGATE EAST
Mansell St.
Middlesex St.
Minories
ALDGATE
Royal Mint St.
E. Smithfield
St. Katharine's Way
Tower Br. Approach
Tower Br.
Widegate St.
Houndsditch
St. Mary Axe
Fenchurch St. Station
TOWER HILL
TRINITY SQUARE
Tower Hill
The Tower
Tower Pier
Liverpool St. Station
Bishopsgate
Old Broad St.
Leadenhall St.
Fenchurch St.
Pepys St.
Seething La.
St. Olave's
Mark La.
Mincing La.
St. Dunstan's
All Hallows
Gt. Tower St.
Lower Thames St.
HMS Belfast
Sun St.
London Stock Exchange
Threadneedle St.
Lloyd's
Leadenhall Market
Lime St.
Gracechurch St.
St. Mary at Hill
Billingsgate Market
South Pl.
Throgmorton Ave.
St. Margaret's Throgmorton St.
Bank of England
Cornhill
Lombard St.
Eastcheap
The Monument
St. Magnus Martyr
MOORGATE
FINSBURY CIRCUS
London Wall
Moorgate
Lothbury St.
BANK
King William St.
MONUMENT
Monument St.
London Br.
Chiswell St.
Ropemaker St.
Moorfields
Coleman St.
Bassinghall Ave.
Princes St.
St. Mary Abchurch
Walbrook
Cloak La.
Southwark Br.
Silk St.
Fore St.
Basinghall St.
Mansion House
Poultry
St. Stephen Walbrook
Temple of Mithras
CANNON
Cannon St. Station
Beech St.
Barbican Centre
St. Giles without Cripplegate
Museum of London
Guildhall
London Wall
King St.
St. Mary le Bow
Wood St.
Watling St.
St. Mary Aldermary
MANSION HOUSE
Queen St.
Aldersgate St.
St. Bartholomew the Great
Little Britain
Gresham St.
Milk St.
Cheapside
Bread St.
New Chance
Cannon St.
River Thames
BARBICAN
Long Lane
West Smithfield
St. Martin's-Le-Grand
ST. PAUL'S
St. Paul's Cathedral
St. Andrew-by-the-Wardrobe
St. Benet's
Puddle Dock
Upper Thames St.
Queen Victoria St.
St. John St.
Cowcross St.
Smithfield Market
Gilspur St.
Holborn Viaduct Station
Warwick La.
Old Bailey
Ludgate Hill
Blackfriars Station
FARRINGDON
Snow Hill
Holborn Viaduct
Fleet La.
Newgate St.
LUDGATE CIRCUS
Fleet St.
St. Bride St.
New Bridge St.
Blackfriars Br.
BLACKFRIARS
Clerkenwell
Farringdon Rd.
Ely Pl.
Shoe Lane
GOUGH SQ.
Tudor St.
Temple Ave.
1/4 mile
Hatton Garden
Greville St.
New Fetter La.
Fetter La.
Temple Church
The Temple
Middle Temple La.
Victoria Embankment
1/4 km
N

Let's Go

BRITAIN & IRELAND

is the best book for anyone traveling on a budget. Here's why:

▓ No other guidebook has as many budget listings.

In Britain & Ireland we list over 6,000 budget travel bargains. We tell you the cheapest way to get around, and where to get an inexpensive and satisfying meal once you've arrived. We give hundreds of money-saving tips that anyone can use, plus invaluable advice on discounts and deals for students, children, families, and senior travelers.

▓ Let's Go researchers have to make it on their own.

Our Harvard-Radcliffe researcher-writers travel on budgets as tight as your own—no expense accounts, no free hotel rooms.

▓ Let's Go is completely revised each year.

We don't just update the prices, we go back to the place. If a charming café has become an overpriced tourist trap, we'll replace the listing with a new and better one.

▓ No other guidebook includes all this:

Honest, engaging coverage of both the cities and the countryside; up-to-the-minute prices, directions, addresses, phone numbers, and opening hours; in-depth essays on local culture, history, and politics; comprehensive listings on transportation between and within regions and cities; straight advice on work and study, budget accommodations, sights, nightlife, and food; detailed city and regional maps; and much more.

▓ Let's Go is for anyone who wants to see Britain and Ireland on a budget.

Books by Let's Go, Inc.

EUROPE

Let's Go: Europe

Let's Go: Austria & Switzerland

Let's Go: Britain & Ireland

Let's Go: Eastern Europe

Let's Go: France

Let's Go: Germany

Let's Go: Greece & Turkey

Let's Go: Ireland

Let's Go: Italy

Let's Go: London

Let's Go: Paris

Let's Go: Rome

Let's Go: Spain & Portugal

NORTH & CENTRAL AMERICA

Let's Go: USA & Canada

Let's Go: Alaska & The Pacific Northwest

Let's Go: California

Let's Go: New York City

Let's Go: Washington, D.C.

Let's Go: Mexico

MIDDLE EAST & ASIA

Let's Go: Israel & Egypt

Let's Go: Thailand

Let's Go

The Budget Guide to

BRITAIN & IRELAND

1995

Daniel George Charles Glover
Editor

Emily Katherine Hobson
Associate Editor

Written by
Let's Go, Inc.
A subsidiary of
Harvard Student Agencies, Inc.

MACMILLAN

HELPING LET'S GO

If you have suggestions or corrections, or just want to share your discoveries, drop us a line. We read every piece of correspondence, whether a 10-page e-mail letter, a velveteen Elvis postcard, or, as in one case, a collage. All suggestions are passed along to our researcher-writers. Please note that mail received after May 5, 1995 will probably be too late for the 1996 book, but will be retained for the following edition.

Address mail to: Or send e-mail to:
  Let's Go: Britain & Ireland   **letsgo@delphi.com**
  Let's Go, Inc.
  I Story Street
  Cambridge, MA 02138
  USA

In addition to the invaluable travel advice our readers share with us, many are kind enough to offer their services as researchers or editors. Unfortunately, the charter of Let's Go, Inc. and Harvard Student Agencies, Inc. enables us to employ only currently enrolled Harvard-Radcliffe students.

Published in Great Britain 1995 by Macmillan, Cavaye Place,
London SW10 9PG.

10 9 8 7 6 5 4 3 2 1

Maps by David Lindroth, copyright © 1995, 1994, 1993, 1992, 1991, 1990, 1989, 1986 by St. Martin's Press, Inc.

Published in the United States of America by St. Martin's Press, Inc.

ISBN: 0 333 62222 7

Let's Go: Britain & Ireland is written by the
Publishing Division of Let's Go, Inc., 1 Story Street,
Cambridge, MA 02138.

Let's Go ® is a registered trademark of Let's Go, Inc.
Printed in the U.S.A. on recycled paper with biodegradable soy ink.

About Let's Go

Back in 1960, a few students at Harvard University got together to produce a 20-page pamphlet offering a collection of tips on budget travel in Europe. For three years, Harvard Student Agencies, a student-run nonprofit corporation, had been doing a brisk business booking charter flights to Europe; this modest, mimeographed packet was offered to passengers as an extra. The following year, students traveling to Europe researched the first full-fledged edition of *Let's Go: Europe*, a pocket-sized book featuring advice on shoestring travel, irreverent write-ups of sights, and a decidedly youthful slant.

Throughout the 60s, the guides reflected the times: one section of the 1968 *Let's Go: Europe* talked about "Street Singing in Europe on No Dollars a Day." During the 70s, *Let's Go* gradually became a large-scale operation, adding regional European guides and expanding coverage into North Africa and Asia. The 80s saw the arrival of *Let's Go: USA & Canada* and *Let's Go: Mexico*, as well as regional North American guides; in the 90s we introduced five in-depth city guides to Paris, London, Rome, New York City, and Washington, DC. And as the budget travel world expands, so do we; the first edition of *Let's Go: Thailand* hit the shelves last year, and this year's edition adds coverage of Malaysia, Singapore, Tokyo, and Hong Kong.

This year we're proud to announce the birth of *Let's Go: Eastern Europe*—the most comprehensive guide to this renascent region, with more practical information and insider tips than any other. *Let's Go: Eastern Europe* brings our total number of titles, with their spirit of adventure and reputation for honesty, accuracy, and editorial integrity, to 21.

We've seen a lot in 35 years. *Let's Go: Europe* is now the world's #1 best selling international guide, translated into seven languages. And our guides are still researched, written, and produced entirely by students who know first-hand how to see the world on the cheap.

Every spring, we recruit over 100 researchers and 50 editors to write our books anew. Come summertime, after several months of training, researchers hit the road for seven weeks of exploration, from Bangkok to Budapest, Anchorage to Ankara. With pen and notebook in hand, a few changes of underwear stuffed in our backpacks, and a budget as tight as yours, we visit every *pensione*, *palapa*, pizzeria, café, club, campground, or castle we can find to make sure you'll get the most out of *your* trip.

We've put the best of our discoveries into the book you're now holding. A brand-new edition of each guide hits the shelves every year, only months after it is researched, so you know you're getting the most reliable, up-to-date, and comprehensive information available. The budget travel world is constantly changing, and where other guides quickly become obsolete, our annual research keeps you abreast of the very latest travel insights. And even as you read this, work on next year's editions is well underway.

At *Let's Go*, we think of budget travel not only as a means of cutting down on costs, but as a way of breaking down a few walls as well. Living cheap and simple on the road brings you closer to the real people and places you've been saving up to visit. This book will ease your anxieties and answer your questions about the basics—to help *you* get off the beaten track and explore. We encourage you to put *Let's Go* away now and then and strike out on your own. As any seasoned traveler will tell you, the best discoveries are often those you make yourself. If you find something worth sharing, drop us a line. We're at Let's Go, Inc., 1 Story Street, Cambridge, MA, 02138, USA (e-mail: letsgo@delphi.com).

Happy travels!

Don't forget to write.

Now that you've said, "Let's go," it's time to say
"Let's get American Express® Travelers Cheques." If they are lost or
stolen, you can get a fast and full refund virtually anywhere you
travel. So before you leave be sure and write.

Contents

■ Maps

◼ Acknowledgments

Cleats and flying *fútbols* of death soon gave way to chronic fatigue syndrome and burst **blood vessels** in the eye. As our desk spaces began to compost, we depended more and more on the kindness of friends at work. Sean & Pete resembled a sallow corpse and bent potato chip those last long lonely hours. May the **demon** that possessed them haunt this building for years to come. Amy & Brian performed proofing miracles, Julie crunched, and Natalie, Such, & Roy walked the night with us. Managing Editor Jahan Sagafi-Nejad fled for Stowe and a flock of **randy** patrician lads—let's hope neither he nor the boys have their hands full with the traumas of pubescence. Jed won Celtic Jeopardy every time and helped locate Emily's **violent** tendencies. Amelia taught us how to say Long Island; Mary picked rocks with us on the Sound.

   Dan will be forever thankful for Emily's graciously warped mind—it helped temper and translate her editor's countless excesses. At home, he flips the bottle cap to Baldy & Fatty, Mike & Kristian. Mom was always too **smart** to drink the Mayo's secret punch, Dad knew what priorities were, and Jamie cackled when the **toothbrush** fell in the Florentine toilet. Matt & Alexis bore with *Speed II* and *the music*, K.P. showed me the way, Cyn & Jen made fun of me, and Mike has a bottle of **wine** to drink. Thanks to Maia, Ben, Kardyhm, & Steve—I *will* clean the sink. **Emily** is grateful for her editor's patience and his willingness to bicker over words; they made the masterwork. She thanks **Zebulon** Books, Laguna Canyon, a mom & pop full of **love** and sound advice, bruddah & mentor Jeff, FUP, Katie, Andy, Susannah, Lucy, Mark, Mai, Moon, Ted, Josh "el Bolivar" Kirshner; many more; and as always, Hannah B., the shining exemplar of all **games** in the park.   ¡GOOOOOOOOOOOL!

STAFF

Editor	Dan Glover
Associate Editor	Emily Hobson
Managing Editor	Jahan Sagafi-nejad
Publishing Director	Pete Keith
Production Manager	Alexis G. Averbuck
Production Assistant	Elizabeth J. Stein
Financial Manager	Matt Heid
Assistant General Manager	Anne E. Chisholm
Sales Group Manager	Sherice R. Guillory
Sales Department Coordinator	Andrea N. Taylor
Sales Group Representatives	Eli K. Aheto
	Timur Okay Harry Hiçyılmaz
	Arzhang Kamerei
	Hollister Jane Leopold
	David L. Yuan
President	Lucienne D. Lester
General Manager	Richard M. Olken

Researcher-Writers

Kelli Rae Patton   *Southwest and Southeast England, Heart of England*
Beset by anxious pigeons and a thousand flowered cities, Kelli Rae emerged from the summer with her Tennessee twang intact. The native dialect proved troublesome at times: Cromwell's bird wasn't all she was cracked up to be, Wookey Hole revealed no inquisitive Chewbaccas, and Henry VIII's coastal erections went soft and fell into the sea after the constant flaying of the salt wind. Kelli's fiery mane disappeared into mock trenches, naval repositories, and tuck shops, always emerging aglow and ready for more, likely a consequence of her ever-itchy trigger finger on B&B coffee machines. In Brighton, she chronicled the dirty weekend and strode the woods by Charleston Farmhouse, scanning Yeats all the while. Kelli takes her act now to UVA for a poetry MFA—perhaps she'll catch up with Seamus Heaney there.

Andy Liu   *Oxford, Southwest England, Wales*
Andy faithfully honored dead golden retrievers wherever his "shoes" took him and revealed his respect for the living with an ever-abiding attention to doggie deals and misogynist parrots in North Wales. His crackling prose intoned safety warnings in God's own voice—you never know when smooth-soled shoes will hasten death in the gorges below. Visitors to Oxford can thank this wily reaper for advice on escaping the bowler-bedecked bouncers into the green glory of the college courtyards. In the throes of a tooth infection, Andy found succor in the home of Eileen Grassby, who was good to him, as she was to R-W Wendy Waldron just two years before. Andy always knew how to make directions *explicit* and where to find the W.C. We promise to return your German dictionary and *Selected Descartes* someday.

Elizabeth Yellen   *Central and Northern England, Southern Scotland*
Liz moved haggis-hungry among polyester lovers at the British Open and, in Hebden Bridge's railway station, evaded drooling men too toothless to share her love for that succulent Drambuie-bathed sheep innards dish. The sound of music sprang from her soul in the central wilds as she considered the sheep she was to later relish in a Scottish feast of kings. Nightly, against a rock jutting from a Pictish moor, our dauntless researcher would scrawl even more haggis price corrections within her flawlessly enthusiastic copy, then dream of jogging until the chilly dawn. Neither vampiric come-ons nor confused strong-bowers could distract Elizabeth from on-the-mark write-ups of Roman ruins or of Robbie Burns schlock-o-rama. She brought the haggis back—in cans, no less—but we'll let it cool for next year's editors.

Tracey Tomlinson   *Scotland*
Last year's editor bequeathed us a beautiful book, then went ahead and relayed us the northern reaches by way of glorious script and cut-outs of midges and corpulent queens. Though a band of Great Skuas tried to pluck her from a barren Shetland shore, Tracey persevered to restore the Orkney Islands to *Let's Go*, so cruelly snatched away last year by the evil goony-birds of typeset changes and Ireland crunches. In her seven-week tour, Tracey danced with island fairies, communed with the dead, and rode the Haggis bus from wee town to wee town. If you run into this newly-minted Marshall Scholar among the dreaming spires next year, she'll never admit to having been the one and only judge in a Hebridean beauty contest, but the marginalia never lies.

Heather Clark   *Western Ireland, Sligo, Lake Districts*
Adam Kirsch   *Dublin, Eastern Ireland, Southeast Ireland*
Jeffrey C. Milder   *Southwest Ireland, Limerick, Southeast Ireland*
Colleen Ryan   *Donegal, Northern Ireland, Isle of Man*
Vivian Lin   *London*
Mimi Schultz   *London*

■ How To Use This Book

As every anxious voyager knows, spontaneity is too important to be left to the last minute. The **Essentials** section runs through things to think about before you go and provides advice useful to planning an itinerary: advice on when and how to travel, on passport and customs rules, on electronic banking and traveler's checks, on camping safety and general health, packing tips, and suggested alternatives to traditional tourism. We give advice to seniors, women, travelers with disabilities, and gay, lesbian, and bisexual travelers; we clue you in on how to seek out greater discounts and make sure you know how to keep in touch with your folks. Be sure to read through all these suggestions *before* you head off. They can save you money; moreover they'll let you relax on the road and *enjoy* your trip.

Of course, travel is much more than exchange rates and ID cards. In the **Life and Times** introductions to each region of the British Isles **(England, Wales, Scotland, Isle of Man, Northern Ireland,** and **The Republic of Ireland),** we've included political and cultural history, social traditions, and notes on local sports and food. Further within regional sections, our courageous researchers have collected details such as tourist offices and bus stations into **Practical Information** listings that ease you in with a minimum of hassle. In our city, town, and national park write-ups, we've tracked down the best hostels, B&Bs, campgrounds, restaurants, cafés, pubs, and shops, with your wallet, toothbrush, and stomach in mind. Note that we list these businesses according to what we think is the best value; those at the top of the list might not be the cheapest, but they do give you the jolliest deal. We also outline the sights and special attractions of the region—both familiar and undiscovered—from museums and castles to nightclubs and festivals. A quick look through these sections before you go will give you an idea of the geography and character of each region. At the end of the book is an appendix with information on telephones and bank holidays and with glossaries of English, Irish, and Welsh terms.

Finally, a note on how *not* to use this book. Retain your independence and wanderlust. Don't let *Let's Go* substitute for your personal travel experience; let it help you head off on your own explorations. There's no need to force yourself to prove how cheaply you can see the world—savor the journey and have fun.

A NOTE TO OUR READERS

The information for this book is gathered by *Let's Go*'s researchers during the late spring and summer months. Each listing is derived from the assigned researcher's opinion based upon his or her visit at a particular time. The opinions are expressed in a candid and forthright manner. Other travelers might disagree. Those traveling at a different time may have different experiences since prices, dates, hours, and conditions are always subject to change. You are urged to check beforehand to avoid inconvenience and surprises. Travel always involves a certain degree of risk, especially in low-cost areas. When traveling, especially on a budget, you should always take particular care to ensure your safety.

Regional

Britain & Ireland: An Introduction

A language of many, sometimes fragmented dialects created by invaded and colonized peoples, English today is also the word of international power. One has only to look back at the history of Britain and Ireland to appreciate this paradox. English has always been a mongrel voice. First considered too common for real scholarship or rule, the tongue later became a tool in England's subjection of Wales, Scotland, and Ireland, and was integral to the creation of the modern British state—from mercantilism to Empire and beyond. Britain and Ireland hold a tight grip on the world's imagination not only because of their myth-laden histories but also because those histories and myths are composed in English—the idiom of tradition.

That tradition is, of course, partly one of cultural innovation and change. Familiar, neatly-clichéd symbols of the Isles—stone-faced Beefeaters standing guard outside Her Majesty's palaces, bagpipes spilling out reels across mist-swirled glens, endless debates in Irish pubs amongst green, green hills—have been slowly transformed. The Beefeaters carry M16s; bagpipers on Edinburgh's street corners are muffled by traffic or are forsaken for contemporary rock; talk in Ireland is now often of Mary Robinson, the Republic's first woman president. Britain and Ireland are lands of the volatile present, as the intense regionalism in their politics and art makes clear.

"England" originally referred to a group of Anglo-Saxon principalities united in the 9th century, though it came to mean the areas of most centralized power. By 1603, the English had established control over Ireland, Scotland, and Wales; the "United Kingdom of Great Britain and Ireland" was proclaimed in 1801. But in the 20th century, this union began to disintegrate, foreshadowing the collapse of the overseas Empire. Most of Ireland won its independence in 1921; Scotland and Wales were promised regional autonomy in 1975. As the ongoing Troubles in Northern Ireland reflect, questions of union and nationalism will likely be contested for years to come—just as they are in Britain's old holdings on more foreign turf. It's been a while since the Union Jack flew over two-fifths of the earth's surface, and the Empire's heirs retain a proud, even arrogant detachment toward the rest of the world. But for all their arrogance, British and Irish can be acutely aware of the inequities in their own lands and articulate in examining them. With a clever wit, passion for introspection, romantic abstraction, and love for the language they claim as *theirs*, the British and Irish have perfected the art of conversation. Any evening in a pub will convince you of that.

Names, like language, hold a certain political force. Deciding just what to call this part of the world can incite local tempers and fuel debates. "Great Britain" refers to England, Scotland, and Wales (and don't call a Scot or Welshman "English"—it's neither accurate nor polite); the political terms "United Kingdom" and "Britain" refer to these regions, Northern Ireland, and the Isle of Man. Because of distinctions in laws and currency, *Let's Go* uses the term "Britain" to refer to England, Scotland, Wales, the Isle of Man, and Northern Ireland, and "Ireland" to refer to the Republic of Ireland. Our use of this terminology does not reflect a political opinion.

Britain and Ireland are small but clearly not homogeneous. For the traveler, such topographical, cultural, and economic difference so close together makes for an extremely rich journey. Allow yourself time to take in both the cities and the isolated, wild hills and sea. The Britain and Ireland of the world's imagination live in both extremes; sometimes, along the way, you can find a place not yet trampled by others claiming the past.

■ Essentials

BEFORE YOU GO

Be smart, not just cheap. Traveling during the low or off-season (mid-Sept. to May) will considerably reduce the damage to your bank account. Airfares will be lower and you won't have to compete with gaggles of garrulous tourists pulling up prices along with their knee socks. However, sights, accommodations (particularly hostels), and tourist offices may close in the off-season, and in some rural areas, local transportation will slow to a crawl if not shut down altogether. The infamous climate of the British Isles may have some bearing on your plans as well (see Climate).

■■■ USEFUL ADDRESSES

The amount of information available to potential travelers to Britain and Ireland from the organizations listed below is astounding—a technicolor sea of enticing pamphlets and brochures. Make your inquiries as specific as possible and assess the information you are given skeptically. Remember, the task of a tourist office is to lure you to a region, not necessarily to objectively present its virtues and flaws.

TOURIST BUREAUS

British Tourist Authority (BTA), 551 Fifth Ave, Suite 701, New York, NY 10176-0799 (tel. (212) 986 2200). Other U.S. branches in **Chicago, Atlanta,** and **Los Angeles.** In **Canada,** 111 Avenue Rd., Ste. 450, Toronto M5R 3J8, Ont. (tel. (416) 925 6326). In **Australia:** The University Centre, 210 Clarence St., Sydney NSW 2000 (tel. (02) 267 4555). Publications include *Stay on a Farm, Stay With a British Family,* detailed hotel, guesthouse, and B&B guides. The British Travel Bookshop in their New York office will send you a catalog.

Irish Tourist Board (Bord Fáilte), 345 Park Ave., New York, NY 10154 (tel. (800) 223 6470 or (212) 418 0800, fax (212) 371 9052). In **Canada,** 160 Bloor St. E., Suite 1150, Toronto, Ont. M4W 1B9 (tel. (416) 929 2777, fax (416) 929 6783). In **Britain,** 150 New Bond St., London W1Y 0AQ (tel. (0171) 493 3201, fax (0171) 493 9065). In **Australia,** Level 5, 36 Carrington Street, Sydney NSW 2000 (tel. (02) 299 6177, fax (02) 299 6323). Ask for the *Ireland Accommodation Guide,* which lists Bord Fáilte-approved B&Bs and campgrounds with prices.

Northern Ireland Tourist Board, 551 Fifth Ave., New York, NY 10176-0799 (tel. (212) 992 0101, fax (212) 922 0099). **Head Office:** 59 North St., Belfast, BT1 1NB, Northern Ireland (tel. (01232) 246609, fax (0232) 231221). In **Britain,** 11 Berkeley St., London W1X 5AD (tel. (0171) 493 0601, fax (0171) 499 3731). In **Dublin,** 16 Nassau St., Dublin 2 (tel. (01) 679 1977, fax (01) 679 1863). In **Canada,** 111 Avenue Rd., Suite 450, Toronto, Ont. M5R 3J8 (tel. (416) 925 6368, fax (416) 961 2175). In **Australia,** 36 Carrington St., Sydney NSW 2000 (tel. (02) 299 6177, fax (02) 299 6323). Or contact any British Tourist Office for Northern Ireland information. Ask for *Where to Stay in Northern Ireland,* a list of all B&Bs and campgrounds with their prices.

Isle of Man Tourist Information, Harris Promenade, Douglas IM1 2HH, Isle of Man (tel. (01624) 686766, fax (01624) 627443).

CONSULATES & HIGH COMMISSIONS

British Consulates: In **U.S.,** British Embassy, 3100 Massachusetts Ave. NW, Washington, DC 20008 (tel. (202) 462 1340); consulates at 845 Third Ave., New York, NY 10022 (tel. (212) 745 0200); Suite 2700, Marquis One Tower, 245 Peachtree Center Ave., Atlanta, GA 30303 (tel. (404) 524 5856); 33 North Dearborn St., Chicago, IL 60602 (tel. (312) 346 1810); First Interstate Bank Plaza, Suite 1990, 1000

Louisiana, Houston, TX 77002 (tel. (713) 659 6270); and 11766 Wilshire Blvd., Ste. 400, Los Angeles, CA 90025-6536 (tel. (310) 477 3322). Call the Embassy for additional addresses. In **Canada,** British High Commission, 80 Elgin St., Ottawa, Ont. K1P 5K7 (tel. (613) 237 1530). In **Australia,** British High Commission, Commonwealth Ave., Yarralumla, Canberra, ACT 2600 (tel. (616) 270 6666). In **New Zealand,** British High Commission, 44 Hill St., Wellington 1 (tel. (644) 472 6049).

Irish Consulates: In the **U.S.,** Irish Embassy, 2234 Massachusetts Ave. NW, Washington, DC 20008 (tel. (202) 462 3939); consulates at: 345 Park Ave., 17th Floor, New York, NY 10154 (tel. (212) 319 2555); Wrigley Building, Rm. 911, 400 N. Michigan Ave., Chicago, IL 60611 (tel. (312) 337 1868); 655 Montgomery St., #930, San Francisco, CA 94111 (tel. (415) 392 4214); 535 Boylston St., Boston, MA 02116 (tel. (617) 267 9330). In **Canada,** contact the Embassy at 170 Metcalfe St., Ottawa, Ont. K2P 1P3 (tel. (613) 233 6281); in **Australia** and **New Zealand,** write to 20 Arkana St., Yarralumla ACT 2600, Australia (tel. (06) 273 3022).

TRAVEL ORGANIZATIONS

Worldwide:

Council on International Educational Exchange (CIEE): 205 East 42nd St., New York, NY 10017 (tel. (212) 661 1414). A private, not-for-profit organization, CIEE administers work, volunteer, academic, and professional programs around the world. They also offer identity cards (including the ISIC and the GO 25) and a range of publications, among them the useful magazine *Student Travels* (free, postage US$1) and *Going Places: The High School Student's Guide to Study, Travel, and Adventure Abroad* (US$13.95, postage US$1.50).

Council Travel: sells charter flight tickets, guidebooks, ISIC, ITIC, GO 25 cards, hostelling cards, and travel gear. Among the 41 U.S. offices are: 729 Boylston St., Ste. #201, **Boston,** MA 02116 (tel. (617) 266 1926); 1153 N. Dearborn St., 2nd floor, **Chicago,** IL 60610 (tel. (312) 951 0585); 6715 Hillcrest, **Dallas,** TX 75205 (tel. (214) 363 9941); 1093 Broxton Ave., Ste. 220, **Los Angeles,** CA 90024 (tel. (310) 208 3551); 205 East 42nd St., **New York,** NY 10017 (tel. (212) 661 1450); 715 S.W. Morrison, Ste. 600, **Portland,** OR 97205 (tel. (503) 228 1900); 530 Bush St., Ground Floor, **San Francisco,** CA 94108 (tel. (415) 421 3473); 1314 Northeast 43rd St., Ste. 210, **Seattle,** WA 98105 (tel. (206) 632 2448). Additional U.S. locations include **San Diego,** CA; **Tempe,** AZ; **Washington,** DC; **Miami,** FL; **Ann Arbor,** MI; **Providence,** RI. In Europe: 28A Poland St. (Oxford Circus), **London** WIV 3DB, England (tel. (0171) 437 7767); 22, rue des Pyramides, 75001 **Paris,** France (tel. (1) 44 55 55 44); and 18, Graf-Adolf-Strasse, 4000 Dusseldorf 1, **Germany** (tel. (211) 32.90.88).

International Student Travel Confederation (ISTC): Store Kongensgade 40H, 1264 Copenhagen K, Denmark (tel. +45 (33) 93 93 03). They offer ISICs. See Youth and Student Identification for further ISIC information. Organizations affiliated with the ISTC include the International Student Rail Association (ISRA), Student Air Travel Association (SATA), ISIS Travel Insurance, and the International Association for Educational and Work Exchange Programs (IAEWEP).

STA Travel: 5900 Wilshire Blvd., Ste. 2110, Los Angeles, CA 90036 (tel. (800) 777 0112 in the U.S.) Over 100 offices around the world offer discount airfares for travelers under 26 and full-time students under 32, railpasses, accommodations, tours, insurance, and ISICs. 297 Newbury St., **Boston,** MA 02116 (tel. (617) 266 6014); 48 E. 11th St., **New York,** NY 10003 (tel. (212) 477 7166); 2401 Pennsylvania Ave., **Washington,** DC 20037 (tel. (202) 887 0912); and 51 Grant Ave., **San Francisco,** CA 94108 (tel. (415) 391 8407). In the U.K.: 86 Old Brompton Rd., **London** SW7 3LQ and 117 Euston Rd., London NW1 2SX (tel. (0171) 937 9921 for European travel). In **New Zealand:** 10 High St., Auckland (tel. (09) 398 9995); in **Australia:** 22 Faraday St., Melbourne VIC 3053 (tel. (03) 349 2411).

In the United States & Canada:

Council Charter: 205 East 42nd St., New York, NY 10017 (tel. (212) 661 0311 or (800) 800-8222). A subsidiary of CIEE, Council Charter offers a combination of inexpensive charter and scheduled airfares from a variety of U.S. gateways to

Britain and Ireland: Points of Interest

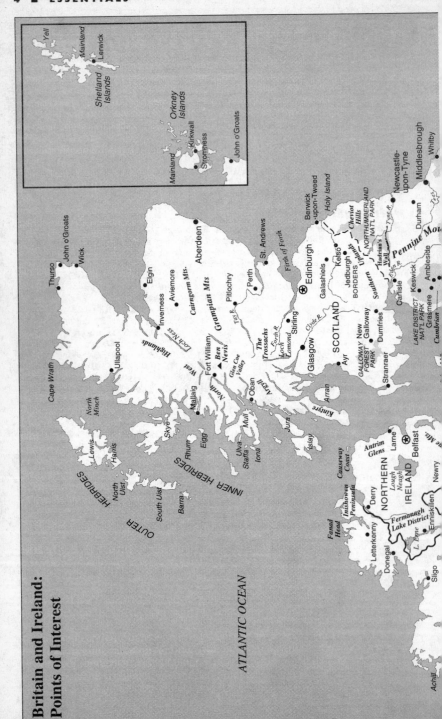

FRANCE

North Sea

IRELAND

GREAT BRITAIN

ENGLAND

WALES

Irish Sea

Celtic Sea

English Channel

North York Moors Natl Park

Yorkshire Dales Natl Park

Peak District Natl Park

Snowdonia Natl Park

Pembrokeshire Coast Natl Park

Brecon Beacons Natl Park

Exmoor Natl Park

Dartmoor Natl Park

Cambrian Mts.

Cotswolds

Chiltern Hills

North Downs

South Downs

Mendip Hills

Salisbury Plain

Stonehenge

The Fens

The Broads

Boyne Valley

The Burren

Connemara

Ring of Kerry

Dingle Peninsula

Beara Peninsula

Knockmealdown Mountains

Lleyn Peninsula

Isles of Scilly

Aran Islands

Ireland: Westport, Clifden, Galway, Roscommon, Athlone, Mullingar, Ennis, Shannon, Limerick, Tipperary, Cashel, Kilkenny, Waterford, Wexford, Rosslare, Rosslare Harbor, Wicklow, Glendalough, Enniskerry, Dublin, Tralee, Killarney, Glengarriff, Bantry, Skibbereen, Kinsale, Cork

Rivers (Ireland): River Shannon, Grand Canal, Nore R., Barrow R., Blackwater R., Lee R., Liffey R.

Great Britain / England / Wales: Douglas, Heysham, Bowness, Windermere, Hull, Beverley, York, Lincoln, Leeds, Bradford, Manchester, Sheffield, Nottingham, Stoke-on-Trent, Chester, Liverpool, Conwy, Bangor, Caernarfon, Holyhead, Anglesey, Betws-y-Coed, Harlech, Machynlleth, Shrewsbury, Llangollen, Aberystwyth, Cardigan, St. Davids, Pembroke, Tenby, Swansea, Cardiff, Brecon, Abergavenny, Monmouth, Chepstow, Worcester, Gloucester, Wells, Glastonbury, Bristol, Bath, Birmingham, Coventry, Stratford-upon-Avon, Cheltenham, Oxford, Cambridge, Peterborough, Ely, King's Lynn, Norwich, Bury St. Edmunds, Ixworth, Harwich, Felixstowe, London, Canterbury, Sandwich, Deal, Dover, Rye, Brighton, Arundel, Chichester, Portsmouth, Winchester, Salisbury, Dorchester, Weymouth, Lyme Regis, Exeter, Bodmin, Tintagel, Padstow, Newquay, St. Ives, Penzance, Falmouth, Plymouth

Rivers (Britain): Humber R., Swale R., Ure R., Ribble R., Mersey R., Dee R., Derwent R., Trent R., Severn R., Wye R., Avon R., Thames R., Gt. Ouse R., Witham R., Welland R., Nene R., Stour R., Parret R., Exe R.

40 miles
40 kilometers
0

N

Britain and Ireland: Transport Map

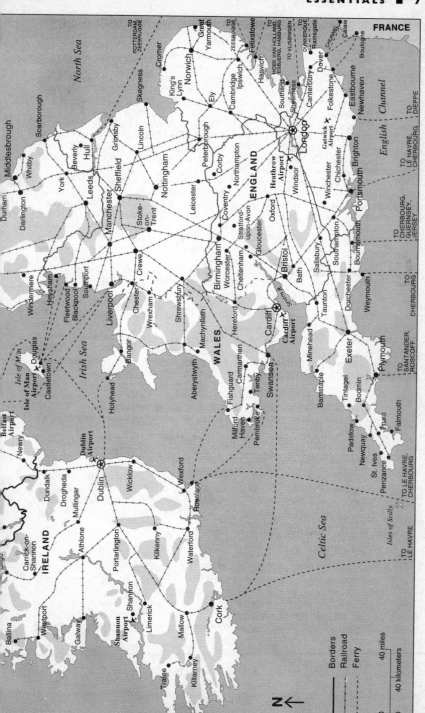

most major European destinations. One-way fares and open jaws (fly into one city and out of another) are available.

Educational Travel Centre (ETC): 438 North Frances St., Madison, WI 53703 (tel. (800) 747 5551, fax (608) 256 2042). Flight information, HI/AYH cards, Eurail and regional rail passes. Write for their free pamphlet *Taking Off.*

International Student Exchange Flights (ISE): 5010 East Shea Blvd., #A104, Scottsdale, AZ 85254 (tel. (602) 951 1177). Budget student flights, BritRail and Eurail passes, traveler's checks, and travel guides, including *Let's Go.* Free catalog.

Let's Go Travel: Harvard Student Agencies, Inc., 53-A Church St., Cambridge, MA 02138 (tel. (800) 5-LETS GO or (617) 495 9649). The world's largest student-run travel agency, Let's Go Travel offers railpasses, HI/AYH memberships, ISICs, International Teacher ID cards, FIYTO cards, guidebooks (all *Let's Go* guides), maps, bargain flights, and budget travel gear. All items available by mail; call or write for a catalog or see the catalog insert.

Travel CUTS (Canadian University Travel Services Limited): 187 College St., **Toronto,** Ont. M5T 1P7 (tel. (416) 798 CUTS, fax (416) 979 8167). Canada's national student travel bureau and equivalent of CIEE, with 40 offices across Canada. Also in the U.K., 295-A Regent St., **London** W1R 7YA (tel. (0171) 637 3161). Discounted domestic and international airfares open to all; special student fares to all destinations with valid ISIC. Issues ISIC, FIYTO, and HI hostel cards, as well as railpasses. Offers free *Student Traveller* magazine, as well as information on the Student Work Abroad Program (SWAP).

University and Student Travel (USTN) specializes in student travel and sell ISICs, GO25 cards, youth hostel cards, STA and CIEE student tickets, USTN student discount plane tickets, Eurail and BritRail passes, student tours, etcetera. Most of the offices are in student unions and in California; none are on the East Coast. In **Berkeley,** their office is Berkeley Northside Travel, 1824 Euclid Ave., Berkeley, CA 94709 (tel. (510) 843 1000).

Unitravel: 117 North Warson Rd., St. Louis, MO 63132 (tel. (800) 325 2222, fax (314) 569 2503). Offers discounted airfares on major scheduled airlines from the U.S. to over 50 cities in Europe. Will hold all payments in a bank escrow until completion of your trip.

In Britain & Ireland:

Campus Travel: 52 Grosvenor Gardens, London SW1W 0AG (tel. (0171) 730 8832; fax (0171) 730 5739). 37 branches in the U.K. Student and youth fares on plane, train, boat, and bus travel. Flexible airline tickets. Discount and ID cards for youths, travel insurance for students and those under 35, and maps and guides. Puts out travel suggestion booklets. Telephone booking service: in Europe call (0171) 730 3402; in North America call (0171) 730 2101; worldwide call (0171) 730 8111. London Student Travel is now affiliated with Campus Travel.

USIT, 19-21 Aston Quay, O'Connell Bridge, Dublin 2 (tel. (01) 677 8117, fax (01) 679 8833). In the USA: New York Student Center, 895 Amsterdam Ave., New York, NY, 10025 (tel. (212) 663 5435). Additional offices in Cork, Galway, Limerick, Waterford, Maynooth, Coleraine, Derry, and Belfast.

WST Charters: 65 Wigmore St., London W1H 9LG (tel. (0171) 224 0504, fax (0171) 224 6142). ISICs and bargain flights worldwide.

BOOKS, GUIDES, CATALOGS, & MAPS

Blue Guides: published in Britain by A&C Black Limited, 35 Bedford Row, London WC1R 4JH, in the U.S. by W.W. Norton & Co. Inc., 500 Fifth Ave., New York, NY 10110, and in Canada by Penguin Books Canada Ltd., 2801 John St., Markham, Ontario L3R 1B4. Blue Guides provide invaluable and unmatched historical and cultural information as well as sightseeing routes, maps, tourist information, and listings of pricey hotels. Several titles covering Britain and Ireland, including *England, Ireland, London, Literary Britain & Ireland,* and *Scotland.*

Bon Voyage!: 2069 W. Bullard Ave., Fresno, CA 93711-1200 (tel. (800) 995 9716, from abroad (209) 447 8441, CompuServe 70754, 3511). Annual mail order catalog offers an amazing range of products for all travelers. Books, travel accessories, luggage, electrical converters, maps, videos, more. All merchandise may be returned for exhange or refund within 30 days of purchase; prices guaranteed; free shipping. They will search their database for items not listed in catalog.

The College Connection, Inc.: 1295 Prospect St., La Jolla, CA 92031 (tel. (619) 551 9770, fax (619) 551 9987). Publishes *The Passport,* a booklet listing hints about every aspect of traveling and studying abroad (distributed free to universities). The College Rail Connection, a division of the College Connection, Inc., sells railpasses with enhancements to college students.

Hunter Publishing: 300 Raritan Center Parkway, Edison, NJ 08818 (tel. (908) 225 1900, fax (908) 417 0482). They offer an extensive catalog of travel books, guides, and maps, including *Britain on Backroads, Explore Britain's National Parks,* and regional guides (Lake District, Scottish Highlands, other regions).

John Muir Publications: P.O. Box 613, Santa Fe, NM 87504 (tel. (505) 982 4078 or (800) 888 7504). Publishes an excellent series of books by veteran traveler Rick Steves, including *2 to 22 Days in Great Britain* (US$10.95). Available in bookstores. See also Specific Concerns: Traveling with Children.

Michelin Travel Publications: Michelin Tire Corporation, P.O. Box 19001, Greenville, SC 29602-9001 (tel. (800) 423 0485, fax (803) 458 5665). Green Guides, for sight-seeing, maps, driving itineraries, and historical information; reliable, detailed Road Maps and Atlases geared towards car travel.

Wide World Books and Maps, 1911 N. 45th St., Seattle, WA 98103 (tel. (206) 634-3453, fax (206) 634 0558). Guides and literature, accessories, and maps. Knowledgeable staff. Phone, fax, and mail orders welcome.

■■■ DOCUMENTS & FORMALITIES

When you travel, always carry two or more forms of **identification** on your person, including at least one photo ID. A passport and a driver's license or birth certificate usually serve as adequate proof of your identity and citizenship. Many establishments, especially banks, require several IDs before cashing traveler's checks. A few extra passport photos will come in handy if you need to have new IDs made. Also see the sections Hostel Membership and Youth & Student Identification, below.

Never carry all your identification in the same place. If you plan to be in Britain and Ireland for an extended stay, register your passport with the embassy or consulate. File all applications for documents weeks or even months in advance of your departure. You might apply in the off-season (Aug.-Dec.) for speedier service.

Be aware of **entrance requirements.** You must have a valid **passport** to enter Britain or Ireland and to re-enter your own country. Canadians, Australians, New Zealanders, and other non-visa Commonwealth nationals also require an **Entry Certificate** to enter Britain, available at the point of entry. Citizens of the U.S., Canada, Australia, and New Zealand may enter both the United Kingdom and the Republic of Ireland without a visa. (Some countries on the European continent do require a visa.) When entering the country, dress neatly and carry proof of your financial independence (such as a visa to the next country on your itinerary, an air ticket to depart, enough money for your stay).

The standard **period of admission** is six months in Britain, three months in Ireland. To stay longer, you must show evidence that you can support yourself for an extended period of time, and a medical examination is often required. Admission as a visitor from a non-EU nation does not include the right to work, which is authorized only by the possession of a work permit (see Alternatives to Tourism, below). Entering either Britain and Ireland to study does not require a special visa, but immigration will want to see proof of acceptance by a British or Irish school, proof that the course of study will take up most of your time in the country, and proof that you can support yourself.

PASSPORTS

Before you leave, *record your passport number,* and keep it apart from the passport itself. If you lose your passport while traveling, tell the local police and your nearest consulate immediately. In an emergency, ask for immediate temporary traveling

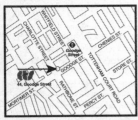

papers that will permit you to return to your home country. Carry an expired passport or a copy of your birth certificate in a separate part of your baggage; most importantly, carry a photocopy of your passport, or leave it with someone at home. Your consulate can issue you temporary traveling papers or replace your passport.

U.S. citizens may apply for a passport valid for 10 years (5 if under 18) at any one of several thousand federal or state courthouses or post offices authorized to accept applications, or at a U.S. Passport Agency, located in Boston, Chicago, Honolulu, Houston, Los Angeles, Miami, New Orleans, New York, Philadelphia, San Francisco, Seattle, Stamford, and Washington, DC. Refer to the "U.S. Government, State Department" section of the telephone directory or call your local post office for addresses. Parents must apply in person for children under age 13. You must apply in person if this is your first passport, if you are under age 18, or if your current passport is more than 12 years old or was issued before your 18th birthday. For a U.S. passport, you must submit a completed application form, proof of U.S. Citizenship (a certified birth certificate, naturalization papers, or a previous passport), a signature-photo I.D., and two identical, recent, passport-sized photographs with a white or off-white background taken within the past six months. Bring these items and $65 (under 18 $40) in check or money order. Agencies accept cash in the exact amount. Write your date of birth on the check, and photocopy the data page for your records. You can renew your passport for $55.

Passports are processed according to the departure date indicated on the application form. In March through August, processing may take even longer. **File early.** If you fail to indicate a departure date, the agency will assume you are not planning any immediate travel. Your passport will be mailed to you; you may pay for express mail return. Passport Agencies offer **rush service;** if you have proof that you are departing within five working days (e.g. an airplane ticket), a Passport Agency will issue a passport while you wait. Arrive well before the office opens so you can lead the line, and expect to remain there at least until the end of the day.

Abroad, a **U.S. embassy or consulate** can usually issue new passports, given proof of citizenship. For more information, call the U.S. Passport Information's 24-hr. recorded message (tel. (202) 647 0518), which offers general information, agency locations, and business hours, or call the recorded message of the passport agency nearest you. If your passport is lost or stolen in the U.S., report it in writing to Passport Services, 1111 19th St., NW, Department of State, Washington, DC 20522-1705, or to the nearest passport agency.

Canadian passport application forms in English and French are available at all passport offices and post offices; apply in person at one of 28 regional offices (ask a travel agent). Along with the application form, a citizen must provide citizenship documentation (an original birth certificate or an original certificate of Canadian citizenship), two identical passport photos less than a year old that indicate the photographer, studio address, and the date the photos were taken, and a CDN $35 fee (no personal checks). The application form and one of the photographs must be certified by a guarantor (someone who has known the applicant for two years and whose profession falls into one of the categories listed on the application form). **Canadian citizens residing abroad** should contact the nearest embassy or consulate. You can apply by mail by sending a completed form with documentation and the fee to Passport Office, Foreign Affairs, Ottawa, Ont., K1A 0G3. Processing will take five business days in person, three weeks through the mail. Applicants under age 16 who travel with a parent should use form B and may be included on the parent's passport. A Canadian passport is valid for five years and is not renewable. For additional information, from Canada call the 24-hour number at (800) 567 6868 (or in Toronto call 973 3251, in Montreal call 283 2152. *Bon Voyage, But . . .* offers information for travelling Canadians and a list of Canadian Embassies, High Commissions, and consulates abroad. It is available free of charge from any passport office or from: Info-Export (BPTE), Foreign Affairs, Ottawa, Ontario, KIA 0G2.

Australian citizens must apply for a passport in person at a local post office, a passport office, or an Australian diplomatic mission overseas. An appointment may be necessary. Passport offices are located in Adelaide, Brisbane, Canberra, Darwin, Hobart, Melbourne, Newcastle, Perth and Sydney. A parent may file an application for a child who is under 18 and unmarried. Along with your application, submit proof of citizenship (a birth certificate, a citizen's certificate from the Immigration Service, or an expired passport), proof of your present name, two identical, signed small photos less than six months old, and other forms of ID (driver's license, credit card, rate notice, etc.). Application fees are adjusted every three months.

Applicants for **New Zealand passports** must contact their local Link Centre, travel agent, or New Zealand Representative for an application form, which they must complete and mail to the New Zealand Passport Office, Documents of National Identity Division, Department of Internal Affairs, Box 10-526, Wellington (tel. (04) 474 8100). With a completed application you must submit proof of citizenship, proof of identity, and two certified photos. The standard processing time is 10 working days from receipt; applications marked "urgent" receive priority. The application fee is NZ$80 or an application submitted in New Zealand and NZ$130 for one submitted overseas (if under age 16, NZ$40 and NZ$65 respectively). Citizens applying from overseas should send the passport application to the nearest embassy, high commission, or consulate authorized to issue passports.

South African citizens can apply for a passport at any Department of Home Affairs Office. Two photos, either a birth certificate or an identity book, and a R38 fee must accompany a completed application. For further information, contact the nearest Department of Home Affairs Office.

CUSTOMS

Don't be alarmed by customs procedures. The many regulations of customs and duties hardly pose a threat to the budget traveler. **Persons entering Britain and Ireland** must declare at the point of entry the three great aromatic luxuries: alcohol, tobacco, and perfume. A duty is placed on excessive quantities of these substances. Britain also has very strict restrictions on imports: among those goods prohibited are controlled drugs, horror comics, fireworks, meat and poultry, fruits and vegetables, plants and plant material, and wood with bark attached. All animals brought into the country are subject to a six-month quarantine at the owner's expense. Neither Britain nor Ireland limits the amount of currency you may bring in, though Ireland restricts the amount taken out of the country—no more than IR£150 in Irish currency, plus no more than the value of IR£1200 in foreign currency. Goods obtained that have had duty and tax paid in another EU country, within certain limits set out for personal use, will not be subject to additional customs duty.

Upon returning home, you must declare all articles acquired abroad and pay a duty on those articles that exceed the allowance established by your country. Holding onto receipts for purchases made abroad will help you establish values when you return home. It is wise to make a list (including serial numbers) of any valuables that you take with you from home; if you register this list with customs at the airport before departing, you'll avoid being charged import duties upon your return. Like the U.K. and Ireland, the U.S., Canada, Australia, and New Zealand all prohibit or restrict the import of firearms, explosives, ammunition, fireworks, plants, animals, lottery tickets, obscene literature and film, and controlled drugs. To avoid problems when carrying prescription drugs, make sure bottles are clearly marked, and have a copy of the prescription ready to show the customs officer.

Keep in mind that goods and gifts purchased at duty-free shops abroad are not exempt from duty or sales tax at your point of return; you must declare these items along with other purchases. For a complete list of what can and cannot be brought back home, contact your local customs service.

For information about **U.K. customs,** contact Her Majesty's Customs and Excise, Custom House, Heathrow Airport North, Houslow, Middlesex, TW6 2LA (tel. (0181) 750 1603; fax (0181) 750 1549). *HM Customs & Excise Notice 1* explains the allowances for people traveling to the U.K. For more information on **Irish Customs,** contact The Revenue Commissioners, Dublin Castle, Dublin 1 (tel. (01) 679 2777).

EU nationals who travel between EU countries no longer need to declare the goods they purchase abroad.

U.S. residents returning from abroad must declare all merchandise acquired abroad, including gifts, articles bought in duty-free shops, and purchases for others. The first $400 worth of merchandise for personal or household use may be entered duty free. You may include in your personal exemption one liter of alcoholic beverages, but must be over 21 to bring in any alcoholic beverages—including **Guinness**). This $400 duty-free exemption is good once every 30 days, provided you have been out of the country for at least 48 hours. The next $1000 worth of merchandise will be subject to a flat 10 percent duty rate; beyond that $1400, different duty rates will apply. You must declare all purchases, so it's wise to keep sales slips handy in carry-on luggage, in case Customs inspectors wish to verify items on your customs declaration. For more information on what to expect when clearing American customs, call or write for a copy of *Know Before You Go* from the U.S. Customs Service, Box 7407, Washington, D.C. 20044l (tel. (202) 927-6724).

United States citizens may **mail home** unsolicited gifts free of duty if they are worth less than $100. You may not send gifts of alcohol, tobacco, or perfume through the mail. If you send a gift back to the U.S., be sure to mark on the outside of your gift package the items it contains, the fact that the contents are unsolicited gifts, and the value of the gift or of each gift. If your gift package exceeds the duty-free limit, the U.S. Postal Service will collect customs duties and handling charges in the form of "postage due" stamps. Duty on gifts or other packages mailed from abroad cannot be prepaid. If you are mailing home personal items of American origin, mark clearly on the outside of the wrapping, "American goods returned" to avoid paying duty. Somewhat different regulations apply to **foreign nationals living in the U.S.** These individuals should get a copy of *Customs Hints for Visitors (Nonresidents)* by writing or calling the same address or phone number above.

Canadian citizens who remain abroad for at least one week may bring back up to CDN $300 worth of goods duty-free once every year; goods that exceed the allowance will be taxed at 12%. You are permitted to ship goods home under this exemption as long as you declare them when you arrive. Citizens over the legal age of the province they are entering may import in person (not through the mail) up to 200 cigarettes, 50 cigars, 400g loose tobacco, 1.14L wine or alcohol, and 355ml beer; the value of these products is included in the CDN$300 allowance. For more information, write to Canadian Customs, 2265 St. Laurent Blvd., Ottawa, Ontario, K1G 4K3 (tel. (613) 993 0534). Or call (800) 461-9999 from within Canada.

Each **Australian** citizen over age 18 may bring into Australia 1 liter of liquor and 250 cigarettes or 250 g of tobacco products duty/tax free. In addition, a duty/tax free allowance or AUS$400 (under 18, AUS$200) is available for other goods intended as gifts. There is no limit to the amount of cash that may be brought into or taken out of Australia. However, amounts of AUS$5000 or more or their equivalent must be reported. For further information contact the Australian Customs Service, 5 Constitution Ave., Canberra, ACT 2601 (tel. (6) 275 6255; fax (6) 275 6989).

Each **New Zealand** citizen may import up to NZ$700 worth of gifts or goods intended for personal use duty-free. The concession is 200 cigarettes (1 carton), 250g of tobacco, or 50 cigars, or a combination of all three not to exceed 250g. You may also bring in 4.5L of beer or wine and 1.125L of liquor. Only travelers over 17 may bring tobacco or alcoholic beverages. For more information, get *New Zealand Customs Guide for Travelers* from customs offices, or contact New Zealand Customs, 50 Anzac Avenue, Box 29, Auckland (tel. (09) 377 3520; fax 309 2978).

Each **South African** citizen may import duty-free 400 cigarettes, 50 cigars, 250g tobacco, 2L wine, 1L of spirits, 250mL toilet water, 50mL perfume, and other items up to a value of R500. Amounts exceeding this limit are fully dutiable. Golf clubs and firearms do not fall within the duty-free allowance for travelers absent less than six months; goods acquired abroad and shipped separately do not qualify for allowances. You may not export or import South African bank notes in excess of R500. For information or advice concerning customs and excise duties, write to The Com-

DOCUMENTS AND FORMALITIES

TOP 5 Ways to Save Money While Traveling

5. Ship yourself in a crate marked "Livestock." Remember to poke holes in the crate.

4. Board a train dressed as Elvis and sneer and say "The King rides for free."

3. Ask if you can walk through the Channel Tunnel.

2. Board the plane dressed as an airline pilot, nod to the flight attendants, and hide in the rest room until the plane lands.

1. Bring a balloon to the airline ticket counter, kneel, breathe in the helium, and ask for the kiddie fare.

But if you're serious about saving money while you're traveling abroad, just get an ISIC—the International Student Identity Card. Discounts for students on international airfares, hotels and motels, car rentals, international phone calls, financial services, and more.

International Student Identity Card
Carte Internationale d'Etudiant/Carnet Internacional de estudiante

GRAHAM
DONNA
10/29/70   7/5/94
USA
U OREGON
STUDENT

For more information:
In the United States:

 Council on International Educational Exchange
205 East 42nd St.
New York, NY 10017
1-800-GET-AN-ID
Available at Council Travel offices (see inside front cover)

In Canada:

 Travel CUTS
243 College Street,
Toronto, Ontario M5T 2Y1
(416) 977-3703
Available at Travel CUTS offices nationwide

missioner for Customs and Excise, Private Bag X47, Pretoria, 0001. This agency distributes the pamphlet *South African Customs Information* for visitors and residents who travel abroad. South Africans in the U.S. should contact the South African Mission to the IMF/World Bank, 3201 New Mexico Ave. #380, NW, Washington, DC 20016 (tel. (202) 364-8320/1; fax 364-6008).

HOSTEL MEMBERSHIP

Hostelling International (HI) is the name adopted by the former International Youth Hostel Federation (IYHF). The 6,000 HI youth hostels worldwide normally display the HI logo alongside the national hostel association symbol. Despite the name, you need not be a youth; travelers over 25 pay only a slight surcharge for a bed. Some hostels do not sell them on the spot.

HI also offers an **International Booking Network,** which allows you to make confirmed reservations at any of the HI hostels in the U.S. and abroad for only US$2 (in addition to the regular overnight fee). Reservations can be made at hostel association headquarters for up to three consecutive nights for groups of up to nine people, and changes can be made up to three or more days before the date of the reservation. Credit card (MC or Visa) guarantee is required. For more details on youth hostels, see Accommodations, below. One-year hostel membership cards are available from some travel agencies (see Useful Addresses) and from the following organizations, all of which are national HI affiliates and comply with HI regulations:

Hostelling International (HI): headquarters and information, 9 Guessens Rd., Welwyn Garden City, Hertfordshire AL8 6QW, England (tel. (01707) 332487).

American Youth Hostels (AYH): 733 15th St. NW, Ste. 840, Washington, DC, 20005 (tel. (202) 783 6161, fax (202) 783 6171). HI-AYH is comprised of 39 local councils. Membership cards cost US$25, renewals $20, under 18 $10, over 54 $15, family cards $35. Membership valid for 12 months from date of issue.

Australian Youth Hostels Association (AYHA), Level 3, 10 Mallett St., Camperdown, New South Wales, 2050 Australia (tel. (02) 565 1699, fax (02) 565 1325). Fee AU$40, renewal $24, under 18 fee and renewal $12.

Hostelling International—Canada (HI-C): 400-205 Catherine St., Ottawa, Ontario, Canada K2P 1C3 (tel. (613) 237 7884, fax (613) 237 7868). One-year membership CDN$26.75, under 18 $12.84, two-year $37.45.

Youth Hostels Association of England and Wales (YHA): Trevelyan House, 8 St. Stephen's Hill, St. Albans, Hertfordshire AL12DY (tel. (01727) 855215; or 14 Southhampton St., Covent Garden, London WC2E 7HY (tel. (0171) 836 1036. Enrollment fees are £9 adult, £3 under 18, £3 for 2-day introductory membership over 18; children 5-18 enrolled free when parent joins.

An Óige (Irish Youth Hostel Association): 61 Mountjoy Sq., Dublin 7, Ireland (tel. (01) 830 4555, fax (01) 830 5808). Membership for one year IR£7.50, under 18 IR£4, family IR£15. Pronounced "ann OY-ga."

Scottish Youth Hostels Association (SYHA): 7 Glebe Crescent, Sterling FK8 2JA, Scotland (tel. (01786) 451181, fax (01786) 450198).

Youth Hostels Association of New Zealand (YHANZ), P.O. Box 436, 17 Gloucester St., Christchurch 1, New Zealand (tel. (03) 379 9970, fax (03) 365 4476). Annual memberships: senior (adult) NZ$34, youth (15-17) NZ$12, under 15 free. Rates are lower for 2- and 3-year memberships. Life membership NZ$240. New Zealand memberships not renewable overseas.

Youth Hostels Association of Northern Ireland (YHANI): 22-32 Donegall Rd., Belfast BT12 5JN, Northern Ireland (tel. (01232) 324733, fax (01232) 439699).

The HI guides (*Vol. 1: Europe and the Mediterranean* and *Vol. 2: Africa, America, Asia, Australia, and New Zealand;* each US$10.95, $3 postage and handling) list up-to-date information on HI hostels. Get them at bookstores or from HI.

YOUTH & STUDENT IDENTIFICATION

Many costs, particularly for transportation and sights, can be substantially reduced with a student ID. The **International Student Identity Card (ISIC)** is the most widely recognized form of student ID. The ISIC gets you discounts on sights, theater tickets, museums, accommodations, trains, ferries, flights, and other services. Ask about discounts when none are advertised. The ISIC provides accident insurance of up to US$3,000 per accident, $10,000 for emergency medical evacuation, and $100 per day of in-hospital care for up to 60 days, among other benefits. Cardholders have access to a toll-free Traveler's Assistance hotline whose staff can help in medical, legal, and financial emergencies overseas.

Many student travel offices issue ISICs (see Useful Addresses). The accompanying *ISIC Handbook* lists by country some of the available discounts. You can also write to CIEE for a copy (again, Useful Addresses). **To apply** you need a current, dated proof of your degree-seeking student status (a photocopied grade report, a letter on school stationery signed and sealed by the registrar, or a Bursar's receipt with school seal that indicates full payment for the applicable semester); a passport-size photo with your name printed and signed on the back; proof of your birthdate and nationality; and the name, address, and phone number of a beneficiary (if you die, insurance payment will go to this person). To apply you must be at least 12 years old and a high school or post-secondary student. The fee is US$15; the card is valid from September 1 to December 31 of the next year. Because of the proliferation of phony and improperly issued ISIC cards, many airlines and some other services now require **double proof** of student identity.

The US$16 **International Teacher Identity Card (ITIC)** offers identical discounts, but because of its recent introduction many establishments are reluctant to honor it. The application process is the same as for an ISIC. The **Federation of International Youth Travel Organisations (FIYTO)** issues a discount card to travelers under 26 (students or not). Known as the **International Youth Discount Travel Card** or the **GO 25 Card,** this one-year card offers many of the same benefits as the ISIC. Most organizations that sell the ISIC also sell GO 25. Proof of birthdate (copy of birth certificate or passport or a valid driver's license) and a passport-sized photo with your name printed on the back are required. The fee is US$10, CDN$12, or £4. For more information, contact the **Federation of International Youth Travel Organisations (FIYTO),** Bredgade 25 H, DK 1260 Copenhagen K, Denmark (tel. +45 (33) 33 96 00; telex 31 239; fax 93 96 76).

■■■ MONEY

CURRENCY AND EXCHANGE

US$1 = British pounds £0.65	£1 = US$1.54
CDN$1 = £0.48	£1 = CDN$2.10
AUS$1 = £0.49	£1 = AUS$2.06
NZ$1 = £0.39	£1 = NZ$2.55
S.A.R = £0.18	£1 = S.A.R5.51
UK£1 = IR£1.02	IR£1 = UK£0.98
US$1 = Irish Pounds IR£0.69	IR£1 = US$1.44
CDN$1 = IR£0.53	IR£1 = CDN$1.90
AUS$1 = IR£0.45	IR£1 = AUS$2.21
NZ$1 = IR£0.38	IR£1 = NZ$2.63
S.A.R = IR£0.18	IR£ = S.A.R5.42

A Note on Prices

The information in this book was researched during the summer of 1994. Inflation and the Inivisible Hand may raise the prices we list by 10%. In the chapters on England, Wales, Scotland, and northern Ireland, the symbol £ denotes British pounds. In the chapter on the Republic of Ireland, it denotes Irish pounds.

Follow the fluctuation of rates for several weeks before your trip. If the trend is toward a stronger pound, exchange a significant amount of money at the beginning of your trip. It's more expensive to buy foreign currency than domestic—pounds will be less costly in Britain and Ireland than at home. It is essential, however, that you exchange a small amount of money before you get on the plane. Airport exchange rates will swindle you, and you won't want to be stuck in a long line to change money after your long flight. Generally, you should bring enough English or Irish currency (depending on where you will arrive) to last for the first 24-72 hours of a trip (keep in mind that exchanging currency will be difficult over a weekend).

Observe commission rates closely when abroad; check newspapers to get the standard rate. Bank rates are generally preferable to those of travel agencies, tourist offices, restaurants, hotels, and the dubious *bureaux de change*. Avoid changing money at a post office (their rates are the worst of all). Since you lose money with every exchange transaction, convert in large sums (provided the exchange rate is either staying constant or deteriorating), but not more than you will need. Planning a travel budget with a daily allowance is a good idea.

The **pound sterling** (£) is the main unit of currency in **Great Britain.** It is divided into 100 pence (p), issued in standard denominations of 1p, 2p, 5p, 10p, 20p, 50p, and £1 in coin, and £5, £10, £20, and £50 in notes. (Scotland uses a £1 note.) The old 10p coin is no longer legal tender and vending machines will not accept it; the new 10p coin is like a thin nickel. A pound is often called a "quid," as in "ten quid" (not "quids"). Northern Ireland, Scotland, the Isle of Man, and the Channel Islands have their own bank notes, which are identical in value to other British notes and can be used interchangeably with standard currency. However, you may have difficulty using Scottish £1 notes outside Scotland, and Northern Ireland currency is not accepted in the rest of Britain. The monetary unit of **Irish currency** is the Irish pound or "punt". Irish and British currencies are issued in the same denominations, but the the Irish pound buys about 9% less.

Most banks are closed on Saturday, Sunday, and all public holidays. Britain and Ireland enjoy **"bank holidays"** several times a year (see Appendix). Usual weekday hours in Britain are Monday through Friday 9:30am to 3:30pm, though many banks are opening Saturdays. These hours apply in Scotland and Northern Ireland, though some banks close for lunch and some banks in Scotland are open later one evening per week (usually Thursday). Banks in Ireland open Monday through Friday from 10am to 12:30pm and 1:30pm to 3pm, closing later on Wednesday or Thursday.

TRAVELER'S CHECKS

Traveler's checks are the safest way to carry large sums of money. Their value can be reimbursed if they are lost or stolen, and the major brands can be exchanged at virtually every bank in Britain and Ireland, sometimes without a commission. Traveler's checks are also accepted at the great majority of B&Bs, shops, and restaurants, though many smaller establishments, especially in remote towns, only take cash. Along with replacement services, many issuing agencies offer services such as refund hotlines, message replaying, travel insurance, and emergency assistance.

Sign your checks immediately when you purchase them; copy the **serial numbers** down and keep them in a safe place (*not* in your wallet or with the checks). Countersign checks *only* when you are ready to use them and when the store cashier is watching; carry your passport when you plan to use checks. To accelerate the refund process for lost or stolen checks, keep **check receipts** and a **record of which checks you've cashed** separate from the checks themselves. Leave a photocopy of check serial numbers with someone at home as back-up. Always keep a few extra pounds handy in case of theft or loss. Buying checks in small denominations (US$20 checks rather than US$50 ones or higher) is safer and more convenient—otherwise, after a small purchase, you'll still be carrying around a large amount of cash.

Major brands are sold at agencies and banks everywhere. Of these, **American Express** Traveler's Cheques are perhaps the most widely accepted. U.S. Platinum Card members and members of the American Automobile Association (AAA) can buy American Express cheques commission-free. In Britain, though, **Barclays** and **Thomas Cook** checks are just as widely recognized; Barclays may be the best

choice if you are traveling only in Britain and Ireland. If you will be visiting other countries in addition to Britain and Ireland, you should buy your checks in U.S. dollars: few currencies are as easily exchanged worldwide and you will save yourself the cost of repeatedly converting currency. In Britain, sterling travelers checks are easier to cash. (Barclays will cash any sterling check for free, regardless of the issuer). Few establishments will take checks issued in foreign currency without taking a hefty bite for themselves. Contact the following companies for checks:

American Express: Call (800) 221 7282 in the U.S. and Canada, (0800) 521313 in the U.K., (1800) 626000 in Ireland, (008) 251902 in Australia, (0800) 441068 in New Zealand, and (612) 886-0689 in Sydney with questions or to report lost or stolen Cheques. Elsewhere, call U.S. collect (801) 964 6665) or Sydney collect (612) 886 0689. Cheque and cardholders can call the Global Assist Hotline (tel. (202) 783 7474 collect from overseas, (800) 554-2639 in the U.S.) for emergency medical, legal, and financial services and advice. Other services include mail-holding, assistance with lost documents, temporary IDs, and reservation help. Services and offices are described in *The American Express Traveler's Companion* (free for customers; order in advance). Cheques available in nine currencies.

Barclays Bank: Sells Visa traveler's checks. Commision varies by bank (1-3%). **Any brand of Visa Travelers Checks can be reported lost at the general Visa number:** in the U.S. or Canada call (800) 227 6811; in the U.K. call (0171) 937 8091; from eisewhere call New York collect at (212) 858 8500. For Barclays info specifically, call (800) 221 2426 in the U.S. and Canada and (202) 671212 from the U.K. Barclays banks will cash Visa checks for free. Many branches throughout Britain. Checks in four currencies (including US dollars and British pounds).

Citicorp: Sells Visa traveler's checks (currencies include US dollars, Australian dollars, British pounds). For Citicorp information and to report lost checks, call (800) 645 6556 in the U.S. and Canada, (0171) 982 4040 in Britain, or collect from elsewhere (813) 623 1709. Commission varies by bank (1-2%). Check holders automatically enrolled for 45 days in Citicorp's **Travel Assist Hotline** (tel. (800) 523 1199), which provides English-speaking doctor, lawyer, and interpreter referrals along with traveler's check refund assistance. Citicorp's World Courier Service guarantees hand-delivery of traveler's checks anywhere in the world.

Mastercard International: Sells Mastercard Travelers Checks in 11 currencies (including US, British, Canadian, Australian). In the U.S., Canada, or Mexico, call (800) 223 9920 in the U.S., Canada, or Mexico, or collect (609) 987 7300; from overseas call (44) 733 502995. Participating banks show Mastercard logo on windows. Commission varies by bank (1-2%). Thomas Cook may sell at a lower rate.

Thomas Cook: Also sells Mastercard Traveler's Checks. Commissions nonexistent to low (0-2%). In the U.S. call (800) 223 7373 for refunds, (800) 223 4030 for orders. From elsewhere call collect (212) 974 5696.

ELECTRONIC BANKING

Automatic Teller Machines (ATMs), operated by bank or credit cards, are quite prevalent in England and Wales but scarce elsewhere. *Let's Go* lists ATMs only in Scotland, Northern Ireland, the Republic, and when they are rare in England and Wales. Most ATMs are connected to an international money network, either **Cirrus** (tel. (800) 424 7787) or **Plus** (tel. (800) 843 7587). Depending on the system that your bank at home uses, you will probably be able to access your bank account whenever you wish. Cirrus does not operate in Ireland. Withdraw from ATMs with bank cards instead of credit cards to avoid hassle with bills. Cirrus charges $5 to withdraw non-domestically, but ATMs get the wholesale exchange rate, which is 5% better than the rate with bank tellers. Before you go, memorize your **PIN** numerically rather than alphabetically.

For the budget traveler, **credit cards** may be useful only in emergencies. You must get a PIN code from your bank beforehand to use your credit card at ATMs. Note that the British "Barclaycard" and "Access" are equivalent to Visa and Mastercard respectively. You can often reduce conversion fees by charging instead of changing traveler's checks. Additionally, with credit cards such as American Express, Visa,

Believe it or not, you can run out of green in Ireland.

If you run out of money in Ireland, you don't have to run around looking for the pot of gold. With Western Union you can receive money from the States within minutes, in case the situation arises. Plus, it's already converted into pounds.

Just call either our number in Britain, 0 800 833 833*. Ireland, 1 800 395 395*, or the United States, 1 800 325 6000*. Then pick up your money at any Western Union location in these countries.

After all, you can't always rely on the luck of the Irish.

WESTERN UNION | MONEY TRANSFER

The fastest way to send money worldwide.℠

and Mastercard, associated banks will give you an instant **cash advance** in local currency as large as your remaining credit line. Unfortunately, in most cases you will pay mortifying rates of interest. To report a **lost credit card** overseas, call American Express at (0800) 892333 (U.K. only) or (1800) 557321 (Republic of Ireland); Visa at (410) 581 7931; or Mastercard at (314) 275 6690.

American Express has a hefty annual fee (US$55) but offers a number of services to cardholders. AmEx cardholders can cash personal checks at AmEx offices abroad (US$1000-$5000 every seven days). See Travelers Checks for details. **Mastercard** (tel. (800) 999 0454) and **Visa** (tel. (800) 336 8472) credit cards are sold by individual banks, and each bank offers different services in conjunction with the card.

GETTING MONEY FROM HOME

Do your best to avoid having money sent to you on the road; instead, carry a bank card, credit card, or a separate stash of emergency traveler's checks. If someone feeds money into your bank or credit card account back home, you'll be set. In an emergency, **wire money** through **Western Union** (tel. (800) 325 6000 in North America, (0800) 833833 in Europe) or **American Express** (tel. (800) 543 4080 in the U.S., (800) 933 3278 in Canada). Fees correspond to the amount being sent and, for AmEx, the speed (10 minutes, overnight, 3-5 days). Western Union is generally cheaper but may take longer: US$29 to send $250, $40 for $500, $50 for $1000. U.S. Citizens can also have money sent to them abroad in dire emergencies by the **State Department's Citizens' Emergency Center** (tel. (202) 647 5225, after hours (202) 647 4000). The State Department will cable a modest amount of money to consular offices for dispersal. To send money through the State Department, a person can drop it off there or cable money to the department through Western Union.

VAT (VALUE-ADDED TAX)

Both Britain and Ireland charge value-added tax (VAT), a national sales tax on most goods and some services. The British rate is 17.5% on many services (hairdressers, hotels, restaurants, and car rental agencies) and on all goods save books, medicine, and food. In Ireland, VAT ranges from 0% on most food and clothing to 12% in restaurants and 21% on such luxury items as watches, jewelry, and cameras. Prices stated in *Let's Go* include VAT unless otherwise specified. Visitors to the United Kingdom can get a **VAT refund** through the Retail Export Scheme. Ask the shopkeeper from whom you buy your goods for the appropriate form, which customs officials will sign and stamp when you take your purchases through customs in your carry-on baggage. Once home, send the form and a self-addressed, British-stamped envelope to the shopkeeper, who will then send your refund. In order to use this scheme, you must export the goods within three months of purchase.

DISCOUNTS (CONCESSIONS)

Discount rates for students, seniors, and children are frequently grouped together under the catch-all term "concessions." All U.S. and Canadian travelers should consider joining the **The Royal Oak Foundation,** the U.S. affiliate of the **National Trust,** a British charity dedicated to preserving "places of historic interest or natural beauty" in England, Wales, and Northern Ireland. Members receive free entry to over 240 Trust sites in Britain and to over 100 properties in Scotland. Membership may be renewed (US$40 per individual, $65 per household). A handbook with brief descriptions of properties in England, Wales, and Northern Ireland is included with membership. A handbook of the Scottish properties is available at a nominal charge. For details, U.S. citizens and Canadian residents should contact The Royal Oak Foundation, 285 West Broadway, #400, New York, NY 10013-2299 (tel. (800) 913 6565 or (212) 966 6565). All others should contact the National Trust Membership Department, P.O. 39, Bromley, Kent BR1 1NH, England (tel. (0181) 464 1111) well in advance of traveling (memberships are £24 per individual, £44 per household).

The Irish government offers a **National Heritage Card,** which allows free access to the 31 national parks, monuments, and gardens maintained by the Office of Public Works (£10, seniors £7, students and children £4). Purchase it in the Republic at any sight. The card is only worthwhile if you plan to visit more than seven sites.

■ ■ ■ HEALTH

GENERAL ADVICE

The general police and medical **emergency** number for most of Britain and Ireland is **999,** a free call from any phone. This number may not work in some rural areas, however; if another emergency number is used, we list it in that town or region's Practical Information section. Late-night pharmacies are scarce, even in larger cities. In the case of an accident, your **passport** should list the names, phone numbers, and addresses of anyone to contact, any allergies or pre-existing medical conditions you would want doctors to be aware of, and any insurance information. If you wear **glasses or contact lenses,** take an extra pair and know your prescription. If you wear contacts, take glasses in case you lose or tear a lens, and bring extra solution, as it can be pricey abroad. Always bring any regular **medication** you may need while traveling and a copy of the prescription, especially if you will be bringing insulin, syringes, or narcotics. It is always a good idea to see a doctor before traveling, especially if you will be abroad for more than a month or two, if you will be hiking or camping a good deal, or if you have any serious preexisting conditions.

Let's Go should not be your only guide to common health problems while traveling, hiking, or camping. Call or write for the *First-Aid and Safety Handbook* ($14.95), **American Red Cross,** 61 Medford St., Somerville, MA 02143 (tel. (617) 623 0033). In the United States, the Red Cross also offers many well-taught and inexpensive first-aid and CPR courses; consider taking one before you go.

Eat well, drink lots of **fluids,** get enough sleep, and don't overexert yourself on the road—in other words, listen to your body. Your may feel fatigue and discomfort not because of any specific illness but simply because your body is adapting to a new climate, food, water quality, or pace when you arrive. If symptoms persist or worsen, of course, they may be signs of a serious disease. You'll need plenty of protein and carbohydrates, so bring quick-energy foods along with you as you travel. Take care of your **feet:** bring moleskin for blisters (the U.S. brand 2nd Skin is most effective), wear comfortable shoes with an arch, and change your socks often.

For minor health problems, a compact **first-aid kit** should suffice. The following items are advisable (the italicized ones are more necessary): *bandages, a painkiller (aspirin, acetomenophin, or ibuprofen), antiseptic soap or antibiotic cream, a thermometer with a sturdy case, a Swiss Army knife with tweezers, moleskin,* a decongestant, motion sickness remedy, medicine for diarrhea or stomach problems, *sunscreen, insect repellent,* burn ointment.

EVERYTHING YOU WERE AFRAID TO ASK

Reliable **contraception** is available in most areas, though you may need to ask by name at pharmacies. Women on the Pill should bring enough to allow for possible loss or extended stays, and should bring a copy of the prescription, since forms vary. If you use a diaphragm, be sure that you have enough contraceptive jelly on hand. Availability and quality of **condoms** vary, so bring them along.

Abortion is legal in England, Scotland, and Wales but illegal in Northern Ireland and the Republic (though women can now travel from Ireland to Britain expressly to obtain an abortion). The **U.K. Family Planning Association** can provide you with information on contraception and abortion in Britain; write to 27-35 Mortimer St., London W1N 7RJ (tel. (0171) 580 9360, fax (0171) 436 3288). You can also call the United States' **National Abortion Federation hotline** (tel. (800) 772 9100; Mon.-Fri. 9:30am-5:30pm). Alternatively, you can contact your embassy to receive a list of doctors who perform abortions.

All travelers must be concerned about **sexually transmitted diseases (STDs),** especially **HIV,** the virus that leads to **AIDS** (Acquired Immune Deficiency Syndrome). If you are HIV positive, rest assured that neither Britain nor Ireland prohibit HIV positive individuals from entering the country. To protect yourself from HIV infection and other STDs, **use a latex condom lubricated with spermicide (nonoxynol-9)** during vaginal and anal sex, and an unlubricated one for oral sex on a man or a woman (a condom can be cut into a square or saran wrap can be used as a **dental dam** on a woman or during oral-anal contact). Never use lambskin condoms and use only water-based lubricants such as K-Y jelly or Aqualube. Also **never share needles, syringes, or any drug works** and do not share tattooing or piercing equipment. If you have any questions about HIV and AIDS and keeping yourself safe, you can call the U.S. **Centers for Disease Control (CDC)'s** main **AIDS hotline** number (English tel. (800) 342 2437, 7 days, 24-hrs.; TTD (800) 243-7889, Mon.-Fri. 10 am-10 pm; or Spanish tel. (800) 344 7432; 7 days, 8am-2am).

CONCERNS SPECIFIC TO WOMEN

Women travelers may be vulnerable to **urinary tract and bladder infections,** common and uncomfortable bacterial diseases which cause a burning sensation and painful, sometimes frequent, urination. Drink lots of vitamin-C-rich juice, plenty of water, and urinate often—especially right after intercourse. If untreated, these problems can lead to kidney infections, which can lead to sterility and death. If symptoms persist, see a doctor. If you often develop **vaginal yeast infections,** take medicine along with you; treatments may not be available elsewhere.

OTHER RESOURCES

Travelers with conditions that cannot be easily recognized (diabetes, epilepsy, heart conditions, allergies to antibiotics, etc.) may want to join the **Medic Alert Foundation,** P.O. Box 1009, Turlock, CA, 95381-1009. Call the 24-hour hotline at (800) 432 5378. Membership provides the Medic Alert Identification Tag, an annually-updated wallet card, and hotline access. The cost of membership begins at US $35 for the tag's stainless steel model. The **American Diabetes Association,** 1660 Duke St., Alexandria, VA 22314 (tel. (800) 232 3472) provides copies of the article *Travel and Diabetes* and diabetic ID cards, which carry messages in 18 languages explaining the carrier's status. In the U.S., contact your local ADA office for details. Or contact **Diabetic Travel Services, Inc.,** which provides worldwide information on diabetic treatment and physicians (39 East 52nd St., New York, NY 10022).

■■■ HIKING & CAMPING

SAFETY

The first thing to preserve in the wilderness is you—**health, safety, and food** should be your primary concerns when you camp. A guide to outdoor survival is *How to Stay Alive in the Woods,* by Bradford Angier (Macmillan, $8). Regardless of the weather when you set out, be prepared for the worst—warm, sunny days in this area of the world can turn to sleeting rain faster than you can say "aaagghhh!"; Gore-Tex or waterproof nylon and wool are musts. Always bring a compass (and know how to use it), sturdy shoes, a first-aid kit, a flashlight, and, for long distance hikers, a whistle. *Never go camping or hiking by yourself for any significant time or distance.* If you're going into an area that is not well-traveled or well-marked, let a ragner or hostel warden know where and how long you're hiking in case you fail to return on schedule or need to be reached. The distress signal is six blasts on a whistle (or anything loud) repeated at regular intervals (reply is three long blasts)..

Be careful about the water you drink outdoors: **do not drink directly from a stream, lake, or river.** Parasites (notably **giardia**) and in some cases pollutants make water unsafe. Many backpackers and campers not scrupulous about their water get infections that can stay with them for years. Symptoms of parasitic infections include swollen glands or lymph nodes, fever, rashes or itchiness, digestive problems, eye problems, and anemia. The most reliable source of water on the trail is

HIKING AND CAMPING

water you boil (it does no good to simply heat it) for at least five minutes. You can make it taste better by adding a little salt or pouring it into another container. Second most reliable, and less tasty, is water that you treat with **iodine** or other chemicals such as Potable-Aqua. Water purifiers can also be useful, but are expensive and not guaranteed for all bacteria and parasites. If you are camping or hiking *anywhere*, bring plenty of water with you or boil or purify the outside water you drink or brush your teeth with.

If the weather's good or if you are at high latitudes such as in Scotland (where the ozone layer is thinner) you may need to be careful about **sunburn.** If you burn easily, carry sunscreen with you (it's often more expensive abroad) and apply it liberally and often. **Extreme cold** is a far greater danger than heat in Britain and Ireland, especially for hikers. **Hypothermia** can occur even in July, especially in rainy or windy conditions or at night. The signs are easy to detect: body temperature drops rapidly; you may shiver, have poor coordination, feel exhausted, or have slurred speech, sleepiness, hallucinations, or amnesia. Do not let hypothermia victims fall asleep— they may lose consciousness and die; seek immediate medical help. To prevent hypothermia, keep as dry as possible and stay out of the wind, which carries heat away from the body. Wear wool, especially in wet weather—it retains heat even when soggy. Polypropylene dries quickly when wet and allows you to stay warm. Nearly all other fabrics make you colder when wet; if you have hypothermia, remove wet non-wool or non-polypropylene clothing (especially cotton). Dress in layers, and remember that most loss of body heat is through your head—always carry a wool hat. In freezing temperatures, **frostbite** may occur. The affected skin will turn white, then waxy and cold. The victim should drink warm beverages, stay or get dry, and gently and slowly warm the frostbitten area in dry fabric or with steady body contact. *Never* rub frostbite. Take serious cases to a doctor ASAP.

Lyme disease is a bacterial infection caused by the bite of certain small, infected ticks, and is characterized by a angry red circular band on the skin that is lighter in the center. Along with the rash often come flu-like symptoms of fever, headache, fatigue, or aches and pains. If untreated, Lyme disease can lead to heart, joint, and nervous system problems and even death. There is no vaccine, but Lyme can be treated effectively with antibiotics if caught early on. Ask rangers whether the areas you will be in contain ticks, and if they do, be careful to **prevent tick and other insect bites:** while hiking, periodically stop and check to brush ticks off. If you find a tick attached to your skin, grasp the tick's head parts with tweezers as close to your skin as possible and apply slow, steady traction. Do not attempt to get ticks out of your skin by burning them or coating them with nail polish remover or petroleum jelly. Wear long pants that tuck into socks, long sleeves (fabric need not be thick or warm), and shoes, and avoid sleeping without a tent or bednet in forested areas. Use **insect repellents**—but sparingly and not near mucous membranes. Repellents containing DEET are effective but can be harmful. Taking garlic pills and vitamin B-12 may also keep bugs away.

CAMPING

The second thing to protect while you are outdoors is the **wilderness.** The thousands of outdoor enthusiasts that pour into parks every year threaten to trample the land to death. Because firewood is scarce in popular parks, campers are asked to make small fires using only dead branches or brush; using a **campstove** is the more cautious way to cook. Check to see if the park prohibits campfires. To avoid digging a rain trench for your tent, pitch it on high, dry ground. Don't cut vegetation and don't clear campsites. If there are no toilet facilities, bury human waste at least four inches deep and 100 feet or more from any water supplies and campsites. Never bury tampons or pads; instead, seal them in plastic bags and carry them out. *Biosafe* soap or detergents may be used in streams or lakes. Otherwise, don't use soaps in or near bodies of water. Always pack up your trash in a plastic bag and carry it with you until you reach the next trash can; burning and burying pollute the environment. Remember, if you **carry it in, carry it out.**

Britain has over 2500 campsites, more than most countries on the Continent. Most campsites are open from April through October, though some stay open year-round. While a few youth hostels have camping facilities (the charge is usually half the hostel charge; hostel card required), most campsites are privately owned and designed for people with caravans rather than tent-dwellers. You can legally set up camp only in specifically marked areas unless you get permission from the owner on whose land you plan to squat. It is legal to cross private land by **public rights of way;** any other use of private land without permission is considered trespassing. For more information about camping in Britain, send for the British Tourist Authority's free brochure *Caravan and Camping Parks* (see Useful Addresses above). Camping in State Forests and National Parks is not allowed in **Ireland,** nor is camping on public land if there is an official campsite in the area. Caravan and camping parks provide all the accoutrements of bourgeois civilization: toilets, running water, showers, garbage cans, sometimes shops, kitchen and laundry facilities, restaurants, and game rooms. In addition, many have several caravans for hire at the site. The price varies wildly and is sometimes free. **Show respect** for the domestic and wild animal population. Be particularly careful not to contaminate livestock water supplies and close every gate you open so animals can't wander through. Also respect fellow campers. Keep light and noise to a minimum, particularly if you arrive after dark.

PUBLICATIONS

Automobile Association, Norfolk House, Basingstoke, Hampshire RG24 9NY ENGLAND (tel. (01256) 20123, fax (01256) 492440) publishes *Camping and Caravanning in Europe* (£7.99).

The Mountaineers Books, 1011 Klickitat Way, Suite 107, Seattle, WA 98134 (tel. (800) 553 4453 or (206) 223 6303, fax (206) 223 6306). Bountiful information on hiking (the *100 Hikes* series), backpacking, climbing, biking, natural history, and environmental conservation all over the world.

Sierra Club Bookstore, 730 Polk St., San Francisco, CA 94109, (tel. (415) 923 5500). Books include *Wild Britain* ($16). Ask for their *Annual Outing Catalog* (US$2). Shipping is $3 for orders up to $20, $5 for orders up to $40, and $7 for any amount over $40.

Wilderness Press, 2440 Bancroft Way, Berkeley, CA 94704-1676, (tel. (800) 443 7227 or (510) 843 8080, fax (510) 548 1355), publishes *Backpacking Basics* ($11), *Backpacker's Sourcebook,* and *Backpacking with Babies and Small Children* ($11), among other guides.

EQUIPMENT

Prospective campers will need to invest money in good camping equipment and energy carrying it on their shoulders. Spend time skimming catalogues and a questioning salespeople before buying anything. Use mail-order firms to gauge prices; order from them if you can't do as well locally. In the fall, last year's merchandise may be reduced as much as 50%. Purchase your equipment before you leave. See Packing for a detailed assement of backpack options. Most of the better **sleeping bags**—down (lightweight and warm) or synthetic (cheaper, heavier, more durable, lower maintenance, and warmer when wet)—have ratings for specific minimum temperatures. Sleeping bags are rated according to the lowest outdoor temperature at which they'll keep you warm. If a bag's rating is a seasonal description, keep in mind that "summer" translates to a rating of 30-40°F, "three-season" means 20°F, and "winter" means below 0°F. The lowest prices for good sleeping bags are $65-80 for a summer synthetic, $135-180 for a three-season synthetic, $170-225 for a three-season down bag, and upwards of $270-550 for a down sleeping bag you can use in the winter. **Sleeping bag pads** range from US$15-30, while **air mattresses** go for about US$25-50. The best pad is the Thermarest (US$50-90), which is light, comfy, and self-inflating. Watch out for big, bulky air mattresses—a pain if you're planning on doing much hiking.

When you select a **tent,** your major considerations should be shape and size. The best tents are free-standing with their own frames and suspension systems. They set

up quickly and require no staking (though staking will keep your tent from blowing away). Low profile dome tents are the best all-around. When they are pitched, their internal space is almost entirely usable; this means little unnecessary bulk. Be sure your tent has a rain fly. Good two-person tents start at about $135; $200 fetches a four-person. You can, however, often find last year's version for half the price. Back-packers and cyclists prefer especially small, lightweight models (US$145 and up). **Sierra Design,** 2039 4th St., Berkeley, CA 94710, sells excellent tents, including the 2-person "Clip Flashlight" model (US$160) that weighs less than 1.76 kg (4 lbs.).

Other camping basics include a battery-operated **lantern** (*never* gas) and a simple plastic **groundcloth** to protect the tent floor. When camping in autumn, winter, or spring, bring along a "space blanket," a technological wonder that helps you retain your body heat (US$3.50-13; doubles as a groundcloth). Large, collapsible **water sacks** will significantly improve your lot in primitive campgrounds and weigh prac-tically nothing when empty, though they can get bulky. **Campstoves** come in all sizes, weights, and fuel types, but none are truly cheap (US$30-85). Consider GAZ-powered stoves (a brand name), which come with bottled propane gas that is easy to use and widely available in Europe. Beware: stove gas can be heavy and bulky if you bring too much. A waterbottle (canteens don't pack well), Ace bandage, Swiss army knife, insect repellent, and waterproof matches are other essential items.

REI, P.O. Box 1700, Sumner, WA 98352-0001 (tel. (800) 426 4840). Stores all over the U.S. (grandmother store in Seattle). Stocks a wide range of the latest in camp-ing gear and holds great seasonal sales. An absolutely huge selection; many things are guaranteed for life (not including normal wear and tear). Very knowledgable staff, all of whom have outdoors experience.

Campmoor, PO Box 700, Saddle River, NJ 075458-0700 (tel. (800) 526 4784, fax (201) 447 5559). Monstrous selection of equipment at low prices for a variety of backpacking and travel needs. One-year guarantee for unused or defective goods.

Eastern Mountain Sports, One Vose Farm Rd., Peterborough, NH 03458 (tel. (603) 924 7231) has stores from Colorado to Virginia to Maine. Though pricey, they provide excellent service and guaranteed customer satisfaction (a full refund if you're unhappy) on all items sold.

L.L. Bean, Casco St., Freeport, ME 04033 (tel. (800) 878 2104, outside U.S. and Canada (207) 865 3111, fax (207) 878 2104). Overpriced goods for preppies, but some good stuff. Camping equipment is better priced. Freeport store is open every minute of the year. Complete mail order service; 100% guarantee.

Sierra Design, 2039 4th St., Berkeley, CA 94710 (tel. (510) 843 0923) has a wide array (all seasons and types) of especially small and lightweight tent models including the 2-person "Clip Flashlight" model (US$160) which weighs less than 1.76 kg (4 lbs.) You can often find last year's version for half the price.

■■■ INSURANCE

Beware of unnecessary coverage—your current policies might well extend to many travel-related accidents. Medical insurance policies, especially those from universi-ties, often cover costs incurred abroad, though Medicare's coverage is not valid most places. Canadians are protected by their home province's health insurance plan up to 90 days after leaving the country. Australians are covered by Medicare in Britain; consult Medicare's *Health Care for Australians Travelling Overseas* or write to the Commonwealth Dept. of Health, Housing and Community Services, GPO Box 9848, Canberra.

ISIC and ITICs provide US$3000 worth of accident and illness insurance, $100 per day up to 60 days of hospitalization, and up to $10,000 coverage for emergency medical evaluation; they also give you access to a toll-free Traveler's Assistance hot-line whose staff can provide help in medical, legal, and financial emergencies over-seas. In the United States, call (800) 626 2427; from abroad call collect (713) 267 2525. **CIEE** offers an inexpensive Trip-Safe plan, with options covering medical treatment and hospitalization, accidents, baggage loss, and even charter flights

INSURANCE

missed due to illness. If you are ineligible for the ISIC or ITIC, Trip-Safe extends coverage of the insurance you have. **STA** offers a more expensive and comprehensive plan; **American Express** cardholders receive car-rental and flight insurance on card purchases (see Useful Addresses and Money). Other perks in travel insurance packages are often not worth the expense. Referral to physicians and lawyers can be obtained through a consulate; a major credit card will get you cash in case of theft.

Insurance companies usually require a copy of the police report for thefts or evidence of having paid medical expenses (doctor's statements, receipts), and may have time limits on filing. Homeowners should list the goods they take on their policy before they leave; otherwise coverage for theft or damage may be denied. Always carry your policy numbers and proof of insurance. Note that some of the plans listed below offer cash advances or guaranteed bills. If your coverage does not include on-the-spot payments or cash transferrals, leave space in your budget for emergencies. If you have less than perfect faith in your travel plans, consider **trip cancellation or interruption insurance,** which protects you in case your airline or tour operator leaves you stranded at the final hour. Check the yellow pages and newspapers, and consult your travel agent. Expect to pay US $2-5 per US $100 coverage for cancellation and interruption insurance.

The following firms offer insurance against theft, loss of luggage, injury, or other emergency: **Access America** (tel. (800) 294 8300); **ARM Coverage, Inc./Carefree Travel Insurance**(tel. (800) 323 3149); **GlobalCare Travel Insurance** (tel. (800) 821 2488); **Travel Guard International** (tel. (800) 826 1300). If you have no medical insurance, or if your policy does not extend overseas, **Travel Assistance International,** by Worldwide Assistance Services, Inc., 1133 15th St. NW, Ste. 400, Washington, DC 20005-2710 (tel. (800) 821 2828), provides on-the-spot medical coverage (US$15,000-$90,000) and unlimited medical evacuation insurance, 24-hr. emergency assistance hotline, and a worldwide local presence. Trip cancellation/interruption, baggage and accidental death and dismemberment are also offered.

■■■ PACKING

Pack lightly. That backpack or suitcase may be light as a feather when you buy it or take it out of the closet, even manageable all the way to the airport, but overseas it will turn into a itchy, monstrous beast. To paraphrase Emerson, "Though we travel the world over to find the beautiful, we must carry it with us whether we find it or not." Before you leave, pack your bag (one only!) and take it for a half-hour walk. If the walk feels like a trudge, unpack several things. A good rule is to pack only what you absolutely need, then get rid of half the clothes and bring more money. Remember that you can find virtually all the supplies you might need in Britain and Ireland.

A **backpack** is ideal if you plan to cover a lot of ground, hike, or camp; get one with several external compartments. **Frame backpacks** (US$125-300) are far more spacious than others. **Internal-frame** packs mold to your back, keep a low center of gravity, and have enough flexibility to follow you through your contortions. They are also more manageable and less easily mangled. **Conversion packs** are internal-frame backpacks which transform into suitcases. **External-frame** packs don't travel as well; bring an empty duffel to protect yours in baggage compartments. Make sure your belt has a strong, padded hip belt, which transfers weight to your legs. Any serious backpacking requires at least 54,000 cubic cm of space and longer trips demand around 65,400 cubic cm. Buy a pack with one large pocket and use stuff sacks to separate your gear. Make sure to test-walk for comfort. **Suitcases** and **duffels** are best suited for people who plan to stay only in cities and large towns. They're the worst for schlepping from city to city. Packing a smaller **daypack** inside your pack or in addition to your suitcase allows you to leave your big bag in the hostel while you see town. Get one with secure zippers and closures.

If you stay in **hostels,** you'll want a **sleepsack,** which is a sheet sewed up like a sleeping bag. Sleepsacks may be available for the night in some hostels, at least in England, Wales, and Scotland, but linen hire can be expensive and gross. Sleeping bags are not allowed for use in hostels except in some unheated simple hostels in England and Wales during winter months. Pillows and blankets are provided.

Guard your money, passport, railpass, and other important articles in a **moneybelt** or **neck pouch** and keep it with you at all times. Be especially cautious about theft while on trains or buses; pickpockets will steal from you in your sleep. The best mix of convenience and invulnerability is the nylon, zippered pouch with belt that should sit *inside* the waist of your pants or skirt. Moneybelts are available at any good camping store. Don't use a fanny pack; it's a ridiculously visible invitation to thieves, and may offend Brits, who regard fannies in a different light altogether. *Never* store all your valuables or important documents in one place.

Bringing a **camera,** while sacred to most tourists, can invite a lot of extra worry. Between the stressful temptation to jam every notable event down your lens, the high cost of film, equipment, and developing, and the ever-present paranoia about loss or theft, you could end up chucking your Nikon in the North Sea. If you're having trouble deciding whether to take or leave your camera, try carrying it with you everywhere you go at home for a week. Like it? Take it—you'll be happy. If you're undecided, a less cumbersome option is a disposable camera, available at most supermarkets and drug stores. These glorified pieces of film let you take 24-36 pictures and then throw away the camera, which is really a paper box. **Camera film** is on the whole quite expensive in Britain and Ireland, so you'll probably be better off buying your rolls at home. Airport x-rays generally don't harm film below 1000 ASA; if you're worried, buy a protective film pouch at a camera store. Impatient sorts in Britain for more than a few weeks can take advantage of the **post office's** developing service: major branches will process your rolls for a competitive price (£2 for 24 prints) and then send them to another branch for free. Visit a post office for details.

Britain and Ireland are notorious for rain. Shoot for something that will cover you *and* your pack at a moment's notice. A compact umbrella plus a longish **waterproof** (perhaps Gore-Tex) jacket plus a backpack rain cover will do nicely, though at a cost. A rain poncho can be unmanageable and will provide less wind protection than a good jacket, but is also lighter and cheaper. Temperatures in the Isles are by and large moderate—rarely above the 60s and 70s (in °F) in the summer, rarely below the 30s and 40s in winter. In the northernmost reaches of Scotland, however, wintery temperatures (sometimes near 0°F) and wind prevail even in summer.

Avoid wearing shorts, short skirts or dresses, jeans, or other very casual clothing in churches. Some regions—most notably northern Scotland—are more conservative than others, but for the most part you should not have to worry much about your **attire.** When packing, keep in mind that laundry services are quite accessible; take fewer clothes and wash them more often. Comfortable **shoes** are a must. A double pair of socks—light absorbent cotton inside and thick wool outside—will cushion feet, keep them dry, and help prevent blisters. Bring a pair of light flip-flops for protection against the fungal floors of some station and hostel showers.

In most European countries, **electricity** is 220 volts AC, enough to fry a 110V North American appliance. Visit a hardware store for an **adapter** (which changes the shape of the plug) and a **converter** (changes the voltage). Don't make the mistake of using only an adapter—you'll melt your radio. Travellers who heat-disinfect their contact lenses should consider switching to a chemical disinfection system.

The following is a **checklist** of items you may need: pocketknife, tweezers, small flashlight, needle and thread, string, safety pins, rubber bands (to roll clothes), waterproof matches, a sturdy plastic water bottle, electrical tape (to repair tears), a travel alarm clock, earplugs, a cold-water soap (Dr. Bronner's Castile Soap, available in camping stores, claims to work as everything from detergent to toothpaste), clothespins and line, towel or chamois (super-absorbant tiny towel), moleskin (for blisters), bags that seal shut (for damp clothing, soaps, or messy foods), a squash ball (to use as a sink plug), and a padlock.

■■■ SAFETY & SECURITY

Surprise, surprise—naive, hapless tourists are particularly vulnerable to crime. You must try to be less trusting than normal and more alert about your belongings, surroundings, and companions. Some reasonable precautions and a general degree of street smarts will ward off most bad fortune; sleepless vigilance and twitching paranoia accomplish little. Britain and Ireland are safer for the traveler than many other European countries; still, exercise caution, particularly in the larger cities.

Muggings are usually impromptu, not planned, so walking with nervous, over-the-shoulder glances can be a tip that you have something valuable to protect. Keep all valuables on your person, preferably stowed away in a **money belt** or necklace pouch, which hide your money from prying eyes. In some cities, such as Dublin, watch out for bands of gypsy children who may distract you and pinch your belongings. A firm shout should make them think twice. If you do feel nervous, walking purposefully into a cafe or shop and checking your map there is better than doing so on a street corner. **Stay near busy and well-lit areas,** and do not attempt to cross through parks, parking lots, or any other large, deserted areas, especially after dark.

Don't put money in a wallet in your back pocket. Women should sling **purses** over the shoulder and under the opposite arm. Carry all your treasured items (including your passport, railpass, traveler's checks, and airline ticket) either in a **money belt** or **neck pouch** stashed securely inside your clothing. Never count your money in public and carry as little as possible. Also, be alert in public telephone booths. If you must say your calling-card number, do so very quietly; if you punch it in, make sure no one can look over your shoulder.

Try to **keep your valuables on your person.** Consider this an ironclad rule in the dorm-style rooms of some hostels. Even a trip to the shower can cost you a wallet or a camera. At night, you may want to sleep with your worldly goods under your pillow, and put the straps of your bag around the leg of your bed. Lockers at bus and train stations are safe. You may need to bring your own padlock. Label all your belongings with your name, address, and home phone number, and keep a record of all serial numbers on valuables. **Making photocopies of important documents** (passport, ID, driver's license, health-insurance policy, traveler's checks, credit cards) will allow you to replace them in case they are lost or stolen. Leave another copy at home. Safes are fine in higher-quality hotels of international repute, but in guest houses, beware of leaving your prized possessions with the owner.

You may be interested in taking a self-defense class. **Model Mugging,** a national organization with offices in several major cities, teaches a very effective, comprehensive course on self-defense (course prices vary from US $400-500). Women's and men's courses are offered. Call Model Mugging in the U.S. at (617) 232 7900) on the east coast, (312) 338 4545 in the midwest, or (415) 592 7300) on the west coast. **Community colleges** frequently offer self-defense courses more cheaply. For an official **Department of State Travel Advisory** on Ireland or the United Kingdom, call the 24-hour hotline at (202) 647 5225. "Security" in Northern Ireland includes knowing how not to run afoul of the Army and how to avoid certain areas; that's covered in Northern Ireland: Safety.

DRUGS

Every year, hundreds of travelers are arrested in foreign countries for illegal possession of drugs. If you are caught with any quantity of illegal or controlled drugs in Britain or Ireland, one of two things may happen: you may be arrested and tried under British or Irish law; or you may be immediately expelled from the country. Your home government is powerless to shield you from the judicial system of a foreign country. If you are imprisoned, consular officers can visit you, provide you with a list of local attorneys, and inform your family and friends, but that's it. The London-based organization **Release** (tel. (0171) 729 9904) advises people who have been arrested on drug charges; that's about all they can do.

■■■ ALTERNATIVES TO TOURISM

WORK

There is no better way to submerge yourself in a foreign culture than to become part of its economy. It's very easy to find a temporary job abroad; the bad news is that it will rarely be glamorous and may not even pay for your plane ticket over.

Officially, you can hold a job in European countries only with a work permit, applied for by your prospective employer (or by you, with supporting papers from the employer). Many countries are tight-fisted with work permits; often, an employer must demonstrate that a potential employee has skills that locals lack. The real catch-22 is that normally you must physically enter the country in order to have immigration officials validate your work permit papers and note your status in your passport. This means that if you can't set up a job from afar and have the work permit sent to you, you must enter the country to look for a job, find an employer and have them start the permit process, then *leave* the country until the permit is sent to you (up to six weeks), and finally reenter the country and start work.

In practice, it's rarely so complicated. Friends in Europe can help expedite work permits or arrange informal work-for-lodgings swaps. Many permitless agricultural workers go untroubled by authorities, who recognize the need for seasonal help. European Union citizens can work in any other EU country without papers, and if your parents or grandparents were born in an EU country, you may be able to claim dual citizenship or at least the right to a work permit. Students can also check with their universities' foreign language departments for job openings abroad.

If you are a full-time student at a U.S. or Canadian university, the cleanest, simplest way to get a job abroad is through work permit programs run by CIEE and its member organizations. For a US$125 application fee, CIEE can procure three- to six-month work permits (and a handbook to help you find work and housing) in Britain and other countries. Then you can just hop on the plane, land, and start job-hunting.

The best tips on jobs for foreigners come from other travelers. Hikers who merely asked to sleep in a barn have found work on dairy or sheep farms in Great Britain.

Menial jobs can be found anywhere; ask at pubs, cafés, restaurants, and hotels. (*Be aware* of your rights as an employee; it'll help if you have a written confirmation of your agreement.) Youth hostels frequently provide room and board to travelers willing to stay a while and help run the place. *Au pair* baby-sitting and household jobs abound in Great Britain. Look for newspaper ads and bulletin board notices. CIEE publishes the helpful brochure *Work Abroad* and the book *Work, Study, Travel Abroad: The Whole World Handbook* (US$14.95, postage $1.50), available at Council Charter locations or through CIEE (see Useful Addresses). The following is a list of other helpful publications and organizations:

Addison Wesley publishes *International Jobs: Where They Are, How to Get Them,* by Eric Kocher. Request it from your local bookstore or write to Addison-Wesley, Order Department, Jacob Way, Reading, MA 01867 or call (new phone number) (tel. (800) 358 4566). The new edition costs US$14.95.

Childcare International, Ltd. arranges *au pair* and nanny placements throughout Europe in selected host families. Provides information on qualifications required and helps to arrange work in the country of your choice. The organization prefers a long placement but does arrange summer work. Application fee £60. Write to Childcare International, Ltd., Trafalgar House, Grenville Place, London NW7 3SA (tel. (0181) 959 3611 or (0181) 906 3116, fax (0181) 906 3461).

Peterson's Guides, 202 Carnegie Center, Princeton, NJ 08543 (tel. 800-338-3282 or (609) 243-9111), publishes The *1993 Directory of Summer Jobs in Britain* (US$15.95), which lists 30,000 jobs in Scotland, Wales, and England and *Work Your Way Around the World* (US$17.95), a compendium of information and tips. The *1993 Directory of Overseas Summer Jobs* (US$14.95) is distributed by Peterson's. These books can be requested from a good bookstore or ordered directly from Peterson's (postage $5.75 for the first book and $1 for each additional one).

The Office of Overseas Schools, A-OS, Room 245, SA-29, Department of State, Washington DC 20522 (tel. (703) 875 7800), maintains a list of schools and agencies that arrange teaching positions for Americans.

Vacation Work Publications, 9 Park End St., Oxford, OX1 1HJ, England (tel. (01865) 241978, fax 790885), publishes a number of directories with job listings for summer and year-long employment around the world. Ask for a catalog.

World Trade Academy Press, 50 East 42nd Street, New York, NY 10017 (tel. (212) 697 4999) publishes *Looking for Employment in Foreign Countries* (US$16.50), which lists federal, commercial, and volunteer jobs abroad.

STUDY & EXCHANGE

It's not difficult to spend a summer, a term, or a year studying in Britain or Ireland under the auspices of a well-established program. Enrolling as a full-time student, however, is somewhat more difficult; the requirements for admission can be hard to meet unless you attended a British secondary school, and often only a limited number of foreign students are accepted each year. For initial information on studying in Britain, contact the British Council office in your home country. You might also turn to CIEE's publications *Work, Study, Travel Abroad: The Whole World Handbook* or *Going Places: The High School Student's Guide to Study, Travel, And Adventure,* available at Council Charter or through CIEE (see Useful Addresses). The following organizations and programs will deluge you with information:

The American Institute for Foreign Study organizes academic year, semester, summer, and quarter study abroad. London programs include internships, art and design at the Royal College of Art, a theater program at the London Academy of Music and Dramatic Art, and an MBA program at Richmond College, and are open to interested adults. Minority and merit scholarships. Write to the American Institute for Foreign Study, College Division, 102 Greenwich Avenue, Greenwich CT 06830 (tel. (800) 727 2437). For high school programs, call (800) 888 ACIS.

Association of Commonwealth Universities (ACU), John Foster House, 36 Gordon Square, London WC1H 0PF (tel. (0171) 387 8572). Administers the British Marshalls and publishes information about Commonwealth universities.

Cambridge Summer Program, University of New Hampshire, Hamilton Smith Hall, Durham, NH 03824 (tel. (603) 862 3962, fax (603) 862 3563). UNH sponsors a 6-week program in July and August at Gonville and Caius College, one of the 30 colleges comprising Cambridge University. A distinguished British and American faculty; courses in English, history, and the humanities. Transfer credit for U.S. students. Applicants must have completed first undergraduate year.

Institute of International Education (IIE), 809 United Nations Plaza, New York, NY 10017-3580 (tel. (212) 964 5412, fax (212) 984 5358) publishes *Academic Year Abroad* (US$42.95) and *Vacation Study Abroad* ($36.95), detailing over 3600 programs offered by U.S. colleges and universities.

Institute of Irish Studies, 6 Holyrood Park, Dublin 4, Ireland (tel. (01) 269 2491). On the campus of Trinity College Dublin; offers two-week courses in Irish civilization in June, July, and Aug. which cover Irish history, literature, culture, and politics (£750). Monastic study tour in March, in which students survey the massive monastic heritage of Ireland (£975).

UKCOSA/United Kingdom Council for International Education, 9-17 St. Albans Place, London N1 0NX (tel. (0171) 226 3762, fax (0171) 226 3373). Advises prospective and current students on immigration, finance, and more .

Universities Central Council on Admission, P.O. Box 28, Cheltenham, Glos. GL50 3SA (tel. (01242) 222444). Provides information and handles applications for admission to all fulltime undergraduate courses in universities and their affiliated colleges in the United Kingdom. Write to them for an application and the extremely informative *How to Apply for Admission to a University* handbook.

University College Dublin, Newman House, 86 St. Stephen's Green, Dublin 2, Ireland (tel. (01) 752004). Offers the **Semester in Irish Studies** every fall semester for college juniors and seniors of all majors with solid academic records. Courses in Irish history, literature, politics, and folk culture. Applications due in April. Its **International Summer School** offers a 2½-week course in July on Irish tradition and contemporary culture for students 18 years and older.

University of Dublin Offers a 1 to 4 year program of high-quality undergraduate courses for non-degree seeking students. Write to International Student Affairs, Art Building, Trinity College, University of Dublin, Dublin 2 (tel. (01) 702 2011).

Youth for Understanding International Exchange (YFU), 3501 Newark St., Washington DC 20016 (tel. 800-TEENAGE or (202) 966 6800, fax (202) 895 1104), places U.S. high school students for summer, semester, or year homestays.

VOLUNTEERING

Volunteer jobs are available almost everywhere and may be your only hope. You may receive room and board for your labor, and the work can be fascinating. The following organizations and publications can help you to explore possibilities. Organizations that arrange placement often charge high application fees in addition to workcamps' charges for room and board. Check listings in Vacation Work's *International Directory of Voluntary Work* (£8.95; see address in Work, above) or in CIEE's *Volunteer! The Comprehensive Guide* (US$13.95, postage $1.50).

The Service Civil International-Voluntary Service (SCI-VS), Route 2, Box 560B, Crozet, VA 22932 (tel. (804) 823 1826), arranges placement in workcamps in Europe and the U.S. Registration fees range from US$40 (U.S.) to US$200.

Volunteers for Peace Inc. (VFP), 43 Tiffany Rd., Belmont, VT 05730 (tel. (802) 259 2759, fax (802) 259 2922, contact Peter Coldwell) has been coordinating workcamps since 1981. VFP publishes the International Workcamp Directory, which is updated every year and can be ordered directly from them for US$10 (deductible from future program fees), and a free newsletter. Placement is quick. Register in spring. Work with 10-15 volunteers from around the world on environmental projects, construction or renovation of buildings or monuments, or painting houses, schools, or murals. Workcamps' fees are $150-$175.

■■■ SPECIAL CONCERNS

WOMEN & TRAVEL

Women exploring any area on their own inevitably face additional safety concerns. It's always best to trust your instincts: if you'd feel better somewhere else, don't hesitate to move on. You may want to consider staying in hostels which offer single rooms with locks on the inside or religious organizations that offer rooms for women only. Stick to centrally-located accommodations and avoid late-night treks or tube rides. Hitching is *never* safe for lone women, or even for two women traveling together. Choose train compartments occupied by other women or couples.

Your best answer to verbal harassment is no answer at all (a reaction is what the harasser wants). Wearing a conspicuous wedding band may help ward off oversexed slimeballs. Don't hesitate to seek out a police officer or a passerby if you are being harassed. Memorize the emergency numbers in Britain and Ireland—it's 999 and free—and carry change for the phone and enough extra money for a bus or taxi. Carry a whistle or an airhorn on your keychain, and don't hesitate to use it in an emergency. These warnings and suggestions shouldn't discourage women from traveling alone. Don't take unnecessary risks, but don't lose your spirit of adventure either. The following are potentially useful publications:

Index/Directory of Women's Media, published by the Women's Institute for the Freedom of the Press, 3306 Ross Place NW, Washington DC 20008 (tel. (202) 966 7793). Lists women's publishers, bookstores, theaters, and news organizations.

A Journey of One's Own, by Thalia Zepatos. Eighth Mountain Press, US$14.95. The latest thing on the market; interesting and full of good advice, plus a specific and manageable bibliography of books and resources.

Women Going Places, a women's travel and resource guide emphasizing women-owned enterprises. Geared towards lesbians, but offers advice appropriate for all women. US$14. Order from Inland Book Company, PO Box 12061, East Haven, CT 0651 (tel. (203) 467-4257) or from a bookstore.

OLDER TRAVELERS AND SENIOR CITIZENS

Proof of senior citizen status is required for many discounts listed, so prepare to get carded. Seniors are eligible for a wide array of discounts on transportation, museums, movies, theater, concerts, restaurants, and accommodations. The terms "concessions," and additionally "OAPs" (old-age pensioners) in Ireland, indicate discounts for seniors. You may want to look for the book *Unbelievably Good Deals and Great Adventures That You Absolutely Can't Get Unless You're Over 50,* by Joan Rattner Hellman (US$7.95).

AARP (American Association of Retired Persons), 601 E St. NW, Washington, DC 20049 (tel. (202) 434 2277). U.S. Residents over 50 and their spouses receive benefits, including the AARP Travel Experience from American Express (tel. (800) 927 0111), the AARP Motoring Plan from Amoco (tel. (800) 334 3300), and discounts on loding, car rental, and sightseeing. Annual fee is US$8 a couple.

Elderhostel, 75 Federal St., 3rd floor, Boston, MA 02110-1941 (tel. (617) 426 8056). You must be 60 or over and may bring a spouse. Programs at colleges and universities in over 47 countries on varied subjects which generally last a week.

Gateway Books, 2023 Clemens Road, Oakland, CA 94602 (tel. (510) 530 0299, fax (510) 530 0497). Publishes *Get Up and Go: A Guide for the Mature Traveler* (US$10.95) and *Adventures Abroad* (US$12.95), which offer general hints for the budget-conscious senior who is considering a long stay or even retiring abroad. For credit card orders in the U.S. call (800) 669 0773.

Pilot Books, 103 Cooper St., Babylon, NY 11702 (tel. (516) 422 2225). *The International Health Guide for Senior Citizens* (US$4.95, postage US$1) and *The Senior Citizens' Guide to Budget Travel in Europe* (US$5.95. postage US$1).

BISEXUAL, GAY, & LESBIAN TRAVELERS

As is true elsewhere, people in rural areas of Britain and Ireland may not be as accepting as those in big cities. (Though some may, like Mom in the short film *Came Out, It Rained, Went Back in Again*, scream with glee "She's gay! Yipeeee! She's gaaaay!") Attitudes will range from friendly to aggressively hostile. Public displays of affection in Ireland and most of Britain will bring you certain verbal harassment. The gay scene will range between regions from low-key (prompting the question "hey, are you *sure* this is a gay pub?") to flashy. Our sections on Brighton, London, Belfast, and Dublin reflect the relatively sizable gay scenes in those places. Sex between consenting men and consenting women is legal in both Britain and the Republic of Ireland. In Britain, the age of consent for hetero sex or sex between women is 16, while the age of consent between men was recently lowered to 18. Get it right, guys! In Ireland, the age of consent between anyone is 17. Below are several resources intended specifically for the BGL traveler:

Are You Two...Together? A Gay and Lesbian Travel Guide to Europe, by Lindsy van Gelder and Pamla Robin Brandt. Random House, available at bookstores (US$18). A funny, very well-written travel guide filled with entertaining anecdotes and handy tips; sections on Brighton and Wales. Includes overviews of regional laws, lists of gay/lesbian organizations in various countries, and country- and city-specific lists of bars, hotels, and restaurants that cater to gays and/or lesbians or are friendly or indifferent.

Ferrari Publications, PO Box 37887, Phoenix, AZ 85069, tel. (602) 863 2408. Publishers of *Ferrari's Places of Interest* (US$16), *Ferrari's Places for Men* (US$15) , *Ferrari's Places for Women* (US$13), and *Inn Places: US and Worldwide Gay Accommodations* (US$14.95). Available in bookstores, or by mail order (postage US$3.50 for the first item, $0.50 for each additonal item).

Gay's the Word, 66 Marchmont St., London WC1N 1AB, England (tel. +44 (0171) 278 7654). A gay and lesbian bookshop. Mail order service available. No catalogue of listings, but they will provide you with a list of titles on a given subject. Open Mon-Fri. 11am-7pm, Sat. 10am-6pm, Sun. and holidays 2-6pm.

Spartacus International Gay Guides, published by Bruno Gmunder, Postfach 301345, D-1000 Berlin 30, Germany (tel +49 (30) 25 49 82 00). Lists hotlines, bars, restaurants, hotels, and bookstores around the world catering to gay men. Available in the US from Giovanni's Room and other bookstores (US$29.95).

TRAVELERS WITH DISABILITIES

Transportation companies in Britain and Ireland are remarkably conscientious about providing facilities and services for travelers with disabilities. Advance booking is strongly recommended; if you notify the bus or coach company of your plans ahead of time, they will have staff ready to assist you and assure room for a wheelchair. **British Rail** offers a **disabled person's railcard,** available at major British Rail stations and travel agencies. If you do not have a railcard and are traveling in your own wheelchair, or are blind and traveling with a companion, you are eligible for the same discounts. Not all stations are accessible; write for the pamphlet *British Rail and Disabled Travellers,* which explains services available. **National Express (coach travel)** offers similar discounts as British Rail. Guide dogs are always conveyed free, but both the U.K. and Ireland impose a six-month quarantine on all animals entering the country and require that the owner obtain an import license (consult a British or Irish Consulate). Ireland is much less wheelchair-accessible than is Britain. Write to the British Tourist Authority or the Bord Fáilte for free handbooks and access guides. Other helpful sources of information are:

Directions Unlimited, 720 North Bedford Rd., Bedford Hills, NY 10507, tel. (800) 533 5343, (914) 241 1700, fax (914) 241 0243. Specializes in arranging individual and group vacations, tours, and cruises for those with physical disabilities.

Facts on File, 460 Park Ave. S., New York, NY 10016, te. (800) 829 0500, (212) 683 2244 in AK and HI. Publishers of *Access to the World* (US$16.95), a guide to accessible accommodations and sights. Available in bookstores or by mail order.

Graphic Language Press, PO Box 270, Cardiff by the Sea, CA 92007, tel. (619) 944 9594. Publishers of *Wheelchair Through Europe* (US$12.95, postage included). Comprehensive advice for the wheelchair-bound traveler, including advice and resources in various European cities–accessible hotels, museums, etc.

Mobility International, USA (MIUSA), PO Box 10767, Eugene, OR 97440, tel. (503) 343 1284 voice and TDD, fax (503) 343 6812; and 228 Borough High St., **London** SE1 1JX, tel. (0171) 403 5688. Information on travel programs, international work camps, lodgings, access guides, and organized tours. Membership US$20/year, newsletter US$10. They sell *A World of Options: A Guide to International Educational Exchange, Community Service, and Travel for Persons with Diabilities* (US$14, nonmembers US$16).

Moss Rehabilitation Hospital Travel Information Service, 1200 W. Tabor Rd., Philadelphia, PA 19141, tel. (215) 456 9603. A telephone information center on international travel accessibility and other travel-related concerns. Will refer callers to other agencies if they cannot provide information.

Society for the Advancement of Travel for the Handicapped, 347 Fifth Ave., Suite 610, New York, NY 10016, tel. (212) 447 7284, fax (212) 725 8253. Publishes quarterly travel newsletter SATH News and information booklets (US$3 for nonmembers), which contain advice on trip planning. Annual membership is US$45, students and seniors US$25.

Twin Peaks Press, PO Box 129, Vancouver , WA 98666-0129, tel. (206) 694 2462, orders only (MC and VISA) (800) 637 2256, fax (206) 696 3210. Publishers of *Travel for the Disabled,* which provides tips and lists of accessible tourist attractions, in addition to providing advice on other resources for disabled travelers (US$19.95). Also publishes *Directory for Travel Agencies of the Disabled* ($19.95), *Wheelchair Vagabond* (US$14.95), and *Directory of Accessible Van Rentals* ($9.95). Postage $2 for first book, $1 for each additional book.

TRAVELERS WITH CHILDREN

Children under two generally fly free on domestic flights and for 10 percent of the adult fare on international flights (this fare does not necessarily include a seat). 2 to 12 usually fly half price. Most sights and many accommodations in Britain and Ireland have reduced fees for children, sometimes listed under the name "concessions." Always have children carry a passport or other ID in case of emergency or if they get lost. You may want to refer to *Sharing Nature with Children* and *Backpacking with Babies and Small Children* (US$10.95) by **Wilderness Press,** 2440 Bancroft Way, Berkeley, CA 94704 (tel. (800) 443 7227). **John Muir Publications,** P.O. Box 613, Santa Fe, NM 87504 (tel. (800) 285 4078) produces *Kidding Around: London* an educational, distracting illustrated book (US$9.95 to 12.95; postage under US$4.25). **Mason-Grant Publications,** P.O. Box 6547, Portsmouth, NH 03802 (tel. (603) 436 1608, fax (603) 427 0015) publishes *Take Your Kids to Europe* by Cynthia W. Harriman (US$13.95), a cartoon-filled budget family guide.

KOSHER & VEGETARIAN TRAVELERS

National tourist offices often publish lists of kosher and vegetarian restaurants. The following organizations can offer advice on how to meet your specific dietary needs while traveling. Vegetarian and wholefoods restaurants and markets are fairly common in Britain, if not in Ireland. **Jewish Chronicle Publications,** 25 Furnival St., London EC4A 1JT England (tel. (0171) 405 9252, fax (0171) 831 5188), publishes *The Jewish Travel Guide,* which lists synagogues, kosher restaurants, and Jewish intsitutions in over 80 countries (US$11.95, postage $1.75); contact Jewish Chronicle Publications or Sepher-Hermon Press, 1265 46th St., Brooklyn, NY 11219 (tel. (718) 972-9010). The **Vegetarian Society of the UK,** Parkdale, Dunham Rd., Altringham, Cheshire WA14 4QG (tel. (0161) 928 0793), publishes the *International Vegetar-*

ian Travel Guide (£3). The **Vegetarian Times** (tel. (800) 435-9610) publishes, in addition to the *Times*, the *European Vegetarian Guide to Restaurants and Hotels*.

■■■ CLIMATE

The weather in Britain and Ireland is subject to frequent changes but few extremes, with an average temperature in the low to mid-60s in the summer and in the low 40s during the winter. Throughout the islands, you should expect unstable weather patterns; a bright and cloudless morning sky is often followed by intermittent drizzle throughout the afternoon. May and June have the best weather; days can be cloudless with temperatures in the 70s, even in the north.

Scotland is generally soggy; you should be prepared with warm, waterproof clothing at all times of year. The northernmost reaches are especially cold, often below freezing even in summer. From early August through September, heather paints the mountains a brilliant purple. Unfortunately, warm weather also brings midges (gnats). Though Ireland gets the most publicity for its wet weather, Wales also suffers through 200 rainy days a year. April is the driest month in Ireland, especially on the east coast near Dublin. May and June are the sunniest months, particularly in the south and southeast, and July and August are the warmest. December and January have the worst weather of the year—wet, cold, and cloudy.

Dublin, Ireland
Jan. max. temp. 8°C, 47°F; min. temp. 1°C, 34°F
July max. temp. 20°C, 68°F; min. temp. 11°C, 52°F
Edinburgh, Scotland
Jan. max. temp. 6°C, 43°F; min. temp. 1°C, 34°F
July max. temp. 18°C, 65°F; min. temp. 11°C, 52°F
London, England
Jan. max. temp. 7°C, 45°F; min. temp. 2°C, 36°F
July max. temp. 22°C, 72°F; min. temp. 13°C, 56°F
Swansea, Wales
Jan. max. temp. 8°C, 47°F; min. temp. 3°C, 36°F
July max. temp. 22°C, 72°F; min. temp. 13°C, 56°F

GETTING THERE

Airfares are complex and sometimes deliberately confusing. Call every toll-free number and ask about discounts. Travel agents might not want to do the legwork to find the cheapest fares (for which they receive the lowest commissions). Have a knowledgeable budget travel agent guide you through the options; better yet, use several. Students and people under 26 should never need to pay full price. Seniors can also get mint deals; many airlines offer senior traveler club deals or airline passes and discounts for companions. Travel sections in Sunday newspapers often list bargain fares from the local airport. Outfox airline reps with the phone-book-sized *Official Airline Guide* (at large libraries); this monthly guide lists every scheduled flight in the world with prices. George Brown's *The Airline Passenger's Guerilla Handbook* (1990) is a more renegade resource.

Most airlines' fare structures peak between mid-June and early September. Midweek (Mon.-Thurs.) flights are 10-20% cheaper than weekend ones. Leaving from a travel hub such as New York, Boston, Atlanta, Dallas, Chicago, Los Angeles, San Francisco, Vancouver, Toronto, Sydney, or Melbourne will win you a more competitive fare, though the gains are not as great when departing from travel hubs monopolized by one airline.

Return-date flexibility is usually not an option for the budget traveler; except on youth fares purchased through the airlines, traveling with an "open return" ticket can be pricier than fixing a return date and paying to change it. Avoid one-way tickets: the flight to Europe may be economical, but the return fares can be outrageous. The commercial airlines' lowest regular offer is the **APEX** (Advance Purchase Excursion Fare); specials advertised in newspapers may be cheaper, but have correspondingly more restrictions and fewer available seats. APEX fares provide you with confirmed reservations and allow "open-jaw" tickets (landing in and returning from different cities). Reservations must usually be made at least 21 days in advance, with 7- to 14-day minimum and 60- to 90-day maximum stays and hefty cancellation and change-of-reservation penalties. For summer travel, book APEX fares early; by May you will have difficulty getting the departure date you want. Whenever flying internationally, pick up your ticket in advance of the departure date and arrive at the airport two to three hours before your flight.

STUDENT TRAVEL AGENCIES

Students and youth fares are rarely available from airlines or travel agents, but instead from student travel agencies like **Council Travel, STA, Travel CUTS, University Travel Network** and **Let's Go Travel** (see Useful Addresses). In 1994, peak season round-trip rates from the east coast of North America to even the off-beat corners of Europe rarely topped US$700, and off-season fares were considerably lower. Return date change fees also tend to be low (around US$50). Most of their flights are on major airlines, though in peak season some seats may be on less reliable chartered aircraft. Student travel agencies can also help non-students and people over 26, but may not be able to get the same low fares.

■■■ FROM NORTH AMERICA

COMMERCIAL AIRLINES

Flying to London is usually the cheapest way across the Atlantic. If you plan to travel through Europe, flying through Amsterdam, Luxembourg, or Brussels can be your cheapest option. In 1994, the high-season, roundtrip fares to London rarely topped US$650, and off-season rates were much lower, often hovering around US$250.

Most airlines no longer offer standby fares, once a staple of budget travel. Standby has given way to the **three-day-advance-purchase youth fare,** a cousin of the one-day variety in Europe. It's available only to those under 25 (sometimes 24) and only within three days of departure—a gamble that often pays off but could backfire if the airline's all booked up. Return dates are open, but you must come back within a year, and once again can book your return seat no more than three days ahead. Youth fares in summer aren't really cheaper than APEX, but off-season prices drop deliciously. **Icelandair** (tel. (800) 223 5500 from the U.S.) is one of the few airlines which offer this 3-day fare. Check with a travel agent for details.

A few airlines offer other discounts. Look into flights to relatively less popular destinations or smaller carriers. Icelandair also offers a "get-up-and-go" fare from New York to Luxembourg (US$299 weekdays, US$329 weekends; Oct.-May US$268 weekdays, US$288 weekends). Reservations can be made no more than three days before departure. After arrival, Icelandair offers discounts on trains and buses from Luxembourg to other parts of Europe. **Virgin Atlantic** (tel. (800) 862 8621 from the U.S.) offers a "Visit Europe" plan in conjunction with British Midland Airways to various cities in Europe. A one-way ticket is US$109. Major British and Irish destinations are Belfast, Dublin, Edinburgh, and London.

CHARTER FLIGHTS AND TICKET CONSOLIDATORS

Ticket consolidators resell, at heavy discounts, commercial and charter airlines' unsold tickets. Look for tiny ads in weekend papers (in the U.S., the Sunday *New York Times* travel section is best) and start calling. Unlike tickets bought through an airline, you won't be able to use these tickets on another flight if you miss yours, and you will have to go back to the consolidator—not the airline—to get a refund.

Phone around and pay with a credit card; you can't stop a cash payment if you never receive tickets. Find out everything you can about an agency and insist on a **receipt** with full details about the tickets, refunds, and restrictions; if they don't want to give you a clear summary or seem clueless, use a different company.

It's best to buy from a major organization that has experience in placing individuals on charter flights. One of the most reputable is the CIEE-affiliated **Council Charter,** 205 E. 42nd St., New York, NY 10017 (tel. (800) 800 8222); their flights can also be booked through Council Travel offices. Another good organization is **Unitravel,** 1177 N. Warson Rd., St. Louis, MO 63132 (tel. (800) 325 2222); they will hold all payments in a bank escrow until completion of your trip. Also try **Interworld Travel,** Douglas Entrance, 800 Douglas Rd. Suite 140, Coral Gables, FL 33134-3138 (tel. (800) 331 4456, in Florida (305) 443 4929); **Rebel,** 25050 Avenue Kearney Suite 215, Valencia, CA 91355 (tel. (800) 227 3235); **Bargain Air,** 655 Deep Valley Dr. #355, Rolling Hills, CA 90274 (tel. (800) 347 2345, (310) 377 6349 in California, fax (310) 877 1824)—don't be afraid to call every number and hunt for the best deal. The **Air Travel Advisory Bureau,** Strauss House 41-45, Goswell Rd. London EC1V7DN, England (tel. (0171) 636 2908), puts travelers in touch with the cheapest carriers out of London. **Brendan Tours,** 15137 Califa St., Van Nuys, CA 91411-3021 (tel. (800) 421 8446, in California (818) 785 9696, fax (818) 902 9876), allows you to buy as little as one day in advance; savings are greatest if you stay for less than 7 or more than 30 days. **AirTech Unlimited,** 584 Broadway Suite 1007, New York, NY 10012 (tel. (212) 219 7000, fax 219 0666), requires you to be flexible about cities and dates; they also offer a courier service for one-week visits.

The theory behind **charter flights** is that a tour operator contracts with an airline (usually a fairly obscure one) to use their planes to fly passengers to peak-season destinations. Charter flights thus fly infrequently, have more restrictions, and may be changed or canceled at the last minute. Shoot for a scheduled air ticket if you can and pay with a credit card. You might also consider traveler's insurance. **Airhitch,** 2641 Broadway, New York, NY 10025 (tel. 212) 864 2000) and 1415 Third St., Santa Monica, CA 90410 (tel. (310) 394 0550) advertises a similar service: you choose a five-day date range in which to travel and a list of preferred destinations. Check all flight times and departure sites only with Airhitch, but read *all* the fine print they send you and compare it to what people tell you. The Better Business Bureau of New York received complaints about Airhitch a few years ago; they still don't recommend them, but they don't discourage you from using them, either.

Last minute **discount clubs** and **fare brokers** offer members savings, including charter flights and tour packages. Research carefully. **Last Minute Travel Club,** 1249 Boylston St., Boston, MA 02215 (tel. (800) 527 8646 or (617) 267 9800) is one of the few travel clubs that does not require a membership fee. Other clubs are **Discount Travel International** (call (800) 555 1212 to find out their new (800) number; it has changed), **Moment's Notice** (tel. (212) 486 0503; US$25 annual fee), and **Traveler's Advantage** (tel. (800) 835 8747; US$49 annual fee). For US$25, **Travel Avenue** will search for the lowest international airfare and then discount it 5-17% (tel. (800) 333 3335.) The often labyrinthine contracts for all these organizations bear close study; you may prefer not to stop over in Luxembourg for 11 hours.

COURIER FLIGHTS

Those who travel light should consider flying to Europe as a courier. The company hiring you will use your checked luggage space for freight; you're left with the carry-on allowance. Watch for restrictions: most flights are round-trip only with fixed-length stays (usually short), you may not be able to travel with a companion, and most flights are from New York or Boston. Round-trip fares to Western Europe from the U.S. range from US$199-349 (during the off-season) to US$399-549 (during the summer). **Now Voyager,** 74 Varick St. #307, New York, NY 10013 (tel. (212) 431 1616), acts as an agent for many courier flights worldwide from New York, although some flights are available from Houston. They also offer special last-minute deals to such cities as London, Paris, Rome and Frankfurt which go for as little as

US$299 round-trip. **Halbart Express,** 147-05 176th St., Jamaica, NY 11434 (tel. (718) 656 8279), **Courier Travel Service,** 530 Central Avenue, Cedarhurst, NY 11516 (tel. (516) 374 2299), and **Able Travel** (tel. (212) 779 8530) are other courier agents to try. If you have travel time to spare, **Ford's Travel Guides,** 19448 Londelius St., Northridge, CA 91324 (tel. (818) 701 7414), lists **freighter companies** that take passengers for trans-Atlantic crossings. Ask for their *Freighter Travel Guide and Waterways of the World* (US$15, $2.50 postage if mailed outside U.S.).

Check your bookstore or library for The *Courier Air Travel Handbook* (US$10.70), which explains courier travel and contains names, telephone numbers, and contact points of courier companies; order it from Thunderbird Press, 5930-10 W. Greenway Rd., Ste. 112, Glendale, AZ 85306, or call (800) 345-0096. Big City Books, P.O. Box 19667, Sacramento, CA 95819, sells *The Air Courier's Handbook*.

■■■ FROM DOWN UNDER

Travelers from Australia or New Zealand are best advised to visit a local branch of one of the specialty organizations listed for North America. **STA Travel** is probably the largest international agency you will find: they have offices in **Melbourne** (tel. (03) 349 2411), 222 Faraday St., VIC 3053 and **Auckland** (tel. (09) 398 9995), 10 High St. STA fares between Sydney and London were AUS$1179 each way in 1994; STA in London may be able to find cheaper fares. **British Airways** (tel. (0181) 564 1449 or 564 1450) and **Qantas** both fly direct from Australia to Britain, but you'll pay for the convenience: in the summer of 1994, the Sydney-London return route was AUS$2699 on B.A. The Irish airline **Aer Lingus** has great deals for travelers from Australia and New Zealand who fly directly to England, providing free shuttle service from London to Dublin. Flying direct is but one (very expensive) way of getting to the British Isles. Any national airline between Australia and Britain can offer somewhat cheaper connecting flights on one part of the route; most travelers reportedly take **Singapore Air** or other Far East-based carriers during the initial leg of their trip.

■■■ FROM CONTINENTAL EUROPE

Eurolines provides extensive, flexible **coach (bus) service** between Britain, Ireland, and Europe; most of the time buses go directly on ferries. Book tickets in Britain at National Express offices or by credit card (tel. (0171) 730 8235 in London, (0121) 622 6226 in Birmingham). Write to Eurolines (UK) Limited, 23 Crawley Road, Luton LU1 1HX, England. **Bus Éireann,** the Irish national bus company, connects coach service to Paris from any city in Ireland, circumventing Britain. Fares are IR£65 single, IR£110 return; call them in Cork (tel. (021) 508188) or try a travel agent.

In May 1994, the **Channel Tunnel (Chunnel)** was completed, connecting England and France (the horror!/*l'horreur!*). **Eurotunnel** is the name of bi-national Franco-British company that built and owns the Chunnel. Eurotunnel's **Le Shuttle** service carries passengers with cars, buses, or campers. Car passenger service should open in October 1994, coach service in March 1995. Also by spring 1995, the limited *Discovery* train service between London and Paris/Brussels through the Chunnel will give way to a full *Eurostar* service with approximately fifteen daily departures to either destination. It has yet to be determined what rail passes (BritRail or Eurail) will be accepted for the journey. Consult Thomas Cook's European timetable or, in the U.K., call (01233) 617575 for information.

As a rule, **air travel** is prohibitively expensive across much of Europe. Look for student fares and holiday charters through budget travel agents and local newspapers and magazines. **STA Travel** and **CIEE** offices are good contacts.

FERRIES

Almost all sailings in June, July, and August are controlled sailings, which means that you must book the crossing ahead (a day in advance). If you're traveling with a car in July or August, reserve through a ferry office or travel agency. Some people ask car drivers to let them travel as one of the four free passengers that a car gets. Arrive an hour in advance, and remember your passport. Ask ahead where to board the ferry, and arrange connections so that you might spare yourself from the misery of sitting by an empty wharf for ten hours because you forgot to book a bus ticket from Pembroke Dock to London. Always ask about reduced fares—flashing an HI card or ISIC with Travelsave stamps might win a 25-50% discount on your fare.

France to England

Calais, France to Dover: Stena Sealink (tel. (01233) 647047 or 240280) and **P&O** (tel. (01233) 203388) both serve Calais (25 and 20/hr., respectively). Stena fares at peak season are: July-Sept. adult single £26; seniors and students £22, children £14; adult return £50, seniors and students £42, children £26. P&O fares are: adult single/5 day return £25, children £15; adult return £50, children £26. **Hovercraft** leave from Dover's Hoverport (tel. 208013; reservations 240241), at the Prince of Wales Pier for Calais or **Boulogne** (35min.). Book a few days in advance (single £26, 3-day return £26, 5-day return £38).

Dunkerque, France to Ramsgate: Sally Ferries, Argyle Centre, York St., Ramsgate (tel. (01843) 595522) sails five times daily year-round. 3½hrs.

Le Havre, France to Portsmouth/Southampton: P&O Ferries (tel. (01705) 827677) floats Francewards two to three times daily year-round. 8hrs.

Northern Europe to England

Routes to England include:

Hook of Holland, Belgium to Harwich: Stena Sealink Line (tel. (01233) 647047) leaves twice daily year-round. Return £35-39.

Oostende, Belgium to Ramsgate (near Dover): Sally Ferries, Argyle Centre, York St., Ramsgate (tel. (01843) 595522). Six per day year-round. 6hrs.

Zeebrugge, Belgium to Felixstowe: P. & O. Ferries (tel. (01304) 203388) leaves one to two times daily year-round. 6½hrs. Return £48, seniors £40, children £25.

Esbjerg, Denmark to Newcastle: Scandanavian Seaways (tel. (01255) 240240) leaves twice weekly from Easter-Oct. 20hrs.

Esbjerg, Denmark to Harwich: Scandanavian Seaways (tel. (01255) 240240) leaves three times per week year-round. 21hrs.

Hamburg, Germany to Newcastle: Scandanavian Seaways (tel. (01255) 240240) leaves twice weekly from Easter-Oct. 24½hrs.

Hamburg, Germany to Harwich: Scandanavian Seaways (tel. (01255) 240240) leaves three times per week year-round. 20 hrs.

Bergen, Norway to Newcastle: Color Line (tel. (01255) 240240) leaves two to three times per week year-round. Single £43-93. 25hrs.

Göteborg, Sweden to Newcastle: Scandanavian Seaways (tel. (01255) 240240) leaves weekly from June 10 to September 9. 22hrs.

Göteborg, Sweden to Harwich: Scandanavian Seaways (tel. (01255) 240240) leaves one to two times per week year-round. 23hrs.

France to Ireland

Ferries also run **between Ireland and the rest of Europe.** The main companies are **Brittany Ferries,** Tourist House, 42 Grand Parade, Cork (tel. 277801); and **Irish Ferries** at 2-4 Merrion Row, Dublin 2 (tel. (01) 661 0511, fax (01) 661 610743); and at Rosslare Harbor (tel. (053) 33158). **Eurail Passes** grant passage but not a berth between Rosslare and Cherbourg/Le Havre.

Roscoff to Cork: Brittany Ferries crosses Mar.-Sept. 2/week; 14hrs.

St. Malo to Cork: Brittany Ferries crosses May-Sept. 1/week; 18hrs.

Le Havre to Rosslare: Irish Ferries crosses 1-3/week; 21hrs.

Cherbourg to Rosslare: Irish Ferries crosses 1-4/month; 17hrs.

■■■ BETWEEN THE ISLES

BUSES AND PLANES

Supabus bus/ferry rates start at IR£30 for a return fare from Dublin to London. Bus tickets that include ferry connections between Britain and Ireland are available as package deals through ferry companies, travel agents, and USIT offices. Arrival and departure times are inconvenient, however. Supabus connects in London to the Eurolines network (contact Bus Éireann in Cork, tel. (021) 508188).

If you're traveling between the Isles you might look into the many **flights** between Gatwick, Heathrow, Luton, Manchester, Birmingham, Liverpool, and Glasgow (Britain); Dublin, Shannon, Cork, Knock, and Waterford (Ireland); Belfast and Derry (Northern Ireland); and Ronaldsway (Isle of Man). British Airways, Aer Lingus, British Midlands, and Ryan Air are some of the companies offering service to Ireland. Students can fly one-way from London to Dublin for £52 if they book through USIT. **British Midland Airways** (Dublin Office: Nutley Hall, Merrion Rd., Dublin 4; tel. (01) 283 0700; Belfast Office: Ste. 2, Fountain Centre, College St.; tel. (01232) 241188) and **British Airways** (Befalst Office: 9 Fountain Centre, College St.; tel. (01345) 222111) both fly eight times a day from London to Belfast (1¼hr.; Midland UK£69, return £85; Airways UK£73, return £88). **Manx Airlines** (tel. (01345) 256256) flies four times a day to Belfast with other service in Ireland and Britain.

FERRIES BETWEEN THE ISLES

This section comprises all of the services between the British Isles, save for ferries from the Scottish mainland to the Highlands and Islands; consult town and island listings for more details on these services.

Wales to Ireland

Two main lines link Wales and Ireland by ferry. The **B&I Line** accepts bookings only at its Dublin or Cork office. Call the B&I office in London (tel. (0171) 734 4681) or Dublin at 16 Westmoreland St. (tel. (01) 679 7977). For after-hours information in England call (0161) 236 3936, in Ireland (01) 660 6666. Try **Stena Sealink** at 15 Westmoreland St., Dublin 2 (tel. (01) 280 8844; recorded info tel. 280 0338).

Pembroke Dock to Rosslare, Ireland: B&I ferries sail twice daily from (Depart Pembroke Dock at 2:45am and 2:15pm; depart Rosslare 8:30am and 8:30pm. 4¼hr. Walk-on passengers £20 each way; £198 return with car. Children under 16 half-fare, under 5 free.

Fishguard Harbor to Rosslare, Ireland: Sealink ferries sail twice daily to Rosslare from Fishguard Harbor, accessible from Pembroke Dock. (Depart Fishguard at 3:15am and 3pm; depart Rosslare at 9am and 9:50pm. 3½ hrs. Foot passengers single £20; under 14 £9; under 4 free; car with 5 passengers £104.) Sealink runs four **catamarans** from Fishguard to Rosslare daily (depart 7am, 11:30am, 4pm, 8:30pm; £23; car with 5 passengers £102).

Holyhead, Wales to Dublin: B&I leaves Holyhead daily (2/day; 4hrs.; £16-26 each way). **Sealink** (tel. (01407) 766765) sails to **Dun Laoghaire** (3½hrs.) with bus connections to Dublin. (May- Dec. 4/day; 4hrs.; £16-26 each way). Sealink runs a high-tech catamaran between Holyhead and Dun Laoghaire (3-4/day; 1¼hr.; £23-30 each way).

Swansea, Wales to Cork: Cork-Swansea Ferries (Swansea tel. (01792) 271166) leave from Keys Dock in **Swansea** for **Cork** in Ireland (1/day except Tues., Sept.-May 4/week; departs at 9pm; 10hr; foot passengers £20-26, bikes £7).

England to Ireland

Supabus bus/ferry rates start at IR£30 for a return fare from Dublin to London. Bus tickets that include ferry connections between Britain and Ireland are available as package deals through ferry companies, travel agents, and USIT offices. Arrival and departure times are inconvenient, however. Supabus connects in London to the Eurolines network (contact Bus Éireann in Cork, tel. (021) 508188). **Slattery's** travel agency, based in Tralee at 1 Russell St. (tel. (066) 21611) runs a cheap combined bus/ferry deal with **B&I Line** to London: buses leave Cork daily and end up in London at 7am the following morning.

Scotland to Northern Ireland

Located on the most western peninsula of Dumfries and Galloway, **Stranraer** is *the* place to get a ferry to Northern Ireland—don't ask for more. **Train** service from London's Euston Station to Belfast's York St. Station via Sealink takes about 12 hours.

Stranraer, Scotland to Larne: Sealink ferries (tel. (01776) 702262 or (01233) 647047) leave for Larne, Northern Ireland (7-10/day, 2¼hr.; £18-20, seniors, students, and children £10; bikes free). Show up 45 minutes before scheduled departures; ferries will occasionally leave early depending on weather conditions.

Stranraer, Scotland to Belfast: The **Seacat Hoverspeed,** dubbed "the vomit comet" by locals (tel. 702255), shudders through the Irish Sea to Belfast (4-5/day; 1½hr.; £20-22, seniors and students £13-14, children £11-12; bikes free). Students should check with the student travel offices at Glasgow University for cheap fares to Dublin via Stranraer.

To the Isle of Man

You can easily combine a ferry across the Irish Sea with a stopover on the **Isle of Man.** The **Isle of Man Steam Packet Co.,** in Douglas (tel. (01624) 661661; open Mon.-Sat. 7am-9pm, Sun. 9am-9pm), shuttles from Liverpool to Douglas (June 3-9/ wk., April, May, and Sept. 1-2/wk., Sept.-March 1/wk.). Also to and from: **Belfast** (May-Sept. 2-4/week, mostly on Mon., Fri., and Sun.; 2½hr. by SeaCat, 4½hr. by ship); **Dublin** (May-Sept. 2-4/week, mostly on Thurs. and Sun.; 2½hr. by SeaCat, 4½hr. by ship); **Heysham** (June-Sept. 1-2/day, Jan.-March Mon-Fri. 1/day; 3¾hr.); **Ardrossan,** Scotland (in cooperation with Caledonian MacBrayne; June-Aug. 1/ week Sat.-Sun.; 8hr.). Single fares run from £20-28; students and seniors £15-28.

ONCE THERE

■■■ GETTING ABOUT

In general, fares on all modes of public transportation in Britain and Ireland are either **single** (one way) or **return** (round-trip). **Period returns** require you to return within a specific number of days; **day return** means you must return on the same day. A **supersaver** (return) won't allow you to travel on Fridays or most Saturdays and often not before 9am, but is often cheaper. An **APEX** (return) is a cheaper rate and must be purchased at least a week beforehand; a **Super APEX** (return) is the cheapest (up to 60% off standard return) and must be purchased at least two weeks before traveling. Always keep your ticket when you travel, as it will sometimes be inspected on the journey or collected at the station when you arrive.

Roads between cities and towns have official letters and numbers ("N" and "R" in the Republic, "M," "A," and "B" in Britain), though in Ireland most locals refer to them by destination ("the Kerry Road"). In Ireland, most signs are in English and Irish; some destination signs are only in Irish. Road signs in Britain use the metric system; additional white signs in Ireland show distances in miles.

BUSES & COACHES

The British and Irish distinguish between **buses,** which cover short local routes, and **coachesb,** which cover long distances with few stops. For practical purposes, *Let's Go* usually uses the term "buses" to refer to both of these services. Long-distance coach travel in Britain is more extensive than in most European countries and the cheapest option. **National Express,** the principal operator of long-distance coach services, can be reached through Eurolines (UK) Limited, 23 Crawley Road, Luton, LU1 1HX, England, or in person in London (tel. (0171) 730 0202), Dover, or Birmingham. Each region also has local companies. Some coaches require advance reservation. **Seniors'** (over 60) and **Young Persons' Discount Coach Cards** (ages 16-25) are £7 and reduce standard fares on National Express by about 30%.

In a partnership with YHA and SYHA, the **Slow Coach** (tel. or fax (01249) 891959) offers a service aimed at rambling hostellers: £69 buys a round trip ticket on a clockwise circuit of London, Windsor, Bath, Stratford-upon-Avon, the Lake District, Edinburgh, York, and Cambridge, ending back in London. Sensibly enough, four coaches per week stop at hostels along the way, allowing packers to stow their bags before rumbling into a strange city. The tickets are transferable and valid for two months, allowing travelers pause as long as they wish in each city and sell or give away any unused portions at the end of the period. Those who buy their ticket overseas receive a book of hostel discounts, including £5 off their first two nights at a London YHA hostel and £1 off their first night at every hostel the Slow Coach visits. Get the ticket at any of the YHA/SYHA hostels on the route, or by calling the above number. In Scotland, **Go Blue Banana Bus** and **Haggis Backpackers** run similar deals (consult Scotland: Getting About for specific details).

Ireland's national bus company, **Bus Éireann,** operates both long-distance **Expressway** buses, which link larger cities, and **Provincial** buses, which serve the countryside and smaller towns. The bus timetable book (50p) is available at Busáras in Dublin and at many tourist offices. A mélange of **private bus services** are faster and cheaper than Bus Éireann; most of these services link Dublin to one or two towns in the west. In Donegal, private bus providers provide local service.

Bus Éireann's discount **Rambler** tickets aren't worth buying. The **Road Rambler** ticket offers unlimited official bus travel within Ireland on eight out of 15 or 15 out of 30 (IR£60-90). A combined **Rail and Road Rambler** ticket good for unlimited travel on rail and bus lines on any eight of 15 days costs £105. Purchase these from the Irish Rail information office, 35 Lower Abbey St., Dublin 1 (tel. (01) 836 3222).

Ulsterbus, Oxford St., Belfast (tel. (01232) 320 011), runs throughout **Northern Ireland.** Pick up a regional timetable (25p) at any station. Again, the bus discount passes won't save you much money: a **Freedom of Northern Ireland** bus pass costs UK£9 for one day, UK£25 for seven consecutive days; under 16 UK£4.50, UK£12.50. The **Emerald Card** offers travel for eight out of 15 consecutive days (UK£100, children UK£50) or 15 out of 30 consecutive days (UK£171, children UK£85.50). Hostelers might take advantage of the **Go as You Please pass** which offers seven days unlimited bus travel and six nights in YHANI hostels (from UK£49), available through YHANI (see Accommodations, above).

Local intra-city services (mostly fast and frequent minibuses) in both Britain and Ireland are provided by local companies together with county councils. In towns where two or three intra-city rural-service companies link up (such as Glastonbury), the confusion can be incredible, so head for the local tourist office or bus station for help. Also be on the look-out for regional coach passes, which offer unlimited travel in a certain area for a certain number of days; these are usually known as Rovers, Ramblers, and Explorers, and we often list them in relevant sections.

TRAINS

Britain's nationalized **British Rail** service is extensive but somewhat pricey. If you plan to travel a great deal within Britain, the **BritRail Pass** is a good buy. (Eurail-passes are *not* valid in Britain.) BritRail Passes are only available in the U.S. and Canada; *you must buy them before traveling to Britain.* They allow unlimited travel in England, Wales, and Scotland. British Rail does not operate in Northern Ireland or the Republic of Ireland. Passes are not valid for ferry, jetfoil, or catamaran transportation, although British Rail does offer fare packages for rail service combined with one or more of these options. In 1994, BritRail standard class Passes cost US$219 for eight days, $339 for 15 days, $425 for 22 days, and $495 for one month. Senior citizens pay US$199, $305, $379, and $445 respectively. Those between 16 and 25 pay US$179, $269, $339, or $395; children ages 5-15 pay half the adult fare. BritRail Travel also offers **Flexipasses,** which allow travel on a limited number of days within a specific time period (4, 8, or 15/mo.; 16-25-year-olds can also buy a special 15 days/2mo. pass). Passes and additional information on discounts are available from most travel agents or **BritRail Travel International's Reservation Centre,** 1500 Broadway, 10th Floor, New York, NY 10036-4015 (tel. (212) 575 2667, fax (212) 575 2542). In Canada, write to 2161 Yonge St., Suite 812, Toronto, ON M4F386 (tel. (416) 484 0571).

The **Young Person's Railcard** (£16, valid for one year) offers 33% off most fares and discounts on Sealink Stena Line to Continental and Irish ports. Buy this pass at major British Rail Travel Centres in the U.K. You must prove you're either between 16 and 23 (with a birth certificate or passport), or a full-time student over 23 at a British school, and submit two passport-sized photos. Those 60 and over can purchase a **Senior Railcard** (£16) taking up to 33% off most fares; these are also available at major British Rail Travel Centres. Families have their own Railcard, as do wheelchair-bound travelers (see Special Concerns: Travelers with Disabilities).

While the **Eurailpass** is *not* accepted in Britain, it *is* accepted in Ireland. However, Eurailpasses are not economical for use in Ireland, since rail routes in the Republic of Ireland are not extensive enough to make the cost of the pass pay off. If you plan to visit other countries in Europe that use Eurail, limit your pass use to when you get there. If anything, get a Flexipass (5 days within 2 months; begins US$348) or Youth Pass (for those under 26; US$398 for 15 days, US$768 for 2 months; youth Flexipass US$255) and begin using it on the ferry to Europe.

Trains run by **Iarnród Éireann** (Irish Rail) branch out from Dublin to larger cities, but there is limited service between these cities (main office: 35 Lower Abbey St., Dublin). For schedule information, pick up a InterCity Rail Travellers Guide (50p), available at most train stations. By far the most useful travel pass for students on trains and buses in Ireland is the **Travelsave stamp,** available at any USIT with an ISIC card and IR£7. Affixed to your ISIC card, this stamp decreases single fares by 50% on national rail and allows you to break your journey to visit at any stop on the way to your final destination (valid for one month). It also provides 15% discounts on bus fares over IR£1. The **Boomerang** return fares offer return travel for single price on certain routes, for Tues.-Thurs. travel only. A **Faircard** can get anyone under 26 up to 50% the price of any InterCity trip. Those over 26 can get the less potent **Weekender card** (up to a third off, Fri.-Tues. only).

Northern Ireland Railways (Belfast tel. (01232) 899411, Britrail enquiries tel. (01232) 230671) service is not extensive but covers the Northeastern coastal region well. The major line connects Dublin to Belfast (4-6/day, 3 hr., UK£27.50) and runs north through Antrim. When it reaches Belfast, this line splits, with one branch ending at Bangor and one at Larne. There is also rail service from Belfast and Lisburn west to Derry and Portrush, stopping at three towns between Antrim and the coast. British Rail passes are not valid here, but Northern Ireland Railways offers its own discounts. A valid **Travelsave stamp** will get you 50% off all trains and 15% discounts on bus fares over UK£1. The **Rail Runabout** ticket allows seven consecutive days of travel between April and Oct. (UK£25.00, seniors and children UK£12.50).

DRIVING

The advantages of car travel speak for themselves. Disadvantages include high gasoline prices (around UK£2.30, or US$4.60, per gallon in 1992), the villainous exhaust that results from lax British emissions standards, and the fact that **they drive on the left.** Be particularly cautious at roundabouts (rotary interchanges); give way to traffic from the right. In both countries, the law requires drivers and front-seat passengers to wear seat belts; in Britain, rear-seat passengers are also required to buckle up when belts are provided. In Ireland, children under 12 must not sit in the front seat.

Britain is covered by a skeletal but adequate system of limited-access **expressways** ("M-roads" or "motorways"), connecting London with Birmingham, Liverpool, Manchester, Cardiff, and Southern Scotland. The M-roads are supplemented by a tight web of "A-roads" and "B-roads" in England, Scotland, Wales, and Northern Ireland. **Speed limits** are 60mph (97kmph) on single carriageways (non-divided highways), 70mph (113kmph) on motorways (highways) and dual carriageways (divided highways), and usually 30mph (48kmph) in urban areas. (Speed limits are always marked at the beginning of town areas; upon leaving, you'll see a circular sign with a slash through it, signaling the end of the speed restriction.) Speed limits aren't rabidly enforced, but note that many British roads are sinuous and single-track; use common sense, especially in rural or mountainous areas.

In **Ireland,** roads numbered below N50 are primary routes that connect all major towns; roads numbered N50 and above are secondary routes, similar to Britain's A-roads; regional R-roads are comparable to Britain's B-roads. Most of these are two-lane. The general **speed limit** is 55mph (90kmph) on the open road and either 30mph (50kmph) or 40mph (65kmph) in town. Signs on roadways are usually in both English and Irish, sometimes only Irish for destination signs.

Hiring (renting) an automobile is the least expensive option if you drive for a month or less. For more extended travel, you might consider **leasing.** Major rental companies with agencies almost everywhere in Britain and Ireland include **Avis, Budget Rent-A-Car, Geoffrey Davis Europcar, Hertz, Kenning,** and **Swan National.** Prices are £150 to £300 a week with unlimited mileage plus VAT; for insurance reasons, renters are required to be over 21 and under 70. In Ireland, you won't get anything cheaper than IR£25 per day. **Europe by Car** (see below), however, will rent to younger people if the paperwork is done in advance, in the U.S. All plans require sizable deposits unless you pay by credit card. Make sure you understand insurance before you rent; some agreements make you pay for damages you may not have caused. Automatics are generally more expensive than stick shifts.

Several U.S. firms offer rental or leasing plans for Britain and Ireland; try **Kemwel Group,** 106 Calvert St., Harrison, NY 10528-3199 (tel. (800) 678 0678); **Auto Europe,** #10 Sharp's Wharf, P.O. Box 1097, Camden, ME 04843 (tel. (800) 223 5555, fax (207) 236 4724); or **Europe by Car,** Rockefeller Plaza, New York, NY 10020 (tel. (800) 223 1516 or (212) 581 3040; student and faculty discounts available). In Ireland, people under 21 can't rent; those under 25 often encounter hassle.

Try **Budget Rent-A-Car,** 151 Lower Drumcondra Rd., Dublin (tel. (01) 837 9611). One book to help plan car travel is *Moto Europa,* by Eric Bredeson (US$19.95, CDN$22.95, US$3 shipping, $7 postage overseas), available in bookstores or from Seren Publishing, P.O. Box 1212, Dubuque, IA 52004 (tel. (800) EUROPA-8).

If you plan to stay in the country longer than three months, you will need an **International Driver's Permit** (an American or Canadian license is valid until that time). Contact any **American Automobile Association (AAA)** office by writing to its main office, AAA Florida, Travel Agency Services Department, 1000 AAA Drive (mail stop 28), Heathrow, FL 32746-5080 (tel. (800) 222 4357 or (407) 444 4245, fax (407) 444 7823) or any **Canadian Automobile Association (CAA)** office by writing to CAA Toronto, 60 Commerce Valley Dr. East, Thornhill, Ontario L3T 7P9 (tel. (905) 771 3000, fax (905) 771 3046).

RIDESHARING

Freewheelers is a National lift share agency which can match passengers and drivers together. Membership is required (£5 per passenger, free to drivers). Each match-up costs £1; the price of the trip itself is agreed between passenger and driver, though the agency recommends a passenger contribution of 3.5 pence per mile (£6.90 London to Manchester). Members must abide by a safety procedure to confirm each others' identity; the agency keeps records of all members and matches. Single-sex matching is available. Freewheelers does not take responsibility for members' safety: you are still getting in a car with a stranger. Call (0191) 222 0090 or write to Freewheelers, 25 Low Friar St., Newcastle upon Tyne, NE1 5UE.

BIKING

Imagine gliding down a deserted country road in the cool morning air. Imagine sitting on something really small for five hours at a time. Today, biking is one of the key elements of the classic budget Eurovoyage. Everyone else in the youth hostel is doing it, and with the proliferation of mountain bikes, you can do some serious natural sightseeing. **Mountaineers Books,** 1011 Klickitat Way #107, Seattle, WA 98134 (tel. (800) 553 4453) puts out detailed bike tour books on Ireland and England, as well as *Europe by Bike,* by Karen and Terry Whitehall (US$14.95). *Cycling Europe: Budget Bike Touring in the Old World,* by N. Slavinski (US$12.95) is also useful. If you're nervous about bicycling alone, **College Bicycle Tours** (tel. (800) 736 2453 in the U.S. and Canada) arranges co-ed bike tours and discounted airfare. **Bike Nashbar,** 4112 Simon Rd., Youngstown, OH 44512 (tel. (800) 627 4227) offers boffo prices on equipment. Cyclists can consult tourist offices or books on cycling in Britain and Ireland for touring routes. Rodale Press, 33 E. Minor St., Emmaus, PA 18098 (tel. (215) 967 5171), publishes *Mountain Biking Skills* (US$4.95) and other general publications on prepping yourself and your bike. The Cyclists' Touring Club, Cotterell House, 69 Meadrow, Godalming, Surrey GU7 3HS, England (tel. (01483) 417217, fax (01483) 426994) provides information, maps, and a list of bike rental firms in Britain. Annual membership is £24, under 18 £12, and family £40.

Much of Britain's countryside is well suited for cycling; many roads are not heavily traveled. Ireland is largely similar, although one *Let's Go* reader points out that after a while it seems that the country is all uphill. Even well-traveled routes will often cover highly uneven terrain. We recommend that you take some reasonably long rides before you leave, both to get in shape and to assure yourself you're not in over your head. You must pack an absolute minimum of luggage. Be sure the gear range on your bike is adequate; you'll need extremely low gears to get a loaded bike up a steep hill. Have a reputable, well-equipped shop tune up your bike before you go.

Bringing a beloved bike from home involves worry, work, and expense. Every airline has its own regulations. Some carriers will include your bike as part of your baggage allowance if it is under a certain size (usually 62 inches), but some charge a fee. Contact your airline for specifics. Make sure your bike conforms to British law; at night there must be a white light at the front of the cycle and a red light and red reflector on the back. A better option is to buy a bike in Britain and Ireland and sell it before you leave. A bike bought new overseas is subject to customs duties if brought into your home country; used bikes, however, will not be taxed. Whatever the origin of the bike, be sure to purchase adequate **touring equipment**. At about US$50-60, the best **helmets**—a Bell V1Pro or Bell Tourlite are frequently suggested—are an investment but cheaper than critical head surgery or a tastefully appointed funeral. You should also obtain a U-lock and **panniers** (non-equestrian saddlebags). A waterproof poncho is a must in this wet corner of the world.

If you plan to explore several widely separated regions, you can combine cycling with train travel. British Rail lets you put your bike in the luggage compartment of most trains free of charge and store your bike at most stations for a nominal fee. In addition, bikes ride free on all ferries leaving Britain and Ireland. *The Rail Traveler's Guide to Biking by Train* is available from British Rail and most stations; the maze of regulations and restrictions look scary, but in real life are not always enforced.

Renting a bike is preferable to bringing your own if your touring will be confined to one or two regions. In Ireland, you can rent 3-, 5-, and 10-speed bikes from **Raleigh Rent-a-Bike** shops almost anywhere in the country for IR£7 per day, IR£30 per week, plus IR£10-40 deposit. They'll often collect your bike for about IR£12. A list of Raleigh dealers is available at most tourist offices and bike shops. Tourist offices sell *Cycling Ireland* (with map, IR£1.50). Check specific town listings for Britain and Ireland for bike rental shops, or contact the Irish Tourist Board for a list of more than 100 dealers in Ireland who rent bikes; if you call or write ahead of time, you can arrange to have a bike waiting for you at Shannon Airport.

HITCHHIKING

> *Let's Go* urges hitchers to seriously consider risks before deciding to hitchhike. **Let's Go does not recommend** hitchhiking as a means of transport, and the routes listed below and elsewhere in this book are not intended to do so.

Not everyone can be an airplane pilot, but most every **bozo** can drive a car, and hitching means **entrusting your life** to a randomly selected person who happens to stop beside you on the road, risking theft, assault, sexual harrassment, and unsafe driving. In spite of this, the gains are many: favorable hitching experiences allow you to meet local people and get around, especially in northern Europe and Ireland, where public transportation is particularly sketchy. The choice, however, remains yours. Hitching is inherently risky; this advice may make it less so.

Depending on the circumstances and the norms of the country, groups of men and women and lone male travelers might consider hitching to locations beyond the scope of bus or train routes. **If you're a woman traveling alone, *don't hitch.*** It's just too dangerous. Two women alone shouldn't hitch either. A man and a woman are a safer combination; two men will have a harder time finding a ride; three will go nowhere. Britain and Ireland may be the easiest places in Western Europe to get a lift: a wait of more than an hour is reportedly rare on major roads in summer.

Where you stand is vital. Experienced hitchers pick a spot outside of built-up areas, where drivers can stop, return to the road without causing an accident, and have time to look over potential passengers as they approach. Hitching on hills or curves is hazardous and unsuccessful. Hitching (or even standing) on super-highways is generally illegal: you may only thumb at rest stops, or at the entrance ramps to highways—*in front* of the nifty blue and white superhighway pictograph (a bridge over a road). In the Practical Information section of many cities we list the tram or bus lines that will take travelers to strategic points for hitching out.

Those hitching in Ireland line the roads like floats at a parade; the result is stiff competition for rides. In more remote areas, many follow bus routes so they can wave down buses when their luck runs out. In general, more rides are given on the East coast than in the Northwest, and Sundays are particularly slow. In Ireland, *never* hitch in County Armagh, especially in Crossmaglen.

Vacation Work Publications (see address in Alternatives to Tourism, above) publishes the *Hitch-Hikers' Manual: Britain,* which contains practical information on hitching laws, techniques, and the best places to hitch in 200 British towns (£3.95).

Finally, your success will depend on **what you look like.** Successful hitchers travel light and stack their belongings in a compact but visible cluster. Most Europeans signal with an open hand, rather than a thumb; many write their destination on a sign in large, bold letters and draw a smiley-face under it. Drivers like hitchers who are neat and wholesome, yet dynamic. No one stops for a **grump,** or for anyone wearing sunglasses. When a car does pull up, don't dawdle.

Safety issues: avoid getting in the back of a two-door car and never let go of your backpack. Hitchhiking at night can be particularly dangerous; stand in a well-lit place and expect drivers to be leery of nocturnal thumbers. When you get into a car, make sure you know how to get out again in a hurry. Couples may avoid hassles with male drivers if the woman sits in the back or next to the door. If you ever feel threatened, insist on being let off, regardless of where you are. If the driver refuses to stop, act as though you're going to open the car door or vomit on the upholstery.

■■■ ACCOMMODATIONS

Tourist offices can provide invaluable aid. These offices often have free or inexpensive lists of vacancies, which they will post on their doors after hours. For about £1.50, most offices will book a place to stay. Calling direct can pay off in your pocket, since some proprietors inflate prices in response to finder's fees. Most offices also offer a "book-a-bed-ahead" service; for about £2.50 (less in Wales), they'll reserve a room in the next town you visit. In many places, tourist offices only list proprietors who've paid a hefty fee to belong to the tourist board organization; other owners may have chosen to remain independent and are less visible. The best way to get good deals is to talk to other travelers.

Securing advance reservations with a deposit will greatly lessen the anxiety of arrival, especially in the summer. Write to a hotel or hostel specifying the date of arrival and the length of your stay (commit yourself only to a minimum stay, since you may wish to switch lodgings). The proprietor will write back to confirm availability, whereupon you should send a deposit of one night's rent, preferably as a signed traveler's check in pounds. Some places accept a personal check or money orders in dollars (possibly for a fee). You may want to phone before leaving home to confirm. A few hostels accept credit card reservations over the phone.

HOSTELS

For those eager to meet fellow travelers of all ages and nationalities, ease the burden on their budgets, or recreate fond memories of summer camp, hostels are the way to go. Though curfews, lockouts, communal showers, and single-sex, dorm-style rooms might dissuade the less-seasoned traveler, hostels are generally clean, well-managed, and reasonable in price. As the undisputed capitals of the budget-travel subculture, they're great places to swap stories and tips or just meet people. Youth hostels aren't just for kids; senior travelers and families are almost always welcome. Some hostels are strikingly beautiful (housed in castles and historic mansions), while others are little more than run-down barracks. Hostels and their grounds usually close from 10am to 5pm; many enforce an 11pm curfew. Hostels require sleep sacks; most prohibit sleeping bags for hygienic reasons. These regulations are often not strictly enforced. Many hostels have laundry facilities, ranging from washing machines to troughs in the backyard (in Scotland, only those marked "Grade 1" have such facilities; see Scotland: Accommodations for an explanation of the grading system). Most large hostels offer dinner; almost all provide kitchens and utensils at no extra charge. Some sell canned goods and camper's food.

The worldwide network of hostels is **Hostelling International (HI).** The associations in Britain and Ireland are: **YHA** (Youth Hostel Association of England and Wales), **SYHA** (Scottish Youth Hostel Association), **YHANI** (Youth Hostel Association of Northern Ireland), and **An Óige** in Ireland. All hostel association addresses are under Useful Addresses, above. Britain and Ireland have 400 HI-affiliated hostels. To stay in an HI hostel, you must be a member of one of the national member organizations of Hostelling International. Nonmembers may ask at hostels for an "International Guest Card." An overnight fee plus one-sixth of the annual membership charge buys one stamp; a card with six stamps is proof of full membership.

In Ireland, the two significant non-HI, non-governmental hostel organizations recently merged to form **IHH.** IHH hostels have no lockout or curfew, accept all ages, require no membership card, are closer to cities and towns than An Óige's, and have a more mellow atmosphere; all are Bord Fáilte-approved. Pick up a free booklet with complete descriptions of each at any IHH hostel. Get in touch with IHH by writing via the IHH Office, U.C.D. Village, Belfield, Dublin 4 (tel. (01) 260 1634, fax (01) 269 7704). Independent hostels in Britain have no distinct organization, but may present a better deal and friendlier quarters.

BED & BREAKFASTS

The bed and breakfast is native to Britain, though the concept has now spread the world over. Conceived as a cheap alternative to hotels, B&Bs are usually homes whose owners have room to spare. The hospitality of British bed-and-breakfast establishments is celebrated the world over—with good reason. Outside London, most B&Bs have fewer than four rooms, but since they often cluster together in one neighborhood, owners will direct you nearby when their own rooms are full.

B&Bs are usually quite clean, particularly in rural areas. Most of the places *Let's Go* lists have central heating, but if you are traveling in the fall or winter, be sure to ask about its existence and nature. (At the very least, secure yourself a hot water bottle.) Before committing yourself to a place, see the room and test the bed. Also make sure the charges are clear to you; quoted fees may conveniently exclude VAT. Solitary travelers may have trouble finding space in rural areas, where proprietors try to fill their doubles with two people who know each other, waiting until the last minute to offer their rooms as singles. In large cities, strangers may be put in the same room to alleviate the problem. Expect to pay £16-60 in London (almost always in advance) and £10-12 in the rest of Britain. Some proprietors grant considerable rate reductions to guests who pay in advance or by the week and will grant discounts between September and May. An "English breakfast" should include eggs, bacon or sausage, toast, and tea or coffee, while a "Continental" breakfast includes only some form of bread and hot caffeine. **Aunties (Great Britain) Limited,** 56 Coleshill Terrace, Llanelli, Dyfed, Wales SA15 3DA (tel. (01554) 770077) will scout out B&Bs in London suburbs and other areas of England, Scotland, and Wales and caters to vegetarians. Their family B&Bs range from £13-20/person (under 13 half price). **Bed and Breakfast (GB),** P.O. Box 66, Henley-on-Thames, Oxon, England RG9 1XS (tel. (01491) 578803; fax (01491) 410806), covers London, England, Scotland, Wales, and Ireland for £14 and up per night. In the U.S., call **Hometours International** in New York (tel. (800) 367 4668, fax (212) 689 0679).

Singles in Irish B&Bs run IR£10-15, doubles IR£20-26. The breakfasts—eggs, bacon, sausage, bread, cereal, orange juice, and coffee or tea—are often filling enough to get you through until dinner. B&Bs displaying a shamrock are officially approved by the Irish Tourist Board (Bord Fáilte); they charge the prices quoted in the 1994 edition of *Guest Accommodation,* published by the Tourist Board and available at tourist offices (IR£4). Tourist offices will book you a room for IR£1 plus a 10% deposit. Approved B&Bs pay a membership fee for this honor; unapproved B&Bs may be of similar quality and less expensive.

Cheap hotels, or guest houses as they are often called, can sometimes offer even better bargains than B&Bs. The quality of these establishments varies widely, but hotels offer fewer restrictions and more flexible arrangements than B&Bs.

ALTERNATIVE ACCOMMODATIONS

More than 50 British **universities** provide accommodations for groups, individuals, or families during the vacation periods (mainly July-Sept., sometimes during Easter and Christmas vacations). Most of these are single-study bedrooms, but some universities can provide self-catering flats or family rooms. B&B or full board is available. Write well in advance for information to Carole Formon, British Universities Accommodation Consortium (BUAC), Box Number 956, University Park, Nottingham, England NG7 2RD (tel. (01602) 504 571, fax (01602) 422 505).

Another option is **homestay. Academy Travel** will find you a place in homes around England and in Edinburgh and Cardiff, starting at £22.50 per night B&B with a 3-night minimum stay. This arrangement can be more friendly than a standard B&B; the hosts will treat you as a family guest. Discounts are available for stays of more than 4 weeks and for students and trainees. Write for more information to Academy Travel, P.O. Box 645, London SW16.

Other organizations can help you find short- or long-term, if pricey, places to stay. **Home Exchange,** PO Box 567, Northhampton, MA 01061 offers a registry service (US$50) linking homeowners all over the USA and United Kingdom. Subscribers' homes are listed in the *Home Exchange Directory*. **Barclay International Group**, 150 East 52nd Street, New York, NY 10022 (tel. (800) 845 6636 or (212) 832 3777, fax (212) 753 1139) arranges short-term apartments in London and Edinburgh. Rentals are pricey and perhaps only feasible for groups: two-person apartments start at $499/week off-season. **Europa-Let,** 92 North Main Street, Ashland, Oregon 97520 (tel. (800) 462 4486 or (503) 482 5806, fax (503) 482-0660) offers a similar service.

■■■ HIKING TRAILS

The **British** maintain an extensive system of long-distance paths that range from the gently rolling footpaths of the South Downs Way to the rugged mountain trails of the Pennine Way. These paths are well-marked and maintained, and in many cases run a day's walk between hostels. Explorers will enjoy the Ordnance Survey 1:25,000 Second Series maps, which mark almost every house, barn, standing stone, graveyard, and pub. Less ambitious hikers will want the 1:50,000 scale maps. Several specific organizations provide information for the self-propelled traveler. The **Ramblers' Association,** 1-5 Wandsworth Rd., London SW8 (tel. (0171) 582 6878), publishes a *Yearbook* on walking and places to stay, as well as offering free newsletters and color magazines (membership £15, family £19). The **Backpackers' Club,** P.O. Box 381, Reading, Berkshire RG3 4RL England (tel. (01491) 680684; 24 hr.) offers its members (membership £17) site and pitch lists for most distance paths in the U.K., a quarterly magazine, camping equipment, insurance services, and best of all a Clothpatch to sew on your gear, identifying you as a Backpacker to all the world. For more information on national trails and recreational paths, contact the **Countryside Commission,** P.O. Box 124, Walgrave, Northampton NN6 9TL, England (tel. (01604) 781 848; fax (01604) 781 752). Be sure to ask for *Walking in Britain, Out in the Country,* and *Heritage Coasts of England and Wales*.

There are many long-distance rural paths in **the Republic of Ireland,** though without the sophisticated infrastructure of England. The **Wicklow Way,** a popular trail through mountainous Co. Wicklow, is an exception, with hikers' hostels within a day's walk of each other. A series of handouts published by Bord Fáilte describe trails, some of which (the **Munster Way**) are almost as good as Wicklow while others exist mainly in theory. The best hillwalking maps are the Ordnance Survey ½"-to-1-mi. series; IR£3.70 each. Consult *Dublin and the Wicklow Mountains—Access Routes for the Hillwalker* (IR£2.80), and the tourist office's pamphlet *Walking in Ireland* (IR£1.50). Also contact the **Federation of Mountaineering Clubs of Ireland,** 20 Leopardstown Gardens, Blackrock, County Dublin (tel. (01) 881266), for a list of hillwalking and rock-climbing guide books.

The **Ulster Way** encircles **Northern Ireland** with 560 mi. of marked trail. For detailed maps and leaflets on the Ulster Way and other trails, contact the **Sports Council for Northern Ireland,** House of Sport, Upper Malone Rd., Belfast BT9 5LA (tel. (01232) 381222). For walks in and among the Glens of Antrim, contact the **Ulster Rambling Federation,** 27 Market Rd., Ballymena, Co. Antrim (tel. (01266) 44685); for walks in the Mourne Mountains, contact **Heart of Down Accommodations Association,** Down District Council, 74 Market St., Downpatrick, Co. Down (tel. (01396) 614331). Get an up-to-date weather report anywhere in the North by calling (01891) 505327) before setting out, and dress for the worst.

■■■ KEEPING IN TOUCH

MAIL

Mail can be sent internationally through **Poste Restante** (the international phrase for General Delivery) to any city or town; it's well worth using and much more reliable than you might think. Mark the envelope "HOLD" and address it, for example, "Hannah <u>TASHJIAN</u>, Poste Restante, Liverpool, England." The last name should be capitalized and underlined. Between the U.S. and Europe airmail averages a week to 10 days. The mail will go to a special desk in the central post office, unless you specify a post office by street address or postal code. As a rule, it is best to use the largest post office in the area; when possible, it is quicker and more reliable to send mail express or registered. Bring ID to pick up your mail. If the clerk insists that there is nothing for you, try checking under your first name as well. *Let's Go* lists post offices in the Practical Information section for each city and most towns.

Many U.S. city post offices offer **International Express Mail** service, which sends packages under 8 oz. to major overseas cities in 40-72 hours for US$11.50-14. Sending mail c/o **American Express** offices is quite reliable; they will hold your mail for free if you have AmEx traveler's checks or a card. To have mail held for over 30 days, write "Hold for x days" on the envelope. Again the sender should capitalize and underline your last name (e.g., Mike <u>HOFER</u>), marking the envelope "Client Letter Service." Check the Practical Information sections of the areas you plan to visit; we list AmEx offices for most large cities. A complete list is available for free from AmEx (tel. (800) 528 4800) in the booklet *Traveler's Companion.*

Private mail services provide the fastest, most reliable overseas delivery. **DHL** (tel. (800) 225 5345 in the US and Canada; (0181) 890 9393 in London; (02) 317 8300 in Sydney; (09) 636 7124 in Auckland; (01) 844 4744 in Dublin; (11) 921 3600 in Johannesburg) covers nearly every country in Europe. Mail to Western Europe costs at least US$30 and takes 2-3 days. **Federal Express** (tel. (800) 238-5355 in the U.S. and Canada; (0181) 844 2344 to London, (0800) 123800 from outside London; (800) 021021 in New Zealand and Australia; (01) 847 3473 in Dublin, (800) 535800 from outside Dublin; (11) 921 7500 in Johannesburg) can send an express letter from North America to London for $26-28.50 in 2-3 days.

Surface mail is by far the cheapest and slowest way to send mail. It takes one to three months to cross the Atlantic, appropriate for sending large quantities of items you won't need to see for a while. It is vital, therefore to **distinguish your airmail from surface mail** by labelling it boldly with the words "air mail" and "par avion."

TELEPHONES
See Appendix for phone information.

TELEGRAMS & FAXES
To send a **telegram** to the U.K. and Ireland from the U.S., Western Union (tel. (800) 325 6000) charges a base fee of US$8, plus US$.56 per word, including name and address. "Mailgrams" can be sent for $18.95 (fifty words) and arrive on the next mail day. Major cities across Europe also have **fax bureaus.**

Overseas Access is a verbal message serviceoffered by EurAide, P.O. Box 2375, Naperville, IL 60567 (708) 420 2343. Between May 2 and Octoberfest, travelers can have phone messages collected in Munich. They can then call and retrieve their messages at any time. Overseas Access is particularly useful for those travelers without a set itinerary. The cost is $15 per week or $40 per month plus a $15 registration fee For an additional $20, EurAide will forward mail sent to Munich at any address.

England

LIFE & TIMES

A short time ago, the esteemed London booking organization William Hill discerned a vital shift in English life. For as long as most could remember, the odds on the fall of the House of Windsor, the British monarchy, had stood at a stately 100-to-1. But as commoners watched the royals flaunt and abuse the ancient prestige of Europe's most famous monarchy, Hill calculated that there is now a one-in-six chance that the Windsors will soon be out of a job.

Most of the world knows England from just this kind of crash of past and present: the royal family at the mercy of flashy tabloids and fickle bookies, modern-day druids dancing around the fences of Celtic Stonehenge, twenty-year-olds raving til dawn under the shadow of Industrial Revolution cotton mills. England doesn't put its past only into museums or rope it all off into National Landmarks; much of history is assumed into daily life. The stones under your feet might be ancient Roman roads, the shoulder of a superhighway, or exquisite 12th-century tile—you can step on them all in the space of an hour.

That past and its effects continue to shape English life, and now, after eons of Empire, the world has turned around and colonized English culture. The land that gave us fish and chips, William Shakespeare, Bass Ale, and fodder for umpteen Merchant-Ivory films is now equally familiar with falafel, CNN, and McPizza. Yet despite the pervasiveness of outside influence (and internal thrusts for change), the English keep a firm hold on their quirky traditions. American travel writer Paul Theroux writes in *The Kingdom by the Sea* of the often comical idiosyncrasies of English culture: "They wallpaper their ceilings! They put little knitted bobble-hats on their soft-boiled eggs to keep them warm! They don't give you bags in supermarkets! They say sorry when you step on their toes!... They live in Barking and Dorking and Shellow Bowells! They have amazing names, like Mr. Eatwell and Lady Inkpen and Major Twaddle and Miss Tosh! And they think *we're* funny?"

England's diversity belies its size and isolation. The British Empire's legacy has brought large communities of former colonials, infusing the island with a wide range of cultures and attitudes, from Indian to Caribbean. Within the island, England's regions maintain distinct identities, from the dramatic coastline and moors of the Southwest to the megalopolis of Central England, from the downs and resorts of the Southeast to the peaks and coal-pits of the North, from London's sprawling splendor to the Cotswolds' village charm.

■■■ HISTORY

Long before the much-maligned Chunnel once and for all linked England to the rest of the world, foreign tourists had already scattered all over the isle of Britain. While Stonehenge and the stone circles of Avebury bear mute witness to the Isles' earliest inhabitants, recorded history began with the Celts, who battled Caesar's army in the first century AD. The Romans occupied southern Britain until the middle of the 5th century AD; they were turned back by Scottish tribes and built Hadrian's wall across today's North England between AD 117 and 138 to keep the *barbarii* at bay, along with the Celts in Wales and Cornwall in the west. But Christian missionaries made more progress, proselytizing beyond the limits of the Empire into Scotland and Ireland. With the dawning of the Christian era, the regions currently defined as England, Scotland, Wales, Northern Ireland, and Ireland began to develop divergent identities. Upon the decline of the Roman Empire in the 4th century, Britain was raided from northern Europe, mainly by the Angles (hence "England"), Saxons, and Jutes. These tribes established settlements and kingdoms alongside those of the resilient Celts (also known as Britons) in Wales and Cornwall. In this time, a rudimentary system of laws developed, mostly involving wound-compensation—rip a two-inch hole in the back of your neighbor's head? One shilling, please. So you bit off his ear, too? That'll run ye thirty more. Anglo-Saxon adultery laws carried the same grim charm—if a man slept with his neighbor's wife, he'd be forced to pay a fine and buy the neighbor a new one. Some archaeologists hypothesize that kings in this age were chosen for the strangeness of their names: witness the judicious reigns of Egbert and Ethelbert and the less notable tenures of Ethelwulf and Ethelbald. Though it seemed briefly that Alfred the Great and his son Edward would restore the crown to those who deserved it for more meritocratic reasons, rulers like Eadwig, Ethelred the Unready, and Harthacnut wrested it away amidst chaos brought about by Danish coastal raids. Time would wait until the Battle of Hastings for the English monarchy to assert its right to a good, simple English name.

And in October of the year 1066, that time came when Duke William of Normandy ventured across the Channel and defeated Harold II's forces in a fierce struggle. William the Conqueror promptly set about cataloguing his recent acquisitions in the epic sheepskin *Domesday Book,* and Norman influence burgeoned during the next three centuries. French became the language of the nobility, while English splintered into hundreds of dialects in villages around the island—hence the atrocious and sometimes arbitrary rules of spelling and grammar which remain today.

Henry II ascended to the throne in 1154, initiating the conquest of Ireland. Soon after that expansion of power, King John was forced by the nobility to sign the Magna Carta in 1215. The document's emphasis on preserving the rights of the Church and royal respect for laws set the precedent for the U.S. Constitution and other democratic charters. The first Parliament convened in 1265, and Wales became a principality of the English crown in 1284.

The Wars of the Roses pitted the house of Lancaster against that of York in a battle for supremacy of the nobility which lasted from 1455-85. Henry Bolingbroke usurped the throne from Richard II in 1399, putting the Lancaster (or Plantagenet) house in Buckingham Palace, and giving Shakespeare something decent to write about. Henry V, perhaps England's most beloved king, conquered France in the legendary Battle of Agincourt, a victory for the English underdogs which soon became legendary. His son, Henry VI, blew it, letting Richard III get his murderous paws on the crown. It was Henry VII who restored law and order, inaugurating the rule of the House of Tudor, which survived until 1603. Henry VIII waged wars against France and Scotland, and proclaimed himself king of Ireland in 1542. In the meantime, in an infamous battle with the Pope over his many marriages, Henry converted England from Roman Catholicism to Protestantism, establishing the Anglican Church. During the reign of Elizabeth I, Henry's daughter, the English defeated the Spanish Armada to become the leading Protestant power in Europe and established themselves as a colonial empire.

The unification of England, Wales, and Scotland effectively took place in 1603, when Protestant James VI of Scotland ascended to the throne as James I of England. The Stuart kings began to irk Parliament with their Catholic sympathies and usurpations of Parliament's financial prerogatives. Tensions came to a head in the English Civil War (1642-48), when Parliament cut off Charles's. In the aftermath, the monarchy was abolished, and a Puritan Commonwealth was founded in 1649. Upon Cromwell's death, his son Richard succeeded him as Lord Protector, but lacked the qualities that kept his father's tenuous grip on the republic. Less than two years later, Charles II was returned to the throne unconditionally, to general relief.

The relatively bloodless Glorious Revolution erupted in 1688 to ward off the possibility of James II achieving a Catholic monarchical dynasty; Protestant William of Orange and his wife Mary were crowned when they assented to the Bill of (Parliamentary) Rights that, after a century of violent upheaval, quietly revolutionized the relationship between Crown and Parliament. This triumph brought Parliamentary leadership to the fore, and over the 18th century, the Prime Minister gradually eclipsed the monarch as the head of government.

The 18th century saw one of the greatest social changes in English history: massive portions of the rural populace migrated to towns, pushed off the land by Enclosure Acts, and attracted by industrial employment. During the next century, industrialization insidiously and irreversibly altered the texture of English as well as global society as England expanded into Empire.

By the 1830s, industrial conditions were visibly poor enough to spur the beginnings of domestic regulation. While the Whigs inaugurated their century of moderate reform in 1832, working-class activists clamored for more. The Chartist movement dramatically pressed for universal manhood suffrage, but modest reforms and a boom in the forties effectively curbed more radical reform till a good while later. Trade-union organization, however, continued, assuming its modern form during the strike of the East London dockers in 1889 and finding a political voice in the Labour Party at the turn of the century. Despite labor gains, urban ills only grew in visibility. The Victorians, emboldened with new faith in "scientific" methods, took up poverty as their next problem to solve, paving the way for a slew of welfare programs begun by the Liberal government in 1910. The peers drew the line at Lloyd George's "people's budget," provoking a constitutional crisis. Herbert Asquith traded support for Irish Home Rule for the votes of the Home Rule party, only to face the possibility of civil war in Ireland—a threat interrupted by the explosion of World War I.

The Great War, Britain's first continental action in a century, scarred the British spirit with the loss of a generation and dashed Victorian dreams of a peaceful, progressive society. Abroad, the second Empire reached its peak and immediately lost its power: the English and French divided the German and Turkish Empires for themselves, only to lose them to the forces of democracy anad national determinism which the Allies themselves had unleashed. Hopes for a new beginning *within* England after the war were derailed—although women gained suffrage at this time—as a sense of aimlessness overtook the nation's politics. A succession of amusing mediocrities came to power: Bonar Law, Ramsay MacDonald, and Stanley Baldwin. The 1930s saw depression and mass unemployment, inertially presided over by Baldwin's National government, as well as the appeasement of Hitler, led by Neville "peace in our time" Chamberlain.

Britain withstood Hitler's potent threats in World War II. Britain's WWI enemies had never been able to seriously threaten Britain itself, except for a few zeppelin raids on the southern shore. But this time, fire and rubble ravaged the sitting room as well as the French field; the German Blitz ravaged London's homes and cities, with citizens proudly resisting. The fall of France precipitated the end of the Chamberlain government and creation of a war cabinet firmly led by Winston Churchill.

The post-war era's growing affluence and diversity propelled Britain to the center stage of international popular culture, and gave rise and fall to countless subcultures clustered around pop music and fashion, as well as a striking confidence in the "modern" and "new." At the same time, Harold Wilson's government introduced a number of crucial social liberalizations, including reform of divorce and homosexuality laws and the abolition of capital punishment. Wilson also sought to drive the nation forward with the "white heat" of technological advance, but toward the end of the 60s became mired in the government's decreasingly "consensual" relationship with organized labor, which now represented middle-class clerical workers as much as railwaymen and Durham miners.

England gradually gave up most of its colonial holdings in Africa, the Middle East, and South Asia, and retreated embarrassingly in the Suez Canal crisis. Visionary Conservative Harold Macmillan heard "the winds of change" blowing and paved the way for the denouement of Empire, hoping to win Britain its place in the European Community, a task completed in 1974 by Edward Heath.

Increasing economic problems in the 70s led to a boom in the theorization of "decline." The discovery of oil in the North Sea lifted hopes, only to be hit hard by plummeting prices. Government after government wrangled with the unions, culminating in a series of public-service strikes in early 1979, the "Winter of Discontent," which stymied the Labour government. "Crisis? What crisis?" Callaghan was misquoted as saying upon return from a tropical vacation.

It was against this backdrop that Britain grasped at what looked like a chance at change: the admonishing "Victorian values" and nationalism of Margaret Thatcher. Her first term seemed doomed by a painful recession, but by 1983, the victory in the Falklands and embarrassing disarray in the Labour Party could ensure another term. She claimed to turn from the won war to "the enemy within," a bitter miners' strike in 1983-84, while denationalizing and dismantling the welfare state with disarming quips like "There is no such thing as society." Meanwhile, Neil Kinnock, once of the party left, piloted Labour's "modernization"—an awkward leap to the right in search of electability. By 1987, the Tories won over a contented sector of the affluent working class with such popular policies as the sale of public housing to its occupants, even as others shuddered at the mention of "that bloody woman's" name. Thatcher's policies brought dramatic prosperity to many, but sharpened the divide between those who benefitted from the changes and those who didn't.

Thatcher prided herself on her "politics of conviction," but her stubbornness was her undoing, as she clung to the unpopular (and unconscionable) poll tax and resisted European integration. A 1990 leadership challenge led to her resignation and the election of circus clown's son John Major as party leader and Prime Minister. Major quietly jettisoned the poll tax and stepped more carefully around Europe. His "Citizen's Charter" tries to continue the reform of public services less radically, gently speaking of Health Service "customers" and promising to refund delayed rail passengers. But Major's cabinet has been more occupied with predicting the end to a deep recession resulting partly from the credit-fueled 80s boom. In 1993, the British pound toppled out of the EC's monetary regulation system, embarrassing Major's government and casting doubt on whether Britain would be able to keep its place in the Community. Finally, in August of the same year, after severe division between Major and anti-treaty rebels within the Conservative Party, Britain became the last member of the EC to ratify the Maastricht Treaty on closer European Union. Even with these Conservative debacles, Labour failed again to shed the image gained in the 70s and propagated furiously by Mrs. Thatcher, and the Tories won another five years in April 1992. Labour's defeat spurred the election of a new leader, Scotsman John Smith, and the pursuit of reform, including, in February 1994, a proposal to lower the age of sexual consent between men from 21 to 16 (the same as that for lesbians and heterosexuals; the final, compromise amendment lowered the age of consent between men to 18). Yet the Labour Party, and the nation, was shaken up yet again by the beloved Smith's death of a heart attack on May 13, 1994.

■■■ LITERATURE

> Leonard was trying to form his style on Ruskin.... Something told him
> that these modifications would not do; and that something, had he
> known it, was the spirit of English Prose. "My flat is dark as well as
> stuffy." Those were the words for him.
>
> —*E.M. Forster*, Howards End

An understanding of English beauty comes more easily when accompanied by a familiarity with the legends and literature, and the society, that frame it. To attempt a two-page summary of English literature is, of course, absurd, but we'll try it anyway. We will suggest a limited and eccentric list of works—some masterpieces, some lesser-known—that begin to recreate the English literary experience.

Beowulf is always a terrific beginning, no matter what anybody tells you—it's a sonorous, rhythmic testament of an Anglo-Saxon culture at the close of the Middle Ages. Geoffrey Chaucer, the first court poet to write in English, revealed the language to be spirited and musical; his *Canterbury Tales* (c. 1387) remain some of the funniest, raciest stories in the English canon. The anonymously authored *Gawain and the Green Knight* (c. 1375) plays out a simple tale of chivalry in a mysterious, forbidding landscape. A more recondite medieval masterpiece is William Langland's *Piers Plowman* (1367-1386), which turned the theme of pilgrimage into an intense, often tortured allegory. His poem criticized the increasing decadence of the rich in the face of common suffering; much of the best work of this period deals with the injustice of class stratification.

A great project of this time began with the first translation of the Bible into English by John Wyclif and his followers in the 1380s. Edition after edition came out of the authoritative word, followed by hurlyburly over exactly how authoritative that word really was. The translator William Tyndale fled to the continent to finish his Biblical work, but loyalists of Henry VIII soon martyred him for his pains. A Geneva English edition rose in the mid-16th century as a steadfastly-Protestant version of the Bible, prompting King James to set forty-seven translators to bring forth a Word of God the King could live with. The result rumbles with magnificent pace and rhetoric, and is a monument the following centuries could scarcely touch.

Those who equate Shakespeare with an English-class avalanche of whithers and wherefores would do well to know that the Bard had perhaps the filthiest feather ever to scrawl the English language. We provide a handy table for you to adapt his words to curses and putdowns you may wish to use in your everyday travels:

My, they're horny!	*they're* "as prime as goats, as hot as monkeys, as salt as wolves in pride."
to have sex	*to make the* "beast with two backs"
This guy's a fat pain-in-the-ass!	"This sanguine coward, this bed-presser, this horse-back-breaker, this huge hill of flesh."
You suck!	"The devil damn thee black, thou cream-faced loon."
This guy from Iceland's a moron, and I hate him	"Pish for thee, Iceland dog! Thou prick-ear'd cur of Iceland!"
A guy in a bar wants to fight you	"Brass, cur! Thou damned and luxurious mountain goat, thou offer'st me brass?"
You kicked his butt, and want to tell your friends all about it	"I took by the throat the circumsized dog, and smote him, thus."

Christopher Marlowe and Ben Jonson tag-teamed their way through the end of the 16th century: Marlowe lost his life to a dagger in a pub brawl and Jonson spent spells in jail for acts as varied as insulting Scotland and killing an actor in a swordfight. None of this prevented Marlowe from guiding Dr. Faustus and Tamburlaine into the world of English letters or Jonson from lashing some of the most arcane Greek and Latin forms to an admirably spare, plain-spoken verse. John Donne (1572-1631), the pastor of London's St. Paul's Cathedral, wrote dramatic, devotional poetry; "Jack Donne," as he is also known, penned intense and ardent erotic verse on the side. Author of the pious Holy Sonnets and the uplifting words, "No man is an island, entire of itself," Donne also wrote a controversial defense of suicide. The quintessential work of this period isn't *Hamlet* (considered inferior until the 18th century), but Robert Burton's *Anatomy of Melancholy* (1621), which gives insight into Renaissance intellectual life. George Herbert's *The Temple* (1633), a volume of simply titled, simply phrased lyrics, might be the most moving collection of Christian poetry in English. The English Puritans, like their American counterparts, produced a huge volume of obsessive and beautiful literature; blind John Milton unclasped some of the Bible's most compressed and allusive verses, and released them into a boundless epic landscape. In *Paradise Lost,* Satan, Adam, and Eve take on a flesh and complexity the Bible would not grant them, allowing Milton "to justify God's ways to man," as he put it. Another Puritan vision arose from John Bunyan, a self-taught Nonconformist pastor whose *Pilgrim's Progress* charts the

Christian's quest for redemption in a world awaiting the apocalypse. After the monarchy regained full power, English writers like Pope and Dryden led a neo-classical revival, which yielded a new keen satire of English social and political life.

William Blake's mock-evangelical "proems" seem to prophesy both the rise and fall of English might; the soaring spirit of "Jerusalem" (which became an anthem of the Victorian era) coexists with the dark, grimy reality of "London." William Wordsworth's immense blank-verse poem *The Prelude* (1798-1850) contains some of the greatest word-painting in the language, and helped make Wordsworth the leader of the Romantic literary movement in England. John Keats, who died at the age of 26 with the words "I always made an awkward bow," was the finest of the Romantic poets; "To Autumn," with its imagery of ripening before death, may well be the most perfect poem in English. Tennyson ground out gorgeous verse for over a half-century; frustrated poets will be soothed to know that writer's block sunk its teeth hard into this Poet Laureate, releasing him only by the agony of revision. Jane Austen's *Pride and Prejudice* (1813) criticizes provincial self-importance somewhat more harshly than it is often remembered to, while Matthew Arnold (1822-88) rebelled against the industrialization of literature, attempting to reinforce elitist culture against the anarchy of mass rule. His "Dover Beach" resonates still to cynical, literary youth on both sides of the Atlantic.

Charles Dickens's often biting, sometimes sentimental works draw on the bleakness of his childhood as well as the more severe destitution of others'; in some ways, his writing was to the abolition of child labor in England what *Uncle Tom's Cabin* was to slavery in the United States. In *Wuthering Heights,* Emily Brontë matches the average but limp pancake of a man, Edgar Linton, against the exquisitely ferocious, socially unmanageable Heathcliff, and makes it quite clear who has the superior soul.

Thomas Hardy (1840-1928) brought the Victorian Age to an end on a dark note with the fate-ridden Wessex landscapes of *Jude the Obscure* and *Tess of the d'Urbervilles*. His poetry is often underappreciated, though he wrote what may be the best break-up poem of all time ("The smile on your mouth was the deadest thing/ Alive enough to have strength to die;/ And a grin of bitterness swept thereby/ Like an ominous bird a-wing..."). Like Hardy, George Eliot (Mary Ann Evans) lost her religious faith; her skepticism drew her to the security of traditional village life. Her depictions are never sentimental; her relentlessly critical voice in *Middlemarch* makes you wonder at first if she sympathizes with any of her characters.

Gerard Manley Hopkins (1844-89) revolutionized English poetry with his "sprung rhythm" verses; he is considered the chief forerunner of poetic modernism. Writing privately and patiently in his Jesuit monastery, he never expected his poetry to be published. An intense religious certainty shines through the thickets of a dark world in poems like "The Wind-Hover" and "The World is Charged with the Grandeur of God."

London in the first third of the 20th century became the home of artistic movements like *Blast!* and the Bloomsbury Group, pulling the world's intellects into its midst. Like Huck Finn, T.S. Eliot is a Missouri boy, but Tom relocated to England later in life. It didn't help; *The Waste Land* (1922), one of the most important poems of this century, is a picture of a fragmented, motionless, precious world waiting for the end. *Four Quartets* (1935-44), Eliot's final poetic testament, is far more ambiguous; a Christian frame of reference returns with a vengeance, and even with the faint light of hope. In *To the Lighthouse,* Virginia Woolf explores English culture and the private, ineffable yearnings of the individual mind; in *Orlando,* she unsettles not only language but also history and gender. E.M. Forster's half-critical, half-abashedly romantic works, among them *A Passage to India* and *Howards End,* makes obvious the links between English repression, class hypocrisy, and wet dreams of Empire. Contemporary fascination with his vision, revealed by the extraordinary success of Merchant-Ivory films, tells us a good deal about our own confused idealism. Language and politics take on a frightening obscurity in George Orwell's World War II era writing: in *1984,* fascism and communism have converged into a raven-ous totalitarian state which strives to strip the world of memory and words of meaning. Lawrence Durrell fled to Greece and Alexandria, and built himself a palace of words in *The Black Book* and *The Alexandria Quartet*—all the phthisises and littorals and litoteses will drive you to buy an OED, and will probably drive you crazy anyway.

The contemporary English temper has yet to emerge clearly in literature, leaving other media, including film and pop music, to pick up the slack. Instead, English literature, like every other sort, has splintered in a thousand brilliant directions. W.H. Auden, often misunderstood, emerged as Eliot's successor in the mainstream of English literature, yet his disjointed and ironic meditations belong outside the broad literary current. The minimally furnished poems of Philip Larkin explore the aftermath of modernism, questioning the value of its psychic destruction and searching for a new home for the tired spirit. Tom Stoppard, originally Czech, pushes Pirandellian comedy to new limits; grim yet hysterical plays like *Rosencrantz and Guildenstern are Dead, Jumpers,* and *Travesties* challenge the very idea of theater and communication in a post-certainty age. Jeanette Winterson's wry, nimble voice emerged in the late '80s, vaulting between topics as far-flung as Deuteronomy, lesbianism, and Napoleon's chickens.

England's greatest test to relativity flamed forth in Bradford in 1988, when Muslim protesters burned Salman Rushdie's *The Satanic Verses* under the BBC's watchful eye. The act spurred a riptide of protest that culminated in the Ayatollah Khomeini's *fatwa* (death sentence) against the author. Heinrich Heine's famous dictum, "Once they burn books, they'll end up burning people" seems sadly relevant here—a scant few have spoken against this tyranny over words, as politicians refuse to see him or support him in public, bending to polls and mortal fears while Rushdie spends his fifth year in hiding.

England has produced a great number of "minor" writers whose works give expression to contemporary trends and values. The hilarious novels and stories of P.G. Wodehouse (Bertie Wooster and his butler Jeeves), and the elegant mystery novels of Dorothy L. Sayers and Agatha Christie affectionately satirize the figure of the useless English aristocrat. James Herriot (Alf Wight), author of *All Creatures Great and Small,* recently faced backlash from a flock of steadfastly unanthropomorphized sheep: they trampled him and broke his leg. Sue Townsend's *Diaries of Adrian Mole* sets brilliant adolescence in Thatcherite England and we love her for it. The popular allegories of Richard Adams (such as *Watership Down*) depict England as a wondering nation searching for new myths and new heroes, while J.R.R. Tolkein's engrossing fantasies prove that old English mythologies remain vibrant sources for the present.

■■■ THE MEDIA

In a culture not yet completely addicted to the telly, the influence of papers is enormous. *The Sun,* a daily Rupert Murdoch-owned tabloid better known for its page-three pinup than for its reporting, was widely credited with delivering victory to Margaret Thatcher in her re-election campaign (no, she did not pose). Ambitious English journalists aspire to finish their apprenticeships in the provinces and join "the Fleet Street hacks " (who now inhabit the old Wapping docks). With the exception of the Manchester-born *Guardian,* national papers originate from London.

The Financial Times, printed on orange paper, does more elegantly for the City what the *Wall Street Journal* does for Manhattan. *The Times,* for centuries a model of thoughtful discretion and mild infallibility, has turned Tory under the leadership of Rupert "Buy It" Murdoch. The *Daily Telegraph* (dubbed "Torygraph") is fairly conservative and old-fashioned, but rigorously fair. The *Independent* lives up to its name. *The Observer* is a polished Sunday paper. Of the screaming tabloids, *The Daily Mail, The Daily Express,* and *The Standard* (the only evening paper) make serious attempts at popular journalism, while *News of the World,* the *Star,* the *Daily*

Mirror, and *Today* are as shrill and lewd as *The Sun.* The best international news shows up in *The Times, The Guardian,* and *The Independent.*

On Sundays, *The Sunday Times, The Sunday Telegraph, Independent on Sunday,* and the highly polished *Observer* publish multi-section papers with glossy magazines, detailed arts, sports, and news coverage, together with a few more "soft bits" than their daily counterparts. Sunday papers, although they share close association with their sister dailies, are actually separate newspapers, with a subtly distinctive look and style.

The magazine *Punch,* dating from the days of Dickens, parodied England and the world with eccentric delight until its slow decline was mercifully terminated a few years ago. Its long-time devotees may find some consolation in the new semi-weekly *Oldie. Private Eye* is subversive, hilarious, and overtly political. The immensely popular *Viz* parodies modern prejudices and hypocrisies with unashamedly outrageous comic-strips. World affairs are covered with a surreptitious wit by *The Economist. The New Statesman* on the left and *The Spectator* on the right cover politics and the arts with verve and sense. *British GQ* displays all the best of English public school humor: one of their writers recently renamed sex "the pigskin bus pulling into Tuna Town."

England boasts some of the best music rags in the world: *Melody Maker* and *New Musical Express* trace the latest trends with often hilarious wit (check these for concert news), while *Q* covers a broader spectrum in excellent detail. *Grammophone* focuses on classical music, *Folk Roots* does the folk and trad bit, and *i-D* and *The Face* cover pop culture in general. The indispensable London journal *Time Out* is the most comprehensive calendar/guide to the city and features fascinating pieces on British life and culture.

The BBC established its reputation for fairness and wit with its radio services: BBC1 has ceded responsibilities of news coverage to its cousin BBC4, but continues to feature rock and roll institution John Peel. BBC2 has easy listening and light talk shows; BBC3 broadcasts classical music (undoubtedly the finest station of its kind anywhere). AM is called Medium Wave (MW) in England. Each town and region in England is equipped with a variety of local commercial broadcasting services.

TV-owners in England have to pay a tax; this supports the advertisement-free activities of BBC TV. Close association with the government has not hampered innovation. Home of *Monty Python's Flying Circus,* BBC TV broadcasts on two national channels. BBC1 carries news at 1, 6, and 9pm as well as various Britcoms. Sheep-dog trials are telecast on BBC2, along with cultural programs. ITV, Britain's established commercial network, carries much comedy along with its own McNews. Channel 4, the newest channel, has highly respected arts programming and a fine news broadcast at 7pm on weeknights—Salman Rushdie once worked for them. This web of national programming is supplemented by local stations. *The Simpsons* now play every night and twice on Sundays. Bart has a new British friend: his name is Blobby, and we make no attempt to understand him. Parliament was introduced to television in late 1989: try to catch a session of Question Time, the regular, refreshingly hostile, parliamentary interrogation of the prime minister. You'll have to reserve a seat with your embassy months in advance, but it's worth it.

■ ■ ■ MUSIC

England was long called "a land without music," a tag which is not entirely deserved. Queen Elizabeth I funded all the arts: William Byrd wrote magnificent pieces for both Anglican and Roman churches. Morley, Weelkes, and Wilbye revamped madrigals; John Dowland wrote lachrymose works for lute. Henry Purcell was England's best-known composer for centuries; his opera *Dido and Aeneas* is still performed. English hospitality welcomed Handel, Mozart (who wrote his first symphony in Chelsea), and Haydn (whose last was named "London"). Gilbert and Sullivan's operettas have been loved since the late 19th century for puns, social satire, farce, and pomp; though the pair were rumored to hate each other, they collaborated on such chestnuts as *The Mikado, H.M.S. Pinafore,* and *The Pirates of Penzance.* Serious music began a "second renaissance" under Edward Elgar, whose bombast is outweighed by moments of quiet eloquence, like "Nimrod" in his *Enigma Variations.* Delius redid impressionism, while Gustav (*The Planets*) Holst adapted neoclassical methods and folk materials to his Romantic moods.

William Walton and Ralph Vaughan Williams brought musical modernism to England; Walton's *First Symphony,* Vaughan Williams's *Sixth,* and Havergal Brian's *Gothic* are three of this century's finest scores. Benjamin Britten's *Peter Grimes* turned a broader audience on to opera; his long string of operas ends with *Death in Venice.* Michael Tippett wrote operas, four symphonies, and the oratorio *A Child of Our Time,* for which he asked T.S. Eliot to write the words; Eliot told Tippett he could do a better job himself. Peter Maxwell Davies, Harrison Birtwistle, Brian Ferneyhough, and Robert Simpson are important postwar composers.

After World War II, imported American rock and jazz led to the first wave of "British Invasion" bands. The Beatles spun out the songs your mother should know and seemed at the front of every musical and cultural trend; the Rolling Stones became their nastier, harder-edged answer, while the Kinks voiced horror at the American vulgarity that seemed, to them, to have crushed Little England. The Who began as Kinks-like popsters, then expanded into "rock operas" like *Tommy* (lately a Broadway hit) and the better *Quadrophenia,* which chronicled the famous fights in Brighton between "rockers" (who liked leather jackets and America) and "mods" (who liked scooters, speed, androgyny, and the Who).

Psychedelic drugs and high hopes produced a flurry of great tunes by bands like the short-lived Creation from '66 to '68. White British adapters of African-American blues—most famously the Yardbirds—spawned guitar heroes such as Eric Clapton (Cream) and Jimmy Page (Led Zeppelin), who dominated mass markets in the early '70s. The same period's "art-rock "(Yes, Pink Floyd, Roxy Music) was at times exciting, at times dreadful. Working-class "skinheads" adopted the sounds and aggression of Jamaican reggae and ska; later skins would split into socialist, anti-racist and right-wing, neo-fascist factions, both propelled by stripped-down rock called "oi." While David Bowie flitted through personae, "pub rock" groups tried to return rock to the people–and in London, a King's Road entrepreneur organized the Sex Pistols to get publicity for his boutique, "Sex."

With "Sex's" clothes, Johnny Rotten's snarl, the Pistols changed music and culture forever. The Clash made their punk explicitly, anti-Thatcherite, political; the all-female Slits mixed theirs with reggae. When the Pistols cursed out presenter Bill Grundy on national TV in December '76, newspapers rushed to condemn this "punk rock," which only gave it more steam. "Do it yourself" was the order of the day: untouched, and often untouchable, by the big corporations, the second wave of punks started their own clubs, record labels, distributors, and studios, making the International Pop Underground that persists to this day. Teenaged Marion Elliot ran away, renamed herself Poly Styrene, and started X-Ray Spex; ex-X Ray Spex sax player Lora Logic found her niche at Rough Trade, a record label with unconventional rock like the influential Fall, the dissonant Swell Maps, the feminist Raincoats, and the suave Monochrome Set.

Industrial unemployment gave Northerners the time to form bands and a harsh landscape to inspire them. The fans who sent it up the charts were surprised to learn that the Buzzcocks' Pete Shelley wrote "Ever Fallen in Love?" about a man. Joy Division and Factory Records made Manchester echo with gloomily poetic rock and graphic design. Leeds's Mekons stayed true to punk's roots, and Gang of Four's *Entertainment!* chewed up funk and reggae to spit out a profound Marxist critique of capital, work, and sex. Birmingham's Au Pairs asked feminist questions over a hooky backbeat, and that grim city's leftist ska bands, like the Selecter and the Specials, took their "two-tone" style to the people. Elvis Costello, Squeeze, and the Jam found that punk and ska had cleared the ground for smart pop, which stayed persistently and bitingly English even as it took over world charts.

Melancholy stylishness like Felt and Eyeless in Gaza passed sadly unnoticed through the 80s, but Manchester mope-tops the Smiths shook teens everywhere. Bristol's Subway Records sent Flatmates, Razorcuts, and Rosehips spinning winsomely across the land. King of the Slums bowed and scraped before the electric violin; sweetly-loud My Bloody Valentine were much-copied in '91-92. Oxford's Tallulah Gosh idealized childhood in million-mile-an-hour pop; regrouped as Heavenly, they, and Bristol-based Sarah Records, inspired self-proclaimed "boys" and "girls" to cast aside volume and swagger for clean tunes and last-chance tries at innocence.

Even current dance trends spring from punk: the Human League and Cabaret Voltaire (whose native Sheffield had no clubs to play in) learned to play synths to make assaultive noise before they used them to shake up clubgoers. Yaz, Depeche Mode, and New Order soon joined them. A decade later, unemployed kids and easy access to the drug Ecstasy created rave culture's all-night, all-day, sweaty, anaesthetic gatherings and the faceless electronic music that accompanied them.

National trends are made and unmade by London-based music weeklies. An unknown band can make "single of the week," graduate to the papers' covers, sell 600,000 CDs and then vanish. The big trend for 1994 was "the New Wave of New Wave," of which Action Painting! are this book's pick. After 16 years, the TV Personalities have kept their brilliant babyfaced charm. Other Sarah-ish bands to see are the Fat Tulips, Blueboy and Boyracer. The popular, but still-inspiring, Wedding Present pound out throaty angst.

■■■ FOOD

> English cooking, like the English climate, is a training for life's
> unavoidable hardships.
>
> —R. P. Lister

English cuisine's deservedly modest reputation redeems itself in the few specialties without which the world's palate would be sadly incomplete. Chances are you will leave the island an addict to rice pudding (a creamy dessert), Yorkshire pudding (not a creamy dessert), Flake bars, shortbread, roast potatoes, sausage rolls, and the inestimable chocolate-covered Hobnob.

The English are a nation of **carnivores,** and the best native dishes are roasts—beef, lamb, and Wiltshire hams. Many proprietors will prepare vegetarian meals on request, if the incessance of meat is too much for you. Vegetables, usually boiled into a flavorless, textureless, colorless mass, are the weakest part of the meal; ask for a salad instead. Meat isn't just for dinner anymore; the English like their breakfasts meaty and cholesterol-filled. The famous English breakfast, still served in the best B&Bs, consists of orange juice, eggs, bacon, sausage, toast, butter, marmalade, grilled tomatoes and mushrooms, kippers, and (in winter) porridge. You will probably want to choose tea to wash all this down; unlike its French and Italian counterparts, English coffee is not exceptional.

The English like their desserts exceedingly sweet, but even if you shy from sugar, you should try one of the glorious English puddings. "Boiled in a pail, tied in the tail of an old bleached shirt, so hot that they hurt," some of the best varieties are Christmas pudding, treacle tart, Spotted Dick, and steamed castle pudding, all served with thick jams and syrups. Perhaps the most blatant misnomer in the English language is trifle, a wondrous combination of the best things in life—cake, custard, jam, whipped cream, and fresh fruit (strawberries are best). Crumpets, scones, Jaffa cakes, and rich Dundee fruitcake are all tasty side-effects of the English sweet tooth.

Pub grub (food served in bars) is fast, filling, and a good option when all else is closed or vandalishly expensive. Hot meals vary from Cornish pastries (meat and vegetable wrapped in pastry) to steak and kidney pie with vegetables. The inexpensive "ploughman's lunch" is simply cheese, bread, pickle, chutney, and a tomato; contrary to common belief, it is not traditional English country fare but the product of a 60s advertising campaign. Fish and chips, traditionally served in newsprint and dripping with grease, now face competition from McNuggets and Whoppers.

In **restaurants,** watch the fine print: a perfectly inexpensive entree may be only one item on a bill supplemented with side dishes, shamefully priced drinks, VAT, minimum per-person charges, and an occasional 50p-£2 cover charge. You don't have to tip in those restaurants that include service charge (10-12½%) on the bill. And if the service has disappointed you, you can complain to the manager and then legally subtract part or all of the service charge.

For a cheaper alternative to restaurant dining, try a meal in a **caff**—the traditional British equivalent of a U.S. diner. Caffs serve an odd mix of inexpensive English and Italian specialties (£4.50-6 for a full meal). Interiors range from serviceable to dingy, and tables may be shared, but the food is often very good. **Sandwich shops** are handy for a quick bite and differ little from their kind in any country. Many serve filling, inexpensive breakfast foods all day. If you're not ordering take-away, order at the counter and sit down; someone will bring your food to you. You leave your plate on the table and pay on your way out. No tip is necessary.

Outdoor markets and **supermarkets** (Safeway, Sainsbury, the Co-Op, and Tesco) sell suitable fare for picnics. Buy some cheese (Stilton—very, very sharp; Double Gloucester—very sharp; or Cheddar—sharp and cheap), apples (Cox's pippins are good), and a package of Hobnobs (oaty biscuits dipped in chocolate), then find a suitably picturesque view. As an alternative to English food, try Chinese, Greek, and Indian cuisines. English restaurants (especially those in London and Birmingham) serve some of the best *tandoori* food outside of India.

TEA

English "tea" refers both to a drink and to a social ritual. Tea the drink is served strong and milky; if you want it any other way, say so. Tea the social ritual centers around a meal. Afternoon high tea includes cooked meats, salad, sandwiches, and pastries. Fans of Victorianism will appreciate the dainty cucumber sandwiches served at classy tea joints like Harrods and Fortnum and Mason. Outside of London, dinner moves to noontime and tea becomes the evening meal, often served with a huge pot of the liquid. Cream tea, a specialty of Cornwall and Devon, includes toast, shortbread, crumpets, scones, and jam, accompanied by delicious clotted cream (a cross between whipped cream and butter). Most Brits take short tea breaks each day, mornings ("elevenses"), and afternoons (around 4pm). Sunday takes the cake for best tea day; the indulgent can while away a couple of hours over a pot of Earl Grey, a pile of buttered scones, and the Sunday supplements.

■■■ PUBS AND BEER

What three things does drink especially provoke?—Marry, sir, nose-painting, sleep, and urine.

—The Porter in Macbeth

"As much of the history of England has been brought about in public houses as in the House of Commons," said Sir William Harcourt. You may not witness history in the making, but you will certainly absorb the spirit of the land with a stop at a local tavern. The pub's importance as a social institution is reflected in its careful furnishings. Mahogany walls appear ancient and are often intricately carved; velvet-covered benches face a crackling fireplace under brass ceiling fans and chandeliers. Indeed, such establishments resemble the private living rooms they have come to replace. Many pubs are centuries old, and each has a distinctive history, ambience, and clientele. Pub crawls are the English equivalent of bar hopping; buy drinks at the bar—bartenders are not usually tipped.

Beer is the standard pub drink, and it is "pulled" from the tap into pint glasses (nearly 20 oz., enough to inebriate a small horse) or the more modest (but less common) half-pints. A request for "a beer" will get you a full pint, and it won't be the blond fizzy lager to which Americans are accustomed. **Bitter** is the staple of English beer, named for its sharp, hoppy aftertaste. Fullers and Youngs are slightly fruity in taste, while Abbot and Ruddles are dark and full-bodied. Other worthy brews include Courage, Directors, Tetleys, John Smith, and Samuel Smith. "Real ale," naturally carbonated (unlike most beers) and drawn from a barrel, retains a die-hard cult of connoisseurs in the shadow of giant corporate breweries. Brown, pale, and India pale ales—less common varieties—all have a relatively heavy flavor with noticeable hop. The Campaign for Real Ale (CAMRA) publishes a guide to pubs that serve real ale; those true to the cause should write to 34 Alma Rd., St. Albans, Herts., England AL1 3BR. Be warned, though, that CAMRA also insists that "Darts is French;" the mere suggestion is clearly tantamount to heresy. **Stout** is rich, dark, and creamy; try standing a match on the silky foam head of a **Guinness.** Most draught ales and stouts are served at room temperature, so if you can't stand the heat, try a **lager,** the European equivalent of American beer. German, Dutch, American, and even Mexican imports are steadily gaining acceptance, especially among trendier crowds (watch the limeys stick limes in their Corona bottles). **Cider,** a fermented apple juice served sweet or dry, is one potent and tasty alternative to beer. Especially succulent brands include Bulmer's Woodpecker, Red Rock, Strongbow, and Diamond White. A **shandy** is a refreshing combination of beer and fizzy lemonade; **black velvet,** a mating of stout and champagne; **black and tan,** stout and beer (layered like a parfait); and **snakebite,** a murky mix of lager and cider.

Those who don't drink alcohol should savor the pub experience all the same; Cidona, a non-alcoholic cider, and BritVic fruit juices are served. Along with food and drink, pubs often host games. Traditional pub games include darts, pool, and snooker (billiards played on a larger table with smaller balls). More recently, a brash and bewildering array of video games, fruit (slot) machines, and extortionate CD jukeboxes has invaded many pubs.

Visitors will learn to their dismay that pubs close relatively early. Generally, drinks are served from 11am-11pm Monday to Saturday, noon-10:30pm on Sunday (though most take a closing break from about 3-7pm on Sundays). A bell 10 minutes before closing time signifies "last orders." T.S. Eliot knew the special agony of pub closings: many a drunkard has argued that the most painful words in all *The Waste Land* come in its second part, with the publican-god's cry, "HURRY UP PLEASE ITS TIME." Whether or not patrons consider the existential implications of the call, it does signal 20 minutes remain for them to finish their beers before chairs go up and lights go down.

■■■ SPORTS

The English take their sports seriously. **Football** (known as soccer in the U.S.) is a chaotic and rowdy spectacle of chanting, fierce loyalties, and sudden violent outbursts; it is also the best game in the world. It is bet upon energetically. **Cricket,** a game of great subtlety and languorous civility, involves England and former members of its empire in intricate matches that last either one or five days. **Croquet,** chess on the grass, requires the careful attention that the leisured class can afford to provide. **Rugby**—"rugger" to its players—is a melée of blood and drinking songs, incomprehensible to the outsider. **Horse-racing** is integral to English leisure; the Grand National Steeplechase in Liverpool in March, and the Royal Ascot and the Derby in June are the highlights of the equestrian year. **Tennis** remains immensely popular despite England's inabilty to produce even a half-decent club player for Wimbledon since Virginia Wade. If English sports leave you bored, take solace in the fact that Monday Night Football is now often relayed from the U.S. to television screens all over Britain.

London

A man who is tired of London is tired of life; for there is in London all that life can afford.

—Samuel Johnson

At first, London is kind to the expectations of visitors stuffing their mental baggage with bobbies and Beefeaters, nursery rhymes and "Masterpiece Theatre," Sherlock Holmes and history books. The Thamescape is still bounded by the over-familiar Big Ben in the west and the archetypical Tower Bridge in the east; St. Paul's and the Tower of London pop up in between. The relatively small area embraced by the Underground's Circle Line seems filled to bursting with the big sights. But even the most timid of tourists will notice that for some reason, those tube lines spider out a long way from the Circle Line—central London is just a speck on the Greater London map. What makes London not just interesting but enthralling can be found partly in this tension between the close quarters of central London and the expansive boroughs; between the cluttered, familiar, and sometimes fictional past of the heritage industry and a riotously modern present.

■■■ ORIENTATION

■ GETTING IN & OUT OF LONDON

FROM THE AIRPORT

With planes landing every 47 seconds, **Heathrow Airport** (tel. (0181) 759 4321), in Hounslow, Middlesex, is the world's busiest international airport. The *bureaux de change* in each terminal are open daily: Thomas Cook, Terminal 1 (tel. (081) 897 3351; open 24 hr.); International Currency Exchange, Terminal 2 (open 6am-11pm); and Travellers' Exchange Corporation, Terminals 3 (tel. (081) 897 3501) and 4 (tel. (081) 759 4449; both open 24 hr.). The easiest way to reach central London from Heathrow is by **Underground** (Piccadilly line; 45 min. to central London), with one stop for terminals 1, 2, and 3 and one for terminal 4. To reach **Victoria Station,** transfer at Gloucester Rd. or South Kensington to a District Line or Circle Line train heading east. At Victoria, you'll find a blue **Tourist Information Centre** with an accommodations service, more currency exchange, and information about transportation connections (see Getting About below).

London Regional Transport's **Airbus** (tel. 222 1234) makes the trip from Heathrow to central points in the city, including hotels. The Airbus A1 runs to Victoria, stopping at Hyde Park Corner, Harrods, and Earl's Ct. tube station. Airbus A2 runs to Russell Sq., with stops at Euston Station, Baker St. station, Marble Arch, Paddington station, Queensway station, Notting Hill Gate station, and Holland Park. (Both buses run daily 6:30am-3pm 3/hr.; 3-8pm 2/hr.; 1hr.; £5, children £3.) The double-decker Airbuses have plenty of room for luggage, and most are wheelchair accessible. A **National Express** bus (tel. 730 0202) goes from Heathrow to Victoria coach station (5:30am-8:30pm 2/hr., 1 hr., £6.50).

Most charter flights land at **Gatwick Airport** in West Sussex (tel. (0293) 535 353). A number of 24-hr. restaurants and *bureaux de change* are located in both the North and South Terminals. From Gatwick, take the BR Gatwick Express train to Victoria Station (35 min.; daily 5:30am-8pm 4/hr.; 8pm-1am 2/hr.; 1-4am 1/hr. on the hr.; £8.50, under 15 £4.25). Council Travel in London sells tickets for the Gatwick Express for £7.50, cheaper than at BR's ticket window—you get the convenience and speed of train travel at the same price as the bus. **National Express coaches** run between Gatwick and Victoria (5:30am-11pm 1/hr.; 1/hr., £7.50).

Taxis are not advisable, especially during rush hour. Fares from central London to Heathrow run at least £30; from central London to Gatwick, expect to pay £50-60. Travelers loaded down with bulky bags should consider using **London Airways,** a private chauffeur service (tel. 403 2228). For a flat rate, London Airways will take up to four people from either airport to any central London destination (£15/car from Heathrow, £25/car from Gatwick; call for airport pickup in 15 min.).

Flights from the U.S. go into both Gatwick and Heathrow. Check which airport your flight serves before you leave. Starting with American Airlines' service from Chicago, major international flights are now arriving in upstart **Stansted Airport,** northeast of London in Stansted, Essex (tel. (01279) 680500). Stansted is served by British Rail's **Stansted Express** to Liverpool St. Station (40 min.; Mon.-Fri. 5:30am-11pm 2/hr.; Sat. 6:30am-11pm 2/hr.; Sun. 7am-11pm 2/hr.; £10, under 15 £5).

FROM THE TRAIN STATIONS

If you are leaving London by train, find out from which of the eight major stations (Charing Cross, Euston, King's Cross, Liverpool St., Paddington, St. Pancras, Victoria, or Waterloo) you will depart. The Underground links these stations, and its stops bear the same names as the train stations. For information about particular destinations in the U.K. and Ireland, call the numbers listed below.

> To East Anglia, Essex, Southern England, Northeast, East, and South London: tel. 928 5100.
> To the South Midlands, West of England, South Wales, West London, and Republic of Ireland via Fishguard: tel. 262 6767.
> To the East and West Midlands, North Wales, Northwest England, Scotland via West Coast, Northwest London, Northern Ireland, and Republic of Ireland via Holyhead: tel. 387 7070.
> To East and Northeast England, Scotland via East Coast, and North London: tel. 278 2477.
> To Europe: tel. (0891) 888731

British Rail runs **Travel Centres** at its mainline stations and at 12-16 Regent St. (tube: Piccadilly Circus); The Strand (tube: Charing Cross); Victoria St.; and King William St. (All open Mon.-Fri. 9am-5pm.)

FROM THE BUS STATIONS

Victoria Coach Station (tube: Victoria), located on Buckingham Palace Rd., is the hub of Britain's denationalized coach network. **National Express coaches** (tel. 730 0202) service an expansive network which links cities big and small. Coaches are considerably less expensive than trains but also take longer. National Express offers a **Discount Coach Card** (£7) to students, youths 16-25, seniors, and disabled persons (30% discount).

Much of the commuting area around London, including Hampton Court and Windsor, is served by **Green Line** coaches, which leave frequently from Eccleston Bridge behind Victoria Station. (For information, call (0181) 668 7261 Mon.-Fri. 8am-8:30pm, Sat.-Sun. 9am-5pm; or try the information kiosk on Eccleston Bridge.)

BY THUMB

Anyone who values safety will take a train or bus out of London. Hitchers often check the University of London Union's ride board, on the ground floor of 1 Malet St., WC1 (tube: Russell Sq.), or ask at youth hostels. Hitching can be difficult within central London and reasonably easy from places like Cambridge and Oxford to the city. Let's Go does not recommend hitchhiking as a safe means of transportation.

■ LAYOUT

Greater London is a colossal aggregate of distinct villages and anonymous suburbs, of ancient settlements and modern developments. As London grew, it swallowed

London

Regent's Park

Euston Station

Maida Vale

Abbey Rd.
Abercorn Pl.
Grove
Wellington Rd.
Circus Rd.
Hall Rd.
End Rd.
Prince Albert Rd.
Outer Circle
Chester Rd.
Inner Circle
Albany St.
Eversholt St.
Hampstead Rd.

St. John's Wood Rd.
Lisson Grove
Park Rd.
Outer Circle
Euston Rd.
Gower St.
Tottenham Court Rd.

Clifton Rd.
Bloomfield Rd.
Edgware Rd.
Marylebone Rd.
Devonshire St.
Gt. Portland St.
Portland Pl.
Harley St.
Cleveland St.
Universi
Lond

Harrow
Rd.
Marylebone Flyover
Crawford St.
Gloucester Pl.
Upper Montague St.
Seymour Pl.
Baker St.
Marylebone High St.
Wigmore St.
Berners St.
Dean St.

Bishop's Bridge Rd.
Paddington Station
Praed St.
Sussex Gdns.
Edgware Rd.
Manchester Square
Duke St.
Oxford Circus
Oxford
St.
Regent St.
Brewer St.
Shafte

Queensway
Craven Hill
Marble Arch
Bayswater Rd.
N. Carriage Dr.
Oxford St.
Brook St.
Grosvenor St.
Bond St.
Berkeley Square
Piccadilly Circus
Regent market

Bayswater Rd.
Speaker's Corner
U.S. Embassy
Grosvenor Square
Sth. Audley St.
Curzon St.
Jermyn St.

Kensington Gardens
W. Carriage Dr.
The Serpentine
Hyde Park
Park Lane
Piccadilly
St. James's Palace
The Mall
Pall Mall

Kensington Palace
Kensington Rd.
Kensington Gore
S. Carriage Rd.
Kensington Rd.
Knightsbridge
Hyde Park Corner
Constitution Hill
Green Park
St. James's Park
Birdcage Wa
We

Cromwell Rd.
Palace Gate
Gloucester Rd.
Queen's Gate
Royal Albert Hall
Prince Consort Rd.
Victoria & Albert Museum
Exhibition Rd.
Natural History Museum
Brompton Rd.
Walton St.
Basil St.
Pont St.
Sloane St.
Cadogan Pl.
Belgrave Square
Grosvenor Pl.
Buckingham Palace Rd.
Eaton Square
Victoria Station
Coach Station
Victoria
ton Rd.
Warwick Way
Belgrave Rd.
Vauxhall b

Old Brompton Rd.
Draycott Ave.
Sloane Ave.
Sloane Sq.
Pimlico Rd.
Sutherland St.
Lupus St.

Redcliffe Gdns.
Finborough Rd.
Fulham Rd.
xworth Pl.
Cale St.
Sydney St.
Old Church St.
Flood St.
King's Rd.
Royal Hospital Rd.
Ebury Br. Rd.
Chelsea Br. Rd.
Grosvenor Rd.

Carlyle's House
Beaufort St.
Oakley St.
Cheyne Walk
Royal Hospital
Chelsea Embankment
Chelsea Br.
Albert Br.

River Thames

Battersea Park

Nine

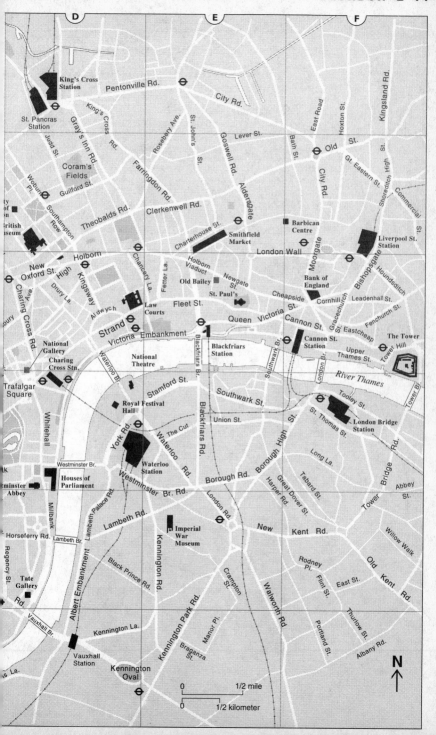

King's Cross Station
St. Pancras Station
Pentonville Rd.
City Rd.
Grays Inn Rd.
King's Cross Rd.
Judd St.
Woburn Pl.
Coram's Fields
Guilford St.
Southampton Row
Farringdon Rd.
Rosebery Ave.
St. John's St.
Goswell Rd.
Lever St.
Bath St.
City Rd.
Old St.
Gt. Eastern St.
Shoreditch High St.
Kingsland Rd.
East Road
Hoxton St.
Commercial St.
Theobalds Rd.
Clerkenwell Rd.
Aldersgate
Moorgate
Barbican Centre
Liverpool St. Station
Bishopsgate
Houndsditch
British Museum
Holborn
New Oxford St.
High Holborn
Kingsway
Drury La.
Chancery La.
Charterhouse St.
Smithfield Market
London Wall
Holborn Viaduct
Fetter La.
Old Bailey
Newgate St.
St. Paul's
Cheapside
Bank of England
Cornhill
Leadenhall St.
Fenchurch St.
Gracechurch St.
St. Eastcheap
Charing Cross Rd.
Aldwych
Law Courts
Fleet St.
Strand
Queen Victoria St.
Cannon St.
The Tower
Victoria Embankment
National Gallery
Charing Cross Stn.
Blackfriars Br.
Blackfriars Station
Southwark Br.
Cannon St. Station
Cannon St.
London Br.
Upper Thames St.
Tower Hill
Trafalgar Square
Waterloo Br.
National Theatre
River Thames
Tower Br.
Whitehall
Royal Festival Hall
Stamford St.
Southwark St.
Tooley St.
London Bridge Station
York Rd.
The Cut
Waterloo Rd.
Union St.
Blackfriars Rd.
Borough High St.
St. Thomas St.
Long La.
Abbey St.
Westminster Br.
Houses of Parliament
Westminster Abbey
Waterloo Station
Westminster Br. Rd.
Borough Rd.
London Rd.
Great Dover St.
Tabard St.
Tower Bridge Rd.
Millbank
Lambeth Palace Rd.
Lambeth Rd.
New Kent Rd.
Harper Rd.
Willow Walk
Horseferry Rd.
Lambeth Br.
Imperial War Museum
Rodney Pl.
Old Kent Rd.
Regency St.
Tate Gallery
Albert Embankment
Black Prince Rd.
Kennington Rd.
Kennington Park Rd.
Crampton St.
Manor Pl.
Walworth Rd.
East St.
Flint St.
Thurlow St.
Portland St.
Albany Rd.
Vauxhall Br.
Kennington La.
Braganza St.
Vauxhall Station
Kennington Oval

0   1/2 mile
0   1/2 kilometer

N

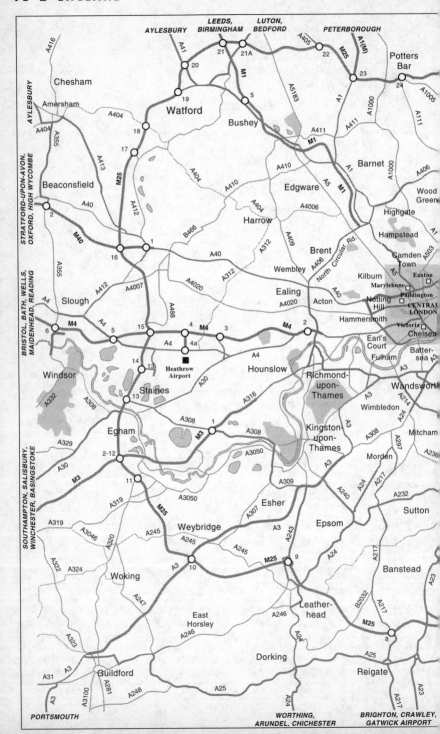

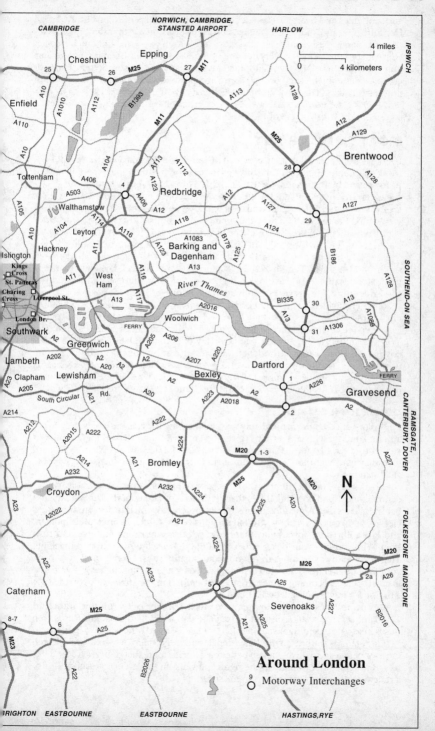

Around London

○ Motorway Interchanges

adjacent cities and nearby villages, chewed up the counties of Kent, Surrey, Essex, Hertfordshire, and Middlesex. Names such as the "City of Westminster" are vestiges of this urban imperialism. "The City" now refers to the ancient, and much smaller, "City of London," which covers but one of the 620 sq. mi. of Greater London. London is divided into boroughs and into postal code areas (whose letters stand for compass directions). The borough name and postal code appear at the bottom of most street signs. The most useful navigational aids are street atlases, such as *London A to Z* ("A to Zed," as streetwise Londoners call it), *ABC Street Atlas,* or Nicholson's *London Streetfinder* (from £2).

■ GETTING ABOUT

London's public transit system, operated by **London Regional Transport (LRT),** is fabulously comprehensive. The **Underground** (known as the tube) is supplemented by **buses** and by **British Rail (BR).** Call 222 1234 for 24-hr. bus and tube info.

Pick up free maps and guides at **London Transport's Information Centres** (look for the lowercase "i" logo at information windows and on signs). You can find these well-staffed booths with information on buses, Underground trains, the Docklands Light Railway (DLR), British Rail's London routes, and night buses at Heathrow Airport, Euston and Victoria rail stations, and the following major tube stops: King's Cross, Piccadilly Circus, Oxford Circus, St. James's Park, Liverpool St., Hammersmith, and Heathrow Terminals 1, 2, 3 station (most open weekdays 8am-6pm; central London stations also have weekend hours). For information on how the buses and Underground trains are currently running, phone 222 1200 (24-hr.).

London is divided into six concentric transport zones. Central London, including most of the major sights, is covered by zone 1; Heathrow Airport takes off in zone 6. Fares depend on the distance of the journey and the number of zones crossed. The **Travelcard,** because of its price and flexibility of both its duration and the zones it covers, has been a must for budget travelers. It can be bought for one day, one week, or one month's worth of travel. Most tourists will find the zones 1&2 cards the most useful and economical. All Travelcards can be used on the Underground, regular buses, British Rail (Network SouthEast), and the Docklands Light Railway.

UNDERGROUND

The color-coded **Underground** railway system, or the **tube,** is the easiest way to get around London, with 273 stations (give or take) on 11 lines (Bakerloo, Central, Circle, District, East London, Hammersmith and City, Jubilee, Metropolitan, Northern, Piccadilly, and Victoria). Small but invaluable "Journey Planner" maps are available at all stations.

Fares depend on the number of zones passed through—a journey wholly within central zone 1 will cost much less than a trip to a distant suburb. On Sundays and Bank Holidays (see Appendix), trains run less frequently. All transfers are free. Bicycles are allowed on the above-ground sections of the Circle, District, Metropolitan, and Piccadilly lines for a child's fare except during morning and evening rush hours. You can buy your ticket either from the ticket window or from a machine. The ticket allows you to go through the automatic gates; keep it until you reach your final destination, where it will be collected by another machine. Be aware that inspectors are becoming rather strict about enforcing the tube's new on-the-spot £10 fine for travel without a valid ticket.

Most tube lines' **last trains** leave Central London between midnight and 12:30am; service resumes around 6am. The gap is bridged by Night Buses (see Buses below). Some distant stations close on Sundays and other off-peak periods.

Many stations feature labyrinthine tunnels and steep staircases, so if you're carrying a lot of luggage, you might fare better on a longer route that requires fewer transfers. And remember to stand to the right, and walk on the left on escalators, or risk a rude tumbling from commuters in full stride.

BUSES

If you're in a hurry, don't take a bus. Take the tube; it's faster, easier, and generally more consistent. However, riding the buses is a great way to orient yourself to the city's layout, and to soak up its atmosphere and its sights. A number of buses in central London (notably #11 and 14) provide excellent sight-seeing at discount rates. Unfortunately, double-decker **Routemaster** buses, with their conductors and open rear platforms, are being replaced to save money. On modern double-deckers and on single-deck "hoppa" buses, you pay your fare to the driver as you board, and you must have exact change. On Routemasters, take a seat and wait for the conductor, who can tell you the fare and let you know when to get off. **Bus stops** are marked with route information; at busy intersections or complicated one-way systems, maps tell where to board each bus. A warning: each stop is marked with route numbers and only those buses stop there. On stops marked "request," buses stop only if you flag them down (to get on) or pull the bell cord (to get off). While waiting, you must form a queue (line up); bus conductors may refuse some passengers at the stop with withering looks of scorn during crowded periods. Service is sporadic in daytime; it is perfectly common to wait 20 minutes, only to be greeted by a procession of three buses in a row. Regular buses run from about 6am to midnight.

Night buses (the "N" routes) now run frequently throughout London from 11pm until 6am. When the tube goes to sleep (last trains run between midnight and 12:30am), night buses provide an inexpensive and convenient alternative to taxis. All night bus routes pass through Trafalgar Square, and many stop at Victoria as well. London Transport's information offices put out a free brochure about night buses, which includes times of the last British Rail and Underground trains. Call London Transport's 24-hr. information line (tel. 222 1234) for fares and schedules.

The bus network is divided into four zones. In and around central London, one-way **fares** range from 60p to £1.20, depending on the number of zones you pass through. Travelcards purchased for the Underground are valid on buses.

If you're planning on utilizing the bus network, London Transport issues a free bus map for London called the *All-London Bus Guide,* which is available at most tube stations and LRT information offices. The *Central Bus Guide* is a more manageable pamphlet, describing only bus routes in zone 1. To find out whether buses are running on schedule, or whether routes have changed, call 222 1200. Wheelchair accessible **Mobility Bus** routes, numbered in the 800s and 900s, service most of London. **Stationlink,** a wheelchair accessible bus, travels hourly between the major train stations. For information on either service, call 918 3312.

DOCKLANDS LIGHT RAILWAY

The Docklands Light Railway (DLR), London's newest transport system, connects the flashy developments of the old docks with the City of London. The tube's zone system applies to the DLR, and DLR lines appear on all tube maps. Fares are the same as the tube's. The **red line** runs north-south (connecting with the tube at Bow Church and Stratford), the **green line** west-east (connecting with the tube at Bank, Shadwell, and Tower Hill/Gateway), and the **Beckton line** starts at Poplar Station (on the red line) and extends five miles east. (Trains run Mon.-Fri. 5:30am-11:30pm; buses travel the routes Mon.-Fri. 11:15pm-12:50am, Sat. 5:30am-midnight, and Sun. 7:30am-11:30pm.) Bus #D8 covers the red line and #D9 the green line. Call the 24-hour **Docklands Travel Hotline** (tel. 918 4000) for information.

BRITISH RAIL

Most of London is fully served by buses and the tube. Some districts, however, notably southeast London, are most easily reached by train. The North London Link, stretching across north London from North Woolwich to Richmond, often deposits travelers closer to sights (such as Keats's house) than the tube: trains (3/hr.) scoot from Hampstead Heath to Kew in 25 minutes. However, BR is used by most visitors for its service from Gatwick Airport to Victoria (see Getting In and Out of London). Information on Network South East services is available at all mainline stations. The massive Victoria train station, the terminus for most Network South East lines, offers timetables on large revolving spindles for your perusal. At the travel and information center at Waterloo (tel. 620 1032; open Mon.-Sat. 7:30am-9pm, Sun. 9am-9pm), you can buy your own copy of any timetable (30p for each section of London, £7.50 for the full timetable). *London Connections,* a map of all tube and Network South East lines, is free and available at any tube station or information office. For 24-hr. information on Network South East, call 928 5100.

TAXICABS

In order to earn a license, London taxicab drivers must pass a rigorous exam called "The Knowledge" to demonstrate that they know the city's streets by heart; the route taken by a cabbie is virtually certain to be the shortest and quickest. A taxi is available if its yellow light is aglow. You can catch a cab yourself or call a radio dispatcher for one (tel. 272 0272 or 253 5000, or look in the Yellow Pages under "Taxi"); beware that you may be charged extra for ordering a cab by phone. Drivers are required to charge according to the meter for trips under 6 mi., but for longer distances you must negotiate the price. A 10% tip is expected, with a surplus charge for extra baggage or passengers. Taxis in London are notoriously expensive. If you believe that you have been overcharged, get the driver's number.

Apart from the licensed cabs, there are countless **"minicab"** companies, listed in the Yellow Pages. *Ladycabs* (tel. 272 3019) has only female cabbies (Mon.-Wed. 7:30am-midnight, Thurs. 7:30am-1am, Fri.-Sat. 8:30am-2am, Sun. 10am-midnight), as does *My Fare Lady* (tel. (0181) 458 9200).

CARS

Renting a car will not save you time, money, or hassle in London. Drivers must be over 21 and under 70. Read the insurance agreement carefully before you rent; some agreements require you to pay for damages you may not have caused. If you pay by credit card, check to see if your company provides any free insurance. Oh, and everything about England's roads is backwards. You have been warned.

BOATS

The **River Thames** no longer commands as much traffic as in the Middle Ages, but if you venture out in a boat you can still sense the pulse of a major lifeline. **Catamaran Cruisers** (tel. 987 1185) offers cruises with commentary. Tours run from Charing Cross to Tower and Greenwich piers (2/hr. 10:30am-6:15pm; Tower £2.50 each way, Greenwich £3 each way, children ½-price).

The following destinations are served by **Westminster Pier** (tube: Westminster):

Tower of London: 3/hr., 10:40am-5pm (tel. 930 4097; £3.60, £4.60 return).
Greenwich: 2/hr. 10:30am-5pm; 40-50min. (tel. 930 4097; £4.60, £5.60 return).
Thames Barrier: daily at 10am, 11:15am, 12:45, 1:45, and 3:15pm; 75min. (tel. 930 3373; £4, £5.70 return, children £2.30, £2.85 return).
Kew: daily 10:15am, 11am, 11:45am, 12:30am, 2, 2:45, and 3:30pm; 90min. (tel. 930 4721; £5, £7 return).
Richmond: daily 10:30am and noon; 3hrs. (tel. 930 4721; £6, £8 return).
Hampton Court: daily 10:30am and noon; 3-4½hrs. (tel. 930 4721; £7, £9 return).

Regent's Canal runs along the north rim of Regent's Park. **Jason's Trip,** opposite 60 Blomfield Rd., Little Venice, W9 (tel. 286 3428; tube: Warwick Ave.), runs daily motor barges on the canal to Camden Lock and back. (June-Aug. and Easter 4/day; otherwise 2/day; return £5; under 14 £3.50 return.) **Jenny Wren,** 250 Camden High St., NW1 (tel. 485 4433). Tube: Camden Town. Drifts from Camden Lock to Little Venice and back. (Mon.-Sat. 2/day; Sun. 3/day; 1½-hr. £4 return, children £3 return).

■■■ PRACTICAL INFORMATION

TOURIST OFFICES

London Tourist Board Information Centre: Victoria Station Forecourt, SW1 (tel. (0839) 123 432, recorded message only, 48p/min.). Tube: Victoria. Information on London and England, a well-stocked bookshop, theatre and tour bookings, and an accommodations service (a hefty £5 booking fee, plus 15% refundable deposit). Expect to take a number and wait at peak hours. Their cheapest rooms cost about £22, but most run around £25-30. Open daily 8am-7pm; Dec.-March Mon.-Sat. 8am-7pm, Sun. 8am-5pm. Additional offices located at **Heathrow Airport** (open daily 9am-6pm; Dec.-March 9am-5pm), **Harrods,** and **Selfridges** department stores.

British Travel Centre: 12 Regent St., SW1. Tube: Piccadilly Circus. Down Regent St. from the Lower Regent St. tube exit. Ideal for travelers heading outside of London. It has the same rates for currency exchange as the main AmEx office, but shorter lines. For its accommodations service, you pay a booking fee (£5) and a deposit (either 1 night's stay or 15% of the total stay; does not book for hostels). Also sells maps, theatre tickets, books, and pamphlets translated into many languages. Open Mon.-Fri. 9am-6:30pm, Sat. 9am-5pm, Sun. 10am-4pm; Nov.-April Mon.-Fri. 9am-6:30pm, Sat.-Sun. 10am-4pm.

City of London Information Centre: St. Paul's Churchyard, EC4 (tel. 606 3030). Tube: St. Paul's. Specializes in information about the City of London but answers questions on all of London. Helpful, knowledgeable staff. Open daily 9:30am-5pm; Nov.-March Mon.-Fri. 9:30am-5pm, Sat. 9:30am-12:30pm.

London Transport Information Offices: (24-hr. information line, tel. 222 1234). At the Heathrow, Victoria, Piccadilly Circus, Oxford Circus, Euston, Liverpool St., and King's Cross tube stops. Underground and bus travel, free maps.

BUDGET TRAVEL OFFICES

The organizations listed below specialize in student discounts and youth fares. All sell ISIC cards. Avoid going after noon, especially on Saturday.

STA Travel: 86 Old Brompton Rd. SW7 3LQ (tube: South Kensington) and 117 Euston Rd. NW1 2SX (tel. 937 9921 for European travel). Open Mon.-Fri. 8am-8pm, Sat. 10am-4pm, Sun. 10am-2pm.

YHA Travel Office: 14 Southampton St., WC2 (tel. 836 8541). Tube: Covent Garden. Branch at 174 Kensington High St., W8 (tel. 938 2948; tube: High St. Kensington). Both branches open Mon.-Wed. 10am-6pm, Thurs.-Fri. 10am-7pm, Sat. 9am-6:30pm.

Council Travel: 28a Poland St., W1 (tel. 437 7767). Tube: Oxford Circus. Open Mon.-Wed. and Fri. 9am-6pm, Thurs. 9am-7pm, Sat. 10am-5pm.

Travel CUTS: 295a Regent St., W1 (tel. 637 3161). Tube: Oxford Circus. Canadian equivalent of Council. Open Mon.-Fri. 9am-6pm, Sat. 10am-5pm.

Trailfinders: 42-50 Earl's Ct. Rd., W8 (tel. 937 5400). Tube: High St. Kensington. Huge clearing house for cheap airline tickets within Europe and to the rest of the world. Info section for those using London as stopover for long flights. Open Mon.-Wed. and Fri.-Sat. 9am-6pm, Thurs. 9am-7pm; Sun. (phone only) 10am-2pm.

Campus Travel: 52 Grosvenor Gdns., SW1 (tel. 730 8832). Open Mon.-Tues. and Thurs.-Fri. 9:30am-5pm, Wed. 10am-5pm.

EMBASSIES & HIGH COMMISSIONS

All embassies and High Commissions close on English national holidays. Check the telephone book for other nationalities.

United States Embassy: 24 Grosvenor Sq., W1 (tel. 499 9000). Tube: Bond St. Someone will always answer the phone. **Embassy Travel Services** at 22 Sackville St., W1 (tel. 439 7433). Tube: Piccadilly Circus. Travel Service office open Mon.-Fri. 10am-4pm.

Australian High Commission: Australia House, The Strand, WC2 (tel. 379 4334; in emergency, tel. 438 8181). Tube: Aldwych or Temple. Visa and passport inquiries tel. 438 8818. Open Mon.-Fri. 10am-4pm.

Canadian High Commission: MacDonald House, 1 Grosvenor Sq., W1 (tel. 629 9492). Tube: Bond St. or Oxford Circus. Visas Mon.-Fri. 8:45am-2pm.

Irish Embassy: 17 Grosvenor Pl., SW1 (tel. 235 2171). Tube: Hyde Park Corner. Open Mon.-Fri. 9:30am-5pm.

New Zealand High Commission: New Zealand House, 80 Haymarket, SW1 (tel. 930 8422). Tube: Charing Cross. Open Mon.-Fri. 10am-noon and 2-4pm.

South African Embassy, South Africa House, Trafalgar Sq. WC2 (tel. 930 4488). Tube: Charing Cross.

FINANCIAL SERVICES

Don't be lured by *bureaux de change* signs touting "No Charge—No Commission;" these establishments make up for the loss simply by offering obscene exchange rates. Exchange traveler's checks at the bank from which you bought them. American Express, Thomas Cook, and Visa all have agencies or banks that will change checks with no fee (Visa and Thomas Cook checks can be exchanged at Barclays at no cost, and AmEx at Lloyds Bank). Expect banks and AmEx to be closed or have limited hours on weekends. Be aware of Bank Holidays (see Appendix). Automated Teller Machines (ATMs), known as "holes-in-the-wall," are rapidly multiplying, and may be the cheapest way to change your dough.

American Express, 6 Haymarket, SW1 (tel. 930 4411). Tube: Piccadilly Circus. Message and mail services open Mon.-Fri. 9am-5pm, Sat. 9am-noon. Currency exchange open Mon.-Fri. 9am-5:30pm, Sat. 9am-6pm, Sun. 10am-5:45pm. Bring ID to pick up mail (60p; free for AmEx Cheque or cardholders). Other offices at Victoria Station (147 Victoria St., SW1; tel. 828 7411); Cannon St. (54 Cannon St., EC4; tel. 248 2671); Knightsbridge (78 Brompton Rd., SW3; tel. 584 6182); and at the British Tourist Centre. Lost or stolen Traveler's Cheques should be reported immediately (tel. 0800 52 1313; 24-hr.).

Late Night Currency Exchange: You'll find *bureaux de change* at airports, major rail stations, and central London tube stations. Most are open 8am-9pm, but the following have later opening hours: **Thomas Cook,** 15 Shaftesbury Ave., WC2. Tube: Piccadilly Circus. Open until 11pm. **Exchange International,** Victoria Station. Tube: Victoria. Open until 10pm. **Chequepoint** offers 5 24-hr. locations: opposite Marble Arch tube station; Coventry Street, tube: Piccadilly Circus; 220 Earl's Ct. Rd., tube: Earl's Ct.; Victoria Station; 2 Queensway, tube: Queensway. Expect to pay a hefty fee.

EMERGENCY, SOCIAL, & SUNDRY SERVICES

Emergency medical care, psychological counseling, crash housing, and sympathetic support can often be found in London free of charge.

Emergency (Medical, Police, and Fire): Dial 999; no coins required.

Police: Stations in every district of London, including: Headquarters, New Scotland Yard, Broadway, SW1 (tel. 230 1212; tube: St. James's Park).

Hospitals: In an emergency, you can be treated at no charge in the A&E ward of a hospital. You have to pay for routine medical care unless you work legally in Britain, in which case NHS tax will be deducted from your wages and you will not be charged. Socialized medicine has lowered fees, so don't ignore any health problem merely because you are low on cash. **Westminster Hospital,** Dean Ryle St., Horseferry Rd., SW1 (tel. 746 8000; tube: Pimlico); **Royal London Hospital,** Whitechapel Rd., E1 (tel. 377 7000; tube: Whitechapel); **Royal Free Hospital,** Pond St., NW3 (tel. 794 0500; tube: Belsize Park or BR: Hampstead Heath); **St. Thomas' Hospital,** Lambeth Palace Rd., SE1 (tel. 928 9292; tube: Westminster). For others consult "Hospitals" in the gray Businesses and Services phone book.

Pharmacies: Every police station keeps a list of emergency doctors and chemists in its area. Listings under "Chemists" in the Yellow Pages. **Bliss Chemists** at Marble Arch (5 Marble Arch, W1; tel. 723 6116) is open daily, including public holi-days, 9am-midnight. **Boots Chemists** has branches throughout London: look in **Sainsbury** supermarkets.

Samaritans: 46 Marshall St., W1 (tel. 734 2800). Tube: Oxford Circus. Highly respected 24-hr. crisis hotline helps with all sorts of problems, including suicidal depression. A listening rather than advice service.

AIDS: National AIDS Helpline (tel. 0800 567 123; 24 hr.). Toll-free for informa-tion on testing, health care, or simply to answer questions and listen.

Women's Aid: 52-54 Featherstone St., EC1 (tel. 251 6537; 24 hr.). Will answer questions on issues of concern to women.

Rape Crisis Line: London Rape Crisis Centre, P.O. Box 69, WC1 (tel. 837 1600; 24 hr.). Call anytime, emergency or not, to talk to another woman, receive legal or medical information, or obtain referrals. Will send someone to accompany you to the police, doctors, clinics, and courts upon request.

Family Planning Association: 27-35 Mortimer St., W1 (tel. 631 0555). Tube: Oxford Circus. Informational services: contraception, pregnancy test and abor-tion referral. Open Mon.-Thurs. 9:30am-5pm, Fri. 9:30am-4:30pm. For abortion and family planning clinics, see "Medical Services" in *Time Out's* classifieds.

Alcoholics Anonymous: 11 Redcliffe Gdns., SW10 (tel. 352 3001). Tube: West Brompton. Information on meeting locations and times. Hotline answered daily 10am-10pm; answering machine from 10pm-10am.

Narcotics Anonymous tel. 498 9005. Hotline answered daily 10am-8pm.

Information for Travelers with Disabilities: Phone the **Disability Information and Advice Service** (tel.275 8485), **RADAR** (tel. 637 5400), the **Disability Information Service** (tel. 630 5994; Mon.-Fri. 10am-4pm), or the **Greater Lon-don Association for the Disabled** (tel. 274 0107) for general information.

Bisexual, Gay, and Lesbian Information: see Bisexual, Gay, and Lesbian London.

Salvation Army: 18 Thanet St., WC1 (tel. 383 4822). Tube: King's Cross/St. Pan-cras. Good reputation for advice and emergency short-term shelter.

Legal Advice: Release, 388 Old St., EC1 (tel. 729 9904; 24-hr. emergency number 603 8654). Tube: Liverpool St. or Old St. Specializes in criminal law and advising those who have been arrested on drug charges. Open Mon.-Fri. 10am-6pm.

Automobile Breakdown: AA Breakdown service, tel. 0800 887 766; 24-hr. RAC Breakdown Service, tel. 0800 828 282; National Breakdown, tel.499 0039.

St. Mary's Hospital Special Clinic, Praed St., W2 (tel. 725 1697). Tube: Padding-ton. Free and confidential drop-in clinic for STDs, including AIDS and HIV. Open Mon.-Tues., Thurs.-Fri. 9am-6pm and Wed. 10am-6pm.

Shelter Nightline: tel. (0800) 446 441. A volunteer-run helpline offering free advice on emergency accomodations. Open Mon.-Fri. 6pm-9am, Sat.-Sun. 24 hrs.

■■■ ACCOMMODATIONS

With a bit of perseverance, finding a safe, clean, convenient place to spend the night in London is not terribly difficult. Plan ahead to nab one of the more desirable rooms, particularly in July and August, as they are likely to fill up quickly. Almost all budget accommodations in London provide a bed and some form of breakfast. The **Tourist Information Centre Accommodations Service** at Victoria Station bustles during high season. In the listings below, all prices are given per room, while prices for a bed in a dorm are listed per person.

■ HI HOSTELS

The cheerful staff members, often international travelers themselves, keep London HI hostels clean and refreshingly well-managed. London hostels are exceptionally crowded; during the summer, beds fill up months in advance. In recent years, hos-tels have not always been able to accommodate every written request for reserva-tions, much less on-the-spot inquiries. But hostels frequently hold some beds free until a few days before—it's always worth checking. To secure a place, show up as early as possible and expect to stand in line. With a Visa or Mastercard, you can book in advance by phone. Or you can write to the warden of the individual hostel. There is a new **central reservations number** for all London hostels (tel. 248 6547; open Mon.-Sat. 9:30am-5:30pm).

All hostels are equipped with large **lockers** that require a padlock. Bring your own or purchase one from the hostel for £2.50. London hostels do not charge for a sheet sleeping bag. Most have laundry facilities and some kitchen equipment. Theatre tickets and discounted attraction tickets are available.

Oxford Street, 14-18 Noel St., W1 (tel. 734 1618; fax 734 1657). Tube: Oxford Circus. Walk east on Oxford St. and turn right on Poland St.; hostel stands next to a 1989 mural entitled "Ode to the West Wind." Bang in the heart of London and Soho, it fills up in a flash. Reception open 7am-11pm. 24 hr. security; no curfew. 89 beds in small rooms of 2-4, with pink walls and worn blue carpets. £16.70, under 18 £13.70. Breakfast £2.70. Book 2-3 wks. in advance; full payment required. MC, Visa. Not much fun for those who have trouble climbing stairs.

Hampstead Heath, 4 Wellgarth Rd., NW11 (tel. (0181) 458 9054; fax (0181) 209 0546). Tube: Golders Green, then bus #210 or 268, or on foot by turning left onto Wellgarth after a ½-mi. walk along North End Rd. Despite its peaceful surroundings, this hostel can fall victim to school parties. No curfew. 200 beds in surprisingly nice dorms. £13.90, under 18 £11.80. Restaurant (breakfast £2.60). Kitchen, laundry. Partial wheelchair access. MC, Visa.

City of London, 36 Carter La., EC4 (tel. 236 4965; fax 236 7681). Tube: St. Paul's. From the City Information Centre on the opposite side of St. Paul's Cathedral, go left down Godliman St. Take the first right onto Carter Lane. Crisp beige walls adorned with posters, new carpeting, and custodians striding purposefully through the halls contribute to the orderliness of this centrally located modern hostel. Reception open daily 7am-11pm. Single-sex rooms available. Single or double £22, under 18 £18.50. Triple or quad £19, under 18 £16.50. Standard dorm (5-8 beds) £18.90, under 18 £15.90. Economy dorm (10-15 beds) £14, under 18 £11. Special weekly rates available Sept.-Feb. Breakfast included.

Earl's Court, 38 Bolton Gdns., SW5 (tel. 373 7083; fax 835 2034). Tube: Earl's Ct. Exit from the tube station onto Earl's Ct. Rd. and turn right; Bolton Gdns. is the fifth street on your left. A converted townhouse in a leafy residential neighborhood. 155 beds in rooms of 4-16. Reception open 7:30am-10:30pm. No curfew. Triple-decker bunk beds uniform to London hostels work particularly well in these airy rooms. All rooms single-sex. £16.90, under 18 £14.90. Currency exchange. 24-hr. security. Cafeteria meals available 5-8pm. Kitchen, laundry.

Holland House (King George VI Memorial Youth Hostel), Holland Walk, W8 (tel. 937 0748; fax 376 0667). Tube: High St. Kensington. The ½ mi. walk from High St. Kensington is *much* safer than the walk from Holland Park. Turn left when you exit the Kensington High Street station; continue walking and turn right onto Holland Walk. Pass the playing field and enter the park through the entrance on your left; a quick right leads you to the hostel. One half of the hostel is a restored Jacobean mansion, but you're just as likely to be sleeping in the other half, a late 60s cement block. Reception open 24 hrs. No curfew or lockout. Single-sex rooms fit 1-20; most have cramped bunk beds. £16.90, under 18 £14.90, breakfast included. *Bureau de change,* kitchen, laundry. Dinner (£2-3).

Highgate, 84 Highgate West Hill, N6 (tel. (0181) 340 1831). Tube: Archway. From the Archway stop take bus #210 or 217 to Highgate Village, or, on foot, leave the Junction Rd. tube exit, turn left immediately onto Highgate Hill, which leads to Highgate Village (¾ mi.). At Highgate Village, turn left onto South Grove (where the triangular bus bay is), a street that becomes St. Michael's Terr. and merges with Highgate West Hill. About 40min. from central London. Reception open 8:45am-10am, 1pm-7pm, and 8pm-11:30pm. Midnight curfew; no lockout. 69 beds, 4-16 beds per room. Bathrooms have flowery curtains and pink floors. £11.75, under 18 £7.85. Early breakfast £2.60. Kitchen. MC, Visa.

Rotherhithe, Island Yard, Salter Rd., SE1 (tel. 232 2114). Tube: Rotherhithe on the East London line. A 15-min. walk down Brunel Rd. then onto Salter. Welcome to *2001, A Space Odyssey.* No curfew. Small, immaculate rooms, most 2- or 6-bed. £16.50, under 18 £13.50. Breakfast £2.60. Wheelchair access. AmEx, MC, Visa.

■ PRIVATE HOSTELS

Private hostels, which do not require an HI card, generally have a youthful clientele and usually have single-sex dorm rooms. Some have kitchen facilities. There are almost never curfews.

BLOOMSBURY

Central University of Iowa Hostel, 7 Bedford Pl., WC1 (tel. 580 1121; fax 580 5638). Tube: Holborn or Russell Sq. From Russell Sq., head left and turn left onto Southampton Row, then turn right onto Russell Sq.; Bedford Pl. is the first left. On a quiet B&B-lined street near the British Museum. No curfew. Reception open 8am-1pm and 3-8pm. Bright, spartan rooms with bunk beds, wood furniture, and bookshelves. Dorms (2-4 beds) £15.50. Continental breakfast. Laundry, kitchen. 2-week max. stay. Open mid-May to mid-Aug. MC, Visa.

Astor's Museum Inn, 27 Montague St., WC1 (tel. 580 5360; fax 636 7948). Tube: Holborn, Tottenham Ct. Rd., or Russell Sq. Off Bloomsbury Sq. International grunge. Bathrooms are clean with temperamental showers. Reception open 24 hrs; no curfew. Co-ed dorms (2-8 beds) £13-18, £57-67/week. Discounts from Oct.-March. Continental breakfast. Kitchen. If full, they will direct you to 1 of 2 other Astor's hostels and pay for the tube. MC, Visa.

Tonbridge School Clubs, Ltd., corner of Judd and Cromer St., WC1 (tel. 837 4406). Tube: King's Cross/St. Pancras. Follow Euston Rd. to the site of the new British Library and turn left onto Judd St.; the hostel is 3 blocks down. Students with non-British passports only. For the true budget traveler, a clean place for sleep and hot showers. No frills and no privacy, but dirt cheap. Lockout 9:30am-10pm; use caution when walking in the area at night. Midnight curfew. Men sleep in basement gym, women in karate-club hall. Blankets and foam pads provided. Storage space for backpacks during the day, but safety is not guaranteed. £3!

PADDINGTON & BAYSWATER

Palace Court Hotel, 64-65 Prince's Sq., W2 (tel. 229 4747 or 4412; fax 727 9228). Tube: Bayswater or Notting Hill Gate. From Bayswater head left out of the station. Take a left on Moscow Rd. and then turn right onto Hereford Rd. From Notting Hill Gate head north up Pembridge Gdns., turn right on Pembridge Sq., then take a left on Hereford Rd. The hostel is on the corner of Hereford Rd. and Prince's Sq. Alternately, call ahead and arrange for the *complimentary shuttle service* to pick you up at Victoria Station and ferry you directly to the hostel. 100 beds. With free keg parties every Wed. night, a late-night TV lounge, and an outdoor patio area, this well-located hostel will doubtless play host to much raucous activity. Bed in a 6-bed room £9, in a 4-bed room £10, in a double £12; weekly rates are £50, £55, and £60. Sheets and cozy duvets are included. English breakfast.

Centre d'Echanges Internationaux, 61-69 Chepstow Pl., W2 (tel. 221 8134; fax 221 0642). Tube: Notting Hill Gate or Bayswater. From Notting Hill Gate, head up Pembridge Gdns., turn right on Pembridge Sq., then turn left on Chepstow Place. From Bayswater, head west on Moscow Rd., then turn right onto Chepstow Place. 180 beds. Bilingual staff welcomes an international clientele, half of whom hail from France. Rooms are spacious and well-kept. Lockout 10am-5pm. No curfew. Dorm (8-12 beds) £14. Singles £25. Doubles £20. Triples £17.50. Off-season discounts. Stay a week and you'll only be charged for 6 nights. Breakfast included. Pay an extra £5/night for a strange in-room shower that looks, and feels, like a closet. Elevators, but narrow hallways prevent the hostel from being entirely wheelchair accessible. Reservations are strongly recommended. AmEx, MC, Visa.

KENSINGTON, CHELSEA, & EARL'S COURT

Albert Hotel, 191 Queens Gate, SW7 (tel. 584 3019; fax 823 8520). Tube: Gloucester Rd, or bus #2 from South Kensington. From the tube, it's a substantial walk for those carrying luggage; take a right on Cromwell and a left on Queen's Gate. The hotel is approximately ¼ mi. up Queen's Gate on your right, in tantalizing proximity to Hyde Park. The bus, which stops by the Royal Albert Hall on Kensington Gore, is much quicker. A porch with a portico leads into an elegant wood-paneled corridor. Stately lounges. 24-hr. reception. No lockout or curfew. Rooms range from large dorms to intimate twins. Dorm £9.50-12. Twins £32. Quads £12. Single-sex and mixed dorms. Continental breakfast. Laundry. No credit cards.

Curzon House Hotel, 58 Courtfield Gdns., SW5 (tel. 581 2116; fax 835 1319). Tube: Gloucester Rd. Turn right onto Gloucester Rd., right again on Courtfield Rd., and right on Courtfield Gdns. Most rooms have tall ceilings and mammoth windows that overlook a gracious park. Singles £26. Doubles £38. Triples £45. Dorm £13. Weekly and seasonal discounts. Single-sex dorms only. Continental breakfast. Kitchen. Luggage storage.

Court Hotel, 194-196 Earl's Court Rd., SW5 (tel. 373 0027; fax 244 9870). Tube: Earl's Ct. Sister hostel at 17 Kempsford Gardens (tel. 373 2174). Very clean Australian-managed hostel. All single, double, and twin rooms have TV and tea/coffee set. Linens provided. Singles £18, £119/week. Doubles £14, £154/week. Triples or more £12, £177/week. Off-season and long-term discounts. Kitchen. Safe available for valuables. Key deposit £5. Reservations not accepted; call for availability.

The Inchmont Hotel, 25 Collingham Place, SW5 (tel. 370 2414; fax 244 8301). Tube: Earl's Court or Gloucester Rd. Refreshed backpackers hit the hostel party circuit, leaving soporific quiet in their wake. Most rooms have 2 or 3 bunkbeds, large windows, and wash basins. Dorm £10/day, £50/week, £47.50 if you stay 2 wks. or more. Doubles £15. Kitchen well-used; guests shop at nearby Sainsbury's.

Chelsea Hotel, 33-41 Earl's Ct. Sq., SW5 (tel. 244 6892 or 7395; fax 244 6891). Tube: Earl's Ct. Turn right onto Earl's Court Rd., then right again at Earl's Court Sq. 300 dorm beds in a mammoth succession of connected houses. 24-hr. reception. No lockout or curfew. Stark rooms generally feature bunk beds. Dorm £9. Doubles £11.50, with shower £12.50. Triples £12. Quads £11. Winter rates £1 lower; weekly rates 7 nights for the price of 6. Continental breakfast. Laundry.

O'Callaghan's Hotel, 205 Earl's Court Rd., SW5 (tel. 370 3000). Tube: Earl's Court. This hotel doesn't aim to impress; with prices this cheap, it doesn't have to. O'Callaghan's thrives by simply providing a solid mattress and unlimited coffee. 24-hr. reception. Garishly colored rooms with big windows. Single-sex rooms only. Doubles/twins £10/person. Quads £8/person, £49/week. Key deposit £5.

NORTH LONDON

International Student House, 229 Great Portland St., W1 (tel. 631 3223; fax 636 5565). Tube: Great Portland St. At the foot of Regent's Park, across the street from the tube station's rotunda. Unattractive 60s exterior hides a thriving international metropolis with its own films, concerts, discos, study-groups, athletic contests, expeditions, and parties. No curfew. 400 beds in doubles and singles. Singles £23.40. Doubles £19.75. Triples £16.60. Quads (some with bunk beds) £12.35. Discounts for HI members. Special monthly and long-term rates also available (about 250 beds are occupied by long-term residents.) English breakfast. Laundry, money changing (£3 flat fee). Key deposit £10. Reserve through main office on Great Portland St. at least 1 month ahead, earlier during academic year. Letter of confirmation required for long-term stays. MC, V. Foreign currencies accepted.

■ HALLS OF RESIDENCE

London's university residences often take visitors for periods from July to August and during Christmas and Easter breaks. These halls aren't gorgeous, but they offer privacy at low rates. Write ahead to the bursar of the hall; conference groups tend to snatch up rooms early. (Contact individual halls for London University residences.)

BLOOMSBURY

Carr Saunders Hall, 18-24 Fitzroy St., W1 (tel. 580 6338). Tube: Warren St. Turn right off Tottenham Ct. Rd. onto Grafton Way, then left onto Fitzroy St. A newer London School of Economics building. 134 single study bedrooms, 12 doubles. Singles £20.50. Doubles £41. English breakfast. Self-catering 2-5 person suites also available across the street; all are fully furnished. Min. stay 4 nights. Doubles £33. Triples £48. Quads £62. Quints £75. Under 12 half price.

Connaught Hall, 36-45 Tavistock Sq., WC1 (tel. 387 6181; fax 383 4109). Tube: Russell Sq. Head left from the station and turn right onto Woburn Pl.; the first left is Tavistock Sq. Graceful London University Hall with laundromat, reading rooms, private garden, and an elegant green marble lobby. Reception open Mon.-Sat. 8am-11pm, Sun. 9am-11pm. 200 small, single study bedrooms with wardrobes, desks, and tea-making facilities. Singles £19.50. English breakfast. Open July-Aug.

John Adams Hall, 15-23 Endsleigh St., WC1 (tel. 387 4086; fax 383 0164). Tube: Euston. Heading right on Euston Rd., take first right onto Gordon St., and first left onto Endsleigh Gdns.; Endsleigh St. is the second right. Elegant London University building. Some rooms have small balconies overlooking street. 124 singles, 22 doubles. Reception open daily 7:30am-10pm. Singles £21.40. Doubles £37. English breakfast. Laundry facilities, TV lounge, ping-pong table, and quiet reading room. Open July-Aug., Easter. MC, Visa.

KENSINGTON, CHELSEA, & EARL'S COURT

The **King's Campus Vacation Bureau,** 552 King's Rd., London SW10 OUA (tel. 351 6011; fax 352 7376), controls bookings for a number of residence halls where students of **King's College** live during term-time. Rooms available from early June to mid-September and during Easter. 24-hour security, breakfast, linen, soap, towel, and laundry facilities. Any form of student ID will get guests a discount of approximately £5 per night; 10% discount open to *all* individuals staying 7 nights or longer.

Ingram Court, 552 King's Rd., SW10 (tel. 351 6513). Tube: Sloane Sq. or Fulham Broadway. From Sloane Sq., take the #11 or 22 bus to Lot's Rd. (in front of campus); or walk 10 min. from Fulham Broadway. This site, once a part of Sir Thomas More's estate, approximates an accommodations utopia. A green lawn and ornamental fish pond in a beautiful courtyard. Singles £19.50, twin £15.25.

Wellington Hall, 71 Vincent Sq., Westminster, SW1 (tel. 834 4740; fax 233 7709). Tube: Victoria, walk 1 long block along Vauxhall Bridge Rd.; turn left on Rochester Row. Charming Edwardian hall on quiet square. Convenient to Westminster, Big Ben, Buckingham Palace, and the Tate Gallery, this hall is the most central and expensive of the King's College halls. Singles £21.50, twin £16.25. Open Easter.

Lightfoot Hall, Manresa Rd. at King's Rd., SW3 (tel. 333 4898 or 351 6011 for booking; fax 333 4901). Tube: Sloane Sq. or South Kensington. From South Kensington, take bus #49; from Sloane Sq., bus #11 or 22. Prime location in an institutional block. With student ID, singles and doubles are £13/person. Singles £20. Twins £16. Rooms may be available during school year.

NORTH LONDON

Hampstead Campus, Kidderpore Ave., NW3 (tel. 435 3564; fax 431 4402). Tube: Finchley Rd. or West Hampstead, or bus #13, 28, 82, or 113 to the Platt's Lane stop on Finchley Rd. Turn onto Platt's Lane then take an immediate right on Kidderpore Ave. Reserve through King's Campus Vacation Bureau (see above—Kensington, Chelsea, and Earl's Ct.). Beautiful surroundings and unparalleled prices (obscene with a student discount), with buildings ancient and modern. Herb gardens. Singles £13.25, twins £11.25.

Walter Sickert Hall, 29 Graham St., N1 (tel. 477 8822). Tube: Angel. Exit the station heading left. Turn left onto City Rd.; Graham St. will be on the left. This ex-office building opened as a new City University dorm in March 1994. About 50 singles and 4 twins. Singles £25. Doubles £40. Prices subject to change, so call ahead. Continental breakfast. Laundry, 24- hr. security. Open July-Sept.

■ BED & BREAKFASTS

BLOOMSBURY

Despite its proximity to the West End, Bloomsbury manages to maintain a fairly residential demeanor. Gracious, tree-filled squares and a prime location (within Zone 1 on the tube) cause hotel prices to be a pound or two higher here—it's worth it.

Most accept major credit cards (Visa and MasterCard). Budget hotels line one side of Gower St. (tube: Goodge). Rooms vary wildly in size, so look at one before paying.

Regency House Hotel, 71 Gower St., WC1 (tel. 637 1804; fax 323 5077). Tube: Goodge St. Well-decorated, color-coordinated rooms with telephone, hot pot, TV. Spotless bathrooms. Enclosed patio with solid teak benches. Singles £27, with shower £37. Doubles £37, with shower £52. Triples £52, with shower £65. Quads £60. Quint £68. Winter discounts. Book in advance. MC, Visa.

Arran House, 77-79 Gower St., WC1 (tel. 636 2186 or 637 1140; fax 436 5328). Tube: Goodge St. The relatively large rooms come with TVs and hot pots and are embellished with elegant moulding, Japanese lanterns, and non-working fireplaces. Well-lit hallways and spotless bathrooms. Visitors have access to the tidy garden, laundry facilities, and a cable TV lounge which feels like a private living room. Singles £28, with shower £33, with bath £38. Doubles £42, with shower £47, with bath £55. Triples £55, with shower £60, with bath £70. Quads £64, with shower £69, with bath £80. Quints £70. English breakfast. MC, Visa.

Ridgemount Hotel, 65-67 Gower St., WC1 (tel. 636 1141 or 580 7060). Tube: Goodge St. Bright, rooms with cheery pink bedspreads on firm beds. Owners have recently doubled their capacity by taking over the hotel next door. Radiantly clean throughout. Rooms with TV. Laundry facilities, a garden in back, and free tea and coffee in the TV lounge. Singles £26, with bath £35. Doubles £38, with bath £47. Triples £51, with bath £60. Quads £60, with bath £70. Quints £68. English breakfast. Call well in advance. No credit cards.

Garth Hotel, 69 Gower St., WC1 (tel. 636 5761; fax 637 4854). Tube: Goodge St. Some rooms charmingly furnished, others (mostly smaller) more standard. All come with TV; hot pot available upon request. Hallways and dining room are decorated with old wooden signs from inns and pubs—read the fine print for amusement. Singles £28, with bath £38. Doubles £40, with shower £50. Triples £52, with shower £60. Quads £64, with shower £70. Weekly rates about £5 cheaper/night. Full English breakfast or traditional Japanese breakfast. MC, Visa.

Thanet, 8 Bedford Pl., WC1 (tel. 636 2869 or 580 3377; fax 323 6676). Tube: Russel Sq. A dependable hotel. The well-kept rooms are simply furnished and spacious, and come with TV, radio, phone, and hot pot. Rooms in the back overlook a peaceable patio. Singles £37, with bath £47. Doubles £49.50, with bath £62. Triples with bath £75. Quads with bath £85. Extensive English breakfast. MC, Visa.

Ruskin Hotel, 23-24 Montague St., WC1 (tel. 636 7388; fax 323 1662). From the Holborn tube station take Southampton Row, then the second left onto Great Russell St.; Montague St. is the second right. Scrupulously well-kept rooms sport motel-type furnishings and hot pots. TV lounge with books and elegant glass lamps. Across the street from the British Museum. Singles £36. Doubles £52, with bath £64. Triples £64, with bath £74. English breakfast. AmEx, MC, Visa.

Cosmo House Hotel, 27 Bloomsbury Sq., WC1 (tel. 636 4661 or 636 0577). From the Holborn tube station take Southampton Row, then the second left onto Bloomsbury Pl. Clean, comfortable rooms with color TVs and fringed pink lampshades that look like Rococo Batman logos. Rooms in the back overlook a tree-filled garden; some in the front have small balconies looking out onto the square. Singles £27. Doubles £40. Triples £50. English breakfast. AmEx.

Euro Hotel and George Hotel, 51-53 and 58-60 Cartwright Gdns., WC1 (tel. 387 8777; fax 383 5044). Tube: Russell Sq. Large rooms with cable TV, radio, hot pot, and phone. White walls and furnishings give the rooms a bright, airy feel. Euro Hotel contains the main dining room and reception; because the George Hotel is in a separate building (about 30 seconds away from the Euro), rates are about £3 cheaper. Full English breakfast. Euro rates: singles £32.50; doubles £45.50; triples £57; quads £70; under 13 £9.50 Mon.-Fri. George rates: singles £29.50, with shower £34.50, with bath £39.50; doubles £42, with shower £46.50, with bath £49.50; triples £52.50, with shower £58.50, with bath £65.50. Quads £66, with shower £70; quints with shower £80; children under 13 £8.50 each Mon.-Fri.

Jenkins Hotel, 45 Cartwright Gdns., WC1 (tel. 387 2067; fax 383 3139). Tube: Russell Sq. Petite, genteel, family-run B&B featured in the BBC's "Poirot." Pastel wallpaper, floral prints, phones, teapots, TV, and fridges. Singles £33, with bath £46. Doubles £46, with bath £56. Triples with bath £76. English breakfast. MC, Visa.

Crescent Hotel, 49-50 Cartwright Gdns., WC1 (tel. 387 1515; fax 383 2054). Tube: Russell Sq. Family-run with care. Attractive and homey. Tea/coffee makers in each room, hair dryers and alarm clocks on request. TV lounge. Singles £34.50, with shower £38.50. Doubles £50.50, with bath £60.50. Quad £72, with bath £80. Discounts past one week. English breakfast. MC, Visa.

NEAR VICTORIA STATION

Victoria Station is a traveler's purgatory. In exchange for your penance in fairly expensive accommodations, you will be blessed with an ideal location, within walking distance from London's major attractions. In the summer, prudent travelers make reservations at least two weeks in advance.

Forage on **Belgrave Road** (tube: Victoria or Pimlico), a noisy thoroughfare south of the station; **St. George's Drive,** parallel to Belgrave Rd. and one block south; **Warwick Way,** which crosses them both near Victoria Station; or historic **Ebury St.,** west of the station in the heart of Belgravia. Some suggestions: **Melbourne House,** 79 Belgrave Rd., SW1 (tel. 828 3516; fax 828 7120); **Luna and Simone Hotel,** 47-49 Belgrave Rd., SW1 (tel. 834 5897 or 828 2474); **Marne Hotel,** 34 Belgrave Rd., SW1 (tel. 834 5195); **Alexander Hotel,** 13 Belgrave Rd., SW1 (tel. 834 9738); **Dover Hotel,** 44 Belgrave Rd., SW1 (tel. 821 9085); **Belgrave House Hotel,** 30-32 Belgrave Rd., SW1 (tel. 834 8620); **Easton Hotel,** 36-40 Belgrave Rd., SW1 (tel. 834 9738); **Sidney Hotel,** 74-76 Belgrave Rd., SW1 (tel. 834 2738 or 834 2860; fax 630 0973); **Georgian House Hotel,** 35 St. George's Dr., SW1 (tel. 834 1438); **Collier's Hotel,** 95-97 Warwick Way, SW2 (tel. 834 6931 or 828 0210).

PADDINGTON & BAYSWATER

Slightly decrepit B&Bs cluster around Norfolk Sq. and Sussex Gdns. As you travel west, the hotels gain character (tube: Paddington). The picks of the litter: **Compton House and Millard's Hotel,** 148-152 Sussex Gdns., W2 (tel. 723 6225 or 723 2939); **Ravna Gora,** 29 Holland Park Ave., W11 (tel. 727 7725; tube: Holland Park); or **Hyde Park House,** 48 St. Petersburgh Pl., W2 (tel. 229 1687; tube: Queensway).

EARL'S COURT

The area feeds on the budget tourist trade, spewing forth travel agencies, souvenir shops, take-away eateries, and *bureaux de change.* The accents of tireless, globetrotting Australians fill the neighborhood, sometimes known as "Kangaroo Court," and the area also has a significant gay population (tube: Earl's Court). The best are the **White House Hotel,** 12 Earl's Ct. Sq., SW5 (tel. 373 5903). The **Mowbray Court Hotel,** 28-32 Pennywern Rd., SW5 (tel. 373 8285 or 370 3690) offers tourists many services. Philbeach Gardens, a quiet tree-lined crescent north of the exhibition hall, offers the best B&B in the area, including two gay B&Bs. Leave Earl's Ct. at the exhibtion hall's west exit. Check out: **York House Hotel,** 27-29 Philbeach Gdns., SW5 (tel. 373 7519; fax 370 4641) and **Philbeach Hotel,** 30-31 Philbeach Gdns., SW5 (tel. 373 1244, 373 3907, or 373 4544), the largest gay B&B in England.

KENSINGTON & CHELSEA

These hotels prove convenient for worshippers at the stunning array of museums on the southwest side of Hyde Park. Prices are high, but hotels here tend to be more comfortable than at Earl's Court. Vicarage Gate lies off of Kensington Church St.

Abbey House Hotel, 11 Vicarage Gate, W8 (tel. 727 2594). Tube: Notting Hill Gate. A gracious entrance hall and wrought-iron banisters lend the feel of an elegant Victorian conservatory to this hotel. Palatial rooms with color TVs, washbasin, Holofil pillows, fresh towels and soap, and billowing curtains. Bathrooms (none en suite) decorated with Laura Ashley furnishings. Singles £32. Doubles £52. Triples £62. Quads £72. Quints £82. Winter discounts. Weekly rates. English breakfast. Reserve a month ahead if possible. No credit cards.

Vicarage Hotel, 10 Vicarage Gate, W8 (tel. 229 4030). Tube: Notting Hill Gate. The entrance hall here is spotless, with classy red velvet and gold framing a sweeping staircase. The stately breakfast room is only surpassed by the small, comfortable, and immaculate bedrooms, which contain fancy wooden wardrobes and antique mirrors. Singles £32. Doubles £54. Triples £66. Quads £72. Negotiable winter rates. Ample English breakfast. Reserve. No credit cards.

Still farther south you can stay in trendy **Chelsea,** but you'll have trouble finding moderately priced hotels south of King's Rd. Consider lodging at the **Oakley Hotel,** 73 Oakley St., SW3 (tel. 352 5599 or 6610; fax 727 1190), one of the best bargains in London. Just steps away from Cadogan Pier, Albert Bridge, Battersea Park, and shopping on King's Rd. Lovely bedrooms with large windows, matching bedspreads, and lots of fresh air. Incredibly amiable staff invites guests to use the kitchen at all hours. (Singles £18. Twins £32. Triples £42. Quads £50. Dorms (women only) £11, £65/week. Winter and long-term discounts. English breakfast. Reserve ahead. No credit cards. Tube: Sloane Sq. or Victoria, then bus #11, 19, or 22; or, Kensington, then bus #49. Turn left onto Oakley St. from King's Rd, at the Chelsea Fire Station.)

NORTH LONDON

Dillons Hotel, 21 Belsize Pk., NW3 (tel. 794 3360). Tube: Belsize Park, then bus #268. Or head right on Haverstock Hill and take the 2nd left onto Belsize Ave., which becomes Belsize Pk. Spacious B&B in a tree-lined suburb. Right around the corner from a lane of shops, little restaurants, a laundromat, and a post office. 15 large, well-furnished rooms. Singles £22, with shower £27. Doubles £31, with bath £36. Discounts Nov.-March. Continental breakfast. Book one month ahead.

Frank and Betty Merchant, 562 Caledonian Rd., N7 (tel. 607 0930). Tube: Caledonian Rd., then 8-min. walk left out of station through dreary bit of north London. Easy tube and bus access to center of London. Three bedrooms available in a private house with no sign but a garden out front. Friendly proprietors. Guests tend to be repeat custormers who have gotten to know each other well over the years. Room for 5-8 people only. £15/person. English breakfast. Book ahead.

■■■ FOOD & DRINK

■ FOOD

London has few rivals in its range of food—Lebanese, Greek, Indian, Chinese, Thai, Italian, Cypriot, African, and West Indian. London is perhaps most famous for its **Indian restaurants;** dishes here are spicier than their milder American counterparts. In general, Indian restaurants are cheaper around Westbourne Grove (tube: Bayswater) and Euston Square, and cheaper still on Brick Lane in the East End.

London's wealth of international restaurants shouldn't deter you from sampling Britain's own infamous cuisine. **Pubs** are a solid choice for meat pastries ("Cornish pasties" and "pies"), potatoes, and shepherd's pie (a meat mixture topped with mashed potatoes and baked). **Fish-and-chip shops** and **kebab shops** can be found on nearly every corner. They vary little in price but can be streets apart in quality. Look for queues out the door and hop in line. The **Restaurant Switchboard** (tel. (0181) 888 8080; Mon.-Fri. 9am-8pm, Sat. 10am-4pm) will provide good advice in choosing a restaurant for the price of a phone call, although their idea of a budget restaurant may not be yours. Budget travelers should remember that it is always cheaper to eat **take-away,** rather than having a sit-down meal.

THE WEST END

Soho, Piccadilly, and Covent Garden offer an endless jumble of food. Prices for restaurants in the West End are high; take-away prices are considerably lower. Free seating can be found at at Leicester Sq., Trafalgar Sq., and Piccadilly Circus. Piccadilly Circus, Leicester Sq., Covent Garden, and Charing Cross tube stations are all within easy walking distance of most of the West End.

Soho & Piccadilly Circus

Scads of unimpressive pizza and fast food joints cluster around Piccadilly Circus. A trip a few blocks down Shaftesbury Ave. and left onto Wardour or Dean St. rewards the hungry with the smart cafés and cheaper sandwich shops of Soho. **Old Compton St.**, Soho's main drag, lies off Wardour St. one block north of and parallel to Shaftesbury Ave. For fresh fruit, check out old **Berwick Market** on Berwick St.

The Stockpot, 18 Old Compton St., W1 (tel. 287 1066), by Cambridge Circus. Tube: Leicester Sq. or Piccadilly. Beloved by locals, who pack the sidewalk tables, it's the cheapest place in Soho to soak up some style. A simply marvelous value. Omelettes £2.10-2.25. Entrees £2.10-3.85. Divine apple crumble drowned in hot custard 85p. Open Mon.-Sat. 8am-11:30pm, Sun. noon-11pm. Also at 40 Panton St.

Pollo, 20 Old Compton St., W1 (tel. 734 5917). Tube: Leicester Sq. or Piccadilly Circus. This restaurant/madhouse serves some of the best Italian values in Soho. Delicious tortellini with a variety of sauces £3.20. *Risotto* £3.15. Pizzas £3.30. Cold gazpacho £1.40. Open Mon.-Sat. 11:30am-11:30pm.

Gaby's Continental Bar, 30 Charing Cross Rd., WC2 (tel. 836 4233). Tube: Leicester Sq. Low on atmosphere. Don't be put off by the steaming food photos out front; great Middle Eastern and vegetarian food lies within. Deservedly famous salt beef sandwich £2.80. Hefty falafel sandwich and a large selection of salads, around £1.80. Open Mon.-Sat. 8am-midnight, Sun. 11am-10pm.

Lorelei, 21 Bateman St. W1 (tel. 734 0954). Tube: Tottenham Ct. Rd., Leicester Sq., or Piccadilly Circus. Dim wall lamps reveal a tidy Italian restaurant with a wistful mermaid mural. Lorelei is the perfect place for an inexpensive oven-baked pizza and a bottle of red wine. Mushroom pizza £3.90. The *Poorman* (tomato, garlic, and oregano) caters to the budget diner (£2.95). Open daily noon-11pm.

Presto, 4-6 Old Compton St., W1 (tel. 437 4006). Tube: Leicester Sq. Highly trendy caff/café combo where Derek Jarman reputedly eats his bubble and squeak. Very crowded at dinner; harried waitstaff serves up pastas £3-4. Breakfast from £2.50. Open Mon.-Sat. 9am-1am, Sun. 11am-midnight.

Rabin's Nosh Bar, 39 Great Windmill St., W1 (tel. 434 9913). Tube: Piccadilly Circus. Off Shaftesbury Ave. right by the Circus. Teensy restaurant serving tasty New York-style deli food. Preferred halting spot for cabbies and comedians. Fried *gefilte* fish £2.40. Bagel sandwiches £2-2.65. Open Mon.-Sat. 11am-8pm.

The Wren at St. James's, 35 Jermyn St., SW1 (tel. 437 9419). Tube: Piccadilly Circus or Green Park. Wholefood/vegetarian delights served in a Christopher Wren church. Tranquil and gorgeous for lunch or tea and cake in the shady courtyard. Casserole of the day with brown rice £3.25. Carrot cake £1.40. Pot of tea 80p. Open Mon.-Sat. 8am-7pm, Sun. 10am-5pm.

Chinatown

Dozens of traditional, inexpensive restaurants cram into London's Chinatown (tube: Leicester Sq.), which occupies the few blocks between Shaftesbury Ave. and Leicester Sq. Gerrard St., the pedestrian-only backbone of Chinatown, is one block south of Shaftesbury Ave. Because of the Hong Kong connection, Cantonese cooking and language dominate. Most restaurants serve *dim sum* every afternoon.

Chuen Cheng Ku, 17 Wardour St., W1 (tel. 437 1398). Some consider it one of the planet's best restaurants. Certainly one of the longest menus. *Dim sum* dishes (served until 6pm) £1.65. Dried and fried *Ho-Fun* noodles with beef £4.20. Open daily 11am-midnight. AmEx, MC, Visa.

Wong Kei, 41-43 Wardour St., W1 (tel. 437 3071). Three stories of notoriously harried waiters and the best value Chinese food in Soho. A waterfall trickles on the first floor and dumbwaiters zoom food up to the other floors. Solo diners should expect to share tables. Roasted pork and egg rice £2.40. Set dinner for £6. Heaping noodle dishes only £2. Open daily noon-11:30pm.

Covent Garden

Covent Garden offers an enticing but expensive array of eateries to playgoers and tourists in the heart of London's theater district. Tucked away from the tourist labyrinth, **Neal's Yard** (off Neal St.) overflows with sumptuous vegetarian digs amongst herbal healers and colorful window boxes. These restaurants close relatively early; keep an eye out for the inconspicuous brasseries that dot the area when searching for late evening dining options (tube: Covent Garden.)

Neal's Yard Soup and Salad Bar, 3 Neal's Yard, WC2. Take-away only from this simple vegetarian's fantasy land. 3-4 hot entrees daily, from eggplant pasta to *dal* dishes, £2.25-4. Tempting mix 'n' match salads from £1.20. If summer means anything, it's the opening of the frozen yogurt annex which creates multi-layered fresh fruity parfaits. Open Mon.-Sat. noon-6pm, Sun. noon-5pm.

Food for Thought, 31 Neal St., WC2 (tel. 836 0239). Verdant foliage decorates this tiny basement restaurant offering large servings of excellent vegetarian food at moderate prices. Soups, salads, and stir-fries. Tasty daily specials from £3.25. Take-away. Open Mon.-Sat. 9:30am-8pm, Sun. 10:30am-4:30pm.

Neal's Yard Dining Room, 14-15 Neal's Yard, WC2 (tel. 379 0298). Above the blue Remedies shop. A touch more expensive than the neighbors, but it's got indoor seating. Wide, intercontinental selection. Mexican tortilla heaped with cheese £3.10. Open Mon.-Fri. noon-8pm, Sat. noon-6pm.

Neal's Yard Bakery and Tea Room, 6 Neal's Yard, WC2 (tel. 836 5199). Sourdough, cheese and herb, and two-seed breads all go for 90p for a small loaf. No smoking. Open Mon.-Fri. noon-8pm, Sat. noon-6pm.

Crank's, 1 Market Place, WC2. This branch of the extremely popular and affordable vegetarian chain has a terrace overlooking one of the most happening piazzas in London. Most entrees, like penne pasta with salad or roasted vegetables with tofu and ginger, are under £4. Open Mon.-Sat. 9am-8pm, Sun. 10am-7pm.

Spreads of Covent Garden, 15A New Row, WC2 (tel. 379 0849 or 836 5359). This cramped pre-theater establishment is packed on Sat. evenings—go early, because they close early. Generous "Main Event" dishes, like the Texas Super Cheeseburger or fried cod with fries and salad, don't exceed £3 . Open Mon.-Sat. 8am-8:30pm, Sun. 10am-6pm.

Piazza, 93 St. Martin's La., WC2 (tel. 379 5278). At the corner of Cecil Ct. and St. Martin's La. Bags of pasta suspended from the ceiling, Italian opera, outdoor seating, and a gourmet buffet satisfy the voracious. No skimping—they grate the parmesan before your eyes, and the pasta is homemade. Lasagna £5. Capuccino. Breakfast served. Open Mon.-Thurs. 8am-midnight, Fri. 8am-1pm, Sat. 8am-2pm.

BLOOMSBURY & EUSTON

Superb Greek, Italian, and vegetarian restaurants line Goodge Street, close to the British Museum. Northwest of Bloomsbury, around Euston Sq., a vast number of what many Londoners consider the city's best and most traditional Indian restaurants ply their trade. Avoid the restaurants on Woburn Pl., Southampton Row, and Great Russell St. that cater to swarms of tourists. Instead, look for the cheap eateries on and around Theobald's Rd., between the Russell Sq. and Holborn tube stops.

Near Goodge Street

Cranks Health Food, 9-11 Tottenham St., W1 (tel. 631 3912). London's original health food restaurant, founded in 1961. Crisp blond wood and white brick interior; frosted glass atrium ceiling in rear. Large portions of vegetarian and vegan dishes made with fresh ingredients, including free-range eggs and organic flour. Salad platter (quiche or vegetable tart with 2 salads) £3.45. Carrot cake £1.15. Take away available. No smoking. Open Mon.-Fri. 8am-7:30pm, Sat. 9am-7:30pm.

Greenhouse Vegetarian Restaurant, 16 Chenies St. basement, WC1 (tel. 637 0838). Luscious aromas of fresh pastas, salads, bean stews, and quiches waft through this demure restaurant of dark wooden tables, black chairs, and candles. Entrees £3.85, thick pizza £2.10, desserts 75p-£1.50. BYOB. Open Mon. 10am-7pm, Tues.-Fri. 10am-9pm, Sat. 10am-8pm, Sun. noon-3pm.

Trattoria Mondello, 36 Goodge St., W1 (tel. 637 9037). Zesty, but pricier, pasta dishes served in a rustic dining room with open-beam ceilings and discreet seating alcoves. Pastas and pizza about £4.20; specialties cost more. Cappuccino 90p. Open Mon.-Fri. noon-3pm and 5:30-11:30pm, Sat. noon-midnight. MC, Visa.

Cosma's Taverna, 29 Goodge St., W1 (tel. 636 1877). The basement *taverna* features a dance floor where patrons can join a belly dancer and smash plates late into the night. Former U.S. presidential hopeful Michael Dukakis once entered the fray here. Tasty lamb kebab £5.80. *Ouzo* £1.60. *Moussaka* £5.50. Open Mon.-Sun. noon-3pm and 5:30pm-midnight. *Taverna* open Wed.-Sat. 6pm-2am.

Champagne, 16 Percy St., W1 (tel. 636 4409). Popular Chinese restaurant with wax candles and wax roses at every table. Meditative sages and serene waterfalls grace the walls. Filling 3-course lunch special £4.50, £4.10 take-away. All-you-can-eat buffet £2.99 (Mon.-Fri. noon-2:30pm). Open Mon.-Sat. noon-midnight.

Near Euston

Wot The Dickens, 3 Woburn Walk, WC1 (tel. 383 4813). Tube: Euston. Head right down Eversholt St., cross Euston Rd., and Woburn Walk will be on the left off of Upper Woburn place. White tiled and modern, this slick café draws lively crowds at lunchtime. Strong espresso and large sandwiches. Shaded sidewalk seating. Smoked salmon plate £2.40. Croissant and coffee take-away £1. Open Mon.-Fri. 7am-6:30pm, Sat. 9am-4pm.

Chutney's, 124 Drummond St., NW1 (tel. 338 0604). Tube: Warren St. A cheerful café serving vegetarian dishes from Western and Southern India. Bright paintings and spiral brass lamps decorate the walls. Lunch buffet Mon.-Sat. noon-2:45pm and Sun. noon-10:30pm, £3.95. *Dosas* (filled pancakes) £2.45-3.50. Take-away available 6pm-11:30pm. Open daily noon-2:45pm and 6-11:30pm.

Around Russell Square

Wagamama, 4 Streatham St., WC1 (tel. 323 9223). Tube: Tottenham Ct. Rd. Go down New Oxford St., taking a left onto Bloomsbury St. Streatham St. is the first right. A smash hit when it opened in 1992, this noodle bar still packs the customers in, so prepare to queue. Fast food with a high-tech twist: waitstaff take your orders on hand-held electronic radios which transmit directly to the kitchen. Strangers sit elbow-to-elbow at long tables slurping happily from their massive bowls of ramen, like extras from the set of *Tampopo*. Pan fried noodles, rice dishes, and vegetarian soup bases also available. Noodles £3.80-5.70. No smoking. Open Mon.-Fri. noon-2:30pm and 6-11pm, Sat. 1-3pm and 6-11pm.

October Gallery Café, 24 Old Gloucester St., WC1 (tel. 242 7367). Tube: Holborn. A high-ceilinged café with wood floors and wicker seats. Adjacent to a gallery which features the work of young international artists. Entrees £3.50. Gallery open Tues.-Sat. 12:30-5:30pm, lunch served in the café 12:30-2pm.

Leigh St. Café, 16 Leigh St., WC1 (tel. 387 3393). Tube: Russell Sq. A bright student and local-filled café serving creative sandwiches and pastries. Elegant decor and marble tables inside, garden seating in back. Watch the four-person team prepare your food behind the counter. Brie sandwich with walnuts, California sultana, and cucumbers, £1.95, £2.15 with salad. Groups of 5 or more students can call ahead and receive a discount. Take-away available. Open Mon.-Sun. 8am-9pm.

VICTORIA, KENSINGTON, & CHELSEA

Victoria

Culinary prospects in Victoria (tube: Victoria) are bleak. The avenues radiating north and east from the station (Buckingham Palace Rd., Victoria Rd., and Vauxhall Bridge Rd.) are populated with mediocre sandwich shops and chain restaurants with tourists on the brain. Follow the suits to find the cheapest lunch spots.

City Harvest, 38 Buckingham Palace Rd., SW1 (tel. 630 9781). A fresher sandwich bar than most in the area, with chalkboard specials and a busy lunch take-away scene. Conventional sandwiches £1-1.40, fancy sandwiches £2.30-3. Several set breakfasts available for less than £4. Open Mon.-Fri. 7am-5pm, Sat.-Sun. 9am-3pm.

The Snack Box, 326 Vauxhall Bridge Rd., SW1. Directly across from the Apollo Victoria. A certain source of sustenance. If you've just stumbled out of Victoria Station, this may be your rude awakening to the "English breakfast"—set breakfast of one fried egg, bacon, beans, sausage, and toast £2.50. Stuffed potatoes £1.40-2.30. Large coffee 50p. Open Mon.-Sat. 6:30am-6:30pm.

Knightsbridge & Hyde Park Corner

Epicurian stomachs-on-a-budget enticed by the sumptuous outlay of the Harrods food court may growl with disappointment here. Knightsbridge Green, northwest of Harrods off Brompton Rd., offers several sandwich shops, in addition to fresh fruit and vegetable stands where you can procure provisions for a picnic.

Mima's Sandwiches and Salads, 9 Knightsbridge Green, SW1 (tel. 589 6820). Understandably packed during lunch hours. Practically every sandwich under the sun, each £2 or less. Open Mon.-Sat. 7am-5:30pm.

Knightsbridge Express, 17 Knightsbridge Green, SW1 (tel. 589 3039). Proprietor George looks after the crowds who pack this upbeat eatery. The upstairs seating area is more placid. Most sandwiches £1-2. Sandwich platters with cole slaw and potato salad under £4. Open Mon.-Sat. 6:30am-5:30pm.

Arco Bars, 46 Hans Crescent, SW1 (tel. 584 6454). Cheap and relatively plentiful Italian food. Lunch special of pasta, wine, and coffee £4.25. Generous sandwiches on excellent bread (£1.75-3). Open Mon.-Fri. 7am-6pm, Sat. 8am-6pm.

South Kensington

For budget dining, Old Brompton Rd. and Fulham Rd. are the main thoroughfares in this graceful area of London; although beware that there are few budget restaurants on Fulham Rd. between the station and Drayton Gardens. South Kensington tube station lies closest, but some of the restaurants below require a substantial hike from there; others can be easily reached from the Earl's Ct. tube station.

Ambrosiana Crêperie, 194 Fulham Rd., SW10 (tel. 351 0070). Airy storefront with cane chairs and small tables. Gourmet but friendly. Savory crêpes £4.60-6 (try the combination of salami, asparagus, onions, and cheese). Sweet crêpes slightly cheaper (peaches, *crème de caçao*, and ice cream £3.65). Open Mon.-Fri. noon-3pm and 6pm-midnight, Sat.-Sun. noon-midnight.

Jules Rotisserie, 6-8 Bute St., SW7 (tel. 584 0600; fax 584 0614). This lively restaurant with indoor and outdoor seating serves roasted free-range poultry in various permutations. ¼ chicken with potatoes or green salad £4.95. Daily vegetarian salad specials (small £2, large £3.75). Fresh-squeezed orange juice £1.20. Open daily 11:30am-11:30pm.

Bar Escoba, 102 Old Brompton Rd., SW7 (tel. 244 8662). Lively Spanish restaurant and bar; just a 10min. walk from the South Kensington tube. A comfortable place with indoor and outdoor seating, pseudo-Mexican decor, and an Indiana Jones pinball machine. *Tapas* £1.50-4. Grilled chicken breast with lemon and chili sauce, chips, and salad £8. Gazpacho £1.95. Full bar. Open daily noon-11pm.

High St. Kensington

There are few appealing options for eating in the area. If you've got more time than you have money, walk uphill to Notting Hill Gate, where the range of food options is noticeably wider and less expensive.

Phoenicia, 11-13 Abingdon Rd., W8 (tel. 937 0120). Save this acclaimed Lebanese restaurant for a special night. Small and down-to-earth; food in huge helpings. All-you-can-eat luncheon buffet (£8) served 12:15-2:30pm. Cover charge £1.40. Service charge 15%. Open Mon.-Sat. noon-midnight.

Chelsea

When hunger pangs strike during a promenade down **King's Road,** you can either sate your desires on the spot or consider a jaunt down a neighboring thoroughfare, where affordable restaurants abound. Buses #11 and 22 run the length of King's Rd. from the Victoria or Sloane Sq. tube stations. Alternately, turn right onto Sydney St. or Edith Grove and head towards Fulham Rd., which runs parallel to King's Rd.

Chelsea Kitchen, 98 King's Rd., SW3 (tel. 589 1330). 5-10min. walk from the tube. Locals rave about the eclectic menu of cheap, filling, tasty food: chicken mushroom fricassee, *spaghetti bolognese*, and a Spanish omelette are each £2.30 or less. Cozy booth seating. When the weather is amenable, grab one of the front tables and watch the Sloanies pass you by. Breakfast served 8-11:25am. Open Mon.-Sat. 8am-11:30pm, Sun. noon-11:30pm. No credit cards.

The Stock Pot, 273 King's Rd., SW3 (tel. 823 3175). The minimum per person is £2.20, but most meals won't cost you more than that anyway. All entrees, from lamb chops to fillet of trout, under £3.50. Itching for roughage? Large salads with exciting embellishments like avocado, cottage cheese, or pineapple under £3. Open Mon.-Sat. 8am-midnight, Sun. 10am-midnight.

Planet Poppadum, 366 King's Rd., SW2 (tel. 823 3368 or 3369). This Balti brasserie and bar manages to incorporate seemingly incommensurate elements of Eurochic, Indian take-away, and futuristic modern styling into a spicy new-wave South Asian synthesis. Tikka-take away served up unfailingly from behind the restaurant's sushi-sleek counter. Most vegetarian and chicken dishes under £5. All entrees include complimentary salad, yogurt, mango chutney, mixed pickle sauce, and, from a galaxy far, far away, poppadum. Renowned *nan* bread £1.50. Open Mon.-Wed. 4pm-midnight, Thurs.-Sun. noon-midnight. MC, Visa.

Earl's Court

Earl's Court, a take-away carnival, revolves around cheap, palatable food. Groceries abound and shops stay open late and on Sunday. Look for coffee shops and Indian restaurants on Gloucester Rd. north of Cromwell Rd. (especially by Elvaston Pl.).

Perry's Bakery, 151 Earl's Court Rd., SW5 (tel. 370 4825). Amiable Bulgarian-Israeli management prides itself on a somewhat eclectic menu and phenomenal fresh baked goods. Great for eat-in, but less expensive for take-away. Flaky *borekas* (cheese-filled pastry) makes a indulgent snack (with spinach, £1.40). Straight from Israel come *Mitzli* juices (60p) and falafel (£2). For breakfast try their croissant plus all-you-can-drink tea or coffee for £2. Open daily 6am-midnight.

Troubador Coffee House, 265 Old Brompton Rd., SW5 (tel. 370 1434). Near the junction of Earl's Ct. and Old Brompton Rd. Copper pots and mandolins dangle from the ceiling, and whirring espresso machines steam the windows in this community café. Bob Dylan played here early in his career. Assorted snacks, soups, and sandwiches, under £4. Open daily 9:30am-11pm.

Season's, 111 Gloucester Rd., SW7 (tel. 244 8454). Tube: Gloucester Rd., or a 10-15 min. walk from Earl's Court area. A member of the National Federation of Fish Fryers. Popular 50s-style fish and chips joint fries only in pure groundnut oil to produce "the finest fish and chips available." Bustling counter serves everything from fried cod, plaice, and haddock (£2.50-2.70) to lemon sole (£3). They also do burgers, salads, sandwiches, cappuccino, and espresso. Open daily 6am-11pm.

NOTTING HILL & BAYSWATER

This area is chock-full of high-quality, reasonably priced restaurants, especially around Notting Hill Gate. Head to Westbourne Grove (tube: Bayswater or Royal Oak) for large concentrations of decent, if rather unremarkable, South Asian places.

The Garden, 1 Hillgate St., W8 (tel. 727 8922, fax 727 8944). Tube: Notting Hill Gate. A small, tasteful establishment that serves the cheapest lunches around, The Garden feels like an old neighborhood institution even though it just opened. Plants, a fireplace, and a bookshelf tucked away tidily behind the espresso machine create an inviting atmosphere in which hip local youth seem to feel right at home. Go crazy and try the most expensive thing on the menu; it's not likely to exceed a trifling £2.50. Sandwiches on your choice of breads range from £1-1.95; try one of the creative tuna salads. Open Mon.-Sat. 8am-4pm.

Oporto Patisserie, 62a Golborne Rd., W10 (tel. (0181) 960 9669). Tube: Ladbroke Grove. A thriving enclave of Portuguese culture, this *pastelana* serves delectable pastries crafted from Iberian ingredients. Order a steaming toasted cheese croissant (85p) and enjoy concourse with the gods. Miraculously, these inexpensive baked goods can make a full meal. Open 8am-8pm daily.

The Belair Diner, 23 All Saints Road, W11 (tel. 229 7961). Tube: Westbourne Park or Ladbroke Grove. Behind a rust-red exterior, sample dishes from a variety of international cuisines while listening to a mix of funk and jazz music. The menu of this candle-lit restaurant is a jumble of well-prepared West Indian, South American, and African dishes. The *roti* dishes, lovingly envelop curried beef, chicken, or vegetables in a large pancake (£5.75 with side salad). Fried plantains £1.95. Open Mon.-Sat. noon-midnight, Sun. 6pm-midnight.

Khan's, 13-15 Westbourne Grove, W2 (tel. 727 5240). Tube: Bayswater. Cavernous, noisy, and crowded, Khan's persists as the best bargain around for delicious Indian cuisine. The menu explains to diners that the distinctive flavor of each dish "cannot come from the rancid ambiguity called curry powder," but only from "spices separately prepared each day." They're not kidding—the chicken *saag* (chicken cooked with spinach, £2.95) contains piquant spices that are well complemented by flat *nan* bread (95p) or rice (£1.40). If you dip into one of the chutneys sitting expectantly on your table when you arrive, you will be charged 30p. Chicken *tikka masala* £3.50. Open daily noon-3pm and 6pm-midnight.

THE CITY

This area is splendid for lunch (when food is fresh for the options traders) and disastrous for dinner (when the expense accounts go home and the food goes stale). Pick up some fresh fruit from a vendor in **Leadenhall Market** on Gracechurch St.

The Place Below, in St. Mary-le-Bow Church crypt, Cheapside, EC2 (tel. 329 0789). Tube: St. Paul's. Attractive and generous vegetarian dishes served to hip suits in the unexpectedly light atmosphere of a stone church basement. Menu changes daily. Quiche and salad £5.25. Savory tomato, almond, and saffron soup £2.70. Meals about £1.50 cheaper take-away or 11:30am-noon. Dinner runs £15 for a two-course meal and coffee. Open Mon.-Fri. 7:30am-3pm, dinner Thurs.-Fri. 6:30-10:30pm. £3.50 min., noon-2pm.

Croissant Express, Unit 20-22, Leadenhall Market, EC3 (tel. 623 8804). Tube: Bank. (Also at the Moorgate tube station.) Business-people consume fresh baked goods and look at their watches. Plain croissant 40p, sandwiches £1.55-2.10. Take note of the bargain Croissant Express special: 2 mini plain croissants, 2 mini *pains au chocolat*, and 2 mini *pains au raisins,* £1. Open Mon.-Fri. 7am-5pm.

The East-West Restaurant, 188 Old St., EC1 (tel. 608 0300). Tube: Old St. Sublime macrobiotic cooking. Original artwork enlivens the white walls. Blond wood furnishings provide a setting commensurate to the vivacious crowd which congregates here. Menu changes daily. Main meals come with vegetables and salad, in small (£4.50) or large (£6) portions. Open Mon.-Thurs. 11am-9pm, Fri.-Sat. 11am-10pm, Sun. 11am-4pm. Major credit cards.

THE EAST END

London's East End is a bustling jumble of neighborhoods filled with restaurants serving a wide variety of traditional foods. The large number of South Asian restaurants differ greatly in decor, quality, and price.

The Cherry Orchard Café, 247 Globe Rd., E2 (tel. (081) 980 6678). Tube: Bethnal Green. A lovely un-Chekhovian restaurant run by Buddhists. Photo portraits line the peach and turquoise walls. A tranquil garden awaits in back. Entrees (like broccoli and almond filo pie) average £3.50. Mixed salads, cakes, and desserts available all day. Hot meals served Mon. and Thurs.-Fri. noon-3pm, Tues.-Wed. noon-7pm. Open Mon. and Thurs.-Fri. 11am-4pm, Tues.-Wed. 11am-7pm.

Bloom's, 90 Whitechapel High St., E1 (tel. 247 6001). Tube: Aldgate East. (Also at Golders Green.) A London institution, this traditional kosher restaurant sells good salt (corned) beef sandwiches for £3.20. *Haimishe* family atmosphere. The take-away counter also sells canned food. Popular on Sun. Open Sun.-Thurs. 11am-9pm, Fri. 11am-2pm.

Nazrul, 130 Brick La., E1 (tel. 247 2505). Tube: Aldgate East. Although the plush red booths are inviting, the rapid service means that you don't have to linger if you're pressed for time. The meat served here is bought from a local halal shop and cooked fresh daily. Considering the size of the portions, prices are terrifically cheap; chicken dishes £2.35-2.80. 10% discount Sun. noon-5pm. No bar, but you may bring your own alcohol. Open Mon.-Thurs. noon-3pm and 5:30pm-midnight, Fri.-Sat. noon-3pm and 5:30pm-1am, Sun. noon-midnight.

ISLINGTON

Café Olé, 119 Upper St., N1 (tel. 226 6991). A hip pasta bar/café adorned with col-orful ceramic plates and painted floral borders on the salmon walls. Endless breakfast: egg, bacon, sausage, tomato, mushroom, black pudding, bubble and squeak, and toast £3.80. Vegetarian breakfast also available. Lunch menu offers pasta (£3.50) and salads (£3.50), in addition to sandwiches (£1-2.50). The selec-tion of pastas and salads expands at dinner; all are offered in small (£3.95) or large (£4.95) portions. Open Mon.-Sat. 8am-11pm.

The New Culture Revolution, 42 Duncan St., N1 (tel. 833 9083). A dumpling and noodle bar with slick black tables, plush chairs, and Matisse prints. Dumplings and noodles come either fried or in soup base, cooked with different meats, fish, or vegetables. Dumplings £3.50-4. Noodles £3.50-5.50. Open Mon.-Fri. noon-2:30pm and 6-11pm, Sat. 1-11pm. 20% off if you pay before 7pm. AmEx, MC, Visa.

Indian Veg Bhelpoori House, 92-93 Chapel Market, N1 (tel. 837 4607 or 833 1167). An unmistakable bargain—all-you-can-eat lunch buffet of 18 vegetarian dishes and chutneys for a startling £3.25. Dinner buffet £3.50. If it's good enough for Miss Asia, who dined here with Miss Philippines in 1991, it's good enough for you. Open noon-3pm and 6-11pm. MC, Visa.

CAMDEN TOWN

Camden Town can be a bit grotty, especially in the wake of the weekend markets; however, glamourous cafés and international restaurants are magnetically attracted to **Camden High Street,** which runs south from the Camden Town tube station to Mornington Crescent, and north to Chalk Farm, becoming **Chalk Farm Road.**

Parkway Pizzeria, 64 Parkway, NW1 (tel. 485 0678). Exit the station to the right, then head left along Camden High St.; Parkway is the immediate right. Juicy piz-zas served in a welcoming pizzeria off of the main thoroughfare. Parquet floor and cool Art Deco mirrors; the partially marbled green walls match the marble table tops. Pizza with capers, pine nuts, tomato, and mozzarella, £3.65. Take away available. £3 min. when the restaurant is full. Open daily noon-midnight.

Bar Gansa, 2 Inverness St., NW1 (tel. 267 8909). A small *tapas* bar with cream-col-ored walls, decorated with bright prints and festive Spanish ceramics. Hip clien-tele of all ages linger over food, coffee, and wine. Ham, eggs, and chips £3.95. *Tapas* £1.95-3.50. Grilled goat cheese sandwich £4. Outdoor seating. Open Mon.-Thurs. 10:30am-11:45pm, Fri. Sat. 10:30am-midnight, Sun. 10:30am-11pm.

Le Petit Prince, 5 Holmes Rd., NW5 (tel. 267 0752). Tube: Kentish Town. French/Algerian cuisine served in a whimsically decorated café/bar/restaurant. Illustra-tions from Saint-Exupéry's *Le Petit Prince* dot the walls, which are painted to sim-ulate a cartoon-purple night sky. Generous plantain sauté starter £2.95. Vegetarian couscous £4.95. Lamb, chicken, and fish dishes are slightly more expensive, but come with unlimited couscous and vegetable broth. Lunch menu includes crêpes (£4.25-4.40) and a coriander, guacamole, and melted goat cheese sandwich (£3.95). Open daily noon-3pm and 7-11:30pm.

HAMPSTEAD

Crêpe Van, 77 Hampstead High St., NW3. Outside the King William IV pub. A Hampstead institution. Paper-thin Brittany crêpes made in front of your eyes by a real French crêpe-maker in the tiniest van imaginable. Both sweet fillings (including banana and Grand Marnier) and savory (spinach and garlic cream, mushroom and cheese) £2-3. Open Mon.-Sat. 1-11pm, Sun. 1:30-11pm.

Everyman Café, Holly Bush Vale, NW3 (tel. 431 2123). The hip café-cum-restaurant of the renowned repertory movie house, the Everyman Cinema. Have a croissant or muffin (£1) before catching Orson Welles's *Othello*. Or, try an omelette (£4), truffle-oil poached eggs with wild mushrooms (£5.50), or warm chicken and oyster mushroom salad (£6.50) after taking in an odious Wim Wenders flick. Open Mon.-Fri. noon-midnight, Sat. 11am-midnight, Sun. 11am-11pm.

SOUTH OF THE THAMES

Jacaranda, 11-13 Brixton Station Road, SW9 (tel. 274 8383). A lot of homecooked food for very little money. Main dishes like *fusilli* dripping with cheese, fresh tomatoes, and broccoli, or vegetarian gumbo with rice and okra £2-4. 4 kinds of foccacia, £2.75 each. Open Mon.-Sat. 9:30am-9pm, Sun. 11am-6pm.

■ GROCERIES & SUPERMARKETS

The most economical source of food is the **supermarket.** Besides groceries, they sell excellent deli and bakery goods and satisfying prepared dishes. Avoid shopping from 6-8pm and weekend afternoons, when lines are longest. Supermarkets include: **Sainsbury,** Victoria Rd. (near Victoria Station); Cromwell Rd. (tube: Gloucester Rd.); Camden Rd. (tube: Camden Town); gargantuan "Hypermarket" in Merton (tube: Collier's Wood); **Europa,** a ubiquitous small grocery store; **Harrod's,** Brompton Rd. (tube: Knightsbridge), whose enormous food halls offer everything under the sun at out-of-this-budget-world prices; visit if only to gawk; and **Marks & Spencer,** Oxford St. (tube: Marble Arch); Poland St. (tube: Oxford Circus); Liverpool St. (tube: Camden Town); Kensington High St. (tube: High St. Kensington).

■ PUBS & BARS

> *"Did you ever taste beer?"*
> *"I had a sip of it once," said the small servant.*
> *"Here's a state of things!" cried Mr. Swiveller, "She never tasted it—it can't be tasted in a sip!"*
>
> *—Charles Dickens, The Old Curiosity Shop*

London's 7000 pubs are as colorful and historic as their counterparts throughout England, with clientele varying considerably from one neighborhood to the next. Pubs in the City pack in tourists and pinstripes at lunch. The taverns up in Bloomsbury tend to draw a mix of tourists and students, while those in Kensington and Hampstead cater to the trendy element. Around the wholesale markets, tradespeople grab pints as early as six in the morning.

Avoid pubs within a half-mile radius of an inner-city train station (Paddington, Euston, King's Cross/St. Pancras, and Victoria). They prey upon tourists by charging 20-40p extra per pint. For the best prices, head to the East End. Stylish, lively pubs cluster around the fringes of the West End. Many historic alehouses lend an ancient air to areas swallowed by urban sprawl, such as Highgate and Hampstead. Some pubs have serious theater groups performing upstairs; others are meeting places for community groups, literary workshops, and other cultural organizations. Buy drinks at the bar—bartenders are not usually tipped. A pint should set you back £1.60-2.10.

THE WEST END

Lamb and Flag, 33 Rose St., WC2, off Garrick St. Tube: Covent Garden or Leicester Sq. Rose St. is off Long Acre, which runs between the 2 tube stops. In days of yore, a mob of angry readers seized Augustan poet John Dryden and nearly beat him to death—just one of the events that earned this pub the title "Bucket of Blood." Today a fun local crowd spills onto the alley streets in the evenings.

The Porcupine, Great Newport St. at Charing Cross Rd., WC2. Tube: Leicester Sq. Young folks on the first floor generate smoke and noise, while their parents peck at tasty pre-theater pub meals (£4.50-7) upstairs.

Riki Tik, 23-24 Bateman St., W1 (tel. 437 1977). Tube: Leicester Square, Tottenham Ct. Rd., or Piccadilly Circus. A hyped, hip, and tremendously swinging bar specializing in flavored vodkas (£2/shot). Try white chocolate or, for the brave, aniseed. Open Mon.-Sat. 11am-11pm; closed Sun.

Freud's, 198 Shaftesbury Ave., WC2 (tel. 240 9933). Tube: Tottenham Ct. Rd. or Covent Garden. A downstairs bar with leftover late-80s decor: concrete walls, slate tables, and art for sale. *The* place to discuss Oedipus; remains comfortable despite itself, even for the single traveler without a mother complex. Beer £1.95-2.75. Cocktails £3.10-4.55. Limited selection of snack foods. Live jazz Sun. eve. Open Mon.-Sat. 11am-11pm, Sun. noon-10:30pm.

KENSINGTON, CHELSEA, & EARL'S COURT

World's End Distillery, on King's Rd. near World's End Pass (before Edith Grove). Tube: Sloane Sq. This pub isn't wedged shamefacedly into a street corner like most others; it stands alone, grandiose and cathedralesque. If the universe collapsed and nothing but the World's End remained, we would not weep. Rather, we would lounge in a soft leather booth and play one of the many board games offered here, or sit on a green velvet stool and peruse one of the old books shelved near the candle-lit mirror. Live music on Thurs. and Sun. nights.

Admiral Codrington, 17 Mossop St., SW3. Tube: South Kensington. This old, handsomely pub with a patio off the back brims with girls in platform shoes and boys in baggy suits. An impressive stash of single-malt whiskey.

The Chelsea Potter, 119 King's Rd., SW3. Tube: Victoria then bus #11, 19, or 22. This pub's name marks its history as a haven for ramshackle Chelsea artists throwing pots and living on their trust funds. Noisy outdoor tables. Enthusiastic patrons watch sports on TV. Pints of Carlsberg lager under £2.

The Australian, 29 Milner St., SW3. Tube: Sloane Sq. This cricket pub is especially appealing during the summer season, when enthusiasts can watch the Test Match while sipping a pint of bitter.

The King's Head, Hogarth Pl., SW5. Tube: Earl's Ct. From Earl's Ct. Rd., head east on Childs Walk or Hogarth Pl. Large and popular pub, but quieter than most in Earl's Ct. Besides real ale, this pub has a passable wine list.

BLOOMSBURY

The Old Crown, 33 New Oxford St., WC1 (tel. 836 9121). Tube: Tottenham Ct. Rd. A thoroughly nontraditional pub. Mustard yellow walls, faded pine-green bar, green plants, and funky brass crowns suspending the light fixtures from the ceiling. The lively mixed crowd spills out onto the outdoor seating, creating a babble of voices above the upbeat rock music playing in the background; quieter seating upstairs. Also a restaurant/café serving salads, hummus, tea, and Mexican specialites. Open Mon.-Sat. noon-11pm. Major credit cards.

The Lamb, 94 Lamb's Conduit St., WC1 (tel. 405 0713). Tube: Russell Sq. E.M. Forster and other Bloomsbury luminaries used to do their tippling here. Discreet cutglass "snob screens" render this pub ideal for dangerous liaisons and illicit assignations. Limited outdoor seating. Hot food served noon-2:30pm.

The Sun, 63 Lamb's Conduit St., WC1 (tel. 405 8278). Tube: Holborn. One of London's largest selections of real ales on tap at this busy pub on a street of cafés and sandwich shops. Stately cast-iron fireplaces and hardwood floors; the wood furniture has a comfortably worn feel. Standard, relatively cheap pub fare. Mixed crowd of business people, older locals, and students.

Grafton Arms, 72 Grafton Way, W1 (tel. 387 7923). Tube: Warren St. Off the tourist trail, near Regent's Park. One of the best central London pubs for a relaxed pint. Caters to a lively London University student crowd. 8 real ales. Standard pub fare sold all day. Wine bar on rooftop patio. MC, Visa.

Museum Tavern, 49 Great Russell St., WC1 (tel. 242 8987). Tube: Tottenham Ct. Rd. High coffered ceiling; spacious, plush atmosphere. Karl Marx sipped *Bier* here after banging out *Das Kapital* across the street in the British Museum reading room. 17 beers on tap.

The Water Rats, 328 Grays Inn Rd., WC1 (tel. 837 9861). Tube: King's Cross/St. Pancras. Ordinary appearance belies radical historical connections—this used to be one of Marx and Engels' favorite haunts. Average pint £2.10. Moonlights as the Splash Club Wed.-Sat. nights, a venue for indie rock, punk, and occasional acoustic gigs. 3 bands a night. £5, concessions £3.

THE CITY & EAST END

Black Friar, 174 Queen Victoria St., EC4 (tel. 236 5650). Tube: Blackfriars. Directly across from the station. The entire edifice stands as an Art Nouveau monument to the medieval monks whose vestments are celebrated in the pub's name. Intriguing nooks and crannies. Witty advice can be read from the walls of the back room, called "The Side Chapel." Average pint £1.90.

Cartoonist, 76 Shoe La., EC4 (353 2828). Tube: Chancery La. Headquarters for the Cartoonist Club of Great Britain. Decorated with hilarity, but the current pinstriped clientele are themselves ripe for caricature. Limited outdoor seating.

Ye Olde Cheshire Cheese, Wine Office Ct., 145 Fleet St., EC4 (tel. 353 6170). Tube: Blackfriars or St. Paul's. Once on Fleet St., watch out for Wine Office Ct. on the right; a small sign indicates the alley. A 17th-century pub which has retained the small-rooms layout characteristic of that era. Famous as Dr. Johnson's and Dickens's hangout—artifacts and pictures highlight events that shaped this pub/restaurant's 300-year history. 5 bars and 3 restaurants contained in "the Cheese."

Sir Christopher Wren, 7 Paternoster Sq., EC4 (tel. 248 1708). Tube: St. Paul's. Tremendous smoked glass windows grant this pub/restaurant instant atmosphere. Plush booths inside, picnic tables outside. Food prices reflect the pub's proximity to Wren's masterpiece, not the food's scrumptiousness. Daily special £4.80. Average pint £1.85. Open Mon.-Fri. 11am-9pm, Sat.-Sun. 11:30am-3pm.

The Blind Beggar, 337 Whitechapel Rd., E1 (tel. 247 8329). Tube: Whitechapel. You may be sitting where George Cornell sat when he was gunned down by rival Bethnal Green gangster Ronnie Kray in 1966. Spacious pub with a conservatory and a garden. Middle-aged locals tipple here.

Clutterbuck's, 89 Whitechapel High St., E1 (tel. 247 5393). Tube: Aldgate East. Newly redone, the decor remains traditional, with a dark wood bar and patterned carpeting. Opens out onto the street, where locals sit around small tables. Students welcome. A pint of Clutterbuck's ale £1.10. Bottomless homemade soup with fresh nob £1.95. Open Mon.-Sat. 11am-11pm, Sun. noon-3pm.

CAMDEN TOWN & ISLINGTON

Slug and Lettuce, 1 Islington Green, N1. Tube: Angel. Upper St. changes its name to Islington Green as it passes by the Green. Patrons of the Screen on the Green across the street conduct earnest dissections of *Casablanca*. Good observation post for spotting Islington trendies (inside or outside).

Engine Room, 78-9 Chalk Farm Rd., NW1 (tel. 916 0595). Tube: Chalk Farm. A rock-oriented bar frequented by local band members. Painted black outside, with grafitti art on the windows; inside, the walls are plastered with old music posters, vinyl platters, and movie ads. Pool table. Cheap pub fare.

HAMPSTEAD & HIGHGATE

The Holly Bush, 22 Holly Mount, NW3. Tube: Hampstead. The quintessential snug Hampstead pub in a quaint cul-de-sac, serving real ale. The maze of glass and wood makes this place ideal for an illicit assignation.

King William IV, 77 Hampstead High St., NW3. Tube: Hampstead. Outside: the famed Crêpe Van (see Restaurants). Inside: the famed gay pub, very trendy for people of all ages.

Spaniards Inn, Spaniards End, NW3. Tube: Hampstead, bus #210 along Spaniards Rd. Upscale pub on Hampstead Heath, providing garden in summer and hearth in winter since 1585. Shelley, Keats, and Byron were patrons. Intriguing aviary.

The Bull and Bush, North End Way, NW3. Tube: Golders Green, then bus #210, or Hampstead tube and bus #268. Immortalized in the classic music hall song "Down at the Old Bull and Bush," though the spiffy young gentlemen who crowd the bar today seem unlikely to break into chorus.

■ TEA

London hotels serve afternoon set teas, often hybrids of the cream and high varieties, which are expensive and sometimes disappointing. You might order single items from the menu instead of the full set to avoid a sugar overdose. Cafés often serve a simpler tea (pot of tea, scone, preserves, and butter) for a lower price.

Louis, 32 Heath St., NW3 (tel. (01) 435 9908). This intimate Hungarian confectionary and tea room thrills with finger-licking Florentine (a candy conglomerate of almonds, cherries, and chocolate)£1.80. A variety of cakes, tarts, and teas are also available. Open daily 9:30am-6pm.

Georgian Restaurant, Harrods, Knightsbridge, SW1 (tel. 730 1234). Tube: Knightsbridge. A carefully staged event. Revel in bourgeois satisfaction as you demurely enjoy your expensive set tea inside or out on the terrace (£10.50). Tea served daily indoors 3:30-5:15pm.

The Muffin Man, 12 Wrights La., W8 (tel 937 6652). Tube: High St. Kensington. Everything you dreamed a tearoom could be: ruffled white curtains, flowered tablecloths, ferns galore, and a side patio. Simply delightful. Set cream tea £3.80. High tea £4.70. Min. £1.50 from 12:30-2:30pm. Open Mon.-Sat. 8am-5:30pm.

The Orangery Tea Room, Kensington Palace, Kensington Gardens, W8 (tel. 376 0239). Tube: High St. Kensington. Light meals and tea served in the marvelously airy Orangery built for Queen Anne in 1705. Two fruit scones with clotted cream and jam £3.15. Pot of tea £1.35. Trundle through the gardens afterward, smacking your lips. Open daily 10am-6pm.

■■■ SIGHTS

The landmarks of London that attract those on foot and in ever-lengthening coaches face an onrush of up to five million visitors a year. These stampedes thicken from the late morning onwards, so try to get started as early as possible. Pacing any assault will allow a much more thorough exploration of the districts that make up the city. Hidden in and around the main sights can be found a serene chapel or an immense carnival, a museum of clocks, a deer park, an Indian film festival, or an exhibition of Masai arms. Modern-day tourists are only the latest in a long line of arrivals to try to find out how the city fits together, and where they fit into the puzzle.

Touring

A good city tour can introduce you to the highlights of London, enabling you to decide where to focus your energies. The **London Transport Sight-seeing Tour** (tel. 222 1234) provides a convenient, albeit cursory, overview of London's attractions from a double-decker bus. Tours lasting 1½ hrs. depart from Baker St., Haymarket (near Piccadilly Circus),Marble Arch (Speaker's Corner), and Victoria St. (near the station), and include Buckingham Palace, the Houses of Parliament, Westminster Abbey, the Tower of London, St. Paul's, and Piccadilly Circus. (Tours daily 2/hr. 9:30am-5:30pm; £9, under 16 £5. Pay the bus conductor.) London Transport also operates **London by Night,** which whizzes by London's floodlit landmarks. It departs 7pm or 9pm from Victoria Station (£6, under 14 £4). Several ordinary buses also give a stunning view of the city; bus #15 is an especially good bet.

Walking tours can fill in the specifics of London that bus tours run right over; with a good guide, a tour can be as entertaining as it is informative. Among the best are **The Original London Walks** (tel. 624 3978; £4, £3 for students and HI members, accompanied children under 15 free); **Historical Tours of London** (tel. (0181) 668 4019; £4.50, seniors, students, and children £3.50); and **City Walks of London** (tel.

700 6931), whose tours include the Londons of Shakespeare, Dickens, or the Beatles, "Legal London," and "The Trail of Jack the Ripper" (£4, concessions £3, accompanied children under 12 free). Leaflets for these and others are all too available in hotels and tourist information centers. For meeting times and details, see the "Around Town" section of the weekly *Time Out* magazine.

If glancing at London from the top of a bus is unsatisfactory, and locomotion by your own two feet seems daunting, a tour led by **The London Bicycle Tour Company** (tel. 928 6838) may be the solution. They offer two Sun. tours: the morning Greenwich Market excursion and the afternoon East End tour. Both depart from 56 Upper Ground, SE1 (Sun. 10am and 2:30pm; 3hrs.; £9.95; independent bike £7.)

WESTMINSTER ABBEY

> Think how many royal bones
> Sleep within this heap of stones;
> For here they lie, had realms and lands,
> That now want strength to stir their hands.
>
> —Francis Beaumont

Neither a cathedral nor a parish church, Westminster Abbey (tube: Westminster) is a "royal peculiar," controlled directly by the Crown and outside the jurisdiction of the Church of England. As both the site of every royal coronation since 1066 and the final resting place for an imposing assortment of sovereigns, politicians, poets, and artists, the Abbey functions as a cross between a national church and a national honor roll. Burial in the abbey is the greatest and rarest official honor in Britain.

Consecrated by Edward the Confessor on 28 December 1065, only the Pyx Chamber and the Norman Undercroft (now the Westminster Abbey Treasure Museum) survive from the original structure. Most of the present abbey was erected by Henry III during the 13th century to honor Edward. However, most of the stone visible in in the Abbey today is actually refacing which dates from the 18th century.

In the Abbey's narrow **nave,** the highest in all of England, a slab of Belgian marble marks the **Grave of the Unknown Warrior,** the one part of the Abbey no one may tread upon. Here the body of a World War I soldier is buried in soil from the battlefields of France. A piece of green marble engraved with the words "Remember Winston Churchill" sits nearby. Parliament placed it here 25 years after the Battle of Britain, perhaps prompted by pangs of regret that Churchill's body lay buried in Bladon and not in the Abbey's hall of fame. At the foot of the **Organ Loft,** a memorial to Sir Isaac Newton sits next to the grave of Lord Kelvin. Franklin Roosevelt, David Lloyd George, Lord and Lady Baden-Powell of Boy Scout fame, and the presumptive David Livingstone number among the elect remembered in the nave. "Rare Ben Jonson" is buried upright; on his deathbed he proclaimed, "Six feet long by two feet wide is too much for me. Two feet by two feet will do for all I want."

To see the rest of the abbey, visitors must enter through a gate at the end of the north aisle of the nave and pay admission (see below). **Musicians' Aisle,** just beyond this gate, contains the graves of the Abbey's most accomplished organists, John Blow and Henry Purcell, as well as memorials to the composers Elgar, Britten, Vaughan Williams, and William Walton. **Statesmen's Aisle,** in the early Gothic north transept, has the most eclectic collection of memorials. Prime Ministers Disraeli and Gladstone couldn't stand each other in life, but in death their figures stand in symmetry flanking a large memorial to Sir Peter Warren, alongside Peel, Castlereagh, Palmerston, and others. The **High Altar,** directly south of the north transept, has been the scene of coronations and royal weddings since 1066. Anne of Cleves, Henry VIII's fourth wife, lies in a tomb on the south side of the sanctuary, just before the altar.

Beyond these chapels stands the **Chapel of Henry VII** (built 1503-12), perhaps England's most upstanding piece of late perpendicular architecture. Every one of its magnificently carved wooden stalls, reserved for the Knights of the Order of the Bath, features a headpiece bearing the chosen statement of its occupant. The lower sides of the seats, which fold to support those standing during long services, were the only part of the design left to the carpenters' discretion; they feature cartoon-like images of wives beating up their husbands and pagan stories. Latter-day members of the order include bellicose Yankees Ronald Reagan and Norman Schwarz-kopf. The chapel walls sport 95 saints, including the once-lovely Bernadette, who after praying to be saved from a throng of suitors, grew a beard overnight. Charles II exhumed Oliver Cromwell's body from this part of the Abbey in 1661 and had it hanged and beheaded. Today only a simple memorial to Cromwell remains. The **Royal Air Force (RAF) Chapel,** at the far east end, commemorates the Battle of Britain. A hole in the wall in the northeast corner of the Air Force memorial, damage from a German bomb, has been deliberately left unrepaired.

Behind the High Altar, in the **Chapel of St. Edward the Confessor,** rests the Coronation Chair, on which all but two (Edward V and Edward VIII) English monarchs since 1308 have been crowned. The chair rests on the ancient **Stone of Scone** ("skoon"), rumored to be inextricably linked to the government of Britain. The legendary stone was used in the coronation of ancient Scottish kings; James I took it to London to represent the Union, and in the 1950s it was briefly reclaimed by Scottish nationalists. Numerous monarchs are interred in the chapel, from Henry III (d. 1272) to George II (d. 1760). Edward I had himself placed in an unsealed crypt here, in case he was needed again to fight the Scots; his mummy was carried as a standard by the English army as it tried to conquer Scotland. An engraving by William Blake commemorates the moment in 1774 when the Royal Society of Antiquaries opened this coffin in order to assess the body's state of preservation.

Visitors befuddled by the graves of arcane English monarchs may find the names on the graves and plaques in the **Poets' Corner** more recognizable. This little shrine celebrates those dead, canonized, and anthologized in the annals of English literature. It begins with Geoffrey Chaucer, who was originally buried in the abbey in 1400—the short Gothic tomb you see today in the east wall of the transept was not erected until 1556. The lower classes of the dead poets' society, and those leading "unconventional" life-styles, often lingered before getting a permanent spot in the Abbey; even the Bard remained on the waiting list until 125 years after his mortal coil was shuffled off. Oscar Wilde will be honored with a long overdue monument in Poet's Corner in 1995, the centenary of his conviction for homosexual activities. Floor panels commemorate Tennyson, T.S. Eliot, Dylan Thomas, Henry James, Robert Browning, Lewis Carroll, Lord Byron, and poets of World War I, all at the foot of Chaucer's tomb. The south wall bears tributes to Edmund Spenser, John Milton, and Ben "Johnson." A partition wall divides the south transept, its east side graced with the graves of Samuel Johnson and actor David Garrick, its west side with busts of William Wordsworth, Samuel Taylor Coleridge, and Robert Burns, in addition to a full-length Shakespeare which overshadows the tiny plaques memorializing Jane Austen and the Brontë sisters. On the transept's west wall, Handel's massive memorial looms over the resting place of prolific Charles Dickens.

The Abbey's tranquil **cloister** reposes in a special peace of its own. The entrance in the northeast corner dates from the 13th century, the rest from the 14th. The **Chapter House,** east of the cloister, has one of the best-preserved medieval tile floors in Europe. The King's Great Council used the room as its chamber in 1257, and the House of Commons used it as a meeting-place in the 16th century. Even today, the government administers the Chapter House and the adjacent **Pyx Chamber,** once the Royal Treasury and now a plate museum. Royal effigies (used instead of actual corpses for lying-in-state ceremonies) live in the **Westminster Abbey Treasure Museum.** The oldest, that of Edward III, has a lip permanently warped by the stroke that killed him. The museum also includes an exhibit on the Abbey' history and a few ancient oddities. (Chapter House open daily 10am-5pm; Pyx Chamber and museum open daily 10:30am-4pm. £1, concessions 80p, children 50p.)

Enter through the cloisters on Great College St. to visit the 900-year-old **College Garden,** the oldest garden in England. (Open April-Sept. Tues. and Thurs. 10am-6pm; Oct.-March Tues. and Thurs. 10am-4pm; 20p; band concerts July-Aug. 12:30-

2pm.) The **Brass Rubbing Centre** (tel. 222 2085) in the cloisters may also be worth a visit (open Mon.-Sat. 9am-5pm).

Those who enjoy amazingly informative discussions about architecture, fun gossip about the dead, and just a little sermonizing should take the excellent, all-inclusive Abbey Guided Super Tour (1½hr., £7) which takes visitors to otherwise inaccessible parts of the Abbey. (Tours depart from the Enquiry Desk in the nave Mon.-Fri. at 10am, 10:30am, 11am, 2pm, 2:30pm, and 3pm (except Fri.); Sat. at 10am, 11am, and 12:30pm.) To book one, inquire at the Abbey desk, call 222 7110, or write to Super Tours, 20 Dean's Yard, London SW1P 3PA. Portable tape-recorded commentaries in assorted tongues are available for £6. Photography is permitted only on Wednesday 6-7:45pm. (Westminster Abbey nave open Mon.-Sat. 7:30am-6pm, Wed. 6-7:45pm, Sun. in between services; free. Chapels and transepts open Mon.-Fri. 9am-4:45pm, also Wed. 6-7:45pm, Sat. 9am-2:45pm and 3:45-5:45pm; £4, concessions £2, children £1; all parts of the abbey free Wed. 6-7:45pm.)

WESTMINSTER

Close to Westminster Abbey, **St. Margaret's** has served as the parish church of the House of Commons since 1614, when Protestant MPs feared Westminster Abbey was about to become Catholic. John Milton, Samuel Pepys, and Winston Churchill were wed here. The stained-glass window to the north of the entrance depicts a blind Milton dictating *Paradise Lost* to one of his dutiful daughters, while the stunning east window, made in Holland in 1501, honors the marriage of Catherine of Aragon to Prince Arthur. The post-WWII John Piper windows to the south provide a contrast; entitled "Spring in London," they aptly consist of shades of gray. Beneath the high altar lies the headless body of Sir Walter Raleigh, who was executed across the street in 1618 (open daily 9:30am-5pm when services are not being held).

On the south side of the abbey cluster the buildings of the **Westminster School,** founded as a part of the Abbey in 1560. The arch in Dean's Yard is pitted with the carved initials of generations of England's most privileged schoolboys, among them Ben Jonson, John Dryden, John Locke, Christopher Wren, and A.A. Milne.

The **Victoria Tower Gardens,** immediately south of the Houses of Parliament, offer a secluded view of the Thames. Militant suffragettes Emmeline Pankhurst and her daughter are memorialized in the northwest corner of the gardens. Any flurry of activity around Smith Square, offMillbank at the south end of the Victoria Tower Gardens, is likely to be connected with no. 31, where the Central Office of the Conservative Party lurks, ready to swing into re-action.

THE HOUSES OF PARLIAMENT

The Houses of Parliament (tube: Westminster), oft-imagined in foggy silhouette against the Thames, have become London's visual trademark. Like the government offices along Whitehall, the Houses of Parliament occupy the former site of a royal palace. Only Jewel Tower and Westminster Hall (to the left of St. Stephen's entrance on St. Margaret St.) survive from the original palace, which was destroyed by a fire on October 16, 1834. Sir Charles Barry and A.W.N. Pugin won a competition for the design of the new houses. From 1840 to 1888, Barry built a hulking, symmetrical block that Pugin adorned with tortured imitations of late medieval decoration.

The immense complex blankets eight acres and includes more than 1000 rooms and 100 staircases. Space is nevertheless so inadequate that Members of Parliament (MPs) cannot have private offices or staff, and the archives are stuffed into Victoria Tower, the large tower to the south. A flag flown from the tower (a signal light after dusk) indicates that Parliament is in session.

You can hear **Big Ben** in the slightly smaller northern tower but you can't see it; it's actually neither the tower nor the clock but the 14-ton bell that tolls the hours. Each of the Roman numerals on the clock face measures two feet in length; the minute hands, 14 feet. The mechanism moving the hands is still wound manually.

Unfortunately, access to Westminster Hall and the Houses of Parliament has been restricted since a bomb killed an MP in 1979. To get a **guided tour** (Mon.-Thurs.) or a seat at **Question Time** when the Prime Minister attends (Mon.-Thurs. 2:30-3:30pm), you need to obtain tickets—available on a limited basis from your embassy—or an introduction from an MP. Because demand for these tickets is extremely high, the most likely way of getting into the building is to queue to attend a debate when Parliament is in session. Tours for overseas visitors can also be arranged by sending a written request to the Public Information Office, 1 Derby Gate, Westminster, SW1. The **House of Commons Visitors' Gallery** (for "Distinguished and Ordinary Strangers") is open during extraordinary hours (Mon.-Thurs. 2:30-10pm, Fri. 9:30am-3pm). The **House of Lords Visitors' Gallery** is often easier to access (open Mon.-Wed. 2:30pm-late, Thurs. 3pm-late, Fri. 11am-4pm). Visitors should arrive early, and be prepared for an endless line by St. Stephen's Gate (on the left for the Commons, on the right for the Lords; free). Those willing to sacrifice the roar of the debate for smaller, more focused business can attend meetings of any of the various committees by jumping the queue and going straight up to the entrance. For times of committee meetings each week, call the House of Commons Information Office (tel. 219 4272). Both houses' business is announced daily in the major newspapers, and in a weekly schedule by St. Stephen's Gate. The Visitors' Galleries close when the Houses are not in session: Easter week, summer recess (end of July-mid-Oct.), and a three-week winter recess during Christmas time.

After entering St. Stephen's Gate and submitting to an elaborate security check, you will be standing in St. Stephen's Hall. This chapel is where the House of Commons used to sit. In the floor are four brass markers where the Speaker's Chair stood. Charles I, in his ill-fated attempt to arrest five MPs, sat here in the place of the Speaker in 1641. No sovereign has entered the Commons since.

To the left from the Central Lobby and up the stairs is the **House of Commons' Strangers' Gallery.** Destroyed during the Blitz, most traditional features remain in the rebuilt version, such as two red lines fixed two sword-lengths apart, which debating members may not cross. The Government party (the party with the most MP's in the House) sits to the Speaker's right, and the Opposition to his left. Members vote by filing into **division lobbies** parallel to the chamber: ayes into the west, nays into the east.

To enter the Lords' Gallery, go back through the Central Lobby, and pass through the Peers' corridor. The ostentation of the **House of Lords,** dominated by the sovereign's Throne of State under a gilt canopy, contrasts with the sober, green-upholstered Commons' Chamber. The bewigged Lord Chancellor presides over the House from his seat on the Woolsack, stuffed with wool from all nations of the Kingdom and Commonwealth. The upper chamber is not entirely vestigial; it may amend bills and serves as the final court of appeal.

Outside the Houses is the Old Palace Yard, site of the untimely demises of Sir Walter Raleigh and the Gunpowder Plotter Guy Fawkes (the palace's cellars are still ceremonially searched before every opening of Parliament). To the north squats **Westminster Hall** (rebuilt around 1400), where high treason trials, including those of Thomas More, Fawkes, and Charles I, were held until 1825.

WHITEHALL

Whitehall was born in 1245 as York Place, residence for the Archbishops of York. Cardinal Wolsey enlarged York Place into a palace he thought fit for a king. Henry VIII agreed, and, after beheading Wolsey for treason, moved into his new London apartments of state, rechristened Whitehall in 1530. This gargantuan palace stretched all the way to Somerset House on the Strand, but William II resented an unnamed diplomat's description of Whitehall as "the biggest, most hideous place in all Europe," and relocated to a shiny new Kensington Palace. The forlorn palace burned in 1698, and since then "Whitehall" (tube: Westminster or Charing Cross), has become a synonym for the British civil service.

Ten Downing Street lies just steps up Parliament St. from the Houses. Sir George Downing, ex-Ambassador to The Hague, built this house in 1681. Sir Robert Walpole made it his official residence (as Prime Minister) in 1732. The exterior of "Number Ten" is decidedly unimpressive, but behind the famous door spreads an extensive political network. The Chancellor of the Exchequer forecasts economic recovery from No. 11 Downing St., and the Chief Whip of the House of Commons cracks at No. 12. Visitors may not enter Downing St.

The **Cabinet War Rooms** lurk at the end of King Charles St., near Horse Guards Rd. (see Museums). The rigorously formal **Cenotaph** honoring the war dead, usually decked with crested wreaths, stands where Parliament St. turns into Whitehall. **New Scotland Yard,** 6 Derby Gate, will probably fall short of crime-hounds' expectations. The second of three incarnations of the lair of those unimaginative detectives humbled by Sherlock Holmes and Hercule Poirot is only two government offices connected by an arch. The original Yard sat on Great Scotland Yard, and the current New Scotland Yard is on Victoria St. In 1953, the government built the massive **Ministry of Defense Building** (nicknamed the Quadragon), just to the north. The cellar had to be dug deeper into the ground to squeeze in the new structure.

The 1622 **Banqueting House** (corner of Horse Guards Ave. and Whitehall), one of the few intact masterpieces of Inigo Jones, was the first true classical Renaissance building in England, and the only part of the original palace to survive the fire that consumed Whitehall. The Stuart kings held elaborate and narcissistic masques and feasts here, but the festivities ended on January 27, 1649 when King Charles I, draped in black velvet, was led out its doorway and beheaded. The allegorical paintings on the 60-foot-high ceiling (ironically the story of the happy reigns of James I and Charles I) are Rubens's handiwork. A cautious James II supposedly placed the weather vane on top of the building to see if a favorable wind was blowing for William of Orange. From 1724 to 1890, the Banqueting House served as a Chapel Royal. These days the hall witnesses no executions, just state dinners behind bulletproof glass and the occasional concert. (Tel. 839 7569; open Mon.-Sat. 10am-5pm, but closed for government functions. £2.90, concessions £2.25, children £1.90.)

On the west side of Whitehall north of Downing St. stand the **Horse Guards,** where two photogenic mounted members of the Household Cavalry keep watch daily from 10am to 4pm, though it is unclear what they are guarding. (The head guard meticulously inspects the troops Mon.-Sat. at 11am and Sun. at 10am. The guard dismounts, with some fanfare, daily at 4pm. Crowds are usually thinner here than at Buckingham Palace. Closed Sat. in June.) **Beating the Retreat,** a must for lovers of pomp and circumstance, takes place here three or four evenings a week during the first two weeks of June (call 930 4466 for dates and ticket information).

TRAFALGAR SQUARE & CHARING CROSS

Unlike many squares in London, **Trafalgar Square** (tube: Charing Cross), sloping down from the National Gallery at the center of a vicious traffic round-about, has been public land ever since the razing of several hundred houses made way for its construction in the 1830s. **Nelson's Column,** a fluted granite pillar, commands the square, with four majestic, beloved lions guarding the base. The monument and square commemorate Admiral Nelson, killed during his triumph over Napoleon's navy off Trafalgar in Spain (the monument's reliefs were cast from French cannons).

At the head of the square squats the ordering façade of the **National Gallery,** Britain's collection of Old Masters (see Museums). A competition to design a new extension to the gallery ended in Prince Charles's denouncement of the winning entry as a "monstrous carbuncle" on the face of London, and the subsequent selection of a new architect. The church of **St. Martin-in-the-Fields,** opposite the National Gallery, dates from the 1720s. Designer James Gibbs topped its templar classicism with a Gothic steeple. St. Martin, which has its own world-renowned chamber orchestra, sponsors lunchtime and evening concerts, as well as a summer festival in mid-July (lunchtime concerts begin 1:05pm; box office in bookshop open Mon.-Sat. 11:30am-7:30pm, Sun. 11am-6pm; bookings tel. 702 1377 daily 12:30-2:30pm and 4:30-6:30pm; tickets £4-14). The crypt has been cleared of all those dreary coffins to make room for a gallery, a book shop, a brass rubbing center, and a café (café open Mon.-Sat. 10am-9pm, Sun. noon-6pm; church open daily 7:30am-7:30pm).

The original **Charing Cross,** last of 13 crosses set up to mark the stages of Queen Eleanor's royal funeral procession in 1291 ("charing" comes from "beloved queen" in French), was actually located at the top of Whitehall, immediately south of the present Trafalgar Square. Like many things, it was destroyed by Cromwell, and a replica now stands outside Charing Cross Station, which is just uphill from the Victoria Embankment. This spot used to be the pulsing heart of London life, as well as the geographical center of the city. "Why, Sir, Fleet Street has a very animated appearance," Samuel Johnson once remarked, "but I think the full tide of human existence is at Charing Cross." The full tide of traffic now engulfs the place.

THE MALL & ST. JAMES'S

Just north of Buckingham Palace and the Mall, up Stable Yard or Marlborough Rd., stands **St. James's Palace,** the residence of the monarchy from 1660 to 1668 and again from 1715 to 1837 (tube: Green Park). The scene of many a three-volume novel and Regency romance, over the years this palace has hosted tens of thousands of the young girls whose families "presented" them at Court. Ambassadors and the elite set of barristers known as "Queen's Counsel" are still received "into the Court of St. James's." You can visit Inigo Jones's fine **Queen's Chapel,** built in 1626, by attending Sunday services at 8:30 and 11:15am (Oct.-July). King Charles I slept for four hours in the palace's guardroom before crossing St. James's Park to be executed at the Banqueting House in 1649.

The high-rent district around the palace has also come to be called St. James's. Bordered by St. James's Park and Green Park to the south and Piccadilly to the north, it begins at an equestrian statue of notorious madman George III on Cockspur St. off Trafalgar Sq. **St. James's Street,** next to St. James's Palace, runs into **Pall Mall**—the name derives from "pail-mail," a 17th-century predecessor of the noble game of croquet. Until Buckingham Palace was built, today's **Mall** (rhymes with "pal") was merely an endless field for the King to play the game on. Lined with double rows of plane trees, the Mall grandly traverses the space from Trafalgar Sq. to Buckingham Palace (tube: Charing Cross).

Along the north side of the Mall lie the imposing façades of grand houses, starting with **Carlton House Terrace,** demolished, rebuilt, and remodeled since Nash erected it along the Mall as part of the 18th-century Regent's Park route. The building became the office of the Free French Forces from 1940 to 1945 under the leadership of General Charles de Gaulle. It now contains the avant-garde **Institute of Contemporary Arts** (see Museums). On the other side of St. James's Palace from Marlborough House at Stable Yard Rd. is **Clarence House,** the official residence of the Queen Mother.

Pall Mall and St. James's St., together with Jermyn St., parallel to Pall Mall to the north, flank what is perhaps the last bastion of the classic, dressed-to-oppress upperclass English man. Escape the patrician solemnity of the area at Alfred Dunhill, 30 Duke Street (entrance on Jermyn); lurking upstairs above the staid merchandise is a riotously sublime **tobacco museum** (tel. 499 9566; open by appointment).

These Regency storefronts rub elbows with a number of famous London coffeehouses-turned-clubs. The coffeehouses of the early 18th century were transformed by the 19th century into exclusive clubs for political and literary men of a particular social station. The chief Tory club, the Carlton, at 69 St. James's St., was bombed by the IRA not long ago. The chief Liberal club, the Reform at 104 Pall Mall, served as a social center of Parliamentary power.

Around the corner from St. James's Palace stand royal medallists Spink's, and Christie, Manson, and Wodds Fine Art Auctioneers—better known as **Christie's,** 8 King St. (tel. 839 9060; tube: Green Park). Auctions, open to the public, are held most weekdays at 10:30am. **Sotheby's** also holds fine arts auctions, at 34 Bond St. (tel. 493 8080; tube: Bond St. or Oxford Circus). Amuse yourself on a rainy afternoon by watching the dealers do their bidding.

Between aristocratic Jermyn St. and Piccadilly, you can enter **St. James's Church** (tube: Green Park or Piccadilly Circus), a postwar reconstruction by Sir Albert Richardson of what Wren considered his best parish church. Blake was baptized here, in the typical Wren single room interior, with galleries surrounding the main space. The work of Grinling Gibbons, Wren's master-carver, can be seen in the delightful flowers, garlands, and cherubs of the reredos, organ casing, and font (church open Mon.-Sat. 10am-8pm, Sun. noon-6pm).

BUCKINGHAM PALACE

I must say, notwithstanding the expense which has been incurred in building the palace, no sovereign in Europe, I may even add, perhaps no private gentleman, is so ill-lodged as the king of this country.
—Duke of Wellington, 1828

When a freshly crowned Victoria moved from St. James's Palace in 1837, Buckingham Palace, built in 1825 by John Nash, had faulty drains and a host of other leaky difficulties (tube: Victoria, and walk up Buckingham Palace Rd.; Green Park and St. James's Park are also convenient). Home improvements were made, and now, when the flag is flying, the Queen is at home, and you can visit her home.

After a recent debate about the proper way to subsidize the monarchy's senselessly posh existence—and because funds are needed to rebuild Windsor castle, which went up in flames in November 1992—Buckingham Palace finally opened to the public. For two months a year for the next four years, the palace will remain open to hordes of tourists. Visitors are able to stroll through the Blue Drawing Room, the Throne Room, the Picture Gallery, the Music Room, and other stately rooms. The monarch scuttles off to Balmoral to avoid the plague of tourists descending upon her residence (palace open Aug.-Sept.; £8, seniors £5.50, children £4). Nasty-looking spikes and barbed wire atop the walls are designed to stop occasional forays by the Queen's admirers or potential assassins.

The chart-topping Kodak Moment for London tourists is the **Changing of the Guard,** which takes place daily from April to July, and only on alternate days from August to March. The "Old Guard" marches from St. James's Palace down the Mall to Buckingham Palace, leaving at approximately 11:10am. The "New Guard" begins marching as early as 10:20am. When they meet at the central gates of the palace, the officers of the regiments then touch hands, symbolically exchanging keys, et voilà— the guard is changed. In wet weather or on pressing state holidays, the Changing of the Guard does not occur. To witness the spectacle, show up well before 11:30am and stand directly in front of the palace. You can also watch along the routes of the troops prior to their arrival at the palace (10:40-11:25am) between the Victoria Memorial and St. James's Palace or along Birdcage Walk.

In the extravagant **Trooping the Colour** ceremony, held on the Queen's official birthday, a Saturday in early June, the colors of a chosen regiment are paraded ceremonially before her and her family. The actual ceremony takes place at Horse Guards Parade, followed by a procession down the Mall to the Palace, where she reviews her Household Cavalry and appears on the balcony for a Royal Air Force fly-by. Tickets for the event must be obtained well in advance through the mail from Household Division HQ, Horse Guards, SW1. If you don't get a ticket for the event, you may receive one for one of the rehearsals on the two preceding Saturdays. Since the Queen does not need to rehearse, these tend to be noticeably less crowded.

Down the left side of the Palace, off Buckingham Gate, an enclosed passageway leads to the **Queen's Gallery.** The exhibition changes every few months, but you can usually catch a few of Charles I's Italian masters, George IV's Dutch still-lifes, Prince Albert's primitives, and occasionally some of the Leonardo da Vinci drawings from Windsor. Also off Buckingham Gate stands the **Royal Mews Museum** (tel. 493 3175), which houses historic royal riding implements (For both museums, call for opening times; £3, seniors £2, under 17 £1.50, family £7.50; combined pass £5, seniors £3.50, under 17 £2.20, family £12.) Nearby, you can drop in on the **Guards Museum** (tel. 930 4466, ext.#3271) at Wellington Barracks on Birdcage Walk, off Buckingham Gate (open Mon.-Thurs., Sat.-Sun. 10am-4pm; £2, concessions £1.20).

PICCADILLY

All of the West End's major arteries—Piccadilly, Regent Street, Shaftesbury Avenue, The Haymarket—merge and swirl around Piccadilly Circus, the bright, gaudy hub of Nash's 19th-century London. Today the Circus earns its place on postcards with lurid neon signs, hordes of tourists, and a fountain topped by a statue everyone calls "Eros," though it was intended to be the Angel of Christian Charity in memory of the reformer, the Earl of Shaftesbury. Akin to New York's Times Square, silly Piccadilly overflows with glam, glitz, and commerce.

The Circus was ground zero for Victorian popular entertainment, but only the façades of the great music halls remain, propped up against contemporary tourist traps. **London Pavillion,** 1 Piccadilly Circus, is a historic theatre recently converted into a mall. Inside the Pavillion lurks the nefarious **Rock Circus** (tel. 734 7203), a waxwork museum and revolving theatre dedicated to the history of rock-and-roll (open Sun.-Mon. and Wed.-Thurs. 11am-9pm, Tues. noon-9pm, Fri.-Sat. 11am-10pm; £7, students and seniors £6, children £5, family of 4 £18.85).

The massive **Trocadero,** 13 Coventry Street (tel. 439 1791), also specializes in charging hapless tourists exorbitant rates for contrived entertainments. Inside, rapt hordes rush from the Guiness World of Records (tel. 439 7331), to Quasar—Serious Fun with a Laser Gun (tel. 434 0795), and Planet Hollywood (tel. 287 1000).

Aristocratic mansions once lined Piccadilly, a broad mile-long avenue stretching from Regent St. in the east to Hyde Park Corner in the west. The name derives from Piccadilly Hall, the 17th-century home of Robert Baker, an affluent tailor who did brisk business in the sale of "pickadills," frilly lace collars that were much in fashion in his day. The only remnant of Piccadilly's stately past is the showy **Burlington House** (across from 185 Piccadilly), built in 1665 for the Earls of Burlington and redesigned in the 18th century by Colin Campbell to accommodate the burgeoning **Royal Academy of Arts** (tel. 439 7438; tube: Piccadilly or Green Park; see Museums). The ambitious **Museum of Mankind** backs onto Burlington House behind the Royal Academy (see Museums).

An easily overlooked courtyard next to the Academy opens onto the **Albany,** an 18th-century apartment block renowned as one of London's most prestigious addresses. Built in 1771 and remodeled in 1812 to serve as "residential chambers for bachelor gentlemen," the Albany evolved into an exclusive enclave of literary repute. Lord Byron wrote his epic "Childe Harold" here. Other past residents include Macaulay, Gladstone, "Monk" Lewis, J.B. Priestley, and Graham Greene.

Piccadilly continues past imperious Bond Street, past the Ritz Hotel with its distinctive arcade and light-bulb sign, past the Green Park tube station, and past a string of privileged men's clubs on the rim of Green Park. At the gateway of the **Wellington Museum** in **Apsley House,** the avenue merges into the impenetrable Hyde Park corner. Apsley House was built by Robert Adam in the 1780s as the home of the Duke of Wellington. It will house an important collection of Spanish, Dutch, and Italian Old Masters (ransacked from Spain's Royal Collection when Wellington defeated the Bonapartes) when it opens in early 1995.

Running north from Piccadilly Circus are the grand façades of (upper) **Regent Street,** leading to Oxford Circus; today the street is known for the crisp cuts of Burberry raincoats and Aquascutum suits.

SOHO, LEICESTER SQUARE, & CHINATOWN

For centuries, Soho was London's red-light district of prostitutes and sex shows. Though most of the prostitutes were forced off the streets by 1959 legislation, the peep shows and porn shops concentrated along Brewer St. and Greek St. ensure the continuation of a licentious tradition. Far from defining the flavor of Soho, however, the sex industry adds merely one small ingredient to the incredible cosmopolitan stew which is Soho today.

Loosely bounded by Oxford St. in the north, Shaftesbury Ave. in the south, Charing Cross Rd. in the east, and Regent St. in the west (tube: Leicester Sq., Piccadilly Circus, or Tottenham Ct. Rd.), Soho first emerged as a discrete area in the 1681 with the laying out of **Soho Square** (tube: Tottenham Ct. Rd., just off of Oxford St.). Grand mansions quickly sprang up as the area became popular with a fashionable set, famed for throwing extravagant parties. By the end of the 18th century, however, the leisure classes moved out, replaced by the leisure industries.

Soho has a history of welcoming immigrants of various nationalities to its streets. The district was first settled by French Huguenots fleeing religious persecution after the revocation of the Edict of Nantes in 1685. In more recent years, an influx of settlers from the New Territories of Hong Kong have forged London's Chinatown south of Soho. A strong Mediterranean influence can also be detected in the aromas of espresso, garlic, and sizzling meats wafting through the area's maze of streets.

Perhaps contemporary Soho's most salient feature, especially on sunny days, is its vibrant **sidewalk café** culture. An *alfresco* mecca, today's Soho overflows with media types (mostly in the film and TV industries), artists, writers, and club kids. The area has a visible gay presence; a concentration of gay-owned restaurants and bars has turned the region's central avenue, **Old Compton Street,** into the big gay heart of London.

Attracted by the scent of money, large corporations and chain stores are moving in for the kill, threatening to destroy the area's distinct character. Construction on what will be the biggest restaurant in Europe is currently underway. Slated to open in Sept. 1995, the 600-seater will take up two floors of what used to be the Marquee Club on Wardour St., a hotbed of rock celebrity in the 60s and 70s.

The eerie ruins of **St. Anne's Soho** on Wardour Street, which runs north through the offices of Britain's film industry from Shaftesbury Ave., remain from World War II. Leveled by German bombers in 1940, only Wren's anomalous tower of 1685 and the ungainly, bottle-shaped steeple added by Cockerell in 1803 emerged unscathed.

Since the 1840s, **Berwick St. Market** (parallel to the north end of Wardour St.) has rumbled with trade. The market is famous for the widest and cheapest selection of fruits and vegetables in central London (open Mon.-Sat. 9am-6pm).

Running parallel to Regent St. is **Carnaby Street,** a notorious hotbed of 60s sex, fashion, and Mods. It witnessed the rise of youth culture and became the heart of what *Time* magazine called "Swinging London." Chic boutiques and parading celebrities have long since left the area, which has lapsed into a lurid tourist trap.

Leicester Square, just south of Shaftesbury Ave., between Piccadilly Circus and Charing Cross Rd. is an entertainment nexus. Amusements range from expensive, mammoth cinemas, to the free performances provided by the street entertainers.

On the north side of the square, at Leicester Place, the French presence in Soho manifests itself in **Notre-Dame de France** (tel. 437 9363). This church may not be architecturally distinctive, but those who venture inside will be rewarded with the exquisite Aubusson tapestry lining the inner walls. The tiny chapel built into the western wall features an arresting 1960 mural by Jean Cocteau (Masses in French Sat. 6pm, Sun. 10 and 11:30am). On the south side of the square, a small hovel and endless queue mark the **SWET half-price ticket booth,** where theatre tickets are sold for half price on the day of the show (see Theatre).

Cantonese immigrants first arrived in Britain as cooks on British ships, and London's first Chinese community formed around the docks near Limehouse. Now, however, London's **Chinatown** (known in Chinese as *Tong Yan Kai,* "Chinese Street") lies off the north side of Leicester Sq. Chinatown swelled with arrivals from Hong Kong in the 50s, and 50,000 more immigrants to Britain are expected as the colony's transfer to China approaches. Between the theatres of Shaftesbury Ave. and the cinemas of Leicester Sq., street signs in Chinese and pagoda-capped telephone booths spring up. **Gerrard Street,** the main thoroughfare, runs closest to Leicester Square tube station; the street where poet John Dryden once lived is now a pedestrian avenue framed by scrollworked dragon gates. Chinatown is most vibrant during the year's two major festivals: the **Mid-Autumn Festival,** at the end of September, and the **Chinese New Year Festival,** around the beginning of February. For further information on festivals or Chinatown call the **Chinese Community Centre** at 44 Gerrard St., 2nd floor (tel. 439 3822).

MAYFAIR

The long-time center of London's blue-blooded *beau monde* was named for the 17th-century May Fair, held on the site of Shepherd's Market, a notorious haunt of prostitutes. Modern Mayfair has a distinctly patrician atmosphere; it is the most expensive property in the British version of *Monopoly.* In the 18th and 19th centuries, the aristocracy kept houses in Mayfair where they lived during "the season" (the season for opera and balls), retiring to their country estates in the summer. Mayfair is bordered by Oxford St. to the north, Piccadilly to the south, Park La. to the west, and Regent St. to the east (tube: Green Park, Bond St., or Piccadilly Circus).

Near what is now the Bond St. tube station, Blake saw mystical visions for 17 years on South Molton St. On busy Brook St., home to ritzy Claridge's Hotel, Handel wrote the *Messiah.* The reigning queen was born in a house (recently demolished) at no. 17 Bruton St. Laurence Sterne ended his life on haughty Bond St. (no. 39).

Bond St. is the traditional address for the most prestigious shops, art dealers, and auction houses in the city. Starting at the New Bond St. end, **Sotheby's,** 34 New Bond St. (tel. 493 8080), displays everything from Dutch masters to the world's oldest condom before they're put on the auction block (open Mon.-Fri. 9am-4:30pm). Modern art aficionados should also note the rugged Henry Moore frieze high up on the crest of the **Time/Life Building,** corner of Bruton St. At the **Marlborough Gallery** (entrance by Albemarle St.), the biggest contemporary names are sold; **Agnew's,** 43 Old Bond St., and **Colnaghi's,** 14 Old Bond St., deal in Old Masters.

Running west off Bond St., Grosvenor St. ends at **Grosvenor Square,** one of the largest of its breed in central London. The square, occasionally known as "little America," has gradually evolved into a U.S. military and political enclave since future President John Adams lived at no. 9 while serving as the first American ambassador to England in 1785. From here you can see the humorless and top-heavy **U.S. Embassy** rising in the west, where protesters occasionally assemble to denounce the latest Yankee indiscretion. West of Grosvenor Sq., a walk down **Park Lane,** the western border of Mayfair at Hyde Park, will take you past the legendary hotels that are sadly no longer quite up to *Let's Go* standards. The Hilton, Grosvenor House Hotel, and the Dorchester can be found here.

Tucked into the southwest corner where Park La. meets Piccadilly is **Shepherd's Market,** once the site of the rowdy May Fair. During the 60s this tiny village-like area briefly revisited its rambunctious past, but has since been regentrified, teeming with swish pubs and shops. South of Hanover Sq. and just to the west of Regent St., The name **Savile Row** is synonymous with the elegant "bespoke" (custom-fitted and hand-sewn) tailoring that has prospered there for centuries..

HYDE PARK & KENSINGTON GARDENS

Totalling 630 acres, **Hyde Park** and the contiguous **Kensington Gardens** constitute the largest open area in the center of the city. At the far west of the Gardens, you can drop your calling card at **Kensington Palace** (tel. 937 9561; tube: Kensington High St. or Queensway), originally the residence of King William III and Queen Mary II and recently of Princess Margaret. Currently, the Princess of Wales, the little princes, and other stray members of the royal family live in the palace. A museum of uninhabited royal rooms (the State Apartments) and regal memorabilia includes a Court dress collection, with Di's wedding gown prominently displayed (palace open Mon.-Sat. 9am-5:30pm, Sun. 11am-5:30pm; £3.75, concessions £3).

The Round Pond east of the palace plays the ocean to a fleet of toy sailboats on weekends. The **Serpentine,** a lake carved in 1730, runs from these fountains in the north, near Bayswater Rd., south towards Knightsbridge. From the number of people who pay the £2.50 (children £1) to sunbathe at the fenced-off Serpentine beach (the Lido), one would think the sun shone more brightly there than anywhere else in London. (Parks open Mon.-Fri. 10am-6pm, Sat.-Sun. 10am-7pm; off-season Mon.-Fri. 10am-dusk, Sat.-Sun. 10am-4pm; free).

On the southern edge of Kensington Gardens, the Lord Mayor had the **Albert Memorial** built to honor Victoria's beloved husband, whose death Victoria mourned for nearly 40 years. Considered a great artistic achievement when first unveiled in 1869, the extravagant monument now seems an embarrassing piece of imperial excess. Unfortunately, you will be unable to judge for yourself since the Albert Memorial will be under designer scaffolding for another five years as it undergoes restoration. Across the street, the **Royal Albert Hall,** with its ornate oval dome, hosts the Promenade Concerts (Proms) in summer (see Entertainment). Rotten Row (a corruption of *Route du Roi,* "king's road") was the first English thoroughfare to be lighted to prevent crime. However, this east-west path through southern Hyde Park, like the rest of the park, remains dangerous at night.

Speakers' Corner, in the northeast corner of Hyde Park (tube: Marble Arch, not Hyde Park Corner), is the finest example of free speech in action anywhere in the world. The **Marble Arch** is built on the exact site where the public gallows of Tyburn rested until 1783. Nowadays, on Sundays from late morning to dusk, and on summer evenings, soapbox revolutionaries, haranguers, madmen, and evangelists scream about anything from Kierkegaard to socialism to knitting.

NOTTING HILL

Notting Hill is one of London's most diverse neighborhoods. On the area's lively streets, trendy places to eat and shop ply their trade among dilapidated stores, wafts of incense, and Bob Marley posters.

Irish and Jewish immigrants were the first to occupy the poor areas of "Notting Dale" in the late 19th century, but the 1930s saw the arrival of Fascist demonstrations against Jews and local immigrant groups. Inter-ethnic tension culminated in the 1950s when Teddy-Boy gangs engaged in open warfare against Afro-Caribbean immigrants; the devastating riots that ensued are depicted in Colin MacInnes's novel *Absolute Beginners* (later made into a movie musical starring David Bowie). Today the multi-ethnic area sees little racial animosity. **Golborne Road** is home to North African and Portuguese communities, and the area is dotted with many traditional bakeries and family restaurants.

Presently, it's the **Portobello Market** (tube: Ladbroke Grove) every Saturday that brings additional energy to the area. Starting on the southern end near Notting Hill Gate, various antique stores and thriving galleries line Portobello Road. As the idler wanders further north, antiquarians give way to fresh fruit, vegetable, and baked goods stalls. Finally, near Lancaster Road and the Westway (the overhead highway), stalls sell second-hand clothing (including second-hand Doc Martens in really good condition for as little as £5-10), collector's vinyl, and various desirable trinkets.

In between Ladbroke Grove and Portobello Road, running parallel to both, is **Kensington Park Road,** home to eccentric specialty shops and (occasionally contrived) trendy restaurants. Here the encouragingly eclectic character of the neighborhood is quite visible; the self-congratulatory Body Shop is right across the street from a tattoo parlor and the Anglo-Yugoslavian Butcher.

Notting Hill celebrates its vital existence more than usual on the August Bank Holiday Monday and the preceding Sunday, during the **Notting Hill Carnival,** Europe's biggest outdoor festival. A parade of steel drummers, fantastic costumes, skanking followers, and dancing policemen is the highlight. African-Caribbean music reverberates through the streets. The more highbrow **Portobello Festival** in early June celebrates film, theatre, art, and music in the area (tel. 229 7981 for information)

KENSINGTON, KNIGHTSBRIDGE, & BELGRAVIA

Kensington, a gracious and sheltered residential area, reposes between multi-ethnic Notting Hill to the north and chic Chelsea to the south. **Kensington High Street,** which pierces the area, has become a shopping and scoping epicenter. Obscure specialty and antique shops fill the area along Kensington Church Street to the north, Victorian-era museums and colleges dominate South Kensington, while the area around Earl's Court has mutated into something of a tourist colony while retaining a substantial gay population.

Take the tube to High St. Kensington, Notting Hill Gate, or Holland Park to reach **Holland Park,** a gracious peacock-peppered garden. Holland House, a Jacobean mansion built in 1606 lies on the park's grounds. Destroyed in World War II, the house has since been restored and turned into a youth hostel. Holland Park also contains formal gardens, an open-air amphitheater, cricket pitches, public tennis courts, and the Kyoto Gardens, a traditional Japanese garden. Two petite exhibition galleries featuring (free) displays of work by local artists, the **Ice House** and the **Orangery,** blossom in the middle of the park.

The curious **Leighton House,** 12 Holland Park Rd. (tel. 602 3316), lies a block west. Devised by the imaginative Lord Leighton in the 19th century, the house is a presumptuous yet amusing pastiche. The Arab Hall, with inlaid tiles, a pool, and a dome, is a hodgepodge of plundered Middle Eastern art. Now a center for the arts, Leighton House features concerts, receptions, and other events in the evenings, as well as frequent contemporary art exhibitions. An excellent taped commentary (£2.25) helps you find your way around (house open Mon.-Sat. 11am-5pm; free).

To reach the grandiose **South Kensington museums,** take the tube to the South Kensington station or the #49 bus from Kensington High St. The **Victoria and Albert Museum** and the **Natural History Museum** (both on Cromwell Road), and the **Science Museum** (on Exhibition Road) all testify on a grand scale to the Victorian mania for collecting, codifying, and cataloguing.

Patrician **Knightsbridge** is defined most of all by London's premier department store, **Harrods.** Founded in 1849 as a grocery store, by 1880 Harrods employed over 100 workers. In 1905 the store moved to its current location; today it requires 5000 employees to handle its vast array of products and services. Besides an encyclopedic inventory, Harrods also contains a pub, an espresso bar, a champagne and oyster bar, a juice bar, and, naturally, a tourist information center (see Shopping).

Belgravia was first constructed as an area to billet servants after the building of Buckingham Palace in the 1820s, but soon became the haughty bastion of wealth and privilege it is today. Belgravia lies south of Hyde Park, ringed by stately Sloane St. to the west, Victoria Station to the south, and Buckingham Palace Gdns. to the east. The spacious avenues and crescents of the district center on **Belgrave Square,** the setting for *My Fair Lady.*

CHELSEA

Chelsea has always been one of London's flashiest districts—Thomas More, Oscar Wilde, and the Sex Pistols have all been resident at one time or another. It used to be that few streets in London screamed louder for a visit than the **King's Road.** Mohawked UB40s and pearl-necklaced Sloane Rangers gazed at trendy window displays and at each other. While the hordes still flock here on Saturday afternoons to see and be seen, most ertswhile scenesters look like they are desperately trying to recapture a past that they have only read about. While no longer the epicenter of the punk rock youthquake, Chelsea remains a brilliant area for strolling. If you're pressed for time, be aware that you'll have to rely on **buses** (#11 or 22).

Any proper exploration of Chelsea begins at **Sloane Square,** named for Sir Hans Sloane (1660-1753), one of three collectors whose artifacts made up the original collections of the British Museum. King's Road, stretching southwest from Sloane Sq., is a commercial thoroughfare where overpriced restaurants, historic pubs, and the **Chelsea Antique Market** (253 King's Road) lurk amid many boutiques.

Off King's Rd., Chelsea becomes cozier, the closest thing to a village in central London. By the river stands Wren's **Royal Hospital** (1691), founded by Charles II for retired soldiers and still inhabited by 400 army pensioners. Former soldiers, in uniforms changed only slightly from 18th-century versions, welcome visitors to the splendid grounds (open Mon.-Sat. 10am-noon and 2-4pm, Sun. 2-4pm; free). East of the Hospital lie the **Ranelagh Gardens** (usually open until dusk). The **Chelsea Flower Show** blooms here the third week in May (Tues.-Fri.), but even Royal Horticultural Society members have trouble procuring tickets for the first two days. The **National Army Museum** stands west of the hospital, along Royal Hospital Rd.

Cheyne (pronounced "chainy") **Walk, Cheyne Row,** and **Tite Street** formed the heart of Chelsea's artist colony at the turn of the century. Watch for the blue plaques on the houses; J.M.W. Turner moved into a house in Cheyne Walk, and Edgar Allan Poe lived nearby. Mary Ann Evans (a.k.a. George Eliot) moved into no. 4 just before her death. Dante Gabriel Rossetti kept his highly disreputable *ménage* (which included peacocks and a kangaroo) in no. 16, where he doused himself with chloral hydrate and hammered the image of the artist as nonconformist into the public mind. Nos. 19 to 26 cover the ground that used to be Chelsea Manor, where Queen Elizabeth I once lived. Both Mick Jagger and Keith Richards got satisfaction on the Walk in the 60s. The area's arbiter of the aesthetic, Oscar Wilde, reposed stylishly at 34 Tite St. from 1884-1895 and was arrested for homosexual activity at Chelsea's best-known hotel, the Cadogan (75 Sloane St.). John Singer Sargent, James MacNeill Whistler, Radclyffe Hall, and Bertrand Russell also lived on Tite St. Today, fashionable artists' and designers' homes line the street, though the area is too expensive for it to remain a true bastion of bohemian culture.

Chelsea's famed resident Thomas Carlyle crafted his magnificent prose on Cheyne Row. On this miraculously quiet street colored by flowers and tidy houses, **Carlyle's House,** 24 Cheyne Row (tel. 352 7087), has remained virtually unchanged since the Sage of Chelsea expired in his armchair. Inside this small Queen Anne home, glass cases shield his books and manuscripts; family portraits and sketches ornament the walls—which he had doubled in thickness, vainly hoping to keep out noise. In his attic study Carlyle wrote and rewrote *The French Revolution* after John Stuart Mill's chambermaid accidentally burned his first draft (open April-Oct. Wed.-Sun. 11am-5pm; £2.75, children £1.50; last admission 4:30pm).

MARYLEBONE

Located between Regent's Park and Oxford St., the grid-like district of Marylebone (MAR-lee-bun) is dotted with decorous late-Georgian town houses. The name derives from "St. Mary-by-the-bourne," the "bourne" referring to the Tyburn or the Westbourne stream; both now underground. The eternally dammed Westbourne now forms the Serpentine in Hyde Park.

There's little to see in this well-kept, well-bred region of residences and office buildings. The area's most fondly remembered resident is Sherlock Holmes who, although fictitious, still receives about 50 letters per week addressed to his 221b Baker St. residence. The Abbey National Building Society currently occupies the site and employs a full-time secretary to answer requests for Holmes's assistance in solving mysteries around the world. The **Sherlock Holmes Museum,** located at 239 Baker St. (marked "221b") will thrill Holmes enthusiasts with the meticulous re-creation of the detective's lodgings.

Ever since the redoubtable **Madame Tussaud,** one of Louis XVI's tutors, trekked from Paris in 1802 carrying wax effigies of French nobles decapitated in the Revolution, her eerie museum on Marylebone Rd. (with an adjacent Planetarium) has been a London landmark (see Museums).

Oxford Street, the southern border of Marylebone, passes through Oxford Circus, Bond St., and Marble Arch tube stations. Arguably London's major shopping boulevard, it's jam-packed with shops (ranging from cheap chainstores to the posh boutiques around Bond St.), crowds, and fast-food stands. Off Oxford St., pleasant **James's St.** (tube: Bond St.) lures passersby with one café after another—a good place for people-watching from a sidewalk table. Off James's St., Manchester Sq. holds the **Wallace Collection,** a must-see for fans of Dutch art.

CAMDEN TOWN & REGENT'S PARK

Camden Town started to develop with the opening of the Regent's Canal in 1820. By the 19th century, Camden Town was a solid working-class district, spliced with railways and covered in soot. Charles Dickens spent his childhood here, crowded in a four-room tenement with his extended family at 16 (now 141) Bayham St. Waves of Irish, Cypriot, Greek, Italian, and Portuguese immigrants followed.

Contemporary Camden Town is a stomping ground for trendy youth of all subcultural affiliations. Trends are instigated and abandoned at the **Camden Markets,** now London's fourth-largest tourist attraction, which draws 200,000 funky visitors each weekend (tube: Camden Town; see Shopping). Though the area is renowned for its shoes and boots, anything and everything can be found here, and the clientele reflects the diversity of the goods.

Although parts of Camden Town have turned into genteel residential enclaves, the area has for the most part resisted gentrification, as the scruffy storefronts on High St. and dilapidated warehouses along Regent's Canal will attest. The market crowds leave behind a recurrent wake of litter that lines the curbs, and Arlington House, the largest dole house in Europe, stands around the corner from the tube.

Just south of Camden Town lies the 500-acre **Regent's Park** (tube: Regent's Park, Great Portland St., Baker St., or Camden Town; open 5am-dusk). Larger than either Hyde Park or Kensington Gardens, and full of lakes, promenades, and Dakotan open spaces, the park has become a popular spot for family cricket and football matches. On Sundays from June through August, you can hear tubas and trumpets entertain at the bandstand, or see performances in the **Open Air Theatre** near Queen Mary's Gardens (see Entertainment). Take a boat ride on the park's lake (£1.25), or, if you're feeling romantic, navigate your own (rowboat for max. 4 people £5.50, available daily 10am-dusk).

Laid out in 1812 by John Nash for the Prince Regent (the future George IV), the park is edged on three sides by majestic Nash terraces. The cream-colored porticoed and pillared buildings have been home to the likes of H.G. Wells (17 Hanover Terrace) and Wallis Simpson (7 Hanover Terrace). **Regent's Park Canal,** part of the Grand Union Canal, dips around the unprotected north side of the park and into neighboring Paddington. From "Little Venice" (Tube: Warwick Avenue), you can take a leisurely trip down the canal. The park's most popular attraction is the privately owned **London Zoo** (tel. 722 3333; tube: Camden Town, or Baker St.; bus #274 from either station takes you almost to the door), located in the northeast quadrant. (Open daily 10am-5:30pm; Oct.-March daily 10am-4pm. £6.50, concessions £5, under 15 £4, families £17.50.)

Within the park's Inner Circle, the delightful **Queen Mary's Gardens** erupt in color in early summer. The rose garden, which stays open until dusk, dazzles with 20,000 blooms. North of Regent's Park stands **Primrose Hill,** long a favorite spot for picnics and kite-flying. (It is also the site of a pagan rite conducted by druids on the Autumn Equinox.) On a clear day you can see as far as the Surrey Downs.

ISLINGTON

Islington first became "trendy" during the late 17th century when its ale houses and cream teas made it a popular hang-out for the wealthy. In more recent times, Islington was one of London's first areas to undergo regentrification; it established itself as an academic and artistic haven by the 1930s, serving as home to writers such as George Orwell, Evelyn Waugh, Douglas Adams, and Salman Rushdie.

Today, Islington is one of the hottest neighborhoods in London. The area is favored by trendy, style-conscious, and well-to-do Londoners, who live alongside several ethnic communities including Turkish, Irish, Italian, and Bengali residents. As the number of gay pubs in the area attests, Islington is also home to a large gay community. (Chris Smith, the only voluntarily out Member of Parliament, was elected from this area.) Many renowned fringe theatres provide entertainment.

A refurbished 19th-century chapel at 44a Pentonville Road now houses the **Crafts Council,** the national organization for the promotion of contemporary crafts. (Tel. 278 7700. Tube: Angel; exit the station to the left and take the first right onto Pentonville Rd. Open Tues.-Sat. 11am-6pm, Sun. 2-6pm. Wheelchair accessible. Free.)

To the north, well-attended street markets **Chapel Markets** and **Camden Passage,** to the left and right of Upper St., offer fresh produce and cheap clothing, and expensive antiques, respectively (see Shopping). Those interested in the history of Islington should visit the **Museum Gallery** at 268 Upper St. (tel. 354 9442), which sponsors local history (and local artists') exhibitions. (Open Wed.-Fri. 11am-3pm, Sat. 11am-5pm, Sun. 2-4pm. Tube: Highbury and Islington.) Also indispensible is the **Islington Tourist Information Centre** at 44 Duncan St. (tel 278 8787), with its friendly staff, free pamphlets, reference books, and information on local guided walks. (Open Mon.-Sat. 10am-5pm. Tube: Angel; exit right and take the first right.)

BLOOMSBURY

During the first half of the 20th century, Bloomsbury gained its reputation as an intellectual and artistic center, due largely to the vitalizing presence of the famed Bloomsbury Group, which included biographer Lytton Strachey, novelist E.M. Forster, economist John Maynard Keynes, art critic Roger Fry, painter Vanessa Bell (sister of Virginia Woolf), and, hovering on the fringe, T.S. Eliot, the eminent British poet from St. Louis. Although very little of the famed intellectual gossip and high modernist argot still emanates from 51 Gordon Square, where Virginia Woolf lived with her husband Leonard, the area maintains an earnestly intellectual atmosphere.

Today, the British Museum and the **University of London** guarantee a continued concentration of cerebral activity in the area. The **British Museum** makes an appropriate Bloomsbury centerpiece; forbidding on the outside but quirky and amazing within, it contains the remains of 2 million years' worth of world history and civilization, in addition to sheltering the enthralling British Library until construction is completed on its controversial new home in St. Pancras (see Museums).

To the north stands the **Percival David Foundation of Chinese Art,** 53 Gordon Sq. (tel. 387 3909; tube: Russell Sq. or Goodge St.), a connoisseur's hoard of fabulously rare ceramics. Be sure to save time for the illuminating Ming Gallery on the top floor (open Mon.-Fri. 10:30am-5pm; free).

Up St. Pancras Rd., **St. Pancras Old Church** sits serenely in its large and leafy garden. Mary Godwin first met Shelley here in 1813 by the grave of her mother, Mary Wollstonecraft. Rumor has it that believing her mum died during her birth, Godwin insisted that Shelley make love with her on the grave.

Directly northeast of the British museum, at **Russell Square,** T.S. Eliot, the "Pope of Russell Square," hid from his emotionally ailing first wife at no. 24 while he worked as an editor and later director of famed publishing house Faber and Faber.

Bernard Street leads east to Brunswick Square, sight of the **Thomas Coram Foundation for Children** (40 Brunswick Square, tel. 278 2424; tube: Russell Square). Thomas Coram, a retired sea captain, established the Foundling Hospital for abandoned children here in 1747. In order to raise funds, he sought the help of prominent artists, including William Hogarth, who, in addition to serving as a governor of the hospital, donated paintings and persuaded his friends to do the same. Although the hospital was torn down in 1926, its art treasures remain, displayed in a suite of splendidly restored 18th-century rooms. Several canvases by Hogarth mingle with works by Gainsborough, Benjamin West, and Roubiliac, a cartoon by Raphael, and a signed manuscript copy of the *Messiah.* The adjacent Governor's Court Room, with its ornate ceilings and rococo plaster work, houses a poignant collection of tokens and trinkets left with the foundlings admitted to the hospital before 1760 (open Mon. and Fri. 1:30-4:30pm; £1, art students and seniors 50p).

Across from the Foundation lies **Coram's Fields** (93 Guilford St., tel. 837 6138), 7 acres of old Foundling Hospital grounds which have been preserved as a children's park, complete with a menagerie of petting animals, an aviary, and a paddling pool for kids under five. No dogs allowed—no adults, either, unless accompanied by a child (open Easter-Oct. daily 9am-8pm, Nov.-March daily 9am-5pm; free).

Charles Dickens lived at 48 Doughty St. (east of Russell Sq., parallel to Gray's Inn Rd.) from 1837 to 1839, scribbling parts of *The Pickwick Papers, Nicholas Nickleby, Barnaby Rudge,* and *Oliver Twist.* Now a four-floor museum and library of Dickens paraphernalia, the **Dickens House** (tel. 405 2127; tube: Russell Sq. or Chancery La.) holds an array of prints, photographs, manuscripts, letters, and personal effects (open Mon.-Sat. 10am-5pm, last entry 4:30pm; £3, students £2, children £1, family £6).

St. Giles-in-the-Fields, a modest rectangular church surmounted by a beautiful Flitcroft tower (1731), rises above a 1687 Resurrection relief and a lush churchyard on St. Giles High St. John Wesley and his brother Charles preached from the pulpit here between 1743 and 1791 (open Mon.-Fri. 9am-4:30pm).

COVENT GARDEN

The outdoor cafés, upscale shops, and slick crowds animating Covent Garden today bely the square's medieval beginnings as a literal "covent garden" where the monks of Westminster Abbey grew their vegetables. When Henry VIII abolished the monasteries in 1536, he bestowed this land upon John Russell, first Earl of Bedford. The Earl's descendants developed it into a fashionable *piazza* (designed by Inigo Jones) in the 1630s, giving London its first planned square.

Jones's **St. Paul's Church** now stands as the sole survivor of the original square, although the interior had to be rebuilt after bring gutted by a fire in 1795. Known as "the actor's church," St. Paul's is filled with plaques commemorating the achievements of Boris Karloff, Vivien Leigh, Noel Coward, and Tony Simpson ("inspired player of small parts"), among others. The church can only be entered through a little churchyard with entrances on Bedford, King, and Henrietta Streets (open Mon. 8:30am-2:30pm, Tues.-Fri. 9:30am-4:30pm). The Victorian Flower Market building in the south-east corner of the piazza now contains the **London Transport Museum** (see Museums).

The **Theatre Royal** and the **Royal Opera House** represent a long tradition of theatre in the Covent Garden area. The Theatre Royal (entrance on Catherine St.), was first built in 1663 as one of only two legal theatrical venues in London. The present building dates from 1812. The Royal Opera House (on Bow St.) began as a theater for concerts and plays in 1732, and now houses the Royal Opera and Royal Ballet companies. The **Theatre Museum** sits to the south, on the corner of Russell and Wellington streets (see Museums). Nearby, a blue plaque at 8 Russell St. marks the site of Boswell's home, where he first met Dr. Johnson in 1763.

On Great Newport St. to the west **The Photographers' Gallery** holds its reputation as one of London's major venues for contemporary photographic exhibitions. Further up, Neal St. leads to **Neal's Yard,** a healthy hub of stores selling whole foods, cheeses and yogurts, herbs, fresh-baked breads, and homeopathic remedies. At the northern section of St. Martin's Lane, six streets converge at the **Seven Dials** monument (the seventh dial is the monument itself as a sundial).

HOLBORN & THE INNS OF COURT

The historical center of English law lies in an area straddling the precincts of Westminster and the City and surrounding long and litigious High Holborn, Chancery Lane, and Fleet Street. The Strand and Fleet St. meet at the **Royal Courts of Justice** (tel. 936 6000; tube: Temple or Aldwych—rush hours only), a wonderfully elaborate Gothic structure designed in 1874 by architect G.E. Street for the Supreme Court of Judicature. While historical legal costumes are on display, most visitors come to view the courts in action (courts and galleries open to the public Mon.-Fri. 9am-4:30pm; court cases start at 10:30am).

Barristers in the City are affiliated with one of the famous **Inns of Court** (Middle Temple, Inner Temple, Lincoln's Inn, and Gray's Inn), four ancient legal institutions which provide lectures and apprenticeships for law students and regulate admission to the bar. The Inns are organized like colleges at Oxford, each with its own gardens, chapel, library, dining hall, common rooms, and chambers. Most were founded in the 13th century when a royal decree barred the clergy from the courts of justice, giving rise to a new class of professional legal advocates. Today, students may seek their legal training outside of the Inns, but to be considered for membership they must "keep term" by dining regularly in one of the halls.

South of Fleet St., the labyrinth of the **Temple** (tube: Temple) encloses the prestigious and stately Middle and Inner Temple Inns. They derive their name from the clandestine, elusive Order of the Knights Templar, who embraced this site as their

English seat in the 12th century. The secretive, bellicose order dissolved in 1312, and this property was eventually passed on to the Knights Hospitallers of St. John, who leased it to a community of common law scholars in 1338. Virtually leveled by the Germans in the early 1940s, only the church, crypt, and buttery of the Inner Temple survive intact from the Middle Ages.

Held in common by both the Middle and Inner Temples, the **Temple Church** is the finest of the few round churches left in England. It contains gorgeous stained-glass windows, a handsome 12th-century Norman doorway, an altar screen by Wren (1682), and ten arresting, armor-clad stone effigies of sinister Knights Templar dating from the 12th and 14th centuries (open erratically Wed.-Sat. 10am-4pm, Sun. 1-4pm). According to Shakespeare (*Henry VI*), the red and white roses that served as emblems throughout the War of the Roses were plucked from the Middle Temple Garden. **Fountain Court** contains its 1681 namesake, restored in 1919.

Back across Fleet St., on the other side of the Royal Courts, **Lincoln's Inn** (tube: Holborn) was the only Inn to emerge unscathed from the Blitz. The lawyers of Lincoln's Inn were mocked by John Donne's rhyming couplets in his *Satire: On Lawyers.* New Square and its cloistered churchyard (to the right as you enter from Lincoln's Inn Fields) appear today much as they did in the 1680s. The **Old Hall,** east of New Sq., dates from 1492; here the Lord High Chancellor presided over the High Court of Chancery from 1733 to 1873. **Gray's Inn** (tube: Chancery La.), dubbed "that stronghold of melancholy" by Dickens, stands at the northern end of Fulwood Pl., off High Holborn. Reduced to ashes by German bombers in 1941, Gray's Inn was restored to much of its former splendor during the 1950s. The Hall, to your right as you pass through the archway, retains its original stained glass (1580) and most of its ornate screen. The first performance of Shakespeare's *Comedy of Errors* took place here in 1594. Francis Bacon maintained chambers here from 1577 until his death in 1626, and is the purported designer of the magnificent gardens.

Of the nine Inns of Chancery, only **Staple Inn's** building survives (located where Gray's Inn Rd. meets High Holborn; tube: Chancery La.). The half-timbered Elizabethan front, with its easily recognized vertical striping, dates from 1586. Devoted son Samuel Johnson wrote "Rasselas" here in one week to pay for his mother's funeral. Those who can't get enough of the fascinating Inns of Court can try "Legal London" **walking tours** (Mon. 2pm and Wed. 11am; tel. 624 3978; £4, students £3).

THE STRAND & FLEET STREET

Hugging the embankment of the River Thames, **The Strand** (tube: Temple or Aldwych—rush hours only) has fared ill through London's growth. Once lined with fine Tudor houses, today this major thoroughfare curves from Trafalgar Square through a jumbled assortment of dull commercial buildings.

Somerset House, a magnificent Palladian structure built by Sir William Chambers in 1776, stands on the site of the 16th-century palace where Elizabeth I resided during the brief reign of her sister Mary. Formerly the administrative center of the Royal Navy, the building now houses the exquisite **Courtauld Collection** (see Museums) and the less exquisite offices of the Inland Revenue.

Just east of the Courtauld, **St. Mary-le-Strand's** slender steeple and elegant portico rise above an island of decaying steps in the middle of the modern roadway. Designed by James Gibbs and consecrated in 1724, the church overlooks the site of the original Maypole, where London's first hackney cabs assembled in 1634. The intricate floral moldings were crafted by brothers John and Chrysostom Wilkins, who received a mere 45p for each elaborate bloom (open Mon.-Fri. 11am-3:30pm). Across the street, newsreaders pompously intone "This is London" every hour from Bush House, the center of the **BBC**'s worldwide radio services.

To the east stands handsome **St. Clement Danes** (tel. 242 8282), whose melodious bells get their 15 seconds of fame in the nursery rhyme "Oranges and lemons, say the bells of St. Clement's." Children get their 15 minutes of fruit when oranges and lemons are distributed in a ceremony near the end of March. Designed by Wren in 1682, the church was built over the ruins of an older Norman structure reputed to be the tomb of Harold Harefoot, leader of a colony of Danes who settled the area in the 9th century. In 1720, Gibbs replaced Wren's original truncated tower with a slimmer spire. Although German firebombs gutted the church in 1941, the ornately molded white stucco and gilt interior has been restored, contrasting beautifully with the rich darkness of the wooden pews. This official church of the Royal Air Force has marble floors inlaid with brass squadron medallions. A crypt-*cum*-prayer-chapel houses an eerie collection of 17th-century funerary monuments (open daily 8am-5pm). Outside the front entrance, the recently erected "Bomber" Harris memorial has attracted controversy; Col. Arthur Harris masterminded the devastating firebombing of civilian Dresden in World War II.

Twining's Teas (tel. 353 3511) brews at 216 The Strand, near the Fleet St. end of the road. It is both the oldest business in Britain still operating on original premises and the narrowest shop in London (open Mon.-Fri. 9:30am-4:30pm). Just east stands the only Strand building to survive the Great Fire, the **Wig and Pen Club,** 229-230 The Strand, which was constructed over Roman ruins in 1625. Frequented by the best-known barristers and journalists in London, the Wig and Pen is, in the sage words of the *Baltimore Sun,* "a window through which you can see Fleet Street in all its aspects." The club is open to members only.

The **Temple Bar Monument** stands in the middle of the street where The Strand meets Fleet St., marking the boundary between Westminster and the City. The Sovereign must still obtain ceremonial permission from the Lord Mayor to pass the bar and enter the City here.

Once a hive of journalistic activity, Fleet Street (tube: Blackfriar's or St. Paul's) is now just a famous name and a few (vacated) famous buildings. In 1986 the *Times,* which moved to cheaper land at Wapping, Docklands, initiated a mass exodus from the street. The *Daily Telegraph* abandoned its startling Greek and Egyptian revival building, moving to Marsh Wall in 1987. The *Daily Express,* once the occupant of an Art Deco manse of chrome and black glass on Fleet St., now headlines in Blackfriars. Rupert Murdoch's *The Sun* also moved to Wapping at this time, using the move as an excuse to shift to non-union labor.

The tiered spire of Wren's **St. Bride's** (1675), near 89 Fleet St., became the inspiration for countless wedding cakes thanks to an ingenious local baker. Dubbed "the printers' church" because the first printing press with moveable type was housed here in 1500, it boasts a ceiling adorned with shiny gold rosettes and scrollery. Underground, a musty collection of relics and rocks calls itself a museum, alongside an exhibit detailing the evolution of printing in Fleet St. (open Mon.-Fri. 8:30am-5pm, Sat. 9am-5pm, Sun. 9am-7:30pm).

A few blocks down the street, opposite 54 Fleet St., a large white sign labels the alleyway entrance to Johnson's Court. Inside the alley, more discreet signs point the way to **Samuel Johnson's House,** 17 Gough Square (tel. 353 3745). Follow the signs carefully; Carlyle got lost on his way here in 1832. This dark brick house was Dr. Johnson's abode from 1749 to 1758. Here he completed his *Dictionary,* the first definitive English lexicon, even though rumor falsely insists that he omitted "sausage" (he did, however, omit the word "gullible"). Tours are self-guided, but the knowledgeable curator is eager to supplement your visit with anecdotes about the Great Cham and his hyperbolic biographer, James Boswell (open Mon.-Sat. 11am-5:30pm; Oct.-April Mon.-Sat. 11am-5pm; £3, concessions £2).

A few more blocks down Fleet St., the neo-Gothic **St. Dunstan-in-the-West** holds its magnificent lantern tower high above the banks surrounding it. The chimes of its curious 17th-century clock are sounded on the quarter hour by a pair of hammer-wielding, mechanical giants. In the central archway, you can see a rough carving of poet-priest John Donne. Both Donne and his biographer Izaak Walton maintained close ties with the church of St. Dunstan.

About a block down the street, at no. 17 Fleet St. (tube: Temple), a half-timbered house dating from 1610 perches above the gateway to the Temple Church (see Holborn and Inns of Court). The stairs leading up to **Prince Henry's Room** (tel. (0181) 294 1158) are just to the left of the gate. The one room consists of an ornate but monochromatic 17th-century ceiling (arguably London's finest example of Jacobean plaster-work), richly carved mahogany paneling, and Samuel Pepys memorabilia (open Mon.-Sat. 11am-2pm; free).

THE CITY OF LONDON

Until the 18th century, the City of London was London; all other boroughs and neighborhoods now swallowed up by "London" were neighboring towns or outlying villages. Today, the one-square-mile City of London is the financial center of Europe. Each weekday 350,000 people surge in at 9am and rush out again unfailingly at 5pm, leaving behind a resident population of only 6000. At the center of the City, the massive Bank of England controls the nation's finances, and the Stock Exchange makes the nation's fortune. Proliferating cranes, office building sites, and rising share indices bore witness to the British "economic resurgence" of the late 80s, while the panic in such City stalwarts as Lloyd's of London is testimony to the non-recovery of the early 90s. Terrorist attacks in the recent past have prompted the government to regulate traffic into the City; all vehicles must enter from one of eight streets where they are then checked for bombs.

The City owes much of its graceful appearance to Sir Christopher Wren, who was the chief architect working after the fire of 1666 almost completely razed the area. In his diary, Samuel Pepys gives a moving firsthand account of the fire that started in a baker's shop in Pudding Lane and leapt between the overhanging houses to bring destruction upon the City. Afterwards, Charles II issued a proclamation that City buildings should be rebuilt in brick and stone, rather than highly flammable wood and thatch. Wren's studio designed 52 churches to replace the 89 destroyed in the fire, and the surviving 24 churches are some of the only buildings in the City from the period immediately following the Great Fire. Most of the City's churches have *irregular or random opening times*.

Perhaps the most important secular structures of the City are the buildings of the **Livery Companies.** The companies began as medieval guilds representing specific trades and occupations. These guilds played a role in fixing trade standards; today many also contribute to charity and sponsor educational programs. The 84 **livery halls** are scattered around the square mile. Most halls do not open to the public; those that do require tickets. The City of London Information Centre (see below) receives a batch of tickets in February, but they disappear rapidly.

The **City of London Information Centre,** St. Paul's Churchyard (tel. 332 1456; tube: St. Paul's) can give you up-to-date details on all of the City's attractions. (Open daily 9:30am-5pm; Nov.-March Mon.-Fri. 9:30am-5pm, Sat. 9:30am-12:30pm.) A 24-hour on-line "Leisure Data Base" is located just outside of the Information Centre.

The oldest part of London, the City is home to many municipal traditions. One of the largest is the **Lord Mayor's Show,** on the second Saturday of November, a glittering parade of pomp and red velvet to the Royal Courts of Justice in celebration of London citizens' right to elect their Lord Mayor. Information and street plans are available from the City of London Information Centre starting in mid-October. One of the newer traditions is July's **City of London Festival,** which jam-packs the churches, halls, squares, and sidewalks of the area with music and theater (see Entertainment).

Bank to Ludgate: Eastern Section

The few remaining stones of the Roman **Temple of Mithras,** Queen Victoria St. (tube: Bank or Mansion House), dwell incongruously in the shadow of the Temple Court building. Discovered during construction work and shifted a few yards from its original location, the temple still retains a recognizable outline. Down Queen Victoria St., **St. Mary Aldermary** (so called because it is older than any other St. Mary's church in the City) towers over its surroundings. A rare Gothic Wren, it is especially notable for its delicate fan vaulting. The bells that recalled London's old Mayor Dick Whittington to London rang out from the church of St. Marie de Arcubus, replaced by Wren's **St. Mary-le-Bow,** Cheapside, in 1683.

St. James Garlickhythe, on Upper Thames St., gets its name from the garlic once sold nearby. To the west on Queen Victoria St. stands a rare red-brick Wren church with an elegant cupola, **St. Benet's.** Just across the street, the **College of Arms** rests on its heraldic authority behind ornate gates. The College regulates the granting and recognition of coats of arms. The officer-in-waiting at the Earl Marshal's stately paneled Court Room can assess your claim to a British family coat of arms. (Open Mon.-Fri. 10am-4pm.) Farther west, at 146 Queen Victoria, **St. Andrew-by-the-Wardrobe** (tube: Blackfriars) was originally built next to Edward III's impressive Royal Stores. Now the church cowers beneath the Faraday building, the first building allowed to exceed the City's previously strict height limit.

Queen Victoria St. meets New Bridge St. in the area known as Blackfriars, in reference to the darkly clad Dominican brothers who built a monastery there in the middle ages. Shakespeare acted in James Burbage's theater here in the late 1500s. Ludgate Circus, to the north, is now the noisy site of major redevelopment. A peaceful haven is offered by **St. Martin-within-Ludgate,** a Wren church on Ludgate Hill untouched by the Blitz. The square interior boasts some fine Grinling Gibbons woodwork, and the slim spire still pierces the dome of St. Paul's when seen from Ludgate Circus, just as Wren intended.

Around the corner, the **Old Bailey** (tel. 248 3277; tube: St. Paul's), technically the Central Criminal Courts, crouches under a copper dome and a wide-eyed figure of justice on the corner of Old Bailey and Newgate St. Trial-watching persists as a favorite occupation, and the Old Bailey fills up whenever a gruesome or scandalous case is in progress. You can enter the public Visitors' Gallery and watch bewigged barristers at work (Mon.-Fri. 10am-1pm and 2-4pm; entrance in Warwick Passage off Old Bailey). When court is not in session (July-Sept.), the building is closed. Cameras, large bags, and backpacks may not be taken inside. The Chief Post Office building, off Newgate to the north, envelops the enthralling **National Postal Museum.**

The Barbican & Northern Section

The **Barbican Centre,** which opened in 1972 and covers 60 acres, stands as one of the most impressive and controversial post-Blitz rebuilding projects (tube: Barbican or Moorgate). A city unto itself, the labyrinthine complex of residential apartments and offices shelters the **Royal Shakespeare Company,** the **London Symphony Orchestra,** the **Museum of London,** the **Guildhall School of Music and Drama,** and the **Barbican Art Gallery. St. Giles Church** and the **City of London School for Girls** stand in the complex's unexpectedly verdant central courtyard, whose artificial lakes and planned gardens temper the Barbican's relentless urbanity.

In order to reach **St. Bartholomew the Great,** one must enter through an exceedingly narrow Tudor house located on Little Britain. Parts of the church date from 1123, although 800 years of alteration have much embellished it. (Open Mon.-Thurs. 8am-4:30pm, Fri. 10:45am-4:30pm, Sun. 8am-8pm.) For an early pint, try one of the pubs around **Smithfield,** a meat and poultry wholesale market since the 12th century. (Market open daily 5am-noon; some surrounding pubs open at 7am.)

Charterhouse (tel. 253 9503), a peculiar institution first established as a priory and converted in 1611 to a school and hospital for poor gentlemen, stands on the edge of Charterhouse Sq. The school has moved to Surrey, but the fine group of 15th- to 17th-century buildings still houses around 40 residents, who must be bachelors or widowers over 60. (Tours April-July Wed. at 2:15pm. Nominal charge.)

Bank to the Tower: Eastern Section

The massive windowless walls and foreboding doors of the **Bank of England** enclose four full acres (tube: Bank). The present building dates from 1925, but the eight-foot-thick outer wall is the same one built by architect Sir John Soane in 1788. The only part open to the public is the plush **Bank of England Museum.** Its neighbors, the **Stock Exchange** and the **Royal Exchange** are not open to visitors. **St. Margaret Lothbury** (down Throgmorton St.)

The 1986 **Lloyd's** building and **Leadenhall Market,** off Leadenhall St., supply the most startling architectural clash in the City. The ducts, lifts, and chutes of Lloyd's are straight out of the 21st century. This futuristic setting houses the **Lutine Bell,** which is still occasionally rung—once for bad insurance news, twice for good. In contrast, across a narrow alley the ornate cream and maroon fittings of Victorian Leadenhall Market emerge. A food market has stood here since the Middle Ages.

Behind the imposing, tautological **Mansion House,** home of the Lord Mayor, stands **St. Stephen Walbrook** (on Walbrook). Arguably Wren's finest, and allegedly his personal favorite, the church combines four major styles: the old-fashioned English church characterized by nave and chancel; the Puritan hall church, which lacks any separation between priest and congregation; the Greek-cross-plan church; and the domed church, a study for St. Paul's. The Samaritans, a social service group that advises the suicidal and severely depressed, was founded here in 1953. The mysterious cheese-like object in the center is actually an altar. Sculpted by Henry Moore, it is as controversial as you think it is.

The church of **St. Mary Woolnoth,** at King William and Lombard St., may look odd without a spire, but the interior proportions and the black and gilt reredos confirm the talents of Wren's pupil Nicholas Hawksmoor. The only City church untouched by the Blitz, it "kept the hours" in Eliot's *Waste Land.* **St. Mary Abchurch,** off Abchurch Lane, provides a neat domed comparison to St. Stephen's—its mellow, dark wood and baroque paintings contrast with St. Stephen's bright airy interior.

Before even the most basic rebuilding of the city, Wren designed a tall Doric pillar. Completed in 1671, the simply named **Monument** lies at the bottom of King William St. (tube: Monument). Supposedly, the 202-foot pillar stands exactly that many feet from where the Great Fire broke out in Pudding Lane on September 2, 1666, and "rushed devastating through every quarter with astonishing swiftness and worse." High on Fish Street Hill, the column offers an expansive view of London. Bring stern resolution and £1 to climb its 311 steps. (Open Mon.-Fri. 9am-6pm, Sat.-Sun. 2-6pm; Oct.-March Mon.-Sat. 9am-4pm.)

Over the river near the Monument the current **London Bridge** succeeds a slew of ancestors. The famed version crowded with houses stood from 1176 until it burned in 1758. The most recent predecessor didn't fall down; in 1973 it was sold to an American millionaire for £1.03 million and shipped, block by block, to Lake Havasu City, Arizona.

St. Mary at Hill, Lovat Lane, is a typical Wren church with a surprisingly convincing reworking of the old interior by early Victorian craftsmen, and an even more convincing contemporary reconstruction project. **St. Dunstan-in-the-East,** St. Dunstan's Hill, suffered severe damage in the Blitz; only Wren's amazing spire remains. The ruins have been converted into a gorgeous little garden that makes a fine picnic spot.

Pepys witnessed the spread of the Great Fire from atop **All Hallows by the Tower,** at the end of Great Tower St. Just inside the south entrance is an arch from the 7th-century Saxon church, discovered in 1960. To the left, the baptistery contains a striking wood font cover by Grinling Gibbons. At the tiny **St. Olave's** in Hart St., an annual memorial service is held for Pepys, who is buried here with his wife.

ST. PAUL'S CATHEDRAL

Sir Christopher Wren's domed masterpiece dominates its surroundings even as modern usurpers sneak up around it. The current edifice is the third cathedral to stand on the site; the first cathedral was founded in 604 and destroyed by fire in 1089. The second and most massive cathedral was a medieval structure, one of the largest in Europe, topped by a spire ascending 489 feet. Falling into almost complete neglect in the 16th century, the cathedral became more of a marketplace than a church, and Wren had already started drawing up his grand scheme in 1666 when the Great Fire demolished the cathedral, along with most of London, and gave him the opportunity to build from scratch.

Both the design and the building of the cathedral were dogged by controversy. Like his Renaissance predecessors, Wren preferred an equal-armed Greek cross plan, while ecclesiastical authorities insisted upon a traditional medieval design with a long nave and choir for services. Wren's final design compromised by translating a Gothic cathedral into baroque and classical terms: a Latin Cross floor plan with baroque detailing. Wren's second model received the King's warrant of approval (and is thus known as the "Warrant Model"), but still differed from today's St. Paul's. The shrewd architect won permission to make necessary alterations as building proceeded and, behind the scaffolding, Wren had his way. The cathedral was topped off in 1710; at 365 feet above the ground, the huge classical dome is the second-largest free-standing dome in Europe.

In December 1940, London burned once again. On the night of the 29th, at the height of the Blitz, St. Paul's was engulfed by a sea of fire. This time it survived. Fifty-one firebombs landed on the cathedral, all swiftly put out by the heroic volunteer St. Paul's Fire Watch; a small monument in the floor at the end of the nave honors them. Two of the four high-explosive bombs that landed did explode, wrecking the north transept; the clear glass there bears silent testimony.

Dotted with sculptures, bronzes, and mosaics, St. Paul's makes a rewarding place for a wander. Above the choir, three neo-Byzantine glass mosaics by William Richmond, done in 1904, tell the story of creation. The stalls in the **Choir,** carved by Grinling Gibbons, narrowly escaped a bomb, but the old altar did not. It was replaced with the current marble High Altar, covered by a St. Peter's-like *baldacchino* of oak, splendidly gilded. Above looms the crowning glory, the ceiling mosaic of *Christ Seated in Majesty.* A trial mosaic adorns the east wall of **St. Dunstan's Chapel,** on the left by the entrance. On the other side of the nave in the **Chapel of St. Michael and St. George** sits a richly carved throne by Grinling Gibbons, made for the coronation of William and Mary in 1710. Along the south aisle hangs Holman Hunt's third version of *The Light of the World.*

The **ambulatory** contains a statue of poet John Donne (Dean of the cathedral 1621-1631) in shrouds, one of the few monuments to survive from old St. Paul's. Also in the ambulatory is a modern sculpture of the Virgin Mary and Baby Jesus by Henry Moore. One month after the arrival of Moore's sculpture, entitled *Mother and Child,* guides insisted a name plaque be affixed to the base, as no one knew what it was meant to represent. Britain restored the former **Jesus Chapel** after the Blitz and dedicated it to U.S. soldiers who died during World War II. The graceful and intricate choir gates were executed by Jean Tijou early in the 18th century.

The **crypt,** saturated with tombs and monuments, forms a catalogue of Britain's officially "great" figures of the last two centuries, including Florence Nightingale and sculptor Henry Moore. The massive tombs of the Duke of Wellington and Nelson command attention. A bust of George Washington stands opposite a memorial to Lawrence of Arabia. Around the corner lounges Rodin's fine bust of poet W.F. Henley (1849-1903). **Painter's Corner** holds the tombs of Sir Joshua Reynolds, Sir Lawrence Alma-Tadema, and J.M.W. Turner, along with memorials to John Constable and the revolutionary William Blake. Nearby, a black slab in the floor marks Wren's grave, with his son's famous epitaph close by: *Lector, si monumentum requiris circumspice* (roughly, "If you seek his monument, just look around you").

The display of **models** of St. Paul's details the history of the cathedral in all of its incarnations. In these models you can see how the upper parts of the exterior walls are mere façades, concealing the flying buttresses which support the nave roof (audiovisual presentations 2/hr. 10:30am-3pm; crypt open Mon.-Sat. 8:45am-4:45pm).

Going up St. Paul's proves more challenging than going down: 259 steps lead to the vertiginous **Whispering Gallery,** on the inside base of the dome. Words whispered against the wall whizz round the sides. A further 118 steps up, the first external view glitters from the **Stone Gallery,** only to be eclipsed by the uninterrupted and incomparable panorama from the **Golden Gallery,** 153 steps higher at the top of the dome. Before descending, take a peek down into the cathedral through the glass peephole in the floor. (Tube: St. Paul's. Cathedral open for sightseeing Mon.-Sat. 8:30am-4pm; crypt and ambulatory open Mon.-Sat. 8:45am-4:15pm; galleries open Mon.-Sat. 10am-4:15pm. £3, students £2.50, children £2. Cathedral and galleries £5, students £4, children £3.)

THE TOWER OF LONDON

The Tower of London, the largest fortress in medieval Europe and the palace and prison of English monarchs for over 500 years, is soaked in blood and history. Its intriguing past and striking buildings attract over two million visitors per year. The oldest continuously occupied fortified building in Europe, "The Tower" was founded by William the Conqueror in 1066 in order to protect—and command—his subjects. Not one but 20 towers stand behind its walls, though many associate the image of the **White Tower,** the oldest one, with the Tower of London. Completed in 1097, it overpowers all the fortifications that were built around it in the following centuries. Originally a royal residence, it last housed James I, and has subsequently served as a wardrobe, storehouse, public records office, armory, and prison. Richard the Lionhearted began the construction of defenses around the White Tower in 1189. Subsequent work by Henry III (1216-72) and Edward I (1272-1307) brought the Tower close to its present condition.

Two rings of defenses surround the White Tower. On the **Inner Ward,** the **Bell Tower** squats on the southwest corner. Since the 1190s, this tower has sounded the curfew bell each night. Sir Thomas More spent some time here, courtesy of Henry VIII, before he was executed in the Tower Green. On the first floor of the White Tower nests the **Chapel of St. John,** dating from 1080, the finest Norman chapel in London. Stark and pristine, it is the only chapel in the world with an "aisled nave and encircling ambulatory," a balcony where women were allowed to join the otherwise men-only chapel services. Failed arsonist Guy Fawkes of the Gunpowder Plot was tortured beneath this chapel.

Along the curtain wall hovers the **Bloody Tower,** arguably the most famous, and certainly the most infamous, part of the fortress. Once pleasantly named the Garden Tower, due to the officers' garden nearby, the Bloody Tower supposedly saw the murder of the Little Princes, the uncrowned King Edward V and his brother (aged 13 and 10), by agents of Richard III in 1483. The murder remains one of history's great mysteries; some believe that Richard was innocent and that the future Henry VII arranged the murders to ease his own ascent. Two children's remains found in the grounds in 1674 (and buried in Westminster Abbey) have never been conclusively identified as those of the Princes. Sir Walter Raleigh did time in the prison here off and on for 13 years and occupied himself by writing a voluminous *History of the World Part I.* Before Part II ever happened, James I had him beheaded.

Henry III lived in the adjacent **Wakefield Tower,** largest after the White Tower. The crown kept its public records and its jewels here until 1856 and 1967 respectively, although Wakefield also has its own gruesome past. Lancastrian Henry VI was imprisoned by Yorkist Edward IV during the Wars of the Roses and was murdered on May 21, 1471 while praying here. Students from Cambridge's King's College, founded by Henry, annually place lilies on the spot of the murder.

Counterclockwise around the inner **Wall Walk** come the **Lanthorn, Salt, Broad Arrow, Constable,** and **Martin** towers, the last scene of the self-styled "Colonel" Thomas Blood's bold attempt in 1671 at stealing the Crown Jewels. Martin's lower level now houses a small exhibit of **Instruments of Torture.** The inner ring comes full circle, completed by the **Brick, Bowyer** (where, according to Shakespeare's constantly accurate *Richard III,* the Duke of Clarence died after being drowned in Malmsey wine), **Flint, Devereux,** and **Beauchamp** towers.

Within the inner ring adjoining the Bell Tower lurks the Tudor **Queen's House** (which will become the King's House when Prince Charles ascends to the throne). The house has served time as a prison for some of the Tower's most illustrious guests: both Anne Boleyn and Catherine Howard were incarcerated here by charming hubby Henry VIII; Guy Fawkes was interrogated in the Council Chamber on the upper floor; and in 1941, Hitler's Deputy Führer Rudolf Hess was brought here after parachuting into Scotland. The only prisoners remaining today are the clipped ravens hopping around on the grass outside the White Tower; legend has it that without the ravens the Tower would crumble and a great disaster would befall the monarchy. The ravens even have a tomb and gravestone of their own in the grassy moat near the ticket office.

Although more famous for the prisoners who languished and died here, the Tower has seen a handful of spectacular escapes. The Bishop of Durham escaped from Henry I out a window and down a rope. The unfortunate Welsh Prince Gruffyd ap Llewelyn, prisoner of Henry III in 1244, apparently had not learned his knots properly—his rope of knotted sheets broke and he fell to his death.

Prisoners of the highest rank sometimes received the honor of a private execution rather than one before the spectators' benches of Tower Hill, just east of the present tube station. A block on the Tower Green, inside the Inner Ward, marks the spot where the axe fell on Queen Catherine Howard, Lady Jane Grey, Anne Boleyn, and the Earl of Essex, Queen Elizabeth's rejected suitor. Sir Thomas More, "the king's good servant but God's first," was beheaded in public. The nearby **Chapel of St. Peter ad Vincula** (St. Peter in Chains) was once called "the saddest place on earth" by Lord Macaulay; the remains of prisoners were transported here after their executions. The decapitated bodies of Henry VIII's two executed queens lie beneath the altar and in the crypt. (Entrance to the chapel by Yeoman tour only. See below.)

The prisoners may be gone, but the weapons and armor remain. An expansive display from the **Royal Armouries,** testifying to Henry VIII's fondness for well-molded metal suits, takes up three floors. To find a glut of arms and weaponry, visit the **New Armouries** to the east.

The prize possessions of the Tower and of England, the **Crown Jewels** pull in the crowds. Oliver Cromwell melted down much of the original royal treasure; most of the collection dates from after Charles II's Restoration in 1660. You may have seen thousands of pictures of the crowns and scepters before, but no camera can capture the dazzle. The **Imperial State Crown** and the **Sceptre with the Cross** feature the Stars of Africa, cut from the Cullinan Diamond. Scotland Yard mailed the precious stone third class from the Transvaal to London in an unmarked brown paper package, a scheme they believed was the safest way of getting it to England.

The Tower is still guarded and inhabited by the Yeoman of the Guard extraordinary, popularly known as the "Beefeaters." (The name does actually derive from "eaters of beef"—well-nourished domestic servants.) To be eligible for Beefeaterhood, a candidate must have at least 22 years honorable service in the armed forces.

Visitors enter the Tower through the **Byward Tower** on the southwest of the **Outer Ward,** which sports a precariously hung portcullis. The password, required for entry here after hours, has been changed every day since 1327. German spies were executed in the Outer Ward during World War II. Along the outer wall, **St. Thomas's Tower** (after Thomas à Becket) tops the evocative **Traitors' Gate,** through which boats once brought new captives.

The whole castle used to be surrounded by a broad **moat** dug by Edward I. Cholera epidemics forced the Duke of Wellington to drain it in 1843. The filled land became a vegetable garden during World War II but has since sprouted a tennis court and bowling green for inhabitants of the Tower.

Free, entertaining tours of about one hour, given every half hour by Yeomen, start outside Byward Tower (tube: Tower Hill; open Mon.-Sat. 9:30am-5pm, Sun. 2-5pm; Nov.-Feb. Mon.-Sat. 9:30am-4pm; £6.70, students and seniors £5.10, children £4.40, families £19). Try to avoid the phenomenal Sunday crowd—queues start around noon. The best times to visit are Mondays and Tuesdays. For tickets to the **Ceremony of the Keys,** the nightly ritual locking of the gates, write in advance to Resident Governor, Tower of London, EC3 (inquiries, tel. 709 0765).

Tower Bridge, a granite and steel structure reminiscent of a castle with a drawbridge, is a familiar sight. (Open daily 10am-6:30pm, Nov.-March 10am-5:15pm. £5, children £3.50.)

THE EAST END

Today London's East End continues a trajectory that began 300 years ago, when the areas directly east and northeast of the City of London first served as a refuge to those who either weren't welcome in the City, or who didn't want to be subject to the City's jurisdictions. During the 17th century, this included political dissenters, religious orders, and the French Huguenots. By 1687, 13,000 Huguenots had settled in Spitalfields, the area northeast of the City of London (which takes its name from a long-gone medieval priory, St. Mary Spital). Most of the Jewish community has moved on to suburbs to the north and west of central London, like Stamford Hill and Golders Green, but notable remnants of the former East End community include the renowned kosher restaurant **Bloom's** (see Food) and the city's oldest standing synagogue, **Bevis Marks Synagogue,** (tel. 626 1274, Bevis Marks and Heneage La., EC3; tube: Aldgate).

Today, scattered deserted warehouse spaces and airy studios house the brushes and oils of the area's 6000 artists. Some of their work, much of which focuses on the experience of the East End's nonwhite population, hangs on the high white walls of the **Whitechapel Art Gallery,** on Whitechapel High St. (tel. 377 0107; open Tues. and Thurs.-Sun. 11am-5pm, Wed. 11am-8pm; free). Around the corner, **Spitalfields Heritage Centre,** 17-19 Princelet St., E1 (tel. 377 6901), is dedicated to research on local immigrant communities. Housed in an 1870 synagogue, it still displays a wooden ark, pulpit, and seats (free; call for opening hours).

Jack the Ripper's six murders took place in Whitechapel; you can tour his trail with a number of different guided walk companies, all of which offer a Jack the Ripper tour every evening (see Sights: Touring). More recently, cockney Capone twins Ron and Reggie Kray ruled the 60s underworld from their mum's terraced house in Bethnal Green. Ron wiped out an ale-sipping rival in broad daylight in 1966 at the **Blind Beggar** pub at Whitechapel Rd. and Cambridge Heath Rd. Along Cambridge Heath Rd. lies the **Bethnal Green Museum of Childhood** (tel. (0181) 980 2415; open Mon.-Thurs. and Sat. 10am-5:50pm, Sun. 2:30-5:50pm; free). North past Bethnal Green, and beyond the wafts of curry on Brick Lane, stretch the expanses of **Hackney** which mesh into **Clapton** and farther north, **Stoke Newington.** Traditionally known as a community of "Londoners' stock," Hackney now ever-adapts to its growing Caribbean, African, and Turkish populations—Brixton without the hype and the tube line. West Indian beef patty shops and thumping night clubs, as well as discount clothing, food, and shoe stores line the main drags of Mare St. and Lower Clapton Rd. The community center at the **Harriet Tubman House,** 136 Lower Clapton Rd., E5 (tel. (0181) 985 6649), acts as a gathering place, an information center, and as the Sam Uriah Morris Society's small black history museum (BR: Clapton).

SOUTHWARK

Across London Bridge from the City lies Southwark (SUTH-uk), a distinctive area with a lively history (tube: London Bridge). The area around the **Borough High St.,** also called "the Borough," has existed—with the exception of minor changes—for nearly 2000 years. Until 1750, London Bridge was the only bridge over the Thames in London, and the highway leading to it had many travelers who liked to stop at the inns lining the road. The neighborhood has historically been associated with entertainment from the days of bear-baiting to the even more vicious pleasures of Defoe's *Moll Flanders*. Shakespeare's and Marlowe's plays were performed at the **Rose Theatre,** built in 1587 and rediscovered during construction in 1989. The remnants are to be preserved and displayed underneath a new *Financial Times* office block at Park St. and Rose Alley. The remains of Shakespeare's **Globe Theatre** were discovered just months after those of the Rose. While privately owned, the remains of the Globe can be viewed under an elevated building on Park street.

A project spearheaded by filmmaker Sam Wanamaker is underway to build a new Globe on the riverbank. The replica will be part of the **International Shakespeare Globe Centre,** a vast complex which will ultimately contain a second theatre, an exhibition gallery, an archival library, an auditorium, and various shops, and will be located directly across the Thames from St. Paul's Cathedral. The **Shakespeare Globe Museum,** 1 Bear Gardens Alley (tel. 928 6342), traces the development of the Elizabethan stage from the first purpose-built playhouse in 1756 to the closing of the Globe in 1642 (open Mon.-Sat. 10am-5pm, Sun. 2-5:30pm; £3, students £2). The Globe Centre will take over from the Globe Museum on August 1, 1995.

At Montague Close near the bridge rises the tower of **Southwark Cathedral** (tel. 407 2939), after Westminster Abbey the most striking Gothic church in the city; it is certainly the oldest. Mostly rebuilt in the 1890s, only the church's original 1207 choir and retro-choir survive. Shakespeare is believed to have rested here between 1599 and 1611. His brother Edmund was buried in the church in 1607 and medieval poet John Gower lies here in a colorful tomb. (Open Mon.-Fri. 10am-4:30pm.)

A couple of blocks southeast, your hair will rise and your spine will chill at **St. Thomas's Old Operating Theatre,** 9a St. Thomas St. (tel. 955 4791), a carefully preserved 19th-century surgical hospital. See the wooden table where unanesthetized patients endured excruciatingly painful surgery, or travel through the herb garret and museum (open Mon., Wed., Fri. 12:30-4pm, or by appointment; £1, seniors, students, and children 60p). If your bloodlust is not sated by the minutiae of early medicine, the **London Dungeon** (tel. 403 0606) awaits buried beneath the London Bridge Station at 28 Tooley St. (open daily 10am-6:30pm, Oct.-March 10am-5:30pm. £6.50, under 14 £6.50, students £5.50). Not for the squeamish, this dank maze of 40 exhibits recreates horrifying tales of European execution, torture, and plague.

Moored on the south bank of the Thames just upstream from Tower Bridge, the World War II warship **HMS Belfast** (tel. 407 6434) led the bombardment of the French coast during D-Day landings. The labyrinth of the engine house and the whopping great guns make it a fun place to play sailor. Mind your head. You can take the ferry that runs from Tower Pier on the north bank to the Belfast whenever the ship is open, or take the tube to London Bridge. Follow Tooley St. from the London Bridge, past the London Dungeon, and look for the signs (open daily 10am-5:20pm, Nov.-March 19 10am-4pm; £4, students £3, children £2, family £10; ferry return £1, students 60p). East of Tower Bridge, the bleached Bauhaus box of the **Design Museum** perches on the Thames.

THE SOUTH BANK

A hulk of worn concrete and futuristic slate, the South Bank gestures defiantly at the center of London from across the Thames. Housing the British terminus of the imminent **Channel Tunnel,** this region is currently poised to become one of London's most dynamic. Major commercial development, which anticipates the Chunnel's eventual flourishing, is currently underway. Waterloo station has been designated the London terminus of the "Chunnel," and Nicholas Grimshaw's spectacular new blue and silver international terminal will be many visitors' introduction to Britain.

The massive **South Bank Centre** is the neighborhood's predominant architectural eyesore, behind which lurks London's most concentrated campus of artistic and cultural activity (tube: Waterloo). The region south of the Thames has long been home to entertainment, much of it bawdy; until the English Civil Wars, most of this area fell under the legal jurisdiction of the Bishop of Winchester, and was thus protected from London censors. Until the post-WWII development began, the area was a den of working-class neighborhoods, dark breweries, smoky industry, and murky wharves through which suburbanites passed on their way into the city.

Contemporary development began in 1951 when the **Royal Festival Hall** was built. An eruption of construction ensued, producing the many concrete blocks that comprise the Centre, including the **National Film Theatre,** the **Queen Elizabeth Hall** complex, and the **Royal National Theatre**.

The 3000-seat Royal Festival Hall and its three auditoriums (Olivier, Lyttleton, and Cottlesoe) are home to the Philharmonia and London Philharmonic Orchestras, the English National Ballet, and host to countless others; its chamber-musical sibling is the Queen Elizabeth Hall. The National Theatre, opened by Lord Olivier in 1978, promotes "art for the people" through convivial platform performances, foyer concerts, lectures, tours, and workshops. Multicolored posters displaying Russian titles and Asian warriors distinguish the entrance to the National Film Theatre (see Entertainment: Film), directly on the South Bank. The Film Theatre also operates the innovative **Museum of the Moving Image** (see Museums). The **Jubilee Gardens,** planted for the Queen's Silver Jubilee in 1977, stretch along the embankment to **County Hall,** a formidable Renaissance edifice with a massive riverfront façade.

Gabriel's Wharf (tel. 620 0544) is a great place to watch original crafts being fashioned while grabbing a snack after a visit to the National Theatre. Beginning in Spring 1995, the newly-renovated **OXO Tower Wharf** will be a frenetic hub of South Bank activity. A meticulously planned potpourri of rooftop cafés, retail outlets, designer workshops, performance spaces, and residential flats make this the most innovative community-minded structure in recent London history.

Numerous pedestrian pathways are being planned for the region which will make it easier to get to the jumbled stalls of the **Cut Street Market** near Waterloo station. Farther along Waterloo Rd., the magnificently restored **Old Vic** (tel. 928 7616), former home of Olivier's National Repertory Theatre, now hosts popular seasons of lesser-known classics and worthy revivals.

Lambeth Palace (tube: Lambeth North), on the Embankment opposite the Lambeth Bridge, has been the Archbishop of Canterbury's London residence for seven centuries. The palace's notable exterior includes the entrance at the 15th-century brick Morton's Tower, and Lollard's Tower, where John Wyclif's followers were thought to be imprisoned (open by prior arrangement only; contact Lambeth Palace, Lambeth Palace Road, SE1). East on Lambeth Road is the **Imperial War Museum** (see Museums).

HAMPSTEAD & HIGHGATE

The urban villages of Hampstead and Highgate, poised on hills north of Regent's Park, seem entirely detached from central London. To get to Hampstead, take the tube to Hampstead or BR to Hampstead Heath. To reach Highgate, take the tube to Archway, then bus #210 or 217 to Highgate Village. Either trip takes at least half an hour from the center of London.

A thousand and five year-old Hampstead has traditionally been a refuge for artists, But nary a one can be found today on its tidy streets lined with Jaguars, designer boutiques, and Georgian townhouses. The sheer affluence of the place overwhelms; half of the restaurants are French, and even the McDonald's has slick Italian black-lacquered chairs. The town exudes old money and refinement, and is still populated by London's elite. Those wealthy enough to live here include former Labour Party leader Michael Foot, authors John Le Carré and Margaret Drabble, earnest thespians Emma Thompson and Kenneth Branaugh, Sting, and George Michael.

The major sight of interest, nestled in the midst of Hampstead, is **Keats House,** Keats Grove, one of London's finest literary shrines. To get there from the Hampstead tube station, head left down High St. for several blocks, turn left down Downshire Hill, and then take the first right onto Keats Grove. (The BR Hampstead Heath station is much closer.) Before dashing off to Italy to breathe his last consumptive breath and die in true Romantic-poet style, John Keats pined here for his next-door fianceé, Fanny Brawne. He allegedly composed "Ode to a Nightingale" under a plum tree here—the distant ancestor of the one growing in the garden today. The house is furnished as it was during Keats's life, complete with his manuscripts and letters (open Mon.-Fri. 2-6pm, Sat. 10am-1pm and 2-5pm, Sun. 2-5pm; Nov.-March Mon.-Fri. 1-5pm, Sat. 10am-1pm and 2-5pm, Sun. 2-5pm; free). The **Keats Memorial Library** (tel. 435 2062) next door contains a unique collection of books on the poet's life, family, and friends (open by appointment only).

The idyllic walk to **Burgh House,** Flask Walk (tel. 431 0144), is much more satisfying than the exhibitions inside. Just a few narrow streets and cobblestone sidewalks away from the High St., the town is transformed into a country village, with flowers everywhere and birds chirping in the boughs of commandingly large trees.

Church Row, off Heath St., retains its 18th-century style and dignified terraces. The painter John Constable lies buried in St. John's churchyard down the row.

Hampstead Heath (tube: Belsize Park) separates the Hampstead and Highgate from the rest of London. Once a hangout for outlaws, it now attracts docile picnickers and kite flyers; however, it is unadvisable to wander the heath alone at night. The heath remains the wildest patch of turf in London; you can get lost here, but dog-walkers will know the way out. On a hot day, take a dip in **Kenwood Ladies' Pond, Highgate Men's Pond,** or the *outré* **Mixed Bathing Pond.** Women may expose their top halves at the Ladies' Pond as long as they remain lying down. In July, 1994, gay protestors held a "strip-off" demonstration at the men's pond to protest the Corporation of London's introduction of a "trunks-on" policy.

Parliament Hill, on the southeastern tip of the heath, marks the southern boundary between Hampstead and Highgate and commands a gorgeous view of London, sweeping from the Docklands to the Houses of Parliament. The height of the hill, some say, owes much to the piles of corpses left here during the Plague. The bones of ancient Queen Boudicca also reputedly lie here. It was toward this hill that Guy Fawkes's accomplices fled after depositing explosives under the House of Commons in 1605, hoping for a good view of the fun.

To get from Hampstead to Highgate, walk across the heath or up Hampstead La. **Highgate Cemetery,** Swains La., is a remarkable monument to the Victorian fascination with death. Its most famous resident, rather inaptly, is Karl Marx, buried in the eastern section in 1883. An unmistakably Stalinist bust, four times life size, was placed above his grave in 1956 and attracts oddly-dressed pilgrims from the far reaches of the earth. Death makes for strange bedfellows; novelist George Eliot lies buried nearby. The magically spooky western section contains some of the finest tombs. (Eastern Cemetery open Mon.-Fri. 10am-4:45pm, Sat.-Sun. 11am-4:45pm. £1.50. Western Cemetery access by guided tour only Mon.-Fri. at noon, 2pm, and 4pm, Sat.-Sun. 1/hr. from 11am to 4pm. £2.)

Waterlow Park, immediately north of the cemetery, affords a gorgeous setting in which you can shed the urban grime of London and the Victorian gloom of the graveyard next door. The sociable ducks never turn down a good feed. By the eastern entrance, **Lauderdale House,** supposedly once home to Nell Gwyn, mistress of Charles II, now serves light snacks and lunches, but no oranges.

Descend from the heights into the depths of the subconscious in South Hampstead. Leaf through the pages of Sigmund's diary at the **Freud Museum,** 20 Maresfield Gdns. (tel. 435 2002; tube: Finchley Rd.; open Wed.-Sun. noon-5pm. £2.50, students £1.50).

DOCKLANDS

London Docklands, the largest commercial development in Europe, has utterly changed the face of East London within the space of 10 years. Londinium, already a prominent port in Roman times, sprouted wharves and quays that spread east from the City during the Middle Ages; Royal Dockyards were established at Deptford and Woolwich in 1515. As London grew in importance, the docks grew with it, stretching miles down the Thames, until they had become the powerful trading center of the British Empire. Then the advent of container transport and modern shipping methods rapidly rendered the docks redundant—by 1982 all had closed, leaving sweeping tracts of desperate dereliction. As part of the Thatcher government's privatization program, redevelopment of the area was handed over to the private sector—in the form of the **London Docklands Development Corporation**—along with a generous helping of public funds. Building has taken place on a phenomenal scale, but populating new office space with businesses lags behind, as Canary Wharf's dire straits demonstrate.

Docklands covers a huge expanse, from the Tower to Greenwich. The best way to see the region is via the **Docklands Light Railway (DLR),** a swish (but slow) semiautomatic railway opened in 1987. (Connect with the tube at Bank, Tower Hill, Shadwell, Bow Rd., or Stratford. Due to extension of the track, the wheelchair-accessible railway is replaced by bus on weekends and after 9:30pm on weekdays. See Getting About.) Getting off at **Shadwell** station, you'll see the old dock community: drab brick housing, dusty streets, traditional pubs, caffs, and pie-and-mash shops. Note the stark contrast between these economically depressed areas and the sleek, newly developed regions; many Londoners believe that this contrast testifies to the largely unregulated LDDC's greed and lack of social responsibility. Southwest of the station, down Cannon St. Rd. and a right onto The Highway, is the turreted **St. George in the East** (1714-26), whose plain façade and tower can be seen from several stops away on the DLR (open daily 9am-5pm).

The Limehouse and Westferry stops cover the historic **Limehouse** neighborhood, where dock and factory workers once lived. The legacy of Limehouse's 19th-century Chinese community can be seen in the Chinese restaurants along West India Dock Rd. The famous Narrow Street along the Thames is an official conservation area, where many Georgian houses can be seen. At 76 Narrow Street, **The Grapes,** the pub Dickens described in "Le Jolly Fellowship Porters," maintains its original ambience. Just east of Narrow street on Ropemaker's fields lies **The House They Left Behind,** a pub famed as a Joseph Conrad haunt. In the 19th century, the docks and factories of the **Isle of Dogs** (not an island, but a peninsula on the Thames named after the hounds of Edward II that once resided here) churned with activity. After its heyday during the Industrial Revolution, it declined along with the rest of the Docklands. Now, however, the most furious building is taking place here, notably the 800-ft. **Canary Wharf** skyscraper, Britain's tallest. The pyramid-topped building, which contains shops, restaurants, a concert hall, and a visitor center, is virtually the emblem of the Docklands (visitor center open Mon.-Sat. 10am-6pm).

The first stop for any tour of the Docklands should be the **Docklands Visitors Centre** (tel. 512 1111; DLR: Crossharbour, then left up the road). Loads of brochures hide behind the information desk, the most useful being the *DLR Tourist Guide,* which includes a map of the area, points of interest, and DLR info. A huge room is devoted to informing visitors about the history of the Docklands and its future, using photos, charts, maps, architects' plans, and a tearfully inspiring propaganda video (open Mon.-Fri. 8:30am-6pm, Sat.-Sun. 10am-4:30pm).

GREENWICH

Greenwich means time, and is pronounced GREN-idge. Charles II authorized the establishment of a small observatory here in 1675 "for perfecting navigation and astronomy." The Royal Naval College, which moved here from Portsmouth in 1873, enhanced Greenwich's strong maritime character. In a nation with a livelihood dependent on the waves, the village became hallowed ground. Today, the village of Greenwich (BR: Greenwich) is filled not only with astronomical sights, but also pubs and cafés, corner markets, and vendors peddling everything from Hendrix CDs to African carvings and leather bomber jackets.

Only select parts of the **Old Royal Observatory** (tel. (0181) 858 1167), designed by Sir Christopher Wren, are open to the public. Flamsteed House, with its unique, octagonal top room contains Britain's largest refracting telescope and an excellent collection of early astronomical instruments—astrolabes, celestial globes, and orreries—displayed with almost comprehensible explanations. The **Prime Meridian** is marked by a brass strip in the observatory courtyard. Jump from west to east in an instant. Greenwich Mean Time, still the standard for international communications and navigation, is displayed on an over-120-year-old clock. The red time ball, used since 1833 to indicate time to ships on the Thames, drops daily at 1pm. In 1894, an anarchist blew himself up while trying to destroy the observatory, and Polish sailor Joseph Conrad used the bizarre event as the seed for his novel *The Secret Agent.* (Open Mon.-Sat. 10am-6pm, Sun. noon-6pm; in winter Mon.-Sat. 10am-5pm, Sun. 2-5pm. £4, concessions £3. Planetarium shows Mon.-Sat. at 11:30am, noon, 12:30, 2, 2:30, 3, 3:30, and 4pm. Planetarium £1.50, children £1.) Just outside the observatory, you can share a splendid view of the Thames with a statue of General Wolfe (conqueror of French Canada) kindly donated by the Canadian government.

By the River Thames in Greenwich, the *Cutty Sark,* one of the last great tea clippers, anchors in dry dock. The ship (whose name, meaning "short shift," comes from Burns's poem "Tam O'Shanter") conveyed 1.3 million pounds of tea on each 120-day return trip from China. The vessel is now filled with the largest collection of ships' figureheads in the world. (Tel. (0181) 858 2698; open Mon.-Sat. 10am-6pm, Sun. noon-6pm; in winter Mon.-Sat. 10am-5pm, Sun. noon-5pm. £3.25, seniors, students, and children £2.25, families £8.)

The most picturesque (and appropriate) passage to Greenwich is by **boat.** Cruises to Greenwich pier depart from the Westminster (tel. 930 4097), Charing Cross (tel. 987 1185), and Tower (tel. (0181) 305 0300) piers (see Getting About for times and prices). Because of changing tides, always call to confirm times. The crew provides valuable commentary on the major sights along the voyage. **Trains** leave from Charing Cross, Cannon St., and London Bridge for Greenwich (less than 20min., day return £2.80). The DLR whizzes from Tower Gateway to Island Gardens (16min., Mon.-Fri. only). From there Greenwich is just a 10-minute walk through the foot tunnel. Bus #188 runs between Euston and Greenwich stopping at Kinsway, Aldwych, and Waterloo. If you plan on seeing all of the major sites, it's a good idea to buy a passport ticket for admission to the Observatory, National Maritime Museum, Queen's House (a 17th-century restrored edifice), and the *Cutty Sark.* The ticket is good for up to one year (£7.95, children £5.45, families £14.95). The friendly **Greenwich Tourist Information Centre,** 46 Greenwich Church St., SE10 (tel. (0181) 858 6376; open daily 10am-5pm; reduced winter hours) will go out of their way to arrange a variety of afternoon tours (£2.50-3, 1½ hr.).

RICHMOND

Ever since Henry I came up the Thames in the 12th century, Richmond has preened its royal pedigree. Although Henry VII's Richmond Palace was demolished during Cromwell's Commonwealth, the town has not lost its dignified sheen; the 18th-century houses around **Richmond Green** make it possibly the most serene park in or around London. The **Richmond Tourist Information Centre,** in the old Town Hall on Whittaker Ave., has complete information on Richmond and surrounding areas (tel. (0181) 940 9125; BR or tube: Richmond; open Mon.-Sat. 10am-6pm, Sun. 10:15am-4:15pm, reduced winter hours).

Richmond Park's 2500 acres were once a royal hunting ground, and are still home to several hundred nervous deer who share the grounds with thousands of tourists and the Royal Ballet School, housed in the Palladian White Lodge. Across Richmond Bridge, on Richmond Rd., the gleaming cube of **Marble Hill House** (tel. (081) 892 5115) perches on the Thames, amid vast trimmed lawns. Like its contemporary Chiswick House, it is a villa inspired by both Palladio and Inigo Jones. The Great Room, on the first floor, is lavishly decorated with gilt and carvings by James Richards and the original Panini paintings of ancient Rome. During the summer, a series of outdoor concerts are held on the grounds. (See Entertainment: Classical Music; house open daily 10am-6pm; Nov.-March Wed.-Sun. 10am-4pm; free.)

KEW GARDENS

After days of sight-seeing in central London, the **Royal Botanic Gardens** (tel. (0181) 940 1171) at Kew provide a restorative breath of fresh air. Yet another example of the Empire's encyclopedic collecting frenzy, the Royal Botanic Gardens at Kew display thousands of flowers, plants, bushes, fruits, trees, and vegetables from the world over, spread over 300 perfectly maintained acres. Inside, not far from the front gate stands **Kew Palace.** Built in 1631 but leased as a royal residence since 1730, this inconspicuous summer home of King George III and Queen Charlotte has evolved into a small museum depicting the vagaries of late-18th-century monarchical life. You can spend hours with the royal toy collection inside or the well-documented herb garden out back (palace open daily 11am-5:30pm. £1, students and seniors 75p). The gardens comprise several buildings and sections, each containing different exhibits. The moist and tropical **Palm House,** a unique masterpiece of Victorian engineering built in 1848, will stun you with the revelation that bananas are in fact giant herbs. Climb the white spiral stairs to the upper gallery for the toucan's-eye view. Although replete with voluptuous fronds, the Palm House is dwarfed by its younger Victorian sibling, the **Temperate House.** The climate here nurtures 3000 species, arranged according to geographical origins in its 50,000 square feet. The lush South American Rainforest species section surpasses all others. The **Princess of Wales Conservatory** allows you to browse through ten different tropical climates; it's just a few steps from a rainforest to an arid desert.

The calming way to reach Kew is by boat from Westminster pier (2/hr. 10:30am-3:30pm, 1½hr., return £9) and the cheapest way is by tube or BR North London line (Kew Gardens station, zone 3). (Gardens open Mon.-Fri. 9:30am-6:30pm, Sat.-Sun. and bank holidays 9:30am-7:30pm; last entry 30 min. before closing. Glasshouses open Mon.-Fri. 9:30am-7:30pm, Sat., Sun., and bank holidays 9:30am-6pm. £4, student and seniors £2, children 5-16 £1.50, under 5 free, last-hour entry £1.50.) **Tours** leave Victoria Gate (Fri.-Wed. 11am and 2:30pm, £1, seniors, students, and children 50p).

HAMPTON COURT

Compared to Buckingham Palace's drab facade, Hampton Court (tel. (0181) 781 9500 or (0181) 781 9666 for recorded information) seems better fit for royalty. Cardinal Wolsey built it in 1514, showing Henry VIII by his example how to act the part of a splendid and all-powerful ruler. Henry learned the lesson well and confiscated the Court in 1525, when Wolsey fell out of favor.

Inside, you can see two curiosities of Renaissance art: the **tapestries** woven from the Raphael cartoons in the Victoria and Albert Museum, and a roomful of grisaille work originally by Mantegna but poorly repainted in the 18th century. You'll also find a selection of paintings from the royal collection. Note the intriguing ceilings, woodwork, and ornaments, especially in the downstairs kitchen and cellars. The **King's Apartments** are newly restored after a 1986 fire; cool down with a snack in Elizabeth I's Privy Kitchen.

Sixty marvelous acres of Palace gardens are open and free, and contain some highly celebrated amusements, including the famous **maze** (open March-Oct.), a hedgerow labyrinth first planted in 1714 that served as the prototype for such later structures as Stanley Kubrick's Overlook Hotel; the great vine planted in 1769 that still produces grapes and now encloses a whole room with its foliage; and the indoor tennis court (built in 1529), still used by "real tennis" purists. Henry's is one of only four courts left in England designed for this early squash-like brand of the game (open March-Oct.). Also note the exhibit of Tijou's ironwork gates, left free-standing for the most part, and admirable from all sides. (Hampton Court open Mon. 10:15am-6pm, Tues.-Sun. 9:30am-6pm; Oct.-March Mon. 10:15am-4:30pm, Tues.-Sun. 9:30am-4:30pm; last admission 45min. before closing. Palace, courtyard, cloister, and maze £7, concessions £5.30, under 16 £4.70, under 5 free, families £19.30. Maze only £1.75, under 16 £1.10.) BR trains run from Waterloo to Hampton Court (2/hr.; 35 min., day return £3.60). From the first Mon. before Easter until the end of Sept., a boat runs from Westminster Pier to Hampton Court (3/morning; 3½hrs; roundtrip £9).

WINDSOR & ETON

Royalty is a national obsession, and **Windsor Castle** (tel. (01753) 868 286 or (01753) 831 118 for 24-hr. information line) contains the majestic ingredients—chivalry and pageantry, ramparts and guardsmen—from which the regal mythology has been constructed. The castle dominates this river town of cobbled lanes and tea shops surrounded by the 4800-acre Great Park, far away from London in the farming country of Surrey. Built by William the Conqueror as a fortress rather than as a residence, it has grown over nine centuries into the world's largest inhabited castle.

You can saunter blithely in and out of its labyrinthine terraces, and enjoy beautiful views of the Thames Valley.

Windsor is notorious to contemporary visitors as the site of a fire which helped make 1992 an *annus horribilis* for the royal family, and reduced the extent to which the public involuntarily subsidizes the royals' senselessly posh existence. The influential conflagration blazed for nine hours on November 20, 1992, and was only extinguished through the efforts of 225 firefighters and 39 fire engines. Six rooms and three towers were destroyed or badly damaged by smoke and flames, although 80% of the state rooms escaped harm. Consequently, admission to the castle grounds has been jacked up in an attempt to raise the funds needed to repair the fire damage; visistors pay once upon entering the grounds, and will pay again if they chose to visit certain wings of the castle. Visitors touring the intact sections of Windsor will see **St. George's Chapel** (tel. (01753) 865 538) rising across the courtyard as they first enter the castle grounds. The chapel is a sumptuous 15th-century building with delicate fan vaulting and an amazing wall of stained glass dedicated to the Order of the Garter (open Mon.-Sat. 10am-4pm, Sun. 2-4pm; £3; students, seniors, and children £1.80; family of 5 £6). Here Henry VIII rests in a surprisingly modest tomb near George V, Edward IV, Charles I, and Henry VI. A ceremonial procession of the Knights of the Garter, led by the Queen, takes place here in June.

Past the gargoyles of Norman Gate, built by Edward III, at the castle's top end, you can visit the elegantly furnished **state apartments** (£4, seniors £2.50, children £1.50). These formal rooms are richly decorated with artwork from the massive Royal Collection, including works by Holbein, Rubens, Rembrandt, and an entire room of Van Dycks. (The state apartments are closed Dec. 22-Jan. 2.) In the same wing is **Queen Mary's dolls' house** and the **Gallery.** Windsor's impressive changing of the guard takes place at 11am. (Grounds open daily 10am-5pm; Nov.-March daily 10am-4pm; state apartments, dolls' house, and gallery open daily 10am-5pm; Nov.-March daily 10am-4pm. Admission to the grounds Mon.-Sat. £8, Sun. £5; over 60 Mon.-Sat. £5.50, Sun. £3.50; under 17 Mon.-Sat. £4, Sun. £2.50; family of 4 Mon.-Sat. £18, Sun. £11.50. Last admission 1 hr. before closing.)

Follow the road that bears left around royal grounds to come to the entrance to **Windsor Great Park,** a huge expanse of parkland where deer graze and the royals ride. The Long Walk leads through the park towards the Copper Horse statue. At the other end of the park lie the Savill Gardens and the Smith's Lawn polo fields, where accident-prone Prince Charles used to play. Windsor's old town is directly across the road from the castle gate.

About 15 minutes down Thames St. and across the river is **Eton College,** the pre-eminent public (that is, private) school founded by Henry VI in 1440. Eton boys still wear tailcoats to every class, and solemnly raise one finger in greeting to any teacher on the street. Wellington claimed that the Battle of Waterloo was "won on the playing fields of Eton": catch a glimpse of the uniquely brutal "Wall Game" and see why. Eton has molded some notable dissidents and revolutionaries—Percy Bysshe Shelley, Aldous Huxley, George Orwell, and even former Liberal Party leader Jeremy Thorpe. John Le Carré taught here, and Denys Finch-Hatton, portrayed in *Out of Africa* by Robert Redford, is memorialized in the bridge by the cricket pitches. The Queen is the sole (honorary) female Old Etonian—although each of Eton's houses has a resident "dame," an elderly matron who possesses domestic skills that Eton boys aren't expected to cultivate (open July-Aug. daily 10:30am-4:30pm; May-June and Oct.-March daily 2-4:30pm; £2.20, children £1.50.) It costs one or two more pounds on a **tour** to see more of the school.

British Rail (tel. 262 6767) serves Windsor and Eton Central station and Windsor and Eton Riverside station, both of which are near Windsor Castle (street signs point the way unmistakably). Trains leave from Victoria or Paddington via Slough or directly from Waterloo to Riverside (2/hr.; 45min.; cheap day return £5). Green Line **coaches** (tel. (0181) 668 7261) #700, 701, and 702 also make the trip from their station on Eccleston Bridge, behind Victoria Station (70-90min., day return £4.35-5.50).

The **tourist office** (tel. (01753) 852 010) is in the Central station (open Easter-Sept. daily 10am-4pm).

■■■ MUSEUMS

Rainy days, although quite numerous here, will not suffice for London's museums—you may find yourself drawn indoors even in the best of weather. Weekday mornings tend to be the most peaceful. Admission is usually free, but many museums, no longer heavily subsidized by the government, now charge or request a £1-2 donation. Most charge for special exhibits and offer student and senior citizen discounts ("concessions"). Many museums sponsor free films and lectures.

BRITISH MUSEUM

The sheer volume of the British Museum's collections stands as a comprehensive document of the political, military, and economic power of the British Empire. Wandering through 2½ mi. of galleries may frustrate even the most die-hard museumgoer. To catch the main attractions, buy the £2.50 short guide. **Guided tours** (£6; 1½hrs.) cover the highlights, and can be booked for groups no larger than 10 at the information desk or by phone at 323 8599.

From the main entrance on Great Russell St., the British Library galleries are to the right. In the **Manuscript Room,** the **English Literature** displays include manuscripts from *Beowulf* (c. 1000) and the *Canterbury Tales* (1410), as well as the scrawlings of various contemporary writers. **Biblical displays** include ravishing illuminated texts and the Celtic *Lindesfarne Gospels.* The **Historical Documents** section proffers epistles by many famous historical figures, and two copies of the *Magna Carta.* **Music displays** show off works by Handel, and Stravinsky.

The **King's Library** contains the Gutenberg Bible and Shakespeare's First Folio. Samples of Chinese calligraphy, early Japanese printed books, manuscripts in Hebrew and Arabic, and Sanskrit scriptures provide glimpses into the role of books in various cultures. Although you'll need a reader's pass in order to study in the circular **Reading Room** where Marx wrote *Das Kapital*, visitors are allowed to see the room briefly Mon.-Fri. at 2:15pm and 4:15pm.

The outstanding **ancient Egypt** collection occupies rooms on the ground and upper floors. Entering the ground floor gallery, the **Rosetta Stone,** discovered in 1799 by French soldiers, rests to the left. Its Greek text enabled Champollion to finally crack the hieroglyphic code. The head of Ramses II, famed for his arrogance towards Joseph and higher beings in Exodus, dominates the northern section of Room 25. In the side gallery 25a, don't miss three of the finest and best known Theban tomb paintings. The central gallery is filled with tributes to the animal world. The upstairs Egyptian gallery contains brilliant sarcophagi and grisly mummies. Delicate papyri include the *Book of the Dead of Ani.*

The **Greek antiquities** exhibits are dominated by the **Elgin Marbles,** 5th-century BC reliefs from the Parthenon, now residing in the spacious Duveen Gallery. In 1810, Lord Elgin "procured" the statues and pieces of the Parthenon frieze while serving as ambassador to Constantinople. Every so often, the Greeks renew their efforts to convince the British government to return the marbles. The marbles comprise three main groups: the frieze, which portrays the most important Athenian civic festivals; the metopes, which depict incidents from the battle of the Lapiths and Centaurs (symbolizing the triumph of "civilization" over "barbarism"); and the remains of large statues that stood in the east and west pediments of the building.

Other Greek highlights include two of the Seven Wonders of the Ancient World. Once crowded by a four-horse chariot, the **Mausoleum at Halicarnassus** and the **Temple of Artemis,** were built to replace the one buried by Herostratus in 356 BC.

Among the many sculptures of the **Roman antiquities,** the dark blue glass of the **Portland Vase,** the inspiration for ceramic designer Josiah Wedgewood, stands out. The **Roman-Britain** section includes the **Mindenhall Treasure,** a magnificent collection of 4th-century silver tableware. Nearby crouches **Lindow Man,** an Iron Age

Celt supposedly sacrificed in a gruesome ritual and preserved by peat-bog. The **Sutton Hoo Ship Burial,** an Anglo-Saxon ship buried in Suffolk complete with an unknown king, is the centerpiece of the **Middle Ages** galleries.

The majority of the museum's **Oriental Collections** reside in the recently refurbished Gallery 33. The gallery's eastern half is dedicated to the Chinese collection, and the western half is filled by Indian and Southeast Asian exhibits, which include the largest collection of Indian religious sculpture outside of India. Upstairs, the collection continues with a series of three galleries displaying Japanese artifacts, paintings, and calligraphy.

1994 witnessed the opening of two new museum galleries: **Renaissance to the 20th Century** and the **Mexican Gallery.**

The museum is located at Great Russell St., WC1 (tel. 636 1555 or 580 1788 for recorded information; tube: Tottenham Ct. Rd., Goodge St., Russell Sq., or Holborn). The rear entrance, with access to certain galleries, is on Montague St. For recorded information on wheelchair accessibility, call 637 7384. Persons who are blind or visually-impaired should enquire about the tactile exhibits; a **touch tour** of Roman sculptures is given in room 84 in the basement—ask about it at the main information desk. (Open Mon.-Sat. 10am-5pm, Sun. 2:30-6pm. Admission is free, but the larger, special exhibits cost £3, seniors and students £2.)

NATIONAL GALLERY

The National Gallery maintains one of the world's finest collections of Western painting, especially strong in works by Rembrandt, Rubens, and Renaissance Italian painters. The Berggruen Collection of works from the turn of this century, including many Impressionist works and a large selection of Picassos, has been temporarily loaned to the National.

You can spend days in this maze of galleries, renovated and rehung in 1992. A helpful guide is the **Micro Gallery,** a computerized, illustrated catalogue which cross-references works, and can print out a free personal tour mapping the locations of the paintings you want to see (open Mon.-Sat. 10am-5:30pm, Sun. 2-5:30pm).

The National's collection is divided into four color-coded sections; paintings within these sections are arranged by school. The collection starts in the new **Sainsbury Wing,** to the west of the main building, with works painted from 1260 to 1510. Paintings from 1510 to 1600 are found in the **West Wing,** to the left of the Trafalgar Sq. entrance. Titian's *Bacchus and Ariadne* displays his mastery of contrast. Stormy El Grecos are featured here as well. Strong collections of Rembrandt and Rubens adorn the **North Wing.** Van Dyck's *Equestrian Portrait of Charles I* headlines the State Portrait room.

The **East Wing,** to the right of the main entrance, is devoted to painting from 1700 to 1920, including a strong English collection. The natural light provides the perfect setting for viewing the paintings; many, such as Turner's *Rain, Steam, and Speed,* seem to acquire a special luminosity. Impressionist works include a number of Monet's near-abstract waterlilies, Cézanne's *Old Woman with Roses,* and Rousseau's rainswept *Tropical Storm with a Tiger.* Picasso's *Fruit Dish, Bottle, and Violin* (1914), the National Gallery's initial foray into the abstract, has since been joined by another room of Picasso's work.

The National Gallery holds frequent special exhibitions in the basement galleries of the Sainsbury Wing, which usually cost £2-4. Free hour-long guided tours which introduce visitors to the collection's major works depart from the Sainsbury wing (Mon.-Fri. at 11:30am and 2:30pm, Sat. at 2 and 3:30pm). The gallery is located in Trafalgar Sq., WC2 (tel. 389 1785 or 839 3526 for recorded information; tube: Charing Cross or Leicester Sq.). Disabled access is on the north side at the Orange St. entrance. (Open Mon.-Sat. 10am-6pm, Sun. 2-6pm. Free.)

NATIONAL PORTRAIT GALLERY

This unofficial *Who's Who in Britain* began in 1856 as "the fulfillment of a patriotic and moral ideal"—namely to showcase Britain's officially noteworthy citizens. The museum's declared principle of looking "to the celebrity of the person represented, rather than to the merit of the artist" does not seem to have affected the quality of the works displayed—many are by such top portraitists as Reynolds, Lawrence, Holbein, Sargent, and Gainsborough. The museum sucessfully melds together different media of portraiture, like sculpture, sketches, caricatures, and photographs.

The 9000 paintings have been arranged more or less chronologically. The earliest portraits hang in the top story. Follow the flow of British history through the galleries: from the War of the Roses (Yorks and Lancasters), to the Civil War (Cromwell and his buddies), to the American Revolution (George Washington), to imperial days (Florence Nightingale), and on to modern times (Margaret Thatcher).

Level four, dedicated to Henry VIII and predecessors, cherishes the Holbein cartoon of the king. Famous geologists, politicians, reformers, and fops populate the Victorian section, along with literary figures. Charming "informal" portraits of the royal family are displayed on the mezzanine.

The first floor is jammed with displays of the 20th century, from Churchill to Peter Gabriel; the modern works take more amusing liberties with their likenesses.

The gallery portrays at St. Martin's Pl., WC2, just opposite St. Martin's in the Fields (tel. 306 0055; tube: Charing Cross or Leicester Sq.; open Mon.-Fri. 10am-5pm, Sat. 10am-6pm, Sun. 12-6pm; lectures Tues.-Fri. 1:10pm, Sat. 3pm; free, except for some temporary exhibits £1-3.) The new Orange St. entrance has a wheelchair ramp, and there is a lift to all floors. Sign-interpreted talks are now regular: call extension #216.

TATE GALLERY

The Tate Gallery opened in 1897 expressly to display contemporary British art. Since then, the gallery has widened its scope, obtaining a superb collection of British works from the 16th century to the present and a distinguished ensemble of international modern art.

The Tate's **British collection** starts with a room at the far end of the gallery devoted to 16th- and 17th-century painting. The parade of Constables includes the famous views of Salisbury Cathedral, and a number of Hampstead scenes. George Stubbs's enlivening landscapes and sporting scenes lead to Gainsborough's landscapes and Sir Joshua Reynolds's portraits. Don't miss the visionary works of poet, philosopher, and painter William Blake. The paintings in each of the 30 rooms of the main gallery are organized chronologically and grouped by theme, offering a clear perspective on the development of British art.

The Tate's outstanding **modern collection** of international 20th-century art emphasizes th erelationship between British and foreign art movements. Sculptures by Henry Moore, Epstein, Eric Gill, and Barbara Hepworth, in addition to Rodin's **The Kiss,** are found in the Cuveen Sculpture Galleries. The works of Monet, Degas, Van Gogh, Beardsley, Matisse, and the Camden Town Group hang to the left of the entrance. Paintings by members of the Bloomsbury Group, Picasso, Dalí, and Francis Bacon, sculptures by Modigliani and Giacometti, and samples of modern art lie to the right of the central hall. The Tate's 300-work J.M.W. Turner collection resides in the **Clore Gallery.** The collection covers all of Turner's career, from early, dreamy landscapes such as *Chevening Park* to the later visionary works.

(Free tours run Mon.-Fri. at 11am for British Art before 1900, noon for Highlights of the Collection (Sat. at 3pm, Sun. 3:45pm), 2pm for Early Modern Art, and 3pm for Later Modern Art. Free lectures Mon.-Sat. at 1pm, Sun. at 2:30pm.) The Tate is located at Millbank, SW1 (tel. 821 1313; tube: Pimlico; open Mon.-Sat. 10am-5:50pm, Sun. 2-5:50pm; free).

VICTORIA & ALBERT MUSEUM

Housing the best collection of Italian Renaissance sculpture outside Italy, the greatest collection of Indian art outside India, and the world center for John Constable studies, the mind-bogglingly inclusive V&A has practically perfected the display of fine and applied arts.

Reopening in late 1995 after extensive renovation, the stars of the **Renaissance collection** (ren-NAY-sonce if you're snooty) are the famed *Raphael Cartoons*—seven of the 10 large, full-color sketches done by Raphael and his apprentices as tapestry patterns for the Sistine Chapel. The endless galleries of Italian sculpture include Donatello's *Ascension* and *Madonna and Child.* The **Medieval Treasury,** in the center of the ground floor, features stained glass and illuminations.

Plaster cast reproductions of European sculpture and architecture occupy rooms 46A-B on the ground floor. Next door, test the knowledge you've gained here to distinguish impostors from the real things in the **Fakes and Forgeries gallery.**

The V&A's formidable **Asian collections** have recently been supplemented by the Nehru Gallery of Indian Art and the T.T. Tsui Gallery of Chinese Art. The **Nehru gallery** contains splendid examples of textiles, painting, Mughal jewelry and decor, and revealing displays on European imperial conduct.

The simply elegant **Tsui gallery** divides its 5000-year span of Chinese art into six areas of life—Eating and Drinking, Living, Worship, Ruling, Collecting, and Burial. Treasures include the Sakyamuni Buddha and an Imperial Throne. The **Toshiba Gallery of Japanese Art** has a prime collection of lacquer art, as well as traditional armor and intriguing contemporary sculpture. The V&A's displays of **Islamic Art** are punctuated by the intricacies of Persian carpets and Moroccan rugs.

The first floor holds the sizeable collection of **British art and design.** International design classics—mostly chairs—grace "Twentieth Century Design." The **jewelry collection** (rooms 91-93—actually a pilfer-proof vault!) includes pieces dating from 2000 BC. The **National Art Library,** located on the first floor, houses Beatrix Potter originals as well as first editions of Winnie the Pooh. The new **Frank Lloyd Wright gallery** on the second floor of the Henry Cole Wing displays the Wright-designed interior of the Kauffmann Office, the V&A's first 20th-century period room. The exquisitely redesigned **Glass Gallery** recently reopened in room C-131.

Photography aficionados will want to visit the **Print Room** (#503 in the Henry Cole Wing). The print collection encompasses both the incipient stages of the medium and the most contemporary products.

The V&A offers scores of special events. (Introductory museum tours Mon.-Sat. 11am, noon, 2, and 3pm, Sun. at 3pm. Theme tours Mon.-Sat. 11:30am, 1:30, and 2:30pm. Numerous free lectures. Fantastic 45-minute tours for children; call for details. The V&A often provides special "gallery trail" guides for children.) The V&A is located on Cromwell Rd., SW7 (tel. 938 8500, 938 8441 for 24-hr. recorded information, or 938 8349 for current exhibitions; tube: South Kensington or buses #C1, 14, and 74; open Mon. noon-5:50pm, Tues.-Sun. 10am-5:50pm; free; suggested donation £4.50, seniors and students £1). Wheelchair users are advised to use the side entrance on Exhibition Rd. Gallery tours and taped tours are available for the visually impaired.

■ OTHER MAJOR COLLECTIONS

Cabinet War Rooms, Clive Steps, King Charles St., SW1 (tel. 930 6961 or 735 8922). Tube: Westminster. Follow the signs from Whitehall. Churchill and his cabinet ran a nation at war from this secret warren of underground rooms. See the room where Churchill made his famous wartime broadcasts and listen to cuts of some of his speeches. Open daily 10am-6pm. Last entrance 5:15pm. £3.90, seniors £3, students £2.80, under 16 £1.90, families £10.

The Courtauld Institute, Somerset House, the Strand, WC2 (tel. 873 2549), across from the corner of Aldwych and the Strand. Tube: Temple or Aldwych (rush hour only). An intimate 11-room gallery displays mostly Impressionist and post-Impressionist masterpieces. The collection features some of the most famous works by Cézanne, Degas, Gauguin, Seurat, and Renoir, plus Van Gogh's *Portrait of the Artist with a Bandaged Ear,* and Manet's *Bar aux Folies Bergère.* The Institute's other collections include early Italian religious works and Oskar Kokoschka's stunning *Prometheus Triptych.* Open Mon.-Sat. 10am-6pm, Sun. 2-6pm. £3, seniors and students £1.50.

The Design Museum, Butlers Wharf, Shad Thames, SE1 (tel. 403 6933 or 407 6261). Tube: London Bridge, then follow signs on Tooley St, or Tower Hill and cross the Tower Bridge. Housed in an appropriately Bauhausy box on the river, this museum is dedicated to mass-produced classics of culture and industry, such as the automotive bombshell dropped by the Citroën DS in the 1950s. Happily, you *can* sit in some of the century's most influential chairs. Open Mon.-Fri. 11:30am-6pm, Sat.-Sun. noon-6pm. £4.50, seniors and students £3.50.

Imperial War Museum, Lambeth Rd., SE1 (tel. 416 5000). Tube: Lambeth North or Elephant & Castle. Do not be misled by the jingoistic resonance of the name; this museum is a moving reminder of the brutal human cost of war. The atrium is filled with tanks and planes; the eloquent testimony to war's horror is downstairs. Gripping exhibits illuminate every aspect of two world wars, in every medium possible. The Blitz and Trench Experiences recreate every sad detail (even smells); veterans and victims speak through telephone handsets. The powerful Belsen exhibit documents the genocide of the concentration camps and the story of the rescue and rehabilitation of survivors. Documents worth seeing include the "peace in our time" agreement that Neville Chamberlain triumphantly brought back from Munich in 1938, and Adolf Hitler's "political testament," dictated in the chancellery bunker. Open daily 10am-6pm. £3.90, students £2.90, children £1.95, families £10.50. Free daily 4:30-6pm.

Institute of Contemporary Arts, the Mall, SW1 (tel. 930 3647 or 930 3647 for recorded information). Tube: Piccadilly Circus or Charing Cross. Entrance is located on the Mall at the foot of the Duke of York steps. Vigorous outpost of the avant garde in visual and performance art. 3 galleries, a cinema featuring first-run independent films, experimental space for film and video, theatre, seminars and lectures (£2-5.50), video library, and readings (call for schedule). Galleries open Sat.-Thurs. noon-7:30pm, Fri. noon-9pm. £1.50.

London Transport Museum, Covent Garden, WC2 (tel. 379 6344). Tube: Covent Garden. On the east side of the Covent Garden piazza. Reopened in Dec. 1993 after 9 months and £4 million worth of renovations, the museum now boasts two new mezzanine floors, two new air-conditioned galleries, and a variety of interactive video displays. In addition to high-tech displays like the subway simulator, low-tech exhibits provide a thought-provoking cultural history: see how the expansion of the transportation system fed the growth of suburbs. London Transport design also features prominently throughout: learn about the history of the Johnston typeface you see everywhere on the tube. Don't miss the excellent temporary exhibits, drawn largely from the museum's photo, map, and poster archives. Opens daily 10am-6pm, last admission 5:15pm. £3.95, seniors and students £2.50, families £10, group rates available. Wheelchair accessible. MC, Visa.

Madame Tussaud's, Marylebone Rd., NW1 (tel. 935 6861). Tube: Baker St. The classic waxwork museum. Models are disconcertingly lifelike. The more macabre exhibits, like the display of famous psycopaths and wife-murderers from English history, are essentially gratuitous titillation designed to keep the crowds rolling in. And roll in they do; one of the U.K.'s top tourist attractions, Madame Tussaud's is best visited in the morning to get a good view of the most popular collections. To avoid the horrific queues, form a group with at least nine fellow sufferers and use the group entrance. Open Mon.-Fri. 10am-5:30pm, Sat.-Sun. 9:30am-5:30pm. £7.40, children £4.75, seniors £5.50, families (2 adults, 2 children) £19.95. A distinctive green dome shelters the adjacent **Planetarium.** £4.20, children £2.60, seniors £3.25, families £11. Combined admission £9.95, children £6.25, seniors £7.55, families £25.95.

Museum of London, 150 London Wall, EC2 (tel. 600 3699 or 600 0807 for 24-hr. info.). Tube: St. Paul's or Barbican. This fabulously engrossing museum tells every aspect of the story of the metropolis from its origins as Londinium to the present. The Nursery Garden flourishes at the museum's center (garden closes at 5:20 pm). Free lectures Wed.-Fri. 1:10pm. Open Tues.-Sat. 10am-6pm, Sun. noon-6pm, last entry 5:30pm. Open Bank Holidays 10am-6pm. £3, students £1.50, families £7.50, free after 4:30pm. Wheelchair accessible.

Museum of the Moving Image (MOMI), South Bank Centre, SE1 (tel. 928 3232 or 401 2636 for 24-hr. information). Tube: Waterloo, or Embankment and cross the

Hungerford footbridge. The entertaining museum charts the development of image-making with light, from Chinese shadow puppets to film and telly. Costumed actor-guides lead you through interactive exhibits—act out your favorite western, read the TV news, or watch your own superimposed image fly over the River Thames. Open daily 10am-6pm; last entry 5pm. £5.50, children 5-16 £4, disabled £4, students with ID £4.70, family £16. Prices are subject to review in 1995.

Natural History Museum, Cromwell Rd., SW7 (tel. 938 9123 or 938 9242 for group bookings). Tube: South Kensington. The museum's personality is split between a glorious but ultimately dull Victorian past (the world's largest collection of metalliferous ores) and a high-tech present (buttons, levers, and microscopes galore). Permanent exhibits include "Discovering Mammals," "Creepy Crawlies," "Ecology: A Greenhouse Effect," "Primates," and the superb dinosaur exhibits, with tantalizing computer displays. The interactive Discovery Centre for children and other hands-on enthusiasts is matchless. Open Mon.-Sat. 10am-6pm, Sun. 11am-6pm. £5, seniors and students £2.50, families (up to 2 adults and 4 children) £13.50. Free Mon.-Fri. 4:30-6pm, Sat.-Sun. 5-6pm. Wheelchair accessible.

Royal Academy, Piccadilly, W1 (tel. 439 7438), across from no. 185. Tube: Green Park or Piccadilly Circus. The academy frequently hosts traveling exhibits of the highest order. The whopping annual summer exhibition is a British institution where the works of established and unknown contemporary artists are reviewed at the deliberate rate of 10/min. Open daily 10am-6pm. £5, students and seniors about £3, under 18 about £2. Summer exhibitions £4.50, students and seniors £3, under 18 £2.25. Advance tickets occasionally necessary for popular exhibitions.

Shakespeare's Globe Museum, Bear Gardens, SE1 (tel. 928 6342). Tube: London Bridge. Theatre memorabilia, balsa-wood replicas of Elizabethan theatres, and a full-size stage upstairs. The museum is also in the midst of an ongoing project to build an exact copy of the Globe Theatre on an adjacent parking lot. Open Mon.-Sat. 10am-5pm, Sun. 2-5:30pm. £3, seniors and students £2.

Sir John Soane's Museum, 13 Lincoln's Inn Fields, WC2 (tel. 405 2107). Tube: Holborn. Soane was an architect's architect, but the home he designed for himself will intrigue even lay persons. Window-sized, inset, and convex mirrors placed strategically throughout the house for lighting effects also create skewed angles and weird distortions. The columns in the Colonnade room support a room-within-a-room above. Famous artifacts on display include Hogarth paintings, the massive sarcophagus of Seti I, and casts of famous buildings and scupltures from around the world. Open Tues.-Sat. 10am-5pm; lecture tour Sat. at 2:30pm (arrive by 2pm). Free.

Theatre Museum, 1e Tavistock St., WC2 (tel. 836 7891). Tube: Covent Garden. Public entrance on Russell St., off the east end of the Covent Garden piazza. This branch of the V&A contains Britain's richest holding of theatrical memorabilia. Exhibits include models of historical and present-day theaters, as well as other stage-related arts, such as ballet, opera, puppetry, the circus, and rock music. Box office just inside the door sells tickets to West End plays, musicals, and concerts with negligible mark-up in most cases. Box office open Tues.-Sat. 11am-8pm, Sun. 11am-7pm. Museum open Tues.-Sun. 11am-7pm. £3; students, seniors, and under 14 £1.50; family £7.

■■■ ENTERTAINMENT

On any given day or night, Londoners and visitors can choose from the widest range of entertainment a city can offer. Suffering competition only from Broadway, the West End is the world's theatre capital, supplemented by an adventurous "fringe." Music scenes range from the black ties of the Royal Opera House to Wembley mobs and nightclub raves. The work of British filmmakers is shown in cinemas all over the city. Dance, comedy, and sporting events can leave you poring in bewilderment over the listings in *Time Out* (£1.50) and *What's On* (£1). **Artsline** (tel. 388 2227) provides information about disabled access (Mon.-Fri. 9:30am-5:30pm).

■ THEATER

ENTERTAINMENT: THEATER

The stage for a national dramatic tradition dating from Shakespeare's day, London maintains unrivalled standards in theatre. The renowned Royal Academy for the Dramatic Arts draws students from around the globe. Playwrights such as Tom Stoppard and Alan Ayckbourn premier their works in the West End; class-conscious political dramas, younger writers, and performance artists uphold a vibrant "fringe" scene; and Shakespearean and Jacobean revenge tragedies are revived everywhere. Tickets are relatively inexpensive; the cheapest seats in most theatres cost about £8, progressing upward to £22 for orchestra seats. Previews and matinees cost a few pounds less, and many theatres offer dirt-cheap **student/senior standbys** (indicated by "concs," "concessions," or "S" in newspaper and *Time Out* listings)—around £7 shortly before curtain with ID (come two hours beforehand to be sure of a seat). **Day seats** are sold to the public from 9 or 10am on the day of the performance at a reduced price, but you must queue up even earlier to snag one. If a show is sold out, returned tickets may be sold (at full price) just before curtain. Most theatres also offer senior citizen discounts on advance ticket purchases for weekday matinees. For the latest on standbys for West End shows, call the **Student Theatreline** (tel. 379 8900; updated from 2pm daily).

The **Leicester Square Ticket Booth** sells tickets at half-price (plus £1.50 booking fee) on the day of the performance, but carries only tickets for the West End, Barbican, and National Theatre. Tickets are sold from the top of the pile, which means you can't choose a seat and the most expensive seats are sold first. Lines are the worst on Saturday (open for matinees Mon.-Sat. noon-2pm, for evening shows 2:30-6:30pm; cash only; max. 4/person). If you schlep to a box office in person, you can select your seats from the theatre seating plan (box offices usually open 10am-8pm). Reserve seats by calling the box office and then paying by post or in person within three days, or by calling the **First Call booking office** (tel. 497 9977; booking fee for some shows) for West End shows. Credit card holders can charge the tickets over the phone but must produce the card when picking up tickets.

London's "West End" of theater consists of forty-odd houses scattered about Covent Garden, Leicester Square, and Piccadilly, plus the following special institutions:

Barbican Theatre, Barbican Centre, EC2 (tel. 628 2295 for 24-hr. information or tel. 638 8891 for reservations). Tube: Barbican or Moorgate. London home of the Royal Shakespeare Company. Tickets for the main theatre, the **Barbican,** £7.50-22; weekday matinees £6-12; Sat. matinees and previews £8-16. Student and senior citizen standbys bookable in person or by telephone from 9am on the day of the performance, £6.50-8 (1/person). Fascinating futuristic auditorium; each row of seats in the Barbican has its own side door through which patrons enter the theatre (there are no aisles). The forward-leaning balconies guarantee that no one sits farther than 65ft. from center stage, and every seat in the house gives a clear view. Stick around at the interval to watch the shiny metal safety curtain seal off the stage. Jacobean, Restoration, and experimental contemporary works in the tiny black-box second theatre, **The Pitt,** evenings and Sat. matinees £15, previews £13, midweek matinees £12. Student and senior standbys available from 9am the day of the performance, £6.50. There are always several signed and audio-described performances during the run of each show. Box office (on Level 5 of the Centre) open daily 9am-8pm. Major credit cards.

Royal National Theatre, South Bank Centre, SE1 (tel. 928 2252). Tube: Waterloo, or Embankment and cross the Hungerford footbridge. The brilliant repertory companies in the **Olivier** and **Lyttleton** theatres (£6-22) put up classics from Shakespeare to Ibsen as well as mainstream contemporary drama. The smaller **Cottesloe** (£6-14) plays with more experimental works like Kushner's *Angels in America*. All 3 theatres are well-raked and have widely spaced rows, so even the rear balcony seats offer an unobstructed view of the stage. 40 day seats in each of the 3 theatres (Olivier, Lyttleton, and Cottesloe) reduced to £7-13 at 10am on day of performance. General standby seats sold from 2hr. before performance at £8-10; student and senior standby 45min. before show £6. **Backstage tours** Mon.-

Sat. £3.50, seniors and students £2.50; call 633 0880 for times. **Box office** open Mon.-Sat. 10am-8pm.

Open Air Theatre, Inner Circle, Regent's Park, NW1 (tel. 486 2431 or 486 1933 for bookings). Tube: Baker St. or Regent's Park. Mostly Shakespeare; sit in the front to catch every word. Bring a blanket and a bottle of wine. Performances in summer Mon.-Tues. and Fri. at 8pm; Wed.-Thurs. and Sat. at 2:30 and 8pm.

London's **fringe,** born in the late 1960s, mixes the intimate with the avant-garde. The renaissance of experimental drama abides in London's fringe theaters, presenting low-priced, high-quality plays. Check the fringe listings in *Time Out* or the *Evening Standard* and phone the theater in advance for details.

Lunchtime theater productions are generally less serious than evening performances, but at £2-4 they're a great way to start the afternoon. (Most productions start around 1:15pm.) The **King's Head,** 115 Upper St., N1 (tel. 226 1916; tube: Highbury and Islington) is probably the most successful at the daytime stuff. **St. Paul's Church,** at the central marketplace in Covent Garden, often has lunchtime theater on its steps..

■ FILM

The degenerate heart of the celluloid monster is Leicester Square, where the most recent hits premiere a day before hitting the chains around the city. Other cinemas have one screen only, and you may find yourself in a converted theater, complete with gilt boxes. *Time Out* includes unbeatable guides both to commercial films and to the vast range of cheaper, more varied alternatives—including late-night films, free films, and repertory cinema clubs. Many reduce prices all day Monday and for matinees Tuesday through Friday. **The Prince Charles** (Leicester Pl., WC2; tel. 437 8181 or 437 7003), shows scads (4/day) of recent Hollywood features sprinkled with classics for only £1.50, evenings and weekends £2 (tube: Leicester Sq.).

Electric Cinema, 191 Portobello Rd., W11 (tel. 792 2020). Tube: Ladbroke Grove or Notting Hill Gate. The first Black cinema in Britain. Past screenings include ground-breakers like *Menace II Society, The Posse* by Mario van Peebles, and *Sankofa,* winner of the 1993 African Cinema Festival. Tickets £5. Discounted tickets (£4) available Mon.-Thurs. for students, seniors, and children; bring ID.

Everyman Cinema, Hollybush Vale, Hampstead, NW3 (tel. 435 1525). Tube: Hampstead. Double and triple bills with a theme. Special seasonal runs; membership 60p/year. Tickets £4.50 Mon.-Fri., £5 Sat.-Sun.; students Mon.-Fri. £3.50.

Gate Cinema, Notting Hill Gate, W11 (tel. 727 4043). Tube: Notting Hill Gate. Recent art films. Tickets £5.50, students matinees Mon.-Fri. £3. Sun. matinees, £4.

Institute of Contemporary Arts (ICA) Cinema, Nash House, The Mall, W1 (tel. 930 3647). Tube: Piccadilly Circus or Charing Cross. Cutting-edge contemporary cinema, plus an extensive list of classics. Frequent special programs celebrating the work of a single director; recent tributes have lauded Rainer Fassbinder and Peter Greenaway. Tickets £6.50; seniors and students, Mon. screenings, and first screenings Tues.-Fri. £5. Experimental films and classics in the *cinémathèque;* £4.

National Film Theatre (NFT), South Bank Centre, SE1 (tel. 928 3232 for box office). Tube: Waterloo, or Embankment and cross the Hungerford footbridge. The NFT is one of the world's leading cinemas, screening a mind-boggling array of film, television, and video in its three auditoria. Home of the London Film Festival, held in Nov. For daily ticket availability, call 633 0274. Tickets £4.35; students, seniors, the unemployed, and registered disabled can buy tickets the day of the performance for £3.15. Box office open daily 11:30am-8:30am.

Notting Hill Coronet, On Notting Hill Gate Rd., (tel. 727 6705). Tube: Notting Hill Gate. Opposite McDonald's. A 396-seater dive with a quirk: it's London's last smoking cinema. Second-run films £6, coughing children £3.

Phoenix, 52 High Rd., N2 (tel. (0181) 883 2233 or 444 6789). Tube: East Finchley. Double bills mix and match European, American, and Asian mainstream hits and classics. Comfortable auditorium. £4.50, afternoons £3, students (Sat. night) £3.

■ MUSIC

Everyone from punk-rockers to opera fiends can exploit the richness of the London music scene. Unparalleled classical resources include five world-class orchestras, two opera houses, two huge arts centers, and countless concert halls. The rock scene is home of the London Underground of the late 60s, birthplace of the Sex Pistols and punk in the 70s, blessed with the Television Personalities and Soul II Soul in the 80s, and lately graced by 90s ragga remixes, Stereolab, and Huggy Bear. Summer is the best time for festivals and outdoor concerts, but the entire calendar offers enough music to satisfy and deafen you. Check the listings in *Time Out*. Keep your eyes open for special festivals or gigs posted on most of the city's surfaces, and for discounts posted on student union bulletin boards.

CLASSICAL

London's five world-class orchestras make the city unique even among musical meccas. Yet they provide only a fraction of the notes that fill London's major music centers, and those are only a fraction of the city's concert venues.

The venerable **London Symphony Orchestra,** led by Michael Tilson Thomas, inhabits **Barbican Hall** in the **Barbican Centre.** (Tube: Moorgate or Barbican; tel. 638 4141 for information. Box office open daily 9am-8pm, tel. 638 8891. Tickets £5-29; student standbys, when available, are sold shortly before the performance at reduced prices.) Klaus Tennstedt's **London Philharmonic** and Giuseppe Sinopoli's **Philharmonia Orchestra** play in the vast **Royal Festival Hall** in the grim labyrinth of the **South Bank Centre.** (Tube: Waterloo, or Embankment and cross the Hungerford footbridge; box office tel. 928 8800; open daily 10am-9pm. Tickets £4-28; student standbys, sold 2 hr. before performance at lowest price.) Vladimir Ashkenazy's **Royal Philharmonic Orchestra** performs at the Barbican and the South Bank, and the **BBC Symphony Orchestra** periodically pops up around town.

Exuberant and skilled, the **Proms** (BBC Henry Wood Promenade Concerts) never fail to enliven London summers. Every day for eight weeks from July to September, an impressive roster of musicians performs routinely outstanding programs including annually commissioned new works in the **Royal Albert Hall.** (Gallery £2, arena £3—join the queue around 6pm; tickets £4-16, sometime £4-21 for special performances.) The last night of the Proms traditionally steals the show, with the massed singing of *Land of Hope and Glory,* and closing with a rousing chorus of *Jerusalem;* a lottery of thousands determines who will be allowed to paint their faces as Union Jacks and "air-conduct" in person. (Box office tel. 589 8212; open daily 9am-9pm. Tube: South Kensington.)

Small, elegant, and Victorian, **Wigmore Hall,** 36 Wigmore St., W1 (tel. 935 2141; tube: Bond St. or Oxford Circus), leans to chamber groups and soloists (tickets £4-20; 1hr. standbys at lowest price) as does **St. John's,** Smith Square, a converted church just off Millbank. (Tickets £4-16, usually reduced for students and seniors. Box office tel. 222 1061. Tube: Westminster.)

Outdoor concerts in summer are phenomenally popular and relatively cheap. The **Kenwood Lakeside Concerts** at Kenwood, on Hampstead Heath present top-class performances, often graced by firework displays. (Tube: Golders Green or Archway, then bus #210, or East Finchley, then free shuttle bus to Kenwood; for information tel. 973 3427; for booking tel. 379 4444—no booking fee.) On Saturdays at 7:30pm, music floats to the audience from a performance shell across the lake. (Reserved deck chairs £10-15, students and seniors £8-12. Grass admission £8.50-11, students and seniors £5.50-9.) If the outdoors are more important to you than the concert, you can listen from afar for free. The grounds of stately **Marble Hill House** also host concerts, on summer Sundays at 7:30pm. (Tube/BR: Richmond, then bus #33, 90, 290, H22, or R70; information tel. 973 3427, booking tel. Ticketmaster, 379 4444—no fee.) Bring a blanket and picnic.

OPERA AND BALLET

London's major opera companies have limited runs in summer. The **Royal Opera,** Box St. (tel. 240 1911 or 240 1066; tube: Covent Garden), performs in the grand old Royal Opera House at Covent Garden. (Tickets run as high as £90; standbys cost £8.25-13 from 10am on the day of the performance; when available, student stand-bys about £10 1hr. before performance; tel. 836 6903 for recorded standby informa-tion; upper slips—on benches with a view of about half the stage—from £2.) Covent Garden has taken up the practice of "surtitling"—subtitling, with a twist—all non-English works in the repertoire. (Box office 48 Floral St., WC2; open Mon.-Sat. 10am-8pm.) The **English National Opera** leans more towards the modern, and all works are sung in English. Seats in the Opera's London Coliseum on St. Martin's La. (tel. 836 6161; tube: Charing Cross or Leicester Sq.) range from £6 to £43; standby tickets £10-15 available from 10am (box office open Mon.-Sat. 10am-8pm).

The **Royal Ballet** performs at the Royal Opera House in Covent Garden. The box office stands around the corner at 48 Floral St., WC2 (tel. 240 1066 or 240 1911; open Mon.-Sat. 10am-8pm). Tickets cost £2.25-54. At 10am on the day of the show, 65 amphitheater seats go on sale (strictly 1/person; lines often long; £6-8.50). When available, standbys for students and senior citizens are sold from one hour before curtain; call 836 6903 for information. In the summer, when the ENO is off, the **English National Ballet** and visiting ballet companies perform in the London Coli-seum, St. Martin's La., WC2 (tel. 836 3161; tube: Leicester Sq.; tickets £8-43. Student and senior citizen discounts available by advance booking only). Visiting companies grace the stage of the **Royal Festival Hall** in the South Bank Centre (tel. 928 8800).

ROCK & POP

Major venues for rock concerts include the indoor **Wembley Arena** and the huge outdoor **Wembley Stadium** (tube: Wembley Park or Wembley Central; tel. (081) 900 1234), the **Royal Albert Hall** (see Classical); the **Marquee,** and the **Town and Country Club** (see below). In the summer, many outdoor arenas such as **Finsbury Park** become the venues for major concerts and festivals. (See also Dance Clubs.)

Brixton Academy, 211 Stockwell Rd., SW9 (tel. 326 1022). Tube: Brixton. Time-honored and rowdy venue for a wide variety of music including rock, reggae, rap, and "alternative." 4000 capacity. Recent gigs include Violent Femmes, Ice Cube, and foxy bachelors Stone Temple Pilots. £9-15. Box office takes cash only—book ahead with a credit card. Box office open Mon.-Fri. 10am-7pm, Sat. 11am-6pm.

Forum, 9-17 Highgate Rd., NW5 (tel. 284 2200). Tube: Kentish Town. Night bus N2. Top notch audio system in a popular venue which was formerly the Town-and-Country Club. Open daily 7-11pm. £7.50-17.50.

Hackney Empire, 291 Mare St., E8 (tel. (0181) 985 2424). Tube: Bethnal Green then bus #253 north or BR: Hackney Downs or Hackney Central. Not much to look at, but its East End location attracts ragga and roots lovers for live tunes and wicked DJs. Also host to popular comic routines like the Caribbean duo Bello and Blacka. £3-12. Hours vary by show.

Hammersmith Apollo, Queen Caroline St., W6 (tel. (0181) 741 4868). Tube: Hammersmith. Big 50s building hosts mainstream rock. £11-25.

London Palladium, 8 Argyll St., W1 (tel. 494 5020). Tube: Oxford Circus. They've hosted Lou Reed. Open 6:45-10:30pm. Music usually starts 7:30. £8.50-29.

The Marquee, 105 Charing Cross Rd., WC2 (tel. 437 6601). Tube: Leicester Sq. or Tottenham Ct. Rd. A loud, busy showcase for the latest bands: hundreds churn through each month. £5-7. Open daily 7pm-midnight.

Mean Fiddler, 24-28 Harlesden High St., NW10 (tel. (0181) 961 5490). Tube: Willesden Junction. Night bus N18. Cavernous club with high balconies and good bars, strangely mixing country & western, folk, and indie rock. £5-10. Open Mon.-Sat. 8pm-2am, Sun. 7:30pm-1am. Music begins 9-9:30pm.

Powerhaus N1, 1 Liverpool Rd., N1 (tel. 837 3218). Tube: Angel. Also accessible by Night buses N92 and N96. Quirky mix of live indie rock and folk music in a converted pub. The recently revitalized Raincoats have played here. £4-6. Open Mon.-Thurs. 8pm-2am, Fri.-Sat. 8pm-3am, Sun. 7-11pm.

Rock Garden, The Piazza, Covent Garden, WC2 (tel, 836 4052). Tube: Covent Garden. Great new bands play nightly. £5, before 11pm. £4, Sun. lunchtime £2. Open Mon.-Sat. 7:30pm-3am, Sun. noon-3pm and 7:30pm-midnight.

Shepherd's Bush Empire, Shepherds Bush Green, W12 (tel. (0181) 740 7474). Tube: Shepherds Bush. Hosts dorky cool musicians like David Byrne and the Proclaimers. 2000 capacity, with 6 bars. £6-20.

The Venue, 2A Clifton Rise, New Cross, SE14 (tel. (0181) 692 4077). Tube: New Cross, Night Bus N77. Getting to be a big indie scene. Dancing goes late into the night. Open Fri.-Sat. 7:30pm-2am; music starts 9:30pm. £5-6.

JAZZ

In the summer, hundreds of jazz festivals appear in the city and its outskirts, including the **Capital Radio Jazz Parade** (July; tel. 379 1066), the **North London Festival** (June-July; tel. (0181) 449 0048), and the **City of London Festival** (July; tel. 248 4260). Ronnie Scott's, Bass Clef, and Jazz Café are the most popular clubs. Jazz clubs often stay open much later than pubs, and so are ideal spots for tippling into the wee hours.

100 Club, 100 Oxford St., W1 (tel. 636 0933). Tube: Tottenham Ct. Rd. Strange mix of traditional modern jazz, swing, and blues. Staged one of the Sex Pistols' first London gigs. Discount for groups of 5 or more. £5-8. Open Mon.-Thurs. 7:30pm-midnight, Fri. 7:30pm-3am, Sat. 7:30pm-1am, Sun. 7:45-11:30pm.

606 Club, 90 Lots Rd., SW10 (tel. 352 5953). Tube: Fulham Broadway, or buses #11 and 22 or Night bus N11. Blossoming talent bops along with household names in diverse styles. Open Mon.-Sat. 8:30pm-2:30am, Sun. 8:30-11:30pm. Music Mon.-Wed. 9:30pm, Thurs. 10 pm, Fri.-Sat. 10:30pm, Sun. 10pm. £4, Fri.-Sat. £4.50.

Jazz Café, 5 Parkway, Camden Town, NW1 (tel. 284 4358 or 916 6000 for box office). Tube: Camden Town, Night bus N93. Top new venue in a converted bank. Classic and experimental jazz. £7-12. Open Sun.-Thurs. 7pm-midnight, Fri. 7pm-3am, Sat. 7pm-1am.

Jazz at Pizza Express, 10 Dean St., W1 (tel. 437 9595). Tube: Tottenham Ct. Rd. Packed, dark club hiding behind a pizzeria. Fantastic groups, and occasional greats; get there early. £3.50-12.50. Music 9:30pm-1am.

Ronnie Scott's, Frith St., W1 (tel. 439 0747). Tube: Leicester Sq. or Piccadilly Circus. The most famous jazz club in London. Expensive food and great music. Candles on every small table, and great faded photographs of jazz legends who've played Ronnie Scott's. Ronnie himself, a bit past his prime, still hosts. Waiters masterfully keep noisy clientele from ruining the music by politely telling them to shut up. Open fabulously late—the music just keeps going. Rock/soul/world music on Sun. £12. Book ahead or arrive by 9:30pm. Music starts 9:30-10pm. Open Mon.-Sat. 8:30am-3am.

FOLK

To a large extent, folk music in London means Irish music. Some variation exists: folk rock, English ballads, and even English country & western. Most of these events are free, but venues welcome donations or, of course, consumption of their goods.

Acoustic Room, at The Mean Fiddler, 24-28 Harlesden Hight St., NW10 (tel. (0181) 961 5490). Tube: Willesden Junction. Superb acoustic rock/folk performers, with a decidedly younger, "alternative" slant. £4-5. Open Mon.-Sat. 8pm-2am, Sun. 7:30pm-1am.

Africa Centre, 38 King St., WC2 (tel. 836 1973). Tube: Covent Garden. African music and dance. More a cultural center than a club. £7. Open Fri.-Sat. 10pm-3am.

Troubadour Coffee House, 265 Old Brompton Rd., SW5 (tel. 370 1434). Tube: Earl's Ct. Acoustic entertainment is served up in a warm café. Bob Dylan played here early in his career. On Wed. the café becomes the "Institute for Acoustic Research." Folk and jazz Fri.-Sat. £4.50, concession £3.50. Open 8pm-11pm.

■ DANCE CLUBS

London pounds to 100% Groovy Liverpool tunes, ecstatic Manchester rave, hometown soul and house, imported U.S. hip-hop, and Jamaican ragga. Check out the 12" bins at record stores for the obscure dub mixes that dominate the playlists. Fashion evolves and revolves: flares and platforms have been supplanted by little-girl t-shirts, silver mini-skirts, and Puma Clydes. The most expensive dance halls get trippy with virtual-reality video shows and cyberpunk games.

Remember that the tube shuts down two or three hours before most clubs and that taxis can be hard to find in the wee hours of the morning. Some late-night frolickers catch "minicabs," little unmarked cars that wait outside clubs. Arrange transportation or acquaint yourself with the extensive network of night buses (tel. 222 1234 for information). Listings include some of the night bus routes that connect beyond central London, but routes change and a quick double-check is recommended. As always, check listings in *Time Out* and *What's On*. Many record stores in Brixton and Soho (on Berwick St.) post handbills advertising dance-club events.

Africa Centre, 38 King St., WC2 (tel. 836 1973). Tube: Covent Garden. On weekends, "Club Limpopo" features DJ Wala's African grooves and a live set. Used to be a Soul II Soul hangout, as mentioned on their hit from *Vol. I.* The Africa Centre is an arts center rather than a full-time club. £6-7. Open 9pm-3am.

The Electric Ballroom, 184 Camden High St., NW1 (tel. 485 9006). Tube: Camden Town. Night bus N2, N29, N90, or N93. Cheap and fun. *Time Out* described Saturdays as "probably London's best rock, Gothic, and Glamour punk night." Most of the clientele here refuse to wear natural fibers. £5, members £4.

The Fridge, Town Hall Parade, Brixton Hill, SW2 (tel. 326 5100). Tube: Brixton. Night bus N2. A serious dance dive with a multi-ethnic crowd. Jazzie B from Soul II Soul got his start here and now he's back every Fri. night. Stylish 21+ crowd. Features Telly psychedelia and twisting dance cages. Immensely popular weekly "Love Muscle" every Sat. night crowds with busy mixed-gay clientele. The Fridge cools down during the summer months. Open 10pm-4 or 6 am.

Gossips, 69 Dean St., W1 (tel. 434 4480). Tube: Piccadilly Circus or Tottenham Ct. Rd. A dark basement club renowned for a wide range of great one-nighters. Anything goes, from heavy metal to ska to psychedelia to reggae. Call ahead for details; music and crowd changes on a nightly basis. Hard Club 92 (Wed.) still claims to be the place for "Euros and trendy weirdos," while the notorious Gaz's Rockin' Blues (now in its 12th year) on Thurs. is highly recommended for its ska, blues, and soul. £3-8. Open Mon.-Sat. 10pm-3:30am.

Iceni, 11 White Horse St., W1 (tel. 495 5333). Tube: Green Park. Off Curzon Street. Three beautiful floors of deep funk. £5-8. Open Wed.-Sat. 10pm-3am.

Maximus, 14 Leicester Sq., WC2 (tel. 734 4111). Tube: Leicester Square. On Thursdays this venue goes back to its roots as a mirrored disco for "Soul Kitchen." £5-10. Open Wed.-Thurs. 10:30pm-3am, Fri.-Sat. 10:30pm-6am, Sun. 9:30pm-3am.

Milk Bar, 12 Sutton Row, W1 (tel. 439 4655). Tube: Tottenham Ct. Rd. Opposite Astoria. Small club with weird white and silver decor. Especially popular on Wed. Crazy drag revue Fri. £4-10. Open Mon.-Sat. 10pm-3am, Sun. 7:30pm-midnight.

Subterania, 12 Acklam Rd., W10 (tel. (0181) 960 4590). Tube: Ladbroke Grove. This is where it's at—directly beneath the Westway flyover. Relaxed, multi-ethnic crowd comes to dance to wicked house and garage music. Club classics and "90s disco." Crucial on Fri. and Sat. midnight onwards. £5-8. Open daily 10pm-3am.

The Vox, 9 Brighton Terrace, SW9 (tel 737 2095). Tube: Brixton. Behind Red Records on Brixton Road. "Institute of Dubology" rages every Thursday night 10pm-3am with dub chemists like Rootsman and Trans-spiritual Express Iyahbingi Drummers. Most nights headline dub, techno, and psycho-trance. £3-6. Open until 3am, Fri.-Sat. until 6am.

The Wag Club, 35 Wardour St., W1 (tel. 437 5534). Tube: Piccadilly Circus. Multi-level complex with bars and an eatery amongst throngs of dancers in platforms. Once clubland's crowning glory, it still hosts one-nighters. Soul on Wed., "Progressive," garage, and house music on Thurs., hip hop/funk on Sat. Mon.-Thurs. £4-6, Fri. £8, Sat. £10. Open Mon.-Thurs. 10:30pm-3:30am, Fri.-Sat. 10:30pm-6am.

■ LITERARY LIFE

Bookstores, especially **Waterstone's** and **Compendium** (see Shopping—Bookstores), hold frequent readings by major authors. The Institute of Contemporary Arts (see Museums—Other Major Collections) also hosts readings. As always, check the "Books and Poetry" listings in *Time Out.*

Brixton Poets, The Prince Albert, Coldharbour Lane, SW2 (tel. 701 9608). Tube: Brixton. Chaotically poetic performance group, new members always welcome. Tues. 9pm. Free.

The Poetry Society, 22 Betterton St., WC2 (tel. 240 0810). Tube: Covent Garden. Along with The Voice Box, the other main venue for readings. £4, students £3.

The Voice Box, Level 5, Red Side, Royal Festival Hall, SE1 (tel. 921 0906). Tube: Waterloo. Frequent readings of international prose and poetry by renowned writers, plus special events and festivals. *Literature Quarterly,* their free listings brochure, has a complete schedule and useful descriptions of the readers. £2.50-£5, students £1.50-3. The **Poetry Library** (tel. 921 0943) has the largest collection of 20th-century poetry in Britain, as well as poetry magazines, audio and video recordings, and an information board where contests and workshops are posted. Open daily 1am-8pm. Membership is free (bring ID and current address).

■ OFFBEAT ENTERTAINMENT

The College of Psychic Studies, 16 Queensberry Pl., SW7 (tel. 589 3292). Tube: South Kensington. Eager for you to become their newest subject. Unlock your true self through graphoanalysis, harness universal wisdom and release life blocks (karmic or otherwise) with regression therapy, or achieve that eternally sought-after harmony between body and spirit through aromatherapy. Open Mon.-Thurs. 10am-7:30pm, Fri. 10am-4:30pm; closed most of Aug.

Conway Hall, Red Lion Sq., WC1 (tel. 242 8032). Tube: Holborn. Spend the day of rest engaged in radical activities. Atheist lectures Sun. morning, chamber music Sun. evening. The evidence suggests that Socialists, New Agers, and other suspicious characters convene here. Free Sun. lectures at 11am, sometimes also at 6:30pm, Oct.-mid-July. Chamber music at 3pm, £3.50

Daily Mail and **Evening Standard,** Northcliffe House, 2 Derry St., W8 (tel. 938 6000). Tube: High St. Kensington. See an issue of one of these tabloids in production. For information write to the Personnel Administrator, Hammondsworth Quays Ltd., Surrey Quays Rd., SE16 1PJ.

Porchester Baths, Queensway, W2 (tel. 792 3980 or 792 2919). Tube: Bayswater or Royal Oak. In the Porchester Centre. A Turkish bath with steam and dry heat rooms and a swimming pool. Built in 1929, the baths are an Art Deco masterpiece of gold and marble. Rates are high (3hr. £15.40), but devoted fans keep taking the plunge. Men bathe Mon., Wed., and Sat.; women bathe Tues., Thurs., and Fri. Open Mon.-Sat. 10am-10pm. Open Sun. 10am-4pm (women only), 4-10pm (mixed couples). Swimwear must be worn at all times.

Vidal Sassoon School of Hairdressing, 56 Davies Mews, W1 (tel. 629 4635). Tube: Bond St. Cuts, perms, and color at the hand of a Sassoony. Cut and blow dry £8.50, with student ID £4.50. All-over tint £10.50. Open Mon.-Fri. 10am-3pm.

■ SPECTATOR SPORTS

ASSOCIATION FOOTBALL

> *Many evils may arise which God forbid.*
> —King Edward II, banning football in London, 1314

Football (soccer) draws huge crowds—over half a million people attend professional matches in Britain every Saturday. Each club's fans dress with fierce loyalty in team colors, and make themselves heard with uncanny synchronized cheering. Mass violence and vandalism at stadiums has dogged the game for years. Ninety-five people were crushed to death in Sheffield in 1989 after a surge of fans tried to push their way into the grounds. Matters have improved; still, visitors may feel more comfortable buying a seat rather than standing on "the terraces."

The season runs from mid-August to May. Most games take place on Saturday, kicking off at 3pm. Allow time to wander through the crowds milling around the stadium. London has been blessed with 13 of the 92 professional teams in England. The big two are **Arsenal,** Highbury, Avenell Rd., N5 (tel. 359 0131; tube: Arsenal) and **Tottenham Hotspur,** 78 High Rd., W17 (tel. (0181) 808 3030; BR: White Hart Lane). But the football scene is very partisan and favorites vary from neighborhood to neighborhood. Tickets are available in advance from each club's box office; many now have a credit card telephone booking system. Seats cost £10-23. England plays occasional international matches at Wembley Stadium, usually on Wednesday evenings (tel. (0181) 900 1234; tube: Wembley Park).

RUGBY

The game was spontaneously created when a Rugby College student picked up a soccer ball and ran it into the goal. Rugby has since evolved into a complex and subtle game. **Rugby League,** a professional sport played by teams of 13, has traditionally been a northern game. The only London side is **Fulham,** Crystal Palace National Sports Centre, SE19 (tel. (0181) 778 0131; BR: Crystal Palace). Wembley Stadium (tel. (0181) 902 8833) stages some of the championship matches in May. A random *mêlée* of blood, mud, and drinking songs, "rugger" can be incomprehensible to the outsider, yet aesthetically exciting nonetheless. The season runs from September to April. The most significant contests, including the Oxford vs. Cambridge varsity match in December and the springtime five nations championship (featuring England, Scotland, Wales, Ireland, and France), are played at **Twickenham** (tel. (0181) 892 8161; BR: Twickenham). First-rate games can be seen in relaxed surroundings at one of London's premiere clubs such as **Saracens,** Dale Green Rd., N14 (tel. (0181) 449 3770; tube: Oakwood), and **Rosslyn Park,** Priory La., Upper Richmond Rd., SW15 (tel. (0181) 876 1879; BR: Barnes).

CRICKET

Cricket remains a confusing spectacle to most North Americans. The impossibility of explaining its rules to an American has virtually become a national in-joke in England. Once a synonym for civility, cricket's image has been dulled. The much-used phrase, "It's just not cricket," has recently taken on an ironic edge. While purists disdain one-day matches, novices find these the most exciting. "First class" matches amble on rather ambiguously for days, often ending in "draws."

London's two grounds stage both county and international matches. **Lord's,** St. John's Wood Rd., NW8 (tel. 289 1615; tube: St. John's Wood), is *the* cricket ground, home turf of the Marylebone Cricket Club, the established governing body of cricket. Archaic stuffiness pervades the MCC; women have yet to see the inside of its pavilion. **Middlesex** plays its games here (tickets £6-7). Tickets to international matches cost £15-40 (booking essential). The **Oval,** Kennington, SE11 (tel. 582 6660; tube: Oval), home to **Surrey** cricket club (tickets £7), also fields Test Matches (tickets for internationals £15-40; book ahead).

ROWING

The **Henley Royal Regatta,** the most famous annual crew race in the world, conducts itself both as a proper hobnob social affair (like Ascot) and as a popular corporate social event (like Wimbledon). The rowing is graceful, though laypeople are often unable to figure out what on earth is going on. The event transpires on the last weekend in June and the first in July. Saturday is the most popular and busiest day, but some of the best races are the finals on Sunday. Public enclosure tickets (£4 for the first two days, £5 for the last three) are available by the river (the side opposite the station) or write to the Secretary's Office, Regatta Headquarters, Henley-on-Thames, Oxfordshire, England RG9 2LY (tel. (01491) 572 153). Take BR from Paddington to Henley, or Green Line coach #390 from Victoria (1½hr., day return £7).

The course of the **Boat Race,** between eights from Oxford and Cambridge Universities, runs from Putney to Mortlake on a Saturday in late March or early April. Old-money alums, fortified by strawberries and champagne, sport their crested blazers and college ties to cheer the teams on. Bumptious crowds line the Thames and fill the pubs (tube: Putney Bridge or Hammersmith; BR: Barnes Bridge or Mortlake). Call (0181) 748 3632 for details.

TENNIS

For two weeks starting in late June, tennis buffs all over the world focus their attention on **Wimbledon.** If you want to get in, arrive early—9am the first week, 6am the second; the gate opens at 10:30am (get off the tube at Southfields or take one of the buses from central London which run frequently during the season). Entrance to the grounds (including lesser matches) costs £5-7, less after 5pm. If you arrive in the queue early enough, you can buy one of the few show court tickets that were not sold months before. Depending on the day, center court tickets cost £10-30, court 1 tickets £9-24. Other show courts (courts #2, 3, 13, 14), where top players play their early rounds, cost £6-16. Other courts have first-come, first-served seats or standing room only. Get a copy of the order of play on each court, printed in most newspapers. If you fail to get center or court 1 tickets in the morning, try to find the resale booth (usually in Aorangi Park), which sells tickets handed in by those who leave early (open from 2:30pm; tickets only £2). Also, on the first Saturday of the 1992 championships, several hundred extra center court tickets were put up for sale; a practice that has since continued. Call (0181) 944 1066 for info during the tournament. For details of the 1995 championships call the All England Club (tel. (0181) 946 2244) or send a self-addressed stamped envelope between August 1 and December 31, 1994 to **The All England Lawn Tennis and Croquet Club,** P.O. Box 98, Church Rd., Wimbledon SW19 5AE. Topspin lob fans mustn't miss the **Wimbledon Lawn Tennis Museum** (tel. (0181) 946 6131), right on the grounds (open Tues.-Sat. 11am-5pm, Sun. 2-5pm; call ahead to check near tournament time).

HORSES

The **Royal Gold Cup Meeting** at **Ascot** takes place each summer in mid-June. An "important" society event, it is essentially an excuse for Brits of all strata to indulge in the twin pastimes of drinking and gambling while wearing silly hats. The Queen takes up residence at Windsor Castle in order to lavish her full attentions on this socio-political vaudeville act. (The enclosure is open only by invitation; grandstand tickets £8.50-20, Silver Ring £3; tel. (01344) 222 11). In July, the popular George VI and Queen Elizabeth Diamond Stakes are run here, and during the winter Ascot hosts excellent steeplechase meetings (BR from Waterloo to Ascot). Top hats, gypsies, and Pimms also distinguish the **Derby** ("darby"), run in early June at **Epsom** Racecourse, Epsom, Surrey (tel. (01372) 726 311; grandstand tickets £9-20). More accessible, less expensive summer evening races are run at **Windsor,** the racecourse, Berkshire (tel. (01753) 865 234; BR: Windsor Riverside; tattersalls and paddock £10), and **Kempton Park Racecourse,** Sunbury-on-Thames (tel. (01932) 782 292; BR: Kempton Park; admission to grandstand £13, Silver Ring £4).

In late June, **polo** aficionados flock to the **Royal Windsor Cup,** The Guards Polo Club, Smiths Lawn, Windsor Great Park (tel. (01784) 437 797; BR: Windsor & Eton Central; £15/car). You can stand on the "wrong" side of the field for free, or hobnob in the clubhouse for a £10 day membership.

■ PARTICIPATORY SPORTS

If you fancy something a little more adventurous than a kickaround in the park or kite-flying on Parliament Hill, then just do it. London provides a satisfyingly wide variety of sporting opportunities. *Time Out's Guide to Sport, Health, & Fitness* (£5.50) can give you more complete information on many sports. For general fitness during your visit, **London Central YMCA,** 112 Great Russell St., WC1 (tel. 637

8131; tube: Tottenham Ct. Rd.), has a pool, gym, weights, and offers weekly membership for £27, off-peak weekly membership (use after 4pm prohibited) £20 (open Mon.-Fri. 8am-10pm, Sat.-Sun. 10am-10pm). **The Sportsline** answers queries on a vast range of clubs and locations (tel. 222 8000; Mon.-Fri. 10am-6pm).

■ SHOPPING

London does sell more than royal commemorative mugs and plastic police helmets.

For department stores and fashion outlets, try Oxford St., Knightsbridge, and Kensington; for expensive designer goods, Sloane St., Bond St., and Regent St.; for hip young clothes, Oxford Circus, Covent Garden, Kensington, and Camden; and for specialty stores, Bloomsbury and Covent Garden. *Nicholson's Shopping Guide and Streetfinder* (£2.95) should suit bargain hunters seeking further guidance. Serious shoppers should read *Time Out's* massive *Directory to London's Shops and Services* (£6) cover to cover.

Prices descend during sale seasons in July and January. *Time Out's* "Sell Out" section has listings of stores having sales. Tourists who have purchased anything over £50 should ask about getting a refund on the 17.5% VAT, although most shops have a VAT minimum. Another option is to save receipts and obtain a refund at the airport—be warned, the commission charged is not small. Many shops stay open late on Thursday. Many stores may be closed on Sunday.

DEPARTMENT STORES

Harrods (tel. 730 1234) says it all with the humble motto *Omnia Omnibus Ubique* ("All things for all people, everywhere"). They can do everything from finding you a live rhinoceros to arranging your funeral. (On Brompton Rd. by Knightsbridge tube; open Mon.-Tues. and Sat. 10am-6pm, Wed.-Fri. 10am-7pm.) **Marks & Spencer** (tel. 935 7954), also known as Marks and Sparks, sells British staples in a classy but value-conscious manner. Everyone British, including Margaret Thatcher, buys their knickers here. (Branches near Bond St., Marble Arch, and High St. Kensington tube stations. Open Mon.-Wed. and Sat. 9am-7pm, Thurs.-Fri. 9am-8pm.) Also near the Bond St. tube station on Oxford St. is **Selfridges** (tel. 629 1234), an enormous pseudo-Renaissance building with a vast array of fashions, homewares, and foods (open Mon., Wed., and Fri.-Sat. 9:30am-7pm, Thurs. 9:30am-8pm).

At the renowned **Fortnum & Mason,** 181 Piccadilly, W1 (tel. 734 8040; tube: Green Park or Piccadilly Circus), liveried clerks serve expensive foods in red-carpeted and chandeliered halls (open Mon.-Sat. 9:30am-6pm).

CLOTHING

Those who'd rather not swap a cherished limb for some new clothes should explore some of London's second-hand clothing stores. **Cornucopia,** 12 Upper Tachbrook St., SW1 (tel. 828 5752; tube: Victoria) is the grande dame of period clothing stores (open Mon.-Sat. 11am-6pm). **Kensington Market,** 49-53 Kensington High St., W8, has some bargains (including second-hand clothes) and a good selection of whatever's trendy at the moment—Pumas and Adidas in '94 (open Mon.-Sat. 10am-6pm; tube: High St. Kensington). Along the same lines, try **Camden Markets** (see *Street Markets*).

For the latest in beat-tapping, inexpensive shoes, try **Shelly's Shoes,** 159 Oxford St., W1 (tel. 437 5842; tube: Oxford Circus; open Mon.-Wed. and Fri.-Sat. 9:30am-6:30pm, Thurs. 9:30am-8pm; branches throughout London), the spiritual home of Doc Marten. **Red or Dead,** 36 Kensington High St., W8 (tel. 937 3837), has been hawking platforms long before Dee-Lite, as well as a solid DM selection. (Tube: High St. Kensington; open Mon.-Fri. 10:30am-7:30pm, Sat. 10am-7pm, Sun. 12:30-7pm; also at 33 Neal St., WC2 in Covent Garden and 186 Camden High St., NW1.)

BOOKSTORES

In London, even the chain bookstores are wonders. An exhaustive selection of bookshops lines Charing Cross Rd. between Tottenham Ct. Rd. and Leicester Sq. and many vend secondhand paperbacks. Cecil Ct., near Leicester Sq., is a treasure trove of tiny shops. Establishments along Great Russell St. stock esoteric and specialized books on any subject from Adorno to the Zohar. The best places to look for maps and travel books are **Stanford's,** 12 Long Acre (tel. 836 1321; tube: Covent Garden; open Mon. and Sat. 10am-6pm, Tues.-Wed. and Fri. 9am-6pm, Thurs. 9am-7pm) and the **Travellers' Bookshop,** 25 Cecil Ct., WC2 (tel. 836 9132; tube: Leicester Sq.; open Mon.-Fri. 11am-7pm, Sat. 11am-6:30pm); also try Harrods and the YHA shop (see Specialty Shops below).

Dillons, 82 Gower St., WC1 (tel. 636 1577), near University of London. Tube: Goodge St. Also on The Strand near Trafalgar Square. The most graceful bookstore in London. Easier to navigate and about as complete as Foyles. Strong on academics, particularly history and politics. Fair selection of reduced-price and secondhand books, plus classical CDs and tapes. Open Mon.-Fri. 9:30am-7pm, Sat. 9:30am-6pm.Trafalgar Square branch open Mon.-Sat. 9:30am-9pm.

Foyles, 119 Charing Cross Rd., WC1 (tel. 437 5660). Tube: Tottenham Ct. Rd. or Leicester Sq. A giant warehouse of books—you'll get lost without a staffer's help. Open Mon.-Sat. 9am-6pm, Thurs. 9am-7pm.

Hatchards, 187 Piccadilly, W1 (tel. 437 3924). Tube: Green Park. Oldest and most comprehensive of London's bookstores, recently expanded. Come in for 10min., stay for 2hrs. Also at 150 King's Rd. (tel. 351 7649); 390 The Strand (tel. 379 6264); 63 Kensington High St., (tel. 937 0858); and Harvey Nichols in Knightsbridge (tel. 235 5000). Open Mon.-Fri. 9am-6pm, Sat. 9am-5pm.

Waterstone's, 121-125 Charing Cross Rd., WC1 (tel. 434 4291), next door to Foyles. Tube: Leicester Sq. A great many reliable branches, including 193 Kensington High St., W8 (tel. 937 8432); 99 Old Brompton Rd., SW7 (tel. 581 8523); 266 Earls Ct. Rd., SW5 (tel. 370 1616); 128 Camden High St., NW1 (tel. 284 4948). An extensive selection of paperbacks; calmer and friendlier than its neighbor, though also a little cramped. They mail books to the U.S. (open Mon. and Wed.-Fri. 9:30am-8pm, Tues. 10am-8pm, Sat. 9:30am-6pm, Sun. 11am-6pm; Kensington High St. open until 10pm Mon.-Fri.)

Art bookstores splatter the streets around the British Museum (tube: Holborn or Tottenham Ct. Rd.) and Christie's (tube: Green Park or Piccadilly Circus), while 50s magazines and film posters clutter **Vintage Magazine Market,** on the corner of Brewer and Great Windmill St. near Piccadilly Circus (tel. 439 8525; open Mon.-Sat. 10am-7pm; Sun. 1-8pm). For theater and opera books, try **Samuel French's,** 52 Fitzroy St., W1 (tel. 387 9373; open Mon.-Fri. 9:30am-5:30pm).

Books for a Change, 52 Charing Cross Rd., WC2 (tube: Charing Cross; tel. 836 2315; open Mon.-Fri. 10am-6:30pm, Sat. 10am-6pm) is a bookstore and information center jointly sponsored by the Campaign for Nuclear Disarmament, Friends of the Earth, the UN Association, and War on Want. **Silver Moon,** at 68 Charing Cross Rd., WC2, is a radical women's bookstore (tube: Leicester Sq.; tel. 836 7906; open Mon.-Fri. 10:30am-6:30pm).

RECORD STORES

If a record can't be found in London, it's probably not worth your listening time. London, for years the hub of the English music scene, has a record collection to match. Corporate megaliths **HMV, Virgin,** and **Tower Records** fall over each other claiming to be the world's largest record store. Don't expect any bargains or rarities, and remember that when it comes to records, "import" means "rip-off." For rarities, secondhand, and specialist records, try the wealth of diverse shops scattered throughout the West End and the suburbs. At **Camden Town, Brixton, Ladbroke Grove,** or Soho's **Hanway Street,** you can have a good afternoon's browse.

Honest Jon's, 278 Portobello Rd., W10 (tel. 969 9822). Tube: Ladbroke Grove. At Honest Jon's, heavily-postered walls declaim slogans like "Hail Caesar, Godfather of Harlem." This jumping joint has extensive Parliament-Funkadelic offerings and a jazz basement in which Blakey, Parker, and Mingus are only the tip of the iceberg. Open Mon.-Sat. 10am-6pm, Sun. 11am-5pm.

Plastic Passion, 2 Blenheim Crescent, W11 (tel. 229 5424). Tube: Notting Hill Gate. New Wave and punkish. Small, but extremely dedicated collectors. Open Fri.-Sat. 10am-6:30pm.

Red Records, 500 Brixton Rd., SW2. Tube: Brixton. Specializes in rhythms and mixes. From Remmy Ongala of Tanzania to the Mighty Sparrows of Trinidad, Red has ragga, hip-hop, soul, motown, or funk faves. Open Mon.-Sat. 9:30am-7pm.

Rough Trade, 130 Talbot Rd., W11 (tel. 229 8541). Tube: Ladbroke Grove. Birthplace of the legendary independent record label. Original snapshots of Johnny Rotten are casually tacked up on the wall next to old posters advertising concerts for Rough Trade bands like The Smiths, The Raincoats, and the X-Ray Spex. Open Mon.-Sat. 10am-7pm.

■ STREET MARKETS

Many street markets sell modern junk or ordinary produce at non-bargain prices; an exceptional handful push offbeat styles and unique trinkets. The open air and an informal atmosphere make the markets livelier and more invigorating than any mall. With some luck and ingenuity, you may find cheap, unusual goods—come prepared to haggle and to participate in some cheerful, often incomprehensible banter.

Listed below is the more entertaining minority of London's 70 markets. Opening times vary considerably—Saturday is usually the busiest and best day.

Brixton Market, Electric Ave., Brixton Station Rd. and Popes Rd., SW2. Tube: Brixton. Covered market halls and outdoor stalls sprawl out from the station. Wide selection of African and West Indian fruit, vegetables, fabrics, and records. Also a remarkable number of stalls vending various colors and styles of hair extension pieces. The two indoor arcades are the Electric Arcade and the Granville Arcade, both with entrances off Atlantic Road. Open Mon., Tues., Thurs., and Sat. 8am-6pm, Wed. 8am-1pm, Fri. 8am-7pm.

Camden Markets, by Regent's Canal and along Camden High St., NW1. Tube: Camden Town. One of the funkiest, trendiest places to tap those Doc Marten soles and buy clothes, shoes, and Manic Panic hair dye. Highlights are the Camden Lock Market (corner of Chalk Farm Rd. and Camden Lock Pl.; open Tues.-Sun.), the Stables Market (past the Lock on Chalk Farm Rd.), and the Electric Ballroom (on the High St.; open Sun. 9am-5:30pm)—all with stalls of cool secondhand garb. Camden Town bootleggers do a roaring trade, but check the quality of the tapes before buying. Open Sat.-Sun. 8am-6pm.

Petticoat Lane, E1. Tube: Liverpool St., Aldgate, or Aldgate East. A London institution—street after street of stalls, mostly cheap clothing and household appliances. The real action begins at about 9:30am. Open Sun. 9am-2pm; starts shutting down around noon.

Portobello Road, W11. Tube: Notting Hill Gate or Ladbroke Grove. High-quality antiques at high prices at the Notting Hill end of the street. Some call this "a place to visit your stolen silver"; others consider it nothing more than a tourist trap. Immortalized by Paddington Bear. Watch out for pickpockets. To the north, tourists thin out as antiques give way to produce and second-hand clothes stalls under the Westway flyover. A number of pricey vintagewear shops operate here. Antique market Sat. 7am-5pm. Clothes market Fri.-Sat. 8am-3pm.

■ BISEXUAL, GAY, & LESBIAN LONDON

London's gay scene ranges from the flamboyant to the campy to the cruisy to the mainstream. Its center is at "the Centre," the **London Lesbian and Gay Centre,** 67-69 Cowcross St., EC1 (tel. 608 1471; tube: Farringdon), a venue for a wide variety of meetings, as well as a disco, bar, restaurant, and gym. Bulletin boards can help you find accommodation or that second-skin leather specialty (open Mon.-Tues. noon-11pm, Wed.-Thurs., and Sun. noon-midnight, Fri.-Sat. noon-3am). The 24-hr. **Lesbian and Gay Switchboard** (tel. 837 7324) is an excellent source of information. The hours of the **Bisexual Helpline** (tel. (0181) 569 7500) are more limited, but when they're on their ears are wide open (Tues.-Wed. 7:30-9:30pm). Legal advice, from basic discrimination to police harassment, is available from **Gay and Lesbian Legal Advice** (tel. 253 2043), Mon.-Fri. 7-10pm. If you can't find a phone or what you need from these services, consult one of the many publications, like *Gay Times, Capital Gay, Pink Paper, Shebang, Diva,* or *Kennedy's Gay Guide to London,* all at **Gay's the Word**, 66 Marchmont St., WC1 (tel. 278 7654), the largest gay bookstore in Britain (open Mon.-Fri. 11am-7pm, Sat. 10am-6pm, and Sun. 2-6pm). Wardrobe expansion begins at **Don't Panic,** 52 Dean St., W1 (tel. 734 5363), for "I can't even think straight" t-shirts (tube: Piccadilly or Leceister Sq.). Small and intimate, the **Clone Zone,** 64 Old Compton St., W1 (tel. 287 3530) sells cards and books and T-shirts (tube: Piccadilly or Leicester Sq.).

Bars particularly popular among gay men are **The Edge,** 11 Soho Sq., W1, and **Comptons of Soho,** 53 Old Compton St., W1; both are fairly touristy (tube: Tottenham Ct. Rd. or Leicester Sq.). **Crews,** 14 Upper St. Martin's La., WC2 (tube: Leicester Sq.) is probably the largest and hottest bar for men in the West End. Drag 'til you drop at **The Black Cap,** 171 Camden High St., NW1 (tube: Camden Town). Fridays and Saturdays at the **First Out Café Bar,** 52 St. Giles High St., WC2 (tel. 240 8042) draw a relaxed crowd of women (tube: Tottenham Ct. Rd.). **Drill Hall Women-Only Bar,** 16 Chenies St., WC1 (tube: Goodge St.) is crowded and friendly on Monday evenings—with cheap drinks. Gay and lesbian pubs include **The Angel,** 65 Graham St., N1 (mixed crowd; tube: Angel), and the women-owned **Duke of Clarence,** 140 Rotherfield St., N1 (tube: Angel then bus #38, 56, or 73). Dine elegantly at the Thai-inflected **Wilde About Oscar,** 30-31 Philbeach Gardens, SW5 (tel. 835 1858 or 373 1244; tube: Earl's Ct.).

But it is the thumping dance clubs of London that bring together the spiciest mix of gays, straights, lesbians, bis, queens, and just folks who want to shake it down.

The Fridge, Town Hall Parade, Brixton Hill, SW2 (tel. 326 5100). Tube: Brixton. "Love Muscle" on Sat. (10pm-6am) is the gay night at this hip club. Totally packed. The former theater's cavernous dance floor (that's for lesbians, not thespians!) still gets sweaty with the crowd of happy men and women dancing to house music. Open 10pm-6am. £9, £6 after 3am, £7 before midnight with flyer.

Heaven, Villiers St., WC2 (tel. 839 3852), underneath The Arches. Tube: Embankment or Charing Cross (Villiers is off of the Strand). Still the oldest and biggest gay disco in Europe. Three dance floors, high-tech lighting, pool tables, bars, and a capacity of 4000. Wed. is the "Fruit Machine," a popular mixed gay night, plus The Powder Room for drag queens. (Open 10pm-3:30am; £6, £4 with flyer or before 11:30pm. Fri. is "Garage," for a mixed gay/straight crowd, plus the Dyke Shed upstairs. (Open 10:30pm-3:30am; £7.50, £6 before 11:30pm, £4 with flyer.) Open 10pm-4am, £8, £7 before 11:30pm.

Turnmills, 63B Clerkenwell Rd., EC1 (tel. 250 3409). Tube: Farringdon. Walk up Turnmill St. and turn right onto Clerkenwell Rd. The Turnmills building plays host to 3 hugely popular clubs. Sat. night is "Pumpin' Curls," a women's night of hard house. Gay men allowed in as guests. (Open 10pm-3am, £5 or £10 joint ticket with "Trade"). At 3am, "Pumpin' Curls" turns into "Trade," a high-energy party for an attractive but no-attitude crowd that grinds to fierce house. Long queues. (Open 3am-noon. £10. Tickets available at Rox on Old Compton St., Trax on Greek St., and the Dispensary on Newburgh St. Joint tickets at Pumpin' Curls and Heaven.) Sun. night at *ff,* music tends to be more techno, the crowd younger, male, and cruisy. (Open 9:30pm-5am. £7, £5 concessions before midnight.)

Up to the Elbow, fortnightly at the Laurel Tree, 113 Bayham St., NW1 (tel. 485 1383). Tube: Camden Town. Exit the station left, then cross to the right; Bayham is parallel to Camden High St. Housed in a small, black-painted, windowless (and hot!) room above the Laurel Tree pub, this club offers a blend of British and L.A. queercore, both DJ's and live. Mixed crowd. Every other Fri. 9pm-late. £3.

SOUTH & SOUTHEAST ENGLAND

Holiday-goers have long been drawn by a warm climate and enthralling landscape to the cities and towns of South and Southeast England, comprising the counties of Kent, Sussex, and Hampshire. Most tourists scatter only Coke cans and Hobnob wrappers; Julius Caesar and William of Normandy left awe-inspiring reminders of their stays in coastal fortifications, most of which lie in ruins. These most threatened icons of England remain to symbolize the shaky durability of British tradition.

Victorian mansions lining Channel shores, rivers lapping along medieval town walls, majestic cathedrals springing from city skylines, and half-timbered houses along roadsides summon up a whirlwind of past voices. Geoffrey Chaucer gave pilgrims on their way to Canterbury both spiritual and bawdy tales to mull over; Charles Dickens grew up in Portsmouth and used his childhood experiences over and over as inspiration for his work. Virginia Woolf, E.M. Forster, John Keynes, and other members of the Bloomsbury group vacationed near Brighton, a seaside resort that has dispensed the dirty weekend to generations of Brits.

GETTING ABOUT

Public transportation pampers the area within 90 mi. of London, facilitating easy exploration of the towns in Southern England. **British Rail** offers day return tickets to many points in the southeast for little more than the cost of single tickets. You can easily make short hops from one town to another, especially along the coast. The **Network Away Break** ticket allows five days of unlimited travel on British Rail Network Southeast at reasonable rates. Almost all local bus companies offer their own travel passes. The **Explorer** ticket (£3.50-5), available from any local ticket office, allows one day of unlimited travel on virtually all **bus** routes in East Kent, Maidenstone, Hastings, and Southdown. The **Freedom** ticket and **Bus Ranger** ticket, available for periods of one, four, and 13 weeks, allow travel on most buses within a defined zone. The **National Bus Company** has offices in all major cities in the southeast; in summer, it's a good idea to reserve seats for Friday and Saturday trips. The **South Coast Express** #316 goes from Canterbury to Brighton, Worthing, and Portsmouth (1/day). Unfortunately, there is no good cheap map of both rail and bus routes. Inquire at tourist offices for detailed timetables and advice.

You can best enjoy the scenically undulating terrain on foot, bike, or moped. Walkers need not carry their packs the entire way; the many fine youth hostels—particularly along the South Downs Way—make excellent bases for day hikes. Tourist offices have regional camping directories.

■■■ CANTERBURY

> Whan Zephyrus eek with his sweete breeth
> Inspired hath in every holt and heeth
> The tendre croppes, and the yonge sonne
> Hath in the Ram his halve cours yronne...
> Thanne longen folk to goon on pilgrimages...
> —Geoffrey Chaucer, Prologue to The Canterbury Tales

"There is no lovelier place in the world than Canterbury," wrote the much-traveled, much-quoted Virginia Woolf. There are those who would disagree, most notably Thomas á Becket, who clashed with Henry II over the clergy's freedom from state jurisdiction. Henry cried in exasperation, "Who will deliver me from this turbulent priest?" In December 1170 four loyal knights answered their king's query and murdered Becket in the Canterbury cathedral. Becket died a martyr and a saint, Henry a mere mortal. In the Middle Ages, the road from London to Canterbury became England's busiest, as pilgrims made their way to Becket's shrine, prompting Chaucer's satire. Come to honor Becket, not to overlook him; visitors today approach

Canterbury Cathedral and the well-preserved village in its shadow for an awe-inspiring and endearing visit to the Southeast.

GETTING THERE

Trains run hourly from London's Victoria Station to Canterbury East Station (the stop nearest the youth hostel) and from Charing Cross and Waterloo stations to Canterbury West Station (1½hr.; £11.70). **Buses** to Canterbury leave London's Victoria Bus Station twice daily (1¾hr.; £6.75). Canterbury is almost as easy to reach from the Continent as from the rest of England; it's on the rail and bus lines from the Dover, Folkestone, and Ramsgate hovercraft terminals.

ORIENTATION & PRACTICAL INFORMATION

Canterbury is roughly circular, enclosed by a ring road around a city wall that has eroded slowly over the centuries. An unbroken street crosses the circle from west to east, taking the names **St. Peter's Street, High Street,** and **St. George's Street.** The cathedral rises from the northeast quadrant. To reach the tourist office from East Station, cross the footbridge, take a left down the hill, then a right on Castle St., which becomes St. Margaret's St. From West Station, walk southwest along Station Rd. West, turn left onto St. Dunstan's St., and walk through Westgate Tower onto St. Peter's St. (which becomes High St.), and then right onto St. Margaret's St.

Tourist Office: 34 St. Margaret's St. CT1 2TG (tel. 766567). Book-a-bed ahead for £3 or 10% deposit of first night's stay. Wide range of maps and guides for Canterbury and the rest of Kent. Those who won't call it quits after a poke through the cathedral should buy *City of Canterbury Guide* (£1.99). Open daily 9:30am-5:30pm; Nov.-March 9:30am-5pm.

Tours: Guided tours of the city depart from the tourist office April-Nov. daily 2pm; additional morning tour at 11am late May-early Sept. Mon.-Sat. On Friday evenings mid-July-late Aug. tours leave from the Buttermarket at 8pm. Tickets and other information available at the tourist center. £2.50, seniors, students, and children £1.80, under 12 free when accompanied by parent.

Financial Services: Banks on High St., including **Lloyd's** and **National Westminster,** close at 3:30 or 5pm. **Midland,** Watling St., opens Mon.-Sat. 9am-3:30pm. **Thomas Cook,** 9 High St. (tel. 781119), opens Mon.-Wed. and Fri.-Sat. 9am-5:30pm, Thurs. 10am-5:30pm. **American Express,** 29 High St. (tel. 784865), offers its full range of services Mon.-Sat. 9am-5pm.

Post Office: 26 High St. (tel. 475280), across from Best Lane. Open Mon.-Fri. 9am-5:30pm, Sat. 9am-12:30pm. *Poste Restante.* **Postal Code:** CT1 2BA.

Telephone Code: 01227.

Train Stations: East Station, Station Rd. East, off Castle St., southeast of town. **West Station,** Station Rd. West, off St. Dunstan's St. (tel. (01732) 770111). Open Mon.-Fri. 6:15am-7:40pm, Sat. 6:30am-7:40pm, Sun. 9:15am-5:30pm.

Bus Station: St. George's Lane (tel. 472082). Open Mon.-Sat. 8:15am-5:30pm. Get there by 5pm to book National Express tickets. **Luggage storage** until 5pm (£1).

Launderette: 36 St. Peter's St., near Westgate Towers. Open Mon.-Fri. 8:30am-5:45pm, Sat. 8:30am-5:30pm, Sun. 9am-1pm.

Market: ¼ mi. north of town along Northgate St. at Kingsmead Rd. opposite Sainsbury's. Open Wed. 9am-2pm.

Hotlines: DIAL (Disabled Informations Advice Line), 9a Gorvell Rd. (tel. 450001 or 462125); open Mon.-Fri. 10am-4pm, also 24-hr. answering service. **Kent Gay Information Line:** tel. (01233) 625395, ext. 2. Open Tues. 7:30-10pm. **Samaritans (crisis):** tel. 457777, on the corner of Love and Ivy Lanes.

Hospital: Kent and Canterbury Hospital: off Ethelbert Rd. (tel. 766877).

Police: Old Dover Rd. (tel. 762055), outside the eastern city wall.

Emergency: Dial 999; no coins required.

ACCOMMODATIONS, CAMPING, & FOOD

Book ahead in summer or arrive by mid-morning to secure rooms recently vacated. B&Bs bunch by both train stations and on London and Whitstable Rd., just beyond

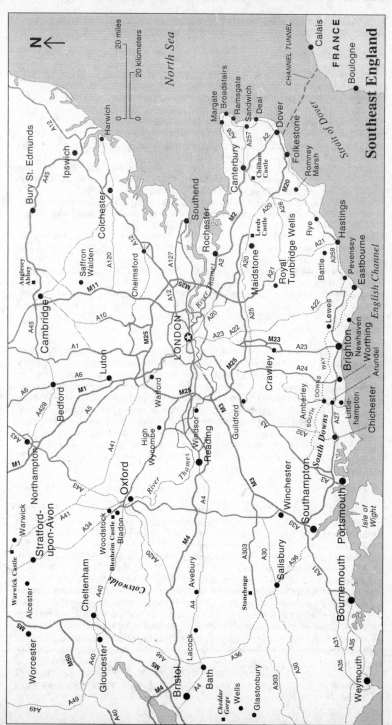

West Station. If you're desperate, head for the more costly B&Bs along New Dover Rd., a ½-mi. walk from East Station, near the youth hostel. Singles are scarce.

HI Youth Hostel, 54 New Dover Rd. (tel. 462911), ¾ mi. from East Station and ½ mi. southeast of the bus station. Turn right as you leave station and continue up the main artery, which becomes Upper Bridge St.; at second rotary, turn right onto St. George's Pl., which becomes New Dover Rd. 91 beds. Victorian villa with good facilities, washers, and hot showers. Doors open 7-10am and 1-11pm. £8.70, under 18 £5.80. Book a week in advance July-Aug. Open Feb.-Dec. daily. Call for off-season openings. When closed, try Dover or Broadstairs HI Youth Hostels.

The Tudor House, 6 Best Lane (tel. 765650), off High St. Clean, bright rooms in a 450-year-old house full of warmth and character. Agreeable owners and a central location. Bikes and boats for hire to guests. £16.

London Guest House, 14 London Rd. (tel. 765860). Run by Shirley and Peter Harris, their mutt Bo, and their ginger kitten Tigger. Spacious Victorian house in immaculate condition. Nicely decorated rooms. £16.

Milton House, 9 South Canterbury Rd. (tel. 765531). 20-min. walk from town center. Two tidy rooms and a warm welcome on a quiet street. Doubles £30. Proprietors will let their rooms go as singles as well.

York House, 22 Old Dover Rd. (tel. 765743), close to East Station, just outside the city wall. Spacious B&B, all rooms with TV. One shower for every 3 rooms. £14.

Alexandra House, 1 Roper Rd. (tel. 767011), a short walk from West Station. TV in all rooms. Upbeat new carpets, quilts, and furniture. Singles £18-25. Doubles £32-34, with shower £34-38, with private facilities £42-45.

Camping: St. Martin's Touring Caravan and Camping Site, Bekesbourne Lane (tel. 463216), off A257 (Sandwich Rd.), 1½ mi. east of city center. Take Longport Rd. from the city wall. 210 pitches for tents and good facilities. £3 pitch fee, £3.30. Open April-Oct.

Bakeries and sweet shops swarm the swart streets around the cathedral. High Street's various pubs, restaurants, and fast food establishments do a good bit of trade as well. On Castle St., **Gambell's Farmshop** deals in fresh fruits and vegetables. Vegetarian **Fungus Mungus,** 34 St. Peter's St., serves great fresh food despite its nasty name. Main dishes cost £4.95; starters run £2.10 (open daily 10am-11pm). **Marlowe's,** 55 St. Peter's St., presents an eclectic mix of vegetarian and beefy English, American, and Mexican food in a friendly setting with theatrical decor. Choose from seven kinds of 6-oz. burgers (£5.75), or stuff down a burrito for the same price (open daily 11am-11pm). **The White Hart,** Worthgate Pl. near East Station, is a congenial pub with homemade luncheon specials (£3-6). Live a little and ask to eat in the rose garden (open for lunch Mon.-Sat. noon-2:30pm).

SIGHTS

An amazingly quiet and near blissful Canterbury greets the early riser; by all means, get up early and enjoy the city before the daytrippers arrive. **Canterbury Cathedral,** England's most celebrated shrine, overwhelms the tiny town from all vantage points. To observe every detail of this soaring 537-ft. building, amble through the grounds of King's School off Palace St. Inside the cathedral, pass through the nave to the left where the dramatic **Altar of the Sword's Point,** the site of the murder, has been restored. The attackers bounded in and out the courtyard door. Explore the vast Norman **crypt,** the oldest part of the cathedral, and emerge into Trinity Chapel, where Becket's body lay enshrined until Henry VIII destroyed the memorial in 1538. (Open Easter-Oct. Mon.-Sat. 8:45am-7pm; Nov.-Easter 8:45am-5pm. Experience the cathedral as it was meant to be at choral evensong Mon. 5:15pm, Sat.-Sun. 3:15pm; 45 min. The cathedral closes two days in July for the University of Kent's graduation. Suggested donation £2. Check nave pulpit for times of guided tours: tickets £2.40, students £1.20. 25-min. walkman tour £1.70. Services Sun. 11am and 6:30pm.)

After making the necessary pilgrimage to the famed cathedral, see Chaucer's equally famous verses brought to life in many languages at **The Canterbury Tales** visitor attraction, St. Margaret's St. (tel. 454888). A swanky walkman-like gadget leads you through a virtual Canterbury pilgrimage land complete with eerie, ugly wax figures, moving sets, even the smells of sweat, hay, and general grime. As if your bus/rail/bike/hitchhiking/car trip to the town weren't enough, the exhibit simulates the journey all over again, and does an excellent job of illustrating the stories. A waxen, black-cloaked Chaucer himself guides you along, bawdy humor and all, like some chortling Virgil in a cosmos of opposites. (Open daily 9am-6pm; £4.75, seniors and students £3.95, children £3.50, family £15.)

The remainder of medieval Canterbury crowds around the branches of the River Stour on the way to the **Westgate,** the only one of the city's seven medieval gates to survive the wartime blitz. A small museum in **Westgate Tower** (tel. 452747) keeps armor and prison relics (open Mon.-Sat. 11am-12:30pm and 1:30-3:30pm; 60p). Several rickety monastic houses perch precariously along the banks of the Stour. For a quiet break, walk over to Stour St. and visit the riverside gardens of the **Greyfriars,** the first Franciscan friary in England, built over the river in 1267. The Franciscans arrived in England in 1224 from Assisi, Italy, two years before Francis died. A small museum and a chapel can be found inside the simple building (open in summer Mon.-Fri. 2-4pm; free). The lovely medieval **Poor Priests' Hospital,** also on Stour St., now houses the **Museum of Canterbury Heritage** (tel. 452747; open Mon.-Sat. 10:30am-5pm; June-Oct. Mon.-Sat. 10:30am-5pm, Sun. 1:30-5pm; £1.30, students £1, children 65p). On St. Peter's Street stand the famous **Weaver's Houses,** where Huguenots lived during the 16th century. Walk into the garden to see an authentic ducking stool (a medieval test for suspected witches) swinging above the river. **Weaver's River Tours** runs cruises from here several times daily (£3.50; row-it-yourself £2.50, children £1.50), except in time of drought. The **Royal Museum and Art Gallery** on High St. showcases struggling local talent. The mind-bogglingly angsty Gallery of the "Buffs" retells the history of the oldest regiments of the British army (open Mon.-Sat. 10am-5pm in the public library building; free).

Near the medieval city wall lie the **Dane John Mound and Gardens** and the massive, solemn remnants of the Norman **Canterbury Castle.** If you fail to encounter the ghost of Canterbury's own Christopher Marlowe "rolling down the streets a-singing," as one local historian put it, you can at least find a statue of his muse in the garden. Not much remains of **St. Augustine's Abbey** (598 AD), but older Roman ruins and the site of St. Augustine's first tomb (605 AD) can be viewed outside the city wall near the cathedral (tel. 767345; open Mon.-Sat. 9:30am-6pm, Sun. 2-6pm; off-season Mon.-Sat. 9:30am-4pm; £1, students 75p). Just around the corner from St. Augustine's on North Holmes St. stands the **Church of St. Martin,** the oldest parish church in England. Pagan King Ethelbert was married here to the French Christian Princess Bertha in 562. Joseph Conrad's heart sleeps in darkness inside the church.

ENTERTAINMENT

The tourist center carries a number of leaflets designed to help you have the night of your life in Canterbury. *Around Canterbury* provides an up-to-date calendar of events; *Fifteen Days,* published biweekly, describes entertainment in all its urban guises. Call 767744 for the recorded "Leisure Line." Buskers (street musicians) blend in with the crowds, especially along St. Peter's and High St. Young bands of impromptu players ramble from corner to corner, acting out the most absurd of Chaucer's scenes. The occasional Fool can be found performing juggling tricks and other joker stunts. But it's the pubs that keep Canterbury awake after dark and asleep till afternoon. The **Miller's Arms,** Mill Lane off Radigund St., offers six draught beers. **Alberry's,** 38 St. Margaret's St., a snazzy wine bar, has live music Monday and Thursday nights (9pm-1am). The bar opens Monday through Saturday from noon to midnight; happy hour is daily from 5:30 to 7pm (drinks 25% cheaper).

The new **Marlowe Theatre,** The Friars (tel. 787787), stages London productions and variety shows (tickets £4-17.50). The **Gulbenkian Theatre,** at the University of Kent, University Rd. (tel. 769075), west of town out St. Dunstan's St., past St. Thomas' Hill, stages a series of amateur and professional productions. (Box office open

Sept.-Dec. Mon. noon-4pm, Tues.-Fri. 10:30am-6pm, until 8pm performance evenings. Tickets £6-10; ask about student and senior discounts.)

The **Stour Music Festival,** a celebration of Renaissance and Baroque music, lasts for ten days at the end of June in Ashford, 5 mi. southwest of Canterbury. Wildly popular, the festival takes place in and around the beautiful **All Saint's Boughton Aluph Church,** accessible by rail from West Station and situated on the A28. Tickets start at £4; enthusiasts are advised to reserve tickets at least a month in advance, if not sooner. Call the Canterbury tourist office at 766567 for details. Ashford's **tourist office,** Lower High St. (tel. (01233) 37311), provides details, or call Forward Bookings at 455600. For information on summer arts events and the **Canterbury Festival**—two full October weeks of drama, opera, cabaret, chamber music, dance, and exhibitions inspired by French culture—call 452853, or write to Canterbury Festival, Christ Church Gate, The Precincts, Canterbury, Kent CT1 2EE.

■ NEAR CANTERBURY

Leeds Castle, 23 mi. southwest of Canterbury on the A20 London-Folkestone road, near Maidstone, was named after the fun-loving chief minister of Ethelbert IV. Henry VIII transformed it into a lavish dwelling. The surrounding 500 acres of woodlands and gardens host some of the world's most unusual waterfowl, including black swans; the castle itself houses a faintly alarming collection of medieval dog collars. From Canterbury, take the train from West Station and change at Ashford. (Open daily 11am-5pm; Nov.-Feb. Sat.-Sun. 10am-3pm; admission to castle and grounds £7, seniors and students £6, children £4.80, family £19.50. Grounds only £5.50, seniors and students £4.50, children £3.30, family £15. Wheelchair accessible; call (01622) 765400). For all information call (01622) 765400 or (01622) 880008.

Chilham Castle stands 6 mi. southwest of Canterbury along the A252. Only the octagonal keep survives from the 800 year-old fortress that was pulled down for use as building stone. The replacement castle represents the pinnacle of large-scale 17th-century architecture. Displays of jousting take place on Sundays, and tournaments of knights on Sundays, Mondays, and bank holidays (open April to mid-Oct. daily 11am-5pm; £3, children £1.50). The castle falconer gives demonstrations (same days). For general inquiries, call 730319.

■ ■ ■ DEAL

Julius Caesar came ashore with an invasion force at Deal in 55 BC, only to be greeted by fierce Britons in primitive galoshes determined to protect their land. Not so territorial these days, Deal's natives don't mind sharing a stretch of their pebbly beach or a space at the pub's counter. Deal deals in subtle merits; visitors will find it almost quiet enough to hear the water lapping at shore far inland.

GETTING THERE

Deal lies 8 mi. north of Dover and 12 mi. southeast of Canterbury; trains and buses stop in Deal on their way to these cities. **Trains** run at least every hour to London (£15) via Dover (return £2.50) and Sandwich (return £1.60). **National Express buses** visit Deal from London Victoria Station (£10.50).

ORIENTATION & PRACTICAL INFORMATION

The town extends from north to south along the coast. Beach St., High St., and West St.—the major arteries—parallel the coast. Deal's **tourist office,** Town Hall, High St. (tel. 369576), pulls in a good catch of leaflets, including the indispensable *Deal Walks,* which details ten 3-8½ mi. walks around the area. For £3 or 10% of the first night's stay, they'll book a room (open Mon.-Fri. 9am-12:30pm and 1:30-5pm, Sat. 10am-3pm; Sept.-mid-May Mon.-Fri. 9am-12:30pm and 1:30-5pm). The **train station** (tel. 852360) stands just west of town off Queen St. To reach Deal's center, turn left onto Queen St. and follow it until you reach the pedestrian precinct of High St. The

bus station (tel. 374088) idles on South St., one block south of Broad St. (office open Mon.-Wed. and Fri. 8:45am-12:30pm and 1:30-5pm, Thurs. and Sat. 8:45am-12:30pm). Rent some wheels at **Park Cycles,** rear of 42 High St. (tel. 366080; £5-8.50/day, £21.50-35/week; deposit from £30; open Mon.-Sat. 8:30am-5:30). **Banks** count their filthy lucre along High St.; **Lloyds** mourns its recent insurance losses at the corner of High and South St. (open Mon.-Fri. 9:30am-4:30pm). **National Westminster** laughs at Lloyds from the corner of High and Queens St. (open Mon.-Tues. and Thurs.-Fri. 9am-4:30pm, Wed. 9:30am-4:30pm). Unaware of it all, the **launderette** bubbles and foams on Queens St. Bring change (open Mon.-Fri. 8am-8pm, last wash 6:45pm; Sat. and Sun. 8am-8pm, last wash 4:45pm). The **post office** (tel. 374216) stirs at 17-19 Queens St. (open Mon.-Fri. 8:30am-5:30pm, Sat. 9am-5:30pm). Deal's **postal code** is CT14 6ET. The **telephone code** is 01304.

ACCOMMODATIONS & FOOD

Deal's utter simplicity and serenity begs a night's stay, though day trips are possible. The nearest youth hostels are in Dover and Canterbury. Be sure to phone B&Bs in advance on weekends. Overseeing Deal Castle, **The Gables,** 10 Gilford Rd. (tel. 347957) hide away cleverly decorated rooms (single £14, doubles £25). Hefty **Cannongate,** 26 Gilford Rd. (tel. 375238), delivers full English breakfast, both carn- and herbivorous (singles £13, doubles £26). From the station take a right down Blenheim Rd.; Gilford Rd. is ten minutes ahead on the left.

Greengrocers glister on High St. **Tesco** supermarket sells the usual stuff on Queens St. (open Mon.-Wed. 8am-6pm, Thurs.-Fri. 8am-8pm, Sat. 8am-5:30pm). Enjoy the Channel view, photos of motley locals with their catch, and '78 flood scenes at the **Lobster Pot** (full English breakfast all day; take-away fish and chips £2.70; open daily 7:30am-10pm). Relax in a plush chair in **Ronnie's,** a beautifully-appointed tea room off High St. at #1B Stanhope Rd. (tel. 374300). Cream tea served for £2.25. **Dunkerley's,** 19 Beach St. (tel. 375016), has an elegant two-course lunch deal for £7 (open Mon.-Fri. 11:30am-3pm and 6-10pm, Sat. 11:30am-3pm and 6-11pm, Sun. noon-10pm).

SIGHTS

A plump, three-tiered wedding cake without frosting, **Deal Castle** (tel. 372762) warded off Catholic invaders from the Continent during the reign of Henry VIII. The largest of Henry's buildings along the Deal coast, the castle sternly surveys its territory. An indomitable fortress rather than an elegant home, Deal Castle was done in the "Tudor Rose" style; it boasts six petals while Walmer Castle's ornamentation has but four (nyaah, nyaah!). Deal Castle stands south of town along the beach at the corner of Deal Castle Rd. and Victoria Rd. (open April-late Oct. daily 10am-6pm; Nov.-late March Wed.-Sun. 10am-4pm; £2, seniors and students £1.50, children £1; limited wheelchair accessibility; free tape tour available). **Walmer Castle** (tel. 364288), rests south of Deal on the A258 to Dover (around ½ mi. from town). The best preserved and most elegant of Henry VIII's citadels, Walmer has been softened by formal gardens and gradually transformed into a country estate. Since the 18th century, it has been the official residence of the Lords Warden of the Cinque Ports, a defensive system of coastal towns. Notable Lords Warden include the Duke of Wellington (whose precious Wellies are on display) and Winston Churchill. The post is currently filled by the Queen Mum. (Open April-Sept. daily 10am-6pm; Nov.-Dec. and March Wed.-Sun. 10am-4pm. Closed when Lord Warden is in residence. £2.70, students £1.90, children £1.30. Wheelchair access to courtyard and gardens.)

If you walk along the Coast to Deal Pier, you'll pass the **Timeball Tower,** a fascinating contraption connected by electric current to Greenwich Observatory. When ships used the Downs as a makeshift port before crossing the Channel, the ball on top of the tower was lowered at precisely 1pm each day to indicate the time to the sailors. Today, the ball drops every hour on the hour. Climb to the top to see a panorama of town and sea (open late spring-early Sept. Tues.-Sun. 10am-5pm; in winter tours offered by arrangement; £1.10, seniors and children 70p). The **Maritime and**

Local History Museum, 22 St. George's Rd. (tel. 369576), located behind the tourist office, delves into Deal's past with seafaring relics as figureheads and stern boards (open late May-late Sept. 2-5pm; 50p, seniors and students 40p, children 20p).

Deal's rowdiest crowd, among it shady figures like Irish Pete and Lascivious Lil, bring to life the town's smuggling past on the streets of Deal. This street theater tour lasts 1½ hrs and includes a pinch of pub-crawling through Old Deal (reserve tickets at the tourist office; £3, children £2.50). If you're in Deal in late July or early August, the **Deal Summer Music Festival** unleashes scores of musical acts. Call the box office (tel. 366077) at the Astor Theatre for tickets (£7-12). A day spent tooling around Deal's old foot paths, along the town streets, and over beachfront property is a day well spent. Refer to the tourist office's free *Deal Walks*.

■■■ SANDWICH

Sandwich (pop. 5500) was northernmost of the Cinque Ports until silt encroached on Kent, drawing the seas a few miles away. Streets narrow enough to prohibit car traffic make this remarkably-preserved village of medieval gateways and half-timbered houses well worth further exploration.

GETTING THERE

Sandwich squeezes 5 mi. north of Deal and 11 mi. east of Canterbury; trains and buses run regularly between these three points. **Trains** depart at least once per hour for Deal (£1.60), Dover (£3.20), and London's Victoria Station (£15.70). **Buses** leave several times daily to Deal but take much longer than the train. Buses make for London once a day (£10).

ORIENTATION & PRACTICAL INFORMATION

Sandwich's **tourist office,** Old Police Waiting Room, Guildhall, New St. (tel. 613565) hands out a free leaflet outlining a self-guided tour of town (open May-Sept. daily 11am-3pm). Also available at the tourist office is the free packet entitled *Sandwich Walks,* which details short, tasteful jaunts about the town and countryside. The **train station** lies just off St. George's Rd. To reach the center of town, bear left on Delfside, turn left on St. George's, then right onto New St. **Buses** stop across from Guildhall on Cattlemarket (tel. 612067; open Mon.-Sat. 9am-12:45pm and 2-5pm). Disgruntled workers at Sandwich's **post office,** 34 King's St., endure opening envelopes filled with rotting meat-and-bread concoctions sent to them as practical jokes (open Mon.-Fri. 9am-5:30pm, Sat. 9am-12:30pm; **postal code** CT139AA). Though they deluge the **police** at Dover (tel. 240055) with complaints, the merciless prankster has never been caught. Sandwich's **telephone code** is 01304.

ACCOMMODATIONS & FOOD

Because Sandwich lacks a youth hostel and any glimmer of nightlife, budget travelers should consider tripping in for the day. Those with an itch to spend the night in this tiny place should call in advance to reserve a guest house room. Check with the tourist office for newly-sprouted B&B and self-catering options. **Manders,** Sunnycot Cottage, 31 Moat Sole (tel. 612057 or 61558), offers homey singles for £15 in a 250-year-old building squished like jelly between newer houses on a quiet residential street. Four minutes from the train station rests **Mrs. Rogers,** 57 St. George's Rd. (tel. 612772). The train-weary will find a friendly couple with two bedrooms in a beautiful home on a meek street (£13). Campers walk along Moat Sole behind Guildhall and over the train tracks to find the **Sandwich Leisure Park Campsite,** Woodnesborough Rd. (tel. 612681), ½ mi. from town (29 pitches; £6.75; open March-Oct.).

Food hasn't been the same since the Earl of Sandwich munched his masterwork. Have a hearty pub lunch at **The Red Cow,** Moat Sole, behind the Guildhall Museum (£3.50-5; open Mon.-Sat.; meals served noon-2pm and 7-9:30pm) At the **16th-Century Tea House,** 9 Cattle Market, across from Guildhall, you can inhale a delicious three-course lunch for £4.95 or indulge in cream tea for £2.75 (open daily 9am-6pm). For a proper tea-making experience around a rustic fireplace, stop by **Cherubs,** 8 Potter St. (open Mon.-Sat. 10am-9:30pm). **Sandwich Continental,** 6 Market St., is an upbeat, family-run restaurant that serves a creative selection of (could it be?) sandwiches from £1.40 and all-day English breakfast (£3.95; open Mon.-Fri. 9am-4pm, Sat. 8:30am-4pm, Sun. 9am-noon).

SIGHTS

A short walk around the town proper reveals quite a bit of history; Strand St. itself boasts perhaps the largest concentration of half-timber Tudor buildings in England. The elevated Butts, Rope Walk, and Mill Wall that once garnished Sandwich's crust now make for a lovely stroll. The **Gazen Salts Nature Reserve** (tel. 611925, evenings only) graces the northwest of town (follow signs across Gallows Field, the former execution site, from the Butts). No trees or shrubs graced the one-time pasture before 1973, when the reserve came into being. The area just borders the marshland which silted over and separated Sandwich from the sea, and hosts numerous birds and other animals (admission free). The River Stour remains a lovely waterway by which to spend the day, dominated by the **Barbican,** built by Henry VIII as part of his coastal defense scheme. The **Guildhall Museum,** beside the tourist office on Cattle Market (tel. 617197), flaunts an extensive, engaging exhibit of Victorian photographs, among other items (open April-Sept. Tues.-Wed. and Fri. 10am-noon and 2-4pm, Thurs. and Sat. 10am-4pm, Sun. 2-4pm; Oct.-March Tues.-Wed., Fri., and Sun. 2-4pm, Thurs. and Sat. 10am-4pm; £1, children 50p, family £2.)

■ ■ ■ DOVER

> The sea is calm tonight.
> The tide is full, the moon lies fair
> Upon the straits;—on the French coast the light
> Gleams and is gone; the cliffs of England stand
> Glimmering and vast, out in the tranquil bay.
> —Matthew Arnold, "Dover Beach"

The grating roar of the English Channel has been drowned out by the puttering of ferries, the hum of hovercraft, and the squabbling of French families *en vacances.* Yet Dover has retained its identity despite the grating roar of tourist traffic. The timeless white chalk cliffs tower above the beach, and Dover's fortress has long outlasted the threats of Napoleon and Hitler. Though the town remains quite ordinary, the dramatic coast, with its darkling plain of lighthouses and Norman ruins, is a stirring reminder of England's history.

GETTING THERE

Trains roar to Dover's Priory Station from London's Victoria, Waterloo, Cannon St., London Bridge, and Charing Cross stations approximately every 45 minutes (2hr., £15.60). Beware when you board at London; many trains branch off en route. From Victoria, express lines continue to the Western Docks Station.

Buses run regularly (2/hr.) from London's Victoria Coach Station; they continue to the Eastern Docks after stopping at the bus station on Pencester Rd. (2¾hr., £10). Buses also make hourly trips to Canterbury (£3), Deal (£1.85), and Sandwich (£2.50); a bus to Folkestone (£1.70) runs every two hours.

Major **ferry** companies operate ships from Dover to Calais, and the Dover tourist office offers a ferry booking service. Ferries to Belgium no longer sail from Dover; ferries to Oostende in Belgium now sail from nearby Ramsgate. **Hovercraft** leave from the Hoverport at the Prince of Wales Pier for Calais or Boulogne. Free bus service leaves Priory Station for the docks and the Hoverport 45 minutes to one hour before sailing time. Several offices, including the Dover tourist office, can book both

Hovercraft and ferry crossings at last-minute notice.(See Essentials: Getting There—From Continental Europe for complete ferry and hovercraft info).

In May 1994, the **Channel Tunnel (Chunnel)** was completed, connecting England and France (the horror!/*l'horreur!*). By spring 1995, the limited *Discovery* train service between London and Paris/Brussels through the Chunnel will give way to a full *Eurostar* service with approximately fifteen daily departures to either destination. It has yet to be determined what rail passes (BritRail or Eurail) will be accepted for the journey. Consult Thomas Cook's European timetable or call (01233) 617575 for information.

ORIENTATION & PRACTICAL INFORMATION

To reach the tourist office from the railway station, turn left onto Folkestone Rd. Continue until York St.; turn right and follow it to the end. Turn left onto Townwall St.; the tourist office is on the left. From the bus station, turn left from Pencester onto Cannon St. Proceed through the pedestrianized city to Townwall St. and turn left. York St., which becomes High St. and eventually London Rd., borders the center of town. Maison Dieu Rd. braces the town's other side.

Tourist Office: Townwall St. (tel. 205108), a block from the shore. The friendly folk who daily greet a whole slew of international arrivals post a list of accommodations after hours and supply ferry and hoverport tickets. Open daily 9am-6pm.

Post Office: 65-66 Biggin St. (tel. 241747). Currency exchange available. Open Mon.-Fri. 9am-5:30pm, Sat. 9am-12:30pm. **Postal Code:** CT16 1BA.

Financial Services: Barclays, Market Sq. Open Mon.-Tues. and Thurs.-Fri. 9:30am-4:30pm, Wed. 10am-4:30pm. **Lloyd's Bank,** Market Sq. (tel. 240808). Open Mon.-Fri. 9:30am-5:30pm. **National Westminster,** Market Sq. Open Mon.-Tues. and Thurs.-Fri. 9:30am-5:30pm, Wed. 9:30am-5:30pm. **Thomas Cook,** 3 Cannon St. (tel. 204215). Open Mon.-Wed. and Fri.-Sat. 9am-5:30pm, Thurs. 10am-5:30pm.

Telephone Code: 01304.

Launderette: Cherry Tree Ave., right off London Rd. beyond the hostel. Change machine. Open daily 8am-8pm; last wash 7:15pm.

Train Station: Priory Station (tel. (01732) 770111), off Folkestone Rd.

Bus Station: Pencester Rd., which runs between York St. and Maison Dieu Rd. (tel. 240024; information (01813) 581333). Purchase tickets on the bus or in the ticket office. Open Mon.-Fri. 8:30am-5:30pm, Sat. 8:30am-2pm.

Hospital: Buckland Hospital (tel. 201624), on Coomb Valley Rd. northwest of town. Take local bus D9 or D5 from outside the post office.

Police: Ladywell St., right off High St. (tel. 240055).

ACCOMMODATIONS & CAMPING

At the height of tourist season rooms are harder to find. Plan ahead; the ferry terminal makes an ugly campground. Several of the hundreds of B&Bs on **Folkestone Road** (by the train station) stay open all night; if the lights are on, ring the bell. During the day, try the B&Bs near the center of town on **Castle Street.**

Charlton House Youth Hostel (HI), 306 London Rd. (tel. 201314), with overflow at 1**4 Goodwyne Rd.** (closer to town center). Hostel is a ½ mi. walk from the train station: turn left onto Folkestone Rd., left onto Effingham St., past the gas station onto Saxon St., and left at the bottom of the street onto High St., which becomes London Rd. Recently refurbished. Kitchen, shower, 70 beds. Lockers available. Lockout 10am-1pm. Curfew 11pm. Overflow building has 60 beds with bathrooms in each room. Kitchen and lounge area. Both hostels £8.80, under 18 £5.95. Breakfast £2.70. You may have to wait a bit for staff at the overflow hostel.

Elmo Guest House, 120 Folkestone Rd. (tel. 206236). A proprietor with a calming presence has airy rooms for £12-16 near the train station.

YMCA, 4 Leyburne Rd. (tel. 206138). Turn right off Goodwyne Rd. Rough it with a pallet on the floor (perfect if you have sleeping bag). Men and women. No curfew. Showers. Reception open daily 9am-noon and 5-10pm. £5 with B&B.

Amanda Guest House, 4 Harold St. (tel. 201711). Well-located house built by a former mayor of Dover. £15, children half-price.

Gordon Guest House, 23 Castle St. (tel. 201894). The management takes cordial where cordial has never gone before. Comfortable rooms, all complete with showers (4 with full bathrooms). From £12-19.

Victoria Guest House, 1 Laureston Pl. (tel. 205140). The Hamblins extend a friendly, family welcome to their international guests. Doubles £26-40, family rooms £48-54. Prices fall in off-season. Special 5-day rates available.

Camping: Harthorn Farm, at Martin Mill Station off the A258 between Dover and Deal (tel. 852658). Large site in a gorgeous rural setting, but a little too close to the railway. 200 pitches. July-Sept. car-and-tent fee (£3.25) plus £3.25/person; without car £3.25/person, ages 10-16 £2. Electricity hook-up £1.62.

FOOD

Despite the proximity of the Continent, Dover's cuisine remains loyally English. Grease fires rage dawn to dusk in the fish-and-chip shops and grocery stores on London Rd. and Biggin St., and a decent pub lunch can be had almost anywhere in the city center. Vegetarians in Dover might check out **The Cabin,** 91 High St. (tel. 206118), or **Topo Gigio,** 1-2 King St. (tel. 201048), for options.

Chaplin's, 2 Church St. (tel. 204870). Grandma meets Charlie in this floral restaurant sprinkled with Chaplin photos and mementoes. Sandwiches come cheap at £1.50 and cheeseburgers with fries cost £2.80. What's this about an all-day English breakfast? £2.95. Open Mon.-Sat. 8:30am-9pm, Sun. 11:30am-5pm.

Jermain's Café, 18 Leighton Rd., on a quiet street off London Rd., just past the hostel; turn onto Beaconsfield Rd., then left into Jermain's. Menu on chalkboards outside. Roast beef, potatoes, and veggies £3.20. Open daily 11:30am-2pm.

Pizza Pronto, 7 Ladywell (tel. 214234). Medium-sized pizzas made while you wait. Good and hot. Plain pizza rings in at £3.50. Open daily 5pm-midnight.

SIGHTS

The view from Castle Hill Rd., on the east side of town, reveals why **Dover Castle** is famed both for its magnificent setting and for its impregnability. (Take bus D77, 90 or 90A from Priory Station; minibus from town center April-Sept. weekends.) Many have launched assaults on it by land, sea, and air: the French tried in 1216, the English during the English Civil Wars in the mid-17th century, and the Germans in World Wars I and II. All efforts failed until 1994, when a phalanx of cyclists under the banner of the *Tour de France* invaded the castle, starting the British leg of cycling's greatest event there. Though workmen established an elaborate plumbing system in the castle, they unfortunately installed lead pipes; look down the long well shaft to discover just how sophisticated their system was. The **castle keep** showcases a queer medley of trivia and relics from the 12th century to the present, including an exhibit entitled "Live and Let Spy," which displays a number of brilliant Bond-like shaving-brushes and dominoes, used to conceal maps and compasses during World War II. The top of the castle, accessible by several staircases, affords an arresting view of the battlements and countryside. Boulogne, 22 mi. across the Channel, can (barely) be seen on clear days; it was from that coast that the Germans launched V-1 and V-2 rocket bombs in World War II. These "doodle-bugs" destroyed the **Church of St. James,** the ruins of which crumble at the base of Castle Hill. The empty **Pharos,** built in 43 BC, sits alongside **St. Mary's,** a Saxon church. The interior of the church is covered with tiles, lending it the appearance of a giant communal shower minus suds and water. The Pharos once served as a beacon for Caesar's galleys. The only Roman lighthouse still in existence and certainly the tallest remaining Roman edifice in Britain, the Pharos' gaping keyhole windows testify to its original purpose. **Hell Fire Corner** is a labyrinth of secret **tunnels** only recently declassified, totalling 3½ mi. Originally built in the late 18th-century to defend Britain from attack by Napoleon, the tunnels were the base for the evacuation of Allied troops from Dunkirk in World War II (Operation Dynamo). The tunnels served various functions for the county government of Kent until the 1980s, when operation costs became prohibitive. Graffiti covers most of the passageways. Though most date from the 1940s, a few inscriptions from the 19th century can be seen. Convince the guides to show you the Napoleonic double helix staircase (open daily 10am-6pm; Nov.-March 10am-4pm; £5.25, seniors and students £3.95, children £2.60, family £15; partially wheelchair accessible).

Recent excavation has unearthed a remarkably well-preserved **Roman painted house** (tel. 203279), New St., off Cannon St. near Market Sq., the oldest Roman house in Britain, complete with wall paintings and under-floor central heating system. The house was dug out from under 20 ft. of soil. (Open July-Aug. daily 10am-6pm; May-June Tues.-Sun. 10am-6pm; April and Sept.-Oct. Tues.-Sun. 10am-5pm. £1.50, seniors and children 50p.) The **Dover Museum,** Market Sq. (tel. 201066), displays curious bits of Victoriana, ship models, and clocks (open daily 10am-6pm; mid-Nov.-Feb. 10am-5:30pm; £1.20, seniors, students, and children 75p; wheelchair accessible). Meet the dark side of Victorian values at the **Old Town Gaol,** Town Hall, Biggin St. (tel. 201200; open Mon.-Sat. 10am-4:30pm, Sun. 2-4:30pm; off-season Wed.-Sat. 10am-4:30pm, Sun. 2-4:30pm; £3.20, seniors and children £1.90).

A few miles west of Dover (25 min. by foot along Snargate St.) sprawls the whitest, steepest, most famous, and least accommodating of the cliffs. Known as **Shakespeare Cliff** (look for the signs), it is traditionally identified with eyeless Gloucester's battle with the brink in *King Lear.* Closer to town on Snargate St. is the **Grand Shaft** (tel. 201200), a 140-ft. triple spiral staircase shot through the rock in Napoleonic times to link the army on the Western Heights and the city center. The first stairwell was for "officers and their ladies," the second for "sergeants and their wives," the last for "soldiers and their women." (Choose your stairwell and ascend May-Sept. Wed.-Sun. 2-5pm, on bank holidays 10am-5pm; £1, children 40p.)

■■■ RYE

Settled before the Roman invasion, Rye's port flourished until the waterways choked with silt. Throughout the 18th century, the town was best known for its bands of smugglers, who darted past royal authorities to stash contraband in an elaborate network of massive cellars, secret passageways, and attics. Today, this townlet on a hill provides the archetypal cushy country weekend to its adoring visitors.

GETTING THERE

Trains roll to London's Charing Cross and Cannon St. stations (1½hr.; £13.30), to Brighton (£9.30) and Eastbourne (£5.20) via Ashford, and to Dover (£7.70) via Hastings. You can also go via Tunbridge Wells, changing at Hastings. **National Express buses** run from London to Rye (£11). Regular bus service runs to points all around southeast England and beyond; schedules flap in the train station's parking lot.

ORIENTATION & PRACTICAL INFORMATION

Pinned in by waterways on three sides, Rye (pop. 4400) resides at the mouth of the River Rother. The **tourist office,** Rye Heritage Centre, The Strand Quay (tel. 226696), distributes the free *Rye: 1066 Country* guide, which lists points of interest, rooms, and eating establishments (open daily 9am-5:30pm; Nov.-March Mon.-Fri. 11am-1pm, Sat.-Sun. 10am-4pm). To reach the tourist office from the **train station**, off Cinque Port St. (tel. (01424) 429325), turn right on Cinque Port St. (it becomes Wish St.). Turn left onto the Strand Quay; the office will be on the left. **Buses** (tel. 223343) stop in front of the train station. To reach the oldest and prettiest part of town, hike up Market Rd. to High St., Lion St., and Mermaid St. **Lloyd's, Barclay's,** and **National Westminster** line High St. The folks at 8/9 Ropewalk Arcade (tel. 223121) rent **bikes** for £7.50/day. A **launderette** spins clothes directly across from the bike shop (tel. 225324; open daily 8:30am-6pm). If you're feeling especially extravagant, have them wash, dry (complete with fabric softener), and deliver your clothing within one hour for £4. Call the **police** at (01424) 425000, or stop by the station on Cinque Port St. **Post office** workers play fervent games of Lite Brite on Cinque Port St. (#22-24; tel. 222163; open Mon.-Fri. 9am-5:30pm, Sat. 9am-12:30pm). Rye's **postal code** is TN31 7AA. Rye's **telephone code** is 01797.

ACCOMMODATIONS & CAMPING

Affluent holiday-goers inflate the prices of some of Rye's B&Bs. Consult the tourist office for listings of spare rooms.

HI Youth Hostel, Guestling, Rye Rd., Hastings (tel. (01424) 812373), 5 mi. down the A259 past Winchelsea on west side of main Hastings-Rye Rd. Take bus #11 or 12 from Rye to the White Hart in Guestling, 200yd. downhill on left from the White Hart. (Mon.-Sat. roughly 1/hr., summer Sun. every 2 hr.; £1.60; last bus around 5pm). You can also take the train to Three Oaks (£1.90) and walk 1¼ mi. 58 beds. Some family rooms available, but book early. £6.90, under 18 £4.60. Open July-Aug. daily; Sept.-Oct. and Feb. 12-March Tues.-Sat.; Nov. Fri.-Sat.; April 11-June Mon.-Sat. Camping pitches also available on 4 acres of surrounding land.

Mrs. Jones, 2 The Grove (tel. 223447), a 3-min. walk from the train station. Turn left through the car park and left again onto Rope Walk, which becomes The Grove just past the train tracks. Well-read landlady who pipes lovely classical music through the house. Plush rooms accompanied by an equally extravagant breakfast, complete with fruit and yogurt. £14.

Mrs. Clifton, 4 Love Lane (tel. 222979). Gorgeous flowers line the walk up to this brick home with large rooms quite near the train station. £14.

Riverhaven Guest House, 60 New Winchelsea Rd. (tel. 223267). Clean and friendly guest house run by the Hollinses. Call for the proprietors to pick you up from train station, especially if you happen to be toting a rucksack. £10-15.

Amberley Bed and Breakfast, 5 New Rd. (tel. 225693). Richard and Jane McGowan run a spotless family B&B. Beautifully furnished, with views of the water. Located on main road from £14-18.

Tillingham Bed and Breakfast, 13 Winchelsea Rd. (tel. 224807). Second generation B&Bers (and their precious toddler) welcome you into their tidy, comfortable home. Big screen TV and VCR in lounge. £15, winter £12.50.

Camping: Old Coghurst Farm, Three Oaks (tel. (01424) 753622), near Guestling and youth hostel. Same buses as hostel. £2.50/2-person tent, £3.60/2+person tent; £1.40/person; under 12 70p. Low season £2.20/2-person tent, £1/person.

FOOD & PUBS

Rye restaurateurs dabble in practically every sort of cuisine and style of serving it. Full-service eateries, take-away joints, and teashops riddle Rye. Pub fare comes cheaper than most. **Ye Olde Tuck Shoppe** on Market St. and **Simon the Pieman** on Lion St. peddle baked goods. The town **market** takes place on Thursday from 8:30am to 3pm. Take care not to go on the wrong day, or you might come away with a live sheep. The **Fish Shop** on Mint St., fries a popular and cheap alternative (open Mon.-Fri. 11:30am-8pm, Sat. 11:30am-9pm, Sun. noon-7pm).

Union Inn, East St., offers a wide selection of foods (£1.70-5.45) in a building erected around the 15th century. Open Mon.-Sat. 11am-3pm and 6-11pm; Sun. noon-3pm and 7-10:30pm.

Fletcher's House, Lion St. (tel. 223101), in front of the church. Dramatist John Fletcher was born here in 1579. Open for morning coffee, lunch, and tea. After a meal, wander upstairs to the 15th-century oak room filled with antiques. Filling lunches £3-5; cream tea £3.40. Open daily 10am-5:15pm.

Jempson's Coffee House and Bakery, Cinque Port St. and Market Rd. Mouthwatering assortment of pastries, and cream teas for £2.25. Open Mon.-Sat. 8am-6pm.

Fu Wing Chinese Restaurant, 2 High St. (tel. 223360). Though dear at dinner, Fu Wing offers a small menu of cheap lunch options: curried vegetables £3.20, beef with green peppers in black bean sauce £3.60. Open Sun.-Mon. and Thurs. noon-2pm and 5:30-10:30pm, Wed. 5:30-10:30pm, Fri.-Sat. noon-2pm and 5:30-11pm.

For a unique pub experience, buy a drink at the **Mermaid Inn** and sit above old smuggling tunnels. For standard pub fare, there are several places to gorge along High St., namely the **Standard Inn.**

SIGHTS

A handful of cobbled streets recall the days when smugglers stole through a sleepy Rye. Extraordinarily well-preserved half-timber homes cover the hill on which much of the town sits. **Lamb House** stands on West St. (at the corner of West and Mermaid St.). Henry James wrote the most insufferable of his later novels while living in the brick home, including *The Wings of the Dove* and *The Golden Bowl* (open April-Oct. Wed. and Sat. 2-5:30pm; £2). Before descending the hill, contemplate **St. Mary's Church,** the huge medieval parish church at the top of Lion St., which houses one of the oldest functioning clocks in the country. The clock's gold-plated "quarter boys,"—they tolled every quarter hour—were forced into early retirement by upstart fiberglass models, and rest in a dignified position on the window sill. In 1377 the French nearly toasted Rye with an immense fire. The church was blackened and its bells were stolen, though some beefy Brits recovered them afterwards. A climb up the tower steps reveals the inner-workings of the clock and the best view of the river valley a pound-and-a-half (75p for children) can buy.

Around the corner from the church rises the **Ypres Tower** above the **Rye Museum.** Originally built to fortify the town against invaders from the sea (c. 1250), the tower has served as a jail and currently contains a haphazard display on reform politics, military paraphernalia, domestic life, and Rye pottery (open April-Oct. daily 10:30am-5pm; £1.50, seniors and students £1, children 50p). A walk down Mermaid St. leads you to the famed **Mermaid Inn,** where smugglers once cavorted until dawn. Not many cavort in Rye these days, though some brush close to it during the week-long **festival,** held in early September. Rye ushers in artists, writers, and musicians for the week (festival booking office tel. 227338; tickets £3.50-8).

■ NEAR RYE: BATTLE, PEVENSEY, BODIAM

Appropriately named after the decisive fight between William of Normandy and King Harold of England that took place here in 1066, **Battle** makes a fine expedition from Rye. To commemorate his victory in the Battle of Hastings, William the Conqueror had **Battle Abbey** (tel. (01424) 773 7921) built in 1094, spitefully positioning its high altar upon the very spot where Harold died. The town grew prosperous enough to survive Henry VIII's closure of the abbey in 1538. Now little remains apart from the gate and a handsome series of 13th-century common quarters (open daily 10am-6pm; Oct.-March. 10am-4pm; £2.70, students £1.90, children £1.30). The battlefield where William's outnumbered band rushed uphill to take Harold's troops by surprise, is now a pasture trampled only by demented sheep. In summer, you can take a tour of the abbey and walk the **battlefield trail,** a 1-mi. jaunt up and down the green hillside.

Battle's **train station** is 30 minutes from **Hastings** on the mainline hourly service from London (for information tel. (01424) 429325). **Bus** #28 runs frequently from Rye to Battle's abbey green in summer; check the timetables on High St. or call (01424) 431770. B&Bs in Battle charge about £17.50 and can be booked by the **tourist office** opposite Battle Abbey, 88 High St. (tel. (01424) 773721; fax 773436; open daily 10am-6pm; Oct.-April Mon.-Sat. 10am-4pm, Sun. 1-4pm). Also try the office in the quiet coastal resort of **Bexhill-on-Sea** (tel. (01424) 212023).

William the Conqueror began his march to Battle from the Roman fortress Anderita. He gave the castle to his brother, who added a Norman keep; around this castle grew **Pevensey,** one of the more delightful towns of the southern coast. (Castle tel. (01323) 762604. Open daily 10am-6pm; Nov.-March Wed.-Sun. 10am-4pm. £1.80, students £1.35, children 90p.) **St. Mary's,** in Westham (tel. (01424) 773649), claims to be the first church built by the Normans after their conquest of England.

The best part of Pevensey owes its origins to commerce rather than conquest. The **Mint House,** High St., begun as a mint under the Normans, was transformed by Henry VIII's physician into a country retreat, and eventually ended up as a smugglers' den, complete with sliding ceiling panels. The antique store teems with Victorian miscellany, stuffed birds, grandfather clocks, and other fascinating oddities—themselves worth the price (open Mon.-Sat. 9:30am-5pm; 80p). Pevensey's **tourist office** stands guard in Pevensey Castle Car Park, High St. (tel. (01323) 761444; open Easter-Sept. daily 10:30am-4:30pm). For **rail** information in the area, call (01424) 429325; for buses call (01424) 722223.

To top off a tour of local castles, head down the A268 to **Bodiam Castle** (tel. (01580) 830436). Built in the 14th century, romance seeps from the castle moat and in sweeping views of the downs. Bring a handful of breadcrumbs for the ducks (castle open daily 10am-6pm; Jan.-March Tues.-Sun. 10am-dusk; £2.50, children £1.30).

■■■ SOUTH DOWNS WAY

The South Downs form a hilly ridge in southern England, parallel to the urban strip sprawling from Eastbourne westward to Portsmouth, and separated from the North Downs by the low-lying Weald. Following the contours of the hills for some 99 mi., the South Downs Way is the oldest long-distance bridle, cycle, and foot path in England.

ORIENTATION & PRACTICAL INFORMATION

Walking the entire path takes about ten days, but public transportation makes it possible to walk just a segment of the trail. Catch a bus or train to one of the major southeastern towns, such as Eastbourne, Brighton or Chichester, and transfer to a local bus which will drop you near the Way. Hourly **train** service runs from London's Victoria Station to Eastbourne (where local service can take you to **Southease,** right on the Way, 5 mi. by bus or thumb along the A275 from Lewes) or **Amberly** (via Horsham), where the path crosses the River Arun. The intersection of Forty Acre Lane and the B2146 is just a short hitch from **Petersfield,** where trains run hourly to London's Waterloo Station. For train information, call Brighton station (tel. (01273) 206755); for **bus** schedules, call Brighton (tel. (01273) 206666) or Chichester (tel. (01243) 783251).

ACCOMMODATIONS

The local tourist offices in Brighton, Chichester, and Eastbourne can supply information on accommodations and points of interest en route. Four **HI Youth Hostels** stretch along or near the Way, each within a day's walk of the next. Alternatively, consider daytrips along parts of the Way, especially from Brighton.

Eastbourne: East Dean Rd., Eastbourne, East Sussex BN20 8ES (tel. (01323) 721081). At start of Way. On the A259, ¼ mi. down a steep hill into Eastbourne, 2 mi. from Beachy Head Cliffe. From the Eastbourne station, turn right and follow A259 (marked Seaford/Brighton). 1½ mi. to the hostel. Lockout 10am-5pm. £7.15, under 18 £4.75. Open July-Aug. daily; Sept.-Oct. and April-June Wed.-Mon.

Alfriston: Frog Firle, Alfriston, Polegate, East Sussex BN26 5TT (tel. (01323) 870423). 1 mi. from Way, 8 mi. from Eastbourne. Lockout 10am-5pm. £8.70, under 18 £5.80. Open July-Aug. daily; Sept.-Oct. and Feb.-June Mon.-Sat.; Nov.-Dec. Fri.-Sat.

Telscombe: Bank Cottages, Telscombe, Lewes, East Sussex BN7 3HZ (tel. (01273) 556196). 2 mi. from Way, 12 mi. from Alfriston. Lockout 10am-5pm. £6.90, under 18 £4.60. Open July-Aug. daily; April-June and Sept.-mid-Oct. Fri.-Wed.

Truleigh Hill: Tottington Barn, Truleigh Hill, Shoreham-by-Sea, West Sussex BN43 5FB (tel. (01903) 813419). At the center of the Way, 10 mi. from Brighton. Modern building on an old barn site on 4½ acres of ground. Lockout 10am-5pm. £7.50, under 18 £5. Open July-Aug. daily; Sept.-Oct. Mon.-Sat.

BRIGHTON

HIKING

The eastern tip of the Way skirts the hairsbreadth of coast touching the **Seven Sisters Country Park** before running behind the seaside resorts to flank the coast. The path begins at the edge of the Downs just west of **Eastbourne,** climbs up toward **Beachy Head,** and passes by the cliffs of the **Seven Sisters;** satisfy yourself with oblique views of the sheer chalk and stay clear of the fatal edges. Head inland along the eastern bank of the River Cuckemere and tramp westwards through small villages to **Firle Beacon,** one of the highest points of the Downs at 712 ft. At **Devil's Dyke,** near **Pyecombe,** the ramparts of a prehistoric fort look down on a steep hollow gouged in the countryside. Further on towards Washington, the route past **Chanctonbury Ring** is a favorite, with its dew pond and eerie views from the steep heights. Unfortunately, fierce gales in the past three years have withered the distinctive trees of the Ring. Continue across the River Arun to **Littleton Down,** with northerly views of the Weald and an occasional glimpse of the North Downs. The spire of Chichester Cathedral marks the beginning of **Forty Acre Lane,** the final arm of the Way which reaches out to touch the West Sussex/Hampshire border.

Horseback riding, the traditional way to travel the Downs, is the business of the **Three Greys Riding School** (tel. (Hassocks) 3536). **Bikes** can be rented at towns along the Way. Bicyclists should be wary, however, of the Way's stony stretches. These routes are meticulously signposted with the words "South Downs Way" or the Countryside Commission's acorn symbol. Due to the terrain, the western section of the Way between Briton and Winchester is closed to both cyclists and riders.

Most useful for serious trekkers are Ordnance Survey 1:50,000 maps #185, 197, 198, and 199. The Ordnance Survey details the route between Rodmell and Stirling. The official Countryside Commission *National Trust Guide* to the Way (£9) is comprehensive and well worth the money for those contemplating more than a brief stroll on the route. It contains the relevant Ordnance Survey map segments. The Society of Sussex Downsmen (tel. (01273) 771906) publishes *Along the South Downs Way* (£2.50) with a brief accommodations guide (both available from area bookshops). For expert guidance call the Sussex Downs Conservation Project (tel. (01243) 777618). Most tourist offices also carry booklets containing Ordnance Survey maps (about £5). For a cheaper aid to finding the Way, check out the *South Downs Way Guide* at any tourist office (30p). Paul Millmore's *The South Downs Way* (£7.95), available from the Countryside Commission, John Dower House, Crescent Place, Cheltenham, Gloucestershire 6L50 3RA (tel. (01242) 521381, fax 584270), provides useful advice for tackling the trail.

■■■ BRIGHTON

> In Lydia's imagination, a visit to Brighton comprised every possibility of earthly happiness.
>
> —Jane Austen, Pride and Prejudice

The undisputed home of the "dirty weekend," Brighton (pop. 145,000) sparkles with a risqué, tawdry luster all its own. According to legend, the soon-to-be King George sidled into Brighton for some hanky-panky around 1784. Having staged a fake wedding with a certain "Mrs. Jones" (Fitzherbert), he headed off to the farmhouse known today as the Royal Pavilion and the Royal rumpus began. Brighton turns a blind eye on some of the more outrageous activity occurring along its shores; holiday-goers and locals alike peel it off—all off—at England's first official beach. Kemp Town, among other areas of Brighton, thrives with one of the biggest gay and lesbian populations in Britain. Foreign students flock to the southern coast (ostensibly to learn English) and join an already immense student population to set the town abuzz with mayhem and frivolity. Nab a stick of "Brighton Rock" (fluorescent hard candy) and naughty postcards on the seafront and nestle down for some fun.

GETTING THERE

Trains slink regularly from London to Brighton (at least 2/hr.; 1¼hr.; £11, day return £17.10). They part for Brighton to other southern locales, including Arundel via Ford (2/hr.; 30min.; £4.90) and Portsmouth (1/hr., 1½hr., £9.30). **National Express buses** head to Brighton from London (8/day, 2hr., return £6.75).

ORIENTATION & PRACTICAL INFORMATION

The train station stands at least 10 minutes from the town center and seafront. To reach the tourist office in Bartholomew Square opposite the town hall, walk south along Queens Rd. towards the water. Turn left onto North St. and continue until you reach Ship St.; then turn right onto Ship and proceed along to Prince Albert St., which leads right up to that dandy little mecca, the T.O.

Tourist Office: 10 Bartholomew Sq. (tel. 326450). The enthusiastic staff will thrust materials on practically any subject down your gullet. Book-a-bed ahead service £2.50 plus deposit; London booking fee slightly higher. Free street map available. Open June-mid-July Mon.-Fri. 9am-6pm, Sat. 10am-5pm, Sun. 10am-4pm; mid-July to late Aug. Mon.-Fri. 9am-6pm, Sat.-Sun. 10am-5:30pm; Sept.-May Mon.-Fri. 9am-5pm, Sat. 10am-5pm, Sun. 10am-4pm.

Financial Services: National Westminster, Midland, and **Lloyd's** scuttle along North St. (between West. St. and Old Steine). **Barclays,** 139 North St., opens Mon.-Tues. and Thurs.-Fri. 9:30am-4:30pm, Wed. 10am-4:30pm, Sat. 9:30am-noon. Look for **American Express,** 66 Churchill Sq., BN1 2EP (tel. 321242), near the Queen's Rd. clock tower. Open Mon.-Tues. and Thurs.-Fri. 9am-5:30pm, Wed. 9:30am-5:30pm, Sat. 9am-5pm. **Thomas Cook,** 58 North St. (tel. 325711) opens Mon.-Tues. and Thurs.-Sat. 9am-5:30pm, Wed. 10:30am-5:30pm.

Student Travel: South Coast Student Travel, 61 Ditching Rd. (tel. 607207).

Post Office: 51 Ship St. (tel. 573209), off Prince Albert St. in the Lanes. Open Mon.-Fri. 9am-5:30pm, Sat. 9am-12:30pm. **Postal Code:** BN1 1BA.

Telephone Code: 01273.

Train Station: (tel. 206755), at the end of Queen's Rd. away from the front. London timetable tel. 27823, Portsmouth timetable tel. 202172.

Bus Station: National Express buses stop at Pool Valley bus at southern angle of Old Steine. Ticket and info booth at south tip of Old Steine Green. Open Mon.-Sat. 8:30am-5:30pm, Sun. 9:30am-4pm. For info call 674881. Get **Local bus** information from **One Stop Travel,** 16 Old Steine at St. James St. Open Mon.-Fri. 8:30am-5:45pm, Sat. 9am-5pm, Sun. 10am-4pm or call 672156 (Brighton and Hove Bus and Coach Co.). A 1-day **Diamond ticket** (£2.95, seniors and children £1.70, family £6), from tourist office, allows unlimited travel on blue buses.

Bike Rental: Harmon Leisure Hire, 21-24 Montpelier Rd. (tel. 205206). £6.15/day, £20/week; deposit £50. Open Mon.-Fri. 8am-5pm, Sat. 8am-2pm. Vendors rent bicycles, rollerblades, and small boats on the seafront near West Pier (not cheap, but convenient).

Launderette: On the corner of St. James Ave. off St. James St. Open daily from 7:30am, last wash 7:30pm.

Public Library: Church St. (tel. 691195), next to the Royal Pavilion. In a fantastic Victorian building, with intriguing exhibits and a good café. King George IV guards the stairs to the reference library on the first floor. Open Mon.-Tues. and Thurs.-Fri. 10am-7pm, Sat. 10am-5pm.

Women's Center: 10 St. George's Mews (tel. 600526). Pregnancy tests available. Open Mon. and Wed.-Thurs. 10:30am-3pm and 7-9pm, Sat. 11:30am-1:30pm.

Hotlines: Rape Crisis: tel. (01293) 511595, Crawley. Open Tues. 6-9pm, Fri. 3-9pm, Sat. 10am-1pm. 24-hr. answering service. **Crisis: Samaritans:** tel. 772277. **Gay Switchboard:** tel. 690825. Referral point for other gay groups. Open Mon.-Fri. 8-10pm, Sat. 6-10pm, Sun. 8-10pm. **Lesbian Hotline:** tel. 603298. **AIDS:** 57166, 8-10pm daily. **Disabled Information:** tel. 203016. Open 10am-4pm.

Hospital: Royal Sussex County, Eastern Rd., parallel to Marine Rd. (tel. 696955).

Police: John St. (tel. 606744).

Emergency: Dial 999; no coins required.

B R I G H T O N

ACCOMMODATIONS

Brighton's best bets for budget lodging are its three hostels, two independent and one operated by HI. B&Bs and cheap hotels cost around £17. Shabbier B&Bs and hotels collect west of West Pier and east of Palace Pier. A number of places to stay can be found in **Kemp Town,** the neighborhood which runs perpendicular to the sea past Palace Pier. Test the beds and smell for dust before signing your night away. Frequent conventions make rooms hard to come by—book early or consult the tourist office immediately upon arrival. Inquire at the tourist office for a list of gay or lesbian owned and operated guest houses. Rooms may be cheaper in Hove, just west of Brighton, and connected by public transport.

Brighton Backpackers Hostel, 75-76 Middle St. (tel. 777717). An independent hostel with an attitude spawned by the two young English chaps who own it and the international crowd which frequents it. Great location (50m from seafront and the fringe of the Lanes) and no curfew. Innovative artwork courtesy of previous guests graces most of the wall space. Kitchen available. Mixed and/or single sex dorms, 4-8/room. £9. Weekly rates negotiable, usually £40/week. Sheets £1. £5 key deposit. Inexpensive breakfast and/or dinner. Laundry facilities available. Rodger and Tim have scored an old hotel around the corner from the hostel on King's Rd. Doubles, twins, and triples at £12.50/person.

Moonrider's Rest, 33 Oriental Place, near West Pier (tel. 733740). The basement entry to the Rest leads into a cool bar with a blue mosaic floor; the hostel takes its clue from these groovy tones. Mixed and single sex dorms available as well as an odd assortment of doubles. No curfew, no lockout. Discounts on windsurfing and bike hire nearby. Laundry facilities. £8/person, £45/week. Doubles £20. Duvets £1. Ask about the "pay for three nights, get one free" promotion.

HI Youth Hostel, Patcham Pl. (tel. 556196), 4 mi. north on the main London road (the A23). Take Patcham bus #773 or 5A (from stop E) from Old Steine to the Black Lion Hotel. Big country house with rooms that look new, though they're 400 years old. A good jumping-off point for the South Downs Way. £7.50, ages 16-20 £6.30. Breakfast £2.30. Sleep sack hire 75p. Often full; call ahead in July-Aug. or show up around breakfast time.

Catnaps, 21 Atlingworth St. (tel. 685193). A kindly, professorly type, the proprietor keeps seven immaculate rooms with decadent high ceilings and a pair of adorable spaniels. Clientele largely gay men, but women welcomed. Full English breakfast. Lounge with TV. Singles up to £17; doubles £35. Will cater to vegetarians; vegans should phone requests ahead.

The Langham, 16 Charlotte St. (tel. 682843 or 682123). Eight neat-as-a-pin rooms situated within walking distance of all major attractions. Pastels predominate, but don't let that dissuade you. £12.50-18.50.

Cavalaire Guest House, 34 Upper Rock Gdns. (tel. 696899). Cheering good value, with TV, tea-making facilities, and assorted electrical appliances in each room. Singles £16-17. Doubles £26-40.

Brighton Marina House Hotel, 8 Charlotte St., Marine Parade (tel. 605349 or 679484). Clean family-run hotel on quiet street off Marine Parade, in the Kemp Town area. Convenient location. Restaurant serves English, Indian, and Chinese cuisine. Some singles. All doubles and triples with private bath. £17-19.

FOOD & PUBS

Wander around The Lanes, a jumble of narrow streets between North St. and Prince Albert St., where the Brighthelmstone fishermen once lived. The cheapest restaurants can be found up the hill between Western and Dyke Rd. **Al Duomo,** 7 Pavilion Buildings (tel. 326741), also serves piping-hot pizza; for Thai try the **Brighton Belle** on Middle St. (tel. 775515). Pick up fruit and vegetables at the open **market** on Saturday mornings on Upper Gardner St. **Safeway** is on St. James St., **Tesco supermarket** in Churchill Sq. Tourists and locals in Brighton and Hove gather around **café** tables inside and out for conversation, coffee, reading, or writing. Especially cool atmospheres include **Sanctuary,** 51-55 Brunswick St. East, Hove (tel. 770002), the **Dorset Bar** at the corner of North St. and Gardener St., and **Brown's,** 3 Duke St. (tel. 323501). Most cafés open early and close around 11pm.

Food for Friends, 17a Prince Albert St. (tel. 202316). Cheap, well-cooked, well-seasoned vegetarian food in a hip, breezy, youthful atmosphere. Daily specials, but the salads send the taste buds straight to heaven. Meals £2.50-4. Open Mon.-Sat. 9am-10pm, Sun. 9:30am-10pm. Also try their patisserie around the corner at 41 Market St. where *al fresco*'s the norm.

The Coffee Company, corner of Meeting House Lane and Prince Albert S. (tel. 220222). England gets immolated by big-time cappucino (£1.10) daily 8am-10pm. Fresh cakes and baguettes every day. Brie baguette £1.95. Also pasta salads (from £1.10). Take away or hang out.

Piccolo, Ship St. Busy even on *late* Monday nights, Piccolo makes good pasta and pizza. Margherita pizza £3.75 (open daily 11am-midnight).

Noori's, 70-71 Ship St. (tel. 329405 or 747109) spices up tandoori and curry dishes. Tandoori chicken goes for £4.45. Vegetarians will take a hankering to Noori's *dal* (£3.45). Open Mon.-Sat. for lunch noon-2:15pm; Mon.-Thurs. 6pm-11:30pm; Fri.-Sat. 6pm-midnight; Sun. 11am-11pm.

Donatello, 3 Brighton Pl (tel. 775477). Open-air Italian restaurant in the heart of the Lanes. Sumptuous salads £3.20, pizza £3.75-5. Open daily 11:30am-11:30pm.

SIGHTS

Brighton's transformation from the sleepy village of Brighthelmstone to England's "center of fame and fashion" was catalyzed by the scientific efforts of one man and the whimsical imagination of another. In 1750, Dr. Richard Russell wrote a Latin treatise on the merits of drinking and bathing in sea water for the treatment of glandular disease. Before that time, sea-swimming had been considered nearly suicidal. The treatment received universal acclaim, and seaside towns like Brighton began to prosper. Thrive as it has, Brighton's still-dignified rowhouses looked on grander days when Victorian holiday-goers paid to strut certain stretches of grass and beach. Recession has hit Britain hard; much of Brighton's real estate stands abandoned. A visit to the city necessitates a visit to the wildly eclectic (and thrice-incarnated) **Royal Pavilion** (tel. 603005) on Pavilion Parade, next to Old Steine. Originally a plain-Jane farmhouse in a dull Brighton, the Pavilion has come to resemble an English princess in a sari. Architect John Nash conjured up the Pavilion's current style between 1815-1822, embellishing Henry Holland's classically-inspired villa. Brighton itself had become fashionable when Royalty graced its streets in the person of George, Prince of Wales. It was at his request that the Pavilion underwent its third round of cosmetic surgery: George in 1811 was named Prince Regent, and his reign as king (1820-1830) saw the complete transformation of his beloved Pavilion.

Not a surface has gone unadorned inside the building. Chinese decorations clutter every inch of floor and wall space, with the exceptions of the King's apartments, which contain bland Regency furniture. A full nine yards high, the chandelier in the opulent Banquetting room sports a silver dragon on top. More serpents and dragons cover the Music Room; rumor has it George wept tears of joy upon first entering it (what was he thinking?). As one might expect, Queen Victoria was less thrilled by the Pavilion; visitors can now peer into her more subdued bedroom. The tiny queen, bless her heart, wasted no time in selling the Pavilion to the city of Brighton in 1850 for next to nothing (open daily 10am-6pm; Oct.-May 10am-5pm; £3.75, seniors and students £2.75, children £2.10; partial wheelchair access). A whimsical shop next door to the Royal Pavilion sells guide books and postcards that suggest royalty may once have had a sense of humor. The well-groomed gardens that surround the Pavilion make a great place to sit a spell.

Around the corner from the Pavilion stands the **Brighton Museum and Art Gallery** on Church St. (tel. 603005). Featuring paintings, English pottery, and an art deco and art nouveau collection wild enough to make viewers spontaneously dance the Charleston, the museum occupies the same buildings as the fantastic public library. Go leer at Salavador Dalí's incredibly sexy, red, pursing sofa, *Mae West's*

Lips. Check out the inkwell molded into the shape of a human face at the fine **Willett Collection of Pottery** (open Mon.-Tues. and Thurs.-Sat. 10am-5:45pm, Sun 2-5pm; free; limited wheelchair accessibility). Before heading to the seafront, stroll where small fishermen's cottages once thrived in the **Lanes.** A bird's nest of 17th-century streets—some no wider than three feet—stretches south of North Street and constitutes the heart of Old Brighton. Sunday **walking tours** leave the tourist office (June-Aug. 2:30pm; £3).

Few people actually swim along the pebbly beaches of Brighton—most spend their time wilting in deck chairs or padding along the stately promenade. The not-as-stately **Palace Pier,** a century old and recently painted, offers a host of amusements, including a museum of slot machines between the piers under King's Road Arches. Just in case you get lucky, the pier's toilets have condom machines dispensing love slickers in an array of colors and flavors. And the deck chairs are free... **Volk's Railway,** Britain's first three-foot-gauge electric train, shuttles along the waterfront (runs April-Sept. daily 10am-dusk; 85p, children 35p). Although England's largest aquarium, **Brighton Sea Life Centre** (tel. 604233), recently freed its dolphins Missie and Silver, many other sea creatures remain trapped in glass tanks for your viewing pleasure. Walk through water in the longest aquarium tunnel in Europe (open daily 10am-6pm; £4.50, children £3.25; wheelchair accessible). The **Grand Hotel,** on the front on King's Rd., has been substantially rebuilt since a 1984 IRA bombing that killed five but left then-Iron Lady Margaret Thatcher unscathed. Farther along, the ghostly **West Pier** stands abandoned out in the sea. The beach in front of the Pier is often a cruisey scene for gay men. A short walk along the coast past West Pier leads to **Hove.** Casual walkers will find numerous examples of Regency architecture in lovely **Brunswick Square.**

Several churches bless Brighton's shores. **St. Nicholas' Church,** Dyke Rd., dates from 1370 and treasures a 12th-century baptismal font some consider to be the most beautiful Norman carving in Sussex. Take bus #5, 5A, or 5B to **St. Bartholomew's Church** on Ann St. First called "The Barn" or "Noah's Ark," this little-known spurt of Victorian genius rises higher than Westminster Abbey, to 135 ft. In the same elaborate tradition as the Pavilion, **Preston Manor** (tel. 603005), a grand house 2 mi. north of Brighton on the A23, preserves the life of Edwardian gentry. (Take same buses as for youth hostel, or #5, 5A, or 59. Open Tues.-Sat. 10am-5pm, Sun. and Bank Holidays 2-5pm; £2.70, children £1.80. Some wheelchair access; call ahead.)

ENTERTAINMENT

Brighton brims with nightlife options, earning it the nickname "London-by-the-Sea." And as surely as the tide turns, clubs and venues go in and out of fashion. The local monthly, *The Punter,* details evening events and can be found at pubs, news agents, and record stores (70p). *What's On,* a poster-sized flysheet, points towards hot and happening scenes. Pub-crawling among the Lanes' free houses is a good bet on any night. Gay and lesbian venues can be discovered in the latest issues of *Gay Times* or *Capital Gay;* the tourist office also offers a brief list of gay owned or operated establishments. Summer brings outdoor concerts and assorted entertainment (mimes, juggling) to the pavilion lawn, the beach deck, and around the Lanes.

Numerous clubs with short half-lives cater to all sensibilities. Most clubs open from 10pm-2pm every day except Sunday. Trendier types dance at **The Escape Club** (tel. 606906) near the pier at 10 Marine Parade. The multi-leveled **Zap Club,** at the King's Rd. arches (tel. 821588), pounds out hardcore rave and house music. The club hosts frequent gay nights. The gaydar blips hard and fast at **Zanzibar,** St. James St. (tel. 622100). **Gloucester,** at Gloucester Plaza (tel. 699068) provides good cheap fun with music (60s, 70s, 80s) varying nightly. **Paradox** (tel. 321628) and **Event** (tel. 732627), both on West. St., admit the masses nightly onto their glitzy dance floors. Get ready to sweat. Beasties that thrive on indie rock will feel at home in the **Underground** at 77 West St. (tel. 327701). Slightly unsightly **Casablanca** on Middle St. (tel. 321817) delivers live jazz to a largely student crowd.

The **Queen's Arms,** 8 George St. (tel. 696873) packs an enthusiastic gay and lesbian crowd into its Sunday night cabaret. On Wednesday and Saturday nights the disco ball sees some action. Bedsteads and vodka bottle chandeliers make **Smugglers** on Ship St. a raucous place to drink. Happy hour from Monday to Friday at 6 to 8pm gets you pints for £1.50. The **Berlin Bar,** also on Ship St., pulls internationals toward its screens, lights, and now's-the-time-we-dahnce floor. Have a jazz lunch (Wed., Thurs., or Sun.) at **The King and Queen,** Marlborough Pl. (tel. 607207).

Brighton Centre, King's Rd., and the **Dome,** #29 New Rd., host Brighton's biggest rock and jazz concerts and events ranging from Chippendales shows to Brighton youth orchestra concerts. Tickets can be acquired at the Brighton Centre **booking office** on Russell Rd. (tel. 202881; open Mon.-Sat. 10am-5:30pm) and at the Dome booking office at 29 New Rd. (tel. 674357; open Mon.-Sat. 10am-5:30pm). The tourist office also vends tickets.

Plays and touring London productions take the stage at the **Theatre Royal,** New Rd., a Victorian beauty with a red plush interior (gallery tickets £4.50-8, circles and stalls £7-18.50; student standbys from 10am on day of performance except Sat. evenings £8-8.50; box office tel. 328488; open Mon.-Sat. 10am-8pm). The latest addition to Brighton's entertainment offerings is **Komedia,** which houses a café bar, theater, and cabaret, all under one roof at 14-17 Manchester St. between Marine Parade and St. James St. (box office tel. 670030). A wide variety of dramatic events grace the Komedia's stage. Tickets range from £4-7.50. Seniors and students discounts available. Stand-by tickets are sold 15 minutes before show-time (all seats £4; box office open 12:30-2pm and 5-9pm daily; café bar open daily 10:30am-11pm).

Hang loose just west of Brighton Marina at the **nude bathing** areas. Be sure to stay within the limits. **Telescombe Beach,** nearly 4½ mi. to the east of Palace Pier, is frequented for the most part by a gay crowd. Look for a sign before Telescombe Tavern marked "Telescombe Cliffs." Numerous sailing opportunities crop up in summer; check bulletin boards at the tourist office.

■ NEAR BRIGHTON

If you are inclined to leave the urban attractions and distractions of Brighton in search of more relaxed pursuits, take a ten-minute train ride to the historic town of **Lewes** (return £1.80). Thomas Paine, author of *Rights of Man* and *Common Sense,* and Gideon Montell, founder of the iguanadon (what?!?), hailed from Lewes. The Norman **Lewes Castle** (tel. 474379) merits a visit, as does the 15th-century **Anne of Cleves House.** Anne received the house from Henry VIII in their divorce settlement by not losing her head. (Castle open Mon.-Sat. 10am-5:30pm; Sun. 11am-5:30pm. £2.80, seniors and students 32.30, children £1.50, family 37.50. Anne of Cleves House open April-Oct. Mon.-Sat. 10am-5:30pm, Sun. 2-5:30pm. £1.60, students £1.30, children 80p, family £4.25. Combined ticket for both sites £3.50, children £1.75, family £9) Just south of Lewes off the A27 is **Charleston Farmhouse.** The intellectual and artistic country home of the Bloomsbury group highlights the domestic decorative art of Vanessa Bell and Duncan Grant (open April-Oct. daily 2-6pm; £1.50). Three mi. east of Brighton rests **The Grange** (tel. (01273) 301004) in the village of Rottingdean. Now taken up largely by an art gallery and museum, the house once sheltered Rudyard Kipling, after whom its gardens are now named (open Mon.-Sat. 10am-4pm, Sun. 2-4pm; free).

■ ■ ■ ARUNDEL

A Merchant-Ivory movie-set of a town, Arundel (pop. 3200) fills with wealthy Brits on holiday and white-vested, pale-thighed cricketers. Entwined with the River Arun and packed in by grassy knolls, its narrow streets gather delightfully distracting bookstores and enticing antique shops beneath the thoughtful brows of a Norman castle and monumental Catholic cathedral.

PRACTICAL INFORMATION

Trains leave London's Victoria Station for Arundel (1/hr.; 1¼hr.; day return £12.30-14.10). Most other train and bus routes require connections at Littlehampton to the south or Barnham to the east. **Bus** #31 goes to Littlehampton hourly, picking up passengers across from the Norfolk Arms on High St. Pick up a free *Town Guide* at the **tourist office**, 61 High St. (tel. 882268; open Mon.-Fri. 9am-5pm, Sat.-Sun. 10am-5pm; off-season Mon.-Fri. 9am-3pm, Sat.-Sun. 10am-3:30pm). Sort things out at the **post office**, 2-4 High St. (open Mon.-Fri. 9am-5:30pm, Sat. 9am-12:30pm). Arundel's **postal code** is BN18 9AD, its **telephone code** 01903.

ACCOMMODATIONS, CAMPING, & FOOD

A glut of tourists take their toll on accommodations during summer; savvy travelers should plan ahead to avoid anxiety and a severe laceration of the wallet. If you're up to a walk, the **Warningcamp Youth Hostel (HI)** (tel. 882204), 1½ mi. out of town, cheerfully offers a place to prop up your feet. From the train station, turn right onto the A27 and take the first left; after 1 mi., turn left at the sign and then follow the other signs (two right turns). (Open April-Aug. daily; Sept.-Oct. and March Tues.-Sat. Breakfast £2.60. Kitchen. Lockout 10am-5pm. Curfew 11pm. £7.15, under 18 £5. Sheets included.) The tourist office maintains an up-to-date list of vacancies; make it your first stop if you haven't booked ahead. Expect to cough up £14 for a B&B along the River Arun. Both the **Arden House,** 4 Queens Lane (tel. 882544), just off Queen St., and **The Bridge House and Cottage,** 18 Queen St. (tel. 882142 or 882779), offer plush facilities with a thousand perks. Doubles at Arden House cost £31-35; singles at Bridge House slip by at £18 to £24 (doubles £34-40). Bridge also has laundry facilities. **Castle View,** 63 High St. (tel. 883029), rents for a pittance compared to other B&Bs in town. All rooms have a bath and cost £14 to £16. Claim a pitch at the **Ship and Anchor Site** (tel. 551262), 2 mi. from Arundel on Ford Rd. (toilet, showers, phone, shops, restaurant; £6.30/tent and 2 people; open April-Sept.).

Arundel's pubs and tea shops usually fall on the wrong side of reasonable. Locals frequent **Belinda's,** 13 Tarrant St. (tel. 882977), a 16th-century tea room with a chirping, bird-filled garden. A barn on the 1560 town map, its only herds today linger over steak and kidney pie (£4.50) and cream teas (£2.95; open Tues.-Sat. 9am-5:30pm, Sun. 11am-5:30pm). They bake scrumptious goods on the premises. Likewise, **The Castle View,** 63 High St. (tel. 883029), bakes a meaty and a veggie lasagna for around £3.80. Snack until your heart's content while gazing at the castle's Norman splendor (open summer daily 10am-5:30pm; winter 10:30am-5pm). Fruit and bread peddlers line High St. For pub grub try the **White Hart,** 12 Queen St. (tel. 882374), which serves food daily noon-2:30pm and 7-9pm. For picnics or late-night snacks, approach the rather incongruous **Circle K,** 17 Queen St. (open daily 6am-10pm). Clearly something strange is afoot in Arundel.

SIGHTS

Arundel Castle (tel. 882173) commands the eye of anyone approaching the town. Ravaged during the Civil War, the castle was restored piecemeal by the dukes who called it home in the 1700s and 1800s. The seat of the Duke of Norfolk, Earl Marshal of England, the castle holds the distinction of being the third oldest in all of England and rivals its elders in opulence. English gentry have graced the home for generations; their presence glints from the well-polished wood floors and stained glass windows of the **baron's hall.** Portraits by Van Dyck and Gainsborough people the hall—don't be surprised if you sense eyes moving behind you. Among the collection housed at the castle are various items owned by Mary, Queen of Scots. Don't overlook the graphically-defined death warrant served against one family member by good-natured Queen Elizabeth I (open April-Oct. Sun.-Fri. 11-5pm; last entry 4pm; £4.50, students and seniors £4, children £3.50). In late August, the castle hosts the **Arundel Festival,** ten days of concerts, jousting, and outdoor theater. A full fringe schedule offers less expensive events. For information call 883690.

Alongside the River Arun across from the castle are the remains of a Dominican priory, **Blackfriars.** A nearby placard recounts the troubled past of a group of monks at the priory. Steep High St. leads on to the **Cathedral of Our Lady and St. Philip Howard.** Decidedly more impressive from the outside, the French Gothic cathedral was designed by Joseph Hansom, inventor of the Hansom Cab. Though executed for cheering on the Spanish Armada in 1588, St. Philip occupies an honored place in the north transept; they've even rolled out the red carpet for him. Should you harbor treasonous thoughts yourself, the priests hear confession twice on Saturdays (cathedral open daily 9am-6pm, in winter 9am-dusk).

The **Arundel Museum and Heritage Center,** 61 High St., chronicles over two millennia of the town's history (open May-Sept. Tues.-Fri. 11am-1pm and 2-5pm, Sun. 2-5pm; also Easter-May and Oct. bank holidays and weekends; £1, seniors 75p, children 50p). Concealed observation enclosures at the **Wildfowl and Wetlands Trust Centre** on Mill Rd., ¾ mi. past the entrance to the castle (tel. 883355), permit visitors to "come nose to beak with nature." Just make sure nature doesn't nip back. Over 12,000 birds roost within the reserve's 55 acres. (Open daily 9:30am-5:30pm, winter 9:30am-4:30pm; last admission an hour before closing; £3.75, seniors and students £2.80, children £1.90; wheelchair accessible; 20% discount available with leaflet coupon from tourist office.)

■ NEAR ARUNDEL

Petworth House (tel. (01798) 42207), 10 mi. from Arundel, showcases the talents of Capability Brown and J.M.W. Turner, among other artists. Brown landscaped the gardens; J.M.W. turned around and painted the landscape. Well-known for exquisitely detailed watercolors, Turner painted some of his best works while secluded in the library of the Third Earl of Egremont, a famous early 19th-century patron of arts and letters. Petworth now retains the artwork produced in the years 1802 to 1812 and 1827 to 1831, and the ground floor visitors' gallery contains some 71 other sculptures and 59 paintings, including two by William Blake. (House open April-late Oct. Tues.-Thurs. and Sat.-Sun. 1-5:30pm, last admission 5pm. Extra rooms shown Tues.-Thurs. Grounds open 12:30-6pm. Deer park open year-round daily 8am-sunset. Ground-floor wheelchair access. House and grounds £4, under 17 £2, deer park free.) Unfortunately, the closest you can get to Petworth by public transportation is Pulborough (a 10-min. train ride from Arundel); you must cover the 2 mi. to the house under your own steam. Ask for directions at the Arundel tourist office.

■■■ CHICHESTER

After centuries of confinement within the remains of Roman walls, the citizens of Chichester (pop. 25,000) seem peculiarly content with their lot, basking in the shade of the immense Norman cathedral and meandering around squat Market Cross in town's center. Chichester conquers other towns hands down when it comes to artistic endeavors, spinning forth a host of dramatic diversions and gallery exhibits. Its slow pace and proximity to both the harbor and the Sussex Downs make day trips and overnight stays equally gratifying.

GETTING THERE

Chichester is 45 mi. southwest of London and 15 mi. east of Portsmouth. **Trains** run to and from London's Victoria Station (2/hr.; 1½hr.; day return £13.40), Brighton (2-3/hr.; 1hr.; day return £6.10), and Portsmouth (2-3/hr.; 40min.; day return £3.80). National Express **buses** run less frequently to London (1/day; period return £12.25); Coastline buses serve Brighton (bus #700 1/hr.; 2hr.; £2.90) and Portsmouth (bus #700 1/hr.; 1hr.; £2.50; #701 2/hr.; 1 hr.; £2.40). If you plan to make forays into the local area by bus, ask about the **Explorer** ticket: £4.40 buys a day's unlimited travel on buses servicing the south of England from Kent to Salisbury (children and seniors

£3.30, families £8.80). The A259 and A27 motorways pass through town on an east-west axis, and the A286 enters Chichester from the north.

ORIENTATION & PRACTICAL INFORMATION

Four Roman streets named for their compass directions divide Chichester into quadrants that converge at Market Cross. The **bus station** (tel. 783251) lies diagonally across from the **train station** (tel. (01273) 206755) on Southgate. To reach the **tourist office** (tel. 775888, fax 539449) from the train station, turn left as you exit onto Southgate, which then turns into South St. (open Mon.-Sat. 9:15am-5:15pm; April-Sept. Mon.-Sat. 9:15am-5:15pm, Sun. 10am-4pm). After closing, a 24-hour computer information guide and updated list of vacancies prove helpful.

Wednesday and Saturday are **market days** in Chichester, and Thursday is **early closing day** for some stores. Spruce up your shirts at the **launderette** on Eastgate (open 7:30am-8pm, last wash 7pm). Change currency at **Thomas Cook** on 40 East St. (open Mon.-Tues. and Thurs.-Fri. 9am-5:30pm, Wed. 10am-5:30pm, Sat. 9am-5pm). Several **banks**, including **Barclays, Lloyd's, National Westminster,** and **Midland** fleece the masses on East. St. The **post office** (tel. 784251) is at 10 West St., across from the cathedral (open Mon. and Thurs. 8:45am-5:30pm, Tues.-Wed. and Fri. 9am-5:30pm, Sat 9am-12:30pm). The **postal code** is PO19 1AB; the **telephone code** is 01243. The **police** play backgammon on Kingsham Rd. (tel. 784433).

ACCOMMODATIONS & FOOD

Rooms for under £15 are a rare breed here; plan on paying £16-17 and expect a 15-minute walk, as most B&Bs are outside city center. Call a few days in advance or arrive early in the day to guarantee yourself a bed. **Hedgehogs,** 45 Whyke Lane (tel. 780022), snuggles close to the town center. The enthusiastic hound Sooty and her affable owners offer cozy rooms complete with warm pricklies (tea, duvets, and hairdryers) and a lovely garden. No smoking, please (£16-17). **Mrs. Gliddon,** 62 Worcester Rd. (tel. 789776), is a ½-hr. walk north of the station and asks £16-17. A Mrs. Wingfield-Hayes runs the **White Lodge,** Lavant Rd., 1½ mi. from downtown, and conducts historical tours by appointment. No smoking (rooms £18-20). Campsites roost at **Southern Leisure Centre,** Vinnetrow Rd. (tel. 787715), a five-minute walk southeast of town (open April-Oct.; £5 pitch fee plus £1.25/person).

Maison Blanc Boulangerie and Patisserie, 56 South St. (tel. 539292), is sure to make even the most resolute Francophobe's mouth water with a fantastic selection of cakes and coffees. Filled baguettes are £1.50 (open Mon.-Fri. 8:45am-5:30pm, Sat. 8:45am-6pm; June-Sept. also Sun. 9am-5pm; table service shuts down ½hr. before shop). **Hadley's,** 4 West St., unabashedly lavishes lasagna (meat or vegetarian for £4.15) and a vast array of sandwiches (£2.50-3.95) on its customers, in full view of the cathedral (open Mon.-Fri. 10am-9pm, Sat. 10am-10pm, Sun. noon-9pm). **The Fountain,** 29 Southgate (tel. 781352), has trouble deciding whether it's a pub or restaurant. There are separate rooms for each, so you pick. Locals provide a congenial atmosphere, filling entrees (menu changes daily), and a wicked homemade apple pie with cream for £1.80. **Noble Pot,** 3 Little London off East St., crouches in 200-year-old well-preserved wine cellars and has been graced by a recent Prime Minister. Expect great food at low prices (Pizza Noble Pot £3.50) and live music on Fridays (open Mon.-Sat. noon-2:30pm, Mon.-Thurs. 5:30-11pm, Fri.-Sat. 5:30pm-midnight); or duck into the adjacent bar (open daily 11am-11pm). **The Medieval Crypt** on 12a South St. (tel. 537033) is actually housed in an 800-year-old undercroft. Guess what—the afterworld has a warm atmosphere and tasty bites for reasonable prices as well as a nifty bar. It's too dear for dinner, but has excellent lunch specials. Try their flapjacks, or their Sussex Cream Tea (pot of tea with scones, clotted cream and jam £2.50; open "breakfast to dinner"). The **Pasta Factory,** 6 South St. (tel. 785764), rolls out fresh pasta twice daily; its *tagliatelle al pesto* will give you pleasant dreams for weeks (£4.75). The hot scent of yeast ebbs from bakeries on North St. as the **Tesco Supermarket** chills on East St. (open Mon., Wed., and Sat. 8:30am-5:30pm, Thurs. 8:30am-7pm, Fri. 8:30-8pm).

SIGHTS

Lunchtime crowds congregate around the close of Chichester's Norman **Cathedral** (tel. 782595), especially during early to mid-July, when the **Chichester Festivities** take their thrilling place. Begun in 1091, the cathedral stands just west of the town center well. Later architectural styles were grafted onto the Norman motifs, creating a strange juxtaposition. A **glorious Marc Chagall stained glass** depiction of Psalm 150 ("let everything that hath breath praise the Lord") crowns the north aisle. A brilliant blizzard of red glass, the window brings worshippers from all walks of life and the animal kingdom into one coherent pattern. Excavations into the cathedral's floor uncovered a **Roman mosaic** (open daily 7:40am-7pm; winter 7:40am-5pm; £1 donation encouraged; tours Easter-Oct. Mon.-Sat. 11am and 2:15pm; evensong Mon.-Fri. 5:30pm, Sun. 3:30pm; wheelchair accessible).

Chichester's other attractions include the Pallants, a city-within-the-city, in the southeast quadrant. Once the special preserve of the bishop, it is now a quiet area with elegant 18th- and 19th-century houses. The **Pallant House,** 9 North Pallant (tel. 774557), a historic art gallery, shelters Walter Hussey's and Charles Kearly's bequests of mainly modern British art in a restored Queen Anne townhouse (open Tues.-Sat. 10am-5:30pm, last admission 4:45pm; £2.50, students £1.70, children £1).

The brown signposted **Walls Walk** winds around the city and bounds the Roman remnants. The most fashionable avenue in town, **North Street,** features a long row of Georgian houses, including **John Nash's Market House,** near the Market Cross called the Butler Market, built in 1807 (closed Thurs. afternoons). Guided walks of town are offered by the tourist office in summer (Mon. 2:30pm, Sat. 11am).

ENTERTAINMENT

Chichester embraces professionals and artists who enjoy tranquil pastimes and cultural events. The gem of Chichesterian nightlife, the **Chichester Festival Theatre** (tel. 781312), lies north of town; walk up North St. which turns into Brogle Rd. and look for signs to your right. Founded by the late Sir Laurence Olivier, it is perhaps the best theater in England outside London, with productions ranging from Restoration comedy to absurd theater. The festival runs from May to October (tickets £6-21; unreserved tickets available at box office 10am on day of performance for £5-6; wheelchair accessible, but phone ahead). If you go in mid-morning, you may get to take a surreptitious peek at rehearsals. The Theater Restaurant and Café caters to patrons from 12:30pm on matinee days and from 5:30pm for evening shows.

The recently added **Minerva Studio Theatre** (tel. 781312) increases the number of dramatic offerings in Chichester and incorporates children's theater into its repertoire (tickets £5-14; half-price just before performance; box office open Mon.-Sat. 10am-8:30pm). During the first two weeks in July, the **Chichester Festivities** enliven the quiet town. In celebration of the cathedral's founding, artists, musicians, and festive individuals from all walks of life collaborate to produce one of the finest spells of concentrated creativity in all of England. Attend concerts in the cathedral, recitals, art exhibitions, films, and outdoor events. Tickets from £2, though artists performing outside don't always charge. Obtain a schedule by writing to The Box Office, The Old Theatre, 43 South St., Chichester, West Sussex PO19 1DX, or by calling 780192 (open May-festival's end Mon.-Sat. 10am-5:30pm.).

Chichester Harbor Water Tours (tel. 786418) get you up close and personal with unusual wildlife. The tours are a leisurely way to see some of the countryside (5/day; 1½hr.; £3.50, children £1.50). Take bus #252 or 253 to Itchenor Crossroads (15min.; return £1.50); from there it is a 2½-mi. hike. If you want to get wet, the new **Westgate Leisure Centre,** Avenue de Chartres (tel. 785651), offers indoor swimming for £1.60 (open Mon. 9am-10:30pm, Tues.-Sat. 7:30am-10:30pm, Sun. 9am-6pm; times may be reserved for schools or members).

■ NEAR CHICHESTER

The **Fishbourne Roman Palace** (tel. (01243) 785859), built in 75 AD, is the largest Roman residence yet excavated in Britain. The palace of local chieftains until 285 AD; the ornate mosaic floors testify to the luxury they enjoyed. Discovered by trench-diggers in 1965, more than three-quarters of the original building remains buried under the houses along Salthill Rd. (Open May-Sept. daily 10am-6pm; March-April and Oct. 10am-5pm; Feb. and Nov.-Dec. 10am-4pm; Jan. Sun. only 10am-4pm. £3.40, students and seniors £2.70, children £1.50, family £8.50.) The **Fishbourne Museum** has an exceptional display of Roman remains. Fishbourne is an easy walk from the Avenue de Chartres roundabout in Chichester; go west along Westgate, which becomes Fishbourne Rd. (the A259) for 1½ mi., or take bus #701 or 700 from Chichester center. Buses let you off at Salthill Rd., a 5-minute walk from the palace.

Three mi. northeast of Chichester stands **Goodwood House** (tel. (01243) 774107), ancestral home of the Duke of Richmond and Gordon. Splendid Canalettos, Reynolds, and Stubbs vie for attention in this 18th-century country abode. (Open Aug. Sun.-Thurs. 2-5pm; May-July and Sept. Sun.-Mon. 2-5pm, as well as Easter Sun. and Mon.; £3.40. Take bus #268, then walk about 1 mi.)

■■■ PORTSMOUTH

> *Don't talk to me about the naval tradition. It's nothing but rum, sodomy, and the lash.*
>
> —Winston Churchill

Set Victorian prudery against a lot of bloody cursing sailors and Portsmouth (pop. 180,000) emerges. 1994 marked both the 50th anniversary of D-Day's launching from Portsmouth and the 900th birthday of this bawdy king of the British maritime. Henry VIII's *Mary Rose,* which sank in 1545 and was raised 437 years later, crowns an incomparable process of naval heritage. Nowhere else would Nelson's triumphant flagship, *HMS Victory,* have to battle to gain notice. Prostitutes and drunkards used to prowl the streets; nowadays, their more civil grandchildren hasten along city thoroughfares to their ancient museum-bound ships.

GETTING THERE

Portsmouth sprawls along the coast for miles—at times, the resort community Southsea, Old Portsmouth, and Portsmouth seem to be altogether different cities. **Trains** from London Waterloo stop at both Portsmouth and Southsea station (town station) and Portsmouth harbor station (2/hr.; 1½hr.; cheap day return £15.70). **National Express buses** rumble from London every 2 hours (2½hr.; £12.25). **Passenger ferries** chug to the Isle of Wight (tel. 827744) from Harbour station (2/hr., winter 1/hr.; 15min.; day return £5.90). Isle of Wight Hovercraft departs from Clarence Esplanade frequently (day return £7.20, child £3.60). For continental services consult Essentials: Getting There—From Continental Europe.

ORIENTATION & PRACTICAL INFORMATION

Major sights in Portsmouth cluster at **The Hard, Old Portsmouth** (near the train station), and **Southsea Esplanade.** A reliable and comprehensive bus system connects the outstretched regions of the city. Tourist offices await year-round on the Hard and on Commercial Rd. in town; two others do business in the high season.

Tourist Office: The Hard (tel. 826722), right by the entrance to historic ships; 102 Commercial Rd. (tel. 838382), next to the train station. *Bureau de Change.* Room booking service. The Hard open daily 9:30am-5:45pm; Commercial Rd. open Mon.-Sat. 9:30am-5:45pm. **Seasonal offices** at the Continental Ferry Port (tel. 838635; open daily noon-2pm and 6:30-10:30pm) and at the Pyramids Resort Centre, Clarence Esplanade, Southsea (tel. 832464; open daily 9:30am-5:45pm).

Budget Travel Office: Travel Shop, University of Portsmouth Union, Alexandra House, Museum Rd. (tel. 816645). Purchase bus, train, and plane tickets here. Open in term Mon.-Fri. 9:30am-5pm. Other times Mon.-Fri. 10am-3pm.

Financial Services: Major banks, including **Lloyd's** and **National Westminster,** clump around the Commercial Rd. shopping precinct just north of Portsmouth and Southsea station. Also look for **Midland** (open Mon. and Wed.-Fri. 9:30am-5pm, Tues. 10am-5pm) and **Barclays** (open Mon.-Tues. and Thurs.-Fri. 9:30am-5pm, Wed. 10am-5pm, Sat. 9:30am-noon). **Thomas Cook,** 29 Cascades (near Commercial Rd.), offers travel-related services, including *Bureau de Change* (tel. 825252 or 851290). Also located at Palmerston Rd. off Kent Rd. in Southsea (open Mon.-Wed. and Fri.-Sat. 9am-5:30pm, Thurs. 10am-5:30pm.

Post Office: Slindon St. (tel. 835201), near the town station. Open Mon. and Thurs. 8:45am-5:30pm, Tues. 9:30-5:30pm, Wed. and Fri. 9am-5:30pm, Sat. 9am-12:30pm. **Postal Code:** PO1 1AB.

Telephone Code: 01705.

Train Station: Portsmouth and Southsea Station, Commercial Rd. Travel center open Mon.-Sat. 9am-4:30pm. **Portsmouth Harbour Station,** The Hard, ¾ mi. away at the end of the line. **Lockers** £1-2. To Cosham, for the hostel, 5/hr.; £1.30, day return from £1.50. Trips between town and harbor cost 80p. Call (01703) 229393 for information about the stations.

Bus Station: The Hard Interchange, The Hard, next to the Harbour station. Local routes (enquiries tel. 738570 or 815452) and National Express services (tel. (01329) 230023). National Express tickets sold at Wight Link office (open July-Aug. daily 8am-5pm; Oct.-June Mon.-Sat. 8am-5pm).

Taxi: Streamline Taxis, tel. 811111. **Mainline Taxis,** tel. 751111.

Hospital: Queen Alexandra Hospital, Southwick Hill Rd. Cosham (tel. 379 451).

Emergency: Dial 999; no coins required.

Police: Winston Churchill Ave. Cosham (tel. 321111).

ACCOMMODATIONS, CAMPING, & FOOD

Moderately priced B&Bs clutter Southsea, Portsmouth's contiguous resort town 1½ mi. east along the coast from the Hard. Many are located along Waverly Rd., Clarendon Rd., and South Parade. Take Southdown Portsmouth bus #6, 43, or 44 to South Parade. Cheaper lodgings lie two or three blocks inland—Whitwell, Granada, St. Roman's, and Malvern Rd. all have a fair sprinkling.

YMCA, Penny St. (tel. 864341), 10min. from the Hard. Basic rooms; those on higher floors look out over the sea wall to the Solent, affording a sublime view. With sleeping bag £6.20. Single B&B £12.35; twin £11.15. Lunch £3.75; dinner £3.75. Confirmation deposit £10, key deposit £1. Students choke it after Sept.

University of Portsmouth Halls of Residence, booking office at Nuffield Centre, St. Michaels Road (tel. 843178), overlooking Southsea common, 15min. from the Hard. Halls are scattered within 3 mi. Single and twin rooms available July 10-Sept. 27. **Burrell House** has small modern rooms with puritanically narrow beds; older **Rees Hall** shows more signs of age and character. £13.50.

HI Youth Hostel, Wymering Manor, Old Wymering Lane, Medina Rd., Cosham (tel. 375661). Take bus #1, 12, or 22 from the Hard or #40, 42, 43, or 44 from Commercial Rd. by Abbey National Bank at Stand D, to Cosham police station and walk left on Medina Rd., or take the train to Cosham, then right out of the station to the police station. The old home of Catherine Parr now houses guests somewhat less likely to be the sixth spouse of a fat English monarch. 58 beds. Lockout 10am-5pm. £7.75, under 18 £5.20. Open July-Aug. and Jan.1-4 daily; March-June Mon.-Sat.; Sept.-Nov. Tues.-Sat.; mid-Jan.- Feb. Fri.-Sat.

Testudo House, 19 Whitwell Rd., Southsea (tel. 824324). Mrs. Parkes fluffs up the pillows in her spick-and-span, pleasantly decorated home, adorned with a proudly-displayed collection of American table mats. £16. Ask about the room with bath and family quarters.

Camping: Southsea Caravan Park, Melville Rd., Southsea (tel. 735070). At eastern end of seafront, 5-6 mi. from The Hard. 2-person tent £8.50, from £5 after Sept. Call ahead.

Restaurants with a dash of style bunch along Osborne, Palmerston, and Clarendon Rd. in the Southsea shopping district. Standard fast-food joints abound near Commercial Rd. and the town station. The town is awash in pubs, especially at The Hard; try **The George** at 85 Queen St. for a hearty fillet of plaice (£3). A **Waitrose** supermarket supplies goods on Marmion Rd. **Country Kitchen,** 59A Marmion Rd., is a hardwood wholefood restaurant with veggie specials hovering around £3 and quiche for £1.60 (open Mon.-Sat. 9:30am-5pm, last order at 4:45pm). The coffee will keep you wide-eyed for days at **Brown's,** 9 Clarendon Rd. The cooks serve solid English food in relaxed low-key surroundings. Daily roast £5.50, omelettes from £2.95-3.50 (open Mon. 9:30am-6:30pm, Tues.-Sat. 9:30am-9:30pm). Munch on something besides mealy pudding and salt beef while touring the boats at the **HMS Victory Buffet,** in Historic Dockyard. Light meals, snacks, and no scurvy 40p-£2.

SIGHTS

Portsmouth overflows with magnificent ships and seafaring relics; the bulk of sights worth seeing anchor near the Hard. Plunge head first into the unparalleled **Naval Heritage Centre** (tel. 839766) in the Naval Base (entrance right next to the Hard tourist office; follow the brown signs to Portsmouth Historic Ships). Henry VIII's best-loved ship, the **Mary Rose** (tel. 750521 or 812931), set sail from Portsmouth in July 1545 only to keel over and sink before the monarch's eyes. Not until 1982 was she raised from her watery grave. Good ships don't die; they just become museums. On display in a special **ship hall,** the not-completely restored hulk is an eerie, compelling sight. An enthralling collection of Tudor artifacts, salvaged with the wreck but displayed in a separate exhibition hall, give a revealing look at 16th-century life.

Two 100-ft. masts lead the way to Admiral Horatio Nelson's flagship **HMS Victory** (tel. 839766 or 822357), the oldest surviving Ship of the Line in the world. The ship won the decisive Battle of Trafalgar against the French and Spanish in 1805. *Victory* conveys a vivid impression of the dismal cramped conditions for press-ganged recruits—just eight toilets for 850 men (guided tours are available of the ship and its toilets). **HMS Warrior** (tel. 822351), though eclipsed by its neighbor, nevertheless provides an intriguing companion to the *Victory.* The pride and joy of Queen Victoria's navy and the first iron-clad battleship in the world, *Warrior* has never seen battle. Nonetheless, a respectful Napoleon III called it "The Black Snake among the Rabbits in the Channel" (open daily 10am-5:30pm; Jul.-Aug. 10am-6:45pm; Nov.-Feb. 10am-5pm; last entry 1 hr. before close). The five galleries of the **Royal Naval Museum** (tel. 733060) fill in the historical gaps between the three ships.

Entrance to the **Historic Dockyard** is free (open 10am-7pm; March-June and Sept.-Oct. 10am-6pm; Nov.-Feb. 10am-5:30pm). But the ships are worth the admission expense: tickets to see one ship are £4.75, seniors £4.25, students and children £3.50, family £15. A combined ticket to explore two ships is £9, seniors £8, students and children £6.50, family £27.50. A Supersaver ticket for all three ships is £13, seniors £11.50, students and children £9.25, family £33.75. Admission to ships includes the fee for the Royal Naval Museum. Admission to the Museum is £2.65, seniors £2.10, students and children £1.85, family £7.50. The cost of other sights can be tacked onto your combined ticket. Allow about 1½ hours for each ship. (All open 10am-6:45pm; March-June and Sept.-Oct. 10am-5:30pm; Nov.-Feb. 10am-5pm. Last admission 1 hr. before closing—a general rule.)

Show up at the jetty by *Warrior* for a 45-minute guided ride (harbor tour only £3.50, seniors £2.75, students and children £2, family £10). Vessels frequent **Spitbank Fort,** which has protected Portsmouth for well over a century. The stern-faced fort faced two world wards and remained relatively unscathed. Boats depart from the Historic Dockyard (open Easter-Oct., weather permitting; crossing 25min.; departures 10:45am, noon, 1:15pm, and 2:30pm; fort trip £5.75, seniors £4.75, students and children £4, family £17). While at The Hard, consider taking **Portsmouth Harbour Tours** (tel. 822584), a more scenic way to make the trek to Southsea Esplanade (tours run Easter-Oct. 11am-5pm; 50min.; return £2.20, children £1.50).

You may want to extend your Hard day into a night at one of the seafront's many pubs; before you do, continue along the water's edge to Clarence Esplanade, the other side of Portsmouth's seaside sights. In the **D-Day Museum** (tel. 827261) on Clarence Esplanade, the Overlord Embroidery, a latter-day Bayeux Tapestry, recounts the invasion of France (open daily 9:30am-5:30pm; £3.50, children and students £2, family £9; wheelchair accessible). Don't let the garish exterior of the **Sea Life Centre** (tel. 734461) fool you—the insides reveal a finful of verve (open daily 10am-9pm; winter 10am-5pm; £4.25, seniors £3.50, students and children £3.25). Also at Clarence Esplanade is **Southsea Castle,** (tel. 827261) yet another coastal fortification built by Henry VIII in 1544. He couldn't bring forth a son, but by Almighty God he could fortress away the seminal sea (open daily 10am-5:30pm; Nov.-March. Sat.-Sun. 11am-5pm; partially wheelchair accessible; 31.50, seniors £1.20, students and children 90p, under 13 free). Tadpoles and bathing beauties will relish the **Pyramids,** Clarence Esplanade, Southsea, a series of water slides and fun pools all housed in pinnacles of power (tel. 826666; open May-June daily 10am-6pm or 7pm, July-Sept. 10am-7pm or 8pm; £3.95, seniors and children £3.10).

Charles Dickens spent his early years here and used the city as inspiration for his masterpieces; he was born in 1812 at 395 Old Commercial Rd., ¾ mi. north of the town station. Morbidly enough, the only authentic Dickens artifact in the Regency style house is the couch on which he died and a lock of his precious hair (open April-Sept. daily 10:30am-5:30pm; £1, seniors 75p, students and children 60p). If Dickens disappointed you, drown your sorrows at the aptly named Oliver Twist, a free house conveniently located at the end of old Commercial Rd.

Because pebbles seem all that Portsmouth has to offer by way of beachfront, reclining on **Southsea Common** is a more pleasing prospect. Well-groomed **Victoria Park,** with an entrance on Edinburgh Rd. near the Commercial Rd. shopping district, will satisfy those in need of a rest.

■■■ WINCHESTER

An axis of ecclesiastical, political, and economic power during the Dark and Middle Ages, Winchester yearns for its former days of glory. The likes of William the Conqueror and Alfred the Great deemed the town the center of their respective kingdoms; monks painstakingly prepared the *Domesday Book* for William himself in Winchester, but royalty has since looked elsewhere. In the more recent past, Jane Austen spent her final days in a small house on College St. Surpassed in pace and prestige, the town hangs on to its nobility for dear life in exclusive residential neighborhoods and costs-of-living that befit a king and his buddies.

GETTING THERE

In the center of southern England, just north of Southampton, Winchester makes an excellent daytrip from less-expensive Salisbury (25 mi.) or Portsmouth (27 mi.). **Trains** run here from London (2/hr.; 1hr.; £13.30-15.90), and leave for Chichester (1/hr.; 1hr.; change at Fareham; £7.60), Portsmouth (1/hr.; 45min.; £5.50), and Bath (1/hr.; 2hr.; change at Southampton or Redding; day return £12.50-£17.50). **National Express buses** run to London via Heathrow (7/day; 2hr.; £7.50-11.50) and also to Oxford and Gatwick. **Hampshire** buses make trips to Salisbury (#68; 6/day; 1½hr.; £3.50), Portsmouth (#69; 13/day; 1½hr.; return £3.50), and Southampton (#47; 2/hr.; 50min.; return £2.55). **Explorer** tickets (£4, seniors and children £2.85, family £8) are available for travel in Hampshire and Wiltshire.

Hitchers heading to Winchester tend to approach it along A34 and M3 from the north, A33 from the south, A31 and A272 from the east, and A272 from the west.

ORIENTATION & PRACTICAL INFORMATION

Winchester proper consists of a compact square bounded by the **North Walls, Eastgate Street** (which runs along the River Itchen), **College Street** (which turns into Canon St.), and **Southgate Street** (which becomes Jewry St.). The train station,

Station Hill, is northwest of the city center, near the intersection of City Rd. and Sussex St.; the city center is an easy 10-minute walk (down City Rd., right on Jewry St., then left on High St.). Winchester's major axis, **High Street,** becomes Broadway as it stretches east past a huge, menacing Alfred the Great.

Tourist Office: The Guildhall, Broadway (tel. 840500 or 848180), near King Alfred's statue. Helpful staff. Several pamphlets (30p-£1) on walking tours. 1½hr. guided tours (May-Sept. Mon.-Sat. 2/day, Sun. 1/day; April and Oct. Mon.-Fri. 1/ day, Sat. 2/day; £2, children 50p). No reliable luggage storage. Pick up a free *What's On* guide. Also get a guide to wheelchair-accessible city attractions. Open June-Sept. Mon.-Sat. 9:30am-6pm, Sun. 11am-2pm; Oct.-May Mon.-Sat. 10am-5pm.

Financial Services: Thomas Cook, 30 High St., The Pentice, across from the Body Shop (tel. 841661 for travel info; 849425 for flight info; 849430 for world travel). *Bureau de Change.* Open Mon.-Wed. and Fri.-Sat. 9am-5:30pm, Thurs. 10am-5:30pm. Major banks cluster around the junction of Jewry and High St.

Post Office: Middle Brook St. (tel. 854004), off High St. Open Mon.-Fri. 9am-5:30pm, Sat. 9am-12:30pm. **Postal Code: SO23 8WA.**

Telephone Code: 01962.

Train Station: Southhampton Station, Station Hill (tel. (01703) 229393), northwest of the city center, near the intersection of City Rd. and Sussex St. Travel Centre open Mon.-Fri. 9am-5pm, in summer also some Sat. 9:10am-4:30pm. Ticket counter open Mon.-Fri. 5:50am-8pm, Sat. 6am-8pm, Sun. 7am-9pm.

Bus Station: Broadway (tel. 852352 for schedule info), across from the Guildhall. All local and Nat. Express. Open Mon.-Fri. 8:30am-5:30pm, Sat. 8:30am-1:30pm.

Taxi: City Cars, tel. 853000 or 840663. They collect in a stand by the Market area.

Market: Chickens fly behind Marks & Spencer on Wed., Fri., and Sat. 8am-5pm.

Crisis: Samaritans, 10 Parchment St. (tel. 860633), off the pedest. area of High St.

Hospital: Royal Hampshire County, Romsey Rd. (tel. 863535), at St. James Lane.

Emergency: Dial 999; no coins required.

Police: N. Walls (tel. 868100), near the intersection with Middle Brook St.

ACCOMMODATIONS & CAMPING

Winchester's B&Bs cluster a ½ mi. southwest of the tourist office, near Ranelagh Rd., on Christchurch Rd. and St. Cross Rd. Buses 29 and 47 journey from the town center to Ranelagh Rd. Many pubs offer accommodations (which sometimes go at cheaper rates than the average guesthouse). Check at the Cricketeer on Bridge St. and in the public houses in the vicinity of the youth hostel.

HI Youth Hostel, 1 Water Lane (tel. 853723). Cross the bridge past the statue of Alfred the Great and turn left before Cricketer Pub. Great location in old 18th-century watermill, flanked by the rushing water of the River Itchen. Expect a 15-min. chore or two. Kitchen. Lockout 10am-5pm. Stringent curfew 11pm. £6.90, under 18 £4.60. Open July-Aug. daily, March-June and Sept. Tues.-Sat. Call ahead.

Mrs. P. Patton, 12 Christchurch Rd. (tel. 854272), between St. James Lane and Beaufort Rd. on a silent street. Breakfast served near a fishpool in the conservatory. Graceful, classy doubles; one has lofty Victorian beds from 1861. £12.50, £10 for multiple nights. Mrs. Patton works during the day; call after 5pm.

The Farrells B&B, 5 Ranelagh Rd. (tel. 869555). Furniture a mother would rave over in a well-kept home 10 min. from town. Cycle shed, no dearth of showers and toilets, and a sprightly proprietor to boot. Tell 'em *Let's Go* sent you. £12-14.

Mrs. Tisdall, 32 Hyde St. (tel. 851621), a 5-min. walk from town (Jewry St. becomes Hyde St.). Large, comfortable rooms and a filling breakfast accompanied by a bowl of fresh fruit. Family house with friendly proprietors. Doubles £24-26. Can be booked as a single for £17. Slight discount for *Let's Go* users.

Camping: River Park Leisure Centre, Gordon Rd. (tel. 869525). a 5-min. walk from town off North Walls, left onto Hyde Abbey, and right onto Gordon Rd. £6.10 for 1- to 2-person tent, £8.40 for larger tents; max. stay 3 nights. Open June-Sept. tents only. **Mornhill,** 2 mi. outside of city center, at top of Alresford Rd. (tel. 869877). Buses from city center stop there. £2 pitch fee, £3.20/person.

FOOD

High Street and St. George's Street are home to several food markets and fast food venues as well as tea and coffee houses. In addition, both **Marks and Spencer** and **Sainsbury Supermarkets** are located on Middle Brooks St., off High St. More substantial restaurants line Jewry St. Most of Winchester's many pubs serve good fare. An upscale clientele fills **The Wykeham Arms,** 75 Kingsgate St., and collected beer mugs festoon the walls (lunches from £3.50, Mon.-Sat. noon-2:30pm; sandwiches noon-6pm). The **Eclipse,** the Square, is Winchester's smallest public house, and the **Royal Oak** off High St. is another of countless English bars that claim fame as the oldest. Descend into the 900-year-old subterranean foundations (See Winchester: Entertainment, below). **Laura,** 17 City Rd. near the train station, serves £2.75-4 breakfasts and cheap sandwiches both on its patio and indoors (open Mon.-Sat. 9am-4pm).

SIGHTS

The **Buttercross,** High St., is a good starting point for a walking tour of the town. Duck through the archway (note the Norman stones from William the Conqueror's palace), pass through the square, and behold **Winchester Cathedral** at 5 The Close. Famed for its nave, the 556-ft. cathedral is the longest medieval building in Europe. Magnificent medieval tiles, roped off for their own preservation, cover much of the floor near the chancel. Jane Austen's grave rests in the northern aisle of the nave. The stained glass window in the rear seems oddly Cubist—Cromwell's soldiers smashed the original window in the 17th century, and though the original glass pieces have been reinserted, the pattern got lost in the shuffle. 1993 marked the cathedral's 900th birthday (tel. 853137; open daily 7:15am-6:30pm, East End closes 5pm; £2 admission in donation's clothing).

The **Norman crypt,** one of the finest in England (supposedly also the oldest in England), can only be viewed in summer by guided tour (Mon.-Sat. 10:30am and 2:30pm, water level permitting; 50p, children 25p). The crypt contains the statues of two of Winchester's most famous figures: Bishop William of Wykeham, founder of Winchester College, and St. Swithun, patron saint of weather. Swithun's remains were interred inside the cathedral against his will, which angered the saint so much that he brought torrents down on the culprits for 40 days. Custom holds that if it rains July 15 (St. Swithun's Day) it will rain for 40 days. It just might do so anyway.

The **Triforium Gallery** at the south transept contains some fine relics including some marvelous 14th-century figures from an altar screen. The 12th-century *Winchester Bible* resides in the library. (Gallery, library open Mon. 2:30-4:30pm, Tues.-Sat. 10:30am-12:30pm and 2:30pm-4:30pm; Oct.-Dec. and March-Easter Wed. and Sat. 10:30am-1pm and 2-4:30pm; Jan.-Feb. Sat. 11am-3:30pm. £1.50, students 50p.)

The **Cathedral Close** clasps a magnificent collection of medieval buildings, including the Deanery, Dome Alley, and Cheyney Court. The Close is open daily when not in use by schoolchildren. Southwards, tiny **St. Swithun's Chapel,** rebuilt in the 16th century, nestles above **King's Gate,** one of the two surviving city gates (the other is Westgate). Check out their newly opened Visitor Centre.

King's Gate leads to **Winchester College,** (tel. 868778) founded in 1382 as England's first "public" school; most of its 14th-century buildings remain intact. The chapel, **War Memorial Cloister,** is open to the public, as are the **Old Cloisters** and chantry during term. (College open daily 10am-1pm, 2-5pm; £2, seniors, students, and children £1.50. Excellent guided tours March-Sept. Mon.-Sat. at 11am, 2pm, and 3:15pm.) At 8 College St. a small sign marks a mustard-colored house in which Jane Austen died; don't dawdle—it's a private residence. A short stroll further down College St. brings you to **Wolvesey Palace** (tel. 854766), where the Bishop of Winchester lives, and **Wolvesey Castle,** where the Norman bishop used to (open April-Sept. daily 10am-1pm and 2-6pm; £1.10, students and seniors £1.10p, children 75p). You can see most of the ruins from the entrance without paying the admission.

At the end of High St., atop Castle Hill, Henry III built his castle on the remains of a fortress erected by William the Conqueror—what remains is the **Great Hall** (open daily 10am-5pm; Nov.-Feb. Mon.-Fri. 10am-5pm, Sat.-Sun. 10am-4pm; free). Beside the close, the **Winchester City Museum** (tel. 863064) deserves a quick peek. Roman relics and mannequins of Winchester tobacconists claim the museum's limited floor space (open Mon.-Fri. 10am-5pm, Sat. 10am-1pm and 2-5pm, Sun. 2-5pm; Oct.-March closed Mon.; free; limited wheelchair access).

ENTERTAINMENT

Weekend nights attract shiploads of artists who dock at bars along Broadway and High St. **Royal Oak,** down Royal Oak passageway and next to Godbegot House on High St., has a splendid antique oak bar, a variety of real ales, and a popular Tuesday night disco (open 11am-11pm, food served noon-4pm). **The Louisiana,** (tel. 870329) at Colebrook St. and High St., across from the hostel, packs hundreds of students indoors and onto a riverside patio. Beer costs a tad more than at drab pubs, but DJ request nights on Tuesday, Thursday, Friday, and Saturday compensate handily (open daily 3-11pm). Public urinals are located near the Guildhall—just in case.

The Edwardian glory of the **Theatre Royal,** Jewry St. (box office tel. 843434; open Mon.-Sat. 10am-8pm), hosts many London-based theatrical companies (£5.25-9.90). The town welcomes a **Folk Festival** in early May. Similarly, the **Hat Fair** in mid-July fills a weekend with theater, street performances, and peculiar headgear.

◼ NEAR WINCHESTER

Jane Austen lived in the meek village of **Chawton,** 15 mi. northeast of Winchester, from 1809 to 1817. In these years she produced *Pride and Prejudice, Emma, Northanger Abbey,* and *Persuasion*—not a bad decade's work. The author's house (tel. (01420) 83262) now displays many of her belongings. Wouldn't Jane be pleased? (Open April-Oct. daily 11am-4:30pm; Nov.-Dec. and March Wed.-Sun. 11am-4:30pm; Jan.-Feb. Sat.-Sun.; £1, children 50p.) Take Alder Valley bus #251 from Winchester (tel. (01252) 83787; Mon.-Fri. 1/hr.; 1hr.; return £3.65).

The **New Forest,** covering 145 sq. mi. of heath and woodland 17 mi. southwest of Winchester, was William the Conqueror's personal hunting ground. The **Rufus Stone** (near Brook and Cadnam) marks the spot where his son William II met an untimely end while pursuing game. The fatal moment occurred when a French courtier aimed an arrow at a stag and missed wildly. The arrow glanced off a tree and impaled the Norman king. The freaked-out Frenchman found God at that precise moment in time, and galloped away to the latest crusade for Jerusalem, leaving William Rufus to gather flies in the woods. The park is now a protected area in which wild ponies, donkeys, and cows frolic freely. Winchester's tourist office can provide a list of campsites within the forest. Bus #900 runs to the forest from Winchester (Sun. 4/day; mid-May to mid-Sept.). The New Forest also has a Museum and Visitor Centre, High St., Lyndhurst (tel. (01703) 282269; open daily from 10am).

Just outside Romsey, a small market town southwest of Winchester along the A31 road, lies the Palladian mansion **Broadlands** (tel. (01794) 516878) once the home of the Victorian Prime Minister Lord Palmerston and the late Lord Mountbatten—the philandering last viceroy of India, uncle of Prince Philip and great uncle to Prince Charles. Visitors can experience the uncanny sensation of being on the inside of a piece of Wedgewood china in the Wedgewood room. Broadlands enjoyed more recent fame as the site of Prince Charles and Lady Diana's honeymoon. Fat lot of good it did them (open Easter-July and Sept. Sat.-Thurs. 10am-4pm; Aug. daily 10am-4pm; £4.50, children £3).

◼◼◼ SALISBURY

Salisbury's small grid of streets (five running north to south and six east to west) didn't grow haphazardly as English towns are wont to do, but was carefully charted by Bishop Moore in the early 13th century. Clean and congenial to the spiritualists, heavy-metal druids, and gawkers who stop here before heading to Stonehenge, Salisbury (pop. 38,000) shouldn't be given short shrift. Its spotless thoroughfares and astounding cathedral grounds rival even the stones situated a few miles northwest. Walled off from the clamor of the busy marketplace and shopping precincts by the buildings around its close, Salisbury Cathedral remains a place for contemplation.

GETTING THERE

Salisbury lies 80 mi. southwest of London. **Trains** depart Salisbury Station for most major towns in the region, including Winchester (2/hr., change at Southampton; 1½hr.; £8), Southampton (2/hr.; 40min.; £5.50), Portsmouth (1/hr.; 1½hr.; £10) and London (1/hr.; £16.90-18.40). **National Express buses** run from Victoria (2/day; 2½hr.; £12.25). **Wilts and Dorset** service #X4 runs from Bath, 40 mi. northwest of Salisbury (6/day; 2hr.; £3.90); buses also drive to Stonehenge (Mon.-Fri. 8/day, Sat.-Sun. 3-5/day, 30min., return £3.75).

ORIENTATION & PRACTICAL INFORMATION

You'll find the Salisbury bus station in the center of town; the train station is a 10-minute walk. To reach the tourist office from the train station, turn left out of the station onto South Western Rd., bear right onto Fisherton St. (which becomes Bridge St.), pass over the bridge, and cross High St. Walk straight ahead onto Silver St., which becomes Butcher Row and then Fish Row. Practically every service a traveler could require is situated within a square mile of town center.

Tourist Office: Fish Row (tel. 334956), in the Guildhall in Market Sq. Extremely helpful. National Express ticket service. Books rooms. Guided tours May-late Sept. 11am and 6pm, £1.50. Open July-Aug. Mon.-Sat. 9:30am-7pm, Sun. 11am-5pm; June and Sept. 9:30am-6pm, Sun. 11am-4pm; Oct.-April Mon.-Sat. 9:30am-5pm; May Mon.-Sat. 9:30am-5pm, Sun. 11am-4pm.

Financial Services: Barclays (tel. (0800) 400100), at High and Silver St. Open Mon.-Tues. and Thurs.-Fri. 9:30am-4:30pm, Wed. 10am-4:30pm, Sat. 9:30am-noon. **Thomas Cook,** 5 Queen St. (tel. 412787). Open Mon.-Tues. and Thurs.-Sat. 9am-5:30pm, Wed. 10am-5:30pm. All other banks are near the town square.

Post Office: 24 Castle St. (tel. 413051), at Chipper Lane. *Poste Restante, Bureau de Change.* Open Mon.-Fri. 9am-5:30pm, Sat. 9am-1pm. **Postal Code:** SP1 1AB.

Telephone Code: 01722.

Train Station: South Western Rd. (tel. Southampton (01703) 229393), west of town across the river. Lockers for **luggage storage** on train station concourse (50p-£1). Information office open Mon.-Fri. 9:30am-4:45pm, Sat. 8:15am-2:45pm.

Bus Station: 8 Endless St. (tel. 336855). It's not an end, it's a beginning. Booking office open Mon.-Fri. 8:15am-5:45pm, Sat. 8:15am-5:15pm. Explorer ticket £4, seniors £2.95, children £2, family £8; good on Wilts and Dorset, Hampshire bus, Provincial, Badger, or Solent Blue.

Taxis: tel. 334343. Taxis throb at the train station and New Canal (by the cinema).

Bike Rental: Hayball and Co., 26-30 Winchester St. just beyond McDonalds (tel. 411378). £9/day, longer periods negotiable; deposit £25. Open Mon.-Sat. 9am-5:30pm.

Launderette: Washing Well, 28 Chipper Lane. Open daily 8am-9pm. Bring change.

Hotlines: Samaritans (crisis): 42 Milford St. (tel. 323355). 24 hrs. **Rape Crisis:** Southampton (tel. (01703) 701213). Mon. 7-10pm, Tues. 10am-1pm, Thurs. 1-4pm, Sun. 7-10pm. **AIDS information:** Dept. of G.U. Medicine (tel. 336212).

Market Days: Tues. and Sat. in Market Sq. (roughly 6am-3pm).

Early Closing Day: Wed. at 1pm (small shops only).

Hospital: Salisbury District Hospital, Odstock (tel. 336212).

Emergency: Dial 999; no coins required.

Police: Wilton Rd. (tel. 411444).

ACCOMMODATIONS & CAMPING

Salisbury's proximity to much-frequented Stonehenge breeds many B&Bs, mostly well-appointed and reasonably priced (around £13). Guesthouses aplenty grace Castle Rd., a short hike north of downtown on Castle St. Many pubs take overnight guests as well (look for signs).

Ron and Jenny Coats, 51 Salt Lane (tel. 327443), just up from the bus station. A welcoming and clean 400-year-old house with warped floors and ceiling beams to prove its age. Mellow, hostel-style 2-, 3- and 6-bed rooms. Centrally located. Mrs. C will lodge you on her floor or at her friends' £11 B&B (tel. 328905) if her beds fill up. Anarchy: no curfew, no rules. £7.50, with breakfast £9-9.50 (depending on how much you eat). Sheets 80p.

HI Youth Hostel, Milford Hill House, Milford Hill (tel. 327572). From the tourist office, turn left on Fish Row, right on Queen St., left on Milford St., and walk ahead a few blocks under the overpass; the hostel will be on the left. A beautiful old house outside with the usual stark hostel interior—walls, thin carpet, bunk-beds. 74 beds; phone ahead. Two acres of garden (camping £4.35/person). Lock-out 10am-1pm. Curfew 11:30pm. £11.30, under-18 £8.40. Breakfast included.

Mrs. Spiller, Nuholme, Ashfield Rd. (tel. 336592), 10 min. from the train station. Bear right out of station, cross the car park straight ahead, turn right onto Church-fields Rd., then turn right again onto Ashfield—a white house on the right. Very friendly place run by an elderly woman who can recite Shakespeare over a cup. £11, students £10.

Camping: Hudson's Field of the **Camping Club of Great Britain,** Hudson's Field, Castle Rd. (tel. 320713). On the way to Old Sarum, with showers and 100 pitches. Curfew for vehicles only 11pm. £4.30/person. Open April-Oct.

FOOD & PUBS

Carbon dating has unequivocally determined that Salisbury's cafeteria steaks existed millennia before Stonehenge was even a twinkle in the eyes of the Old People. Other sorts of food, though, are years fresher. From 6am to 3pm on Tuesdays and Saturdays the town center resounds with vendors hawking clothes, fresh local produce, and homemade jams. **Reeve the Baker** (main branch next to the tourist office, between the town square and Fish Row) stocks all the strolling sightseer could crave, from Cornish pasties to caterpillar meringues. **Salisbury Health Foods,** 15 Queen St., vends life-inducing edibles and squirts frozen yogurt (open Mon.-Sat. 9am-5:30pm). Grocery stores include **Tesco** on Castle St. (open Mon.-Thurs. 8am-8pm, Fri. 8am-9pm, Sat. 8am-6pm)and **Safeway** in the Malting Shopping Centre. At **Mo's,** 62 Milford St. (tel. 331377), on the way to the youth hostel, carnivores can devour cheeseburgers (£4.75) or ribs (£5.95) while vegans consider what "lentil creation" really is, anyway (£4.55). Mo's milkshake (£1.75) is magnificent (open Mon.-Sat. noon-2pm and 6-10:30pm, Sun. 5:30-10:30pm. At **La Gondola,** 155 Fisherton St. (tel 324856), pastas line the windows and phenomenal Italian specialties fill your plate (open daily noon-2:30pm and 6pm-midnight).

Even the most jaded pub dweller will find a pleasing venue among Salisbury's 67-odd watering holes. What's more, most serve cheap food (£2-4), and many offer drink specials and live music. The not-so-**New Inn** forged the way for non-smoking pubs in Britain. **The Pheasant,** Salt Lane (tel. 320 675), serves lunch and sports live music on Thursday night. **Wig & Quill,** One New St. (tel. 335665), offers a traditional interior backed up by a garden with a view and an original cathedral wall section (bar meals £3-4). **Coach & Horses,** Winchester St. (tel. 336254), serves meals (Mon.-Sat. 10am-10pm) and drinks all day (it's also reputed to be Salisbury's oldest pub). **The Old Mill,** atop the river at the end of a ten-minute stroll along Town Path, is *the* scenic setting for an outdoor drink on a summer evening. Share your pint with the ducks closer to town at **The Bishop's Mill** over the creatively named Bridge St. bridge.

SIGHTS

Go to church. Hie thee hither to **Salisbury Cathedral** (tel. 328726), which rises monolithically from its grassy close (the biggest one in England) to a neck-breaking height of 404 ft.The bases of the marble pillars seem to buckle under the strain of

6400 tons of limestone; if a pillar rings when you knock on it, you should probably move away. Nearly 700 years have left the cathedral in need of structural and aesthetic repair. (Sir Christopher Wren calculated that the spire leaned 29.5 in.) Scaffolding will shroud the spire, tower, and west front of the cathedral for years to come. Once inside, say hello to the timber tomb of William Longespee, Earl of Salisbury (d. 1226), rare indeed in a universe of stone sarcophagi. A tiny stone figure rests in the nave; legend has it either that a boy bishop is entombed on the spot or that it covers the heart of Richard Poore, bishop and founder of the cathedral. Framed and sitting in the nave, a flag once hung in Eisenhower's planning office, but was presented to the cathedral in 1944. Tower tours begin at 11:30am and 2:30pm (£2). Bursars lead adventuring souls to the roof area at 11am and 2, 3, and 6pm (£1).

One of four surviving copies of the *Magna Carta* rests in the **Chapter House,** to King John's chagrin. Detailed medieval friezes around the perimeter of the Chapter House narrate stories from Genesis and Exodus. Adam and Eve cower from God's wrath and Cain bludgeons his fair brother's head with what looks like a hammer. Ask a guide for a complete list of the figures in relief (open Mon.-Sat. 9:30am-4:45pm, Sun. 1-4:45pm; Nov.-Feb. Mon.-Sat. 11am-3pm, Sun. 1-3:15pm; 30p, students and seniors 20p). The **cloisters** adjoining the cathedral somehow grew to be the largest in England, though the cathedral never housed any monks. (Cathedral open daily 8am-6:30pm; July 8am-8:15pm. Virtually mandatory donation £2.50, seniors and students £1, children 50p. Evensong Mon.-Sat. 5:30pm, Sun. 3pm.) The open lawns of the **cathedral close** flank some beautifully preserved old homes, including **Malmesbury House,** where Handel once lived and which his ghost now haunts. Shhh! (it's a private residence). Tours available every half-hour (open April-Oct. Tues.-Thurs., Bank Holiday Mon. noon-5pm; £3, children and seniors £2.50).

The **Salisbury and South Wiltshire Museum,** King's House, 65 The Close (tel. 332151) houses a potpourri of artwork (including Turner's exquisite watercolors of the nearby cathedral), handicraft, and random oddities. Exhibits trace the development of Salisbury, show aerial photographs of ancient cities and burial mounds, and present the latest crackpot theories on Stonehenge (open Mon.-Sat. 10am-5pm, Sun. 2-5pm; Sept.-June Mon.-Sat. 10am-5pm; £2.50, seniors £1.75, children 50p). The museum possesses the bizarre Giant and his companion Hob-Nob—a 12-ft. high stuffed behemoth of obscure origins. Purchased in 1873 for 30 shillings, the absurd figure has numerous times greeted royalty; he enjoyed the procession of George V and Queen Elizabeth's coronation, as well as Victoria's Diamond Jubilee.

ENTERTAINMENT

Salisbury's repertory theatre company puts on good shows at the **Playhouse,** Malthouse Lane (tel. 320333), over the bridge off Fisherton St. (Tickets £7; £5.50 seats available 30 min. before curtain, to students from 10am on the day of the show.) The **Salisbury Festival** features dance exhibitions, music and a wine tasting festival at the Salisbury library during, tentatively, May (tickets from £2.50; Festival Box Office, Salisbury Playhouse, Malthouse Lane, Salisbury SP2 7RA.; tel. 320333).

■ NEAR SALISBURY

The germ of Salisbury, **Old Sarum,** lies 2 mi. north of the town. Here, an Iron Age fort evolved into a Saxon town, then a Norman fortress. In the 13th century, church officials moved the settlement and built a new cathedral. Now a lonely windswept mound, Old Sarum was the most notorious of the "rotten boroughs" eliminated by the Reform Act of 1832 (tel. (01722) 335398; open daily 10am-6pm; Nov.-March 10am-4pm; £1.35, seniors and students £1, children 65p). Old Sarum is off the A345, the road to Stonehenge. Buses #5-9 run every 15 minutes from the Salisbury.

Declared by James I to be "the finest house in the land," **Wilton House** (tel. (01722) 743115), 3 mi. west of Salisbury on the A30 and home to the Earl of Pembroke, exhibits paintings by Van Dyck, Rembrandt, Rubens, and others, and has an impressive, almost outrageous interior design devised partly by Inigo Jones (open

April-mid-Oct. daily 11am-6pm; house £5, students £4.20; grounds only £2). Catch bus #60 or 61 outside Marks and Spencer (Mon.-Sat. every 10 min., Sun. 1/hr.).

■■■ STONEHENGE

You may put a hundred questions to these rough-hewn giants as they bend in grim contemplation of their fellow companions; but your curiosity falls dead in the vast sunny stillness that shrouds them and the strange monument, with all its unspoken memories, becomes simply a heart-stirring picture in a land of pictures.

—Henry James

Stonehenge is a reminder that England seemed ancient even to the Saxons and Normans. Surrounded by imperturbable cows and swirled by winds exceeding 50mph, the much-touted stones, only 22 ft. high, may be initially disappointing. Consider, though, that they were lifted by a simple but infinitely tedious process of rope-and-log leverage. Built over many lifetimes, Stonehenge exudes a religious and aesthetic dedication difficult to comprehend today. Forever pelted by sensational theories and outlandish fantasies, Stonehenge has yielded none of its ageless mystery.

The most famous Stonehenge legend holds that the circle was built by Irish stones magically transported by Merlin. (Actually, the seven-ton Blue Stones are made of rock quarried in Wales.) Other stories attribute the monument to giants, Romans, Danes, Phoenicians, Druids, Mycenaean Greeks, and aliens. In any case, whether they traveled by land, water, or spaceship, the Bronze Age builders (ca. 2800-1500 BC) would seem to have possessed more technology than anthropologists can explain. Archaeologists divide the complex into three successive incarnations of the monument. The relics of the oldest are the Aubrey Holes (white patches in the earth) and the Heel Stone (the isolated, rough block standing outside the circle). This first Stonehenge may have been a worship and burial site for seven centuries. The next monument consisted of about 60 stones imported from Wales around 2100 BC to mark astronomical directions. It may once have been composed of two concentric circles and two horseshoes of megaliths, enclosed by earthworks; the present shape dates from 1500 BC.

Many peoples have worshipped at Stonehenge, from late Neolithic and Early Bronze Age chieftains to contemporary mystics. In 300 BC the Druids arrived from the Continent and claimed Stonehenge as their shrine. The Druid Society of London still honors the sun rising over the Heel Stone on Midsummer's Day. The summer of 1988 saw a bizarre confrontation between hippie-pagan celebrants and police. Recently, officials have felt obliged to close access to Stonehenge on the summer solstice, outraging the devout Druid and inconveniencing the romantic tourist.

Stonehenge belongs to everyone—everyone, that is, who can afford to fork over the pricey admission which allows a glimpse only a wee bit better than that offered from the road. Shrewd travelers will do well to photograph the stones from the roadside vantage or on Amesbury Hill, 1.5 mi. up the A303, thereby avoiding the entry fee and the crush of people waiting to be admitted. (Stonehenge open daily 10am-6pm; Nov.-late March 10am-4pm; £2.85, concessions £2.15.)

Getting to Stonehenge takes little effort. **Wilts & Dorset** (tel. (01722) 336855) runs several **buses** daily from Salisbury center and from the train station (return £3.75). The first bus leaves Salisbury at 8:45am (Sat. 8:50am, Sun. 10:45am), and the last leaves Stonehenge at 4:20pm (Sun. 3:50pm; 30min.). Some private operators offer **tours** to Stonehenge and Avebury (£9-10). Those without money to burn may prefer the free tours of Stonehenge offered by **English Heritage.**

The most scenic walking or cycling route to Stonehenge follows the **Woodford Valley Route** through Woodford and Wilsford. Go north from Salisbury on Castle Rd., bear left just before Victoria Park onto Stratford Rd., and follow the road over the bridge through Lower, Middle, and Upper Woodford. After about 9 mi., turn left onto the A303 for the last mile.

SOUTHWEST ENGLAND

Mists of legend shroud the counties of Dorset, Somerset, Devon, and Cornwall in England's **West Country**. King Arthur is said to have been born at Tintagel on Cornwall's northern coast and to have battled Mordred on Bodmin Moor. One hamlet purports to be the site of Camelot, another village claims to be the resting place of the Holy Grail, and no fewer than three small lakes are identified as the final resting place of Arthur's sword, Excalibur. The ghost of Sherlock Holmes still pursues the Hound of the Baskervilles across Dartmoor, in Devon, and St. Michael's Mount at Marazion is believed to have held the terrible giant Cormoran hostage in its well.

It is easy to lose the spirit of legend among "King Arthur" parking lots, "Mayflour" bake shops, and the smoke of industrial cities like Bristol and Plymouth. Still, the terrain is unfailingly beautiful. The cliffs of the coastal path and the moors and wooded valleys of Dartmoor contain the most timeless views of the West Country.

Legends aside, a scattered civilization found a refuge in the West Country's daunting hills. Bronze Age barrows (burial mounds), Stone Age quoits (chamber tombs), and foreign megaliths of unknown purpose litter the countryside. Abbey ruins totter amid the heather and bracken. The Celts maintained a stronghold in Cornwall even as the Saxons and Normans overran the rest of the country. The Gaelic language spoken in Cornwall held out tenaciously against standard English; the last native speaker of Cornish died a few decades ago, but a few committed souls are attempting a revival.

GETTING THERE & GETTING ABOUT

Unfortunately, no single rail or bus pass covers all of the worthwhile spots in the region, as many of the more remote towns are accessible only by local buses. Select a pass that best suits your itinerary, but it will at times be necessary to take a local bus (usually under £3), rent a bike, or walk to a spot of interest.

Trains

British Rail offers fast and frequent service from London and the north. The region's primary east-west line from Paddington Station, London passes through Taunton, Exeter (16/day; 2½hr.; £34), Plymouth (15/day; 3½hr.; £39), and Truro, and ends at Penzance (6/day; 5-6hr.; £46). The north-south line from Glasgow and Edinburgh (Mon.-Sat. 1/day) passes through Bristol, Taunton, and Exeter before ending at Plymouth; it may be easier to travel through London. Branch lines connect St. Ives, Newquay, Falmouth, and Barnstaple to the network.

Special fares make rail travel competitive with bus travel; ask about cheap day-return fares, which, as elsewhere in Britain, are often only marginally more expensive than single fares. British Rail offers a variety of Rail Rover passes in the West Country: the **Freedom of the Southwest Rover** allows unlimited travel for a 7-day period, in the area from Bristol Parkway through Salisbury and down to Weymouth, covering all of Cornwall, Devon, Somerset, and part of Avon and Dorset (£50). The **Devon Rail Rover** is bounded by and includes the Taunton-to-Exmouth line on the east and the Gunnislake-Plymouth line in the west (7 days, £35; **FlexiRover,** valid any 3 of 7 days, £25); the **Cornish Rail Rover** is bounded by and includes the Gunnislake-Plymouth line (7 days, £30; **FlexiRover,** valid 3 of 7 days, £21). For rail information, call British Rail in Bristol at (0117) 929 4255, in Plymouth at (01752) 221300, or in Truro at (01872) 76244.

Buses

National Express buses run to major points along the north coast via Bristol and to points along the south coast (including Penzance) via Exeter and Plymouth. For journeys within the region, local bus service is less expensive and more extensive than the local trains, passing through towns that are too small to have train stations.

All the large regional bus companies—**Western National** (in Cornwall and south Devon), **Southern National** (in Somerset and West Dorset), **Devon General,** and the **Badgerline** (in Avon and Somerset)—offer **Explorer** or **Day Rambler** tickets, which allow a full day's travel on any bus within their region for £4-6. The aptly named **Key West** ticket (£22) is good on all Devon and Cornwall routes for a week; there is also a three-day ticket for £13. For information about regional bus services or National Express buses, call Western National in Penzance at (01736) 69469 or Plymouth at (01752) 222666, or Badgerline in Bristol at (0117) 927 2033. Phone ahead in the off-season; branch-line rail service on Sundays shuts down for the winter, and many bus lines don't run at all between September and March.

Hiking & Biking

Distances between towns are so short in England's southwest that it is feasible to travel through the region on your own steam. The narrow roads and hilly landscape can make biking difficult, but hardy cyclists will find the quiet lanes and countryside rewarding terrain. If you're walking or cycling, on- or off-road, bring along a large-scale Ordnance Survey map and an impregnable windbreaker to shield you from foul weather. If you'll be hiking through countryside, it is important to respect the local residents whose livelihood depends on the land you're crossing.

The longest coastal path in England, the **South West Peninsula Coast Path,** originates in Dorset and passes through South Devon, Cornwall, and North Devon, ending in Somerset. The path, which takes several months to walk in its entirety, winds past cliffs, caves, beaches, ports, and resort colonies; walkers should expect to run into herds of sheep and camera-dependent tourists. Many rivers cross the path on their way to the sea, so you will have to take a ferry or wade through the crossings. Check times carefully to avoid being stranded. Some sections of the trail are difficult enough to dissuade all but the most ambitious; check your route with a tourist official before you set out to make sure that the area you want to visit is well-marked.

The path is divided into four parts based on the national parks and counties through which it passes. The **Dorset Coast Path,** stretching from Lyme Regis to Poole Harbor, can be negotiated in a few days. Accommodations and eats can be gotten along the way. Ordnance Survey maps 1:50,000: 193, 194, 195 and Purbeck Outdoor Leisure Map will enable you to plan your route. The **South Devon Coast Path** picks up near Paighton and continues through Plymouth, winding around spectacular cliffs, wide estuaries, and remote bays set off by lush vegetation and wildflowers. The **Cornwall Coast Path,** which includes some of the most rugged stretches of the route, starts in Plymouth (a ferry service takes you on to Cremyll), rounds the southwestern tip of Britain, and continues up the northern Atlantic coast all the way to Bude. The magnificent Cornish cliffs in this stretch of the path harbor a great range of birds and sealife. The final section, the **Somerset and North Devon Coastal Path,** extends from Bude through Exmoor National Park to Minehead. The least arduous of the four sections, it still offers magnificent coastal scenery in North Devon and the highest seaside cliffs in Southwest England.

Most of the path is smooth enough to cover on a bike; often bike rental shops will suggest three-day to week-long routes along the coast. Journeys of any length are possible along all parts of the path, as buses serve most points along the route, and youth hostels and B&Bs are spaced out at 5 to 25 mi. intervals along it. The Countryside Commission sells extremely useful guides and Ordnance Survey maps covering each section of the path (for address see Essentials: Traveling in Britain and Ireland), as do most tourist offices.

■■■ DORCHESTER

Famed as the inspiration for Thomas Hardy's "Casterbridge," Dorchester (pop. 14,000) is sleepy, bordering on narcoleptic. Neolithic and Roman oddities—notably Maiden Castle and the Maumbury Rings—are sprinkled outside Dorchester, but Hardy's various houses and his church are all that recommend the town itself. A

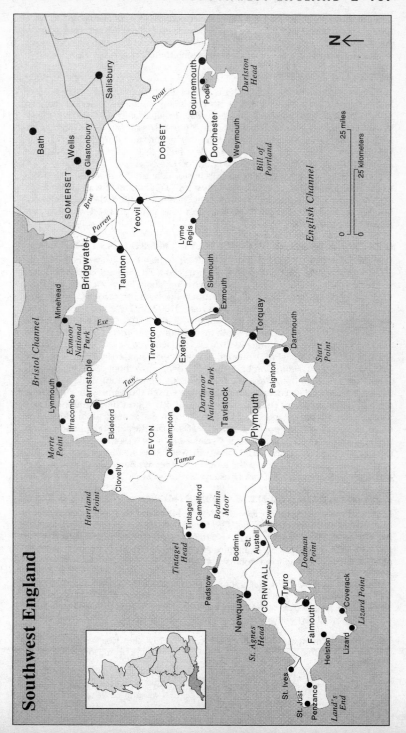

Southwest England

series of footpaths allow access to the Dorset countryside and enable one to trace Hardy's characters as they developed in his imagination. Ramblers and cyclists enjoy the sloping hills, cows chew their cuds in outlying fields, and a smattering of antique dealers and other shops peddle their wares along High St.

GETTING THERE

The county seat of Dorset, Dorchester is 120 mi. southwest of London. Trains leave **South Station** for points north and east, including London's Waterloo (18/day; 2½hr.; return £25.50) and Weymouth (20/day; 15min.; return £1.90). Trains from **West Station** connect to points west. The **Wilts & Dorset bus** (tel. 673555) connects Dorchester with Salisbury, while **Bere Regis,** 7 Bridport Rd. (tel. 262992), provides service within the local perimeter; Bere Regis also sells tickets for **National Express** buses to London's Waterloo Station and Exeter.

Those hitching from Salisbury to Dorchester take the A354 to the A35; from Exeter, the A30 to the A35. From Dorchester to London, most walk down West High St. and over Greys Bridge. To Exeter, hitchers walk west to the intersection of Bridport Rd. and Damers Rd. To Bristol, most head north on The Grove just past Millers Close to New Rd.

ORIENTATION & PRACTICAL INFORMATION

The intersection of High West St. with South St. (which eventually becomes Cornhill St.) serves as the unofficial center of town. The main **shopping district** extends southward along South St. The Top o' Town roundabout lies at the nexus of High West St., Bridport Rd., The Grove, and Albert Rd. Both **rail stations,** Dorchester South (tel. 269748) and Dorchester West (tel. (01202) 292474) are off Weymouth Ave., which runs southwest from the bottom of South St. To reach the **tourist office** (tel. 267992) from the Dorchester South train station, walk straight out of the station onto Weymouth Ave., right onto South Walks and left onto Acland Rd. The office is on your left (open Mon.-Fri. 9am-6pm, Sat. 9am-5pm, Sun. 10am-2pm; Sept.-June Mon.-Sat. 9am-5pm.) From Dorchester West Station, turn left out of the station onto Maumbury Rd., right onto Great Western (which becomes South Walks Rd.), then left onto Acland Rd. Guided walking **tours** leave from the tourist office mid June through mid September (Thurs. 11am; 1½hr.; £1.50). A **post office** grumbles at 43 South St. (tel. 251093). (Open Mon.-Fri. 9am-5:30pm, Sat. 9am-12:30pm; *Bureau de Change, Poste Restante*; **postal code:** DT1 1DN.) Dorchester's **telephone code** is 01305. Rent out a bike at **Dorchester Cycles,** 31A Great Western Rd. (tel. 268787). (Mountain bikes £7.50/day, £20/3 days, £40/week, deposit £100. Open Mon.-Sat. 9am-5:30pm.) Bank and gawk at the same time: **Barclays Bank,** South St., operates in a house where Hardy's Mayor of Casterbridge supposedly lived.

ACCOMMODATIONS & CAMPING

Dorchester has no youth hostels; the nearest **HI hostel** is 10 mi. away at Litton Cheney (tel. (01308) 482340). Beds go for £5.10 (open April-Oct.). Lodging is a king's ransom (£15-18) at the town's scattered boarding houses and pubs (try the Royal Oak on High West St. or inquire at the tourist office); none are especially plush, and most have only two rooms, but they'll do in a rush.

Clovelly, 19 Cornwall Rd. (tel. 266689). Follow Albert Rd. south from the Top o' Town roundabout. Newly renovated, with remote-control TVs and comfortable beds. The proprietress serves meaty breakfasts, but can cater to vegetarians. See if she'll show off her animal kingdom—20-odd birds, two dogs, and a lonely rabbit. Singles £15, doubles £25.

Maumbury Cottage, 9 Maumbury Rd. (tel. 266726). Kind Mrs. Wade keeps two cozy singles close to Dorchester West station and 5 min. from Dorchester South station. £14.

The Old House at Home, Salisbury St. (tel. 268909). Just off High East St. by the Jehovah's Witness building, the Stephensons greet guests in their home, which operated as a pub for well over 200 years. Immaculate, but few rooms. Enjoy a good breakfast (they cater on the side). One room with bath. £14-16/person.

Camping: Giant's Head Caravan and Camping Park, Old Sherborne Rd., Cerne Abbas (tel. (013003) 242), 7 mi. north of Dorchester. Head out of town on The Grove, bear right onto Old Sherborne Rd. Two folks and tent from £4.50. Open March-Oct.

FOOD

Food in all its glorious forms can be enjoyed in eateries along High West and High East St. Several places slice sandwiches for 60p-£1; **County Stile,** 10 Hardye Arcade, creates oversized ones for under £2 (open 8am-4:30pm). The **Borough Arms** at 36 East St. and **Judge Jeffrey's** at 6 High West St. pack in the indigenous for pints. Vegetarians and their more exacting cousins, vegans, won't suffer for lack of food at **Walnut Grove Vegetarian Coffee Shop,** 25 Dungate St., just off South St. (tel. 268882). Indoors and out they serve a vegetarian meatloaf (why?) for £3.50, along with more predictable soups and sandwiches (£1.60-1.90). No smoking (open Mon.-Sat. 10:30am-4:30pm). Also in the area, the **Potter Inn,** 19 Dungate St., serves crunchy wholefood ideal for light lunches, snacks, and tea. Meals (£2-3) are served from noon to 2pm. (Open Mon.-Sat. 9:30am-6pm, Sun. 11am-4pm; Oct.-May Mon.-Sat. 9:30am-6pm.) **Gorge Café,** 39 South St., serves Dorset's finest eggburgers (£2). (Open Mon.-Sat. 7am-7pm, Sun. 9am-7pm.) Wander through the well-stocked aisles of **Waitrose Supermarket** in the Tudor Arcade (also off South St.; open Mon.-Wed. and Sat. 8:30am-6pm, Thurs.-Fri. 8:30am-8pm).

SIGHTS & ENTERTAINMENT

Dorchester's sights are stupefyingly dull; you would do better to hike around outside the village. Two vastly different periods collide in the countryside, Roman Britain and Hardy's Wessex. The traveler with a taste for adventure and, preferably, a bike, can negotiate both in a day and emerge still breathing. Begin in town at the **Dorset County Museum,** High West St. (tel. 262735), where a replica of Hardy's study shines among yawn-producing geological and historical exhibits (open Mon.-Sat. 10am-5pm, Sun. during July-Aug.; £1.95, children under 16 and seniors 95p). **Hardy's Wessex,** on Icen Way (tel. 250525), features a stroll through the village and woodland scenes of Hardy's time (in case you didn't get enough of them in town). Animated figures provide narration along the route (open Mon.-Fri. 10am-5pm, Sat.10am-12:30pm, Sun. 10am-3pm; £2.30, children and seniors £1.15). Before hitting the high road to visit the more pastoral sites of Hardy's youth, take a walk by **Max Gate,** a home Hardy once occupied at Arlington Ave. and Syward Rd.

Next stop on the Hardy adventure is the ever-so-small **Stinsford Church** to the northeast of town in Stinsford village. Follow the London Rd. which eventually becomes Stinsford Hill. At the roundabout proceed straight ahead; after crossing to the continuation of Stinsford Rd., continue walking till you come to the first right. Turn and follow the road over the hill; the churchyard will be straight ahead. Hardy was christened in the church and his family plot can be found in the yard. Oddly enough, Hardy's desire to be entombed in the shadow of the little church was only satisfied in part—only his heart is buried there. Alongside the Hardy graves rests the poet Cecil Day Lewis, who requested he be buried near his beloved Hardy. Though there's no room left by his graveside, you can show your love for Dorchester's favorite son by joining the **Thomas Hardy Society,** which administers the biennial international Thomas Hardy Conference in Dorchester. Contact Helen Gibson, P.O. Box 1438, Dorchester, Dorset DT1 1YH for further information or call 251501.

Upon exiting the churchyard return to the road and turn right to continue along to the village of **Higher Brockhampton** (three mi. east of Dorchester proper), where Hardy was born in 1840. The modest "seven-roomed rambling house" was the setting for his first two novels, *Under the Greenwood Tree* and *Far from the Madding Crowd.* Appointments are necessary to see the house's interior (tel. 262366; £2.50). A delightful flower garden fronts the house; Thorncobe Wood and the Blackheath Trails are at the rear (garden and trails open Fri.-Wed. 11am-dusk). No bus goes to Higher Brockhampton. It's quite a hike but worth the effort.

Dorchester's status as a former Roman stronghold cannot be denied, nor should the several ruins scattered here and there be neglected. Just past the entrance to the Dorchester South railway station on Weymouth Ave. sprawl the **Maumbury Rings,** a bronze age monument similar to Stonehenge and Avebury; the gaping, grassy maw of the amphitheater, later used by the Romans, hedges in as the most noteworthy aspect of the site. The complete foundation and one mosaic floor of a **Roman Town House** are at the back of the County Hall complex near the Top o' Town roundabout. (Enter the parking lot and walk all the way back; the gate is unlocked during daylight hours.) The only remaining fragment of the old **Roman Wall** is on Albert Rd., a short walk to the south. Look sharp, or you'll walk right by. On the way the stone likeness of Thomas Hardy grumpily surveys the roundabout.

The **Borough Gardens** at the corner of Albert Rd. and Cornwall St. provides a breathing space for worn-out tourists and townspeople (open till dusk). The most significant of Dorchester's ancient ruins is **Maiden Castle,** a fortification dating from 3000 BC which was seized by the Romans in 44 AD. The "castle" consists of a hilltop fortified by a series of steep ridges. Today only sheep hold the fort. There is no bus to the site, but the local shuttle to Vespasian Way will take you halfway (every 15 min. from Trinity St.); otherwise, it is a scenic two-mi. hike from the center of town down Maiden Castle Rd.

Dorchester doesn't really dabble in nightlife; most restaurants and shops shut down early. The **Plaza Cinema** on Trinity St. is small but functional and shows first-run flicks (tel. 262488). A short walk northwest. **The Sun Inn,** Lower Burton, Dorchester has wonderful pub grub and friendly folk (tel. 250445; open Mon.-Sat. 11am-2:30pm and 6:30-11pm, Sun. noon-3pm and 7-10:30pm).

■■■ WEYMOUTH

Surrounded by the rolling Dorset hills, Weymouth (pop. 44,000) has depended on the favor of the weather and waves ever since King George III made the town fashionable by gracing the coast. A small resort town with a spectacular sandy beach by English Channel standards, Weymouth still pulls droves of day-trippers into its welcoming waters. Not the spot for a quiet holiday, Weymouth has opportunities aplenty to sea and be seen, but few attractions. Crowds congregate along the streets and automobiles congest the area.

King George's Bathing Machine is the centerpiece of an otherwise mundane collection of artifacts at the **Weymouth Museum,** which now hides in the **Time Walk,** Hope Sq., Brewer's Quay (tel. 777622), Weymouth's most popular attraction after the English Channel. Witness the horrors of the Black Plague, board a Spanish Galleon, and cavort in a smuggler's cove (open daily 9:30am-9:30pm; Sept.-mid-July 9:30am-4:30pm; £3.50, students and seniors £3, children £2.50). Bask in historical splendor at the **Tudor House,** 3 Trinity St. (tel. 782925 or 788168), an authentically furnished early 17th-century merchant's house (open Tues.-Fri. 11am-3:45pm; Oct.-May first Sun. and bank holidays only 2-4pm; £1.50, students £1, children 50p). A 15-minute walk along the harbor lands you in **Nothe Gardens,** a well-manicured park bursting with color. Garden enthusiasts can pick up the leaflet "Welcome to the Gardens of Wessex and the Southwest" for directions to numerous green spots.

In the old harbor, the **Deep Sea Adventure and Shipwreck Centre,** 9 Custom House Quay (tel. 760690), reels in three floors of sleep-inducing exhibits which trace the development of diving and sea salvage techniques from the 17th century. Entry into the cavernous interior does offer a respite from the tourists and sun, and the museum houses a special exhibit on the *Titanic* that proves enlightening if not terribly fascinating (museum open July-Aug. daily 10am-6pm; March-June and Sept.-Oct. 10am-5:30pm; Nov.-Feb. 10am-4:30pm; £3.35, seniors and students £2.80, children £2.35; disabled access).

From the quieter south side, a four-mi. peaceful cliffside stroll along the **Underbarn Walk** leads to the island town of **Portland.** Frequent buses (every 10 min.) run to Portland from the King's Statue near the Weymouth tourist office; pick up an information leaflet at the office before you go. Visitors to the **Portland Bill Conservation Area,** at the southern tip of the island, should climb up the steps of the lighthouse for an eye-popping view and a morsel of respite from the screaming ninnies on the **Esplanade.** From the last week of July to the end of August, Monday nights are filled with exploding fireworks over the water. Grab a blanket and some beach (open daily 11am-dusk; free). **Portland Castle** (tel. 820539) overlooks the harbor. Henry VIII built it in his frenzy to stave off French and Spanish Catholic attacks. More recently, World War II soldiers used the site as a base (open April-late Oct. daily 10am-6pm; £1.80, seniors and students £1.35, children 90p; the bus leaves from Weymouth King's statue every 15min.).

Sunbathing crowds soak up all the rooms in summer; consider making reservations early. B&Bs on the Esplanade cost a pretty penny and fill up quickly. More isolated side streets provide the best bargains—especially **Lennox Street** and **Ranelagh Road** (£12-14). **Seaways,** 5 Turton St. (which runs parallel to the Esplanade, second right off Gloucester Terrace, across from Tourist Office), has centrally located rooms from £14, with breakfast (tel. 771646). Eats are easily found around lunchtime in the Old Town area, surrounding St. Thomas St. You'll Roo the day you don't stop at **The House at Pooh Corner,** 50 St. Mary St. (tel. 770472), which serves pasta and Piglet. Lasagna costs £3.75; Piglet is priceless (open Mon.-Sat. 9:30am-5pm, Sun. 11am-4pm). **Ye Olde Sally Lunne Shoppe,** 9 Upper St. at Albans St., has a variety of Bak'd Goodes to take out to the beach—try the bloomer loaf (47p; open Mon.-Sat. 8:30am-5pm). **Brunches,** 27 Maiden St. (tel. 788900), serves up good seafood and pasta lunches (£3-4) in a relaxed and youthful bistro atmosphere where "he who shouts loudest gets served last!" As day-trippers roll out of town, the brightly lit **White Hart**, at the head of Bond St., turns out cheap pub grub from around noon until 7 or 8pm, depending on the day. The White Hart features live music every Thursday night (Mon. and Fri. as well in summer). Edibles can also be purchased at the **Tesco Supermarket** on St. Thomas St. next to the post office (open Mon.-Fri. 8am-8pm, Sat. 8am-6:30pm). Five pubs make noise on Brewers' Quay, Weymouth's pub central. **The Golden Lion,** at the corner of St. Edmund and St. Mary St., is quieter. Greengrocers, restaurants, and pubs cover St. Thomas St., which is far less hectic than the Esplanade.

The Weymouth **tourist office** (tel. 785747) is on the Esplanade at the King's Statue (open June-July daily 9am-6:30pm, Aug. 9:30am-9pm, Sept.-May 10am-5pm). Their 20p map does not name the streets in the Old Town, so be ready to find your way by asking. The **post office** is at 67 St. Thomas St. (tel. 784828; open Mon.-Fri. 9am-5:30pm, Sat. 9am-12:30pm). Thursday is **market day;** Wednesday is early closing day. The **hospital** on Melcombe Ave. (tel. 772211) offers the best backless gowns south of London. Weymouth's **postal code** is DT4 8HR, and like Dorchester's, its **telephone code** is 01305. **Toilets** are located in the same building as the tourist office. The railway station features glorious **lockers** to suit your luggage size (from £1); use 'em, by God. The Weymouth **Market** opens every Thursday from early in the morning till 4pm, near the station.

The **train station** on Ranelagh Rd. (tel. 773030) connects Weymouth with London (return £27), Chichester (£19.10), Brighton (£24.80), and Dorchester (£1.90). **National Express bus** tickets can be bought at the Southern National office on the Esplanade, across from George III's brightly painted statue (open Mon.-Fri. 9am-5pm, Sat. 9am-3:45pm).

■■■ DORSET COAST: LYME REGIS

Known as the "Pearl of Dorset," Lyme Regis (pop. 3500) perches precariously on the face of a hillside overlooking the Dorset coast. Steep climbs, startling views, and prodigious natural beauty entice both budget travelers and would-be beach bums.

Though the town retains many of the rugged characteristics of an 18th-century fishing village, the Victorians who clambered down Lyme's steep streets to palatial beachfront cottages also made an impression. It was here that Jane Austen worked and vacationed and Whistler painted both *The Master Smith* and *The Little Rose*. (In 1895, when Whistler approached young Rosa Rendall and said he wanted to paint her, she thought he meant to douse her in paint.) More recently, native John Fowles set his neo-Victorian novel *The French Lieutenant's Woman* in Lyme Regis, and part of the movie was filmed on location.

Lyme lives by the sea. The stone **Cobb** curves out from the land to cradle the small harbor. A mere 20p will enable you to peer out to sea (magnified 10X); maybe, just maybe, you can convince yourself you're aboard an 18th-century schooner (no seasickness, please!). Footpaths wind along the coast towards Seaton and over cliff tops to Charmouth. Or navigate down to the beach itself to enjoy the abundant rock pools. Sunbathers and fossil collectors people the beach, though few actually dip into the water. The **Marine Aquarium** on the Cobb (tel. 443039) features local catches such as giant conger eels and luminescent, frighteningly magnified models of plankton. The Mermaid's Purse and Dead Men's Fingers (fish eggs and anemone clusters) amaze even the most jaded (open May-Oct. daily 10am-5pm, July-Aug. until dusk; £1.10, children 60p). The fisherman who runs the aquarium offers "Magical Maritime Mystery" boat tours on the *Donna Marie*. Summer hours depend on the ever-mysterious weather. Tours are £3; check the chalkboard by the aquarium for changes. Chalk board notices on the Cobb also advertise **fishing trips** (night deep-sea angling for about £7). Call the *Predator* (tel. 443297) or *Neptune* (tel. 443659) for details. History buff Richard J. Fox, former town crier, conducts **tours** dressed in military regalia on summer Tuesdays at 3pm. Tours last 1½ hours and cost £1. Inquire at Country Stocks, 53 Broad St. (tel. 443568) or meet at the Guild Hall. Luxuriate in **Langmoor Gardens,** accessible from Pound St. This green expanse looks down onto the beach. Herbert Paul offers guided cruises of the Devon/Dorset coast (tel. 442563; daily 11am-4pm; £3, children £2). Book at Cobb harbor or call ahead. Coombe St. heads inland from the north of the Lym, and boasts its own attractions. **Dinosaurland** on Coombe St. (tel. 443541) presents the dangerous captive cro-magno-lapin and reveals the intimacies of Brontosaurus procreation (open Easter-Oct. 9am-5pm; call for winter times; £2.90, seniors £2.10, children £1.90).

Silver St. (the continuation of Broad St.), Hill Road, and Woodmead sprinkle lodges and B&Bs alongside their curbs (going inland on Silver St., Hill is the first right and Woodmead the second right). Expect to pay £14-18.50. The **Newhaven Hotel,** at the beginning of Pound St. (tel. 442499), has glimpses of ocean view and a cheerful hostess who will cater to any dietary need (£14.50-18.50/person). **The Happy Friar,** 7 Church St. (tel. 442379), is especially well-suited for group accommodations (tel. 442352; check in 8am-10pm. £12.50). Camping costs £7 at **Hook Farm** (tel. 442801), a 15-minute walk from the coast.

Coffee shops and greengrocers line Broad St., the town's main strip, and excellent fish-and-chip shops sizzle where the Cobb meets Marine Parade. Pubs along Broad St. offer generous portions of traditional English food; try the **Royal Lion.** Visit **Lyme's Fish Bar,** 34 Coombe St. (tel. 442375), for fish-and-chips (£2) and neighborhood fun (open daily noon-2pm and 5-10pm). Sneak a Dorset cream tea (£2.60) at the **Smuggler's Restaurant,** 30 Broad St. (tel. 442795; open daily 9am-10pm). The **Pancake Restaurant,** hidden just before Silver St. in the rear of 2616 Sherborne Lane (tel. 442616), serves crêpe and wholefood dinners, along with daily pasta specials (around £4.80; open 6 to 10pm.

The **tourist office** (tel. 442138) sits on Church St. Walk down the hill from the bus stop at the top of Broad St., turn left onto Bridge St. and walk straight (open Mon.-Fri. 10am-6pm, in summer also Sat.-Sun. 10am-5pm). **Early closing day** is Thursday at 1pm. The **postal code** is DT7 3QF, and the **telephone code** is 01297. The **police** debate *habeas corpus* on Hill Rd. (tel. 442603).

Lyme Regis makes a fine day trip from Exeter. **National Express bus** #515 runs once a day in the summer (morning departure; 1hr. 45min.; £7.25, students £4.50) and only on weekends in winter. Visit Exeter bus station for more information. Bus #31/X31 from Axminster (5 mi. north of Lyme Regis on the A35) runs hourly. The easiest way to reach Lyme from Exeter is by train. To get to Axminster, take the London-Exeter **rail** line (from Exeter's St. David's and Central Stations daily every 1-2hr.) Buses stop on **Broad Street,** with its three banks and **post office** (open Mon.-Fri. 9am-5:30pm, Sat. 9am-12:30pm).

■■■ EXETER

Exeter (pop. 103,000) gradually and proudly developed over centuries as the county seat of Devon, only to be flattened in a few perilous days of Nazi bombing in 1942. Frantic rebuilding has made Exeter an odd mixture of the venerable and the banal: Roman and Norman ruins poke from delicatessen parking lots, and atop a medieval catacomb stand the cash registers of a bustling department store.

GETTING THERE

Frequent trains and buses serve passengers traveling from London and Bristol, who transfer here for trips to the rest of Devon and Cornwall. **National Express buses** are the least expensive way to Exeter, especially if you take advantage of a discount student coach card (from London Victoria Coach Station 8/day; 4hr.; £24). **Trains** leave from London (Paddington and Waterloo Stations; 16/day; 3hr.; £34, £22.45 with rail card).

ORIENTATION & PRACTICAL INFORMATION

Bus and train stations are located just outside the city walls. To reach the town center from St. David's Station, where most trains unload, follow the footpath in front of the station and turn right onto St. David's Hill (which becomes Iron Bridge and then North St.), and turn left after the Guild Hall Shopping Centre onto High St. From Central Station, take Queen St. down to High St. Buses stop in the station on Paris St.; walk through the arcade to Sidwell St. and turn left to reach High St. **Nipper buses** shuttle between city areas. A **Freedom of Exeter** pass allows unlimited travel on these buses (£2.05/day, £7.50/week). Stops are frequent, especially around High St., but the Nippers will skip stops unless hailed.

Tourist Office: Civic Centre, Paris St. (tel. 265700). Across the street from the steps at the rear of the bus station. Accommodations service £1.50; list of B&Bs free. Ordnance Survey maps of Dartmoor, Exmoor, Plymouth, Land's End (£4.25); free copies of *Exmoor Visitor, Dartmoor Visitor,* and *What's On.* Open Mon.-Fri. 9am-5pm, Sat. 9am-1pm and 2-5pm. Wheelchair accessible.

Tours: Free walking tours (April-Oct. Mon.-Sat. 4-7/day, 1½hrs.) leave from the Royal Clarence Hotel (call 265212 or get a brochure at the tourist office).

Financial Services: Barclays, 20 High St. (tel. 52288). £5 minimum commission. Open Mon.-Fri. 9:30am-5pm, Sat. 9:30am-noon. **Thomas Cook,** 9 Princesshay (tel. 432371, fax 493214). Open Mon. and Wed.-Sat. 9am-5:30pm, Tues. 10am-5:30pm.

Post Office: Bedford St. (tel. 423401). Open Mon.-Fri. 9am-5:30pm, Sat. 9am-1pm. **Postal Code:** EX1 1AA.

Telephones: Ubiquitous near High St. **Telephone Code:** 01392.

Trains: Exeter St. David's station, St. David's Hill (tel. 433551), several blocks from the center of town. Some trains from London's Waterloo (9/day) go through **Exeter Central Station,** on Queen St. next to Northernhay Gardens. Office open Mon.-Sat. 8:40am-6pm, Sun. 9:30am-5:30pm. No phone.

Buses: Paris St., off High St. just outside the ancient city walls (tel. 56231). Lockers available 24hrs. Open Mon.-Sat. 8:45am-7:30pm, Sun. 8:45am-5pm.

Bike and Camping Rental: Flash Gordon, 1a Old Park Rd. (tel. 58536). 5-speeds £6/day, £22/week; 10-speeds £8/day, £25/week. Insurance 50p. Camping and hiking gear galore. Open Mon.-Sat. 10am-6pm.

Launderette: St. David's Launderette, 24 St. David's Hill. Open Mon.-Sat. 8am-9pm, Sun. 9am-9pm. Last wash 8pm; door locks at 8:30pm.

Hotlines: Samaritans (crisis), 2 Wynards, Magdalen St. (tel. 411711); 24hrs. Also check bulletin board in **Library** (tel. 384201) off High St. on Castle St. **Rape:** tel. 430871; 24hrs. **AIDS helpline:** tel. 411600.

Hospital: Royal Devon and Exeter, Barrack Rd. (tel. 411611). Take Bus H from High St. toward Wonford.

Emergency: Dial 999; no coins required.

Police Station: Heavitree Rd. (tel. 52101). Three blocks past the junction of Heavitree Rd., Western Way, and Paris St.

ACCOMMODATIONS & CAMPING

Exeter's less expensive B&Bs flourish on St. David's Hill between the train station and the center of town.

HI Youth Hostel, 47 Countess Wear Rd. (tel. 873329, fax 876939), 2 mi. southeast of city center off Topsham Rd. Take minibus K or T from High St. to Countess Wear post office (75p). Follow Exe Vale Rd. to the end and turn left. The spacious and cheery hostel is at the top of the hill. Self-catering kitchen. £7.75, July-Aug. £8.70. Hearty English breakfast £2.60; evening meal £3.90. Towels 90p.

University of Exeter, (tel. 211500). Stop-Over Special: accommodations at St. Lukes and other campus buildings during school vacations. Clean, simple rooms. Singles £10. Doubles £17. Breakfast included. Call for availability. Take Minibus G to Cowley Bridge to save the trek from High St.

Telstar Hotel, 77 St. David's Hill (tel. 72466), between downtown and St. David's rail station and next to the connected **Fort Williams Hotel** (run by the same family). Soft and springy beds; TVs available. Singles from £13, doubles from £24. Book a week ahead during the summer, or try one of the B&Bs next door.

FOOD & PUBS

The cathedral area overflows with restaurants; **St. George's Market,** 91 High St., holds several stalls selling produced and meats (most stalls open Mon.-Tues. and Thurs.-Sat. 8am-5pm, Wed. 8am-3pm). The standard supermarket is **Salisbury's,** across the River Exe at Cowick St. (tel. 217129; open Mon.-Thurs. 8:30am-8pm, Fri. 8:30am-9pm, Sat. 8am-7pm, Sun. 10am-4pm. At **Herbies,** 15 North St. (tel. 58473), as in herbivorous, you'll find vegetarian food (£2-5) and peace journals to browse through as you eat. (Open Mon.-Fri. 11am-2:30pm, Sat. 10:30am-4pm; dinner Tues.-Sat. 6-9:30pm.) **Mad Meg's,** in an alley across from 99 Fore St. (tel. 221225) has mammoth meals in medieval mode. Let Madame Rio, not-so-famous clairvoyante, trace your palm. The spirits recommend the lasagne. (Entrees £8-15. 20% discount Sun.-Wed. evenings. Open daily 11:30am-2:15pm and 7pm until late.)

Pubs are on parade in Exeter; find the ones hiding in the alleyways off High St. for the best ale. A plagued skeleton guards the medieval well in the basement of the **Well House Tavern** on Cathedral Close (annexed to the ancient **Royal Clarence Hotel**) while hearty ale flows upstairs. Sir Francis Drake frequented the **Ship Inn** (tel. 72040), on St. Martin's Lane off High St. Beef and veggie burgers cost £1.80 in the pub and snack bar downstairs; the upstairs is more plush and expensive. The **Turk's Head,** 202 High St. (tel. 56680) displays the legless leather stuffed chair of Charles Dickens, who used to install himself here between installments. The chair now molders between a fireplace and a video game machine. Open Mon.-Sat. 11am-11pm, Sun. noon-3pm and 7-10:30pm.

SIGHTS

Exeter Cathedral, low-slung and lovely, overlooks the commercial clutter of High St. The west front holds hundreds of stone figures in sundry states of mutilation, crowned by a statue of St. Peter as a virile naked fisherman. Inside, effigy tombs (including cadavers) line the walls, and shattered flagstones mark the chapel where a German bomb landed in 1942. Tiny details abound: a gilded ceiling boss depicts the murder of St. Thomas à Becket; misericords (small seats against a wall) are carved with elephants and basilisks. The 60-ft. **Bishop's Throne,** made without nails, was disassembled in 1640 and again during WWII to save it from destruction. A collection of manuscripts, donated to the cathedral in the 11th century by the munificent Bishop Leofric and known to modern scholars as the **Exeter Book,** is the richest treasury of early Anglo-Saxon poetry in the world; the book is on display in the cathedral library. (Library open Mon.-Fri. 2-5pm; cathedral open daily 7:15am-5:30pm; £2 donation requested. Free choral evensong services Mon.-Fri. 5:30pm, Sat.-Sun. 3pm. Free guided tours Mon.-Fri. 11:30am and 2:30pm, Sat. 11am. Call cathedral office (tel. 55573, fax 498769) for more information.)

William the Conqueror took Exeter in 1068 after an 18-day siege. To keep the natives in check, he built **Rougemont Castle.** The ruins between High St. and Central Station include a gatehouse from 1070. The immaculate flower beds of the Regency-era **Rougemont Gardens,** on Castle St., surround the remaining castle walls. The castle is open to the public during school terms, but in the summer it is only open for educational visits—unless you've got twenty English schoolkids in tow, you're probably out of luck. The expansive 17th-century **Northernhay Gardens** unfold just beyond the Rougemont and the preserved **Roman city walls.** Medieval authorities dug subterranean ducts to transport water into the city; **underground passages** (tel. 265887) are accessible from Roman Gate Passage, off High St. (open Mon.-Sat. 10am-4:30pm, 2 tours/hr.). Book tickets by noon during July and August. The passages, which are two by six feet and emphatically not wheelchair accessible, contain doors built by Cavaliers from 1642 to 1646 to keep out besieging Roundheads. The 900-year-old **St. Nicholas Priory** (tel. 5870 or 265858) contains a medieval guest hall and kitchen, along with a timeworn toilet seat young Arthur himself couldn't lift. Take the alleyway next to the Mint at 154 Fore St. (Open Mon.-Fri. 10am-1pm, 2-5pm; Sat. 2-5pm.) **The Royal Albert Museum's** only real treasure is a blackened skull from New Guinea with a six-inch blade in the nose, a cork in the right eye, and great tufts of grass bursting from the jaw joints (on Queen St. (tel. 265858); open Tues.-Sat. 10am-5:30pm).

ENTERTAINMENT

Exeter's students hang at the **Double Locks,** Canal Banks towards Topsham from the Exe Bridges (tel. 56947; open Mon.-Sat. 11am-11pm; Sun. noon-3pm and 7-10:30pm). **The Cavern,** in a brick cellar at 83/84 Queen St. (tel. 495370) reverberates to live bands every night. Post-punk underground music. Usually no cover. (Open Mon.-Sat. 11am-11pm, Sun. 7-10:30pm.) Anything goes at the **Timepiece** wine bar (tel. 78070), a second home to throngs of happy University students. The club, near the library on Little Castle St., spins indie and punk music and features occasional live bands (open Wed.-Sat. 7pm-1am; free until 8pm, then £1-2 cover plus £1 "membership"). **Humphrey B's,** 81 Fore St. (tel. 422221) admits only the smartly dressed to its Casablanca-style dance den (open Wed.-Sat. 9:30pm-1am; cover £3-5).

The **Exeter and Devon Arts Centre** at Bradninch Place, on Gandy St. (tel. 421111) and the **Arts Booking and Information Centre** opposite Boots just off High St.(tel. 211080), supply monthly listings of cultural events in the city. The **Northcott Theatre** (tel. 54853) at the **University of Exeter** trots out a fine stable of drama troupes.

■■■ EXMOOR NATIONAL PARK

Once the English royal hunting preserve, Exmoor is among the smallest of Britain's 11 National Parks, covering 265 square mi. on the north coast of England's southwestern peninsula. Dramatic sea-swept cliffs fringe woodlands and moors where sheep and cattle graze in purple heather. Countless ancient bridges span over 300 mi. of rivers full of trout and salmon, and thatched hamlets dot the valleys. Wild ponies still roam here, and the last great herds of red deer graze in woodlands

EXMOOR NATIONAL PARK

between the river valleys. R.D. Blackmore's novel *Lorna Doone* (1869), based on the exploits of a band of smuggling brigands, takes place in the heart of Exmoor; a 6-mi. path leads from Oare, the scene of Lorna's shooting, to the Doone Valley.

Though over 80% of Exmoor is privately owned (as in most British National Parks), the territory is open to respectful hikers, bikers, and nature enthusiasts.

GETTING THERE

Access to Exmoor is made easy by frequent buses and trains from Exeter and Plymouth, the two closest cities, as well as from Bristol and London. Many lines pass through Taunton on their way to the park. The towns of Barnstaple and Minehead are Exmoor's western and eastern gateways; to get into the park you'll probably have to pass through one or the other. Barnstaple, at the end of a branch line from Exeter, is easy to reach by **rail** (5/day; 1hr.; £8.30). By **bus**, catch the Red Express 75/Devon Bus 315 from Exeter to Ilfracombe; Barnstaple is close to the end of the line (Mon.-Sat. 2/day; 2hr.; £4.30). One bus chugs over every afternoon from Bristol (2½hr.; £16). From London, use **British Rail** (8/day; 3hr.) or **National Express** (from Victoria Station; 3/day; 5hr.; about £41.50). From Plymouth, catch the **Western National** #86 (2½hr.) or British Rail (6/day; 2hr.; £14.60). Call the bus station in Plymouth (tel. (01752) 222666) for information.

The surest way to **Minehead,** by rail or by bus, is via Taunton, accessible by the main Penzance-London rail line and by frequent bus services from Exeter and Plymouth. From Taunton, you have several options for reaching Minehead: the hourly **Southern National** bus #28 (12/day, Sun. 4/day; 1¼hr.; £3); **Scarlet's Coaches,** 53 the Avenue (tel. (01643) 704204), which offers competitive prices (Mon.-Fri. 1/day; £2.60, single £1.50); or the **West Somerset Railway** (tel. (01643) 704996), a private line that runs to Minehead from Bishops Lydeard, a town 4 mi. from Taunton (July-Aug. 7/day, May-June and Sept.-Oct. 4/day; 1¼hr; £7.50 return). Buses shuttle to Bishops Lydeard from the Taunton rail station. As bus service to both Minehead and Taunton is erratic, call ahead to confirm routes and times.

GETTING AROUND

Although getting to the outskirts of Exmoor by public transport is easy, exploring the park by bus is a nightmare. Service is erratic, changing from season to season and from year to year. Crossing the park from Barnstaple to Minehead can take all day if you have to wait for the infrequent connecting bus in Lynton. Although it will cost £4-5 extra, you may save time by taking the train to Exeter, changing to a Taunton train, and then taking the Minehead bus from Taunton. The meager offerings of the area's bus companies have been collected in a booklet available at the tourist and park offices.

The park is best toured on foot or by bike. Two long-distance paths are the **Somerset and North Devon Coast Path** for hikers and the **coastal path,** which follows the ghost of the Barnstaple railroad, for bikers. Both of these pass through or near the towns of Barnstaple, Ilfracombe, Combe Martin, Lynton, Portlock Weir, Minehead, and Williton, traveling from west to east (see Exmoor National Park: Sights, below). The new **Tarka Trail** traces a 180 mi. figure-eight (starting in Barnstaple, reaching toward Dartmoor), 31 mi. of which are bicycle-friendly. For those who insist on making quick time on sections of the coastal routes, the following buses run: **Southern National** (tel. (01823) 272033) from Minehead to Ilfracombe (#300; Mon.-Fri. 2/day; 2hr.; £3.80), Williton (Mon.-Sat. 1/hr.; 30min.; 99p), and Dunster (Mon.-Sat. 1/hr.; Williton and Dunsterare a continuation of the Scarlet's Coaches line form Taunton to Minehead). **North Devon Bus** (tel. (01271) 45444) goes from Barnstaple to Ilfracombe (Mon.-Sat. 1/hr) and from Ilfracombe to Combe Martin (1/day).

PRACTICAL INFORMATION

The National Park Information Centres listed below supply detailed large-scale Ordnance Survey maps of the region (about £4) and bus timetables. Also pick up a free copy of the *Exmoor Visitor,* an annual park publication that includes a map and a detailed B&B and camping list. The centers offer guided walks from 1½ to 10 mi. Always be prepared for a sudden rainstorm on Exmoor. Sea winds create volatile weather, and thunderstorms blow up without warning. Be sure to stock up on food and equipment in the larger towns, as supermarkets and camping stores in the tiny villages along the coast have a smaller selection of goods.

Exmoor National Park Information Centres

Combe Martin: Seacot, Cross St. (tel. (01271) 883319), 3 mi. east of Ilfracombe. Open April-June and Sept. daily 10am-5pm, July-Aug. 10am-7pm.

County Gate: Countisbury (tel. (015987) 321), east of Lynton. Open April-Oct. daily 10am-5pm.

Dulverton: Dulverton Heritage Centre, the Guildhall, Dulverton, Somerset (tel. (01398) 23841). Headquarters of Exmoor National Park. Handles all postal inquiries. Open daily 10am-5pm; Nov.-March shortened hours.

Dunster: Dunster Steep Car Park (tel. (01643) 821835), 2 mi. east of Minehead. Open March-Oct. daily 10am-5pm, shortened hours in winter.

Lynmouth: The Esplanade (tel. (01598) 52509). Open April-Oct. daily 10am-5pm.

Tourist Offices

Barnstaple: Library, Tuly St., Devon, EX32 7EJ (tel. (01271) 388583 or 388584). Turn left at bus station and follow signs for library. Open Mon.-Sat. 9am-5pm, till 7pm in summer.

Ilfracombe: The Promenade, EX34 9BX (tel. (01271) 863001). Open Mon.-Fri. 9:30am-5pm, Sat. 10am-5pm, Sun. 10am-4pm; Oct.-March Mon.-Fri. 10am-4pm.

Lynmouth and Lynton: Town Hall, Lynton, EX35 6BT (tel. (01598) 52225). Open Mon.-Sat. 9:30am-5:30pm, Nov.-March Mon.-Sat. 9:30am-1pm.

Minehead: 17 Friday St., TA24 5UB (tel. (01643) 702624), corner of Bancks St. Open Mon.-Sat. 9:30am-5:30pm (July-Aug. also Sun 10am-1pm), Nov.-March. Mon.-Sat. 10am-4pm.

ACCOMMODATIONS & CAMPING

Check tourist office listings for accommodations; the *Exmoor Visitor* includes several pages of detailed listings, including B&Bs (starting at £10-11) scattered through the park. Call to reserve, as hostels and B&Bs tend to fill up quickly, rain or shine. Camping may be the best way to see the park without worrying about accommodations. The *Exmoor Visitor* lists several caravan parks that accept tents, but campsites that don't advertise are easy to find, especially near coastal towns. Before pitching a tent, ask the landowner's permission; most of Exmoor is private property.

Hostels

The quality of hostels varies widely according to proprietor and location. In general, however, guests can expect accommodations with self-catering kitchen, a day lockout (usually 10am-5pm), a curfew (around 11pm-midnight), and no laundry facilities. Hostel schedules change from year to year; check the YHA accommodations guide (or call (01722) 337494 Mon.-Fri. 9am-5pm for up-to-date schedules).

Crowcombe Heathfield: Denzel House, Crowcombe Heathfield, Taunton, Somerset TA4 4BT (tel. (019847) 249), on the Taunton-Minehead road, 2 mi. from village below Quantock Hills. Turn opposite the road marked "Crowcombe Station & Lydeard St. Lawrence"; *don't* make the turn by Flaxpool Garage signposted "Crowcombe Station and Crowcombe Heathfield." *Don't make the turn.* Please! Large house in the woods. £6.50, under 18 £4.35. The opening dates are as odd as the directions-call far in advance or check the YHA handbook. Open April-Aug.; schedule varies from open daily to open only weekends.

Exford: On Withypoole Rd., Exe Mead, Exford, Minehead, Somerset TA24 7PU (tel. (01643) 83288); Southern National bus #39, or Scarlet Coaches from Minehead, next to the River Exe bridge. Superior grade, in the center of the park's moorland. £7.75, under 18 £5.20. Open July-Aug. daily; April-June and Sept. Mon.-Sat.; Jan.-March and Oct.-Nov. Tues.-Sat.

Hartland: Elmscott, Hartland, Bideford, Devon EX39 6ES (tel. (012374) 41367), Extremely difficult to find—get a map before you go. 3 mi. southwest of Hartland village by footpath. £5.30, July-Aug. £5.90. Open July-Sept. 18 daily; April-June Fri.-Wed.

Holford: Sevenacres, Holford, Bridgwater, Somerset TA5 1SQ (tel. (01278) 741224). 1½ mi. past the Alfoxton Park Hotel in Holford—keep right after passing through gate by hotel stables. From Kilze, take Pardlestone Lane opposite post office for 1mi., then follow signs. In forest overlooking Bridgwater Bay, with riding stables nearby. £6.50, under 18 £4.35. Open April-Aug. Mon.-Sat.

Ilfracombe: Ashmour House, 1 Hillsborough Terrace, Ilfracombe, Devon EX34 9NR (tel. (01271) 865337). Take Red Bus #6, 62, or 306 from Barnstaple, just off the main road. Georgian terrace house with view of the Welsh coast. Superior grade. £7.75, under 18 £5.20. Open July-Aug. daily; April-June and Sept. Mon.-Sat.

Instow: Worlington House, New Road, Instow, Bideford, Devon EX39 4LW (tel. (01271) 860394); Take Red Bus #1, 2, or B from Barnstaple and get off at the Quay in Instow. The Victorian house is an exhausting ½-mi. climb from the bus stop. Provides meals, has laundry. £7.75, under 18 £5.20. Open July-Aug. daily; April-June Sat.-Thurs.; Sept.-early Nov. Tues.-Sat.; late Nov.-Dec. 17 Fri.-Sat.

Lynton: Lynbridge, Lynton, Devon EX35 6AZ (tel. (01598) 53237); Red Bus #310 from Barnstaple to Castle Hill Car Park, Lynton. Small former hotel in valley of River Lyn West. Meals provided. £7.15, July-Aug. £8.70. Open July-Aug. daily; April-June Tues.-Sun.; March and Sept.-Oct. Wed.-Sun.

Minehead: Alcombe Combe, Minehead, Somerset TA24 6EW (tel. (01643) 702595), 2 mi. from the town center. Follow Friday St., which becomes Alcombe Rd., turn right on Brook St. and continue to Manor Rd. From Taunton, take Minehead bus to Alcombe stop (1 mi. from hostel). Spacious grounds. £7.15, under 18 £4.75. Open July-Aug. daily; April-June Mon.-Sat.; Sept.-Oct. Tues.-Sat.

FOOD, SIGHTS, & ACTIVITIES

Although **Barnstaple** is not the only good hiking base for the coastal path or the Tarka Trail, it is the largest town in the region (much larger than Minehead), a transportation center, and the best place to get camping and hiking gear, as well as a good pre-trip meal. **La Viennetta**, at 27 Boutport St. (tel. (01271) 25531) and **Heavens Above** at 4 Bear St. (tel. (01271) 77960) both sell good, reasonably priced food (Italian and vegetarian, respectively). There are also daily markets at the **Pannier Market.** Cheap camping equipment can be bought at **Cassie's Surplus**, 19 Tuly St., across from the tourist office (tel. (01271) 45079). Bikes can be hired from **Tarka Trail** (tel. (01271) 24202), conveniently located at the head of the coastal bike path; from the center of town, cross the bridge, take the second left after the bridge at the roundabout, and Tarka's is by the railroad station (£5.50/day; open daily 9am-5pm). The path provides level cycling for 15 mi. along the coast, where the old Barnstaple railroad tracks used to run.

Two good places to begin traipsing into the forest close to Barnstaple are **Blackmoor Gate**, 9 mi. northwest of Barnstaple, and **Parracombe,** 2 mi. further. Both are on the Barnstaple-Lynton bus line.

Minehead is only a mile from the park's eastern boundary. It prides itself on having a **nature trail** designed for disabled visitors that winds past labeled trees and shrubs. A guided trail (25p) begins off Parkhouse Rd. Other well-marked paths weave through North Hill, an easy walk from the town center. Bikes, horses, and fishing boats can be rented on Warren St., along the water, at the **West Somerset Booking Office** (mountain bikes £8/day).

Three mi. east of Minehead lies the village of **Dunster. Dunster Castle** (tel. (01643) 821314) towers over the still-thriving 17th-century yarn market. Home to the Luttrell family for 600 years, the castle has seen its share of battles, especially during the English Civil Wars. The demolished sections were remodeled in the 19th century, but today the elaborate interior includes a not-to-be-missed 16th-century portrait of Sir John Luttrell wading buck-naked through the surf. (Open April-Sept. Sat.-Wed. 11am-5pm; Oct. Sat.-Wed. 11am-4pm. Subtropical gardens and shrubs open daily April-Sept. 11am-5pm; Feb.-March and Oct.-Dec. 11am-4pm. Full admission £4.60, children £2.30; admission to the garden and grounds £2.50, children £1.20.) Buses from Minehead stop at the base of Dunster Village every hour in the summer. Four mi. farther east, near Washford, the ornamentation of the ruined 12th-century **Cleeve Abbey,** Abbey Rd. (tel. (01984) 40377), is still discernible (open daily 10am-6pm; Oct.-March 10am-4pm; £1.80, seniors £1.35, children 95p).

Four mi. west of Minehead, **Selworthy** is a beautiful thatched-roof village built around Selworthy Green. The National Trust owns most of the village and maintains an information booth and shop (tel. (01643) 862745; open Mon.-Sat. 10am-5pm; April-Oct. Mon.-Sat. 10am-5pm, Sun. 2-5pm; the village is open all the time).

■■■ SOMERSET & NORTH DEVON COAST PATH

This coastal stretch is the highest of England's Cliff Walks, but the least arduous of the four sections of the Southwest Peninsula Coast Path, which hugs cliffs and shore all the way around Cornwall and back to South Devon. It runs 87 mi. from Minehead west through Porlock, Lynmouth, Ilfracombe, and Marshland Mouth at the Devon/Cornwall border, passing within 2 mi. of the HI Youth Hostels at Minehead, Lynton, Ilfracombe, Instow, and Hartland. The hostels are about 20 mi. apart, an ambitious but not impossible day's walk. Along the way, the path passes **Culbone,** with England's smallest church, the 100 ft. dunes of **Saunton Sands,** and the precipitously steep cobbled streets of **Clovelly Village** on Hartland Point, with its pubs dating back to the 1500s. Consider hiking or bicycling along the coastline and visiting some of these less-traveled towns. Pick up the Countryside Commission's leaflet on the path at any tourist office, and bring along a large-scale Ordnance Survey map, also available at tourist offices—some stretches of the path are not yet marked.

■■■ DARTMOOR NATIONAL PARK

The lush, green forests and windy moors of the Dartmoor National Park (south of Exmoor, 10 mi. west of Exeter, and 7 mi. east of Plymouth) will make you forget how hard it was to get there. Most of Dartmoor's 365 square mi. are covered by high, wild moorland where historic remains date back to 4000 BC. Ramblers may search for standing stones, chambered tombs, and rock rows tossed mysteriously across the moor. In the midst of this archaeological jumble, the skeleton of a once-flourishing tin-mining industry now rusts in grime and darkness. These abandoned civilizations lend the park a grim charm; Dartmoor's haunting atmosphere oppressed and inspired Sir Arthur Conan Doyle, whose horror story *Hound of the Baskervilles* is set on the misty granite mass.

GETTING THERE & GETTING ABOUT

Most travelers approach Dartmoor from either Plymouth or Exeter. Buses link these two large towns on the peninsula's southern coast with towns on the park's perimeter (such as Ivybridge, Tarrstock, Okehampton, Moretonhampstead, Bovey Tracey, and Ashburton), along with a few in the central moorlands (Princetown and Postbridge).

The **Transmoor Link** (Western National bus #82; 3/day) cuts through the middle of the park on its southwest-northeast route between Plymouth (tel. (01752) 222666) and Exeter (tel. (01392) 382800), passing through Yelverton (at the southwest corner of the park), Princetown, Postbridge, Moretonhampstead, and Steps Bridge (at the park's northeast corner; late July-Aug. 3/day). Devon General #X38/39 also binds Exeter and Plymouth, stopping in Buckfastleigh and Ashburton along the park's southern edge (every hr., Sun. every 2hrs.). Plymouth runs 14 buses to Ivybridge (service X80; every hr.; 30 min.; or Western National #88; every hr. 8am-5pm; 30 min.); to Tavistock, north of Yelverton on the park's western edge, take

#83, 84, or 84A (Mon.-Fri. 3/hr. until 6pm, then every hr.; 1hr.; #98A runs from Tavistock to Plymouth at 9am and the opposite way at 1:10 pm); to Okehampton, on the park's northern edge, catch #86 (passing through Tavistock and Barnstaple; Fri.-Mon. 1-3/day). Services change seasonally, prices are erratic, and routes far from permanent; check schedules at the bus station. For more information, contact the **Exeter bus station** at (01392) 56231; the **Plymouth bus station** at (01752) 664011; the Devon County Council's Public Transportation Helpline (Mon.-Fri. 8:30am-5pm; tel. (01392) 382800); or any National Park Information Centre (see below).

Hike and cycle your way around the park once you've reached its perimeter, as making bus connections requires careful planning. In the winter, snow often renders the park and its torturous roads virtually inviolable. Hitchers report that rides are frequent. *Let's Go* does not recommend hitch-hiking.

ORIENTATION & PRACTICAL INFORMATION

Visitors should not underestimate Dartmoor's capricious weather or treacherous terrain. An Ordnance Survey map scaled 1:50,000 (£4.25) or 1:25,000 (£4.99), a compass, and truly waterproof garb are essential; mists come down without warning, and there is no shelter away from the roads. Footpaths marked on the map are not signposted on the high moor; invest in the better (1:25,000) Ordnance Map with terrain markings. The official **Dartmoor Rescue Group** is on call through the police (call (01626) 62849 for information or help).

Most of Dartmoor's roads are good for cycling, though the dips and hills can send you hurtling head over heels. Fishing, canoeing, and climbing are also popular activities hereabouts; for canoeing arrangements, contact Mr. K. Chamberlain, **Mountain Stream Activities,** Hexworthy (tel. (013643) 215). For horseback riding contact **Smallacombe Farm Riding Stables,** Islington (tel. (01364) 661265); **Cholwell Farm and Riding Stables,** Mary Tavy (tel. (01822) 810526); or **Skaigh Stables,** Sticklepath (tel. (01837) 840429).

> **Warning:** The Ministry of Defense uses much of the northern moor for target practice; consult the *Dartmoor Visitor* or an Ordnance Survey map for the boundaries of the danger area, and then check the weekly firing timetable (available in park and tourist offices, hostels and campsites, police stations, local pubs, and the Friday papers) or call (01837) 52939 from Okehampton, (01752) 701924 from Plymouth, (01803) 294592 from Torquay, or (01392) 70164 from Exeter, for recorded information.

National Park Information Centres

The Dartmoor National Park Authority offers guided walks (2-7hrs., £1.50-£3) departing from many locations in the park. Check the *Dartmoor Visitor* (available at any tourist office); also check the publication's back page for an updated list of Information Centres and a map showing their locations.

> **Dartmoor National Park Tourist Information Centre:** Town Hall, Bedford Square, Tavistock PL19 0AE (tel. (01822) 612938). The main moor center with scads of information about Southwest England. Books accommodations within a 15-mi. radius for £2.50, elsewhere for £3.50. Accommodations list free. Open April-Oct. Mon.-Sat. and Sun. in summer 10am-5pm.
>
> **Ivybridge:** in Ivybridge on the southern edge of Dartmoor (tel. (01752) 897035). Books beds for free within 10 mi., £2 within Devon and Cornwall, £3 elsewhere. Open Mon.-Sat. 9am-5pm, Sun. 10am-4pm; July-Aug. Mon.-Sat. 9am-6pm, Sun. 10am-4pm.
>
> **Okehampton:** 3 West St. (tel. (01837) 53020), in the courtyard adjacent to the White Hart Hotel. Books beds for £2.50 (you must be there in person). Open July-Aug. daily 10am-5pm; April-June and Sept.-Oct. Mon.-Sat. 10am-5pm.
>
> **Newbridge:** (tel. (013643) 303), in Riverside car park. Open April-Oct. daily 10am-5pm.

Parke Barn: (tel. (01626) 832093). Haytor Rd., Bovey Tracey. Headquarters of the Dartmoor park authority. Open April-Oct. 10am-5pm.

Postbridge: (tel. (01822) 88272). In a car park off B3212 Moretonhampstead-Yelverton Road. Open April-Oct. daily 10am-5pm; Nov.-March Sat.-Sun. 10am-4pm. Hours may vary.

Princetown (High Moorland Visitor Centre): (tel. (01822) 890414). In the former Duchy Hotel. Open Mon.-Sun. 10am-5pm, winter 10am-4pm. Disabled access.

Steps Bridge (tel. (01647) 52018), on the Dartmoor side of the River Teign bridge about 5 mi. north of Bovey Tracey. Caravan center in a car park off the B3212. Convenient to the Steps Bridge Youth Hostel. Open April-Oct. 10am-5pm.

ACCOMMODATIONS & CAMPING

B&B signs are frequently hung in pubs and farmhouses along the roads. The Dartmoor Tourist Association runs an accommodations hotline at the Princetown Information Centre (tel. (01822) 890567; 24hrs.). The Dartmoor National Park Information Centres will give you an accommodations list for free, and the Tavistock, Ivybridge, and Okehampton offices will book you a room for £2.50. If you arrive late at an information center, check the "Out of Hours" notice board in the window. If all else fails, call the Dartmoor Tourist Association for help (northwestern area, tel. (0182281) 411; northeastern area, tel. (01364) 52679; eastern area, tel. (01626) 832422; southern area, tel. (0182285) 3501).

Youth Hostels

Steps Bridge (HI), Dunsford, Exeter EX6 7EQ (tel. (01647) 52435), 1 mi. southwest of Dunsford village on the B3212. Take the Exeter-Moretonhampstead bus (359) and get off at Steps Bridge. Simple grade HI hostel; a cabin in the woods. The funky warden makes vegetarian creations and fosters a homey, communal atmosphere. Open July-Aug. daily (£6.50); April-June and Sept. Fri.-Tues. (£5.90).

Bellever (HI), Postbridge, Yelverton, Devon PL20 6TU (tel. (01822) 88227), 1 mi. southeast of Postbridge village on Bus 359 from Exeter. Ask to be let off as close as possible. In the heart of the park. Very popular. Showers, evening meal available. Standard grade. £7.75. Open July-Aug. daily; April-June Mon.-Sat.; Sept.-Oct. Tues.-Sat.

Camping

Although official campsites exist, many travelers camp on the open moor. Dartmoor land is privately owned, so ask permission before crossing or camping on land whose owner is evident. Backpack camping is permitted on the unenclosed moor land more than 100 yards away from the road or out of sight of inhabited areas and farmhouses. Campers may only stay for one night in a single spot. Hikers should not climb fences or walls, nor build fires in the moors; stick to the marked paths.

Ashburton Caravan Park, Waterleat, Ashburton (tel. (01364) 652552). 1½ mi. from town; head north on North St. and follow the signs. £6 for a 2-person tent (July-Aug. £8); £1.50 each additional person (July-Aug. £2.25). Open Easter-Oct.

River Dart Country Park, Holne Park, Ashburton (tel. (01364) 652511). £3.65-4.95 per adult, depending on the season. Open April-Sept.

Okehampton: Yertiz Caravan and Camping Park, Exeter Rd. (tel. (01837) 52281). 1 mi. east of Okehampton on the brow of a hill near the Esso Garage. One person £2, 2 people £2.50. Open all year.

Tavistock: Higher Longford Farm, Moorshop, Tavistock (tel. (01822) 613360). 2 mi. from Tavistock toward Princetown on B3357. One person £4 (£5.50 with car), 2 people £5 (£6.50 with car). Open March-Nov.

SIGHTS

Postbridge and **Princetown** hover at the southern edge of the park's north-central plateau. Dartmoor's forbidding maximum-security prison looms over Princetown, the larger of the two towns. Within its walls once languished Frenchmen from the Napoleonic Wars and Americans fighting to annex Canada in 1812. Prehistoric remains lurk about a nearby moor, at the setting of one of the most famous of Sir Arthur Conan Doyle's Sherlock Holmes tales: the *Hound of the Baskervilles* emerged from an ancient Dartmoor legend of a gigantic, glowing hound. Several peaks crown the northern moor, the highest of which is **High Willhays** (2038 ft.).

The rugged eastern part of the park gathers around **Hay Tor.** Dartmoor's celebrated medieval ruins at **Hound Tor,** where excavations unearthed the remains of 13th-century huts and longhouses, lie 2 mi. north of Hay Tor village. Check the *Dartmoor Visitor* for guided walks on the mound.

Sir Francis Drake was born west of Hay Tor at Tavistock. South of Hay Tor lies **Yelverton,** where Cistercian monks built **Buckland Abbey** (off Milton Combe Rd.) in 1273 (tel. (01822) 853607). Drake later bought the abbey and transformed it into his private palace. Wander the abbey's exterior and grounds, including the huge **Tithe Barn,** but don't bother with the abbey's lusterless Tudor and Georgian interior. Check out the new restaurant in the monk's guesthouse (open April-Oct. Mon.-Wed. and Fri.-Sun. 10:30am-5:30pm).

Dartmoor Letterboxes, each complete with an inkpad, rubber stamp, and visitors book, hide themselves all about the moors, waiting to be discovered by amateur Sherlocks. (Collect as many different stamps as possible; cluebooks available.)

■ ■ ■ PLYMOUTH

Fifty-nine air raids in 1941 left Plymouth a cracked shell of a city. Between the husks of churches, a new street plan had to be laid out because the old streets had disappeared. A half-century later the largest city in Southwest England stands a neat and rectilinear field of concrete: every storefront looks the same, as does every traffic circle, and the city center resembles a giant bus station. But the harbor, which saw Drake and the Mayflower sail, remains untouched. At night Blitz ghosts waltz through adjoining parks, the windy brow of this resolute port faces green hills and the channel beyond, and Plymouth Sound roars ashore below.

GETTING THERE

Plymouth lies on the southern coast between Dartmoor National Park and the Cornwall peninsula, on the east-west rail line between London and Penzance (at England's southwestern tip). **Trains** run at least every hour to: London's Paddington (3½hr.; £39); Bristol (3½hr.; £26.50); and Penzance (1¾hr.; £8.70). **National Express buses** serve London Victoria Coach Station (6hr.; £29) and Bristol (2½hr.; £21). **Devon General** buses connect Plymouth and Exeter by running around Dartmoor (X38; 1¼hr.; single £4), while the Transmoor Link #82 goes through the park during the summer and weekends. Sit on the right-hand side of the X-38 for a supreme view of the glowering mass of Dartmoor. **Ferries** go to Roscoff, France (1-3/day; 6hr.; £23-38, depending on season), and Santander, Spain (2/week; 24hrs.; £75). Check in an hour before departure.

ORIENTATION & PRACTICAL INFORMATION

Plymouth's center, wedged between the River Tamar and Plymouth Sound, sprouts half lush grass and half bleak buildings. The gardens and restored forts of the Hoe (the area along the coastal road and overlooking the harbor) yield to the gray and blocky metropolitan corridors of Royal Parade and Armada Way. **Hoppa** buses shuttle from Royal Parade to most areas of the city (50p-£1.50).

Tourist Office: Island House, 9 The Barbican (tel. 264849, fax 257955). In a new location on Sutton Harbour, south of the bus station. Piles of overpriced pamphlets; city map £1. The new building is said to have housed the Pilgrim Fathers just before their departure on the *Mayflower.* Open Mon.-Sat. 9am-5pm, Sun. 10am-4pm. Hours may change because of disorder from their recent move.

Tours: A *Plymouth Historic Walk* pamphlet (15p at the tourist office) guides you through sites between St. Andrew's Church and the harbor. Daily bus tours leave every 20 min. from stations near the Barbican (tel. 222221; £4, students £3). Boat cruises around the harbor depart sporadically from spots near the *Mayflower* shrine on the Barbican; check boards there for times and prices. The Plymouth Dome on the Hoe sells tickets for daily guided tours of the Royal Citadel, now a commando facility (May-Sept. noon and 2pm; £2.50).

Financial Services: Thomas Cook, 1 Old Town St., by the post office. Thomas Cook checks cashed free, others £3.50. Open Mon. 9:30am-5:30pm, Tues.-Sat. 9am-5:30pm. **American Express,** 139 Armada Way (tel. 228708, fax 260747), in the plaza formed by New George St. and Armada Way. Open Mon. 9am-5pm, Tues. 9:30am-5pm, Wed.-Sat. 9am-5pm.

Post Office: 3 St. Andrew's Cross (tel. 222450). Open Mon.-Fri. 9am-5:30pm, Sat. 9am-12:30pm. **Postal Code:** PL1 1AB.

Telephone Code: 01752.

Bus Station: Bretonside Station, near St. Andrew's Cross at the eastern end of Royal Parade (tel. 222666). **Lockers** on the downstairs platform.

Train Station: Milehorse, North Rd. (tel. 221300), north of city center. Take Western National bus #80 or 81 to the city center, or frequent local buses #16 or 43.

Ferries: Millbay Docks, Brittany Ferries (tel. 221321). Take city bus #34 to docks, to the west of the city center at the mouth of the River Tamar, and follow signs to the ferry stand. Ten-min. walk from the bus stop. Book tickets at least 24 hrs. in advance, though you may need to come only 2 hrs. early if on foot.

Bike Rental: Action Sports, Queen Anne's Battery (tel. 268328). £10/day. Open Mon.-Fri. 9:30am-5:30pm, Sat. 9:30am-6pm.

Launderette: Mayflower Launderette, 93 Mayflower St. W (tel. 229082). Open daily 8am-9pm. Last wash 8pm.

Hotline: Samaritans (crisis), 20 Oxford Place (tel. 221666; 24hrs.), off North Rd. Western Approach. Doors open daily 9am-10pm.

Hospital: Derriford Hospital, Derriford (tel. 777111). About 5 mi. north of the city center. Take bus 50X or X50 from Royal Parade in front of Dingles.

Emergency: Dial 999; no coins required.

Police: Charles St. (tel. 701188), near Charles Cross bus station.

ACCOMMODATIONS & CAMPING

A slew of low-priced B&Bs grace Citadel Rd. and Athenaeum St. between the west end of Royal Parade and the Hoe; all include color TV, tea-making facilities, and continental breakfast. Standards are uniformly high, and prices run from about £10-15. Rooms tend to be small since most B&Bs are in restored 18th-century row houses. Consult *Welcome to Plymouth* for accommodations listings, or check on B&B availability at the tourist office. Book in advance at the hostel, which fills up quickly.

HI Youth Hostel, Belmont House, Devonport Rd., Stoke, Plymouth PL3 4DW (tel. 562189), 2 mi. from city center. Take bus #14, 14A, 15, or 15A from Royal Parade to Molesworth Rd., then left onto Devon port, pass through Stoke Village and the hostel is on your left. Or take bus #33, 33A, 34, or 34A from Royal Parade to Stoke Village, then ask directions. Spacious rooms in former banker's mansion. Curfew 11pm, lockout 10am-4pm. £7.75. Breakfast £2.60, evening meals £3.90.

University of Plymouth, Drake Circus (tel. 232027, fax 232025). Call some time ahead and ask for Nicola Lobb. Dorm rooms, mostly carpeted, on the spectacularly ugly campus. Self-catering kitchens; bathrooms in hallway. Available July-Sept. when the university lies dormant. £10.

YWCA, 9-13 Lockyer St. (tel. 660321), a pebble's toss from the Hoe and the Royal Parade. 40 beds, mostly in spare single bedrooms. Lounges, game room, laundry facilities. Narrow labyrinthine hallways; locks on every door. Reservations usually not needed if you're only staying one night. Singles £10.75. Doubles £6.80/person. Dinner £2.80. £10 key deposit. Reception open Mon.-Fri. 8am-noon and 4pm-9:30pm, Sat. 9am-noon and 4pm-9:30pm, Sun. 10am-8:30pm.

Camping: Riverside Caravan Park, Longbridge Rd., Marsh Mills (tel. 344122). Take bus #21 or 51 from city center toward Exeter(£3/adult with car, £5 for 2 people on foot).

FOOD & PUBS

The city center and the cobbled streets of the Barbican quake with shoppers during the day. At night, locals overflow the pubs; the restaurants in the Barbican (several have signs proclaiming how historic they are) depend largely on tourist cash. Pick up picnic fixings at **Plymouth Market** (tel. 264904) at the west end of New George St. (open Mon.-Tues. and Thurs.-Sat. 8am-5:30pm, Wed. 8am-4:30pm). Check the back of the tourist map for a list of restaurants and food stores.

Plymouth Arts Centre Restaurant, 38 Looe St. (tel. 660060), Kinterbury St. from St. Andrew's Cross. Homemade for herbivores. Fill up on an a la carte meal (£2-4) after catching a flick downstairs (tickets £3.20). Open Mon. 10am-2pm, Tues.-Sat. 10am-8pm, Sun. 5:30-7:30pm.

Cap'n Jaspers, a stand by the Barbican side of the Harbor. Sells local catch to sea-salts and schools of tourists. Puppets pop-up and gizmos bob while you wait. Open Mon.-Sat. 6:30am-11:45pm, Sun. 10am-11:45pm.

The Gorge, Royal Parade (tel. 262552), diagonally across from the Theatre Royal. Gorge yourself on plain but weighty food (ham steak £3.40). In this surreal and spacious melon-colored cavern, Victorian fixtures swing from plaster cave formations. Weepy early-80s American music. Open Mon.-Sat. 7am-6pm, Sun. 7am-5pm.

Crawl through Southside St.'s pubs en route to the Barbican; try **The Ship** or **The Navy** for seaside spirits. **The Abbey,** on Higher Lane, is a popular spot for drinks and dinner. An older crowd frequents the **Queen's Arms** by the harbor.

SIGHTS & ENTERTAINMENT

The blackened shell of **Charles Church,** destroyed by an incendiary bomb in March, 1941, stands in the middle of the Charles Cross traffic circle half a block east of the bus station. The roofless walls are Plymouth's memorial to her citizens killed in the Blitz; grass grows where the altar used to stand. Keys to the ruin are available from the chief inspector's office at the Bretonside Bus Station.

The kernel from which Plymouth grew, a Saxon parish church, stood on the site of **St. Andrew's Church** on Royal Parade. Little remains of the 13th-century structure, which was restored to its 15th-century incarnation after being gutted by bombs in 1941. In a glass case near the altar sits the church's holy relic: a fruitcake in the shape of a Bible open to a plodding version of the 23rd Psalm ("The Lord is my shepherd; therefore I can lack nothing."). **Prysten House,** behind the church, cherishes an 11th-century tapestry. (Open April-Oct. Mon.-Sat. 10am-4pm. 50p, seniors and children 25p.) In 1762, the Jewish community built a **synagogue** on Catherine St. behind St. Andrew's Church; still active today, it is the oldest Ashkenazi synagogue in the English-speaking world. Ring and the caretaker will show you around.

Big wax figures illustrate "Tinker, Tailor, Soldier, Sailor, Rich Man, Poor Man, Apothecary, Thief" in **Merchant's House,** near St. Andrew's. Visiting children have filled the "Poor Man" display with coins. (Open Easter-Oct. Tues.-Fri. 10am-5:30pm, Mon., Sat., and Bank Holiday 10am-5pm; 80p, children 20p).

From the Hoe, climb the spiral steps and leaning ladders to the balcony of **Smeaton's Tower** for ferocious blasts of wind from the Channel and a magnificent view of Plymouth and the Royal Citadel. Originally a lighthouse 14 mi. offshore, the 72-ft. tower was moved to its present site in 1182. (Open Easter-Sept. 10:30am-5pm; 70p.) Legend has it that Sir Francis Drake was playing bowls on the Hoe in 1588 when he heard that the Spanish Armada had entered the English Channel. Displaying classic British phlegm, Drake finished his game before hoisting sail. At the foot of the Hoe, the **Plymouth Dome** (tel. 603300) deploys the latest technology to revive the stench of Elizabethan England—hold your nose and curse the maid emptying a chamberpot overhead. (Open daily 9am-6pm; £3.40, seniors £2.70.)

A plaque on the Barbican marks the spot where the Pilgrims set off in 1620 for their historic voyage to America. Subsequent departures have been marked as well, including Sir Humphrey Gilbert's voyage to Newfoundland, Sir Walter Raleigh's attempt to colonize North Carolina, and Captain Cook's voyage to Australia and New Zealand. Further down on the Barbican, a three-story mural at 58 Southside St. hides the studio of **Robert Lenkiewicz,** containing hundreds of paintings, mostly of naked women in splayed postures. Enter from the back facing the harbor; the voluble painter will show you around his private library of 200,000 volumes from the 15th century to Jacques Derrida. One room of the library holds a shelf full of skulls, along with the desiccated corpses of two frogs who died while fucking.

The **Theatre Royal** on Royal Parade (tel. 267222) sells discount tickets for students and those under 18 (every week, usually Mon.-Thurs.; call box office for details). Student standbys purchased a half-hour before the show cost £4-8. The **Plymouth Art Centre,** 38 Looe St. (tel. 660060), runs art films (£3.20, students £2.70).

■■■ BODMIN MOOR

Bodmin Moor is high country, like Dartmoor and Exmoor to the east, containing Cornwall's loftiest points—Rough Tor (1311 ft.; rhymes with "chowder," believe it or not) and Brown Willy (1377 ft.). Unlike Exmoor and Dartmoor, Bodmin Moor is not a national park, and so technically *any* hiking and camping in this scenic area requires the permission of the private owners of these lands. In practice, hikers keep to designated paths and sheep don't prosecute. The region is rich with remains of ancient history: Bronze Age Cornishmen littered stone hut circles at the base of Rough Tor; some maintain that Camelford, at the moor's northern edge, is the site of Arthur's Camelot and that Arthur bled at his last battle at the Slaughter Bridge a mile north of town.

GETTING THERE & GETTING ABOUT

Bodmin Moor spreads north of Bodmin town towards Tintagel (on the coast), Camelford, and Launceston (both inland from Tintagel). Bodmin is the park's point of entry, accessible from all directions; however, it is not a good place to start hiking. The town is served directly (Mon.-Sat.) by buses from Padstow on the north coast (9/day) and St. Austell on the southern shore (1/hr.). **National Express buses** arrive from farther afield: from Plymouth in the southeast (3/day; afternoons only; 1hr.; £4.10; book in advance) and Newquay in the west (3/day; mornings). For bus information, call the station in Truro (tel. (01872) 40404). **Trains** stop at the Bodmin Parkway Station on the Plymouth-Penzance line (from Plymouth, 1/hr.; 40min.; £5.80). Call (01872) 76244 for train information.

Buses run from Bodmin to various towns on the moor. **Western National** (X3/X4) departs for Camelford from the Mt. Folly bus stop by the post office (2/day; 1 hr.; £1.70). **Fry's Bus Services** (tel. (01840) 770256) connects Bodmin with Camelford, Tintagel, Launceston, and Plymouth (Mon.-Sat. 1/day). For a schedule, look under "Frys Coaches 241" in the back section of the National Express North Cornwall timetable (20p at any bus station).

Since Bodmin is not a national park, it lacks information centers dedicated to the area; ask at the tourist office instead. Hiking is convenient, especially from Camelford, and is the only way to reach the tors which give the grandest views of the boulder-strewn expanse. Bikes can be hired in Bodmin and the surrounding towns.

ACCOMMODATIONS

B&Bs may be spotted across the moor or booked through the Bodmin tourist office (10% deposit). The 13th-century monk's fishery, **St. Anne's Chapel Hayes,** next to the River Camel (tel. 72797) on the road between Bodmin and Wadebridge and on the Camel Trail, will give you a bed and a breakfast for £12.50 any day of the year. **Colliford Tavern** in the middle of the moorland (tel. (012108) 821335) offers campsites, showers, and a pub in the wilderness. (£4.70; £6.45 for 2 adults sharing a tent. Open April-Sept.) Check the Bodmin tourist office for a list of other campsites on or

BODMIN MOOR

near the moor. The nearest youth hostels are on the northern coast of Cornwall, a few miles northwest of the moor.

Boscastle Harbour (HI), Palace Stables, Boscastle PL35 0HD (tel. (01840) 250287); take Fry's bus from Bodmin or Plymouth, or Western National from Bodmin or Wadebridge. Beautiful hostel embedded among steep green hills and flowery riverbanks. Open daily July-Aug. (£7.75); March-June and Sept.-Oct. Wed.-Sun. (£7.15).

Tintagel (HI), Dunderhole Point, Tintagel PL34 0DW (tel. (01840) 770334). Take Fry's Services from Camelford, Launceston, or Plymouth to Tintagel. From Tintagel, walk ¼ mi. past the 900-year-old St. Materiana's Church; then bear left and keep as close to the shore as possible. After 300m look out for the chimney of the hostel, located in a hollow by the sea, and invisible until you come upon it. Self-catering kitchen (no meals served), 27 beds, and one happy owner. £7.50. Open July-Aug. daily (£7.75), April-June Thurs.-Tues. (£7.15).

BODMIN & CAMELFORD

The unremarkable town of **Bodmin** (pop. 13,500) is the last supply stop before venturing onto Arthurian stomping grounds. The helpful **tourist office** at the Mount Folly Car Park (tel. 76616) provides Ordnance maps of the area (£4) and supplementary reading (open Mon.-Sat. 10am-5pm). For food head to Fore St., where grocers and bakers hawk edibles. **Pots Coffee Shop and Restaurant,** 55 Fore St. (tel. 74601), offers a huge variety of fillings for sandwiches or jacket potatoes and makes blackcurrant milkshakes as thick as yogurt (open daily 9am-5:30pm). Saturday is **market** day in Bodmin. The **police station** (tel. 72262) is up Priory Rd., past the ATS car parks, and the **post office** (tel. 72638) is beyond the tourist office (open Mon.-Fri. 9am-5:30pm, Sat. 9am-12:30pm). The **postal code** is PL31 1AA and the **telephone code** is 01208. **Phones** are across from Haywoods Bistro on Mt. Folly Square. Lloyds Bank on Fore St. has an **ATM** (Cirrus and Plus).

To get to the center of town from the **Bodmin Parkway Station,** 3 mi. out of town on A38, hop bus #55, or take a £3 taxi. Efficient two-wheeled transport is available at the **Bodmin Trading Co.** (tel. 72557) in Church Square at the bottom of Mt. Folly and Fore St. (Mountain bikes £5/day, deposit £25. Open Mon.-Fri. 9am-5:30pm, Sat. 9am-5pm.) For accommodations in the town itself, try **Elmsleigh,** 52 St. Nicholas St. (tel. 75976, which provides huge and excellent breakfasts (the best Andy Liu's ever eaten), or one of the other B&Bs on St. Nicholas St. (£12-14). The closest camping to Bodmin is a mile north of the town at the **Camping and Caravaning Club,** Old Callywith Rd. (tel. 73834), equipped with laundry, showers, and shop (£4.11/pitch, open March-Sept.).

Thirteen mi. north of Bodmin, **Camelford** seems not to have grown much since the days when it was Arthur's Camelot (if the legend is to be believed). The tiny and unmarked **Slaughter Bridge** a mile north of town, crudely inlaid with hunks of petrified wood, marks the site where Arthur fell into the dust and was buried. The Camelford tourist office, in the North Cornwall Museum (tel. (01840) 212954), can tell you how to find the inscribed stone marking his grave.

From the center of town, **Rough Tor** is a 1¼-hr. walk through mist and nervous sheep. Take Rough Tor Rd. to the end; the summit looms ahead. The climb is not arduous except for the 300 ft. ascent at the top of the tor, where stacked granite boulders form a natural castle with steps and passageways, offering a wind-ravaged lookout above the moor. Watch out for great clumps of excrement as you climb.

TINTAGEL

Tintagel, 5 mi. northwest of Camelford, is the promontory fortress of Arthurian legend. Roman and medieval ruins cling to a headland under siege from the Atlantic; some have already collapsed into the sea. Climb through the debris to Merlin's cave below—don't try any hocus-pocus else some of Cornwall's steepest cliffs claim you. The site is unfortunately dominated by the only building that is not a ruin: the King Arthur's Castle Hotel and the attached Excali-Bar. (Real castle open daily April-Oct.

10am-6pm, Nov.-March 10am-4pm; £2.10, children £1.05.) Inland is the one-road village of Tintagel, lined with Arthur bistros and Pendragon gift shops. On Fore St. in the center of town stands **King Arthur's Great Hall of Chivalry** (tel. (01840) 770526), built in the 1930s to house the now-defunct Knights of the Fellowship of King Arthur. An antechamber tells Arthur's story with spotlights, a pulsing red laser, and a 'mist of time' laid down by a humidifier; beyond, the stern stone chapel houses not one, but *two* Round Tables. (Open March-Jan. daily 10am-dusk; £2.50, children £1.75.) Down the street toward the castle is the **Old Post Office,** a medieval manor house (mind your head) used as a post office in the 19th century (open May-Oct. daily 11am-5:30pm; £1.90, children 90p). Tintagel has made the bold move of not opening a tourist office. The **HI Youth Hostel** (tel. (01840) 770334) at Dunderhole Point provides seaside lodgings (open daily July-Aug. (£7.75); April-June Thurs.-Tues. (£7.15) or try the B&Bs on Bossiney Rd. Fry's Coaches travel to Tintagel from Plymouth by way of Launceston and Camelford (Mon.-Sat. 1/day in the afternoon).

■■■ FALMOUTH

Two spectacular castles guard the bland town of Falmouth (pop. 18,600), which reclines along the Penryn River next to the world's third-largest natural harbor. Seven rivers flow into this historically divisive port: in the 16th and 17th centuries, Falmouth's ruthless Killigrews built a name on rapine, piracy, and murder. Loyal to none but themselves, one particularly faithless Killigrew even sold Pendennis Castle to the Spanish. Though only souvenir shops skirmish in Falmouth today, the magnificent 450-year-old fortresses of Pendennis and St. Mawes still eyeball each other across the mouth of the harbor, providing two of England's finest perches for sitting and watching the sea.

GETTING THERE

About 60 mi. west of Plymouth along England's southern coast, Falmouth (pop. 18,600) is accessible by **rail** from any stop on the London-Penzance line (including Exeter and Plymouth); change at Truro and go one stop to Falmouth (12/day, 9/day on summer Sundays; 30min.; £5.90). From Truro, **Western National** bus 88A (Mon.-Sat. 3/hr., Sun. 1/hr.; £1.85) runs to Falmouth. By bus, take **National Express** from London (2/day; 6½hr.; £36), Newquay, Plymouth, or Penzance (every 2hrs.). From Penzance, **Western National** #2 rumbles to Falmouth through Helston.

ORIENTATION & PRACTICAL INFORMATION

Falmouth has three train stations, all stops on the Truro-Falmouth line and all platforms in the grass. **Penmere Halt** is a 10-minute walk from town; the **Dell-Falmouth Town** is east of the center and close to budget B&B-land; **Falmouth Docks** is nearest the Pendennis Castle area and hostel. Out-of-town buses and local **Hoppa** buses stop just outside the tourist office at **The Moor,** a large traffic island on Killigrew St., which runs perpendicular to the harbor. The post office and three banks surround The Moor. As elsewhere in Cornwall, streets are narrow; make love to a wall if a car comes by.

> **Tourist Office:** 28 Killigrew St. (tel. 312300), on The Moor. From inland, follow signs to Killigrew Rd. or Kimberley Park Rd., then go downhill toward the river. Open Mon.-Thurs. 8:45am-5:15pm, Fri. 8:45am-4:45pm, Sat. 9am-5pm; Oct.-March closed Sat.
> **Financial Services: Barclays,** Killigrew St., The Moor. Open Mon. and Wed.-Fri. 9:30am-4:30pm, Thurs. 10am-4:30pm. **Lloyds,** 11-12 Killigrew St., The Moor. Open Mon.-Fri. 9:30am-5:30pm.
> **Post Office:** The Moor (tel. 312525). Open Mon.-Fri. 9am-5:30pm, Sat. 9am-12:30pm. **Postal Code:** TR11 3RB.
> **Telephones:** In front of the post office. **Telephone Code:** 01326.

Trains: None of the stations sells tickets; get 'em at Newell's Travel Agency, 26 Killigrew St. (tel. 312620) on the Moor (open Mon.-Fri. 9am-5:30pm, Sat. 9am-4pm).

Bus Station: Buses stop next to the tourist office at The Moor. Call 404 04 for information. For National Express schedules and tickets, contact Newell's Travel Agency, 26 Killigrew St. (tel. 312620). The tourist office carries local schedules.

Boats and Ferries: check signs on Prince of Wales Pier and Custom House Quay. Boat Co. (tel. 313201 or 313813) runs twice-daily cruises around the bay and frequent ferries to St. Mawes (in summer every ½-hr., Sun. every hr., in winter every hr.; 30min.; return £3). You can rent your own boat at the Custom House Quay from Easter until Oct. (tel. 789109).

Bike Rental: Aldridge Cycles, 1 Swanpool St. (tel. 318600), by the Custom House Quay. £5-8/day, deposit £20. Open Mon.-Sat. 9am-5:30pm.

Early Closing Day: Wed. at 1pm; widely violated.

Hotlines: Samaritans (crisis), tel. (01872) 77277; 24hrs. **Women's Aid,** tel. (01736) 50319.

Health Centers: Trescobeas Rd. (tel. 317317) or Trevaylor Rd. Take Falmouth Hoppa B from the library to Trescobea (the centers are close together).

Hospital: Truro City Hospital, Trescobeas Rd., Truro, tel. (01872) 74242.

Emergency: 999; no coins required.

Police: In a blue shack on Quarry Hill, uphill from the Moor, tel. 372231 or (01209) 714881.

ACCOMMODATIONS & CAMPING

The B&Bs on Cliff Rd. and Castle Dr. have spectacular views of the foliage and cliffs that touch the water, but reserve ahead and expect to pay for the thrill (£14-16). B&Bs closer to town, surprisingly, are cheaper. The exceptionally accommodating tourist office will book a bed within your budget.

HI Youth Hostel, Pendennis Castle, Falmouth (tel. 311435). A ½-hr. walk from town ending with an uphill hike by the sea. After 6pm, guests have the star-shaped castle to themselves and can savor the sunset from Elizabethan crenellations. The hostel is often requisitioned by parties of 50 or more schoolchildren; book at least 3 weeks ahead in the summer. £7.75 (July-Aug. £8.70). Breakfast £2.60, dinner £3.90. Reception open 8:30-10am, 5-6:45pm, 8-10:30pm. Curfew 11pm. Open July-Aug. daily; Sept.-June Mon.-Sat.

Castleton Guest House, 68 Killigrew St. (tel. 311072). Comfortable accommodations in a 200-year-old house. Vegetarians may request alternatives to the English breakfast. No singles during high season. £12.

Engleton House, next door to Castleton (tel. 315447) for twins and doubles only, from £12/person.

Tremorvah Tent Park, Swanpool Rd. (tel. 312103), just past Swanpool Beach and reachable by Hoppa #6 (every ½hr). A lovely hillside spot with laundry and showers. £15/week, July-Aug. £18; £2.50/night; car 50p extra.

FOOD, PUBS, & ENTERTAINMENT

Pick up a pasty (the ubiquitous Cornish stuffed turnover) filled with sausage or vegetables for under £1 at any bakery on the waterfront. **De Wynn's 19th Century Coffee House,** 55 Church St. (tel. 319259) delivers exotic teas and baked specialties (open Mon.-Sat. 10am-5pm, Sun. 11am-4pm). Falmouth's pubs serve especially good grub. A local favorite is the plush **King's Head,** on the corner of Church St. Climb the 111 steps of **Jacob's Ladder** (a 45° alley next to Lloyds Bank on the moor) and collect your reward of £1 meal specials at the pub at the top (served noon-2pm and 7-9pm). Falmouth's hip head for the **Pirate Inn** (tel. 311288), on Grove Place, opposite the Killigrew Monument and the Quay, which features local live bands and hand-rolled cigarettes. Evenings rock at **Club International,** upstairs at **St. George's Market** and at **Shades Night Club** on the Quay (both open until 1am).

SIGHTS

Pendennis Castle (tel. 316594), built by Henry VIII to keep French frigates out of Falmouth, now features a walk-through diorama that assaults the eyes with cannon smoke and the ears with the noise of gunners bellowing incoherently. Ignore this foolery and walk the battlements instead; Pendennis commands the sea. (Open daily 10am-6pm, Nov.-March 10am-4pm; admission to grounds £2.10.)

Across the channel from Pendennis stands the magnificently-preserved **St. Mawes Castle** (tel. 270526), built by Henry VIII to blow holes through any Frenchman the gunners of Pendennis spared. A 20-minute ferry ride from Falmouth ends among the thatched roofs and tropical gardens of St. Mawes village in the shadow of the 6-story castle keep, in use as a fort until 1920. No talking dioramas here; tunnels wind past cold cannon down to the rocky shore. (Open daily 10am-6pm, Nov.-March Wed.-Sun. 10am-4pm; £1.35.) Regardless of what the tourist brochure might say, there is not a whit of wheelchair access to this castle.

To taste the surf, head to one of the three beaches on Falmouth's southern shore. **Castle Beach,** on Pendennis Head, is too pebbly for swimming or sunbathing, but low tide reveals a labyrinth of seaweed and tidepools writhing with life. The waters of **Gyllyngvase Beach** are popular with windsurfers and families. **Swanpool Beach,** west of Gyllyngvase, is the sandiest. The town throws a tizzy during the first two weeks of August, when **Carnival Week** and **Regatta Week** hit town.

■ NEAR FALMOUTH: LIZARD PENINSULA

Once a leper's colony, the **Lizard Peninsula** between Falmouth and Penzance still sits in isolation, untrampled by tourists. A scaly line of coastal cliffs and coves ends at Lizard Point, the most southerly prong of England. Inland, the heath of the **Goonhilly Downs** is riven by slices of purple serpentine rock. One-and-a-half mi. from Mullion village on the west coast of the Lizard, waves swirl around offshore rocks at **Mullion Cove,** lined with steep but grassy and climbable cliffs. Hundreds of seabirds nest on **Mullion Island,** 300m off the cove.

A lonely one-pub town (called simply "The Lizard") lines the road down to **Lizard Point,** where perilous cliffside paths wind past tropical plants clinging to the rocks above the waves. The **Most Southerly House** (next to the Most Southerly Cafe and the Most Southerly Gift Shop) offers three bedrooms, breakfast, and a front lawn right on the Point (singles £15 and £18; blasts from the nearby foghorn free; tel. (01326) 290300). In the village, try **The Caerthillian** (tel. (01326) 290019) for luxurious bathroom and a restaurant downstairs. (Singles £14.50-16.50.) The **Tophouse** pub on the village green is open daily until 11pm for meat or vegetarian meals; quaff one of the 19 malt whiskeys, 18 wines, or multiple ales (£1-1.90). The only HI hostel on the Lizard is at Coverack in the southeast; take Truronian bus #326 from Helston, then to Parc Behand on School Hill. (Tel. (01326) 280687; £7.15; Jul.-Aug. £7.75; open April-May Tues.-Sun., June-Sept. daily., Oct. Tues.-Sat.)

Access to the peninsula is through **Helston,** where the tourist office (tel. (01326) 565431) in front of the Coinagehall bus stop offers free copies of *Guide to the Lizard.* Open Mon.-Sat. 10am-noon, 1-5:30pm. Take Western National bus 2 from Falmouth or Penzance to Helston (6/day; 45min.; £2) and one of the **Truronian** lines down to Mullion and the Lizard. The Penzance and St. Ives bus stations provide guided tours of the Lizard on Tuesdays (leaves Penzance 12:30 pm, leaves St. Ives 1pm; £4.70, children £3.10). For information on bus service into the peninsula, call Truro (tel. (01872) 40404) or Penzance (tel. (01736) 69469). Driving access is by the A30383 via A394. A **coastal path** crawls the entire length of the Lizard's shoreline and takes about a week to hike.

■■■ PENZANCE

Old pirate hangouts choke its streets, smuggler's tunnels run beneath its alleys, and buildings still bear scorch marks from 16th-century pirate raids. The sun-showered bay that used to shelter outlaws of all states now laps the feet of thousands of British tourists, who have made Penzance a prime lair for their raids on western Cornwall.

GETTING THERE

Just ten mi. from England's southwesternmost point, Penzance is the last stop on a long train ride from London (5½hr.; £46), via Plymouth (1½hr.; £9.10) and Exeter (2½hr.; £22.80). Change at St. Erth for St. Ives (£2.60); change at Truro for Falmouth (£6.70); change at Par for Newquay (£9). Get a **Regional Railways** timetable at the tourist office, and don't forget about the many long-term Southwest England rail passes (see above).

Eight **National Express Rapide buses** make the trip to London daily (8hr.; £32-40, £27 with a week advance booking; stop at Heathrow). Buses run to Plymouth via Truro (2/hr.; 3hr.; £5.50). Local service runs to St. Ives (4/hr.; 35min.; £2), Land's End (#1, 4 1/hr.; 50min.; £2), Mousehole (MUZ-zle; 2/hr.; 20min.; 95p), Falmouth (Western National bus #2 or 2X every 30min.; 1½hr.; £4.50), and Helston (Hoppa #2 ; 1/hr.; 45min.; £2.60; change here for Lizard Peninsula).

National Express, Western National, and local Cornwall buses offer guided tours of the region and bargain Explorer passes. **Western National** guided tours include weekly trips from Penzance to: King Arthur's County, Boscastle, and Tintagel (Thurs. 9:15am; £6.50), Cornish fishing villages (Fri. 9:15am; £6.50), and Lizard Peninsula (Tues. 12:30pm; £4.70).

ORIENTATION & PRACTICAL INFORMATION

Penzance's rail station, bus station, and tourist office stand conveniently together in the same square, adjacent to both the harbor and the town. **Market Jew Street** rises up from the harbor, laden with well-stocked bakeries and ill-stacked bookstores. **Chapel Street,** the cobblestone row of antique shops and pubs, descends from the town center into a welter of alleys near the docks.

Tourist Office: Station Rd. (tel. 62207), between train and bus stations. Free map of Penzance, books beds for £2.25. Arranges mini-coach **tours** of attractions in west Cornwall, led by the mirthful Harry Safari (Sun.-Fri. 2/day; £10). Open Mon.-Fri. 9am-5pm, Sat. 10am-1pm; extended hours in summer.

Financial Services: Barclay's, 8-9 Market Jew St. (tel. 62271; fax 64297). Open Mon.-Tues. and Thurs.-Fri. 9:30am-4:30pm, Wed. 10am-4:30pm, Sat. 10am-12:30pm.

Post Office: 113 Market Jew St. Open Mon.-Fri. 9am-5:30pm, Sat. 9am-12:30pm. **Postal Code:** TR18 2LB.

Telephone Code: 01736.

Trains: Wharf Rd. (tel. (01872) 76244), at the head of Albert Pier. Office is open Mon.-Fri. 6am-6:40pm, Sat. 6:15am-7:10pm, Sun. 8:30am-5:15pm, but you can board trains at any hour.

Buses: Wharf Rd. (tel. 66055), at the head of Albert Pier. Information and ticket office open Mon.-Fri. 8:30am-4:45pm, Sat. 8:30am-3pm.

Bike Rental: Blewett & Pender, 1 Albert St. (tel. 64157). Mountain bikes £5/day, £8 overnight. Deposit £25.

Early Closing Day: Wed. at 1pm. Suspended during summer.

Launderette: Polyclean, corner of Leskinnick and Market Jew St. Open daily 9am-9pm. Last wash 7:45pm.

Market Day: Tues. and Thurs., at the top of Causeway Rd.

Crisis Hotlines: Samaritans, tel. (01872) 77277; 24hrs. **Women's Aid:** 50319.

Pharmacy: Boots, 100-102 Market Jew St. (tel. 62135). Open Mon.-Sat. 8:45am-5:30pm.

Hospital: West Cornwall Hospital, St. Clare St. (tel. 62382). Bus #D, 10, or 10A to St. Clare St.

Emergency: 999; no coins required.

Police: Penalverne Dr. (tel. 62395), just off Alverton St.

ACCOMMODATIONS & CAMPING

Penzance's tribe of B&Bs occupies the hills above the esplanade and beach mainly on Morrab Rd. between Alverton St. and Western Promenade Rd. Also check out the side streets off Chapel St. and on Alexandra Rd., farther down Western Promenade. Prices range from £13 to £16. Camping areas blanket the west Cornwall peninsula; the tourist office has lists.

HI Youth Hostel, Castle Horneck (tel. 62666). Stroll up Market Jew St. and then Alverton St. (or take Hoppa B and hop off at Pirate Inn), turn right onto Castle Horneck, and take left fork up hill. Barracks-style accommodation on iron-framed beds, in a formerly gracious 18th-century mansion. 800-year-old basement; brand-new bathroom fixtures. Breakfast £2.60; cafeteria dinners £2.20-3.60. Self-catering kitchen available. Open year-round. Reception open 5-11pm; lockout 10am-5pm. £8.70. **Campsites** available in the backyard for £4.35, including use of hostel facilities.

Inyanga, 36 Chapel St. (tel. 60967). A superb B&B at the bottom of Antique Row. Spacious and spotless, with Zimbabwean decor downstairs. English or vegetarian breakfast graciously served. Meson the dog submits to fondling. £12.50/person; July-Aug. £14/person. If full, try **Trelawney** next door or **Trevelyan** up the street at #16 (£13.50/person).

YMCA, Orchard Ct. and Alverton St. (tel. 65016), past the Alexandra Rd. roundabout. Coed dorm accommodations in linoleum-floored rooms, some of which have washbasins. Showers 20p. Lockout 9:30am-2pm. Curfew midnight. With your own sleeping bag £6.30; without £8.50 first night, £6.30 thereafter. Light breakfast £2.25, English breakfast £3.35, evening meal £5.45.

Cornerways, 5 Leskinnick St. (tel. 64645). A block from the rail station. You're in luck—you'll get a warm welcome from the entire royal family, past and present, and on porcelain, yet. Book weeks ahead. £13; optional evening meal £5.50.

Camping: River Valley Caravan Park, Relubbus, Penzance (tel. 763398). Quiet camping in sheltered valley. £7.75/2 people, July-Aug. £8.70.

FOOD & PUBS

Expect to pay at least £7 for Penzance's excellent seafood dinners along the Quay. Market Jew St.'s fare is unexciting and expensive. The best buys are in coffee shops and local eateries on smaller streets and alleys, far from the hustle-bustle of town.

The Turk's Head, 46 Chapel St. Delicious food in a 13th-century pub, sacked by Spanish pirates in 1595. In the 17th century a smuggler's tunnel allegedly wound from the harbor to the inn. Lunch £4-5, seafood dinners from £5. Pricey drinks. Open Mon.-Sat. 11am-2:30pm and 6-10pm, Sun. noon-2:30pm and 7-10pm.

Nelson Bar, in Union Hotel on Chapel St. (tel. 62319). Hearty English pub food between walls crammed with Nelsoniana. The admiral's death at Trafalgar was first announced to Englishmen in this building. Specials and entrees from £4. Food served noon-2pm, 6:30-9pm.

Snatch-a-Bite, 45 New St. (tel. 66866), off Market Jew St. at Lloyd's Bank. Sumptuous salads (under £3.50) and sandwiches (under £2). Open Mon.-Sat. 9am-4pm.

On the waterfront, the **Dolphin Tavern** on The Quay enthusiastically preserves the piratical tradition of heavy drinking. On Chapel St., you can spit and cuss as smugglers once did in the nautical chambers of the 400-year-old **Admiral Benbow** or swill elderberry wine and Cornish mead by candlelight in the medieval dungeon of **The Regent Meadery Restaurant** (tel. 62946; open daily 6:30-10pm). Pubs serve light meals and snacks regularly, but food is usually less expensive elsewhere. Until 1am, try **Club Zero,** on Abbey St., for after-hours drinking and dancing.

SIGHTS

The town's few sights lie on Chapel Street between Market Jew St. and the docks. The bizarre and gaudily-painted **Egyptian House,** near the top of the street, pokes fun at itself and the 1830s craze for Egyptian ornamentation. A stoned sailor greets visitors to the **Maritime Museum** halfway down Chapel St., which simulates the crabbed life of an 18th-century seaman with 5 ft.ceilings, scant lighting, and a gruesome below-docks diorama of dismembered sailors awaiting a lean and swarthy surgeon. (Open June-Oct. Mon.-Sat. 10am-5pm; £1.50, children 75p.)

Across the bay at Marazion rears the offshore **St. Michael's Mount** (tel. 710507), with a church and castle at its peak and a village at its base. The castle is open to the public, but the interior is unspectacular save for a mummified cat on a mantel; visitors can perch on the castle grounds, thirty stories above the surf. Joachim von Ribbentrop, Hitler's foreign minister, had the mountain picked out as his personal residence after the conquest of England. Take bus #2 from Penzance to Marazion (Mon.-Sat. 3/hr.; return 50p). Access to this old monastery is by ferry (return £1.30) since the seaweed-strewn causeway to the island is submerged except during low, low tide. (Open April-Oct. Mon.-Fri. 10:30am-5:45pm, most weekends during summer and clement days during winter; admission to the island £3.)

■■■ PENWITH & THE NORTH CORNISH COAST

You know you've hit the Cornish "Rivera" when every cottage has a name like "Shore Enuf" or "Beachy Keen." England's Southwest tip has some of the broadest, sandiest beaches in northern Europe; the surf is up year-round whether or not the sun decides to break through. The peninsula's riches are no secret. Every year hundreds of thousands of British and foreign tourists jockey for rays on the beaches of Penzance, St. Ives, and Newquay. Penwith is also home to a rich collection of Stone Age and Iron Age monuments—the region has apparently attracted partially naked people for thousands of years.

GETTING ABOUT

By far the best base for exploring the region is Penzance, terminus of **British Rail's Cornish Railways** service and of **Western National's** bus service from Plymouth. The main rail line from Plymouth to Penzance bypasses the coastal towns, but there is connecting rail service to Newquay (change at Par; 5-8/day; £9), Falmouth (change at Truro; 13/day, 9/Sun.; £6.70), and St. Ives (direct or with a change at St. Erth; 1-2 every hr.; £2.60). Trains are frequent, and distances are short enough that you can easily make even Newquay a day trip from Penzance. Pick up the free Cornish Railways timetable at any station, or call British Rail in Truro (tel. (01872) 762 44) for information.

The **Western National** network is similarly thorough, although the interior is not served as well as the coast. Buses run frequently from Penzance to Land's End (#1, 4; 12/day Mon.-Fri., 7/Sat.; £2.70 return), St. Ives (#16, 17; Mon.-Sat. 3/hr.; £2 return), and from St. Ives to Newquay (#57; Mon.-Sat. 2/day), stopping in the smaller towns along these routes. Pick up a set of timetables at any Cornwall bus station. Most buses don't run on Sundays, and many run only from May through September. Summer service varies from year to year, and the starting and ending dates may vary from what's printed on the timetable, so call the Penzance bus station (tel. (01209) 719988) to check. Although fares are already quite low (most Penwith day returns are under £3), **Explorer tickets** are an excellent value for those making long-distance trips or hopping from town to town (£4.40/day, seniors £3.30). Cyclists may not relish the narrow roads, but the cliff paths with their evenly spaced youth hostels make for easy hiking.

■■■ LAND'S END TO ST. IVES

The Penwith Peninsula scrolls into the Celtic Sea at **Land's End** with granite cliffs so dramatic that, once upon a time, the Countryside Commission declared Land's End an "Area of Outstanding Natural Beauty." Unfortunately, the commission's protective efforts could not prevent the area from being purchased and transformed into an area of outstanding commercial booty. Land's End is now a tourist holiday park of rides, historic displays, and other plastic phenomena. Seen from the cliff path that circles the Peninsula, the complex rears up out of the barren landscape like a tortured carousel stallion. A look out to the cliffs and sea, however, will remind you why you came. **Buses** run to Land's End from Penzance (1/hr.;1hr.; £2.70) and St. Ives (3/day).

Bus #10, 10A, 10B, or 11 will take you to **St. Just** (pop. 2700), just north of Land's End on Cape Cornwall. This craggy coast, strewn with cows and cottages, remains unexploited and remarkably beautiful. Small (2-4 mi.) day walks are outlined in leaflets in most tourist offices, but the dramatic cliff path winding around the entire coast unveils the best of Cornwall. The **St. Just Youth Hostel (HI)** at Letcha Vean is said to be among the nicest in the region (tel. (01736) 788437; £7.75, off-season £7.15; open April-Oct. daily; from the bus station's rear exit, turn left, and follow the lane past the chapel and farm to its end).

Inland on the Penwith Peninsula, some of the best-preserved Stone and Iron Age monuments in England lie along the Land's End-St. Ives bus route. Once covered by mounds of earth, the *quoits* (also called cromlechs or dolmens) are believed to be burial chambers dating back to 2500 BC. The **Zennor Quoit** is named for the town where a mermaid, drawn by the singing of a young man, happily returned to the sea with him in tow. The **Lanyon Quoit** (off the Morvah-Penzance road about 3 mi. from each) is one of the best preserved megaliths in the area. The famous stone near Morvah (on the Land's End-St. Ives bus route), with a hole through the middle, has the sensible Cornish name **Mên-an-Tol,** or "stone with a hole through the middle." The big bagel is attributed with magical powers and curative capabilities. Climbing through the aperture supposedly remedies backache, assures easy childbirth, or induces any alteration in physiology your heart could desire. The best-preserved Iron Age village in Britain is at **Chysauster** (tel. (01736) 61889), between Penzance and Zennor (approx. 4 mi. from each). Parts of four pairs of oval stone houses remain erect. Take the footpath off the B3311 near Gulval. (Open daily 10am-6pm; Nov.-March 10am-dusk.) For those unafraid of hills and hell-bent drivers, biking is the best way to tour the region, which is poorly served by local buses. Cycles may be rented in Penzance (about £5/day).

■■■ ST. IVES

These days, it seems more than bigamous men are going to St. Ives, and with good reason. Ten mi. north of Penzance, the town looks over a breathtaking turquoise bay and sandy beaches. Peaked roofs line the hillside and brazen seagulls divebomb the harbor. St. Ives grants a partial reprieve from the rampant commercialization of neighboring towns. When the surf's up, head to **Porthgwidden Beach** or the much larger **Porthmeor Beach** to glimpse roasted Briton loin on display. It's better than pub food, at least.

Although the closest youth hostel and YMCA to St. Ives are in Penzance, **B&Bs** line every alley for £13 and up. Prices are usually lower for rooms farther from the water and higher up the gusty hillside. Try **Clodgy View** and **West Place** for fine sea views. B&Bs also cluster on **Park Avenue** and **Tregenna Terrace.** Bring Monopoly money. **Harbour Lights** (tel. 794817), just 30 ft. from the water on Court Cocking off Fore St., offers a cheap and friendly mooring at £13. Camping is abundant in Hayle—check the tourist office for listings. Try **Trevalgan Camping Park** (tel. 796433), with laundry and cooking facilities, and access to the coastal path.

Fore St. is packed with small bakeries, each with its own interpretation of Cornish pasty (PAH-stee). Minuscule **Ferrell's Bakery,** at 15 Fore St. (tel. 797703), bakes a delicious version as well as a fine saffron bun—reputedly Cornwall's best; the buns run out by early afternoon (open Mon.-Sat. 9am-5pm). **The Café** on Island Sq. (tel. 793621; open daily 10am-3pm and 7-10pm) has vegetarian meals (mushroom stroganoff £6.20). Climb Mt. Zion from The Wharf and sing fat-free hosannas at the top.

Stock up on groceries at **LoCost,** Treganna Place, and **Co-Op Supermarket,** Royal Square. Beer has flowed at **The Sloop** (tel. 796584), on the wharf since 1312; swill ale from 11am-11pm and down yer vittles from noon to 3pm and 6 to 8:45pm. The **beach cafés** at Porthmeor, Porthgwidden, and Porthminster serve inexpensive pastries, sandwiches, and fish lunches.

The **tourist office** (tel. 796297), in the Guildhall on Street-an-Pol, books beds for £2.25 and sells maps of this medieval maze—trust us, you'll need them. (Open Mon.-Sat. 9am-5:30pm; closed Sat. in winter.) **Walking tours** leave from the Guildhall (Tues. and Thurs. at 8pm; £2, children £1.50). Bikes and surfboards can be hired or repaired at **Windansea Surf Shop** at 11 Fore St. (tel. 796560). (Surfboard or wetsuit £5/day, £24/week. Mountain bikes £8-10/day. Deposit £5 on surfing equipment, £15 plus ID on bikes. Open daily 9:30am-6pm.) Across the street, Natural Balance (tel. 793264) gives **surfing lessons** (3hr.; £15; open daily 9am-5:30pm, 9am-10pm in summer).

The small St. Ives branch rail line meets the main Plymouth-Penzance line at St. Erth. **Trains** run during the summer between St. Erth and St. Ives (daily; 2/hr.; 10min.), and St. Erth connects to Penzance (£2.60) and Truro. **Buses** run from Penzance (3/hr.; off-season Mon.-Sat. only), and y **National Express** buses between Plymouth and Penzance stop in St. Ives year-round (6/day). From the bus and train stations, walk down to the foot of Tregenna Hill and turn right on Street-an-Pol to the tourist office. For ailments of the body, visit the **health center** on the Stennade (tel. 796413); for ailments of the spirit, browse among first editions of T.S. Eliot and W.H. Auden at **The Mirror and the Lamp,** 1 St. Andrew's St., off the marketplace. (Open Tues.-Fri. 1-6pm, 11am-4pm in winter.) The **post office** is on Treganna Place at High St. St. Ives' **postal code** is TR26 1AA. St. Ives's **telephone code** is 01736.

■■■ NEWQUAY

Newquay (or "Surf City") is an outpost of surfer subculture, an enclave of neon youth in a region of blue-haired bus tours. On Britain's rainy shores, the endless dayglo "shacks" emit an angry commercial radiance. In 1989, favorite son Martin Potter shredded his way through the pro tour to become Britain's first World Surfing Champion. The town overlooks six beaches, each with its own particular crowd and character. Porth Beach, Lusty Glaze, Tolcarne Beach, Great Western, and Towan Beach are cut off from one another at high tide, when the surfers stir from their beach chaises and hit the water in large numbers.

Getting to or from Newquay (pop. 20,000) by rail from the main London-Penzance line requires a quick stopover in the small town of Par. **Trains** go to Par (5/day; 50min.; £5.20), Plymouth via Par (1/hr.; 2hr.; £7.90) or Penzance via Par (1/hr.; 2hr.; £9.70). By **bus**, catch **National Express** to Plymouth via Bodmin (3/day; 2hr.; £4.35), St. Austell (off-season Mon.-Sat. only; 2/hr.; 45min.; £2.15), or St. Ives (June-Sept. 3/day; 2hr.; £3).

The **tourist office** on Marcus Hill (tel. 871345), ten minutes from the train station and downhill from the bus station, dispenses helpful lists of discos, tide tables, and accommodations. (Open Mon.-Sat. 9am-6pm, Sun. 10am-5pm; shortened hours in winter.) The **post office** (tel. 873364) is on East St. (Open Mon.-Fri. 9am-5:30pm, Sat. 9am-12:30pm). Newquay's **postal code** is TR7 1BU.) Newquay's **telephone code** is 01637. **Trains** steam out of Station Parade, off Cliff Rd. (tel. 877180). (Station staffed Mon.-Fri. 9am-5pm, Sat. 9am-4pm.) The **bus station** is on East St. (office open Mon.-Thurs. and Sat. 9am-8:30pm, Fri. 9am-5pm, Sun. 9am-1pm and 5-8:30pm). For bus information, call Truro at (01872) 404 04. Rent bikes at **Cycle Revolutions,** 7 Beach Rd. (tel. 872364; mountain bikes £10/day, £50/week; ID deposit.) **Bilbo 2000** (tel. 874501) on Cliff Rd., rents surfboards and wet suits (each cost £5/day, £25/week; open Mon.-Sat. 9am-10pm, Sun. 9am-6pm. Dude.)

Despite looking like a B&B colony, Newquay is short on places to stay in July and August; the accommodations list at the tourist office is well worth the 20p. The **HI Youth Hostel** (tel. 876381), with a spacious lounge and a sluggish dog, is at the top of Narrowcliff (eastern extension of Cliff Rd., ten minutes from the bus station). (Open April-Aug. daily; March and Sept.-Oct. Tues.-Sat.; £8.70, children £5.80). **Mrs. W.H. Bragg** (tel. 873631), 3 Grosvenor Ave., and **Quebec House** (tel. 874 430), 34 Grosvenor Ave., are close to Norquay's stations and restaurants (£12 for bed and breakfast in each). **Towan Beach Backpackers,** 15 Beachfield Ave. (tel. 874668), offers cramped and merry quarters for a mere £5 a night. Expect showers, rough-hewn picnic tables, cigarette butts & lotsa beer in the lounge. No curfew. Open year-round. Camping facilities are found at **Trevelgne Caravan and Camping Park** (tel. 873475), Porth (£3-4.60, depending on season) or **Hendra Tourist Park** (tel. 875778), about 2 mi. east of town beyond the Lane Theatre. From Trenance Gardens, go under the viaduct and past the boating lake, then turn left. For families and couples only (£4-5/person, electricity £2.50).

The restaurants in Newquay pour tea and squish pasties into tourists who want a quick, bland, and costly fill-up. Watch out for signs advertising three-course "early bird" specials. **Food for Thought,** on Beachfield Ave., offers take-away "Californian" salads, sandwiches, and meat subs for under £1.50. (Open daily 8:30am-10pm.)

On sunny days, Newquay's streets seethe with tourists and wetsuit-clad surfers headed for the town's 7 mi. of **beaches.** You can avoid the crush if you hit the beaches at low tide; high tide reduces the beaches to one-fourth their maximum size. There are two beach areas at Newquay—**Fistral,** Cornwall's best surfing beach, and the stretch of beach adjacent to the harbor, which at high tide is subdivided into four separate beaches. Surfboards are available for rental all over town.

Newquay is notorious for its after-hours activities; even stores extend their hours well into the night. **Lucifer's,** Tolcarne Rd. (tel. 873894), was recently refurbished and is still crowded. **Steamers,** Marcus Hill (tel. 872194) is black-walled and is more anonymous (open til 1am; cover £3, weekdays £2.50). Almost every hotel offers some type of dancing, and doorways innocuous by day open up onto flashy clubs at night. Follow your ears and look around early to avoid the cover charge, which usu-ally manifests at 9 or 10pm. The **Lane Theatre** (tel. 876945) presents midsummer night's drama (tickets from £4), and comedians and musicians often entertain by the beach.

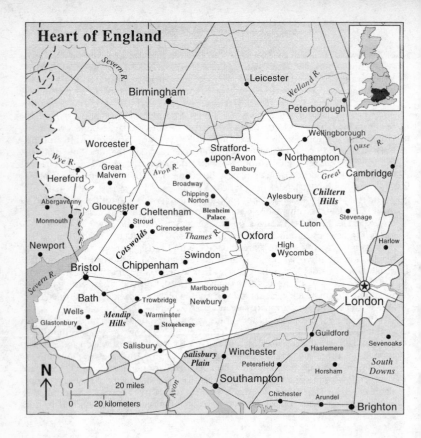

HEART OF ENGLAND

After London, the Heart of England contains the largest number of "must-sees" in England; it is this countryside which captures the essence of English life. Extending from London west to Salisbury and Bath and north to the Cotswolds and Stratford-upon-Avon, the Heart of England centers on Oxford, England's oldest university town. The region is warm and inviting, brightened by light yellow Cotswolds stone. Stratford-upon-Avon still looks like a village—having been saved from the threat of industrialization by Shakespeare's pre-eminence—though the tranquil country scenery and groomed flowerbeds have difficulty peeking out from under the morass of tourists. Bath and Stonehenge, despite being overrun in the hot summer months, retain an air of ancient and unshakable dignity. When possible, spend more than just a day in these towns, so as to roam free of the glut of daytrippers. Only an overnight can provide the wonder of twilight at an English river's edge.

■■■ OXFORD

Shrouded in 800 years of tradition, Oxford shook off those dusty cloths and found itself a city. Beneath its "dreaming spires," trucks rumble, bus brakes scream, and bicycles crush the toes of pedestrians shoving past each other in the streets. The famous walls and spires have a sickly cast: those that have been cleaned look sallow, and those that haven't are black with soot. None of this keeps travelers from stop-

OXFORD

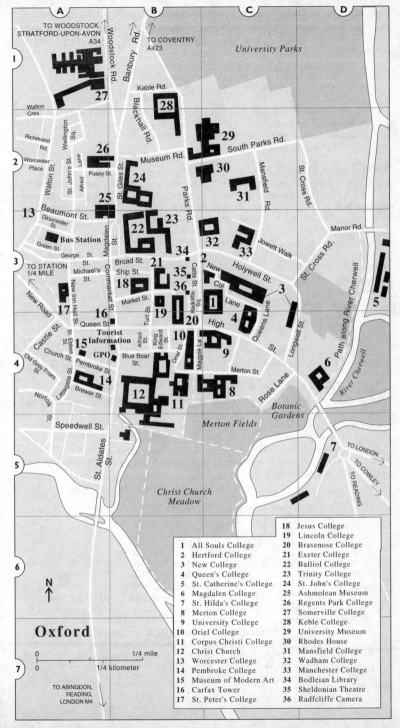

TO WOODSTOCK,
STRATFORD-UPON-AVON
A34

TO COVENTRY
A423

University Parks

Walton
Cres.

Keble Rd.

27

28

Richmond
Rd.

Museum Rd.

29

South Parks Rd.

Worcester
Place

26

30

31

Mansfield
Rd.

St. Cross Rd.

Manor Rd.

13 Beaumont St.

25

24

Gloucester
St.

Green St.

Bus Station

22

23

32

33

Jowett Walk

St. Cross Rd.

5

TO STATION
1/4 MILE

34

2

Holywell St.

Path along River Cherwell

New Road

George   St.
St.
Michael's
St.

Broad St.

21

Ship St.

35

New
Col
Lane

3

River Cherwell

17

18

Market St.

19

36

1

4

Queens Lane

6

16

Queen St.

**Tourist
Information**

20

High

10

St.

Castle St.

Church St.

15

GPO

Blue Boar
St.

St.

9

Merton St.

TO LONDON

14

Brewer St.

12

11

8

Rose Lane

TO COWLEY

Norfolk
St.

Speedwell St.

Merton Fields

*Botanic
Gardens*

7

TO READING

St. Aldates St.

*Christ Church
Meadow*

Oxford

N

0   1/4 mile
0   1/4 kilometer

TO ABINGDON,
READING,
LONDON M4

1 All Souls College	18 Jesus College
2 Hertford College	19 Lincoln College
3 New College	20 Brasenose College
4 Queen's College	21 Exeter College
5 St. Catherine's College	22 Balliol College
6 Magdalen College	23 Trinity College
7 St. Hilda's College	24 St. John's College
8 Merton College	25 Ashmolean Museum
9 University College	26 Regents Park College
10 Oriel College	27 Somerville College
11 Corpus Christi College	28 Keble College
12 Christ Church	29 University Museum
13 Worcester College	30 Rhodes House
14 Pembroke College	31 Mansfield College
15 Museum of Modern Art	32 Wadham College
16 Carfax Tower	33 Manchester College
17 St. Peter's College	34 Bodleian Library
	35 Sheldonian Theatre
	36 Radcliffe Camera

ping here and ducking for a few days into quieter, bikeless quads and cloisters. Oxford remains full of civilized places —the basement room in Blackwell's Bookshop, the impeccable Great Quad at All Souls College—to delight and edify the academic pilgrim.

GETTING THERE

Local trains run hourly from London. **Intercity** trains leave from Paddington (1hr.; day return £12.40). The **Oxford Tube** (tel. 772250) sends buses from Grosvenor Gardens in London (1-6/hr.; 1½hr.; day return £6, seniors, students, and children £5.50). **Oxford CityLink** shuttles between Oxford and Heathrow (1/hr., Sun. 4/day; about 1hr.; day return £10) and between Oxford and Gatwick Airport (5/day, Sun. 2/day; 2hr.; day return £10).

FLITTING ABOUT

The **Oxford Bus Company** (tel. 711312) operates the red double-deckers and lime-green "City Nipper" minibuses, as well as the CityLink service to London; **Oxford Minibus** (tel. 771876) owns the checkered-flag minibuses and the Oxford Tube London service. Masses of minibuses scurry around Oxford, and competition makes for swift and frequent service.

Most local services board on the streets adjacent to Carfax; some longer-distance buses depart from the bus station. Abingdon Rd. buses are often marked "Red Bridge," and some Iffley Rd. buses are marked "Rose Hill." Fares are low (most about 80p single). Some companies issue **Compass** tickets, good for one day's travel (about £4), but companies disdain each other's tickets. You can also purchase weekly bus passes at Carfax travel or at the bus station.

The signs all over town reading "No Cycles Here" do little to prevent cyclists from riding wherever they like, even in heavy traffic. 25p at the tourist office or a bike shop buys a *Cycle into Oxford* pamphlet, with cycling maps of the city and its hinterland. Bikes are banned from Queen and Cornmarket Streets during the day (a rule often violated) and from college parks and quads at all times (never violated).

ORIENTATION & PRACTICAL INFORMATION

Queen, High, St. Aldates, and Cornmarket Streets meet at right angles in **Carfax,** the town center. The colleges surround Carfax to the east along High St. and Broad St.; the bus and train stations lie to the west. Past the east end of High St. over Magdalen Bridge, the neighborhoods of **East Oxford** stretch along **Cowley Road** (marked "To Cowley" on some maps) and **Iffley Road** (marked "To Reading"). To the north along **Woodstock** and **Banbury Roads,** leafier residential areas roll on for miles past some of the more remote colleges.

Tourist Office: St. Aldates Chambers, St. Aldates St. (tel. 726871, after hours 252664). A pamphleteer's paradise. *Welcome to Oxford* (£1) is the official guide; *Vade Mecum* (£1), put out by Oxford undergrads, includes a helpful list of restaurants. Both guides are fairly bland. Accommodations list 40p, comprehensive map 70p. Books rooms for £2.50 and a 10% deposit. Oxbridge Blackcurrant Conserve £2.40/jar. *Bureau de Change.* Open Mon.-Sat. 9am-5pm, Sun. 10am-3:30pm.

Tours: 2-hr. walking tours leave 7 times daily from the tourist office between 10:30am and 4pm (£3.20, children £2). **Spires and Shires** (tel. 513998) runs 1½-hr. tours every hour 11am to 4pm, leaving from the Trinity College gate on Broad St. (£3, children £2). The **Oxford Ghost Tour** will make £3.50 vanish from your wallet, £2 if you're a child; leaves 9pm daily from the Oxfam shop on Broad St. Ubiquitous **tour buses** can be boarded anywhere between the train station and Magdalen College; **The Oxford Tour** (tel. 790522) charges £6.50, students £4.50, children £2. Spires and Shires runs two morning bus tours to Blenheim Palace from the train station (£7.50, children £5). Or take a tour from one of the many **student groups** that offer them (£2.50, students free; tours depart from tourist office). Some students will regale you with stories you won't hear on the official tours and will give you your money back if you're dissatisfied. Others won't. One tour every hour between 9am-5pm.

Budget Travel Office: Campus Travel, 13 High St. (tel. 242067). Eurotrain tickets, ISICs, railcards, discount airfare, bus tickets, and insurance. Open Mon.-Tues. and Thurs.-Fri. 9am-5:30pm, Wed. 10am-5:30pm, Sat. 10am-5pm. **STA Travel,** 36 George St. (tel. 792800). Open Mon.-Wed. and Fri. 9am-6pm, Thurs. 9:30am-6pm, Sat. 10am-4pm.

Financial Services: Banks crowd in on Carfax. **Barclays,** 54 Cornmarket St. (tel. 79133). Open Mon.-Tues. and Thurs.-Fri. 9:30am-4:30pm, Wed. 10am-5:30pm, Sat. 10am-5pm. **National Westminster,** 32 Cornmarket St. (tel. 722621). Open Mon.-Tues and Thurs.-Fri. 9am-5pm, Wed. 9:30am-5pm, Sat. 9:30am-3:30pm. **Lloyds,** 1-5 High St. (tel. 244822). Open Mon.-Fri. 9:30am-5:30pm. **Thomas Cook,** 5 Queen St. (tel. 240441). Open Mon., Wed.-Sat. 9am-5:30pm, Tues. 10am-5:30 pm. **American Express** (Keith Bailey Travel Agency), 99 St. Aldates St. (tel. 790099) Client mail held. Open Mon. and Wed.-Fri. 9am-5:30pm, Tues. 9:30am-5:30pm, Sat. 9am-5pm.

Post Office: 102/104 St. Aldates St. (tel. 814785). Open Mon.-Fri. 9am-5:30pm, Sat. 9am-12:30pm. **Postal Code:** OX1 1ZZ.

Telephones: Phonecard and intercontinental phones gather at Carfax and on Cornmarket St., as well as on St. Aldates St, but are almost inaudible through the roar of cars and buses.

Telephone Code: 01865.

Train Station: Botley Rd. (tel. 722333 for British Rail timetable), west of Carfax. Travel Centre open Mon.-Fri. 8am-7:30pm, Sat. 8am-6pm, Sun. 11am-6pm. Station open Mon.-Fri. 5:50am-8pm, Sat. 6:50am-8pm, Sun. 8am-8pm.

Bus Station: Gloucester Green (follow arrows from Carfax). **Oxford Tube** (tel. 772250); **Oxford CityLink** (tel. 711312, 772250 for timetable); **National Express** (tel. 791579), office open daily 8am-6:30pm. **Carfax Travel,** 138 High St. at Carfax (tel. 726172), books for National Express, as well as for British Rail and ferries. Open Mon.-Fri. 9am-5pm, Sat. 9am-1pm.

Taxi: Radio Taxi, tel. 242424. **ABC,** tel. 770681.

Bike Rental: Pennyfarthing, 5 George St. (tel. 249368). Closest to town center. Rental £5/day; 3-speeds £10/week; deposit £25. Open Mon.-Sat. 8am-5:30pm.

Bookstores: Blackwell's, 48-51 Broad St. (tel. 792792; see Oxford: Sights, below). Oxford's biggest, and one of the world's best. Open Mon.-Sat. 9am-6pm, Sun. noon-5pm. The Blackwell's empire covers most of Broad St. and part of Holywell St.; it includes an **Art and Poster Shop** at 27 Broad St., a **Children's Bookshop** at 8 Broad St., and a **Music and Rare Books** shop at 38 Holywell St. **Oxford University Press,** 116 High St. (tel. 242913). First editions from one of the world's most respected academic publishers. Open Mon. and Wed.-Sat. 9am-5pm, Tues. 10am-5pm. **Dillons,** corner of Broad St. and Cornmarket St. Mon.-Wed and Fri. 9am-7pm, Thurs. 9am-8pm, Sat. 9am-6pm., Sun. 11am-5pm.

Public Library: Westgate Shopping Centre (tel. 815509). Take Queen St. from Carfax. Fine local history collection. Open Mon.-Tues. and Thurs.-Fri. 9:15am-7pm, Wed. and Sat. 9:15am-5pm.

Camping and Hiking Supplies: YHA Adventure Shop, 9-10 St. Clements (tel. 247948), on Magdalen Bridge roundabout. Rents tents. Open Mon.-Wed. and Fri. 9:30am-5:30pm; Thurs. 9:30am-6pm; Sat. 9am-6pm.

Launderette: Clean-o-Fine, 66 Abingdon Rd., South Oxford. Open Mon.-Fri. 8am-9:30pm, Sat.-Sun. 7:30am-9:30pm. Last wash 8:30pm. **Valumatic,** 184 Cowley Rd., across Magdalen Bridge. Open Mon.-Fri. 8:30am-8pm, Sat. 8:30am-4pm, Sun. 8:30am-7pm. Last wash 1 hr. before closing.

Hotlines: Samaritans (crisis): 123 Iffley Rd. (tel. 722122). Phone 24-hr.; drop in daily 8am-10pm. **Gay Switchboard:** tel. 793999. Mon., Tues., Fri., Sun. 7-9pm. **Oxford Lesbian Line:** tel. 242333. Wed. 7-10pm. **Drug and Alcohol Hotline:** tel. 749800. 24-hr. answer phone. **Rape Crisis:** tel. 726295. Open Mon.-Tues. and Thurs. 7-9pm, Wed. 4-6pm, Sun. 6-8pm; answering machine other times; in emergency call **London Rape Crisis Center** at (0171) 837 1600.

Pharmacy: For late-night pharmacies, check the weekly Rota Service listings on pharmacy doors around town.

Hospital: John Radcliffe Hospital, Woodstock Rd. (tel. 741166). Take bus #10.
Emergency: Dial 999; no coins required.
Police: St. Aldates and Speedwell St. (tel. 266000).

ACCOMMODATIONS & CAMPING

Book at least a week ahead, especially for singles, and expect to mail in a deposit. B&Bs line the main roads out of town, all of them a vigorous walk (15-20min.) from Carfax. The No. 300s on **Banbury Road,** fern-laced and domestic, stand miles north of the center (catch a Banbury bus on St. Giles St.). You'll find cheaper B&Bs in the 200s and 300s on Iffley Rd. and from No. 250-350 on **Cowley Rd.,** both served by frequent buses from Carfax. **Abingdon Road,** in South Oxford, is about the same price and distance, though less colorful. Wherever you go, expect to pay at least £15-18/person. If it's late and you're homeless, call one of the following numbers: 241497 (East Oxford), 862138 (West Oxford), 510327 (North Oxford), 725870 (South Oxford).

HI Youth Hostel, Jack Straw's Lane, Headington (tel. 62997). Catch any minibus from the post office just south of Carfax (4/hr., last bus 11:10pm; 55p). One of England's largest hostels (116 beds) and well-equipped, with kitchen, lockers, and food shop. Close quarters and large lounges promote chatter. Offers camping in backyard. Lockout 10am-1pm, curfew 11:30pm (though night guard is on duty to let stragglers in). £8.70, under 18 £5.80.

Tara, 10 Holywell St. (tel. 244786 or 248270). The best B&B in town, situated among the colleges on the oldest medieval street in Oxford. Kind hearing-impaired proprietors, Mr. and Mrs. Godwin, lip-read and speak clearly, so there'll be no communication problems. Desks, basins, TVs, and refrigerators in every room; kitchenette on 2nd floor. Breakfast room a virtual museum of academic regalia, college coats-of-arms, and other Oxford paraphernalia. Singles £25, doubles £38. Open July-Sept.; the rest of the year it fills up with students, but check anyway. Reserve at least 2 weeks in advance for this lost kingdom.

Bravalla, 242 Iffley Rd. (tel. 241326). Sunny rooms hung with soothing, nonintrusive floral patterns and pastels. Dining room has glass walls. Singles £18-20, doubles with bath £36-42. If her B&B is full, the proprietress will help you find a room elsewhere.

Whitehouse View, 9 Whitehouse Rd. (tel. 721626), off Abingdon Rd. Only 10min. from Carfax. The size and decor of the rooms vary; ask to see a selection if you can. Solicitous proprietors and excellent breakfasts. Doubles with TV. £17-18.

Newton House, 82-84 Abingdon Rd. (tel. 240561), a ½ mi. from town center; take any Abingdon bus across Folly Bridge. TVs and dark, hulking wardrobes in every room. Affable proprietor. Doubles £35, with bath £45.

Old Mitre Rooms, 48 Turl St. (tel. 279821). Lincoln College dorm rooms with authentic ripped-down poster decor. One bathroom for every six people. Continental breakfast. Singles £18, doubles £35.20, with bath £38. Open July-early Sept. Inquire at the Mitre Pub and Restaurant at the corner of Turf and High St.

St. Hugh's College, St. Margaret's Rd. off Banbury Rd. (tel. 54642). Bedrooms, some enormous, in Victorian houses on Canterbury Rd. Continental breakfast won't sustain you for the vigorous walk into town. Singles £15-19, doubles £30-36. Open late June-Sept.

Camping: Oxford Camping International, 426 Abingdon Rd. (tel. 246551), behind the Texaco Station. 129 nondescript sites on a manicured lawn. Laundry and warm showers. One person £3.75, 2 people £5.15, car £1.60 extra. **Cassington Mill Caravan Site,** Eynsham Rd., Cassington (tel. 881081), about 4 mi. northwest on the A40. Take bus #90 from the bus station. 83 pitches and hot showers. One person £5-7, £4 if on foot. Open May-Oct. Neither site rents tents. The **HI Youth Hostel** has campsites for £4.35; campers may use the hostel facilities.

FOOD

The swank, bulging swagger of Oxford's eateries seduces students fed up with fetid college food. Expect happiness. For fresh produce, deli goods, breads, and shoe leather, visit the **Covered Market** between Market St. and Carfax (open Mon.-Sat. 8am-5:30pm). Or visit the Wednesday market at Gloucester Green (all day, by the bus station) for amazing deals on produce, pies, cheeses, meats, clothing, and more. The closest supermarket to Carfax is the **Co-op** on Cornmarket St. (open Mon.-Fri. 8am-7pm, Sat. 8am-6pm). For dried apricots and whole grains, head for **Holland & Barrett,** King Edward St. (open Mon.-Sat. 9am-5:30pm, 10% discount for seniors on Wed.). Or if you're staying across Magdalen Bridge, beam yourself over to **Uhuru Wholefoods,** 48 Cowley Rd. (open Mon.-Fri. 10am-6pm, Sat. 9:30am-5:30pm). Eat and run at one of the better take-aways: **Bret's Burgers,** in a shack on Park End St. (tel 245229), near the train station, with delectable burgers and chips from £1.50 (open Sun.-Thurs. noon-11pm, Fri.-Sat. noon-11:30pm); or **Parmenters,** 58 High St. near Magdalen College, recognizable by the line out the door (apricot flapjacks 75p, great chunks of carrot cake £1.15, mighty sandwiches £1.30-2.75; open Mon.-Fri. 8:30am-5:30pm, Sat.-Sun. 9am-5:30pm).

The Nosebag, 6-8 Michael's St. (tel. 721033). More wholesome than the name suggests. Heaping plates of salad and meat dishes served cafeteria-style for under £5, £6.50 at dinner. Open Mon. 9:30am-5:30pm, Tues.-Thurs. 9:30am-10pm, Fri.-Sat. 9:30am-10:30pm, Sun. 9:30am-9pm.

Chiang Mai, in an alley at 130A High St. (tel. 202233). Spicy Thai food in half-timbered surroundings. Extensive vegetarian menu; entrees £4.30-6.50. Reserve ahead, especially on weekends. Drink lots of water. Try the sticky rice dessert for £3.20. Open Mon.-Sat. noon-2:30pm, 6-11pm.

Cherwell Boathouse, Bardwell Rd. (tel. 52746), off Banbury Rd., 1 mi. north of town. Romantically perched on the leafy bank of the Cherwell and run by amiable young proprietors. A good place to propose. Menu offers two 3-course meals—one vegetarian, both unorthodox. Well-loved wine list. Expect to spend the entire evening; book well in advance. Dinner usually under £20, and worth every penny. When you're finished, rent a punt next door (£6; £30 deposit) and drift off into the watery night. Open Tues.-Sat. 6:30-10pm, Wed.-Sun. noon-2pm.

Munchy Munchy, 6 Park End St., (tel. 245710), on way into town from rail station. Stark wooden decor and silly name redeemed by spirited cooking and energetic proprietress. Different dishes daily, all Indonesian or Malaysian, at least 1 vegetable dish (£5-8). Open Tues.-Sat. noon-2pm and 5:30-10pm.

Polash Tandoori Restaurant, 25 Park End St. Delicious Indian cuisine served in a quiet setting near the train station. Vegetable dishes under £2.50. Sunday lunch buffet £7/person. Open Mon.-Thurs. noon-2:30pm and 6-11:30pm, Fri.-Sat. noon-2:30pm and 6pm-midnight, Sun. noon-11:30pm.

Heroes, Ship St. (tel. 723459). Packs in student clientele and serves up yummy sandwiches with a super selection of stuffings, £1.60-2.65. Open Mon.-Fri. 8am-7pm, Sat. 8:30am-5pm, Sun. 10am-5pm. Breakfast 8am-11am.

Bella Pasta, 14-16 George St. (tel. 791032). Simple Italian fare. Pizza (£4-6.50) and pasta (£4-7). Wheelchair access. Live jazz Fri., Sat. nights. Open daily 10am-11:30pm.

For those staying at B&Bs across Magdalen Bridge, there are a number of cheap and tasty ethnic restaurants along the first four blocks of Cowley Rd. **Hi-Lo Jamaican Eating House,** 70 Cowley Rd. (tel. 725984), **Kashmir Halal,** 64 Cowley Rd. (tel. 250165), and **The Pak Fook,** 100 Cowley Rd. (tel. 247958), are all good bets. Or just keep an eye out for the legendary **kebab vans** that roll into town to arm students with skewers after hours—usually at Broad St., High St., Queen St., and St. Aldate's.

PUBS

Pubs far outnumber colleges in Oxford; many consider them the city's prime attraction. Most pubs are open all afternoon and begin to fill up around 4pm. Be ready to crawl—some pubs are so small that a single band of merry students will squeeze out other patrons. *Good Pubs of Oxford* (£2 at bookstores and tourist office) is an indispensable guide to the town's beer dungeons. Buy it, use it, keep it dry.

Turf Tavern, 4 Bath Pl., off Holywell St. A 13th-century building, intimate and relaxed until the student crowd turns it into a mosh pit. Extensive outdoor seating by the ruins of the old city wall. Many many drinks: beers, punches, ciders, and country wines—mead, elderberry, apple, and red-and-white currant.

The Eagle and Child, 49 Giles St. Known to all as the Bird and Baby, this archipelago of pleasant panelled alcoves moistened the tongues of C.S. Lewis and J.R.R. Tolkein for a quarter-century. *The Hobbit* and *The Chronicles of Narnia* were first read aloud here. Very popular with tourists. Good food; soothing Sinatra-era music. Nice glassed-in garden.

The Bear, Alfred St. Medieval austerity since 1242. Plain tables, 6-foot ceiling. 5000 ties from England's brightest and most boastful cover every flat surface but the floor; you can buy your own "The Bear 1242-1992" tie for £6.50. Food served daily noon-3pm, Tues.-Sat. also 6-8pm.

Head of the River, Folly Bridge. Sit on the terrace and watch the Sweet Thames run softly by while buses rumble loudly on the bridge. Lots of tourists.

The Perch, Binsey Village (tel. 240386). From Walton St. in Jericho, walk down Walton Well Rd. and over Port Meadow, cross Rainbow Bridge, head north, then follow the trail west. This pub on the Thames will make your whole vacation worthwhile. Definitely worth the trouble of finding—it does exist, trust us. The lovely garden is ideal for Sunday lunch or twilight drinks. Lunch served noon-2pm, dinner 7:15-9pm. Occasional do-it-yourself barbecues.

Oxford Brewhouse, Red Lion Sq., 14 Gloucester Green. Huge, dark, and faceless, but it packs them in. Live music every Monday.

The Blue Boar, 11 Wheatsheaf Yard, off Blue Boar St. Small with white walls, like a continental café, but the hammering music will drive you out onto the terrace for a fine view of a blackened stone wall. Right behind Christ Church and packed with students.

The Kings Arms, Holywell St. Oxford's unofficial student union, with a few refugee scholars from the New Bodleian across the street. High ceilings; good lighting. Look for the photo of a whale impacted in a rooftop. Open Mon.-Sat. 10:30am-11pm; Sun. 10:30am-3pm, 7-10:30pm.

White Horse, 52 Broad St., between the two wings of Blackwell's. Narrow and crowded, with a decrepit ceiling. Extensive menu of standard English half-edibles (steak & kidney pie, hamsteak, bleh; £3.75-5); lunch daily served noon-2:30pm, dinner Mon.-Thurs. and Sat. 5:30-8pm.

SIGHTS

King Henry II Oxford University (Britain's first) in 1167. Until then, the English had traveled to Paris to study, a fact that never sat well with the Francophobic English king. After his tiff with Thomas à Becket, Archbishop of Canterbury, Henry ordered the return of English students studying in Paris, so that "there may never be wanting a succession of persons duly qualified for the service of God in church and state." Ever in fierce competition with that other university on the Cam, Oxford boasts among its graduates Sir Christopher Wren, Oscar Wilde, Indira Gandhi, and Dudley Moore; Christ Church alone has produced 13 prime ministers.

Oxford has no official "campus." The university's 40 independent colleges, where students live and learn, are scattered throughout the city; central libraries, laboratories, and faculties are established and maintained by the university. At the end of their last academic year, students from all the colleges come together for their "degree examinations," a grueling three-week process that takes place in the Examination Schools on High St. in late June and early July. Each year, university authorities unsuccessfully undertake to prohibit the vigorous post-examination celebrations in the street. The tourist office guide *Welcome to Oxford* (£1) and the tourist office map (20p) list colleges' public visiting hours (usually for a few hours in the afternoon; often curtailed neither with prior notice nor explanation). Christ Church, Magdalen College, and New College charge admission; others may impose mercenary fees during peak tourist times. At Christ Church, don't bother trying to sneak in (even after cleverly hiding your backpack and flaming yellow *Let's Go*): elderly bouncers in bowler hats stationed 50 feet apart will squint at you and kick you out. Other colleges have been known to be less vigilant near the back gates.

Start your walking tour at Carfax, the center of activity, with a hike up the 99 spiral stairs of **Carfax Tower** (tel. 792653) for an overview of the city. Before hitting the heights, get a free map of the rooftops from the attendant at the bottom (open late March-Oct. daily10am-6pm; £1.20, children 60p).

Just down St. Aldates St. stands **Christ Church** (tel. 26492), an intimidating pile of stone that dwarfs the other colleges. "The House" has Oxford's grandest quad and its most socially distinguished, obnoxious students. (Open Mon.-Sat. 9:30am-5:30pm, Sun. noon-5:30pm. Services Sun. 8am, 10am, 11:15pm, 6pm; weekdays 7:15am, 7:35am, 6pm. £2.50; seniors, students, and children £1.) Christ Church's chapel is also Oxford's **cathedral,** the smallest in England. In the year 730, St. Frideswide, Oxford's patron saint, built a nunnery on this site in thanks for two miracles she had prayed for: the blinding of an annoying suitor, and his recovery. The cathedral's right transept contains a stained glass window (c. 1320) depicting Thomas à Becket kneeling in supplication, just before being hacked apart in Canterbury Cathedral. The 20-minute film shown continuously in the vestry (free) gives a concise history of the college and cathedral.

The Reverend Charles Dodgson (who wrote under the name Lewis Carroll) was friendly with Dean Liddell of Christ Church—and friendlier with his daughter Alice—and used to visit them in the gardens of the Dean's house next to the cathedral. From the largest tree in his garden, the Cheshire Cat first grinned and vanished, and the White Rabbit can be spotted fretting in the stained glass of the hall.

Curious and curiouser, the adjoining **Tom Quad** sometimes becomes the site of undergraduate lily-pond-dunking. The quad takes its name from **Great Tom,** the seven-ton bell in Tom Tower, which has faithfully rung 101 strokes (the original number of students) at 9:05pm (the original undergraduate curfew) every evening since 1682. Sixty coats of arms preside over the ceiling under the tower. Nearby, the fan-vaulted college **hall** bears imposing portraits of some of Christ Church's most famous alums—Charles Dodgson, Sir Philip Sidney, John Ruskin, John Locke, and a bored-looking W.H. Auden in the corner by the kitchen. If you can, visit the kitchens and see the spits used for roasting oxen.

Through an archway (to your left as you face the cathedral) lies **Peckwater Quad,** encircled by the most elegant Palladian building in Oxford. Look here for faded rowing standings chalked on the walls and for Christ Church's library, closed to visitors. The adjoining **Canterbury Quad** houses the **Christ Church Picture Gallery** (enter on Oriel Square and at Canterbury Gate), a fine collection of Italian primitives and Dutch and Flemish paintings. (Open April-Sept. Mon.-Sat. 10:30am-1pm and 2-5:30pm, Sun. 2-5:30pm; Oct.-March closes at 4:30pm. £1, students 50p. Visitors to gallery only should enter through Canterbury Gate off Oriel St.) Spreading east and south from the main entrance, **Christ Church Meadow** compensates for Oxford's lack of "backs" (riverside gardens in Cambridge). Across St. Aldates at 30 Pembroke St., the **Museum of Modern Art** (tel. 722733) exhibits works ranging from 10-ft.-high floral hemp structures to photos of people with AIDS. (Open Tues.-Wed. and Fri.-Sat. 10am-6pm, Thurs. 10am-9pm, Sun. 2-6pm. £2.50, seniors, students, and children £1.50, free Wed. 10am-1pm and Thurs. 6-9pm. Wheelchair access.)

Oriel College (real name "The House of the Blessed Mary the Virgin in Oxford") is wedged between High and Merton St. (tel. 276555). Oriel became a hotbed of the "Tractarian Movement" in the 1830s, when college clergy such as Keble and Newman tried to push the Anglican church back toward Rome (open daily 2-5pm). Behind Oriel, **Corpus Christi College** (tel. 276700) surrounds a quad with an elaborate sundial in the center, crowned by a golden pelican (open daily 1:30-4:30pm).

Next door, **Merton College,** off Merton St. (tel. 276310), features a fine garden; the college's 14th-century library holds the first printed Welsh Bible. The college is also home to the **Mob Quad,** Oxford's oldest and least impressive, dating from the 14th century (college open Mon.-Fri. 2-5pm, Sat.-Sun. 10am-5pm). A peaceful stroll down Merton Grove leads to **Merton Fields,** a quiet dab of green adjoining Christ Church Meadow.

The soot-blackened **University College** on High St. (tel. 276602), up the crooked Logic Lane from Merton St., dates from 1249 and vies with Merton for the title of oldest college, claiming Alfred the Great as its founder (open July-Aug. daily 10am-6pm). Percy Bysshe Shelley was expelled from University for writing the pamphlet *The Necessity of Atheism,* but has since been immortalized in a prominent godless monument inside the college (to right as you enter from High St.). Down High St. on the right lies the **Botanic Garden,** a sumptuous array of plants that has flourished for three centuries (open daily 9am-5pm; glasshouses open daily 2-4pm; free).

With flowers lining the quads, a deer park on its grounds, the river watering its flank, and Addison's Walk (a verdant circular path) framing a meadow at one edge, **Magdalen College** (MAUD-lin; tel. 276000) has traditionally been considered Oxford's handsomest. Its spiritual patron is alumnus Oscar Wilde—the place has always walked on the flamboyant side. Edward Gibbon declared the 14 months he spent here "the most idle and unprofitable of my whole career" (open July-Sept. daily 11am-6pm; Oct.-June Mon.-Fri. 2-6pm, Sat.-Sun noon-6pm. £1.50, children and seniors £1).

Just up High St. toward Carfax, a statue of Queen Caroline (wife of George II) crowns the front gate of **Queen's College** (tel. 279120). Wren and Hawksmoor went to the trouble of rebuilding Queen's in the 17th and 18th centuries, with a distinctive Queen Anne style in glorious orange, white, and gold. A trumpet call summons students to dinner; a boar's head graces the Christmas table. The latter tradition supposedly commemorates an early student of the college who, attacked by a boar on the outskirts of Oxford, choked his assailant to death with a volume of Aristotle. The College is closed to the public, except for those on authorized tours.

Next to Queen's stands **All Souls** (tel. 279379), a graduate college with a prodigious endowment. Candidates who survive the terribly difficult admission exams get invited to dinner, where it is ensured that they are "well-born, well-bred, and only moderately learned." The Great Quad, with its fastidious lawn and two spare spires, may be Oxford's most serene, ordered space. (Open Mon.-Fri. 2-4:30pm).

Turn up Catte St. to the **Bodleian Library** (tel. 277000) Oxford University's principal reading and research library with over six million books and 50,000 manuscripts. Sir Thomas Bodley endowed the library's first wing in 1602 on a site that had housed university libraries since 1488; the institution has since grown to fill the immense **Old Library** complex, the round **Radcliffe Camera** next door, and two newer buildings on Broad St. As a copyright library, the Bodleian receives a copy of every book printed in Great Britain—gratis. There are four guided tours a day (£3). Admission to the reading rooms is by ticket only. If you can prove you're a scholar (a student ID may be sufficient, but a letter of introduction from your college is encouraged) and present two passport photos (which can be taken on the spot), the Admissions Office will issue a two-day pass for £2. You still won't be allowed access to the manuscripts division unless you are "formally enrolled in a graduate degree program" and/or have a letter from your institution explicitly specifying the necessity of the Oxford archives. No one has ever been permitted to take out a book, not even Cromwell. Well, especially not Cromwell. (Library open Mon.-Fri. 9am-6pm, Sat. 9am-12:30pm.) Across Broad St. from the Bodleian you can browse at **Blackwell's,** the famous bookstore. The basement room dwarfs the building and undermines the foundations of Trinity College next door; Guinness lists it as the largest room devoted to bookselling anywhere in the world. The literate should set aside a day, or two, or three (see Practical Information above).

The **Sheldonian Theatre** (tel. 277299), set beside the Bodleian, is a Roman-style jewel of an auditorium built by Wren as a university theatre and home of the University Press. Graduation ceremonies, conducted in Latin, take place in the Sheldonian and can be witnessed with permission from one of the "bulldogs" (bowler-hatted university officers on duty). The cupola of the theatre affords an inspiring view of the spires of Oxford (open Mon.-Sat. 10am-12:45pm and 2-4:45pm; Nov.-Feb. until 3:45pm; admission 50p, children 25p).

The gates of **Balliol College** (tel. 277777), across Broad St. (open daily 2-5pm), still bear scorch marks from the immolations of 16th-century Protestant martyrs (the pyres were built a few yards from the college, where a small cross set into Broad St. rattles cyclists today). The martyrs' monument is sometimes identified to gullible tourists as Oxford's "famous sunken cathedral." Housed in flamboyant pink and yellow neo-gothic buildings, Balliol is a mellow place that recently had a Marxist master. Matthew Arnold and the poet Swinburne went here.

Balliol students preserve a semblance of tradition by hurling bricks over the wall at their arch-rival, conservative **Trinity College** (tel. 279900), on Broad St. (open daily 2-5pm). Trinity, founded in 1555, has a perfectly baroque chapel, with a lime-wood altarpiece, cedar lattices, and angel-capped pediments. Trinity's series of eccentric presidents includes Ralph Kettell, who used to come to dinner with a pair of scissors and chop at members' hair that he deemed too long.

Across Catte St. from the Bodleian, New College Lane leads inevitably to **New College** (tel. 279555). So named because of its relative anonymity at the time of its founding by William of Wykeham in 1379, New College has become one of Oxford's most prestigious colleges. The accreted layers of the front quad—compare the different stones of the first and second stories—reveal the architectural history of the college. Look for the exquisitely detailed misericords, carved by sympathetic carpenters into the pews to support monks' bottoms. A peaceful croquet garden is encircled by part of the **old city wall,** and every few years the mayor of the City of Oxford visits the college for a ceremonial inspection to ascertain the wall's good repair. A former head of the college, Rev. Warden Spooner, is now remembered as the unintentional inventor of the "spoonerism." This stern but befuddled Oxford academic would raise a toast to "our queer old dean" or rebuke a student who had allegedly "hissed all the mystery lectures" and "tasted the whole worm" (open daily 11:30am-5pm; school term 2-5pm).

Turn left at the end of Holywell St. and then bear right on Manor Rd. to see **St. Catherine's** (tel. 271700), one of the most striking of the colleges. Built between 1960 and 1964 by the Danish architect Arne Jacobsen, "Catz" has no chapel, and its dining hall was funded by that curmudgeonly eccentric, Esso Petroleum (open daily 9am-5pm). At the corner of St. Cross and South Parks Rd., the **Zoology and Psychology Building** looms like a great concrete ocean liner. Many colleges hold sporting matches nearby on the **University Parks,** a refreshing expanse of green.

Walk through the **University Museum** (tel. 272950), Parks Rd. (open Mon.-Sat. noon-5pm; free) to the **Pitt Rivers Museum** (tel. 270927) and behold a wonderfully eclectic ethnography and natural history collection that includes shrunken heads and rare butterflies (open Mon.-Sat. 1-4:30pm; free). Just up Banbury Rd. on the right, the **Balfour Buildings** house 1400 musical instruments from all over the world, including a working black leather violin (open Mon.-Sat. 1-4:30pm; free).

Keble College (tel. 272727), across from the University Museum, was designed by architect William Butterfield to stand out from the Museum's sandstone background; the intricate and multi-patterned red brick, known as "The Fair Isle Sweater," was deemed "actively ugly" by Sir Nikolaus Pevsner (open daily 2-5pm). Through a passageway to the left, the **Hayward** and **deBreyne Buildings** squat on the tarmac like black plexiglass spaceships ready to take off.

The imposing **Ashmolean Museum,** Beaumont St. (tel. 278000), was Britain's first public museum when it opened in 1683. Its outstanding collection includes drawings and prints by Leonardo da Vinci, Raphael, and Michelangelo; copious French impressionist and Italian works; and Rembrandts, Constables, and assorted Pre-Raphaelites (open Tues.-Sat. 10am-4pm, Sun. 2-4pm; free). Ashmolean's **Cast Gallery,** behind the museum, stores over 250 casts of Greek sculptures (open Tues.-Fri. 10am-4pm, Sat. 10am-1pm; free).

A few blocks up St. Giles, as it becomes Woodstock Rd., stands **Somerville College** (tel. 270600), Oxford's most famous women's college. (The oldest is Lady Margaret Hall.) Somerville's alumnae include Dorothy Sayers, Indira Gandhi, Margaret Thatcher, Ena Franey, and Shirley Williams. Women were not granted degrees until 1920—Cambridge held out until 1948—and they still comprise only 38% of today's student body (open daily 2:30-5:30pm).

At the remote end of Beaumont St., you'll reach **Worcester College** (tel. 278300). Derisively called Botany Bay, the college has attracted some of Oxford's more swashbuckling students, including handsome poet Richard Lovelace and essay fiend and opium addict Thomas De Quincey. Worcester enjoys a large and dreamy garden and a lake shore that stages summertime plays (open daily 2-6pm).

By far the most self-indulgent of Oxford's neighborhoods is the five blocks of **Cowley Road** nearest the Magdalen Bridge roundabout. The area is a living version of the *Whole Earth Handbook,* a fascinating clutter of alternative lifestyles, small bookstores, jumble shops, and scruffy wholefood and ethnic restaurants. Check out **Rainbow's End,** a comic-book shop at 78 Cowley Rd. (open Mon.-Thurs. and Sat. 10am-12:45pm and 1:30-6pm, Fri. 10am-12:45pm and 1:30-5:30pm), and **Jeremy's,** a stamp-collector's, used-paperback, and postcard shop at 98 Cowley Rd. (tel. 241011; open Mon.-Fri. 10am-12:30pm and 2-5pm).

Two museums near Carfax give grand syntheses of Oxford's history. The **Museum of Oxford** on St. Aldates St. (tel. 815559), across from the tourist office, must be the most comprehensive local history collection in Britain. Seemingly endless placards, models, and artifacts outline Oxford's growth from a Roman and Saxon river-crossing to the fortress of intellect it is today (open Tues.-Fri. 9am-4pm, Sat. 10am-5pm; free). **The Oxford Story,** 6 Broda St. (tel. 790055 or 728822), hauls visitors around on medieval-style "desks" through noisy dioramas recreating Oxford's past. Share the simple pleasures of a thirteenth-century student making merry with a wench; hear the cries of the bishops who were burned a few feet away on Broad St. (Open July-Aug. 9am-6:30pm, April-June and Sept.-Oct. 9:30am-5pm, Nov.-March 10am-4pm; £4.50, seniors and students £4, children £3.25.)

ENTERTAINMENT

Oxford shuts down fairly early, and public transit vanishes by 11pm. Posters plastered around town advertise upcoming events and make the best entertainment guide. Check the bulletin boards at the tourist office or pick up a free copy of *This Month in Oxford.* The tourist office also provides a daily information sheet in the summer about Oxford goings-on. Local events have their **ticket office** at 44-46 Cornmarket St. in HMV records (tel. 728190; open Mon. and Wed.-Sat. 9am-6pm; Tues. 9:30am-6pm; Thurs. 9am-7pm; Sun. noon-6pm); to book **Shakespeare** tickets, call (01789) 295623.

The university itself offers marvelous entertainment. Throughout the summer, college theatre groups stage productions in gardens or in cloisters. Music at Oxford is a cherished art; try to attend a concert or an evensong service at one of the colleges, or a performance at the **Holywell Music Rooms,** the oldest in the country. **City of Oxford Orchestra,** the city's professional symphony orchestra (tel. 252365), plays a subscription series ("Beautiful Music in Beautiful Places") in the Sheldonian Theatre and college chapels throughout the summer (shows at 8pm; tickets £7-17, students 25% discount). They also have Sunday coffee concerts. The year-long **Music at Oxford** series plays in halls throughout the city; for information, call 864056 or write to 6A Cumnor Hill, Oxford OX2 9HA.

The annual **Dorchester Abbey Festival** (music, drama, and poetry readings) runs for two weeks beginning in late June in **Dorchester-on-Thames,** 9 mi. south of Oxford. Bus transportation is available from Oxford; call 240 358 or write to Dorchester Abbey Festival, Oxford OX1 2BR. The **Apollo Theatre,** George St. (tel. 244544), presents a wide range of performances, including comedy, drama, rock, jazz, and the Royal Ballet (tickets from £7, students and seniors £2 discount). The **Oxford Playhouse,** Beaumont St. (tel. 798600) puts on bands, dance troupes, and the Oxford Stage Company (tickets from £5, children and seniors £2 discount, students gets best available seat from 2 hrs. before the show for £5, Wed.-Thurs. £3).

The **Oxford Union,** St. Michael's St., and **The Old Fire Station** on George St. (tel. 794494) feature more avant-garde work.

The Phoenix, Walton St. (tel. 54909), shows mostly serious (translation: foreign) films (tickets £2.75). *What's On In Oxford* catalogues the clubs and pubs that play music. The tourist office also provides a free bi-monthly publication, *Recreation Day,* listing activities in Oxford. The **Jericho Tavern,** at the corner of Walton and Jericho St. (tel. 54502), features local rock bands (open Mon.-Sat. 11am-3pm, 6-11pm; cover charge £3.50-5). **The Jolly Farmers,** Paradise St. (tel. 793759), is Oxfordshire's only gay and lesbian pub, featuring occasional comedy, female impersonators, and male strippers. Take Queen St. from Carfax, turn left on Castle St., then right on Paradise St. Open Mon.-Sat. noon-11:30pm; Sun. noon-3pm, 7-10:30pm.

A favorite pastime in Oxford is **punting** on the River Thames (known in Oxford as the Isis) or on the River Cherwell (CHAR-wul). Punters receive a long pole and a small oar, and are advised not to fall into the river. Don't be surprised if you suddenly come upon **Parson's Pleasure,** a small riverside area where men sometimes sunbathe nude. Female passersby are expected to open their parasols and tip them at a discreet angle to obscure the view. Three companies rent punts—long boats like shallow gondolas. **Oxford Punting Co.,** Folly Bridge (tel. (01223) 327280), St. Aldates St., south of Carfax and across from Head of the River pub, rents from June to September (weekdays £4/hr, £20 deposit, weekends £6/hr, £30 deposit) and from March to May (£3/hr. weekdays, £5/hr. weekends). **Riverside Boating Co.,** Folly Bridge (tel. 721600), behind Head of the River pub, rents from April to September (£6/hr, £20 deposit.; open daily 10am-dusk). Or try **Magdalen Bridge Boat Co.,** Magdalen Bridge (tel. 202643), east of Carfax along High St. (£7/hr, £20 plus ID deposit; open March-Nov. daily 10am-9pm). Call **Salter Brothers,** Folly Bridge (tel. 243421) for cruises to Iffley (5/day; 40min.; £3.15, child £1.90) and Abingdon (2/day; 2hrs.; £8.25, children £5.70; open May-Oct. daily 9am-5:30pm). If you won't punt yourself, at least take a seat on the deck of the **Head of the River** pub at Folly Bridge (see Oxford: Pubs, above) and watch braver souls go by.

The university celebrates **Eights Week** at the end of May, when all the colleges enter crews in the bumping races and beautiful people gather on the banks to nibble strawberries and sip champagne. In early September, **St. Giles Fair** invades one of Oxford's main streets with an old-fashioned carnival, complete with Victorian roundabout and whirligigs. Daybreak on May 1 brings one of Oxford's loveliest moments: the Magdalen College Choir greets the summer by singing madrigals from the top of the tower to a crowd below, and the town indulges in morris dancing, beating the bounds, and other age-old rituals of merrymaking—pubs open at 7am.

■ NEAR OXFORD

The largest private home in England (also one of the loveliest) and birthplace of Winston Churchill, **Blenheim Palace** (BLEN-em, tel. (01993) 811325) was built in appreciation of the Duke of Marlborough's victory over Louis XIV's armies at the Battle of Blenheim in 1704, and as a token of Queen Anne's friendship with the Duke's wife Sarah. The palace's rent is currently a single French franc, payable each year to the Crown. Sir John Vanbrugh's design is at once immense and coherent. Blenheim has rambling grounds designed by Capability Brown, as well as a lake and a fantastic garden center. Whilst attending a party here, Churchill's mother gave birth to the future cigar smoker and Prime Minister in a closet. (Palace open mid-March to Oct. daily 10:30am-4:45pm. Grounds open daily 9am-5pm. £6.90, children £3.30, includes a boat trip on the lake.) Blenheim sprawls in **Woodstock,** 8 mi. north of Oxford on the A34; **Thames Transit** (tel. (01865) 727000) runs buses from bay #2 at the Oxford bus station (2/hr; 25 min.). **Spires and Shires** (tel. (01865) 251785) offers daily bus tours to Blenheim from Broad St. and the Oxford train station (2/day, both in the morning; £7.50, children £5). A tidy little village,

Woodstock flutters with shops and pubs. Geoffrey Chaucer once lived here, and Winston Churchill is lain in the nearby village churchyard of **Bladon.**

■■■ COTSWOLDS

Stretching across the west of England, these whimsical hills enfold small towns barely encroached upon by modern life. Hewn straight from the famed Cotswold Stone (termed oolite after the microscopic sea creatures that comprise it), Saxon villages and Roman settlements link a series of trails accessible to walker and cyclist both. Walls of the same stone interlace and delimit rugged fields dotted with sheep and linseed. Rounding a bend in the road it's easy (and disconcerting) to mistake an expanse of purple linseed for a body of water. Townspeople and tourists alike traverse the Cotswold terrain, skirting pastureland and treading near larger cities. The slow flow of honey from a spoon matches the pace of life in these honey-colored stone villages.

GETTING THERE

The Cotswolds lie mostly in Gloucestershire, bounded by Banbury in the northeast, Bradford-upon-Avon in the southwest, Cheltenham in the north, and Malmesbury in the south. The range hardly towers: a few areas in the north and west rise above 1000 ft. but the average Cotswold hill reaches only 600 ft. A 52-mi. long unbroken ridge, **The Edge** (not to be confused with a certain Irish rock musician), dominates the western reaches of the Cotswolds.

Though not readily accessible by public transportation, the Cotswolds demand entry into any itinerary. Trains and buses frequent the area's major gateways (Cheltenham, Bath, Gloucester, and Cirencester), but buses between the villages themselves are few and far between. Several companies which operate under the auspices of the county government cover the Gloucestershire Cotswolds, comprising most of the range. The inclusive and far-reaching *Connection* timetable is free, indispensable, and available from all area bus stations and tourist offices.

Various firms offer **coach tours** of the Cotswolds, departing from Cheltenham, Cirencester, Gloucester, Stroud, and Tewkesbury. The cost of such journeys varies by duration and destination. Inquire at the tourist information centers for more information. **Marchant's Coaches,** 61 Clarence St., Cheltenham (tel. (01242) 522714) offers excursions to 16 Cotswold villages for £3. Call ahead, for such trips are specially scheduled. In addition, **Guide Friday** and **Mad Max** offer guided tours of the area (see Stratford: Practical Information).

PRACTICAL INFORMATION

Tourist offices in the area (listed north to south) include:

- **Chipping Camden:** Woolstaplers Hall Museum, at High St., Glos. GL55 6HB (tel. (01386) 840289). Open April-Sept.
- **Broadway:** 1 Cotswold Court, Worc. WR12 7AA (tel. (01386) 852937). Open April-Sept.
- **Stow-on-the-Wold:** Hollis House, The Square (tel. (01451) 831082).
- **Cirencester:** Corn Hall, Market Pl., Glos. GL7 2NW (tel. (01285) 654180).
- **Cheltenham:** 77 The Promenade, Glos. GL50 1PP (tel. (01242) 522878).
- **Gloucester:** St. Michael's Tower, The Cross, Glos. GL1 1PD (tel. (01452) 421188).
- **Bath:** the Colonnades, 11-13 Bath St., Avon BA1 1SW (tel. (01225) 462831).

ACCOMMODATIONS, CAMPING, & FOOD

The **Cotswold Way Handbook** (£1) lists B&Bs along the Way; they are generally spaced 3 mi. apart in villages and offer friendly lodgings to trekkers. Call ahead in the morning to reserve lodging for the same evening. Savvy backpackers should seek shelter outside the larger towns to enjoy the silence. HI has a number of **hostels** in the area. The distance to the next closest hostel is indicated in parentheses.

Charlbury: The Laurels, The Slade, Charlbury, Oxford OX7 3SJ (tel. (01608) 810202. On the River Evenlode, 1 mi. north of Charlbury, 5 mi. northwest of Blenheim Palace, 13 mi. northwest of Oxford; off the Oxford-Worcester rail line. From town center, follow road sign-posted *Enstone*. At B4022 crossroads, go straight across; hostel is 50 yds. on left. (12 mi. from Stow-on-the-Wold hostel.) £6.30; under 18 £4.20. Open April-Aug. Mon.-Sat.; Feb-March and Sept.-Oct. Wed.-Sun.; Jan. Fri.-Sun.

Cleeve Hill: Rock House, Cleeve Hill, Cheltenham, Glos. GL52 3PR (tel. (01242) 672065), 4 mi. northeast of Cheltenham, just off B4632, next to Redmond's Hotel. Castleways (Winchcombe) bus from Royal Well in Cheltenham stops on request at the hostel gate.; hitchers report frequent rides on the A46. ½ mi. from Way. (14 mi. from Duntisbourne hostel). No meals served, but self-catering facilities are available. Bike rentals. When Cleeve Hill is closed, contact the Duntisbourne Abbots Youth Hostel to book in advance (tel. (01285) 821682). £6.50; under 18 £4.35. Open April-Sept. Tues.-Sun.

Duntisbourne Abbots: Cirencester, Glos. GL7 7JN (tel. (01285) 821682), off the A417, 5 mi. northwest of Cirencester. (14 mi. from Cleeve Hill hostel.) 19th-century rectory set in 2 acres of grounds. Home cooking will make your taste buds happy. £7.15, under 18 £4.75. Open March-early Nov. Mon.-Sat.; Dec. 24-28 daily.

Slimbridge: Shepherd's Patch, Slimbridge, Glos. GL2 7BP (tel. (01453) 890275), across from the Tudor Arms Pub, next to the swing bridge. Comes complete with its own ponds and wildfowl. Off the A38 and the M5, 4 mi. from the Cotswold Way and ½ mi. from the Wild Fowl Trust Reserve and Wetlands Centre. 56 beds; showers and dinner; small store. (22 mi. from Cleeve Hill hostel.) £8.40, under 18 £5.60. Open April-Sept. daily; early Jan.-March and Oct.-Nov. Mon.-Sat.

Stow-on-the-Wold: The Square, Cheltenham, Glos. GL54 1AF (tel. (01451) 30497). On the east side of this hilltop village, between the White Hart Hotel and the Old Stocks. On the A424 highway; Pulham's bus passes about every hr. from Cheltenham (17 mi.), Bourton-on-the-Water, and Moreton-in-Marsh (4 mi.). Comfortable rooms, knowledgeable warden. Call ahead; it's small. (12 mi. from Charlbury hostel.) £6.50,under 18 £4.35. Lockout 10am-5pm. Inexpensive breakfast, packed lunch, and evening meals available. 42 beds. Annex with 18 beds. Self-catering kitchen. Open March-Oct. daily; Feb. and Nov.-Dec. Fri.-Sun.

Campsites congregate close to Cheltenham; the villages Bourton-on-the-Water, Stow-on-the-Wold, and Moreton-on-the-Marsh also provide convenient places to bivouac. When in doubt consult the *Gloucestershire Caravan and Camping Guide*, free (and annually updated) at local tourist centers.

You'll never go hungry in the Cotswolds. Supermarkets, fast food establishments, and full-fledged restaurants call larger towns like Cheltenham and Cirencester home; country pubs crop up every 3 mi. or so in hamlets and villages along the way. For a selection of inns and teahouses in the Cotswolds, check at the local tourist office for the free leaflet *Cotswold Fayre*.

HIKING THROUGH COTSWOLD VILLAGES

Experience England as the English have for centuries by treading well-worn footpaths from village to village. Speed-walking will enable you to see several settlements in a day, which proves especially convenient for daytrippers based in Cheltenham. Those in search of long-distance hiking routes have a choice between a handful of carefully marked trails. B&Bs and pubs rest conveniently within reach of both the **Cotswold Way** and the **Oxfordshire Way.** Local roads are perfect for biking, and the rolling hills welcome casual and hardy cyclers alike; the closely-spaced, tiny villages make ideal watering holes. Check listings for local spring-time festivities like cheese rolling or woolsack races, where participants dash up and down hills laden with 60 pounds.

The more extensive of the two, the Cotswold Way, spans just over 100 mi. from Bath to Chipping Camden. The way affords glorious vistas of hills and dales and thankfully tends to be uncrowded. The entire walk can be done in about a week at a pace of about 15 mi. per day. Due to pock-marks and gravel, certain section of the path are not suitable for biking and horseback riding. What's more, many sections cross pastureland; cyclists and horses disturb Cotswold sheep and cattle, two breeds we're told it's fatal to mess with. Consult the Cotswold Voluntary Warden Service (tel. (01452) 425674) for details. Tourist information centers sell trail guides especially designed for the cyclist. Also available at the centers, the *Cotswold Way Handbook* (£1) provides a basic guide to the area, and Mark Richard's *Cotswold Way: A Walker's Guide* (£3) has maps and explicit directions. For additional reference, consult Ordnance Survey Maps 1:50,000: sheets #151 (Stratford), 150 (Worcester and the Malverns), 163 (Cheltenham), 162 (Gloucester), and 172 (Bath and Bristol). In addition, the Cotswolds Voluntary Warden Service provides guided walks through the Cotswolds. Tourist information centers provide free pamphlets with information about the routes, and how to reserve a spot.

Years back, quiet **Chipping Camden** became the capital of the rampant Cotswold wool trade. Later, the village became a market center ("chipping" means "market"). The town currently gathers in fame for its **Dover Games,** highlighted by the obscure sport of shin-kicking. This sadistic activity was prohibited from 1852 to 1952, but has since been enthusiastically revived in late May and early June to the glee of local bone-setters (tickets available day of game).

Only 3 mi. west of Chipping Campden, restored Tudor, Jacobean, and Georgian buildings scheme to make **Broadway** a museum. Above every street peek traditional roofs of Cotswold tile or thick thatch, jaunting through practically every century. Since it became a bus stop on the London-Worcester route in the 16th century, Broadway has bustled with visitors. **Broadway Tower** enchanted the likes of the decorator/designer/poet William Morris and his pre-Raphaelite comrade Dante Gabriel Rossetti; their antics and artistic temperaments may have unnerved some of the townsfolk, but today Morris is celebrated as a fine artist throughout the Cotswolds. Built in the late-1700s in an attempt to intensify the beauty of the landscape, the tower affords a view of 14 counties (tel. (01386) 852390; open early April-late Oct. daily 10am-6pm; £2.75, children £1.75).

Confirm your suspicion that Cotswold settlers looked no further than their backyards for building materials in **Stow-on-the-Wold,** "where the cold winds blow." Situated on a hillside, many of the town's streets feature fine views of the surrounding fields. Stick your feet into Stow's authentic stocks and snap a photo (everybody else does it). A few yards away from the stocks stands an **HI Youth Hostel** (see Cotswolds: Accommodations, above).

The Oxfordshire Way (65 mi.) runs between the popular hyphen-havens of Bourton-on-the-Water and Henley-on-Thames. A comprehensive *Walker's Guide* can be found in tourist offices. To while away a morning or afternoon, plod over cow paddies to wend your way from Bourton-on-the-Water to Lower and Upper Slaughter along the **Warden's Way.** Parts of the footpaths are hospitable to cyclists, though slightly rut-ridden. Most adventurous souls can continue on to Winchcombe for a total of about 14 mi. In addition, the Cotswolds Voluntary Warden Service provides inexpensive **guided walks** through the Cotswolds. Tourist information centers proffer free leaflets with details about the routes and how to reserve a spot.

Like the proverbial lamb, travel a few mi. southwest to the **Slaughters (Upper and Lower),** a pair of tranquil villages. Fortunately, your visit will be heralded by a whole host of sheep, not an insane butcher. Footpaths connect Upper and Lower Slaughter and also lead to **Bourton-on-the-Water**. Rather inexplicably touted as "Venice of the Cotswolds" (no gondolas, just a stream and a series of footbridges), Bourton hosts its fair share of tourists. The town merits a stopover on any whirlwind tour of the Cotswolds, if only for afternoon cream tea in one of its many tearooms. Many of the larger trails (The Cotswold Way, Oxfordshire Way) converge at Bourton. A tourist information point can be found at the Edinburgh Woollen Mill on High St. (tel. (01451) 820323). Between the heaven and hell of rose-laden gates and fields strewn with sheep dung lies **The Cotswold Perfumery** on Victoria St. (tel. (01451) 820698; open daily 9:30am-5pm, sometimes later in summer; £1.30, seniors and children £1; wheelchair accessible).

West of Stow-on-the-Wold and 6 mi. north of Cheltenham on the A46, **Sudeley Castle** (tel. (01242) 602308) at the home of Lord and Lady Ashcombe dominates **Winchcombe.** Once the manor estate of King Ethelred the Unready, the castle was a prized possession in the Middle Ages, with lush woodland and a royal deer park. The Queens Garden is streamlined by a pair of yew-hedge corridors leading to rose and herb beds; Charles I's four-poster bed sits in carved glory among the rich furnishings, armor, and paintings that ornament the castle's interior. Well-maintained **St. Mary's Church** contains the tomb of Queen Katherine Parr. The castle also schedules falconry shows. (Open April-Oct. daily noon-5pm; £4.75, children £2.50, under 5 free; gardens only £3.10, children £1.40, family ticket £12.)

Prehistoric tracks, Doc Marten prints, and sheep dung prevail across the Cotswolds. Archaeologists have unearthed some 70 habitation sites as well. **Belas Knap,** a gargantuan anthill to the innocent eye, is actually a 4000-yr.-old burial mound. The laterally chambered long barrow stands about 1½ mi. southwest of Sudeley Castle, and is accessible from the Cotswold Way. The **Rollright Stones,** off the A34 between Chipping Norton and Long Compton, comprise a 100-ft.-wide ring of 11 stones. Other sites are scattered throughout the Cotswolds; consult Ordnance Survey Tourist Map #8 (£4.25).

The Cotswolds contain some of the best examples of Roman settlements in Britain—most notably **Cirencester** and **Chedworth** in the center. Sometimes regarded as the capital of the region, Cirencester is the site of Corinium, a Roman town founded in 49 AD and second in importance only to Londinium. Cirencester today largely caters to its older population; the town's small and the pension crowd's large, so a queue forms at the post office ten minutes prior to opening. Stay in Cheltenham and take a daytrip to see the Roman remains. Although only scraps of the ampitheater still exist, the **Corinium Museum,** Park St. (tel. (01285) 655611), has culled a formidable collection of Roman paraphernalia, including a hare mosaic comprised of thousands of tessarae (tiny handworked bits of ceramic) and implements from everyday life (open Mon.-Sat. 10am-5pm, Sun. 2-5pm; Oct.-March Tues.-Sat. 10am-5pm, Sun. 2-5pm; £1.25, seniors and students £1, children 75p). The second longest yew hedge in England bounds Lord Bathwist's mansion in the center of town; the garden behind the home, scattered with Roman ruins, provides the perfect place for an afternoon stroll. On Fridays, the entire town turns into a bedlamic marketplace; a smaller, crafts fair manifests every Saturday inside Corn Hall at the Marketplace (near the tourist office). Stop by the **Golden Cross** on Black Jack St. or the **Crown** at West Market Pl. near the Abbey for a pint. B&Bs cluster a few minutes from downtown along Victoria Rd. Prices are steep, but it is possible to barter.

In the little village of **Painswick,** halfway between Cheltenham and Cirencester, England's oldest post office still sorts mail. In the village churchyard, 99 yew trees grow among the tombstones. According to legend, that is all that the yard will bear; with each 100th tree that is planted, another dies.

Tucked away in the Chedworth hills southwest of Cheltenham is a well-preserved **Roman villa** (tel. (01242) 89256), equidistant from Cirencester and Northleach off the A429. The famed Chedworth mosaics were discovered in 1864, when a gamekeeper noticed fragments of tile uncovered by clever rabbits (open March-Oct. Tues.-Sun. 10am-5:30pm; Nov. Wed.-Sun. 11am-6pm; £2.25).

Slimbridge, 12½ mi. southwest of Gloucester off the A38, is the largest of the Wildfowl Trust's seven centers in Britain. Sir Peter Scott has cached the world's largest collection of wildfowl here, with a total of over 180 different species. All six varieties of flamingos nest here, and white-fronted geese visit from their Siberian homeland. In the tropical house, hummingbirds and tanagers skim through jungle foliage. The visitors center has exhibitions, films, and food, glorious food (tel. (01453) 890065; open daily 9:30am-5pm, in winter until 4pm; £3, children £1.50). The Slimbridge **HI Youth Hostel** (see Cotswolds: accommodations, above) benefits from Sir Peter's aviary efforts, as well, hosting its own flocks of wild birds.

■■■ CHELTENHAM

Cheltenham (pop. 86,500) exudes elegance. Beautifully manicured gardens, expensive shops, and immaculate terraces attest to the town's past as a posh spa. The budget traveler need not be dismayed by the Laura Ashley-esque quality of this town; its flower-lined streets, plush gardens, and free waters offer an affordable respite from the heavily touristed centers of Bath and Stratford or the gloomy industrial megaliths of Bristol and Birmingham.

GETTING THERE

Cheltenham lies 43 mi. south of Birmingham. Trains run regularly to London (1/hr.; 2½hr.; £22.50), Bath (1/hr.; 1½hr.; £9.50), and Exeter (every 2 hr.; 2hr.; £21).

Frequent **buses** pull into **Royal Well,** behind the tourist office. **National Express** runs to London (1/hr.; 3hr.; £16); Bristol (every 2 hr.; 1¼hr.; £6.75), Bath (2/day; 2½hr.; £7.50), and Exeter (every 2 hr.; 3½hr.; £17). **Swanbrook Coaches** (tel. 574 444) also run to Oxford (£3.50) and London (4/day, 2/Sun.; £9). Pick up the tourist office's free edition of *Getting There*.

ORIENTATION & PRACTICAL INFORMATION

The majority of attractions in Cheltenham trickle through a compact square bounded by Albion St. to the north, Bath Rd. to the east, Oriel Rd. to the south, and Royal Well Rd. to the west. The **Promenade** is the main street in town and home to the tourist office. To reach the tourist office from the train station, walk down Queen's Rd. and bear left onto Lansdown Rd. Bear left again at the Rotunda onto Montpellier Walk, which leads to the Promenade. Or jump on one of the frequent F or G buses (54p). From the bus station, Royal Well, walk around the block.

Tourist Office: Municipal Offices, 77 Promenade (tel. 522878), 1 block east of the bus station. Vacancies posted after hours. Open June-Sept. Mon.-Fri. 9:30am-6pm, Sat. 9:30am-5pm, July-Aug. also Sun. 10am-4pm; Oct.-May Mon.-Sat. 9:30am-5pm.

Financial Services: Thomas Cook, 159 High St. (tel. 233601). Open Mon.-Wed. and Fri.-Sat. 9am-5:30pm, Thurs. 10am-5:30pm. **Barclays,** 128 High St. Open Mon.-Fri. 9:30am-4:30pm, Sat. 9:30am-noon. **American Express,** Grosvenor House, 4 Oriel Terrace (tel. 582 642). Open Mon.-Fri. 9am-5:30pm.

Post Office: 227 High St. (tel. 526056). Open Mon.-Fri. 9am-5:30pm, Sat. 9am-12:30pm. **Postal Code:** GL50 1AA.

Telephone Code: 01242.

Train Station: Lansdown Station, Queen's Rd. at Gloucester Rd. (tel. (01452) 529501 for schedules). Ticket office open Mon.-Sat. 8am-8pm, Sun. 9am-6pm.

Bus Station: Royal Well (tel. 584111), Royal Crescent. National Express has a temporary office there, but tickets can also easily be bought at **National Travel World,** 229 High St. (tel. 575606). Open Mon.-Fri. 9am-5:30pm, Sat. 9am-4:30pm. Bus schedules posted.

Taxi: Central Taxi: tel. 526611. **Associated Taxis:** tel. 523523.

Bike Rental: Crabtrees, 50 Winchcombe St. (tel. 515291). Mountain bikes £8/day, £35/wk.; deposit £50. Open Mon.-Sat. 9am-5:30pm, Sun. 10am-4pm.

Launderette: Soap-n-Suds, 312 High St. Open daily 8am-8pm. Last wash 7pm.

Market Day: At the race course; open-air. Sun. 10am-2pm.

Crisis: Samaritans, 3 Clarence Rd. (tel. 515777).

Hospital: Cheltenham General, Sandford Rd. (tel. 222222). Follow the Bath Rd. southwest from town, turn left onto Sandford. Near the college.

Emergency: Dial 999; no coins required.

Police: Lansdown Rd. (tel. 528282 or 521321). From the town center follow Promenade until it becomes Montpellier Walk. Lansdown is on the right.

ACCOMMODATIONS & FOOD

Prices for Cheltenham's B&Bs tend to be high; luckily, the standards are, too. The tourist office publishes a thick booklet to help plan your stay. Though day-trips from Oxford and other locales are possible, Cheltenham makes an excellent stopover for

HEART OF ENGLAND ■ 233

CHELTENHAM

cyclists and walkers traveling the Cotswolds. A handful of B&Bs can be found in the Montpellier area of town and along Bath Rd.

- **HI Youth Hostel,** Rock House, Cleeve Hill (tel. 672065), 4 mi. north of Cheltenham, next to Redmond's Hotel. Castleways buses (tel. 602949) run Mon.-Sat. 1/hr. 8:30am-10pm, Sun. 3/day. Or try Marchant's Coach at the main bus station. The hostel stuffs 44 beds into three rooms. £6.50, under 18 £4.35. Open April-Sept. Tues.-Sun.
- **YMCA,** Vittoria Walk (tel. 524024). At Town Hall, turn left off Promenade and walk three blocks—it's on the right (look for the "Y"). Men and women. Large and well-located with standard rooms and a helpful staff. Office open 24hrs. Porter lets guests in after 11pm. Caters mostly to long-term tenants, but singles are available for £12.25. Continental breakfast included.
- **Hamilton Guest House,** 65 Bath Rd. (tel. 527772). High ceilings, furniture a mother would adore, and TVs. English breakfast, but French, German, Chinese, and Spanish spoken. £16 per person, £18 with bath.
- **Cheverel,** Western Rd. (tel. 517159), at the corner of St. George's Rd. Grandfather clocks and somber furniture. Quiet neighborhood. Bath, no shower (shared facilities). English breakfast. £15 per person.
- **Cross Ways,** 57 Bath Rd. (tel. 527683). Clean rooms, floral inside and out. Informative proprietor. TVs, coffee/tea-making facilities in each room. £16 per person.
- **Camping: Longwillows,** Station Rd., Woodmancote (tel. (01242) 674 113), 3½ mi. off the F3 north of Cheltenham. Take the A435 (Evesham Rd.) north toward Evesham and turn off at Bishops Cleeve onto Station Rd.; it's on the left after the railway bridge. 80 sites. Bar and restaurant on grounds. £5.50/tent. Open March-Oct.

Food in Cheltenham runs the gamut from fast food to haute cuisine; supermarkets and the tautological **Fruity Fruit Store** occupy High St. and Clarence St. **Sainsbury** supermarket sells sundries at 257 High St. (open Mon. 8:30-6pm, Tues.-Wed. 8:30am-7pm, Thurs.-Fri. 8:30am-8pm, Sat. 8am-6pm). **Peppers Vegetarian Restaurant,** 317 High St. (tel. 234232), pampers vegetarians on its outdoor patio (entrees under £4; open Mon.-Wed. 11am-9pm, Thurs.-Fri. 11am-10:30pm, Sat. 10am-10:30pm, Sun. noon-3pm). **Bella Pasta,** 23 Promenade, is a link in a chain that dishes up pasta and pizza for £4-9 (open daily 11am-11pm; children under 12 eat free Sun.). For wholesome food near the theater, try **Tucketts,** 16 Regent St. (tel. 262664; sandwiches and salads from £2.70, larger meals £4-6; open Mon.-Wed. 10am-5pm, Thurs.-Sat. 10am-9pm). Tables are scarce on weekend nights at **Moran's,** 127-9 Bath Rd. (tel. 581411), which combines excellent food and a young, lively atmosphere. Crowded **Montpellier Wine Bar** on Queen's Parade (tel. 527774) also offers tasty bites. The tourist office serves *What's Cooking in Cheltenham* (free), a food guide indexed by type of cuisine and price range.

SIGHTS

Cheltenham proudly possesses the only **naturally alkaline water** in Great Britain. King George III took the waters in 1788, and in the 19th century the Duke of Wellington claimed that the spring cured his "disordered liver." You need not have one of your own to enjoy the diuretic and laxative effects of the waters at the **Town Hall** (open Mon.-Fri. 9am-1pm and 2:15pm-5pm; free) or at the **Pittville Pump Room** in Pittville Park (tel. 512740), which also houses a **Museum** and a rather dull **Gallery of Fashion** (open Tues.-Sat. 11am-3:30pm; May-Sept. also Sun. 11am-4:20pm; museum open June-Sept. Tues.-Sat. 10am-4:20pm, Sun. and bank holidays 11am-4:20pm; pump room free; museum £1.50, children 50p). Thrifty and sensible travelers will do well to see the pump room from the outside and venture in only to taste the water. **Pittville Park** hosts Sunday concerts and brunches in the summer (tel. 261017 for reservations). The Pump Room and Town Hall occasionally serve as the venues for a wide range of entertainment, from symphonies to cabarets to big band music (tel. 523690 for tickets; free May-Sept.).

The **Cheltenham Art Gallery and Museum** (tel. 237431) houses an impressive collection of pottery, mementos of the Arts and Crafts movement, and curious curios like a pewter collection, a late 18th-century Ewbank carpet sweeper, and wooden bird-scares (open Mon.-Sat. 10am-5:20pm; free). The Gallery is on Clarence St., two blocks from the bus station. The **Gustav Holst Birthplace Museum,** 4 Clarence Rd. (not Clarence *Street*, tel. 524846), presents a picture of middle-class family life in the Regency and Victorian periods as worthwhile as the museum's stated purpose, the portrayal of the composer's early life. Born here into a family of musicians, Holst enjoyed only a brief period of astronomical popularity during his lifetime. Follow the signs in the general direction of the bus station, then walk one block farther to Clarence Rd. (open Tues.-Sat. 10am-4:20pm; £1.50, children 50p).

A one-block stroll over from the Promenade immerses you in the city's shopping district. If you're traveling with a Gold Card, stroll down Regent's Arcade between Regent St. and Rodney Rd. For continental ambience, promenade along **Montepellier Walk,** where *caryatids* (female figures used as pillars) guard everything from banks to tobacconists. Sunbathe with bouffants and bikers alike at the **Imperial Gardens,** just past the Promenade away from the center of town. Exquisite blooms indicate why Cheltenham has thrice received the prestigious Britain in Bloom award. The Gardens also provide the mood for Summer Sunday band **concerts** (2:30-4:30pm; free) and occasional open-air **art exhibits** (usually June and July, but check with the tourist office).

ENTERTAINMENT

The monthly *What's On,* posted around town on kiosks and available free from the tourist office, will fill you in on the many concerts, plays, and evening hotspots. **Everyman Theatre** on Regent St. (tel. 572573) is a stop for traveling performers such as dancers from the London City Ballet, though it primarily hosts local professional theater (tickets £4-12.50). The **Playhouse Theatre,** Bath Rd. (tel. 522852), stages amateur productions on Monday nights (open Mon.-Sat. 10am-4pm).

For a relaxing pint and good conversation, try **Peter's Bar** on Montpellier Walk or **Dobell's,** #24 on the Promenade (both open Mon.-Sat. 11am-11pm, Sun. noon-2:30pm and 7-10:30pm). If you'd prefer to dance, head to **Gas,** St. James Square (tel. 527700; cover £3-5; open daily 9pm-2am), or **Ritzy** on the Bath Rd. (tel. 242751). Every day has its own theme (house, funk, 60s, hip-hop, alternative); cover charge and dress code vary with the tunes (£1 to £7; open daily 9pm-2am). **Axiom Centre for the Arts**, 57-59 Winchcombe St. (tel. 253183), provides a venue for activities as diverse as yoga, crafts, and juggling; the center also houses a bar with frequent live music (£1-4 cover), an art gallery, and a theater.

Cheltenham hosts superb cultural events; most notable is the **Cheltenham International Festival of Music** in early July, now celebrating its 50th year of classical music, opera, dance, theater, and professional singers. Fringe concerts feature jazz and folk music. Many of the fringe festivities can be enjoyed for free, including a picnic in the park and a fireworks exhibit. Full details are available in March from the box office (tel. 227979), Town Hall, Imperial Sq., Cheltenham, Glos. GL50 1QA. Tickets are available first come, first serve; prices range from £1.50-19.

The oldest (and longest) in the country, the **Cheltenham Cricket Festival** commences in early August. Tickets can be purchased at the gate (inquire about game times at the tourist office). October heralds the **Cheltenham Festival of Literature,** which runs for a fortnight. Poets, prose writers, and playwrights converge on Cheltenham for readings, lectures, and seminars. Recent writers at the festival include Kingsley Amis, P. D. James, and Stephen Spender. For a full program of events, write to the Town Hall (address above). Tickets can be bought in advance (£1.50-4).

■ NEAR CHELTENHAM: TEWKESBURY

Ten mi. northwest of Cheltenham, on the A38 to Worcester and at the confluence of the Rivers Avon and Severn, lies **Tewkesbury.** Consecrated in 1121, stately

Tewkesbury Abbey (tel. (01684) 850959), is surrounded by expansive grounds that lead out into the countryside. The abbey stands today after townsfolk subscribed £453 to save it from Henry VIII's planned dissolution (open Mon.-Sat. 7:30am-5:30pm, Sun. 7:30am-7pm; in summer, open 30 min. later Mon.-Sat.; abbey services Sun. at 8am, 9:15am, 11am, and 6pm; matins, evensong, and guided tours daily). The **Old Baptist Chapel,** Church St., dating from 1480, is newly restored (open daily 10am-6pm; free). The **Country Park,** Crickley Hill (tel. (012152) 863170), once an Iron Age fort, offers ethereal views and items of archaeological interest.

Museums dot the town: the **Tewkesbury Town Museum,** 64 Barton St. (tel. (01684) 297174), displays models of the town and the Battle of Tewkesbury (open daily 10am-1pm and 2-5pm; 50p, children 25p). The **John Moore Museum,** Church St. (tel. (01684) 297174), has rustic exhibits and emphasizes conservation (open Easter-Oct. Tues.-Sat. 10am-1pm and 2-5pm; 40p, children and seniors 20p). The **Little Museum,** Church St., is a medieval merchant's cottage built in 1450 and restored in 1970 (open Easter-Oct. Tues.-Sat. 10am-1pm and 2-5pm; free).

Stay at Mrs. Warnett's **Crescent Guest House,** 30 Church St. (tel. (01684) 293395), for £16 (all doubles include color TV and washbasin) or Mrs. Wells' **Hanbury Terrace** (tel. (01684) 299911) for £15, or £17 with bath (non-smokers only). Stop by the town's **tourist office,** The Museum, 64 Barton St. (tel. (01684) 295027), with any questions (open Mon.-Sat. 10am-5pm).

Marchant's Coaches (tel. (01684) 522714) run from Cheltenham through Bishop's Cleeve (Mon.-Fri. 5/day, Sat. 2/day, Sun. 4/day; 30min.). **Cheltenham District** buses (tel. (01684) 522021) depart every hour til 5pm (Mon.-Sat.).

■■■ WORCESTER

Those who have grown to love its spicy brown sauce won't find Worcester quite so tasteful. Halfway between Cheltenham and Birmingham, Worcester (WOOS-ter; pop. 90,000) lacks both the gentility of the former and the frenetic pace of the latter. Site of the Civil War's final battle, Worcester spreads out from a captivating cathedral at river's edge.

GETTING THERE

Trains connect Worcester, 25 mi. south of Birmingham, to London (1/hr.; 2½hr.; £24.70), Birmingham (every ½hr. from 9am-6pm; £5), Oxford (1/hr.; 1½hr.; £8.80), and Cheltenham (1/hr.; ¼hr.; £4.80). **Buses** arrive and depart from the station on Angel Pl.: **National Express** runs to London (2/day; 4hr.; £14), Birmingham (1/hr.; 1hr.; day return £8.80), and Bristol (2/day; 1½hr.; day return £4.70). A **Midland Red West Day Rover** ticket (£3.50, seniors £2.70, children £2.10, family £7) allows unlimited one-day travel throughout the region.

ORIENTATION & PRACTICAL INFORMATION

The city center is bounded on the northern end by the train station and by the cathedral on the southern side. A pedestrian street spans the length between the two; this fickle street switches names along the way from The Foregate to The Cross to High St. To reach town from the rail station, proceed south along Foregate St. from the bus station, turn left onto Broad St. and right onto The Cross.

Tourist Office: The Guildhall, High St. (tel. 726311). Quiet and packed with pamphlets for the taking. Open mid-March-late Oct. 10:30am-5:30pm; Nov.-mid-March 10:30am-4pm.

Tours: 1½-hr. tours from the Guildhall (May-Aug. Wed. 11am and 2:30pm.) £2, children £1.

Financial Services: Thomas Cook, 26 High St. (tel. 28228), across from the Guildhall. Open Mon.-Wed. and Fri. 9am-5pm, Thurs. 10am-5pm, and Sat. 9am-5pm. **Lloyds,** The Cross. Open Mon.-Fri. 9:30am-5:30pm. **National Westmin-**

WORCESTER

ster, The Cross. Open Mon.-Tues. and Thurs.-Fri. 9am-5:30pm, Wed. 9:30am-5:30pm, Sat. 9:30am-3:30pm.

Post Office: 8 Foregate St. (tel. 23208), next to the train station. *Bureau de Change. Poste Restante.* Open Mon.-Tues., Thurs.-Fri. 9am-5:30pm, Wed. 9:30am-5:30pm, Sat. 9am-12:30pm. **Postal Code:** WR1 1AA.

Telephone Code: 01905.

Train Stations: Foregate St. (serving travelers going through Birmingham) in the town center, next to the post office. Ticket window open Mon.-Sat. 6:30am-6pm; Sun. 10:15am-5:45pm. Travel Centre open Mon.-Fri. 9am-4pm, Sat. 9am-2pm. Telephone inquiries: (01452) 529501 or (0121) 643 2711. Also **Shrub Hill Station** (mainly serving the southwest), just outside town. To get to town from Shrub Hill Station, take a right onto Shrub Hill Rd., then a left onto Tolladine Rd., which becomes Lowesmoor. Follow Lowesmoor to St. Nicholas St., which intersects Foregate, the town's main drag. A 10-min. walk. British Rail serves both stations.

Bus Station: Angel Place (tel. 25255), off Broad St. Depot at Newport St. For info call **Midland Red West** (tel. 23296 or 24898) or **National Express** (tel. (0121) 623 4373). For local bus info, call **Citibus** (tel. 763888).

Taxis: The Cross and High St. or call Associated Radio Taxis (tel. 763939).

Bike Rental: Peddlers, 46 Barbourne. Rentals £5/day, £25/week, £50 deposit/bike. Open Mon.-Sat. 10am-6pm.

River Trips on the Severn: **Bickerline River Trips** (tel. 25973) from South Quay near the cathedral. Daily 1-hr. trips in the summer 11am, noon, 1, 3:45, and 4:45pm. £2.30/person. Small boats also available for hire along the North and South Quay.

Launderette: Severn Laun-Dri, 22 Barbourne Rd., across from the Esso station. Change machine. Open daily 9am-9pm; last wash 8pm.

Market Day: Shambles Indoor Market with fruits and vegetables open Mon.-Sat. 9am-5:30pm. **Angel Pl.** open Tues.-Sat. 8:30am-4:30pm (Thursday is a bric-a-brac market).

Way Cool Toilet: Try it, you'll like it. Space-age facility automatically sanitizes after each use. Copenhagen St., off High St. 10p.

Hotline: Samaritans: 21121. **Gay and Lesbian Switchboard:** 723097. **AIDS:** 22957.

Hospital: Ronkswood Hospital on Newtown Rd. Bus #29D and 31A (tel. 723333).

Emergency: Dial 999; no coins required.

Police: Deansway (tel. 723888), directly behind the Guildhall, across from St. Andrew's Park.

ACCOMMODATIONS & CAMPING

B&B prices in Worcester are high, as proprietors cater to Londoners looking for a weekend in the country; the beginning and end of summer tend to be the busiest times. Call ahead or try your luck on Barbourne Rd., north of Foregate St. The nearest **HI Youth Hostel** is 7 mi. away in Malvern (see Near Worcester, below). **Osbourne House,** 17 Chestnut Walk (tel. 22296), offers tastefully decorated, dazzlingly-clean rooms with awesome electronic, touch-operated showers, and incredible flora and fauna wildpaper. The best in the city (single £16, £15 for twin/double; wheelchair accessible). Tidy, if eclectically designed and appointed rooms await lovers of vinegary sauces at the **Shrubbery Guest House,** 38 Barbourne Rd. (tel. 26731). Watch the morning news over a nourishing breakfast (sauce optional; B&B £15/person). Campers will have to take a cab to the **Millhouse Caravan and Campsite** (tel. 51283), off A44, north of Worcester (Open April-Oct.; £3.50-4.50/person). The grounds include toilets, lockers, showers, and a shop.

FOOD

You can satisfy your appetite on Friar St. or at **Sainsbury's Supermarket** (open Mon.-Thurs. 8:30am-6pm, Fri. 8:30am-7pm, Sat. 8am-6pm) in **The Shambles** on High St. **Natural Break,** off Foregate St. at The Hopmarket (tel. 26654), sells semivegetarian wholefood at good prices. Another branch pokes out at 17 Mealcheapen St. (tel. 26417). Both stores gyre and gimble Mon.-Fri. 9:30am-4pm, Sat. 9:30am-5pm. **Heroes,** 26-32 Friar St. (tel. 25451), near the Tudor House, stocks a boundless supply of bistro-style cuisine: steaks, pizza, pasta, and Mexican. Wolf mega-burgers (from £3.75; open daily 11am-11:30pm). The **Hodson Coffee House and Patisserie,** 99-100 High St. (tel. 21036), has a cafeteria-style interior and café-style garden. Try the regal coronation chicken (£4.10) or nervous gooseberries with cream (£1.40; open Mon.-Sat. 9:30am-5pm). At the **Farrier's Arms,** 9 Fish St. (tel. 27569), off High St, fresh bar meals are served under wooden beams or in the light and airy beer garden. Try their specialty fish pie (£3.25), or the veggie bake (£2.50; open Mon.-Sat. 10:30am-11pm, Sun. noon-3pm and 7-10:30pm). An always appealing option, **The Balcony Café,** Foregate St. (tel. 724488), reverberates above the Worcester City Museum and Art Gallery in its pleasant marble and stone surroundings. An iced coffee, vanilla ice cream, and whipped cream concoction goes for £1.70; sandwiches and salad from £2.30. (Open Mon.-Wed. and Fri. 9:30am-5:30pm, Sat. 9:30am-4:30pm. Wheelchair accessible.)

SIGHTS

Worcester Cathedral (tel. 28854) towers majestically by the river at the southern end of High St., cloaking a frail internal structure: the buttresses supporting the central nave have deteriorated and the central tower is in danger of collapsing. Though steel rods have been set into the tower's base, renovation efforts fail to detract from the awe-inspiring detail of the nave and choir. Worth a closer look are the pulpit (carved marble), King John's tomb, the cloister garden, the bell display (flick each one with a finger to appreciate the tones), and the tower. From Nash's passage, look over Perry Wood—here, detractors allege, Cromwell danced with the devil under pale moonlight to insure his success in the battle of Worcester. Some believe he would have won anyway (cathedral open daily 7:30am-6:30pm; choral evensong Mon.-Fri. 5:30pm, Sun. 4pm; suggested donation £1.50; free guided tours from information desk May-Sept.; Touch and Hearing Center for the visually impaired, wheelchair accessible). Cromwell's elfin morrice paid off; you can retrace the history of the 1651 Battle of Worcester at the **Commandery,** Sidbury Rd. (tel. 355071), Charles II's former headquarters (open Mon.-Sat. 10am-5pm, Sun. 1:30-5:30pm).

The **Worcester City Museum and Art Gallery,** Foregate St. (tel. 25371), near the post office, evokes the military glories and pitfalls of England and Worcester in an especially well-done regimental exhibit. It's worth the trip, if only for the cool cafe on the balcony (see Worcester: Food, above). (Open Mon.-Wed. and Fri. 9:30am-6pm, Sat. 9:30am-5pm; free). Southeast of the cathedral on Severn St., legions of blue-haired women swarm the **Royal Worcester Porcelain Company,** manufacturer of the tremendously famous and incredibly beautiful blue-red-and-gold-patterned bone-china, the finest in England. A showroom on the premises sells high-quality pieces; bargain-hunters should scour the seconds available in a shop also on the grounds. A few works in the adjacent **Dyson Perrins Museum** (tel. 23221) merit a quick look. The porcelain factory gives 45-minute tours explaining the oh-so-delightful manufacture of porcelain (open Mon.-Fri. 9:30am-5pm, Sat. 10am-5pm; free; tours Mon.-Fri. 10:25am-3:30pm; £3.25, children £2.25).

A trip to Worcester wouldn't be complete without acknowledging the birthplace of the feisty **Worcestershire Sauce,** a blue wash building on Bank St. Lea and Perrins later moved their factory to Midland Rd., near the Shrub Hill rail station. To the south, behind the Guildhall, all that remains of the demolished St. Andrew's Church is the magnificent 245-ft. spire that graces the entrance to the gardens. It is known locally as the **Glover's Needle** because of its comely shape and the area's ties with glove-making (size is everything). Left of the garden, turn onto the riverwalk that leads up the bridge to the **Worcestershire Cricket Ground,** New Road, (tel. 748474). Matches proceed at a slug's pace from 11am to 6:30pm (£7; students, children, and seniors £4; county matches £5, students, children, and seniors £3; second team and friendly matches are free, gloriously free! Call to find out specific dates).

Three mi. south of town lies **Elgar's Birthplace Museum** (tel. 333224), filled with manuscripts and memorabilia. Elgar is touted as England's greatest composer, out-ranking Holst on the classical charts. **Midland Red West** buses #312, 317, and 419/420 make the journey (10min., return £1.10). Otherwise, you can cycle 6 mi. along the Elgar trail, based on routes taken by the composer himself. (Museum open May-late Sept. Mon.-Tues. and Thurs.-Sat. 10:30am-6pm; Oct. to mid-Jan. Mon.-Tues. and Thurs.-Sat. 1:30-4:30pm; mid-Feb.-late April Mon.-Tues. and Thurs.-Fri. 1:30-4:30pm; £3, seniors £2, students £1, children 50p.)

■ NEAR WORCESTER: MALVERN

The name **Malvern** refers collectively to the contiguous towns of Great Malvern, West Malvern, Malvern Link, Malvern Wells, and Little Malvern, all of which hug the base and the eastern side of the Malvern Hills. The tops of the Malvern Hills peek over the A4108 southwest of Worcester and offer the hiker 8 mi. of accessible trails and quasi-divine visions of greenery. The **Worcestershire Way** slips through the Malverns for 36 mi. to Kingsford County Park in the north. The **Countryside Service** (tel. (01905) 766475) in the County Hall in Worcester will inform you on hiking and safety in the area. The Malvern **tourist office** (tel. (01684) 892289) at the Winter Gardens, Grange Rd., assists in hill-navigation (short distance walk pamphlets 30p; open daily 10am-5pm; Oct.-April open Mon.-Sat. 10am-5pm).

Great Malvern was built around an 11th-century parish church. Benedictine monks completely rebuilt the structure in the mid-15th century and added narrative stained glass windows. On the hillside above town, **St. Ann's Well** supplies the famous restorative "Malvern waters" that fueled Great Malvern's halcyon days as a spa town. The **priory** (tel. (01684) 892988) in Little Malvern, noted for its chancel and 15th-century stained glass, also harbors whimsical carvings of three rats attempting to hang a cat. The **Festival Theatre** (tel. (01684) 892277), built in the 1920s, hosts recitals and large-production plays as well as famous celebrities like Frankie "Mule Train" Laine and Prunella "Fawlty Towers" Scales. The **HI hostel** in Malvern, **Hatherly,** sits at 18 Peachfield Rd. in Malvern Wells (tel. (01684) 569131); take citibus #42 from Great Malvern (£6.90, under 18 £4.60; open April-Oct. daily; Feb.-March Thurs.-Mon.). The Malverns are accessible from Worcester via **British Rail** and **bus** (Mon.-Sat. 2/hr., less frequently on Sun.).

■■■ STRATFORD-UPON-AVON

It is something, I thought, to have seen the dust of Shakespeare.
—*Washington Irving*

In 1930, the owners of the Great Texas Fair cabled Stratford-upon-Avon: "Please send earth Shakespeare's garden water River Avon for dedication Shakespeare Theater Dallas Texas July 1," betraying a classic case of Bard obsession. The indoctrinated have craved Stratford's soil ever since David Garrick's 1769 Stratford jubilee—England and this town have made an industry of the Bard, emblazoning him on £20 notes and casting him and all of his long-lost twin brothers in beer advertisements. Yet this rich and strange form of relic worship has more to it than another ill-begotten encounter with Polonius in polyester. Mary Arden's house, described as the home of Shakespeare's mother, may be a complete fiction, but despite—or perhaps because of—its unverifiable or imagined associations, Stratford keeps itself in the tourist limelight. There's no business like Bard business, and this helluva town may even upstage London as the center of England's cultural consciousness.

GETTING THERE

Stratford (pop. 21,000) struts a fretful two and one-quarter hours from London by **Intercity rail** or by the bus/rail **Shakespeare Connection** (departs London Euston Mon.-Sat. 4/day, Sun. 2/day; 2 hr.; £22.50; only Shakespeare Connection operates at night after plays; tel. 294466). **National Express buses** run to and from London's Victoria Station (3/day; 3hr.; day return £13.75). The **Slow Coach** stops here on its circuit of England (consult Essentials: Getting About—Buses & Coaches for details).

ORIENTATION & PRACTICAL INFORMATION

The corner of Waterside and Bridge St., at the Crystal Shop, is as close to a bus station as Stratford gets; National Express and Midland Red South buses stop here. Local Stratford Blue service also stops on Wood St. You can buy tickets for National Express buses at the tourist office.

Tourist Office: Bridgefoot (tel. 293127). Cross Warwick Rd. at Bridge St. towards the waterside park. Books accommodations (they'll do, they'll do, and they'll do!). **American Express** (tel. 415856), is located in the tourist office. Open Mon.-Sat. 9am-6pm, Sun. 11am-5pm; Oct.-March Mon.-Sat. 9am-5pm.

Tours: Mad Max Tours (tel. (01926) 842999) run Thurs. 9am-5pm that depart from the HI hostel. Book there or call. **Guide Friday,** 14 Rother St. (tel. 294466) runs tours of Stratford Town Center daily 4/hr (£6, seniors £4, children under 12 £1.50). They also offer tours of the Cotswolds (£12, seniors £11, children £6).

Royal Shakespeare Theatre Box Office, Waterside (tel. 295623). Standby tickets for students and seniors (£8-13) available immediately before the show at the RST, the Swan, and The Other Place (tel. 292965). **24-hr. ticket information:** tel. 269191. Open Mon.-Sat. 9:30am-8pm, or until 6pm when the theater's closed.

Post Office: 2-3 Henley St. (tel. 414939). *Poste Restante. Bureau de Change.* Open Mon.-Tues. and Thurs.-Fri. 9:30am-5:30pm, Sat. 9am-12:30pm. **Postal Code:** CV37 6AA.

Telephone Code: 01789.

Train Station: off Alcester Rd. (train info tel. (01203) 555211 or (0121) 643 4444). Call **Guide Friday, Ltd.** (tel. 294466) in advance if you plan travel on the late-night Shakespeare Connection. Discount rail fares can be had by purchasing rail and theater tickets from **Theatre and Concert Travel** (tel. (01727) 41115).

Taxi: Main Taxis (tel. 414514). 24-hr. service.

Bike Rental: Clarke's Gas Station, Guild St. (tel. 205057), at Union St. Look for the Esso sign. £5.75/day, £25/week; deposit £50. Open daily 7am-9pm.

Boat Rental: Stratford Marina, Clopton Bridge (tel. 269669). Row boats £4/hr.; 4-seaters £7/hr., 6-seaters £9/hr. **Behind the RST:** rowboats £2/hr. **Next to the Stratford Marina:** £1.50, children £1, group and senior discounts. Helpful guide.

Launderette: Sparklean, Bull St. at the corner of College Lane. Open daily 9am-8pm. Near many B&Bs. Bring change.

Market Day: Fri. 8:30am-4:30pm, at the intersection of Greenhill, Windsor, Rother, and Wood St.

Hospital: Stratford-upon-Avon Hospital, Arden St. off Alcester Rd. (tel. 205831).

Emergency: Dial 999; no coins required.

Police: Rother St. (tel. 414111), up Greenhill St. from American Fountain, turn left.

ACCOMMODATIONS & CAMPING

To B&B or not to B&B? This hamlet has tons of them, but singles are hard to find. In summer, 'tis nobler to make advance reservations by phone. Guest houses (£14-18) line **Grove Road, Evesham Place,** and **Evesham Road.** (From the train station, walk down Alcester Rd., take a right on Grove Rd., and continue to Evesham Place, which becomes Evesham Rd.) If these fail you, try **Shipston** and **Banbury Road** across the river. The tourist office will put you in touch with local farms that take paying guests (£12.50-16); they'll also book B&Bs.

HI Youth Hostel, Hemmingford House, Wellesbourne Rd., Alveston (tel. 297093), 2 mi. from Stratford. Follow the B4086; take bus #518 or 18 from Wood St. (west of the tourist office), or walk. Large, attractive grounds and a 200-year-old building. Many rooms feature superb views. Vegetarian food available. 154 beds in rooms of 2-14. Kitchen. Reception open 7am-midnight, night guard on duty. Curfew midnight. £12, under 18, £8.80. Breakfast included.

The Hollies, 16 Evesham Pl. (tel. 266857). Truly warm and attentive proprietors for whom the guest house has become a labor of love. From the mint walls to the ivy scaling the outer wall, green prevails. All private facilities. TV and tea-making facilities in every room. Spacious doubles; no singles. £15.

Nando's, 18 Evesham Pl. (tel. 204907; fax reservations to the same number). Delightful owners, homey rooms. TVs in each room. Private facilities. Credit cards accepted. £16.50-20.50 per person (singles usually £19).

Ashley Court, 55 Shipston Rd. (tel. 297278). Proprietors welcome you into their spacious, immaculate guest house with rooms filled with all the luxuries. All rooms with private facilities, remote control TV, radio, tea/coffee pots. Half-acre garden in back. Only a 5-min. walk to all the sights. Doubles £38-40. £15 deposit/room required upon booking.

Field View Guest House, 35 Banbury Rd. (tel. 292694). Peaceful and refreshing accommodations with a kindly proprietor. Only an 8-min. walk to town, but less convenient to the train station. Tea and coffee-making facilities in each room. Singles £14. Doubles £28.

Greensleeves, 46 Alcester Rd. (tel. 292131), on the way to the train station. Mrs. Graham will dote on you in her cheerful home. TVs in every room. £14.

Bradbourne Guest House, 44 Shipston Rd. (tel. 204178). Easygoing proprietors offer peace and quiet in charming rooms only ¾ mi. from the center of town. Singles £14-18. Doubles £25-40. Rates lower Oct.-April. TVs and tea-making implements in every room.

Moonraker House, 40 Alcester Rd. (tel. 267115 or 299346; fax 295504). 5-10 min. from town center. Luxury rooms with near-opulent facilities. No singles. All private facilities, from £19.50 per person.

Camping: Elms, Tiddington Rd. (tel. 292312), 1 mi. northeast of Stratford on the B4086. Tent and 1 person £2.50, each additional person £1.50. Open April-Oct. **Avon Caravan Park,** Warwick Rd. (tel. 293438), 1 mi. east of Stratford on the A439. £4.50, each additional person £1.50. Open March-Oct. Both have showers.

FOOD

Faux-Tudor fast food clogs the Bard's hometown. Small grocery stores hover like itinerant minstrels along Greenhill St., and a new-ish Safeway **Supermarket** beckons on Alcester Rd. Take the Avon shuttle from town center, or walk; the store rests just across the bridge past the railway station (open Mon.-Thurs. 8am-8pm, Fri. 8am-9pm, Sat. 8am-8pm, Sun. 10am-4pm).

Café Natural, 10 Greenhill St. Behind a health food store, this acclaimed café serves elaborate vegetarian foods. Tues. discount (10%) for students and seniors. Entrees £2.50-3.15. Open Tues.-Sat. 9am-4:30pm. Full lunch served noon-2:30pm.

Kingfisher, 13 Ely St. A take-away that serves chips with everything (fish, chicken, beans). Cheap, greasy, and very popular; lines form outside. Meals £1.60-3.50. Open Mon. 11:30am-1:45pm and 5-9:30pm, Tues.-Thurs. 11:30am-1:45pm and 5-10:45pm, Fri.-Sat. 11:30am-1:45pm and 5pm-11pm.

Hussain's Indian Cuisine, 6a Chapel St. Probably Stratford's best Indian cuisine with a slew of tandoori specialties. A favorite of Ben Kingsley. 3-course lunch for £6. Open Mon.-Thurs. noon-2pm and 5:15-11:45pm, Fri.-Sat. noon-2pm and 5pm-midnight, Sun. 12:30-2:30pm and 5:30-11:45pm.

Dirty Duck Pub, Southern La. Soothing river view. Indulge. Pub lunch £1-4.25; dinners too much. Ask for sack. Open daily 11am-11:30pm.

Vintner Bistro and Cafe Bar, 5 Sheep St. (tel. 297259). Satisfying salads (£4.75-5) and uncommon desserts. Open Mon.-Sat. 10:30am-11pm, Sun. 10:30am-10:30pm.

Elizabeth the Chef/The Shakespeare Coffee House, Henley St., opposite the Birthplace. Perk up over a pot of tea surrounded by pink. Choices of baked potatoes and sandwiches galore for a cafeteria-style lunch (£1.40-3.30). Open Mon.-Sat. 9:30am-5pm, Sun. 10am-5pm.

SIGHTS

Stratford's sights are best seen before 11am (when the herds of daytrippers have not yet arrived) or after 4pm (when most have left). Bardolatry peaks at 2pm. Five official **Shakespeare properties** grace the town: Shakespeare's Birthplace and BBC Costume Exhibition, Anne Hathaway's cottage, the fictitious Mary Arden's House and Countryside Museum, Hall's Croft, and New Place or Nash House. Diehard Bard fans should purchase the **combination ticket** (£7.50, students £7, children £3.50), a savings of £3.50 if you make it to every shrine. If you don't want to visit them all—dark timbered roof beams and floors begin to look the same no matter who lived between them—buy a **Shakespeare's Town Heritage Trail ticket,** which covers only the three in-town sights (the Birthplace, Hall's Croft, and New Place) for £5 (students £4.50, children £2.30).

The least crowded way to pay homage to the institution himself is to visit his grave in **Holy Trinity Church,** Trinity St., though the little arched door bulges with massive tour groups at peak hours. Visit the churchyard and its painfully old but well-preserved gravestones (50p, students 30p). In town, begin your walking tour at **Shakespeare's Birthplace** on Henley St. (tel. 269890; enter through the adjoining museum). The Birthplace, half period recreation and half Shakespeare life-and-work exhibition, includes an admonishment to Will's father for putting his rubbish in the street. The adjacent **BBC Costume Exhibition** features costumes used in the BBC productions of Shakespeare's plays, complete with photo stills. Avoid this exhibition if the idea of a Disney plastic show turns your stomach—one half-expects the mannequin cast of Hamlet to launch into a chorus of "Zip-a-Dee-Do-Dah" (birthplace and exhibition both open Mon.-Sat. 9am-5:30pm, Sun. 10am-5:30pm; Nov.-Feb. Mon.-Sat. 9:30am-4pm, Sun. 10:30am-4pm; £2.60, children £1.20).

On High St., you can see another example of humble Elizabethan lodgings in the **Harvard House.** Period pieces sparsely punctuate this authentic Tudor building. The caretaker can tell you many truths about how the Rogers family passed the 16th century (open late May-Sept. daily 10am-4pm; £1, students and children 50p). **New Place,** Chapel St., was Stratford's hippest home when Shakespeare bought it back in 1597. Also visit the **Great Garden** at the back (open Mon.-Sat. 9:30am-5pm, Sun. 10:30am-5:30pm; Nov.-Feb. Mon.-Sat. 10am-4pm, Sun. 1:30-4pm; house admission £1.80, children 80p; garden free).

Shakespeare learned his "small Latin and less Greek" at the **Grammar School,** on Church St. To visit, write in advance to the headmaster, N.W.R. Mellon, King Edward VI School, Church St., Stratford-upon-Avon, England CV37 6HB (tel. 293351). The **guild chapel,** next door, is open daily. Shakespeare's eldest daughter once lived in **Hall's Croft,** Old Town Rd., an impressively furnished building with a beautiful garden in tow (hours and admission same as New Place).

Stroll through the **theatre gardens** of the Royal Shakespeare Theatre. You can fiddle with RSC props and costumes at their **RSC Collection** museum (gallery open Mon.-Sat. 9:15am-8pm, Sun. noon-5pm; £2, students and seniors £1.50). Backstage tours, including a review of the RSC Collection, give new perspective on this drama mecca (tel. 296655 for advance booking; daily 1:30 and 5:30pm; £4, students £3). The **RST Summer House** in the gardens contains a **brass-rubbing studio,** an alternative to plastic Shakespeare memorabilia (free, but frottage materials cost 95p-£9, average £2.50; open April-Sept. daily 10am-6pm; Oct. daily 11am-4pm).

Anne Hathaway's Cottage, the birthplace of Shakespeare's wife, lies about 1 mi. from Stratford in Shottery; take the footpath north from Evesham Place or the bus from Bridge St. The cottage exhibits portray the swinging Tudor rural lifestyle. View from outside if you've already seen the birthplace (open Mon.-Sat. 9am-5:30pm, Sun. 10am-5:30pm; Nov.-Feb. Mon.-Sat. 9:30am-4pm, Sun. 6:30am-4pm; £2.20, children £1). **Mary Arden's House,** the farmhouse restored in the style a 19th-century entrepreneur determined to be that of Shakespeare's mother, stands 4 mi. from Stratford in Wilmcote; a footpath connects it to Anne Hathaway's Cottage (open Mon.-Sat. 9:30am-5pm, Sun. 10:30am-5pm; Nov.-Feb. Mon.-Sat. 10am-4pm, Sun. 1:30-4pm; £3, children £1.30, family £7).

ENTERTAINMENT

Settle into a plush (ooh, *plush*) chair at the **Royal Shakespeare Company** and let a sublime performance wash over you in their recently redone theater. To reserve seats (£4.50-41), call the box office (tel. 295623; 24-hr. recording tel. 269191); they hold tickets for three days only. The box office opens at 9:30am. Good matinee seats are often available after 10:30am on the day of a performance. A limited number of tickets get set aside for same-day sale (apply in person; £4.50-10, limit 2/person) and some customer returns and standing-room tickets may turn up later in the day for evening shows (line up 1-2hr. before curtain). Student standbys for £8-13 exist in principle (available just before curtain—be ready to pounce). Beware—the company does not perform in Stratford during February or until the ides of March. The disabled should advise the box office of their needs.

The **Swan Theatre** has been specially designed for RSC productions of plays written by Shakespeare's contemporaries. The theatre is located down Waterside, in back of the Royal Shakespeare Theatre, on the grounds of the old Memorial Theatre (tickets £8-25, standing room £4.50). It's smaller and often more crowded than the RST; line up early for tickets. The Swan also sets aside a few same-day sale tickets (£4.50-£13); standbys are most rare. **The Other Place** is the RSC's newest branch, producing modern dramas and avant-garde premieres (reserved seats £14, unnumbered seats and same-days £12, standbys £8).

The **Stratford Festival** (last half of July), astonishingly celebrates artistic achievement other than Shakespeare's. The festival typically features world-class artists from all arenas of performance (from the conductor Simon Rattle to the anachronistic theatrical troupe Regia Anglorum). Tickets (when required) can be purchased from the Civil Hall box office (tel. 414513), on Rother St. The modern, well-respected **Shakespeare Centre,** Henley St., hosts the annual **Poetry Festival** throughout July and August with readings and/or lectures every Sunday evening. Those putting in appearances at the festival over the past two years include Leo McKern, Seamus Heaney, Elaine Feinstein, Ted Hughes, James Fenton, and Derek Walcott (tickets £4.50-13, call 295623). The Centre also has a library and a bookshop (across the street), opens archives to students and scholars, and holds madrigal concerts (£1 to £1.50; non-festival poetry readings are held Sundays at 8pm for £3.50-5.50). No nose-painting here—nightlife in Stratford is next to nil; go to the theater or go to bed early.

■ NEAR STRATFORD

Within an hour's drive of Stratford gather dozens of stately homes and castles, all children of England's "teeming womb of royal kings." Many historians, architects, and PR hacks regard **Warwick Castle** (tel. (01926) 408000), between Stratford and Coventry, as England's finest medieval castle. Its magnificent battlements loom over gracious, meandering grounds. Wax models by Madame Tussaud occupy the castle's private apartments; the dungeon and torture chamber feature nightmare-inducing exhibits, including a small hole dug in the earth that held especially wicked prisoners. Called the *oubliette*, this chamber restricted the movements of those it was necessary to forget (castle and grounds open daily 10am-5:30pm; Oct.-Feb. 10am-5pm; £5.75, children £3.50). A Midland Red bus journeys from Stratford to Warwick every hour (#18 or X16; 20min.); trains run frequently (£2.60).

Ragley Hall (tel. (01789) 762090), located 2 mi. southwest of Alcester and 8 mi. from Stratford on the Evesham Rd. (A435), houses the Earl and Countess of Yarmouth. Set in a 400-acre park, the estate boasts a fine collection of paintings and a captivating **maze** (open mid-April-Sept. Tues.-Thurs., Sat.-Sun., and bank holidays; house noon-5pm, gardens 10am-6pm; £4.50,children £3.50). Take a bus (Mon.-Sat. 5/day) from Stratford to Alcester, then walk 1 mi. to the gates of Ragley Hall and another ½ mi. up the drive.

Twenty miles northeast of Stratford burgeons the city of **Coventry,** chiefly notable for the reconstruction of its fine cathedral after the devastation of World War II.

Rather than work with the shards left behind, a collective of artists let them stand and helped build a stunning modern cathedral in their wake. In 1962, the building was rededicated to the strains of Benjamin Britten's *War Requiem*, newly filled with artworks such as a gargantuan tapestry by Graham Sutherland and St. Michael and the Devil battling in bronze. The building speaks to peaceful forgiveness, an impressively ungrudging message after the pain of post-war rebuilding.

■■■ BATH

A visit to the elegant Georgian city of Bath (pop. 83,000) remains *de rigueur*, even though it is now more of a museum than a resort. Immortalized by Fielding, Smollet, Austen, and Dickens, Bath once stood only second to London as a social capital of England. Queen Anne's visit to the natural hot springs here in 1701 established Bath as one of the great meeting places for British artists, politicians, and intellectuals of the 18th century. Heavily bombed during World War II, Bath has since been painstakingly restored, so that today, too, every thoroughfare is fashionable, though now more hair salons than literary salons grace its fair streets.

Legend ascribes the founding of Bath to King Lear's leper father Bladud, who wandered the countryside bemoaning his banishment from court. He took work as a swineherd, but his pigs soon caught the affliction. The devoted and decomposing swine led their king to a therapeutic spring; out of gratitude, Bladud founded a city on the site. The Romans built an elaborate complex of baths here early in their occupation of Britain.

GETTING THERE

Bath is served by direct Intercity **rail** service from London's Paddington Station (1/hr., 1½hr., £26), Exeter (22/day, 1¾hr.; £16), and Bristol (60/day, 15min., £3). **National Express** operates **buses** from London's Victoria coach station (9/day, 3hr., return £12.25), Oxford (6/day, 2hr., £12.25), and Salisbury (4/day, 1½hr., £4.30). **Badgerline** buses offer a **Day Rambler** ticket (£4.30), for unlimited travel in the region. The **Slow Coach** stops here on its circuit of England (consult Essentials: Getting About—Buses & Coaches for details).

ORIENTATION & PRACTICAL INFORMATION

The Pulteney Bridge and North Parade Bridge span the **River Avon,** which runs through the city from the east. The Roman Baths, the Abbey, and the Pump Room are all in the city center. The Royal Crescent and the Circus lie to the northwest. The train and bus stations are near the south end of Manvers St., at the bend in the river. From either terminal, walk up Manvers St. to the Orange Grove roundabout and turn left to the tourist office in the Abbey Churchyard.

Tourist Office: The Colonnades (tel. 462831). Extremely efficient staff, though the office gets crowded in summer. Map and mini-guide 25p. Pick up a free copy of *This Month in Bath*. Open Mon.-Sat. 9:30am-6pm, Sun. 10am-4pm; mid-Sept.-mid-June Mon.-Sat. 9:30am-5pm.

Tours: Excellent free 2hr. guided **walking tours** leave from the Abbey Churchyard Sun.-Fri. at 10:30am and Mon., Wed., Thurs. at 2pm, Sun. 2:30pm; evening tours Tues., Fri., Sat. 7pm. City **tour bus tours** (every 15 min., 1hr.; 9:30am-5pm) cost £3. **Mad Max Tours** (tel. (01926) 842999; Mon.-Fri. 9am-5:30pm or call Maddy Mon.-Fri. 6-8pm at (01836) 742857) cater to young hordes eager for day-away bus treks to Wiltshire on Tues. and Thurs. (Stonehenge, Avebury). A 4-person min. required for this day-long escapade (8:45am-5pm; £12). Tours leave from "the statue" on Cheap St. by the Abbey.

Financial Services: Barclays, Stall St. (tel. 462521), behind the Abbey Churchyard. Open Mon.-Tues. and Thurs.-Fri. 9:30am-4:30pm, Wed. 10am-4:30pm, Sat. 9:30am-noon. **Lloyds Bank,** Milsom St. Open Mon.-Fri. 9:30am-4:30pm, Sat. 9:30am-12:30pm. **Thomas Cook,** 20 New Bond St. (tel. 463191). Open Mon.-Wed. and Fri. 9:30am-5:30pm, Thurs. 10am-5:30pm. **American Express,** 5

Bridge St. (tel. 444767), just before Pulteney Bridge. Open Mon.-Fri. 9am-5:30pm, Sat. 9am-5pm.

Post Office: New Bond St. (tel. 825211), at Broad St. *Bureau de Change.* Open Mon.-Fri. 9am-5:30pm, Sat. 9am-1pm. **Postal Code:** BA1 1AA.

Telephone Code: 0225.

Train Station: Railway Pl., at the south end of Manvers St. (tel. 463075). Booking office open daily 6am-9:30pm. Travel Centre open Mon.-Fri. 8am-7pm, Sat. 9am-6pm, Sun. 10:30am-6pm. **Lockers** available.

Bus Station: Manvers St. (tel. 464446). **Lockers** available.

Taxis: Stands near stations. **Abbey Radio:** tel. 465843. **Rainbow:** tel. 460606.

Bike Rental: Avon Valley Bike Hire, Railway Pl. (tel. 461880), behind train station. £4.50-6.50/hr.; £10.50-22.50/day; deposit £20-75. Open daily 9am-6pm.

Boating: Bath Boating Station, Forester Rd. (tel. 466407), about ½ mi. north of town. Punts £3.50/person for 1hr., £1.50/person each additional hr. Canoes £9.50/day single. Open daily 11am-8pm weather permitting.

Launderette: Self Serve Laundry, St. George St. Bring change. Open daily 8:30am-7:45pm.

Hotline: Samaritans (crisis), 2 New King St., tel. 429222. 24hrs.

Gay and Lesbian Information: Gay West: tel. (0117) 942 5927.

Hospital: Royal United Hospital (tel. 428331).

Emergency: Dial 999; no coins required.

Police: Manvers St. (tel. 444343), just up from the train and bus stations.

ACCOMMODATIONS & CAMPING

Bath's well-to-do visitors drive up the prices of the B&Bs—don't try to find a bargain basement room (some are quite frightening). Instead, expect to pay £14-17, and enjoy Bath's gracious style. B&Bs cluster on **Pulteney Road** and **Pulteney Gardens.** From the stations, walk up Manvers St., which becomes Pierrepont St., right on to N. Parade Rd. and past the cricket ground to Pulteney Rd. For a more relaxed setting continue past Pulteney Gdns. (or take the footpath from behind the rail station) to **Widcombe Hill.** The steep climb has prices to match (from £16).

HI Youth Hostel, Bathwick Hill (tel. 465674). From N. Parade Rd., turn left onto Pulteney Rd., then right onto Bathwick Hill. A footpath takes the hardy up the steep hill to the hostel (20-min. walk). Badgerline "University" bus #18 (5/hr. until 11pm, return 75p) runs from the bus station or the Orange Grove roundabout. Gracious, graciously clean Italianate mansion overlooking the city. 119 beds, shower, TV, laundry. No lockout. £8.70; Sept.-May £7.50.

YMCA International House, Broad St. Place (tel. 460471). Walk under the arch and up the steps from Walcot St. across from Beaufort Hotel. Men and women. More central than HI hostel (3 min. from tourist office); free baths/showers. Laundry. Heavily booked in summer. Singles £12. Doubles £22. Triples available. Dorm rooms with continental breakfast £9.50/person; key deposit £5.

Mrs. Guy, 14 Raby Pl. (tel. 465120). From N. Parade, turn left onto Pulteney Rd., then right up Bathwick Hill. Savor this Georgian house with light, cool interiors, and a modern art collection. Fresh seasonal fruits, homemade jams, and yogurts complement a generous English breakfast. Yum. No smoking. Singles £16. Doubles £32.

The Shearns, Prior House, 3 Marlborough Lane (tel. 313587). Great location on the tony west side of town beside Royal Victoria Park. Take bus #14 or 15 from bus station (every 15 min.). Among Bath's best values. Warm, wonderful proprietors. No singles; no smoking. Doubles with full English breakfast £26.

Mrs. Rowe, 7 Widcombe Crescent (tel. 422726). In the southeastern area, up the hill from the stations. The height of elegance—and a view to match. Atmosphere decidedly staid. Blissfully quiet neighborhood. Full bath and TV. Singles £16-20. Doubles £30-36.

Avon Guest House, 1 Pulteney Gdns. (tel. 313009), at Pulteney Rd. Large rooms, full bath, color TV, and tea-making facilities. Friendly owners. Doubles with full English breakfast £34.

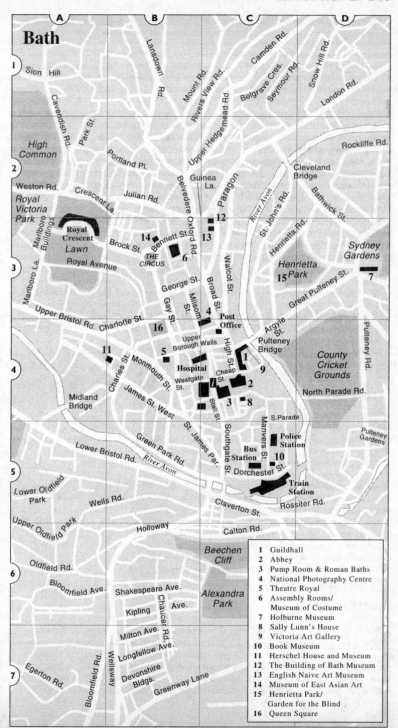

Bath

1 Guildhall
2 Abbey
3 Pump Room & Roman Baths
4 National Photography Centre
5 Theatre Royal
6 Assembly Rooms/
  Museum of Costume
7 Holburne Museum
8 Sally Lunn's House
9 Victoria Art Gallery
10 Book Museum
11 Herschel House and Museum
12 The Building of Bath Museum
13 English Naive Art Museum
14 Museum of East Asian Art
15 Henrietta Park/
  Garden for the Blind
16 Queen Square

BATH

Hunter's Moon Inn, 10 Widcombe Parade (tel. 335454). A variety of rooms above a pub and restaurant. Kindly owner will negotiate price and occupancy. £16 per person. No smoking. Good location.

Camping: Newton Mill Touring Centre, Newton St. Loe (tel. 333909), 3 mi. west of city center off A4/A36. Take bus #5 from bus station (5/hr., return 75p) to Twerton (ask bus driver to let you off at campsite). 105 sites. Laundry; free warm showers. £3.35/person under tent. Bar and restaurant on grounds.

FOOD & PUBS

For fruits and vegetables, visit the **Guildhall Market,** between High St. and Grand Parade (open Mon.-Sat. 9:30am-5:30pm). **Harvest Natural Foods,** 27 Walcot St., stocks a tremendous selection of organic produce, including some exotic items (open Mon.-Sat. 9:30am-5:30pm). **Seasons,** 10 George St. (tel. 469730), has a small deli and offers bountiful natural foods (open Mon.-Sat. 9am-5:30pm). Grab picnic fare at **Waitrose** supermarket in the Podium on High St. across from the post office (open Mon.-Tues. 8:30am-6pm, Wed.-Fri. 8:30am-8pm, Sat. 8:30am-6pm).

On Sundays when food is hard to come by, hit the pubs; many offer Sunday roast three-course lunches at bargain prices. If you're feeling flush, gossip over an elegant cream tea (£4.50) in the **Pump Room,** Abbey Churchyard, a palatial Victorian restaurant (open Mon.-Sat. 10am-5pm) and testament to the luxury tourist facilities developed by professional gambler Richard "Beau" Nash in 1703.

Scoff's, corner of Monmouth and Westgate St. Memorable, freshly baked wholefood pastries and filling lunches served in a warm, woody dining room with high ceilings and a fine view of Kingsmead Sq. Take-away, too (it's cheaper!). Big *tandoori* burger and salad £2. Open Mon.-Sat. 9am-5pm.

The Walrus and The Carpenter, 28 Barton St. (tel. 314684), uphill from the Theatre Royal. Basic bistro served alongside candle-stuffed wine bottles. Good burgers with creative toppings £5-7. Vegetarian entrees as well £5-8. No oysters. Open Mon.-Sat. noon-2:30pm and 6-11pm, Sun. 6-11pm.

The Canary, 3 Queen St. (tel. 424846). Airy tea house serving tasty twists on light meals. Somerset rabbit from 18th-century recipe £4.50. Open Mon.-Fri. 9am-10pm, Sat. 9am-7pm, Sun. 11am-5:30pm.

The Crystal Palace, 11 Abbey Green, behind Marks and Sparks. A sprawling, 18th-century pub and restaurant with an outdoor patio. Ploughman's lunch 6 different ways (£3-4.50). Open for meals daily noon-2:30pm and 6pm-8:30pm.

Café Retro, at Orange Grobe (tel. 339347). Let Ole Blue Eyes croon to you over pastries or burgers. Cool atmosphere. Smoked chicken and orange salad £3.90. Open Mon.-Sat. 10am-10:30pm, Sun. 10am-6pm.

The Boater on Bridge St. overlooks the river with outside seating and a stunning view of the lit-up Pulteney Bridge. Pubs pass time along Walcot St.: locals favor **The Bell,** where the best local bands (from rock to jazz) perform live nightly, and the trendy **Hat and Feather,** with two levels of indie and rave as well as mind-expanding light decorations. Those in search of powerful cider might venture up Broad St. to Belvedere St. and the **Beehive.** Wear grunge and look stoned. Next to the Theatre Royal, the Green Room at **The Garricks Head** is a pleasant gay pub. An inspiration for Dickens's *Pickwick Papers,* the **Saracen's Head,** on Broad St., is Bath's oldest pub, dating from 1713.

SIGHTS

Long before the age of Hanoverian refinement, Bath flourished for nearly 400 years as the Roman spa city of Aquae Sulis. **The Roman Baths** (now with a telephone— call 461111) retain their prominence in the town center. Sewer-diggers first uncovered the site inadvertently in 1880, and recent deliberate excavation has yielded a splendid model of advanced Roman engineering. Make your way through a maze of tunnels interrupted by dripping, fenced-off segments of the bath. Also on display within the corridors lurk a gilded bronze head of Minerva and a heap of Roman pennies tossed into the baths for good luck (open daily March-July and Sept. 9am-6pm; Aug. 9am-6pm and 8-10pm; Nov.-Feb. Mon.-Sat. 9am-5pm, Sun. 10am-5pm; last tickets 30 min. before closing; partial wheelchair access; £5, children £3, family £13). Excellent tours of the baths (2/hr.) leave from the main pool.

Situated next door to the Baths, the 15th-century **Bath Abbey** towers over its neighbors; the tower beckons to visitors across the skyline. An anomaly among the city's first-century Roman and 18th-century Georgian sights, the abbey saw the crowning of King Edgar, "first king of all England," in 973 AD (for a Technicolor Edgar, see the stained glass window near the baptismal font). Tombstones cover every possible surface in the church save the sanctuary and ceiling. Take time to peruse the protruding markers: they reveal the eerie and often mysterious ways various Brits and Yanks met their ends. A stone just inside the entrance commemorates Reverend Dr. Thomas "Dismal Science" Malthus (1766-1834), founder of modern demographics and inspiration to family planners everywhere. Play "Trivial Pursuit: New Testament Edition" with the 56 stained-glass scenes of Jesus' life at the east end (open daily 9am-6pm; £1). While in the vicinity, descend into the Bath Abbey **Heritage Vaults** (tel. 422462) for a "subterranean journey through time." You'll learn more about the church and its site than you ever wanted. And then some (open Mon.-Sat.; wheelchair accessible; £2; seniors, students, and children £1).

A short jaunt up Broad St., away from the tourist-trafficked abbey and baths, rests the **National Centre of Photography**, where visitors can purchase picture-perfect postcards, catch contemporary exhibits, and follow the history and growth of the camera (open daily 9:30am-5:30pm; £3, seniors and students £1.75).

Ever northward of the city center, the **Assembly Rooms,** Bennett St. (tel. 461111), staged fashionable social events in the late 18th century. Although World War II ravaged the rooms, renovations duplicate the originals in fine detail. In the same building, the prestigious **Museum of Costume** traces dressing-up over 400 years. (Open daily 10am-5pm; £3.20, under 19 £2, under 9 free. Joint ticket with Roman Baths £6.60, children £3.50.)

In the city's residential northwest corner, Nash's contemporaries John Wood, father and son, made the Georgian rowhouse a design to be reckoned with. Walk up Gay St. to **The Circus,** which has attracted illustrious residents for two centuries. Blue plaques mark the houses of Thomas Gainsborough, William Pitt, and David Livingstone. Proceed from there up Brock St. to **Royal Crescent** and its up-ended saucer of a lawn. The interior of **One Royal Crescent** (tel. 428126) is painstakingly restored by the Bath Preservation Trust to a near-perfect replica of a 1770 townhouse, authentic to the last teacup and butter knife (open Tues.-Sun. 10:30am-5pm, Nov.-Dec. 10:30am-4pm; £3, children, students, and seniors £2.50). **Royal Victoria Park,** next to Royal Crescent, contains one of the finest collections of trees in the country, and its botanical gardens nurture 5000 species of plants from all over the globe. For bird aficionados, there's an aviary. Observe the obelisk dedicated to Victoria and ask why they chose such an erect shape to honor her Highness (open Mon.-Sat. 9am-dusk, Sun. 10am-dusk; free). Throughout the city scatter stretches of green born to comfort weary limbs (consult a map or inquire at the tourist office).

Amble back down the hill to **Beckford's Tower**, Lansdown Rd. (tel. 338727) for stupendous views to reward the 156 steps to the top (open April-late Oct. Sat.-Sun., and bank holidays 2-5pm). If the climb makes you sing the blues, dally in the denim-swathed **History of Jeans Museum** (Britain's first and only!) at Scallywag next to the Baths (tel. 445040; open daily 9:30am-5:30pm; free). Those with a discerning eye might consider the **Victoria Art Gallery**, Bridge St. (tel. 461111, ext. 2772). Host to a collection of diverse works including Old Masters and contemporary British art, the museum stands next to the Pulteney Bridge—a work of art in its own right (open Mon.-Fri. 10am-5:30pm, Sat. 10am-5pm; wheelchair accessible; free).

Homesick Yankees and those who want to visit the United States vicariously and haven't yet found a McDonald's should stop by the **American Museum** (tel. 460503), perched high above the city at Claverton Manor. Inside is a fascinating series of furnished rooms transplanted from historically significant homes in the

United States. Among the most impressive are a 17th-century Puritan Keeping Room, a Shaker Meeting House, and a cozy Revolutionary War-era tavern kitchen complete with a working beehive oven. Climb Bathwick Hill to reach the manor. (Museum open late March-early Nov. Tues.-Sat. 2-5pm; Sun. and Mon. on bank holiday weekends 11am-5pm; gardens open Tues.-Fri. 1-6pm, Sat.-Sun. noon-6pm; house, grounds, and galleries £5, seniors and students £4.50, children £2.50; grounds, Folk Art, and New Galleries only £2, children £1.) The #18 bus (£1.20) can save you a steep 2-mi. trudge up Bathwick Hill. Upon your descent, lounge in a lawn chair in the **Parade Gardens** as the waters of the River Avon sweep by (open daily 10am-8pm; 60p, children 30p).

ENTERTAINMENT

Classical and jazz concerts enliven the **Pump Room** (see Bath: Food and Pubs, above) during morning coffee (Mon.-Sat. 10:30am-noon) and afternoon tea (2:30-5pm). In summer, buskers (street musicians) perform in the Abbey Churchyard, and a brass band often graces the Parade Gardens. Beau Nash's old pad, the magnificent **Theatre Royal,** Sawclose (tel. 448844), at the south end of Barton St., sponsors an ever-changing dramatic program (tickets £7-30, matinees £7-14; student discounts available for all shows except Wed. matinees and Sat.-Sun. evening performances; box office open Mon.-Sat. 10am-8pm, Sun. 1hr. before show). **The Little Theatre,** at St. Michael's Pl. near the tourist office (tel. 466822), shows offbeat movies and oldies (tickets £3.70, students and children £2.50).

Before a pub-and-club crawl, gather at the Huntsman Inn at North Parade Passage nightly at 8pm for the **Bizarre Bath Walking Tour** (tel. 335124; no advance booking required). Punsters lead locals and tourists alike around Bath pulling pranks for about 1¼ hours (£3, students £2.50.). Bath nights wake up at **The Bell**, 103 Walcot St. (tel. 460426), an artsy pub which challenges its clientele to talk over the live jazz and blues. The Bell's partner in crime, **The Hub** (also on Walcot St.; tel. 446288), starts up late and keeps going with reggae and funk vibes (open Wed.-Sat. 9pm-2am; cover £3-6). Stop by and pick up a listing of upcoming concerts or give 'em a call. at 14 George St., **Moles** burrows underground and pounds out techno and house music. Dress sharp; act smart. The club is members only, but you might get in (open Mon.-Sat. 9pm-2am). High-energy dance tracks draw a young crowd to the **Players Club,** on the corner of Pierrepont and North Parade (open nightly 9pm-2am; cover £5). Check the tourist office or shop windows for monthly club schedules.

The renowned **Bath International Festival of the Arts,** over two weeks of concerts and exhibits, produces merriment all over town from late May to early June. The **Contemporary Art Fair** opens the festival by bringing together the work of over 700 British artists. Musical offerings range from major symphony orchestras and choruses to chamber music, solo recitals, and jazz. For a festival brochure and reservations, write to the Bath Festival Office, Linley House, 1 Pierrepont Pl., Bath BA1 1JY. The concurrent **Fringe Festival** (which also occurs city-wide) celebrates music, dance, and liberal politics—and proves just as much fun as the established gala, with no advance booking required.

■■■ WELLS

Named for the five natural springs at its center, the small town of Wells (pop. 10,000) orbits a splendid Gothic cathedral. Its streets, lined with petite Tudor and golden sandstone shops, fade gently into quiet Somerset meadows.

GETTING THERE

Rail routes leave Wells well enough alone, but **Badgerline buses** run regularly to Bath (tel. (01225) 464446; #173, 1/hr., Sun. every 3hr.; 1hr. 20min.; return £3.30) and Bristol (tel. (0117) 955 3231; #376, #676, 1/hr., Sun. every 3hr.; 1hr.; £3.30); buses #163 and 376 make frequent, short hops to Glastonbury (£1.45; purchase tickets on board). If you'll be skipping from place to place, a **Day Rambler** (£4.50, seniors £3.30) helps cut costs. **Bakers Dolphin coach travel service** (tel. 679000) offers inexpensive (and fast) buses to London (1/day; 2hrs.; £10).

ORIENTATION & PRACTICAL INFORMATION

Buses stop at the **Princes Road Depot.** To reach the tourist office, turn left onto Priory Rd. from Princes. Proceed along Priory, which becomes Broad St. and eventually merges with High St. The Market Place rests at the top of High St.

Tourist Office: Town Hall (tel. 672552), in the Market Place, to the right as you face the cathedral grounds. Area bus timetables free. Open Mon.-Sat. 9:30am-5:30pm; Nov.-March 10am-4pm. Call the fashionably-attired town crier, Freddy Gibbons, at 676139 to arrange a **tour.**

Financial Services: Barclays, Market Place, next to the Conservative Club. Open Mon. and Wed.-Fri. 9:30am-4:30pm, Tues. 10am-4:30pm. **Thomas Cook,** #8 High St., near Market Place. Open Mon.-Thurs. and Sat. 9am-5:30pm, Fri. 10am-5:30pm (tel. 677747). **Lloyds,** High St. Open Mon.-Fri. 9am-4:45pm.

Post Office: Market Place (tel. 73113). Open Mon. and Wed.-Fri. 9am-5:30pm, Tues. 9:30am-5:30pm, Sat. 9am-12:30pm. **Postal Code:** Somerset, BA5 2RA.

Telephones: Four phone boxes including a Phonecard phone in Market Place. Two more by the bus station. **Telephone Code:** 01749.

Bus Station: Badgerline buses from Avon and Somerset stop in the Princes Rd. depot. Call 673084 or pick up a timetable at the tourist center.

Bike Rental: Wells City Cycles, 80 High St. (tel. 675096). Mountain bikes £9/day, 3-speeds £4/50/day; deposit £25-50. Open Mon.-Tues. and Thurs.-Fri. 9am-5:30pm, Wed. 9am-1pm.

Launderette: Wells Laundrette, St. Cuthbert St. Open daily 7am-8pm. Last wash 7pm. Change machine.

Early Closing Day: Wed., at 1pm. Sparsely observed during tourist season.

Hospital: Wells and District Cottage Hospital, St. Thomas St. (tel. 673154).

Emergency: Dial 999; no coins required.

Police: Glastonbury Rd. (tel. 673481).

ACCOMMODATIONS & CAMPING

When in doubt, take a daytrip to Wells from Bath. The closest **HI Youth Hostels** are in Cheddar (10 mi.; see Near Wells: Accommodations, below) and Street (6 mi.; see Glastonbury: Accommodations, below). During the summer, accommodations fill up early. A number of B&Bs (rates about £13-15) line **Chamberlain Street,** and others cluster on **St. Andrews St.,** behind the cathedral.

HI Youth Hostel, Hillfield, Cheddar (tel. (01934) 742494), off the Hayes, 3 blocks from Cheddar bus stop (walk up Tweentown Rd.), and 1 mi. from Cheddar Gorge. Frequent buses from Wells (#126, 826, 827; Mon.-Sat. 1/hr. until 5:40pm; £1.20). Stone Victorian house, a bit worn. Lockout 10am-5pm. £6.30. Breakfast £2.40, evening meal available. Open July-Aug. daily; Feb.-March and Sept.-Oct. Tues.-Sat.; April-June Mon.-Sat.

Richmond House, 2 Chamberlain St. (tel. 676438). Large rooms and friendly proprietors. Great location. Good book selection in lounge—pick up A.S. Byatt's *Possession* for literary bliss. Vegetarian breakfast available. £15. Rooms to accommodate most group sizes. You may very well want to live here forever.

17 Priory Rd. (tel. 677300). Comfortable quarters available in a large Victorian home. Baths only. English breakfast complemented by a hearty selection of homemade breads and preserves. Near the bus station. £15.

The Old Poor House, 7A St. Andrew St. (tel. 675052). One need not be a pauper to stay here. Mrs. Wood is perfectly charming and she'll give you a clean room right up the street from the cathedral. £16.50.

Camping: In **Wookey Hole** and **Cheddar** (see Near Wells: Accommodations, below).

FOOD

Assemble a picnic at the market behind the bus stops (Wed. and Sat. 8:30am-4pm) or purchase drool-producing breads, cheeses, and other provisions at **Laurelbank Dairy Co.,** 14 Queens St. (open Mon.-Sat. 9am-6pm). Health-conscious **Holland & Barrett,** up the block, sells wholefood (open Mon.-Sat. 9am-5:30pm), while **Mount-stevens Bakery and Coffee Shop,** 49 High St., specializes in fattening fare (open Mon.-Sat. 8:30am-5pm). Homemade soups (£1-1.60) and soothing tea await the weary backpacker at **The Good Earth,** 4 Priory Rd. There's an adjoining shop as well (open Mon.-Sat. 9:30am-5:30pm). A popular Tudoresque store, **Raso's Fish and Chips,** 17 Broad St., cooks up cheap daily lunch specials (Mon.-Thurs. noon-2:30pm and 5-10:30pm, Fri. noon-2:30pm and 5pm-midnight, Sat. noon-midnight). Green-grocers straddle busy Broad and High streets and **Tesco** supermarket feeds the town at Princes Rd. (right across from the bus depot; open Mon.-Thurs. 8am-8:30pm, Fri. 8:30am-9pm, Sat. 8am-8pm, Sun. 10am-4pm).

In the evening, step into the **Penn Eating House,** near the Market Place, a pub which serves hot food until 9pm. Or try the Star Hotel's **Brassiere** on High St. (open 11am-11pm). Order pizza (£3.10-4.50) from **Da Luciano Espresso Bar,** 14 Broad St. They also pour coffee so hot it has to be nursed all day long (open Mon.-Sat. 11:30am-11:30pm, Sun. 12:30-10:30pm).

SIGHTS

The 13th-century **Cathedral Church of St. Andrew** in the center of town (tel. 674483) survives as a fantastically-preserved cathedral complex, with a bishop's palace, vicar's close, and chapter house. Atop the fanciful 14th-century astronomical clock in the north transept, a pair of jousting, mechanical knights spur on their chargers and strike at each other every 15 minutes—the same unfortunate rider is unseated every time. Walter Raleigh, Dean of Wells, and nephew to the Sir, was murdered in the deanery where he had been imprisoned for his Royalist ways. Ascend the swerving steps (which may make you think you're a bit dizzy) to the octagonal Chapter House (cathedral open daily 7:15am-8:30pm, until 6pm in winter; not-so-voluntary donation £2.50). Enjoy evensong (Mon.-Tues. and Thurs.-Fri. 5:15pm, Sun. 3pm). The renowned **Wells Cathedral School Choir** performs term-time (Sept.-April); visiting choirs assume the honor through summer break. The cathedral hosts a slew of musical events during the year. Pick up the leaflet *Music in Wells Cathedral* at the cathedral or tourist office for concert details and ticket info.

The 13th-century **Bishop's Palace** (tel. 678691) to the right of the cathedral (entrance from Market Place) evokes the power wielded by medieval bishops. Bishop Ralph of Shrewsbury (1329-63), alarmed by village riots in the 14th century, built the moat and walls to protect himself. Today, with onslaughts unlikely from the common folk, the moat sports a concrete bridge (open Aug. daily 10am-6pm; April-July and Sept.-Oct. Tues. and Thurs. 11am-6pm, Sun. 2pm-6pm; £2). The mute swans in the moat have been trained to pull a bell-rope when they want to be fed. Feeding by tourists is strongly discouraged as it inhibits the Pavlovian tradition. **Vicar's Close,** behind the cathedral, is the oldest street of houses in Europe; the houses date from 1363, their chimneys from 1470.

Just north of the cathedral green and to the left of the cathedral's entrance, the **Wells Museum** preserves the history of Wells' surrounding countryside, the Mendips. On display are human remains found in the caves; these are purported to be those of the legendary Witch of Wookey Hole, though accompanied not by mystical artifacts but only by two tethered goats. The shop of miniature antiques has every detail exquisitely reproduced (open Mon.-Sat. 10am-5:30pm, Sun. 11am-5:30pm, July-Aug. until 8pm; Oct.-Easter Wed.-Sun. 11am-4pm; £1, seniors and children 50p).

■ NEAR WELLS: WOOKEY HOLE & CHEDDAR

You need only venture a short distance from the simplicity and serenity of Wells to encounter a fantastic vale of cheese, in every sense of the word. If you plan to see both Wookey Hole and Cheddar, buy a **Day Rambler** ticket (£4.30).

Disappointing some and delighting few, **Wookey Hole,** only 2 mi. northwest of Wells, is not the home of Chewbacca; still, the **Wookey Hole Caves and Papermill** (tel. (01749) 72243) hold some weird prehistoric animal mutations. The admission (£4.30, £3.80 if bought at the tourist center in Wells) includes the subterranean caves, a tour of the working paper mill, and a spectacular collection of wooden carousel animals. The gold lion is worth over £75,000 (open daily 9:30am-5:30pm; Oct.-April 10:30am-4:30pm). **Camping** is available at **Homestead Park** (tel. (01749) 673022) beside a babbling brook (£8/tent, car and 2 people). For lunch, stop at the **Wookey Hole Inn** (open daily 10:30am-2pm and 7-10:30pm).

Satisfy that craving for **Cheddar** with a ploughman's lunch at a pub wherever you happen to be right now instead of venturing into the town itself. The **Cheddar Gorge,** formed by the River Yeo (YO!) in the hills just northeast of town, *might* justify a daytrip, depending on your sensibilities and toleration for an overcrowded mélange of touristy tea-shops and cheezwizardry. The bus from Wells (Mon.-Sat. every hr.; 20min.; £1.50) lets you off below the thicket of tourists at the gorge's mouth. From the bus stop follow the signs to Jacob's Ladder, a 322-step stairwell to the top (75p, seniors and children 50p). The unsullied view of the hills to the north and the broad expansive plain to the south rewards the climber.

At the foot of the cliffs huddle the **Cheddar Showcaves** (tel. (01934) 742343), the finest show caves in England. Note the different mineral colors of the stalagmites and stalactites: rust-red is iron; green is manganese; and grey is lead. Feast your eyes on the Cheddar Man, a 9000-year-old skeleton typical of the Stone-agers who settled in the Gorge (caves open daily 10am-5:30pm; Oct.-Easter 10:30am-4:30pm; admission to all caves, Jacob's Ladder, and museum £4.90, children £2.90). As in Wookey Hole, discount tickets are available at the Wells tourist office.

The Cheddar library shelves the town's **tourist office** on Union St. (tel. (01934) 742769; open Mon. and Wed. 10am-1pm and 2-5:30pm, Fri. 10am-1pm and 2-7:30pm, Sat. 10am-12:30pm). From June to September, there's another tourist office at the base of Cheddar Gorge (tel. (01934) 744071). The town also boasts an **HI Youth Hostel** (see Wells: Accommodations, above). Camping is available at **Bucklegrove Caravan and Camping Park** in Rodney Stoke near Cheddar (tel. (01749) 870261; £4.50-7.50 for tent and 2 persons).

In 1170 Henry II declared Cheddar cheese the best in England. Wine and cheese enthusiasts can fill their bellies at the **Chewton Cheese Dairy** (tel. (01761) 241666), just north of Wells on the A39. Take the bus toward Bristol and get off at Cheddar Rd., just outside Wells (shop open Mon.-Fri. 8:30am-5pm, Sat. 9am-5pm, Sun. 10am-4pm; Jan.-March Mon.-Fri. 8:30am-4pm, Sat.-Sun. 9am-4pm; cheese-making begins at 7:30am Mon.-Wed. and Fri.-Sat., but call first; the best time to view the cheesemaking festivities is 11:30am-2pm).

■■■ GLASTONBURY

The reputed birthplace of Christianity in England and the seat of Arthurian myth, Glastonbury has evolved into an intersection of Christianity, mysticism, and granola. According to ancient legend, Jesus traveled here with his merchant uncle, Joseph of Arimathea. Other myths hold that the area is the resting place of the Holy Grail, Glastonbury Tor is the Isle of Avalon, with the bones of Arthur and his queen Guinevere safe beneath Glastonbury Abbey, and the Tor contains a passage to the underworld. Grow your hair, suspend your disbelief, and join hands with Glastonbury's subculture of hippies, spiritualists, and mystics.

GETTING THERE

Fast, frequent **Badgerline buses** come from Bristol (#376, 1/hr., Sun. every 3 hr.; 1½hr.; £3.45) and from Wells (#163, 167, 168, 378, or 379; £2.15). From Bath, change at Wells (£3.75). For information on other Badgerline services, call Bristol (tel. (0117) 955 3231), Bath (tel. (01225) 464446), or Wells (tel. (01749) 673084). **Southern National** (tel. (01823) 272033) buses take travelers to points south, such as Lyme Regis and Weymouth. Explorer passes enable you to travel a full day to various locales (£4.50, seniors £3.50, children £2.75).

ORIENTATION & PRACTICAL INFORMATION

Glastonbury lies 6 mi. southwest of Wells on the A39 and 22 mi. northeast of Taunton on the A361. The compact town is bounded by Manor House Rd. in the north, Bere Lane in the south, Magdalene St. in the west, and Wells Rd. in the east.

Tourist Office: The Tribunal, 9 High St. (tel. 832954 or 832949). Open Sun.-Thurs. 10am-5pm, Fri.-Sat. 10am-6pm; Oct.-Easter Mon.-Sun. 10am-4pm.

Financial Services: Barclays, High St. Open Mon.-Tues. and Thurs.-Fri. 9:30am-4:30pm, Wed. 10am-4:30pm. **National Westminster,** High St. Open Mon.-Tues. and Thurs. Fri. 9:30am-4:30pm, Wed. 10am-4:30pm.

Post Office: 35-37 High St. (tel. 831563). Open Mon.-Fri. 9am-5:30pm, Sat. 9am-1pm. *Poste Restante.* **Postal Code:** BA6 9HS.

Telephones: In front of town hall, Magdalene St. **Telephone Code:** 01458.

Bus Station: All buses stop in front of the town hall. **National Express tickets** are sold at the Bakers Dolphin on High St.

Bike Rental: Pedlars Cycle Shop, 8 Magdalene St. (tel. 831117). Bikes £5/day, £20/week; deposit £20. Open Mon.-Sat. 9am-5:30pm.

Launderette: Glastonbury Launderette, 46A High St. Open daily 8am-7pm. Change available next door at the gift shop. Washers may be less than satisfactory.

Market Day: Tues. 8:30am-5:30pm in back of St. John's Church on High St.

Emergency: Dial 999; no coins required.

Police: In the nearby town of Street at 1 West End (tel. (01823) 337911).

ACCOMMODATIONS & CAMPING

Singles don't come easily in Glastonbury. Stop by the tourist office for a free list. **Lambrook St.** and **Chilkwell St.** have a handful of B&Bs. Be forewarned that some occupy the hilly hinterlands of town.

HI Youth Hostel, The Chalet, Ivythorn Hill, Street BA16 OT2 (tel. 42961), 2 mi. south off the B3151 in Street. Take Badgerline bus #376, alight at Leigh Rd., and walk 1 mi. Swiss-style chalet with views of Glastonbury Tor, Sedgemoor, and Mendip Hills. Lockout 10am-5pm. £6.90. Open July-Aug. daily; April-June Wed.-Mon.; Sept.-Oct. Thurs.-Mon.

Tamarac, Mrs. Talbot, 8 Wells Rd. (tel. 834327). A spiffy modern house on a central residential street. Plush, comfortable rooms with color TV and teapots. Primarily doubles, though families can grab the lovely cottage out back. Generous breakfast. From £13.50.

Blake House, 3 Bove Town (tel. 831680). Groovy and conveniently located 17th-century stone house complete with working fireplace. Vegetarians especially welcome in this non-smoking house. Well-traveled owners with superb garden. £15.

The Bolt Hole, 32 Chilkwell St. (tel. 832800), opposite the Chalice Well. Bright, flowery rooms with basins, TVs, and teapots. Proprietor keeps healing well water on hand. One twin and 2 doubles, £13-14. If this B&B is full, you may end up staying with the owner's sister.

Camping: Ashwell Farm House, Ashwell Lane (tel. 832313), Take the 1st left after Ashwell Lane. Impeccably maintained sites with nothing but green void between you and Avalon. From £2.50/person. Electricity hookup £1.

FOOD

Set up for a picnic by the Tor at **Truckle of Cheese,** 33 High St. (open Mon.-Sat. 8:30am-5:30pm). High St. also has green-grocers, two supermarkets, a wholefood store, a bakery, and reasonably priced restaurants. A side dish of simple spiritual nourishment can be obtained with a purchase of incense and crystals.

Rainbows End, 17A High St. No pots of gold, but there's a whole-food buffet served on earthenware. Try the pizza (£1.30) and wear your Birkenstocks. Open Mon. and Thurs.-Sat. 10am-4pm, Tues. 9:30am-4pm, Wed. 10am-2:30pm. Bulletin board refers you to the astrologer/acupuncture/body-aura-reader of your dreams.

Market House Inn, 21 Magdalene St., near the town center. Huge helpings at bargain prices. Dark and sticky with beer, but burgers for £2. Bar food served noon-2:30pm and 6:30-9:30pm daily.

Blue Note Café, High St., near the tourist office. No singing the blues over quiche (£1.75) and coffee. Jazz trills over the loudspeaker; indoor and outdoor dining, but leave your smokes at home. Mon.-Sat. 9am-5pm, Sun. 9am-5:30pm.

Abbey Tea Room, 16 Magdalene St. Quiet, prim, and proper lunch for under £3 and delicious cream teas with scones and jam for £2.60. How can you not go here? Open Mon.-Sat. 10am-5:30pm, Sun. 10:30am-5:30pm, off-season Mon.-Sat. 10am-5pm, Sun. 10:30am-5:30pm.

SIGHTS

Behind the archway on Magdalene St. lurk the ruins of **Glastonbury Abbey** (tel. 834747), the oldest Christian foundation and once the most important abbey in England. All that remains is a lone steeple bordered by the shadow of the old abbey, but the sight is still awe-inspiring, especially in springtime's grassy wash. Joseph of Arimathea supposedly built the original wattle-and-daub church on this site in 63 AD; larger churches were successively raised (and razed) over the next millenium. Erected in 1184, the stone abbey flourished until the Reformation. Its sixth and final abbot, Richard Whiting, refused to obey Henry VIII's order that all Catholic churches dissolve. Not known for his tolerance, Henry had Whiting hanged, drawn, and quartered on Glastonbury Tor.

Two national patron saints, Patrick of Ireland and George of England, have been claimed by the abbey—Patrick is said to be buried here and George to have slain his dragon just around the corner. St. Dunstan hails from Glastonbury where he served the diocese for several decades. King Arthur most captivates the legend-makers—in 1191, the remains of Arthur and Guinevere were discovered just in time for the campaign to rebuild the abbey after a fire; the royal bones were reinterred in 1276 in the presence of King Edward I. The Abbey's 36 acres claim a large portion of the town. A new exhibit leads you by the hand through the history of the sacred space. Marvel at the model of the Abbey which represents it as it looked in 1539 when Henry VIII commenced his antics around Glastonbury. (Abbey open daily 9:30am-6pm; June-Aug. 9am-6pm; £2, children £1). Modern religion finds an outlet in the open-air masses which are periodically held among the ruins—ask at the tourist office.

Present-day pagan pilgrimage site **Glastonbury Tor** towers over Somerset's faltlands. Visible miles away, the Tor was known in its earlier incarnation as St. Michael's Chapel, and is site of the mystical Isle of Avalon, where the Messiah is slated to reappear. From the top of the hill, you can survey the Wiltshire Downs, the Mendips and, on a clear day, the distant spires of Bristol Cathedral. To reach the Tor, turn right at the top of High St. and continue up Wellhouse Lane. Take the first right up the hill. A brilliant view rewards the bewitching climb. Latter-day magicians get their kicks by burning incense in the remaining tower.

On the way down from the Tor, visit the **Chalice Well,** at the corner of Wellhouse Lane, the supposed resting place of the Holy Grail. Legend once held that the well ran with Christ's blood; in these Post-Nietzschean days, rust deposits at the source turn the water red. Water gurgles from the well down through a tiered garden of hollyhocks, climbing vines, and dark, spreading yew trees. People drink the water from the lion's head on the second tier, or after hours, from a tap on the outside wall (open daily 10am-6pm; Nov.-Feb. daily 1-4pm; 60p, children 30p).

Take a short walk down Chilkwell St. to the 14th-century **Abbey Barn,** part of the **Somerset Rural Life Museum** (tel. 31197). Exhibits depict cider-making and peat-digging, among other industries of rural Somerset. The elegant roof in the Abbey Barn supports 80 tons of stone tiles (open Mon.-Fri. 10am-5pm, Sat.-Sun. 2-6pm; Nov.-Easter Mon.-Fri. 10am-5pm, Sat. 11am-4pm; £1.20, seniors 80p, children 30p; free Fri.). Discount tickets for Somerset County Museums, including the Rural Life Museum, the County Museum of Taunton Castle, the Peat Moors Visitors Centre, and Glastonbury Lake Village are available at the tourist center.

Head down Bere Lane to Hill Head to reach **Wearyall Hill,** where legend has it that Joseph of Arimathea's staff bloomed and became the **Glastonbury Thorn.** The Thorn, a grove of trees of a species native to Israel, has grown on Wearyall Hill since Saxon times, and, according to legend, should burst into bloom in the presence of royalty. If you have royal blood, stay away or prepare to be disappointed. Horticul-turists here and abroad (where offshoots of the thorn are planted) have wasted con-siderable time making the trees bloom each time the Queen comes to visit. Citizens of Glastonbury happily hark back to feudal days every Christmas as they send clip-pings from the thorn, according to medieval privilege. Wrap up your visit to Glas-tonbury (trusting you haven't decided to sell all your possessions to commune with the cattle and sheep on the Tor) on High Street. "Welcome to the Glastonbury Expe-rience," a shopping arcade and psychedelic journey, brings acupuncturists, tarot card readers, mystics, medicine men, and Janis Joplin look-alikes together in one peaceful point in space and time. Don't forget the aromatherapy.

EAST ANGLIA

> *When you work with water, you have to know and respect it. When you labor to subdue it, you have to understand that one day it may rise up and turn all your labours to nothing. For what is water, children, but a liquid form of Nothing? and what are Fens, which so imitate in their levelness the natural disposition of water, but a landscape which, of all landscapes, most approximates Nothing?*
>
> —*Graham Swift,* Waterland

The plush green farmlands and dismal watery fens of East Anglia stretch northeast from London, cloaking the counties of Cambridgeshire, Norfolk, and Suffolk. While high-tech industry is modernizing the economies of Cambridge and Peterborough, the college town and cathedral city are still linked by flat fields sliced into irregular tiles by windbreaks, hedges, and stone walls. In the low-lying northwest quarter, rivers course between raised embankments that catch the water from the drained swamps of the Fens. From Norwich east to the English Channel, water long ago drenched enormous areas of medieval peat bogs and created the maze of waterways known as the Norfolk Broads.

Skirting the north coast between Great Yarmouth and Cromer, the **Weaver's Way** led Roman traders through dozens of market towns. Further inland, Norman invaders made their way to the elevated mound at Ely; they built a stunning cathedral from stone transported by boat across the immense flooded fenland. In a minor village to the south, renegade scholars from Oxford set up shop along the River Cam. Eventually granted a royal imprimatur, they thereby built a university.

Centrally-located Cambridge and Norwich offer comfortable hostels and good transit connections, making them ideal bases for exploring the area. Ely and Bury St. Edmunds make easy daytrips from Cambridge, and north of Norwich, dignified natural preserves lie among sand dunes and salt marshes. Along the coast, the fishing towns of Southwold and Aldeburgh live ageless in the salt air. Farther south, the resort towns of Harwich and Felixstowe have a quicker pace and more international feel brought about by frequent ferry traffic.

GETTING ABOUT

An **Anglia Rover** ticket (about £35, discount with Railcard), available only at stations within East Anglia, entitles you to a week's unlimited travel on all rail routes in the region. The **Explorer** ticket (£4.50) is good for a day's travel on all Eastern Counties bus routes in East Anglia, which serve many areas not covered by British Rail. You might end up paying with your time; buses run infrequently.

East Anglia's flat terrain and relatively low annual rainfall please bikers and hikers. Though rental bikes are readily available in Cambridge and Norwich, they can be difficult to find elsewhere. The area's two longest and most popular walking trails, together covering 200 mi., are **Peddar's Way,** which runs from Knettishall Heath to Holme and includes the Norfolk coast path, and **Weaver's Way,** a newly extended trail that traverses the coast from Cromer to Great Yarmouth. Every 10 mi. or so, each walk passes through a town with a bus or rail station. Tourist offices in Norwich, Bury St. Edmunds, and several other Suffolk villages offer route guides for the Weaver's Path. For the Peddar's Way, pick up *Peddar's Way and Norfolk Coast Path* at area bookstores.

■■■ CAMBRIDGE

The town of Cambridge has been around for over 2000 years, but the University got its start a mere 785 years ago when rebels "defected" from nearby Oxford to this settlement on the River Cam. Each term, battalions of bicycle-riding students invade this quintessential university town. Competing in most everything with Oxford, Cambridge loses in years and boat races but wins on charm and energy. In recent years, Cambridge has ceased to be the exclusive preserve of upper-class sons, although roughly half of its students still come from independent schools and only 35% are women. While tradition mandates that students bedeck themselves with cravat and cane, few actually preserve this staid image.

The University itself exists mainly as a bureaucracy that handles the formalities of lectures, degrees, and real estate, leaving to individual colleges the small tutorials and seminars that form a Cambridge education. Since third-year finals shape many students' futures, most colleges close to visitors during the official quiet periods of May and early June. But at exams' end, Cambridge explodes with gin-soaked glee, and May Week (in mid-June, naturally) launches a dizzying schedule of cocktail parties, beginning with a health-threatening number on aptly-named Suicide Sunday.

GETTING THERE

Trains to Cambridge run from both London's King's Cross and Liverpool Street stations (2/hr.; 1hr.; £11.70). **National Express** coaches connect London's Victoria Station and Drummer St. Station in Cambridge (1/hr.; 2hr.; £8.50). National Express buses and **Cambridge Coaches** travel between Oxford and Cambridge every two hours from 8:40am to 5:40pm (3hr.; £12). **Cambus,** the town's bus service, runs regional routes from Drummer St. (fares vary). The **Slow Coach** stops here on its circuit of England (consult Essentials: Getting About—Buses & Coaches for details).

CAMBRIDGE

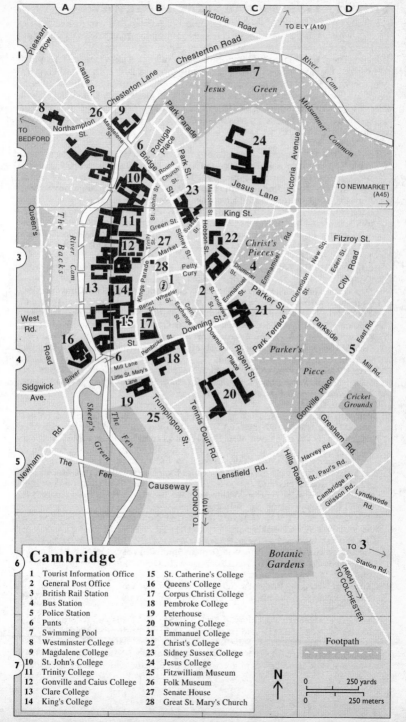

Cambridge

1 Tourist Information Office
2 General Post Office
3 British Rail Station
4 Bus Station
5 Police Station
6 Punts
7 Swimming Pool
8 Westminster College
9 Magdalene College
10 St. John's College
11 Trinity College
12 Gonville and Caius College
13 Clare College
14 King's College
15 St. Catherine's College
16 Queens' College
17 Corpus Christi College
18 Pembroke College
19 Peterhouse
20 Downing College
21 Emmanuel College
22 Christ's College
23 Sidney Sussex College
24 Jesus College
25 Fitzwilliam Museum
26 Folk Museum
27 Senate House
28 Great St. Mary's Church

Footpath

N

0   250 yards

0   250 meters

ORIENTATION & PRACTICAL INFORMATION

Cambridge (pop. 100,000), about 60 mi. north of London, has two main avenues, both of which suffer from amnesia. The main shopping street starts at Magdalene Bridge and becomes Bridge St., Sidney St., St. Andrew's St., Regent St., and finally Hills Rd. The other—alternately St. John's St., Trinity St., King's Parade, Trumpington St., and Trumpington Rd.—is the academic thoroughfare, with several colleges lying between it and the River Cam. The two streets merge at St. John's College. From the bus station at Drummer St., a hop-skip-and-jump down Emmanuel St. will land you right in the shopping district near the tourist office. To get to the heart of things from the train station, go west along Station Rd., turn right onto Hills Rd. and continue straight ahead.

Tourist Office: Wheeler St. (tel. 322640), a block south of the marketplace. Mini-guide 30p. Maps of the town 10p. Open Mon.-Tues. and Thurs.-Fri. 9am-6pm, Wed. 9:30am-6pm, Sat. 9am-5pm, Sun. 10:30am-3:30pm; Nov.-March closes at 5:30pm. Info on Cambridge events also available at **Corn Exchange box office,** Corn Exchange St. (tel. 357851), opposite the tourist office.

Tours: Informative 2-hr. walking tours of the city and some colleges leave the main tourist office daily: April-June 11am and 2pm; July-Sept. every hr. 11am-3pm. Special **Drama Tour** Tues. and Fri. at 6:30pm, led by guides in period dress. Tours less frequent during the rest of the year. Sun. and bank holidays, first tour at 11:15am. £3.50-5.

Budget Travel: STA Travel, 38 Sidney St. (tel 66966). Open Mon.-Fri. 9am-5:30pm, Sat. 10am-4pm. **Campus Travel,** 5 Emmanuel St. (tel. 324283). Open Mon.-Tues. and Thurs.-Fri. 9am-5:30pm, Wed. 10am-5:30pm, Sat. 10am-5pm.

Financial Services: Barclays, Sidney St. branch (tel. 542000) open Mon.-Tues. and Thurs.-Fri. 9:30am-5pm, Wed. 10am-5pm. Market Sq. branch open Mon.-Fri. 9:30am-3:30pm, Sat. 9:30am-noon. **Thomas Cook,** 18 Market St. (tel. 66141). Open Mon.-Sat. 9am-5:30pm. **American Express: Abbot Travel,** 25 Sidney St. (tel. 351636). Client mail held. Open Mon.-Tues. and Thurs.-Fri. 9am-5:30pm, Wed. 9:30am-5:30pm, Sat. 9am-5pm.

Post Office: 9-11 St. Andrew's St. (tel. 323325). Open Mon.-Tues. and Thurs.-Fri. 9am-5:30pm, Wed. 9:30am-5:30pm, Sat. 9am-12:30pm. *Poste Restante* and *Bureau de Change.* **Postal Code:** CB2 3AA.

Telephone Code: 01223.

Train Station: Station Rd. (tel. 311999; recorded London timetable Mon.-Fri. tel. 359602, Sat. tel. 467098, Sun. tel. 353465). Open daily 5am-11pm to purchase tickets. Travel Centre open Mon.-Sat. 4:30am-11pm, Sun. 6am-11pm. To get to Market Square from the train station, take a Citral Link bus (Mon.-Sat. daytime 7/hr., Sun. and evenings 4/hr.; 60p) or walk down Hills Road (25min.).

Bus Station: Drummer St. Station. **National Express** (tel. 460711). **Cambus** (tel. 423554) handles city and area service (40p-£1). Some local routes serviced by **Miller's** or **Premier** coaches. **Whippet Coaches** run daytrips from Cambridge. Travel Centre open Mon.-Sat. 8:15am-5:30pm.

Taxi: Cabco: tel. 312444. **Camtax:** tel. 313131. Both open 24hrs. Or hail one at St. Andrew's St. and Market Sq.

Bike Rental: University Cycle, 9 Victoria Ave. (tel. 355517). £7/day, £15/week; cash deposit £25. Open Mon.-Sat. 9am-5:45pm. **C. Frost,** 118 New Market Rd. (tel. 356464). £5/day, £10/week; deposit £20. Open Mon.-Fri. 9am-1pm and 2-6pm, Sat. 9:30am-1pm and 2-5pm.

Camping: YHA, 6-7 Bridge St. (tel. 353956). The place for camping, hiking, and backpacking equipment. Open Mon.-Tues. and Thurs.-Fri. 10am-6pm, Wed. 10am-7pm, Sat. 9:30am-6pm.

Bookstores: Heffers, 20 Trinity St. (tel. 358351). Get maps and recordings at 19 Sidney St. (tel. 358241), and paperbacks at 31 St. Andrew's St. (tel. 354778). Assorted other branches. Most open Mon.-Sat. 9am-5:30pm. St. Andrew's St. branch open 9am-6:30pm. **V. Galloway and Porter,** 30 Sidney St. (tel. 67876). Cheap second-hand books in great condition upstairs. Open Mon.-Fri. 8:30am-

5:30pm, Sat. 9am-5:15pm. Second-hand bookstalls moulder around St. Edward's passage and the marketplace.

Library: 7 Lion Yard (tel. 65252). Reference library with helpful information desk on 2nd floor. Open Mon.-Fri. 9:30am-7pm, Sat. 9:15am-5pm. Disabled access.

Launderette: Nameless Laundry (look under the painted bull), 44 Hills Rd. Open daily 9am-9pm.

Hotlines: Alcoholics Anonymous: tel. 833900. **AIDS:** tel. 69765. Open Tues.-Wed. 7:30-10pm. **Crime Victims:** tel. 63024. **Rape Crisis:** tel. 358314. 24-hr. answering service. **Samaritans:** tel. 64455. **Young People's Counselling and Information Service:** tel. 316488.

Hospital: Addenbrookes, Hills Rd. (tel. 245151). Catch Cambus #95 from Emmanuel St. (75p).

Emergency: Dial 999; no coins required.

Police: Parkside (tel. 358966).

ACCOMMODATIONS & CAMPING

Cambridge has no shortage of rooms (albeit expensive ones) for visitors, but it's advisable to book ahead during high season. Many of the cheap B&Bs around Portugal St. and Tenison Rd. house students during the academic year and are open to visitors only during the summer. If one house is full, ask for other accommodations in the neighborhood (B&Bs are often not labeled as such). Check the comprehensive list in the tourist office window, or pick up their guide to accommodations (50p).

HI Youth Hostel, 97 Tenison Rd. (tel. 354601; fax 312780), entrance on Devonshire Rd. Relaxed, welcoming atmosphere. Well-equipped kitchen, laundry room, TV lounge. 126 beds, mostly in 3-4-bed rooms; a few doubles. Couples may share a room, space permitting. Small lockers to store valuables available in some rooms; use 'em. Breakfast and sleepsack included. £12, under 18 £8.80. Packed lunch £2.10-2.80; evening meal £3.70. You can book ahead from any HI Youth Hostel on international computer booking system. Crowded March-Oct.; call a few days in advance and arrive by 6pm.

Home from Home B&B, Mrs. Flora Miles, 39 Milton Rd. (tel. 323555). Mrs. Miles welcomes guests into her sparkling, well-decorated home, located 15min. from the bus station and city center. Two doubles and 1 single with TV, wash basins, wonderful showers, and tea and coffee-making facilities. Singles £20. Doubles £32. Full English breakfast included. Call a few days ahead for reservations.

Warkworth Guest House, Warkworth Terrace (tel. 63682). Charming and gracious hostess has 16 sunny rooms in pastels near the bus station. Use of kitchen, laundry facilities, telephone. Singles £17. Doubles £30. Family £45. Breakfast included. Packed lunch on request.

Tenison Towers, Mr. and Mrs. Madeira, 148 Tenison Rd. (tel. 566511). Clean, comfy rooms near train station. Singles in summer £18, in winter £14. Doubles £24-28. Triples £35-39. Quads £44-52. Reductions for long-term stays.

Mrs. McCann, 40 Warkworth St. (tel. 314098). A jolly hostess with comfortable twin rooms in a quiet neighborhood near the bus station. Rates go down after two nights. Singles £15. Doubles £24. Breakfast included.

YMCA, Queen Anne House, Gonville Pl. (tel. 356998). 136 clean, bright dorm-style rooms in a buzzing social center which includes a fitness center and restaurant. Ideal location near the center of town. Singles £19.13. Doubles £31. Breakfast included. Call a week in advance.

Mrs. French, 42 Lyndewode (tel. 316615). Now starring Mr. French. Cramped, functional rooms. Save money here; treat yourself later to compensate. £12.

The tourist office has a list of 16 campsites in the Cambridge area (25p). To reach the **Highfield Farm Camping Park,** Long Rd., Comberton (tel. 262308), head west on A603 for 3 mi., then turn right on B1046 for 1 mi.; or take Cambus #118 from the Drummer St. bus station (every 45min.). Enjoy flush toilets, showers, and a washing machine (£7-8/tent; call ahead; open April-Oct.). The **Camping and Caravanning Club Site,** 19 Cabbage Moor, Great Shelford (tel. 841185), has toilets, showers, a washing machine, and facilities for travelers with disabilities. Head 3 mi. south on A10, then left onto A1301 for ¾ mi., or take Cambus #103 (£3.01-3.37, children £1.28 or free in off-season; call before arrival; open March-Oct.).

FOOD

Market Square has bright pyramids of fruit and vegetables for the budgetarian (open Mon.-Sat. approx. 8am-5:30pm). For vegetarian and wholefood groceries, try **Arjuna,** 12 Mill Rd. (tel. 64845; Mon.-Fri. 9:30am-6pm, Sat. 9am-5:30pm). The local version of **Holland and Barrett,** 6 Bradwell's Court off St. Andrew's St., carries a more extensive and expensive selection (open Mon.-Sat. 9am-5:30pm). Students buy gin and cornflakes at **Sainsbury's,** 44 Sidney St., the only grocery store in the middle of town (open Mon.-Wed. 8:30am-7pm, Thurs.-Fri. 8:30am-8pm). The food section in **Marks and Spencer,** 8 Sidney St., includes gourmet picnic items (open Mon.-Tues. 9:30am-5:30pm, Wed. 9am-8pm, Thurs. 9am-6pm, Fri. 8:30am-7:30pm, Sat. 8:30am-6pm). On Sunday, get groceries at the **Nip-In General Store,** 30 Mill Rd. (tel. 69048; open daily 8am-10pm), **H.T. Cox,** 67 Regent St. (open daily 8am-9pm), or **Spenser's,** 33 Hill Rd. (open daily 8:45am-11:30pm).

Cambridge has some fantastic ethnic foods, including a wealth of satisfying curry restaurants (make sure that the Christ's College football club has not arrived on their ritual curry night out). Both Hills Rd. and Mill Rd., south of town, brim with good, cheap restaurants just becoming trendy with student crowds.

Nadia's, 11 St. John's St. The best bakery in town, and one of the cheapest. Wonderful flapjacks and quiches 55p-£1.30. Take-away only. Open Mon.-Sat. 7:30am-5:30pm, Sun. 7:30am-5pm.

Rajbelash, 36-38 Hills Rd. A bewildering array of curries, *tandooris,* and *biryanis* £2.60-6.40. Love the *murg vindaloo.* Give your mouth some relief with unleavened *naan* bread (£1.20). Take-away and delivery available. Open daily noon-2:30pm and 6pm-midnight. Sunday buffet noon-2:30pm £6.50, children £4.50.

Tatties, 26-28 Regent St. Delectable baked potatoes to please any palate. With roof garden over Downing College. Vegetarians will delight. Hot potato with butter, £1.70. Open Mon.-Fri. 8am-9pm, Sat.-Sun. 10am-9pm.

Corner House Restaurant, 9 King St. Generous portions, friendly service, and low prices make up for the corner-diner atmosphere. Spaghetti and chips £2.95. Open Mon.-Fri. 11:30am-2:30pm and 5-9:30pm, Sat.-Sun. 11:30am-9:30pm.

Clown's, 54 King St. A meeting place for foreigners, bozos, and beautiful people. Affable, entertaining proprietor. Practice your Esperanto over a mean cappuccino (£1), quiche (£1.50), or cake (£1). Open daily 9am-11pm.

Hobbs' Pavillion, Parker's Piece, off Park Terrace. Renowned for imaginative, overpowering, rectangular pancakes. (The English like their pancakes thin, like French crepes.) Mars Bar and cream pancake £3.50—don't expect to feel like eating again for 2 weeks. Open Tues.-Sat. noon-2:15pm and 7-9:45pm.

The Little Tea Room, 1 All Saints' Passage. Not as hopelessly precious as it sounds; tip-top teas served in a teeny basement room. Scone, jam, and cream with tea £2.50. Open March-Dec. Mon.-Sat. 9:30am-5:30pm, Sun. noon-6pm.

Auntie's Tea Shop, 1 St. Mary's Passage, off King's Parade. Lace tablecloths, clinking china, and triangular sandwiches. Egg-and-cress sandwich £1.50, carrot cake £1.35. £1.50 minimum after noon. Don't expect many students. Open Mon.-Fri. 9:30am-6pm, Sat. 9:30am-6:30pm, Sun. noon-5:30pm.

PUBS

Cantabrigian hangouts offer good pub-crawling year-round, though they lose some of their character and their best customers in summer. Most pubs stay open from 11am to 11pm, noon to 10:30pm on Sundays. A few close from 3 to 7pm, especially on Sundays. The local brewery, Greene King, supplies many of the pubs with the popular bitters IPA (India Pale Ale) and Abbott. Students drink at the **Anchor,** Silver St. (by the river), on rainy days, and **The Mill,** Mill Lane off Silver St. Bridge, on sunny ones. The Anchor boasts live jazz bands on Tuesdays and Thursdays (tel.

353554), and at the neighboring Mill you can partake of a pint along the banks of the Cam while punt-and-people watching. At 3-4 King St. wobbles the **Cambridge Arms,** a large renovated brewery. Further along rests the **Champion of the Thames,** 68 King St., a broom closet of a pub—groups of more than five might not even fit. King St. gets a bit dodgy around closing time on Saturday nights, so take care. A favorite with Magdalene men and Cambridge secretarial college women, the **Pickerel** on Bridge St. (where it turns into Magdalene St.) holds the grand distinction of being Cambridge's oldest pub. **The Maypole,** on Portugal Pl. between Bridge St. and New Park St., conjures up cocktails more often than beer; the pub sports a billiards table. Locals and collegiate crew members pack the **Free Press,** on Prospect St. and Prospect Row; tourists might not feel comfortable walking in alone. The **Sir Isaac Newton,** Castle St., is one of the few pubs in town with facilities for travelers with disabilities. Alas, older, professional types sip bitters here and bore one another to tears. The **Burleigh Arms,** 9-11 Newmarket Rd., serves up beer and lager to its primarily gay clientele. Amble down to the **Bird in Hand** (next to the roundabout), where gay men are welcome, and have a pint in the beer garden.

Those who prefer to drink to live music can take their choice of pubs. **Flambard's Wine Bar,** 4 Rose Crescent (tel. 358108), has live blues and jazz on weekends, and to the east, **The Geldart,** 1 Ainsworth St. (tel. 355983), features Irish folk, rock and R&B. **The Junction,** Clifton Rd. (tel. 412600), off Cherry Hinton Rd. south of the town, proves a popular alternative dance venue on Friday nights and hosts top local bands. Popular night spots change constantly; students, bartenders, and the latest issue of *Varsity* will be your best sources of information.

SIGHTS

Cambridge is an architect's dream, packing some of the most breathtaking monuments of English engineering over the last 700 years into less than one square mile. World-famous King's College Chapel is a must-see, but if you explore some of the more obscure courts (quads), you'll discover gems unseen by most visitors.

If you are pressed for time, visit at least one chapel (preferably at King's College), one garden (try Christ's), one library (Trinity's is the most interesting), and one dining hall. Most historic university buildings line the east side of the Cam between Magdalene Bridge and Silver St. On both sides of the river, the gardens, meadows, and cows of the **Backs** bring a pastoral air to Cambridge. If you have time for only a few colleges, **King's, Trinity, Queens', Christ's, St. John's,** and **Jesus** should top your list, though the IthinkI'lldoEuropeinaweek traveler could trample through 12 or 14 colleges in a few hours: most cluster around the center of town.

The University of Cambridge has three eight-week terms: Michaelmas (Oct.-Dec.), Lent (Jan.-March), and Easter (April-June). Visitors can gain access to most of the college grounds daily from 9am to 5:30pm, though many close to sightseers during the Easter term, and virtually all are closed during exam period (mid-May to mid-June). Unlike many U.S. campuses, Cambridge has no armed University police. Plump bowler-bedecked ex-servicemen called Porters maintain security. Look and act like a student (i.e. wear no traveler's backpack, no camera, and, for heaven's sake, no Cambridge sweatshirt) and you should be able to wander freely through most college grounds even after hours (never on the preciously tended lawns). In the summer, a few undergrads stay to work or study, but most skip town, leaving it to hormone-driven mobs of teenage language students. Some university buildings shut down over vacations.

King's College, on King's Parade, is the proud possessor of the university's most famous chapel, a spectacular Gothic monument. In 1441, Henry VI cleared away most of the center of medieval Cambridge for the foundation of King's College, and he intended this chapel to be England's finest. Although Hank wanted the inside to remain unadorned, his successors spent nearly £5000 carving an elaborate interior. If you stand at the southwest corner of the courtyard, you can see where Henry VI's master mason John Wastell (who also worked on the cathedrals of Peterborough and Canterbury) left off and where work under the Tudors began. The earlier stone is off-white, the later, dark. The interior of the chapel consists of one huge chamber cleft by a carved wooden choir screen, one of the purest examples of the early Renaissance style in England. Wordsworth described the fan-vault ceiling as a "branching roof self-poised, and scooped into ten thousand cells where light and shade repose." Stained glass windows depicting the life of Jesus were preserved from the iconoclasm of the English Civil War, allegedly because John Milton, then Cromwell's secretary, groveled on their behalf. Symbols of Henry VI's reign abound; look for the Tudor roses. Behind the altar hangs Rubens' magnificent *Adoration of the Magi* (1639), protected by an electronic alarm since a crazed would-be stonemason attacked it with a chisel several years ago. Free musical recitals often play at the chapel—pick up a schedule at the entrance. (College open June-Oct. Mon.-Fri. 9:30am-4:30pm; Sun. 9am-5pm. £2, students and children £1, under 12 free with adults. Chapel open term-time Mon.-Sat. 9:30am-3:30pm, Sun. 1:15-2:15pm and 4:45-5:15pm; chapel and exhibitions open college vacations 10am-5pm; free). Enjoy the classic view of the chapel and of the adjacent **Gibbs Building** from the river; take a picnic down by the water and graze by the lazy black cows. Moo.

In early June the university posts the names and final grades of every student in the Georgian **Senate House** opposite the King's College chapel, designed by Gibbs and built in the 1720s; about a week later, degree ceremonies are held there. Cambridge graduates are eligible for the world's easiest master's degrees: after spending three and one-third years out in the Real World, a graduate sends £15 to the university to receive one without further ado, provided that said graduate is not in the custody of Her Majesty's Prison Service. It's the ultimate mail-order diploma service.

Trinity College, on Trinity St., holds the largest purse at the University. The college's status as the wealthiest at Cambridge has become legendary—myth-mongers claim that it was once possible to walk from Cambridge to Oxford without stepping off Trinity land. Founded in 1546 by Henry VIII, Trinity once specialized in literature (alums include George Herbert, John Dryden, Lord Byron, and Lord Tennyson), but in this century has instead spat forth scientists and philosophers (Ernest Rutherford, Ludwig Wittgenstein, G.E. Moore, and Bertrand Russell). Inside the courtyard, in a florid fountain built in 1602, Byron used to bathe nude. The eccentric young poet lived in Nevile's Court and shared his rooms with a pet bear, whom he claimed would take his fellowship exams for him. Generations later, the heir adulterant, Prince Charles, was an average student in anthropology. The expanse of Trinity's **Great Court**—the largest yard in Cambridge—encompasses an area so huge that you can almost fail to notice its utter lack of straight lines and symmetry. The great courtyard race in *Chariots of Fire* is set here, although Eton College, a university preparatory school, mimicked it for the movie. What William Wordsworth called the "loquacious clock that speaks with male and female voice" still strikes 24 times each noon. Sir Isaac Newton, who lived on the first floor of E-entry for 30 years, first measured the speed of sound by stamping his foot in the cloister along the north side of the court. Underneath the courtyards lie the well-hidden, well-stocked Trinity wine cellars. Recently the college purchased over £20,000 worth of port that won't be drinkable until 2020.

Amble through the college toward the river to reach the reddish stone walls of the stunning **Wren Library**. Notable treasures in this naturally lit building include A.A. Milne's handwritten manuscript of *Winnie-the-Pooh* and less momentous works such as John Milton's *Lycidas*. The collection also contains works by Byron, Tennyson, and Thackeray. German-speakers certain of the existence of books might look for Wittgenstein's journals. His phenomenal *Philosophical Investigations* was conceived here during years of intense discussion with G.E. Moore and students in his top-floor K-entry rooms. (Library open Mon.-Fri. noon-2pm; free. Trinity's courtyards close at 6pm; college and library closed during exams.) Avoid grumpy guards.

Established in 1511 by Lady Margaret Beaufort, mother of Henry VIII, **St. John's College** is one of seven Cambridge colleges founded by women. The striking brick and stone gatehouse bears Lady Margaret's heraldic emblem. St. John's centers around a paved plaza rather than a grassy courtyard, and its two best buildings stand across the river from the other colleges. A copy of Venice's Bridge of Sighs connects the older part of the college to the towering neo-Gothic extravagance of New Court, likened by philistines to a wedding cake in silhouette (chapel open during term Tues.-Fri. 9am-noon and 2-4pm; Mon. and Sat. 9am-noon; college open daily during vacation; £1, children and seniors 50p, families £2). Next door, you can see more adventurous college architecture, the modern **Cripps Building,** with clever bends that create three distinct courts under the shade of a noble willow. The **School of Pythagoras,** a 12th-century pile of wood and stone rumored to be the oldest complete building in Cambridge, hides in St. John's Gardens (courtyard and some buildings open until 6pm; closed during exams).

Queens' College, was founded not once, but twice—by Margaret of Anjou in 1448 and again by Elizabeth Woodville in 1465. It possesses the only unaltered Tudor courtyard in Cambridge, containing the half-timbered President's Gallery. The **Mathematical Bridge,** just past Cloister Court, was built in 1749 without a single bolt or nail, relying only on mathematical principle. A meddling Victorian took the bridge apart to see how it worked and the inevitable occurred—he couldn't put it back together without using a steel rivet every two inches (college open daily 1:45-4:30pm; during summer vacation also 10:30am-12:45pm; closed during exams; £1, under 14 free).

Clare College, founded in 1326 by the thrice-widowed, 29-year-old Lady Elizabeth de Clare, has preserved an appropriate coat of arms: golden teardrops on a black border. Across Clare Bridge (the most elegant on the river) lie the **Clare Gardens** (open Mon.-Fri. 2-4:45pm; during summer vacation also 10am-4:30pm). Walk through Clare's **Old Court** (open during exams after 4:45pm to groups of less than 3) for a view of the University Library, where 82 mi. of shelves hold books arranged according to size rather than subject. George V called it "the greatest erection in Cambridge;" more recently it appeared in the cinematic masterpiece *Brazil* (college open daily 10am-5pm; £1.50, under 10 free).

Christ's College, founded as "God's-house" in 1448 and renamed in 1505, has won fame for its gardens (open Mon.-Fri. 10:30am-12:30pm and 2-4pm; summer Mon.-Fri. 9:30am-noon) and its association with the poet John Milton; a mulberry tree reputedly planted by the "Lady of Christ's" still thrives here. To reach the gardens, walk under the lovely neoclassical Fellows Building dubiously accredited to Inigo Jones. Charles Darwin dilly-dallied through Christ's before informing man he was little more than a clean-shaven ape with a tie. His rooms (unmarked and closed to visitors) were on G staircase in First Court. **New Court,** on King St., is one of the most stunning, horrific modern structures in Cambridge; its symmetrical gray concrete walls and black-curtained windows look like the whelp of an Egyptian pyramid, a Polaroid camera, and a typewriter. The college closes during exams, save for access to the chapel during services and concerts. (Inquire at the porter's desk.)

Cloistered on a secluded site, **Jesus College** has preserved an enormous amount of unaltered medieval work, dating from 1496. Beyond the long, high-walled walk called the "Chimny" lies a three-sided court fringed with colorful gardens. Through the archway on the right lie the remains of a gloomy medieval nunnery. The Pre-Raphaelite stained glass of Burne-Jones and ceiling decorations by William "Wallpaper" Morris festoon the chapel (courtyard open until 6pm; closed during exams).

Once the recipient of buildings from a 15th-century Benedictine hostel, **Magdalene College** (MAUD-lin), founded in 1524, has more recently acquired an unsavory, aristocratic reputation. Don't forget to take a peek at the **Pepys Library** (ridiculously labeled **Bibliotheca Pepysiana**) in the second court; the library displays the noted statesman and prolific diarist's collection in their original cases. The college dining hall hovers to the left as you walk to the second court. (Library open Mon.-Sat. 2:30-5:30pm; Easter-Aug. 11:30am-12:30pm; free. Courtyards closed during exams.)

Thomas Gray wrote his *Elegy in a Country Churchyard* while staying in **Peterhouse,** on Trumpington St., the oldest and smallest college, founded in 1294. In contrast, **Robinson College,** across the river on Grange Rd., distinguishes itself by being the college's newest. Founded in 1977, this mod-medieval brick pastiche sits just behind the university library. Bronze plants writhe about the door of the college chapel, which features some fascinating stained glass. James Stirling's **History Faculty Building,** between West Rd. and Sidgwick Ave., once provoked much debate about its aesthetic merits; of its leaky roof, there were never any doubts.

Corpus Christi College, founded in 1352 by the common people, contains a dreary but extremely old courtyard forthrightly called Old Court, unaltered since its 1352 enclosure. The library maintains the snazziest collection of Anglo-Saxon manuscripts in England, including the Parker Manuscript of the *Anglo-Saxon Chronicle.* The 1347 **Pembroke College** next door harbors the earliest architectural effort of Sir Christopher Wren (courtyards open until 6pm; closed during exams).

A chapel designed by Sir Christopher Wren dominates the front court of **Emmanuel College.** Emmanuel, founded in 1584, on St. Andrew's St. at Downing St., and **Downing College,** founded in 1807, just to the south along Regent St., are both pleasantly isolated (courtyards open until 6pm; chapel open when not in use). Downing's austere neoclassical buildings open onto an immense lawn (open daily until 6pm; dining hall open when not in use; closed during exams). John Harvard, alleged founder of a certain New England university, attended Emmanuel; a stained glass panel depicting Harvard graces the college chapel.

The **Round Church (Holy Sepulchre),** Bridge St. and St. John's St., one of five circular churches surviving in England, was built in 1130 (and later rebuilt) on the pattern of the Church of the Holy Sepulchre in Jerusalem. The pattern merits comparison with **St. Benet's Church,** a rough Saxon church on Benet St. The tower of St. Benet's, built in 1050, is the oldest structure in Cambridge.

You can easily get caught up in the splendor of the colleges, but try also to take in a few museums. The **Fitzwilliam Museum,** Trumpington St. (tel. 332900), a 10-minute walk down the road from King's College, dwells within an immense Roman-style building. Inside, a cavernous marble foyer leads to a collection that includes paintings by Leonardo da Vinci, Michelangelo, Dürer, Corot, Monet, and Seurat. A goulash of Egyptian, Chinese, and Greek antiquities bides its time downstairs, coupled with an extensive collection of 16th-century German armor. Check out the illuminated manuscripts under their protective cloths. The drawing room displays William Blake's books and woodcuts. (Open Tues.-Fri. ground floor 10am-2pm, upper floor 2-5pm, Sat. both floors 10am-5pm, Sun. both floors 2:15-5pm; free. Call to inquire about lunchtime and evening concerts; guided tours Sat.-Sun. at 2:30pm, £1.50). The **Museum of Zoology** (tel. 336650), off Downing St., houses a fine collection of wildlife specimens in a modern, well-lit building (open Mon.-Fri. 2:15-4:45pm; free; wheelchair accessible). Across the road, opposite Corn Exchange St., the **Museum of Archaeology and Anthropology,** Downing St. (tel. 333516), contains an excellent collection of prehistoric artifacts from American, African, Pacific, and Asian cultures, as well as exhibits from Cambridge through the ages (open Mon.-Fri. 2-4pm, Sat. 10am-12:30pm; free; wheelchair accessible, but call ahead). If you're near Magdalene College, stop by the **Folk Museum,** 2-3 Castle St. (tel. 355159), by Northampton St., an appealing collection dating from the 17th century (open Mon.-Sat. 10:30am-5pm, Sun. 2-5pm; £1, student, seniors, and children 50p). **Kettle's Yard,** at the corner of Castle and Northampton St. (tel. 352124), houses early 20th-century art (house open Tues.-Sun. 2-4pm; gallery open Tues.-Sat. 12:30-5:30pm, Sun. 2-5pm; free). The **Scott Polar Research Institute,** Lensfield Rd. (tel. 336540), commemorates icy expeditions with photographic and artistic accounts, equipment, and memorabilia (open Mon.-Sat. 2:30-4pm; free).

The **Botanic Gardens** (tel. 336265; enter from Hill Rd. or Bateman St.) were ingeniously laid out by Henslow, Sir Joseph Hooker's father-in-law, circa 1846. When the wind gets rolling, the scented garden turns into an perfume factory. Perambulate about the paths and gaze on the recently replanted rose beds. (Open daily 10am-4pm or 6pm, depending on the season; Wed. free; Nov.-Feb. Mon.-Fri. free; otherwise £1.50, under 18 £1.) Guided tours available.

ENTERTAINMENT

On a sunny afternoon, bodies sprawl on the lush banks of the Cam and the river fills with narrow, flat-bottomed **punts,** England's gondola. Punting is the sometimes stately, sometimes soggy pastime of propelling a flat little boat (a punt) by pushing a long pole into the river bottom. If your pole gets stuck, leave it in the mud instead of taking a plunge. Punters seeking calm and charm can take two routes—one from Magdalene Bridge to Silver St., and the other from Silver St. along the River Granta (the name given to the Cam as it passes out of town) to Grantchester. On the first route—the shorter, busier, and more interesting of the two—you'll pass the colleges and the Backs. Punt-bombing, in which students jump from bridges into the river right next to a punt, thereby tipping its occupants into the Cam, has been raised to an art form, hindered only slightly by increased river policing. You can rent a punt from **Scudamore's Boatyards,** at Magdalene Bridge or Silver St. (tel. 359750); hourly rates £6-8 for punts, rowboats, and canoes, plus a £40 cash deposit (open daily 9am-6pm). **Tyrell's,** Magdalene Bridge (tel. 352847), has punts, rowboats, and a canoe for £8 per hour, plus a £30 deposit. Tyrell's offers chauffeured rides (45min.) starting at £15 per group. Most rental agents accept credit cards.

You can expect long lines for punts on weekends, particularly on Sunday—rowboats and canoes are easier to come by. To avoid bumper-punting, go late in the afternoon when the river traffic dwindles, but boats must be returned by 6pm. Guided tours, punted by students, offer a cop-out option to those unwilling to risk a plunge. Inquire at the tourist office.

During the first two weeks of June, students celebrate the end of the term with **May Week** (a May of the mind), crammed with concerts, plays, and elaborate balls that feature everything from hot air balloon rides to sleeping face-down drunk in the street to recuperative breakfasts by the river. Along the Cam, the college boat clubs compete in an eyebrow-raising series of races known as the **bumps.** Crews line up along the river rather than across it and attempt to ram the boat in front before being bumped from behind. Visitors may enjoy the annual fireworks from the vantage of one of the city's bridges. May Week's artistic repertoire stars the famous **Footlights Revue,** a collection of comedy skits; its performers have gone on to join such troupes as Beyond the Fringe and Monty Python. John Cleese, Eric Idle, and Graham Chapman graduated from the Revue.

The third week of June ushers in the **Midsummer Fair,** which dates from the early 16th century and appropriates the Midsummer Common for about five days. The free **Strawberry Fair,** Cambridge's answer to Glastonbury, takes place the first Saturday in June. Address all festival inquiries to the tourist office.

During the rest of the summer, Cambridge caters to tourists more than students, but the **Cambridge Festival** brightens the last two weeks of July with a series of concerts and special exhibits culminating in a huge folk festival. Tickets for the weekend (about £32) include camping on the grounds. (For the main festival, call the Corn Exchange box office, tel. 357851.) The **Arts Cinema,** Market Passage (tel. 352001), screens comedy classics and undubbed foreign films and holds a film festival during the Festival (tickets £2.90-3.80; box office open Mon.-Sat. 10am-9:15pm, Sun. 1-9:15pm). The Cinema box office also handles **ADC Theatre** (Amateur Dramatic Club) ticket sales. The ADC, Park St., offers lively performances and entertainment during the term and the Cambridge Festival—both student-produced plays and movies. The best source of information on student activities is the *Varsity.* You can get an earful of concerts at the **Cambridge Corn Exchange,** at the corner of Wheeler St. and Corn Exchange, a venue for band, jazz, and classical concerts (box office tel. 357851; tickets £7.50-16; 50% off for student standby day of performance for certain concerts; box office open Mon.-Sat. 10am-6pm).

■ NEAR CAMBRIDGE

Not easily visited, **Grantchester** is worth the effort. Immortalized by Rupert Brooke in 1912 with his clumsy verse "Stands the Church clock at ten to three? And is there honey still for tea?" Grantchester is a mecca for Cambridge literary types. When the clock was stopped for repairs in 1985, its hands were left frozen pedantically at ten to three. You can see the church clock tower next to Brooke's home at the Old Vicarage (closed to the public). To reach Grantchester Meadows from Cambridge, take the path that follows the River Granta (about 45min.; the river is the namesake of a British literary magazine). Grantchester itself lies about a mile from the meadows; ask the way at one of the neighborhood shops. If you have the energy to pole or paddle your way, rent a punt or canoe from **Scudamore's Boatyards** (see Cambridge: Entertainment, above). After tying up your boat, follow the signs to the road. Look up. Is it raining? Close the book! Close the book! The **Rupert Brooke,** 2 Broadway (open daily 11am-11pm), and the **Green Man,** High St. (open Mon.-Sat. 11am-3pm and 6-11pm, Sun. noon-3pm and 7-10:30pm), will reward the famished and parched. Before returning to Cambridge, stop by the charmingly weathered **Parish Church of St. Andrew and St. Mary,** on Milway. Some of its fragments date to the 14th century.

Wimpole Hall, Cambridgeshire's most spectacular mansion, done in an elegant 18th-century style, lies 10 mi. southwest of Cambridge. The Hall holds works by Gibbs, Flitcroft, and Joane and gardens sculpted by Capability Brown. (Open July 23-Aug. 30 daily 1-5pm; April-Oct. Tues.-Thurs., Sat.-Sun. 1-5pm; bank holidays 11am-5pm. £4.50, children £2.) **Wimpole's Home Farm** (tel. (01223) 207257), fills with Longhorn and Gloucester cattle, Soay sheep, and Tamworth pigs. (Open April-Oct. Tues.-Thurs. and Sat.-Sun. 10:30am-5pm. Farm only £3.50, children £1.55, hall and gardens only £4.50, children £2.25; joint hall and farm £6.)

Northeast of Cambridge, 12th-century **Anglesey Abbey** (tel. (01223) 811175) has been tastefully remodeled to house the priceless exotica of the first Lord Fairhaven. One of the niftiest clocks in the universe sits inconspicuously on the bookcase beyond the fireplace. In the 100-acre gardens, trees punctuate lines of clipped hedges and manicured lawns. (Open mid-July-mid-Sept. daily 11am-5:30pm; April-mid-July and mid-Sept.-Oct. Wed.-Sun. 1-5:30pm. Gardens open April-July Wed.-Sun. and bank holidays 11am-5:30pm; July 12-Sept. 7 daily 10am-5:30pm; Sept. 8-Oct. 17 Wed.-Sun. 11am-5:30pm. £4.75, gardens only £3, children half-price.) The abbey lies 4 mi. from Cambridge on the B1102 (off the A1303). Buses (#111 or 122) from Drummond St. Station (1/hr.). Ask to be let off at Lode Crossroads.

Dating from the days of the Saxon invasions and possibly the Neolithic and Bronze Ages, the market town of **Saffron Walden** (pop. 13,000), 15 mi. south of Cambridge, retains a medieval street layout that few towns in England can match. Saffron Walden's name comes from the saffron that used to be sold there and from the Anglo-Saxon word for "wooded valley." The town is best known for the "pargetting" (plaster moulding) that adorns many of the town's Tudor buildings. Those who want to lose themselves should head either to the **Bridge End Garden Maze** (closed for hedge growth, but the tourist office can make special arrangements) or to the brick-and-turf maze on the Common. To reach Saffron Walden from Cambridge, take Cambus #22 or 112 (Mon.-Sat. 10min. before every hour; about £20), Cambus #122 (leaves Cambridge Mon.-Sat. at 12:15, 2:40, and 5:35pm; last return 1:05pm), or Cambus #103 (Sun. only; every 2 hrs.; last return 7:10pm). Trains leave Cambridge semi-hourly for nearby **Audley End,** a magnificent Jacobean hall set in grounds designed by Capability Brown (open April-Sept. daily 1-6pm; £4.50, students £3.40, children £2.30).

The **tourist office** at 1 Market Pl., Market Sq. (tel. (01799) 510444) has a good map and guide (20p; open Mon.-Sat. 9:30am-5pm; Nov.-March 10am-5pm; walking tours April-Oct. Sun. at 2:45pm; £2). The **HI Youth Hostel,** 1 Myddylton Place (tel. (01799) 523117), in the north part of town on the A130, occupies one of the oldest buildings in the village. (Lockout 10am-5pm; curfew 11pm; £6.30, under 18 £4.20; open May-July Mon.-Sat.; Aug. daily; Feb. Fri.-Sat.; March-April and Oct. Tues.-Sat.) Within the **Eight Bells** pub on Bridge St. beats the heart of the town's social life.

■■■ ELY

Legend has it that in the area just north of Cambridge, St. Dunstan saw fit to turn the local monks into eels as punishment for their lack of proper piety, a sacred transformation that earned one town the name Ely (EEL-ee). Here too, brave Hereward the Wake defended himself against Norman invaders, earning the title "the last of all the English." While Norman battles are tough to top, the beautiful cathedral and restful atmosphere make for an agreeable one-day stopover between London or Cambridge and cities farther north.

Ely serves as the junction on the train lines between London, King's Lynn, Norwich and Peterborough, with frequent connections to each of these cities. **Cambus** runs often from Market St. to Cambridge (£2.55). **Trains** rumble between Cambridge and Ely (1/hr.; 20min.; day return £3.10) and Norwich (1/hr.; 1½hr.; return £8.90). To reach the cathedral and the tourist office from the train station, walk up Station Rd. and continue onto Back Hill, which then becomes The Gallery. Hitchhikers report Ely and the surrounding areas to be fertile ground for a ride.

PRACTICAL INFORMATION

The **tourist office** shares and operates the Cromwell House. The dedicated staff will book rooms and provide you with free maps and accommodations lists (open daily 10am-6pm; Oct.-March Mon.-Sat. 10am-5:15pm). **Tours** of the town and cathedral leave the tourist office twice a week July through August (Sat. at 11am; £2.75, children £1.80; winter tours of the city and cathedral must be booked in advance). Cromwell House and city tours occur on Thursdays (£1.80, children 90p). Tours of the city alone leave at 2pm on Saturday (£1.50). The **post office** (tel. 669946) is in Lloyd's Chemist on High St. Ely's **postal code** is CB7 4LQ, its **telephone code** 01353. The **police** actively resent Sting's solo career on Nutholt Lane (tel. 662392).

ACCOMMODATIONS, CAMPING, & FOOD

Ely's B&Bs hover slightly out of reach of the budget-minded traveler (£12-15). You might do better at the **HI Youth Hostel,** Ely Sixth Form Centre, St. Audrey's, Downham Rd. (tel. 667423), which occupies a large, clean school building (lockout 10am-5pm; curfew 11pm; £6.30, under 18 £4.20; open mid-May to early Sept.). From the cathedral, follow the Gallery to Egremont St., turn left, then right on Downham Rd.—the hostel is three blocks away on the right. **Mrs. Wheeler,** St. David's, 19a Egremont St. (tel. 662217), offers two single rooms and one double room to non-smokers exclusively (£16, includes full English breakfast). You can camp among spuds and sugarbeet for only £1.50 per tent or £2.50 per caravan at **Braham Farm,** Cambridge Rd. (tel. 662386), off the A10 just past the golf course (toilets and cold water available).

Tea houses abound in Ely. For a bargain meal, stop at one of the numerous takeaway places (be forewarned: many close early). Most shops in the town close down on Tuesday afternoons at about 1pm. On Thursdays (8:30am-4:30pm) stock up on provisions at the general **market** in Market Pl. The **Minster Tavern,** Minster Pl., opposite the cathedral, is a popular spot (lunches £2-5). **The Steeplegate,** on 16-18 High St. across from the cathedral, serves tea and light snacks in two rooms built over a medieval undercroft; fall into a romantic reverie over a pot of Earl Grey (75p; open daily 10am-5pm). **Mother Nature,** High St., purveys wholefoods (open Mon.-Sat. 9am-5pm). Fill yourself on a lunch of roast beef, Yorkshire Pudding, two vegetables, and potatoes (£3.55) at the crowded, in-a-way elegant restaurant above **Bonnet's Bakery,** 13 High St. (lunch only; closes at 5pm). On the banks of the Great Ouse (OOZE), the pub at the **Maltings,** Ship Lane, a restored brewery building, serves bar meals on its patio (£1.50-6.95; open daily noon-2pm and 6-9pm). **Surma,** 78 Broad St., serves good, affordable curries and *tandooris* (£3.50-5; open daily noon-3pm and 6pm-midnight).

SIGHTS

The massive **cathedral,** nicknamed the "Ship of the Fens," was founded in 1081 on the spot where St. Etheldreda had formed a hilltop religious community four centuries earlier. In 1322, the original Norman tower collapsed and the present octagonal **lantern tower** was constructed. Macabre masks grin with bared teeth from the intersection of the inner buttresses (disabled access on the south side). In 1986, Ely was the first city in England to charge admission to its cathedral, earning national notoriety, although bitter Elians claim that the people of Salisbury actually beat them to it by effectively forcing people to make donations. (Cathedral open daily 7am-7pm; Oct.-Easter Mon.-Fri. 7:30am-6pm, Sun. 7:30am-5pm; tours Easter-Oct. Mon.-Sat. 11:15am and 2:15pm; July-Aug. also 3:15pm; evensong Mon.-Sat. 5:30pm, Sun. 3:45pm; £2.80, students £2, free during services; guided tours of tower through booking only; refectory open daily in summer 10am-5pm). The cathedral's separate **stained glass museum** overlooks the nave (open March-Oct. Mon.-Sat. 10:30am-4pm, Sun. noon-3pm; £1.50, students 70p). Admission to the **brass-rubbing center** is free; you pay only for those materials that you use in your frottage (open daily July-Aug. 10:30am-4pm, Sun. noon-3pm).

The monastic buildings that surround the cathedral are still in use: the **infirmary** now houses one of the residentiary canons, and the **bishop's palace** is a home for children with disabilities. The rest of the buildings are used by the **King's School,** one of the older public (i.e., private) schools in England. For a rigorous architectural tour of the town, follow the path outlined by the tourist office's overwhelmingly detailed *Town Walks* pamphlet (45p). The **Ely Museum,** 28d High St. (tel. 666655), tells the engaging story of a fenland city and its people. Ely was an island until the fens were drained in the 17th century (open Tues.-Sun. 10:30am-1pm and 2:15-5pm; last entry 4:30pm; £1, children over 6 50p). Standing in the western shadow of Ely Cathedral, **Oliver Cromwell's House,** 29 St. Mary's Street (tel. 662062), has recently been refurbished in 17th-century decor (£1.80, children and seniors £1.30). Walking around the restructured **marketplace,** open only to pedestrians, provides a moment's escape from the motorized world.

■■■ KING'S LYNN

King's Lynn (pop. 42,000) meets the earth tones of the flat East Anglian countryside with a somber red-brick facade. This dockside city on the banks of the Great Ouse, once a member of the Hanseatic League (a 17th-century EC), borrows its Germanic look from trading partners like Hamburg and Bremen. While King's Lynn makes a perfect stop-over for cyclists exploring the region, the town slumbers early; thrill-seekers need not apply.

PRACTICAL INFORMATION

The **tourist office** (tel. 276 3044), housed in the Old Gaolhouse on the Saturday Market Pl., gives out free accommodations lists and maps, books rooms gratis, provides bus and train info, and houses exhibits (see Sights, below). To get to the office from the train station, turn left onto Blackfriars Rd., take a right onto St. John's Terrace, and a quick left onto St. James Rd. Turn right at St. James St., which will become Saturday Market Place. The tourist office is just past High St. From the bus station, walk out the rear entrance onto Broad St. and turn left. Turn right onto New Conduit St., then left onto High St. (open Mon.-Thurs. and Sat. 9:15am-5pm, Fri. 9:15am-5:30pm, Sun. 10am-5pm). The **train station** (tel. 277 2021) rests on Blackfriars Rd. Trains steam to London's Liverpool Station (20/day; 2½hr.; £20.30), Cambridge (1hr.; £6.70), and Peterborough (£5.80). **Eastern Counties buses** leave from **Vancouver Centre** (tel. 2772343) for Norwich (5/day; £3.70) and Peterborough (4/day; £3.45). **National Express coaches** run once daily to Norwich and to Peterborough. Buy tickets from **Dick Ropas,** a store on St. James St. (tel. 269 2035).The **hospital** (tel.

276 6266) is on Gayton Rd. Send *Let's Go* a postcard from the **post office** at the corner of Broad and New Conduit St. King's Lynn's **postal code** is PE30 1YB.

> On April 16, 1995 ("Phone Day"), the **telephone code** for the Leicester/King's Lynn area will change from 0533 to **0116** and a 2 will prefix all existing local numbers. The new code and numbers can, however, be used as of August 1, 1994, and *Let's Go* lists only these. For further information, see the Appendix.

ACCOMMODATIONS & FOOD

A pleasant, quayside **HI Youth Hostel** (tel. 277 2461) occupies part of the 16th-century Thoresby College, on College Lane, just opposite the tourist office. (Lockout 10am-5pm; curfew 11pm; £7, under 18 £4.60; evening meals available; open June-Aug. Sun.-Tues. and Thurs.-Sat.; Feb. 12-28, April-May, and Sept. Thurs.-Mon.; March and Oct. Fri.-Sat.) The hostel often fills, so call well ahead. **B&Bs** are a hike from the city center; the least expensive span Gaywood Rd., near the hospital. Late arrivals should consult the list of guesthouses posted outside the tourist office.

King's Lynn restaurants operate on their own sweet time—closed Sunday and Monday evenings (look for a take-away or grocer instead). They do stay open Wednesdays, when shops close early. The pink and spacious **La Mama's,** 110 High St. (tel. 269 1512), one of the only places open Mondays, bakes good and filling pizzas (£3.45-10.45, open daily 9:30am-11:30pm; free delivery; credit cards accepted). The **Tudor Rose,** St. Nicholas St. (tel. 276 2824), off the Tuesday Market Pl., has a popular bar menu, including vegetarian specials (£1.60-3.75). For fresh fruits and vegetables, try the **markets** (Tues. and Fri. roughly 8:30am-4pm), held at the larger Tuesday Market Pl. on the north end of High St., or on Saturday at the Saturday Market Pl. across from the tourist office.

SIGHTS

King's Lynn's most interesting buildings snooze by the Ouse on the city's western edge. The huge 15th-century **Guildhall of St. George,** 27-29 King St. (tel. 277 4725), near the Tuesday Market, is said to be the last surviving building in England where Shakespeare appeared in his own play; it now hosts the **King's Lynn Arts Centre** (open Mon.-Fri. 10am-5pm, Sat. 10am-12:30pm and 2-4pm).

The tourist office holds two exhibitions, the **Regalia Room** and **Tales of the Old Gaol House** (wheelchair access). Filled with treasures from King's Lynn's past, the Regalia Room merits a quick peek. Next door, a personal stereo guide leads you through the town's old jail, spinning stories of Lynn's murderers, robbers, and witches. Clamp that Swiss guy who's been following you for three weeks into the stocks, and leave. (Open Easter-Oct. daily 10am-5pm; Nov.-Easter Fri.-Tues. 10am-5pm; last entry 4:15pm. Gaol House £2, seniors and children £1.50; Gaol House and Town House Museum (see below) £2.50, seniors and children £1.80.)

Across the street is **St. Margaret's Church** (tel. 277 2858), bits of which date from the 13th century. **Town House Museum,** 46 Queen St., next to the Guildhall (tel. 277 3450), catalogues the drudgery of life from medieval times through the Victorian Era (open Tues.-Sat. 10am-5pm., Sun. 2-5pm; Oct.-April Tues.-Sat. 10am-4pm; £1, children 50p). Although it looks like a space rocket, the octagonal **Greyfriars Tower,** St. James St., is in fact the final remnant of a 14th-century monastery.

During July's last half, the guildhall hosts the **King's Lynn Festival,** an orgy of classical and jazz music, along with ballet, puppet shows, and films which even the Royal Family may have seen. Get schedules at the Festival Office, 27 King St., PE30 1HA (tel. 277 3578). Tickets cost £2.50-9; look for ½-price student standbys 30 min. before curtain (box office open Mon.-Fri. 10am-5pm, Sat. 10am-1pm and 2-4pm).

■ NEAR KING'S LYNN

The stomping grounds of the wealthy, punctuated by sumptuous mansions, gives way to wildlife country as the road leading north from King's Lynn bends east to flank the northern Norfolk coast. Ten miles north of King's Lynn lies **Sandringham** (tel. (0116) 277 2675), a home of the Royal Family since 1862. Its extensive grounds are open to the public when not in use by the Royal Family. The best time to visit is during the **flower show** in July's final week. (Open late April-Sept. Mon.-Sat. 11am-4:45pm, Sun. noon-4:45pm; grounds open 30 min. before house, close 15min. after; house, grounds, and museum £3.50, seniors and students £2.50, children £2; grounds and museum £2, seniors and students £1.50, children £1.) The house and grounds shut down for part of July; ask the King's Lynn tourist office before you leave. **Eastern Counties bus** #411 serves Sandringham from King's Lynn (Mon.-Sat. 8/day, last return 6pm, Sun. 5/day, last return 8:30pm; 25min.; £1.95).

Closer to King's Lynn, **Castle Rising,** a solidly intimidating keep set atop massive earthworks, was home to Queen Isabella after she plotted the murder of her husband, Edward II (open daily 10am-6pm; Oct.-March Tues.-Sun. 10am-4pm; 95p, seniors and students 85p, children 55p). Eastern Counties buses #410 and 411 run from Lynn (Mon.-Sat. 22/day, plus a few that don't stop at the castle, last return 8:45pm, Sun. 5/day; last return 6:25pm; 15min.).

Built in the mid-18th century for Sir Robert Walpole, the first prime minister of England, **Houghton Hall** (tel. (01485) 528569) is a magnificent example of Palladian architecture, with lavish paintings, tapestries, and "the most sublime bed ever designed." It also houses one of the most impressive collections of model soldiers and militaria in the world, some of whom dance splendidly on tiny tightropes (house open Easter-late Sept. Thurs., Sun., and bank holidays 2-5:30pm; grounds open 1½hr. earlier; gates close 5pm; house and grounds £4, seniors £3.50, ages 5-16 £2, under 5 free). Call ahead, as the hall has been closed for repairs since 1994, and it is not certain that it will be open in 1995. Access the hall (14 mi. northwest of King's Lynn) by **bus** (Mon.-Sat. 2/day, last return 5:30pm; 45min.).

The northern **Norfolk coast,** with its expanses of beach, sand dunes, and salt marsh, stretches from **Hunstanton,** 16 mi. north of King's Lynn, to **Wells-next-the-Sea** and beyond. Bird sanctuaries and nature preserves abound; the **Scolt Head Island Reserve** and the **Holme Bird Observatory** are superb. Buses #410 and 411 run from Vancouver Centre in King's Lynn to Hunstanton (Mon.-Sat. 2/hr., Sun. every 2 hr.; £1.90). An **HI Youth Hostel** (tel. (01485) 532061), 15 Avenue Rd., perches in the center of Hunstanton near the Wash (£7.75, under 18 £5.20; open July-Aug. daily; Feb. 12-28, April-May, and Sept. Thurs.-Mon.; March and Oct. Fri.-Sat.). Holme can be found 3 mi. to the east. Access Scolt Head Island from Brancaster Staithe (an Anglo-Saxon word meaning "pier"), 10 mi. east along the A149.

■■■ NORWICH

One of England's largest cities before the Norman invasion and its most populous until London became the capital, Norwich (NOR-ridge, like porridge) retains traces of its medieval character. An 11th-century cathedral and a 12th-century castle reign over the city's smaller structures, and the weighty remains of the old city's walls girdle the central district. Norwich's puzzling streets, whose twists and ends recall a time when feet and horses were the only transport, wind through a fascinating city which prefers to convert its medieval churches (one church for every day of the year) into commercial enterprises rather than knock 'em down and start anew.

GETTING THERE

Easily accessible by bus, coach, or train, Norwich makes a decent base for touring both urban and rural East Anglia, particularly the Norfolk Broads. **National Express** coaches depart Victoria Station frequently. Explorer tickets (£4.50, children £2.85) offer a day's worth of unlimited travel on **Eastern Counties** buses, which travel to King's Lynn, Peterborough, and other Norfolk villages. Consult timetables at the Surrey St. station or call the Eastern Counties information line (tel. 788890). The tourist office can book National Express coaches which depart from Surrey St., or stop by

Galaxy Travel Office on Surrey St. Coaches run to Cambridge (1/day, Sat. 2/day; 2½hrs.; £8) and London (5/day; 3hrs.; £14.50), among other places.

Regional Railways (tel. 632055) go to Yarmouth (Mon.-Sat. 12/day; Sun. 6/day; 1hr.; £2.60), Peterborough (Mon.-Sat. 15/day, Sun. 8/ day; 2hr.; £11.50), Cambridge (Mon.-Sat. 12/day; £8.50), and London (Mon.-Sat. 12/day; 4hrs.; £25). Those under 16 ride at half-price. Hitching is scarce; most drivers tend not to give rides.

ORIENTATION & PRACTICAL INFORMATION

Although the architect of Norwich's old city had a wobbly hand, most of the city's sights are fairly close together and manageable on foot. Ask often for directions (every corner may not be frequently enough); even former park rangers could lose themselves in this mess. The hostel and many B&Bs lie to the west of the city walls in a much more modern and more easily navigable part of town. A fine view of much of the city can be had from the castle's tiny windows. Avoid the red light district, near the center of town, and the market area at night.

Tourist Office: Guildhall, Gaol Hill, Norwich NR2 1NF (tel. 666071, after hours 761082), on the westward continuation of London St. in front of City Hall. Loads of brochures and books about Norwich and Norfolk, many for free. Accommodations service (10% deposit), free list. City guide/map 30p. **Luggage storage** £2 with £2 key deposit. *Bureau de Change.* Open Mon.-Sat. 9:30am-6pm; Oct.-May Mon.-Sat. 9:30am-5:30pm. 90-min. guided **tours** leave from the tourist office in summer (£1.80, ages 11-16 £1).

Financial Services: Thomas Cook, 15 St. Stephen St. (tel. 621547, fax 766663) and on St. Andrews St. next to Midland Bank. Open Mon., Wed.-Fri. 9am-5:30pm; Tues. 10am-5:30pm. **London Street** is lined with an abundance of major banks, including **Barclays.**

Post Office: 1317 Bank Plain (tel. 220228), near Anglia Television, a rock's toss north of the castle. Open Mon.-Wed. and Fri. 9am-5:30pm, Thurs. 9:30am-5:30pm, Sat. 9am-12:30pm. Large branches reside at 13 Davey Place (tel. 220208) and Queen St. (tel. 220278). All offer *Poste Restante.* **Postal Code:** NR2 1AA.

Telephone Code: 01603.

Train Station: (tel. 632055) at the corner of Riverside and Thorpe Rd., a 15-min. walk uphill to the town center. Lockers for **luggage storage** (£1-3).

Bus Station: Surrey St. (tel. 620491), off St. Stephen St. southwest of the castle. Information center and ticket desk open Mon.-Fri. 8:30am-5pm, Sat. 8:30am-4pm. Additional information at the **Norfolk Bus Information Centre (NORBIC),** 4 Guildhall Hill (tel. 613613), behind the tourist office. Open Mon.-Fri. 9am-5pm.

Taxi: ABC Taxis (tel. 666333). Female drivers available. One wheelchair taxi (tel. 300300).

Bike Rental: Anglia Cycles, 72A Gloucester St. (tel. 632467). From £5/day, £25-30/week. No reservations needed. Call a day or two in advance. Discounts for YHA members. Open Mon.-Sat. 9am-6pm.

Market: In the square facing City Hall and the tourist office. Open Mon.-Sat. 8am-4:30pm. Vendors peddle fresh fruits, vegetables, clothing, and more.

Launderette: Laundromat, 179A Dereham Rd. (tel. 626685). Open Mon.-Sat. 8am-8pm, last wash 6:30pm; Sun. 8am-7pm, last wash 5:30pm.

Hotlines: Samaritans (crisis): tel. 611311; **Rape:** tel. 667687.

Hospital: Norfolk and Norwich Hospital, corner of Brunswick Rd. and St. Stephen's Rd. (tel. 286286).

Emergency: Dial 999; no coins required.

Police: Bethel St. (tel. 768769), around the corner from City Hall.

ACCOMMODATIONS & CAMPING

The most conveniently located and reasonably priced accommodations are the YMCA and YWCA, a few blocks west of the tourist office. Earlham, Unthank, and Eaton Rd. have many pleasant B&Bs in the £12-14 range, but they are at least a 20-minute westward hike from downtown and even further from the train station. From the tourist office, follow St. Giles St. to the Ring Rd. rotary and cross the footbridge; Unthank Rd. branches off to the left, Earlham Rd. to the right. Eaton Rd. is a half mile up the main road. The guesthouses on all three streets appear when house numbers reach the 100s. B&Bs may also be found along Deneham Road; follow St. Benedict's St., which eventually becomes Deneham.

YMCA, 46-52 St. Giles St. (tel. 620269). Central location. Simple and clean singles, doubles, and dorm-style rooms. Separate wings for men and women. Laundry facilities. TV lounge. Weight room. No curfew; porter lets you in after midnight. Free tea at 10:45pm. B&B single £12.50, bed in dorm room £8.50. Key deposit £5.

YWCA, 61 Bethel St. (tel. 625982). Women only. Central location. Rooms are clean and simple. Some rooms feature a nice view of a courtyard. Well-equipped kitchen and laundry room. Min. age 16. Men allowed on main floor until 10pm. No curfew; porter lets you in after 10:30pm. Singles £9.50. Doubles £15.70. Weekly singles £43.80, doubles £73.40. Key deposit £10. Call ahead in summer.

HI Youth Hostel, 112 Turner Rd. NR2 4HB (tel. 627647), 1½ mi. from the center. From the train station, cross the river and either wait at the shelter in front of the Multiyork Furniture Store for bus #19 or 20 (#37 or 38 after 6pm and on Sun.), take a taxi, or drag your bones along Prince of Wales Rd. until Bank Plain. Take a right and continue as the road becomes St. Andrews, Charing Cross, St. Benedict, and finally Deneham Rd. Upon reaching the Earl of Leicester Pub, turn right onto Turner Rd. Clean rooms of varying sizes; satisfying, inexpensive food and good kitchen facilities; luggage storage. Curfew 11pm. Opens 5pm. Open April-Aug. daily; Sept.-Oct. Tues.-Sun.; Nov.-Dec. and Feb. Fri.-Sat.; March Tues.-Sat. £7.75, under 18 £5.20. Family rates available. Often filled July-Aug.; call a month ahead.

Aberdale Lodge, 211 Earlham Rd. NR2 3RQ (tel. 502100), 15-min. walk from the center. A relaxed and unpretentious B&B with, alas, one pressure-poor shower that must accommodate up to 10 guests. £14, children sharing adults' room £9. Mrs. Gibson serves up a full English breakfast to early-waking guests (7-8:30am).

Camping: Closest is the **Lakenham** campsite, Martineau Lane (tel. 620060; no calls after 8pm), 1 mi. south of the center. Eastern Counties #29, 31, 32 stop nearby. Toilets and showers. Facilities for travelers with disabilities. Peak season June-Aug. £2.91, children £1.07; off-peak £2.60, children free; £3 pitch fee for non-members. Family deals available. Open April-Sept. Call ahead. Gates locked to cars at 11pm, though foot traffic permitted. Also near is **Scouts Headquarters,** Eaton Vale, Church Lane, Eaton (tel. 501228), though it's sometimes full. Take bus #1, 2, or 6 from the train station or Castle Meadow to Cellar House Pub and turn left onto Church Lane. £1.50/person, showers 10p. Call ahead in summer.

FOOD & PUBS

Just a stone's throw from the city centre and the castle keep lies one of England's largest and oldest open-air **market**s (Mon.-Sat. roughly 8am-4:30pm). Feast your eyes on it from the steps of the tourist office, then feast your gut on everything from fresh fruit and cheeses to ice cream.

The Waffle House, 39 St. Giles St. (tel. 612790), near the YMCA and YWCA. Stylish family restaurant with wicker galore. Astounding Belgian waffles (wholemeal or white) with fillings ranging from ham, cheese, and mushrooms to tuna and bean sprouts. Prices begin at £1.85. All ingredients are organic. Strawberry wine, fruity milkshakes, and dessert waffles to top it all off. Vegetarians will be happy. Try the Horlicks and your fondest dreams may come true. Open Mon.-Thurs. 11am-10pm, Fri.-Sat. 11am-11pm, Sun. noon-10pm.

The Mecca, 5 Orford Hill, off Bell Ave. (tel. 614829). A good old-style deli, health food grocer, vegetarian restaurant, and coffee/tea shop occupy several floors. Open Mon.-Sat. 8:30am-5:30pm; lunch served noon-2:30pm and tea 2:30-5pm.

The Britons Arms Coffee House, 9 Elm Hill (tel. 623367). Location, location, location. Near the cathedral on a restored, cobbled medieval street. Offers morning coffee, lunch; the perfect place for afternoon tea in a garden. Tea 80p. Cakes from 60p. Open Mon.-Sat. 9:30am-5pm.

The Reindeer Pub, 10 Dereham Rd, just beyond the city walls and near the hostel. The quintessential English pub. Six home-brewed ales, many imports, food, and a lively atmosphere. Often features local bands. They brew their own beer in the back; pints from £1. Usually deserted on Christmas Eve. Open Mon.-Sat. 11am-11pm, Sun. 10:30am-3pm and 7-10:30pm.

The Adam and Eve, Bishopgate (tel. 667423), at the Palace St. end of Riverside Walk, behind the cathedral. Older than sin. The first pub in Norwich (est. 1249) and one of its most pleasant watering holes. Dare you taste the apple cider (£1 for a half pint)? Cheesy jacket potatoes (£2.60) and other foods served noon-7pm. Bar open daily 11am-11pm.

Pizza One—Pancakes Too, 24 Tombland (tel. 621583), by the cathedral. Creative pizza and crepe dishes. Order four-cheese "charity pizza" (£4.25) and 50p goes to charity. Students get 10% off main course. £2 minimum charge. Delivery service. Open Mon.-Sat. noon-11pm, Sun. noon-10pm. Wheelchair accessible.

One of the most charming places for an evening drink isn't a pub. **Take 5,** St. Andrews St. (tel. 622 047), in the old Suckling House, is an exhibition center that includes a movie theater, bookshop, information desk, and a fantastic 14th-century bar. Scope out free jazz on summer weekends in the courtyard and biweekly art exhibits in the restaurant (open Mon.-Sat. 10:30am-11pm, Sun. 5:30-10:30pm). The theater shows second-run and foreign films (check tourist office for schedule).

SIGHTS

The original **Norwich Castle** was a wooden structure built in 1089 by a Norman monarchy intent on subduing the Saxon city. The stone keep was erected in 1160, but its current exterior dates from the 1830s, when it was refaced and restored. It was here that English nobles forced King John to sign the Magna Carta in 1215, thereby curbing the power of the monarchy; the castle was later used as a jail from 1345 until 1887. The **Castle Museum** (tel. 223624), which occupies the castle keep, contains an eclectic jumble of art, archaeology, history, natural history, and some other crap: everything from bits of armor to a prized chunk of 12,500-year-old mammoth poo. While the museum fee (£2.20, children £1, senior citizens and unemployed £1.50) allows you to explore the inside of the keep, only a guided tour (£1.50, children 50p) permits entry into the battlements and dungeons. (Museum open Mon.-Sat. 10am-5pm, Sun. 2-5pm. Tours Mon.-Fri. 4/day, Sat. and holidays 10:30am-3:30pm on the ½-hr.; Sun. 3/afternoon. Wheelchair accessible.) Admission to the museum includes entry to the **Royal Norfolk Regimental Museum** on nearby Castle Meadow (tel. 223649; same hours as Castle Museum). Though the Regimental Museum can also be entered from Castle Meadow, venturing into the trenches via the castle steps tests the courage of even the most valiant soldier.

Two blocks north of the tourist office is **Stranger's Hall** (tel. 667229), a folk museum that displays furnishings and items of daily life since the Tudor period (entrance on Charing Cross west of St. Andrew's St.; open Mon.-Sat. 10am-5pm). Two blocks down St. Andrew's St., in Bridewell Alley, rests the **Bridewell Museum** (tel. 667228). From 1583 to 1828, all kinds of rabblerousers paced the rooms and grounds of this medieval merchant's house when it served as a prison. Prisoners carved dates and initials (still visible) in the far left corner of the courtyard above the bench. Limited disabled access. Further down the alley at no. 3, **Colman's Mustard Shop** (tel. 627889) chronicles the spicy rise and fall of one of Norwich's oldest industries (open Mon.-Sat. 9:30am-5pm). On Princes St., the **St. Peter Hungate Church Museum** holds art, books, and other church artifacts (open Mon.-Sat. 10am-5pm). The **Royal Norfolk Regimental Museum, Bridewell Museum, Stranger's Hall,** and **St. Peter Hungate Church Museum** can all be seen with a single pass. Valid for two days, it is available at any of the museums (£1.40, seniors and students £1.20, children 70p).

The castle and the Norman **Norwich Cathedral** dominate the skyline; follow the cathedral's spire to Tombland. Though it sounds like an amusement park, the area known as Tombland lacks any garish rides or games. Across from the cathedral are buried many victims of the Great Plague. The cathedral itself, built by an 11th-century bishop as penance for having bought his episcopacy, features unusual two-story cloisters (the only ones of their kind in England) and flying buttresses which help support the second tallest spire in the country. The cloister garth and wide expanse of lawn just outside the cathedral entice would-be picnickers and nappers. (Open mid-May to mid-Sept. daily 7:30am-7pm; mid-Sept. to mid-May 7:30am-6pm. Free; guided tours June-Sept. Mon.-Fri. 11am and 2:15pm, Sat. 11am; disabled access.) In the summer, the cathedral frequently hosts orchestral concerts and small art exhibitions. Call the visitors' office for information (tel. 764385).

Out at the University of East Anglia, 3 mi. west of town on Earlham Rd., is the **Sainsbury Centre for Visual Arts** (tel. 56060; Eastern Counties buses on Sat. #12, 14, 23, 26, 27, 15; on Sun. #33, 34 leave from Castle Meadow.; 25min.; 75p). Sir Robert Sainsbury, former chair of the supermarket chain, donated a superb personal collection of 20th-century and primitive art to the university in 1973, including works by Picasso, Moore, Degas, and still-active artists (open Tues.-Sun., noon-5pm; £1, students 50p). **St. John's Roman Catholic Cathedral,** just over the footbridge at Earlham Road, also merits a visit. Though not as old as Norwich Cathedral, it is nonetheless equally imposing. Don't miss the view from **St. James Hill** near **Mousehold Heath,** a large public park about 1½ mi. northeast of the city center, on the other side of the River Wensum. Or ascend **Kett's Heights,** just across Kett's Hill. The **Riverside Walk** follows the curving Wensum from Palace St. to Prince of Wales Rd.

ENTERTAINMENT

Located next to the Assembly House on Theatre St., the **Theatre Royal** (tel. 630000) features professional productions from Shakespeare to ballet to pantomime (wheelchair accessible). The home of the Norwich Players, **Maddermarket Theatre,** 1 St. John's Alley (tel. 620917), has revived high-quality amateur drama, performed in an Elizabethan-style theater (box office open 10am-5pm and also after 7pm performances; tickets £2.50-6.50, students at matinees £3, evening student standby £3; wheelchair accessible). In the summer, Norwich City Council presents free **Theatre in the Parks** (tel. 212137). Norwich's several outdoor parks host a stream of festivals and folk fairs; inquire at the tourist office about times and dates.

A few pubs and clubs offer live music. The **Reindeer** hosts local bands on Tuesdays and any other night they can get 'em (10 Dereham Rd.). **Boswells,** at 24 Tombland near the cathedral, serves up food and drink alongside nightly jazz and blues (tel. 626099; open Tues.-Sat. noon-2am, Sun. 11:30am-6pm, Mon. noon-11pm). **Peppermint Park,** Rose Lane (tel. 627701), is a disco-den frequented by slackers.

■ NEAR NORWICH

The ports along the northeastern East Anglian coast, among England's first, yielded to the iron fists of London and other towns to the south which pirated away much of their trade; despite the loss, folk around here still engage in seafaring adventures. Birds, beasts, and humans alike flock to the **Norfolk Broads,** a watery maze of navigable marsh lands, and the hills looming nearby beckon to nature enthusiasts travelling on foot or on cycle. This Environmentally Sensitive Area, with its abundance of wildlife and natural reserves, can be traversed by foot or by boat. Exercise care when walking about the Broads; continual abuse by humans has tremendously damaged the area. Among the many **nature trails** which pass through the Broads, Cockshoot Broad lets you birdwatch; a circular walk around Ranworth points out the Broad's various flora; and Upton Fen is, oddly enough, popular for its bugs. Pleasure boats of all sizes cruise the canals, and it's possible to sail from one pub to the next all the way from Norwich to Great Yarmouth. The tourist offices in Norwich and villages in the area sell helpful mini-guides to the Broads that describe various trails, waterways, and nature reserves.

Wroxham, 7 mi. northeast of Norwich, provides a good base for exploring the more remote areas of the Broads. Procure information from the **Hoveton tourist office,** Station Rd. (tel. (01603) 782207; open Easter-Oct. 9am-1pm and 2-5pm). The office also has lists of boat-rentals and of the many campsites scattered through the area. The sheer number of guesthouses and hotels (which may be booked through the tourist office) both within Wroxham proper and just outside attests to the popularity of its waterways and byways. While in the tourist office, pick up a free copy of *The Broadcaster,* which outlines happenings in Norfolk Broads. Consider renting a bicycle to explore secluded spots, as access to certain areas is restricted to those with cars. **Just Pedalling,** in Coltishall (tel. (01603) 737201) can accommodate you.

From Wroxham, **Broads Tours,** on the right hand side before the Bridge (tel. (01603) 782207), runs cruises (1-3½hr.) through the Broads (most at 11:30am and 2:30pm; more frequent hours in high season; £4.20-6.50, children £3.20-4.50). In Norwich, **Southern River Steamers,** 65 Trafford Rd. (tel. (01603) 624051), offers cruises to Surlingham Broad in the summer and autumn, departing from quays near the cathedral and train station (leave Elm Hill Quay 2:15pm; leave Foundry Bridge Quay (near train) 2:30pm; 1½hr.; disabled access; £5.20-5.75, children £2.90-3.50). **Strumpshaw** is particularly popular among birdwatchers. Inquire at the Royal Society for the Protection of Birds, 97 Yarmouth Rd. Norwich (tel. (01603) 661662).

To reach the Broads, take a **train** from Norwich, Lowestoft, or Great Yarmouth to the smaller towns of Beccles, Cantley, Lingwood, Oulton Broad, Salhouse, or Wroxham. From Norwich, **Eastern Counties buses** leave from St. Stephen's St. and Surrey St. to: Wroxham (#717: Mon.-Fri. 5/day, Sat. 4/day; #718: Sun. 3/day; 30 min.; £1.35), Horning (45min.; £1.40), Potterheigham (1hr.; £2), and other Broads towns (#705: Mon.-Fri. 1/day in the evening).

■■■ SUFFOLK COUNTY

A thriving center of wool production and trade in days gone by, Suffolk County now serves as a testament to the alarming amount of wealth accumulated in the past. Its numerous small towns boast imposing houses, halls, and magnificent "wool churches." But despite the obvious impact humans have made on this region, the green hills maintain the rustic beauty that inspired the landscape paintings of natives Constable and Gainsborough. Bury St. Edmunds' nationally acclaimed flowers bloom at the center of this pastoral county, surrounded by the villages of Lavenham, Long Melford, Woodbridge, and Sudbury. The frenetic pace of life in southeast East Anglia has slowed in recent years, leaving an air of quiet serenity amongst the hundreds of crooked timber-framed buildings.

GETTING THERE & GETTING ABOUT

A short hop from metropolitan London, Suffolk enjoys frequent train and coach service. Bury St. Edmunds makes an excellent daytrip from either Norwich or Cambridge, especially if you include a jaunt to Lavenham, Sudbury, Lona, Melford, or any of the other historic villages scattered throughout Western Suffolk. The region is eminently explorable by bike, but recently instituted local laws have made rentals extinct. Still, if you have your own or can borrow one, go for it.

Trains leave London's Liverpool St. Station for Bury St. Edmunds via Ipswich (£16); Felixstowe (£17.50); and Colchester (£11). Trains also run between Cambridge and Norwich via Bury (1/hr.; Sun. every 2 hrs.). Some change at Stowmarket (1¼hr.; £8.90). **National Express** (tel. (01223) 460711) coaches leave from London's Victoria Station for Bury St. Edmunds (£12.50). **Cambus** #X11 runs on weekdays every two hours (Sun. every 3 hrs.) from Drummer St. Station in Cambridge to St. Andrew's Station in Bury (50min.; return £3.50). You may find it difficult to get information from the National Express number (the one listed here is based in Cambridge); instead, seek out National Express ticket agents in town.

Regional bus service is provided by **Eastern Counties** (tel. (01284) 766171). Eastern Counties' #141, 142, 143, and 144 leave Bury's St. Andrew's Station to Horringer and Ickworth (Mon.-Sat. 6/day; 15min.; day return £1.25; last return from Horringer Mon.-Fri. 4:30pm, Sat. 5:30pm). **H.C. Chambers** buses #20 and 27 leave Bury from St. Andrew's station for Lavenham (Mon.-Sat. 7/day; 20min.; £1; call (01787) 227233 for information); Sudbury is 10 mi. further along this bus route. An H.C. Chambers bus also leaves Bury for Melford (Mon.-Sat. 7/day; 45min.; £1.15). Bury lies on the A45, and Melford is reputedly an easy 12-mi. hitch south of Bury on the A134.

ACCOMMODATIONS

B&Bs provide a comfortable base from which to explore the area, and there are several conveniently located youth hostels. The 15th-century **George and Dragon** (tel. (01787) 71285), in Long Melford, offers bed and board above a country pub (single £20, twin/double £35, family room with facilities £45-50). The elegant, Edwardian **Cottage**, 1 Melford Rd., Sudbury (tel. (01787) 881184), welcomes all to its exquisite gardens (£15, doubles £25, family £35). In **Alpheton** there is a simple-grade **HI Youth Hostel** at Monk's Croft, Bury Rd. (tel. (01284) 828297), on the A134 (£5, under 18 £3); open April-Oct. Wed.-Mon.). The hostel, 3 mi. north of Long Melford, 4 mi. northwest of Lavenham, and 10 mi. south of Bury St. Edmunds, makes a good base for touring the region if you have a bicycle. **Colchester,** famed as England's oldest town, is home both to England's finest cricketer, Gregory St. John Munby, and an **HI Youth Hostel** at East Bay House, 18 E. Bay (tel. (01206) 867982). This large Georgian house is often crowded with ferry-riders. (£6.90, under 18 £4.60. Open March-Aug. daily; Sept.-Oct. Tues.-Sat. Lockout 9am-1pm; July-Aug. 9am-5pm. Call ahead, though no phone reservations taken if hostel is nearly full.) There's also a simple-grade **HI Youth Hostel** in Castle Hedingham, Halsted (tel. (01787) 60799) at 7 Falcon Sq., located near Cambridge and Colchester and south of Bury St. Edmunds on the A131 (lockout 9am-5pm; £7.50, under 18 £5; evening meals served; wheelchair accessible; open July-Oct. and April-June Mon.-Sat.).

BURY ST. EDMUNDS

Bury St. Edmunds stands above the site where invaders beheaded Saxon King Edmund in 869 AD after tying him to a tree and using him for target practice. According to besotted legend, a voice crying "Here I am!" led Edmund's faithful subjects to the place in the brush where his severed head rested between the paws of a wolf. The busy commercial and administrative center which grew up around Edmund's mythical burial place attracts few travelers, in welcome contrast to the milling centers of Cambridge and Norwich.

A few hours of whimsical wandering will reveal Bury's modest charms. Along Crown St., across from the tourist office on the soggy banks of the River Lark, lies the beautifully ruined **abbey,** home to cadres of foraging ducks. Only low crumbling walls and three massive pillars remain where 25 English barons met in 1214, a year before they forced King John to sign the *Magna Carta*. The elaborate formal gardens next to the remains of the abbey won a special award in the annual "Britain in Bloom" competition; go in mid- to late June when the flowers blossom. The English Rose Garden, enclosed by towering shrubs, allows for an especially contemplative moment. On the outer edge of the grounds birds chirp from a small aviary. While still on the grounds of the abbey visit the ruins of an old Norman tower, which guards a decadently overfoliated cemetery (abbey and gardens open daily 7:30am-sunset; free). Next door, the 16th-century **St. Edmundsbury Cathedral** (free) sports a recently repainted hammerbeam roof—a cross between a gingerbread house and a cuckoo clock, in red, green, yellow, and other colors of childhood—flanked by guardian angels. The cherub overhanging the entrance, allegedly pilfered years before, was rediscovered by a Bury businessman in a Belgium antiques shop. Inquire at the tourist office about summer organ concerts. The **Manor House Museum,** which houses the Gershom Parkington Collection of Clocks and Watches, borders the abbey gardens to the south. This elegant Georgian house contains dozens of synchronized timepieces, including a replica of the first rolling-ball clock (open Mon.-Sat. 10am-5pm, Sun. 2-5pm; £2.50, children £1.50). The **Moyses' Hall Museum,** Corn Hill, in the marketplace, houses a wonderful collection of historical junk, including a violin made out of a horse's skull and a 19th-century jukebox (open Mon.-Sat. 10am-5pm, Sun. 2-5pm; free). Bury comes alive on market days—£700 (or a handful of magic beans) will buy you a cow at Wednesday's cattle market, if your pack can hold it (open Wed. and Sat., 8am-4pm).

The Baker's Oven, 11 Abbeygate St., sells excellent, cheap sandwiches, salads, and rolls (60p-£2) in a comfortable cafeteria and busy take-away (open Mon.-Sat. 8am-5pm). £1.54 will buy you a pint at the pint-sized **Nutshell** (Abbeygate at the Traverse), the smallest—it often seems the most popular—pub in England.

Laid out according to its original 12th-century street plan, Bury's streets are easier to untangle than those of its East Anglian neighbors. The **tourist office,** on the corner of Angel Hill and Abbeygate St. (tel. (01284) 764667), distributes maps and leaflets galore, as well as the voluminous *Bury and District Visitor Guide* (99p; open Easter-May and Oct. Mon.-Fri. 9:30am-5:30pm, Sat. 10am-3pm; June-Sept. also Sun. 10am-3pm; Nov.-Easter Mon.-Fri. 10am-4pm, Sat. 10am-1pm). The tourist office books B&Bs in town or on a nearby farm (£12.50-15). To reach the office from the train station, follow Outnorthgate past the roundabout onto Northgate St. Turn right onto Mustow St. and walk up to Angel Hill. From the bus station, follow St. Andrew's St. past the library to Brentgovel St. Turn right at Lower Baxtel St. and then left onto Abbeygate St. The **post office** can be found at 17-18 Cornhill St. (open Mon.-Fri. 9am-5:30pm, Sat. 9am-12:30pm). The **postal code** is IP33 1AA.

Near Bury St. Edmunds

Just 3 mi. southwest of Bury in the village of **Horringer** is **Ickworth** (tel. (01284) 735270), the massive home of the Marquis of Bristol. Dominated by a 106-ft. rotunda, the opulent 19th-century state rooms are filled with 18th-century French furniture and more than a few portraits (some by Reynolds and Gainsborough) of the mansion's founding family, the Herveys. The classical Italian garden is predictably splendid, considering its proximity to the florid glory of Bury. (House open May-Sept. Tues.-Wed., Fri.-Sun., and bank holidays 1:30-5:30pm; April and Oct. Sat.-Sun. and bank holidays only; last entry 5pm; park open daily 7am-7pm; £4.30, children £2. Park and garden £1.50, children 50p. House £3.50, children £1.75; wheelchair accessible.)

The medieval village of **Lavenham** lies 10 mi. south of Bury on the A1141. **Lavenham Guildhall,** originally the hall of the Guild of Corpus Christi, in the marketplace (tel. (01787) 247646), displays an exhibition on the 700-year wool trade under its 450-year-old timbers (open April-Oct. daily 11am-5pm; £2.40, first two children free, then children 60p). The **tourist office,** Lady St. (tel. (01787) 248207) provides information on sights in and around the village (open April-Oct. Mon.-Thurs. 10am-4:45pm; Fri.-Sat. 10am-5:45pm).

Along the bus route 8 mi. further is the village of **Sudbury** and **Thomas Gainsborough's House,** 46 Gainsborough St. (tel. (01787) 372958), where the artist was born. Feast your eyes on the largest collection of Gainsborough's paintings anywhere in the world. Temporary exhibitions of historic and contemporary art and crafts also brighten this 18th-century setting. Look for the 15th-century mulberry tree in the town garden (open Tues.-Sat. 10am-5pm, Sun. 2-5pm; Nov.-Easter Tues.-Sat. 10am-4pm, Sun. 2-4pm; £2.50, students and children £1.25).

Turrets and moats await those who visit **Long Melford,** a mile-long Suffolk village well-known for its Tudor architecture. **Melford Hall** (tel. (01787) 880286), a Tudor mansion, has been maintained in style over the past century. The most impressive display, the Chinese porcelain, was stolen from a Spanish galleon. The octagonal garden house is, well, octagonal. (Principal rooms and garden open May-Sept. Wed.-Thurs. and Sat.-Sun. 2-5:30pm; April and Oct. Sat.-Sun. only; bank holidays also 2-5:30pm; £2.60, children £1.30; wheelchair accessible.) Just north of the village green stands another red brick Tudor mansion, **Kentwell Hall** (tel. (01787) 310207), braced by a broad moat. Hours are schizo (£4, children £2.50; gardens and farm only £2.25, children £1.50).

Just 8 mi. south of Cambridge on the A505 and southwest of Bury, **Duxford Airfield** (tel. (01223) 835000) exhibits aircraft, military vehicles, tanks, and guns used during the Battle of Britain (open daily 10am-6pm; off-season 10am-4pm; hangars and exhibition areas close 15 min. early; £5.95, seniors £3.95, children, students, and disabled £2.95, children under 5 free). Unspoilt **Woodbridge,** on the bank of the River Deben to the southeast of Bury, boasts a rare 19th-century **Tide Mill** (tel. (01473) 626618). When the tide comes in you can see the mill grind the meal into flour. (Open May-Sept. daily 11am-5pm; Oct. Sat.-Sun. only 11am-5pm; 80p, students and children 40p.)

HARWICH & FELIXSTOWE

Continent-seeking travelers should head south to Harwich (HAR-idge), a popular ferry depot for trips to Holland, Germany, and Scandinavia, and to Felixstowe, where boats sail to Belgium. **Sealink, Scandinavian Seaways, and P. & O. Ferries** operate from these twin ports. Consult Essentials: Getting There—From Continental Europe for all ferry information.

The **Harwich tourist office** (tel. (01255) 506139) doles out info on cheap accommodations in the area, as does the **Felixstowe tourist office** (tel. (01394) 276770). In Harwich, take bus #604 from the ferry terminal to Parkston Quay to reach the tourist office. In Felixstowe, follow signs for the leisure center on Undercliffe Rd. West; the tourist office is right next door.

Central England

CENTRAL ENGLAND

The 19th century swept into central England in an industrial sandstorm, revolution-izing quiet village life. By the end of the 1800s, the "dark satanic mills" that William Blake foresaw indeed overran the Midlands. But prominence and prosperity fol-lowed these smokestacks and their soot; towns rapidly became cities, and cities the workshops of the world's wool textiles, armaments, and autos. The region remains the industrial heart of England despite growing unemployment and a dwindling population, but the description "industrial" should not disqualify this region from your route: cities like Lincoln and Chester tell some of their stories in Latin, and many once-grim urban centers like Manchester and Liverpool are now home to innovative music and arts scenes as well as some of the UK's most vibrant nightlife. Commercial necessity spilled an efficient series of rail lines into the Liverpool-Manchester-Leeds-Sheffield metropolis and the adjoining Peak District, but the tour-ist trade has not followed; many of these metropoli lack hostels and cheap B&Bs.

■■■ SHREWSBURY

Wales used to be something of a Wild West to the English, and the rough, tough bor-der town of Shrewsbury (pop. 91,000) saw some horrific bloodshed. Dafydd, the last Welsh Prince, was hanged, drawn, beheaded, and quartered in the town center in 1293; 120 years later, the corpse of Harry Hotspur was ground between two millstones, beheaded, then quartered on the same site. Tour buses now drip oil where Dafydd's trunk was left to bleed, and visitors gape at the well-maintained Tudor buildings and exclaim, "Ah, how lovely! How nice it would have been to live here!"

GETTING THERE

Shrewsbury is a whirlpool of rail, with **trains** spinning out to London (1/hr.; 3hr.; £35), Machynlleth and Aberystwyth (every 2 hrs., Sun. 4/day; to Machynlleth £9.70), Wolverhampton (every 2 hrs., Sun. 3/day; 50min.; £5.80), Swansea (4/day; 4hr.; £21.40), and most of North Wales. **Buses** servicing the surrounding area are frequent and far less expensive. **Midland** buses (tel. 344028) tread most local routes. **Shearing** buses also blanket Shrewsbury and its suburbs, while **National Express** buses go farther afield; call 241166 for details on either company. All bus and train schedules are unified in the **Public Transport Guide,** available at the bus station.

ORIENTATION & PRACTICAL INFORMATION

The **River Severn** enters Shrewsbury from the north and embraces the town center on three sides. The Welsh and English Bridges tie to the outskirts, and the castle sits defensively at a narrow point between two branches of the river, next to the train station. Uphill lie **Pride Hill** and **Butcher's Row,** where in medieval times slaughterers turned their trade; these remain the town's shopping and business areas.

Tourist Office: Music Hall, The Square, across from the Market Building (tel. 350761). Free town maps, oversized town trail leaflets (80p), and the beautiful *Shrewsbury Guide* (95p). Piles of literature: Charles Darwin, Wilfred Owen, and the Brother Cadfael mystery series. Summer **tours** of Shrewsbury's historic streets and structures (May-Oct. daily 2:30pm, also Sun. 11am; Nov.-March Sat. 2:30pm; April Sat.-Sun. 2:30pm; 1½hrs.; £1.60, children 80p). Office open Mon.-Sat. 9:30am-6pm, Sun. 10am-4pm; Nov.-Easter Mon.-Sat. 9:30am-5:30pm.

Financial Services: Barclays, 44-46 Castle St. (tel. 232901). The site where Dafydd and Hotspur were dismembered. Cheerful staff despite it all. Open Mon.-Fri. 9:30am-4:30pm. **Lloyds,** 1 Pride Hill (tel. 235051). Open Mon.-Fri. 9:30am-5:30pm, Sat. 9:30am-12:30pm. **Thomas Cook,** 36 Pride Hill (tel. 231144). Open Mon.-Wed. and Fri.-Sat. 9am-5:30pm, Thurs. 9:30am-5:30pm. **American Express,** 27 Claremont St. (tel. 236387). Open Mon.-Tues. and Thurs.-Fri. 9am-5:30pm, Wed. 9:30am-5:30pm, Sat. 9am-5pm.

Post Office: St. Mary's St. (tel. 362925). Open Mon.-Fri. 9am-5:30pm, Sat. 9am-12:30pm. **Postal Code:** SY1 1ED.

Telephone Code: 01743.

Train Station: In a splendid neo-Gothic building on Castle St. Ticket office open Mon.-Sat. 5:30am-10pm, Sun. 7:45am-8:30pm. Info booth open Mon.-Sat. 8:10am-5:45pm, Sun. 9:10am-5:50pm. Call 364041 for train information.

Bus Station: Raven Meadows (tel. 244496). Open Mon.-Sat. 8:30am-5:30pm.

Taxi: Access Taxis, tel. 360606.

Launderette: New Monkmoor Road Launderette, Monkmoor Rd. over English Bridge. Open daily 7:30am-7:30pm. Last wash 6:30pm.

Hotline: Samaritans (crisis): tel. 369696; 24hr. **Victim Support:** tel. 362812.

Hospital: Shrewsbury Hospital, Copthorne Rd. (tel. 261000).

Emergency: Dial 999; no coins required.

Police: At Raven Meadows and Roushill (tel. 232888). Open Mon.-Sat. 8:30am-5pm.

ACCOMMODATIONS

The **Shrewsbury Youth Hostel,** The Woodlands, Abbey Foregate (tel. 360179), lies about 1 mi. from the rail station. From town, cross the English Bridge, pass the abbey, and go straight down Abbey Foregate; or catch bus #8 or 26 from the town center. Housed in a large Victorian ironmaster's house, the hostel offers laundry facilities, video games, a mini-pool table, and an atrocious piano (£7.75; open mid-March to Oct. Mon.-Sat.; mid-Feb. to mid-March and Nov.-Dec. Fri.-Sat.). B&Bs in town are expensive (£14-18), and even the smaller ones are hotel-style rather than homey. They cluster on Abbey Foregate and Monkmoor Rd. across the English Bridge. **Sunbeams,** 1 Bishop St. off Monkmoor Rd. (tel. 357495), will brighten your day; its tellies take over at sunset. **Abbey Lodge,** 68 Abbey Foregate (tel. 235832), has patches of peeling paint in the hallways and austerely decorated rooms, but it's cheap (single £13, twin £13-18, double £15-18). Breakfast is served at an evil hour.

FOOD

Though Shrewsbury's streets display every kind of fast food imaginable, slower food is also in good form. The **Good Life Wholefood Restaurant,** Barracks Passage, Wyle Cop (tel. 350455), occupies a restored 14th-century building in an alley between the Lion Hotel and the house where Henry VII stayed on his way to Bosworth Field in 1485. Delicious salad combinations and hot specials appear magically before you (everything under £2.05; open Mon.-Fri. 9:30am-3:30pm, Sat. 9:30am-4:30pm). **The Little Gourmet,** 21a Castle St., butters superb French bread sandwiches from £1; the hot pork with stuffing, applesauce, and crackling makes a meal (£1.60; open Mon.-Sat. 8am-4pm). Pubs cry timber all over town; check out **The King's Head,** a pregnantly-bowed inn on Mardol St. with a medieval wall painting of the Last Supper uncovered during renovation. **The Hole in the Wall** provides Gullet Passage with a cavernous tummy. **The Dun Cow Pie Shop** on Abbey Foregate serves meal regularly in its cozy and crazy den.

SIGHTS

Shrewsbury overflows with stone buildings, timber-frame neighborhoods, and huge Georgian townhouses that all claim to have sheltered famous men, including Charles Darwin. The daily tour from the tourist office (£1.60) drags you through old alleyways (called "shuts" because they were used to keep out strangers) to the castle grounds, administering soporifics along the way. The **Shrewsbury Castle** (tel. 358516), just up from the train station, was built by Roger of Montgomery in 1083 only to be stripped of its stones for town building projects. The interior held a regimental museum until an incendiary bomb gutted it three years ago; the castle plans to reopen by the spring of 1995. Shakespeare's fine filed phrase floats across the castle garden the third week in July; tickets for the open-air performances are available from the box office in Music Hall next to the tourist office (tel. 350763).

Shrewsbury's biggest attraction is undoubtedly its architecture. Quirky Tudor-esque houses dot the central shopping district and rally in full force at the **Bear Steps,** near the town center. According to local law, sheep are free to graze in the grassy patches of the town; ignoring the protests of nearby bakers and grocers, a number even infiltrate the churchyard at **St. Mary's,** across from the post office. The church boasts stained-glass windows from all over the world.

Beyond the English Bridge, the wine-red **Shrewsbury Abbey** (tel. 232723) holds a shrine to St. Winefride, a 7th-century princess who was beheaded but survived to become an abbess (open daily 9:30am-5:30pm; Nov.-Easter 11am-2pm). Across the way at the faux-medieval **Shrewsbury Quest** (tel. 243324), you can stroll by deferential monks and make rubbings of illuminated manuscripts while tracking the 12th-century sleuth Brother Cadfael, whose bestselling chronicles are set at the Abbey (open Mon.-Sat. 10am-5pm, Sun. noon-5pm; £3.50, seniors £2.80, under 12 £2).

Stuart supporters with cars may want to swing by nearby **Boscobel House,** on a minor road between the A41 and A5, past Telford. A nearly 300-year-old direct descendant of the famous **Royal Oak,** in whose branches the future Charles II hid from pursuing Roundheads, stands proudly on the grounds. Unfortunately, you're not allowed to climb it. (House open April-Oct. daily 10am-6pm; Nov.-Dec. and Feb.-March Wed.-Sun. 10am-4pm. £3.15, students and seniors £2.35, children £1.55.)

■■■ BIRMINGHAM

Birmingham, the "big heart of England" and the country's second largest city, needs a bypass surgery. The city met its Armageddon in a hail of Nazi bombs, waking to a

BIRMINGHAM

sick afterlife of convention centers and industrial machines. Though a distinguished symphony and ballet company play bravely within its black mist, "Brummagem" has nothing to offer the budget traveler besides scattered trash, moody crowds, crime, and suffocating traffic. For those who have no choice but to travel here, our coverage follows.

GETTING THERE

Birmingham snares a clutch of train and bus lines between London, Central Wales, Southwest England, and all points north. Most trains arrive at **New St. Station;** the remainder pull into **Moor St. Station** (rail info tel. 643 2711; disabled information tel. 654 4288). **Trains** flee for London's Euston Station (2/hr.; 2hr.; £19), Manchester's Picadilly Station (1/hr., £13), Liverpool's Lime St. Station (1/hr.; 1½hr.; £12), Nottingham (1/hr.; 1¼hr.; £9.40), and Oxford (1/hr.; 1¼hr.; £13). **National Express** (tel. 622 4373) and **West Midlands bus** services run out of **Digbeth Station** on New St. (luggage storage £1-3, open daily 6:50am-10pm). National Express buses drive to London (1/hr.; 2½hr.; £13.75), Manchester (every 2 hr.; 2¼hr.; £12), and Cardiff (5/day; 2¼hr.; £16). For bus information, ring 622 4373, or dial (01345) 212555 for Midland Red West information—all calls are at Birmingham local rates. Hitching into town is very difficult. Birmingham is surrounded by major highways (M90, M5, M6, M54) on which hitching is dangerous and nigh impossible; bus travel is a necessity.

ORIENTATION & PRACTICAL INFORMATION

To reach the city center from Digbeth Bus Station, turn left as you exit and follow the signs up the hill to the New St. Rail Station. The Bull Ring market will be on your left. New Street culminates in Victoria Square; Corporation Street and Colmore Row run perpendicular to it, cutting across New St. at the rail station. Travellers would do well not to venture through the ominous streets beyond the central district; as always, take special care after nightfall.

Tourist Office: 2 City Arcade (tel. 643 2514). A ticketing office. Provides scads of information on the arts scene. Books rooms. Open Mon.-Sat. 9:30am-5:30pm.
Financial Services: Barclays, 56 New St. (tel. 632 5721). Open Mon.-Tues. and Thurs.-Fri. 9:30am-4:30pm, Wed. 10am-4:30pm. **Thomas Cook,** Corporation St. (tel. 236 9711) or 99 New St. (tel. 643 3120). Open Mon.-Wed. 9am-5:30pm and Fri.-Sat. 9am-5:30pm, Thurs. 10am-5:30pm. **American Express,** 17 Martineau Sq. (tel. 233 2141). Open Mon.-Fri. 8:30am-5:30pm, Sat. 9am-5pm; Oct. to mid-April, Mon.-Tues. and Thurs.-Fri. 9am-5:30pm, Wed. 9:30am-5:30pm, Sat. 9am-5pm.
Post Office: 1 Pinfold St., Victoria Sq. (tel. 643 5542). *Bureau de change.* Open Mon.-Fri. 9am-5pm, Sat. 9am-noon. **Postal Code:** B2 4AA.
Telephone Code: 0121.
Train Station: New St. or **Moor St.** (all rail info, tel. 643 2711; disabled booking 654 4288). Most trains go through New St. **Public Transportation Office:** in the New St. Station (information tel. 200 2700). Local transit map and bus schedules. Day bus and train pass £3.10; bus only £1.80. Open daily 6am-11pm. Passes can be purchased from the bus driver.
Bus Stations: Digbeth Station (tel. 622 4373), and at Colmore Row and Bull Ring. **West Midlands** (tel. 236 8313) serves Coventry and Wolverhampton. Office open Mon.-Sat. 9am-5pm.
Hotlines: Samaritans (crisis): tel. 666 6644. **Rape Crisis:** tel. 233 2122, Mon.-Fri. 10am-10pm, or the **Rape Crisis Center:** tel. 766 5366. **AIDS:** toll-free tel. (0800) 567123.
Hospital: General Hospital, Steelhouse Lane (tel. 236 8611).
Emergency: Dial 999; no coins required.
Police: Lloyd House, Colmore Circus, Queensway (tel. 626 5000).

ACCOMMODATIONS & FOOD

So you're staying in Birmingham—sucks to be you! Hotels in the city cater to convention-goers, and budget B&Bs are rare. Try to book through the tourist office, or try the ones lining Hagley Road. Call ahead to reserve a place at the YMCA or YWCA, since they are often booked solid.

HI Youth Hostel, Cambrian Halls, Brindley Dr. off Cambridge St. (tel. 233 3044). Take any bus (50p) from Rackham's (#3, 10, 21, 22, 23, 25, 29) to the Botanical Gardens; ask to be let off at the Polytechnic. Single rooms with keys and private facilities, and dorms with gourmet kitchens. Lockout 10am-5pm. £9.50; key deposit £5. Open mid-July-mid-Sept. To book before July 9, call the Stratford-Upon-Avon hostel (tel. (01789) 297093).

YMCA: 300 Reservoir Rd. (tel. 373 1937). Take bus #104 to Six Ways in Erdington. £13.70/person. **200 Bunburg Rd.** (tel. 475 6218). Take bus #61-63 to Church Rd., Northfield. Women and men. Singles £13.92. Breakfast included, dinner £3. Weekly with full board £67.93.

YWCA: Alexandra Residential Centre, 27 Norfolk Rd. (tel. 454 8134). Take bus #9 or 19 from Colmore Row. Women and men. Singles £6, weekly £38; key deposit £10; required membership fee 50p. **5 Stone Rd.** (tel. 440 2924; £8). Take bus #61-63 to the stop after Belgrave Rd. (ask the bus driver to announce the stop if possible; it's not clearly marked). Women and men. Single, semi-sanitary rooms. Lockout (12:30-5pm). Be wary in the neighborhood, especially after dark.

Grasmere Guest House, 37 Serpentine Rd., Harborne (tel. 427 4546). Take bus #103, 21, 22 or 23 from Corporation St. Tidy rooms, breakfast included. Singles £12-20, doubles £24-30, some with private bathrooms.

Lyby, 14/16 Barnsley Rd., Edgbaston (tel. 429 4487). Spacious and well-equipped rooms; no private bath. Take bus #9 from Corporation St. to King's Head Pub, walk 50m back, and turn left at the New Talbot. £12.50, breakfast included.

Birmingham's eateries conjure some expensive up culinary delights as well as the requisite, cheap, crusty cod. Bakeries and fruit stores surround the markets. A **Holland and Barrett** vegetarian supermarket resides at #54 in the Pallasades Shopping Centre, close to the New St. station (tel. 633 0104; open Mon.-Fri. 8:30am-6pm, Sat. 9am-6pm). At **The Charters,** 106 New St., **Bella Pasta** (tel. 643 1548) dishes out trendy Italian and has festive music to feast by (lunch specials 11am-4pm for £3.95; open Sun.-Thurs. 10am-11pm and Fri.-Sat. 10am-midnight). The **Burlington Bar and Restaurant** in the Burlington Arcade, between New and Stephenson St. (tel. 643 2601) features continental fare; a hodgepodge of vegetarian dishes, fish, and sandwiches cost around £3-4. The **Little Pub Company** (not to be confused with a public house) has outlets everywhere and boffo burgers (£3.50-5.50).

SIGHTS & ENTERTAINMENT

Amid the clinking and clanking of metals artisans work in the historic **Jewellery Quarter** at the end of Newhall St. Never mind the Crown Jewels—the development of Birmingham's metalworking past and flourishing jewelry trade are showcased at the **Jewellery Quarter Discovery Centre,** 77-79 Vyse St., Hockley (open Mon.-Fri. 10am-4pm and Sat. 10am-5pm; wheelchair accessible). The **City Museum and Art Gallery** at Chamberlain Sq. off Colmore Row (tel. 235 2834), boasts **Big Brum,** a northern cousin to London's Big Ben. The museum includes a pre-Raphaelite art and these oh-so-engaging local history artifacts (open Mon.-Sat. 11am-5pm, Sun. 11am-5:30pm; free; wheelchair accessible). The **Barber Institute of Fine Arts** (tel. 472 0962), at the University of Birmingham, Edgbaston Park Rd., displays stunning works by artists as diverse in country and era as Rubens, Gainsborough, and Magritte. Take bus #61, 62, or 63 from the city center (open Mon.-Sat. 10am-5pm, Sun. 2-5pm; free; wheelchair accessible). **Aston Hall,** Trinity Rd. (tel. 327 0062), features a "long hall" of Jacobean architecture flanked by heavy tapestries; cannon marks scar the Great Staircase. Take bus #7, 65, 67, 102, 104-5, 114, or 440 (open late March to late Oct. daily 2-5pm).

The **Hippodrome Theatre,** Hurst St., applauds Birmingham's rich theatrical tradition. Originally a variety music hall that featured big-name vaudevillians, the theater recently underwent major renovations and is now one of Britain's leading opera houses (box office tel. 622 7486; open Mon.-Sat. 10am-6:30pm; tickets £5-20; call about the many discounts). A less grandiose but justly celebrated theater in Birmingham is the **Birmingham Repertory Theatre,** Centenary Sq. on Broad St. (box office tel. 236 4455; open Mon.-Sat. 10am-8pm; student tickets on weekdays). The experimental theater and cinema at the **Midland Arts Centre,** Cannon Hill Park (box office tel. 440 3838), shows avant-garde art as well as music from Africa and the Caribbean, and an occasional children's play (tickets £3.75-6.50). Ticket information for all Birmingham theaters is available from the **Convention and Visitor Information Bureau** (tel. 643 2514). Pick up the free *What's On* or leaflets at the tourist office.

The **Birmingham Jazz Festival** brings over 200 jazz bands, singers, and instrumentalists to town during the first two weeks in July. (For information, tel. 454 7020.) The world-class **City of Birmingham Symphony Orchestra,** in the new Symphony Hall at the Convention Centre, is conducted by the extremely talented Simon Rattle (tel. 213 3333; tickets £5-18; family, seniors, students, and children's discounts on select performances). Bobby Brown's **The Club,** 52 Gas St. (tel. 643 2573), attracts an energetic student crowd. Industrial cities breed good music; the leaflets plastered all over town are the best guide to local bands.

■■■ NOTTINGHAM

Robin Hood is gone from Nottingham, even if advocates of income redistribution are not. Remnants of a lace industry and a working canal prove that there was life in Sherwood Forest after Friar Tuck and Maid Marian. Situated on the highest navigable point of the Trent, the city has much more to recommend it than the memory of a proto-socialist, anti-Tory bowman (though tourist officials would disagree).

GETTING THERE

Trains run to Lincoln (24/day, Sun. 11/day; £3.50), Sheffield (1/hr.; £9.50), and London's St. Pancras (1/hr.; 2hr.; £28.50). **Buses** run to London (7/day, 2:20am-6:05pm; £16.50), Sheffield, Manchester, and other destinations.

ORIENTATION & PRACTICAL INFORMATION

Nottingham is a bustling, modern city without streets to match. Its hub is **Old Market Square,** a paved and fountain-filled plaza near the stately Council House (beware the pigeons). Maid Marian Way skirts the western edge of this central district and in the northwest crosses Parliament St. **Buses** stop at Victoria Shopping Centre (tel. (01332) 585317) on the north side of town. The **train station** (tel. (01332) 32051) is on Carrington St. across the canal from city center.

On April 16, 1995 ("Phone Day"), Nottingham's **telephone code** will change from 0602 to **0115** and a 9 will preface all existing 6-digit local phone numbers. The new code and numbers can, however, be used as of August 1, 1994, and *Let's Go* lists only these. For a further explanation, see the Appendix.

Tourist Office: City Information Centre, 1-4 Smithy Row (tel. 947 0661), just off Old Market Sq. Ask for the bountiful free goodies behind the counter. Staff will book rooms 9am-4:30pm; hotel list posted outside. Open Mon.-Fri. 8:30am-5pm, Sat. 9am-5pm, Sun. 10am-4pm; Nov.-March Mon.-Fri. 8:30am-5pm, Sat. 9am-5pm.
Budget Travel: STA Travel, Shakespeare St., near Nottingham Trent University (tel. 952 8802). Open Mon.-Fri. 10am-5pm.
Financial Services: Thomas Cook, 16 Clumber St. (tel. 947 0311). Open Mon. and Wed.-Sat. 9am-5:30pm, Tues. 10am-5:30pm. **American Express,** 2 Victoria St. (tel. 950 8846 or 924 1777). Open Mon.-Tues. and Thurs.-Fri. 9am-5:30pm, Wed. 9:30am-5:30pm, Sat. 9am-5pm. **Barclays,** Old Market Sq. (tel. 980 6200). Open Mon.-Tues. and Thurs.-Fri. 9:30am-4:30pm, Wed. 10am-4:30pm.
Post Office: Queen St. (tel. 947 4626). Open Mon.-Fri. 9am-5:30pm, Sat. 9am-1pm. *Bureau de Change, Poste Restante.* **Postal Code:** NG1 2BN.

Bookstores: Dillon's, 25 Wheeler Gate (tel. 947 3531). Bargain books in back, as well as the entire *Let's Go* series. Open Mon.-Sat. 9am-5:30pm.
Launderette: Brights, 150 Mansfield Rd. (tel. 948 3670, by the hostel). Open Mon.-Fri. 8:30am-7pm, Sat. 8:30am-6pm, Sun. 9:30am-5pm; last wash 1 hr. before close.
Hotlines: Samaritans: 941 1411. **Rape crisis:** 941 0410.
Hospital: Queen's Medical Center, Derby Rd. (tel. 942 1421).
Emergency: Dial 999, no coins required. **Police:** North Church St. (tel. 948 2999).

ACCOMMODATIONS

B&Bs are scattered throughout the central city and also in neighboring villages to the north and south. Along Goldsmith Rd. (near Nottingham Trent University) a number of guesthouses cluster. Expect to pay £13-15 per person.

YMCA, 4 Shakespeare St. (tel. 947 3068), located north of the bus and train stations on a thriving street corner. Lots of spartan rooms in a high-rise tower. Fitness gym. B&B £13; £4 key deposit. Weekly B&B £42. Call 2 weeks ahead.
Central Nottingham Tourist Hostel, a.k.a. Igloo, 110 Mansfield Rd. (tel. 947 5250). Operated by an experienced, affable backpacker and located in a partially-restored 150-year old building with clean bunkbeds and hot showers. Lounge area with TV. Complimentary tea and coffee served. Self-catering. Lockout 10am-4:30pm. Sleepsacks available and necessary. Best buy north of the city center. £8.
Langley Guest House, 82-84 Goldsmith St. (tel. 947 4992). Bargain rates for decent rooms across from Nottingham Polytechnic. Lounge area. Shared toilet and shower. Small, but sparkling clean. Singles £11. Doubles £20.
Newcastle Arms, 68 N. Sherwood St. (tel. 947 4616). Eleven basic and comfortable bedrooms above a pub frequented by students. Each room equipped with a wash basin. Shared shower and toilet. Includes breakfast. £14-16. Call ahead.
Mr. Gent, 16 Clinton Ct. (tel. 947 2414), off N. Sherwood St. Ask your host to recount his *Let's Go* adventures before you head off to sleep in a bedroom, covered patio, or pull-out couch. £11, breakfast included.

FOOD

Let no one say that Nottingham seems too British; its food selections are, well, so… international. Pizza places and other fast-food chains abound, as do Chinese and Indian restaurants, especially on Milton St./Mansfield Rd. Around Goose Gate and environs gather many delicious sandwich shops and take-out joints (the area caters largely to a young crowd). The shelves of a **Tesco supermarket** bulge in Victoria Shopping Centre (open Mon.-Tues., Thurs. 8:30am-6:30pm, Wed. 8:30am-8pm, Fri. 8:30am-7pm, Sat. 8:30am-5:30pm). With many eateries packed into the city center, searching for the ultimate eating experience on foot proves quite painless.

Salutation Inn, Spaniel Row (tel. 950 4627). Journey through medieval caves (1200 AD) before enjoying a pint of bitter upstairs in a 550-yr.-old pub. Open Mon.-Sat. 10:30am-11pm, Sun. noon-3pm and 7-10:30pm. Food till 7pm.
Hiziki Wholefood Collective, 15 Goose Gate (tel. 948 1115). Divine vegetarian and vegan food. Peruse the numerous anti-fur broadsides while enjoying spicy aubergine fritters in a lemon and coriander sauce (£2.25), chick-pea and veggie balls with salad (£2.10), or gorgeous cakes (60-75p). Open Mon.-Tues. and Thurs.-Fri. 9:30am-6pm, Wed. 9:30am-5:30pm, Sat. 9am-5:30pm.
Whitwell Delicatessen, 7-9 Ilkeston Rd. (tel. 978 2517). An old-style deli and wholefood shop. Delicious mozzarella, basil, and tomato sandwich on brown baguette £1. Open Mon.-Thurs. 8am-5pm, Fri. 8am-6pm, Sat. 8:30am-6pm; sandwiches 10am-3pm only.
Amigo's, 29 Pelham St. (tel. 948 4954). Take-away shish kebab (£2.20) or a chili burger (£1). Open daily 11:30am-3pm and 7pm-midnight; Thurs.-Sat. until 3am.

SIGHTS

Nottingham Castle today is not the Nottingham Castle of yesteryear. In fact, Prince John's famous home was demolished in the 17th century (and rebuilt) and burned in the 19th century (and repaired). Between annihilations, it was the staging ground for seminal medieval events, divine-right monarchist confrontations, and democratic revolutions; it was here that Charles I raised his standard against Parliament and began the Civil War. The current building (some call it a palace) houses the **Castle Museum** (tel. 948 3504), complete with exhibits on the history of Nottingham, some mediocre Victorian art, and the regimental memorabilia—medals, uniforms, and trophies—of the Sherwood Foresters. (Museum open daily 10am-5pm; Oct.-March 10am-4:45pm. Grounds open Mon.-Fri. 8am-dusk, Sat.-Sun. 9am-dark. Museum and grounds free Mon.-Fri.; Sat.-Sun. and bank holidays £1, children 50p.)

Across Castle Rd. at 51 Castle Gate is the **Museum of Costume and Textiles** (tel. 948 3504). The museum displays several furnished rooms with mannequins dressed in period costume, as well as an exhibit of hundreds of pieces of lace from the Continent and Nottingham, where the production of lace was mechanized at an early date (open daily 10am-5pm; free). Nearby, at the base of the castle's hill, the **Brewhouse Yard Museum** (tel. 948 3504, ext. 3600) stocks items of everyday life from the past 300 years—see how toothpaste was packaged during the reign of Queen Victoria (open daily 10am-5pm; Mon.-Fri. free; Sat.-Sun. £1, children 50p; free). Lacelovers will take to the **Lace Centre** (tel. 941 3539, opposite the Robin Hood statue on Castle Rd.). The staff demonstrates the lace-making process on Thursdays in the summer (open daily 10am-5pm; Jan.-Feb. 10am-4pm; free).

ENTERTAINMENT

Nottingham-by-night offers an array of paths to venture down—laser games, art film houses, theaters, pubs, and dance clubs. Many student-oriented establishments border the Polytechnic University near Sherwood St. and Parliament St. Other wateringholes and clubs occupy turf northeast of the Broad Marsh Centre. **Nottingham Playhouse,** Wellington Circus, features musicals, dramas, comedy, and other performances from September until mid-July (box office tel. 941 9419; tickets from about £6; Sat. matinee £1.50 off). **Cooperative Arts Theatre,** George St., presents amateur drama, opera, pantomime, and musicals from October to June (box office tel. 947 6096; open Mon.-Sat. noon-2pm; tickets from £3.50, discounts available). Looking for artificial fun? Head to **Megazone** for a laser game, 1 Hockley Rd. (tel. 958 9178; open Sun.-Fri. 11am-10pm, Sat. 9am-10pm).

The **Hippo,** 45 Bridlesmith Gate (tel. 950 6667), dishes out food and disco-dancing in its many rooms. **Garage,** 41 St. Mary's Gate (tel. 950 1251), shelters a largely student crowd for dancing. **Rock City,** Talbot St. (tel. 941 2544), hosts bands (international and otherwise) frequently. Slackers, whether rock or alternative music fans, will be at home. **The Filly and Firkin,** Mansfield Rd., frequently offers live rock. The upper level consists of a student crowd while the downstairs fills with die-hards.

■ NEAR NOTTINGHAM

North of Nottingham, in the village of Linby, stands **Newstead Abbey** (tel. (01623) 793557), the gorgeous green ancestral estate of Lord Byron. Inside, visitors enjoy access to the poet's living quarters and manuscripts. (Grounds open daily early April to late Sept. 9am-8pm; early Oct. to late March 9am-5pm. House open daily from early April to late Sept. noon-5pm. Admission to house and grounds £3.50, seniors and students £2, under 16 £1. Grounds only £1.60, seniors, students, and children £1.) Even farther to the north is the famous **Sherwood Forest,** considerably thinned since the 13th century. The **Sherwood Forest Visitor Centre** (tel. (01623) 823202) is the bull's eye of all things Robin-Hoody and Maid-Mariany, but Costner paraphernalia is outlawed, thank Tuck (center open daily 10:30am-5pm; Oct.-March daily 10:30am-4:30pm). The **Robin Hood Festival** occurs each August (call (0115) 977 4212 for information).Call the **Nottinghamshire Buses Hotline** (tel. (0115) 924 0000) for information on public transit to these sites.

Another of Sherwood Forest's merry men, D.H. Lawrence, was a Nottinghamshire native and schoolteacher who went on to write blessedly dirty books of prose and

LINCOLN

poetry. Once he was banned from the bookshelves; now he's buried in Westminster. Who knew? There's a **D.H. Lawrence Birthplace Museum** at 8a Victoria St., Eastwood (tel. (01773) 763312; open daily 10am-5pm; Nov.-March 10am-4pm). Fans of *Sons and Lovers* might want to explore the home where young Lawrence and family lived from 1887 to 1891. It's called the **Sons and Lovers Cottage,** and it's on 28 Garden Rd., Eastwood, and open by appointment (tel. (01773) 719786).

■■■ LINCOLN

Although Lincolnshire-born Lord Tennyson found poetic inspiration in the rolling wolds and low-lying fens of his youth, travelers with a keen interest in history might be more impressed by the country's charming hilltop city of Lincoln. To explore it is to unfold the quilt of English history since Roman times. Medieval streets climb their cobbled way past half-timbered Tudor houses to Lincoln's imposing 12th-century cathedral. The towering Minster and the Norman castle which crown the hill are relative newcomers to a city first built as a settlement for retired Roman legionnaires (not unlike North Miami Beach). Because the main attractions sit on the top of a hill, separate from Lincoln's center, the town enjoys a relative freedom from milling tourists, lending it a relaxed aura.

GETTING THERE

Lincoln sits on a rail route connecting Doncaster and London. **Trains** run to London's King Cross station via Newark (about 3/day, Sat. 1/day; £30), to York (Mon.-Sat. roughly 1/hr., Sun. 10/day; 1½-3½hr., £14.50), and to other cities as well. **National Express** sends **buses** to London (2/day, 5hrs., £22).

ORIENTATION & PRACTICAL INFORMATION

Roman and Norman military engineers were attracted to the summit of **Castle Hill;** later engineers who constructed the railway preferred its base. As a result, Lincoln is somewhat split between the historic and affluent acropolis to the north and the lower town which largely consists of cottages built near the railway. Regrettably for backpackers, the tourist office perches on the top of Castle Hill; store your things at the train station or take them to your lodgings before attempting the climb.

Tourist Office: 9 Castle Hill, LN1 3AA (tel. 529828). Books rooms and posts list outside upon closing. Open Mon.-Thurs. 9am-5:30pm, Fri. 9am-5pm, Sat.-Sun. 10am-5pm; Oct.-March same weekday hrs., Sat.-Sun. 11am-3pm. **Tours:** July-Aug. daily 11am and 2pm from tourist office (£1, children 75p).

Financial Services: Thomas Cook, 4 Cornhill Pavement (tel. 532294). Open Mon.-Thurs. and Sat. 9am-5:30pm, Fri. 10am-5:30pm. **Barclays,** 316 High St. (tel. 532 311). Open Mon.-Tues. and Thurs.-Fri. 9:30am-4:30pm, Wed. 10am-4:30pm, Sat. 9:30am-noon.

Post Office: 19/20 Guildhall St. (tel. 532288). *Bureau de change.* Open Mon.-Fri. 9am-5:30pm, Sat. 9am-12:30pm. **Postal Code:** LN1 1AA.

Telephone Code: 01522.

Train Station: Central Station, St. Mary's St. (tel. 539502). Lockers 50p-£1. Travel Center open Mon.-Sat. 9am-5pm.

Bus Station: National Express (tel. 534444), as well as regional and local buses, stop at the **City Bus station** off St. Mary's St. opposite the railway station. For information on local/regional bus service, contact the bus office on St. Mark St. (tel. 532424; open Mon.-Fri. 8:30am-5pm, Sat. 8:30am-4:30pm.)

Launderette: Maytag, 8 Burton Rd., at Westgate near the cathedral. Open daily at 8:30am; Mon.-Fri. last wash 7pm, Sat.-Sun. last wash 4pm.

Hotline: Samaritans (crisis): tel. 528282.

Hospital: County Hospital, St. Anne's Rd. (tel. 512512).

Emergency: Dial 999; no coins required.

Police: Beaumont Fee, near City Hall (tel. 529911).

ACCOMMODATIONS

B&Bs line Carline Rd. and Yarborough Rd., just west of the castle and cathedral. Most can be had for £12-18 per person. Call ahead in summer, as rooms fill quickly. Also pick up *Where to Stay* (free) at the tourist office.

HI Youth Hostel, 77 S. Park (tel. 522076), opposite South Common at the end of Canwick Rd. Take bus #51 from train station, or veer right from station, then right onto Pelham Bridge (becomes Canwick Rd.). Take the first right after the traffic lights at South Park Ave. A top-notch hostel across the street from a park, removed from the main tourist area. Reception closed 10am-5pm. Curfew 11pm. £7.75, under 18 £5.20. Cafeteria meals7pm (£3.90). Open July-Aug. daily; April-June Mon.-Sat.; mid-Feb.-March and Sept.-Oct. Tues.-Sat.; Nov.-mid-Dec. Fri.-Sat.

Mayfield Guest House, 213 Yarborough Rd. Entrance on Mill Rd. (tel. 533732), 15-min. walk from train station. Run by a grandmother with a sensational house on the hill. No smoking. £15, with a private toilet and shower.

Admiral Guest House, Mrs. Robertson, 18 Nelson St. (tel. 544467), in lower part of town. Follow Newland, which becomes Newland St. W. after the Avenue; pass the Vine Inn; turn left. Cheery proprietor has small, pleasant rooms. B&B £13-15.

Bradford Guest House, 67 Monks Rd. (tel. 523947). Terraced house on a busy, gray street, 5 min. from High St. Enthusiastic proprietor and immaculate rooms. TVs and tea/coffee-making facilities in every room. Singles £15. Doubles £26.

FOOD

Sincil St. Markets, by the bus station, sell fresh produce, clothing, and other goods (open Mon.-Sat. 8:30am-about 4:30pm). A variety of restaurants, tearooms, and take-aways grace High St. Lincoln natives and tourists alike take time to take tea.

Stokes High Bridge Café, 207 High St. (tel. 513825). Busy tearoom in a house built on a medieval bridge. Sit by a window for a marvelous river view. Savory quiche or steak pie £3.70. £3-4 lunchtime specials (11:30am-2pm). Open Mon.-Wed. 9am-5pm, Thurs.-Sat. 9am-5:30pm.

Lion and Snake, 79 Bailgate, up by the cathedral. An alluring pub setting for a restorative pint and meal (£4.50-5). Open Mon.-Sat. 11am-11pm, Sun. noon-3pm and 7:30-10:30pm. Food served Mon.-Fri. noon-2pm and 6-8pm.

Wig and Mitre, 29 Steep Hill (tel. 535190), near the cathedral in a 14th-century building. Downstairs, sandwiches and breakfast items for £2-5. Open 8am-11pm.

The Spinning Wheel, 39 Steep Hill (tel. 522463), 1 block south of tourist office in a leaning, half-timbered building. Basic entrees (£4-7); mind-blowing desserts. May be your only chance to eat in a fireplace. Open daily 11am-9pm.

SIGHTS

All roads lead to the spectacular Gothic cathedral (or so it seems). Built beginning in the 12th century on the ruins of a Norman structure, **Lincoln Minster** (tel. 544544) was for many centuries the tallest building in Europe, and its position at the top of Castle Hill makes it visible as far away as Boston on clear days, and some twenty miles to the south). Don't miss the cloisters, with their humorously carved wooden vaulting, and the library designed by Christopher Wren. (Open Mon.-Sat. 7:15am-8pm, Sun. 7:15am-6pm; winter Mon.-Sat. 7:15am-6pm, Sun. 7:15am-5pm. Near-obligatory donation £2.50, seniors and students £1, children 50p. **Tours** Mon.-Fri. 11am, 1 and 3pm; March-April and Oct.-Dec. Mon.-Fri. 11am and 2pm; Jan.-Feb. Sat. 11am and 2pm.) Roof tours (£2.50) must be booked in advance.

Near the cathedral, on the south side of Minster Yard, stand the remains of Lincoln's medieval **Bishop's Palace** (tel. 527468), which, while no longer magnificent itself, still offers splendid views of the city and outlying countryside. Built in the 12th century as the seat of England's largest diocese, the palace fell into ruins after extensive damage wrought by the Civil War. The thrifty traveler might do well to take a surreptitious peek through the doorway into the yard and beyond (open April-Sept. daily 10am-6pm; 85p, seniors and students 65p, children 40p, under 5 free).

William I was a practical conqueror, as conquerors go, so he only granted a charter for a cathedral in 1072, four years after he had ordered the construction of **Lincoln Castle** (tel. 511068). Though heavily restored, the Norman walls remain, enclosing a vast area and the best of the four copies of the *Magna Carta*. Visitors can walk along the battlements, and the panoramic view from Observatory Tower includes the cathedral, the river, and most of Lincolnshire. Guided tours start daily Easter through October at 11am and 2pm (castle open Mon.-Sat. 9:30am-5:30pm, Sun. 11am-5:30pm; Nov.-March Mon.-Sat. 9:30am-4pm; last entry 30 min. before closing; £2; children, seniors, and students £1.20).

ENTERTAINMENT

Club names in Lincoln change constantly. **Kiss,** on Newland Ave. (tel. 520598), and **Ritzy,** Silver St. (tel. 522314), currently supply music and a flat surface. For a full summer arts listing and calendar of activities in the castle, pick up a copy of *Lincoln Castle Events* at the tourist office. The **Theatre Royal,** Clasketgate (tel. 525555 or 534570), between High St. and Broadgate, stages drama year round (tickets £2.50-6.50; student discounts sometimes available; box office open daily 10am-6pm).

Like most English towns, Lincoln has its fair share of festivals. The **Arts Festival** in May features exhibitions and touring theater companies. You can sample wines from Neustadt, Lincoln's German sister city, at the **Wine Festival,** usually held the first week in June, and crafts at the **Christmas Market,** held you know when. Lincoln's attempt to recreate the front of your grandmother's Christmas card: carolers, roasting chestnuts, and luminary trees galore.

■ NEAR LINCOLN

It was in **Grantham**, about 25 mi. south of Lincoln, that Sir Isaac Newton attended the **King's School** on Brook St. and carved his schoolboy signature into the window-sill (visitors by appointment; tel. (01476) 63180). The **Grantham Museum** (tel. (01476) 68783), St. Peter's Hill by the tourist office, features exhibits on Newton's life and work, as well as a video exhibit on another Grantham prodigy, Margaret Thatcher (open Mon.-Sat. 10am-5pm; Oct.-March Mon.-Sat. 10am-12:30pm and 1:30-5pm; 50p, children 25p; wheelchair accessible). The Thatchers' legendary grocery store (owned by dad) is now the **Premier** restaurant on North Parade (tel. (01476) 77855). Seven mi. south in Colsterworth is **Woolsthorpe Manor** (tel. (01476) 860338), Newton's birthplace. It was here under an apple tree that the scientist was first struck by the idea of gravity and also here (on a 1665 visit to escape the plague in Cambridge) that he dreamt up calculus, the bane of precocious teenagers everywhere (open April-Oct. Wed.-Sun. 1-5:30pm; £2.30, children £1.10). Trains from Lincoln reach Grantham via Newark upon Trent (1/hr.; 1hr.; day return £6.60) or by **Lincolnshire Road Car** from St. Mark's Bus Station (1/hr.; 1¼hr.; day return £3).

East of Grantham, near the mouth of the River Witham, life goes on in tiny **Boston** despite the departure of a band of Puritans for New England in 1630. Originally planning to depart for Holland in 1607, they were betrayed by their captain (leaving the country was a crime) and imprisoned in the **Guildhall** (now a museum). Holding no grudges, they named their quite remarkable new settlement on Massachusetts Bay after the Lincolnshire town that had held them prisoner. Boston can be reached by **rail** from Lincoln, changing at Sleaford (1/hr.; 1hr.; day return £7.10). The refreshingly happy folk in the **tourist office,** Blackfriars Arts Centre, Spain Lane (tel. (01205) 356656), can give you information about the area.

■■■ SHEFFIELD

God gave man teeth and fingers, but Sheffield gave him cutlery. While Manchester was clothing the world, Sheffield was setting the table, first with hand-crafted flatware, then with mass-produced goods and eventually stainless steel, which was invented here. The city's population soared in the boom years of the mid-19th century, and Sheffield remains England's fourth-largest city. It is a task-and-a-half for an aging industrial beast to transform itself into a cosmopolitan, attractive, and inviting destination, and Sheffield gets points for trying. A massive mill and England's largest dancefloor now occupy the hilly landscape beside vestiges of Sheffield's heyday.

GETTING THERE

Sheffield lies on the M1 Motorway, about 30 mi. east of Manchester and 25 mi. south of Leeds. It is connected by frequent direct train service to Manchester (through the Peak District's Hope Valley), Liverpool, York, and Birmingham. For the Lake District and the northwest, change at Preston or Stockport; for Chester, change at Stockport. **Trains** run to Manchester (2/hr., Sun. 1/hr.; 1-1½hr.; £7.50), Birmingham (14/day, Sun. 12/day; 2hr.; £15.50), and London's St. Pancras (17/day, Sun. 11/day; 2-3hr.; £36.50). **National Express Rapide bus** service isn't as frequent as the hourly inter-city trains to London, but it's cheaper. National Express buses run to London (every 2 hr.; 3½hr.; £10), Birmingham (roughly every 2 hr.; 2hr.; £13), and Nottingham (every 1-2 hr. all night; 1hr.; £6.25). All buses leave the Sheffield Interchange.

ORIENTATION & PRACTICAL INFORMATION

Buses arrive at the marvelously designed **Sheffield Interchange** between Pond St. and Sheaf St. (tel. 275 4905; **lockers** £2; open Mon.-Thurs. 8am-5:30pm, Fri. until 6pm). The **train station** is a block south on Sheaf St. (24-hr. train information, tel. 272 6 411). The **Transport Executive Office** (tel. 276 8688) is located in the Interchange opposite the bus office and has news on local buses (open Mon.-Sat. 8am-6pm, Sun. 9am-5pm). You can also get bus info from **South Yorkshire's Transport,** Exchange St. (tel. 275 5655). Sheffield's central district is not large, but it has been so heartlessly lacerated by divided highways that walking becomes tortuous, traffic congested, and parking expensive; pedestrian underpasses and a new tram system promise to ease this transportation chaos, but currently only the line to the gigantic Meadowhall Shopping Centre has been completed.

Sheffield harbors two **tourist offices**. The main one, Town Hall Extension, Union St. (tel. 273 4671), distributes accommodations lists and information on the town and its surroundings. After hours, a lodgings list is posted in the window (office open Mon.-Fri. 9:30am-5:15pm, Sat. 9:30am-4:15pm; room booking closes 1 hr. earlier). Another full-service office awaits at the train station (tel. 279 5901).

Traveling letters lug their way to the **post office** at Fitzalan Sq. (tel. 273 3525), uphill from the Interchange (open Mon.-Tues. and Thurs.-Fri. 8:30am-5:30pm, Wed. 9am-5:30pm, Sat. 8:30am-12:30pm). Sheffield's **postal code** is S11 AB. Cash your Traveler's Cheques at **American Express Travel Service,** 20 Charles St. (tel. 273 7606; open Mon.-Fri. 9am-5pm, Sat. 9am-4pm; client mail held). Wash the smog from your clothes at **Abbey Glen Cleaners,** 1 Crookes Rd. (tel. 266 3307), near Tapton Hall. The adjacent dry-cleaner's provides change (open Mon.-Sat. 8am-10pm, last wash 8:30pm; Sun. 8:30am-9pm, last wash 7pm). The **police** can be reached at 276 8522, but in an **emergency** dial **999;** no coins required. The **Royal Hallamshire Hospital** is on Glossop Rd. (tel. 276 6222).

On April 16, 1995 ("Phone Day"), Sheffield's **telephone code** will change from 0742 to **0114** and a 2 will preface all existing 6-digit local phone numbers. The new code and numbers can, however, be used as of August 1, 1994, and *Let's Go* lists only these. For a further explanation, see the Appendix.

ACCOMMODATIONS

Pick up the thorough *Where to Stay in Sheffield* guide at the tourist office. It's free, unlike the pricey B&Bs scattered around town, which cost at least £15 per night. Most places are a hilly westward hike-and-a-half from the city center and fill up quickly, especially during summer weekends. Call in advance.

YMCA, 20 Victoria Rd. (tel. 268 4807) between Broomhall and Victoria Rd. Take bus #60 to Hallamshire Hospital; bear left on Clarkehouse Rd. to Park Lane and turn left again. Or take buses #81-86 from Pinestone St. to Collegiate Crescent, then walk up and turn right on Victoria Rd. Spare, clean, and comfortable rooms on a quiet street a few blocks from the University. Men and women. Singles £14. Doubles £22. Continental breakfast included. Evening meals at in-house cafe £2, students £1.50. Laundry and kitchen facilities. Key deposit £5.

Mr. and Mrs. Chambers, 17 Sale Hill (tel. 266 2986). Take bus #60 to the beginning of Manchester Rd., then climb 1 block to Sale Hill. Charming hosts and flower garden above the city make the hike worthwhile, despite the mildly malevolent orbit of two wee foldy dogs. No smoking. Singles £17. Doubles £32.

University of Sheffield: Halifax Hall, Endcliffe Vale Rd. (tel. 266 4196), 2½ mi. west of the city center; take bus #60 from the train station or buses #81-86 from Pinstone St. Clean and basic dorm rooms available with kitchen and laundry facilities, TV, room, and bar. Open mid-March to mid-April, July-Sept. and mid-Dec. to mid-Jan. B&B £17.75, students £11. **Tapton Hall,** Crookes Rd. (tel. 266 4309), offers similar accommodations for the same price. To reserve a room in advance, write to Bed and Breakfast Reservations, Octagon Centre, University of Sheffield, Sheffield S10 2TQ (tel. 282 4080); £5 deposit required.

Camping: Fox Hagg Farm, Lodge Lane (tel. 230 5589), about 4 mi. from town, off Manchester Rd. Take bus #51. Open April-Oct. £3.50-5/person.

FOOD & DRINK

Most of the offerings around the Moor shopping area are unexciting. For more stimulating nourishment, check out the studenty area around Division St. and Ecclesall Rd. To cater your own feast, head for **Castle Market** on Exchange St. for meats; **Sheaf Market,** across the street, has fruit and vegetables (both open Tues.-Wed. and Fri.-Sun. 8am-5pm). **Gateway Supermarket** resides in the city center at 33-34 Pine St. (open Mon.-Fri. 8am-6:30pm, Sat. 8am-6pm). Its enormous evil twin, **Safeway,** glowers at the corner of Hanover Way and Ecclesall Rd. (open Mon.-Sat. 8am-8pm, Sun. 10am-4pm).

Bekash Indian Cuisine, 349-351 Ecclesall Rd. (tel. 266 4168). Scrumptious entrees (£5-6) of varying spiciness; "very hot" is wicked hot. Open Tues.-Thurs. and Sun. noon-2pm and 6pm-midnight, Fri.-Sat. noon-2pm and 6pm-1:30am.

Mamas and Leonies, 111-115 Norfolk St. (tel. 272 0490). Serves pasta, burgers, and smoked haddock and cottage cheese quiche to suits. Is this you? Entrees around £4.50. Some veggie options. Open Mon.-Sat. 10am-11:30pm.

Chubby's, 26 Cambridge St. (tel. 275 3875). Offers a variety of burger and kebab options; the nectar-like cheese on the burgers is a local treasure (£2). Look for daytime burger specials. Open Mon.-Sat. 11am-3am, Sun. 11am-1am.

The Frog and Parrot, 64 Division St. (tel. 272 1280). A lively, traditional pub known for its mettle-testing selection of home-brewed lagers; mighty livers might dare to try "Roger and Out." Lunch served noon-2:30pm. Open Mon.-Sat. 11am-11pm, Sun. 7-10:30pm.

Yankees, 418 Ecclesall Rd. (tel. 268 0828), if you can't get the New World off your hungry mind. More than just hot dogs and peanuts. Main courses £3-5. Open daily 11:45am-midnight.

SIGHTS & ENTERTAINMENT

The **Kelham Island Industrial Museum,** Alma St. (tel. 272 2106), houses a clutter of iron and steel, most of it bent into engines and silverware in Sheffield itself. Its section on steelmaking documents the depressing working and living conditions over the past 300 years. The museum also displays a working 12,000 horsepower steam engine (Britain's most powerful), in full use until 1978. (Open Mon.-Thurs. 10am-4pm, Sun. 11am-4:45pm; £2.50, seniors and children £1.25.) Take bus #47 or 48 from the Interchange (1/hr.); alight at Nursery St., turning left on Corporation St. Take a right on Alma St. and wind 200 yd. through a black-lunged industrial park to the museum on the right.

In 1875, Victorian critic and artist John Ruskin established a museum to show the working class that "life without industry is guilt, and industry without art is brutality." What emerged was the Guild of St. George Collection: rocks, flora, and fauna, complemented by watercolors, illuminated manuscripts, and architectural details. This miscellany is now displayed in the **Ruskin Gallery,** Norfolk St., by Tudor Square (tel. 273 5299). The local crafts gallery is also worth a once-over (both open Mon.-Sat. 10am-5pm; free). Nearby is the **Graves Art Gallery,** Surrey St. (tel. 273 5158), on the top floor of the Central Library building, which hosts revolving exhibits from the museum's permanent collection of Dutch and British art, mingled with a good selection of Far Eastern jade and ivory (open Mon.-Sat. 10am-5pm; free).

Two museums share a building in the beautifully landscaped Weston Park, west of the city center and adjacent to the university. The **Mappin Art Gallery** (tel. 272 6281) holds a large collection of Victorian paintings (open Tues.-Sat. 10am-5pm, Sun. 1-5pm; free; wheelchair access). The **City Museum** (tel. 276 8588), focuses on ancient British artifacts, many from the Bronze Age, and has a roomful of cutlery from Sheffield and elsewhere (open Tues.-Sat. 10am-5pm, Sun. 11am-5pm; free; disabled access). Take bus #52 from High St. to the Children's Hospital.

At night, the **Crucible Theatre** and the recently revamped **Lyceum Theatre** (both on Arundel Gate, Tudor Sq., with a joint box office on Norfolk St., tel. 276 9922) stage musicals, plays, dance performances, and concerts. Students with ID can get tickets for £3 after 10am on day of performance at the Lyceum, and theatergoers of all ages can get same-day tickets at both theaters for £4. After the show, cross the street (via the subterranean walkway) to the **Roxy** (tel. 272 1927), home to the largest dance floor in Britain and an otherworldly lighting system. Dance until 2am with 3,000 or so fellow chart-busters. For a more intimate (and mature) milieu, try **The Leadmill** (tel. 275 4500), near the train station. A favorite among local students, it hosts live rock concerts, a comedy cabaret, and regular house-music club nights. Funky rhythms also emanate from **The Palais,** 33 London Rd. (tel. 279 9022). *The Gig Guide* will tell you where and when to catch these and other nighttime happenings; inquire at the tourist office about where you can pick up a copy.

■■■ PEAK NATIONAL PARK

Covering 555 sq. mi., Peak National Park lies at the southern end of the Pennines, with Manchester, Sheffield, Nottingham, and Stoke-on-Trent at its corners. Devoid of towering peaks, the area in fact derives its name from the Old English *peac,* meaning hill. In the northern Dark Peak area, deep groughs (gullies) gouge the hard peat moorland against a backdrop of gloomy cliffs. Gray stone villages and patches of woodland break up rolling hills in the limestone plateau of the southern White Peak. Here the landscape is pastoral rather than wild, with chest-high stone walls meandering through fields of grass well-nibbled by sheep and Friesian cattle. In the Derbyshire Dales, rivers have chiseled the white limestone into deep gorges, or dales.

Wedged between large urban centers, the Peak receives over 22 million visitors per year, more than any other national park in Europe. Although nature is the cardinal attraction, some head peakward for the annual "well-dressing" festivals. *Haute couture* is not the theme. Rather, Derbyshire Dales residents press elaborate mosaics of flower petals onto clay slabs near local wells as thanksgiving for another year's supply of water. These venerations of a pagan life source are scheduled according to the church calendar (ah! such lovely irony!), and exact dates (ranging from June to late September) are published in *Peakland Post,* the park's invaluable and free newspaper, available from tourist centers after February, when high season begins.

Public transport and commercial bus tours move the mobs on sunny summer weekends; for a more tranquil visit, try to catch the infrequent buses to the bleaker northern moors, out of the reach of commuter-rail lines. Although protected from development by national park status, the land is still privately owned, so be respectful and stay on designated rights-of-way. Ramblers' guidebooks and other useful publications are available at National Park Information Centres, and can be ordered

Peak District National Park

1 Wessenden Moor
2 Wessenden Head Moor
3 Saddleworth
4 Dick Hill
5 Thurlstone Moor
6 Longsett Moors
7 Shining Clough Mass
8 Margery Hill (elevation 1793)
9 Broomhead Moor

10 Hobson Moss
11 Hope Woodlands
12 Birchinlee Pasture
13 Black Ashop Moor
14 Derwent Moors
15 Edale Moor
16 Kinder Low (elevation 2077)
17 Edale Head
18 Jacob's Ladder

19 Blue John Cavern
20 Treak Cliff Cavern
21 Peak Cavern
22 Hartington Upper Quarter
23 Shining Tor (elevation 1854)
24 Raven's Low
25 Axe Edge Moor
26 Middle Hills
27 Thor's Cave

by mail. Write to Peak Park Joint Planning Board, National Park Office, Aldern House, Bakewell DE4 1AE for a list of publications. For an information pack on the park, write to the Tourism Officer, Town Hall, Matlock, Derbyshire, DE4 3NN.

GETTING THERE & GETTING ABOUT

Many would say that walking is the essence of the park and that your feet are all you need to get from one village to the next. But for those who enjoy keeping skin on their soles, local bus companies provide fairly good service between the villages. Derbyshire County Council's *Peak District Timetable* (50p) is an invaluable invest-ment; it includes all bus and train routes and comes with a large map. You can buy it at the Transport Executive in the Sheffield interchange and at most Peak tourist offices. The Council also staffs a bus info line (tel. (01298) 23098, daily 7am-8pm). Coverage of certain routes actually improves on Sundays, especially in summer.

Rail service to the park is, at best, limited. Two **rail lines** originate in Manchester and enter the park from the northwest: on one line trains terminate at Buxton near the park's western edge, while the Hope Valley line continues across the park to Sheffield (via Edale), Hope (near Castleton), and Hathersage. Both rail lines (1/hr.) enter the park at New Mills—the Buxton line at Newtown Station and the Hope Val-ley line at Central Station (20 min. will get you from one to the other on foot). A third rail line leaves Nottingham and runs north via Derby to Matlock on the south-eastern edge of the Peak District.

Bus #R1, the "Transpeak," winds through the park for 3½ hours from Manchester to Nottingham every two hours, stopping at Buxton, Bakewell, Matlock, Matlock Bath, Derby, and towns in between; this mainline service is a counterpart to the north's Hope Valley rail line. Evening buses may not cover the whole route, so check the timetable. Several buses also trundle regularly into the Peaks from Shef-field; bus X23 serves Bakewell and Buxton and bus #272 hits Castleton. **National Express** makes the four-hour journey to Buxton form London (1/day; £21).

Those who plan to ride frequently should buy a **Derbyshire Wayfarer** (£6.50, seniors and children £3.25). It covers virtually all rail and bus services within the Peak District and to and from Sheffield for a day. If you're traveling strictly within the park, the ticket will pay for itself if you board three or more buses or trains. The **Trent Explorer** ticket (£4.50; one child travels free with each adult) gives you one-day access to all Barton and Trent buses (buy tickets on board). The **East Midland Day Rover** is good for one day of travel on East Midland, Mansfield, and Disrict buses (£5.75). Yet another **Wayfarer** pass allows one day of travel east of Matlock, Ashborne, and Crich, covering the area up to and around Manchester. Plan in advance; you may need to take several buses to reach your destination.

ORIENTATION & PRACTICAL INFORMATION

Facilities in the Peak District generally stay open through the winter, due to the proximity of large cities. Some B&Bs and youth hostels stay open into December.

Tourist Offices

Ashbourne, 13 Market Pl. (tel. (01335) 343666). Open Mon.-Sat. 9:30am-5:30pm, Sun. 9:30am-5pm; Nov.-Feb. daily 10am-4pm.

Bakewell, Old Market Hall at Bridge St. (tel. (01629) 813227). From the bus stop walk past Sandringham Fabrics' right flank. Also a National Park Information Cen-tre. Comprehensive exhibit on local life and the park's history. Sells a good selec-tion of maps and guides. Open daily 9:30am-5:30pm; Sat., Sun., bank holidays, and Aug. 9:30am-6pm; Nov.-Feb. Fri.-Wed. 9:30am-5pm, Thurs. 9:30am-1pm.

Buxton, The Crescent (tel. (01298) 25106). Open daily 9:30am-5pm; Nov.-Feb. Fri.-Wed. 9:30am-5pm, Thurs. 9:30am-1pm.

Matlock Bath, The Pavilion (tel. (01629) 55082), along the main road. Open daily 9:30am-5:30pm; Nov.-Feb. 10am-4:15pm.

National Park Information Centres

These centers display the park's symbol of a circle resting atop a rectangle. All carry detailed walking guides and other park fun-facts.

Bakewell, See Tourist Offices, above.

Castleton, Castle St. (tel. (01433) 620679), near the church. From the bus stop, follow the main road into town and turn left at the youth hostel sign. Open daily 10am-5:30pm; Nov.-Easter Sat.-Sun. 9am-5pm.

Edale, Fieldhead (tel. (01433) 670207), between the rail station and village. Open daily 9am-5:30pm; Nov.-Easter daily 9am-1pm and 2-5pm.

Fairholmes, in Upper Derwent Valley, near Derwent Dam (tel. (01433) 650953). Open daily 10:30am-5:30pm; Oct.-March Sat.-Sun. 10:30am-5pm.

Hartington, in the signal box at Hartington Old Station, 1½ mi. from the village. Open Easter-Sept. weekends and bank holidays approximately 11am-5pm.

Langsett Barn, near Stocksbridge (tel. (01226) 370770). Open March-Sept. weekends and bank holidays 10:30am-5:30pm.

Torside, in Longdendale Valley. Open March-Sept. weekends and bank holidays approx. 11am-5pm.

ACCOMMODATIONS & CAMPING

Park information centers and tourist offices distribute free park-wide and regional accommodations guides; a camping guide costs 35p. B&Bs are plentiful and cheap (from £10), as are youth hostels (about £7). Matlock Bath is especially full of inexpensive B&Bs. Many farmers allow camping on their land, sometimes for a small fee; remember to leave the site just as you found it.

HI Youth Hostels

Most hostels are within an easy day's hike of one another, and each sells maps that detail routes to neighboring hostels. Most hostels in the Peak District cost between £5.70 and £8.40, and have a 10am to 5pm lockout and 11pm curfew. Hostels often fill with rambunctious kiddies; so call ahead and invest in earplugs.

The hostels and their telephone numbers are: **Bakewell** (tel. (01629) 812313), **Bretton** (tel. (0114) 288 4541), **Buxton** (tel. (01298) 22287), **Castleton** (tel. (01433) 620235), **Crowden-in-Longdendale** (tel. (01457) 852135), **Dimmingsdale** (tel. (01538) 702304), **Edale** (at Rowland Cote; tel. (01433) 670302), **Elton** (tel. (01629) 650394), **Eyam** (tel. (01433) 630335), **Gradbach Mill** (tel. (01260) 227625), **Hartington Hall** (tel. (01298) 84223), **Hathersage** (tel. (01433) 650493), **Ilam Hall** (tel. (0133529) 212), **Langsett** (tel. (0114) 288 4541), **Matlock** (tel. (01629) 582983), **Ravenstor** (tel. (01298) 871826), and **Youlgreave** (tel. (01629) 636518). The **Meerbrook** and **Shining Cliff** hostels can be contacted through the Elton hostel. For more information, contact the YHA Central Region Office, P.O. Box 111, Via Gellia Mills, Bonsail, Matlock DE4 2HA (tel. (01629) 825850).

Camping Barns

The 11 park-operated **camping barns** are simple night shelters for hikers and bikers, providing a sleeping platform, water tap, and toilet for £2.25 per person. A comprehensive leaflet with map is available at all tourist centers. You can book and pay ahead with the **Peak National Park Centre,** Losehill Hall, Castleton, Derbyshire S30 2WB (tel. (01433) 620373).

Abney: Mr. and Mrs. Chadwick, Ivy House Farm, about 5 mi. southwest of Hathersage. Sleeps 8.

Bakewell: Mr. and Mrs. Lawton, Bank Top House Farm. Sleeps 13.

Bakewell: Mr. and Mrs. Hodgson. Near the head of Edale. Well situated for exploring Kinder Scout and ridgewalking above Edale. Sleeps 12.

Birchover: Mrs. Heathcote, Barn Farm, between Bakewell and Matlock off the B5056. Sleeps 10.

Butterton: Mr. and Mrs. Renshaw, Fenns Farm. Two camping barns near the southern end of the park, along the Manifold track. Sleeps 21.

Colin Hugh's: Mr. Graham, Tanyard Farm, close to the village of Old Glossop in the Northern Peaks. Sleeps 12.

Edale: Mr. and Mrs. Gee, Catefield Farm, close to one endpoint of the Pennine Way. Sleeps 8.

Losehill: Losehill Hall, near Castleton. Sleeps 8.

Nab End: Mr. and Mrs. Cox. Between Hollinsclough and Longnor. Sleeps 16.

Old Glossop: Mr. Graham. In the northern part of the park, near the terminus of a rail line to Manchester. Sleeps 12.

One Ash Grange: Mr. and Mrs. Wells. Above Lathkill Dale National Nature Reserve. Sleeps 12.

Taddington: Mr. Gillott, The Woodlands, in the center of Taddington village, at an altitude of 1000 ft. and midway between Buxton and Bakewell. Sleeps 10.

HIKING & BIKING

The central park is marvelous territory for rambling or light hiking. Settlement is sparser, and buses are fewer north of Edale in the land of the Kinder Scout plateau, the great Derwent reservoirs, and the gritty cliffs and waterlogged peat moorlands. From Edale, the Pennine Way runs north to Kirk Yetholm, across the Scottish border. The Peak District is on the same latitude as Siberia and Labrador, and people have died in the mist on Bleaklow and Kinder Scout, just a half-hour outside two large cities; be sure to dress warmly.

The park authority operates seven **Cycle Hire Centres** (listed below), where you can rent a bike (£6/day, £3.80/3hr.; under 16 £4.30/day, £3.30/3hr.; deposit £10; 10% discount for YHA members and Wayfarer ticket holders; centers open in summer daily 9:30am-6pm, varying hours the rest of the year).

Ashbourne: Mapleton Lane (tel. (01335) 343156).

Derwent: Near the Fairholmes information center (tel. (01433) 651261).

Hayfield: Near New Mills on Station Rd. in the Sett Valley (tel. (01663) 746222).

Middleton Top: Near Matlock on the High Peak Trail (tel. (01629) 823204).

Parsley Hay: At the meeting of the Tissington and High Peak Trails (tel. (01298) 84493).

Shipley Country Park: Near Heanor off the A608 (tel. (01773) 719961).

Waterhouses: Between Ashbourne and Leek on the A523 near the southern end of the Manifold Truck (tel. (01538) 308609).

SOUTHERN PEAK DISTRICT: BAKEWELL

Cause and effect are unclear, but two things are true: the Southern Peak is more accessible than the Northern Peak and also more trampled.

Fifteen mi. southwest of Sheffield and 30 mi. southeast of Manchester, **Bakewell** is the best base for exploring the southern portion of the park and a transfer point for more elaborate bus trips. Located near several scenic walks through the White Peaks, the town itself is best known for its delicious Bakewell pudding, created when a flustered cook in the Rutland Arms tried to make a tart by pouring egg mixture over strawberry jam instead of mixing it into the dough. **All Saints Church,** on the hill above town, lies in a crowded park of Anglo-Saxon gravestones and carved-cross fragments, accented with shade trees and benches. Nearby, a 16th-century house that has been aptly transformed into the **Old House Museum** (tel. (01629) 813647) with displays of ancient tools for wheel-making, cotton-weaving, and leather-working (open April-Oct. daily 2-5pm; £1.80, children 80p). Bakewell's **well-dressing festival** occurs during the last week of June.

Bakewell has an intimate and comfy **HI Youth Hostel** (tel. (01629) 812313) on Fly Hill, a three-minute walk from the tourist office (Open Fri.-Wed; lockout 10am-5pm). B&Bs here are more costly than in Matlock Bath (see below); many lie on or near Haddon Rd., the continuation of Matlock St. On Rutland Sq., **The Old Original Bakewell Pudding Shop** (tel. (01629) 812193) sells lunches and delicious desserts in a paneled restaurant above the shop. Skip lunch and order the full afternoon tea, which includes sandwiches, two huge fruit scones, with jam and cream, a Bakewell pudding, and the mandatory pot of tea (shop open daily 8:30am-9pm; Sept.-June Mon.-Thurs. 9am-6pm, Fri.-Sat. 8:30am-9pm, Sun. 8:30am-6pm).

Bakewell's **tourist office,** at the intersection of Bridge and Market St., doubles as a National Park Information Centre and displays informative exhibits on the history of Bakewell and the Peaks. The **post office** resides at 8 Portland Sq. (tel. (01629) 814427; open Mon.-Fri. 9am-5:30pm, Sat. 9am-12:30 pm).

Just five miles north of Bakewell, the hamlet **Eyam** underwent a self-imposed quarantine during the plague years 1665 and 1666, in which 250 of its 360 residents died a miserable bubonic death. Plaques on old houses tally the numbers that died in each. Tiny **Eyam Museum**, on Hawkhill Rd., (tel. (01433) 631371), commemorates all the grisly details (open Tues.-Sun. 10am-4:30pm; £1.25, seniors and children 75p). A hundred yards west of the church on the main drag, **Eyam Hall** (tel. (01433) 631976) traces the owner's family history in a 17th-century manor house. The Hall boasts a wall-to-wall tapestry room, an eight-line love stanza carved into the library window, and a 1675 pop-up human anatomy textbook (open March-Oct. Wed.-Thurs., Sun. and Mon. bank holidays 11am-4:30pm; £3.25, seniors and students £2.75, children £2.25.). The 60-bed **HI Youth Hostel** perches 800m above the town on Hawkhill Rd. (tel. (01433) 630335) in an old castle-like building. Rooms are clean and somewhat worn. The hostel has a lockout from 10am-5pm, and curfew comes at 11:30pm. (£7.15, breakfast £2.60, other meals available.) The hostel is open year-round, but occasionally closes on Sundays. Bus #65 hits Eyam on its route between Buxton and Sheffield (7/day, Sun. 3/day).

NORTHERN PEAK DISTRICT

The northern Dark Peak area contains some of the wildest, most rugged hill country in England, with vast areas like **Kinderscout** and **Bleaklow** entirely undisturbed by motor traffic. In these desolate mazes of black peat hags and deep groughs, even paths are scarce, and sparse towns and villages huddle in valleys. These towns provide little but provisions, shelter, and solace for bone-weary hikers. Less-experienced hikers may wish to stick to Edale and the southern paths.

Cradled in the deep dale of the River Noe, with gentle, gray-green hills sweeping up on two sides, **Edale** has little in the way of civilization other than a church, café, pub, school, and nearby youth hostel. Its environs, however, are arguably the most spectacular in Northern England. On summer weekends this tranquil village brims with hikers and campers readying themselves to tackle the **Pennine Way** (which passes out of the Peak District and into the Yorkshire Dales after a 3-4 day hike) or trek one of the shorter (1½-8½ mi.) trails closer to Edale proposed by the National Park Authority's *8 Walks Around Edale* (75p). The 7½-mile path to Castleton and back affords a breathtaking view of both the dark gritstone Edale Valley (Dark Peak) and the lighter limestone Hope Valley (White Peak) to the south. A new flagstone detour on the ridge between these valleys runs its environmentally-friendly way as far as **Mam Tor**. This decaying Iron Age hillside fort is visited by more than 250,000 walkers a year. Cliffs on three sides beckon fearless hang-gliders from near and far. The trip should take about 6½ hours at an easy pace. Stop at the huge **National Park Information Centre** (see listing above) for weather forecasts, free videos of the Hope Valley, and training with a map and compass.

Unless you reserve centuries ahead, your tent could be your best friend in this town where the only accommodations lie within the 140-bed **HI Youth Hostel** (tel. (01433) 670302), in which the population grows considerably more youthful and temperamental on summer weekends. (Ask at the Park Centre about the 30-min. shortcut through the fields to the hostel.) **Ollerbrook Farm** (tel. (01433) 670235), five minutes across the fields, is cheap at £1 per person. Near the school, **Cooper's Camp and Caravan Site** (tel. (01433) 670372), Newfold Far, asks £1.25. **The Field-head Campsite,** next to the **National Park Centre,** tops them all at £2.35 (children

£1.55). Edale lies on the Hope Valley rail line between Manchester and Sheffield, and is served every two hours (from Sheffield, £2.90, day return £5.50).

Two mi. southeast of Edale, **Castleton** is the least crowded and—dare we say—loveliest of the area's villages. Its main attractions include several caverns and Blue John, a rich blue-and-brown variety of spar mined here and found nowhere else in the world. The **Blue John Cavern** (tel. (01433) 20638) and **Treak Cliff Cavern** (tel. (01433) 620571) are about 1½ mi. west of town on the A625. (Blue John open 9:45am-6pm; in winter 9:45am-about 4pm; closed Jan.-Feb. £4, seniors £2.50, children £2. Treak Cliff open 9:30am-5pm; Nov.-Easter 9:30am-4pm. £3.80, seniors £3, children £1.90.) Also on A625, **Spreewell Cavern** (tel. (01433) 620512) features a boat tour of a partially-flooded mine. (Open 9:45am-6pm, closes earlier in winter. £4, seniors £2.50, children £2.) All of the caverns have student and YHA discounts. Tours leave frequently—call for times. Gigantic **Peak Cavern** (tel. (01433) 620285), right in town, features the second-largest aperture in the world (the first is in New South Wales, Australia), unfortunately obscured by the entrance structures. Decorously known in the 18th century as the "Devil's Arse," the cavern now features tours by guides pale from spending altogether too much time in Old Harry's Sphincter (open Easter-Oct. daily 10am-5pm; closed Mon. in winter; £3, children and seniors £2, discount with flier from tourist office). The **National Park Information Centre** in town offers guided walks through Castleton on Monday at 2pm from June-Sept. (£1.85, children 20p). The Centre also distributes free accommodations listings. Hikers looking for a more strenuous challenge can set off southwards on the 26 mi. **Limestone Way Trail** to Matlock.

The super-duper **HI Youth Hostel** (tel. (01433) 620235) by the castle entrance has an open lounge (£9.75/night includes a nice meaty breakfast). The several guest houses nearby include Mr. and Mrs. Skelton's **Cryer House** (tel. (01433) 620244), across from the tourist office (£14.50). The tearoom downstairs is a great place for lunchtime tea or a home-baked scone. Castleton lies 2 mi. west of the Hope rail station. Bus #272 runs daily from Sheffield Interchange to Castleton via Hathersage and Hope (departs Castelton hourly).

■■■ MANCHESTER

The northern hub of Manchester (pop. 600,000) has always tackled modern life with a vengeance. Once a vigorous leader in the Industrial Revolution, Manchester eventually developed into a center of liberal politics, and now savors its reputation as one of the hippest spots in England to live or to visit. Once derided by Ruskin as a "devil's darkness," the city recently declared itself "a nuclear-free city," and countless placards and posters reveal that labor movements and environmentalism are the norm among today's Mancunians. Although the dearth of budget accommodations in the city center often forces travelers to lodge in neighboring towns, Manchester is well worth a visit, if not a stay.

GETTING THERE

After Heathrow and Gatwick, **Manchester International Airport** is the third airport in England to serve North America. Bus #757 (2/hr.; return £2.75) connects the airport with Piccadilly Bus Station, Piccadilly Rail Station, and Victoria Rail Station, all in the center of town.

Manchester is served by **two main rail stations:** Piccadilly (primarily for trains from the south and east) and Victoria (primarily for trains from the west and north). They are connected by Metrolink trams (every 6-10min., 15min. on Sun.; 70p). **Trains** run to London's Euston Station (1/hr.; 2½hr.), Liverpool (2/hr.; 45min.; £5.70, day return £6.50), Chester (1/hr.; 1hr.; £6.20), and York (2/hr.; 1hr.; £11.50). A third rail station, Manchester Oxford Rd., near the university, is served mostly by local and regional trains. **Buses** stop in the Chorlton St. Coach Station. **National Express** serves Birmingham (8/day; 2-3hr.; £9.50, £10.50 on Fri.), Sheffield (7/day;

1½hr.; £5.50), Glasgow (5/day; 4½-5hr.; £18, £22 on Fri.), London (9/day from 7:30am-11:50pm; 4hr.; £24-42), and Edinburgh (5/day; 6hr.; £18.50-22.50).

Metrolink **trams** run every 5-10 minutes (Sun. 4/hr.). They connect Altrincham in the Southwest with Bury in the northeast. Manchester proper boasts eight of the 24 stops in between. Ticket prices vary with distance traveled.

ORIENTATION & PRACTICAL INFORMATION

The city center lies mostly within the triangle formed by Deansgate to the south, Victoria Station to the north, and Piccadilly station to the east. This area is fairly compact, and several pedestrian streets make getting around on foot easy, but the myriad by-ways and side-streets necessitate a good map. The **tourist office** is across the street from Town Hall.

Tourist Office: Manchester Visitor's Center, Town Hall Extension on Lloyd St. (tel. 234 3157 or 234 3158). Pick up copies of *Manchester Accommodation Guide* and *Manchester Food and Drink Guide* (both free). *Manchester Visitor Guide* gives hours, prices, disabled access and other practical information on most of the city's sites (80p). *What's On* (free) lists local events. Open Mon.-Sat. 10am-5:30pm and Sun. 11am-4pm.

Tours: The Visitor's Center offers dozens of guided walks (£2; seniors, students, and children £1) on such topics as "Murders and Mysteries of Manchester" and "Feminine Influence." One tour on one topic is usually given every day May-Sept.; less frequently other months. Pick up a free schedule with full details about walking and bus tours (£5-12.50). Most tours leave from the Visitor's Center.

Budget Travel Office: YHA Adventure Centre, 166 Deansgate (tel. 834 7119). Hostel memberships, ISIC, Travelsave stamps. Camping and hiking supplies. Open Mon.-Wed. and Fri. 10am-6pm, Thurs. 10am-7pm, Sat. 9:30am-6pm.

Financial Services: Thomas Cook, 2 Oxford St., off Peter Sq. Open Mon.-Wed. and Fri. 9am-5:30pm, Thurs. 10am-5:30pm, Sat. 9am-5pm. **Barclays,** 51 Mosley St. Open Mon.-Wed. and Fri. 9:30am-4:30pm, Thurs. 10am-4:30pm. **American Express:** 10-12 St. Mary's Gate, at Deansgate and Blackfriars. Client mail held. Open Mon.-Fri. 8:30am-5pm, Sat. 9am-4pm.

Post Office: 26 Spring Gardens (tel. 839 0697), near Market St. *Poste Restante* (separate entrance; tel. 834 0697) open Mon.-Fri. 6am-6pm, Sat. 6am-12:45pm. Main office Mon.-Tues., Thurs.-Fri. 8:30am-6pm, Wed. 9am-6pm, Sat. 8:30am-1pm. **Postal Code:** M2 1BB.

Telephone Code: 0161.

Train Station: Piccadilly Station, on London Rd. Travel Centre open daily 9am-6pm. **Victoria Station,** on Chapel St. Travel Centre open Mon.-Sat. 8:30am-6pm. Both stations open 24 hrs. For 24-hr. information call 832 8353.

Bus Station: Piccadilly Bus Station consists of about 50 bus stops around Piccadilly Gardens. Immense fold-out route map (free) can be had at the information desk in the station. Regular bus service til 11:30pm, night service on weekends til 2:30am. Call 228 7811 for more information. Piccadilly Information Office open Mon.-Sat. 7am-6:30pm; information line open daily 8am-8pm. **National Express** rolls into **Chorlton St.** (tel. 228 3881), 2 blocks south and 1 block east of Piccadilly Bus Station. Office hours Mon.-Sat. 7:15am-6:15pm, Sun. 8:30am-6:15pm. **Luggage storage** £1 (it's the only place in town), open 8:30am-6pm daily.

Bookstore: Waterstone's, 91 Deansgate (tel. 832 1992), between St. Ann's St. and King St. Large selection of everything good, including *Let's Go* guides. Fantastic section of real travel memoirs. Open Mon.-Fri. 8:45am-9pm, Sat. 8:45am-7:30pm, Sun. 10:30am-6:30pm.

Launderette: Mr. Bubbles, 246 Wilmslow Rd., near university and Didsbury (tel. 257 2640). Open daily 8am-10pm. Change and soap available.

Gay Community Center: Gay Centre, Sidney St. (tel. 274 3814). Drop-in center with coffee bar, meeting room, and phonelines.

Hotlines: Samaritans (crisis): tel. 834 9000; 24hr. **Rape crisis:** tel. 228 3602; Tues. and Fri. 2-5pm, Wed.-Thurs., Sun. 6-9pm.

Pharmacy: Cameolord, 7 Oxford St. (tel. 236 1445), off St. Peter's Sq. Open daily 8am-midnight.

MANCHESTER

Hospital: Royal Infirmary, Oxford Rd. (tel. 276 1234). Buses #42-49 run southward down Oxford Rd.

Emergency: Dial 999; no coins required.

Police: Chester House, Boyer St. (tel. 872 5050).

ACCOMMODATIONS

According to the economic theories of the Manchester School, a high demand for cheap rooms in Manchester should have produced an abundant supply. No such luck. While there are plenty of business hotels with potted ferns and fax machines, budget travelers will want to take a bus outside of town to more economical lodgings. Potted ferns are so kitschy, anyway. The highest concentration of budget lodgings is found 2 or 3 mi. south of the city center in the suburbs of **Fallowfield**, **Withington,** and **Didsbury;** take bus #40, 42, 45, or 49 to reach any of the small hotels, B&Bs, and university residence halls which abound in these areas. YHA plans to complete a 150-bed **hostel** on Potato Wharf, Castlefield, Manchester by March 1, 1995; book via their Central Reservations Office (tel. (0171) 248 6547). The disabled-access hostel will be open 24-hr., charging between £6.50-£12 per person.

University of Manchester, St. Gabriels Hall, 1-3 Oxford Pl., Victoria Park (tel. 224 7061). Self-catering dorm available during school vacations. Singles £10, students £6. Twins £20, £12. Reserve 2 or more weeks in advance. If full, try **Woolton Hall,** Wilmslow Rd., Fallowfield (tel. 224 7244); room only £8, with breakfast £10.40. For more information on these and other residence halls, contact the university-wide Accommodation Office, Precinct Centre, Oxford Rd., Manchester M13 9RS (tel. 275 2888; open Mon.-Fri. 9:30am-5pm).

Mrs. Matheson, 41 Atwood Rd., Didsbury (tel. 434 2268). Large, comfortable rooms in an uncommercialized, suburban house. Take bus #40, 42, or 45 to Didsbury Village. Singles £12, doubles £20. Up School St. a short block, left on Beaver Rd., then right onto Atwood Rd.

Mrs. Lambros, 34 Brunswick Rd., Withington (tel. 445 1823). Take any 40's bus to the Arosa Hotel, turn left into Mauldeth Rd.; Brunswick is the second on the right. Chat about Victorian writers with the friendly proprietor of this old house. Minimum stay 2 nights. B&B £12; £65/week.

FOOD & PUBS

Downtown offers numerous fast-food places and cheap, charmless cafés. Chinatown, bounded by Portland, Mosley, Charlotte, and Oxford St., is a disappointingly uniform agglomeration of pricey Cantonese restaurants, though you can save a few quid by eating a multi-course "Businessman's Lunch," offered by most Monday through Friday (noon-2pm; £4-7.50, with or without the briefcase). A more heartening source of ethnic food is the Rusholme area, before the university on bus #40, where numerous Middle Eastern and Indian (including some *halal* and vegetarian) restaurants and take-out counters line Wilmslow Rd.

Cornerhouse Café, 70 Oxford St. near the city center. On second floor of arts center. Trendy crowd. Panoptical view of street and its crawling inhabitants. Quiche and salad £2.40, hot vegetable dishes and salad from £2.70. Scrumptious desserts from 70p. Hot meals served noon-2:30pm and 5-7pm. Open daily 11am-8:30pm. Check out bulletin board by bar downstairs for information on local arts and entertainment events. The **Cigar Store** building across the street is a cappucino bar and continuation of the Café (open Mon.-Sat. 9am-8:30pm, Sun. 1-9pm).

French Window, 31 King St. (tel. 831 7119). Busy take-away serving a wide selection of baguette sandwiches (£1-2) and filled croissants (60p-£1.65). Fresh and tasty. Open Mon.-Sat. 7:30am-5:30pm.

Camel One, 107 Wilmslow Rd. (tel. 257 2282), in Rusholme. Snazzier than its take-away brethren, with a more interesting menu. £3 gets you a kebab or curry and a fluffy naan, to take away or eat at the counter. Open daily 11am-5am.

Royal Exchange Theatre Café, Cross St. Great atmosphere; elegantly busy and cluttered. Cold salads £1.95, sandwiches from 85p. Open Mon.-Sat. 10am-7:30pm.

Manchester is a bastion of real ale. Join the lively crowd at the **Lass O'Gowrie Brewhouse** (tel. 273 6932) on Charles St., where can you can watch your bitter brew. The **Green Room Theatre,** 54-56 Whitworth St., and the **Cornerhouse** (see above) break from the "Ye Olde" tradition and cater to would-be artists and students. The **Dry Bar** on Oldham St., famous for its association with British alternative music, was founded by Factory Records and New Order. Rub elbows with Ian McCulloch and the Happy Mondays, or simply relax in the mellow ambience with the up-and-coming of the Manchester scene.

SIGHTS

Towering over the city, the **Manchester Town Hall** is an awesome neo-Gothic building designed by Alfred Waterhouse and opened in 1877. Behind the building, the postage-stamp-sized **Peace Garden** attests to Manchester's freedom from things nuclear, if not to its horticultural ingenuity. Behind the Town Hall Extension is Manchester's jewel, the **Central Library.** One of the largest municipal libraries in Europe, it was opened by George V in 1934. The domed building houses, among other fine collections, a music and theater library, an exceptional language and literature library, and England's most extensive Judaica collection outside London (open Mon.-Wed. and Fri. 10am-8pm, Sat. 10am-noon and 1-5pm). In the **Museum of Science and Industry** (tel. 832 1830 or 832 2244), on Liverpool Rd., working steam engines and looms provide a more dramatic vision of the awesome speed, power, danger, and noise of Britain's industrialization than any diagram or description ever could. (Open daily 10am-5pm. £3.50, students, seniors and disabled £1.50; includes entrance to all galleries for one day, which may not be enough.)

The **City Art Galleries** (tel. 236 5244) consist of two adjacent buildings with entrances on different streets. The Mosely St. gallery gives a whirlwind tour of western art from 14th century Italian religious painting to modern art, with a focus on a few excellent pre-Raphaelite works. The Princess St. building next door houses touring shows and other temporary exhibitions (both buildings open Mon.-Sat. 10am-5:45pm, Sun. 2-5:45pm; free; disabled access). The Spanish and Portuguese Synagogue turned **Jewish Museum,** 190 Cheetham Hill Rd. (tel. 834 9879), north of Victoria Station, traces the history of the city's sizeable Jewish community (open Mon.-Thurs. 10:30am-4pm, Sun. 10:30am-5pm; £1.75, seniors, students, and children £1; disabled access ground floor only).

ENTERTAINMENT

Among certain cities, it is a badge of the cosmopolitan to induce Andrew Lloyd Webber and his evil, money-grubbing minions to put on *Cats* or some other suitably banal production. And indeed, Manchester has attracted that blight of a musical, *Phantom of the Opera*. Nod cheerfully if a Mancunian beats his chest about it, and proceed to culture with a longer half-life. The **Royal Exchange Theatre,** Cross St. (tel. 833 9833), performs an exciting and diverse program in a space-age theater-in-the-round inside the 1809 Exchange Building. (Box office open Mon.-Sat. 10am-8pm or until performance begins. Tickets from £5; can be purchased up to 3 days in advance. Student standbys £5, child, senior, and disabled person discounts (also £5) available Wed. and Sat. matinee.) The **Library Theatre** (tel. 236 7110), in the intimate former lecture hall of the Central Library, St. Peter's Sq., is an active and offbeat professional company (Sept.-July). The **Palace Theatre,** Oxford St. (tel. 242 2503), caters to more bourgeois tastes in theater, opera, and ballet. Buses run to outlying areas regularly until 11pm; less frequent night service runs until 2:30am.

The Free Trade Hall, Peter's St., houses the superb **Hallé Orchestra** from October to May (booking office in Heron House on Albert Sq., tel. 834 1712). Pop, jazz, and classical concerts are frequently held at the **G-Mex** (Greater Manchester Exhibition and Event Centre; tel. 834 2700), a renovated former train station on Lower Mosley St. Students stampede at **Band on the Wall,** 25 Swan St. (tel. 832 6625), to hear quality jazz, blues, reggae, and rock performed Monday through Saturday.

Manchester's club scene remains a national trend-setter, and it centers on the notorious **Hacienda,** 11-13 W. Whitworth St., close to G-Mex (cover £6-12). The club that launched The Smiths, New Order, and the Stone Roses continues to host Ecstatic house music raves, a gay night on the last Wednesday of every month, and "Transform" night the third Thursday of every month (for concert information call 236 5051; open 9pm-2am). If indy rock and 80s new wave are your thing, try **The Venue,** also on Whitworth St. (tel. 236 0026; open 10pm-2am; cover £1-3). **The Number One Club,** 1 Central St., and the recently opened **Paradise Factory,** 112-116 Princess St. (tel. 273 5422), spin groovy tunes for a mixed gay and straight crowd. Although most clubs shut around 2am, bold ravers might ask around about after-hours clubs and parties held in venues as diverse as airplane hangars and grassy meadows. Check at **Eastern Bloc Records** or the **Arcade** (a.k.a. Afflecks Palace), both on Oldham St., for listings and passes for these events. Let go man, just let go.

■■■ CHESTER

With fashionable shops tucked away in medieval houses, guides in full Roman armor leading tours around the city's walls, and a Barclays bank occupying a wing of the cathedral, Chester (pop. 60,000) at times resembles an American theme-park pastiche of Ye Olde English Village. Originally the Roman fortress of Deva on the River Dee, the town thrived between the 5th and 10th centuries after the Romans departed. Chester withstood sieges, became a base for Plantagenet campaigns against the Welsh, and expanded its web of trading connections all the way to the Baltic, France, Spain, Portugal, and the Low Countries. Over the course of the 17th century, the silting-up of the River Dee interfered with Chester's harbor and rival Liverpool supplanted it as a commercial center, and Chester was left to age gracefully. Crowded but charming, the city now conspires to keep foreigners inside its fortified walls, while keeping a watchful eye on Wales just a few miles away.

GETTING THERE

Chester serves as a rail gateway to North Wales; one line hugs the north coast, another branches down into Snowdonia. You can travel by **train** from Chester via Shrewsbury to central and south Wales. Frequent Merseyrail rail service makes Chester a nice day trip from Liverpool (2/hr.; 45min.; £2.80). **British Rail** trains run to London's Euston (1/hr.; 3hr.; £38.50), Holyhead (2/hr.; £12.60), Manchester's Piccadilly station (1/hr.; 1hr.; £6.20), Birmingham (2/hr.; 2hr.; £12). **National Express buses** run to London (5/day; 4½hr.; £22.50), Birmingham (4/day; 2½hr.; £8.25), Manchester (7/day; 2hr.; £4.35), and Liverpool (1/hr. 6am-5pm; 1hr.; £2.10).

ORIENTATION & PRACTICAL INFORMATION

Chester's city center is encircled by a medieval **city wall,** which in turn is breached by seven gates. The rail and bus stations are both to the north, outside the walls. From the rail station, which is about ¾ mi. out of town, cross the road in front of the station and proceed straight ahead down City Rd. At the roundabout, take the subterranean passage towards the city center, exit onto Foregate Street (which becomes Eastgate street at the city wall) and turn left at St. Peter Cross 2 blocks past the wall to get to the city center and main tourist office. From the bus station, trundle left onto Upper Northgate St. and patter through Northgate to the tourist office. Frequent buses (20p) run from both stations to the Market Square Bus Exchange, near the tourist office. Otherwise, it's a 15-minute walk from the rail station.

Tourist Office: Town Hall, Northgate St., Chester (tel. 318356 or 313126). Open Mon.-Sat. 9am-7:30pm, Sun. 10am-4pm; Oct.-April Mon.-Sat. 9am-5:30pm, Sun. 10am-4pm. Two smaller branches are located at the train station (tel. 322220; open daily 10am-8pm), and at the **Chester Visitor Centre,** Vicars Lane, opposite the Roman amphitheater (tel. 351609; open daily 9am-6pm). At all three you can purchase city maps (£1). The cuter, less useful, pop-up ones are only 75p.

Tours: A legionnaire, sweating in his full armor, leads the **Roman Tour** (from Town Hall, June-Sept. Thurs.-Sat. 11:30am and 2:30pm; £1.80, students, seniors, children £1); beings ghoulish and ghastly lurk on the **Ghost Hunter Trail** (May-Oct. Thurs.-Sat. 7:30pm; £2). Let us know if you see any.

Financial Services: Barclays, in the west wing of cathedral and at 35 Eastgate St. Open Mon., Wed., Fri. 9:30am-4:30pm, Tues. 10am-4:30pm, Sat. 9:30am-noon. **American Express:** 23 St. Werburgh St. (tel. 311145). Client mail held. Open Mon.-Fri. 9am-6pm, Sat. 9am-5pm (foreign exchange open Sun. 10am-4pm).

Post Office: 2 St. John St. (tel. 348315). Open Mon.-Tues. and Thurs.-Fri. 9am-5:30pm, Wed. 9:30am-5:30pm, Sat. 9am-12:30pm. **Postal Code:** CH1 1AA.

Telephone Code: 01244.

Train Station: City Rd. (tel. 340170). Enquiry office open Mon.-Fri. 8:10am-5:30pm, Sat. 8am-6pm, Sun. 9:40am-6pm. **Luggage** lockers are £1-3.

Bus Stations: Delamere St. (tel. 381515), just north of the city wall, off Northgate St. Long-distance and county coaches and buses. Office open Mon.-Sat. 9am-5pm. Some intercity buses stop on Delamere St.; most stop at the **bus exchange** in Market Sq., around the corner from the town hall. Call 602666 (Mon.-Fri. 8am-6pm, Sat. 9am-1pm) for information about all local services in Chester and Cheshire.

Bike Rental: Davies Bros. Cycles, 6-8 Cuppin St. (tel. 319204), off Grosvenor St. near Bridge St. Mountain bikes £10/day, £50/week; £100-150 deposit. Open Tues.-Sat. 9am-5:15pm, Mon. 9:30am-5:15pm.

Laundry: The Launderette, 71-77 St. Anne St., near Northgate Arena. Bring change. Open Mon.-Fri. 8:30am-7pm, Sat. 8:30am-6pm, Sun. 10:30am-3:30pm.

Hospitality Service: Chester at Home. Overseas visitors can visit in an English home (8-10:30pm) free of charge, and enjoy tea, biscuits, and conversation. Phone any day 5:30-7pm; Mr. and Mrs. Richardson (tel. 678868) or Mr. and Mrs. Brockley (tel. 380749) will find you a host. Pick-up from hotel arranged.

Hotlines: Samaritans (crisis): 36 Upper Northgate (tel. 377999). **Rape Crisis:** (tel. 317922). Open Mon. 7:30-10pm, Fri. 2-6pm.

Hospital: Countess of Chester (West Chester) Hospital, St. Martin's Way (tel. 365000). Bus #100 stops nearby on Liverpool road, or take #40A from the station, #3 from the bus exchange. **Police:** Grosvenor Rd. (tel. 350222).

Emergency: Dial 999; no coins required.

ACCOMMODATIONS

The highest concentration of decent B&Bs (average price £12) is along **Hoole Road,** a five-minute walk from the train station (turn right from the exit, climb the steps to Hoole Rd., and turn right over the railroad tracks). Buses #21, C30, and C53 run to this area from the city center.

HI Youth Hostel, Hough Green House, 40 Hough Green (tel. 680056), 1½ mi. from the city center. Cross the river on Grosvenor Rd. and turn right at the round-about (45min.), or take bus #7, 8, 16, 19, or any bus headed for "Mold." A beautiful recently renovated Victorian house on a quiet street. Exceptionally jovial staff and thunderous showers restore lost youth and vitality. Lockout 10am-3pm. £11.90, under 18 £7.80. Open Jan.-Nov.

YWCA, 49 City Rd. (tel. 320127), a 2-min. walk from the train station. For women at least 16 years old. Adequate, small, clean rooms. No meals, but a well-stocked kitchen, washer and dryer, free baths, and TV. No curfew. £10.

Davies Guest House, 22 Cuppin St. (tel. 340452), off Grosvenor St. near Bridge St. Fine rooms with floral decor. Six rooms located on the better side of the city walls—inside. £12.50.

Laburnum Guest House, 2 St. Anne St. (tel. 380313). Smallish, standard rooms one block from the bus station. £15. Doubles £28.

FOOD & PUBS

All the indoor shopping malls off Northgate, Eastgate, and Bridge Streets contain supermarkets and bakeries. For cheeses and fresh produce, stop at the indoor **market** beside the Town Hall. A covered market is held by the bus exchange on Princess

St. Mon. to Sat. from 8am-5pm. Expect lotsa raw, drippy, bloody meat and the men who slice it. **Dutton's Health Foods,** 8 Godstall Lane (tel. 316255), near the cathedral entrance, has packed lunches—a roll with cheese or paté, apple, and Brazil nuts—for a pittance (open Mon.-Sat. 8:30am-5:30pm). For a smaller range of the same (and free pastry samples to boot), try **Owen Owen,** on Bridge St. (open Mon.-Wed. and Fri. 9am-5:30pm, Thurs. 9am-8pm, Sat. 9am-6pm).

Chester Rows, 24 Watergate Row (tel. 316003), on the upper tier of Watergate. Eat cheap at this swanky joint by ordering the early bird special: a delicious entree, including bread and vegetables, plus starter or dessert, all for £7.50 (order it before 7pm, Mon.-Fri.). Open daily noon-2:30pm and 6-10pm. Disabled access.
Hattie's Tea Shop, 5 Rufus Ct., off Northgate. Scrumptious homemade cakes and inexpensive lunchtime snacks. The "giant topless" ham salad sandwich (£3.25) turns on porcine fetishists. Perhaps as a result, the staff is exceptionally jovial. Open Mon.-Sat. 9:30am-5pm. Disabled access.
The Hungry Pilgrim, 39-41 Watergate St. Omelettes and vegetarian dishes downstairs in garishly renovated cheese cellars. Spinach and veggie lasagna £3.80. Open Mon.-Fri. 9:30am-4pm, Sat. 9:30am-5pm.

Chester has 30-odd pubs to assuage thirst and hunger; many parrot Ye Olde English decor. The concentration of comfortable and interesting watering holes is highest along Lower Bridge and Watergate St. **The Falcon,** 6 Lower Bridge St., and **Ye Olde King's Head,** 48-50 Lower Bridge St. (tel. 324855), peer out from restored 17th-century family houses; across the street, **Claverton's** has a large array of salads and sandwiches (tel. 319760; open Mon.-Sat. 11:30am-11pm, Sun. noon-3pm and 7-10:30pm). **The Watergates,** 13 Watergate St. (tel. 321515), offers a traditional English "Monk's menu" (£3-6). Gobble the Tilly Pie beneath the vaulted stone ceiling. The **Boat House** glitters along the River Dee at night, while **Telford's,** by the canal, is favored by grungier university students.

SIGHTS

The architectural hodgepodge here (some of the buildings that seem medieval are actually Victorian pastiches) effectively masks the fact that the center of Chester is really one vast outdoor shopping mall. On summer Saturdays, the already thick crowds coagulate, and a bizarre variety of street musicians, from cowpoke trios to accordion-wielding matrons, sets up shop. The famous **city walls** completely encircle the town, and you can walk (or drive your chariot) on them for free.

Many pathways slither over and under the walls and pass through unimaginatively named gates. The original **Northgate,** with a fine-grained view of the Welsh hills, was rebuilt in 1808 to house the city's jail, 30 ft. below ground level. The bridge outside the gate, dubbed the Bridge of Sighs, connected the jail with the chapel to prevent convicts from escaping on the way to their last service.

Chester's brooding and massive gothic **cathedral** began its life in the 11th century as the burial place for St. Werburgh, a Mercian abbess and one of the early founders of the northern monasteries. Her shrine became a center for pilgrimages during the Middle Ages. Look for the Norman arches hidden in the north transept. In the choir, decorative ledges along the back walls supported aged, infirm, or fidgety monks during the lengthy services. Check out the carvings *under* the choir seats (cathedral open daily 7am-6:30pm).

Just outside Newgate lies the half-unearthed base of the largest **Roman amphitheater** in Britain. Excavated in 1960, it once accommodated the 7000-strong Roman legion at Deva (open daily 10am-6pm; Oct.-March Tues.-Sun. 10am-1pm and 2-4pm; free). Chester's streets are credited to the Romans, but their character is medieval. The **rows** of Bridge St., Watergate St., and Eastgate St. are unique to Chester; above the street-level shops, a walkway gives access to another tier of storefronts. Some historians theorize that Edward I imported the idea from Constantinople, which he had visited while on crusade.

LET'S GO®
TRAVEL

C A T A L O G

1995

WE GIVE YOU THE WORLD... AT A DISCOUNT

Discounted Flights, Eurail Passes,
Travel Gear, Let's Go™ Series Guides,
Hostel Memberships... and more

Let's Go Travel

a division of

Harvard Student
Agencies, Inc.

**Bargains
to every
corner of
the world!**

Travel Gear

A Let's Go T-Shirt..$10

100% combed cotton. Let's Go logo on front left chest. Four color printing on back. L and XL. Way cool.

B Let's Go Supreme..........$175

Innovative hideaway suspension with parallel stay internal frame turns backpack into carry-on suitcase. Includes lumbar support pad, torso, and waist adjustment, leather trim, and detachable daypack. Waterproof Cordura nylon, lifetime gurantee, 4400 cu. in. Navy, Green, or Black.

C Let's Go Backpack/Suitcase....................$130

Hideaway suspension turns backpack into carry-on suitcase. Internal frame. Detachable daypack makes 3 bags in 1. Waterproof Cordura nylon, lifetime guarantee, 3750 cu. in. Navy, Green, or Black.

D Let's Go Backcountry I..$210

Full size, slim profile expedition pack designed for the serious trekker. New Airflex suspension. X-frame pack with advanced composite tube suspension. Velcro height adjustment, side compression straps. Detachable hood converts into a fanny pack. Waterproof Cordura nylon, lifetime guarantee, main compartment 3375 cu. in., extends to 4875 cu. in.

E Let's Go Backcountry II............................$240

Backcountry I's Big Brother. Magnum Helix Airflex Suspension. Deluxe bi-lam contoured shoulder harness. Adjustable sterm strap. Adjustable bi-lam Cordura waist belt. 5350 cubic inches. 7130 cubic inches extended. Not pictured.

Discounted Flights

Call Let's Go now for inexpensive airfare to points across the country and around the world.

EUROPE • SOUTH AMERICA • ASIA • THE CARRIBEAN • AUSTRALIA •

AFRICA

Eurail Passes

urailpass (First Class)

days	$498
month (30 days)	$798
months (60 days)	$1098

Unlimited rail travel anywhere on Europe's 100,000 mile rail network. Accepted in 17 countries.

Eurail Flexipass (First Class)

A number of individual travel days to be used at your convenience within a two-month period.

Any 5 days in 2 months	$348
Any 10 days in 2 months	$560
Any 15 days in 2 months	$740

urail Youthpass (Second Class)

days	$398
month (30 days)	$578
months (60 days)	$768

All the benefits of the Eurail Pass at a lower price. For those passengers under 26 on their first day of travel.

Eurail Youth Flexipass (Second Class)

Eurail Flexipass at a reduced rate for passengers under 26 on their first day of travel.

Any 5 days in 2 months	$255
Any 10 days in 2 months	$398
Any 15 days in 2 months	$540

uropass (First & Second Class)

rst Class starting at	$280
cond Class starting at	$198
r more details	CALL

Discounted fares for those passengers travelling in France, Germany, Italy, Spain and Switzerland.

Hostelling Essentials

F Undercover Neckpouch............$9.95
Ripstop nylon with soft Cambrelle back. Three pockets. 6 x 7". Lifetime guarantee. Black or Tan.

G Undercover Waistpouch.........$9.95
Ripstop nylon with soft Cambrelle back. Two pockets. 5 x 12" with adjustable waistband. Lifetime guarantee. Black or Tan.

H Sleepsack................................$13.95
Required at all hostels. 18" pillow pocket. Washable poly/cotton. Durable. Compact.

I Hostelling International Card
Required by most international hostels. For U.S. residents only. Adults, $25. Under 18, $10.

J Int'l Youth Hostel Guide.......$10.95
Indispensable guide to prices, locations, and reservations for over 4000 hostels in Europe and the Mediterranean.

K ISIC, ITIC, IYTC..........$16, $16, $17
ID cards for students, teachers and those people under 26. Each offers many travel discounts.

800-5-LETSGO

Order Form

Please print or type — Incomplete applications will not be processed

Last Name	First Name	Date of Birth

Street	(We cannot ship to P.O. boxes)	

City	State	Zip

Country	Citizenship	Date of Travel

( )   -

Phone	School (if applicable)

Item Code	Description, Size & Color	Quantity	Unit Price	Total Price
			SUBTOTAL:	

Domestic Shipping & Handling		
Order Total:		Add:
Up to $30.00		$4.00
$30.01 to $100.00		$6.00
Over $100.00		$7.00
Call for int'l or off-shore delivery		

Shipping and Handling (see box at left):	
Add $10 for RUSH, $20 for overnite:	
MA Residents add 5% tax on books and gear:	
GRAND TOTAL:	

MasterCard / VISA Order

CARDHOLDER NAME _____

CARD NUMBER _____

EXPIRATION DATE _____

Enclose check or money order payable to:
Harvard Student Agencies, Inc.
53A Church Street
Cambridge, MA 02138

Allow 2-3 weeks for delivery. Rush orders guaranteed within
one week of our receipt. Overnight orders sent via FedEx the same afternoon.

Missing a Let's Go Book from your collection?
Add one to any $50 order at 50% off the cover price!

Let's Go Travel
1-800-5-LETSGO

(617) 495-9649   Fax: (617) 496-8015
53A Church Street
Cambridge MA 02138

The **Grosvenor Museum,** 27 Grosvenor St. (tel. 321616), flaunts Chester's archaeological and natural history, with an extensive collection of Roman artifacts. The museum spills over into the adjoining building; each room is a reconstruction of a period in Chester's history (Roman, Georgian, Victorian, etc...) Don't miss the human hair mourning necklace on the second floor (open Mon.-Sat. 10:30am-5pm, Sun. 2-5pm; free). Wander through a re-creation of Roman Chester and visit an actual archaeological dig at the recently opened **Deva Roman Experience** (tel. 343407), Pierpoint Lane, off Bridge St. (open daily 9am-6pm, last admission 5pm; £3.80, seniors £3, under 16 £1.90). Visit the **Toy Museum,** 13A Lower Bridge St. Row (tel. 346297), to see which match-box cars you were missing—the museum has the largest collection in the world (open daily 10am-5pm; £1.50, seniors, students, and children 70p).

ENTERTAINMENT

During the last week in June and the first week of Luly, Chester is home to the **Sports and Leisure Fortnight.** Celebrations center around a river carnival and raft race down the winding Dee. Write the tourist office or contact Joan Houghton, Holly Cottage, Nomansheath, Malpas (tel. (0194) 885325). On sporadic spring and summer weekends, England's oldest horse races are held counter-clockwise on the **Roodee** (tel. 327371), formerly the Roman harbor. Lodgings fill up quickly on these weekends; write to the tourist office for schedules and advance booking. An event begun in the 18th century as a forum for Chester's minstrels to audition, the **Chester Summer Music Festival** draws orchestras and musical groups from across Britain during the third week of July. Contact the Chester Summer Music Festival Office, Gateway Theatre, Hamilton Pl., Chester CH1 2BH (tel. 340392).

Rendezvous, 12-16 Northgate St. (tel. 327141; open Thurs.-Sat. 9:30pm-2am), and **Blimper's,** City Rd. (tel. 314794; open Wed.-Sat. 9:30pm-2am), blast a good variety of music, both live and recorded. Cover £5. **The High Society,** Forest House, Love St. (tel. 340754) keeps up with university trends—check for alternative nights (open Mon.-Sat. 9pm-2am). Cover £1-4.

■■■ LIVERPOOL

Athens had its Piraeus, Rome its Ostia, and Manchester has its Liverpool. Liverpool (pop. 450,000) was on its way to becoming an important port as early as 1715, when it opened England's first commercial dock, but it was the growth of the Lancashire cotton industry that allowed Liverpool to export more cargo than London by 1900. After World War I, both the decline of the British Empire and the advent of air travel dealt serious blows to the city's once-prosperous shipping industry. Economic hardship is still evident here, and most areas of the city should be explored with a measure of caution. Despite certain grim segments, Liverpool is a remarkably pleasant place to visit, with docklands recently transformed to attract tourists—not vessels—and two enormous and distinctive cathedrals. The city that clings tightly to its status as the birthplace of the Beatles maintains a thriving cultural life that has diminished little since the 1960s, when Allen Ginsberg described it as "the center of human consciousness."

GETTING THERE

Trains connect Liverpool to most major cities in North and Central England. They run to Manchester (2/hr.; 1½hr.; £5.70), Birmingham (1/hr.; 2hr.; £16), and London's Euston Station (1/hr.; 3hr.; £47). APEX return fares to London are available on certain trains; buy a week early at Lime St. station or with a credit card by calling 709 2894. **Buses** run to London's Victoria Station (6/day; 4-5hr.; £21.50); Manchester (1/hr.; 1hr.; £3.35); and Birmingham (5/day; 2½hr.; £8.75). The **Isle of Man Steam Packet Company** ferries from Liverpool to the Isle of Man but can be prohibitively expensive. See Essentials: Getting There—Between the Isles for details.

L
I
V
E
R
P
O
O
L

ORIENTATION & PRACTICAL INFORMATION

Although Liverpool is part of a vast metropolitan area that sprawls across the **River Mersey,** its central district is pedestrian-friendly. Two clusters of museums flank the central shopping district: those on William Brown St. near the main train station at Lime St., and those at Albert Dock, on the river. Train and bus stations are both centrally located, and most everything is within a 20-minute walk from either of them.

Tourist Office: Merseyside Welcome Centre, in the Clayton Sq. Shopping Centre (tel. 709 3631). From the train station at Lime St., exit onto Skelhorne St. and turn right. Clayton Sq. is the brick building with horizontal bands of sandstone. From the bus stop, walk downhill and turn right on Lime St.; walk about a block until you see a green and blue "W." Pick up the *Pocket Guide to Liverpool and Merseyside* (25p), which contains lists of things to see in the county and a map of the city. Open Mon.-Sat. 9:30am-5:30pm, 10am-5pm on bank holidays. A smaller branch at **Atlantic Pavilion,** Albert Dock (tel. 708 8854), has much of the same information (open daily 10am-5:30pm).

Tours: 1-hr. Beatles "Magical History Tour" leaves from Albert Dock at 2:20pm and from the Welcome Centre at 2:30pm (2hrs.; £5). Request a Japanese-speaking Beatleguide for an alternative linguistic perspective on the Fab Four. 20-odd bus tours (from £3) and thirtysomething walking tours (£1) rotate throughout the summer; the tourist office has the leaflets if you have the feet.

Travel: Merseytravel, 24 Hatton Garden (tel. 236 7676). Provides details on buses, trains, and ferries throughout Merseyside. Information is available at the Welcome Center (see Tourist Office), at the Ferries Center on the docks, and elsewhere. Their phone line is open daily 8am-8pm.

Budget Travel Office: Campus Travel, Student Union, 2 Bedford St. N. (tel. 708 0721). Open Mon.-Tues. and Thurs.-Fri. 9:30am-5pm, Wed. 10:30am-5pm.

Financial Services: Thomas Cook, 75 Church St. (tel. 709 3825). Open Mon.-Wed and Fri.-Sat. 9:30am-5:30pm, Thurs. 10am-5:30pm. **Barclays,** 9-11 Whitechapel (tel. 236 5428). Open Mon.-Tues. and Thurs.-Sat. 9:30am-5pm, Wed. 10am-5pm. **American Express,** 54 Lord St. (tel. 708 9202). Client mail held. Open Mon.-Fri. 9am-5pm, Sat. 9am-4pm.

Post Office: 22-23 Whitechapel (tel. 242 4165). Disabled access. Also at Bold St. Both open Mon.-Fri. 9am-5:30pm, Sat. 9am-12:30pm. **Postal Code:** L1 4DD.

Telephone Code: 0151.

Train Station: Lime St. Station. Make schedule inquiries at Lime Street Travel Centre (tel. 709 9696) in the station. Open daily 9am-7pm. **Moorfields** and **Central** train stations serve mainly as transfer points to local Merseyrail trains (which include service to Chester and Crewe).

Bus Station: "Office" is a shack on the Brownlow Hill sidewalk up the street from Adelphi Hotel (tel. 709 6481). Open Mon.-Sat. 8am-5:30pm, Sun. 9am-5:30pm.

Bookstores: W.H. Smith, 10-16 Church St. at Williamson St. (tel. 709 1435). Paperback writers and others. Open Mon.-Wed. and Fri. 9am-5:30pm, Thurs. and Sat. 9am-6pm. **News From Nowhere,** 112 Bold St. (tel. 708 7270). Feminist bookshop run by a women's cooperative with a wide selection of literature and gay and lesbian periodicals, and a bulletin board with various gay and lesbian groups and events posted. Information and tickets are available from the friendly, helpful staff. Disabled access. Open Mon.-Sat. 10am-6pm.

Launderette: The YMCA has somewhat reliable machines (see Liverpool: Accommodations, above). For the genuine laundromat experience, take bus #9 or 10 to **Fabricare Dry Cleaners,** 134 Kensington (tel. 263 1533). Change and soap available. Open Mon.-Fri. 8am-8pm, Sat.-Sun. 8am-7pm.

Friends of Merseyside: tel. 336 6699.

Hotlines: Samaritans (crisis): tel. 718 8888. **Gay/Lesbian: Friend:** tel. 708 9552; daily 7-10pm. **Rape Crisis:** tel. 727 7599; 24hr.

Late-Night Pharmacy: Em-Ess Chemist, 68-70 London Rd. (tel. 709 5271). Open daily 9am-11pm.

Hospital: Royal Liverpool Hospital, Prescot St. (tel. 709 1041 or 706 2000), ½ mi. from the train station.

Emergency: Dial 999; no coins required. **Police:** Canning Place (tel. 709 6010).

ACCOMMODATIONS

Your best bet for cheap accommodations lies east of the city center. **Lord Nelson Street,** adjacent to the train station, is lined with very modest hotels, and similar establishments are found along **Mount Pleasant,** one block from Brownlow Hill and the bus stop. Stay only at tourist-office-approved places. Demand for rooms is highest in early April when jockeys and gamblers gallop into town for the Grand National Race; call ahead for reservations.

YWCA, 1 Rodney St. (tel. 709 7791). Single women only. Recently renovated rooms are sparking clean, attractively decorated, and surprisingly spacious, with firm beds. Kitchen and laundry facilities (no soap or change). Singles £9.50. Doubles £16. Discounted weekly rates. Key deposit £15 for stays above 5 nights.

Embassie Youth Hostel, 1 Falkner Sq. (tel. 707 1089), in the southeast part of town, at the end of Canning St. Recently opened hostel in a beautiful old house has spacious dormitory style rooms and facilities galore (TV lounges, laundry, kitchen, pool hall, darts). Yes, you've seen this place before: *In the Name of the Father* was filmed in Falkner Sq. Ask the energetic staff for pub-crawling tips. No curfew. £8.50 (discounts for extended stays). Staff recommends that you walk from the bus or train stations (15-20min.) or take a taxi (£2); bus drop-off points are too far away to make the bus worthwhile.

University of Liverpool: Roscoe and Gladstone Hall (tel. 794 6405), on Greenbank Ln., 2½ mi. from city center. B&B £15, students £9. **Mulberry Court,** Oxford St. (tel. 794 3298), offers self-catering accommodations for £13.50. Ring the university-wide conference office (tel. 794 6440) for information on other halls open to travelers.

YMCA, 56-60 Mt. Pleasant (tel. 709 9516), near the city center. Men and women. The rooms are all right (ask for a refurbished one), the common areas less attractive: the smell of cigarettes lingers in the corridors, and the laundry facilities have been known to be out of order. Singles £12.50. Doubles £21.50. Full breakfast included. Key deposit £2.

Atlantic Hotel, 9 Lord Nelson St. (tel. 709 1162). Clean rooms a bit worse for wear but in a good location. Full or vegetarian breakfast. Singles £15. Doubles £25.

Camping: Wirral Country Park, Thurstaston (tel. 648 4371). Take Mersey Ferries across the river to Woodside, then take bus #71 (2/hr.), which passes within 1 mi. of the site. £2.50, ages 5-18 £1.25. **Abbey Farm,** Dark Ln., Ormskirk (tel. (01695) 572686), on the northern rail line from Lime St. Station. £4.70 for 2-person tent. Caravans £6. Enjoy the free showers. Disabled toilet and bathing facilities.

FOOD & PUBS

Try **St. John's Market** (above the St. John's shopping mall) for fresh produce and local color. **Holland & Barrett,** 15-17 Whitechapel (open Mon.-Tues. and Thurs.-Sat. 9am-5pm, Wed. 9:30am-5:30pm), has a large selection of health foods and yummy granola. **Matta's,** 51 Bold St. (tel. 709 3031), sells foods from all corners of the earth (open Mon.-Sat. 9am-6:30pm, Sun. 11:30am-5pm). **Kwik Save** is a budget supermarket located at 58 Hanover St. (open Mon.-Sat. 7am-6pm). Liverpool has many an ethnic restaurant, especially along Hardman St.

Everyman Bistro, 9-11 Hope St. (tel. 708 9545), off Mt. Pleasant by the university. A bouncy allegorical hangout below the theater. Interesting herbs and preparation set this bistro apart from standard cafeterias. A large vegetarian selection. Hot meals run about £3-6. Open Mon.-Sat. noon-midnight.

Kirkland's, 13 Hardman St. (tel. 707 0132). Lunch and dinner of various ethnic origins (vegetable lasagne swimming in cheese £3). Ceiling fans and a long bar provide the quintessential "pleasant" atmosphere. Open Mon.-Sat. 11am-noon, also Mon. til 12:30am, Tues. til 2am, Thurs. and Fri. til 1am.

Black Horse & Rainbow, 21-23 Berry St., near Chinatown. A feisty pub named after the two bitters brewed on the premises. Open Mon.-Sat. 11:30am-2am, closed Sun. Disabled access.

SIGHTS

Liverpool has two 20th-century cathedrals, both southeast of the city center. The Anglican **Liverpool Cathedral** (tel. 709 6271), begun in 1904 and completed in 1978, is *vast*. A Trumpian wonder, it has the highest Gothic arches ever built (107 ft.), the largest vault and organ (9,704 pipes), and the highest and heaviest bells in the world. Climb to the top of the tower for a view to north Wales. (Cathedral open daily 7:45am-6pm; tower open daily 10am-3:30pm, weather permitting. Admission to tower £1.50, children £1. Free organ recitals in summer Fri. 12:30pm.) The cathedral refectory, overlooking the quarry, serves delicious teas and brunches (open Mon.-Sat. 10am-4:30pm, Sun. noon-5pm). In sharp contrast, the inside of the Roman Catholic **Metropolitan Cathedral of Christ the King** (tel. 709 9222), dubbed "Paddy's Wigwam" by local blasphemers, looks more like a rock concert hall than the setting for a mass. Steel and concrete walls encircle a dramatic stained-glass Lantern Tower. The interior explodes into multicolored rays when the sun is shining (open daily 8am-6pm; winter Mon.-Sat. 8am-6pm, Sun. 8am-5pm; disabled access).

Albert Dock is an open rectangle of Victorian warehouses that has been transformed into a modern-day shopping mall replete with offices, restaurants and museums. The **Tate Gallery** (tel. 709 3223), a branch of the London institution, rests imposingly in the corner between the dock and the harbor, and contains scads of modern art, including pop, op, and kinetic. By prior arrangement, the cheery, knowledgeable staff will fit the visually-impaired with special gloves to allow them to touch some of the art. (Museum and café open Tues.-Sun. 10am-6pm; free, but some special exhibitions £1, concessions 50p. Wheelchair access.)

The **Merseyside Maritime Museum** explains every detail of ships, shipping, shipbuilding, shipwrecks, sailors, and all else shippy, a fitting tribute to Liverpool's historic dependence on the sea (open daily 10:30am-5:30pm; last entry 4:30pm; £3; concessions £1.50). The same ticket will get you into the **Museum of Liverpool Life** (tel. 207 0001), right next door. It holds an interesting, if somewhat confusing, array of sound-bite displays on a range of subjects from local soccer to the women's movement at the turn of the century to pop music today. (Times and prices are the same as those for the Maritime Museum.)

Also at Albert Dock is **The Beatles Story** (tel. 709 1963). Shed a tear on John Lennon's white piano before you leave (open daily 10am-6pm, Oct.-March 10am-5pm; £4.25, concessions £2.95). For more Beatle-theme locales, pick up the **Beatles Map** (£1.50) at the tourist office: it takes you down to Strawberry Fields and Penny Lane without the acid. Nearby, the **Beatles Shop,** 31 Mathew St. (tel. 236 8066), is stuffed to the gills with souvenirs and memorabilia (open Mon.-Sat. 9:30am-5:30pm). There's more than just the Beatles to Liverpool's musical history—Flock of Seagulls, Frankie Goes to Hollywood, and Teardrop Explodes are all Liverpudlians. And who could forget the Groovy Train? The museums on William Brown St., near the train station, are more stately than those on Albert Dock. The **Walker Art Gallery** is the home of the famous "And When Did You Last See Your Father," a picture of Cromwell interrogating a child, which continues to hang in many a proper British nursery. The collection dates back to 1300, and houses some wonderful High Victorian Classical and Pre-Raphaelite paintings.

ENTERTAINMENT

Liverpool's oft-grim demeanor is brightened by a thriving arts scene and an energetic nightlife. *L: Scene,* available at the tourist office and at newsstands, is a monthly entertainment guide laden with articles and listings (£1). For local alternative events, check the bulletin board in the Everyman Bistro (see Food), where they often host bohemian happenings in their own **Third Room.** The *Liverpool Echo,* a local evening newspaper sold by streetcorner vendors, has the most up-to-date arts information as well as local news and warmed-over royal family gossip (25p).

Fight your way inside **Flanagan's Apple,** Matthew St., which offers the best Irish music in town nightly. **Daley's Dandelion,** 25 Dale St., has launched a few local bands in its day, including the popular Mojo Filter. Like a moth to a flame, the fluorescent orange and blue facade of the **Baa Bar,** 43-45 Fleet St., attracts a trendy and far from sheepish crowd for cappucino during the day and cheap beers at night.

A **Beatles Convention** in August draws pop fans and bewildered entomologists from all over. The **Cavern Club** on Matthew St. (tel. 236 9091), where the Fab Four first gained prominence, features live music Wednesday and Thursday nights and a 60s disco Wednesday through Saturday (free before 9pm).

If you prefer to shake to something of this decade, Liverpool's nightclubs should serve you well. Get down to some classic disco and funky house on the flashing, Saturday-Night-Fevery dance floor at the **Beat Bar,** Mount Pleasant (tel. 708 9128; open Mon.-Sat., gay/mixed on Tues.; £2-4). **The Academy Annexe,** Wolstenholme Sq. (tel. 708 0945), packs in the city's young hipsters on Friday and Saturday nights with its blend of soulful house vibes. Check in *L: Scene* for current news on clubs or look for passes at the trendy shops at the **Liverpool Palace,** 6-10 Slater St.

The **Royal Liverpool Philharmonic Orchestra,** one of the finest English orchestras outside of London, performs at Philharmonic Hall (tel. 709 3789), Hope St. (Tickets from £7.75, 25% student discount, half-price on day of performance). The **Liverpool Empire,** on Lime St. (tel. 709 1555), hosts drama and comedy, welcoming such famous troupes as the Royal Shakespeare Company. (Box office open Mon.-Sat. 10am-8pm. 50% student discounts sometimes available week of performance. Prices start at £5. Wheelchair access).

■■■ LEEDS

As the U.K.'s third-largest metropolitan district, luv'ley Leeds is home to over 700,000 people. Leeds's textile prosperity blossomed in the late Victorian period, an era fond of ornament; building façades reflect that time with a curious cast of stone lions, griffins, and cherubs. Leeds has several interesting museums, an exciting nightlife, and boasts intriguing current bands Boyracer, Hood, and the Wedding Present; yet the city's flashy shops and office buildings leave little room for budget lodgings. For those unwilling to stay in suburban guesthouses 2-3 mi. outside the city center, a daytrip here from York or Manchester proves most economical.

Leeds's main museums and galleries cluster conveniently on the Headrow, near the massive, Victorian, and somewhat grim (the lions have eroded) **Town Hall.** Just across Calverley St. stands the **Leeds City Museum** (tel. 247 8275), a natural history museum and the resting place of an Egyptian mummy and stuffed Bengal tiger (open Tues.-Fri. 10am-5:30pm, Sat. 10am-4pm; free). The **City Art Gallery** (also known as the Headrow Gallery; tel. 247 8248) in the next building over, features one of the best permanent collections of 20th-century British art outside London. (Open Mon.-Tues. and Thurs.-Fri. 10am-5:30pm, Wed. 10am-9pm, Sat. 10am-4pm; free.) The adjacent **Henry Moore Centre for the Study of Sculpture** (tel. 247 8277) displays Moore's pioneering abstract sculpture in stone and bronze, as well as works by his student Barbara Hepworth (open Mon.-Fri. 10am-5:30pm, Sat. 10am-4pm).

Mr. and Mrs. D. Hood, 17 Cottage Rd., Headingly (tel. 275 5575) will charm you with conversation over coffee and home-baked gingerbread. Clean, beautifully furnished rooms £15 (take bus #93 or 96 from the city square). **Mrs. Clayton,** Parklea, 66 Avenue Hill (tel. 262 3394; £9), offer comfortable accommodations. Headingly seems safer than Avenue Hill. Leeds's huge Asian community offers the traveler a welcome respite from traditional English cooking—head to the north end of Vicar Lane where ethnic restaurants abound. **New Asia,** 128 Vicar Lane (tel. 234 3612) serves affordable Indian, Chinese, and Vietnamese dishes.

The **tourist office** (tel. 247 8301 or 247 8302) is at 19 Wellington St. From the train station turn left and continue 2 blocks down Wellington St. The bus station is another block further down Wellington. Plunder the plethora of free leaflets and useful bus maps. The office offers room bookings for a £1.25 fee (open Mon.-Fri. 9:15am-4:50pm, Sat. 9:15am-3:45pm). The tourist office hopes to move to the train station in 1995 and become "Gateway Yorkshire." The **post office** is on the City

Square (tel. (01345) 223344; open Mon.-Tues. and Thurs.-Fri. 9am-5:30pm, Wed. 9:30am-5:30pm, Sat. 9am-12:30pm). Leeds' **postal code** is LS1 2UH.

> On April 16, 1995 ("Phone Day"), Leeds' **telephone code** will change from 0532 to **0113** and a 2 will preface existing local phone numbers. The new code and numbers can be used as of August 1, 1994, and *Let's Go* lists only these. For further explanation, see the Appendix.

Leeds is about 50 mi. northeast of Manchester and 10 mi. east of Bradford, midway between the South Pennines and the Yorkshire Dales. Direct **trains** run to Leeds from most major cities, including Bradford (every 15min.; 20min.; 65p-£1.40), Manchester (2/hr.; 1½hr.; £7.40), York (every 10min.;2/hr.; £4.30), and London's King Cross Station (1/hr.; 2½hr.; £43-46.50). **National Express buses,** more reasonably priced, serve Manchester (9/day; 1½hr.; £3.85), London (9/day; 4hr.; £10), and most other major cities. Both stations have **luggage lockers** for £1-3.

■■■ BEVERLEY

English common law nowhere decrees that travelers must follow the hackneyed route north to Scotland via London, Stratford, and York. A detour through the restful market town of Beverley is as legal as afternoon teatime. Thirty mi. southeast of York and 9 mi. north of maritime Hull, Beverley rests snugly between the Yorkshire Wolds and the coastline, serving as a pitstop for cyclists and a haven for travelers. The train station and attractions lie within ¼ mi. of the pedestrianized town center.

Beverley Minster, constructed from 1220 to 1440, is not a cathedral, not enormous, not so famous, but appealingly packaged in all three English Gothic styles (early, decorative, and perpendicular: the differences can be seen in the construction of the windows); it proudly presents itself as England's largest parish church. (Open daily 9am-8pm, may close after morning service until 2:30pm on Sun.; closes at dusk in winter). Northwest of the Minster, **Butcher Row,** the pedestrian city center, beckons to hungry tourists with delicious bakeries and numerous sandwich shops. A few blocks beyond, **St. Mary's Church** houses a small, unobtrusive carving that became the inspiration for the White Rabbit in *Alice in Wonderland.* Enter by the side door, proceed to the nave and look at the door on your left; the carving is at altar level. Take a pill or drink from a strange vial and hear it whisper "The Duchess! The Duchess! Oh my dear paws! Oh my fur and whiskers! She'll get me executed, as sure are ferrets are ferrets!" When you reappear in this world, seat yourself among tourists in the fancy atrium at the pricey-but-worth-it **Tea Cosy** (open Mon.-Sat. 10am-5pm, Sun. noon-5pm; often open later if crowded). An ever-reliable **Safeway** is on Butcher Row (open Mon.-Fri. 8:30am-8pm, Sat. 8am-8pm).

Twenty-five yards from the Minster, a restored medieval friary houses the 34-bed **Youth Hostel** (tel. 881751) on Friar's Lane, ¼ mi. from the rail station (lockout 10am-5pm, 11pm curfew; £6.50, under 18 £4.35; breakfast £2.69, evening meal £3.90; open July-Aug. daily; April-June and Sept.-Oct. Thurs.-Sat. and Mon.-Tues.) Also within smelling distance of Wednesday's **cattle market** (slaughter is on Tues., steer clear) are **Mrs. Bromby's** clean and recently redecorated rooms, 37 Morton La. (tel. 868087; £12.50). For a library's worth of information about Beverley, including a free city map, and much of Yorkshire and Humberside, visit the **tourist office** (tel. 867430) at the **Guildhall,** itself a building dating to the 15th century (office open Mon.-Fri. 9:30am-5:30pm, Sat. 9:30am-5pm, Sun. 10am-2pm; Oct.-Easter Mon.-Fri. 9:30am-5pm, Sat. 10am-4pm). Beverly's **telephone code** is 01482.

Various regional **bus** services connect Beverley to York and to Hull. #744 and 746 run via Beverley between Hull and York (12/day towards York, Sun. 3/day; 1hr.; 10/ day towards Hull, Sun. 4/day; 30min.). Call 27146 9am-12:30pm on Saturdays or York's bus schedule office other times (see York: Getting There, below). **National Express** buses (tel. 212644) run to London (1/day; 5hr.; £29).

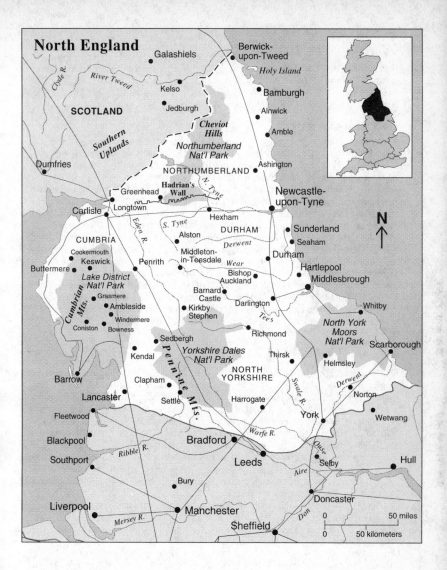

NORTH ENGLAND

Even before the Victorians invented tourism, local and foreign travelers were drawn to this quiet area between Central England's industrial belt and the rugged wilderness of Scotland. Bisected by the Pennine Mountains, North England's main attractions lie in four national parks and several calm coastal areas. Walkers and ramblers flock here, and no trail tests their stamina more than the Pennine Way, the country's first official long-distance path and still its longest. Extensive systems of shorter paths traverse the grey and purple moors that captured the imagination of the Brontës, the emerald green dales that figured so prominently in the stories of James Herriot, and the stunning crags and lakes that inspired Wordsworth's philosophy of the sublime. Isolated villages along the trails continue a pastoral tradition that contrasts with the polluted din of many cities to the south.

Food addicts know North England for Yorkshire pudding, Cumberland sausage, Wensleydale and Cheshire cheeses, and "fat rascal" scones, all delicious and highly caloric. Northumbria's Craster kippers redefine seafood, and the Lake District's Kendal Mint Cake is a quick sugar jolt for climbers. Eccles cakes (raisins and spices wrapped in flaky pastry) are unique to Lancashire and Yorkshire.

GETTING ABOUT

Two north-south rail lines traverse the far north: York to Newcastle (east of the Pennines) and Crewe to Carlisle (west of the Pennines). From Carlisle, an east-west line connects to Newcastle. Express Intercity trains pass en route to London and Scotland. For regional travel, **British Rail Rover** tickets pay for themselves after a few trips. The **North East Rover** (£57) offers a week of unrestricted travel on all British Rail-operated lines in the rectangular region bounded by Sheffield, Carlisle, Newcastle, and Cleethorpes (including the scenic Settle-Carlisle line). The **North West Rover** (£43) bounded by Carlisle, Leeds, Manchester, Liverpool, and the coast, includes fewer lines. **Flexi-Rover** passes, about £10 less, permit 3 to 4 days of travel within 7 to 8 days. Day returns may prove cheaper than single tickets, especially near major cities. **Buses** run between some of the scattered hamlets of agricultural England, though less frequently than their urban counterparts; plan detailed itineraries and check with transport officials to avoid being stranded for a week in Hebden Bridge. Local **bus** offices issue **Wayfarer, Explorer,** and **Day Rambler** tickets (each about £5) for a day's travel on all bus companies' routes within a given region, and often on rail routes as well; some companies sell their own.

■■■ PENNINE WAY

The Pennine (PEN-nine) Peaks form, as the common anthropomorphism goes, England's spine, arching south to north up the center of Britain from the Peak National Park to the Scottish border. The 250-mi. Pennine Way crowns the central ridge of the watershed. Beginning at Edale, it traverses the massive, boggy plateau atop **Kinder Scout** in the south, then passes into the craggy Yorkshire Dales at Malham to reemerge at the formidable Pen-y-Ghent peak. The northern section crosses the **High Pennines,** a 20-mi. stretch from below Barnard Castle to Hadrian's Wall and terminates at Kirk Yetholm, just across the Scottish border. Turbulent rivers have slit gentle dales into the mountainsides, from the southernmost Derwent Valley to Teesdale, Weardale, and Allendale, begetting spacious moorland and arbored slopes, now dotted with stone villages.

Hikers (with a capital H) have completed the hike in ten days, but most walkers spend three weeks on the long, often remote trail before they can rightfully purchase a "My mother finished the Pennine Way, but all she brought back was this striking T-shirt" T-shirt for their offspring. Countless shorter loops along the route can cut the mileage considerably but will cost you the chemise. The unusual limestone formations in the Yorkshire Dales and the lonely moor of Kinderscout are especially captivating, though any two wayfarers might recommend five different best stretches.

The classic Wainwright's *Pennine Way Companion* (£6.50), a pocket-sized volume available from bookstores, is a worthwhile supplement to Ordnance Survey maps, which run about £5 from Peak Information Centres. Sudden mist and rain on the Peaks can reduce visibility to under 20 ft. After a storm, the low-level paths become boggy and some paths will leave you knee-deep (or worse) in peat. At some points (especially in the Yorkshire Dales) and in ominous weather you should stay on the narrow roads that run nearby. Those in the know recommend staying away from the Pennines in the wintertime unless you are, in truth, a Hiker. Whatever the weather, bring a good map and compass and know how to use them together. Complete rain gear, warm clothing, and extra food are also essential.

ACCOMMODATIONS

HI Youth Hostels are spaced within a day's hike (7-29 mi.) of one another; note which ones are closed on certain nights. YHA now offers a handy **Pennine Way Package:** you can book a route of 18 or more hostels along the walk (50p/hostel) and obtain useful advice on paths and equipment. Send a self-addressed envelope to YHA, Northern Region, P.O. Box 11, Matlock, Derbyshire DE4 2XA (tel. (01629) 825850). Any **National Park Information Centre** can supply details on trails and alternate accommodations. The *Pennine Way Accommodations and Catering Guide* (90p) could prove as valuable as moleskin.

The following hostels are arranged in a south-north progression along the Pennine Way in the order of the most direct route possible. Lockout is 10am to 5pm unless otherwise noted.

Edale Youth Hostel, Rowland Cote, Nether Booth, Edale, Derbyshire S30 2ZH (tel. (01433) 670302), 2 mi. from Edale. YHA activity center; opens 1pm. £8.70, under 18 £5.80. Dinner and breakfast. Open daily early Jan.-early Dec.

Crowden-in-Longdendale Youth Hostel (Peak National Park), Crowden, Hadfield, Hyde, Cheshire SK14 7ZH (tel. (01457) 852135), 15 mi. from Edale. Evening meal, breakfast, and shop. £6.50, under 18 £4.35. Open April-Oct. Thurs.-Tues.; March and Nov. Fri.-Sat.

Mankinholes Hall Youth Hostel, Mankinholes, Todmorden, Lancashire OL14 6HR (tel. (01706) 812340), 24 mi. from Crowden. Evening meal, breakfast. Store. £6.50, under 18 £4.35. Open April-Aug. Mon.-Sat., Sept.-Oct. Tues.-Sat. and mid-Feb.-March Fri.-Sat.

Haworth Youth Hostel, Longlands Hall, Longlands Drive, Lees Lane, Haworth, Keighley, West Yorkshire BD22 8RT (tel. (01535) 642234), 18 mi. from Mankinholes. Evening meal, breakfast. Store. £7.75, under 18 £5.20. Open April-Sept. daily; mid-Feb.-March Mon.-Sat.

Earby Youth Hostel, Glen Cottage, Birch Hall Lane, Earby, Colne, Lancashire BB8 6JX (tel. (01282) 842349), 17 mi. from Haworth. No meals served. £5.90, under 18 £3.95. Open April-Sept. Fri-Wed.

Malham Youth Hostel (John Dower Memorial Hostel), Skipton, North Yorkshire BD23 4DE (tel. (01729) 830321), 15 mi. from Earby. Evening meal and breakfast available. £7.75, under 18 £5.20; Open April-Sept. daily; Oct. Mon.-Sat.; Nov.-late Dec. and late Feb. Tues.-Sat.

Stainforth Youth Hostel, Taitlands, Stainforth, Settle, North Yorkshire BD24 9PA (tel. (01729) 823577), 8 mi. from Malham. Evening meal, breakfast. Store. £7.15, under 18 £4.75. Open May-Aug. daily; April and Sept.-Oct. Mon.-Sat.; March and Dec. Fri.-Sat.

Hawes Youth Hostel, Lancaster Terrace, Hawes, North Yorkshire DL8 3LQ (tel. (01969) 667368), 19 mi. from Stainforth. Evening meal, breakfast. Store. £7.75, under 18 £5.20. Open April-June Mon.-Sat.; July and Aug. daily; Sept.-Oct. Tues.-Sat.; Jan.-March Fri.-Tues.

Keld Youth Hostel, Keld Lodge, Upper Swaledale, Richmond, North Yorkshire DL11 6LL (tel. (01748) 86259), 9 mi. from Hawes. Evening meal, breakfast. Store. £6.50, under 18 £4.35. Open June-Aug. Mon.-Sat.; Sept.-Oct. Thurs.-Mon.; Nov. and Feb.-March. Fri.-Sat. and April-May Thurs.-Tues.

Baldersdale Youth Hostel, Blackton, Baldersdale, Barnard Castle, Co. Durham DL12 9UP (tel. (01833) 50629), 15 mi. from Keld. Shop, evening meal. £6.50, under 18 £4.35. Open mid-March-Aug. Mon.-Sat.; Sept.-Oct. Tues.-Sat.

Langdon Beck Youth Hostel, Langdon Beck, Forest-in-Teesdale, Barnard Castle, Co. Durham DL12 0XN (tel. (01833) 22228), 11 mi. from Baldersdale. Evening meal, breakfast. Store. £7.75, under 18 £5.20. Open May-July Mon.-Sat.; Aug. daily; Sept.-Oct. and March-April Tues.-Sat.; Nov. and Feb. Fri.-Sat.

Dufton Youth Hostel, Redstones, Dufton, Appleby, Cumbria CA16 6DB (tel. (017683) 51236), 12 mi. from Langdon Beck. Evening meal, breakfast. Store. £7.15, under 18 £4.75. Open daily July-Aug. and mid-March-mid-April; mid-Jan.-March Thurs.-Mon.; mid-April-June Wed.-Mon.

Alston Youth Hostel, The Firs, Alston, Cumbria CA9 3RW (tel. (01434) 381509), 22 mi. from Dufton. Evening meal, breakfast. Store. £7.15, under 18 £4.75. Open mid-March-mid-Sept. Mon.-Sat.; mid-Sept.-Oct. Tues.-Sat.; Jan.-mid-March Fri.-Sat.

Greenhead Youth Hostel, Greenhead, Carlisle, Cumbria CA6 7HG (tel. (016977) 47401), 17 mi. from Alston. Evening meal, breakfast. Store. £6.50, under 18 £4.35. Open July-Aug. daily; Sept. to mid-Nov. and mid-Feb. to March Thurs.-Mon.; April-June Mon.-Sat.

Once Brewed Youth Hostel, Once Brewed, Military Road, Bardon Mill, Hexham, Northumberland NE47 7AN (tel. (01434) 344360), 7 mi. from Greenhead. Store open after 1pm. Evening meal. £7.75, under 18 £5.20. Open April-Oct. daily; Nov. and Feb. Tues.-Sat.; March Mon.-Sat.

Bellingham Youth Hostel, Woodburn Road, Bellingham, Hexham, Northumberland NE48 2ED (tel. (01434) 220313), 14 mi. from Once Brewed. No store or meals. £5.90, under 18 £3.95. Open mid-July-Aug. daily; March-mid-July and Sept.-Oct. Mon.-Sat.

Byrness Youth Hostel, 7 Otterburn Green, Byrness, Newcastle Upon Tyne NE19 1TS (tel. (01830) 520519), 15 mi. from Bellingham. Café and store nearby. No meals. £5.90, under 18 £3.95. Open late July-Aug. daily; April-late July and Sept. Wed.-Mon.

Kirk Yetholm Youth Hostel, Kelso, Roxburghshire, TD5 8PG Scotland (tel. (01573) 420631), 27 mi. from Byrness (you're almost there!). Grade 2. Curfew 11pm. £5.05, ages 5-17 £4.15. Open late March-Sept.

SOUTH PENNINES

The bleakness of the gorse-strewn moorlands and scattered towns of the South Pennines is overwhelming. The desolation that drove the Brontës to write layered dramas of anguish draws innumerable hikers and walkers who traverse the peaks and valleys via the Pennine Way or sundry short-distance footpaths. In the midst of this land, the tiny villages **Haworth** and **Hebden Bridge** provide brief dots of civilization from Leeds or Manchester.

The Haworth tourist office boasts a wide selection of trail guides. One of the trails, the **Worth Way,** traces the 5½ mi. from Keighley and Oxenhope; ride the steam-train back to your starting point. The private **Keighley and Worth Valley Railway** chugs from Oxenhope to Keighley and passes through Haworth (all-day Rover £5.50). From the Manchester-Leeds mainline trains, change at Keighley (KEETH-lee). To hike to Hebden Bridge, choose either an 8-mi. or 12-mi. trail as mapped out in the tourist office's *Two Walks Linking Haworth and Hebden Bridge* (30p).

Yorkshire Rider operates infrequent bus service between Hebden Bridge and Haworth (#500; 4/day; Oct.-late May Wed. and Sat.) and between Bradford and Haworth; call (01535) 603284 for information. Single bus fares within West Yorkshire are all 55p except during weekday rush hours; rail fares are also discounted. A **Day Rover** ticket is good for a day's unlimited bus and rail travel in West Yorkshire after 9:30am weekdays and all day weekends (train and bus £2.20, children £1.10; bus only £2, children £1).

Hebden Bridge

A historic gritstone village built on the side of a hill, Hebden Bridge lies in Calderdale, close to the Pennine Way and the 50-mi. circular Calderdale Way. In medieval times, the bridge gained fame as an important crossing over the Hebden water for goods en route to Halifax. Today, Hebden Bridge is an excellent starting point for day or longer hikes, though not a terribly exciting destination in itself. **Calder Valley Cruising** (tel. 845557), in Hebden Bridge, gives horse-drawn boat-trips along the recently restored Rochdale Canal and stops at the **Walkley Clogs** working mill for all your trendy wooden footwear needs. (Office open Mon.-Sat. 10am-5pm, Sun. 10am-5:30pm, shorter in winter; departs Hebden Bridge Marina at 1 and 3pm; times may vary so pick up a schedule at the tourist office; £4.95, seniors £4, children £2.50; longer and charter cruises available. Clog factory tel. 842061, open daily 10am-5pm.) From Hebden Bridge, you can make day-hikes to the nearby villages of

Blackshaw Head, Cragg Vale, or Hepstonstall, where you'll find the ruins of a 13th-century church and a 1764 octagonal church, the oldest Methodist house o' worship in the world. Grab a copy of the helpful *Hepstonstall History Trail* guide (75p) at the Hebden Bridge tourist office.

The **Birchcliffe Centre,** in a former Baptist chapel on Chapel Ave. at the top of the hill off Birchcliffe Rd. (tel. 843626), allows travelers who call ahead to fill beds not needed by groups. All rooms have 4 beds with bathrooms (£11-15). **Watergate Tea Shop,** 9 Bridge Gate near the tourist office, is worth breaking into (meals from £1.60). **St. George's Square** brims with inexpensive bakeries and sandwich shops and several more pricey pubs. What the **Fox & Goose** at Hepstonstall Rd. lacks in atmosphere, it makes up for in cheap quality pub grub (£1-3). The **tourist office** at 1 Bridge Gate (tel. 843831) is equipped with maps (25p) and free walking guides and leaflets (open Mon.-Sat. 9am-5pm, Sun. 10am-5pm; Oct. to mid-March daily 10am-4pm). The Hebden Bridge **post office** is at Holme St. (tel. 842366); the **postal code** is HX7 8AA and the **telephone code** is 01422. Hebden Bridge is about halfway down the Manchester-Leeds rail line, with service in both directions every hour, and is also served by the Transpennine Express, which runs between Newcastle-upon-Tyne, Manchester, and Liverpool (every hour 7am-9pm, fewer Sundays).

Haworth

> *I can hardly tell you how the time gets on at Haworth. There is no event whatever to mark its progress. One day resembles another...*
> —Charlotte Brontë

Those underwhelmed by Brontë-sister stories might be a bit bored by Haworth. The town is plain, the shops on Main Street fall well short of quaint, and the whole area is enveloped in a death shroud of tourists. If you're out to make the rounds of Brontënalia, begin at the **parsonage** (tel. 642323) near the tourist office, where Emily, Charlotte, and Anne lived with their father and their brother Branwell. The bleak Georgian building is now an excellent museum that houses such relics as postage-stamp-sized books written and illustrated by the Brontës in their childhood years (open daily 10am-5pm; Oct.-March 11am-4:30pm; £3.60, seniors and students £2.60, ages 5-16 £1.10). On your way to the parsonage take a look at the village church, the final resting place of Charlotte and Emily. Behind the church, a footpath leads up the hill toward **Brontë Falls,** a 2½-mi. hike over the moor. The tourist office's *Three Walks* leaflet lists alternative routes; the second, a 6½-mi. walk through Brontë country, boasts farmhouses and halls that appeared in their novels.

The **YHA Youth Hostel,** Longlands Dr. (tel. 642234), tops another hill 1 mi. from the tourist office. It's a lovely Victorian mansion with red carpets, wood paneling, and stained glass, but you don't have to marry wealth to get inside (sleeps 90; 11pm curfew; 11:30pm lights out; lockout 10am-5pm or pay £1.50 for day access; breakfast £2.60, evening meal £3.90; £7.75, under 18 £5.20; open March-Oct. daily; mid- to late-Feb. and Nov. Sun.-Thurs.). B&Bs for about £16-17 are at #4, 6, and 8 Main St. and all up the hill to the tourist office. **Ebor House,** Lees Lane (tel. 645869), off Mill Hey on the opposite side of Haworth Park from Main St., is a large house with B&B for £12.50. Head to Mill Hey for nourishment, as the pubs and tea shops lining Main St. are generally overpriced. **Wild's Bakery,** 7 Mill Hey, has take-away sandwiches (about £1) and pizza slices (42p; open daily 8:45am-5:30pm). **Snowdon's,** 29-31 Mill Hey (tel. 642279), is a small supermarket (open daily 7am-9pm) with another branch near the tourist office on Main St.

The **tourist office,** 2 West Lane (tel. 642329; open daily 9:30am-5:30pm; Nov.-March 9:30am-5pm) at the summit of Main St., stocks plenty of maps and guides. Most useful to the daytripper are *Three Walks from the Centre of Haworth* and the town's mini-guide (both 25p). The **post office** is at 96 Main St., Haworth, West Yorkshire (open Mon.-Fri. 9am-5:30pm, Tues. closes 1pm, Sat. 9am-1pm). Haworth's **postal code** is BD22 8DP, its **telephone code** 01535. **West Yorkshire bus** #663-5 runs a lumpy route every 20 minutes between Haworth and Keighley.

HIGH PENNINES

The area known as the **High Pennines** stretches north to south about 20 mi. west of Durham City, from below Barnard Castle in the south to Hadrian's Wall in the north. The vast landscape straddles the counties of Cumbria, Durham, and Northumbria and gives rise to the great northern rivers: the Tees, Tyne, Derwent, and Wear, whose sources lie high in the moorlands. Unlike the neighboring Yorkshire Dales and Lake District, access to this region is limited, and therefore it remains largely untouched by the frenetic tourist trade. Wide open moorland, tree-lined slopes, quiet stone villages, and turbulent rivers and waterfalls greet the visitor in the Derwent Valley and the region's other dales: Teesdale, Weardale, and Allendale. The Pennine Way crosses each dale as it winds up to Hadrian's Wall and then the Scottish border. The leaflet *The High Pennines,* available from the Northumbrian National Park Centres, provides a good introduction to the area.

Getting There & Getting About

The area is best suited to **hiking;** cars can successfully navigate the roads but buses tackle the region with distressing hesitancy. Those inclined to use wheels at all should consider bikes, given the livestock-laden pastures and relatively level roads that greet the High Pennines explorer. Four motorways bound the region: the A66 in the south, hugging Darlington's latitude, the A6 or M6 from Penrith to Carlisle in the west, the A69 from Carlisle to Newcastle to the north, and in the east the A167 from Newcastle through Durham and Darlington. The B6277 cuts a diagonal through this, running northwest from Barnard Castle through Middleton-in-Teesdale to Alston. **United bus** #75 runs hourly from Darlington's rail and bus stations to Middleton, via Barnard Castle. An Explorer **North East Day Rover** ticket allows one day of unlimited travel within the Tyne/Wear area on most local bus companies. An **Explorer** pass covers a larger area, from Berwick and Newcastle down to Whitby, and from Barnard Castle across to Sunderland. Both tickets are good for travel on weekdays after 9am, all day on weekends, and all day every day June through August (Day Rover £3, Explorer £4.50, seniors and children under 14 £3.50. Call (01324) 468771 for info.) **Primrose Coaches** run the 1½ hr. route from Newcastle to Barnard Castle June-Oct. (tel. (0191) 232 5567). Or, for those traveling from the Northwest, **OK Travel's** service X74 connects Carlisle and Penrith to Barnard Castle (2/day, 1/Sun.), and **United's** summer service #495 from Kendal and Keswick in the Lake District stops at Barnard Castle on its journey to the northeast coast (1/day Mon. and Fri.-Sat.; mid-June-mid-Sept.).

Sights

Twenty mi. southwest of Durham along the River Tees, the bustling market town of **Barnard Castle** makes an excellent base for exploring the castles of Teesdale and the peaks and waterfalls of the North Pennine Hills. Along the river, the ruins of the 13th-century Norman **castle** sprawl over six acres (open daily 10am-6pm; Oct.-March Tues.-Sun. 10am-1pm, 2-4pm; £1.80, under 16 90p), but the major attraction in town is the anomalous **Bowes Museum** (tel. 690606), a 17th-century-style French chateau set in a landscaped garden. Built in the 19th century by a wealthy local businessman and his French wife, the museum purports to bring French culture to the heart of England. Why? (Open May-Oct. Mon.-Sat. 10am-5:30pm, Sun. 2-5pm; March-April and Oct. Mon.-Sat. 10am-5pm, Sun. 2-5pm; Nov.-Feb. Mon.-Sat. 10am-4pm, Sun. 2-5pm. £2.30, seniors and children £1.30. Free tours June-early Sept. Tues.-Fri. 11:15am and 2pm, Sat. 2pm, Sun. 2:15pm.) The Museum will be closed for rewiring from November 1994 to April 1995. Many of Barnard Castle's most affordable accommodations are found in the hotels and pubs on **Market Place** (£12-18). Ask to see the rooms first, however, as they can be a bit worn and grotty. Or walk to **Mrs. Fry's** sublime gardens on 66 Newgate (tel. 37240) and experience B&B for £13. Most pubs and restaurants along the Bank and Market Place serve lunch and dinner. Five gracious, witty women manage the small but well-stocked **tourist office,** 43 Galgate (tel. 690909). Guided walks of the town leave from here

(Thurs. July-Sept. 2:30pm; 1½hr.; £1, seniors and children 50p), while "Guided Rambles," 3 to 4 mi. of extended walks, depart Tuesday (2:30pm; late July-Sept.; £1, seniors and children 50p). Dickens nuts won't want to miss the chance to follow the master's footsteps on **Dickens Drive,** a 25-mi. circular path tracing the route Dickens followed in 1838 while researching *Nicholas Nickleby.* The tourist office has free pamphlets describing transportation along the route. The **post office** licks stamps at 2 Galgate (open Mon.-Fri. 9am-5:30pm, Sat. 9:30am-12:30pm). Barnard Castle's **postal code** is DLI 28BE; its **telephone code** is 01833.

Just northeast of Barnard Castle along the A688 looms **Raby Castle** (RAY-bee; tel. 660202), an imposing 14th-century fortress with a superb medieval kitchen and gardens (open July-Sept. daily, May-June Wed. and Sun., castle 1-5pm, park and gardens 10am-5pm; no admission to either after 4:30pm; £3.30, seniors £3, children £1.50, seniors and children £75p).

A pleasant 12 mi. hike northwest along the **Pennine Way** lies **Middleton-in-Teesdale,** a mining town. The *Teesdale Accommodation Guide,* free at the **tourist office** (open daily 9:30am-5pm; reduced hrs. in winter), lists dozens of B&Bs in town. The **Hudeway Centre hostel** (HEWD-way), Stacks Lane (tel. (01833) 40012), has 22 beds *plus* underground exploration, climbing, and canoeing options; it caters mostly to groups, but is open to individuals if at least 12 people show up (£7, with breakfast £8). Return to Barnard Castle by bus #75, or carry on along the River Tees for the next 9 mi. of the Pennine Way to the **Langdon Beck Youth Hostel (HI),** Forest-in-Teesdale, Barnard Castle (tel. 22228; £7.75, under 18 £5.20; open Aug. daily; April-June and Sept.-Oct. Tues.-Sat.; March Tues.-Sat.; Feb. and Nov. Fri.-Sat.). During this idyllic stroll in the Tees Valley past **High Force Waterfall,** one of England's most spectacular falls, follow Wainwright's advice and "tarry long in the presence of beauty, for so much in life is barren" (viewing platform 35p, children 15p). **United Bus** #75 runs near the High Force Waterfall from Barnard Castle.

■■■ YORKSHIRE DALES NATIONAL PARK

The stunning emerald beauty of the Yorkshire Dales National Park extends to the rim of the sky. Formed by swift rivers and lazy glacial flow, the kelly-green valleys and misshapen hills will steal your breath; don't miss towering white limestone pinnacles, plummeting waterfalls, and subterranean caverns below the cascades. Scenery is not all that the park can offer: the Old People left their mark on these hills as well. Bronze and Iron Age tribes traced winding "green lanes" (footpaths that remain upon the moorland tops), while Romans built straight roads and stout hillforts and Vikings influenced the local dialect. The park lies between the Peak District to the south, the Lake District to the west, Northumberland National Park to the north, and the North York Moors to the east. For a true taste of the Dales, try some Yorkshire pudding, parkin, or curd tarts.

GETTING THERE & GETTING ABOUT

The size of the Dales demands that you have a car or several days and good hiking and camping equipment to get around. Compasses are a must. In the south of the park, semi-industrial **Skipton** serves as a transportation hub and provides goods and services not available in the smaller villages. **Grassington** and **Linton,** farther north, are more scenic bases for exploring southern Wharfedale. Malham is a sensible starting point for forays into western Wharfedale and Eastern Ribblesdale. To explore Wensleydale and Swaledale in the north, move out from **Hawes.**

The most convenient way to enter the park is to take a bus or train from Bradford, Leeds, or Lancaster to Skipton, then switch to a local bus that ventures into the smaller villages. **Trains** run from Bradford and Leeds to Carlisle, Morecambe, and Lancaster via Skipton (Mon.-Sat. 1/hr., Sun. 3/day; 40min.; Bradford -Skipton £2.70, day return £3.70; Leeds-Skipton £3.50, day return £5.20.) **Keighley & District** buses

#666 to 669 connect Bradford to Skipton (Mon.-Sat. about 3/hr., Sun. 1/hr; 1½hr.); **Yorkshire Rider** bus #784 and X84 provides access to Skipton from Leeds (1/hr.; 1½hr.). Other options for reaching Skipton include a bus from York that runs to the Lake District via Skipton, Settle, and Ingleton (**Mountain Goat Bus Co.;** tel. (017687) 73962; mid-April to Oct. Mon., Wed., and Fri.-Sat. 1 each direction), or the daily **National Express Rapide** bus from London (£32.50, return £34-44).

From Skipton, **Pride of the Dales** line (tel. (01756) 753123) bus #72 connects to **Grassington** (Mon.-Sat. 1/hr., Sun. 5/day; £2, return £3.50) and occasionally Kettlewell. **Pennine Motors and Bibby's** (tel. (01756) 749215) bus #580 joins Skipton to **Settle** (every hr., 5/day on Sun.), and to **Ingleton** (Mon.-Fri. 2/day, 4/day on Sun.). Their bus #210 runs from Skipton to **Malham** (#210; 3/day; Sun. in summer). Most of these companies sell a daily **Wayfarer** ticket for £3-4 on their own routes. Settle also receives some Carlisle-bound trains from Leeds. The train from Skipton to **Windermere** (with transfers at Oxenholme and Lancaster) is just as fast as the Mountain Goat bus from York.

Other villages are served less regularly. Inter-village buses tend to be infrequent, often running only on certain days of the week; some bus service is by post bus, which only runs once a day to scheduled towns. All public transport devotees must procure the *Dales Connection* timetable, free at any tourist office or National Park Information Centre. Note that in the winter, bus service fairly well hibernates.

Hitchers often suffer thumb sprains from unreliable pickups and settle for rides that carry them only part way. If you miss your bus, you may well get stuck walking.

PRACTICAL INFORMATION

The following **National Park Information Centres** are staffed by well-informed Dales devotees. The centers sell maps, guidebooks, and leaflets. Many also offer guided walks; call for details. Pick up the annual park guide, *The Visitor* (free). As a rule, the following centers are open from April to October daily at least from 10am to 4pm; in winter, hours vary according to the weather: **Aysgarth Falls,** Wensleydale, less than a mile east of the village (tel. (01969) 663424); **Clapham,** in village centre (tel. (015242) 51419); **Grassington,** Hebden Rd., Wharfedale (tel. (01756) 752774); **Hawes,** Station Yard, Wensleydale (tel. (01969) 667450); **Malham,** southern end of village, Malhamdale (tel. (01729) 830363); **Sedbergh,** Main St. (tel. (015396) 20125).

ACCOMMODATIONS & CAMPING

Hostels, converted barns, tents, and B&Bs dot the dales. The *Yorkshire Dales Accommodation Guide* (30p) is available at National Park Information Centres and at the York tourist office. The Centres also stock the *Yorkshire and Humberside Caravan & Camping Guide*. See also Pennine Way: Accommodations for more information.

Twelve **HI Youth Hostels** play host in the Yorkshire Dales area. Hawes, Keld, and Malham lie on the Pennine Way. Ingleton, on the western edge of the park, is a good jump-off point to the Lake District. Linton, Stainforth, Kettlewell, Dentdale, Aysgarth Falls, and Grinton Lodge all lie a few miles off the Pennine Way (Stainforth is (3½mi. from the Pennine Way and 2mi. from Settle). Ellingstring, near Ripon, and Kirkby Stephen, north of Hawes and served by rail, lie farther away from the trail.

Hawes: (tel. (01969) 667368), £7.75, under £5.20, open July-Aug. daily, April-June Mon.-Sat., Sept.-Oct. Tues.-Sat., Nov.-mid-Dec. and Feb.-March Fri.-Tues.

Keld: (tel. (01748) 86259), £6.50, under 18 £4.35, open June-Aug. Mon.-Sat., Feb.-March and Sept.-Nov. Fri.-Sat.

Malham: (tel. (01729) 830321), £7.75, under 18 £5.20, open April-Sept. daily, Feb.-March Tues.-Sat., Oct. Mon.-Sat.

Ingleton: (tel. (015242) 41444), £6.50, under 18 £4.35; open July-Aug. daily, April-June Mon.-Sat., Sept.-Dec. and Jan.-March Tues.-Sat.

Linton: (tel. (01756) 752400), £7.75, under 18 £5.20; open April-Aug. Mon.-Sat., Sept.-Oct. Tues.-Sat. Edgar lives here no more...good riddance.

Stainforth: (tel. (01729) 823577), £7.15, under 18 £4.75; open May-Aug. daily, April and Sept.-Oct. Mon.-Sat., March, Nov., and Feb. Fri.-Sat.

Kettlewell (tel. (01756) 760232), £7.15, under 18 £4.75, open April-Sept. daily, Oct.-mid.Dec. and mid-Feb.-March Mon.-Fri.

Dentdale (tel. (015396) 25251), £7.15, under 18 £4.75, open April-Aug Fri.-Wed., Sept.-Oct. Fri.-Tues., Feb-March. Fri.-Sat.

Aysgarth Falls (tel. (01969) 663260), £7.15, under £4.75, open July-Aug. daily, April-June Mon.-Sat., Nov. and Feb.-March Fri-Sat.

Grinton Lodge (tel. (01748) 84206), £6.50, under 18 £4.35, open April-Aug. daily, Sept.-Oct. and Jan.-March Tues.-Sat.

Ellingstring (tel. (01677) 460216), £5.30, under 18 £3.50, open July-Aug. daily, March-June and Sept.-Oct. Fri.-Tues.

Kirkby Stephen (tel. (017683) 71793), £7.15, under 18 £4.75, open July-Aug. daily, mid-March-June Weds.-Mon., Sept.-mid Dec. and Feb.-mid March Weds.-Sun.

Numerous **Dales Barns** offer cheap accommodations: £3-6 per night in dorm rooms in converted barns (up to 30 people/barn; expect an empty bunkhouse). The barns cater to small groups but are also ideal for hikers exploring the Pennine or Dales Way. Book to individual barns, weeks in advance: **Airton** (tel. (01729) 830263), **Catholes** (tel. (015396) 20334), **Chapel-le-Dale** (tel. (015242) 41477), **Dub Cote** (tel. (01729) 860238, £5.75/night), **Grange Farm** (tel. (01756) 76059, £5/night), **Halton Gill** (tel. (01756) 770241), **Hill Top Farm** (tel. (01729) 830320), and **Skirfare Bridge** (tel. (01756) 752465).

Campgrounds are difficult to reach on foot, so consider asking farmers if you can sleep on their bit of moor. The following official campgrounds are available: at **Hawes, Bainbridge Ings,** Hawes, N. Yorks. DL8 3NU (tel. (01969) 667354) is open from April to October. In **Richmond,** try **Brompton-on-Swale Caravan Park,** Richmond, N. Yorks. DL10 7EZ (tel. (01748) 824629; open April-Oct) or **Swaleview Caravan Park,** Reethe Road, Richmond, N. Yorks. DL10 4SF (tel. (01748) 823106; open March-Oct). In **Skipton, Dalesway Caravan Park,** Marton Rd., Gargrave, Skipton, N. Yorks. BD23 3NS (tel. (01765) 749592) is open from April to October.

HIKING

> **Warning:** Be aware that all the Dales are filled with shake holes, small depressions similar to grassy potholes that indicate underground caverns. *Don't step on them*—they can give way and kill you if the cavern is large. Especially on the smaller, unmarked trails, Ordnance Survey maps and a compass are essential. See Essentials: Hiking & Camping for other important tips.

Since the bus service is scant, the hitching abysmal, and the scenery breathtaking, hiking remains the best way to traverse the Dales. The park's six National Park Information Centres can help you prepare for a trek along one of the three long-distance footpaths through the park. The **Pennine Way** curls from Gargrave in the south (on the rail line just west of Skipton) to Tan Hill in the north, passing Malham, Pen-y-ghent, Hawes, Keld, and most of the major attractions in the Dales. The **Dales Way** edges from Bradford and Leeds past Ilkley, through Wharfedale via Grassington and Whernside, and by Sedbergh on its way to the Lake District; it crosses the Pennine Way near Dodd Fell. The **Coast-to-Coast Walk** stretches through the top of the park from Richmond to Kirkby Stephen, sweeping through Reeth and Keld. Eighteen additional informal information points are housed in shops and post offices; ask about these at the six main Centres.

Countless trail guides, for sale at the Centres, detail less crowded routes of varying lengths. The park authority encourages you to keep to its designated walks so as to protect grasslands and avoid falling into hidden mineshafts. They offer leaflets (40p) describing over 30 of these unmarked walks. A multitude of trail leaflets (40p) describe better marked trails; they begin at Ingleton, Longstone Common, Malham, Aysgarth Falls, Grassington's Centre, and Clapham's Centre. The Centres also supply route cards that detail the Yorkshire Dales Cycleway, a series of six 20-mi. routes connecting the dales, and list cycle hire locations. The area is hilly, though feasibly explored by bike. Detailed Ordinance Survey maps are available for most of the smaller paths; purchase them for £4.25 at any Centre.

SKIPTON

Skipton (pop. 13,000) shines as a transfer point, but a number of sights, armadas of ducks, and plenty of B&Bs make it a desirable destination in its own right. The empty **Skipton Castle** (tel. 792442) is the well-preserved medieval home of the Earls of Cumberland, with plenty of arrow slits and a good field of fire (please refrain from attacking the other visitors; castle open Mon.-Sat. 10am-6pm, Sun. 2-6pm; Oct.-Feb. Mon.-Sat. 10am-4pm, Sun. 2-4pm; £2.90, ages 5-18 £1.40). Meander through Skipton's canals in a narrow barge rented from **Pennine Boat Trips,** Coach St. (tel. 790829). Cruises leave in July and August, usually at 11:30am, 1:30pm, 3pm, and 4:30pm daily (1¼hr.; £2.50, seniors £2.20, children £1.50).

For friendly lodging, head to **Mrs. Wright's,** Ringwood House, 1 Salisbury St. (tel. 791135). Complete with bathtub, bidet, rocking chair, and toasty towel-rack, the mauve W.C. is as luxurious as the bedrooms (£15 first night, £14/night for stays of more than one night, £13/night for stays of a week). **Bourne House,** 22 Upper Sackville St. (tel. 792633), has modern, sparkling rooms for £13-14/person. Call ahead to pitch your tent at Mr. Harrison's **Sixpenny Syke Farm,** Carlton (tel. 792025), about 1½ mi. outside of Skipton.

Load up on fresh fruit and vegetables at the **market,** which makes High St. and other streets nigh impassable (all day Mon., Wed., and Fri.-Sat.). At 5 Albert St., **Rag Albert's** (tel. 796216) dishes out hearty meals and vegetarian options amid rustic decor for £3-5 (open Mon.-Sat. 10am-3pm, Wed.-Sat. also 7-10pm). **Hong Kong,** 27 Water St., packs mostly meat into a take-away tin of chicken with mushroom (£2.30) and other basic dishes (open Mon. and Weds.-Sat. 5:30pm-midnight, Sun. 5:30-11:30pm). Consider picnicking with quacks along the canal. Every Tuesday night at 8:30pm, performers from the **Skipton Folk Club** sing between pints at **Rose and Crown** on Coach St. Most beers, especially local Yorkshire brews, cost 10-20p less per pint than elsewhere. Bottoms up!

Ewe will find the **tourist office** at 9 Sheep St., a ¼mi. from the train station (tel. 792543, open daily 10am-5pm, Nov.-Easter 10am-4:30pm). **Keighley & District Travel,** on Keighley Rd. at the bus station (tel. 795331), books **National Express coaches** and stores piles of *Dales Connections* (open Mon. and Wed.-Fri. 8:45am-4:15pm, Tues. 1-4:15pm, Sat. 8:45am-12:15pm). For mountain bike rental and repairs, try **Eric Burgess Cycles,** 3/5 Water St. (tel. 794386; £11.75/day, £50/week, tandems £20/day; open Mon.-Fri. 9am-5:30pm, Sat. 9am-4:30pm). Stock up on camping and hiking supplies at **The Dales Outdoor Centre** on Coach St. (tel. 794305; open Mon. and Wed.-Fri. 9:30am-5pm, Sat. 9am-5:30pm, Sun. 11am-4pm). Wash your bandannas and socks at the **Laundromat,** 22 Sackville St. (open Mon.-Fri. 8am-6pm, Sat. 8am-noon, winter Mon.-Fri. 8am-7pm, Sat. 8am-noon; change and soap available). Skipton's **post office** is at Sunwin House, 8 Swadford St. (tel. 792724; open Mon.-Thurs. 9am-5:30pm, Fri. 9am-6pm, Sat. 9am-4pm). The **postal code** for Skipton is B23 1UR; the **telephone code** is 01756.

GRASSINGTON & WHARFEDALE

With an information center, nearby trails, and regular bus service to Skipton, **Grassington** (pop. 1500) makes a good base from which to explore the southern part of the Dales region. The **National Park Information Centre,** on Hebden Rd. across from the bus station, books rooms for free and offers two- to three-hour guided walks (March-Oct.; £1.50, children 70p) on varying days of the week (open daily 9:30am-5:15pm; Nov.-April Sat.-Sun. 11am-4pm). The **telephone code** for Grassington and Wharfedale is 01756.

Florrie Whitehead, 16 Wood Lane (tel. 752841), supplies excellent B&B and legendary hospitality for £11. If this haven is full, you should try **Burtree** (tel. 752442), a stone country cottage a few steps from the Information Centre (£13). Numerous pubs and tea shops along Main St., such as **Picnic's Cafe** (open daily 9am-5:30pm, winter Mon.-Fri. 10am-3pm, Sat.-Sun. 9am-5:30pm) serve sandwiches, soups, and hot traditional meals (£1.250-4). **The Mountaineer** in Pletts Barn Centre behind Craven Cottage at the top of Main St. (tel. 752266), sells camping gear and rents mountain bikes (£6 half day, £10 day) and hiking boots (£5/day; open Tues., Thurs. 9:30am-3pm, Sat. 9:30am-5pm, Sun. 10am-4:30pm).

Spectacular **Kilnsey Crag** is a 3½-mi. walk from Grassington towards Kettlewell. Wharfedale Walk #8 will guide you through a deep gorge, Bronze Age burial mounds, and stunning views of Wharfedale. **Stump Cross Caverns** (tel. 752780), adorned with beautiful stalagmite columns and glistening curtains of rock, are a 5-mi. walk east from Grassington toward Pateley Bridge; some travelers choose to hitch along the B6265. Dress warmly; it gets chilly down under (caverns open daily 10am-5pm; Nov.-Feb. Sat.-Sun. 11am-4pm; £2.90, under 13 £1.45).

Linton, a picturesque one-church, one-street village, is less than 10 mi. north of Skipton and 2 mi. south of Grassington. Wharfedale Walk #6 takes you on a circular route from Grassington through Linton, mainly through pastures and along the drug store walls. The church by the river features an unusual stile that kept livestock from nibbling at the poisonous yew on the grounds. An **HI Youth Hostel** (tel. 752400) occupies the town's 17th-century rectory. (£7.75, under 18 £5.20; open April to Aug. Mon.-Sat.; Sept.-Oct. Tues.-Sat.) Address inquiries to the Old Rectory, Linton-in-Craven, Skipton, N. Yorkshire BD23 5HH.) The Skipton-Grassington bus #72 (see above) passes near the hostel. **Kettlewell,** 10 mi. north of Grassington, is another fine base for touring the Dales. In the center of the village is an **HI Youth Hostel,** Whernside House (tel. 760232; £7.15, under 18 £4.75; open April-Sept. daily; mid-Feb. to March and Oct. to mid-Dec. Mon.-Fri.).

MALHAMDALE & RIBBLESDALE

Sights in **Malham** are consistently spectacular, largely because humans haven't touched them. Climb to the stunning limestone pavement of **Malham Cove** and then walk through "Dry Valley" with its Iron Age caves to **Malham Tarn,** Yorkshire's second-largest natural lake. Two mi. from Malham is equally impressive **Gordale Scar,** cut in the last Ice Age by a rampaging glacier. You can catch all of these beauties on the park's *A Walk in Malhamdale* (leaflet #1, about 4hrs.).

Malham contains a **National Park Information Centre** (tel. (01729) 830363) and a superior-grade **HI Youth Hostel** (tel. (01729) 830321), thronged by Pennine Way groupies (£7.75, under 18 £5.20; open daily April-Sept.; Oct. Mon.-Sat.; Feb.-March Tues.-Sat.). **Townhead Farm** (tel. (01729) 830287) provides tent sites for £2 per person. For B&B in town, try **Mrs. Harrison,** Friars Garth (tel. (01729) 830328), where you can bed down for £10 in a single or £9 per person in a double. North of Malham, the high peaks and cliffs of **Ingleborough, Pen-y-ghent,** and **Whernside** form the so-called "Alpes Pennina." The 24-mi. **Three Peaks Walk** connecting the Alpes begins and ends in **Horton-in-Ribblesdale** at the clock of the **Pen-y-ghent Cafe,** a hiker's haunt with mammoth mugs of tea.

The best place to break your journey is **Ingleton** (meaning "Fire Town"; pop. 2000), where the local **tourist office** books rooms (tel. (015242) 41049, open April-Oct. 10am-4:30pm daily). Several small B&Bs on Main St. charge about £12. Or, walk a mi. to **Stacksteads Farm** (tel. (015242) 41386), where farmhouse lodging costs £14. In town lies the **HI Youth Hostel,** Greta Tower (tel. (015242) 41444; £6.50, under 18 £4.35; open July-Aug. daily, April-June Mon.-Sat.; Jan.-March and Sept.-late Dec. Tues.-Sat.). From Ingleton, consider following the stunning 4-mi. "Falls Walk."

WENSLEYDALE

As you venture north into Wensleydale, the landscape of potholes, caves, clints, and grikes melds into a broad strath of fertile dairyland. Charles Kingsley described Wensleydale as "the richest spot in all England, this beautiful oasis among the mountains." And he should know. Base your forays in **Hawes,** which has a **National Park Information Centre** (tel. (01696) 667450). Farther west along Ingleton Rd. sits the **HI Youth Hostel** (tel. (01969) 667368; breakfast, evening meal, and shop; £7.75, under 18 £5.20; open July-Aug. daily; April-June Mon.-Sat.; Sept.-Oct. Tues.-Sat.; Nov. to mid-Dec. and mid-Feb. to March Fri.-Tues.).

Hardrow Force, England's highest above-ground waterfall, spits and hisses 1 mi. north along the Pennine Way. To see this overrated natural sight, hand over 20p at the Green Dragon Pub. More worthwhile are the **Aysgarth Falls** to the east— which roll in successive tiers down the craggy Yoredale Rocks—and the natural terrace of the **Shawl of Leyburn.** A **National Park Information Centre** idles in the car park above Aysgarth Falls; a **tourist office** (tel. (01969) 23069) sits in the center of **Leyburn.** Both Aysgarth and Leyburn are served by **United** #26 and sporadically by **Keighley & District** #800, both from Hawes. Information centers are open only in summer. Aysgarth boasts an **HI Youth Hostel** (tel. (01969) 663260) in a former private school ½ mi. east of the village (£7.15, under 18 £4.75; open July-Aug. daily, April-June Mon.-Sat., Feb.-March and Nov. Fri.-Sat.).

■ ▓ ■ YORK

With well-preserved city walls that have foiled many a marauding invader, today York's impressive fortifications welcome equally stubborn hordes of tourists. Their quarry is a city strewn with medieval cottages and Georgian townhouses, presided over by Britain's largest Gothic cathedral. In 71 AD the Romans founded "Eboracum" as a military and administrative base for Northern England; the town remained important as Anglo-Saxon "Eoforwic" and Viking "Jorvik" (Norse for "Hey, this town's got some serious tourist potential"), growing steadily until the Norman conquest. William permitted York's Archbishop to officiate at his consecration, anointing the city as England's second greatest. In 1069, York thanked him by joining with the Danes to massacre 3,000 men in the Conqueror's garrison, producing some of the many ghosts in the self-proclaimed "most haunted city in the world." Fresh shades spilled in during the War of the Roses (1455-1485), during which enemy heads were severed and spiked by the walls on Micklegate Bar. These days, untold brochures sway camera-packing aggressors with little touches, noting at every turn details like "Margaret Clitherow, crushed to death on Ouse Bridge, 1586."

GETTING THERE

York is on the main London-Edinburgh Intercity rail line. **Trains** run to London, King's Cross Station (2/hr.; 2hr.; £47), Manchester's Piccadilly (2/hr.; 1½hr.; £11.50), Newcastle (4/hr.; 1¼hr.; £17.50), Scarborough (1/hr.; 1hr.; £7.20, return £11), and Edinburgh (1/hr.; 3-4hr.; £39.50). **National Express buses** run less frequently to London (4/day; 4hr.; £30), Manchester (3/day; 3hr.; £8), and Edinburgh (1/day; 5hr.). The **Slow Coach** stops here on its circuit of England (consult Essentials: Getting About—Buses & Coaches for details).

ORIENTATION & PRACTICAL INFORMATION

York is a fairly compact city, with most attractions lying within the walls or just at the edge of enemy territory. Surrounding the tangle of pedestrian streets at the city center are a few relatively straight thoroughfares. The half-mile long thoroughfare formed by Station Rd., the Lendal Bridge, Museum St., and Duncombe Pl. (street names change just about every block) leads from the rail station to the **Minster.** The other important chain runs perpendicular to this. Running southeast from the Minster, another multi-block avenue named High Petergate, Low Petergate, then Colliergate leads towards the shops and restaurants in the crowded city center.

There is a small tourist office in the train station, a privately owned one on Rougier St. which shares an office with National Express, and a main tourist information center near the Minster in city center. From the train station, turn left down Sta-

YORK

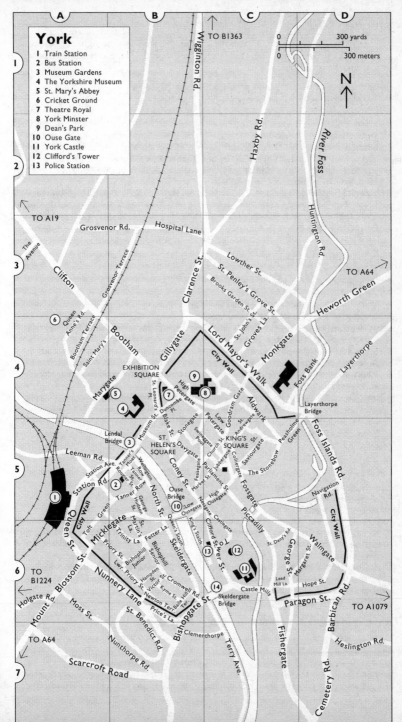

York

1 Train Station
2 Bus Station
3 Museum Gardens
4 The Yorkshire Museum
5 St. Mary's Abbey
6 Cricket Ground
7 Theatre Royal
8 York Minster
9 Dean's Park
10 Ouse Gate
11 York Castle
12 Clifford's Tower
13 Police Station

TO B1363

0   300 yards
0   300 meters

N

TO A19

Grosvenor Rd.   Hospital Lane

The Avenue

Clifton

Lowther St.

St. Penley's Grove St.

Brooks Garden St.

Clarence St.

Groves La.

St. John's St.

Huntington Rd.

River Foss

TO A64

Heworth Green

Queen Anne's Rd.

Bootham Terrace

Saint Mary's

Grosvenor Terrace

Bootham

Gillygate

Lord Mayor's Walk

Monkgate

city wall

Marygate

EXHIBITION SQUARE

High Petergate

Foss Bank

Layerthorpe

Lendal Bridge

Museum St.

St. Leonard's Pl.

Duncombe Pl.

Blake St.

Stonegate

Low Petergate

Goodram Gate

Aldwark

St. Andrewgate

Layerthorpe Bridge

ST. HELEN'S SQUARE

Davygate

Church St.

Swinegate

Pool

Parliament St.

KING'S SQUARE

Colliergate

Fossgate

Peasholme Green

Leeman Rd.

Station Ave.

Coney St.

Jubbergate

Market St.

Saviourgate

The Stonebow

Foss Islands Rd.

city wall

Station Rd.

Tanner Row

Wellington

North St.

Ouse Bridge

Low Ousegate

High Ousegate

Piccadilly

Navigation Rd.

Queen St.

City Wall

Micklegate

Toft Green

Trinity La.

Tanner's

Row

Priory St.

George Hudson St.

Martin La.

Fetter La.

Skeldergate

Clifford St.

Nunnery Lane

Bishophill Junior

Bishophill Senior

Hampden St.

Lwr. Priory St.

Victor St.

Cromwell Rd.

Kyme St.

Newton Terr.

Castle Mills

Lead Mill La.

St. Deny's Rd.

Walmgate

George St.

Margaret St.

Barbican Rd.

TO A1079

Holgate Rd.

Mount Blossom St.

Moss St.

St. Benedict Rd.

Price's La.

Baile Hill Terr.

Bishopgate St.

Skeldergate Bridge

Clementhorpe

Terry Ave.

Hope St.

Paragon St.

Heslington Rd.

TO B1224

TO A64

Nunthorpe Rd.

Scarcroft Road

Fishergate

Cemetery Rd.

tion Rd. and cross under either arch of the city wall; with the wall on your left, cross over the river on Lendal Bridge. Rougier St. and the bus station are on the right just before the bridge. As you walk onto the bridge, the Minster is straight ahead; turn left one block before it onto crescent-shaped St. Leonard's Place to reach Exhibition Square and the main tourist office.

Tourist Offices: The main **Tourist Information** is in De Grey Rooms, Exhibition Sq. (tel. 621756). The office will find you a room for the night for a £2 fee (£2.70 to book a bed ahead). A multitude of free leaflets sit behind the counter; just ask. Tours usually need to be booked from a tourist office. Open Mon.-Sat. 9am-7pm, Sun. 10am-1pm; Sept.-June Mon.-Sat. 9am-5pm, Sun. 10am-1pm. A **smaller branch** awaits in the train station (tel. 643700, open Mon.-Sat. 9:30am-5:30pm, Sun. 11am-5pm). The **York Visitor and Conference Bureau,** 6 Rougier St. by the bus station, offers similar services, with a £3.50 room booking fee (open Mon.-Sat. 9am-6pm, Sun. 10am-5pm).

Financial Services: Barclays, 2 St. Helen's Sq. (tel. 631333). Open Mon.-Tues. and Thurs.-Fri. 9:30am-4:30pm, Wed. 10am-4:30pm. **Thomas Cook,** 4 Nessgate (tel. 639928). Open Mon.-Thurs. 9am-5:30pm, Fri. 10am-5:30pm, Sat. 9am-5pm. **American Express,** 6 Stonegate (tel. 611727). Open Mon.-Fri. 9am-5:30pm, Sat. 9am-5pm; Nov.-March same weekday hrs., Sat. 9am-1pm. Currency exchange also open April-Oct. Sun. 10am-4:30pm.

Post Office: 22 Lendal (tel. 617285). Open Mon.-Fri. 9am-5:30pm, Sat. 9am-4pm. **Postal Code:** YO1 2DA.

Telephone Code: 01904.

Trains: Station Rd. (tel. 642155). Information office open Mon.-Sat. 9:30am-5:30pm, Sun. 11am-5pm. Travel center open Mon.-Fri. 9am-6pm, Sat. 9am-5pm, Sun. 10am-4pm. **Luggage lockers** 50p-£2.

Bus Station: Offices and stops at Rougier St. tourist office. **National Express** (tel. (0113) 246 0011). **Rider York** local buses (tel. 624161). Open Mon.-Fri. 8am-5pm, Sat. 9am-4:30pm. Board buses here, at the train station, or on Piccadilly. Buses to Scarborough, Harrowgate, and Castle Howard board at Rougier St. **York-Pullman,** Exhibition Sq. (tel. 622992), runs day tours to Castle Howard, Moors, and Dales from ABC Cinema, Piccadilly.

Boats: Several companies along the River Ouse near Lendal, Ouse, and Skeldergate Bridges offer 1-hr. cruises for about £3 (tel. 705812 or 704442). **York Marine,** Skeldergate Bridge (tel. 704442), rents motorboats (£8-12/hr., deposit £10). Open daily 9am-6pm.

Bike Rental: Bob Trotter (tel. 622868), 13 Lord Mayor's Walk. £5 for half day rental, £9.50 for a full day. Open Mon.-Wed. and Fri.-Sat. 9am-5:30pm, Thurs. 9am-7pm.

Early Closing Day: Wed., approx. 1pm. Smaller shops only.

Launderette: Haxby Road Washeteria, 126 Haxby Rd. (tel. 623379). Change and soap available. Open Tues.-Thurs. 8am-6pm, Mon. and Fri. 8am-8pm, Sat. 8am-5:30pm and Sun. 8am-4:30pm.

Market: Mon.-Sat. 8am-5pm between Shambles and Parliament St. Take Jubbergate to Little Shambles. Stalls and stalls of imitation name-brand bras.

Hotlines: Samaritans (crisis): 89 Nunnery Lane, tel. 655 888. **Gay and Lesbian Switchboard:** tel. 411399, Thurs. 7-11pm. **Rape Crisis:** tel. 610917, Thurs. 6:30-10pm; the **police rape hotline** is (0800) 181505, 24-hr. and no coins required.

Hospital: York District Hospital, Wiggonton Rd. (tel. 631 313). Bus #1, 2, or 3.

Emergency: Dial 999; no coins required.

Police: Fulford Rd. (tel. 631321).

ACCOMMODATIONS & CAMPING

Competition for inexpensive B&Bs (from £12) can be fierce from June through August. Bring a tire-iron or a black belt. The tourist office posts a list of accommodations outside after hours. B&Bs are most concentrated on the sidestreets along **Bootham/Clifton** (Bootham becomes Clifton at Grosvenor Terrace). Or try **The Mount** area (out past the train station and down Blossom St.), **Haxby Road** (take bus #2A, or walk from the tourist office out to the end of Gillygate and take the right fork). Book weeks ahead during the summer, even for hostels and camping sites.

Queen Anne's Guest House, 24 Queen Anne's Rd. (tel. 629389), a short walk out Bootham from Exhibition Sq. Spotless single, double, and family rooms with TV. Filling breakfast. £14.

The Old Dairy, 10 Compton St. (tel. 623816). Walk ½ mi. up Bootham from Exhibition Sq or take bus to Clifton Green. Look for the doorway with the *Let's Go* sign. Charming chambers with wrought-iron bedsteads. £12, breakfast included.

HI Youth Hostel, Water End, Clifton (tel. 653147), 1 mi. from town center. From Exhibition Sq. tourist office, walk about ½ mi. out Bootham/Clifton; or take bus to Clifton Green and walk ¼ mi. Superior-grade hostel with excellent facilities: members' kitchen, TV room, blazing hot showers, laundry. But at B&B-level prices, is it worth the lack of privacy and the long hike? 156 beds with 4-8 beds/room; often fills with groups. Reception open 7am-11:30pm. Bedroom lockout 10am-1pm. No curfew. £12.90, under 18 £9.40, includes breakfast. Open mid-Jan.-Dec.

York Youth Hotel, 11-13 Bishophill Senior (tel. 625904 or 630613). Turn left out of train station and follow Station Ave. Cross under the walls and continue onto Rougier, then George Hudson St., until you reach Micklegate. Turn right and take next left onto narrow St. Martin's Lane, which leads to Bishophill. 20-bed Room #12 is an excellent place to meet fellow travelers; rest of building often booked by youth groups. Bar open 9pm-1am, after pubs close. Bike rental £4.50. Dorm beds £8-11 (sheets £1). Singles £13-16.50. Twins £24-30. Continental breakfast £1.30, full breakfast £2.50. Laundry available. 24hr. reception. Sleeps 140.

Clifton View Guest House, 118/120 Clifton (tel. 625047), ¾ mi. from town. Soft-spoken Mrs. Oxtoby offers 13 comfortably furnished rooms and a hearty breakfast. Laundry facilities available. Singles £14-15. Doubles £27, cheaper in winter.

Avenue Guest House, 6 The Avenue, (tel. 620575), off Bootham/Clifton. Enthusiastic hosts provide rooms with soft beds. A step up without the usual step up in price. On a quiet, residential sidestreet. Some family rooms with baths are available. No smoking. 7 rooms. £15-20, £13-15 in winter.

Alemar Guest House, 19 Queen Anne's Rd. (tel. 652367), off Bootham/Clifton. Lovely rooms and happy hosts. Singles £16. Doubles £30. Less in winter.

Camping: Riverside Caravan and Camping Park, 1 Ferry St., Bishopthorpe (tel. 704442), 3 mi. south of York off the A64. Riverside site. Take bus #15 to Bishopthorpe. Tent and 2 people £6, 1 person £4.50. Open Easter-Sept. **Old Post Office Site** (tel. 706288), 4 mi. south of York off the A64, by the river. Take any Acaster Malbis bus. Frame tent, car, and 2 people £4.50. Additional person 75p. Open April-Oct. **Poplar Farm** (tel. 706548), downriver from Post Office Site. Tent and 2 people £6. Additional person £1. Syke's bus leaves Skeldergate every 2 hrs. until 5:45pm, stopping outside the grounds en route.

FOOD & PUBS

Expensive tea rooms, medium-range bistros, and cheap eateries bump elbows in even the most remote alleyways of York. Fruit and vegetable grocers peddle their wares at the **market** behind the Shambles (open Mon.-Sat. 8am-5pm), and **Holland & Barrett** shelves their ever-reliable wholefoods at 39 Parliament (tel. 641 232; open Mon.-Sat. 9am-5:30pm). **Jackson's** is a small supermarket at 25 Bootham, near the city center (tel. 623558; open daily 8am-10pm).

La Romantica, 14 Goodramgate (tel. 636236). Enjoy delicious pasta (£4-5) in plush and elegant candlelit setting. Subtle name—atmosphere to match. Open Mon.-Sat. noon-2:30pm and 5:30-11:30pm, Sun. 5:30-11:30pm.

Oscar's Wine Bar and Bistro, Little Stonegate, off Stonegate (tel. 652002). Load up a massive plate with salads and meats (£5-7)—enough to keep you going for a week. Swank courtyard, a varied menu, and a lively mood. Open daily 11am-11pm. Happy hour Mon.-Fri. 5:30-6:30pm; live jazz and blues on Mon. nights.

St. William's Restaurant, 3 College St. Cafeteria inside 15th-century building and quiet cobbled courtyard outside St. William's College. Small but tasty portions. Hot dishes about £3, soups £1.45. Luscious desserts 85p. Open daily 10am-5pm.

Gillygate Vegetarian Restaurant, Millers Yard, off Gillygate. Tasty and inventive meatless hot dishes (£2.50-3), sexy fruit pies (£1.50), and vegan ice cream (40p/scoop). Open Mon.-Fri. 10am-4:30pm, Sat. 10am-5pm; winter Mon.-Fri. 10am-4pm, Sat. 10am-4:30pm.

Theatre Royal Café Bar, St. Leonard's Pl. Sandwiches (£1-2), salads, and quiches (£3) in an attractive, windowed, theaterside location designed for people-watching. Open Mon.-Sat. 10am-8pm.

There are more **pubs** in the center of York than gargoyles on the east wall of the Minster. Whether Tudor, Victorian, or something in between, most are packed on weekend nights and all serve bar meals during the day. The **King's Arms** draws lively folk into its royal embrace. The **Roman Bath** (tel. 620455), St. Sampson's Sq., serves pints among the ruins. The **Punch Bowl** (tel. 622307), Stonegate, is one of York's handsomest pubs, and its neighbor the **Old Starre** (tel. 623063) is the city's oldest, with a license that goes back to 1644. The Old Starre also has the best pub meals. The **Black Swan,** Peasholme Green, is more sedate—come here to avoid the droves of teenagers who queue up for a pint of shandy outside the pubs closer to St. Sampson's Sq.

SIGHTS

York Visitor Cards (£1) are available at the tourist office and offer discounts on many of the museums and buildings in York. The card will pay for itself if two adults use it at just one or two sites. The best introduction to York is a 2½-mi. walk along its medieval walls. Beware the tourist stampede, which weakens only in the early morning and just before the gates close at dusk. At the tourist office, ask for the useful brochure *Historic Attractions of York,* or rent a walkman with an excellent **recorded tour** called *Yorspeed* for £4 a day. Of the bewildering array of **organized tours,** a few merit attention: the free two-hour **walking tour,** offered by the Association of Voluntary Guides, emphasizes York's architectural glories (meet in Exhibition Sq.; April-Oct. daily at 10:15am and 2:15pm; June-Aug. also at 7pm), and a fascinating **haunted walk** covers some of York's ghostlier spots (meet at King's Arms Pub, King's Staith, 8pm; £2.50, children £2; tel. 646463). Excellent *Yorspeed* self-guided tours let you linger as you choose; walkmans can be rented from the tourist office (£4). For information on the narrated open-top **Guide Friday bus tour** (£5), call 640896. In an effort to dispel the king's allegedly undeserved reputation as a humpbacked, scheming murderer, the Friends of Richard III (tel. 762492) gives a tour of **Richardian York** every Sunday at 2pm (he ruled out of York for 12 years; meet at Library Sq., Museum St., £2, children under 16 free). Consult the offbeat book *Snickelways of York* by Mark W. Jones (£4.50), an excellent guide to the city.

Everyone and everything in York converges on **York Minster,** the largest Gothic cathedral in Britain. The present structure, erected between 1220 and 1470, was preceded by the Roman fortress where Constantine the Great was hailed emperor in 306 and the Saxon church where King Edwin converted to Christianity in 627. An estimated half of all the medieval stained glass in England glitters and holds the walls together. The **Great East Window,** constructed from 1405 to 1408 and depicting the beginning and the end of the world in over a hundred small scenes, is the largest single medieval glass window on earth. Scaffolding will cover some part of the exterior until the next century (open daily 7am-8:30pm; off-season 7am-5pm; recommended donation £1.50).

It's a mere 275 steps up to the top of the **Central Tower,** from which you can stare down at the red roofs of York. The Tower is open daily from 9:30am-6:30pm, but there is only a five minute window every 30 minutes during which you may ascend (the stairs don't allow two people to pass; £2, children £1). Join one of the frequent, free **tours** for an informative overview (usually 9:30am-3:30pm), but explore the **crypt** (open Mon.-Fri. 9:30am-4:30pm, Sat. 9:15am-3:30pm, Sun. 1-3:30pm; 60p, children 30p), the **chapter house** (same hours as tower; 70p, children 30p), the **foundations** and **treasury** (same hours as tower; £1.80, children

70p), and **Minster Library** at the far corner of the grounds (open Mon.-Thurs. 9am-5pm, Fri. 9am-noon; free) at your own pace.

Nearby, **York City Art Gallery,** in Exhibition Sq. across from the tourist office, has a mixed bag of Continental work and a better selection of English painters (open Mon.-Sat. 10am-5pm, Sun. 2:30-5pm; last entry 4:30pm; free; wheelchair access). The **Yorkshire Museum,** hidden deep within the Museum Gardens, contains a variety of artifacts dug out of local soil, including a bust of Constantine the Great, Roman pottery, and ichthyosaur fossils. A thorough, detailed history of York accompanies them (open daily 10am-5pm; Nov.-Easter Mon.-Sat. 10am-5pm, Sun. 1-5pm; £3; seniors, students, and children £1.75; disabled access). In the museum gardens that slope down to the river, peacocks strut among the haunting and romantic ruins of **St. Mary's Abbey,** once the most influential Benedictine monastery in northern England. York has retained so many of its old buildings and streets that structures dating back 600 years seem run-of-the-mill. The **guildhall** in St. Helen's Sq. (tel. 613161), built in 1466 but partly destroyed by bombs in 1942, has been largely restored to its medieval state (open Mon.-Thurs. 9am-5pm, Fri. 9am-4:30pm, Sat. 10am-5pm, Sun. 2-5pm; Nov.-April closed Sat.-Sun.; 40p, children 20p).

Housed in a former debtor's prison, huge York **Castle Museum** (tel. 653611), by the river and Skeldergate Bridge, the tormented brainchild of eccentric collector Dr. Kirk, and contains everything from excavations to, quite literally, the kitchen sink. Visit **Kirkgate,** an intricately reconstructed Victorian shopping street, and the **Half Moon Court,** its Edwardian counterpart (museum open Mon.-Sat. 9:30am-5:30pm, Sun. 10am-5:30pm; Nov.-March Mon.-Sat. 9:30am-4pm, Sun. 10am-4pm; £3.95, seniors, students, and children £2.85). Across from the Castle Museum is the strange, squat silhouette of **Clifford's Tower** (tel. 646940), one of the last remaining pieces of York Castle and a reminder of the worst outbreak of anti-Semitic violence in English history. In 1190, Christian merchants tried to erase their debts to Jewish bankers by destroying York's Jewish community. On the last Sabbath before Passover, 150 Jews took refuge in a tower that previously stood on this site and, faced with the prospect of starvation or butchery, committed collective suicide (tower open daily 10am-6pm; Oct.-March daily 10am-4pm; £1.20, seniors and students 90p, children 60p).

ENTERTAINMENT

For the most current information, pick up the weekly *What's On* guide and the seasonal *Evening Entertainment* brochure from the tourist office. The free, bi-monthly *Artscene* is a good resource for arts information throughout Yorkshire.

The **Black Swan Inn** (tel. 625236), Peasholme Green, hosts folk artists on Thursday nights and live jazz and blues on Sunday nights (cover £2-4). Housed in a beautifully preserved 15th-century merchant's house, this pub is worth visiting anytime. At the **Punch Bowl,** 7 Stonegate, Saturday-night jazz, Monday-night hootenanny, Wednesday-night folk, and Thursday-night blues are all free and begin at 9pm. The drinking atmosphere is particularly jolly here (maybe it's the excellent pub food). In **King's Square** and on **Stonegate,** barbershop quartets and recorder ensembles share the pavement with jugglers, magicians, politicians, and evangelists. In addition, the Minster and local churches host a series of summer concerts. Next to the tourist office on St. Leonards, the **Theatre Royal** (tel. 623568), stages Broadway-esque productions (box office open Mon.-Sat. 10am-8pm tickets £3-12.50; student standbys 30min. before show £3-4; wheelchair access).

■ NEAR YORK

Castle Howard (tel. (0165384) 333), still inhabited by the Howard family, made its TV debut in the grandiose soap opera *Brideshead Revisited.* The famous hall is a lavish example of the English Baroque—horses of the sun tumble out of the sky on the painted ceiling. Outside, formal gardens stretch through fountains and lakes to Hawksmoor's mausoleum, warehouse for the Howard bones. The stables have recently been remodeled into a **Costume and Regalia Gallery,** the largest private collection of its kind. (Castle and galleries open mid-March to Oct. 11am-4:30pm, grounds open from 10am. Call for winter opening hours. £5.50, seniors and students £5, children £3). **Yorktour Coaches** (tel. 645151) conducts afternoon tours to Castle Howard (£6).

■■■ NORTH YORK MOORS NATIONAL PARK

Those who have sampled the English countryside and determined that *moor* is a four-letter word (along with *rain* and *peat*) may not find the paths here any less boggy or the rain any less maddening than in the Peak District or the Lake District, whatever the statistics may insist. For those in search of moody romanticism, the mists of the moors will take you directly to the 19th century; these are the very acres where the morose Mr. Rochester met Jane Eyre and Heathcliff stood on the heath screaming, howling, nay, ripping his lungs out for his lost love.

The North York Moors National Park is a kidney-shaped assortment of heather-covered moorland, rock-walled farms, and wooded dales; it includes 26 mi. of coast from above Whitby south to Scarborough, and extends westward almost to Thirsk. Topographically, the park includes the Vale of Pickering in the south, the Vales of York and Mowbray in the west, the flat Cleveland and Teeside Plains in the north, and the rugged North Sea coastline in the east.

The moors are unrelentingly bleak, except during August and September, when heather erupts with a purple flourish and the moors sprout a solid groundcover of tourists. The moors are undoubtedly at their best under a shroud of early-morning mist, haunted by the spirits that inspired the Brontë sisters, Bram Stoker, and Sir Arthur Conan Doyle. Bring your laminated copy of *Wuthering Heights,* pull up a spot of moor, and brood. Thirteenth-century flagstone paths (known as "trods" or "pannierman's tracks"), once used by monks on business trips, still thread the moors, and wayfarers still find their way by the famous stone moorland crosses. **Lilla Cross,** on Fylingdales Moor, is the oldest Christian monument in northern England—a tribute to the servant Lilla who in 626 AD used his own body to shield King Edwin from an assassin's dagger. The landscape is dotted with castles (at Helmsley, Pickering, and Scarborough) and the ruins of many medieval abbeys and hermitages. Some of the highest cliffs in England line the park's coastal border, interspersed with tiny harbors such as Staithes and Robin Hood's Bay.

The park, about 30 mi. north of the city of York, is fringed by Middlesbrough and Guisborough to the northwest, Whitby to the northeast, Scarborough to the southeast, Pickering and Helmsley to the south, and Thirsk to the southwest. While any of these towns make good bases for park exploration, coastal **Whitby,** with its innumerable B&Bs and two hostels, and **Pickering,** which lies in the south-central section at the junction of A169 and A170, prove the most hospitable.

GETTING THERE & GETTING ABOUT

No single town serves as an obvious transport hub—Malton and Pickering, near the southern edge of the park, and Middlesbrough to the north all have good connections. **Scarborough District bus** #128 connects Scarborough and Pickering about every hour. **Buses** #93, 93A, 93C, and X93 link Middlesbrough, Whitby, and Scarborough about every hour. Yorkshire Coastliner buses #840, 842, and 843 connect Malton and Scarborough to York and Leeds (1/hr.; Sun. 7/day), while buses #840, 842, and X40 run between Malton, Whitby, York, and Leeds (1/hr.; Sun. 1/day). Make sure you check the destination before boarding since the same numbers run different routes. Check *Moors Connections* for **Moorbus** schedules; they provide extensive service to most attractions on Sundays only.

British Rail's Esk Valley Line runs from Darlington to Whitby through Middlesborough, Danby, and Grosmont (4/day). A **Tees Day Ranger** allows a day's unlimited rail travel along this route (£9, children £4.50). Another line connects York and Scarborough through Malton (1/hr.; 9/day on Sun.) From Grosmont (GROW-mont), the private, steam-powered **North Yorkshire Moors Railway** chugs south through Newtondale Gorge to Pickering (May-Oct. 5/day, more in Aug.; all day ticket £7.90, children £4). Tees Bus #99 links Whitby and Grosmont from July to mid-September, timed to connect with most trains (tel. (01947) 602146; single £1.20).

The essential document for transport within the park is the *Moors Connections* pamphlet, which covers both bus and rail service in great detail (available free at information centers or for 50p from Elmtree Publications, The Elms, Exelby, Bedale, North Yorkshire DL8 2HD). A **Tees Explorer** (£4.25, seniors and children £3.25) is good for unlimited travel in the area bounded by Bishop Auckland, Darlington, Sunderland, and Whitby. Scarborough, East Yorkshire, and Primrose Valley share their own **Explorer** ticket (tel. (01751) 473530; £4.20, seniors £2.75, children £2.40).

The approach to the moors on **bicycle** is tough, but on the plateau the paths are pleasantly level. **Keldy Castle Trekking Centre** in Cropton (tel. (01751) 472982) offers short **horseback** rides from Easter to Oct.; £5/hr. The Pickering tourist office (see below) has comprehensive cycle and horse hire lists.

PRACTICAL INFORMATION

Along with the free *Moors Connections,* the *North York Moors Visitor* (40p) is as crucial as good shoes for exploring the park. Available at all information centers, it lists attractions, events, and accommodations.

National Park Information Centres

Danby: The Moors Centre, YO21 2NB (tel. (01287) 660654). Largest National Park Information Centre in the area with a similarly colossal amount of information. 20 min. by foot from the train station. Turn left out of the train station lot, then right at the cross road before the Duke of Wellington Pub. The Centre is ½ mi. ahead on the right. On Sundays, Tees buses #700 and 740 shuttle between Malton and Pickering, stopping at Danby. Open daily 10am-5pm; Nov.-Easter 11am-4pm weekends only.

Sutton Bank: Near Thirsk (tel. (01845) 597426). Open daily 10am-5pm; Nov.-March 11am-4pm weekends only.

Helmsley: Market Place (tel. (01439) 770173). Open daily 9:30am-6pm; Nov.-March Sat.-Sun 10am-4pm.

Tourist Offices

Pickering: Eastgate Car Park Y018 7DP (tel. (01751) 473791). Winner of the 1991 and 1993 Best Tourist Centre in England award. Posts accommodations list after hours. Open daily 9:30am-6pm; Nov. to mid-March Mon.-Sat. 10am-5pm.

Malton: Old Town Hall, Market Place (tel. (01653) 600048). Open Easter-Oct. daily 9:30am-5:30pm.

Scarborough: St. Nicholas Cliff (tel. (01723) 373333). Open daily 9:30am-6pm; Oct.-April daily 10am-4:30pm.

Whitby: Langborne Rd. (tel. (01947) 602674). Open daily 9:30am-6pm; Nov.-Feb. daily 10am-4:30pm.

ACCOMMODATIONS

Local tourist offices will book accommodations for a small fee or a 10% deposit. Ten **Youth Hostels** provide lodging in the moors (with a reservation):

Boggle Hole (tel. (01947) 880352). £7.75, under 18 £5.20, closed Dec.-Jan.

Helmsley (tel. (01439) 770433). £7.17, under 18 £4.75. Open July-Aug daily, Feb.-June and Nov.-Dec. Fri.-Sat., Sept.-Oct. Tues.-Sat.

Lockton (tel. (01751) 460376). £5.30, under 18 £3.50. Open April-Sept. Mon.-Sat. No meals available.

Malton (tel. (01653) 692077). £6.50, under 18 £4.35. Open March-Sept. Tues.-Sat.

Osmotherley (tel. (01609) 883575). £7.15, under 4.75. Open Nov.-Feb. Laundry with soap and change available.

Scarborough (tel. (01723) 361176). £6.50, under 18 £4.35. Open April-July Mon.-Sat., Sept.-Oct. Tues.-Sat., Feb.-March and Nov. Fri.-Sat.

Thixendale (tel. (01377) 288238). £5.30, under 18 £3.50. Open June-Sept. Weds.-Mon., Easter-May Fri.-Sat. No meals or showers.

Wheeldale (tel. (01947) 896350). £5.30, under 18 £3.50. Open July-Aug. Thurs.-Tues., April-June and Sept. Fri.-Tues. No showers.

Whitby (tel. (01947) 602878). £6.50, under 18 £4.35. Open May-Sept. daily, April-May Mon.-Sat., Nov.-Dec. and Feb.-March Fri.-Sat.

HIKING

Hiking is really the only way to travel these vast, lonely moors. Ambitious hikers might consider tackling one of the three official, or one of the many unofficial, long-distance footpaths in the park. The 93-mi. **Cleveland Way,** the 79-mi. **Wolds Way,** the famous **Lyke Wake Walk,** and the shorter and unofficial **White Rose Walk** and **Crosses Walk** each pose unique challenges and rewards.

Not all the trails are well-defined or well-marked, and many intersect cunningly. Always carry a detailed map and a compass. The Ordnance Survey *Tourist Map 2* (£4.25) covers the whole park, but may be too general for hikers; the 1:25,000 *Outdoor Leisure* sheets #26 and 27 (£5) are more precise. The amount of literature on the north moors is astounding—browse through information offices for the pamphlet or book that best suits you. See Essentials: Hiking & Camping for safety advice, but definitely also pick up the free *Moorland Safety* pamphlet, available from Helmsley, Danby, or Sutton Bank. The moors can be horribly hot or bitterly cold in the summer—sudden changes in weather make for unquiet slumbers. Check the weather forecast beforehand (tel. (01891) 500418), but be aware that it reports on all of northeast England; the weather can vary dramatically even within the park.

THE NORTHERN PARK

The walk to **Danby's** information center from the train station will refresh the cathedral-weary with ungodly beauty; woods and meadow, farms and scattered houses are chastened by windblown, heathery peaks. Several hiking trails (from 2-8 miles long) stem from the center into the Esk Valley and moors. All are clearly marked, family-oriented, and require no special equipment. *Waymark* guides (3p each) are available for a wide variety of walks with varying degrees of difficulty throughout the park. Ascend the 1400 foot **Danby Rigg** (ridge) to the top of **Danby High Moor,** or try **Castleton** or **Glaisdale Riggs** (these are also accessible from the train stations at Castleton, Glaisdale, or Lealholme).

Danby Castle, visible from the outside only and at some distance, is an early 14th-century fortress built by the house of Latimer. The castle itself is quite unspectacular, but the easy two-hour walk across the valley and back will inspire you to romp across the fields and sing "I Feel Pretty" to the attentive sheep. Farther afield, you can walk from the Little Ayton rail station (on the Esk Valley line) or from Newton-under-Roseberry (accessible by bus) to the summit of **Roseberry Topping** (not a dessert), governing over the wide expanse of the western moors.

THE SOUTHERN PARK

Pickering (pop. 7500), beyond the park's southern border, makes an ideal base for jaunts to the park and nearby coast, though the village itself is rather typical. Built in the time of William the Conqueror, **Pickering Castle** was once a vacation home for monarchs who hunted boar and deer in a nearby royal forest. Commoners can use it as a picnic ground (castle open daily 10am-6pm; Oct.-March Tues.-Sun. 10am-4pm; £1.70, seniors and students £1.30, children 85p; disabled access).

In Pickering, stay with the **Bennetts,** 4 Westgate (tel. (01751) 476776), who will assure you that their home is as much yours as it is theirs (£12.50-13.50). **Wayside Caravan Park** (tel. (01751) 472608) will let you camp in a tent for £5.70 in summer. The tourist office also has a regional **farmhouse** leaflet. Enjoy tea and inexpensive sandwiches (£1.30) in an oversized dollhouse called the **Forget-Me-Not Tea**

Room, 37 Burgate, on the road up to the castle (open daily 10am-5:30pm; Nov.-March closed Tues. and Thurs.). For good, cheap, hot meals head around the corner to **The Concorde Café,** Willowgate (tel. (017151) 47278, £1-4, open Mon., Tue., Thurs. 9:30am-5pm, Wed. 10am-3pm, Thurs. 9:30am-5pm, Sat. 9:30am-7pm, Sun. 10am-7pm, Oct.-March closed Wed.).

Ryedabike rents mountain cycles (£12.50/day, £8/day for 3 or more days; panniers and most equipment included). Call (01653) 692835 in Malton; free delivery available throughout Ryedale. Or try **S. Taylor & Son** (tel. (01751) 472143), £12/day, £40/week for a mountain bike). The **post office,** 7 Market Place (tel. (01751) 72256), wields a big letter stamper (open Mon.-Fri. 9am-5:30pm, Sat. 9am-1pm). Pickering's **postal code** is YO1 87AA.

From **Helmsley,** 10 mi. directly west of Pickering, roads and footpaths lead to the magnificent ruins of the **Rievaulx** (REE-vo) **Abbey,** 3 mi. northwest of Helmsley. Founded in the 12th century by monks from Burgundy, the abbey was once one of the finest and largest Cisterian abbeys in England. Rievaulx's daughterhouses (spin-offs) include the once-great Melrose Abbey in southern Scotland. An incredible valley setting and well-trimmed lawn circling the ruins give Rievaulx the aura of Narnia, post-White Witch (open daily 10am-6pm; Oct.-March 10am-4pm; £2.20, seniors and students £1.65, children £1.10; wheelchair access). Recently opened **Duncombe Park** (tel. (01439) 771115), 1 mi. from Helmsley center, features an 18th-century estate with a Baroque mansion and 100 acres of beautifully landscaped gardens and forests, most of which were recently incorporated as a National Nature Reserve (open July-Aug. daily, May-June and Sept. Sun.-Thurs., April and Oct. Wed. and Sun. all 11am-4:30pm; admission to house and grounds £4.40, seniors and students £3.75, children £2; grounds only £2.75, children £1.50).

From the Newtondale or Levisham stations on the scenic North Yorkshire Moors Railway, explore the **Newtondale Gorge,** lined with ferns and pine forests, or stroll through the lush **Newtondale Forest.** Gorge-gazers can lodge at the **HI Youth Hostel,** near Levisham in **Lockton** at the Old School. From Pickering take York City District buses #840 and 842 (tel. (01904) 624161). Three mi. southwest of the Moors Railway stop at **Goathland** (past **Mallyan Spout,** a beautiful waterfall) is the secluded **Wheeldale Youth Hostel (HI)** (tel. (01947) 896530).

WHITBY

Whitby (pop. 13,588; we told you we update every year) offers more than commercial sandy-beach-resort tourism, though fish-and-chip establishments and tacky gift shops abound. Auspicious alignment renders Whitby one of two English towns where, during the two weeks surrounding summer solstice, the sun both rises and sets over the sea.

In summer, the skeletal remains of **Whitby Abbey,** the inspiration for Bram Stoker's *Dracula,* is an ideal spot for sungazing or seaviewing. After dark, large blackbirds roost in its arched windows. Dracula arrived on a boat one stormy night from Transylvania; no one saw him leave (abbey open daily 10am-6pm; Oct.-March daily 10am-4pm; £1.50, seniors and students £1.10, brave children 75p). Beware of local vampiric come-ons. A short walk carries you to lighthouses and the scenic **Captain Cook's Monument** at the edge of West Cliff on the bank, Johnny Walker's 300-year-old house, now the **Captain Cook Memorial Museum,** Grape Lane (tel. 601900), contains an outstanding collection of ship models, letters, and drawings by artists who traveled on Cook's voyages (open April-Oct. daily 9:45am-5pm, last entry 4:30pm; March and Nov. Sat.-Sun. 11am-3pm; £1.50, seniors and children £1). Whitby hosts a **folk week** the week before the August bank holiday, with 200 hours of dance, concerts, and workshops. Contact Malcolm Storey, 26 Marine Ave., North Ferriby, East Yorkshire HU14 3DR (tel. (01482) 634742) for more information.

The hilltop **YHA Youth Hostel** (tel. 602878) occupies the old stable block, hence the 12th-century triangular ceilings and wooded beams. The town, harbor, and Abbey views compensate easily for the steps. (Open late May-Aug. daily; April-late May and Sept.-Oct. Mon.-Sat.; mid-Feb to March Fri.-Sun.; Nov.-early Dec. and early Feb. Fri.-Sat.) Moor-bound school groups often fill the place until mid-July, so call ahead. Or head for its cozier independent competition, **Harbour Grange,** Spital Bridge, ½ mi. inland on the eastern bank (tel. 600817; no lockout; curfew 11:30pm, 26 beds, kitchen facilities; £6.50; sheets £1.40, open all year). Enjoy riverside splendor, fewer screeching schoolchildren, and views of the 199 steps you didn't have to climb. There are two campsites about four mi. south on the A171 in High Hawkser, with toilets, shower, laundry facilities, and a shop (both open April-Oct.) **Northcliffe Caravan Park** (tel. 880477) charges £5.50-8/night, one free night if you reserve at least a week in advance); **York House Caravan Park** (tel. 880354) charges £5.50 a night. Camping on the Abbey Plain is not permitted; the fierce winds would tip over your tent anyway. Hudson St. and Normanby Terrace, back-to-back streets, and neighboring blocks brim with £13-15 beds; most **B&B** proprietors post rates outside. Whitby always runs out of beds in August—call ahead throughout the summer. Pick up basic victuals at **Peter's,** 1 Mulgrave Pl. off Skinner St. (open daily 6:30am-8:30pm). **Monks Haven** (tel. 604608), a tea house on 148 Church St. near the abbey steps, offers sandwiches (£1.25-2) and significant takeaway discounts (open May-June and Sept. 10am-5pm; July-Aug. 10:30am-6pm). Whitby's **tourist office,** Langborne Rd., has free accommodations and more park and local information than you could ever use (tel. 602674, open daily 9:30am-6pm, Oct.-April 10am-4:30pm). The **telephone code** in Whitby is 01947.

■■■ DURHAM CITY

The presence of England's greatest Norman cathedral lets Durham add "city" to its name, but "university town" or "overgrown village" might be more appropriate. From their strategic cliff-top location on a hairpin bend of the River Wear, the cathedral and adjacent University of Durham rule this small and gracious city. Windy, medieval streets, inconspicuous alleyways, walking bridges, and restricted vehicle-access make Durham a foot-friendly and lively town, even when students give way to tourists in the summer months.

GETTING THERE

Durham lies 20 mi. south of Newcastle on the A167 and an equal distance north of Darlington. **Trains** from Newcastle stop frequently at the main railway station, on a steep hill just north of town, en route to York and London. Trains run to London's King's Cross (roughly 1/hr.; 3hr.; £55, return £56-67, APEX return £37), York (roughly 2/hr.; 1hr.; £15, return £17-23), and Newcastle (at least 2/hr.; 15-30min.; £2, day return £3.50). A real bargain, the **Tyne Valley Day Ranger** ticket offers one day's unlimited train travel across northern England, from Durham and Sunderland in the northeast to Carlisle and Whitehaven in the northwest (£13, children £6.50).

A large number of **bus** companies serve local routes, stopping at the station on North Rd. **National Express** goes regularly to London (4/day; 5hr.; £17.50-25, return £25). **Northern** and **United** run a frequent, joint service from the Durham bus station to Worswick St. station in Newcastle (every 10-20min.; 50min.; £1.93, day return £3.35).

ORIENTATION & PRACTICAL INFORMATION

The **River Wear** surrounds Durham City, and plentiful footbridges connect this semi-isle to the mainland. The **bus station** (tel. 384 3323) squats on North Rd. in a slightly seedy area to the west of the castle. (National Express and United information office open Mon.-Fri. 9am-5pm, Sat. 9am-4pm.) The **rail station** (tel. 232 6262) also lies west of town; to reach the **tourist office** at Market Place (tel. 384 3720), descend the hill on Station Approach and take the steps down to Castle Chare, following the signs for the city center. Take Millburngate to the right at the roundabout, then left at Silver St., which crosses the Wear on Framwellgate Bridge and leads up the hill to Market Place (tourist office open Mon.-Sat. 9:30am-6:30pm, Sun. 2-5pm; June and Sept. Mon.-Fri. 10am-5:30pm, Sat. 9:30am-5:30pm; Oct.-May Mon.-

Fri. 10am-5pm, Sat. 9:30am-1pm.) The **post office** (tel. 386 4644) can be found at 33 Silver St. (open Mon.-Fri. 9am-5:30pm, Sat. 9am-12:30pm). Durham's **postal code** is DH1 3RE, and its **telephone code** is 0191, the same as Newcastle. **Dave Heron Cycles,** 6 Neville St. (tel. 384 0287), rents road and mountain bikes for £15 per two days or £30-45/week, and panniers for £1 per day. He asks a deposit of £40, and has a 10% discount for *Let's Go* readers (open Mon.-Tues. and Thurs.-Sat. 9am-5:30pm).

ACCOMMODATIONS & CAMPING

A great boon for travelers is the large supply of inexpensive dormitory rooms (breakfast included) that ring the cathedral, available from July to September and during school vacations. The **HI Youth Hostel** located at Durham Sixth Form Centre, The Sands, Providence Row (tel. 384 2217) performs Durham's version of musical beds; check the tourist office for the hostel's current location. (£6.30, under 18 £4.20. Open late July-Aug.) **University College,** Durham Castle (tel. 374 3863), provides bed and breakfast at far less than a king's ransom (£17.50). Dorms include a castle with display cases of historic weapons, statues, and a massive dining hall. On a quiet cobbled street behind Durham Cathedral, **St. John's College,** 3 South Baily (tel. 374 3566), offers B&B for £15.50. Vie for a room in the spacious theology students' section or in riverside Cruddas House. **St. Chad's College,** 18 N. Bailey (tel. 374 3370), is blessed with front room views of the cathedral, and rear window ones of the garden and river. (Singles and doubles £11.70, non-students £15, add £3.50 for rooms with bathroom, ages 5-12 half-price. Limited disabled access with prior arrangement.) The camping is good at the **Grange,** Meadow Lane, Carrville (tel. 384 4778), on the A690 off the A1, 2½ mi. away. (£5/tent and 2 people; arrive by 8pm.)

FOOD

Bakeries with £1 sandwiches and pizzerias peddling £3 pies occupy prime Durham real estate near places of interest. For local specialties, try Lindisfarne mead, still made on Holy Island to the north. Most bakeries in town sell stottycakes, flat brown loaves for jumbo sandwiches. Fruits and vegetables fill the stands of the weekend **market** near the tourist office (open Thurs.-Sat.). University students congregate at **Vennel's** quiet, hidden courtyard to discuss Rimbaud or rowing over fresh items such as a brie and walnut sandwich off a blackboard menu (£2-4; open daily 9am-5pm; entrance next to Waterstone's bookstore). The bright, airy **Almshouses Café,** Palace Green, near cathedral and castle, serves light, elegant meals. (Lunch served noon-2:30pm; open daily 9am-8pm; Oct.-May 9am-5:30pm.) **Rajpooth,** 80 Claypath, cooks up *tandoori* specials. (10% student discount Mon.-Thurs. Open Mon.-Sat. noon-2pm and 6pm-midnight, Sun. 6pm-midnight.)

SIGHTS

Durham's tourist attractions are sparse but spellbinding. Built in 1093, **Durham Cathedral** is the greatest Norman cathedral in England. Described by Sir Walter Scott as "half church of God, half castle 'gainst the Scot," the cathedral has withstood the siege both of northern warriors and time itself since it was founded by monks from Holy Island in 875 (open Mon.-Sat. 7:15am-8pm, Sun. 8am-8pm, closes at 6pm from Oct.-April; free). A pamphlet on the layout, history, and architecture of the cathedral (30p) is invaluable. Behind the choir is the **tomb of Saint Cuthbert,** for whom the cathedral was erected. His body remained pristine for 400 years after his death. At the other end of the church lies the **tomb of the Venerable Bede,** author of *Ecclesiastical History of the English People.* Note the strip of black marble that separates the Bede's tomb and the eastern from the main part of the church; women had to stay behind this strip during the period that the church was used as a monastery. The spectacular view from the top of the **Tower** merits the 325 steps it takes to get there (open same hours as cathedral in summer; £1, child 50p). The **Monk's Dormitory,** off of the cloister, is an enormous hall with an impressively timbered roof that houses a grab-bag of elaborately carved stones and stone crosses (open Mon.-Sat. 10am-4pm, Sun. 12:30-3:30pm and 4:30-6pm, 50p, children under

14 20p). Further along the cloister, the **Treasury** houses precious religious metal-ware, manuscripts, and robes (open Mon.-Sat. 10am-4:30pm, Sun. 2-4:30pm; £1, child 80p, seniors 20p). Next to the treasury, the **Refectory** offers bread, water, and delicious cakes and hot drinks for £1-2 (open Mon.-Sat. 10am-5pm, Sun. 11am-5pm, lunch served daily noon-2pm). All of the cathedral is open to the public, but you must write in advance to receive a guided tour (£2). Across the palace green is **Durham Castle.** Once a key defensive fortress against Scotland, it has become in these quieter times a residence for students at the University of Durham. (Tours daily 10am-noon and 2-4pm; Oct.-June Mon., Wed., and Sat. 2-4pm; £1.50, children £1). Below the cathedral on the riverbank, decipher the inscriptions on carved Roman stones in the **Museum of Archaeology** with the Latin you've spent years cultivating. the second floor houses changing exhibits on local topics (open daily 11am-4pm, Nov.-March 12:30-3pm; 80p, seniors and students 40p, children 20p).

ENTERTAINMENT

After-hours entertainment in Durham is inextricably intertwined with the university; when students depart, most nightlife follows suit. A young crowd fills the popular **Brewer and Firkin,** Saddler St., where a pub upstairs and a dance club downstairs accommodate ale-takers and limb-shakers alike. The trendy, riverside, and gosh-darn enormous **Coach and Eight,** Framwelgate Bridge, has music on Friday and Saturday nights (open Mon.-Sat. 11am-11pm, Sun. noon-3pm and 7-10:30pm). **Traveller's Rest,** Claypath St., attracts locals with its wide selection of beer and real ale. For a cheap evening under the stars, £2 buys an hour in a **rowboat** from **Brown's Boathouse Centers,** Elvet Bridge (tel. 386 3779, £1 children). Wind around the horseshoe curve of the River Wear, dodging scullers and ducks.

Durham holds a **folk festival** during the first weekend in August, with singing, clog dancing, mimes, and musicians from all over the country—all free. Get a leaflet at the tourist office. This is the only time when you can camp free along the river (Fri.-Sun.), so pitch your tent early. (Weekend festival tickets £12; call Jean Longstaff at 384 4445 for more information.) Other major events include the **Durham Regatta** in the middle of June, and a massive, sodden **beer festival** (the second biggest in the country) during September's first weekend.

■■■ NEWCASTLE UPON TYNE

Hardworking Newcastle (pop. 296,000) wants attention, billing itself as a city of firsts. Beyond such constructive contributions to civilization as the hydraulic crane and the steam locomotive, this gritty industrial capital also brought us the world's first beauty contest and dog show. Not to mention Sting, the first human to invoke Vladimir Nabokov in a pop song. Newcastle lacks the splendor of York and Durham to the south, and with their oft-incomprehensible nasal accents Newcastle Geordies are the butt of many jokes. But it's a mistake to dismiss this strangely grand city. Down a few and dance till dawn before staggering onto a coach for Edinburgh.

GETTING THERE

Newcastle is the last English stronghold before crossing the Scottish border. It lies 1½ hours north of York on the A19 and about 1½ hours east of Carlisle on the A69. Edinburgh is a straight run up the coast along the A1, or through pastures and mountains via the A68.

Trains leave Newcastle's **Central Station** for York (2/hr.; 1hr.; £17.50), London's King's Cross (1/hr.; 3hr.; £60), Edinburgh (Mon.-Sat. 22/day, Sun. 17/day; 1½hr.; £25), and Carlisle (Mon.-Sat. 15/day, Sun. 8/day; 1½hr.; £7.10). Several train passes sweep the area around Newcastle: the **Northeast Flexi Rover** offers four days of travel out of eight consecutive days for £44. The **North Country Flexi Rover** does the same for the region north of Bradford and south of Hexham. For more restricted but cheaper wanderings, try the **Tees Day Ranger** (£9), good for one day of unlimited travel Monday through Friday after 9am or all day on Saturday or Sunday.

Most **buses** depart **Gallowgate Coach Station. National Express** runs to London (7/day; 5-6hr.; £17.50) and Edinburgh (3/day; 3hr.; £6). **Northeast** also sends buses to London from Gallowgate (2-4/day; 5½hr.; £17). From the Haymarket Station, the local **Northumbrian Line** goes to Berwick-upon-Tweed (#501, 505, 515, 525; Mon.-Sat., roughly 1/hr., Sun. 4/day; 2½hr.; £3.40).

Ferries to the Continent set afloat from **Tyne Commission Quay.** Bus #327 serves all departures, leaving Central Station 2½ hrs. and 1¼ hrs. before each sailing. For complete listings, see Essentials: Getting There—From Continental Europe.

ORIENTATION & PRACTICAL INFORMATION

The tourist office's free, full-color map of Newcastle is essential; streets switch direction and name every few blocks. When in doubt, remember that the waterfront is at the bottom of every hill. The center of town is **Grey's Monument,** a filthy, 80-ft. stone pillar dedicated to Charles, Earl of Grey, who nudged the steep 1832 Reform Bill through Parliament and who mixed glorious bergamot into Britain's bleak tea.

Tourist Office: Central Library, off New Bridge St. (tel. 261 0691). Open Mon. and Thurs. 9:30am-8pm, Tues., Wed., and Fri. 9:30am-5pm, Sat. 9am-5pm. Also try the office at **Central Station** (tel. 230 0030). Open Mon.-Sat. 10am-8pm, Sun. 10am-5pm; Oct.-May Mon.-Sat. 10am-5pm. **Tours: City tours** leave Mon.-Sat. from the Central Library (July-Sept. 2pm; £1.50).

Travel Office: Union Society Travel Bureau, Newcastle University Student Union Bldg., Kings Walk (tel. 232 1798). Open Mon. and Wed.-Thurs. 9:30am-5pm, Tues. 10am-5pm, Fri. 9:30am-4:30pm; non-school term, closes 4:30pm.

Financial Services: Barclays, Grainger St. (tel. 261 7676), at Market St. Open Mon.-Tues. and Thurs.-Fri. 9:30am-5pm, Wed. 10am-5pm, Sat. 9:30am-noon. **Thomas Cook,** 6 Northumberland St. (tel. 261 2163) at New Bridge St. W. Open Mon.-Wed. and Sat. 9am-5:30pm, Thurs. 9am-7pm, Fri. 10am-5:30pm.

Post Office: 33 Mosley St. (tel. 232 2134). Open Mon.-Fri. 9am-5:30pm, Sat. 9am-12:30pm. **Postal Code:** NE1 AA.

Telephone Code: 0191.

Trains: Central Station, Neville St. (tel. 232 6262; 24hr.). Travel Center open Mon.-Fri. 5:30am-8pm, Sat. 5:30am-7pm, Sun. 6am-8pm. **Lockers** £1-3.

Buses: National Express (tel. 232 4211 or 261 6077) and **Northeast** (tel. 232 3377 or toll-free (0800) 591568) operate from **Gallowgate Coach Station,** off Percy St. **Northumbria** (tel. 232 4211) runs from the bus stand at **Haymarket Bus Station** beside the Metro Stop.

Ferries: Ferries leave from **Tyne Commission Quay;** take bus #327, taxi (£8), or Metro to Percy Main (£1) and walk 20 min. to the quay.

Bike Rental: Newcastle Cycle Centre, 165 Westgate (tel. 222 1695). Rents bikes for £10/day, £35/week, £50 deposit. Open Mon.-Fri. 9am-5:30pm, Sat. 9am-5pm.

Hotlines: Samaritans (crisis): tel. 232 7272. **Rape Crisis Centre:** tel. 232 9858. **Gay and Lesbian Line: Friend to Newcastle:** tel. 261 8555.

Hospital: Royal Victorian Infirmary, Queen Victoria Rd. (tel. 232 5131).

Emergency: Dial 999; no coins required.

Police: Market St. at Pilgrim St. (tel. 232 3451).

ACCOMMODATIONS

Many costlier lodgings neighbor the Youth Hostel and YMCA in **Jesmond,** just northeast of town via a 35p Metro ride (3 min.). Slightly less expensive alternatives are scattered along bus routes, many a few blocks to the north of Jesmond on Osborne Rd. If you can't get into the youth hostels or YMCA, you'll have to pay at least £15, more for singles, so call in advance to secure a room.

HI Youth Hostel, 107 Jesmond Rd. (tel. 281 2570). From Jesmond Metro station, turn left, then left again onto Jesmond Rd., and walk past the traffic lights—it's on the left. Funky old townhouse attracts global backpackers. Kitchen a bit archaic but manageable; carob granola bars at desk (45p). Breakfast and packed lunch available. Curfew 11pm, lockout 10am-5pm. £6.50, under 18 £4.55. Breakfast

£2.60, evening meal £3.90. Sheets free. Overrun by ferry traffic, so call several days in advance. Open March-Oct. daily; Feb. and Nov. Wed.-Sun.

YMCA, Jesmond House, on Clayton Rd. (tel. 281 1233). Turn left just beyond the youth hostel onto Akenside Terr., then take the second left onto Clayton; it's on the right, behind lovely gardens. Affable and immaculate, with evening meal available. Men and women. B&B £15.50; £80.80/week includes evening meal. Night key deposit £5. Call days ahead.

Newcastle University, Leazes Terrace Student Houses, 10 Leazes Terr. (tel. 222 8150). Convenient to center; just steps from St. James Metro stop and two blocks north of Gallowgate Bus Station. Commonplace dorms within converted townhouses that retain their grandeur despite the departure of the bourgeoisie. £14.85 for B&B, £11 for room only; students £31.50/week.

FOOD

Every other restaurant offers inexpensive pasta and pizza, and those in between serve *tandoori* specialties popular with the late night crowd, enchiladas, veggie burgers, and peanut butter casserole. Chinese eateries line Stowell St. near Gallowgate. **Health Fayre,** opposite Haymarket Station, sells wholefood groceries, little pots of hummus (50p), and take-away sandwiches (open Mon.-Fri. 8am-5pm, Sat. 8am-3pm). For just about everything else, head for the **Cloth Market/Bigg Market** area, northwest of the cathedral. **Don Vito's,** 82 Pilgrim St. (tel. 232 8923) gives amazing value for amazing food. Generous pastas and pizzas with glorious toppings and inventive sauces cost only £2.20 with delicious bread. Try the *gnocchi* (open Mon.-Fri. noon-2pm and 5-10pm, Sat. 5-11pm). Expect cheap food and a dreary interior at the **Super Natural Vegetarian Restaurant,** Princess Sq, which offers entrees for £1.90-2.95 (10% student discount on main courses; open Mon.-Sat. 10am-8pm).

SIGHTS

Newcastle wears its monuments and towers particularly well. Between Central Station and the architectural masterpiece that is **Tyne Bridge** lingers the **Castle Keep,** remaining from the New Castle built in 1080 by Robert Curthose, bastard son of William the Conqueror. (Museums open Tues.-Sun. 9:30am-5:30pm; Oct.-March daily 9:30am-4:30pm; £1; seniors, students, and children 30p). **Grey's Monument** is the steepest tower and can be climbed every Saturday for a view of the city (40p). The most elegant tower in Newcastle crowns the **cathedral** on Nicholas St. This set of small towers around a double arch, called "The Lantern," is meant to resemble Jesus's crown of thorns (cathedral open Sun.-Fri. 7am-6pm, Sat. 8am-4pm; free).

The Side Gallery, 5 The Side (tel. 232 2208), features one smallish room of first-rate photographs. Exhibits rotate every six weeks, and often feature such notables as Graciela Iturbide, Robert Doisneau, and Martin Chambi. Enter it through the eclectic Newcastle Bookshop (gallery open Mon.-Sat. 10am-5pm, Sun. 11am-3pm.). One of the city's newest attractions, **Newcastle Discovery,** Blanford House, Blanford Sq. (tel. 232 6789), set to open in early 1995, houses a science museum, exhibits on local history, and galleries for fashion and costume and photography, all in one massive complex (open Mon.-Sat. 10am-5pm; free).

ENTERTAINMENT

Newcastle has a thriving club and theater scene. Unfortunately, hostelers with an 11pm curfew will enjoy little of it. Pubbing starts early, peaking at midnight when revelers tumble downhill from the closing pubs of Bigg Market to the Quayside club scene. Most pubs offer happy hours between 4 and 8pm (Sundays 7-8pm). Revel in postmodern decor at **Yel!** at 3 Cloth Market off Bigg Market (no sneakers on weekends), but don't tap a foot or undulate to the music's infectious beat—Newcastle pubs don't hold dance licenses, and restrictions are enforced by the police, if you can believe it. **Redhouse** and its neighbor **Offshore 44** both pack a youngish crowd into nautically-themed, multi-level bars on Sandhill, Quayside. **The Village,** a pub, and **Powerhouse,** a wild nightclub, share the corner of Waterloo St. and Sunderland

St. (tel. 261 8874) and cater to lesbian and gay crowds. The latest underground bands from both sides of the Atlantic surface at **Riverside,** 57-59 Melbourne St. (tel. 261 4386). On Fridays, flocks of trendies shimmy to industrial; Thursdays feature charty pop (open 8pm-1am; cover £2.50, £1.50 before 9:30pm). Ravers won't want to miss the "Soulful Funky" vibes on Fridays and Saturdays at the recently opened **Global Village,** Park Terrace, Whitley Bay.

If you fancy entertainment of a lazier variety, treat yourself to some Shakespeare or Tchaikovsky at the lush red velvet and gold **Theatre Royal**, 100 Grey St. (tel. 232 2061; box office open Mon.-Sat. 10am-8pm; tickets from £5, discounts for seniors, students, and children for some performances—call for details).

■■■ NORTHUMBERLAND

Forever battered by the sea, and until recent times by the Scots, Northumberland endures on the English frontier. It feels ancient (maybe it's all the ruins), war-torn (must be the forts), rugged (probably the hilly, boggy landscapes), and stoic (the weather). The 1030-sq.-km **Northumberland National Park** stretches south from the grassy Cheviot Hills near the Scottish border through the Simonside Hills to the dolomitic crags of the Whin Sill, where it digests part of Hadrian's Wall. When Romans ruled, this line marked the northern limit of the empire; later, the Anglo-Saxon kingdom of Northumberland extended over the valleys and woodlands from above the river Humber to southern Scotland.

East of the park, in the northernmost corner of England, the coast yields to rocky cliffs, gusty winds, and frigid water—an awe-inspiring combination. High above the water the land bears Roman, Norman, and non-imperial ruins. As North as it gets, around Berwick and the Holy Islands, car- and train-loads from Newcastle revel in rugged coastlines and squawking gulls, crashing at a salty rest stop before the next day's one-hour journey to Edinburgh.

GETTING THERE & GETTING ABOUT

If you don't own a car or bicycle, staying overnight in Berwick-upon-Tweed with its mainline train service is your best bet. From there, buses depart to most coastal hotspots. A punctilious planner can depart Newcastle in the morning with an Explorer ticket, see two or three coastal sights, and lodge that night in Berwick—though a more relaxed agenda allows for extended sea-gazing. The essential *Northumberland Public Transport Guide* (£1.30) is available at any tourist office or bus station or by sending £1.75 to "Public Transport Officer, County Hall, Morpeth NE61 2EF." Those who eschew this transport bible risk being stranded in a village populated by two pricey B&Bs, a barber shop, 15 mountain goats, and a border collie named Bill.

British Rail runs from Newcastle to Berwick (15/day, Sat. 17/day, Sun. 12/day; 1hr.; £8.20); Edinburgh is a half-hour farther north (Mon.-Sat. 22/day, Sun. 17/day; £25). Considerably less comfortable but half the price is the #505 **bus** from Newcastle to Berwick via Alnwick (1/hr.; 2hr.; single £3.40). Bus #X18 runs from Newcastle's Haymarket Station to Warkworth (1/hr.; 1¼hrs.; approx. £3), terminating inland at Alnwick. From there, bus #501 leaves every two hours for Craster, continuing up the coast to Dunstanburgh Castle, Seahouses, and Bamburgh Castle. Smart travelers will invest in a Northeast **Explorer** ticket (£4), which allows unlimited use of most local bus services for one day.

As **buses** run more frequently up the coast than between national park towns and villages, Newcastle, Alnwick, and Berwick make the best bases for park exploration. On the park's border, Rothbury (southwest of Alnwick) and Wooler (northwest of it) enjoy the most frequent connections, halfway between "slightly accessible" and "left for dead" on Ye Olde Access Meter. Postbuses creep like snails leaving a slime of junk mail on somewhat erratic schedules; contact the post office to find connections for a ride on one of those red Royal Mail trucks that drive through snow or rain or rain or rain. You may find it easier to stick with the **Northumbria** line. Bus #464

NORTHUMBERLAND

connects Wooler and Berwick (3-4/day); buses #470 and 473 connect Wooler to Alnwick (10/day), where buses for Newcastle can be caught. Service #516 runs from Newcastle to Morpeth and Rothbury (Mon.-Sat. 7-9/day, Sun. 3/day).

NATIONAL PARK ACCOMMODATIONS & SIGHTS

The northernmost section of the Pennine Way penetrates the park beginning at **Greenhead,** a meek village on Hadrian's Wall 25 mi. east of Carlisle and 40 mi. west of Newcastle, and ending in Scotland. The path winds 7 mi. east to **Once Brewed,** home of the **Once Brewed Youth Hostel (HI),** Military Rd., Bardon Mill, Hexham NE47 7AN (tel. (01434) 344360). The hostel is situated ½ mi. from the Wall, 9 mi. from Vindolanda, and 3 mi. from Househeads Fort (£7.75, under 18 £5.20; wheelchair accessible; open April-Oct. daily, Nov.-Dec. and Feb. Tues.-Sat., March Mon.-Sat.) From there, the path continues 14 mi. northeast to **Bellingham** (BELL-in-jum), due west of Morpeth. In town rests the **Bellingham Youth Hostel (HI),** Woodburn Rd., Bellingham, Hexham, NE48 2ED (tel. (01434) 220313; no smoking, no meals; £5.90, under 18 £3.95; open mid-July-Aug. daily, March-mid July and Sept.-Oct. Mon.-Sat.). The Bellingham **tourist office** in the Fountain Cottage on Main St. (tel. (01434) 220616) details nearby walks, including a 1-mi. stroll through a woodland ravine to the **Hareshaw Linn Waterfall** (office open Mon.-Sat. 10am-1pm and 2-6pm, Sun. 1-5pm; Nov.-March Tues.-Sat. 2-5pm). After your stroll, return to the Fountain Cottage to enjoy a scrumptious snack at the **Tea Rooms,** adjacent to the tourist office (open Mon.-Sat. 10am-5pm; Sun. 10:30am-5pm).

From Bellingham, bus #814 runs west to **Kielder** (Mon.-Fri. 2-7/day, Sat. 2/day; 30 min.), located on the northern tip of **Kielder Water,** the largest man-made lake in Europe. Built in 1775 by the Earl Percy, Duke of Northumberland, **Kielder Castle** now houses the Kielder Forest Visitor Centre which brandishes the park's flora and fauna (tel. (01434) 250209; open Aug. 10am-6pm; Sept.-July 10am-5pm). The **tourist office** at Tower Knowe (tel. (01434) 240398), near the village of Falstone, on the lake's southeastern shore, acquaints travelers with the lay of the lake (open March-Oct. daily 10am-6pm). **Kelder Water Cruises** (tel. (01434) 240436) depart from five docks along the lake (mid-March to Oct. 11am-5:45pm; £3.30, seniors £2.75, children £2.20). The **Leaplish Waterside Park** (tel. (01434) 250203), located centrally on Kielder's southern shore, offers a wide range of water sports, including sailing, canoeing, and windsurfing. Don't forget your insulated wetsuit. Bus #814 stops at Falstone, Tower Knowe, and Leaplish.

High hills to the east and dense forests to the west accompany the 15-mi. Pennine stretch from Bellingham northwest to **Byrness,** home to an **HI Youth Hostel** (tel. (01830) 520519) and its god-given drying room (£5.90, under 18 £3.95; open mid-July-Aug. daily, April-mid-July and Sept. Wed.-Mon.). Bus #915 runs between Bellingham and Byrness (Mon.-Fri. 2/day; 45 min.). The homestretch of the Pennine Way, unserved by hostels, runs an uneven, boggy 27 mi. through the Cheviots from Byrness to **Kirk Yetholm** in Scotland. The **Border Hotel** (tel. (01573) 426237) marks the official end of the Pennine Way and offers a free half-pint to anyone who has completed the Way and is carrying Wainwright's *Pennine Way Companion.*

At the northern boundary of the park, **Wooler,** miles from the Pennine Way and decent bus service, can serve as a base for less strenuous day trips into the **Cheviots,** especially around the Glendale and Kyloe areas. Barring possession of a cycle or car, serious hikers should grab a taxi to the trailheads at Dunsdale, Mounthooly, and Hethpool, each over 8 mi. away. Contact Peter Park's **taxi** and **minibus** service (tel. (01668) 81246; open all year; £4-5). A wonder-warden runs the revamped **Wooler hostel (HI),** 30 Cheviot St., Wooler NE71 6LW (tel. (01668) 81365), with full wheelchair access, enviable bathrooms, and comfortable dormitories 300 yd. uphill from the bus station on 30 Cheviot St. (£7.15, under 18 £4.75; open mid-July-Aug. daily, April-mid-July and Sept.-Oct. Mon.-Sat., March and Nov. Fri.-Sat.). Camp at **Highburn House** in Wooler (tel. (01668) 81344; £5-7.50). The breadbox of a **tourist office** can be found in the bus station (tel. (01668) 281602) and details uphill climbs in the

Cheviots and gentler, low-level walks through the Happy and College Valleys. (Open daily Easter-Oct. 10am-1pm and 2-6pm).

The nearest **National Park Visitor Centre** (tel. (01665) 78248) is 7 mi. south of Wooler in **Ingram** (open mid-March to Sept. daily 10am-6pm). **Gold Leaf Travel bus** #940 runs a circular route between Wooler and Ingram twice daily on school days at 7:30am and 3:35pm (bring ear plugs). During summer vacation, take bus #473 to Wooperton (Mon.-Fri. 10/day, Sat. 5/day) and hike the 4 mi. to Ingram.

Twenty-five mi. farther south of Wooler off the A697 on the B6341, the village of **Rothbury** sits in a narrow, densely wooded valley carved by the River Coquet halfway to Bellingham. Another **National Park Visitor Centre,** networked with a tourist office, on Church St. (tel. (01669) 20887), describes beautiful walks on either bank of the river, posts the weather, and directs adventurers to rock-climbing locales (open daily April-Aug. 10am-6pm and Sept. 10am-5pm).

COASTAL ACCOMMODATIONS & SIGHTS

Twenty mi. north of Newcastle, the evocative ruins of **Warkworth Castle** (tel. (01665) 711423) guard the mouth of the River Coquet. Best viewed from the river, the magnificent 15th-century keep, foundation rubble, and largely intact curtain wall come to life in an excellent, self-guided walkman tour (£1.50, children 75p; open daily 10am-6pm, Nov.-March 10am-4pm; £1.80, seniors and students £1.35, under 16 90p). Shakespeare set much of *Henry IV Part I* here; the enchanting 14th-century hermitage carved out of the Coquet cliffs is the reputed site of Harry Hotspur's baptism. The staff at the castle will row you across to the hermitage on selected days from April to September; call ahead for exact dates and times (£1, seniors and students 75p, children 50p). On summer afternoons, you can rent **rowboats** below the castle, although visitors aren't allowed to dock at the Hermitage (tel. (01665) 711416); follow the narrow path by the side of the castle (£1.50/person/hr., children 75p; last boat 5:30pm).

About 7 mi. northwest of Warkworth off the A1 trunk road is the tiny town of **Alnwick** (AN-ick) and the magnificently preserved **Alnwick Castle** (tel. 510777), another former Percy family stronghold. This rugged Norman fortification gives way to an ornate Italian Renaissance interior, Titians and Van Dycks, and numerous likenesses of the Duke and Duchess of Northumberland. Over the years an eccentric line of duchesses have swamped the castle with items such as Cromwell's nightcap and sash, a scrap of the bedsheet in which he died, King Charles II's nightcap, and, egad! yet another cap made entirely of hair plucked from Mary, Queen of Scots (open Easter-Oct. daily 11am-5pm, last entry 4:30pm; £4, seniors £3.50, children £2.20). Near the castle, at 8 Bondgate Without, friendly **Mrs. Givens** and her affectionate mutt offer B&B in their 300-year-old house (tel. 604473; £12.50 if you mention *Let's Go*). Alnwick's **tourist office,** The Shambles market place (tel. 510665), rests at the town's vortex (open Mon.-Sat. 9am-6:30pm, Sun. 9am-5pm; Sept.-Oct. and March-June Mon.-Fri. 9am-5pm and Sat.-Sun. 10am-5pm; Nov.-Feb. Mon.-Sat. 9am-5pm). Across from the **bus station office** (tel. 602182; open Mon.-Fri. 9am-5pm and Sat. 9am-4pm) is a **launderette,** 5 Clayport St. (tel. 604398; open Mon.-Fri. 8am-7pm, Sat.-Sun. 9am-5pm; bring change). Alnwick's **telephone code** is 01665.

Just off the coast—halfway between Bamburgh Castle and Berwick-upon-Tweed—lies romantically lonely and wind-swept **Holy Island.** The missionary Aidan came here from the Scottish town of Iona to found England's first Christian monastery, **Lindisfarne Priory** (tel. (01289) 89200), seven years after Northumberland's King Edwin converted (open daily 10am-6pm; Nov.-March 10am-4pm daily; £2.20, seniors and students £1.65, children £1.10). Check tide tables at any tourist office before embarking. You can traverse the 2¾-mi. causeway only at low tide; otherwise you'll have to swim. Bus #477 runs from Berwick to Holy Island via Beal (Feb.-Aug. schedules vary from day to day). Just south of the Scottish border is **Berwick-upon-Tweed** (BARE-ick), which has nationalized and denationalized more often than just about any town in Britain: 14 times between 1100 and 1500 alone. Most of its once-prominent castle is buried beneath the present railway station, although the

13th-century Breakneck Stairs still absorb sun rays. To get a feel for Berwick's turbulent history as a border town, walk along the **Elizabethan Walls**, which encircle the Old Town; the astounding view of Berwick and the River Tweed from **Meg's Mount** is even better now that the arrows have stopped flying. **Berwick's tourist office** (tel. (01289) 330773), next to the Castlegate car park, houses literature on *everything*, near or far.

■■■ CARLISLE

By dint of some foolish boundary-setting, Carlisle became and remains Britain's largest city, spreading out over 398 sq. mi. Nicknamed "The Key of England," Carlisle unlocks the history of this frontier culture and serves as the main base from which to climb Hadrian's Wall. Once there, **Cumberland** (tel. (01946) 63222) offers bus excursions to the Lake District, Northumberland, and Scotland (£5-5.50).

Everything to see in Carlisle is trapped inside the remains of the **city walls,** built in the 12th century to enclose the Roman town of Luguvallium. The **Castle,** built in 1092 by William II using stones from Hadrian's Wall, stands at the heart of the city. Tickets (tel. 591922; £2, seniors and students £1.50, children £1) include access to a museum of regimental history and an exhibition of over 900 years of Carlisle's history. Free tours start at 11am and 2pm daily in July and August and on selected days during the rest of the year (open daily 10am-6pm, Nov.-March 10am-4pm.)

The **Tullie House Museum and Art Gallery,** Castle St. (tel. 34781), has lots of things to poke, listen to, and play with; don't miss the crawl-though mine exhibit or quotes from Romans who tended Hadrian's Wall, such as "Another son... joined the Army—centurion bait, his brains half-cudgelled out whenever he leaned on his spade." To the left of the tourist office, the **Guildhall Museum** is a 14th-century building that houses a farrago of queer things from looms to rare chests to musical instruments. The 20-minute self-guided walkman tour is free with admission and recaptures the feel of the old guildhall and life in Carlisle (open April-Sept. Tues.-Sat. 11am-4pm, Sun. noon-4pm; 50p, seniors, students, and children 25p).

Carlisle's **cathedral** was built in 1122 by Henry I. Though more of a large church than a cathedral, the stained glass is magnificent and the ceiling over the nave is beautifully painted with gold stars and sun in a blue sky. The **treasury** (free) caches a small, well-chosen set of religious items from carved walrus tusks to an intricate Indian communion set (cathedral and treasury open Mon.-Sat. 7:45am-6:15pm, Sun. 7:45am-5pm). The park just outside is a quiet spot for a rest or picnic.

If you've had enough of air-conditioned archaeology, consider touring some of Cumbria's less traveled areas via the circular **Cumbria Cycle Way.** The 259-mi. route runs from Carlisle in the north around the outskirts of the Lake District. Pick up the pamphlet (£1.50) from the tourist office, which includes a map, information on hostels, trains, and buses, as well as addresses of bike shops in each town along the road. The closest **bike** rental to Carlisle dwells 12 mi. away at a lake called Talkin Tarn. Clearly there is an entrepreneurial opportunity here.

Carlisle welcomes travelers at its many B&Bs, most within ½ mi. or so of the tourist office. **Cornerways Guest House,** 107 Warwick Rd. (tel. 21733) sports a graceful, skylit staircase and three floors of comfortable rooms (B&B £12.50, key deposit £5). Large, centrally located **Park View,** 38 Aglionby St. (tel. 33599), offers pleasant one-to-four bed rooms (£12.50/person). Within the Carlisle Antique Centre on Cecil St., an indoor re-creation of a Tudor neighborhood complete with housefronts and streetlamps, you'll find **Penny Farthing** (tel. 21970); enjoy basic teahouse fare at reduced costs in a miniaturized story-book setting (open Mon.-Sat. 9am-4pm).

You can leave your backpack at the museum-like **tourist office** in the Old Town Hall, Green Market (tel. 512444), for only 30p and join one of the office's guided **walkabouts** (1½hr.; May-Sept. daily 1:30pm; £1.50, children 50p; office open June and July 9:30am-6pm daily, Aug. 9:30am-6:30pm, Sept.-May Mon.-Sat. 9:30am-5:30pm). To get there from the train station, turn left on English St. and walk through town; from the **bus station** at the corner of Lowther and Lonsdale St.

(National Express and local bookings; open Mon.-Fri. 8:45am-5pm, Sat. 8:45am-4:15pm), cross Lowther St. and walk through the shopping center, then look right. Carlisle's **train station** (tel. 44711) lies near the southern end of English St. (ticket office open Mon.-Sat. 5:30am-midnight, Sun. 9:30am-midnight). Trains depart for Newcastle (1/hr., Sun. 8/day; 1½hr.; £7.10), Leeds (8/day, Sun. 3/day; 2¾hr.; £14), Settle (8/day, Sun. 4/day; 1½hr.; £10.50), and Glasgow (about 1/hr., Sun. 10/day; 2½hr.; £10.50). Stash your pack in a locker on the platform (£1-2). **Cumberland bus** #555 (Mon.-Sat. 4/day; 1¼hr.; £3.25) and bus X5 (4/day, Sat. 3/day, Sun. 1/day) drive to Keswick in the Lake District. Carlisle's **telephone code** is 01228.

■■■ HADRIAN'S WALL

> *Over the heather the wet wind blows, I've lice in my tunic and a cold in*
> *my nose. The rain comes pattering out of the sky, I'm a Wall soldier, I*
> *don't know why.*
>
> —W.H. Auden, *"Roman Wall Blues"*

When Roman Emperor Hadrian visited Britain in 122 AD, he quickly decided that any barbarians who painted themselves blue and fought as fiercely as the Picts were too much trouble to rule. So he found the narrowest part of Britain and built a wall across it—first a 27-ft.-wide V-shaped ditch, then a stone barrier 15 ft. high and eight-to-nine ft. across, wide enough for a chariot. Seventeen forts (milecastles), 34 turrets (watchtowers), 5500 cavalrymen, and 13,000 infantrymen later, Hadrian could rest easier. The wall originally stretched unbroken from coast to coast; today's ruins are visible as far west as Lanercost and nearly to Newcastle in the east. The highest concentration of visible remains scatter along the southern edge of the Northumberland National Park.

GETTING THERE & GETTING ABOUT

Bus and trains stations all lie 1½ to 4 mi. from the wall, so be prepared to hike to the nearest stones. From Carlisle, Sunderland-bound **trains** (Mon.-Sat. 9/day, Sun. 3/day) stop at spots close to the major attractions: Brampton (access to Lanercost 2 mi. and Birdoswald 5 mi.; 20 min.; £1.70) and Bardon Mill (access to Vindolanda 2 mi. and Housesteads 3 mi.; 40 min.; £3.30). Trains depart more frequently for Haltwhistle (access to Cawfields 2 mi.; Mon.-Sat. 17/day, Sun. 8/day; 35 min.; £2.90). **CMS bus** #685 runs from Carlisle's bus station to Brompton, Haltwhistle, and Bardon Mill (16/day, Sun. 4/day). Bus #682 runs much closer to the wall, stopping at Brampton, Lanercost, Birdoswald, the Roman Army Museum, Once Brewed, Vindolanda and Hartwhistle, but runs only twice a day in each direction.

ACCOMMODATIONS & SIGHTS

Use **Carlisle** as a base when exploring Hadrian's Wall; it runs circles around the next best alternative, Hexham. The easiest, most informative, and least creative approach to wall sight-seeing is to join a 3-hr. guided **bus tour** that leaves the Carlisle tourist office at 1pm (June-Sept. on Mon., Thurs., and Sat., Aug. Mon., Tues., Thurs., Sat.; £7, under 14 £4; includes entry into Birdoswald Fort). Foregoing a bus tour will add adventure, if it doesn't save money; a self-guided tour of the Wall can turn costly, since many of the more important museums and forts charge admission fees of £2-3.

Two **HI Youth Hostels** lie close to the wall. **Greenhead Youth Hostel (HI)**, Carlisle, Cumbria CA6 7HG (tel. (016977) 47401), sits in a converted chapel 16 mi. east of Carlisle and a mi. Hadrian Wall's 12-mi. "high point." (Lockout 10am-5pm, evening meal available; £6.50, under 18 £4.35; open July-Aug. daily; April-June Mon.-Sat.; mid-Feb.-March and Sept.-mid-Nov. Thurs.-Mon.) **Once Brewed Youth Hostel (HI)**, Military Rd., Bardon Mill, Hexham NE47 7AN (tel. (01434) 344360), only ½ mi. from the Wall and 1 mi. from Vindolanda, rents binoculars (check-in after 1pm; £7.75, under 18 £5.20; open April-Oct. daily; March Mon.-Sat.; Feb. and Nov.-Dec. Tues.-Sat.). Once Brewed is 2½ mi. northwest of Bardon Mill's train station.

The main part of the surviving wall stretches for 7 mi. along the Pennine Way from Once Brewed to the excellent **Roman Army Museum** (tel. (016977) 47485) at **Carvoan,** just ½ mi. north of the Greenhead hostel. (Open daily July-Aug. 10am-6:30pm; May-June 10am-6pm; April and Sept. 10am-5:30pm; March and Oct. 10am-5pm; Feb and Nov. Sat. and Sun. 10am-4pm. £3, seniors and students £2.25, children £1.75.) Several well-preserved milecastles and bridges lie between Greenhead and the **Birdoswald Roman Fort,** 4 mi. to the west (open April-Oct.).

From Bardon Mill, take the 1½-mi. footpath to **Vindolanda,** a fort and civilian settlement whose timber foundations predate the wall. Extensive excavations have revealed hundreds of written wooden tablets that give insight into Roman life. Examples include "I have sent you socks and two pairs of underpants" and "June 24th AD 100: Wine 15 litres, Celtic beer 25 litres; Fish sauce ½ litre; Pork fat 8 litres." Tickets (£3, seniors and students £2.25, children £1.75) include admission to the museum on the grounds. Supersaver tickets (£4.50, seniors and students £3.60, children £2.75) are good for one admission each at Vindolanda and the Roman Army Museum. (Vindolanda open daily July-Aug. 10am-6:30pm, May-June 10am-6pm, April and Sept. 10am-5:30pm, March and Oct. 10am-5pm, Nov.-Feb. 10am-4pm. The museum is only open March-Oct.)

■■■ LAKE DISTRICT NATIONAL PARK

Although rugged hills make up much of England's rural landscape, only in the northwest corner do sparkling waterholes fill the spaces in between. In the Lake District, mortarless cottages, livestock, literary legacy, and even tourists fade in the reflections of jagged peaks, windswept fells, and primeval forests. The major lakes diverge like spokes of a wheel from the hub town of **Grasmere,** south of Keswick and north of Ambleside on the A591. **Lake Derwentwater,** by Keswick, is perhaps the most beautiful of the lakes; halfway between Grasmere and the coast, **Wastwater** bewitches travelers with its wildness; **Lake Windermere** reigns spectacular despite man's best attempts to bludgeon it with condos and marinas. Grasmere and the remote town of **Borrowdale** rank with the Peak District's Vale of Edale at the top of the awe seismograph.

Windermere, Ambleside, Grasmere, and Keswick all make convenient bases for exploring the Lake District. To enjoy the best of the region, though, ascend into the hills and wander through the smaller towns, especially those in the more remote northern and western areas; the farther west you go from the busy bus route serving the towns along the A591, the more countryside you'll have to yourself. In summer, hikers, bikers, and boaters are almost as many as sheep and cattle. The ratio is particularly disastrous in July and August, when an exhaustive cloud of tour buses spew their contents onto the lakeshores.

GETTING THERE

The best way to reach the Lake District is to take public transport straight to Windermere and Keswick and then make your way to removed pockets of the park; you can also cross the park's edge at Oxenholme or Penrith and connect from there.

British Rail trains run to London's Euston station (7/day, 5/day on Sun.; 4hr.; £43) and Manchester (11/day, 5/day on Sun.; 3hr.; £14.50), and via Oxenholme (rail station tel. (01539) 720397) to Edinburgh (10/day, 5/day on Sun.; 3hr.; £23.80). Twice daily, **National Express** buses leave the Lake District from Keswick via Windermere and strike out for Manchester (3hr.; £14), Birmingham (5½hr.; £23), and London (eight long hours—bring a book; £30.50). Get info on National Express buses from the Windermere tourist office (tel. (015394) 46499). **Stagecoach Cumberland** bus #555 runs from Keswick to Carlisle (4/day; 1½hr.; £3.75); bus #X9 runs to York (1/day on Wed., Fri. and Sat. only; 4hr.; £12). The **Slow Coach** stops here on its circuit of England (consult Essentials: Getting About—Buses & Coaches for details). Two

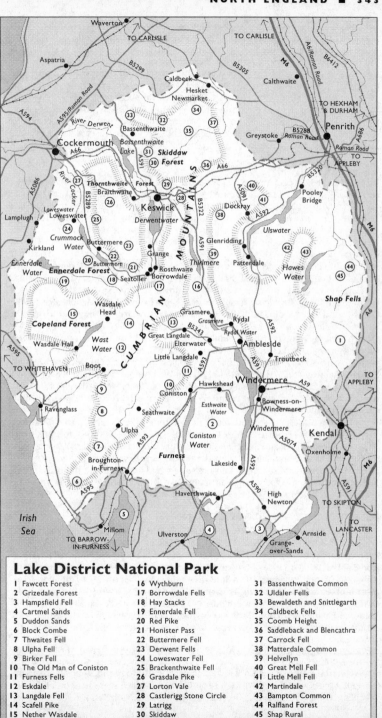

Lake District National Park

1 Fawcett Forest	16 Wythburn	31 Bassenthwaite Common
2 Grizedale Forest	17 Borrowdale Fells	32 Uldaler Fells
3 Hampsfield Fell	18 Hay Stacks	33 Bewaldeth and Snittlegarth
4 Cartmel Sands	19 Ennerdale Fell	34 Caldbeck Fells
5 Duddon Sands	20 Red Pike	35 Coomb Height
6 Block Combe	21 Honister Pass	36 Saddleback and Blencathra
7 Thwaites Fell	22 Buttermere Fell	37 Carrock Fell
8 Ulpha Fell	23 Derwent Fells	38 Matterdale Common
9 Birker Fell	24 Loweswater Fell	39 Helvellyn
10 The Old Man of Coniston	25 Brackenthwaite Fell	40 Great Mell Fell
11 Furness Fells	26 Grasdale Pike	41 Little Mell Fell
12 Eskdale	27 Lorton Vale	42 Martindale
13 Langdale Fell	28 Castlerigg Stone Circle	43 Bampton Common
14 Scafell Pike	29 Latrigg	44 Ralfland Forest
15 Nether Wasdale	30 Skiddaw	45 Shap Rural

rail lines flank the park: the **Preston-Lancaster-Carlisle line** (trains connect with Leeds at Lancaster) runs from south to north along the eastern edge of the park, while the **Barrow-Carlisle line** serves the western coast. If your first destination is the remote western or southern area, hiking from one of the stations along the Barrow-Carlisle line might be your best bet. Otherwise, catch the Preston-Carlisle line to either Oxenholme or Penrith. From **Oxenholme,** a short branch line covers the 10 mi. to Windermere (1/hr.; 20min.). Stagecoach Cumberland supplies regular service from Windermere to the north on #555 (Mon.-Fri. 11/day, Sat. 9/day, Sun. 5/day; 15min. to Ambleside, 30min. to Grasmere, 1hr. to Keswick). If you decide to disembark at **Penrith,** just south of Carlisle, bus #X5 runs westward to Keswick; Mon.-Fri. 6/day, Sat. 4/day, Sun. 2/day; 1½hr.; £2.45).

GETTING ABOUT

Bus, rail, and lake steamer transport serve the park. **Stagecoach Cumberland buses** serve Hawkshead, Coniston, and Newby Bridge, and connect Keswick with Penrith, Carlisle, Seatoller, Whitehaven, Buttermere, and Cockermouth. The free *Explore Lakeland by Bus* presents a list of timetables, available at tourist offices. An **Explorer** ticket (£5, seniors and children £3.75) gives one-day travel on all CMS buses and discounted admission to a few sights; £13 (seniors and children £9) buys the same deal for four consecutive days. If you want one-day travel on coastal rail services and lake steamboats, a **Cumbrian Coast and Lakes Day Ranger** costs £8, seniors and children £4. **British Rail** serves the rugged western coast with its Carlisle-Barrow route and offers a **North West Rover** ticket (£43), good for a week's unlimited travel in the coastal region bounded approximately by Manchester, Leeds, Carlisle, and Liverpool. The **Lakeside and Haverthwaite Railway** (tel. (015395) 31594) can take you through the scenic River Leven Valley by steam locomotive (March-Sept. 6-7/day; return £3, children £1.80). The 15-minute trip runs between Lakeside, a town on the southwest shore of Lake Windermere that connects by ferry with Bowness Pier, and Haverthwaite via Newby Bridge. The **Ravenglass and Eskdale Railway** (tel. (01229) 717171) is England's oldest and narrowest (15 in.) narrow-gauge railway, affectionately known as "t'laal Ratty" (6-15/day, Nov. to early April Mon.-Fri. 1-2/day; 40min.; return £5.60, children £2.80). Ravenglass meets British Rail's Barrow-Carlisle line.

For those who wish to explore the park with minimal effort, **Mountain Goat** (tel. (015394) 45161) organizes a series of friendly, if bizarre, minibus and bus tours (such as "Wordsworth and Beatrix Potter Country" and "Goat and Boat") which cost £4.50-19.50 for full and half-day tours. **Lakes Supertours,** 1 High St., Windermere, offers similar half- and full-day minibus tours for £11-19, including the daily "Afternoon Eight Lakes Spectacular." Book at any Lake District tourist office or by calling (0151394) 42751 or (01534) 88133 (open 8am-9pm).

PRACTICAL INFORMATION

Many information centers, B&Bs, and nearly all campgrounds close for the winter. For an introduction to the Lake District, including exhibits, talks, films, and special events, visit the beautifully landscaped grounds and house of the **National Park Visitor Centre** (tel. (015394) 46601) in **Brockhole,** halfway between Windermere and Ambleside (open July-Aug. 10am-8pm; Easter-June and Sept.-Oct. 10am-5pm; free). Most Ribble or CMS buses will drop you off at the site. The free newspaper, *Lake District Guardian,* includes a calendar of guided walks and events. The following **National Park Information Centres** provide expert information on the Lakes, sell a camping guide (95p), and book accommodations. North to south, the Centres are:

Pooley Bridge: the Square CA10 2NP (tel. (017684) 86530). Open April-Oct. daily 10am-5pm.
Keswick: 31 Lake Rd. CA12 5DQ. Open daily 9:30am-5:30pm, Nov.-March 10am-4pm. Free 3½hr. guided walks Wed. and Sun. at 2pm.

Ullswater: Main Car Park, Glenridding, Penrith CA11 0PA (tel. (017684) 82414). Open April-Oct. daily 9:30am-5pm, Nov.-Christmas 9:30am-5pm Fri.-Sun.

Seatoller Barn: Borrowdale CA12 5XN at the foot of Honister Pass (tel. (017687) 77294). Open April-Sept. daily 10am-5pm.

Grasmere: Red Bank Rd. LA22 9SW (tel. (015394) 35245). Open April-Sept. 10:30am-5:30pm.

Ambleside (Waterhead): tel. (015394) 32729. Open March-Nov. 9:30am-5:30pm. Free warden-guided walks every Mon. at 10:30am. Write to National Park Information, Waterhead, Ambleside, Cumbria LA22 0EN.

Hawkshead: Main Car Park LA22 0NT (tel. (015394) 36525). Open Easter-July daily 9:30am-5:30pm and Aug.-Sept. 9:30am-6pm.

Coniston: 16 Yewdale Rd. LA12 8DU (tel. (015394) 41533). Open daily March-Oct. 10am-5pm. Hopes to move in April 1995 to Tilberthwaite Ave. in the car park.

Bowness Bay: Glebe Rd. LA23 3HJ (tel. (015394) 42895). Open July-Sept. 9:30am-7:30pm, April-June 9:30am-5:30pm.

BIKING, CLIMBING, & HIKING

Hilly terrain comes with the territory in the Lake District; psych yourself up for a challenge if you decide to bike. A selection from Ambleside, Keswick, and Windermere is mentioned below, but any local tourist office will print complete listings:

Ambleside Mountain Biker, Scotts Café, Waterhead, by the lake and hostel (tel. (015394) 32014). £12.50/day, £10/day for YHA members, about £60/week, deposit ID. Open for hiring 9-11am; return cycle by 5pm. Call ahead.

Trackers Cycle Hire, 66 Main St. in Keswick (tel. (017687) 71372). High-quality cycles, professional staff. King of the mountain bike shops. £14/day (includes rucksack, helmet, lock, route map), £8/½day. Guided tours daily at 10am (free sauna and steam bath at the end of day; tours £7.50). Open daily 9am-5pm.

Keswick Motor Co., Lake Rd. in Keswick (tel. (017687) 72064). £11/day, £6/4hr.; deposit £20. Open Mon.-Fri. 8:30am-5:30pm, Sat. until 5pm, Sun. by appt.

Windermere Cycles, corner of Lake Rd. and S. Terrace in Bowness (tel. (015394) 44479). Panniers £1.50/week. Mountain bikes £11/day, £55/week, deposit £20. Open daily 9am-5:30pm.

Lakeland Leisure, in front of the rail station in Windermere (tel. (015394) 44786). 21-speed mountain bikes £13/day, £11/day in winter, £70/week, deposit £20. Guided tours on Sun. £10. Packed lunch £2.75. 10% YHA discount. Open daily 9am-5pm.

Coniston Mountain Bikes, 14 Yewdale Rd. in Coniston (tel. (015394) 41212). 21-speeds £12.75/day, £9/½day, deposit £20. Open Easter-Sept. daily 9am-5pm.

Grizedal Mountain Bikes (tel. (01229) 860369), in Hawkshead. £12.50/day, £8/½day, deposit £20. Open March-Oct. daily 9:30am-5pm.

The Lake District is both a climber's fondest dream and worst nightmare, presenting superb rock faces and treacherous, loose shale. Every town has climbing stores, such as **John Gaynor Sports,** near Barclays in Ambleside (tel. (015394) 33305; open Mon.-Sat. 9am-6pm, Sun. 10am-5pm), and **Stuart's Sports,** 32 Lake Rd. between North and South Terraces in Bowness (tel. (015394) 43001; open daily 9am-9pm; Sept.-mid-July 9am-5:30pm). Any such store can describe the best climbs, advise on the necessary precautions, and give current weather reports. A few establishments also rent boots and backpacks. In Keswick, try **Keswick Mountain Sports,** 73 Main St. (tel. (017687) 73843; boots, baby papooses, and knee-gouging ice axes £5/week, no deposit; backpacks £3/week, deposit £10; open daily 9am-5:30pm). In Ambleside, **The Climber's Shop,** on the corner of Rydal Rd. and Compston Rd. (tel. (015394) 32297), rents boots (£1.50/day or £7/week; deposit £20). (Open daily 9am-5:30pm). If you plan to take a long or difficult hike, check with the Park Service, call for weather information (tel. (015394) 45151; 24hr.), and leave a plan of your route with your B&B proprietor or hostel warden before you set out.

ACCOMMODATIONS & CAMPING

Although B&Bs line every street in every town (£13-15) and the Lakes have the highest concentration of HI youth hostels in the world, lodgings in the Lake District do fill in July and August; book as far ahead as possible; most places hold beds until 6pm. Campers should pick up the National Park Authority's guide (95p), which includes listings of **camping barns** (£3-5). The following lists **HI Youth Hostels.** Lockouts are from 10am-5pm except for Derwentwater, Grasmere (Butterlip How), Hawkshead, and Windermere, which open at 1pm, and Ambleside and Patterdale, which open all day. Evening meals are available everywhere except Skiddaw House.

Ambleside: Waterhead, Ambleside, Cumbria LA22 0EU (tel. (015394) 32304), 1 mi. south of Ambleside on Windermere Rd. (the A591), 3 mi. north of Windermere on the Lake's shores. Impersonal attention, and no wonder; they have 240 beds. A distinctive country club feel—you can even swim off the pier. Windermere bus #555 stops in front. Wash (drying room included) 50p. £8.40, under 18 £5.60. Open April-Aug. daily; Sept.-mid-Dec. and mid-Feb.-March Thurs.-Tues.

Arnside: Oakfield Lodge, Redhills Rd., Arnside, Carnforth, Lancashire LA5 0AT (tel. (01524) 761781). This 72-bed hostel lies 1 mi. south of this coastal town on the region's southern tip. £7.75, under 18 £5.20. Open daily April-Sept.; Oct. and mid-Feb.-March Mon.-Sat.

Black Sail: Black Sail Hut, Ennerdale, Cleator, Cumbria CA23 3AY (no phone). Between Grasmere and the coast, but otherwise in the middle of nowhere. Warden is a charming mountaineer who serves plenty of coffee, tea, and simple meals. CMS #79 runs from Keswick to Seatoller and the hostel is another 3½-mi. walk from there. No smoking, car access, or showers. 18 beds. £5.90, under 18 £4. Open mid-April-Oct. Tues.-Sun.

Buttermere: King George VI Memorial Hostel, Buttermere, Cockermouth, Cumbria CA13 9XA (tel. (017687) 70245). Overlooking Lake Buttermere, ¼ mi. south of the village on the B5289. 17 beds. £7.75, under 18 £5.20. Open mid-March-mid-Sept. daily; Jan.-mid-March Wed.-Sat.

Carrock Fell: High Row Cottage, Haltcliffe, Hesket Newmarket, Wigton, Cumbria CA7 8JT (tel. (016974) 78325). Between Caldbeck and Mosedale in the northern area of the District. Good views of the Carrock Fell. 18 beds. £6.50, under 18 £4.35. Open July-Aug. Tues.-Sun; Sept.-Oct. and mid-March-June Wed.-Sun.

Cockermouth: Double Mills, Cockermouth, Cumbria CA13 0DS (tel. (01900) 822561), in the town center. Converted 17th-century water mill with 28 beds. £6.50, under 18 £4.35. Open July-Aug. Thurs.-Tues.; Sept.-Oct. and mid-March-June Thurs.-Mon.

Coniston (Holly How): Far End, Coniston, Cumbria LA21 8DD (tel. (015394) 41323), ¼ mi. north of Coniston village on the Ambleside Rd. Good cooking, including hearty vegetarian options. 70 beds. £7.15, under 18 £4.75. Open mid-March-mid-Sept. daily; mid-Sept.-Oct. and Jan.-mid-March Mon.-Sat.

Coniston Coppermines: Coppermines House, Cumbria LA21 8HP (tel. (015394) 41261), 1 mi. west of the village overlooking the water. No need to venture into the hills; the rugged, uphill, streamside journey to the mines is itself a scenic challenge. 31 beds. £6.50, under 18 £4.35. Open July-Aug. Thurs.-Tues.; late March-June and Sept.-early Nov. Fri.-Tues.

Derwentwater: Barrow House, Borrowdale, Keswick, Cumbria CA12 5UR (tel. (017687) 77246). Two mi. south of Keswick on the B5289. Take the Borrowdale bus (CMS #79) to Seatoller (1/hr.). It's worth the inconvenience to stay in this 200-year-old house with a splendid view of Derwentwater, extensive grounds and trails, home-cooked meals, and its own 108-ft. waterfall. YHA activity center. Opens at 1pm. 95 beds. £8.70, under 18 £5.80. Open daily mid-Feb.-mid-Sept.; mid.-Sept.-early Nov. Mon.-Sat.; Jan.-mid-Feb. Thurs.-Tues.

Elterwater: Ambleside, Cumbria LA22 9HX (tel. (015394) 37245), 1 mi. west of High Close. Near lots o' falls. CMS bus #516 from Ambleside passes less than 1 mi. from the 46-bed hostel. £7.50, under 18 £4.75. Open daily mid-March-mid-Sept.; mid-Sept.-Oct. Tues.-Sun.; Nov.-Dec. and mid-Feb.-mid-March Fri.-Sat.

Ennerdale: Cat Crag, Ennerdale, Cleator, Cumbria CA23 3AX (tel. (01946) 861237). Tough to get to. 1 ¼ mi. west of Ennerdale water. Nearest bus drops 7 mi. away at Kirkland (bus #17 from Whitehaven) or at Seatoller (#79 from Keswick). From May-Oct., buses from Keswick come within 3 mi. (for information call (01946) 63222). 24 beds. £6.50, under 18 £5.20. Open July-Aug. Fri.-Wed.; mid-March-June and Sept.-Oct. Fri.-Tues.

Eskdale: Boot, Holmrook, Cumbria CA19 1TH (tel. (019467) 23219). In a quiet valley 1½ mi. east of Boot on the Ravenglass/Eskdale railway. Pool and ping-pong tables. 54 beds. £7.75, under 18 £5.20. Open early April and July-Aug. daily; late April-May Mon.-Sat.; mid-Feb.-March and Sept.-mid-Dec. Tues.-Sat.

Grasmere: Butterlip How, Grasmere, Ambleside, Cumbria LA22 9QG (tel. (015394) 35316). Victorian house with flowering gardens north of Grasmere village; follow road to Eastdale for 150 yd., then turn right down sign-posted drive. 96 beds. Reception opens at 1pm. £7.75, under 18 £5.20. Open daily mid-March-mid-Sept.; mid-Sept.-early Nov. and Jan.-mid-March Tues.-Sun.

Grasmere: Thorney How, Ambleside, Cumbria LA22 9QW (tel. (015394) 35591). A converted farmhouse with 46 beds; follow Easedale road, turn right at the fork, then turn left. £7.75, under 18 £5.20. Open daily mid-March-mid-Sept.; mid-Sept.-Oct. Wed.-Sun.; Nov.-mid-Dec. Wed.-Sat.; mid-Feb.-mid-March Fri.-Sat.

Hawkshead: Esthwaite Lodge, Ambleside, Cumbria LA22 0QD (tel. (015394) 36293). Overlooking the lake (Esthwaite), this was the home of novelist Francis Brett Young; books from his library make for good bedtime reading. Near hiking and cycling trails. Bus #505 from Ambleside drops off at Hawkshead, 1 mi. north. 117 beds. Reception opens at 1pm. £8.70, under 18 £5.80. Open daily mid-March-early Nov.; Nov.-mid-Dec. and mid-Feb.-mid-March Tues.-Sat.

Helvellyn: Greenside, Glenridding, Penrith, Cumbria CA11 0QR (tel. (017684) 82269). Stands 900 ft. up and a mere 1½ mi. from Glenridding village, 3 mi. from Ullswater Lake. Buses from Keswick and Windermere will stop at Glenridding. 64 beds. £7.15, under 18 £4.75. Open daily Easter week and July-mid-Aug.; April-June Mon.-Sat.; mid-Aug.-Oct. and early March Wed.-Sun.; Jan-mid.March Fri.-Sat.

High Close: Langdale, Loughrigg, Ambleside, Cumbria LA22 9HJ (tel. (015394) 37313). Lies 4 mi. north of Loughrigg and semi-accessible by bus #516 from Ambleside; go ¾ mi. south of Elterwater, and the hostel is another ¾ mi. to the west. Comfortable and seldom full. Pool table, ping-pong. 91 beds. £7.75, under 18 £5.20. Open daily mid-March-mid-Sept.; mid-Sept. and Feb.-mid-March Mon.-Sat.; mid-Jan.-mid-Feb. Fri.-Sat.

Honister Hause: Seatoller, Keswick, Cumbria CA12 5XN (tel. (017687) 77267). At the summit of **Honister Pass,** an easy trek from Keswick, 9 mi. north. Bus #79 from Keswick to Seatoller gets you within 1½ mi. of hostel. 30 beds. £6.50, under 18 £4.35. Open July-Aug. Fri.-Wed.; late March-June and Sept.-early Nov. Fri.-Tues.

Kendal: 118 Highgate, Cumbria LA9 4HE (tel. (01539) 724906). Right in town, convenient to both the bus and train stations. £7.75, under 18 £5.20. Open daily mid-March-mid-Sept., mid-Sept.-Dec. and Jan.-mid-March Thurs.-Tues.

Keswick: Station Rd., Keswick, Cumbria CA12 5LH (tel. (017687) 72484). From tourist office, bear left down Station Rd.; find YHA sign on left. Former hotel has balconies over river, spanking new rooms, lenient staff, and decent kitchen. Opens 1pm. Curfew 11:30pm. 91 beds. £8.70, under 18 £5.80. Open daily mid-March-Oct. and late Dec.; Nov.-mid-Dec. and mid-Feb.-mid-March Wed.-Sun.

Longthwaite: Borrowdale, Keswick, Cumbria CA12 5XE (tel. (017687) 77257). On the River Derwent's shores. The village of Rothswaite is a mi. north. Bus #79 from Keswick drops you nearby. 94 beds. £7.15, under 18 £4.75. Open daily mid-March-Oct. and late Dec.; Nov.-mid-Dec. and mid-Feb.-mid-March Wed.-Sun.

Patterdale: Goldrill House, Patterdale, Penrith, Cumbria CA11 0NW (tel. (017684) 82394). Only 1 mi. south of Ullswater and just off the A592, ¼ mi. south of the village. No lockout. 82 beds. £8.70, under 18 £5.80. Open daily mid-March-mid-Sept.; mid-Sept.-Oct. Fri.-Wed.; mid-Feb.-mid-March and early Dec. Fri.-Tues.

Skiddaw House: Bassenthwaite, Keswick, Cumbria CA12 4QX (for information, call Carrock Fell hostel at (016974) 78325). A pair of shepherd's cottages 1550 ft. above sea level. Basic and isolated. No one loony enough to trek this far will be turned away. No access by car (4½ mi. from Threlkeld and 5 mi. from Bassenthwaite on foot). £5.30, under 18 £3.50. Open daily mid-March-Oct.

Tebay: The Old School, Penrith, Cumbria CA10 3TP (tel. (015396) 24286). No kitchen, but they've got a dryer. In Tebay village on the A685. 46 beds. £7.15, under 18 £4.75. Open mid-Feb.-Nov. Fri.-Wed.

Thirlmere: The Old School, Stanah Cross, Keswick, Cumbria CA12 4TQ (tel. (017687) 73224). This 33-bed hostel, 5 mi. south of Keswick off the A591, is about as simple as they come (no showers). No smoking. £5.30, under 18 £3.50. Open mid-June-Sept. Tues.-Sun.; Easter-mid-June and Oct.-mid-Nov. Wed.-Sun.

Wastwater: Wasdale Hall, Wasdale, Seascale, Cumbria CA20 1ET (tel. (019467) 26222). Right on the water in quality climbing territory. Bus #12 from White-haven to Seascale stops 5 mi. away in Gosforth. 50 beds. £7.75, under 18 £5.20. Open daily mid-March-mid-Sept.; mid-Sept.-early Nov. and mid-Jan.-mid-March Thurs.-Mon.

Windermere: High Cross, Bridge Lane, Troutbeck, Windermere, Cumbria CA23 1LA (tel. (015394) 43543). One mi. north of Windermere off the A591. Spacious house with lovely grounds and panoramic views, but few showers. Ambleside bus stops in Troutbeck Bridge; walk remaining ¾ mi. to hostel. 80 beds. Reception opens at 1pm. £7.15, under 18 £4.75. Open daily mid-March-mid-Sept.; mid-Sept.-early Nov. and Jan.-mid-March Wed.-Mon.

WINDERMERE & BOWNESS

Windermere and Bowness (pop.8500) fill to the gills with vacationers in July and August when water-skiers swarm the water. Pleasant enough to visit, the towns' real popularity stems from their proximity to spectacular Lake Windermere and their **rail station** (call Oxenholme for information; tel. (01524) 32333). Store your pack for £1.50 at the British Rail counter (Mon.-Sat. 7am-5pm, Sun. 10:45am-5pm). To reach Bowness and its famous pier, turn left from Windermere's station onto High St., then right on Main St. and walk through downtown to New Rd., which becomes Lake Rd. and leads you pierwards after a 1½-mi. downhill walk. You can also catch the **CMS Lakeland Experience** bus to Bowness from the rail station (5/hr.; 75p).

The nearest **HI Youth Hostel** is in **Troutbeck,** 2 mi. north of Windermere (see Lake District: Accommodations and Camping, above). Both Windermere and Bowness are chock-full of B&Bs, all convenient to train and town. Nevertheless, those who neglect to book ahead risk bedding down in a cold, lonely field amidst cow pies and wool tufts. **Brendan Chase,** 1-3 College Rd. (tel. 45638), is made up of two converted Victorian townhouses with airy, attractive rooms, antique furnishings, and a dedicated, lively proprietress (£10-13/person). Mention *Let's Go* at the **Old Bakery,** High St. (tel. 42512) and get £1 off your room with breakfast in bed (£11-12/person). Other good B&Bs are **The Haven,** Birch St. (tel. 44017), **Dalecote,** Upper Oak St. (tel. 45121; £12.50-15), and **Ferndale,** 32 Queens Dr. (tel. 44014), halfway between Windermere and Bowness (£13.50). The nearest campground, **Limefitt Park** (tel. 32300), lies 4½ mi. south of Bowness on the A592 and has all the necessary amenities, except (ugh!) public transport (2-person tent £5-6).

Next door to the laundromat, cheery pink decor brightens the simple, tasty offerings at the espresso-sized **Coffee Pot,** 15 Main Rd. (cottage pie and salad £3.25, apple pie with cream £1.30, homemade lemonade 95p; open Mon.-Sat. 9:30am-6:30pm). In Bowness, try the **Hedgerow Teashop,** on Lake Rd. above Cumbria Books, and enjoy tasty sandwiches in a beautiful, wooden, "old-tyme" setting (open daily 10:30am-5pm; Nov.-Easter Wed.-Mon. 10:30am-5pm).

Bowness Bay Boating (tel. 43360) rents rowboats near the pier (£3/person/hr.; open Easter-Oct. 9am-5pm). Along with its daughter enterprise, **Windermere Iron Steamboat** (tel. 43360), it runs cruises from the pier at Bowness. Both charge the same rates. From Easter to October, boats sail north to Waterhead pier in Ambleside (about 2/hr. 10am-6pm; return £5, ages 5-15 half-price) and south to Lakeside (2/hr., 10am-6:30pm; return £5, ages 5-15 half-price). Evening cruises from Bowness cost £4.95. Swans, gulls, choughs, and tourists waddle along the public pier. BYOB (bring your own bread); nearby grocers sell it cheaply. For a shorter walk to a more deserted chunk of lakeshore away from the pier, turn right from New Rd. and follow Birthwaite Rd. to its end near Queen Adelaide's Hill.

Avoid wasting £2.85 to visit **The World of Beatrix Potter,** Crag Bow (tel. 88444). Fresh country scents and soothing music accompany smarmy-cutesy 3-D Jemima Puddleducks and Peter Rabbits. Two short films provide information about Potter and the Lakes, but you may be better off rereading the books and keeping your childhood memories intact.

Tourist information is available in both towns: the **Windermere tourist office** near the rail station (tel. 46499; open daily 9am-6pm; Nov.-Easter daily 9am-5pm; disabled access) and the **National Park Information Centre** beside the Bowness Pier (see Lake District: Practical Information, above) are fair game for questions. In Windermere, you can pick up a *Vegetarian Directory* (40p), a guide to the area's food, a guide to lake walks (20-25p), book **National Express** buses, and exchange foreign currency for a £2.50 commission. Let your belongings regain their manure-free luster at **Windermere Laundry,** Main Rd. (open Mon.-Fri. 9am-6pm, Sat., 9am-5pm, change and soap available. Windermere's **post office** resides at 2 St. Martins Parade (tel. 46964, open Mon.-Fri. 9am-5:30pm, Sat. 9am-12:30pm). The **telephone code** for these towns is 015394.

CONISTON

Separated from the larger lake and the busy towns of Windermere and Ambleside by a 5-mi. trek through the Grizedale Forest, Coniston makes a phenomenal base for hikers and cyclists, as multiple trails begin and end a few yards from the sleepy town center. Coniston is accessible by **bus #505** (the "Coniston Rambler"), which starts in Kendal and travels via Windermere (Bowness Pier), Ambleside, and Hawkshead to the lake (from Ambleside 8/day, Sun. 3/day; 45min.).

On Yewdale Rd., near Coniston, the **John Ruskin Museum** preserves relics of this writer-philosopher-art-critic's life (tel. (015394) 41164; open Easter-Oct. Weds.-Sun. 10am-1pm and 2-4pm; £1, children 50p). The High Lords of Tourism situated **Brantwood** (tel. (015394) 41396), Ruskin's manor house from 1872, perfectly between Coniston and Hawkshead; it contains Ruskin's art and works by some of his lesser admirers (Tolstoy, Gandhi, and Proust; open daily 11am-5:30pm; mid-Nov. to mid-March Wed.-Sun. 11am-4pm; £3, students £1.50, under 18 free). Stay at the **Holly How Youth Hostel (HI)** or the delightful **Coniston Coppermines Youth Hostel (HI).** (See Lake District: Accommodations and Camping, above.) Those heading to the trails will find their ideal B&B hosts at classy **Holmthwaite,** Tilberthwaite Ave. (tel. (015394) 41231; £15.50). Coniston's **tourist office** (tel. (015394) 41533) opens its doors from April to early November (daily 10am-1pm and 1:30-5pm).

The small village of **Hawkshead,** several miles east of Coniston, was the boyhood home of William Wordsworth. A **Theatre in the Forest** offers folk and classical music and drama amid a snarl of pine-trees and nature trails (tel. (01229) 860291; box office open Mon.-Sat. 11am-4pm). The **Hawkshead Youth Hostel (HI)** overlooks the lake (see Lake District: Accommodations and Camping, above). Two mi. southeast of Hawkshead, in the hamlet of **Near Sawrey** on the shores of Esthwaite Water, Beatrix Potter's 17th-century house **Hilltop** (tel. (015394) 36269) contains her furniture, china, and pictures. Take the ferry from Bowness and walk about 1½ mi. (open April-Oct. Sat.-Wed. 11am-5pm, last entry 4:30pm; £3.30, children £1.70).

AMBLESIDE

Only four mi. from the town of Windermere, at Lake Windermere's northern tip, Ambleside (pop. 3353) is more handsome and less frenetic than its neighbor. Frequently served by buses and full of reasonably priced B&Bs and restaurants, the town makes a solid base for exploring more remote areas.

Ambleside's only worthwhile sight is the tiny **House on the Bridge,** off Rydal Rd.; actually, house and bridge are one and the same. About four paces long and one pace wide, it was once inhabited by a basket weaver, his wife, and six children; now it serves as a National Trust Information Center. You can view the surrounding fells most vividly from the middle of the lake; rent a boat at the Waterhead pier (£3/hr., £4 for 2 people) and drift under the splendor of the Horseshoe Falls.

If a B&B falls in the woods and nobody's there, does it make a sound? Without accommodations, Ambleside would hardly exist: almost as many **B&Bs** and guesthouses reside here as private residences. Most B&Bs cost about £14.50 and fill up quickly in summer; call ahead in July and August, or at least arrive early in the day to hunt down a room. Some B&Bs cluster on Church St. and Compston Rd.; others line the busier Lake Rd. leading in from Windermere.

Ambleside's **HI Youth Hostel** resides near the steamer pier, a pleasant 1½-mi. walk from the town center (see Lake District: Accommodations and Camping, above). In town, the **YWCA,** Old Lake Rd. (tel. 32340), is open to both women and men. Though they cater predominantly to school groups, the wardens take the bunks down in July and August to create a B&B (closed for school groups Easter-early July, call ahead; £13, £12 for a dorm room). **Linda's B&B and Shirland,** on Compston Rd. near the bus stop (tel. 32999) has four rooms (doubles, triples, and quads) for £12.50-13/person, a cramped attic space for three, a private bunkhouse (both £6-9/person). Hospitable Mr. and Mrs. Richardson run **3 Cambridge Villas,** on Church St. next to the tourist office (tel. 32307), and will make vegetarian breakfasts on request (£14.50, doubles £13.50). Upscale, uphill **Raaesbeck,** Fair View Rd. (tel. 33844), a fascinating 250-year-old country cottage with solid oak floors, beams, and beds, occupies a tranquil, secluded spot ideal for R&R (£15). Ask the proprietress why mill workers are short. Camp at the basic **Hawkshead Hall Farm** (tel. 36221), five mi. south of Ambleside off the B5286 (£1/person; £1/tent; open March-Oct.).

Ambleside's eateries are miles ahead of the rest of the Lake District. **The Old Smithy,** The Slack, off Market Pl. at the Queen's Hotel, serves cheap and excellent fish and chips and boasts lengthy lines to prove it (open daily 11:30am-2pm and 5-8:30pm). Bohemian **Rock and Run Cafe** is literally on the Cheapside, behind Barclays; well-known among climbers, who grab hummus on toast (90p) or a cheese veggie burger (£1.90) en route to the fells (open Mon. and Weds.-Fri. 9am-4:30pm, Tues. 9:30am-4:30pm, Sat. 9am-5pm, Sun. 10am-4:30pm). The **Golden Rule** has good local beer and a loyal following among residents. Young people frequent the **Sportsman** on Compston Rd., which has a disco and serves pizza daily from 7 to 11pm (open Mon.-Sat. 11am-11pm, Sun. and 7-10:30pm). A local band plays Sunday evenings at 9pm at **Unicorn** on North Rd.; the pub is largely empty other times.

The **tourist office,** Church St. (tel. 32582), offers free but serious 4-8 mi. walks with a park warden every Friday at 10:30am from mid-June to September; bring lunch (office open daily 9am-5pm; Oct.-Easter Fri.-Sat. 9am-5pm). A second office at Waterhead offers exchange (£2.50/transaction). Change money in the **post office,** Market Place, LA22 9AA (tel. 32267; open Mon.-Fri. 9am-5:30pm, Sat. 9am-12:30pm; Oct.-June Mon.-Tues. and Thurs.-Fri. 9am-12:30pm, Wed. 1:30-5:30pm, Sat. 9am-12:30pm). Ambleside's **telephone code** is 015394. If you know the magic word, cash will spill out of the gaping maw of a **Cirrus ATM** at **Barclays** on Market Place (open Mon.-Wed. and Fri. 9:30am-4:30pm, Thurs. 10am-4:30pm). **Buses** arrive and depart on King St., serving many areas in the Lake District. **Lakeslink** buses #555-556 run hourly to Grasmere and Windermere (£1.33) and Keswick (£2.85). Bus #505 joins Hawkshead and Coniston (10/day, Sun. 3/day).

Near Ambleside

Although you can't go wrong hiking in any direction out from Ambleside, hidden trail markings, steep, slippery slopes, and reliably unpredictable weather that can quickly limit visibility to 5 feet make a good map, a compass, and the ability to use them a necessity (ask at the tourist or National Park Information offices for the best maps). The mountain rescue service averages two to three crises per day in this area; don't let one be you. Inexperienced hikers might try one of the excellent warden-guided walks which leave from Ambleside's and Grasmere's National Park and tourist information offices (1/week from each, call individual offices for routes and details). Bring a sweater, rain gear—*it will rain!*—sturdy walking shoes or boots, and a hearty lunch to fuel you for the four to six hour rambles of varying degrees of difficulty. Most wardens are volunteers who have lived in the area for many years and know it well; you'll receive an enthusiastic education. The hike to **Trout Beck** via **Jenkin Crag** and **Wansfell Pike** is an easy 5 mi. with unbelievable views of Lake Windermere and beyond. Serious hikers can tackle the path from **Rydal** (halfway between Ambleside and Grasmere) to **Legburthwaite** (near Kendal) in one full and athletic day. This route passes by several of the highest peaks in the area including **Great Rigg** and the spectacular **Helvellyn.** Bus #555 will return you to Ambleside (about 1/hr) or you can stay at the basic **Thirlmere** hostel (see Lake District: Accommodations and Camping, above). A shorter, 2½ mi. stroll north up the road by the stream leads to a bucolic, Wordsworthian stepping-stone bridge and to Rydal where bus #555 or your own happy feet will deposit you in Ambleside. From Grasmere, a steep two-hour climb will bring you to **Helm Crag,** dubbed by locals "the lion and the lamb." Can you find the magic angle? Hint: the lion is lying beside the lamb. The way is well marked, with excellent views of Grasmere and Borrowdale all the way up, even on misty days when cloud cover frustrates postcard photographers.

GRASMERE

Grasmere is a rather bland little town, populated by wealthy, retired aficionados of garage-sale landscapes. Every establishment tries, in relatively good taste, to cash in on William Wordsworth's legacy, occasionally falling back on the more easily digested Beatrix Potter. Though framed cross-stitches of *Daffodils* and excerpts from *The Prelude* can be seen just about everywhere, the sublimity of the splendid lake and hills at Grasmere ultimately speaks for itself.

The early 17th-century **Dove Cottage** (tel. 35544), where Wordsworth lived with his wife, his sister Dorothy, Samuel Taylor Coleridge, Thomas De Quincey, and up to a dozen assorted children, opium-eaters, and literati from 1799 to 1808, is a relatively primitive affair. Its current caretakers will load you with as much Wordsworth lore as you can bear during their 20-minute guided tour. Tickets to the cottage (£3.90, children £2) also cover admission to the museum next door, with an excellent exhibit on the life of Wordsworth and manuscripts and portraits of Wordsworth, Coleridge, De Quincey, and Southey (cottage open mid-Feb. to mid-Jan. daily 9:30am-5:30pm; last entry 5pm). The Wordsworth trail continues back toward Ambleside and the poet's last and most comfortable home, **Rydal Mount,** where he lived from 1813 until his death in 1850. The attic study is now a showcase for his books, letters, and portraits, and family tree (tel. 3302; estate open daily 9:30am-5pm; Nov.-Feb. Wed.-Mon. 10am-4pm; £2, children 80p). The Wordsworths' graves are in the yard of St. Oswald's Church in Grasmere village.

Grasmere is ideal walker's country. Ambitious climbers might tackle the **Rydal Fells** or **Langdale Fells,** but even the paths around Rydal Water and Grasmere are scenic. Hydrophiles might walk down Langdale Rd. and hire a boat to row on the deep green lake (in summer daily 10am-5pm; £4/person/hr., deposit £15). The **National Park Information Centre** (tel. 35245) lies in town on Red Bank Rd. The staff of experienced hikers will answer your questions and exchange your foreign currency for £2.50 per transaction. Grasmere's **telephone code** is 015394. There are two **HI Youth Hostels** within a mile of Grasmere. **Butterlip How** is a large stone house north of the village; **Thorney How** is ½ mi. northwest and planted squarely between several desirable walking routes. (See Lake District: Accommodations and Camping, above.) All B&Bs in town cost at least £15, but **Eller Close** (tel. 35786), 1½ mi. northeast in a cow-infested idyll off the A591, provides streamside tranquility. Vegetarian cuisine is available. (Small double £25-29 if you mention *Let's Go*.) Grasmere makes a good daytrip from Windermere, Ambleside, or Keswick.

Grasmere's restaurants are surprisingly good but relatively expensive. **Baldry's,** in the village center, serves Wensley rarebit (£3.25) and delicious Cumberland Rum Nicky, a pie laced with rum and filled with dates, roast ginger, and eggs (open daily 9:30am-5:30pm; Nov.-March weekends 10am-4pm). Sarah Nelson's famous Grasmere Gingerbread is a bargain at 20p per slice in **Church Cottage,** just by St. Oswald's (open Mon.-Sat. from 9:30am-5:30pm, Sun. 12:30-5:30pm, Dec.-Feb. Mon.-Sat. 10am-4:30pm, Sun. 1-4:30pm).

LAKE DISTRICT NATIONAL PARK

KESWICK

Sandwiched between towering Skiddaw peak and the northern edge of Lake Derwentwater, Keswick (KEZ-ick) rivals Windermere as the Lake District's tourist capital; in summer, visitors indulging their Kendal Mint Cake fetish outnumber permanent residents. This former mining center is a hiker's springboard for the central and northern lakes; most of the lakes lie within a 10-mi. radius of the town and are accessible by road or hiking trail.

Located 1½ hr. southwest of Carlisle and 17 mi. west of Penrith on the A66, Keswick (pop. 4700) is northernmost in the string of gorgeous towns stretching south from Carlisle through Ambleside, Grasmere, and Windermere that are well-served by public transport (see Lake District: Getting There, above). The **tourist office** at Moot Hall, behind the clock tower, Market Sq. (tel. 72645), sells a lodgings booklet (90p) and a map (20p), and will find you B&Bs for no charge (open daily 9:30am-7pm; April-June and Sept.-Oct. 9:30am-5:30pm; Nov.-March 10am-4pm). The tourist office provides a list of pony trekking centers, boat rentals, and hiking trails in the area. Many walks leave from the tourist office, including the popular, lengthy "Keswick Rambles," leaving daily at 10:15am (bring a packed lunch and rain gear; £2.50, children £1). Serious climbers should inquire about taking a daytrip with one of Lakeland's finest, **Ray McHaffie.** The National Park's **Information Center,** 31 Lake Rd. (tel. 72803), offers similar services and **currency exchange** (open daily 9:30am-5:30pm; Nov.-Easter 10am-4pm). Free 3½-hour guided walks leave the Discovery Centre (July-Aug. Wed. and Sun. 2pm). Book **National Express** buses and get local bus information and tickets at the **Mountain Goat Office** in the car park (tel. 73962; open Mon.-Sat. 9am-5pm, Sun. 9:30am-12:30pm, Nov.-March Mon.-Fri. 9am-4pm). Saturday is **market day** from 9am to 4pm. Let Mom call you in Keswick by dialing its **telephone code,** 017687. The **Cirrus ATM** at **Barclays** on Marketplace shall extrude cash for you, and it might even force some out (open Mon.-Tues. and Thurs.-Fri. 9:30am-4:30pm, Wed. 10am-4:30pm).

The Keswick and Derwentwater **hostels** grace this small town. (See Lake District: Accommodations and Camping, above.) Vast quantities of B&Bs sandwich between the A591, Station St., St. John St., and Ambleside Rd. Though the July and August crowds munch at this supply, you will be able to find a vacancy unless Wordsworth rises from the dead and wanders over here for a one-time-only Greatest Hits Literary Revival Show. **Bridgedale,** 101 Main St. (tel. 73914), sits outside the bus station; noisy buses rumble by. (£10, with continental breakfast £11, with cooked breakfast £12). **Century House,** 17 Church St. (tel. 72843), has pristine peach and white bedrooms in a Victorian-style house run by friendly Mrs. Hutton (£14/night, £20 deposit). Pitch a two-person tent for £3/person at the **Dalebottom Holiday Park** (tel. 72176), 2 mi. southeast of Keswick off the A591 (open April-Oct.) or **Castlerigg Hall** (tel. 72437), 1 mi. southeast of Keswick (open April-Nov.) Both sites have phones, flush toilets, showers, and lie on the Windermere bus route. Another campsite rests right by the lake, a 15-min. walk from the bus station (£4.50/night).

Most pubs in town serve luncheon and supper. **Mayson's,** Lake Rd., serves heaping plates of veggie lasagna and stir-fry (£4-6) under a thicket of hanging plants (free samples of sweets; open daily 10:30am-9pm, Nov.-June 10:30am-4pm.) When the thirst for pub-crawling hits you, join the Lost Generation at **Queen's Head,** also on Main St. **Lakes** is an enormous supermarket next to the bus station (open Mon.-Sat. 9am-7pm, to 8pm on Fri., Sun. 10am-5pm).

Near Keswick

The best ridge hike in the entire Lake District starts only 1 mi. from Keswick. Ascend the **Cat Bells** from the west shore of Derwent Water at Hawes End and take a gentle 3-mi. stroll atop the ridge, passing **Maiden Moor** and **Eel Crags** on the way to **Dale Head,** one of the highest peaks in the area. Descend via the saddle-shaped Honister Pass to get to Seatoller. For another excellent daytrip, walk southwest through the quiet village of **Portinscale,** over the rugged Derwent Fells, and past the forested shores of Derwentwater to **Buttermere.** The easy **Castlehead Walk** from

Keswick's Market Place leads to spellbinding **Friar's Crag,** praised by Ruskin, Wordsworth, and other luminous literati. The "Borrowdale Bus" to Seatoller follows an arresting route along Derwentwater and through the dramatic Jaws of Borrowdale Pass. Also consider visiting the **Castlerigg Stone Circle,** in a sheep-laden field a half-hour walk east of Keswick. It's not quite Stonehenge, but dates back about 5,000 years, and lacks the surly guards, screeching children, and steel fences of its more famous kin. Cyclists love Keswick's gentle hills and wide, sweeping valleys—consider taking a day to cruise around the lake and see the stone circle.

WESTERN LAKE DISTRICT

A 9-mi. hike south of Keswick and Derwent Water lies the harrowing **Honister Pass,** leading to the wildest parts of the Lake District: Wasdale, Eskdale, and Langdale. Noses grow a little each third Thursday in November at **Santon Bridge,** a village near Eskdale, which hosts its "Biggest Liar in the World" competition; until his recent death, Richard Nixon terrorized the competition for over three decades, his streak interrupted only by Ollie North in 1987. Catch **CMS bus** #79 from Keswick to Seatoller (5-9/day; 30min.), south of Keswick on the B5259 and 1½ mi. east of the pass. At the summit of the pass poses the **Honister Hause Youth Hostel (HI)** (See Lake District: Accommodations and Camping, above).

Set in a splendid valley beside an icy mountain lake, **Buttermere,** 4 mi. northwest of the pass, makes a smashing base for touring the area and a remote fishing hole. Access the town by CMS bus #77 (see Lake District: Getting About, above). Nearby **Sour Milk Gill Falls** plummet from the slopes of Red Pyke. The hike to the top of **Haystacks** is difficult, but the summit delivers bone-chilling views of surrounding mountains. **Red Pyke, High Style,** and **High Cragg** are the three main challenges for ambitious hikers in the area. Others might take an afternoon constitutional up **Ranadale Knotts,** just behind the village. The **Buttermere HI Youth Hostel** grants a hiker's reprieve (see Lake District: Accommodations and Camping, above). If the hostel is full, stay at **Syke Farm** (tel. (017687) 70222) for B&B (£15; stay two or more nights at £13) or camping (£2.50/person, £1/car); or spend the night at **Crag Foot Cottage** (tel. (017687) 70220), a wonderfully friendly B&B (£15).

Wasdale cowers beneath solemn **Great Gable** (2949 ft.) and its bulky twin, **Green Gable** (2628 ft.). The 3½-hour climb from Honister to the summit is steep and invigorating. A mi. from the base of Green Gable is **Black Sail Youth Hostel (HI),** one of England's most remote hostels. Equally charming and inaccessible is the **Ennerdale Youth Hostel (HI),** in a valley just off the Smithy Beck trail. The Ravenglass-Eskdale railway (tel. (01229) 717171) stops in Boot, 1½ mi. from the **Eskdale Youth Hostel (HI).** (See Lake District: Accommodations and Camping, above.)

B&Bs cluster at **Wasdale Head;** try **Mrs. K. Naylor,** Row Head Farm (tel. (019467) 26244), who rents rooms for £15, or **Mrs. S. Naylor,** Middle Row (tel. (019467) 26306), for friendly lodging for £14. Facing the famous and forbidding **Wastwater Screes,** a jumble of loose rock, is the standard-grade **Wastwater Youth Hostel (HI).** (See Lake District: Accommodations and Camping, above.) Climb the nearby **Whin Rigg** or venture over to the many waterfalls of **Greendale Valley.** No serious mountain climber's Lakeland experience would be complete without a hike up nearby **Scafell Pike** in the magnificent Langdale Fells. At 3221 ft., it is the highest peak in England. Ring CMS (tel. (01946) 63222) or inquire at any tourist office for information on public transportation nearby.

Wales (Cymru)

Lady Percy: Lie still, ye thief, and hear the lady sing in Welsh.
Hotspur: I had rather hear the Lady, my brach [bitch-hound], sing in
Irish.

I Henry IV, III. i. 232-33.

Wales borders England, but if many Welsh had their way, it would be floating miles away. Since England's bloody execution of Wales' last Prince in 1283, relations between the two have been marked by a powerful unease. Until late in the 19th century, schoolchildren were forbidden to speak Welsh in the classroom; those who did were made to wear a "Welsh Knot" around their necks, which was passed around to the next child who dared speak Welsh, and whoever was wearing the knot at the end of the day would get some kind of punishment. Against this conquering presence, Wales clings steadfastly to its Celtic heritage, continuing a struggle for independence that has been surging for over a millennium. Especially in the North, Welsh endures in conversations, in commerce, and through a fiercely-revived literature. As churning coal and steel mines fall victim to Britain's tumbling economy, the unemployment rate has risen, and Wales has turned its economic eye from heavy industry to tourism. Visitors and natives alike enjoy miles of sandy beaches, grassy cliffs, and inland mountains. Considering it all, the Welsh endure it well: the nationalists confine themselves to spray-painting the English halves of bilingual signs and many recall proudly the rule of Welshmen Henry VII and Lloyd George over all Britain. Avoid calling the Welsh "English" at all costs.

GETTING THERE & GETTING ABOUT

Possessed by a split personality, the same Welsh bus network that will make you coin new curses in the south will render you speechless in the north. In the south, take all bus schedules with a grain of salt—buses are usually late. **Cardiff Bus** (tel. (01222) 396521) blankets the area around Cardiff; **Red and White** (tel. (01291) 622947) buses serve the routes from Gloucester and Hereford in England west through the Wye Valley, past Abergavenny and Brecon in the north. **South Wales Transport** (tel. (01492) 475511) operates between Swansea and Haverfordwest in South Pembrokeshire. South Wales Transport also operates **Expresswest** buses, running from South Wales to Bristol with stops in Haverfordwest, Milford Haven, Pembroke, Tenby, Carmarthen, Swansea, and Cardiff. These buses run less frequently (6/day), but tend to be much faster than local service between towns. **TransCambria** (tel. (01222) 398700) is a north-south bus line. On it, you can travel easily from Cardiff or Swansea north to Aberystwyth, Machynlleth, and Bangor. Seniors receive a 25% discount, students and YHA/HI members 15%.

Private bus companies fill in some of the gaps. **Silcox Coaches** (tel. (01834) 2189) covers south Pembrokeshire, and a branch of South Wales Transport, locally called **Cleddau** (KLETH-eye; tel. (01437) 763284), covers the Haverfordwest area. **Richard Bros.** (tel. (01239) 613756) connects Haverfordwest north to St. David's, Fishguard, and Cardigan, where you can hook up with **Crosville** for travel north. Pick up a *Public Transport Map* for the area in which you will be traveling. Most local buses do not run on Sunday, though Expresswest does operate twice in the morning and twice in the afternoon on summer Sundays.

Passes simplify the bus fare system in the south. The **Roverbus** pass, which can be purchased from any driver, is valid for unlimited travel for one day on all South Wales Transport buses (£4, seniors and under 16 £2.85). For seven days of consecu-

Wales

TO DUN LAOGHAIRE, DUBLIN

Irish Sea

Amlwch

Wallasey
Birkenhead   Liverpool
Hoylake

Prestatyn

Holyhead   ANGLESEY   *Conwy Bay*   Llandudno
Holy   Conwy   Rhyl   *R. Mersey*   Ellesmere
Island   Beaumaris   Colwyn   Holywell   Port
Bangor   Bay
Trefriw   Bodnant   Denbigh   Chester
Caernarfon   *Menai Strait*   Garden
Llanberis   Capel   *Brenig*   Ruthin
Snowdon   Curig   *Resevoir*   Wrexham
Betws-y-Coed

Caernarfon Bay   Blaenau   Corwen
Ffestiniog   Llangollen   Chirk
LLEYN PENINSULA   Porthmadog   Ffestiniog   *Dee*   Glyn   Ellesmere
Pwllheli   Bala   Ceiriog   Wem
Harlech   *Lake Bala*   *Ceriog*
Aberdaron   Absersoch   *Snowdonia*   *Lake*
Forest and   *Vyrnwy*   *Tanat*   *Severn*
National Park   Llanfyllin   Shrewsbury
Barmouth   Dolgellau
Cadair   Powis Castle   Welshpool
Idris   Montgomery   Church
Tywyn   *Dovey*   Stretton
Cardigan   Machynlleth   *Severn*   Newton
Bay   Borth   Llanidloes   Bishop's
Aberystwyth   *Wye*   Castle   Ludlow
Llywernog Silver   Knighton
Lead Mine   Rhayader   Presteigne
Aberaeron   Newbridge-   Llandrindod
New Quay   on-Wye   Wells
Lampeter   Builth Wells   Clyro   Hereford
Cardigan   *Teifi*   Llanwrtyd   Hay-on-Wye
Fishguard   Newcastle   Wells   *Wye*   Llanthony
Mynydd   Emlyn   Llandovery   Brecon   Priory
Preseli   Tretower   Monmouth
St. David's   Llandeilo   *Black Mountain*   Court
Solva   Carmarthen   *Brecon*   Abergavenny
St.   *Beacons*   Ebbw Vale   *Wye*
Brides   Haverfordwest   Merthyr   Abertillery   *Valley*
Bay   Narberth   Kidwelly   Tydfil   Pontypool   Tintern
Amroth   Ammanford   Aberdare   Cwmbran   Abbey
Pembroke   Tenby   Burry Port   Neath   Mountain   Chepstow
Manorbier   Llanelli   *Tawe*   Ash   Newport
Carmarthen   Swansea   Port Talbot   Cardiff   Bristol
Bay   *GOWER*   Mumbles   Bridgend   *Mouth*
TO CORK   *PENINSULA*   *Swansea*   Porthcawl   Cowbridge   *of the*
Bay   Barry   *Severn*
Penarth

TO ROSSLARE HARBOR

PEMBROKESHIRE COAST NATIONAL PARK

CAMBRIAN MOUNTAINS

Black Mountains

Bristol Channel

0   30 miles
0   30 kilometers

N

tive travel on these buses, buy a **Weekly Roverbus** (£12.90, children and seniors £8.50; also good on Expresswest West buses); the pass must be bought at a South Wales Transport office in a local bus station. (Bring a passport-sized photo.)

The efficiency of the **North Wales** bus service will amaze you. Close your gaping mouth and buy a **Crosville Rover** ticket, good north of Aberystwyth and as far east as Chester. (**Week Rover** £14-18; **Day Rover** £4.70.) Bear in mind that few bus routes operate on Sunday. Pick up the Crosville bus timetables for all of north and mid-Wales at any bus station or tourist office.

Two main rail lines in the south and two in the north connect the coast with many towns in England. Originating in Cardiff, one rail line sticks to the coast; another runs inland across the peninsula, stopping in Carmarthen and terminating at Fishguard on the peninsula's northern coast. Of the two northern lines, one runs from Holyhead on the Isle of Anglesey along the northern coast to Chester; the other begins in Pwllheli on the Lleyn Peninsula and runs along the Cambrian coast south to Aberystwyth. Other **British Rail** lines run from Llandudno Junction near Conwy on the north coast to Blaenau Ffestiniog; and from Machynlleth on Cardigan Bay east across Wales to Shrewsbury in England.

Rail passes help lessen the costs of travel. The seven-day **Freedom of Wales Rover** (£45) is good on the whole Welsh network plus Chester to Abergavenny via Crewe. In the south, the **Valley Lines Day Ranger** (£4.60) is valid on branches radiating from Cardiff to Barry, Penarth, Rhymney (via Caerphilly), and Treherbert, Aberdave, and Merthyr Tydfil (via Pontypridd). And in the north, the **Cambrian Day Ranger** takes care of travel between Machynlleth, Aberystwyth, and Pwllheli (£15). The **North and Mid-Wales Rover** is valid for all travel within the Aberystwyth-Shrewsbury-Crewe area, including free travel on the Ffestiniog Railway (trains and buses £34; three out of seven days £22). Call the British Rail offices at Cardiff (tel. (01222) 228000) or Swansea (tel. (01492) 467777) for information.

While *Let's Go* does not recommend **hitchhiking** anywhere, many people choose this form of transport in the summer. Cars stop easily for hitchers who stand in lay-by (pull-off) areas along narrow roads.

HIKING & BIKING

Wales has hundreds of well-marked **footpaths**. Long-distance hikers should buy 1:50,000 Ordnance Survey maps and bring along proper equipment. For further advice, check the booklets *Walking in Wales*, available in Welsh tourist offices, and *Wales: Walking* (£1.10), available from the British Tourist Authority. The Offa's Dyke Path and the Pembrokeshire Coast Path are popular long-distance walks through glorious and often remote countryside. For more information, write to the Countryside Commission Dispatch Dept., Prinworks Lane, Levenshulme, Manchester, England M19 3JP. The £1.20 tourist map available at all tourist offices and most bookstores gives a good sense of the layout of the region, as well as train and road lines. Be sure to read Essentials: Hiking & Camping before heading out to the wild.

Bikers should obtain a copy of the indispensable *Cyclists Guide to North Wales* at tourist offices; bicycles can be rented from the occasional dealer. Betws-y-Coed, Llanberis, and Shrewsbury all make good biking bases.

LIFE & TIMES

HISTORY

As the western terminus of many waves of emigration, Wales has felt the influence of a wide array of invaders. The compact build and dark complexion of many Welsh people is a legacy of the Iberians, the area's original inhabitants. Tall, fair Celts conquered them and took over all the British Isles in 800 BC. When the Romans invaded Britain, Welsh resistance compelled the Romans to station two of their three legions at the border. The Romans departed in 410 AD, and for 700 years the Welsh were left to themselves. The Saxons pushed them back and built Offa's Dyke, a 168-mi.-long earthwork, to keep the Welsh in their hilly land. But even the Saxons could not subdue these Celtic tribes—they were foiled, perhaps, by the daring military tactics of the legendary Arthur. After a long campaign, Edward I of England finally conquered the rebellious country in 1282 by recapturing the bride of Llewelyn ap Gruffydd, the Prince of Wales. Edward constructed a series of massive castles—the fortresses of Conwy, Caernarfon, Harlech, and Beaumaris—at strategic points along the northern and western coasts.

In the 15th century, the bold guerilla warfare of Owen Glendower (Owain Glyndwr) temporarily freed Wales from English rule. "The great magician, damn'd Glendower," as Shakespeare's Henry IV calls him, succeeded in reigniting Welsh nationalism and rousing his compatriots to arms, but after 1409 he disappeared into the mountains, leaving only a legend to guide his people. Full union with England came in 1536, at which time Welsh customs, laws, and language were outlawed; ironically, the reigning Tudors were of Welsh descent.

In the early 19th century, the discovery of rich coal veins in the south catapulted Wales into modernity. The handsome area of Glamorgan was soon covered with ash, grit, and dust-covered workers; Carlyle described it as "a vision of Hell." The harshness of the era fermented a grim sobriety that paralleled the rise of religious fundamentalism. The organization of labor found perhaps its purest expression in the soaring men's choirs still found in many Welsh towns. Crushingly rapid industrialization in Wales contributed to the formation of a strongly leftist political consciousness. David Lloyd George, leader of Liberal reform in the first decade of the 20th century, began his career as a rabble-rousing Welsh rad-boy. During his tenure as Prime Minister, Winston Churchill violently smothered a Welsh coal-miners' strike by sending in the British Army; many here still mutter his name in darkness.

A vigorous campaign to retain one of Europe's oldest living languages is part of the recent, sometimes prickly, revival of Welsh nationalism. A few years ago, a majority of Welsh community councils voted to make Wales a nuclear-free zone, a move that was as much a reaction against England as a protest against nuclear development. Prince Charles's office wrote a letter to the councils "denying the request," and the liberal Welsh have continued their crusade against conservatism and English who treat Wales like a summer holiday playground.

LLITERATURE

Like other Celtic countries, Wales has a long bardic tradition. The 12th-century *Mabinogion* contains the three tales that became the famous Arthurian romances of Chretien de Troyes and the 14th-century poetry of Dafydd ap Gwilym. In 1568, Queen Elizabeth was so concerned with the "intolerable multitude of vagrant and idle persons calling themselves minstrels, rhymers, and bards" that she issued a Royal Commission for the establishment of an Eisteddfod where dawdlers could be put to the test. Today the National Eisteddfod in Llangollen is a huge annual festival and competition of singing, storytelling, and skits, the culmination of hundreds of smaller local and school *eisteddfodai*.

Welsh literature has retained a compelling self-consciousness in addressing problematic questions of identity and national ideals. R.S. Thomas's incisive poetry treads a fine line between a fierce defense of his proud heritage and a bitter rant against its claustrophobic provincialism. Kate Roberts's short stories and novels, such as *The Chains Around My Feet*, dramatize Welsh fortitude in the face of dire poverty. The best-known Welsh writer is, of course, Dylan Thomas, who has become something of a national industry. His sonorous poetry and works like *A Child's Christmas in Wales* chronicle his homeland with nostalgia, humor, and a vein of bitterness.

FFOOD

Traditional Welsh cooking relies heavily on potatoes and onions, dairy products, mutton and pork, and fish and seaweed. Welsh rarebit is buttered toast topped with a thick cheesy mustard beer sauce. Griddle cakes *(crempog)* are made with sour cream and topped with butter. Wales abounds with unique and tasty breads—try *laver*, made with seaweed, or the scrumptious *bara brith*, a fruit and nut bread (always ask for butter with it). *Cawl* is a thick, complex broth, served with a slab of bread. Soups are thick with leeks and generous helpings of lamb and beef.

LLANGUAGE

The word "Welsh" comes from the Old English *wealh*, or "foreigner," and the language does indeed seem utterly alien to English-speakers. A full 500,000 people speak Welsh out of a total population of just under three million, and most of those who do speak Welsh speak it as a first language. North of Aberystwyth, Welsh becomes the language of the shops and streets and buses. Try to familiarize yourself with Welsh's lovely lilt by learning the mechanics of its pronunciation. *Ch* is the deep, guttural "kh" heard in "Bach" or "loch." *Ll*—the oddest of Welsh consonants—is produced by placing your tongue against the top of your mouth, as if you were going to say "l," and blowing. If this technique proves baffling, just say "hl" (Hlan-GO-hlen for "Llangollen") and bus drivers will know where you want to go. Another common consonant *dd*, is said like the "th" in "the." *C* and *g* are hard. *W* is generally used as a vowel and sounds like the "oo" in "drool," and *y* sounds either like the "u" in "ugly" (especially between hyphens) or the "i" in "ignoramus." *F* is spoken like a "v," as in "vavoom," and *ff* sounds exactly like the English "f." Emphasis usually falls on the next to last syllable, and there are no silent letters in Welsh.

Most Welsh place names are quite sensibly derived from prominent features of the landscape. *Llan* or *betws* means church, *chepe* market, *stowe* town, *afon* river, *mynydd* mountain, *ffordd* road, *glyn* glen or valley, *pen* top or end, and *caer* fort. *Mawr* is big, *fach* is little. The Welsh call their land *Cymru* and themselves *Cymry*. The appendix lists some essential Welsh phrases to help you in your travels. Oh, and don't be discouraged if the language escapes you—it did us.

SOUTH WALES

The transition from England to Wales is smoothest in the South, where the culture is particularly British and gritty harbors and market towns meld with the peaceful landscape. Unemployment remains high, public transportation has been cut back alarmingly, and coal-mining strikes ravage morale. It is in the North, many say, that the true Wales lives on, and the traveler may find the Welsh translations of every street sign, rugby memorabilia in every pub, and red dragons in every window of South Wales occasionally contrived. But the Southerners' pride in their country is as firm as any Welshman's, and North Wales does not hold a monopoly on Welsh natural beauty. The Wye Valley forms a rich and tranquil shelter shared by England and Wales, while rugged hills, forests, limestone caves, and moorlands stud Brecon Beacons National Park, north of Cardiff. Both the Gower Peninsula, jutting south at Swansea, and the far larger Pembrokeshire Peninsula to the west flaunt unmatched coastal scenery and fine beaches.

■■■ CARDIFF (CAERDYDD)

The only urban center in a land of small villages and the youngest capital in Europe, Cardiff (pop. 300,000) has a modern flair and a youthful culture. Its intense Welsh pride expresses itself in a lively arts scene and the beautifully restored architecture of both public buildings and homes. Residential buildings spread out around a center containing one of Britain's most lavish castles, the enormous Bute Park, and classical buildings that house government offices and the National Museum. Cardiff's style of shopping in arcades results in some of Britain's most varied and affordable markets.

GETTING THERE

National Express Rapide buses (tel. 344751) careen between Cardiff and London's Victoria Station (6/day; 3hr.; £21), Heathrow (10/day; 2¾hr.; £24.50), Gatwick Airport (9/day; 4hr.; £27.50), and Glasgow (3/day; 8½hr.; £45). **British Rail** trains are faster and more frequent, leaving from London's Paddington Station (1/hr.; 2hr.; £34.50) and stopping in Cardiff before heading west to Pembroke/Haverford and Fishguard. Trains also speed from Bath (via Bristol; 1hr.; £9.90), Glasgow and Edinburgh (via Birmingham; 1/hr.; 7hr.; £66), and Birmingham (2½hr.; £24.50). British Rail services several other lines through Wales departing from Cardiff. **Cardiff Bus** and **South Wales Transport** both offer **Rover** day passes and week passes, and British Rail offers a **Freedom of Wales Rover.**

ORIENTATION & PRACTICAL INFORMATION

The castle stands triumphantly in the city center, with massive Bute Park stretching out behind it; to the east are the Civic Centre, university buildings, and the National Museum. Shops, pedestrian walks, and indoor arcades line the rest of the city. The bus and train stations face each other south of the city center. The purple-and-white map given out at the tourist office is deceptive: it leaves out many side streets and makes distances seem shorter than they really are.

    Cardiff Bus (Bws Caerdydd) runs an extensive network of orange buses in Cardiff and environs. Buses run less frequently Sunday mornings, and almost never after 11pm (ask about the "night owl" at 11:20pm). Regular fares run from 28p-£1.15; take advantage of the reduced fares Monday through Friday (9:15am-3:45pm; seniors and persons with disabilities half-fare, day tickets £2.80, children £1.60; purchase on bus). Cardiff Bus also runs a daily **Cambrian Express** to Aberystwyth via Swansea (4hr.; £10, students £8.50, children and seniors £6.75). Stop by the Cardiff Bus office across from the station at St. David's House, Wood St. (tel. 396521) and pick up a thick timetable for 35p. Local buses do not give change; if you drop in too much, the extra money goes to charity.

Tourist Office: Cardiff Central Railway Station, smaller branch 8-14 Bridge St. (tel. 227281). Helpful staff and a handsome leaflets. Free accommodations list and free booking (10% deposit). Open Mon.-Sat. 9am-6:30pm, Sun. 10am-4pm.

Tours: The Cardiff Experience (tel. 522202) runs bus tours Mon.-Sat. from the bus station (1/hr. 11am-3pm; £4, seniors and children £2.50). Includes Cardiff Castle, National Museum, Llandaff Cathedral, and Maritime Museum.

Budget Travel: Students' Union, Park Pl., 1st Floor, Cardiff University (tel. 382350). Books British Rail, National Express, ferries, charter flights, etc. Student discounts. Open Mon.-Thurs. 9:30am-4:30pm, Fri. 10am-4:30pm.

Financial Services: Barclays, 114/116 St. Mary St. (tel. 239055, ext. 2046; fax 239055). Open Mon.-Tues., Thurs.-Fri. 9:30am-4:30pm, Wed. 10am-4:30pm. **Thomas Cook,** 16 Queen St. (tel. 224886). Open Mon.-Thurs. and Sat. 9am-5:30pm, Fri. 10am-5:30pm. **American Express,** 3 Queen St. (tel. 668858). Open Mon. and Wed.-Fri. 9am-5:30pm, Tues. 9:30am-5:30pm, Sat. 9am-5pm.

Post Office: 2-4 Hill St., off The Hayes (tel. 232410). Open Mon.-Fri. 9am-5:30pm, Sat. 9am-12:30pm. **Postal Code:** CF1 2ST.

Telephones: At Queen St. shopping precinct and St. David's Hall.

Telephone Code: 01222.

Train Station: Central Station, Wood St. (tel. 228000), south of the city center and behind the bus station. **Lockers** £1-3. Tickets open Mon.-Sat. 5:45am-9:30pm, Sun. 6:45am-9:30pm. Travel desk open Mon.-Sat. 9am-6pm, Sun. 1-5pm.

Bus Station: Wood St. (For National Express, call 344751.) Booking office and Travel Centre open daily 7:15am-5pm. **Cardiff Bus** information office across Wood St. in St. David's House (tel. 396521).

Taxi: Metro Cabs: tel. 464646; 24hr. **Supatax:** tel. 226644; 24hr. Taxi stands in front of train station and on Wood St. in front of bus station.

Bike Rental: Freewheel, 9 Castle St. (tel. 667049). £7/day, £30/week; £15-30 deposit. Open Mon.-Sat. 9:30am-6pm.

Bookstore: Waterstone's, 2A The Hayes (tel. 665606). Open Mon.-Fri. 9am-7pm, Sat. 9am-6pm, Sun. 11am-5pm.

Camping Equipment: YHA Adventure Shop, 13-15 Castle St. (tel. 399178). A herring barrel's worth of backpacking, camping, and hiking gear. Open Mon.-wed. and Fri. 9:30am-5:30pm, Thurs. 9:30am-6pm, Sat. 9am-6pm. Shares space with **Campus Travel,** which books student fares.

Launderette: Launderama, 60 Lower Cathedral Rd. (tel. 228326). Open Mon. 9am-4:30pm, Tues.-Wed. and Fri. 9:30am-5:30pm, Thurs., Sat.-Sun. 9am-5pm.

Hotlines: Samaritans (crisis): Cowbridge Rd., opposite St. David's Hospital (tel. 344022). Drop-in daily 8am-10pm; phone manned 24hrs. **AIDS Line:** tel. 223443; open Mon.-Fri. 7-10pm. **Gay Switchboard:** tel. 340101; open Tues.-Sat. 8-10pm. **Rape Hotline:** 108 Salisbury Rd., tel. 373181; open Mon. and Thurs. 7-10pm. **Women's Aid:** tel. 460566.

Sunday Pharmacy: Boots, 5 Wood St. (tel. 234043), around the corner from the stations. Open Mon.-Fri. 8am-8pm, Sat. 9am-6pm, Sun. 6-7pm.

Hospital: Royal Infirmary, Newport Rd. at Glossop Rd. (tel. 492233).

Emergency: Dial 999; no coins required.

Police: Cathay's Park, Civic Centre (tel. 344111).

ACCOMMODATIONS & CAMPING

Budget accommodations are scarce at the center of Cardiff, but the tourist office lists reasonably priced B&Bs (£13-15) on the outskirts and will book you a room for free if you leave a deposit. Most of the B&Bs in the courtly Victorian houses along Cathedral Rd. are graciously decorated but often indecorously priced (£18-22). The smaller neighborhoods around Cathedral Rd. are the best bet for less expensive B&Bs (bus #32, 62, or a 15-min. walk from the castle). Across town, Newport Rd. harbors the **YWCA** and several large guest houses and hotels.

Cardiff Youth Hostel (HI), 2 Wedal Rd., Roath Park (tel. 462303), 2 mi. from the city center; take bus #78, 80, or 82 from Central Station. Comfortable, roomy dormitory with individual bed lights in each bunk. Helpful warden knows the bus timetable and stops by heart, but will brook no talk about Winston Churchill. Good meals available. Lockout 10am-3pm; check-in after 3pm. Curfew 11pm. £8.70, under 18 £5.80. Open March-Oct. daily; Jan.-Feb. and Nov. Mon.-Sat.

Annedd Lon, 3 Dyfrig St. off Cathedral Rd. (tel. 223349). Pure and elegant non-smoking household with a Victorian touch. All rooms with tea/coffee and color TV, some with shower. Mottled cat and mottled carpet. Warm proprietress will house *Let's Go* users for £14, or across the street for £12.

Ty Gwyn, 7 Dyfrig St., off Cathedral Rd. (tel. 239785). Big and well-sunned rooms, with nice panelled bathrooms. Some doubles have shower in a corner of the bedroom. Singles £13.50, doubles £26.

Plasturton House, 1 Plasturton Ave. (tel. 383188), off Cathedral Rd. Turn left at the Beverly Hotel onto Plasturton Place, right onto Plasturton Gardens and continue past the small park. £13, double £24. Three children, the goldfish in the backyard, and relics of a deceased golden retriever will give you a down-home welcome in a house littered with toys. The proprietor can also give you tips on clog-dancing.

Bon Maison, 39 Plasturton Gardens (tel. 383660). White walls everywhere, with a draped honeymoon suite. TVs in every room. Look for the little placard of a boy pissing into a pot. Single £16, double £28.

Camping: Acorn Camping and Caravaning, Rosedew Farm, Ham Lane South, Llantwit Major (tel. (01446) 794024). Has showers and laundry. Open April-Oct. £3 pitch + £1.35/person, electricity £1.60. No extra charge for a car.

FOOD

Although the Welsh take on English fare tends to be just as meaty and fattening as the original, Cardiff is waking up to health food. A number of wholefood groceries ply their wares in the city center, including **Beanfreaks,** 3 St. Mary St. by the High St. (open Mon.-Fri. 7am-6:30pm, Sat. 8am-6pm, Sun. 8am-5pm). Or try **Wally's Deli-**

catessen in the Royal Arcade between St. Mary St. and the Hayes. Enough herbs to faze a Frenchman, enough oats to burst a horse (open Mon.-Sat. 8am-5:30pm). **Central Market,** in a ground arcade between St. Mary and Trinity St., is a fantastic farrago of food—from peaches to octopi (open Mon.-Sat. 8am-5:30pm). Behind the library on Charles St. simmers an **open-air market** (open Mon.-Sat. 9am-5pm). Cardiff virtually shuts down on Sundays, leaving visitors to search high and low for nourishment; try the fish bars or buy provisions on Saturday.

Crumbs, 33 David Morgan Arcade (tel. 395007), between St. Mary St. and The Hayes. Locals pack this vegetarian restaurant serving enormous, delicious salads (£2.30) and homemade breads in its wee wooden den. Open Mon.-Fri. 9:30am-3pm, Sat. 9:30am-4pm.

Celtic Cauldron Wholefoods, 47-49 Castle Arcade, across from the castle on, you guessed it, Castle St. (tel. 387185). Traditional Welsh faggots (misshapen meatballs dunked in gravy, £3.70) and wholefood served among the obligatory plants and lattices. Open Mon.-Sat. 8:30am-6pm.

The Homade, 26 Dumfries Pl., at the end of Queen St., and **Bistro One,** 4 Quay St., off St. Mary St. near the castle. Large rolls enlivened by a variety of fillings and salad—try the Spanish omelette (£1.10). Both open Mon.-Sat. 7:30am-6pm.

Dorothy's and **Tony's Fish Bar,** both on Caroline St., an alley that runs between St. Mary St. and The Hayes next to the mighty Brains Brewery complex. Fish and not a few chips £2.45. Pasties, pies, and curries under £2. Open Mon.-Sat. 10am-3:30am, Sun. 10am-2:30am.

SIGHTS

The preposterously opulent interior of **Cardiff Castle** (tel. 822083) is no less flamboyant than the peacocks that mewl inside the gates and pester tourists for food; the third Marquess of Bute employed the 4-foot tall William Burges, most lavish of Victorian architect-designers, to restore and gild the castle in the 19th century. (Castle open May.-Sept. daily 10am-6pm, 5 tours/hr. 10am-12:40pm and 2-5pm; Oct.-Nov. and Feb.-April less frequently. £3.30, seniors and children £1.70.) Though the castle's interior draws the attention, the gardens, Norman keep, and military museum are also worth a look (museum and grounds £2.20, seniors and children £1.10).

Across North Rd. stands Cardiff's **Civic Centre,** a grassy expanse containing everything appropriate to a provincial capital that wants to look impressive: monumental white buildings, ceremoniously inscribed rocks, statues with hair the pigeons have dyed white, and, in the middle of it all, a colonnaded, roofless **War Memorial.** The giant asparagus stalk is the belfry of Cardiff's **City Hall,** which houses a "Hall of Welsh Heroes" promenading in marble for the edification of the people (including an unusually healthy-looking Harri Tewdwr—Henry VII). The domed grandeur of the **National Museum of Wales** (tel. 397951) overwhelms its collection, which includes a hoard of pastoral paintings and Impressionists, as well as exhibits outlining the history of Wales since the Mesozoic era. (Open Tues.-Sat. 10am-5pm, Sun. 2:30-5pm; £2.50, students, seniors, and disabled £1.85, children £1.25.)

ENTERTAINMENT

Cardiff's signature odor emanates from **Brains Brewery** in the middle of the city. Its specialty is Brains S.A. (Special Ale), known to locals as "Brains Skull Attack" and served proudly by many pubs in the city center. Tuesday and Thursday nights vie with each other as Student Night in Cardiff, and discounts and happy hours are to be found all over town. Head to the **Four Bars Inn** on Castle St. and Womanby St. for a Brains booze-fest—most other people seem to. Although the bottom floor of the pub is strictly for chatting and chugging, the upstairs houses one of Britain's only all-jazz clubs outside of London. Performances begin nightly around 9pm (cover £3-4, student discounts 50p) and Thursday nights feature big-name musicians from around the country (£6-7). Exercise your dancing feet at **The Loop,** 8-10 High St., a new techno/industrial club with occasional live performances. The chic brood at the **Stage Door,** 25 The Parade (tel. 838145). **Philharmonic** at 76 St. Mary's St. pours pints upstairs while a nightclub rocks downstairs from 9:45pm to 2am; go to the pub early to avoid a £4 cover. (Live jazz Sunday nights. Pub open Mon.-Sat. 11am-2am, Sun. noon-3pm, 7-10:30pm.) Gays and lesbians gather at the **Exit Bar,** 48 Charles St. (tel. 378866; open Mon.-Tues. 6pm-2am, Wed.-Sat. 6pm-midnight, Sun. 7pm-midnight). **The Student Union** on Park Place behind the Civic Centre (tel. 396421) is probably the best bet for music and company (as well as cheap meals); on weekends go early or have a student take you in as a guest—also check the university for theatrical performances. The weekly newspaper *South Wales Echo* (25p) provides information on social events and hotspots; look under "Night Out." Avoid the city's docks while you're wandering through Cardiff; solo travelers won't find the wharf a safe place to spend an evening. As always, don't hesitate to hail a cab.

If you'd rather sit back and spectate, pick up a copy of *The Buzz* or the Cardiff *Entertainments* guide, free at the tourist office. The **Chapter Arts Centre,** Market Rd. in Canton (tel. 399666), features an eclectic program of dance, drama, gallery exhibitions, and film (from Joel Silver to *Help I'm Being Crushed to Death by a Black Rectangle).* The first-floor café is relaxed, and the Downstairs Bar has music nightly. (Open Mon.-Sat. 10am-11pm, Sun. noon-11pm. Late-night films Thurs.-Sat. at 11pm. Take bus #12 or 19 from Castle St. up Cowbridge.)

Adornments on the **John Bachelor Statue,** at the corner of Hill St. and The Hayes, are a happy gauge of the festive atmosphere in Cardiff. Scarves and hats signify rugby or football matches, and a clumsily held can of Brains S.A. is a sure sign of bacchanalia. Rugby is beyond doubt the national religion of Wales. Games are played in the September through April season in Cardiff at the **National Rugby Stadium,** Westgate St. (ticket office tel. 390111). While tickets for international games theoretically sell for £6-15, the only way the masses can obtain seats is by smooth-talking hawkers, who have been known to sell at as much as £200 for one seat. Try your luck at club games next door at the **Cardiff Rugby Club** (tel. 383546; £3-7).

■ NEAR CARDIFF

The **Welsh Folk Museum** (tel. 569441) shares the 100 acres of **St. Fagan's Park,** 4 mi. west of Cardiff, with native trees and sculpted hedges. Nearly 20 buildings— ranging from a late 15th-century farmhouse to the 1760 Esgair woolen mill—have been transported piece by piece from different parts of Wales and reassembled here. Someone (often a professional artisan) at each of these exhibits is eager to answer questions and demonstrate a skill such as handweaving, leather-tanning, or blacksmithing (open daily 10am-5pm; Nov.-March Mon.-Sat. 10am-5pm; £4, seniors and students £3, children £2). Take the hourly bus #32 from Central Station, or the hourly bus #56 from Castle St.

Two mi. northwest of the city center, near the River Taff, **Llandaff Cathedral** was built by the Normans, used by Cromwell as an alehouse, restored by the Victorians after the roof fell in, and gutted by a German land mine in 1941. It is now an architectural mince pie: a stern and solid Norman arch behind the altar is overshadowed by an intrusive reinforced-concrete arch from 1957, surmounted by a floating Christ shaped like a Pez dispenser. Off the Cathedral stands a ruin the Victorians would have loved for its tidy decrepitude: the broken, ivy-covered arches of the Castle of the Bishops of Llandaff, now a manicured park where schoolchildren flirt. Take bus #25 from Castle St. or #62 from the station (2/hr., Sun. 1/hr.), or walk down Cathedral Rd. and through Llandaff Fields.

The third Marquess of Bute and the diminutive architect William Burges (the same pair who renovated Cardiff Castle) struck again at **Castell Coch** (tel. 810101), piling up a toy castle atop 13th-century ruins, with dungeons for very bad, naughty children. The interior is like the nursery of an overgrown, profligate child; the walls are covered with scenes from Aesop and coloring-book figures of monkeys and maidens. The wooded site is good for picnics. Take bus #26 (1/hr.) up A470 to the village of **Tongwynlais,** where a brisk 15-min. walk up the hill brings you to the castle; or bus #136 (Mon.-Fri. 5/day) unloads you at the castle gate. Open daily 9:30am-6:30pm, Oct.-March Mon.-Sat. 9:30am-4pm, Sun. 11am-4pm; £2, seniors, students, and children £1.50, taped tours 50p).

Eight mi. north of Cardiff, sprawling **Caerphilly Castle** (tel. 883143) dwarfs the surrounding town. With 30 acres of man-made lakes and walls built by the 13th-century Norman warlord Gilbert de Clare, Caerphilly is Europe's largest fortification after Windsor Castle. Cromwell was inspired to drain the lakes and blow up the towers; the famous leaning tower of Caerphilly, with a top-to-bottom crack through which one can climb and scrape one's shirt, is said to be testimony to his failure (to a less fervent eye, it seems the ground subsided, but look at what he did to Llandaff Cathedral). Take the hourly bus #26 from Cardiff Central and get off in the shadow of the endless curtain wall. (Castle open daily 9:30am-6:30pm; Nov.-March Mon.-Sat. 2-4pm, Sun. 11am-4pm; £2, students, seniors, and children £1.50, audio tours £1.)

Cardiff Bus runs sporadic services to **Barry Island** to bask on sandy beaches and promenade through lush gardens just 11 mi. outside of the city.

■■■ WYE VALLEY

The wonder is that such a small stream could cut such a deep and gorgeous valley. The River Wye (Afon Gwy) winds down from the hills of central Wales in intestinal curves to its confluence with the broad and muddy River Severn just south of **Chepstow**. Below **Monmouth** it forms the border between England and Wales, and flows among the steep and lofty cliffs, orchard-tufts and pastoral farms, that William Wordsworth limned in 1798. The Normans built a chain of castles, now ruined, on the west side of the river to launch wars of conquest against the Welsh lowlands. Wordsworth thought he heard here "the still, sad music of humanity." These days the music might come from a car radio, though great stretches of the valley have slept through the Age of Industry.

GETTING THERE & GETTING ABOUT

The valley is best entered from the south, at Chepstow; both **buses** and **trains** run to Chepstow from Cardiff or Newport, 20 mi. east of Cardiff (by bus: #64 and 74; 4/hr.; 1¼hr.; £2; by train:14/day; 30min.; £3.40 from Newport, £4.40 from Cardiff). **National Express** buses ride to Chepstow from Cardiff (9/day; 50min.; £3.35), Newport (9/day; 25min.; £2.35), London (5/day, Sun. 4/day; 2¼hr.; £17.50), and Heathrow (9/day; 1¾hr.; £20). Trains chug from Cardiff or Newport to Hereford, north of Chepstow in England (1/hr.; 1hr.; £10.10).

Red and White Buses (tel. (01633) 266336) are the primary means of transport in the Wye Valley; be forewarned that there is no Sunday service. Bus #69 loops through Chepstow, Tintern, and Monmouth every two hours, and bus #416 runs 6 times per day from Monmouth to Hereford and Hay-on-Wye. A **Roverbus** pass (£4) will save you money if you plan to take more than one bus in a given day (See Wales Getting About). Hitchhikers say the going is good on the A466 in the summer; some stand near the entrance to Tintern Abbey or by the Wye Bridge in Monmouth.

HIKING

The valley yields walks of all difficulties and lengths. The **Wye Valley Walk** runs between Chepstow and Monmouth along cliffs, wooded hills, and farmland; the beautiful abbey and cathedral at Tintern and Hereford provide an hour's diversion. Across the river, **Offa's Dyke Path** runs the entire length of the English-Welsh border, offering 177 mi. of hiking trails (Chepstow-Tintern, 5 mi.; Tintern-Monmouth, 11 mi.; Monmouth-Symonds Yat, 6 mi.). From Symonds Yat, the walk continues north to Hay-on-Wye and ends at Prestatyn in the far north. "Offa's Dyke" itself is an 8th-century earthwork of uncertain origin; the English say it was built to keep the Welsh in, the Welsh say it was built to keep the English out. The path is awful for bikes and horses. East of Symonds Yat, the 20,000-acre **Forest of Dean,** once the happy hunting ground of Edward the Confessor and Williams I and II, now lies open to lords and villains alike. It is no longer fatal to be mistaken for a stag. For information on the forest, contact **Forest Enterprise** (tel. (01594) 833057) on Bank St. in Coleford, or the Coleford tourist office, 27 Market Place (tel. (01594) 836307). A variety of trails leads to the Wye Valley Walk or Offa's Dyke Path; tourist offices sell pamphlets of these 1.5 to 10 mi. walks. A 1:25000 Ordinance Survey map (£5) shows every path, pit, and remarkable rock in the lower Wye Valley and the Forest of Dean. For information on Offa's Dyke Path, write to the Offa's Dyke Association, West St., Knighton, Powys, Wales LD7 1EW or call (01547) 528753.

CHEPSTOW (CAS-GWENT)

Chepstow's strategic position at the mouth of the River Wye and the base of the English/Welsh border made it an important fortification and commercial center in Norman times. Its stature has since diminished. **Chepstow Castle** (tel. 624065), which commands the ancient entrance to the valley, contains a rectangular Norman keep that makes it Britain's oldest stone castle. It is also one of Britain's longest, with dozens of 700-year-old apertures along the clifftop for gazing upon a sometimes muddy Wye River. (Open daily 9:30am-6:30pm; mid-Oct. to March Mon.-Sat. 9:30am-4pm, Sun. 11am-4pm. £2.90; students, seniors, and children £1.80.) The old **town wall,** in some places as thick as 7 feet and as high as 15 feet, was designed as an extension of the castle for the collection of tolls and nighttime protection from vagabonds. The **Chepstow Festival,** held throughout July in even-numbered years, features open-air Shakespeare and musical events punctuated by the clash of full armored battles in the castle.

The **HI Youth Hostel** at **St. Briavel's Castle** (tel. (01594) 530272), 4 mi. northeast of Tintern, fills a 12th-century castle that has a dungeon through a trapdoor in the floor. (Don't break curfew.) One stone bedroom holds poignant inscriptions carved in the walls by prisoners through the centuries. From A466 (bus #69 from Chepstow) or Offa's Dyke, follow signs for 2 mi. from Bigsweir Bridge to St. Briavels. (Kitchen and meals. No laundry, but sells wine. Lockout 10am-5pm, curfew 11:30pm. Open daily March-Oct.; £7.75, under 18 £5.20.) In Chepstow, **Lower Hardwick House,** on Mt. Pleasant 300 yds. up the hill from the bus station (tel. 622162), is a 200-year-old mansion run by the delightful and wonderfully solicitous Eileen Grassby (£17, doubles £26).The large landscaped garden accommodates campers (£5/tent, English breakfast £3.50) as well as sculptures by Eileen's son—look for the tree ringed with severed heads. Or try **Langcroft,** 71 St. Kingsmark Ave., which has a massage bathtub (tel. 625569; singles £15, doubles £28). For more **camping** options, try **Beeches Farm,** Tidenham (tel. 689257), 5 mi. north of Chepstow and just east of Offa's Dyke Path, particularly convenient for walkers (£1.50/person; no showers or laundry).

Chepstow's **train station** is on Station Rd. **Buses** stop above the town gate in front of the **Somerfield** supermarket in Albion Sq. (Supermarket open Mon., Tues., Sat. 8:30am-6pm; Wed. 8:30am-7pm; Thurs., Fri. 8:30am-8pm; Sun. 10am-4pm.). Both stations are unstaffed, but you can ask about National Express tickets at **Fowler's Travel,** 9 Moor St. (tel. 623031; open Mon.-Fri. 9am-5:30pm, Sat. 9am-4pm). Chepstow's **tourist office** (tel. 623772) confronts the castle from its car park (open in season daily 9am-5pm). Chepstow's **telephone code** is 01291.

TINTERN

Five mi. north of Chepstow on A466, the roofless walls of **Tintern Abbey** (tel. (01291) 689251) shade crowds of tourists in the summer. Tintern was built by Cistercian monks in the 12th and 13th centuries as a center for religious austerity; this did not keep it from being the richest abbey in Wales until Henry VIII dissolved it. On wet days, the abbey can still look mystical and touchingly decayed from certain perches in the surrounding hills, when bushes block out the parking lot and the postcard shack next door. (Open daily 9:30am-6:30pm, mid-Oct. to mid-March Mon.-Sat. 9:30am-4pm, Sun. 11am-4pm. £2; seniors, students, and children £1.50.) An unofficial information service (tel. (01291) 689566) operates out of the Old Station a mile north of the abbey on A466; the office will book beds for a 10% deposit (open April-Oct. daily 10:30am-5:30pm). If crowds in Tintern village overwhelm you, cross the iron footbridge and head for the hills. Waymarked paths lead to **Offa's Dyke** (45min.) and **Devil's Pulpit** (1hr.), an enormous stone from which Satan is said to have tempted the monks as they worked in the fields.

As the path winds through Tintern village, it passes the 400-year-old **Wye Barn Bed and Breakfast,** which enjoys a lovely view (from £17; space is limited). Right off A466 at the village, **The Old Rectory** (tel. (01291) 689519) clings to a hill just a few feet from the Wye (£13.50/person). Or try **Home Farm** (tel. (01291) 689559), 2 mi. east of town (single £13, double £28). It's hard to find; call ahead for directions. The Old Station information office lists accommodations, with color photos.

MONMOUTH (TREFYNWY)

The market town of Monmouth sits snagged in the fork of the Rivers Wye and Monnow, eight miles north of Tintern. Fascinated by its own long past, the town is the birthplace of Geoffrey of Monmouth, who gave a shred of historical credibility to King Arthur and Merlin in his *History of the Kings of Britain*. People are forever digging up some slice of Monmouth's turf; whenever a shop changes hands, archaeologists go wild, unearthing Roman walls and medieval wells. The famous 13th-century **toll bridge** still glowers intact at visitors crossing the Monnow, but time has so ruthlessly ruined the Norman **castle** (where Henry V was born in 1387) that it barely rises above its parking lot, a single cluttered hill past the town center.

Monmouth's **HI Youth Hostel** (tel. 715116) occupies the 15th-century Priory St. School near the center of town. Self-catering kitchen; no meals served. (Lockout 10am-5pm, curfew 11pm, last booking 10:30pm. Open daily March-Oct. £6.50, under 18 £4.35.) The **Coleford tourist office** (tel. (01594) 836307), across the river in England, will help lay you down to sleep in the Forest of Dean. In Monmouth, B&Bs lie mostly along Hereford Rd. and in St. James' Square. **Wye Avon,** Dixton Rd. (tel. 713322), provides board in a typically beautiful Monmouth mansion at a typically high Monmouth price (£14, double/twin £28). **Mrs. Emblem,** 91 Hereford Rd. (tel. 713591), stands for a glorious view of green hills, and represents a 15-minute walk from town (£15). A **tourist office** (tel. 713899) hides in Shire Hall on Agincourt Sq. beneath the statue of Henry V (Open April-Oct. daily 10am-6pm). The **telephone code** in Monmouth is 01600. Buses stop in a lot near the fortified bridge. Monmouth is the last stop for bus #69 from Chepstow and Tintern (see above); bus #60 goes to Newport. Ask for a timetable at the tourist office or call (01633) 266336.

HEREFORD, ENGLAND

Eighteen mi. north of Monmouth, Hereford is easily accessible by British Rail; the city lies in England, but it makes a good springboard for a trip through Wales. The town still confines itself to the ruins of its old Norman walls, built in AD 676 (self-guided tour of walls takes two hours). A great pile of purple sandstone, the 13th-century **cathedral** (tel. 359880), guards the world's only complete medieval world map. The **Mappa Mundi** was drawn around 1290 and hangs now in a dim crypt; look for a splendidly naked Lot's wife turning into salt as Sodom and Gomorrah sink behind her. Troy and Babylon still stand, and Britain is as big as China. (Cathedral open daily; Mappa Mundi open Mon.-Sat. 10am-4:15pm, Nov.-Easter 10:30am-3:30pm; admission to map £2.60, students, seniors, and children £1.20.) The vertiginous 218-step cathedral tower opens for climbing some Saturdays and holidays. The **Old House,** Broad St. (tel. 268121 ext. 225), recreates 17th-century Hereford life while **Churchill Gardens,** Venn's Lane (tel. 267409), displays Georgian and Victorian rooms and furniture. (Churchill Gardens open Tues.-Sun. 2-5pm, in winter Tues.-Sat. 2-5pm; £1, seniors, students, and children 40p. Old House open Mon. 10am-1pm, Tues.-Sat. 10am-1pm, 2-5:30pm; in winter Sat. 10am-1pm. 80p, seniors, students, and children 40p.) Adjacent to the Cider Brandy Distillery on Whitecross Rd., the **Cider Museum,** Pomona Place (tel. 354027), tells the story of traditional cider-making from the 17th century to the present (open daily 10am-5:30pm; Nov.-

March Mon.-Sat. 1-5pm). Art and music create a carnival atmosphere during the **Festival** of the first two weeks of August. In late October, a crafts exhibition arrives.

Accommodations in town are sparse and expensive. Try the **Tenby Guest House,** 8 St. Nicholas St. (tel. 274783), for huge rooms with particle board decor and a lounge with papsan chairs (single £16, double £30, twin £28). Whitecross Rd., the noisy extension of Eign St., has several B&Bs. **YMCAs** at 107 Whitecross Rd. (tel. 272452) and 61 Newtown Rd. (tel. 354341) have small, bare rooms and self-catering kitchens 15 minutes from the cathedral. (Men and women. No breakfast; no curfew.) You can windowshop along cobblestoned **Church Street,** or march to **Victory,** 88 St. Owen St. (tel. 274998), to toss back beer aside a ship-shaped bar (open Mon.-Sat. 11am-11pm, Sun. noon-3pm, 7-10:30pm). Behind **The Barrels** (tel. 274968), the **Wyevalley Brewery,** 69 St. Owen St., offers free tours if you call ahead. Metal casks clatter on the cobblestones.

The **tourist office,** 1 King St. in front of the cathedral (tel. 268430) books beds for a 10% deposit (open daily 9am-5pm, Oct.-April Mon.-Sat. 9am-5pm). Walking tours leave from the tourist office mid-May to mid-Sept. Mon.-Sat. at 10:30am, Sun at 2:30pm (£1, seniors and children over 12 50p, under 12 free). **Trains** from London arrive every hour and leave for London 1-2 times per hour (3hr.; £31). They also run to Abergavenny (1/hr.; 25min.; £4.90), Shrewsbury (1/hr.; 1hr.; £9.60), Cardiff (1/hr.; 1hr.; £10.10), and Chepstow via Newport (£11.50). Hereford is connected by **Red and White bus** routes to the other Wye Valley villages as well as to Brecon, Abergavenny, and Newport (Red and White Rover Pass, £4). Sundays, **Yeoman's** Bus #40 runs twice to Brecon via Hay-on-Wye. The **train station** and **bus station** are at the end of Commercial Rd., near the **County Hospital,** Union Walk (tel. 355444); any Hopper bus will take you there. Hereford's **telephone code** is 01432.

HAY-ON-WYE

Presided over by a stubby town clock that rings hollow chimes, Hay-on-Wye seeds its confusing streets with the world's largest clutter of second-hand book stores. After weathering eight centuries of border wars, fires, and neglect, Hay's Norman fortress fell to the relentless sellers of yellowing paperbacks. Its mighty walls now buttress books and cash registers, joining Hay's movie theater among the recently vanquished. Each year at May's end, the town throws a 10-day literary festival, during which luminaries like Derek Walcott and Maya Angelou give readings and Salman Rushdie darts nervously about. Befitting its status as a literary Never-Never Land, Hay elected to secede from Britain on April 1, 1977; as yet, London has treated the act as a grandiose April Fool's joke, choosing not to launch a punitive air raid to defend its hard-won territory.

The **HI Youth Hostel** nearest to Hay-on-Wye lies 8 mi. out of town at **Capel-y-Ffin,** along Offa's Dyke Path (tel. (01873) 890650; £6.50; open March-Oct. Thurs.-Tues.; Nov. and Feb. weekends only). Ideal for walkers of the path, bikers, or those who don't mind paying for the taxi from Hay (taxi £8.50; tel. 821266), the road to the hostel climbs up breathtaking **Gospel Pass,** where part of *An American Werewolf in London* was filmed. The tourist office has an excellent list of Hay's many B&B's; expect to pay at least £15 for a single in town. The delightful low-ceilinged **Jasmine Cottage,** on Brook St. behind the Wheatsheaf pub (tel. 821168), displays a 500-year-old dresser in a breakfast-room crammed with antiques (single £15, double/twin £27). **Belmont House,** on Belmont Rd. (tel. 820718), has huge rooms and healthy old furniture (single £16, double/twin £25). It's easy to camp near Hay along the Wye Valley walk or Offa's Dyke. **Radnor's End Campsite** (tel. 820780) is the closest to town; cross Bridge St. and go 300 yards to the left towards Clyvo (£2/person). The famished should stop by **The Granary,** Broad St. (tel. 820790), which bakes Welsh specialties like *Bara Brith* (a delicious buttered fruitcake) fresh every day (open daily 10am-5:30pm). Hay's oldest pub, the **Three Tuns** on Broad St., has one bench and one table. It's open when the chatty proprietress feels like it.

The **tourist office** on Oxford Rd. next to the bus stop (tel. 820144) has binders of information on hang-gliding, ballooning, pony trekking, and other pricey excursions, as well as free lists of accommodations and booksellers. They book beds for £1 and speak twice as slowly as you do. (Open daily 10am-1pm, 2-5pm; Oct.-March 11am-4pm.) The nearest **bike rental** is **Black Mountain Hire** 4 mi. west of town at Glasbury-on-Wye (tel. 847897); mountain bikes £12.50/day. (The Wye Valley Path accommodates bikes; Offa's Dyke Path doesn't.) Black Mountain Hire also rents canoes (£9-16/day). The closest train station is Hereford. **Red and White** bus #39 runs between Hay, Hereford, and Brecon (Mon.-Sat. 5/day; £2-2.70). On Sundays, Yeoman's Bus #40 runs twice between Brecon, Hay, and Hereford (£1.50-2.50). Hay-on-Wye's **telephone code** is 01497.

ABERGAVENNY (Y-FENNI)

The bushy marker town of Abergavenny (pop. 10,000) styles itself the "traditional gateway to Wales," yielding to the Black Mountains in the eastern third of Brecon Beacons National Park. In 1175, the Norman knight William de Breos invited the Welsh lords to his table at Abergavenny castle, and then killed them while they were well-fed and unarmed. Dining out in Abergavenny hasn't been the same since, though markets try to fill the culinary void. William's **castle** is now an inscrutable ruin with scattered wall fragments and stairs leading nowhere; near the dungeon stands the **Abergavenny Museum,** which displays a flaked mural taken from the chapel of two local priests who were hanged, disemboweled, and burned by an anti-Catholic mob in 1678 (open Mon.-Sat. 11am-1pm, 2-5pm, Sun. 2-5pm; £1, students and seniors 50p, under 18 free with an adult—you may need one). The **Abergavenny Town Trail** (pamphlet 60p) rambles through medieval streets and courtyards.

Budget-breaking B&Bs (£15-20) lie in wait on Monmouth Rd. near the tourist office; the closest youth hostel is at **Capel-y-Ffin,** 16 mi. out of town and inaccessible by bus. The tourist office distributes a free list of accommodations, most of them wonderful rooms in farmhouses within 5 mi. of the city center, near the park. Some proprietors will arrange to pick you up in town if you call ahead. The **Ivy Villa Guest House,** 43 Hereford Rd. (tel. 852473), has no ivy but flaunts its poinsettia carpet. The proprietors mourn the recent death of their huge, wooly mammoth (£13.50). **Mrs. Bradley,** 10 Merthyr Rd. (tel. 852206), at the end of Frogmore St., has beds of varying hardnesses—find one that suits. £10 with continental breakfast, £12 with cooked breakfast. On Tuesday, Friday, and Saturday, the **market** proffers produce, cheese, baked goods, and live sheep. For dead meat, try the **Safeway** on Cibi Walk off Frogmore St. (open Mon.-Thurs. 8am-8pm, Fri. 8am-9pm, Sat. 8am-7pm, Sun. 10am-4pm). For quiche and lasagna at a decent price (about £2), head to **Focus,** 53 Frogmore St. (open Mon.-Sat. 9:30am-4:45pm). **Pinch the Baker** at 16 Frogmore St. sells jelly doughnuts so sugary they crunch (open Mon.-Sat. 8am-5pm).

The **tourist office** shares space with the **National Park Information Centre** (tel. 853254) on Monmouth Rd. by the bus station. (Tourist office open daily 10am-6pm, National Park Office open Easter-Oct. daily 9:30am-5:30pm.) **Dave Brook Bikes,** 9 Brecon Rd. (tel. 857066), rents mountain bikes for £10 per day; they'll negotiate weekly rates (open Mon.-Sat. 9:30am-5:30pm). Piles of camping supplies may be admired and then purchased at **Trekitt,** 37 Cross St. (tel. 853302; open Mon.-Sat. 9am-5:30pm). **Rail** tracks run north from Abergavenny to Hereford (£4.90) and Shrewsbury (£13.50) and southwards to Newport (£4.20), with connections to Cardiff (£6.20), Chepstow (£7.20), Bristol (£6.50), and London (£27.50). **Red and White Buses** run Monday through Saturday to Hereford (#20, 4/day; £2.48), Brecon (#21; 6/day; £2.26), Newport (#20 and 21 in the other direction; 12/day; about 1hr.; £2.42), and to Merthyr, continuing to Cardiff (#X4, 9/day; 2¼hr.). Hitchers say the A40 between Abergavenny and Brecon is unreliable, but not impossible. The **train station** is on Station Rd. off Monmouth Rd. The **bus station** bows at the foot of Monmouth Rd., near the castle. Get National Express information at **Gwent Travel,** Frogmore St. (tel. 857 666; open Mon.-Fri. 9am-5:30pm, Sat. 9am-4pm) or at the tourist office. Abergavenny's **telephone code** is 01873.

Near Abergavenny

Abergavenny's real attraction lies in the hills around it. **Blorenge** (1811 ft.) is by far the most massive, a looming hump 2½ mi. southwest of town, perfect for launching hang-gliders. **Skysports Hangliding School,** 36 Hatherleigh Rd. (tel. 856112) teaches two, five, and seven-day courses for novices and intermediate students (£90-210). A path begins off the B4246, traversing valley woodlands to the upland area; it climbs the remaining 1500 ft. in 4½ mi. Climbers adore the sharp, arresting **Sugar Loaf** (1955 ft.), 2½ mi. north; the trailhead to the top starts about 1 mi. west of town on the A40. Many say hitching a ride to the car park and beginning your hike from there is the best way to save your legs for the difficult but rewarding hike to the summit. The path to **Skirrid Fawr** (1595 ft.), northeast of town, starts about 2 mi. down the B4521. *Over Thirty Walks in the Southern Black Mountains* (£1), available from the park office, details mountain climbs as well as gentler walks in the valleys. Pony trekking is popular in the farmlands around Abergavenny; pick up the free brochure on Outdoor Activities from the tourist center.

All of the megaliths in the Black Mountains are believed to point toward the ruined 12th-century **Llanthony Priory,** perhaps to help errant friars find their way home. Founded by a group of dissenting Augustinian priests led by William de Lacy, the priory has been roofless and abandoned since the 16th century. Take the Hereford bus (#20) or the A465 to Llanfihangel Crucorney, where the B4423 begins. Most walk or hitch the last 6 mi. to the priory. The **Capel-y-Ffin Youth Hostel (HI)** is an additional 4 mi. along. (See Hay-on-Wye.)

At the **Big Pit Mining Museum** (tel. (01495) 790311), in Blaenavon, 5 mi. southwest of Abergavenny (take the B4246, then the B4248), you can ride a 300-ft. shaft to the subterranean workshops, stables, and coal faces of a 19th-century colliery that remained in operation until 1980. Ex-miners work as guides, and tell stories as grim and chilling as the mine. (Open March-Dec. daily 10am-3:30pm, call for winter hours; £5, students and seniors £4.50, children £3.50, under 5 not admitted.)

■■■ BRECON (ABERHONDDU)

Although not actually in the mountains, Brecon (pop. 7100) is the best base for hiking through the craggy Brecon Beacons to the south. Accessible from the south coast via Abergavenny or Hereford, Brecon is a market town with ample and inexpensive accommodations, a supremely competent National Park Information Centre, shops where you can stock up for your outdoor adventures, frequent craft and antique fairs, and an exceptional Jazz Festival (mid-August).

GETTING THERE

Brecon has no bus or train station, but **buses** arrive regularly from other spots in the area. Inquire about bus schedules and routes at **Holiday World,** 7 The Bulwark (tel. 625678; open Mon.-Sat. 9am-5:30pm) or **The Travel Centre,** 99 The Struet (tel. 625858; open Mon.-Fri. 9am-5:30pm, Sat. 9am-1pm). **Silverline** bus #63 (tel. (01685) 382406) connects Brecon with Swansea (2-3/day, Sun. 1/day). Service #43 meets trains from Cardiff at Merthyr Tydfil (6/day, Sun. 3/day); the scenic drive highlighted by waterfalls every 100 yd. is worth the £2 ticket. **Red and White Buses** (tel. (01633) 266336) runs four or five buses (Mon.-Sat.) to Hereford via Hay-on-Wye (#39), Abergavenny, and Newport (#21). Red and White #X4 runs to Merthyr every hour from Abergavenny and from Cardiff; to get to Brecon from Merthyr, you must rely on Silverline buses. Based in Brecon, **Williams Buses** (tel. 730289) makes two morning trips to Abergavenny. Along the A40 from Abergavenny or the A470 from Merthyr Tydfil, most hitchers stay near intersections where lorries can stop.

ORIENTATION & PRACTICAL INFORMATION

Buses stop at the **Bulwark,** Brecon's main strip, which fans out into St. Mary St., Church Lane, High St. Inferior, and Lion St.; these streets empty into a stretch dubbed, successively, Wheat St., High St. Superior, and the Struet. The Watton leads out of town towards the youth hostel.

Tourist Office: Cattle Market Car Park (tel. 622485 or 625692). Take Lion Yard off Lion St. to the car park, or follow the mooing from the doomed cows nearby. Books beds for a 10% deposit; the booklet *Where to Stay in Brecon Beacons National Park* is free. Sells excellent town maps for 10p. Open daily 10am-6pm; Oct.-Easter 9:30am-5:30pm.

Brecon Beacons National Park Information Centre: Cattle Market Car Park (tel. 623156), 10 ft. from the tourist information center. Ordnance survey maps (£5) and good advice. Open April-Oct. daily 9:30am-5:30pm. Main Park office around the corner on Glamorgan St. Send National Park inquiries to 7 Glamorgan St. (enclose self-addressed envelope plus an International Reply Coupon).

Financial Services: Barclays, 9 The Bulwark (tel. 855911). Open Mon.-Wed. and Fri. 9:30am-4:30pm, Thurs. 10am-4:30pm. **Lloyds,** 38 High St. (tel. 623761). Open Mon.-Sat. 9:30am-5:30pm. Both charge £3 commission on traveler's checks.

Post Office: 6 Church Lane (tel. 611113) off St. Mary St. Sells stationery, candy bars, and jigsaw puzzles. Open Mon.-Sat. 9am-5:30pm. **Postal Code:** LD3 7AS.

Telephone Code: 01874.

Bus Station: Buses leave from The Bulwark, opposite St. Mary's Church. Schedules posted in three nearby locations, or ask at an information center.

Bike Rental: Crickhowell Adventure Gear, 1 High St. (tel. 810020). Mountain bikes £12/day. Open Mon.-Sat. 9am-5:30pm, occasionally on Sun.

Camping Supplies: Crickhowell Adventure Gear, 1 High St. (tel. 810020) and 21 Ship St. (tel. 611586). Gear galore: climbing equipment, hiking boots, outdoor books. Rents bikes. Open Mon.-Sat. 9am-5:30pm, occasionally on Sunday.

Launderette: Washeteria, Lion Yard, between car park and Lion St.; follow signs to toilets. Wash £1.50. Ineffectual dryers. Change given at Joy's, 3A High St. Open Mon.-Fri. 9am-6pm, Sat. 9am-4pm, Sun. 9am-1pm. Last wash 1hr. before closing.

Early closing day: Wednesday at 1pm.

Hospital: Brecon War Memorial, Cerrichion Rd. (tel. 622443). Open daily 8am-8pm.

Emergency: Dial 999; no coins required.

Police: Lion St. (tel. 622331).

ACCOMMODATIONS & CAMPING

Only a three-minute walk from town, the Watton is ripe with B&Bs (£14-15). If you plan to visit during mid-August, book far in advance—the Jazz Festival will claim every pillow in town.

Ty'n-y-Caeau Youth Hostel (HI) (tin-uh-KAY-uh; tel. 86270), 3 mi. from town, on a lane leading from the A470 through the hamlet of Groesffordd to the A38 (Hay Rd.). A 2½-mi. footpath from Brecon reduces the distance; ask at the tourist office. The Brecon-Abergavenny bus stops right outside Groesffordd; from there, follow the signs. You may also be able to arrange a pick-up with the warden. A large country house, popular with cyclists and fell-walkers, which the friendly and helpful warden runs by the book. £6.50, under 18 £4.35. Open March to mid-July and Oct. Mon.-Sat., mid-July to mid-Sept. daily.

Walker's Rest, 18 Bridge St. (tel. 625993), across the Usk bridge. Rustic decor and rooms so huge you get breakfast in your bedroom—or in your bed, if you prefer. The bathroom has a fireplace. No TVs. Single £15, double £13.50 per person.

Mrs. J. Thomas, 13 Alexandra Rd. (tel. 624551) behind the tourist office. The proprietress has traveled in 25 countries, lived in 15, and collected exotic memorabilia from each. A squashed tiger threatens breakfasting guests from the floor. Large rooms, some with inlaid tiles. £15, doubles £14 per person.

Camping: Brynich Caravan Park (tel. 623325), 1½ mi. east on the A40 and sign-posted from the A40/A470 roundabout. £3 per person. Showers and laundry. Open Easter-Oct.

FOOD

Gather ye camping supplies while ye may at the **Top Drawer,** 15 Ship St., which specializes in dried food and snacks (open Mon.-Tues. and Thurs.-Sat. 9:30am-5:30pm, Wed. 9:30am-1pm). For fresh produce, head to **Top Drawer 2,** High St., or one of the supermarkets on High St. **St. Mary's Bakery,** 4 St. Mary's St., has shelves of puffy bread, custards, and pastries (open Mon.-Fri. 7:30am-5pm, Sat. 7:30am-2pm). **Brown Sugar Restaurant and Tea Garden,** 12 The Bulwark (tel. 625501). Light and tasty homemade sandwiches at light and tasty prices (£1-1.60). Open Mon.-Sat. 9:30am-9:30pm, Sun. 10am-9:30pm; Sept.-May Mon.-Sat. 10am-6pm). **Sarah Siddons Inn,** 47 High St. (tel. 622009). Sandwiches and hot entrees; pigeon in red wine £4.25. Sarah Siddons, "England's most famous actress," was born in the pub in 1755 (open Mon.-Sat. 11am-11pm, Sun. noon-3pm, 7-10:30pm).

SIGHTS & ENTERTAINMENT

Brecon's **cathedral** squats in a pleasant grove on a hill by the River Honddu. The 13th-century church is heavy-set and poorly lit; oddly, the west side lacks a door. The **Brecknock Museum** (tel. 624121), at the end of The Bulwark seems mainly designed to teach children about the region's history—little blue-and-yellow banners read, "Normans invade England" and "Normans attack Wales." The cozy Edwardian naturalist's study may make you homesick (open Mon.-Fri. 10am-5pm, Sat. 10am-1pm, 2-5pm, and also April-Sept. Sun. 10am-1pm, 2-5pm; free). Further down The Watton, the **Borders Military Museum** (tel. 623111) has a Zulu war room filled with guns and uniforms (open Mon.-Sat. 9am-5pm; Oct.-March Mon.-Fri.; £1). **Dragonfly Cruises** (tel. (01831) 685222) glides through the Monmouth and Brecon Canal for 2½-hour mountain tours (Aug. Wed.-Thurs., Sat.-Sun. 3pm; Sept.-Jul. Wed., Sat.-Sun. 3pm; £3.50, seniors and children £2.50).

   Brecon draws crowds to its **antique fairs** on the last Saturday of every month, and craftspeople from all over South Wales hawk their wares in Market Hall on High St. at the **craft fairs** on the third Saturday of every month. The **Jazz Festival,** held in mid-August, subtitles itself "the only festival in Britain bigger than the town itself" as it packs the streets for the likes of Gerry Mulligan and Cecil Taylor. Additional campsites open on the farms during the festival, and buses provide extra service to Cardiff. For more information, contact the Festival Office, Watton Chambers, Brecon, Powys, Wales LD3 7EF (tel. 625557).

■■■ BRECON BEACONS NATIONAL PARK

Brecon Beacons National Park (Bannau Brycheiniog) encompasses 519 sq. mi. of barren peaks, well-watered forests, and windswept wastes. The park divides into four regions: the rugged country around the remote western Black Mountain; Fforest Fawr, containing the spectacular waterfalls of Ystradfellte; the Black Mountains to the east; and the impressive Beacon peaks where King Arthur's mountain fortress was once thought to have stood. The market towns on the fringe of the park, especially Brecon and Abergavenny, make pleasant touring bases. The park's beauty is a well-kept secret, making the region much less crowded than northern Snowdonia, and the bus service much patchier.

GETTING THERE & GETTING ABOUT

The Paddington Station (London)-South Wales **rail** line runs via Cardiff to Abergavenny at the park's southeastern corner, and to Merthyr Tydfil on the southern edge. (Check a *Valley Lines* brochure from Regional Railways for the hourly Merthyr Tydfil connection.) Train lines also connect to Newport, Chepstow, and Bristol on the coast, and Hereford and Shrewsbury inland. The Central Wales rail line passes through Llandeilo and Llandovery, towns in the more remote Black Mountain region. **Silverline** buses regularly cross the park en route from Brecon, on the northern side of the park, to Merthyr Tydfil (7/day, Sun. 2/day; 35min.; £2-3), or to Swansea, west of Cardiff along the coast (3/day; Sun. 2/day; 1½hr.; £2-3). **Red and White** buses stop in Abergavenny, Hay-on-Wye, and Brecon. For bus information, call Red and White (tel. (01633) 266336) or Silverline (tel. (01685) 382406). For rail schedules, call (01222) 228000. Information offices in the area will also provide timetables. Hitchers say the going is tougher on A470 than on minor roads, where drivers often stop just to enjoy the view.

PRACTICAL INFORMATION

Stop at a **National Park Information Centre** (listed below) before venturing forth. While tourist offices are helpful in planning a route by car or bus, the park centers provide pamphlets and advice on hiking, including updated weather reports. Free maps of the park are available, but the 1:25000 scale Ordnance Survey maps #11, 12, and 13 (£4.99) are indispensable, both for serious exploring and for reaching safety in bad weather. You can buy leaflets outlining suggested walks in almost any region of the park (15p-£1.25). A £1 pamphlet guides you through plane crash sites in the Beacons mountain range. The National Park staff offers free walks of varying difficulties between April and November; ask a tourist office for a brochure. Yellow trail cards are available at the Libanus Mountain Centre; consider leaving one with the police before setting out on a hike. The free *Summer Walks and Events* outlines an assortment of lovespoon-carving and sheepdog demonstrations.

National Park Information Centres

Abergavenny: Monmouth Rd. (tel. (01873) 853254), opposite bus station in the tourist office. Open Easter-Oct. daily 9:30am-5:30pm.

Brecon: Cattle Market Car Park (tel. (01874) 623156), next to the tourist information office, off Lion St. Open April-Oct. daily 9:30am-5:30pm. Main Park office around the corner on Glamorgan St.

Llandovery: Broad Street (tel. (01550) 20693). Open May-Sept. daily 9:30am-5:30pm; Easter-May Mon.-Sat. 10am-5:30pm, Sun. 2-5:30pm.

Libanus National Mountain Park Visitor Centre (Mountain Centre), Brecon Beacons (tel. (01874) 623366). Catch the Silverline Brecon-Merthyr bus #43 to Libanus, 5 mi. southwest of Brecon (7/day, Sun. 2/day; 8 min.), and walk the remaining 1½ mi. uphill. Disabled access. Open July-Aug. daily 9:30am-6pm; March-June and Sept.-Oct. daily 9:30am-5:30pm, Nov.-Feb. daily 9:30am-4:30pm.

Craig-y-nos: Pen-y-cae (tel. (01639) 730395). Open daily 9:30am-5:30pm; July-Aug. Mon.-Thurs. 10am-6pm, Fri.-Sun. 10am-7pm; winter daily 10am-4pm.

You can load up on gear in the market towns (see Brecon and Abergavenny) or south of Brecon at the **Tal-y-Bont Venture Centre** (The Old Shop), Tal-y-Bont-on-Usk, Brecon Powys LD3 7JD (tel. (01874) 87458). Tal-y-Bont offers access to the Beacons by way of an enjoyable 6-mi. hike alongside the reservoir. The rivers flowing into it form an impressive string of waterfalls which rival those in Ystradfellte.

SAFETY

The mountains are unprotected and in places difficult to scale. Air masses clash and cloud banks slam down over the Beacons, breeding storms within minutes. Do not shelter in caves or under isolated trees in violent weather, since they tend to draw lightning. A **compass** is essential: much of the park is trackless waste, and landmarks get lost in the sudden mists. Never hike alone. If you hit trouble and can reach a telephone, call **mountain rescue** in Brecon at (01874) 622331 or dial 999. Otherwise, the standard six blasts on your whistle should summon help. (Three are the reply.) Please review Essentials: Hiking & Camping for advice on keeping safe in the wilds.

ACCOMMODATIONS & CAMPING

Like towns and people, B&Bs are sparse within the park; the Brecon tourist offices's free *Where to Stay in Brecon Beacons National Park* lists a few. Five **HI Youth Hostels,** including Brecon's (see Brecon above) are scattered about the park.

Llwyn-y-Celyn HI Youth Hostel (HLOOEEN-uh-kel-in; tel. (01874) 624261), 8 mi. south of Brecon, 2 mi. south of Libanus, and 1 mi. north of the Storey Arms car park on the A470. Take Silverline bus #43 from Brecon or Merthyr Tidfil (7/day, 2/day Sun.). Very convenient to Pen-y-Fan and the rest of the Beacons range. Traditional Welsh farmhouse full of the warden's own creations; look for the chunky chess set and records made into clocks. Excellent dinners (£3.90) and breakfasts (£2.60). Lockout 10am-5pm, but a rain shed keeps you dry while you wait. £6.50, under 18 £4.35. Open July-Aug. daily; March-June and Sept.-Oct. Mon.-Sat.

Ystradfellte HI Youth Hostel (tel. (01639) 720304), south in the woods and waterfall district. A 3-mi. walk or drive from the A4059 along a paved road; 4 mi. from the village of Penderyn and a 5-min. walk from the Porth-yr-Ogof cave. This delightful hostel in two small cottages will heal your thorn wounds and bruises from exploring cave and waterfall country. Self-catering kitchen. £5.90, under 18 £3.95. Open April-Oct. Fri.-Wed.; Nov.-March for groups of 10 or more only.

Llanddeusant HI Youth Hostel (tel. (015504) 634 and 619), in the isolated Black Mountain area around Llangadog village, reached by the Trecastle-Llangadog mountain road. £5.90, under 18 £4. Open daily Easter-Sept., year-round for advance booking. Reservations advised.

Capel-y-ffin HI Youth Hostel (tel. (01873) 890650), near the River Honddu, at the eastern edge of the Black Mountains. Hay-on-Wye is the closest town; catch Red and White Bus #39 from Hereford to Brecon, stop before Hay and walk uphill. A beautiful base for ridge-walking. No smoking. Meals available. Allows camping on its grounds. £6.50, under 18 £4.35. Open April-Sept. Thurs.-Tues.

Commercial campsites are plentiful and fairly evenly dispersed, but often difficult to reach without a car. The free brochure *Camping and Caravan Sites* maps 30 sites in the park, complete with grid references. Many offer laundry and shopping facilities, and all have parking and showers; prices range from £1.75-5 per tent. Farmers may let you camp on their land if you ask first and promise to leave the site as you found it; be prepared to make a donation toward feeding the sheep.

THE BRECON BEACONS

At the center of the park, the Brecon Beacons lure hikers with their pastoral slopes and barren peaks. A splendid view of the range complements an exhibit on its history at the **Mountain Centre** outside Libanus (see Practical Information, above). From the Mountain Centre, an hour-long stroll among the suicidal sheep leads to the scant remains of an Iron Age fort and more views of the surrounding valleys and hills. The most convenient route to the top of **Pen-y-Fan** (pen-eh-van), at 2907 ft. the highest mountain in South Wales, begins at **Storey Arms,** a large parking lot and bus stop 5 mi. south of Libanus on the A470. Unfortunately, the paths to the peak are so popular that they have been eroded, scree (loose rocks) shaking underfoot.

A far more pleasant hiking route starts in nearby **Llanfaes,** a western suburb of Brecon, and follows leafy roads up to trails past streams and waterfalls. Walk or drive the first 3 miles from Llanfaes down Ffrwdgrech Rd. to the parking lot (take the middle fork after the first bridge). From the car park, a trail to the peak passes **Llyn** (Lake) **Cwm Llwch,** a glacial pool 2000 ft. high in the shadow of **Corn Ddu** peak. A hundred feet from the path near Corn Ddu stands an obelisk marking the site where the body of 5-year-old Tommy Jones was found a month after he lost his way one night in 1900. No one knows how he climbed so high before dying of cold. Sheep cluster at the top of Pen-y-Fan and pester picnickers for food; feeding one draws more. An arduous ridge path leads on from Pen-y-Fan to other peaks in the Beacons.

The touristy **Brecon Mountain Railway,** Pant Station, Merthyr Tydfil (tel. (01685) 722988), gives a glimpse of the southern side of the Beacons. Take the narrow gauge steam train north to Pontsticill, where the station provides information on specific walks in the area. (Train runs daily Easter week and June-Sept. 11am-4pm on the hour; £3.90, children £2, accompanied children £1, dogs 70p.) **Silverline Coaches** runs a Beacons Rambler daily in the summer starting from Merthyr, stopping in Brecon and Talybont before returning to Merthyr. Guided walks link up with the bus route, or you can walk part of the Taff Trail on your own; walks booklet provided with the ride (£2.85, seniors and children £1.70).

THE WATERFALL DISTRICT (FFOREST FAWR)

Forest rivers tumble through rapids, gorges, and spectacular falls near **Ystradfellte** (uh-strah-FELTH-tuh), about 7 mi. southwest of the Beacons. At **Porth-yr-Ogof** ("mouth of the cave"), less than a mile from the Ystradfellte HI hostel, the River Mellte ducks into a cave at the base of the cliff and emerges as an icy pool. Swimming is risky: the stones are slippery, the pool deepens alarmingly in the middle, and at least two people drowned here recently. Another pool 200 yards downstream offers slightly safer swimming. Porth-yr-Ogof offers no solitude—litter and the people who drop it crowd the banks. A **footpath** follows the River Mellte from the cave area past cliffs and waterfalls. As it penetrates deeper into the forest, the path fades until walkers have to wade through mud and swing from tree branches. A 1:25,000 scaled map is necessary but insufficient. The rocks are treacherous, and smooth-soled shoes may hasten death in the gorges below. The few signs merely warn people that "fatal accidents have occurred here." Remote but worth the sweat is the **Sgwdyr Elra** waterfall on the River Hepste a third of a mile from its confluence with the Mellte; you can stand behind the thundering water in a hollow in the cliff-face and keep dry. Follow the river path to the end, or else take the flat and easy "advised path" (yawn) from the Porth-yr-Ogof parking lot straight to the falls.

Hikers can reach the waterfall district from the Beacons by crossing A470 near the Llwyn-Celyn hostel, climbing Craig Cerrig-gleisaid cliff and Fan Frynych peak, and descending by way of a rocky Roman road. The route crosses a nature reserve, as well as some of the park's most trackless heath. Just north of the falls, the village of Ystradfellte has a pub to make you vigorous again (pub open Mon.-Fri. in good weather noon-2pm and 7-11pm, Sat.-Sun. 11am-2pm and 6:30-11pm).

Near **Abercrave,** midway between Swansea and Brecon off the A4067, the **Dan-yr-Ogof Showcaves** (tel. (01639) 730284) are huge and stunning, with enormous stalagmites. From the Ystradfellte Youth Hostel, 10 mi. of trails pass by Fforest Fawr (the headlands of the Waterfall District) on their path to the caves. **Silverline Coaches** (tel. (01685) 382406) pause at the hostel on their way from Brecon. Walk along the cemented pathways inside the caves, or slalom down the dry-ski-slope outside (3/day; tours last 2 hrs; open daily 10am-5pm, last tour 4-4:30pm, slightly later in peak season; £5.50, children £3.75). A large camping site nearby has full facilities (£2/tent). Relax from your adventures at the **Craig-y-nos Country Park** (tel. (01639) 730205), a half-mile away, upon which scatter picnic tables, ponds, meadows, paths, and opera singer Adelina Patti's personal castle, complete with restaurant (admission to park free; Sun. lunch served every week to Welsh music).

THE BLACK MOUNTAINS

The Black Mountains, in the easternmost section of the park, are a group of long and lofty ridges that offer 80 sq. mi. of solitude. Such summits as **Waun Fach,** the Black Mountains' highest point (2660 ft.), may seem dully-rounded and boggy, but the ridge-walks are unsurpassed. A 1:25,000 Ordnance Survey Map #13 is essential.

Crickhowell, on the A40 and the bus route between Brecon and Abergavenny (Red and White bus #21, Mon.-Sat. every 2-3hr.), is the easiest starting point for forays into the area. **Pony-trekking** centers based in Crickhowell and Abergavenny charge £10-14 per day; pick up the pony-trekking pamphlet (20p) at any information center. You can also explore by bus: the route linking Brecon and Hay-on-Wye (Red and White #39, from Brecon to Hereford) descends the north side of the Black Mountains. **Gospel Pass,** the highest mountain pass in the park, often reveals sunshine above the cloud cover. Nearby, **Offa's Dyke Path** (see Wye Valley, above) sprints down the eastern boundary of the national park. The ridge valleys are dotted with a handful of impressive churches, priories, castles, and other ruins. Those who use public transportation will find these sights more accessible from Abergavenny.

■■■ SWANSEA (ABERTAWE)

Native son Dylan Thomas called Swansea "this ugly lovely town." After Wales' second-largest city was blitzed by the Germans, even this assessment seemed generous. Judicious planning has made Swansea a place of broad shopping avenues and condos by the bay, with the cranes and smokestacks well out of sight. No doubt it's a lovely city in which to live, but everyone save urban renewal nuts will be bored.

The rebuilders triumphed at the **marina** a block down Bathwurst St. from Oystermouth Road. A derelict dock a few years ago, the area now contains breezy apartments, stained-glass workshops, a restaurant housed in a gaudily-painted man-o-war, and the **Maritime and Industrial Museum** (tel. 650351), which holds old engines, boats, and a working mill that brings Kafka's harrow to life in wood and iron (open Tues.-Sun. 10:30am-5:30pm; free). In front of the museum, climb aboard the lightship **Helwick** and admire the stained-wood bunks, far plusher than anything hostels offer. A thick-lipped and dropsical **Dylan Thomas** presides over the end of the marina, where a square bears his name. (A free brochure from the tourist office guides poetry groupies along the **Dylan Thomas Uplands Trail** past the poet's boyhood haunts.) Wedged between an office tower and a laser-gun emporium, Swansea's ruined **castle,** on Castle St. north of the marina, has no gift shop, no admission charge, and no entrance. The nearby **Phantasia** (tel. 302454), in the Parc Tawe complex off the Strand, incubates 700 varieties of plants in a glass pyramid. Sleepy piranha guard the gift shop (open Tues.-Sun. 10:30am-5:30pm; £1, students, seniors, and children 75p; wheelchair access; don't feed the fish).

The new **Dylan Thomas Theatre** (tel. 475715), along the marina, stages large-scale musical productions (ticket prices vary according to performance). The **Grand Theatre,** on Singleton St. next to the tourist office (also tel. 475715), puts on operas, ballets, and musicals. Student standby discounts are available for opera performances on the day of the performance. The **Taliesin Arts Center** (tel. 296883) on the University College campus, plays host to films, dramatics, and dances from September through July (films: £2.75, students £1.75). For the entire month of October, the **Swansea Festival** (tel. 302432) presents a variety of concerts and recitals; a simultaneous **Fringe Festival** offers cheaper, wackier stuff. In mid-August, the area moans and pines with folk musicians from all over the world attending the **Pontardawe International Music Festival,** held in the village of **Pontardawe,** 8 mi. north of Swansea (take bus #120 or #125).

The B&Bs begin on the bayside **Oystermouth Road** just past His Majesty's Prison, a 10-minute walk from the bus station, and continue almost unbroken for 600 yards. Between #358 and #396 Oystermouth Rd. stand 15 B&Bs in a row, all with loud signs and all charging £12-13 for a single and £20 for a double or twin. Farther up the hillside, **Harlton Guest House,** 89 King Edward's Rd. (tel. 466938), has bright rooms and narrow hallways for £10/person, single or double. In July and August, the **YMCA,** 1 The Kingsway (tel. 652032), opens its newly-renovated rooms to backpackers for £8-9. The closest youth hostel to Swansea is the **HI Port Eynon Hostel,** about one hour out of town by bus (see Gower Peninsula, below). In high season, many opt to camp along the peninsula. **Deep Pan Pizza,** in the Parc Tawe complex next to Phantasia, has an all-you-can-shove down pizza, pasta, and curry buffet for £3.25 from 5-10pm on Mondays and Tuesdays (open Mon.-Thurs. 11:30am-11pm, Fri.-Sat. 11:30am-midnight, Sun. noon-11pm). The city waxes agricultural in the **Swansea Market,** across the quadrant from the bus station. Try the gooseberries or laver bread, an ancient dish made from boiled seaweed which some locals eat with cockles or lightly-fried bacon, while others plug their noses and declare it unfit for human consumption. (Market open Mon.-Sat. 9am-5:30pm.)

The **tourist office,** Singleton St. (tel. 468321), supplies free maps of Swansea, Mumbles, and the Gower Peninsula (ask for the black and white version) and a thousand glossy guides (open Mon.-Sat. 9:30am-5:30pm). The **post office** is at 35 The Kingsway; open Mon.-Thurs. 9am-5:30pm, Fri. 9:30am-5:30pm, Sat. 9am-12:30pm. The **postal code** is SA1 5LF, and the **telephone code** is 01792. The **police** are at the corner of Orchard St. and Alexandra Rd. (tel. 456999). Swansea has direct connections to most major cities in Britain. **British Rail** (tel. (01222) 228000) leaves the station on High St. for Cardiff (2/hr.; 1hr.; £6.60), Birmingham (1/hr.; £27), and London (1/hr.; 2¾hr.; £33). **National Express buses** (tel. 470 820) depart every two hours for London (4hr.; £24.50), Birmingham (4hr.; £19.50), Manchester (7hr.; £29.50), and Cardiff (1¼hr.; day return £6.75). **South Wales Transport** buses cover the Gower Peninsula and the rest of south Wales; a shuttle runs every hour to Cardiff (1 hr.; £5). A bus runs between the train station and the Quadrant Bus Station (tel. 475 511) every half-hour (25p). Various Rover Tickets are available; the **Rover Bus** ticket covers most trajectories (£3.95/day). **Cork-Swansea ferries** leave for Cork, Ireland (see Essentials: Getting There—Between the Isles for complete information). **Cruises** leave from Swansea to Ilfracombe and other spots on the Bristol Channel from May to October; call (01446) 720656 for information.

■■■ GOWER PENINSULA

The stumpy 18 mi. phallus of the Gower Peninsula pokes westward from Swansea. The first place in Britain to be designated an Area of Outstanding Natural Beauty, the Gower boasts a southern coast lined with sheer cliffs, headlands, and lovely bays and beaches. Good roads and green hills make the peninsula a popular place to enjoy nature without the hardship of a hike.

GETTING ABOUT

Buses overrun the peninsula from Swansea's Quadrant Station; an exceptionally competent local bus information desk at the station will help you find your patch of sand. South Wales Transport buses #1, 1A, 2 and 3 depart for Oystermouth Sq. in Mumbles (20/hr.; 20min., return £1.85). Bus #18 runs to Oxwich every two hours (40min.) and #18A lurches through the hills to Rhossili every two hours by way of Port Eynon (1hr.; return £3.40). Almost all buses shut down on Sunday. A **Roverbus** ticket (£3.95) allows unlimited travel for a day anywhere in South Wales Transport's domain, extending as far west as Pembroke and Haverformwest. Hitchhiking is reported to be often quicker than public transport, and it allows hikers to see more of the coast since most buses follow inland routes. The **Swansea Bikepath** leads directly to Mumbles pier; the booklet **Gower Walks** by Ruth Ridge (£2.40) outlines scenic rambles, as do free leaflets available at tourist offices.

ACCOMMODATIONS & CAMPING

The farther west you go on Gower, the more likely you are to find camps not swarming with tents and caravans. B&Bs in Mumbles charge £12.50-15 and cluster on Mumbles Rd. and in the South End area; singles can be hard to find. **Rock Villa,** 1 George Bank, on the waterfront (tel. 366794), offers plush rooms, sea views, and tellies (£14-16). **Three Cliffs Bay Caravan Park,** North Hills Farm, Penmaen, (tel. 371218) has clean showers and a beautiful campsite overlooking Three Cliffs Bay between Mumbles and Port Eynon (£3/person). An on-site shop will meet all your camping needs. Port Eynon, west of Mumbles, offers both a no-frills hostel and beachside camping. Book ahead for the busy **HI Port Eynon Hostel** (tel. 390706), a former lifeboat house on the beach (£7.15, under 18 £4.75; open April-Sept. Mon.-Sat.; Feb.-March and Nov. Fri.-Sat.). The **Carreglwyd Camping Site** (tel. 390795) offers somewhat noisy camping amid arcades (£3-5/person). Way out west, Rhossili has several B&Bs for £15. **Richards B&B,** on The Green at Rhossili (tel. 390509), offers well-buffed bathrooms and views of the sea and an old stone church (£12.50).

SIGHTS

In the southeast corner of the Gower Peninsula rests **Mumbles,** a quiet fishing village by day and a raving Gomorrah of student indulgence by night. The short stretch of Mumbles Rd. at Mumbles Head is lined with 14 pubs, some of them former haunts of the area's most famous dipsomaniac, Dylan Thomas. To hang out on Mumbles Rd. is, in University of Swansea parlance, to "go mumbling," while to start at one end and have a pint at each of the pubs on the road is to "do the Mumble Mile." Flower's, Usher's, Buckley's, and Felin Foel are the local real ales. The people at the **Lovespoon Gallery,** 492 Mumbles Rd. (tel. 360132), will give you advice on what it means when a wild-eyed Welshman comes lurching after you with a big wooden spoon in his fist. (It means he loves you, silly!) Lovespoons average £5. (Open Mon.-Sat. 9am-5:30pm, Dec.-Feb. 9am-5pm.) On a hill overlooking Mumbles, beheaded **Oystermouth Castle,** off Newton St., was built around 1280 by the De Breos family, the same clan that in 1175 killed the Welsh lords at Abergavenny Castle (open April-Oct. daily 11am-5pm; 80p, children 40p).

The Mumbles **tourist office** (tel. 361302) and the **bus stop** stand abreast (open Mon.-Sat. 9:30am-5:30pm; Easter-Sept. Mon.-Sat. 10am-4pm; July-Aug. also open Sun. 10am-4pm). The **telephone code** for the Gower Peninsula is 01792. You can rent bikes from **Mumbles Cycle Hire,** in a green shack by the water across from the Antelope on Mumbles Rd. (tel. 814290; £12/8hrs.; open May-Sept. daily 10am-9pm). Various water rides are available all along the Promenade. Head to the **Seaview Tandoori Restaurant,** Mumbles Rd., for a £5.50 all-you-can-feast special (Sun.-Thurs. 6-10pm, Fri. 6-9pm). **Roots Café,** 2 Woodville Rd. (tel. 366006), adopts the BYOB (no, not broccoli) philosophy of enjoying vegetarian cuisine (lunch £3-4; dinner under £7.50; open Tues.-Fri. 10am-2:30pm, 6:30-9pm and Sat. 9:30am-9pm).

Tourist offices in the area offer free guides to Gower's beaches, and 1:25,000 scale maps of the peninsula (£4.30). **Three Cliffs Bay** and **Southgate-on-Pennard,** on the south coast between Swansea and Port Eynon, are particularly quiet beach areas. From Pennard, a 20-minute walk along the Coast Path brings you to Three Cliffs, a secluded, cave-ridden, and stupefyingly beautiful beach. **Caswell Bay** and **Oxwich Bay** are quite popular. **Llangannith** beach, north of Rhossili, draws surfers from all over Wales into its wild waves. On the peninsula's western tip, green cliffs clutch the sexy curve of **Rhossili Beach,** whose sandy expanse makes overcrowding impossible. At low tide, a causeway of tortured rock gives foot-breaking access to **Worms Head,** which actually resembles a snail. The National Trust Shop in Rhossili has tide tables for Worms Head, as well as a cautionary mannequin of a drowned sailor being dragged from the water.

The **Gower Festival** during the last two weeks of July fills the peninsula's churches with string quartets and Bach chorales. Call 468321 for information or contact the Civic Information Centre, Singleton St., Swansea SA13QG.

■■■ PEMBROKESHIRE COAST NATIONAL PARK

The Pembrokeshire Coast National Park offers 225 square mi. of lovely coast broken only by little harbors, stone villages, and Milford Haven's towering oil refineries. Pre-Cambrian cliffs, sheltered beaches, natural sea arches, and islands spotted with wild birds and seals line the 186-mi. coastal path from Amroth to Cardigan. Inland, swaths of farmland cleave small towns like Tenby and St. Davids, where Welsh bakers and craftsmen labor among the country's ancient and reverend shrines.

GETTING THERE & GETTING ABOUT

The best place from which to enter the region is centrally located **Haverfordwest,** on the main **rail** line from London (£48) and Cardiff (£12.10; 7/day). A rail line also runs to Fishguard, on the north coast (change at Clarbeston Rd.), and to Tenby and Pembroke Dock, on the south coast (change at Whitland). **Buses** offer more frequent and wide-ranging service than the speedy trains that venture into this area. Although many different operators run the services, schedules are compiled in the Bws Dyfed timetable booklets, available from tourist offices in the region. From Haverfordwest, inexpensive **Richards Brothers** and **Southwest Transport** buses run to St. Davids (#340; Mon.-Sat. 1/hr.; 50min.), Tenby (#358/359; Mon.-Sat. 1/hr.; 1½hr.) and Pembroke (#358; 1/hr.; 15min.). Tenby bus #361 runs to Pembroke Dock (Mon.-Sat. every 2hr.; 1hr.).

The Dale Peninsula, southwest of Haverfordwest, is rather poorly serviced by public transport. Your best bet is bus #315 or #316 from Haverfordwest. Buses serve the northern portion of the park more frequently, from Broad Haven and Little Haven to Poppit Sands. A-roads lead from Tenby west through Pembroke and then north to Haverfordwest and St. Davids. Many hitchers rave about this area. *Let's Go* does not recommend hitch-hiking.

PRACTICAL INFORMATION

The **National Park Information Centres** listed below sell 10 annotated maps covering the entire coastal path, printed on plastic cards (25p, complete set £2.50). Other pamphlets outline less demanding walks and pony trails in the area (10-20p). The park authorities publish their own coastal path mileage chart and *A Guide for Disabled Visitors* (£1.50). The free newspaper *Coast to Coast* has details on walks and tours (half day £1.50, full day £2.50), and on boat trips, park events, riding, fishing, and tide tables. Also available are the indispensable Ordnance Survey maps (£4-4.25). For walking, try Brian John's *The Pembrokeshire Coast Path* (£9). National Park officers help plan hikes and will book you into area hostels. Write for brochures to National Park Information Services, County Offices, Haverfordwest, Dyfed, Wales SA61 1QZ (tel. (01437) 764591, ext. 5133). For **weather information,** call any park office; dialing 999 puts you in touch with rescue rangers.

National Park Information Centres:
   Broad Haven: National Park Car Park (tel. (01437) 781412); open late March to Sept., and Oct. 22-30; daily 10am-5pm.
   Haverfordwest: The Old Bridge (tel. (01437) 763110); open Mon.-Sat. 10am-5pm.
   Newport: Bank Cottages, Long St. (tel. (01239) 820912); open late March to Sept. Mon.-Sat. 10am-5pm.
   Pembroke: Drill Hall, Main St. (tel. (01646) 682148); open Easter-Oct. Mon.-Sat. 9:30am-5:30pm.
   St. Davids: City Hall (tel. (01437) 720392); open Easter-Oct. Mon.-Sat. 9:30am-5:30pm.
   Saundersfoot: The Harbour Car Park (tel. (01834) 811411); open daily 9:30am-5:30pm.
   Tenby: The Croft (tel. (01834) 842404); open Easter-Oct. daily 10am-5pm, July-Aug. 10am-9pm.

Tourist Information Centres:
   Fishguard: Hamilton St. (tel. (01348) 873484); open daily 10am-6pm.
   Milford Haven: 94 Charles St. (tel. (01646) 690866); open Mon.-Sat. 10am-5pm.

The park is also aflutter with **Outdoor Activity Centres,** which rent canoes, kayaks, ponies, bicycles, and other archaic vehicles (£5-15/day). Pick up two extremely helpful brochures at the tourist office: *Sporting Preseli* and *Preseli on the Water.* Mountain bikes are great for the park's paved one-lane roads, many of which lead straight to the most secluded beaches. Do not, however, ride on the coastal path itself; it is not only illegal, but extraordinarily dangerous to boot. **Mr. Codd,** Cross Inn Garage, Broadmoor, Saundersfoot (tel. (01834) 813266), rents bikes for £4/day (open Mon.-Tues. and Thurs.-Sat. 8am-7:30pm, Wed. 8am-1pm). Or try **Preseli Mountain Bikes** (tel. (01348) 837709), near the village of Mathry on the coast between Fishguard and St. Davids (bikes and helmets £16/day), which also offers sea kayaking with instruction (£33/day, £18/half-day) and "activity weekends" with instruction (£75-95). Call in advance; hours are flexible.

ACCOMMODATIONS

HI Youth Hostels are conveniently spaced along the coastal path. The following are all within a reasonable day's walk of one another:

Pentlepoir (tel. (01834) 812333), north of Tenby. £6.50 (see Tenby).

Manorbier (tel. (01834) 871803), the new space station near Manorbier Castle. £7.75 (see Near Tenby). Wheelchair access.

Marloes Sands (tel. (01646) 636667), near the Dale Peninsula. No laundry. Curfew 11:30pm; lockout 10am-5pm, but access to kitchen and lounge. £6.50, July-Aug. £7.15 Open July-Aug. daily; mid-March-June and Sept.-Oct. Mon.-Sat.

Broad Haven (tel. (01437) 781688), on St. Bride's Bay. Best facilities on the Walk. 60 beds; laundry facilities; wheelchair access. Curfew 11pm; lockout 11am-5pm. £7.75, July-Aug. £8.70 Open mid-March-Sept. daily; Oct. Mon.-Sat.

St. Davids (tel. (01437) 720345), near St. David's Head. Beds in a converted stable. Curfew 11:30pm; lockout 10am-5pm, but the dining hall is open. £5.90; July-Aug. £7.10. Open April-Oct. Fri.-Wed.

Trevine (tel. (01348) 831414), between St. Davids and Fishguard. £6.50. July-Aug. £7.15. Open July-Aug. daily; March and Oct. Tues.-Sat.; April-June and Sept. Mon.-Sat.

Pwll Deri (tel. (013485) 233), on breathtaking cliffs just around Strumble Head from Fishguard. £6.50; July-Aug. £7.15. Open July-Aug. daily; April and Oct. Mon.-Fri.; May-June and Sept. Mon.-Sat.

The **Poppit Sands hostel** (tel. (01239) 612936) is 30 mi. past Pwll Deri near Cardigan at the sign of a bush in the form of a snail. (Open daily year-round. Curfew 11:15pm; lockout 10am-5pm.Camping and washers. £6.50; July-Aug. £7.15.) Book ahead in July and August; if you plan out your route in advance, you can book at all of the hostels through the **West Wales Booking Bureau,** YHA Llaethedy, St. Davids, Haverfordwest, Dyfed SA62 6PR (tel. (01437) 720345; booking £2.20).

The roads between Tenby, Pembroke, and St. Davids teem with B&Bs which run from £10 for a basic bed to £16-20 for a fancy farmhouse. Despite the quantity, B&Bs can be hard to secure in Pembrokeshire, especially in the summer. The coast is lined with **campsites,** as many farmers convert fields that are lying fallow into tent sites in summer (usually about £3/tent). Use common sense; always ask first. The youth hostels at Manorbier, Poppit Sands, and Pwll Deri also allow camping.

HIKING

For short hikes, stick to the more accessible St. Davids Peninsula, in the northwest. Otherwise, set out on the coastal path, which is marked with acorn symbols and covers mostly manageable terrain. The path begins in the southeast at Amroth and continues westward through Tenby to St. Govan's Head, the southernmost point in Pembrokeshire. From here to Elegug Stacks, birds cling to every nook in the rocks; the path passes natural sea arches, mile-wide lily pools at Bosherton, and great limestone stacks. Unfortunately, the 6-mi. stretch from St. Govan's Head past the Stacks to Freshwater West is sometimes used as a shooting range; it is closed to hikers except on weekends and certain evenings. (Contact Pembroke National Park Office at (01646) 682148 for times.)

From Freshwater West to Angle Bay, the coastline is relatively easy to walk and exceptionally pretty. There is a small break in the path at Milford Haven at the mouth of the extensive waterway, a channel which runs for over 25 mi. inland. Geologists call it a "ria" (a drowned river valley).

From the Dale Peninsula, the path passes by the long, clean beaches of St. Bride's Bay, turns up to Newgale, and arrives at the ancient St. David's Head, the site of pre-Cambrian formations and the oldest named feature on the coast of Wales. The spectacular trail continues—past Abereiddy's trilobite fossils, the quarry at Porthgain, the Strumble Head Lighthouse, and on to Fishguard along some of the highest cliffs in Britain. From Fishguard it runs up past Dinas Head and Newport Bay almost all the way to Cardigan, ending at the cliffs of Poppit Sands, just beyond Cemaes Head at the mouth of the River Teifi.

A number of islands freckle the coast. On **Grassholm,** farthest from the shore, 35,000 pairs of gannets nest and raise their young. **Dale Sailing Company** (tel. (01646) 601636) runs daytrips from Martin's Haven (June-Aug. Mon. only; £19; departs at 10am and 2pm, stops on island for 45min.; reservations required). On Fridays from April to September, weather permitting, Dale runs cruises around, not to, the island (depart at noon; 2½hrs., £16). They also sail to the island of **Skomer,** a marine reserve and breeding ground for auks and puffins (April-Sept. Tues.-Sun.; £5, children £3; landing fee £5; no booking necessary). Serious bird enthusiasts sing the praises of **Skokholm Island,** accessible on Mondays on cruises run by the National Park (from £1.50; reservations required; contact any National Park Information Center or call (01437) 781412 for details). Seals and rare seabirds live on **Ramsey Island,** farther up the coast. On the east side of the island lurk **The Bitches,** a chain of offshore rocks where sailors have come to grief. You can hire a boat in almost any harbor; owners who don't officially run services often bow to requests.

ST. DAVIDS

Near the western extremity of the coast path sleeps St. Davids, the largest and richest diocese in medieval Wales and now Britain's smallest city. The **cathedral** slumps in a hollow below the village; its rough-hewn stones, squat round arches, and massive crumbled buttresses give an impression of must and ancientness. The site has been holy ground since the 6th century, and some pillars still lean from an earthquake in 1248. A chest holds the bones of St. David, the patron saint of Wales, and his friend St. Justinian, who was killed on nearby Ramsey Island but carried his head back to the mainland for burial (£1 suggested donation). The **Bishop's Palace** a few yards away (tel. 720517) resembles a castle, as indeed it had to—in 999 and again in 1078, marauding Danes sacked St. Davids and killed the reigning bishop. The arcaded parapets of the ruin now provide a pendent bed and procreant cradle for grass and nesting birds (open daily 9:30am-6:30pm; Nov.-March Mon.-Sat. 9:30am-4pm, Sun. 11am-4pm; £1.50, seniors, students, and children £1). A half mile south of town, the ruined seaside walls of **St. Non's Chapel** mark the site of St. David's birth around 500 AD; the water from the nearby well cures all ills. Take Goat St. downhill from the town and follow the signs to health and happiness.

St. Davids' **HI Youth Hostel** (see Pembrokeshire Coast: Accommodations, above) is 2 mi. northwest of town near the 500-million-year-old St. David's Head. Take the B4583 and follow signs to the hostel, or else **Tony's Taxis** (tel. 720931; 24 hrs.) will take you there for £2-3. B&Bs in the village charge £12-15. **Penalbro Bed and Breakfast,** 18 Goat St. (tel. 721865), has TVs and stereos in every room; the doubles have art deco fireplaces and wedding-cake canopies on the beds (£12/person the first night, £10 each night thereafter). The **National Park Information Centre and Tourist Office** in the City Hall on High St. (tel. 720392) will book you a bed for a 10% deposit (open Easter-Oct. daily 9:30am-5:30pm). **Buses** run to St. Davids from Haverfordwest (#340; Mon.-Sat. 1/hr.; 50min.) and from Fishguard (#411, Mon.-Sat. 7/day; 50 min.). St. Davids' **telephone code** is 01437.

■■■ TENBY (DINBYCH-Y-PYSGOD)

Nicknamed the "Welsh Riviera" (is there *any* coastal resort that isn't somehow likened to the Riviera?), Tenby lacks only a decent Bordeaux, *provençale* cuisine, and sexy nude bathers. The stern medieval stone wall, from which Welsh flags fly triumphantly, now keeps out no one: families with squabbling children and gray and fat pensioners flood the golden sandy beaches. Even the monastery on nearby Caldey Island finds its grounds overrun by picnickers searching for sun.

GETTING THERE

Bus routes in Pembrokeshire are slightly easier to untangle than those further east. The *Bws Dyfed* booklet (available at tourist offices) lists bus schedules around Tenby. **South Wales Transport** buses #358/359 arrive hourly from Haverfordwest via Pembroke (Mon.-Sat. until 5pm; £2). Buses #X11 and X30 from Swansea link up at Carmarthen with buses #333 and 359, which go to Tenby and Haverfordwest (3-4/day Mon.-Sat; Swansea to Tenby 2½hr.). **Silcox** buses (tel. 842189) cover most local routes in conjunction with SWT.

    Trains are a good alternative—five chug in every Sunday, ten on Saturdays, and eight on weekdays. **British Rail's** southern line through Swansea branches at Carmarthen and continues to Pembroke Dock. Trains ride from Cardiff (2½hr.; £12.10), Swansea (1½hr.; £7.40), Pembroke (30min.; £2.50), and Carmarthen (45min.; £3).

ORIENTATION & PRACTICAL INFORMATION

Despite its medieval birth, Tenby has an orderly street plan. The old town, encircled by the stone wall, hugs the cliffs above the beach and bay; High St. and Upper Frog St. run parallel both to the waterfront and to the wall. The main passage through the wall is at the **Five Arches** on St. Georges St., which in fact has six arches. If you walk from the rail station up Warren St. until you see the beach, the tourist information center will be to the left, shops to the right.

Tourist and National Park Information Centre: The Croft (tel. 842404), overlooking North Beach. Street map of Tenby and Pembroke (15p); Ordnance Survey maps (£4), and shelves of coastal path info. Free lodgings list; books beds (10% deposit). Open Easter-June and Sept.-Oct. daily 10am-5pm; July-Aug. 10am-9pm.

Financial Services: Barclays, 18 High St. (tel. 844614). Open Mon.-Wed. and Fri. 9:30am-4:30pm, Thurs. 10am-4:30pm.

Post Office: Warren St. at South Parade (tel. 843213). Open Mon.-Fri. 9am-5:30pm, Sat. 9am-3pm. **Postal Code:** SA70 7JR.

Telephones: On South Parade on Warren St. and next to the tourist office. **Telephone code:** 01834.

Train Station: At the bottom of Warren St. Unmanned. **Tenby Travel** in the Tenby Indoor Market between High St. and Upper Frog St. (tel. 843214 or 843664) handles train inquiries.

Bus Station: Buses leave from the **multi-story car park** at Upper Park Rd. Get info from posted schedules, or Silcox Coaches in the Arcade between South Parade and Upper Frog St. (tel. 842189 or 842459).

Taxi: Tudor Taxis, 28 Warren St. (tel. 844310 or 844544), 24hr.

Launderette: Washeteria, Lower Frog St. (tel. 842484). Has change machine. Open daily 8:30am-9pm, last wash 8:30pm; Sept.-May daily 10am-6pm.

Hospital: Doctor's Surgery: The Norton, Tenby (tel. 844161). Open Mon.-Fri. 9am-5:30pm, Sat. 10am-noon. **Tenby Cottage Hospital,** Church Park (tel. 842040).

Emergency: Dial 999; no coins required.

Police: Jones Terrace, Warren St. (tel. 842303), near the church off White Lion St.

ACCOMMODATIONS

Ask at the tourist office for the *Tenby and South Pembrokeshire Holiday Accommodation Guide.* **Warren Street,** just outside the town wall near the train station, has several B&Bs in the £12-14 range; **Greenhill Avenue** and its sidestreets, as well as the streets off Esplanade and Trafalgar Rd., are almost as well-endowed. Almost all B&Bs post their prices on the door, so shopping is easy. Should these fail you, take a short bus ride to Saundersfoot for a plethora of B&Bs.

Pentlepoir Youth Hostel (HI), The Old School, Pentlepoir (tel. 812333). 4 mi. north of Tenby near Saundersfoot. Take the Kilgetty bus from Tenby and ask the driver to let you off at the cheery hostel (30min.; 80p). £6.50, under 18 £4.35.

Open April-Oct. Fri.-Tues., July-Sept. daily. Phone ahead from Nov. to March and on days when they're closed—they might stay open just for you.

Somerville, Warren St. (tel. 843158). An iridescent carpet and huge windows. Small single with breakfast £10.50, doubles £23.

Lundy Villa, Warren St. (tel. 843571). Splendid breakfasts and a very attentive hostess. £12/person.

Hazlemere, Warren St. (tel. 844691). Sun-baked rooms, like all the others on the street, and a comfy carpeted bathroom. No TVs. £11.50-12.

Camping: Meadow Farm (tel. 844829), at the top of The Croft, beyond the tourist office and overlooking North Beach. Has showers. Plenty of other sites in the area. Follow The Croft up the hill. £3, car free.

FOOD

Tenby has plenty of restaurants. Most of them are so expensive you'll be tempted to eat the ketchup just to get your money's worth. Avoid paying £6 for pub grub by taking a picnic to the tiny garden behind St. Mary's Church. You can buy raw meat, veggies, and bread at the **Tenby Market Hall** between High St. and Upper Frog St. (open Mon.-Sat. 8:30am-5:30pm). **Somerfield,** Upper Park Rd., will fill your pack with goodies (open Mon.-Thurs 8:30am-8pm, Fri. 8:30am-9pm, Sat. 8am-8pm, Sun. 10am-6pm). Hidden in an alley connecting Bridge St. and St. Julians St., the **Plantagenet,** Quay Hill (tel. 842350), serves excellent continental and vegetarian cuisine in a house with an 800-year-old chimney, under which you can sit. The women's toilet has a lovely view; the men's has nary a window (entrees £8-15; open daily 10am-late, Nov.-March Fri.-Sun. only). **Pam Pam,** 2 Tudor Sq. (tel. 842946), slaps down huge portions (£4-6) to the tune of live music four nights a week (open daily 10:30am-10pm). And there's more to **Candy,** High St. and Crackwell St. (tel. 842052), than its name suggests—go for salads and sandwiches in full view of the ocean (£4-6; open April-Oct. daily 9am-8:30pm). Or for those willing to trade in health and happiness for a full stomach, there's always fish and chips—**Pipers** on St. George St. is cheaper than most and as greasy as any (open Sun.-Thurs. 11:30am-11:30pm, Fri.-Sat. 11:30am-midnight).

SIGHTS

On a sunny day, catatonia will lap your feet on sandy **North Beach** by The Croft or **South Beach,** beyond the Esplanade. If you're feeling adventurous, try **Castle Beach** at the southern tip of Tenby for cliffs and coastal caves. Just off Castle Hill sits the craggy spur of **St. Catherine's Island,** which bears an abandoned fort once used as an early warning outpost. A variety of trips offered around the bay leave from the harbor (prices range from £5-7; check the boards for the offerings or call 843179).

Three perfume-drenched miles to the south lies **Caldey Island,** site of an active monastery founded in the 6th century, sacked by the Vikings, refounded around 1100, sacked by Henry VIII, and refounded again early this century. Now the land holds fish ponds, medieval buildings, and a community of 17 Cistercian monks who produce perfume, dairy products, and chocolate, sold on an island shop. Anyone may visit the island, but only men can enter the monastery (and they can never leave—mwa ha ha!!). Twice a day, usually at 11:30am and 3pm, free informal tours are given of the cloister, where the monks run laps in the winter to keep warm. The twin tortoises Glasnost and Perestroika (formerly Abelard and Heloise) prowl the courtyard. The island's post office (postal code SA70 7UH) dispenses information and fake stamps. **Caldey Boats** (tel. 842296) sail from Tenby harbor to the island (late May-Sept. 4/hr. Mon.-Fri. 10am-3pm; last boat from Caldey Island 5pm, 6pm July-Aug.; 20min.; £5 return). Check at the quay on Castle Hill for 4-hour **deep-sea fishing trips** (tackle included in prices; £8.50; call 843545 for details).

■ NEAR TENBY

Five mi. northwest of Tenby, between Pembroke and Tenby, rest the imposing ruins of **Carew Castle** (tel. (01646) 651782). A strange, handsome stronghold built in the late 11th-century, it was enlarged in the 15th century for use as a dwelling. Nearby, a **tidal mill** dating from 1558 (one of three in Britain) turns quietly alongside a medieval bridge and a 13-ft. 11th-century Celtic cross. (Open Easter-Oct. Mon.-Sat. 10am-5pm. Mill and castle £2, children £1.20. Castle only £1.50, seniors 90p.) Take Silcox bus #361 from Tenby to Carew Cross (Mon.-Sat., every 2hr.).

B&Bs and camping sites line the roads between Tenby and Pembroke. In **Jameston,** the village next door to Manorbier, the **Elm House,** on the main road in the center of the village, will make you feel right at home; it is the least expensive B&B in Pembrokeshire (singles £10, doubles £16). The national park organizes guided walks in the area, outlined in their free seasonal publication *Coast to Coast,* available at information centers in the main towns.

Five mi. southwest of Tenby stands the superbly preserved **Manorbier Castle** (tel. 871394), A Norman baron's palace with a garden in the keep and a beach below the ramparts. The gatehouse holds a mannequin of a gatekeeper sunk in lassitude; the dungeon's plaster prisoners look far worse. (Open Easter-Sept. daily 10:30am-5:30pm; £1.50, seniors and children 70p.) Bus #358/359 shuttles (1/hr. Mon.-Sat.) between Tenby, Manorbier, and Pembroke; or trains run every two hours from Tenby, Pembroke, and Haverfordwest to the slightly more remote, unmanned train station. **Manorbier** also has a new space-age, deluxe **Youth Hostel (HI)** at Skrinkle Haven (tel. 871803). Spotless laundry facilities and rigorously hot showers might make a traveler wonder how this complex landed in the middle of the desolate Pembroke farmland (camping and laundry facilities available; open July-Aug. daily; mid-Feb. to June and Sept.-Oct. Mon.-Sat.; £7.75, July-Aug. £8.70). From the Manorbier train station, walk up past the A4139 to the castle, make a left onto the B4585 and then a right up to the army camp and follow the hostel signs. Dylan Thomas spent the last 16 years of his life in the **Boat House** (tel. (01994) 427420) in Laugharne (LARN) at the mouth of the River Taf, about 15 mi. east of Tenby. The boat house displays a collection of Thomas' photographs, art, and books (Open Easter-Oct. daily 10am-5pm, Nov.-Easter 10:30am-3:30pm; £1.60, children £1.10). Take SWT bus to St. Clear's and then bus #222 from St. Clear's to Laugharne.

■■■ PEMBROKE & PEMBROKE DOCK

Bounded by a towering Norman castle and the crumbling hangover of 14th-century walls, Pembroke looks preposterously tiny compared to the structures built to guard it. Castle and town boast a 902-year existence; nearby Pembroke Dock lacks their blue blood, the ferry to Rosslare, Ireland being its greatest attraction today. Both towns are stepping stones to the Pembrokeshire National Park, but Pembroke is the more popular place to stay.

GETTING THERE

Silcox buses #358/359 (tel. (01646) 683143) leave from the front of the castle in Pembroke for Water St. in Pembroke Dock every hour (Mon.-Sat.; last bus around 7pm). Bus #358/359 also runs to Tenby. **Cleddau Buses** (tel. (01437) 763284), the local branch of South Wales Transport, connects the Pembrokes with Haverfordwest more frequently, less expensively, and infinitely more slowly than Expresswest. Pembroke Dock lies at the end of a British Rail western branch line that splits at Whitland. **Trains** run daily from Pembroke Dock to destinations in England, passing through Pembroke and Tenby (Mon.-Sat. 8/day, Sun. 4/day). Wait at the unstaffed Pembroke station at the end of Main St. and the Diamond St. E., Pembroke Dock (tel. 684896). Buses stop in Pembroke on the Commons and across from the castle, and in Pembroke Dock at the **Silcox Garage** (tel. 683143; call Mon.-Fri. 9am-5pm). **B&I** and **Stena Sealink** sail **ferries and catamarans** from Pembroke Dock and nearby **Fishguard** (tel. (01646) 684161) to Rosslare, Ireland. See Essentials: Getting There: Between the Isles for complete information.

ORIENTATION & PRACTICAL INFORMATION

Pembroke may be thought of as a great flat fish with the castle as the head, the Great Keep as the eye, Main St. as the spine, and the Mill Pond and the 14th-century town wall as the sides. Main St. winds uphill from the castle; it ends at the train station and the road to Tenby and the rest of Pembrokeshire. The **National Park Information Centre** (tel. 682148) just below the castle entrance in Drill Hall, dispenses park publications and goodwill (open Easter-Oct. Mon.-Sat. 9:30am-5:30pm). At the new **tourist office** (tel. 622388), located in a former slaughterhouse on Commons Rd. below the old town wall, you can have your picture taken as the lovely Welsh Princess Nesr, mistress of Henry I (open daily 10am-5:30pm; Nov.-Easter Tues., Thurs., and Sat. 10am-4pm). An **ATM** yields its bounty from **Barclays**, 35 Main St. (tel. 684996; open Mon.-Wed. and Fri. 9:30am-4:30pm, Tues. 10am-4:30pm). **Camping** supplies await at **John Bull,** 41 Main St. (tel. 683128; open Mon.-Sat. 9am-5:30pm). Pembroke's **post office** sorts mail at 49 Main St. (tel. 682737; open Mon.-Sat. 9am-5:30pm). Its **postal code** is SA71 4JT, its **telephone code** 01646.

ACCOMMODATIONS & FOOD

B&Bs in Pembroke are sparse and widely dispersed; book ahead. The charming **Merton Place House,** 3 East Back (tel. 684796), has a foyer of faded grandeur, a rose garden in the back, and a slightly imperious proprietress, the offspring of Lord Nelson and Mrs. Claus. No TVs. (£13-15, sometimes £12 in winter.) With its three "B&B" signs, one of them enormous, **Eirlyn**, 20 Lower Lamphey Rd. (tel. 682768), is impossible to miss. Pink accents, soft beds, and TVs glow within. Tread lightly in the dining room, which is covered with precariously hung porcelain (£11/person if sharing, £14 single, £2 packed lunches). The nearest hostel is at Mansbrier, on the bus line between Tenby and Pembroke (see Near Tenby, above).

The restaurants in Pembroke know very well that hungry tourists will gobble anything within reach. Skip the "best fish and chips" next to the castle and check the faded lunch menu at the **King's Arms Hotel** (tel. 683611), down the street. Enjoy shark in soy sauce or fried whitebait with brown bread for £4 (open daily noon-2pm and 6:30pm-closing). The **Watermans Arms** pub just across the bridge on Northgate St. offers seating by Mill Pond with a view of swans and the occasional carousing otter (open Mon.-Sat. 11am-3pm and 6-11pm; Sun. 7-10:30pm; food served noon-2pm and 7:30-9:30pm). **Gateway** supermarket on Main St. opens its doors Mon.-Wed. and Sat. 8:30am-6pm, Thurs.-Fri. 8:30am-7pm.

SIGHTS

Pembroke Castle (tel. 684585), at the head of Main St., is among the most impressive fortresses in South Wales and the birthplace of Henry VII. Its 75-ft. keep dates from the 13th century. The cavernous **Great Keep** is now home to the Greater Horseshoe Bat; **Wogan Cavern** is down 53 spiral steps from the Northern Hall. The mill pond, directly beneath the castle walls, amuses coots and cormorants. During the first week in August, troupes stage Shakespearean plays in the courtyard. (Castle open daily 9:30am-6pm; March and Oct. daily 10am-5pm; Nov.-Feb. Mon.-Sat. 10am-4pm. £2, children and seniors £1.20. Summer tours daily, 4/day; 50p.) Pembroke swells with churches: have a look at 12th-century **St. Daniel's Church,** St. Daniel Hill, by the train station; **St. Mary's Church,** on Main St., with its 13th-century windows, or **Monkton Priory Church,** Monkton St., which has a hagioscope—a wall-slit that enabled leprous monks to watch the service at the altar.

In the **Museum of the Home,** 7 Westgate Hill (tel. 681200) past the castle, masses of household gadgets trace the history of the common home from the 16th century to the present. Items include an ivory and tortoise-shell tongue-scraper "for removing excesses of poor claret" (open May-Sept. Mon.-Thurs. 11am-5pm; £1.20, seniors and children 90p).

NORTH WALES

North Wales is even more fiercely nationalistic and linguistically independent of England than is South Wales. Even the topography of the region seems to pronounce its distinctiveness. From atop the hills of Snowdonia, the vast English flatlands appear soft and placid, in sharp contrast with the jagged and uneven Welsh hills to the west. You can avoid the crowded castles and resort towns of the northern coast by heading inland to the mountain footpaths and hamlets of Snowdonia National Park, which covers the larger part of North Wales. Mount Snowdon itself, at 3560 ft., is the highest, barest, and most precipitous peak in England or Wales. Other ranges, such as the Glyders or Carder Idris, challenge blissfully smaller numbers of serious hikers. To the southwest of Snowdonia, the largely unspoiled Lleyn Peninsula invites visitors to its sandy beaches; to the northwest the Isle of Anglesey sends ferries to Ireland. The lush Vale of Conwy languishes to the east. Llangollen, near the English border, hosts the International Musical Eisteddfod in July, a week-long singing festival attended by people from over 30 countries.

■■■ ABERYSTWYTH

At the center of Cardigan Bay's shallow sweep, the elaborate pier and promenade of Aberystwyth (abber-IST-with) hark back to the town's heyday as a Victorian seaside resort. When Aberystwyth's not-so-Victorian students vanish in summer, the town grows melancholy and still, gray sea bumping against empty, decaying houses and castle ruins. In the fall, the present revives itself at the National Library and in the country's first college.

GETTING THERE

Aberystwyth is a hub for travel by bus or train to all of Wales. The city rests at the western end of the mid-Wales **rail** line that cuts across to Shrewsbury (every 2 hrs., Sun. 4/day; 2hr.; £12.60). To rail destinations north along the coast, change at Machynlleth (11/day, Sun. 5/day; 30min.; £3.50). **Crosville Buses** (tel. 617951), headquartered in Aberystwyth, run south to Cardigan (#550, hourly until 6:30pm; £2.65) and north to Machynlleth (#94 and 514; 7/day, Sun. 3/day; £2.40). Crosville offers **Day Rover** tickets (£4.70; one dog rides free), valid all the way to Snowdonia, and packages of ten tickets for £11; a single **Transcambria** bus runs daily from Cardiff (£9.40). The **North and Mid-Wales Rail Rover** and **North and Mid-Wales Day Ranger** are valid on both buses and trains everywhere north of the imaginary Aberystwyth-Shrewsbury line.

ORIENTATION & PRACTICAL INFORMATION

Pier St. and **Terrace Rd.,** which contain most of Aberystwyth's shops and eateries, rise uphill from the flat and kelp-strewn beach. **Great Darkgate St., North Parade,** and **Alexandra Rd.** run parallel to the waterfront; buses stop outside the train station on Alexandra Rd. **Penglais Rd.** climbs a hill to the east, atop which stand the university and the National Library in white stone.

Tourist Office: Lisbourne House, Terrace Rd. (tel. 612125). Chipper, helpful staff. Dossiers of B&B photos and current rates. Open daily 10am-5pm; July-Aug. 10am-6pm, June 10am-5:30pm.

Financial Services: Barclays, 26 Terrace Rd. (tel. 612731). Open Mon. and Wed.-Fri. 9:30am-5pm, Tues. 10am-5pm.

Post Office: 8 Great Darkgate St. (tel. 612536). Open Mon.-Thurs. 9am-5:30pm, Fri. 9:30am-5:30pm, Sat. 9am-12:30pm. **Postal Code:** SY23 1AA.

Telephone Code: 01970.

Train Station: British Rail, Alexandra Rd. (tel. (01654) 702311). Information office open Mon.-Fri. 8:45am-5:25pm; Sat. 8:45-11:30am, 12:30-3:20pm; Sun.

So, you're getting away from it all.

Just make sure you can get back.

AT&T Access Numbers
Dial the number of the country you're in to reach AT&T.

*AUSTRIA†††	022-903-011	*GREECE	00-800-1311	NORWAY	800-190-11
*BELGIUM	0-800-100-10	*HUNGARY	00◇-800-01111	POLAND†◆²	0◇010-480-0111
BULGARIA	00-1800-0010	*ICELAND	999-001	PORTUGAL†	05017-1-288
CANADA	1-800-575-2222	IRELAND	1-800-550-000	ROMANIA	01-800-4288
CROATIA†◆	99-38-0011	ISRAEL	177-100-2727	*RUSSIA¹ (MOSCOW)	155-5042
*CYPRUS	080-90010	*ITALY	172-1011	SLOVAKIA	00-420-00101
CZECH REPUBLIC	00-420-00101	KENYA†	0800-10	S. AFRICA	0-800-99-0123
*DENMARK	8001-0010	*LIECHTENSTEIN	155-00-11	SPAIN•	900-99-00-11
*EGYPT¹ (CAIRO)	510-0200	LITHUANIA◆	8◇196	*SWEDEN	020-795-611
*FINLAND	9800-100-10	LUXEMBOURG	0-800-0111	*SWITZERLAND	155-00-11
FRANCE	19◇-0011	F.Y.R. MACEDONIA	99-800-4288	*TURKEY	00-800-12277
*GAMBIA	00111	*MALTA	0800-890-110	UKRAINE†	8◇100-11
GERMANY	0130-0010	*NETHERLANDS	06-022-9111	UK	0500-89-0011

Countries in bold face permit country-to-country calling in addition to calls to the U.S. **World Connect℠** prices consist of **USADirect®** rates plus an additional charge based on the country you are calling. Collect calling available to the U.S. only. *Public phones require deposit of coin or phone card. ◇Await second dial tone. †May not be available from every phone. †††Public phones require local coin payment through the call duration. ◆Not available from public phones. • Calling available to most European countries. ¹Dial "02" first, outside Cairo. ²Dial 010-480-0111 from major Warsaw hotels. ©1994 AT&T.

Here's a travel tip that will make it easy to call back to the States. Dial the access number for the country you're visiting and connect right to AT&T. It's the quick way to get English-speaking AT&T operators and can minimize hotel telephone surcharges.

If all the countries you're visiting aren't listed above, call **1 800 241-5555** for a free wallet card with all AT&T access numbers. Easy international calling from AT&T. **TrueWorld Connections.**

These people are only a third of the 150 students who bring you the *Let's Go* guides. With pen and notebook in hand, a few changes of underwear stuffed in our backpacks, and a budget as tight as yours, we visited every *pensione*, *palapa*, pizzeria, café, club, campground, or castle we could find to make sure you'll get the most out of *your* trip.

We've put the best of our discoveries into the book you're now holding. A brand-new edition of each guide hits the shelves every year, only months after it is researched, so you know you're getting the most reliable, up-to-date, and comprehensive information available.

But, as any seasoned traveler will tell you, the best discoveries are often those you make yourself. If you find something worth sharing, drop us a line. We're at Let's Go, Inc., 1 Story Street, Cambridge, MA 02138, USA (e-mail: letsgo@delphi.com).

HAPPY TRAVELS!

9am-1pm, 2-5:30pm. **Vale of Rheidol Railway** (tel. 625819 or 615993) in the BR
Station. Open daily 10am-2:30pm, late July-Aug. Mon.-Thurs. until 4pm.
Bus Station: Buses stop on Alexandra Rd. in front of the train station. Information
desk at **Crosville Buses** garage, Park Ave. (tel. 617951), open Mon.-Fri. 10am-
12:30pm and 1:30-4pm.
Taxi: Express, tel. 612319; 24hr. Taxi stand next to the train station.
Market: Market Hall, St. James' Sq., Mon.-Sat. 9am-5:30pm.
Early Closing Day: Wed. at 1pm, generally violated except by jewelers.
Hotlines: Samaritans (crisis): 5 Trinity Rd. (tel. 624535). **Women's Aid:** tel.
625585. **Rape Crisis:** Hereford at (01432) 341494 or Telford at (01952) 504666.
Hospital: Bronglais General Hospital, Caradog Rd. (tel. 623131), a 5-min. walk
up Penglais Rd. Reception open 24 hrs.
Emergency: dial 999; no coins required.
Police: Boulevard St. Breiuc (tel. 612791), at the end of Park Ave.

ACCOMMODATIONS & CAMPING

Expensive B&Bs (£16-30) rub dormers with student housing on the waterfront.
Bridge St. still has a small B&B cluster, and a few cheap establishments scatter on
South Rd., Sea View Pl., and Rheidol Terrace.

HI Youth Hostel, 9 mi. north in Borth (tel. 871498). Surrounding beaches are set
in beautiful landscape, but the hostel is often full. Sand-yachting courses for £95.
Take the train to Borth Station (Mon.-Sat. 10/day, Sun. 5/day; 10min.) or Crosville
bus #511, 512, 520, or 524 from Aberystwyth. From the train station, turn right
and walk for 5 min. £7.75. Open April-Aug. daily, Sept. Mon.-Sat., Oct. Tues.-Sat.
Mrs. E. V. Williams, 28 Bridge St. (tel. 612550). Large rooms with very heavy pillows. Kind proprietress bakes delicious Welsh cakes and can teach you to pronounce "Machynlleth." £11.
Mrs. P. E. Thomas, 8 New St. (tel. 617329). Scattershot decor—Chinese paintings, bottled ship models, and a giant harp. All rooms with TV. £11.
Linda Davis, 28 South Rd. (tel. 612115). Two big rooms jammed with overstuffed
furniture and floral designs. Has TVs. Single £14, double £12.50/person.
Camping: Midfield Caravan Park (tel. 612542), 1½ mi. from town center on the
A4120, 200 yd. uphill from the junction with the A487. The most pleasant campsite in the area, with an excellent view of town and the hills. No laundry facilities.
£3.50/person. Walkers and cyclists may be charged less.

FOOD & PUBS

On Pier St., take-away places are cheap and open on Sundays. Try the two Chinese
restaurants or **Bridgend Restaurant**, 40 Bridge St. (take away cod and chips £2;
open Mon.-Sat. 11am-11pm, Sun. noon-7pm). The **Lo-Cost Supermarket,** Terrace
Rd. (open Mon.-Thurs. 8:30am-5:30pm, Fri. 8:30am-7pm, Sat 8:30am-5pm), and the
much larger **Somerfield** (open Mon.-Thurs. and Sat. 8am-8pm, Fri. 8am-9pm, Sun
10am-4pm), behind the railway station, sell napkins to blot the grease.

Y Graig Wholefood Café, 34 Pier St. (tel. 611606). Tie-dyed T-shirts and political
postcards in a hole in the wall. Wholefood for vegans, vegetarians, and carnivores
for under £4. Chili con Tofu £4.30, dandelion coffee 65p. CYMRU DDI NIWCLIAR
(Nuclear Free Wales)! Does evil exist in this world of ours? The owner may have
an answer. Open Mon.-Sat. 9am-midnight, Sun. 2pm-midnight; hours erratic.
Connexion, 19 Bridge St. (tel. 615350). Macramé, Aubrey Beardsley, stone walls,
and scorched timber—ask to sit in the cozy attic, where thick chains swing from
the ceiling. Vegetarian dishes £5.50-6.50; lunch baguettes with ham or prawns
£2. Open daily noon-3pm and 6:30-10pm.
The Cabin Coffee Bar, Pier St. (tel. 417398) at Eastgate. The walls read like a history of Hollywood machismo—Bogie and Cagney stare intently into your gourmet
coffee. Welsh spoken here. Sandwiches £1-2, including a good chicken *tikka* version. Open Mon.-Sat. 9am-5:30pm; July-Aug. also Sun. 9am-5:30pm.

You might be pleased to learn that at last report there were 42 **pubs** in Aberystwyth. **The Bear Necessities of Life,** on Marine Terrace, downstairs at the Marine Hotel, serves all beers for £1.05. **Porky's** on Bridge St. (open until 1am Thurs. and Fri.) is a disco as well as a pub. And what a name.

SIGHTS

Aberystwyth's charming *fin-de-siècle* pier has been battered by the scourges of the tourist trade: arcades and unappealing restaurants. The beachfront and promenade remain much as they were in Victorian times, though the salt air has peeled their paint a bit, and pastel townhouses still lend the town a peaceful, aristocratic air. At the south end of the promenade stands the university's **Old College,** a Neo-Gothic patchwork structure opened in 1877 as Wales' first university. Prince Charles was drilled in Welsh here before being crowned Prince of Wales in 1969. Next door stands **St. Michael's Church,** where you can climb the tower for a view of Cardigan Bay. Pass the time while waiting for a train at the **Aberystwyth Yesterday** exhibit above the train station. Once a city dance hall, the building now houses sepia photographs, women's dresses in fantastic profusion, archaic underwear strewn about, and rotting wooden dolls laid out like victims of a massacre. There's even a stereoscope you can try (open daily 10am-5pm; free).

Edward I built **Aberystwyth Castle** in 1277 after defeating the last native Prince of Wales, Llywelyn ap Gruffydd. Cromwell dropped by in 1649 and made quick work of the diamond-shaped fortress. The ruins on the hill are perfect for climbing, hiding, and seeking, and they offer a free view of the coastline. An odd little churchyard idles between St. Michael's Church and the Castle. Its borders contain gravestones, 19th-century tombs covered with graffiti, picnic tables, a playground, and public toilets, all jumbled together without fences to mark off holy ground from the septic tanks. Savor a more conventional view from **Pen Dinas Hill,** near the end of Bridge St. At the other end of the promenade, the **Electric Cliff Railway** (tel. 617642) will whisk you to the top of **Constitution Hill** to see the *camera obscura* gazebo, an enormous wide-lens telescope which offers dizzying views of the town. (Open daily 10am-9pm; Sept.-June 10am-6pm; 6 trains/hr. Last entry to *camera obscura* 5:30pm. Railway fare return £1.85, students and seniors £1.60, ages 5-16 £1, under 5 free. Camera Obscura free.) Check at the pier for coastal fishing trips (30min.-8 hr.), or call Sunshine Boat Trips at 828844.

The **National Library of Wales** (tel. 623816), off Penglais Rd. past the hospital, houses almost every book or manuscript written in or pertaining to Wales. A well-designed gallery displays, in rapidfire, the first Welsh written text (c. 800), the first Welsh printed book (1546), the first Welsh dictionary (1547), the first Welsh map (1573), the first Welsh "Beibl" (1588), and the first Welsh magazine (1735), which managed one feeble issue and folded forthwith. In another corner of the library, scalded toutes and lusty bachelers rise from the pages of the earliest surviving manuscript of the *Canterbury Tales,* dating to the early 15th century. (Open Mon.-Fri. 9:30am-6pm, Sat. 9:30am-5pm; free.) A short climb farther up the hill brings you to **Theatre Y Werin** (tel. 623232), which sponsors fine Welsh repertory and film.

■ NEAR ABERYSTWYTH

The **Vale of Rheidol Railway** (tel. (01970) 625819) chugs and twists its way by steam locomotive from Aberystwyth to the waterfalls and gorges of **Devil's Bridge** (Easter-Sept. 2/day; late July and Aug. Mon.-Thurs. 8/day; 3-hr. round-trip; £9.90, children £5, accompanied children £1, dogs 80p). The two upper bridges were constructed over the waterfalls in 1708 and 1901; the lower bridge, attributed to the Architect of Evil, was probably built by Cistercian monks from the nearby **Strata Florida Abbey** in the 11th century. The paths are turnstile operated, so take some change. The rungs of **Jacob's Ladder** (£1) descend into the depth of the **Devil's Punchbowl** gorge, cross the torrent on an arched footbridge, and climb back beside the waterfall to the road. The hostel closest to the gorge is the **Ystumtuen Youth**

Hostel (HI) (tel. (0197085) 693), near the end of the railway off the A44 in Ponterwyd, with simple-grade accommodations. Take bus #501 from Aberystwyth (Mon.-Sat. 7/day; last bus 5:40pm) and ask to be dropped off near the hostel. A 1½ mi. walk (signposted "Ystumtuen") from A44. (£5.30; open April-Nov. daily.)

■■■ MACHYNLLETH

> At my nativity,
> the front of heaven was full of fiery shapes,
> Of burning cressets, and at my birth
> The frame and huge foundation of the earth
> shaked like a coward.
>
> —I Henry IV III. i. 13-17

Owain Glyndwr, the long-prophesied savior of Wales, rose from birth to the cry of bloodied horses, and soon commanded the hopes and fears of a rebellious Wales. By 1404, the Crown's strongholds had fallen at Aberystwyth and Harlech, and it seemed Glyndwr was on the verge of claiming an independent Wales. Here at Machynlleth, he summoned four men from every commot in the territory to a vast open-air parliament. (A commot is an old Welsh administrative unit that corresponds roughly to 50 hamlets, each typically containing nine houses, one plow, one oven, one churn, one cat, one cock, and one herdsman. We do not jest.) Before the approving eyes of Charles VI of France, a new Prince of Wales was born. Then the delegates departed, the rebellion fell apart, and Machynlleth (mach-hun-hleth, pop. 2000) collapsed into the slumber from which it has not yet awakened. The **Owain Glyndwr Interpretive Centre,** Maengwyn St. (tel. 702827), occupies a primitive stone building with spikes in the windows on the site of Glyndwr's conclave; visitors can read the placards tracing the rebel's career or make brass rubbings of British historical figures (open Easter-Sept. Mon.-Sat.10am-5pm, winter by appointment; 95p-£3 to rub). The weekly Wednesday **market** lines the town's two main streets with vendors selling food, crafts, underwear, and much, much, more.

High on a hill 3 mi. north of town, the **Centre for Alternative Technology** (tel. 702400) is a giant summer camp whose counselors never leave. A water-powered railway drags visitors (including those in wheelchairs) up a 200-ft. cliff into a green village of cabins, lily ponds, wind turbines, and energy-efficient houses. Placards extol the joys and benefits of conservation, clean power, and the communal living practiced on-site. A wholefood **cafe** serves excellent vegetarian lunches for about £3; behind the cafe, men are urged to "PEE HERE" into a Urine Bank used to activate compost. The bookshop sells aromatherapy oils, solar torches, and water-divining rods. (Centre open Easter-Oct. daily 10am-5pm, phone ahead in winter; £4.50, students and seniors £3.50, children £2.50, under 5 free. HI members get a 10% discount; visitors arriving by bike get a 50% discount.) Take Gwynedd bus #30 or 34 (Mon.-Sat. every 2 hrs.) and demand to be let off at the center.

While Machynlleth lacks a hostel, the privately-run **Old School** (tel. 761686) on Old Corris Rd. in Corris is just 15 min. away on bus #94A, 34, or 30. Laundry facilities, meals, and three campsites are available. (Open May-Aug. daily, March-April and Sept.-Oct. Tues.-Sun.; £7.15, under 18 £4.75). B&Bs flourish in town. **Brooklyn,** Heol Powys (tel. 702662), has an extraordinarily vigorous 84-year-old hostess and a carpeted bathroom more spacious than any of the bedrooms (£12). Turn off Maengwyn St. at New St., then take the first left onto Heol Powys. **Melin-y-Wig** (tel. 703933), on Aberystwyth Rd. near the high school, has TVs, attractive color schemes in every room, and a dog whose front paws never touch the floor (£14/person). Off A487 3 mi. north of town next to the Centre for Alternative Technology, **Llwyngwern Farm** (tel. 702492), offers showers and campsites among the sheep (open Easter-Sept.; £3.50/1 person, £5.50/2 people, dogs £1).

Machynlleth pubs offer nothing spectacular in the way of affordable gluttony, but cheap and healthy pig-outs can be had at the pine table of the **Quarry Shop Cafe,**

MACHYNLLETH TO HARLECH

13 Maengwyn St. (tel. 702624; shop open Mon.-Sat. 9am-6pm; cafe open Mon.-Sat. 9am-4:30pm; both close at 2pm on Thurs. from Sept.-June). A **Lo-Cost** supermarket flaunts its prosperity on Maengwyn St. past the tourist office (open Mon.-Wed. and Sat. 8:30am-6pm, Thurs.-Fri. 8:30am-8pm, Sun. 10am-4pm).

At the poorly-signposted **tourist office** (tel. 702401) in the Owain Glyndwr Centre on Maengwyn St., down the road from the Clocktower, you can stock up on local guides and literature (open daily 9am-6pm; Oct.-Easter Mon.-Fri. 9am-5pm). From the rail station, follow Doll St., veer right at the church onto Penrallt St., and continue until you see the clock tower. Maengwyn St. is on the left. You can rent **bikes** in all their permutations at **Joyrides** (tel. 703109), in a stone cottage behind the train station (touring bikes and mountain bikes £9/day, £47/week; open daily 9am-5:30pm, Easter-June and Sept.-Dec. Fri.-Wed. 10am-5:30pm, Jan.-Easter Mon.-Wed. and Fri.-Sat. 10am-5pm). Crosville bus passes are available at the **post office,** at the head of Maengwyn St. (open Mon.-Tues. and Thurs.-Fri. 9am-1pm and 2-5:30pm, Wed. 9:30am-1pm and 2-5:30pm, Sat. 9am-12:30pm). Machynlleth's **postal code** is SY20 8AF, and its **telephone code** is 01654.

British Rail (tel. (01654) 702311) chugs to Machynlleth from Birmingham (7/day, Sun. 2/day; 2½ hrs.; £20.50), Shrewsbury (7/day, Sun. 4/day; 1½hr.; £9.70), Aberystwyth (8/day, Sun. 6/day; 30min.; £3.50), and Harlech (7/day, Sun. 3/day; 1½hr.; £6.90, buy a Cambrian Coast Day Rover for £5.20 instead). **Crosville** bus #94/514 winds from Aberystwyth (7/day, Sun. 3/day; 40min.; £2.40); the scenic ride along the A487 is worth the extra 10 minutes. Bus #94A swerves inland to Dolgellau on an even lovelier route (6/day, summer Sundays 2/day; £2.55), and a **Transcambria** bus rattles in daily from Cardiff (£12.10).

■■■ MACHYNLLETH TO HARLECH

Deep in the conifers of the Idris mountain range, the endless dark stone buildings of **Dolgellau** (dol-GETH-high) give the Mawddach Estuary a fierce and gloomy aspect. The town lies in the shadow of **Cader Idris,** literally "seat of Idris" and home to the Grey King (Brenin Llewyd) of Susan Cooper's *Dark is Rising* series. Dolgellau is a good base for a number of scenic walks: the **Precipice Walk** begins 3 mi. north of Dolgellau, near Llanfachreth; and the **Penmaen Pool Walk,** 3 mi. from town, leads down the river's estuary to a bird observatory.

For further information on area walks, contact the **tourist office** at Eldon Sq. (tel. (01341) 422888) by the bus stop, which doubles as a Snowdonia National Park Information Centre. The office books B&Bs (£12 and up) and provides excellent free brochures and maps (open daily 10am-6pm; Oct.-Easter Wed.-Mon. 10am-5pm). Four mi. away at Kings is an **HI Youth Hostel** (tel. (01341) 422392); take bus #28 (Mon.-Sat. 6/day) from Dolgellau (£6.50). Two B&Bs with spectacular views of the Idris range cling to the heights just north of Dolgellau. **Arosfyr,** Pen-y-Cefn (tel. (01341) 422355), offers huge rooms and stout furniture in an old farmhouse (£15 single, £13.50 double). Cross the bridge, turn left, and turn right at the school. **Dwy Olwyn,** Coed-y-Fronallt (tel. (01341) 422822), has a colorful hillside garden to clamber through (single £15, double £13.50). Cross the bridge, turn right, and follow the sign that says "B&B 400m." Camping is available at the hostel and at **Tanyfron Caravan and Camping Site** (tel. (01341) 422638), a five- to 10-minute walk south of town off the A470. (1 person £3.50, 2 people £5.50, car 50p, open year-round.) Bus #94A follows a winding scenic route through the mountains to Dolgellau from Machynlleth (Mon.-Sat. 6/day, summer Sun. 2/day; £2.55) and Aberystwyth (£4.95). The **Transcambria** bus stops by daily on its way to Cardiff (£13.60).

For some reason, tourists fill the streets of **Barmouth,** an amusement park town 10 mi. south of Harlech where Beethoven's Fifth blares with a backbeat from the beachfront. A **bilingual talking garbage can** at Beach Rd. and High St. used to thank visitors for keeping the town tidy; now it doesn't even bother. Inebriated revelers used to be locked up in **Ty Crwn,** The Round House, built under a 1782 Act of Parliament in the south end of town as a jail for drunken sailors (open in summer Sun.-

Fri. 10am-6pm). The **Three Peaks Yacht Race,** held during the third week of June, is the current inspiration for town-wide drinking. Racers push off from Barmouth and work their way up the British coast, landing in Caernarfon (Wales), Ravenglass, and Fort William (Scotland) and climbing a mountain each time they disembark (Mount Snowdon, Scafell Pike, and Ben Nevis respectively).

Most B&Bs in Barmouth charge over £12; the cheapest stand on Marine Rd. and King Edward St. The Barmouth **tourist office** (tel. (01341) 280787), directly across from the railroad station on Jubilee Rd., provides the usual with a smile (open Easter-Oct. daily 10am-1pm, 2-6pm). **Bikes n' Boards** (tel. (01341) 281263), on King Edward St. opposite the Job Centre, rents riders for £14 per day and a £25 deposit (open daily 9am-5pm). Trains serve Barmouth every two hr. on the Machynlleth-Pwllheli line (from Machynlleth £5.30, from Harlech £2.40). The open-top bus "Happy Dragon" #102 runs eight times per day to Llanbedr, snorting happy flames along the way. Buses #37 and 94 link Barmouth and Dolgellau (Mon.-Sat. 1/hr., summer Sun. 4/day; £3.20); #38 flees to Harlech (Mon.-Sat. 4/day).

Just 1½ mi. south of Harlech on the A496 near Llanfair lie the **Old Llanfair Quarry Slate Caverns** (tel. (01766) 780247). Although tiny compared to their Snowdonian cousins at Blaenau-Ffestiniog, these caves are less crowded and more memorable. The "crypt" cavern delivers you to the "cathedral"; try to arrive in the afternoon, when sunshine filters through the ceiling (open Easter to mid-Oct. daily 10am-5pm; £2.30, children £1.30). Take bus #38 from Harlech to Llanfair (Mon.-Sat. 3-4/day).

■■■ HARLECH

The tiny town of Harlech hovers just shy of the Lleyn Peninsula, about 50 mi. north of Machynlleth along the coastal road. Recluses and refugees from busy Barmouth will find solitude and sea breezes amid the grassy dunes at Harlech beach, a 20-minute walk from town. **Harlech Castle** (tel. 780552), Edward I's third in-your-face fortress, crowns a 200-ft. rock with sweeping views of prefabs, caravan parks, the Snowdonian mountains, and the sea. A walk through the gatehouse, where traces remain of the two barred gates and three portcullises that used to slam down on the uninvited, will make you wonder how in the world Owain Glyndwr took it in 1404. From the outer bailey, 151 steps cling to the cliff as far as the train station, where the sea used to be. (Open daily 9:30am-6:30pm, Nov.-March Mon.-Sat. 9:30am-4pm, Sun. 11am-4pm; £2.90, seniors, students, and children £1.80.) From the splendid overhanging garderobe on the castle's south wall, gape across the moat at the equestrian statue that illustrates a tragic tale from the *Mabinogion* with a contorted horse, dismembered rider, and a dead child. **Theatr Ardudwy,** Coleg Harlech (tel. 780667), is the town's cultural axis, hosting films, plays, concerts, and exhibitions. (Some concerts are free; other performances range from £2.50-£10; students, seniors, and children get a £1-2 discount.)

The **Llanbedr hostel (HI;** tel. (0134123) 287) is the closest hostel to Harlech, only 4 mi. south; take the train or bus #38 and ask to be let off at the hostel (£6.50; open July-Aug. daily; April-June Mon.-Sat.; March and Oct. Tues.-Sat.; Feb. and Nov. weekends only). Good B&Bs in and around Harlech should save you the trip. **Mrs. Williams,** Ael-y-Garth, 6 Rock Terrace (no telephone), offers a full breakfast and friendly chatter (but no shower) for £8. From the castle, turn right onto High St. and left at the TV store beyond the tourist office. Farther up Rock Terrace, **Pant Mawr** (tel. 780226) occupies a tobacco-free farmhouse with big rooms and a view even better than the castle's, since it includes the castle. The owners can arrange to pick you up from the station—take them up on it (£12.50). **Clogwyn Villa** (tel. 780950), on High St. at the foot of Rock Terrace, has TV in all rooms and serves breakfast in a stone-walled restaurant. If you mention *Let's Go,* you can leave in the morning hungry for £8 or stuffed for £10.50. For camping, try **Min-y-Don Park,** Beach Rd., with showers and laundry (tel. 780286; open Mar.-Oct. £2/person).

The **Yr Ogof Bistro** (tel. 780888), on High St. left from the castle, offers the best cuisine in town, with a wide range of homemade entrees and creative vegetarian dishes (£4-8). Call ahead to reserve a table (open Easter-Sept. daily 5-10pm, Oct.-Nov. daily 7-10pm, Nov.-Easter Wed.-Sat. 7-10pm). The view from the **Plas Cafe,** High St. (tel. 780204), demands afternoon tea (savory chicken and fish dishes £5, nightly vegetarian special £5; open daily 9:30am-8:30pm; reservations recommended). Cheap, simple food can be had at the **Lion Hotel's bar** for £3-4 (food served daily noon-3pm, 6-9pm; light refreshments 3-6pm). The **tourist office,** Gwyddfor House, High St. (tel. 780658), doubles as a **National Park Information Centre,** offering maps and pamphlets about Harlech and Snowdonia (open Easter-Oct. daily 10am-6pm). The **post office** (tel. 780231) on High St. won the 1993 award for the "Brightest and Best Post Office in Gwynedd;" the small bookstore inside is strong on poetry and recent highbrow fiction (open daily 9am-5:30pm, closed weekends in winter). Harlech's **postal code** is LL46 2YA, and its **telephone code** is 01766.

Harlech lies mid-way on the Cambrian coastal rail line; its **train station,** just below the castle, is a spirit-breaking 15-minute walk from town. Trains arrive from Shrewsbury (7/day, Sun. 3/day; 3hrs.; £14) and Machynlleth (7/day, Sun. 3/day; 1½hrs.; £6.90), connecting to Pwllheli and other spots on the Lleyn Peninsula (every 2 hr.; Sun. 3/day). If you're coming from Machynlleth or Aberystwyth, a Cambrian Coast Day Rover (£5.20) is cheaper than the single fare. **Bus** #38 links Harlech to Barmouth in the south and Blaenau Ffestiniog in the north (Mon.-Sat. 4/day).

■■■ LLEYN PENINSULA (PENR HYN LLYN)

Lleyn has thrived on tourism since the Middle Ages, when crowds of religious pilgrims tramped through on their way to Bardsey Island off the peninsula's western tip. Latter-day English imperialists have established colonies of *tai-haf* (summer houses) to better enjoy the sandy beaches between Pwllheli and Abersoch, the cliff-lined coast west of Abersoch, and the breakers at southerly Hell's Mouth, where the waves wash surfers and other sea debris ashore. But much of the hilly region is remote and unsullied like the ancient village of Aberdaron in the west; the two Phonecard booths at Porthmadog are the only ones on the peninsula.

GETTING THERE & GETTING ABOUT

The northern end of **British Rail's** Cambrian Coast line reaches through Porthmadog and Criccieth (KRIK-key-ith) to Pwllheli (pooth-ELLY), stopping at smaller towns in between. The line begins in mid-Wales at Aberystwyth; change at Machynlleth for northern destinations (Mon.-Sat. 6/day, Sun. 3/day; Machynlleth-Pwllheli £10). The **Cambrian Coast Day Rover** allows travel to any stops for £5.20/day. Porthmadog is the starting point of the justly famous **Ffestiniog Railway** (tel. (01766) 512340), which runs northeast through the Ffestiniog Valley into the hills of Snowdonia, terminating in Blaenau Ffestiniog (March-Oct. 2-8/day; 1hr.; return £4.50-11.40). British Rail's **Conwy Valley** line links up with the Ffestiniog Railway at Blaenau Ffestiniog and continues via Betws-y-Coed to Llandudno on the northern coast; this line in turn connects to Manchester and Bangor (Mon.-Sat. 6/day; Manchester-Porthmadog return £21.20, Bangor-Porthmadog return £13.80, Llandudno-Porthmadog return £11.80).

A daily bus from London arrives in Pwllheli in the evening and departs Pwllheli for London the next morning (£26), with service extending to Caernarfon, Aberdaron, and Porthmadog. The **Crosville Transcambria** bus #701 connects Porthmadog once a day with Aberystwyth, Carmarthen, Swansea, and Cardiff (to Cardiff 6½hr., £16). **Bus Gwynedd** serves most spots on the peninsula with reassuring haste for £1-2. Bus #1 connects Porthmadog to Caernarfon (Mon.-Sat. 1/hr.; 50min.; £1.65), and bus #12 connects Pwllheli to Caernarfon (Mon.-Sat. 1/hr., Sun 4/day; 50min.; £1.90). Crosville runs the open-top "Happy Dragon" bus #103 nine times per day in the summer from Porthmadog to Pwllheli via Criccieth. A **Gwynedd Red Rover,** bought from the driver, is good for a day throughout the peninsula and the rest of

Gwynedd County (£4, child £2). Sunday buses run infrequently or not at all; the unwieldy **Gwynedd Public Transport Guide** tells all you need to know.

ACCOMMODATIONS & SIGHTS

Porthmadog (port-MAD-dok), resort town and travel hub, is the southeastern gateway to the peninsula. Though the town's principal attraction is the Ffestiniog Railway, you can splatter paint or torture clay *behind* the largest mural in Wales at **Porthmadog Pottery,** Snowdon St. (tel. 512137; open daily 9am-5:30pm; 50p, under 14 free; £2.50 to throw a pot or paint a plate). Look for David Lloyd George and Bertrand Russell arguing politics in the top right corner of the mural.

Check for small B&B signs in windows along Madoc St. and Snowdon St. in Porthmadog—rooms are generally uninspiring but reasonably priced. **Vro Gain,** Bank Place (tel. 513125), charges students £12.50 for full breakfast and orange curtains that give the bedrooms a twilight glow in the morning (non-students £14). Two B&Bs occupy one building at the corner of Avenue Rd. and Meadow Drive behind the train station. **Lleiron,** 1 Meadow Dr. (tel. 512064), has a bilious green sheepskin in the lounge and a Rorschach-blot hide of unknown origin in the dining room (£13.50). **The Nest,** 2 Meadow Dr. (tel. 512519), incubates TVs and a friendly semi-retired couple (£14). Porthmadog's **post office** is at the corner of High St. and Bank Pl. (tel. 512010; open Mon.-Fri. 9am-5:30pm, Sat. 9am-12:30pm). The **postal code** is LL49 9AD, and the **telephone code** 01766. The **tourist office** is at the end of High St. (tel. 512981; open daily 10am-6pm, Nov.-Easter Fri.-Wed. 10am-5pm). **Buses** stop at various points along High St.; check posted schedules.

An eccentric landmark of Italy-fixation, the private village of **Portmeirion** stands 2 mi. east of Porthmadog, a project of the late potter Sir Clough Williams-Ellis from 1925 to 1972. A grassy piazza flaunts ruined columns, evergreens trimmed to look like cypresses, and a Baroque triumphal arch built on a budget. Dogs can't enter the village, but they go the way of all flesh at the **dog cemetery** deep in the nearby woods, where cairns are raised to Pepys (1965-76, "a brave and much loved cavalier") and Dearest Darling Woofy (1977-94, "a very exceptional dog and mother of Softy"). Take a bus to Minffordd (#3 is the most frequent) and then follow signs to the village, a 15-minute walk away (tel. (01766) 770 228; open daily 9:30am-5:30pm, Nov.-March 10am-5pm; £3, seniors £2.40, children £1.30.

Above the coastal town of **Criccieth,** 5 mi. west of Porthmadog, stand the remains of **Criccieth Castle** (tel. 522227), built by Llewelyn the Great in 1230 and destroyed by Owain Glyndwr in 1404. Its gatehouse, silhouetted against the skyline, glowers over Tremadog Bay, with Snowdonia to the northeast and Harlech across the water (open daily 9:30am-6:30pm; Nov.-March Mon.-Sat. 9:30am-4pm, Sun. 11am-4pm; £2, seniors, students, and children £1.50). Bus #3, which connects Criccieth to Porthmadog and Pwllheli, also stops at **Llanystumdwy,** a tiny town 1½ mi. north of Criccieth and the boyhood home of David Lloyd George, liberal Prime Minister and Welsh-village-boy-made-good. The town preserves the house where he grew up, the school where first he made his mischief, and his grave by the river Dwyfor. The **Lloyd George Museum** (tel. 522071), on the village's only street, displays relics from his career, including the pen he used to sign the Treaty of Versailles and his working copy of the treaty (open Easter-Sept. Mon.-Fri. 10:30am-5pm, Sat.-Sun. 2-5pm; Oct. Mon.-Fri. 11am-4pm; £2.10, children and seniors £1.35). A short hop away, 1000 bunnies breed liberally at the **Dwyfor Ranch Rabbit Farm** (tel. 523136). Pony rides are free for children with admission (open Easter-mid-Sept. Sun.-Fri. 10am-6pm, Sat. 9am-noon; £2.50, children and seniors £1.50). In Criccieth, B&Bs (£12-14) are scattered on Wellington Terr. on the way to the castle. **Dan-Y-Castell,** 4 Marine Terr. (tel. 522375), serenades both castle and sea (£12); or try **The Rhoslyn,** 8 Marine Terr (tel. 522685; £11.50, Jul.-Aug. £12). Despite the signpost at the bus stop, Criccieth has no tourist office. **Trains** stop in the town on their way to and from Pwllheli. Criccieth and Llanystumdwy share a **telephone code** of 01766.

Pwllheli (pooth-ELLY), 8 mi. west of Criccieth, has little to attract the traveler besides the station that spews buses to every corner of the peninsula and beyond.

The town has two **beaches:** sandy Abererch beach to the east, and pebbly South Beach. A short walk from the tourist office, **Bank Place Guest House,** 29 High St. (tel. 612103), has spacious rooms and huge breakfasts (£10). Across the street, **Mrs. Jones** (tel. 613172) offers well-decorated rooms with TV for £12 and coin-op showers. **Hendre** (tel. 613416) offers **camping** near Pwllheli, on the road to Nefyn at Efailnewidd (£7/tent; laundromat and showers available; open March-Oct.); **Cae Bach Site** (tel. 612536) lies ¾ mi. from Pwllheli (£3-6; showers; open mid-June to Sept.); **Abererch Sands** (tel. 612327) is on the main road between Pwllheli and Butlin's Starcoast World (1 person £4.50, high season £5.50; 4 people £6.75-7.75; showers included; open March-Oct.). The **post office** is open Mon.-Thurs. 9am-5:30pm, Fri. 9:30am-5:30pm, Sat. 9am-12:30pm; the **postal code** is LL53 5ND, and the **telephone code** 01758. The **tourist office,** Station Sq. (tel. 613000), books B&Bs (open March-Sept. daily 10am-6pm). Go halfsies on a bicycle-built-for-two in Pwllheli at the **Llyn Cycle Centre** (tel. 612414) on Lower Ala Rd. near the post office (10-speeds £10/day, £30/4 days, £45/week; deposit £25; open Mon.-Wed. and Fri.-Sat. 9:30am-5pm). A friendly red dragon welcomes trains pulling into the station at Station Sq. (from Machynlleth Mon.-Sat. 7/day, Sun. 3/day; £10). Buses #3 and 69 connect Porthmadog and Pwllheli (Mon.-Sat. 1/hr.; summer Sun. 2/day; £1.15).

Farther west along the peninsula, **Abersoch** is a slightly snooty resort with an overabundance of leisure boats and a paucity of cheap accommodations. Almost all the B&Bs charge over £14 and jack up their prices in the summer; **Doris Jones,** Lon Hawen (tel. (01758) 712755), holds her price at £12.50. Walk for 10 minutes up High St., which becomes Lon Sarn Bach as it passes the expensive guest houses, and turn right at the **second** sign reading "Lon Hawen." The **tourist office** (tel. (01758) 712929) on Lon Gwydryn off High St. offers advice on bedding down, but will not book rooms (open Easter-Sept. daily 10am-5pm). Take bus #18 from Pwllheli (Mon.-Sat. 1/hr.; £1.15). The last stop for pilgrims on their way to Bardsey Island, the beautiful village of **Aberdaron** on the peninsula's western tip holds nothing crass to distract visitors from the wind and the gray-blue sea. The plain stone church by the beach surrounds the oldest doorway in North Wales and two 5th-century gravestones carved in Latin; **Y Gegin Fawr** café has fortified pilgrims since AD 1300. Water in the wishing well 1½ mi. west of town stays fresh even when the tide crashes over it. **Bryn Mor** (tel. (01758) 86344) crowns a high hill above the village and the bay (B&B £13.50). Bus #17 runs from Pwllheli (Mon.-Sat. 6/day; £1.45), and #17B follows a scenic coastal route once a day from Pwllheli to Aberdaron via Abersoch. Off the southwest corner of the peninsula, 20,000 saints sleep beneath **Bardsey Island,** one of the last Welsh Druid strongholds and a seaswept open-air hostel for migratory birds. **Elwyn Evans** (tel. (01758) 83654; 6-person min.) sails from Aberdaron (£14, under 10 £7); **David Thomas** makes the trip from Criccieth by arrangement (tel. (01766) 522239; 12-person min.; £14, under 16 £10).

Tre'r Ceiri (trair-KAY-ree), on the peninsula's north shore, is home to Britain's oldest fortress and city wall, dating back some 4000 years. Take the Pwllheli-Caernarfon bus to Llanaelhaearn, 7 mi. from Pwllheli (#12; Mon.-Sat. 12/day, Sun. 4/day), then look for the public footpath signpost 1 mi. southwest of town on the B4417. The remains of over 200 circular stone huts are clustered within a double defensive wall. Wear warm clothing to protect yourself from the crosswinds at the top.

■■■ SNOWDONIA FOREST & NATIONAL PARK

Stretching from Machynlleth in the south to Bangor and Conwy in the north and covering the larger part of northern Wales, Snowdonia is the reason you came to Wales. All of 840 sheep-dotted square miles in total, the park sweeps through the coast as well as the rugged hills of the interior. Myriad crooked paths lead visitors through the mountains, while the Snowdon Mountain Railway and the slate mines of Llanberis and Blaenau Ffestiniog lure visitors out of the woods to the little towns where everyone speaks Welsh. Phenomenal popularity notwithstanding, the towns and the park remain largely unsullied by touristic excess; you can always find solitude somewhere in the mountain vastness.

GETTING THERE & GETTING ABOUT

The **Snowdon Sherpa,** a service of Crosville bus lines on which all Crosville and Gwynedd County passes are valid, offers relatively easy access to the various Snowdon trailheads. A **Red Rover ticket** (£4, children £2) buys unlimited travel on the Sherpa buses and on any other bus in Gwynedd; individual trips tend to cost about £1.50. Most routes are serviced by one bus every two hours, even on Sundays. Inform the driver if you intend to switch buses; connections often fail due to late or impatient buses. Buses run to the interior from towns near the edge of the park, such as Porthmadog and Caernarfon at the root of the Lleyn Peninsula to the west, Conwy on Wales' north coast, and Betws-y-Coed, just south of Conwy.

  Narrow-gauge railway lines running through Snowdonia let you enjoy the countryside without enduring a hike. The **Snowdon Mountain Railway** (tel. (01286) 870223), opened in 1896 and still operated by seven coal-fired steam locomotives, travels from Llanberis to the summit of Snowdonia (2hr. round-trip; 30min. at the peak). Weather conditions and passenger demand rule the schedule from July to early September; on a clear day the first train leaves Llanberis at 9am (if there are at least 25 passengers), with subsequent trains about every half-hour until mid-afternoon (single £9.50, return £13.20; weary hikers can try for a £5 standby back down). The **Ffestiniog Railway** (tel. (01766) 512340) romps through the mountains of Snowdonia from Porthmadog to Blaenau Ffestiniog, where the mountains of discarded slate that ring the town rival those of Snowdonia (return £7.60-11.60). You can travel part of its route to Minffordd, Penrhyndeudraeth, Tanybwlch, or Tdnygrisiau (4-11/day, Oct. and March 2-6/day). At Porthmadog, the narrow-gauge rail connects with the Cambrian Coast service from Pwllheli south to Aberystwyth in mid-Wales; at Blaenau Ffestiniog, it connects with the Conwy Valley Line to Llandudno via Betws-y-Coed and Llanrwst. **Llanberis Lake Railway** (tel. (01288) 870549) jaunts a short and scenic route from Gilfach Ddu station at Llanberis through the woods (5-11/day; 40min.; £3.60; March-Oct. 4/day, £3).

PRACTICAL INFORMATION

Tourist offices and National Park Information Centres stock leaflets on walks, drives, and accommodations, as well as Ordnance Survey maps. Contact the **Snowdonia National Park Information Centre** (tel. (01766) 770274), Penrhyndeudraeth (pen-rin-DOY-dryth), Gwynedd, Wales LL48 6LS for details. The annual **Snowdonia Star,** stacked to the roof at tourist offices across North Wales, has fistfuls of information on the park and overenthusiastic writeups of selected attractions.

  Snowdonia National Park Study Centre, Plas Tan-y-Bwlch, Maentwrog, Blaenau Ffestiniog, Gwynedd, Wales LL41 3YU (tel. (01766) 85324), offers courses on naturalist favorites such as wildlife painting and geology. For canoeing, photography, rock climbing, and first-aid courses, call a month ahead to the **Pen-y-Pass Youth Hostel (HI),** Mountain Centre, Nant Gwynant, Gwynedd, Wales LL55 4NY (tel. (01286) 870428, fax 872434).

NATIONAL PARK INFORMATION CENTERS

  Betws-y-coed: Royal Oak Stables (tel. (01690) 710665 or 710426). The busiest and best-stocked. Open April-Oct. daily 10am-5:45pm, Nov.-March daily 10am-4pm.

  Blaenau Ffestiniog: High St. (tel. (01776) 830360). In the shadow of Ffestiniog Railway's slate heaps and smoke clouds. Open Easter-Sept. daily 10am-6pm.

  Dolgellau: Eldon Sq. by the bus stop (tel. (01341) 422888). Crowded with sedentary tourists in cars, as well as climbers assaulting Cadair Idris. Open daily 10am-6pm; Oct.-Easter Wed.-Mon. 10am-5pm.

  Harlech: Gwyddfor House, High St. (tel. (01766) 780658). A small, quiet office in an untrampled region of the park. Open Easter-Oct. daily 10am-6pm.

Aberdyfi: The Wharf (tel. (01654) 767321). Open April-Sept. daily 10am-6pm.

Bala: Penllyn Leisure Centre, Pensarn Rd. (tel. (01678) 521021). Open Easter-mid-Oct. daily 10am-6pm.

ACCOMMODATIONS & CAMPING

The eight **HI Youth Hostels** in the mountain area are some of the best in Wales. They are marked clearly on Gwynedd bus schedules and on the more legible transport map. Summer school excursions can make getting into the hostels a challenge.

Llanberis (tel. (01286) 870280). Plenty of sheep, cows, and bulls keep hostelers company as they take in the splendid views of Llyn (Lake) Peris and Llyn Padarn below and Mt. Snowdon above. No washers. £7.75. Open April-Sept. daily; Feb.-March and Oct. Fri.-Tues.; Nov.-Dec. Fri.-Mon.

Bryn Gwynant (tel. (0176686) 251), at the trailhead of the Watkin's path to Snowdon, above Llyn Gwynant and along the road from Pen-y-Gwryd to Beddgelert (4 mi. from Beddgelert). Take bus #11 from Caernarfon (summer 4/day, winter Mon.-Sat. 1/day). Washing machine. £7.75. Open March-Aug. and mid.-Sept.-Oct. daily; Jan.-Feb. Tues.-Sat.

Pen-y-Pass (tel. (01286) 870428), 6 mi. from Llanberis and 4 mi. from Nant Peris. Commands the most unusual and spectacular position of any hostel in Wales: 1170 ft. above sea level at the head of Llanberis Pass between the Snowdon and Glyders peaks. Open the door to the Pyg track or the Llyn Llydaw miner's track to the Snowdon summit in your hired walking boots. They also rent waterproofs and ice axes. No washer. £8.70. Open April-Oct. daily; Feb.-March and Nov. Tues.-Sat.

Snowdon Ranger, Llyn Cwellyn (tel. (01286) 650391). The base for the grandest Snowdon ascent—the **Ranger Path.** Bus #11 stops here. No washer, but has spin dryer. £7.75. Open April-Sept. daily; Feb.-March and Oct. Thurs.-Mon.

Ffestiniog (tel. (01766) 762765), in Ffestiniog (*not* Blaenau Ffestiniog). Only 2 mi. from the famous slate quarries and narrow-gauge railway. Take bus #1 or 3 from Porthmadog or Blaenau Ffestiniog, #35 from Dolgellau, or #38 from Barmouth or Harlech. No washers. £6.50. Open April-Aug. Mon.-Sat.

Capel Curig (tel. (016904) 225), 5 mi. from Betws-y-Coed on the A5. At the crossroads of many mountain paths. Bus #19 and 65 stop nearby. No washers. £7.75. Open April-Aug. and Oct. daily; Sept. Wed.-Sun.; Nov. Wed.-Sat.

Idwal Cottage (tel. (01248) 600225), just off the A5 at the foot of Llyn Ogwen in northern Snowdonia. Within hiking distance of Pen-y-Pass, Llanberis, and Capel Curig. Buses come here less frequently than the other hostels—check the bus #65 timetable. £6.50. Open July-Aug. daily; April-June and Sept.-Oct. Mon.-Sat.; Jan.-March Fri.-Tues.

Lledr Valley (tel. (016906) 202), only 5 mi. from Betws-y-Coed on the rail line between Llandudno Junction and Blaenau Ffestiniog. The hostel is 1 mi. from the train station. No washers. £7.15. Open May-Aug. daily; April and Sept.-Oct. Mon.-Sat.; Jan.-March Tues.-Sat.

The land in Snowdonia is privately owned—stick to public pathways and campsites or ask the owner's consent. In the high mountains, **camping** is permitted as long as you leave no mess, but the Park Service discourages it because of a recent and disastrous erosion. In the valleys, owner's consent is needed to camp. Public camping sites dot the roads in peak seasons; check listings below for sites in specific towns.

HIKING

Weather on the exposed mountains shifts quickly, unpredictably, and wrathfully; arm yourself to battle the elements. Please review Essentials: Hiking & Camping, and be sure to pick up the Ordnance Survey maps of Snowdonia National Park (£4-5) and individual path guides (six at 20p each)—all available at Park Centres and most bookstores. Call **Mountaincall Snowdonia** (tel. (01839) 500449) for the local forecast, ground conditions, and a national three- to five-day forecast (36-48p/min.). Weather forecasts are tacked on the doors of the National Park Information Centers.

Park rangers lead day walks near Betws-y-Coed, Nant Gwynant, and elsewhere (£3, seniors £2, children 50p). Contact tourist offices and National Park Information Centres for more options, and check the free newsletter, the *Snowdonia Star*, for goings-on and walking advice. Private mountain guides and other companies also advertise in the local youth hostels.

Lesser ranges, such as the **Glyders** or **Cader Idris,** will challenge any serious climber, but the highest peak, **Mount Snowdon** (Yr Wyddfa, or "burial place"), at 3560 ft., remains the most popular; half a million climbers reach the summit every year and descend to tell the world via "I Climbed Mt. Snowdon" T-shirts. Because multiple trails make the mountain accessible to hikers of all strengths, Mt. Snowdon has become eroded and its ecosystem disrupted. Park officers request that all hikers stick to the well-marked trails to avoid further damage. Since other climbs will be less crowded and probably more scenic, it might be wise to skip Snowdon altogether and try a hike up **Tryfan** or nearby **Devil's Kitchen.**

Six principal paths lead up Snowdon. The **Llanberis Path** is the easiest, the longest (a 5-mi. ascent), and by far the most popular. The path begins on the first side road above the Snowdon railway station at the edge of Llanberis and takes five hours round-trip. The **Snowdon Ranger Path** is, like the Llanberis Path, one of the easier ways up Snowdon. The 3.1-mi. trek begins beside the Snowdon Ranger Youth Hostel, on the northern shore of Llyn Cwellyn, and takes five hours round-trip. The **Watkin's Path,** with an ascent of 3300 ft., is the most arduous and also the most beautiful attack on the summit. The 3.4-mi. hike takes five hours up and three hours down; it begins at Pont Bethania on the A498, 3 mi. northeast of Beddgelert (on the Snowdon Sherpa bus line). The spectacular sunsets above the **Rhyd Ddu Path** make it a popular end-of-the-day descent. The trailhead of this five-hour path is at the end of the car park south of Rhyd Ddu on the Snowdon Sherpa line between Beddgelert and Caernarfon. Two other paths are the **Miner's,** easy only as far as Llyn Glaslyn, and the **Pyg Path,** a tough trail at the top. Both of these paths are 2.8 mi. and begin at Pen-y-Pass. Bicycle-riding through mountain pastures is not looked upon kindly by farmers and local landowners. Follow trails, close each gate you open, and give walkers and horseback riders the right of way. A cycling pamphlet available at tourist offices has details on bike routes and a cheerful admonishment.

LLANBERIS

Toss your pack over your fleece jacket, pull on your purple waterproof pants, and join the crowd of walkers and climbers who populate **Llanberis,** the largest town in the park's northwest sector and the best place to stock up on gear and food. The **Museum of the North** gives tours of Dinorwig Power Station inside a mountain and shows a film on electric power that will shake your earwax loose (open daily June-Sept. 9:30am-6pm; March-May and Sept.-Nov. 10am-5pm; £5, children £2.50). To reach the ruins of nearby **Dolbadarn Castle,** follow the River Hwch until the path crosses the footbridge and leads up through woods to the castle. From the castle, you can gaze at the industrial scabs on the shores of Llyn Peris. To reach **Ceunant Mawr,** one of Wales's most impressive waterfalls, take the public footpath on Victoria Terrace by Victoria Hotel, then the first right and first left (about 1 mi.). The path leads past smaller falls and pools to the tracks of the Snowdon Mountain Railway. **Craft workshops** (tel. 351427) dot the park, and craftspeople demonstrate brass-molding (on request), harp manufacturing, screen printing, flower pressing, woodburning, and slate art (open Easter Week daily 9:30am-5:30pm; May-Sept. daily 9:30am-6:30pm). The **Llanberis Lake Railway** (tel. 870549) slides 2 mi. along Llyn Padarn (£3.60; see above). The **Snowdon Mountain Railway** (tel. 870223) whisks you up Mt. Snowdon from Llanberis (return £13.20; see Snowdonia: Getting There and Getting About, above).

The town has flocks of B&Bs (£12 and up) and the **Llanberis Youth Hostel (HI),** ½ mi. up Capel Coch Rd. (see Snowdonia: Accommodations and Camping, above). **The Heights Hotel,** 74 High St. (the town's only street; tel. 871179), has 24 bunk beds packed hostel-style into big rooms—but these beds are stained wood, and the showers are nice (£7, with breakfast £10). The restaurant serves pizzas and burgers for £2-4 (open daily breakfast-10pm; Oct.-April Sun.-Thurs. 6-10pm, Fri.-Sat. breakfast-10pm). **Hugh and Judy Walton** (tel. 870744), experienced climbers, run a bunkhouse 2 mi. from town on the Caernarfon road (£5, with three meals/day £14); groups can hire guides for £80/day). Campers can head 2 mi. north to the mammoth **Snowdon View Caravan Park** (tel. 870349), which has great facilities and a heated swimming pool (£4-6/tent), or ride a bit further on bus #88 to **Pritchard's Camp Site,** opposite the hotel in Nant Peris (tel. 870494; toilets and showers; £2/person). Llanberis's restaurants have adapted their fare to the healthy demands (and appetites) of hikers. You can stoke your engine or break it down with a dose of awe-inspiring chili (£3.90) or a vegetarian mixed grill (£4.20) at **Pete's Eats** (tel. 870358; open daily 9am-8pm; off-season Mon.-Fri. 9am-6:30pm, Sat.-Sun. 8am-8pm).

The **tourist office,** Museum of the North building (tel. 870765), in the bypass at the end of High St., doles out tips on hikes and sights, in addition to running an accommodations-booking service (open Easter-Sept. daily 10am-5:45pm). Plan your hike and pick up gear at **Joe Brown's Store** (tel. 870327) on High St., owned by one of the world's greatest pioneer climbers (open Mon.-Sat. 9am-6pm, Sun. 9am-5pm; winter closing 5:30pm). Address the **post office** (open Mon.-Tues. and Thurs.-Fri. 9am-noon and 1-5:30pm, Wed. and Sat. 9am-noon) with **postal code** LL55 4EU. Llanberis's **telephone code** is 01286.

Situated on the western edge of the park, Llanberis is a short ride from Caernarfon; catch **Crosville bus** #88 from Caernarfon (Mon.-Sat. 2/hr., Sun. 1/hr.; return £1.20), bus #77 from Bangor (Mon.-Sat. 7/day), or one of the **Sherpa** buses.

■■■ CAERNARFON

The castle and walled city at Caernarfon (can-AR-von), across the estuary from the Isle of Anglesey, once served as the center of English government in North Wales. For centuries, the Welsh were forced to live outside the walls, but during a tax revolt in 1294 they managed to break in to sack the town and massacre the English settlers. Caernarfon withstood two sieges by Owain Glyndwr during the Welsh Rebellion of 1401-14. Even now the legacy of British dominion lives on: Prince Charles was invested as Prince of Wales at the castle in 1969. As a gesture, he studied the tongue-tying tongue for a while at Aberystwyth.

The appalling size and splendor of **Caernarfon Castle** (tel. 677617) led one Welshman to call it "this magnificent badge of our subjection." Begun by Edward I in 1283, the castle features the rapid-arrow slits and decorative bands of colored stone he discovered while fighting infidels in the Levant. These arrow slits are arranged so as to allow three archers to fire from a single aperture; Caernarfon has the world's only surviving examples. For all its swagger, the fortress was left unfinished, and its garrison never exceeded 28 men. In the summer, choirs, musicians, and *Mabinogi* actors often perform here, and a "Fire and Fantasy" light show sparkles from time to time. The distinctive garbage cans inside were specially designed by Lord Snowdon, the constable of the castle. Entertaining and cynical tours are available for £1. The castle also contains the regimental museum of the **Royal Welsh Fusiliers** (famous in the U.S. for suffering ignominious defeat at Bunker Hill; the museum avoids that particular). The museum holds spoils of war from Waterloo to Peking and the stuffed regimental goat "Billy." (Open daily 9:30am-6:30pm; Nov.-March Mon.-Sat. 9:30am-4pm, Sun. 11am-4pm; £3.50, seniors, students, and children £2.50, regimental museum free with admission.) On a hill just across the river, a crenellated **folly** (a picnic house built to look like a castle) forms an absurd counterpoint to the real castle below and offers fine views of the mountain to the east. Most of Caernarfon's 13th-century **town wall** survives, and a short stretch between Church St. and Northgate St. is open for climbing the same hours as the castle. Those curious to see what youth hostels will look like in 2000 years can inspect the 15 ruined barrack blocks at **Segoritium Roman Fort** (tel. 675625), which cuts rudely across a residential area up the Beddgelert road (open Mon.-Sat. 9am-6pm,

Sun. 2-6pm; March-April and Oct. Mon.-Sat. 9:30am-5:30pm, Sun. 2-5pm; Nov.-Feb. Mon.-Sat. 9:30am-4pm, Sun. 2-4pm; £1, seniors, students, and children 60p). Caernarfon's **war memorial** on Castle Sq. is striking in a country full of them: among the names are 17 sets of brothers and a single father-son pair killed in the Great War.

Testimonials of the here and now in Caernarfon are rare. On some Saturday nights during the summer, folk musicians play at **Parc Glynllifon,** a craft, amusement, and nature park outside of Caernarfon. (Take bus #91 to Dinas Dinlle.) Check at the quay opposite the Castle Gift Shop for 40-minute **cruises** to the southwest entrance of the Menai Strait (£2.75), or call 672902 during the day, 672792 in the evening.

Budget lodgings are scarce in Caernarfon, though you can enjoy great comfort for £13.50 to £15 on St. David's Rd., off the Bangor roundabout a 10-minute walk from the castle. If you don't mind bathing, **Mrs. Hughes,** Pros Kairon, Victoria Rd. (tel. 676229), should be your first port of call. If you make it in, you will be treated like one of the family (£11). Follow Pool St. to the end and take the first left onto Dinorwic St. off the road to the Roman fort; Victoria Rd. is straight ahead. Pricey but delightful, **Brynltyfryd** on St. David's Rd. (tel 673840) has color TVs, a broadly smiling hostess, and a huge snorting black cat named (Mike) Tyson (£13.50, July-midSept. £15, dead of winter £11.50). Or try **Marianfa** (tel. 675589), in the same row of yellow townhouses, for large, subdued rooms and an obstreperous dog, fortunately small (single £15, double £25-32). Other guest houses (£13-15/person) line Church St., inside the old town wall. Camp ½-mi. from town at **Cadnant Valley,** Llanberis Rd. (tel. 673196); expect lots of caravans in the summer (tents £3.30-4.40/person).

For picnics, try Pool Street's bakeries and **Lo Cost Supermarket** (open Mon.-Wed. 9am-5:30pm, Thurs. and Sat. 9am-5pm, Fri. 9am-6pm), or the **Tesco's** on Eastgate St. (open Mon.-Wed. and Sat. 8:30am-5:30pm, Thurs. 8:30am-7pm, Fri. 8:30am-8pm). **Stones Bistro,** 4 Hole-in-the-Wall near Eastgate (tel. 671152), is candlelit and crowded on weekends. The Welsh lamb costs £8.95 and is worth wounding your wallet—you get a vast limb, sweet and tender (vegetarian entrees £6.35; open daily 6-11pm, Jan.-Feb. Tues.-Sat. only). Should your conscience withstand the styrofoam trays, **Crempogau,** Palace St. (tel. 672552), serves dinner pancakes stuffed with chili or in mushroom sauce (£2.10; open daily 10am-about 6pm; 10am-4pm in winter).

The **tourist office,** Castle Pitch, Oriel Pendeitsh (tel. 672232), cowers opposite the cavernous castle gate; its town trail pamphlet (50p) is actually worth following (open daily 10am-6pm; Nov.-March Thurs.-Tues. 10am-5pm). Castle Sq. and its tributary streets sell everything you need; in the winter, shops shut down on Thursdays at 1pm. For a huge hoard of **camping** gear, head to **14th Peak,** 9 Palace St. (tel. 675124; open Mon.-Wed. and Fri.-Sat. 9am-5:30pm, Thurs. 9am-5pm, Sun. 1-5pm). An all-day **market** on Saturday fills the square (which is, of course, a triangle); and another market slows traffic on Mondays in summer. The **post office** (tel. 2116) flanks the square (open Mon.-Thurs. 9am-5:30pm, Fri. 9:30am-5:30pm, Sat. 9am-12:30pm; **postal code** LL55 2ND). Caernarfon's **telephone code** is 01286. In a medical emergency, contact **Bangor General Hospital (Ysbyty Gwynedd;** tel. (01248) 384384); Bangor bus #5, 5A, or 9 will take you right there from Castle Sq. Otherwise contact the **police** at Castle Ditch (tel. 673333), on the quay.

Caernarfon is the well-greased pivot for **buses** from mid Wales and the Lleyn Peninsula swinging northeast to Bangor and the Isle of Anglesey; buses #5, 5A, and 9 flit between Caernarfon and Bangor via the Ysbyty Gwynedd (4/hr.; 30min.; £1.05), and to Holyhead via Bangor (£3.50). **Snowdon Sherpa** bus #11 loops through Beddgelert to Llanberis (Mon.-Sat. every 2 hr., Sun. 1/day), and Sherpa bus #19 treads to Llanduno via Llanberis, Betws-y-Coed, and Conwy (daily every 2 hr.). Buses #1 and 2 run to Porthmadog (Mon.-Sat. 1/hr., Sun. 2/day; £1.65), and bus #12 twists and rocks to Pwllheli (Mon.-Sat. 1/hr., Sun. 3/day; £1.90). A lone **Transcambria** bus strikes off daily for Cardiff (£16.70). Caernarfon has no train station, but **trains** leave Bangor for Holyhead, Chester, and beyond, and leave Porthmadog and Pwllheli for other spots on the Cambrian coast. All buses from Caernarfon leave from Penllyn, a block from Castle Sq. Before you depart, bid adieu to the Caernarfon's gulls, who cry here more incessantly than anywhere else in Wales.

B
A
N
G
O
R

■■■ BANGOR

Huddled in a valley by the Menai Strait, this university town makes the best bus base for forays into all the corners of North Wales. The city itself has little to offer travelers: most of it is pleasant and parklike, with townhouses strewn indifferently among the trees; and even the venerable cathedral makes no attempt to soar to heaven, but rather stares down glassy-eyed at its congregation.

GETTING THERE

Bangor is the transportation depot for the Isle of Anglesey to the north, the Lleyn Peninsula to the southwest, and Snowdonia to the southeast. **Crosville** bus #4 leaves Bangor for Llangefni and Holyhead via Llanfair P.G. (Mon.-Sat. 2/hr.; £2.45); for Conwy and Llandudno (bus #5; 3/hr.; £3.05); to Caernarfon (2/hr.; £1.05); and to the Snowdonia towns by various Sherpa bus routes. Switch at Caernarfon for buses to Porthmadog and Pwllheli on the Lleyn Peninsula. The **Transcambria** bus runs daily to Cardiff (£17). Bangor is on the North Wales Coast **rail** line that connects Holyhead (£4.60) with Chester (1/hr.; to Chester £9; to Holyhead £4.60).

ORIENTATION & PRACTICAL INFORMATION

Bangor's two main streets—**Deiniol Rd.** and **High St.**—run parallel to each other and bisect the city. Deiniol Rd. becomes **Garth Rd.** as it turns, laden with B&Bs, up to Bangor Pier on the Menai Strait. **Upper Bangor,** up the hill from Deiniol Rd., marks the edge of the university area with hip shops and cheap health food.

Tourist Office: Theatr Gwynedd, on Deiniol Rd. (tel. 352786). Gleeful staff accompanied by loads of bus schedules, maps, brochures, train schedules, souvenirs, and other good things. Open Easter-Sept. daily 9:30am-5pm.

Financial Services: Barclays, 273 High St. (tel. 370070). Open Mon.-Tues. and Thurs.-Fri. 9:30am-4:30pm, Wed. 10am-4:30pm, Sat. 9:30am-noon. **Lloyds,** 268 High St. (tel. 370132). Open Mon.-Fri. 9:30am-4:30pm, Sat. 9:30am-12:30pm.

Post Office: 60 Deiniol Rd. (tel. 373329). Open Mon.-Thurs. 9am-5:30pm, Fri. 9:30am-5:30pm, Sat. 9am-12:30pm. **Postal Code:** LL57 1AA.

Telephone Code: 01248.

Train Station: Holyhead Rd., at the end of Deiniol Rd. (tel. (01492) 585151). Ticket office open daily 5:30am-6pm.

Bus Station: Garth Rd., down the hill from the town clock. A **Crosville** office at the station (tel. 370295) opens Mon.-Fri. 8am-4:15pm, Sat. 9am-5pm. The **National Express** agent is Brian Kellet Travel, 364 High St. (tel. 351056), open Mon.-Fri. 9am-5pm, Sat. 9am-4pm.

Taxi: Ace Cabs, tel. 351324.

Camping Equipment: The Great Arete, College Rd., Upper Bangor (tel. 352710). Reasonably-priced, reasonably-stocked climbing shop run by folks in the know. Open Mon.-Tues. and Thurs.-Sat. 9:15am-5:30pm, Wed. 9:15am-5pm.

Market Day: Fri., at the bottom of High St.

Early Closing Day: Wed. at 1pm.

Hotline: Samaritans (crisis): 7 Abbey Rd. (tel. 354646); 24-hr. **Gay Line:** tel. 351263, Fri. 7-9pm. **Lesbian Line:** tel. 351263, Tues. 7-9pm. Or write: Gay Youth, 1 Trevelyan Ave., Bangor.

Hospital: Ysbyty Gwynedd (tel. 384384), off Penrhos Rd. Bus #9, 5, or 5A.

Emergency: Dial 999; no coins required.

Police: At the corner of Garth Rd. and Well St. (tel. 370333).

ACCOMMODATIONS & FOOD

Finding a room in Bangor during the University College of North Wales' graduation (the second week of July) is a nightmarish prospect unless you book many months ahead. The best B&Bs occupy handsome Victorian townhouses on Garth Rd.

Tany y Bryn Youth Hostel (HI), (tel. 353516), ½ mi. from town center. Follow High St. to the water and turn right uphill, turning right again at the house with 3-

headed dog at base of window. Aristocratic view of Penrhyn Castle; Vivien Leigh and Sir Laurence Olivier always chose Room Seven. Lockout 10am-5pm, curfew 11pm. Meals available. £7.75; open daily March-Jan.; Feb. Tues.-Sat.

Mrs. Sloane, 4 Greenbank, at the very end of Garth Rd. by the pier (tel. 364426). High ceilings and a garden with lily pond overlooking the sea; on a clear day you can see Llandudno. £13. Or try **Glan Menai,** three houses down at 1 Greenback (tel. 352802), for a huge mint-colored family room above the sea and a loo with a view. Singles £13, doubles £24.

Mrs. Jones, Bro Dawel, near the end of Garth Rd. (tel. 355242). Winter colors, a sooty dog named such, and an old, well-placed print of happy couples making out. TVs in all rooms. £13.

Mrs. S. Roberts, 32 Glynne Rd. (tel. 352113), between Garth Rd. and High St. A bustling house you'll share with metronomically-barking Lucky and Rusty. £12.

Camping: Dinas Farm, Halfway Bridge (tel. 364227), 2 mi. from town on the A5. Sheltered sites on the bank of the River Ogwen. £2/person. Open March-Oct.

The **Student Union** on Deiniol Rd. next to the Theatr Gwynedd, opens term-time (Mon.-Tues. 9am-8pm, Wed.-Sat. 9am-11:30pm) for coffee, salads, and burgers (75p!) in the lounge upstairs (in summer Mon.-Fri. 11am-2pm). Grab a baguette behind the sleek black storefront of **The Fat Cat** on High St. near the cathedral (open Mon.-Sat. 10am-11pm, Sun. noon-3pm and 7-10:30pm) or bite bleeding burgers (£2.70-3.65, ½lb. £4-4.75) at nearby **Cane's,** an upbeat student hangout (open Mon.-Sat. 9am-10pm, Sun. 11am-9pm).

SIGHTS & ENTERTAINMENT

The **University College of North Wales,** on the hill overlooking the town, is Bangor's most visible feature. For 1400 years, **Bangor Cathedral** (tel. 353983), small and lacking a steeple because of its weak foundations, has been the ecclesiastical center of one quarter of Wales, keeping aggressive barkers in their place with cast iron "dog tongs" (open daily 10am-7pm, Thurs. until 8:30pm). Lovers fondle in the "Bible Garden" out front. The nearby **Museum of Welsh Antiquities and Art Gallery** (tel. 353368), on Ffordd Gwynedd, models 19th-century Welsh costumes and antique furniture alongside such modern contributions as beer-can sculptures and beer-towel murals (open Tues.-Fri. 12:30-4:30pm, Sat. 10:30am-4:30pm; free). The onion-domed Victorian **pier** at the end of Garth St. is open daily until sunset (admission 20p, fishing rod rental £1).

Just outside Bangor, where the A55 splits off the A5 (walk about 2 mi. or catch any bus heading north), stands **Penrhyn Castle** (tel. 353084), a 19th-century neo-Norman structure grotesquerie. Many of the furnishings were made from local slate, and the results are staggering—one bed weighs over a ton. (Open July-Aug. Wed.-Mon. 11am-5pm; April-June and Sept.-Oct. noon-5pm. Grounds open 11am-6pm. £4.40, children £2.20.)

The modern **Theatr Gwynedd** on Deiniol Rd. at the base of the hill (tel. 351708) houses a thriving company that performs in both Welsh and English. (Box office open Mon.-Sat. 10am-5pm; additional hours on performance days Mon.-Sat. 8:30pm showtime, Sun. 6-8:30pm. Films £3, students £2.50; plays £4.50-7. Tickets available at most tourist offices on the north coast.) When school is in session, **The Student Union's** basement bar often jams with rock, pop, folk, and reggae concerts (see Food, above). Check the Union and Cob Records on High St. Concerts can be heard year-round at the **Victoria Hotel and Pub** (tel. 712309) just over the straits in Menai Bridge—a taxi can run you back to Bangor after the show for about £3.

■■■ ISLE OF ANGLESEY (YNYS MÔN)

Separated from the rest of Wales by the Menai Strait, Anglesey found itself a particularly easy target for English domination. Edward I built castles on the mainland at

Caernarfon and on the island at Beaumaris to cut off Welsh supplies and isolate the region. Bronze Age and Roman ruins are common, especially near Holyhead and on the coast facing Caernarfon, but it is the beaches and resorts along the northeast and southwest coasts that lure most tourists to the isle. Today, private farms cover most of the island, and Ireland-bound ferries sail into the mists off Holyhead. CADW Welsh Historic Monuments puts out a guide to Anglesey's ancient monuments (£2), available at most tourist offices in North Wales.

GETTING THERE & GETTING ABOUT

Bws Gwynedd spins a web around the island. Buses #4 and 44 run from Bangor to Holyhead via Llanfair P.G. and Llangefni (Mon.-Sat. 2/hr., Sun. 4/day; 1¼hr.; £2.45). Bus #53 and 57 hug the southeast coast from Bangor to Beaumaris (Mon.-Sat. 2/hr., Sun. 2/day; 30min.; return £1.95), and #56 shuttles between Penrhyn Castle (near Bangor) and Beaumaris (Mon.-Sat. 1/hr.; 1hr.). Bus #62 runs northwest from Bangor to Amlwch, on the northern coast (2/hr., Sun. 2/day; £2.45). From Amlwch, bus #61 cruises across northwestern Anglesey and into Holyhead (Mon.-Sat. 5/day, Sun. 2/day). Bus #32 runs north from central Llangefni to Amlwch (Mon.-Sat. 5/day; £1.10). Bus #42 from Bangor curves along the southwest coast as far as Aberffraw, then heads north to Llangefni (Mon.-Sat. 1/hr.; £1.50). **British Rail** runs from Bangor to Holyhead (express 1-3/hr.; 30min.; £4.60); some of these trains stop at Llanfair P.G.

SOMEWHAT PRACTICAL INFORMATION

Telford's **Menai Suspension Bridge** (1826) links Bangor with **Llanfairpwllgwyngyllgogerychwyrndrobwllllantysiliogogogoch,** the longest-named village in the world. Devised in the 19th century to attract attention, the name translates as "Church of Mary in the Hollow of the White Hazel near the Rapid Whirlpool at the Church of Tysilio by the Red Caves." Sensibly, the town's war memorial reads "Llanfair P.G." so as not to overwhelm the roll call of the dead; the spot is also known locally as "Llanfairpwll." It boasts one of Anglesey's two **tourist offices** (tel. (01248) 713177; open Mon.-Sat. 9:30am-5:30pm, Sun. 10am-5pm; Oct.-April closes at 5pm; the other is at Holyhead), as well as a Pringle woollens factory mobbed by tourists having photos taken under the sign with the town's name. Puts antiecclesiodisestablishmentarianism in the lexicographical dustbin.

BEAUMARIS

Four mi. northeast of the Menai Bridge on the A545 stands the tourist town of Beaumaris (bew-MAR-is; don't you dare say it the French way). The main draw is of course **Beaumaris Castle** (tel. (01248) 810361), which squats ignobly in a marsh at the end of Castle St. Planned on too lavish a scale by Edward I and never finished, the moat-ringed fortress would have been Britain's deadliest concentric castle. The dark, slippery passages and countless hidden latrines promote dangerous games of hide-and-seek (open daily 9:30am-6:30pm; Nov.-March Mon.-Sat. 9:30am-4pm, Sun. 11am-4pm; £1.50, seniors, students, and children £1). Those of twisted mind should enjoy the whipping room, shackles, and "walk to the scaffold" at the **Beaumaris Gaol** (tel. (01286) 679098), a dank Victorian lockup on Bunker's Hill (open June-Sept. daily 11am-5:30pm; £2.80, seniors and children £2.10). The **Museum of Childhood,** 1 Castle St. (tel. (01248) 712498), is a house full of things that would have made you happy many birthdays ago—like a hand-held trench football game whose object is to tilt a metal ball through a winding trench into the Kaiser's gaping mouth (open Easter-Oct. Mon.-Sat. 10am-5:30pm, Sun. noon-5pm; last admission 1 hr. before closing; £2.50, seniors £1.50, children £1.25). Beaumaris hosts a week-long **Gŵyl Beaumaris Music Festival** at May's end, which includes concerts, opera, theater, jazz, and street performances (programs £2).

The closest **Youth Hostel** to Beaumaris is in Bangor (tel. (01248) 353516; £7.75). B&Bs in Beaumaris are quaint and comfortable, if pricey (from £16). Institutionalized camping is best at **Kingsbridge Caravan Park,** 3 mi. out of town towards Llangoed (tel. (01248) 490636; £1.80/person). Piping-hot pizzas (£4-6) prove perfectly palatable at busy **Bottle's Bistro,** on Castle St. Though Beaumaris can support the majestic Seaside Royal Anglesey Yacht Club, it refuses to invest in a tourist office. A case outside Town Hall on Castle St. usually contains **tourist brochures,** and unofficial advice is best obtained from **Janet** in the **Nut House** (tel. (01248) 810930), a health food store at 44 Castle St. (open Mon.-Sat. 9am-5pm).

HOLYHEAD (CAERGYBI)

A narrow strip of land attached to the Isle of Anglesey by a causeway and a bridge, Holy Island has only one sure lure for the traveler: Holyhead and its **ferries to Ireland.** The town has weakly resisted the austerity of other ferry ports and the harbor has a grim collection of houses rotting beneath tin bandages. If you have time, explore the many paths of Holyhead Mountain. Its **North** and **South Stacks** are good for birdwatching, and the closed lighthouse looks longingly out to sea.

B&I and **Stena Sealink** operate ferries and catamarans to **Dublin** and its suburb, **Dun Laoghaire.** See Essentials: Getting There—Between the Isles for more information. For off-season trips, **Mona Travel,** 20 Market St. (tel. (01407) 764556) in Holyhead, has fare, schedule, and booking information (open Mon. and Wed.-Fri. 9am-5pm, Tues. and Sat. 9am-1pm). Only car-ferry parties leave from the docks; foot passengers embark at the rail station. Arrive an hour early and remember your passport.

If you arrive in Holyhead too late to continue on your route, check B&B vacancies (from £12) posted at Holyhead's poorly-marked **tourist office** (tel. (01407) 762622), Marine Sq., Salt Island Approach, in a caravan down the main road from the terminal (open daily 10am-6pm; winter 9:30am-5pm). The Sealink staff at the car dock and railway station also has a B&B list. If you call ahead, B&B owners can arrange to let you in the middle of the night, but don't, of course, go ringing their doorbells unannounced in the wee hours. **Roselea,** 26 Holborn Rd. (tel. (01407) 764391), just up from the station, will give you a packed lunch in lieu of the 3am breakfast you didn't eat (£12-14). **Mrs. Octavia,** 66 Walthew Ave. (tel. (01407) 760259), will also pack your lunch; she has TVs to tranquilize you in the evening and a huge cereal selection to crunch you awake in the morning (£12). Go up Thomas St., which becomes Porth-y-Felin Rd. as it passes the school, and turn right onto Walthew Ave.

Holyhead can be reached from landward by **Crosville bus** #4 and 44 from Bangor via Llanfair P.G. and Llangefni (Mon.-Sat. 2/hr., Sun. 4/day; 1¼hr.; £2.45), and **National Express** hits Holyhead from most major cities (from London £27.50). The town is also the terminus of the North Wales Coast **rail** line with hourly trains to Bangor (30min.; £4.60), Chester (1½hr.; £12.60), and London (6hr.; £49). **British Rail** runs from Holyhead to Cardiff (£45.90).

■■■ CONWY

At times, it seems like Conwy made a blood pact with Mephistopheles and the National Trust to laminate itself forever, stamp Ye Olde in its forehead, and build the world's smallest and tackiest house to draw in the mighty vacationer buck. Too bad: if left to crumble, the 13th-century castle and town wall would make some of Britain's most beautiful ruins.

GETTING THERE

Crosville buses #5 and 5A climb the northern coast from Caernarfon to Llandudno, stopping in Bangor and Conwy along the way (2/hr., Sun. 1/hr.; Bangor-Conwy £1.80). Sherpa bus #19 circles back to Caernarfon via Betws-y-coed and Llanberis (4/day), with connection to the Lleyn Peninsula. **National Express** buses leave for London (7hr.; £23.50) and Birmingham (4hr.; £14.50).

ORIENTATION & PRACTICAL INFORMATION

Old Conwy is contained behind the long town wall. One-way traffic on Castle St. brushes the foot of the castle and then crosses the Conwy River on the way to Llandudno. Rosehill St. ascends from the castle and crosses High St. at Lancaster Square by the post office and police fortress; it continues out the town's main gate on the way to Bangor.

Tourist Office: Conwy Castle Visitor Centre (tel. 592248), at the entrance to the castle. Open daily 9:30am-6pm; Nov.-Easter 10am-4pm.

Financial Services: Barclays, High St. (tel. 592881). Open Mon. and Fri. 9:30am-4:30pm, Tues.-Thurs. 9:30am-3:30pm. **National Westminster,** Castle St. near the castle (tel. 592444). Open Mon.-Tues. and Thurs.-Fri. 9am-4:30pm, Wed. 9:30am-4:30pm.

Post Office: Lancaster Sq., near the top of High St. in the VG Store (tel. 573990). Open Mon.-Fri. 8:30am-6pm, Sat. 9am-5:30pm. **Postal Code:** LL32 80A.

Telephone Code: 01492.

Train Station: Off Rosehill St. Buy tickets on train. **Llandudno Junction train station,** tel. 585151. **Lockers** 30-50p. Booking office open Mon.-Sat. 5:30am-6:45pm, Sun. 11:25am-6:30pm.

Bus Station: Buses stop at various points on the major streets; check pasted schedules or the tourist office. **National Express** information from Conwy Travel Service, 5b High St. (tel. 592573; open Mon.-Fri. 9am-5:30pm, Sat. 9am-1pm).

Market: In the train car park Tues. (April-Aug.) and Sat. (year-round) 8:30am-5pm.

Early Closing Day: Wed. at 1pm (Sept.-April).

Hospital: Llandudno Hospital, Maesdu Rd. Take bus #19.

Emergency: Dial 999; no coins required.

Police: Lancaster Sq. (tel. 517171, ext. 5081).

ACCOMMODATIONS, CAMPING, & FOOD

B&Bs crowd the **Cadnant Park** area, a 10-minute walk from the castle. Leave the town wall by the post office and turn left into the greenery. If you have trouble finding a room, try the **Rowen Youth Hostel (HI)**, 5 mi. south of Conwy in the Conwy Valley (see Vale of Conwy: Accommodations, below).

Colwyn Bay Youth Hostel (HI), Foxhill, Nant-y-Glyn (tel. 530627), about 8 mi. from Conwy and 1mi. from Colwyn Bay. Buses run to Colwyn Bay (#13, 14, 16, 22, or 26; Mon.Sat. 2/hr.; Sun. 1/hr.). Beg the use of warden's own laundry facilities. £6.50. Open daily July-Aug.; Sept.-late Oct. Tues.-Sat.; mid-Feb.-March Fri.-Sat.; April-June Mon.-Sat.

Glan Heulog, Llanrwst Rd. (Woodlands) (tel. 593845). Huge house on a hill with talkative proprietors and TVs in every room. Yogurt and fresh fruit available for breakfast. £13, £14.50 with bath. Breach the town wall at the Morfa Bach Car Park behind the Visitor Centre, then turn right and walk 10 min. down Llanrwst Rd.

Cadwern, 5 Cadnant Park (tel. 593240). Sunny 1st-floor rooms braced by gardens and a riotous proprietress. Includes a mammoth, lilac-filled purple room with bay window for 3-4 people. £12.50.

Llwyn Guest House, 15 Cadnant Park (tel. 592319). A hearty welcome and thick carpets that trap dust. The shower looks antiquated but isn't—you can control it to the nearest Celsius degree. £12.50.

Camping: Conwy Touring Park, Llanrwst Rd. (tel. 592856). A steep mile or so out of town on a ridge overlooking Conwy Valley. Follow Llanrwst Rd. and posted signs. Equipped with launderette and showers. 2-person tent £4.10-7. No single-sex groups accepted. Open Easter-Oct.

Most Conwy restaurants cater to the tourist crowd, serving ordinary grub at extraordinary prices. Sip afternoon tea beneath the glowering timber beams of the 419-year-old **Pen-y-Bryn Tearooms,** on High St. at Lancaster Square (tel. 596445). Soups and light fare run £1.85-3.50 here (open daily 11am-5pm; Nov.-Easter Tues.-Sun. 11am-5pm). Herds of broccoli gazelles graze on big vegetarian or vegan meals (£2-4) at **The Wall Place,** Chapel St. (tel. 596326); you can drop right in from the town wall parapet (open daily 11am-9pm; winter 11am-7pm).

SIGHTS

Edward I built **Conwy Castle** (tel. 592358) to protect the English settlers cowering at its base. The castle chapel witnessed Henry "Hotspur" Percy's betrayal of Richard II in 1399, and the prison tower saw many prominent Normans and English rot beneath its false bottom. The grassy east barbican is the town's best vantage point—Telford's elegant **suspension bridge** and the Conwy River lie before you, the castle walls behind. (Open daily 9:30am-6:30pm; Nov.-March Mon.-Sat. 9:30am-4pm, Sun. 11am-4pm. £2.90, seniors, students, and children £1.80. Tours £1.) The **Conwy Festival,** held in late July, calls local musicians, dancers, and medieval performers into streets and castle courtyard. Both bridge and castle can be seen by boat; vigorous bellowing heralds the departure of the **Queen Victoria** from the quay at the end of High St. (30min.; £2.50, children £1.50). A steep section of the ¾-mi. **town wall,** built together with the castle, is open for climbing between Rosehill St. and Berry St.

Head down High St. and onto the quay to bang your head on **Ty Bach** (tel. 593484), Britain's smallest house. With a frontage of 72 in., the two-story cell housed a couple on a twin mattress (their sex rocked the house) and then one 6'3" fisherman (open July-Aug. daily 10am-9pm; Easter-June and Sept.-Oct. 10am-6pm; 50p, students and children 30p, payable to Ye Quaintly Dressed Lady out front). The **Teapot Museum** on Castle St. (tel. 593429) displays 300 years of miniature teapots, giant teapots, and teapots shaped like Gladstone, Reagan, and Donald Duck. Look for the teapot showing nymphs being ravaged, kept a respectable distance from Donald (open April-Oct. daily 10:30am-5:30pm; £1, children and seniors 50p).

In the 14th-century **Aberconwy House,** High St. and Castle St. (tel. 592246), tilted floors and windows frame displays of armor and period furnishings, and a narrated slide show recounts the town's history (open April-Oct. Wed.-Mon. 11am-5:30pm, last entry 5pm; £1.80, children 90p). Awash in unkempt grass and sinister tombstones, the ancient walled enclosure of **St. Mary's Church** broods behind Conwy's loud streets. The **Conwy Butterfly Jungle** (tel. 503149), in the park outside the town wall at Berry St., sets swarms of butterflies flapping in a greenhouse. Some frightening specimens (a "giant armored jungle nymph," 8 in. long with spikes) are locked in cages. (Jungle open April-Sept. daily 10am-5:30pm; Oct. 10am-4pm; £2.50, seniors and students £1.75, children £1.50.)

■■■ VALE OF CONWY

Kermit the Frog had it wrong—it's not easy *seeing* green, so much of it, everywhere. Well-watered by the river and the rain, the Conwy Valley casts a spear of chlorophyll from northern Llandudno into the wooded mountains around Betws-y-Coed in the south. Cyclists enjoy the flat roads and gentle hills, but may find all turning red after the green receptors in their eyes burn out by blasts of foliage.

GETTING ABOUT

Most chartered coaches stop only at the two end-point cities, Betws-y-Coed and Llandudno, leaving the valley itself unchartered. As usual, the **Gwynedd Red Rover** (£4, children £2) is an economical way to see the region, allowing unlimited bus travel for one day. Hop on bus #19—the route winds from Betws-y-Coed up to Conwy and Llandudno and stops in most of the valley's tiny villages. The **British Rail North Wales Day Ranger** ticket gives you a day of unlimited rail travel between Llandudno and Blaenau Ffestiniog, south of Betws-y-Coed, but you'll have to scurry like a squirrel on a hotplate to make it pay off (£11, £7.25 with railcard).

BETWS-Y-COED

Situated at the southern tip of the Vale of Conwy and the eastern edge of the Snowdonia Mountains, Betws-y-Coed (BET-us uh COYD) makes a convenient though crowded base from which to hike or bike either area. The houses and churches of navy blue hillstone, the continuous gurgle of moving water, and the surrounding tree-covered bluffs all hold their charm against the stiffest summer odds. The eight bridges in Betws deserve a look, especially the elaborate suspension bridge off Old Church Rd. that rocks when you walk on it, and Telford's 1815 **Waterloo Bridge,** built in the same year as the battle that brought Napoleon's demise.

B&Bs in town charge £12.50 and up. The cheapest are **Gwynant** (tel. 710372), on the main road next to the Cotswold outdoor shop, with bland but big and airy rooms (£12.50), and the nearby **Maelgwyn House,** next to the Cafe Veronica (tel. 710252) which serves a smaller-than-average breakfast and brooks no smoking (£13). A line of B&Bs charging £13.50-16 holds down the other end of the town's main road, or check for pleasantly ensconced properties near the Vicarage behind the post office (£14-17). Call ahead to the local hostels. **Lledr Valley hostel (HI)** (tel. (016906) 202) is on a bluff 5 mi. west of town just past Pont-y-Pant train station and 2 mi. away from the majestic square tower of Dolwyddelan Castle (£7.15; open daily April-Aug.; March and Sept.-Oct. Mon.-Sat.). Ten **Sherpa** buses (#19 or 65) per day head 5 mi. west along the A5 to the **HI Capel Curig** (tel. (016904) 225), a favorite with climbers (£7.75; open April-Aug. and Oct. daily; Sept. Wed.-Sun.). **Riverside Caravan Park** (tel. 710310) suns beside a crowded cemetery in the back of Betws rail station (tenting or caravanning £4/person; open March-Oct.). The **Dol Gam Campsite** (tel. 710228), midway between Betws-y-Coed and Capel Curig on the A5, charges £2.50 per person. Some people camp unofficially along the roads, banking on security in numbers.

Most of the 30 restaurants in Betws-y-Coed are overpriced. Try the less formal hotels near Pont-y-Pair Bridge (lunch specials about £4), or stock up at the bakeries and small grocery stores lining Holyhead Rd. Take-away food is prohibited in Betws, as it is a National Park village; plastic containers and other litter are not welcome here (not that they are anywhere else).

The cheerful and tireless staff at the self-proclaimed busiest **tourist office** in Wales (tel. 710426 or 710665) provides sight information, bus and train timetables, a well-stocked bookshop, and the occasional lecture. On rainy days the tourist office will point to indoor activities in Blaenau Ffestiniog. If you are bent on seeing Betws in the rain, wear your wellies. (Open April-Oct. daily 10am-5:45pm; Nov.-March 10am-4pm.) You can escape from the mob at the office by heading behind the **bus** and **train** stations to the 14th-century **St. Michael's Church,** which has one of the plainest, barest, quietest interiors in Wales. Betws-y-Coed means "chapel in the woods;" this is the chapel. Two giant emporia on the main road sell mountaineering supplies, books, and canoe equipment: **Cotswold** (tel. 710234; open daily 9am-6pm or 9am-7pm, depending on the season) and **Climber and Rambler** (tel. 710555; open Mon.-Thurs. 9am-6pm, Fri.-Sun. 9am-7pm). Rent bicycles from **Beics Betws** (tel. 710766), behind the post office and across from the Vicarage (mountain bikes £5/hr., £14/day; tool kit, and helmet included; open daily 9am-5:30pm). The town's **postal code** is LL24 0AA, and its **telephone code** is 01690. There is a Midland Bank at Betws, but the nearest cashpoint is at Llanrwst.

Sherpa bus #19 connects Betws-y-Coed with Llanrwst, Conwy, and Llanberis, stopping at most of the area hostels five times a day (from Conwy £2.04). Betws-y-Coed lies halfway down the Conwy Valley line between Llandudno and Blaenau Ffestiniog—**trains** pass through six times a day Monday through Saturday (Sun. 2/day in high season); winter Sundays are practically silent.

VALLEY VILLAGES

Chilean Fire Bush flirts shamelessly with eucrypheas and hydrangea at **Bodnant Gardens** (tel. (01492) 650460), 8 mi. south of Llandudno off the A470 (open mid-March to Oct. daily 10am-5pm; £3.90, children £1.95). The entrance is by the Eglwysbach Rd.; take **Crosville bus** #25 from Llandudno (6/day) or the **Conwy Valley** line to Tal-y-Cafn Station (6/day).

On the other side of the River Conwy and farther south, the town of **Trefriw** lies along the River Crafnant. **Lake Crafnant,** 3 mi. uphill from town (along the road opposite the Fairy Hotel), is surrounded by some of the highest peaks in Snowdonia.

You can hire a rowboat at the small quay during the summer or look on from the lakeside farmhouse café. Dustballs fly at the **Trefriw Woolen Mills** (tel. (01492) 640462), on the banks of the River Crafnant, where workmen demonstrate the weaving of tapestries and tweeds (open Mon.-Fri. 9am-5:30pm; free). A 20-minute walk from town north along the main road, a rust grotto offers up the "richest charlybeate" spa waters at the **Trefriw Wells Spa** (tel. (01492) 640057). Originally found to be healthy treatment for anemia, today the water is used to treat rheumatism, indigestion, and homesickness. A month's supply sells for £5 and tastes like rancid chicken broth. (Open daily 10am-5:30pm; Nov.-Easter Mon.-Sat. 10am-5pm, Sun. noon-5pm. £2.65, seniors £2.40.) B&Bs (£13.50-16) line Trefriw's long main street. To get to Trefriw, take **Crosville Sherpa bus** #19 from Conwy, Llandudno, or Llandudno Junction (from Conwy £1.44).

Tuesday is **market day** in nearby **Llanrwst,** the area's financial capital (it has more than one bank). Just across the Llanrwst Bridge on the bank of the Conwy River, **Tu-Hwnt-i'r-Bont** is a pile of ivy that serves grand Welsh teas under a viciously low ceiling. Before banging your head, check the timbers for graffiti in all languages (tea with scone and *bara brith* £3; open Easter-Oct. Tues.-Sun. 10am-5:30pm). A 15-minute walk past the tea house deposits you at **Gwydir Castle** (tel. (01492) 648261), the 16th-century manor house of Sir John Wynne. The slightly unkempt grounds shelter peacocks and a yew tree good for sitting under and contemplating life's transience (£2, seniors and children £1). The Betws-y-Coed tourist office sells leaflets tracing walks through nearby oak forests (25p-£2). The rustic **HI Youth Hostel** in **Rowen** (tel. (01492) 530627), just north of Llanrwst, is a great place to rest your weary bones, free of screaming school groups (£5.30; open May-Aug.). **Snowden Sherpa bus** #19 stops in Rowen village; the hostel is 1 mi. up a steep hill.

■■■ LLANGOLLEN

Near the English border, Llangollen (hlan-GOTH-len) is a plain patch of red brick in a hollow in the hills. Its most noteworthy architectural feature is the 14th-century bridge on the River Dee with four arches of varying size. Walkers gently tread the surrounding hills on their way to Horseshoe Pass, and white-water canoeists slash through nearby streams on weekends. Each August, the town is woofed awake by the Sheepdog Trials at Glyn Ceiriog, which pits farmers and their dogs against pens of recalcitrant sheep.

Every summer, the town's population of 3000 swells to 80,000 during the **International Eisteddfod** (ice-TETH-vod)—July 4-9 in 1995. Competitors from 50 countries sing, shout, and dance until the fields and hills can take no more. Book tickets and rooms far in advance through the International Musical Eisteddfod Office, Llangollen, Clwyd, Wales LL20 8NG (tel. 860236, fax 861300). (Office open Mon.-Fri. 9:30am-12:30pm and 1:30-4:30pm. Unreserved seat and ground admission day of performance £3, seniors and children £1.50. Concert tickets £6-8).

Up Hill St. from the town center stands **Pla Newydd,** former home of the two "Ladies of Llangollen" who eloped from Ireland dressed as men in 1778 and denied all their lives that they were lesbians. Wellington, Wedgwood, Walter Scott, and Wordsworth all visited the Ladies in their fancifully-carved house, where their double bed still smells perfumed. Repression theorists can gloat over the bushes of suggestive shape and the oddly twisted and truncated pillars (open May-Sept. Mon.-Sat. 10am-7pm, Sun. 10am-5pm; April and Oct. Mon.-Sat. 10am-5pm, Sun. 10am-4pm; £1.70, children 75p). The Ladies' tomb stands proudly outside **St. Collens Church** on Church St., and some of their autographed letters can be seen at the **Sarah Posonby Pub** on Mill St. across the bridge.

A 30-minute walk from Llangollen along Abbey Rd., the ruins of 13th-century **Valle Crucis Abbey** (tel. 860326) grace a leafy valley. Restored with the utmost taste, with empty arches framing trees and sky, the abbey would be beautiful were it not for the giant caravan park that surrounds it and slithers up to the cloister (open daily 9:30am-6:30pm; Nov.-March Mon.-Sat. 9:30am-4pm, Sun. 2-4pm; £1.50, seniors, students, and children £1). Across the caravan park stands the 9th-century **Pillar of Eliseg,** once a cross until its arms fell off.

Perched on a hill overlooking the town are the lyrical ruins of **Dinas Brân** (Crow's Castle). The footpath up the hill begins behind the canal museum, and the walk takes about an hour each way. The view from the castle stretches from the mountains near Snowdonia to the flat English Midlands.

The friendly wardens at the **HI Hostel,** Tyndwr Hall (tel. 860330), 1½ mi. out of town, frequently organize "activity weekends" with climbing, archery, water sports, and mountain biking (about £74; call 2 weeks ahead; bike rental £12/day). Expect to share this newly-renovated 124-bed activity center with a group of some sort. From town, follow the A5 towards Shrewsbury and bear right up Birch Hill (£7.75; open mid-Feb. to Oct.). In town, **Bryant Rose,** 31 Regent St. (tel. 860389), has TVs in big rooms with flowers and a warm hostess (£12.50). **Bryn y Coed,** 66 Berwyn St. (tel. 860339), ushers you into peach rooms on a noisy road (£12.50); **One Bodwen Villas,** Hill St. (tel. 860882), offers sunlit spaces on a quieter road (£13.50, with bath £16). A bell outside the bathroom warns occupants to be done in a hurry. **Campsites** abound; investigate **Tower Farm,** Tower Rd. (tel. 860798), at the far end of Eisteddfod campgrounds (£2/person, £6/caravan) or **Wern Isaf Farm,** Wern Rd. (tel. 860632), with sites ¾ mi. from town. Take Wharf Hill to Canal, then turn right up Wern Rd. (£2/person, £6/caravan). The most exciting of Llangollen's many restaurants is **The Good Taste,** Market St. (tel. 861425), which serves healthy portions for £3.50 or less. The African parrot Jason likes men but disdains women. (Open March-Dec. Fri.-Wed. 10am-6pm.) At **Café and Books,** Castle St., you can thumb thousands of used volumes upstairs while they fry your fish and chips downstairs, using less grease than usual (open daily 9am-7pm; Oct.-May 9am-5pm).

The **tourist office,** Town Hall, Castle St. (tel. 860828; open daily 9am-6pm; Oct.-May 10am-5pm), and Eisteddfod office keep an emergency list of accommodations, although some are as far away as 15 mi. Bikes may be hired from **Llansports,** 10 Berwyn St. (tel. 860605; £3/hr., £15/day, helmet and map included; open daily 9am-5:30pm). The town's **postal code** is LL20 8RW; its **telephone code** is 01978.

For such a booming tourist town, Llangollen is virtually inaccessible to the carless and coachless. Most public transport from outside Wales comes as far as Wrexham, 30 minutes from Llangollen; trains connect Wrexham with Shrewsbury, Birmingham, and London, and **National Express buses** depart for Birmingham and London (1/day). **Gwynedd bus** #94 connects Llangollen to Wales's west coast at Barmouth via Dolgellau (Mon.-Sat. 5/day; Sun. 3/day); **Crosville** buses travel north from Wrexham to Chester (4/hr.). Local **Bryn Melyn** buses (tel. 860701) leave Llangollen for Chirk and Wrexham (Mon.-Fri. 1/hr. 9am-5pm; return £1.50-2).

Isle of Man

The Isle of Man (or "Mann" to its friends) is a pint-sized anomaly floating in the middle of the Irish Sea, equidistant from Ireland and Britain. Why an anomaly? Well, the 70,000 Manx are British and swear allegiance to Queen Elizabeth, but they aren't part of the United Kingdom—the Isle of Man has its own legislature (the world's oldest), its own flag (a pinwheel with feet), its own currency, and its own post office, which complement its own fauna (weird cats and sheep), its own language (now nearly dead), and its unique approach to human rights legislation (illegal homosexuality and corporal punishment—weird and weirder!).

It would take a lot more than legislation to rob Mann of its charms. The island is beautiful: ringed by cliffs, sliced by deep valleys, and criss-crossed by lovable antique trains. The Manx language, a close cousin to Irish, is taught in schools and in newspaper columns, and is still heard when Manx laws are proclaimed on July 5 on Tynwald Hill. Manx (tailless) cats are bred on the island, as are the terrifying, four-horned Manx Loghtan sheep. The three legs of Man emblem appears on every available surface, asserting the Manx identity with the slogan "Quocunque Jeceris Stabit": whichever way you throw me, I stand (like a weeble-wobble). The Isle of Man has rolled through the political and cultural changes on either side of the Irish Sea without losing its independence or its moxie: visitors will come to cherish the fierce and indomitable Manx spirit the three legs represent.

The Isle of Man shares the international phone code of 44 with Britain. All British pounds (from England, Scotland, or Northern Ireland) are accepted in the Isle of Man; however, Manx bills and coins are not accepted outside the Isle. Exchange before you leave, or save your freaky Manx currency for souvenirs. The Isle of Man issues its own stamps; British stamps are not valid.

> Perhaps the finest book ever written on the subject, *Let's Go: Ireland* offers the budget traveler an even more in-depth look at the Isle of Man.

GETTING THERE

The **Isle of Man Steam Packet Company** has a monopoly on ferry service to the island, with sailings between Douglas and Heysham, Liverpool, and Fleetwood, England; Ardrossan, Scotland; and Belfast and Dublin. Heysham and Liverpool are the only routes covered all winter. In 1994, a high-speed SeaCat catamaran replaced the ferry for most sailings to and from Belfast, Dublin, Liverpool, and Fleetwood, cutting the sailing time almost in half. Consult Essentials: Getting There—Between the Isles for fares, frequencies, and useful contacts.

GETTING AROUND

The seven-day **Freedom Ticket** allows you to ride any public transport on the island for £22.90, a bargain if you plan to see the whole island in this manner. The Freedom Ticket, other tickets, and a full bus/train timetable (30p) can be found at bus and train stations, newsagents, and the tourist office in Douglas.

Buses

A **three-day Bus Rover** discount ticket allows unlimited bus travel for three days out of seven for £9.50, a good deal if riding on old trains doesn't interest you. The one-day Bus Rover ticket (£4.10) is worthwhile only if you spend a lot of time on the bus that day. The **Tours (Isle of Man) Bus Tour Company** (tel. 676105) provides transportation from Douglas to specific events, such as concerts and parades, as well as daytrips to towns and sights around the island. They drop you off in the morning or before the event, and pick you up in the afternoon or after the event (round-trips £1-

3.50). Check their schedules at the Douglas tourist office or at the Crescent Leisure Center, Central Promenade, Douglas. Tours leave from in front of the Center.

Trains

The unique Isle of Man Railways, all at least 100 years old, run up and down the east coast, from Port Erin in the south to Ramsey in the north. A separate line of the electric railway branches off at Laxey, 6 mi. north of Douglas, heading northwest to the top of Snaefell, the island's highest peak. The **Steam Railway,** dating from 1873, used to cover much of the island, but only the line south from Douglas to Port Erin is still running. The newer **Electric Railway** (dating from 1893) runs from the other end of Douglas north to Ramsey. The 2 mi. between the Steam and Electric Railway Stations is covered by bus, or by quaint but slow **horse-drawn trams** which travel along the seaside Promenade in Douglas. The Electric Railway runs from 10am to 6pm (April-Oct. 5/day, increasing to 14/day in July-Aug.). The Steam Railway runs from 10am to 5:30pm (April-Sept. and the last week of October 4/day, increasing to 6/day Mon.-Thurs. in July-Aug.).

By Bike or Thumb

The island's small size makes it easy to bike. The southern three-fourths of the island is covered in rolling hills that present a manageable challenge to cyclists. Bike rental is available but expensive in Douglas and Ramsey; the ferry carries bikes for free, so import them. Some of the walking trails described below are open to bikes, many are not. But the back roads are fairly quiet. Hitching is legal and socially acceptable here. The scarcity of hitchhikers on the island probably relates more to the lack of budget travelers and the ease of public transport than to any difficulty in getting lifts. While *Let's Go* does not recommend hitch-hiking, locals claim that the Isle of Man is among the safest places in the world, for hitching or just about any other activity.

By Foot

The Isle of Man is a walker's paradise. The short distances between towns and sights make it feasible to walk from place to place. Three long-distance **hiking trails** are marked and maintained by the Manx government, making walking even more pleasant. **Raad ny Foillan,** or "The Road of the Gull," is a 90-mi. path, marked with seagull signs, which goes all the way around the island's coast, passing all the major towns and stunning scenery. **Bayr ny Skeddan,** or "The Herring Road," marked with signs of (guess what?) a herring, covers the somewhat less-spectacular 14 mi. between Peel in the west and Castletown in the east. The end of this trail overlaps with the **Millennium Way,** which begins at Castle Rushen in Castletown and goes north to Ramsey, following the course of an ancient highway for 28 mi.

EVENTS

Consider avoiding the Isle of Man during these times; crowds get huge and raucous.

T.T. (Tourist Trophy) Race Weeks. First 2 weeks in June; all kinds of crazy events, and huge crowds.

Manx Heritage Festival. Week of July 5. Music recitals and flower displays in the island's churches, with Tynwald Fair and the pronouncement of new laws on July 5, a public holiday.

Southern "100" Motorcycle Races. Late July. Call 822546 for info.

International Football Festival. Last week in July. Gangs of large, noisy, beer-drinking men from across Britain (*very* international) play ball. Info tel. 661930.

Manx Grand Prix Motorcycle Races and Vintage Motorcycle Rally. Last weekend in August. Race info tel. 627979.

The T.T. Race has spawned a local tradition: islanders often give directions in relation to the "T.T. Circuit," the route the motorcycles tear through at 120 m.p.h.

■■■ DOUGLAS

The capital of a none-too-large country, Douglas really is a grape-sized metropolis. Douglas grew in the Victorian era, after it was named the capital of the island; the Victorian tourist boom dominates the present-day landscape. Remains include the railway and horse tram network, the promenades, and the Gaiety Theater. The turn of the century can be seen as Douglas' high point, unless one wants to include its dubious honor of hosting the British offshore financial industry today.

GETTING THERE & GETTING AROUND

The **ferry/SeaCat terminal** lies at the southern end of Douglas, near the bus station and shopping area. Walk north along the seaside to reach the promenades, or follow the signs to the tourist information office. During the summer, **horse-drawn trams** run along tracks up and down the Promenade every few minutes. **Buses** also run along the Promenade every few minutes, connecting the Bus and Steam Railway stations with the Electric Railway and Onchan (bus station to Electric Railway 55p). Local buses are covered by the Bus Rover **passes,** and both buses and horse trams are covered by the seven -day Freedom Ticket. The £1.10 "Ride-A-Day" ticket offers just that on the horse trams for a week.

ORIENTATION & PRACTICAL INFORMATION

Douglas stretches for 2 mi. along the seafront, from Douglas Head in the south to the Electric Railway terminal in the north. Just north of the river, the shopping district spreads around Victoria St., which turns into Bucks Rd., and pedestrianized Strand St., which runs parallel to Loch Promenade. The Promenade itself is a wide street, running between the long crescent of beach and a continuous row of grand but slightly tatty Victorian terrace houses.

Tourist office: Harris Promenade (tel. 686766). Follow the signs on a 10-min. walk from the bus station or ferry terminal. Bus and rail timetables and passes here. Open daily 9am-7:30pm; Sept. to mid-May Mon.-Fri. 9am-5pm, Sat. 9am-1:30pm.

Travel Agent: Not a budget travel agency, but **Lunn Poly Holiday Shop,** 83 Strand St. (tel. 612 848), offers cheap flights. Open Mon.-Sat. 9am-5:30pm.

Financial Services: Thomas Cook, Strand St. (tel. 626288). Open Mon.-Wed. and Fri.-Sat. 9am-5:30pm, Thurs. 10am-5:30pm. **American Express: Palace Travel,** Central Promenade (tel. 662662), in the Palace Hotel. **A.T. Mays Travel Agents,** 1 Regent St. (tel. 623330). *Bureau de change;* convenient to the ferry terminal for trading your Manx money for English bills before you leave. Open Mon.-Fri. 9am-5:30pm, Sat. 9am-5pm.

Bank: Isle of Man Bank, (tel. 637100), corner of Regent St. and Strand St. ATM. Open Mon.-Fri. 9:30am-3:30pm.

Post Office: Regent St. (tel. 686130). Post shop has wide range of unique Manx stamps (check out the "tailless cats" series), stationery, and packing materials. Open Mon.-Fri. 9am-5:30pm, Sat. 9am-12:30pm.

Telephone code: the code for the whole island is 01624.

Taxis: A-1 Taxis (tel. 674 488). 24-hr. service to the whole island.

Car rental: E.B. Christian and Co., Bridge Garage (tel. 673211). Fords. Ages 21-75 may rent. £24/day; £124/week. Under 22 must leave a £100 deposit.

Bike rental: Eurocycles, 8a Victoria Rd. (tel. 624909), off Broadway. Mountain bikes £10.50/day, £49/week; sports bikes £7/day, £25/week. ID deposit.

Launderette: Broadway Launderette, 24 Broadway (tel. 621511). £2.50 wash, dryers 20p per brief time interval.

Bisexual, Gay, and Lesbian Info: Carrey-Friend (tel. 611600), Thurs. 7-10pm. **Ellan Vannin Gay Group,** P.O. Box 195, Douglas IM99 1QP (no phone).

Pharmacy: Flynn's Pharmacy, Strand St. (tel. 673925). 24-hr. service.

Crisis Hotline: Samaritans, 5 Victoria Pl. (tel. 663399), near Broadway. Drop-ins 10am-10pm; hotline 24 hrs.

Hospital: Nobles Hospital, Westmoreland Rd. (tel. 663322).

Emergency: dial 999, no coins required. **Police:** tel. 631212.

D
O
U
G
L
A
S

ACCOMMODATIONS

Inexpensive guesthouses (in the £10-12 range) can be found on the promenades, but the majority of them cluster on Church Rd. (next to the tourist office), around Broadway, on Castle Mona Ave. (off Central Promenade), and around Mona Drive (halfway up Central Promenade). The Mona Drive area is the quietest, but least convenient to the center of town.

Merridale Guest House, 30 Castlemona Ave. (tel. 673040). Large, clean bedrooms with sinks and coffee/teapots. Open March-Dec. Sometimes fills up weeks in advance for June-Aug. £12/person.

Pat's B&B, 27 Derby Rd. (tel. 623689), off Broadway to the left. Small and cozy, with a well-maintained garden. Fresh flowers on the tables. The cheapest place in town. Open March-Oct. £10/person.

Glen View, 7 Stanley Terrace (tel. 674360), part of Broadway, about 200 yds. from the Promenade on the right. The house itself is quiet, but the neighborhood is not. Clean, basic rooms with sinks. £11/person; min. stay 2 nights.

Sea Nook, 10 Empire Terrace (tel. 676830). Turn off Central Promenade next to the Imperial Hotel, go 50 yds., and turn right onto Empire Terrace. Small but pleasant rooms, come with views of Douglas Bay. All have sinks and teapots. Open June-Sept. Singles £14. Doubles £22.

Nobles Park Grandstand Campsite, on the site of the T.T. races' start and finish line. Only campground in Douglas. For reservations, call the Douglas Corporation (tel. 621132) Mon.-Fri. 9am-5pm. Site open June-Sept. except during the races (first 2 weeks in June). Showers £1, toilets £1. Site £4.

FOOD

Groceries can be found at the enormous **Safeway,** Chester St., near the Manx Museum (open Mon.-Thurs. and Sat. 8:30am-8pm, Fri. 8:30am-9pm). Fresh and cheap fruits and vegetables tempt the palate at **Robinson's,** Strand St. **Holland and Barrett Health Food Store** sells things that crunch when you step on them. (Open Mon.-Tues., and Thurs.-Sat. 9am-5:30pm, Wed. 9:30am-5:30pm.)

Crusoe's, North Quay (tel. 663337). Offers pizza, simple meals, and a salad bar amidst tropical decor, complete with fake palm trees. Chicken dinner £5.50, pizzas £4. Open daily noon-10pm.

Taylor's, Castle St. (tel. 624561). Victorian tea room specializing in veggie burgers (choice of 4 types; with salad and pasta, £3.70) and pancakes with lots of toppings (£1.80). Banana milkshake £1.20. Open daily 10am-6pm.

La Brasserie, Central Promenade (tel. 661155), in the Empress Hotel. Large menu with cheap veggie dishes (stuffed zucchini £4.35). Open daily 6:45am-10:45pm.

Green's Vegetarian Buffet, Steam Railway Station, Bank Hill (tel. 629129). Small but tasty menu of tea and cakes 9am-5pm; pizzas, salads, etc. noon-2:30pm. Lunches around £4.

PUBS

Manx pubs are not known for their music. While many pubs are busy and fun every night of the week, entertainment generally falls into either the disco or country-singer categories. In summer, hordes of young people roam the streets until the wee hours, while the hotel bars generally fill with older people.

Bushy's Bar (a.k.a. Sammy Webb's), (tel. 675139), at the intersection of Loch Promenade and Victoria St. Prime location, live rock bands on weekends (cover £3), and tasty Bushy's beer. The friendly crowd spills out into the square in front of the bar on most summer evenings. Open till 11:45pm Mon.-Sat.

Cul-de-Sac Bar and Pizzeria, 3 Market Hill (tel. 623737). Youthful crowds munch cheap lunch specials (prawn salad and garlic bread £3; available Mon.-Fri. noon-2pm, Sat. noon-6pm). Closed Sun. in winter.

Quids Inn, 56 Loch Promenade (tel. 611769). A money-saver for serious drinkers: pay £1 to get in and £1 per drink. Closed during the day in winter.

Palace Hotel and Casino, Central Promenade (tel. 662662). Enormous complex with nightclub, bars, and casino. Bars open until 3:30am. All kinds of people, from local teens to elderly tourists.

SIGHTS

Just past the Villa Marina on Harris Promenade sits one of the most impressive reminders of the island's Victorian heyday, the **Gaiety Theater** (tel. 625001). Among the theater's three purported ghosts is a little old lady sitting in seat D-14. (Tours every Sat. at 10:30am, plus July-Aug. Thurs. 2:30pm. Tea and scones afterwards. Free; donation encouraged.) Just south of the Gaiety Theater, the shopping district begins. From here, signs lead to a parking garage with an elevator to the **Manx Museum** (tel. 675522). The terrific museum, which takes about three hours to see properly, chronicles the natural and human history of the island, from the Ice Age to the present. The museum also contains the **National Art Gallery,** a shop with a wide range of books on Manx subjects, and a library stoked with every book on Manx there could be. (Museum and library open Mon.-Sat. 10am-5pm; free.)

The thing that looks like a little castle sitting on a rock in Douglas Bay (the ferry goes past it on the way to the dock) is the **Tower of Refuge.** The tower was built in 1832 to provide a protected place for shipwreck survivors to wait out the storm until they were rescued. The southern end of Douglas is marked by **Douglas Head** jutting out into the sea. To reach Douglas Head on foot, go across the Swing Bridge (actually a sturdy metal footbridge connecting North and South Quays), turn left, and walk along the water for about 600 yds. Turn right after the gas tanks, and head up the hill past the Coast Guard station. At the end of this road, a hefty set of steps leads up to the top of the Head, past the lighthouse and another relic of Victorian tourism, the **Camera Obscura.** The blinking lights along the Promenade, which look so horribly tacky up close, assume a more pleasing sparkle when viewed at night from the top of Douglas Head.

ENTERTAINMENT

Visitors to the Isle of Man want to be entertained rather than enlightened. At least, that seems to be the principle that venue owners use when hiring performers. As a result, the arts and entertainment scene here tends to be heavy on hypnotists and country crooners, and low on good music.

The splendid **Gaiety Theater** (tel. 625001) is the only theater of note on the island, but it does its best to fill the hole in the Manx arts scene. The theater's season runs from March through December, but its busiest period is from July to October, when there are plays most nights. (Box office open Mon.-Sat. 10am-4:30pm and performance nights; tickets £4-12; discounts for seniors and children.) The self-explanatory Hour of Popular Classical Music at **St. Thomas' Church,** Church Rd., showcases local talent (mid-May to mid-Sept. Wed. 7:45pm; free). Douglas pubs, including **Bushy's Bar** and the **Cul-de-Sac Bar,** often have live, seldom-outstanding rock and folk in summer. **Smuggler's** (tel. 629551), in the Admiral Hotel, Loch Promenade, has folk music (April-Sept. Thurs. 8:40pm; cover £1.50).

The **Palace Hotel Complex** has a popular nightclub and a casino, both open until 4am. **Paramount City,** Queens Promenade (tel. 622447), has a nightclub called **The Dark Room** on Wed., Fri., and Sat. from 9am-2am, and the **Director's Bar,** which serves until 2am. **The Tardis,** Barrack St. (tel. 661547), is an indication of the frightening number of Doctor Who fans on this island. (Open Mon.-Sat. 10pm-1:45am. Mon.-Thurs. free, Fri.-Sat. £2 cover.)

■ NEAR DOUGLAS

On the western edge of Douglas, about 2 mi. from the Douglas bus station, the village of **Braddan** has two sights of interest to visitors. The old church, next to the old cemetery, houses a major collection of Viking-era **Manx crosses,** along with a few Celtic-period crosses. In a more southerly direction, 3 mi. out the Castletown Rd.

CASTLETOWN

from Douglas, fields full of happy old horses draw visitors to the **Isle of Man Home of Rest for Old Horses** (tel. 674594), Bulhrenny. The horses, most of whom used to pull the trams back and forth across Douglas, are happy because the Home has saved them from the slaughterhouse, and a museum shows exactly how this came about. (Open June-Sept. Mon.-Wed. 10am-4:50pm.)

To the northeast of Douglas along the coast, on the Electric Railway line, the rocky, forested **Groudle Glen** leads down to the sea. A miniature steam railway (tel. 622138) carries passengers through the glen out to the rocky headland and back during a few hours each week. (Runs May-Sept. Sun. 11am-4:30pm; July-Aug. Wed. 7-9pm; £1.20).

Laxey is a quiet, picturesque village which seems to have changed very little since its heyday as a mining and mill town in the second half of the 19th century. The town's main attraction is the old mine itself, with its giant (72 ft. in diameter), restored waterwheel, said to be the largest in the world, called the **Great Laxey Wheel (a.k.a. Lady Isabella).** (Wheel open Easter-Sept. daily 10am-5pm; £1.80). The way to the Wheel from the railway station is well-signposted, leading past the tiny **tourist office** and craft shop (tel. 862007; open Easter-Oct.). Laxey is easily accessible by **train** from Douglas (11/day; 30 min.; £2) or Ramsey (11/day; 45 min.; £2.30), or by bus, car, bike, or foot on the main coast road.

Laxey is also known to tourists as the beginning of the Snaefell Mountain Railway, a separate Electric Railway line which climbs the rattly, creaky 5 mi. to the 2036-ft. summit of **Snaefell,** the highest point on the island. Even when the weather is nice in the valley below, Snaefell is always windy, often cold, and usually shrouded in mist. Even if the view from the top is less than perfect, the ride on the 100-year-old train along the precipitous hillside, and the views of the neighboring valleys and Sulby Reservoir are worth the trip. Plus, the train stops at **Murray's Motorcycle Museum** (tel. 861719) just before the summit, allowing bikers and fans the chance to peek at the 120 vintage machines on the way up or down the mountain. (Open mid-May to Sept. daily 10am-5pm; £2.) (Trains depart Laxey for the summit Easter-Sept. daily 10:30am-3:30pm; return from Laxey £5, from Douglas £6.10.)

■■■ THE SOUTH & WEST

CASTLETOWN

Nine mi. south of Douglas, Castletown retains its energy and history from its stint as the old capital of the island. The Square and the narrow streets to the north and west of it contain most of the town's history and businesses, including the **IOM Bank,** 3 Market Sq. (tel. 822503; open Mon.-Wed. and Fri. 9:30am-3:30pm, Thurs. 9:30am-5:30pm; ATM) and the **post office,** Arbory St. (tel. 822516; open Mon.-Fri. 9am-12:30pm and 1:30-5:30pm, Sat. 9am-12:30pm). From the castle, a short walk towards the pier leads to the Old Grammar School, built as a church around 1200 and now is a well-stocked **tourist office** (tel. 675522; open Easter-Sept. Tues.-Sun. 10am-5pm). **Buses** from Port Erin/Port St. Mary (20/day; 25 min.; £1.05) and Douglas (20/day; 35 min.; £1.35) stop by the castle. The **Steam Railway** station is a 5-min. walk toward Ballasalla. (4-6/day; to Douglas, 40 min.; to Port Erin, 20 min.)

Accommodations, Food, & Pubs The cheapest place to stay in town is **Sandymount,** Bowling Green Rd. (tel. 822521), a large, well-loved house near the beach. From the Castle, go across the footbridge, walk right along the sea to Bowling Green Rd., and head to its other end. From the railway station, turn left (away from town center), go 200 yds. to the rotary, and turn right. The house is 10 yds. on the left (open April-Sept. £14.50/person). The only year-round option is **The Rowans,** Douglas St. (tel. 823 210), facing the beach (£16/person).

Simple meals, omelettes (£2.85-3.40), baked potatoes (£2-3), and sandwiches (£1.30-2.30) are available at **Ye Olde Bakery Café,** 31 Malew St. (tel. 823092), or more substantial fayre can be had from the affordable "snacks" menu at **Bunter's**

Bistro, Parliament Sq. (tel. 822400), next to the old House of Keys (parliament) building. Lasagna £3.25. (Open Mon.-Fri. noon-2pm and 7-10pm, Sat. 7-10pm.) The lively, friendly **Glue Pot,** overlooking the harbor, sticks to drinkers from all over the island.

Sights In summer, guided **walking tours** of Castletown leave from the tourist office on Tuesdays at 11am (£1.50 for 1¼-hr. tour; for info, call 823209). The former seat of the Lords of Mann, **Castle Rushen** dominates the center of town as both the major sight and the major landmark. Certain rooms have been reconstructed as they would have appeared during various historical periods, such as the banquet hall in which a 15th-century Lord of Mann feasts on 15th-century food, surrounded by 15th-century furniture. Look for the guard sitting on the garderobe (toilet), with appropriate sound effects. (Open Easter-Sept. daily 10am-5pm; £2.80.)

From the castle, a short walk towards the pier, across the footbridge and around the corner leads to the small **Nautical Museum,** with its 18th-century yacht and replica ship's cabin. (Open Easter-Sept. daily 10am-5pm; £1.80.)

PORT ERIN

A pretty little town near the southern tip of the island, Port Erin lost its competition with Douglas to replace Castletown as the island's major port when its breakwater fell into the sea in 1884. As a result, it has remained small and quiet, despite its preponderance of tourist accommodations.

The **tourist office** is on Station Rd. (tel. 832298; open Mon.-Fri. 9am-5pm, Sat. 9am-noon), by **IOM Bank.** (Open Mon.-Wed. and Fri. 9:30am-3:30pm, Thurs. 9:30am-5:30pm. ATM.) The **post office** stamps down Church Rd. (tel. 833119; open Mon.-Wed. and Fri. 9am-1pm and 2-5:30pm, Thurs. 9am-1pm, Sat. 9am-12:30pm.) **Trains** bip to Douglas (4-6/day; 1/hr.; £3.50); **buses** bop to Douglas (20/day, 1/hr., £1.65), and to Peel (3/day, 50 min., £1.75).

Accommodations & Food A very friendly welcome will be yours at **York House,** The Promenade (tel. 832 440). Enjoy clean, simple rooms with teapots and sinks and huge, tasty breakfasts (£13). **Epworth,** Church Rd. (tel. 832431), off the Promenade near the center of town, is popular and comfortable. (Open May-Sept. £13/person.) **Anchorage,** Atholl Park (tel. 832355), has great, green views of a glen from many bedrooms. (Open March-Oct. £15/person.)

Port Erin will keep you well-fed. If you tire of inexpensive restaurants, try the **Shoprite Supermarket,** Orchard Rd., behind the bus stop (Open Mon.-Tues. 9am-5:30pm, Wed.-Fri. 9am-8pm, Sat. 8:30am-5pm). **Cozy Nook Café,** Lower Promenade (tel. 835 020), has an incredible setting on the beach with views of the bay and Mourne Mountains, well-suited for summer evenings. Cook-your-own-barbecues from a choice of veggie burgers, steak, chicken, or other meat, with baked potato, salad, and bread for £3-5.50. (Open daily 10:30am-10pm; Oct.-March Fri.-Sun. 10am-6pm.) **DaVinci's Brobourne House,** The Promenade (tel. 834 124), offers interesting pasta dishes, pizza, steaks, and seafood. (7" pizzas from £2.30, pasta £4-5. Open daily 7-10pm.)

Sights Port Erin's major attractions are natural ones. Cruises to the **Calf of Man,** the small island and bird sanctuary off the southern tip of Mann, leave from the Port Erin pier daily during the summer in good weather. Visitors can choose between a 1¼-hr. cruise around the Calf, with good views of the cliffs, seals, and countless sea birds, or a ferry service. The ferry allows anywhere from an hour to a whole day to explore the island up close, with its bird observatory and herds of native, four-horned Loghtan sheep (the demonic sheep can also be found at the Cregneash Folk Museum and around the island). (Tel. 832339. Summer only. Cruises leave 10:15am daily; ferries leave 10:15, 11:30am, and 1:30pm daily; £6 return.)

The 1½-mi. road to Cregneash, past the strange Neolithic **Meayll Circle** (a chambered burial mound) makes a nice walk. The **Cregneash Village Folk Museum** (tel.

675522) is a fascinating preservation of 19th-century life in a farming village. Farmers and craftspeople in traditional dress demonstrate their skills for the visitors. (Open Easter-Sept. 10am-5pm; £1.80.) The 6-mi. portion of the coastal walking path (Raad ny Foillan) between Port Erin and the fishing village of **Port St. Mary** to the east is a manageable walk with stunning views of cliffs and sea. (Buses run back to Port Erin frequently.) The *Southern Walks* pamphlet, free from tourist offices, describes these walks and more.

PEEL

The "most Manx of all towns" is a beautiful fishing town on the west coast of the island. Narrow streets and small stone buildings have hardly changed since the days when its fishers sailed from Kildare to the Hebrides. The town is the headquarters of the big-time Manx kippers industry; except for connoisseurs of brine, visitors to Peel will more likely go bananas for its cathedrals and coastal walks.

The **tourist office,** Town Hall (tel. 842341), has pamphlets with self-guided walking tours. (Open Mon.-Thurs. 9am-5:15pm, Fri. 9am-4:30pm.) **IOM Bank,** Atholl St. (tel. 842122), has an ATM. (Open Mon.-Wed. and Fri. 9:30am-3:30pm, Thurs. 9:30am-5:30pm.) The **post office** sits in Market Pl. (tel. 842282; open Mon.-Wed. and Fri. 9am-12:30pm and 1:30-5:30pm, Thurs. and Sat. 9am-12:30pm.) **Buses** go to Douglas (30/day, 40 min.), Ramsey (10/day, 40 min.), and Port Erin (3/day; 1hr.).

Accommodations, Food & Pubs The **Haven Guest House,** 10 Peveril Ave. (tel. 842585), is non-smoking; since all rooms have teapots, TVs, and bathrooms, you've no need to leave your room. (£15/person.) The vegetarian breakfasts at **Seabourne House,** Mount Morrison (tel. 842 71), are an escape from kipperdom. (£14/person.) **Kerrowgarrow Farm,** Greeba (tel. 801871), is a dairy farm 4 mi. from Peel on the Douglas Rd. (£13/person.) **Peel Camping Park** (tel. 842341) has laundry, a game room, and a disabled-accessible bathroom. (Open May-Sept.)

There's not much decent food to be found in Peel; everyone's too focused on their kippers. **Peel Wholefoods,** 5 Douglas St., sells health food to crafty eaters. (Open Fri.-Wed. 9:30am-5pm, Thurs. 9:30am-7pm.) The best bet for food is the **Creek Inn Pub,** The Quay (tel. 842216), which serves meals all day (crab salad £5; food served Mon.-Sat. 11am-11pm, Sun. noon-1:30pm and 8-10pm), but the best place to drink is the **White House Hotel,** a former farmhouse, on the Tynwald Rd.

Sights **Peel Castle** is located on **St. Patrick's Isle,** now connected to the mainland by a causeway, where the first Christian missionaries (followers of St. Patrick) landed around 450. The castle has a ghost, in the form of a black dog, the **Moddey Dhoo,** which supposedly frightened one of the resident soldiers to death in the 17th century. Inside the castle are a 10th-century Irish-style round tower, built as a place of refuge for the monks during Viking raids, and the 13th-century **Cathedral of St. German.** The damp, eerie **Bishop's Dungeon** under the cathedral was used for hundreds of years to punish sinners for terrible offenses such as missing church. **Odin's Raven Boat House** (tel. 842852), on the opposite quay from the one that leads to the castle, holds a two-thirds scale replica of a Viking longship found in Norway. (Open April-Oct. daily 10am-5pm, last admission 4:30pm; £1.60.) Learn about taste-bud-pleasing foodstuffs at **Davisons' Chocolate Factory,** 1 Douglas St. (tel. 84324), which does have tours (2/hr. Mon.-Fri. 11am-4pm).

Near Peel: St. John's

St. John's is three mi. from Peel, on the Douglas Rd. All Peel/Douglas buses stop here (30/day). **Tynwald Hill** is an ancient site of the original Tynwald (parliament) from Norse times, and is still the site of Tynwald Fair, where Manx laws are proclaimed on July 5. Acts which are passed by Tynwald and the Governor (a rubber-stamp representative of the Queen) are read in Manx and English at the open-air meeting, which makes them into law. "Tynwald" comes from the Norse for "assembly field," which is where they have met since at least the 9th century.

Scotland

Scotland at its best is a world apart, a defiantly distinct nation within the United Kingdom with a culture and worldview all its own. Glasgow celebrates just about everything with a mind-bending nightlife, Aberdeen's grand buildings and manicured gardens sprawl regally at the mouth of two rivers, and Edinburgh, the epicenter of Scottish culture, pulls out all the stops during its famed International Festival in August. A little over half the size of England but with a tenth of its population, Scotland revels in stark and open spaces—the Scottish highlands contain some of the last great wilderness in Europe. The heather-covered mountains and glassy lochs of the west coast and luminescent mists of the Hebrides demand worship, while the farmlands to the south and the rolling river valleys of the east coast and Orkney in the north display a gentler beauty.

Most Scottish folk will welcome you with geniality and pride; as in the other few unharried corners of the world, hospitality and conversation are valued highly. Before reluctantly joining with England in 1707, the Scots commanded their independence with the broadsword for over 400 years. Since the union, they have continued to nurture a separate identity, retaining control over a number of social and political institutions, such as schools, churches, and the judicial system. Don't offend a Scot by calling him or her "English," but refer to a Scot correctly as "British" (better) or "Scottish" (best). While the kilts, bagpipes, haggis, and find-your-own-clan kits of Glasgow, Edinburgh, and Aberdeen may grow cloying, a trip to the lesser touristed regions of Scotland will reveal these definitively Scottish objects in their natural habitat and in daily usage, in heather and lupin blanketed valleys, thatch-roofed black houses that smell of centuries of peat fires, and among the snow-capped peaks of Scotland's many black granite mountains.

GETTING THERE

The cheapest way to Scotland from outside Britain is usually through London. Although the **bus** trip from London's Victoria Station takes more than seven hours, fares are one half that of trains. Recently combined, **Scottish Citylink** and **National Express** (tel. (0171) 730 0202)—look for either logo—serve Scotland via Glasgow and Edinburgh (£29.50, return £36-38, one-week APEX return £25). Buses depart London before 1pm (day service) and after 9pm (overnight). The cheapest options are Citylink's **Londonliner** or the independent **Night Rider** (tel. (0171) 833 4472). Both depart King's Cross at 11pm (each £15, return £22). Make reservations in advance. Scottish Citylink and National Express offer student and youth (23 and under) discount cards for £7, which reduce all fares (except APEX) by one-third.

From London, **trains** to Scotland take only five to six hours, but fares are steep: trains to Edinburgh (14-19/day, most from King's Cross Station) and to Glasgow Central (9-16/day, most from Euston Station) both cost £57 (return £57-67). Overnight trains carry sleeper berths for an extra £25. **Stagecoach** (tel. (01738) 300 08) runs overnight trains to many Scottish cities including Edinburgh, but not Glasgow (London Euston-Edinburgh £33.50, return £67, APEX return £44). Holders of British Rail's Discount Railcards (see Essentials: Getting Around, above) and Scottish Citylink or Caledonian Express discount bus cards receive one-third off all Stagecoach fares (except APEX).

Air travel is expensive. **British Airways** (tel. (0181) 897 4000), **British Midland** (tel. (01345) 589 5599), and **Air UK** (tel. (01345) 666777) sell a limited number of APEX return tickets for £75-77 (you must stay over a Saturday night; call far in advance). Air UK's **Skylink Singles** (from Gatwick £70, standby £67) are the choicest one-way fares. Air UK also flies to Aberdeen from London's Stanstead Airport.

Scotland is also linked by **ferry** to Northern Ireland (see Larne or Stranraer), the Isle of Man (see the Isle of Man) and to Norway and the Faroe Islands (see Thurso and the Shetland Islands).

Before you leave London, visit the **Scottish Tourist Board** office at 19 Cockspur St. (tel. (0171) 930 8661; tube: Charing Cross or Piccadilly Circus). They have gads of books and free brochures and can book train, bus, and plane tickets at their travel desk (open Mon.-Fri. 9am-6pm).

ONCE THERE

GETTING ABOUT

The *Touring Map of Scotland* (£3.75 at any tourist office) provides a good overall view for planning any sojourn into Scotland. Train or bus travel within the Lowlands (south of Stirling and north of the Borders) is much like travel in England. Rail connections are frequent, buses run almost everywhere, and transportation is relatively cheap. In the Highlands, though, trains snake slowly north on a few restricted routes, bypassing almost the entire Northwest region. Normally extensive and frequent, even bus service declines in the Northwest Highlands and grinds to a standstill on Sundays. Even if you intend to do all your sightseeing by bus and train, it may not be physically possible to make the various rail and bus special deals profitable; no single company offers a network comprehensive enough that their pass allows sufficient freedom or flexibility. A possible exception is the **Scottish Travelpass** (£99 for 8 days, £139 for 15 days), which allows unlimited travel on ScotRail trains and almost all Caledonian Macbrayne west coast ferry services, as well as providing discounts on P&O ferries to Orkney and Shetland and one-third off bus fares on some buses. Purchase the pass at almost any train station.

Bus travel in Scotland is a steal. Tickets often cost as little as half the train fare, and service is usually more frequent and almost as fast and comfortable, especially in the Highlands, though non-smokers may find the smoggy buses less hospitable than non-smoking train cars. Intense competition in some regions makes for some extremely low fares. **National Express** and **Scottish Citylink** have merged; their prices are the same and tickets may be bought at either counter, but routes still run under separate names. Unfortunately, neither company prints a full timetable. Bus stations are often closed or non-existent, but tickets are always sold on board. In rural areas, wave to signal the driver to stop.

Scottish Rail trains are clean and punctual, if not especially cheap. Their comprehensive timetable is 40p and available at all stations; alternatively, pick up free timetables to services in particular regions. The £16 **Student Coach Card** (actually ages 16-25, regardless of student status), available at major stations, reduces all fares by one-third for one year; bring two photos. Rail Rovers abound, but even the most frenetic rider of the rails will find it difficult to make these passes pay off.

Two minibus services provide the cheapest and most flexible way for hostellers to see Scotland: for those with limited time, the excellent **Go Blue Banana** minibus (tel. (0131) 220 6868), office at 28 North Bridge Rd. near the Edinburgh tourist office, provides outstanding three days tours of Scotland, taking in over 500 miles of scenery and sights of the Grampians, Loch Ness, the Northwestern Highlands, and Glencoe (among other places) for only £39. Their **hop-on, hop-off tour** allows hostellers to complete a circuit from Edinburgh through Perth, Pitlochry, Kingussie, Aviemore, Loch Ness, Loch Lochy, Skye (Kyleakin), Fort William, Glen Nevis, Glencoe, Oban, Inverary, Glasgow, and Loch Lomond in an unlimited amount of time for £55. The bus completes the circuit every day except Wednesday, picking up at hostels and campsite with advance notice. The newer **Haggis Backpackers** minibus (tel. (0131) 557 9393) provides a similar high-quality hop-on, hop-off service from Edinburgh through Perth, Pitlochry, Aviemore, Inverness, Loch Ness, and Ratagan

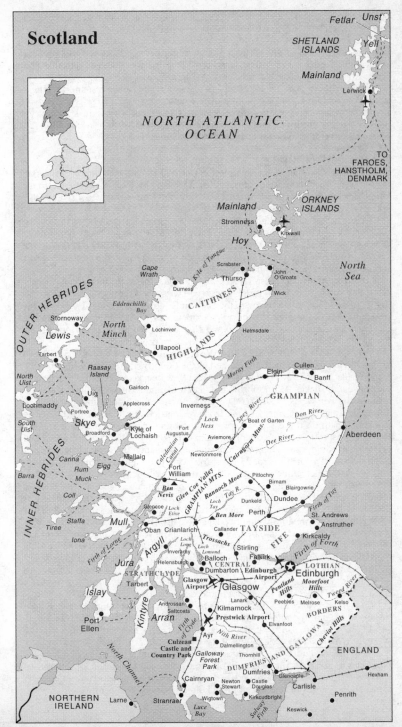

Scotland

to Skye daily except Thursday, and from Skye through Fort William, Glencoe, Oban, Inverary, Loch Lomond, and Glasgow daily except Friday (£55).

Air travel is predictably expensive between major cities, but British Airways offers a decent deal in the north: a 30-min. flight between Orkney and Shetland costs about the same as the 8-hr. ferry, providing that you spend a night in a B&B after arriving (see Shetland Islands: Getting There, above).

Many **hitchhike** in Scotland, except in places like the Northwest and Inverness, where cars crammed full of namby-pamby tourists make up a large percentage of the traffic. Hitchers report that drivers tend to be most receptive in the least-traveled areas. Far to the northwest and in the Western Isles, the Sabbath is strictly observed, making it difficult or impossible to get a ride on Sundays.

Biking And Hiking

Scotland offers scenic, challenging terrain for biking. You can usually rent bikes even in very small towns and transport them by ferry for little or no charge. In the Highlands, even major roads often have only one lane, and locals drive at high speeds—keep your eye out for the passing zones.

Bringing a bike to the Highlands by public transportation can be as difficult as pedaling there. Many Scottish Rail trains carry only four or fewer bikes; reservations (£3) are essential. Beginning in April, the **Bike Bus** (tel. (0131) 229 6274) will take you and your bike from Edinburgh to different points north and south on summer weekends (£18, plus £2 if you need to rent a bike).

Both the northern and western isles are of a negotiable scale and terrain for bicyclists. Fife and regions south of Edinburgh and Glasgow offer gentle country pedaling. Touring or mountain biking in the Highlands allows a freedom of access to the remote beauty of this area which easily compensates for the physically demanding cycling. *Mountainbiking in the Scottish Highlands* (£6) by Frances Fleming outlines many rides with meticulous maps and gradient profiles.

Two long-distance footpaths, the **West Highland Way** and the **Southern Upland Way,** were planned and marked by the Countryside Commission under the Countryside Act of 1967. The West Highland Way begins just north of Glasgow in Milngavie and snakes 95 mi. north along Loch Lomond, through Glencoe to Fort William and Ben Nevis ("from Scotland's largest city to its highest mountain"). The Southern Upland Way runs 212 mi. from Portpatrick on the southwest coast to Cockburnspath on the east coast, passing through Galloway Forest Park and the Borders. Most tourist offices distribute simple maps of the Ways as well as a list of accommodation options along the routes. For information on these paths, write or call the Scottish Tourist Board, 23 Ravelston Terr., Edinburgh EH4 3EU (tel. (0131) 332 2433). Detailed guidebooks to both paths are available at most bookstores.

Scottish mountaineering is dominated by the frequently obsessive practice of Munro Bagging. Hugh T. Munro compiled the original list of Scottish peaks over 3000 ft. in 1891; today about 280 are recorded. Any addition sends thousands of hikers scrambling up previously unnoticed peaks to maintain their distinction of having "bagged every Munro." Some people accomplish this feat over a lifetime of hiking; others do it in a frenetic six months. Thankfully, only one Munro, the Inaccessible Pinnacle on Skye, requires technical rock-climbing skills. *The Munros* (£15), put out by the Scottish Mountaineering Club, presents a full list of the peaks along with climbing information. In *The First Fifty Munro Bagging Without a Beard* (£13), the irreverent Muriel Gray presents a humorous account of this compulsive sport.

Mountain areas like the Cuillins, the Torridons, Glen Nevis, and Glencoe all have hostels situated in the midst of the ranges, providing bases for spectacular round-trip hikes. You can also walk along mainland Britain's highest sea cliffs at Cape Wrath or ramble across eerie moors of the Outer Hebrides and the Northwest.

One of the most attractive aspects of hiking in Scotland is that you can often pick your own route across the heather (you should check first with the local ranger or landowner). The wilds do pose certain dangers. Cairns (stone markers) can be unreliable, and expanses of open heather will often disorient. Heavy mists are always a possibility, and blizzards can surprise you even in July. Never go up into the mountains without the proper equipment: sturdy, well-broken-in boots, a 1:50,000 Ordnance Survey map, a compass, adequate waterproof gear and clothing to withstand freezing temperatures, an aluminized mylar blanket, insect repellent, and an emergency food supply. Leave a copy of your planned route and timetable at the hostel or nearest mountain rescue station. From mid-August to mid-October, always ask the hostel warden or innkeeper about areas in which deerstalkers might be at work. For information on walking and mountaineering in Scotland, consult Poucher's *The Scottish Peaks* (£10) or the introductory Tourist Board booklet, *Walk Scotland.*

ACCOMMODATIONS

SYHA hostels, part of the Hostelling International handbook, are the most economical lodgings in Scotland; hostel standards are perhaps the best in the world. The price range is low (£3.15-9.80, including breakfast), and there are hostels in or near almost every city and region described in our Scotland section. SYHA regulations are quite strict; curfews and lockouts are tightly enforced, and in grade 2 and 3 hostels, guests must do a brief chore, such as sweep out a room, before their membership card is returned in the morning. (Those planning an early departure should request evening duties.)

Hostels are carefully inspected and graded: grade 1 hostels have laundry facilities, free hot showers, shorter lockouts, and a microwave in the kitchen. Most grade 2 hostels have hot showers, more primitive clothes-washing facilities, and lockouts until 5pm. Grade 3 hostels, usually more remote, lack hot showers and clothes washers, but compensate with coziness and lenience. A sleepsack (rentable for 60p) and an HI membership card (purchasable as you go) are required at all grades. The *SYHA Handbook* (£1.50) is extremely useful; it lists all telephone numbers and opening dates, and its excellent maps might save hours of aimless wandering. From June to August, advance booking is *essential.* Hostels generally accept telephone reservations between 7 and 10pm (never on the same day as arrival) and hold them until 6pm (or sometimes later if you can specify a train or bus arrival time). The SYHA has introduced a **faxbooking system** between its most popular hostels (mostly grade 1); 70p plus the prepaid unrefundable overnight fee assures you of a bed up to 10pm on your date of arrival. Many hostels close in October and reopen in March, April, or May.

Many travelers prefer the growing Scottish network of **independent hostels.** Their atmosphere and rules are usually more relaxed than those at SYHA hostels, though kitchens are sometimes cramped and bathrooms tiny. The independent hostels in Edinburgh, Inverness, Skye, Oban, Stornoway (Lewis), Stromness (Orkney), Fort William, and Glasgow are particularly well-run, friendly, and atmospheric. Try to pick up a copy of the *Scottish Independent Hostels* leaflet at one of the independents. The Scottish Tourist Board publishes an extremely useful booklet, *Scotland Tir Nan Og—"The Land of the Ever Young"—Youth Accommodation*, which lists most of the available budget accommodations in Scotland by place.

B&Bs are a comfortable but more expensive alternative. For less than £14, you can have privacy and the luxury of sleeping late. It's best to book B&Bs using tourist office literature. Most tourist offices charge £1 for local booking (with a 10% deposit), except in Edinburgh where the same service costs £2.50. By booking independently, you save both the tourist office fee and a surcharge which some B&B owners add to their prices to compensate for the 15% taken by the tourist offices. In addition, all tourist offices participate in the Book-a-Bed-Ahead scheme which allows you to reserve a room in any other region in Scotland for a £2.50 fee; they do all the phoning. All tourist offices issue glossy regional accommodations directories that become increasingly important resources as the summer tourist season heats up.

You can camp free on all public land, but make sure you know which areas are restricted (*i.e.,* preserves or other protected land). Always ask the landowner's permission if you suspect you're on privately owned land. Private sites, usually geared to caravans, charge £4-7 per tent and vary widely in quality; a good investment is

Scotland: Camping and Caravan Parks (approximately £4) available at any tourist office. Beware Scotland's often wet and cold weather. You should use a sleeping-bag with artificial insulation, rather than down (which deflates unpleasantly when wet). Gore-Tex jackets are strongly recommended.

LIFE & TIMES

HISTORY

Unlike their English neighbors, Scotland's Celtic tribes successfully repelled Roman incursions. (Only, of course, to fall prey to the English themselves a millenium later.) Emperor Hadrian sagely built a wall across the north of England to fend off the pitch-fork-tossing farmers of the north. The invading tribes from the continent, however, were more successful, and by 600 AD the Scottish mainland was inhabited by four groups: the Picts, Scots, Britons, and Angles. The Pict-Scot kingdom formed under the leadership of Kenneth MacAlpin (Kenneth I) in about 843 AD to ward off Viking conquerors. By 1034, the Angles and Romanized Britons of the Lowlands had been incorporated into this united kingdom; James IV subjugated Caithness and Sutherland, and received Orkney and Shetland as a gift from Christian I of Denmark.

The increasingly powerful English monarchy posed an intermittent but considerable threat to Scottish independence throughout the Middle Ages and well into the 16th century. After a century-long peace under Alexanders II and III, Scotland was attacked by Edward I who sought to reimpose English rule. Arachnophilic Robert the Bruce emerged as Scotland's leader (1306-1329) after the Wars of Independence. During the 15th- and early 16th-century the monarchy set nobles against one another in an attempt to preserve its own waning position, and the Reformation further split allegiances within the country: Scottish objections to Roman supremacy in the church merely reinforced English power.

In the midst of this turmoil, Mary Queen of Scots (1542-1567), prompted a civil war that lasted until 1573. Her ambitious son James VI was crowned King James I of England in 1603, uniting both countries under a single crown. James ruled from London, and his half-hearted attempts to reconcile the Scottish domains were tartly resisted. Scottish Presbyterians supported Cromwellian forces against James' successor, Charles I, in the English Civil War. When the English Parliament executed Charles in 1649, though, the Scots named his son Charles II as King. Oliver Cromwell readily defeated him as well, but in a conciliatory gesture gave Scotland representation in the English Parliament. Although this body did not last, the political precedent of representation endured.

England and Scotland were permanently united when England engaged in the War of Spanish Succession (1701-1714) and requested the support of its neighbor. Scotland, forced to choose between England and its long-suffering ally, France, decided that its Presbyterian interests were safer with Anglicans. The 18th century proved to be the most culturally and economically prosperous in Scotland's history, producing such luminaries as Adam Smith and David Hume.

The civil wars of the 18th century pitted Highlanders against Lowlanders and Roman Catholics against Presbyterians. Though 19th-century political reforms did much to improve social conditions, economic problems in both the 19th and 20th centuries induced large-scale emigration.

Today Scotland has 72 seats in the United Kingdom's House of Commons and is largely integrated into the British economy. Nevertheless, the Scottish National Party (SNP), which received about one-quarter of the Scottish vote in the 1992 general election, regularly demands autonomy or independence. You'll greatly offend a Scot by using the term "England" for what should be called "Britain" or "the U.K." (and here, "Scotland"). While demands for constitutional change persist, Conservative Prime Minister John Major argues that a slight increase in the Conservative vote in Scotland in 1992 signified a vote for a strong union, and plans no significant change in Scotland's status. Scotsman John Smith succeeded Welshman Neil Kinnock as leader of the Labour Party in July 1992, but his life and leadership were cut short by a heart attack this past year. He now is laid to rest in a simple grave on the isle of Iona; a red rose tops his grave.

LITERATURE & MUSIC

Scottish literature in English starts in the 1400s, with Robert Henryson and William Dunbar, sensitive, underrated followers of Chaucer. You'll hear plenty about Robert Burns (1771-1832) whose lyrics glorified love, friendship, country life, and the Scots dialect itself; "Auld Lang Syne" and "My luv is like a red, red rose" are his, but so are many more complex verses. Sir Walter Scott won huge followings with his novels of chivalry; Robert Louis Stevenson did the same for his stories. Hugh MacDiarmid and Edwin Morgan are *the* Scottish poets of this century, so far; Scottish verse now spans three languages, Scottish Gaelic, Scots (like Burns') and English. Novelists Lewis Grassic Gibbon and Nell Gunn (*Silver Darlings*) kept up the nation's prose tradition; more recent star novelists are Alasdair Gray (*Lanark, Unlikely Stories Mostly, Janine 1984*) , Tom Leonard, and sharp newcomer Janice Galloway.

Forget, for a minute, bagpipes: Scotland's rock music can be just as impressive. The Rezillos (c. 1978) were a drinking man's punk band, whose power and humor shone through their zoot suits in numbers like "Somebody's Gonna Get Their Head Kicked In Tonight." The Skids slid from poetic to pathetic when their guitarist left to form Big Country, while Altered Images singer Clare Grogan gathered listeners with her childlike charm. Angrier, artier new wavers (Scars, Fire Engines, Restricted Code) flocked to the great FAST and Pop:Aural record labels. More poetic, catchier, and more influential were Glasgow's Orange Juice, Edinburgh's Josef K, and their record label, Postcard, which favored Byrdsy guitar chimes and winsome, coy boy singers. (Aztec Camera's early Postcard singles are genuinely heartbreaking.)

Postcard had shot its wad by 1984; in their place at Scottish-rock central were Glasgow's unassuming, poppy Pastels and their 53rd & 3rd Records, which helped inspire the Shop Assistants and the Soup Dragons, the sex-obsessed Vaselines, and Rote Kapelle, whose *No North Briton* is an underrated showcase of glittering, tortured pop. Edinburgh native Alan McGee and his Creation Records shot Glasgow's Jesus and Mary Chain into international chart orbit; onstage, it was said, the Marychain could never get enough feedback, or enough malt. Another Creation gem was Aberdeen's craftsmanlike, Postcard-y Jasmine Minks. And another thing altogether were the crunchy, noisy, political, Fire Engines-descended bands, like Badgewearer and Dawson; the best of those, the trumpet-wielding, feminist Dog-Faced Hermans, are alive (and stunning live) and now living in Amsterdam. The cute-smart-pop tradition continues in the Wake, the Orchids, Aberdeen's Kitchen Cynics and the reclusive Golden Dawn and Besotted, while Teenage Fanclub demonstrate that heavy guitars, charm, long hair and chart success can coexist in one band.

FOOD & DRINK

Scotland's whisky (spelled without the "e") is as justifiably famous as its cuisine is not. A few dishes invoke the good old days of the tartan clans and cavorting livestock—most notably black pudding, made with sheep's blood, and the infamous *haggis,* (sheep's or calf's heart and liver minced with oats and boiled in the animal's stomach). They sound more exotic than they taste. Ubiquitous tea and coffee shops provide the cheapest meals at lunch, but often sell only soup, sandwiches, and french fries. "Salad" here means something strange and awful: asking for it may get you anything from dressing to mayonnaise to nasty pickled beets. Pub meals are more substantial and cost £3.50-4 (usually served noon-2pm and 6-9pm; often the only option on a Sunday). The biggest supermarket chains are Presto, Wm. Low, Safeway, and the Co-op.

Scotch whisky is either "malt" (from a single distillery), or "blended" (a mixture of several different brands). The malts are all good and distinctive; the blends are the same as those available abroad. Due to heavy "sin taxes" on all alcohol sold in Britain, Scotch may often be cheaper at home than in Scotland. True to their character, the Scots know when not to call it a night; more generous licensing laws than England keep the pubs open Monday to Saturday 11am to 11pm, Sunday 12:30pm to 2pm and 6:30 to 11pm. Bars in big cities often stay open as late as 4am.

FESTIVALS, GATHERINGS, & GAMES

Weekend clan gatherings, bagpipe competitions, and Highland games occur frequently during the summer. Check at the tourist office and in the local newspaper for dates of local events. The Scottish Tourist Board publishes *Scotland Events: January-December*. Traditional Scottish games originated from local competitions in which participants could use only common objects, such as hammers, rounded stones, and tree trunks. Physical prowess combines with technical skill; although "tossing the caber" (a pine trunk) looks easy, it requires a good deal of talent and practice and is not recommended for the home.

A slew of events featuring folk and classical music, general mirthfulness, and revelry occurs throughout the summer. June and July's drunken **Common Ridings** in the Borders and raucous **Up-Helly-Aa** in Shetland on the last Tuesday in January are among the best-known; the **National Gaelic Mod** (different locations in Oct.) is a feast of all things Celtic. For more information, see listings in specific areas.

Above all events towers the **Edinburgh International Festival,** (August 13-September 2, 1995), the largest international festival in the world. The concentration of musical and theatrical events in the space of three weeks is dizzying; Edinburgh's cafés and shops open to all hours and pipers roam the streets. While plenty of drag-out-your-Tux events run a hefty bill, many more casual and just as entertaining ones are in the range of the budget traveler. Be sure to enjoy the **Festival Fringe,** the much less costly sibling of the Festival. Literally hundreds of performances appear on the Fringe each day, including Shakespeare, musicals, comedy acts, jazz, and a bit of the bizarre. Be warned—the Festival season is not the time to see Edinburgh itself; the great city is momentarily buried under vendors, bleachers, and vast milling crowds. For crying out loud, reserve a room ahead. For info, contact either the Edinburgh International Festival, 21 Market St., Edinburgh EH1 1BW (tel. (0131) 225 5756), or the Festival Fringe Society, 180 High St., Edinburgh EH1 1QS, respectively.

SOUTHERN SCOTLAND

Scotland's gentle slope up from England belies the historic violence between the two. Monuments and ruins reveal past struggle among Picts, Romans, English, and Scottish; Dumfriesshire is rich in tales of Robert the Bruce, born in nearby Lochmaben, who successfully led the cause of Scottish independence to victory at Bannockburn in 1314. Regional hostility and crumbling stone draw big tourist bucks, but the less urban areas of Southern Scotland are traveled at least as much for their hiking paths as for their rubble. Edinburgh and the smooth hills south of it may seem to lack the urban or natural rawness that benefits other areas of Scotland. Still, they shouldn't be overlooked. Walkers and bikers will find the Borders and Dumfries and Galloway both accessible and calming, and Edinburgh, once a fountainhead of Enlightenment, continues to shine as the home of several international festivals.

■■■ EDINBURGH

Scotland's magnificent capital is less a city than an event, a meeting of natural rock and hewn stone, wild landscapes and terraced gardens, the distant skirling of bagpipes and the closer beeping of carhorns. Natural splendor and human art intersect—a castle-crowned volcano rises abruptly from the city's center, across elegant green parks lace through a drained loch, and Arthur's seat looms over Hollyrood Pal-

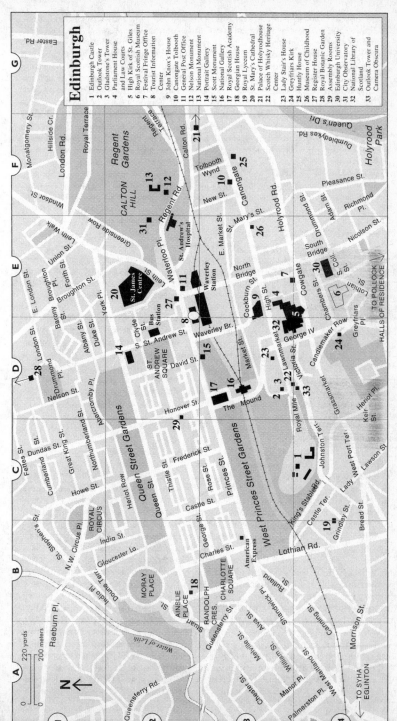

Edinburgh

1 Edinburgh Castle
2 Outlook Tower
3 Gladstone's Tower
4 Parliament House and Law Courts
5 High Kirk of St. Giles
6 Royal Scottish Museum
7 Festival Fringe Office
8 Tourist Information Center
9 John Knox's House
10 Canongate Tolbooth
11 General Post Office
12 Nelson Monument
13 National Monument
14 Portrait Gallery
15 Scott Monument
16 National Gallery
17 Royal Scottish Academy
18 Georgian House
19 Royal Lyceum
20 St. Mary's Cathedral
21 Palace of Holyroodhouse
22 Scotch Whisky Heritage Center
23 Lady Stair's House
24 Greyfriars Kirk
25 Huntly House
26 Museum of Childhood
27 Register House
28 Royal Botanic Garden
29 Assembly Rooms
30 Edinburgh University
31 City Observatory
32 National Library of Scotland
33 Outlook Tower and Camera Obscura

ace. Edinburgh boasts a heady year-round mixture of superb museums, bookstores, and pubs, and transforms into a gallery of thrills during August's festival season.

In the early 18th century, the dark alleys of this Calvinist Kingdom of God saw an outpouring of philosophical and literary talent that made Edinburgh a capital of the Enlightenment. The philosopher David Hume presided over a republic of letters that produced the invisible hand of economist Adam Smith, the poetry of Allan Ramsay and Robert Fergusson's poetry, and the literary wanderings of Tobias Smollett, Sir Tristan Busch, Robert Louis Stevenson, and Sir Walter Scott. But the Age of Reason did not completely dismantle the narrow, winding alleys and dark, huddled buildings. The Old Town's tenements, closes, and wynds, immortalized by native son Robert Louis Stevenson in *Dr. Jekyll and Mr. Hyde,* remain a contrast and complement to the graceful symmetry and orderly gridwork of Georgian New Town.

GETTING THERE

Edinburgh lies 45 mi. east of Glasgow and 405 mi. northwest of London on Scotland's east coast, on the southern bank of the Firth of Forth. Edinburgh is a major hub of Scotland's **bus** network; see the Scotland: Getting There and Getting About, above for information on discounts and companies. **Scottish Citylink** service runs from **St. Andrew Square Bus Station** to Glasgow (#500, 501; at least 1/hr.; £4), Aberdeen (#564, 565, 568, 569; 1/hr.; £11.70), Inverness (#555, 557; 1/hr.; £11.20), and Thurso (change at Inverness; from Inverness #558, 559; £9). **National Express** stretches to London (£29.50). You might also want to try Scottish Citylink's **Londonliner** bus services to London (£15; departs at 9am and 9pm). Edinburgh forms the northern limit of the **Slow Coach tour** (consult Essentials: Getting About— Buses & Coaches for details).

Trains leave Edinburgh's **Waverley Station** for Glasgow (at least 2/hr.; £5.50), Stirling (at least 1/hr.; £3.70), Aberdeen (1/hr.; £26), Inverness (5/day direct, 4/day connect at Glasgow; £23), Thurso (3/day; £30.50), Oban (3/day; £20), and London (£44 APEX return). Call Scotrail at 556 2451. Hitchers often take public transit out of city center. For points south (except Newcastle and northeast England), most ride bus #4 or 15 to Fairmilehead and then the A702 to Biggar. For Newcastle, York, and Durham, many take bus #15, 26, or 43 to Musselburgh and the A1. North-seekers catch bus #18 or 40 to Barnton for the Forth Road Bridge and beyond.

ORIENTATION & PRACTICAL INFORMATION

Edinburgh's small distances and quiet streets make it an ideal walking city. Princes St. is the main thoroughfare in the New Town, the northern section of Edinburgh; "The Royal Mile" (Lawnmarket, High St., and Canongate) connects **Edinburgh Castle** and **Holyrood Palace** and is the major road in the Old Town in the southern half of the city. Three bridges—North Bridge, Waverley Bridge, and The Mound—connect these two areas. Waverly train station lies between North Bridge and Waverly Bridge, in what used to be the loch that protected the old town to the north. St. Andrew Square bus station is a short three blocks from the east end of Princes St.

Although your feet will often suffice, Edinburgh does have an efficient and comprehensive (though confusing) bus system. There are two main companies. **Lothian Regional Transport** or **LRT** (maroon doubledecker buses; tel. 220 4111 for information, 226 5063 for bookings) was Edinburgh's only bus company before privatization and still provides the best service. At their **Ticket Centre** on Waverley Bridge, you can buy a one-day **Silver Freedom Ticket** (£2, children £1.40), as well as longer-term passes (open daily 8am-7pm). Consider buying an **Edinburgh Explorer Ticket** for £2 on any of the green and cream buses of **SMT** (tel. 558 1616). If you don't want a pass, ask your driver for the price of your destination, and be sure to carry coins: *drivers do not carry change.* The **Travel-line** (tel. 225 3858; open Mon.-Fri. 8:30am-4:30pm) will give you information on either busline.

Tourist Office: Edinburgh and Scotland Information Center, Waverley Market, 3 Princes St., Edinburgh EH2 2QP (tel. 557 1700), next to the Waverley train station behind the statue of the three grovellers. Busy but efficient accommodations service (£2.75-3); a 24-hr. computer outside gives updates on availability. Pick up *The Essential Guide to Edinburgh* (25p), the calendar *Day by Day* (free), and a free Edinburgh accommodations booklet. Bus, theatre, and other tickets sold. Rates at the *bureau de change* in the tourist office are 3%, min. charge £3 on foreign currency and travellers cheques 2.5%, min. charge £2.50 on sterling cheques. Open Mon.-Sat. 9am-8pm, Sun. 10am-8pm; May-June and Sept. Mon.-Sat. 9am-7pm, Sun. 11am-7pm; April and Oct. Mon.-Sat. 9am-6pm, Sun. 11am-6pm; Nov.-March Mon.-Sat. 9am-6pm.

Budget Travel Services: Edinburgh Travel Centre, Potterow Union, Bristo Sq. (tel. 668 2221). Also at 196 Rose St. (tel. 226 2019) and 92 S. Clark St. (tel. 667 9488). Affiliated with Council and STA Travel. Open Mon.-Fri. 9am-5:30pm; Rose St. and S. Clark St. also open Sat. 10am-1pm. **Campus Travel,** 53 Forrest Rd. (tel. 225 6111). Open Mon.-Tues. and Thurs.-Fri. 9am-5:30pm, Wed. and Sat. 10am-5pm. Both sell ISIC, railcards, and budget airfares. **SYHA District Office,** 161 Warrender Park Rd. (tel. 229 8660), near Bruntsfield Hostel. Sells hostel memberships (£9) and a range of camping and hostel supplies, including sleeping sacks and stylish SYHA badges. Open Mon.-Fri. 9am-5pm, Sat. 9am-12:30pm.

Consulates: U.S.: 3 Regent Ter. (tel. 226 8315), open Mon.-Fri. 10am-noon, and Mon.-Wed. and Fri. 1-4pm. Call for an appointment. **Australia:** 80 Hanover St. (tel. 226 6271), open Mon.-Fri. 10am-4pm.

Financial Services: Go to just about any bank or the currency exchange desk in the tourist office, which is open on Sundays (hours same as the office, listed above). **American Express:** 139 Princes St. EH2 4BR (tel. 225 7881), 5 long blocks from Waverley Station. Holds mail. Open Mon.-Fri. 9am-5:30pm, Sat. 9am-4pm. There is an **ATM** at the Barclays 42 South St. Andrews St.

Post Office: 2-4 Waterloo Place (tel. 550 8253), at North Bridge and Princes St. Open Mon.-Fri. 9am-5:30pm, Sat. 9am-12:30pm. **Postal Code:** EH1 1AA.

Telephone Code: 0131.

Airport: LRT's Airlink 100 (tel. 220 4111; £3) and the Edinburgh Airbus Express (tel. 556 2244; £3.20) both depart from Waverley Bridge for Edinburgh Airport. Journey time is about 25 min.

Train Station: Waverley Station, in the center of town. For 24-hr. information, call 556 2451. Office open daily Mon.-Sat. 8am-11pm, Sun. 9am-11pm. Young Person's Scot Cards (£16) sold Mon.-Sat. 8am-6pm, Sun. 9am-6pm. Free bike storage at the back of the main Travel Centre. Lockers £2-4.

Bus Station: St. Andrew Square Bus Station, St. Andrew Square. For Scottish Citylink information call 557 5717; for SMT information call 654 0707; for National Express information call 452 8777. After hours, or to avoid crushing lines, buy your ticket on the bus. The information office for SMT and National Express is by Platform A in the bus stop. Open Mon.-Tues. and Thurs.-Sat. 8:40am-5pm, Wed. 9am-5pm. The Scottish Citylink office is across the station by Platform D. Open Mon.-Sat. 9am-5pm, Sun.9am-4pm. **Lockers** £1-3.

Taxi: Taxi stands at both stations and on almost every corner on Princes St. Or call **City Cabs** (tel. 228 1211) or **Central Radio Taxis** (tel. 229 2468).

Car Rental: Get a list of agencies at the Tourist Office. Most, including the following, have a min. age of 21 or 23 and rates from £30/day, £150/week with unlimited mileage; try **Carnie's Car Hire** (tel. 346 4155) or **Alexanders of Edinburgh** (tel. 229 3331).

Bike Rental: Central Cycle Hire, 13 Lochrin Place (tel. 228 6333), off Home St. in Tollcross near Cameo Cinema. 12-speed town bikes £8/day, 21-speed touring bikes £10/day, mountain bikes £15/day. £60/week. Open Mon.-Sat. 10am-5:30pm; Sept.-May Mon. and Wed.-Sat. 10am-5:30pm.

Bookstores: Waterstone's, 83 George St. (tel. 225 3436). A great store for browsing, with superb fiction and travel sections. Open Mon.-Sat. 9:30am-10pm, Sun. 11am-6pm.

Camping Supplies: Camping Outdoors Centre, 77 South Bridge (tel. 225 3339). Has all the essentials. Open Mon.-Sat. 9am-5:30pm.

Sports Center: Meadowbank Sports Centre, 139 London Rd. (tel. 661 5351). Buses #4, 15, 26, or 44. Full exercise and gymnasium facilities, including a track and a velodrome. Charge varies according to activity.

EDINBURGH

Launderette: Bruntsfield Laundrette, 108 Bruntsfield Pl. (tel. 229 2669), near Bruntsfield hostel. Wash £2, dry 20p. Open Mon.-Fri. 9am-5pm, Sat. 9am-4pm, Sun. 10am-4pm.

Public Showers: In the "Superloo" at the train station. Super clean. 65p for 20min. Free towel (£1 deposit). Condoms £1. Open Mon.-Sat. 6am-midnight, Sun. 7:30am-midnight.

Lesbian, Gay, and Bisexual Services: West and Wilde Bookshop, 25a Dundas St. (tel. 556 0079). Open Mon.-Fri. 9am-9pm, Sat. 9am-7pm, Sun. noon-6pm. **Gay Switchboard:** tel. (556 4049), daily 7:30-10pm. **Lesbian Line:** tel. (557 1751), open Mon.-Thurs. 7:30-10pm. Pick up a copy of *Gay Scotland*, ask the tourist office for their information sheet, or drop by the **Bisexual Resource Center** (tel. 556 1471), downstairs from **The Edge,** 60 Broughton St. (open Tues. 10:30am-4:40pm, Thurs. noon-7pm, Sat. 11-5pm). The Edge and the **Blue Moon Café,** also on Broughton St., dispense pastries, coffee, and terrifically friendly, up-to-date advice on nightspots.

Services for Disabled: Lothian Coalition of Disabled People, 13 Johnston Ter. (tel. 220 6855). Information available on disabled access to restaurants and sights.

Hotlines: Nightline: (tel. 557 4444); daily 6pm-8am. **Rape Crisis Center:** (tel. 556 9437); Mon. 7-9pm, Tues. 1-4pm, Thurs. 6-8pm; answering machine all other hours. **Women's Aid:** (tel. 229 1419); Wed. 6-8pm, Thurs. 1-3pm. **AIDS Information:** (tel. (0800) 567123).

Hospital: Royal Infirmary of Edinburgh, 1 Lauriston Pl. (tel. 229 2477). From the Mound take buses #23 or 27.

Emergency: Dial 999; no coins required.

Police: Headquarters are on Fettes Ave. (tel. 311 3131).

ACCOMMODATIONS

The *Where to Stay 1995* register (free at the tourist office) gives exhaustive listings of Edinburgh's gargantuan B&B population, the largest outside London. For a prince's fortune (£3), the booking service at the tourist office will find you a room, but the private service in the train station will do the same for free (open Mon.-Sat. 8am-8pm, Sun. 9:30am-7:30pm). During the festival season (in 1995, Aug.13-Sept.2), there are few rooms available anywhere in the city. Try to book through the tourist office a few months in advance for B&Bs, or write hostels early in the summer. B&Bs cluster in three well-stocked colonies. The **Bruntsfield** district lies south of the west end of Princes St.; take bus #11, 15, 16, or 17 and try around Gilmore Pl., Viewforth Ter., or Huntington Gardens. **Newington** is south of the east end of Princes St. Hunt along Dalkeith Rd. and Minto St.; take bus #3, 8, 18, 31, 36, 62, 69, 80, 81, or 89. **Leith** lies northeast of the east end of Princes St. Try Pilrig St.; take Leith Walk from the east end of Princes St. or bus #11 or 14. Most of the hundreds of **B&Bs** in the city open between May and September and cost £11-16. Slightly more elegant **guest houses** run £15-25 and remain open year-round.

Edinburgh's hostels are cheap and convenient but fill up fast. Students looking for long-term residence (a month or more) should stop by the **Student Accommodation Service,** 30 Buccleuch Pl. (tel. 667 0151 or 650 4669; open Mon.-Fri. 9:30am-12:30pm and 2-4:30pm). Also check the notice boards in the basement of David Hume Tower and on the ground floor of Teviot Row Union, both near Bristo Sq.

High Street Hostel, 8 Blackfriars St. EH1 1NE (tel. 557 3984). From Waverley Station, turn right up North Bridge to the Royal Mile (High St.), then turn left down the hill and take the second right. Hostel paradise. Located just off the Royal Mile, this well-managed friendly hostel fills up fast. Some call this the best independent hostel in Great Britain. Videos nightly. Reception 24hrs. Check-out 10:30am. No curfew. 140 beds, 4-16/room. Coed bathrooms. Vigorous private showers. £8.50, seventh night free. Continental breakfast £1.20. Laundry service (£2.50) and kitchen facilities. Storage. Phone reservations with credit card payment for first night. Opening in the spring of 1995, the **Backpackers' Royal Mile Hostel,** 117 High St. (tel. 557 6120), will hold 30 beds and be run by the High Street Hostel management. All High St. services apply (£8.90). Look for tartan curtains.

14 Argyle Pl. (Iolaire), EH9 1JL (tel. 667 9991), south of the Meadows and the Royal Mile. From High St. turn left on South Bridge, continue as it changes into Nicolson and then Clerk Sts., turn right on Hope Park Terrace and follow it onto Melville Dr., then take a right on Argyle Place. Heather and Jed Dignan have lovingly renovated two old houses. A welcoming cup of tea and excellent advice on sights. 2- to 4-person rooms; capacity 50-55 people. No curfew. At £9-10, it's a bargain. TVs in rooms and in lounge; unlimited kitchen access. Try the bathtubs.

Belford Youth Hostel, 6-8 Douglas Gardens EM4 3DA (tel. 225 6209). About 1 mi. west of town center, near Haymarket train station. Take bus #3, 4, 12, 13, 22, 26, 28, 31, 33, or 44 from Princes St. to Palmerston Pl., which turns into Douglas Gardens at its end. The Hunter family has spared no effort to convert this elegant, 100-yr.-old church into a clean, welcoming, modern hostel—you'll wake under stained glass windows. Reception open 8am-11pm. Check-out 10am. No curfew. 90 beds in 4- to 6-person "hives" £8.50, including linen. 6 doubles with private bathrooms £25/room. Snooker, ping-pong, and videos nightly; weekly pub crawls, barbecues, theme nights. Kitchen, laundry. Phone and post reservations accepted. Bus will pick up groups from train or bus stations with prior notice.

HI Hostel Eglinton, 18 Eglinton Crescent EH12 5DD (tel. 337 1120), about 1 mi. west of town center, near Haymarket train station. Near Belford Youth Hostel; before Douglas Gardens turn left on Eglinton Crescent, the second left on Palmerston Place. Pleasant views. Sumptous Victorian decor. Be careful walking back late. Video-monitored buzz-in front gate. Reception 7am-2am. Check-out 10am. Curfew 2am. 184 beds in 4- to 22-bed dorms. £9.80; under 18 £8.45. Evening meal £3.55. Laundry machines, good kitchen, luggage storage, good-natured staff. Sheets 60p/week. Paid advance reservations urged Easter-Sept. Open Jan.-Nov.

HI Hostel Bruntsfield, 7 Bruntsfield Crescent EH10 4EZ (tel. 447 2994), about 1½ mi. south of the West End of Princes St. Take bus #11, 15, 16, 17, 23, or 45, or walk down Lothian Rd. to 24 Earl Grey St.—at the large intersection bear right on Leven Home, turn left on Whitehouse, and turn right on Bruntsfield Crescent. A trek, but the sparkling facilities, amiable staff, and wonder-dog Jedda make it all worthwhile. Reception open 7am-11:30pm. Curfew 2am. 168 beds in 8- to 24-bed rooms. £7.25, under 18 £5.95. Kitchen, laundry, TV lounge. Open Feb.-Dec.

Christian Alliance Frances Kinnaird Hostel, 13-14 Coates Crescent EH3 7AF (tel. 225 3608). Follow Princes St. west to Shandwick Pl., then bear right on Coates Crescent. Women and married couples. A staid, quiet B&; clean rooms and washbins. Curfew midnight, Festival 1:30am. Reception open 8:30am-11:45pm. Check-out 10am. B&B from £10-16.50. Dinner £4. Laundry; luggage storage. Post reservations accepted with payment for first night (during Festival, full amount).

HI Hostel Merchiston, North Merchiston Boys' Club, Watson Crescent. Grade 2. Take bus #9 or 10 to Polwarth and then #30 or 43 to Dundee St. Long hike from the city center but provides 100 beds at the peak of summer. £4.80. Hot showers, full kitchen. No advance bookings accepted—just show up. Take precaution when returning to the neighborhood late at night. Open July-early Sept.

Camping: Silverknowes Caravan Park, Marine Drive, by the Forth (tel. 312 6874). Take bus #1 from North Bridge (70p). Tents from £4.70. Space for 150 tents. Toilets, showers and a shop in the campground. Open April-Oct.

FOOD

Most traditional Scottish fare in Edinburgh is served in restaurants that will put you in the alms house, but you can get haggis at many inexpensive cafés. Perhaps out of extreme revulsion for this dish, affordable restaurants here tend to serve mainly or exclusively vegetarian food. Indian food is generally cheap, and the most reasonably priced Chinese fare is available from several take-out shops on South Clerk St. **Littlewoods Department Store,** 92 Princes St., has a basement supermarket, Iceland Food Hall, with salad bar (£1.19-2.59; open Mon.-Wed. 9:30am-5:30pm, Thurs. 9am-7pm, Fri.-Sat. 9am-6pm). Other supermarkets include **Wm. Low,** 94 Nicolson St. (open Mon.-Sat. 8:30am-7:30pm, Sun. 9am-5pm), and **Scoopamarket,** a wholefood haven at 112 Nicolson St. (open Mon.-Sat. 9am-5:20pm).

Corner Stone Coffee House, Lothian Rd. (tel. 229 0212), at Princes St., hidden beneath St. John's Church. Savory vegetarian meals £3.05. Picnic by a graveyard. Open Mon.-Sat. 10am-4:30pm, during Festival Mon.-Sat.10am-6:30pm.

Teviot Restaurant, Teviot Row Union, the dark stone building in Bristo Sq. The best of the university unions. Main dishes £2. Open Oct.-June Mon.-Fri. 8:30am-6:45pm, Sun. 12:30-6:30pm. During the Festival, it becomes the **Fringe Club.**

Kalpna, 2 St. Patrick's Sq. (tel. 667 9890). Superb Indian vegetarian fare in a smoke-free setting. Buffet lunch £3.50. Curry, *korma,* and wildly exotic vegetable dishes, £3.25-7. Reserve for dinner . Open Mon.-Fri. noon-2pm and 5:30-11pm.

Larry's Diner, 26 Nicolson St. (tel. 667 5712). Bright and clean. Good chips. Steak pie and chips (£2.50), fish and chips (£2.75). Set lunch served noon-2pm includes soup, main dish, chips, and tea (£2.50). Open Mon.-Sat. 8am-5pm, Sun. 9am-2pm.

Seeds Café, 53 W. Nicolson St. (tel. 667 8673). Hardcore vegetarian fare. Open Mon.-Sat. 10am-9pm, Fri. 10am-10pm; during the Festival daily 10am-midnight. Daily specials under £3. Super hummus 65p.

Kebab Mahal, 7 Nicolson Sq. (tel. 667 5214). The best of Edinburgh's many kebaberies. Kebabs £2-4, hummus £1.55, and lamb curry £3. Open Sun.-Thurs. noon-midnight, Fri.-Sat. noon-2am.

Parrots, 3-5 Viewforth (tel. 229 3252). A faithful clientele flocks to the parrot-theme dining room for tasty dishes (and good vegetarian selection). Aubergine and mushroom moussaka (£3.25), seafood gratia (£4.25), plum pudding with brandy (£2.25). Open Sun.-Thurs. 6-10:30pm, Fri.-Sat. 5-10:30pm; under 18 admitted only on Fri-Sat. from 5-7pm. Closing hours flexible; call if arriving after 10:30pm. Non-smoking. Reservations strongly recommended.

Henderson's Salad Table and Wine Bar, 94 Hanover St. (tel. 225 2131), between George and Queen St. About the only cheap place in New Town without golden arches. Heaping dishes—*paella* to eggplant pasta, £3.20. Live piano and guitar music nightly from 7pm. Open Mon.-Sat. 8am-10:45pm, also Sun. 9am-9pm during the Festival. Farm shop upstairs sells lots of good organic stuff.

PUBS

It is difficult to find yourself without a pub in view anywhere in Edinburgh, but *The List* (£1.30), available at any news agent, will direct you to the most authentic ones and to the loci of student nightlife. Licensing laws are much more liberal than in England, so you can sample a pint of McEwan's real ale or Tennent's lager at just about any time of the day; most pubs open at 11am and remain open until at least 11pm, sometimes closing only at 4am.

Royal Mile pubs attract an older crowd, but **Scruffy Murphy's,** 49 George IV Bridge near St. Giles, and **The Ceilidh Bar** off High St. at South Bridge, are exceptions: students enjoy the nightly Irish and Scottish folk music. **Deacon Brodie's Tavern,** 435 Lawnmarket, pays homage to the multiple-personalitied Scot who inspired *Dr. Jekyll and Mr. Hyde;* prices are steeper, the atmosphere touristy.

Some of the best pubs in the Old Town are clustered around the university. Students booze it up to live music by the base of Candlemaker Row at the **Grassmarket.** Many also toast at the **Pear Tree,** 38 W. Nicolson St., with a large outdoor courtyard, and **Greyfriars Bobby's Bar,** 34 Candlemaker Row. Greyfriars Bobby himself, the loyal dog who guarded his master's grave for 14 years, is buried at the entrance to the cemetery next door. Look for his statue in the street median. Under the medieval arches of Cowgate, which runs parallel to the Royal Mile, you'll find **Bannermans,** 55 Niddry St. (try the fruit-flavored beer), and **The Green Tree,** 182-84 Cowgate, with cobbled interior arches. Try **Sneeky Pete's** at the west end of Cowgate for an after-hours pint. **The Laughing Duck,** 24 Howe St. (tel. 225 6711), offers a hectic gay and lesbian scene on Thursday nights. Just off Queen St., **The New Town Bar,** 26b Dublin St. (tel. 556 3971), is a frequent stop-over on the way to **Chapps** (see Entertainment, below). Near Broughton St. (the city's gay neighborhood) at Northumberland Place is the friendly **Star Tavern** (tel. 539 8070).

The adventurous may want to try the traditional pub crawl on **Rose Street,** in the New Town parallel to Princes St. The area has a dodgy reputation, so women especially should take care; to hear the locals, the devil himself drinks there at night. Traditionally, the pubs lining Rose St. brew their own, and the beer is much more alcoholic. Just across St. Andrew's Sq., the well-preserved **Café Royal Circle Bar,** 17a W. Register St., entertains Edinburgh yuppies and rugby fans amid antique portraits and a pre-Paleolithic hand-carved walnut gantry.

SIGHTS

Princes St. Gardens now occupy the drained loch which once protected the Old Town, the medieval center of Edinburgh. The **Royal Mile** (Lawnmarket, High St., and Canongate) spills downhill through the middle of the Old Town, from Edinburgh Castle to the Palace of Holyrood. Lined with historic buildings, the Mile is one of the great tourist walks in Britain. Today the Old Town has little to fear except perhaps a yuppie invasion from New Town; this classically Georgian area north of town center houses much of the municipal, professional, and financial life of the city.

Try to take an Old Town walking tour. Student-run evening tours tend to be the most humorous and informative. **Mercat Tours** (tel. 661 4541) offers a variety of routes and themes, one of the most interesting of which plays on the witchhunt obsession that King James VI (of Scotland) and I (of England) brought from the continent to Scotland after his marriage to Anne of Denmark (£4, student £3.50, children £2). Walks leave from the Mercat Cross before St. Giles Cathedral at 11am and 2pm and from the tourist office at Waverly Station at 10:30am and 1:30pm. The **Ghost and Ghouls** horror walk (daily 7 and 8pm; Oct.-May 8pm only; 1½hr.) departs from Mercat Cross (Satan's ancient rendezvous) and ends with refreshments at a local inn (£4; with drink £5). **Robin's Tours** (tel. 661 0125) will also take you around the Royal Mile and Old Town (history by day, horror by night; £4, students £3.50, children £2; 2-hr. walk; disabled access). Neither Mercat nor Robin's require advance reservations. **The Witchery's** *Ghosts and Gore and Murder and Mystery* evening tours (£5) require advance booking (24-hr. info tel. (01839) 202 066; booking tel. 225 6745), but are well worth it (they're led by officially deceased guides). **Guide Friday's** open-top Edinburgh bus tour sweeps you off your feet as a guide points from the roof of a doubledecker to sights including the cemeteries where the notorious bodysnatchers, Burke and Hare, practiced their craft (£5.50, students and seniors £4). Tours leave from Waverly Bridge, and tickets may be used all day to get around town and obtain discounts at many area sights.

The Royal Mile

At the top of the Royal Mile, **Edinburgh Castle** (tel. 225 9846) glowers over the city from the peak of an extinct volcano. Those willing to pay royally at the gate will find the Scottish Crown Jewels within, as well as a view north all the way to Fife from the battlements. (If you're running low on funds, know that this view is available at other prominent spots in the city, such as the Nelson monument, without the admission fee and the hour-long wait common on summer afternoons at the castle.) Tours leave every 15 minutes just inside the walls. Tour guides revel in recounting how many Englishmen fell in various attempts to take the stronghold. Inside the castle is **St. Margaret's Chapel,** a Norman church that dates back to the 12th century and is believed to be the oldest structure in Edinburgh. The Scottish Crown Regalia (crown, scepter, and sword of state), the oldest in Europe, was hidden from Oliver Cromwell and eventually rediscovered in 1818 by the ubiquitous Sir Walter Scott. The state apartments include Queen Mary's bedroom and the French prison where prisoners from Napoleon's armies scratched *graffiti français* on the ancient walls. (Open Mon.-Sun. 9:30am-6pm, last admission 5:15pm; Oct.-March Mon.-Sun. 9:30am-5pm, last admission 4:15pm. £4, children £1.)

The walk along the **Royal Mile** from the castle to the palace passes some of Edinburgh's most quintessential old houses and attractions. Because space on the Royal Mile was limited, shopfronts are narrow and buildings rise to five and six stories. The 1620 tenement **Gladstone's Land** (tel. 226 5856), behind the sprawling pig at 483 Lawnmarket, is the oldest surviving house on the route; inside, everything remains as it was almost 400 years ago, right down to the piebald rat and the wooden ceilings painted with bouncing citrus fruits. (Open April-Oct. Mon.-Sat. 10am-5pm, Sun. 2-5pm, last admission 4:30pm. £2.40, students £1.20.) Through the passage at 477 Lawnmarket is **Lady Stair's House,** a 17th-century townhouse. It is now the home not of Lady Stair but of **The Writer's Museum** (tel. 529 4901), a reliquary of memorabilia and manuscripts belonging to three of Scotland's greatest literary figures—Robert Burns, Sir Walter Scott, and Robert Louis Stevenson. (Open Mon.-Sat. 10am-6pm, during Festival also Sun. 2-5pm; Oct.-May Mon.-Sat. 10am-5pm. Free.) If you drift over George IV Bridge you'll come to the 1620 **Greyfriars Kirk,** in a beautiful churchyard beyond the gates atop Candlemaker Row; linguistics mavens can hear Gaelic services here Sundays at 12:30pm (disabled access). Look for the grave of that loyal dog Greyfriars Bobby in front of the Church.

Where Lawnmarket becomes High St., the Mile is dominated by the principal church of Scotland: **St. Giles Cathedral** (tel. 225 9442), properly called the High Kirk of St. Giles. For two brief spells in Scotland's turbulent religious history, this church was pressed into service as an Episcopal cathedral, against the will of some of the local citizens. From the pulpit of St. Giles, John Knox delivered the fiery Presbyterian sermons that drove Mary Queen of Scots into exile. A series of spectacular stained-glass windows provide a little light in the nearly 800-year-old church—its crown spire is one of Edinburgh's hallmarks (open daily 9am-7pm; Sept.-Easter 9am-5pm; free; donation requested in Thistle Chapel).

Behind St. Giles in Parliament Sq. is the old **Parliament House** (tel. 225 2595), known for its unique dropped-beam ceiling and fine stained glass. The building now houses the Supreme Court of Scotland, and you can drop by in the morning to see bewigged barristers plead criminal cases before red-robed judges (open Tues.-Fri. 9:30am-4:30pm; free). A few more blocks along the Mile is **John Knox House,** 45 High St. (tel. 556 9579), a rigid and austere example of old Edinburgh housing. Restoration has revealed the original walls, fireplaces, and painted ceiling (open Mon.-Sat. 10am-4:30pm; £1.25, students and seniors £1, children 75p.)

Canongate isn't just the fall of great books. It's also the last segment of the Royal Mile. It was once a separate burgh and a part of the Augustinian abbey that gave the royal palace its ecclesiastical name. Sixteenth-century **Huntly House** (tel. 225 2424, ext. 4142), a nobleman's mansion, contains Edinburgh's chief museum of local history and tableware. The **Museum of Childhood,** 42 High St. (tel. 225 2424, ext. 4142)—"the noisiest museum in the world"—displays dolls, games, rods, and canes, and also sketches children's health and education through the centuries (same hours as Huntly House; also free). **Canongate Tolbooth** (1591), with its beautiful clockface projecting over the Royal Mile, houses **The People's Story Museum** (tel. 225 2424, ext. 4057), which honors the workers who built Edinburgh with reconstructions of settings from everyday life in the past, including a pub and a prison cell. All Canongate museums are open Mon.-Sat. 10am-6pm, during Festival also Sun. 2-5pm; Oct.-May Mon.-Sat. 10am-5pm. All are free.

The spectacular **Palace of Holyroodhouse** (tel. 556 7371), at the eastern end of the Royal Mile, abuts Holyrood Park and the peak of Arthur's Seat (see Gardens and Parks below). This ancient Stuart palace dates from the 16th and 17th centuries and served as the home of Mary Queen of Scots; it remains Queen Elizabeth II's official residence in Scotland (open Mon.-Sat. 9:30am-5:15pm, Sun. 10:30am-4:30pm; Nov.-March Mon.-Sat. 9:30am-3:45pm; closed during official residences in late May and late June-early July; £3.50, seniors £3, children £1.80, family £9).

When in residence, royalty attend services at **Canongate Kirk,** a lovely 17th-century chapel up the Mile and opposite Huntsly House. The economist Adam Smith and Robert Burns' beloved Clarinda, though unlikely bedfellows, lie together in the kirkyard. Get keys to the church at the Manse, towards Holyrood Palace on the left.

South of the Mile on Chambers St. is the Old College of **Edinburgh University,** with numerous exhibits and events year-round. Nearby, the **Royal Museum of Scotland** (tel. 225 7534) has a large collection of decorative art, exhibits on archaeology, geology, and natural history, and free gallery talks (open Mon.-Sat. 10am-5pm, Sun. noon-5pm; free).

The New Town

Edinburgh's **New Town** is a masterpiece of Georgian planning. James Craig, a 23-year-old architect, won the city-planning contest in 1767 with his rectangular, symmetrical gridiron of three main parallel streets (Queen, George, and Princes) linking two large squares (Charlotte and St. Andrew). Queen and Princes, the outer streets, were built up only on one side to allow views onto the Firth of Forth and the Old Town, respectively. The **New Town Conservation Centre,** 13A Dundas St. (tel. 557 5222), will answer your questions about the area and direct you on your merry way. They also provide a number of thoroughly researched booklets: *4 Walks in Edinburgh New Town* (free) and *New Town Guide,* by Colin McWilliam (£2) are especially well-conceived (open Mon.-Fri. 9am-1pm and 2-5pm).

For a self-guided tour, start at **St. Andrew Square** and walk west up George St. to the subtly labeled **Georgian House,** 7 Charlotte Sq., an restored townhouse where guides named George dedicate themselves to recalling how late 18th-century aristocrats hung their hats, entertained their guests, and even relieved themselves. (Open April-Oct. Mon.-Sat. 10am-5pm, Sun. 2-5pm. £3, children and students £1.50.) Nearby, at no. 19, gawk from the pavement at the **birthplace of Alexander Graham Bell.** West of Charlotte Sq. and across Queensferry St. is the **West End,** another elegant Georgian neighborhood; the impressive neo-Gothic **St. Mary's Episcopal Cathedral** on Palmerston Place (tel. 225 6293) merits a visit (open Mon.-Fri. 7:30-9pm, Sat. 7:30am-5:30pm, Sun. 7:30am-4pm; free).

The chandliered **Assembly Rooms** (tel. 220 4348), east of Charlotte Sq. on George St., shine as one of the glories of classical Edinburgh. They host all kinds of performances in the Festival and during summer. On Princes St. between The Mound and Waverley Bridge is the **Walter Scott Monument** (tel. 225 2424, ext. 4068), a grotesque Gothic spire once called "a steeple without a church." Climb the winding 287-step staircase for £1 and get an eagle's-eye view of Princes St. Gardens, the castle, and Old Town's Market St. (open Mon.-Sat. 9am-6pm; Oct.-March Mon. and Sat. 9am-3pm). Statues of Scott and his dog sit inside the spire.

At the eastern end of the New Town, Robert Adam's 1774 **Register House** (tel. 556 6585) guards the busy intersection of Princes St. and North Bridge. The Register House was one of the first structures erected on the north side of the loch, which, drained of its 12 million gallons of water, now forms Princes St. Garden and Waverley Sq. (exhibition open Mon.-Fri. 9am-4:30pm; free). Beyond Register House is **Calton Hill,** from which the 143-step **Nelson Monument** (tel. 556 2716; open Mon. 1-6pm, Tues.-Sat. 10am-6pm; Oct.-March Tues.-Sat. 10am-3pm, Mon. 1-3pm; £1) provides as fine a view of the city and the Firth of Forth as you will get at the Edinburgh Castle (where it will cost you £4). Calton Hill also supports an *ersatz* Parthenon built, oddly enough, to commemorate those killed in the Napoleonic Wars, and the **City Observatory** (tel. 556 4365), where you can see a 20-minute 3-D video on Edinburgh's history (every 30 min.; open July-Aug. daily 10:30am-5:30pm; £1.70; showings April-June and Sept.-Oct. Mon.-Fri. 2-5pm, Sat.-Sun. 10:30am-5pm; students, children and seniors £1). Unfortunately, the builders of the observatory ran out of money and failed to build the planned telescope.

Galleries

The *Edinburgh Gallery Guide* at the tourist office will lead you through the marble halls of Edinburgh's vast and varied, though somewhat musty, collections. On The Mound between the two halves of Princes St. Gardens, the **National Gallery of Scotland** (tel. 556 8921) stashes a small but superb collection of works by Renaissance, Romantic, and Impressionist masters, including three Raphaels, two stern-looking Bernini busts, and Gainsborough's ravishing Mrs. Graham. The lower floor houses a fine spread of Scottish art. (Open Mon.-Sat. 10am-5pm, Sun. 2-5pm; during Festival Mon.-Sat. 10am-6pm, Sun. 11am-6pm; free.) Draped in yellow gorsebushes,

Queen Victoria perches atop the **Royal Scottish Academy** (tel. 225 6671) next door at Princes St. and The Mound (same hours; admission £1-3 depending on traveling exhibit). Summer travelers inclined to splashes and dashes, spots and dots will enjoy the annual exhibits of Scottish modern art. Beneath The Mound down Market St. are galleries of a similarly newish bent. The **FruitMarket Gallery** flaunts cheeky modern artworks (open Tues.-Sat. 11am-6pm; free). Explore material and space at **The City Art Centre,** 2 Market St. (tel. 529 3541), where exhibits of Scottish modern artwork slip away faster than Dali's clocks.

The **Scottish National Portrait Gallery,** 1 Queen St. (tel. 556 8921), north of St. Andrew Sq., mounts the mugs of famous Scots. The standing exhibition on the royal house of Stewart includes a fingerbone of Robert the Bruce and a sensuous portrait of the young, hot, and corpulent Queen Anne (open Mon.-Sat. 10am-5pm; free).

West of the New Town, Palmerston Pl. leads down the hill past Douglas Gardens to the medieval village of **Dean,** on the banks of Leith Water (to the right) and which is preserved within the confines of the city. Several pleasant paths lead along the water to Belford Rd. to reach the Scottish **National Gallery of Modern Art** (tel. 556 8921), an excellent rotating collection that includes works by Braque, Matisse, and Picasso, as well as a disturbingly life-like statue of two American tourists. Take bus #13 if you don't want to walk the mile or so from Princes St. to Belford Rd. (same hours as National Gallery; free).

Gardens and Parks

Just off the eastern end of the Royal Mile, you can get a wee wink at the Highlands with a stroll through **Holyrood Park,** or a manageable 45-minute climb up **Arthur's Seat** (823 ft.)—the exposed volcanic summit offers a stunning view. The **Radical Road,** named for the politically extreme unemployed weavers who built it, allows a shorter walk up to the steep Salisbury Crags on the cityward side of Arthur's Seat. The park is best accessed from Holyrood Road, by the Palace, where a small tourist center displays information on the variegated history, geology, and wildlife of the park. Experts on natural history lead free walks every Sunday at 1:30pm beginning in late April (call 557 5762 for discussion topics and information on where to meet). More general walks leave on Wednesdays at 1:30pm from the Holyrood Lodge.

Hidden away from the city, the sleepy village of **Duddingston,** at the foot of Arthur's Seat, makes a great grazing stop—try the **Sheep's Heid Inn** (tel. 661 1020; take bus #42 or 46 from The Mound), Scotland's oldest licensed drinking establishment, with an ancient outdoor garden (open daily 11am-11pm). A smaller refuge, located directly in the city center, is **Princes St. Gardens,** a lush, green park where the castle's moat once festered. Lie out on the grass and listen to one of the numerous Scottish bands perform on early summer afternoons. The Scottish equivalent of miniature golf—minus the dinosaurs and windmills—is available at **Princes St. Putting** (open daily mid-April to mid-Sept. 10am-7:30pm; 18 holes £1.30, children and seniors 55p). Rent clubs at the tiny building in the Southwest corner of the main green. Those fond of hitting small objects with long sticks can also head to the **Meadows,** an enormous grassy park in southern Edinburgh that contains an impromptu golf course as well as public football fields and tennis courts. Melville Dr. bisects the park and connects with both Brougham St. (in the west) and South Clerk St. (in the east).

Edinburgh's requisite romantic oasis is the **Royal Botanic Gardens** on Inverleith Row (tel. 552 7171). Take bus #23 or 27 from Hanover St. and stroll around the splendid rock garden and plant houses (open daily 10am-8pm; March-April and Sept.-Oct. 10am-6pm; Nov.-Feb. 10am-4pm). The **Edinburgh Zoo,** 134 Corstorphine Rd. (tel. 334 9171), lies just outside the city to the west. Its extensive grounds offer penguins on parade in the summer daily at 2pm. (Open Mon.-Sat. 9am-6pm, Sun. 9:30am-6pm; Nov.-March Mon.-Sat. 9am-4:30pm, Sun. 9:30am-4:30pm. £4.80, children and seniors £2.50. Take bus #2, 26, 31, 69, 85, or 86.)

ENTERTAINMENT

The summer season overflows with music in the gardens, theater and film events, and *ceilidhs* (KAY-lees; bouts of country dancing, singing, and drinking)—and that's all *before* the Edinburgh International Festival comes to town. In winter, shorter days and the crush of students promote a flourishing nightlife. For details, no one does it better than *The List* (£1.30), a bi-weekly comprehensive guide to events in Glasgow and Edinburgh, at any local bookstore, newsstand, or record shop. Also useful is *Day by Day*, free from the tourist office.

King's Theatre, 2 Leven St. (tel. 229 1201), in Bruntsfield, sponsors touring productions of musicals and plays. The **Royal Lyceum Theatre,** Grindlay St. (tel. 229 9697), presents well-known comedies; the **Traverse Theatre,** Cambridge St. (tel. 228 1404), performs innovative, sometimes controversial drama. The **Playhouse Theatre,** Greenside Place (tel. 557 2590), often hosts musicals. Tickets for these theaters run £5-25. The **Netherbow Arts Centre,** 43 High St. (tel. 556 9579), stages more informal but equally delightful productions each week. Edinburgh University's **Bedlam Theatre,** 2 Forrest Rd. (tel. 225 9873), presents excellent student productions of both straight-laced and experimental drama in a converted church with a bedlam-red door. The best cinema in Edinburgh is the **Filmhouse,** 88 Lothian Rd. (tel. 228 2688), which shows a wide variety of classic and artfully obscure films (tickets from £1.50-3.60, weekday matinées students £1.50).

Thanks to an overabundance of university students who never let books get in the way of a good night out, Edinburgh's music scene is alive and well. Excellent, impromptu or professional folk sessions abound at almost every pub in Edinburgh. For jazz and blues, head to **Preservation Hall,** 9A Victoria St. (tel. 226 3816; open daily 1pm-1am). If you're going to keel over drunk, do it backwards, and look up at the humorous quotes from such odd characters as Woody Allen and Prince Philip. Jazz can also be found at **L'attache,** below **Platform 1,** Rutland St. (tel. 225 2433), **Navaar House Hotel** on Mayfield Gardens, and **McKirdy's,** 43 Assembly St. (tel. 553 6363). For a complete run-down of Edinburgh's jazz scene, pick up the *Jazz News* at the Jazz Festival Office, 116 Canongate (tel. 557 1642). For rock and progressive shows, try **The Venue** (tel. 557 3073) and **Calton Studios** (tel. 556 7066), both on Calton Rd. **Ripping Records,** 91 South Bridge (tel. 226 7010), and the **Virgin Megastore,** 131 Princes St. (tel. 225 4583), have calendars of most rock, reggae, and popular performances in Edinburgh, and sell tickets as well. Many of the university houses also sponsor live shows; look for flyers on walls near Bristo Sq. **Negociant's,** 45-47 Lothian St. (tel. 225 6313), is a pub with a wide range of Continental beers upstairs and frequent live shows downstairs, not to mention the best cappuccino in Edinburgh (open daily 9am-3am). The **Chapps Club,** 22 Greenside Pl. (tel. 558 1270; open 9:30pm-4am), and **The Sunday Club,** 12 Shandwick Pl. (open Sun. 11pm-4am), are popular night spots for gay men. Every Saturday night, the Calton comes out as **Joy,** Scotland's largest gay club (11pm-late, £3 before midnight, £5 after). For cabaret, The **Blue Moon Café,** Broughton St., and **Madisons** on Greenside Place are good gay and lesbian meeting places. (Madisons becomes the women-only **Women's Network Disco** on the first Friday of every month.)

The "Scottish Evenings" sponsored by many of the larger hotels are about as genuine as vegan haggis. Try the **Edinburgh Folk Club** (tel. 339 4083), which stages authentic performances on Wednesday nights at the **Café Royal Circle Bar** on West Register St. (shows at 8pm; £3). Scottish folk sessions just as good and £3 cheaper (free!) heat up nightly at the **Ceilidh Bar** (see Pubs, above). You'll also find Scottish bands and country dancing most evenings at the **Ross Open-Air Theatre** (tel. 529 7905), under the tent in Princes St. Gardens (usually begins about 7pm), and at a number of smaller local pubs. Edinburgh's **Folk Festival** is usually held in mid-April; for more information, try the **Edinburgh Folk Festival Society,** 16a Fleshmarket Close (tel. 224 2148).

EVENTS

The extraordinary **Edinburgh International Festival** (Aug. 13-Sept. 2 in 1995) ignites a massive bonfire of music, art, drama, and dance. For tickets and a full schedule of events, contact the **Festival Box Office,** 21 Market St. EH1 1BW (inquiries tel. 226 4001; bookings tel. 225 5756, fax 226 7669). Tickets (£2-44) are sold by phone and over the counter starting in the third week in April, and by post or fax from the second week in April. You can also get them at the door for most events. Look for half-price tickets in the Princes St. Gardens (1-5pm on day of performance).

Around the established festival has grown a more spontaneous **Festival Fringe,** which now includes over 500 amateur and professional companies presenting theater, comedy, children's shows, folk and classical music, poetry, dance, mime, opera, revue, and various exhibits. You may find the Fringe more whimsical and interesting than official offerings. Reviews of a few of the 1000-odd Fringe productions appear in most papers, *The List* (at any newsstand), and the *Festival Times* (free at the Fringe Festival Office). Or get the scoop on the best shows at some main haunts: the Fringe Club at the Teviot Row Union, the Pleasance Theatre on Pleasance St., the Gilded Balloon on Cowgate, the Assembly Rooms, the Theatre Workshop, and the Traverse Theatre. You can sometimes get free tickets from actors who give them away outside the Fringe Festival Office. Tickets are seldom over £6.

The *Fringe Programme* (available from the end of June) and the *Daily Diary* list necessary information on performances; get brochures and tickets by mail from the **Fringe Festival Office,** 180 High St., Edinburgh, Scotland EH1 1QS. (From outside Britain, include £1 (from EU countries) or £2 postage; cash, stamps, and foreign currency accepted; from within Great Britain, 60p.) Bookings can be made by post starting June 26, by phone (with a credit card) beginning July 3, and in person from Aug. 1 (inquiries tel. 226 5257, bookings tel. 226 5138; box office open Mon.-Fri. 10am-6pm; in Aug. and during the Festival daily 10am-7pm).

A number of other festivals also center around the same dates. Concurrent with the Edinburgh International Festival is the **Military Tattoo** (August 4-26 in 1994), performed nightly except Sunday in the Esplanade—a spectacle of military bands, bagpipes, drums, often featuring participants from other Commonwealth countries. Be prepared to sit next to a middle-aged couple from Maryland. For tickets (£7.50-15), contact the **Tattoo Office,** 22 Market St. EH1 1QB (tel. 225 1188; phone and post bookings from Jan. 1; open from first Mon. in July Mon.-Fri. 10am-4:30pm, Sat. 10am-12:30pm; on performance days, open until start of the show).

The **Edinburgh International Film Festival** also comes to town in August. For information, write to **Filmhouse,** 88 Lothian Rd., Edinburgh EH3 9BZ (tel. 228 2688). The Filmhouse box office sells festival tickets starting in early August. The **Edinburgh International Book Festival** emerges during August in odd-numbered years. Contact Waterstone's (tel. 225 3436) at 83 George St. for information.

The **Edinburgh International Jazz Festival** (Aug. 5-12 in 1994) opens with a day of free outdoor jazz at the Princes St. Gardens. Tickets (£8-15) are available at the **Ticket Centre** on Waverley Bridge from five days before the festival, by phone (tel. 557 1642; credit card required) and by post from the **Festival Office,** 116 Canongate EH8 8DD. The office stocks complete listings of events and venues.

The **Beltane Fires** is a primal festival occurring every May Day on Calton Hill. This pagan event begins with coal jumping around Calton Hill and then moves to Arthur's Seat at sunrise where, legend has it, those who wash their face with the morning dew will receive eternal youth (no tickets, no office, no towels).

■ NEAR EDINBURGH

Edinburgh's extensive bus service permits numerous daytrips from the city. South of the city, enjoy Scotland's beautiful countryside at **The Braids,** where a trail cuts through the woods around Braid Burn. From Braid Burn you can head up to **Blackford Hill** for a smashing view of the city. The **Braid Hermitage Nature Trail** is accessible from Braid Rd.; take bus #18, 40, or 41 from The Mound. The **Royal**

Observatory (tel. 668 8405), at the top of Blackford Hill, has Scotland's biggest telescope; take bus #40 or 41 (open Mon.-Fri. 10am-4pm, Sat.-Sun. noon-5pm; Oct.-Dec. Sat.-Thurs. 1-5pm, Fri. 1-9pm; Jan.-March. daily 1-5pm; £1.50, children 75p).

Bus #41 from Frederick St. runs to the placid, white-washed fishing village of **Cramond. Lauriston Castle,** 2a Cramond Rd. S. (tel. 336 2060), a mansion with a 16th-century tower house and 19th-century additions, exudes Edwardian privilege. Its gardens offer a good view of the Firth of Forth. (Guided tours only; open Sat.-Thurs. 11am-5pm; Nov.-March Sat.-Sun. 2-4pm; £2, seniors, students, and children £1.)

In **South Queensferry,** about 10 mi. west of the city center, stand two grandiose homes. **Hopetoun House** (tel. 331 2451) is the more spectacular, considered by most to be Scotland's stateliest "Adam" mansion, designed by 18th-century Scottish architect William Adam and his sons Robert and John. The house has a roof-top viewing platform which provides a panoramic vista of the Firth of Forth and its bridges (open mid-April-Sept. daily 10am-5:30pm, last entry 4:45pm; £3.80, students £3.10, children £1.90). **Dalmeny House** (tel. 331 1888), the first Tudor Gothic-style building in Scotland, boasts a grand hammer-beamed hall. Its **Napoleon Room** holds furniture that propped up the great general at the height of his glory and later in the despair of his exile on St. Helena. The **Rothschild Collection,** acquired through a strategic marriage, includes remarkable 18th-century French furniture, tapestries, and porcelain (open May-Sept. Mon.-Tues. noon-5:30pm, Sun. 1-5:30pm; £3.20, students £2.50). Take a bus from St. Andrew Sq. to Chapel Gate in the center of South Queensferry, then walk 1 mi. up the drive.

In **Penicuik,** 7 mi. south of Edinburgh, you can watch glass being blown and cut at the **Edinburgh Crystal Visitors Centre** (tel. (01968) 75128); take bus #81 or 87 from North Bridge or call to check whether the bus from Waverley Bridge is running (open Mon.-Sat. 9am-5pm, Sun. 11am-5pm; £2, ages 8-18 and seniors 50p, children under 8 deemed too clumsy). East of Penicuik in **Roslin** is the **Rosslyn Chapel.** Its exotic stone carvings raised eyebrows in late medieval Scotland. Venture past the simple exterior to the delightfully confused rib-vaulting of the Eastern chapels and the stone carvings of the Seven Acts of Mercy, the Seven Deadly Sins, the Dance of Death, and the Bagpiping Angels. The most famous part of the church is the pier known as Prentice Pillar, supposedly the work of an apprentice who was later killed by the jealous master mason (chapel open April-Oct. Mon.-Sat. 10am-5pm, Sun. noon-4:45pm; £2, students £1.50, children 75p). Roslin lies by the **Pentland Hills,** a superb hiking area and haunt of the stripling Robert Louis Stevenson.

■■■ THE BORDERS

Until 200 years ago, this 1800-square-mile region was caught in a tug-of-war between Scotland and England—ever since blue-painted Picts repelled Hadrian and his legions in the 2nd century. Signs of strife remain: fortified houses and castles brace the region and spectacular abbeys at Dryburgh, Jedburgh, Kelso, and Melrose lie in ruins. The fertile Borders region looks best when the sun brings out warm colors or when mists follow the soft rises of the land. As in Dumfries and Galloway, the narrow winding roads and spectacular hill paths of the Borders belong to walkers and cyclists.

While border disputes are a thing of the past, locals have not forgotten the key defensive role their villages played in Scottish history. Practically all villages hold annual **common ridings,** where "principals" lead their followers on horseback around the town limits to ensure that no encroaching clans have shifted a border-forming fence or stone. Spirits run high during these week-long festivals—pubs close for only two hours each day, and the locals go "stone mad." Definitely try to hit one of the common ridings—Hawick (first weekend in June); Selkirk, Peebles, or Melrose (second week in June); Jedburgh (first week in July); Kelso (mid-July); or Lauder (late July).

GETTING THERE & GETTING ABOUT

Trains don't run in the Borders, but **bus** service is frequent and cheap. Buses leave Edinburgh for Galashiels (16/day, Sun. 8/day; 1¼hr.; £3.15), connecting there with Melrose (frequent service; 15 min.; 98p); Jedburgh (14-15/day, Sun. 5/day; 45 min.; £2.35); and Kelso to the southeast (13-15/day, Sun. 5/day; 45min.; £2.35). Services also connect with the train at Berwick-upon-Tweed (£3.90), just across the English border on the east coast. No roads lead directly to Dumfries and Galloway in the west. To reach those areas from the Borders most efficiently, take bus #95 (Mon.-Sat. 7/day, Sun. 3/day) from Galashiels to Carlisle (£5.50), just across the English border on the west coast, then rail from Carlisle to Dumfries (£5.90).

Citylink/National Express no longer stop at Galashiels on their way from London to Edinburgh. The only way to get to Galashiels from the south is via Newcastle (**National Express #375**; Newcastle to Melrose is £4.75). Otherwise, you must head up to Edinburgh and then south to Galashiels on National Express #591 (London to Edinburgh to Galashiels; £32.65 single).

The regional **Reiver Rover** ticket allows one day's unlimited travel (£4.70, children £2.65; week £18, children £9) in the area delineated by Penicuik in the northwest, Dunbar in the northeast, and Berwick in the south. The **Waverley Wanderer** (£8; 1-week £23, children half-price) is valid within the Reiver area, extending north to Edinburgh (via routes from Penicuik, Galashiels, and Dunbar), and south to Carlisle. All area tourist offices provide free regional bus schedules. Single-day bus passes can be purchased from bus drivers or at bus stations.

Hitchers report the lethargy of Border hitching is least intense along the main roads; the A699 runs east-west between Selkirk and Kelso, the A68 connects Edinburgh to Newcastle via Jedburgh, and the A7 runs south through Galashiels and Selkirk en route to Carlisle. The labyrinth of B roads are even less traveled.

ACCOMMODATIONS

The six **HI Youth Hostels** of the Borders are strategically dispersed. Two of them provide footholds for an ascent into the Tweedsmuir Hills: **Broadmeadows,** west of Selkirk off the A708 (tel. (01750) 76262; grade 3; curfew 11pm, lockout 10:30am-5pm; £3.85, ages 5-17 £3.15; open April-Sept.) and **Snoot,** at Robertson, west of Hawick on the B711 (tel. (01450) 880259; grade 3; curfew 11pm; £3.85, ages 5-17 £3.15; open April-Sept.). The hostel at St. Abbs Head, just outside of **Coldingham** near the ocean, surveys the entire east coast and the eastern end of the Southern Upland Way (tel. (018907) 71298); grade 2; lockout 10:30am-5pm; curfew 11pm; £5.05, ages 5-17 £4.15; open April-Sept.). Ten mi. east of Coldingham, the **Abbey St. Bathans** hostel lies on the Southern Upland Way opposite the site of a 12th-century Cistercian priory (tel. (01361) 840311; grade 1; curfew 11:30pm; £6.50, ages 5-17 £5.50; open all year). Those hiking north from England on the Pennine Way must cry out the border password to the proprietor of the hostel in **Kirk Yetholm** (tel. (01573) 420631; grade 2; curfew 11pm; £5.05, ages 5-17 £4.15; open late March-Sept.), right on the border at the junction of B6352 and B6401 (served Mon.-Sat. by 5-7 buses/day, Sun. 3/day, from Kelso; ½hr.; £1.35, day return £2.30). The sixth hostel holds the town center in **Melrose** (see Melrose, below).

HIKING & BIKING

The Borders welcomes hikers of all levels and motivations; take a late afternoon stroll in the hills or wander the wilds for days at a time. Trails weave through the **Tweedsmuirs** (all over 2500 ft.) to the west along the A708 towards Moffat, as well as the **Cheviot Hills** to the southeast. Closer to Edinburgh, the **Moorfoots** and **Lammermuirs** offer gentler day walks. Ninety mi. of the 212-mi. **Southern Upland Way,** Scotland's longest footpath, wind through the Borders. The Way is clearly marked, and the Countryside Commission for Scotland annually publishes a free pamphlet with route and accommodations information. Retrace ancient footsteps along ways such as **Dere Street, Girthgate** (a pilgrimage from Edinburgh to Melrose Abbey), or **Minchmoore.** D.G. Moire tracks these trails in his booklet *Scottish Hill Tracks—Southern Scotland.*

Local tourist offices provide plenty of trail guides, including "walk cards" (20p) and Ordnance Survey (scale 1:50,000) Map Sheets #66, 67, 72-75, 78, 79, and 80 (£4.25), which provide a detailed overview of terrain. The **Scottish Borders Tourist Board offices** in Jedburgh (Murrays Green; tel. (01835) 63435 or 63688) and Selkirk (in the Municipal Buildings on High St.; tel. (01750) 20054) are quite helpful.

Both on- and off-road **biking** are ideal means of exploring the area. **Scottish Border Trails,** on Venlaw High Rd. in Peebles (tel. (01721) 722934), offers guided half-day and day tours (£10 and £16 respectively) and can organize accommodations. You can rent bikes at almost all the significant Border towns; the following cycle shops rent a range of bikes (£3.50-7.50), and give advice on routes: **Coldstream Cycles,** Gaurds Rd. Industrial Park (tel. (01890) 883456; **Hawick Cycle Centre,** 45 North Bridge St., Hawick (tel. (01450) 373352); **George Pennel Cycles,** 3 High St., Peebles (tel. (01721) 720844; open Tues.-Sun.); **On Yer Bike,** Dunsdale Rd., Selkirk (tel (01750) 20168); **Gala Cycles,** 58 High St., Galashiels (tel. (01896) 757587).

While a bit pricey, horseback riding is yet another good means of experiencing the Borders. The **Border Way Riding Center,** Yethouse Farm, Newcastleton (tel. (013873) 75642), will provide horses for trekking (£5/hr., £12/half day), as will **Bowhill Riding Center,** Bowhill, Selkirk (tel. (01750) 20192; from £4/hr.; open Easter-Oct.). The **SYHA Snoot hostel,** 7 Globe Crescent (tel. (01786) 51181), also arranges riding in July and August.

GALASHIELS

Tweed-bound professors and plaid-clad preppies can come home to "Gala," the birthplace of tartan and tweed and center of the woolen-weaving industry since the 13th century. A visit to **Peter Anderson's Woolen Mill and Museum,** Huddersfield St. (tel. 2091), will quench your curiosity about the history and manufacture of these famous fabrics, adored by lumberjacks, golfers, and kilt-clad Scots alike (open April-Oct. Mon.-Sat. 9am-5pm; also June-Sept. Sun. noon-5pm; tours Mon.-Fri. at 10:30 and 11:30am, 1:30 and 2:30pm; £1.50, under 14 free). The seasonal **tourist office** (tel. 55551) will help with transport connections (open July-Aug. Mon.-Sat. 10am-6:30pm, Sun. 1-5:30pm; April-May Mon.-Sat. 10am-5pm; June Mon.-Sat. 10am-5:30pm, Sun. 1-3pm; Sept. Mon.-Sat. 10am-5:30pm; Oct. Mon.-Sat. 10am-4:30pm). Or check with the tremendously friendly and helpful folks at the **bus station,** across Gala Water (tel. 752237; open Mon.-Fri. 9am-5pm, Sat. 9am-noon). Galashiels, the focal point for transportation in the Borders, sends buses west to Peebles (13-16/day, Sun. 6/day; 1hr.; £2.35), east to Kelso via Melrose (13-14/day, Sun. 5/day; 45 min.; £2.35), and north to Edinburgh (16/day, Sun. 8/day; 1¼hrs.; £3.15). You may want to be on one of them. Galashiels's **telephone code** is 01896.

PEEBLES

Fifteen mi. west of Galashiels on the A72 and the River Tweed lies **Peebles,** a quiet and extraordinarly clean town and a good base for exploring the forests of **Tweed Valley, Glentree,** and **Cardrona,** as well as **Lindinny Wood.** Each forest has paths of varying lengths and degrees of difficulty; some can be tackled by mountain bike. (Check the tourist office for brochures.) The park-lined banks of the river also make for a pleasant picnic or stroll. Peeble's main thoroughfare is **High St.,** pressed in by innumerable old and immaculate buildings and woolen-wear shops. The **Tweeddale Museum** displays a rotating collection of Victorian and natural history knick-knacks; its **Secret Room** contains two enormous plaster ancient-style friezes, and the secret, appropriately enough, is still a secret. Upstairs, the **Art Gallery** houses temporary exhibits of surprisingly good contemporary art, often by local artists. All three museums are located at the Chambers Insitute on High St. (tel. 720123; open Mon.-Fri. 10am-1pm and 2-5pm, Sat-Sun. 2-5pm; Oct.-Easter Mon.-Fri. 10am-1pm and 2-5pm; free). Two houses with famous former occupants book-end High St.: Mungo Park, the explorer and missionary of Africa, lived at the corner of High and

Broad-gauged, and John Buchan, whose novels include *The Thirty-Nine Steps*, lived in a house on the street's west end. On Cross Rd., the 13th-century ruins of **Cross Kirk** in a small wooded park evoke Ivanhoe-spiked daydreams. Across town in the Cemetery stands **St. Andrew's Tower,** the ruins of which were used as stables by Cromwell's troops. At **Neidpath Castle** (tel. 720333), 1 mi. west of town on the A72, you can visit the dungeon or relish great views of River Tweed (open Easter-Sept. Mon.-Sat. 11am-5pm, Sun. 1-5pm; £2, seniors £1.50, ages 5-15 £1).

Rest up, for tomorrow is another day, at **Mrs. O'Hara's,** Rowanbrae, 103 Northgate (tel. 721630; £14). Campers find comfort at the **Rosetta Camping and Caravan Park,** (tel. 720770; £3/person; open April-Oct.), a 10-minute walk from town center on the wooded grounds of the Rosetta House. The former owner of the House accompanied Abercromby to Egypt to secure the Rosetta Stone for England. The **Sunflower Restaurant,** 4 Bridgegate, offers home-made gourmet meals that, for the lucky few, hark back to summer in Provence. Pricey but delicious, with blackcurrant and ginger coulis or tomato and basil quiche for £5 (open Tues.-Sat. 9am-5:30pm and 7:30-8:45pm, Sun. noon-2:30pm and 7-8:30pm, Oct.-Easter Tues.-Wed. 9am-5:30pm, Thurs.-Sat. 9am-5:30pm and 7:30-8:45pm, Sun. noon-2:30pm and 7-8:30pm). At **Big Eb's,** across the road at 14-16 Northgate, the friendly proprietor ladles out a healthy dollop of travel experience with his excellent fish and chips (£3.90 for sit-down, £2.35 for take-away; open daily until 11:30am-11pm).

The **tourist office** (tel. 20138), in the Chambers Institute on High St. sells a slew of local maps and walking guides; the *Peebles Tour Walk* (10p) is a good place to start (open July-Aug. Mon.-Sat. 9am-7pm, Sun. 1-6pm; April-May Mon.-Sat. 10am-5pm, Sun. 2-4pm; June and Sept. Mon.-Sat. 10am-5:30pm, Sun. 1-5pm; Oct. Mon.-Sat. 10am-12:30pm, Sun. 1:30-4:30pm). **Buses** edge from Edinburgh to Peebles (£2.55). Peebles's **telephone code** is 01721.

MELROSE

One of the loveliest of the region's towns, Melrose makes a solid touring base. Bike routes fan out from the town, and the **Eildon Hills,** an easy 4-mi. walk away, supply sweeping views across the Borders. Centerpiece of the town, **Melrose Abbey** was begun in 1136, destroyed in the early 12th century by the English, rebuilt in an ornate and Gothic style, then demolished again in 1545. Despite all this, the walls of the abbey are remarkably intact. Search amid the extensive foundations for a plaque marking the spot where Robert the Bruce's embalmed heart lies in a leaden casket (abbey open Mon.-Sat. 9:30am-6:30pm, Sun. 2-6:30pm; Oct.-March Mon.-Sat. 9:30am-4:30pm, Sun. 2-4:30pm; last admission 30 min. before closing; £2.50, seniors £1.50, children £1). Towards the B6361, gorgeous vintage autos and motorcycles, antique oil cans, cast-iron toy cars, and a very funky 24 horsepower Albion from 1909 jam the **Melrose Motor Museum** (open Easter to mid-Oct. daily 10:30am-5:30pm; £2, seniors and students £1.50, children 50p). Sir Walter Scott settled into his mock-Gothic **Abbotsford** estate, 2 mi. west of Melrose (tel. 752043), to write most of his Waverley novels (open mid-March to Oct. Mon.-Sat. 10am-5pm, Sun. 2-5pm; £2.60, children £1.30). For a rockin' good time, visit Melrose at the beginning of September for the annual **Melrose Music Festival.**

The well-equipped **HI Youth Hostel** (tel. 822521; grade 1) off High Rd., looks out of a magnificent stone mansion at Melrose Abbey. Magnificently equipped kitchens, laundry facilities (ask for change and soap at reception), and energetic, outgoing staff make you wish there were more reasons to stay. (Curfew 11:30pm. £6.50, under 18 £5.50, open all year). If you prefer B&B accommodations, stop by **Mrs. Aitken's Orchard House** (tel. 822005) at 17 High St. (£14). Camp at **Gibson Park Caravan Club Park,** High St. (tel. 822969; off-season booking (01342) 329644; £2-3.50/tent; arrive by 8pm; open April-Sept.). Though not known for its budget fare, Melrose does have the cafeteria-style **Abbey Mill Coffee Shop,** above the Abbey Mill Woolen Shop, Annay Rd. Homemade soups and hot dishes change daily (£1.20-3; open June-Oct. 9am-5pm). The charming pink **Melrose Station Restaurant,** Palma Place, in a renovated railway station, serves filled French baguettes (from £1.55) and stocks a salad bar (£1.75-2.50) at lunch (open Tues.-Sat. 10am-2pm and for dinner Thurs.-Sat. after 6:45pm, Sun. 10:30am-2pm). The seasonal **tourist office** (tel. 822555) is tucked away in a tiny garden across from the abbey on Abbey St. (open July-Aug. Mon.-Sat. 9:30am-6:30pm, Sun. 2-6:30pm; June and Sept. same days until 5:30pm; Oct. until 4:30pm; April-May Mon.-Sat. 9:30am-5pm). Melrose's **telephone code** is 01896.

JEDBURGH

Thirteen mi. south of Melrose bustles the town of Jedburgh (JED-burra), complete with abbey, castle gaol, and town trail. Founded in 1138 by King David I and dedicated to St. Mary, the **Jedburgh Abbey** suffered repeated attacks from 1237 until 1546, when the Earl of Hertford reduced it to rubble (open Mon.-Sat. 9:30am-6:30pm, Sun. 2-6:30pm; Oct.-March Mon.-Sat. 9:30am-4:30pm, Sun. 2-4:30pm; last admission 30 min. before closing; £2.50, seniors £1.50, children £1). Down Smiths Wynd on Queen St., the home of **Mary Queen of Scots** survives as one of the few remaining examples of a 16th-century fortified house. Mary lived here at the height of her popularity in 1566 when she came to confront the notorious outlaw Border Reivers and suffered a serious illness. Several years later, facing imprisonment and death, she is said to have wished aloud, "Would that I had died at Jedworth." Look for signs of bandaging on her gruesome death mask, used to hold her head together for the cast after it was messily hacked off. (Open March-mid-Nov. daily 10am-5pm; £1.20, seniors, students, and children 60p.) The **Castle Gaol** (tel. 63254) stands on Castlegate. Built in 1823 as a model prison, it failed miserably and is now a museum of social history (open Easter-Sept. Mon.-Sat. 10am-5pm, Sun. 1-5pm; 80p).

B&Bs pepper the town; look for the ubiquitous Scottish Tourist Board B&B signs. Across the street from Mary, Queen of Scots' House at 7 Queen St., **Mrs. Elliott** (tel. 862482), offers B&B (£12.50, £14 single). Star-gazers can camp at the **Jedwater Caravan Park** (tel. 840219), 4 mi. south of town center on the A68 and down an unposted road—keep your eyes peeled and don't forget to make a wish (£6.50-8.50/tent; arrive by midnight; open Easter-Oct.). You should not go hungry in handsome Jedburgh. Try the sweet **Brown Sugar Coffee Shop and Bakery,** 12 Canongate. Their quick snacks include burgers (£1.10-1.75), filled rolls (£1-1.70), and baked potatoes (95p-£1.50).

The **tourist office** (tel. 863435 or 863688) on Murrays Green, opposite the abbey, dispenses information (open July-Aug. Mon.-Sat. 9am-7pm, Sun. 10am-7pm; Sept-mid-Dec. Mon.-Sat. 10am-5pm, Sun. 2-5pm; Christmas-March Mon.-Fri. 10am-5pm, Sun. 2-5pm; April Mon.-Sat. 10am-5pm; May-June Mon.-Sat. 9:30am-5pm, Sun. 2-5pm). A **post office** rests at 37 High St (open Mon.-Fri. 9am-5:30pm, Sat. 9am-12:30pm). The **postal code** is TD8 6DG, and the **telephone code** 01835.

MAJESTIC HOMES OF THE BORDERS

The 800-year-old **Traquair House** (tel. (01896) 830323), the most ancient inhabited house in Scotland, stands 16 mi. west of Melrose off the A72 and then 1½ mi. from Innerleithen on the B709. The family treasures of the Stuarts of Traquair, including manuscripts, embroideries, and letters of the better-known Stuarts of Scotland, are displayed upstairs. Catherine Maxwell Stuart, the present resident, brews her own ale in the 200-year-old brewery below the chapel (beer tasting June-Sept. Fri. 3-4pm). The main gates to Traquair are permanently closed; legend has it that the Earl of Stair swore after Prince Charlie's defeat at Culloden in 1745 that they would not be reopened until another Stuart took the throne (open July-Aug. daily 10:30am-5:30pm; May-June and Sept. 12:30-5:30pm; last admission 5pm; £3.75, seniors £3.25, children £1.50). Ten mi. north of Melrose on the A68 near Lauder stands **Thirlestane Castle** (tel. (01578) 722430), easily accessible by bus. One of the most beautifully restored castles in Scotland, Thirlestane is worth a visit if only to relive its bloody history. Jealous nobles hanged a host of King James III's low-born supporters here in 1482. (Castle open July-Aug. Sun.-Fri. 2-5pm; May-June and Sept. Sun., Wed., and Thurs. 2-5pm; last entry 4:30pm. Grounds open May-Sept. noon-6pm; same days as the castle. £3.50; grounds only £1.) Five mi. southeast of Melrose idles **Dryburgh Abbey** (tel. (01835) 822381), where Sir Walter Scott is buried near his favorite overlook (open Mon.-Sat. 9:30am-6:30pm, Sun. 2-6:30pm; Oct.-March Mon.-Sat. 9:30am-4:30pm, Sun. 2-4:30pm; last admission 30 min. before closing; £2, seniors £1.25, children 75p).

Due east of Melrose in the town of Kelso, the home of the Duke of Roxburghe, **Floors Castle** (tel. (01573) 223333), endures the tourist masses. A yew in the gardens memorializes the site where James II was killed while inspecting a cannon. Try not to make the same mistake. (Open July-Aug. daily 10:30am-5:30pm; mid-April to June and Sept. Sun.-Thurs. 10:30am-5:30pm; Oct. Sun. and Wed. 10:30am-4:30pm. £3.40, seniors £2.60, children £1.70. Grounds only £1.60, children free.) Nearby on the A6089 is the Georgian **Mellerstain House** (tel. (01573) 410225), begun in 1725 by William Adam and later completed by his son Robert (open July-Aug. Sun.-Mon. 12:30-5pm; Easter, May-June, and Sept. Weds., Fri., and Sun. 12:30-5pm; £3.50, seniors and students £3, children £1.50). From Galashiels, bus #65 stops at Mellerstain House on its way to Kelso (Mon.-Fri. 3/day).

You haven't really experienced ornate until you've walked the sumptuous halls of **Manderston House** (tel. (01361) 883450), north of Kelso and 2 mi. east of the town of Duns on the A6105. The doors unclasp to a silver staircase, silk wallpaper, and a marble dairy and tower (open early May to Sept. Thurs. and Sun. 2-5:30pm; £3.90, children £1; grounds only £2, children 50p). The 18th-century Neo-Palladian **Paxton** mansion (tel. (01289) 386291) lies 5 mi. east of Berwick-upon-Tweed (open Easter-Oct. daily noon-5pm; last admission 4:15pm; £3.50, seniors £3, children £1.75).

■■■ DUMFRIES & GALLOWAY

The southernmost region of Scotland, Galloway derives its name from Welsh neighbors who, during the Middle Ages, dubbed the area *Galwyddel* ("Land of the stranger Gaels"). Dumfries tagged along in the 1974 county divisions, merging the town with the ancient kingdom. Through the centuries, the region has passed through the hands of stranger Romans, Vikings, and English feudal lords; independence was finally won in 1314 by Dumfrieshire native Robert the Bruce who returned from Ireland to wage a successful seven-year war against the English.

Although the region is known as Scotland's "quiet country," Dumfries and Galloway locals know how to celebrate as well as any Scots. Dumfries' **Guid Nychburris Festival** (geed NEE-burs) on the third Saturday in June lasts a full week. The **Dumfries and Galloway Arts Festival,** held throughout the region in various venues at the end of May, offers a variety of music, dance, and drama.

Public transportation here is notoriously expensive. Several bus companies crisscross the area; call **Western Scottish** at (01387) 53496, **McEwan's Service** at (01387) 710357, and **Nelson's Bus Company** at (01848) 330376 for schedule information or pick up local bus timetables at any area bus station or tourist office. Bikers will find the Galloway coast among the best touring areas in Scotland. Those hitching often try the A75.

STRANRAER

Located on the most western peninsula of Dumfries and Galloway, Stranraer (stren-RAHR) is *the* place to get a ferry to Northern Ireland—don't ask for more. Though not particularly interesting, the town is well-stocked with B&Bs; check the supplies on the A75 towards Newton Stewart (London Rd.). If you happen to get a hunger pang while waiting for your ferry/bus/train, don't despair. **Romano's,** 36-38 Charlotte St., has good, quick food at reasonable prices (open Mon.-Wed. 7:30am-10pm, Thurs.-Sat. 7:30am-11pm, Sun. 9am-9:30pm; Oct.-June Mon.-Sat. 8am-9:30pm, Sun. 9am-9:30pm). If you fancy some munchies for the ride, **Wm. Low Supermarket** is next door to the ferry terminal and offers much better deals than the rip-off cafeteria aboard ship (open Mon.-Wed. 8:30am-6pm, Thurs.-Fri. 8:30am-8pm, Sat. 8:30am-5:30pm, Sun. 10am-5pm). The beautiful gardens at **Castle Kennedy** (tel. 2024), 3 mi. east of Stranraer on the A75, merit a fly-by (gardens open April-Sept. daily 10am-5pm; £2, seniors £1.50, children £1; disabled access). Frequent buses run from Stranraer to the castle (#430; 17/day, Sun. 2/day; 56p).

The **tourist office** (tel. 702595) at 1 Bridge St. posts a list of B&Bs (open June-Sept. daily 9:30am-6pm, April-May and Oct. 9:30am-5pm.) Stanraer's **telephone code** is 01776. **Sealink ferries** leave for Larne, Northern Ireland and the **Seacat Hoverspeed** shudders through the Irish Sea to Belfast (see Essentials: Getting There—Between the Isles for complete information). From Stranraer, **buses** run to Dumfries (#500; 3/day, Sat. 2/day; 3hr.; £6.30) and Ayr and Glasgow (#303; 5-6/day, Sun. 4/day; change at Girvan; 2 hrs. to Ayr, £4.90; 4 hrs. to Glasgow, £6.60). Buses #920 and 921 lumber one to two times daily to London (9½hr.) via Carlisle (3hr.), Manchester (6hr.), and Birmingham (7½hr.).**Trains** connect Glasgow to Stranraer (7/day, Sun. 4/day; 2½hr.; £17.30).

WESTERN GALLOWAY

Western Galloway splits time between two peninsulas. On the eastern one, 8 mi. southwest of Stranraer on the A77, is the one-good-hour-should-do-it village of **Portpatrick.** On weekends, wealthy yacht owners sail here from Northern Ireland for Sunday lunch—you can stroll by the harbor with your crusty bread and overladen pack and lust after the good life. **Dunskey Castle** lies on a spectacular cliff overlooking the ocean, and the 1-mi. hike from Portpatrick harbor is at least worth a few yards of film. On the left side of the harbor as you face the water, a long flight of steps leads up to the path to the castle.

Portpatrick also marks one end of the **Southern Upland Way,** a 212-mi. footpath that cuts across the country to Cockburnspath, about 30 mi. east of Edinburgh. Long stretches of the Upland Way wind through uninhabited forest and barren moors. The path passes by **HI Youth Hostels** at **Kendoon, Wanlockhead, Broadmeadows,** and **Melrose;** you can also camp or find accommodations at small villages along the route (see area listings below for details). Write to the Dumfries Tourist Information Center, Whitesands, Dumfries DG1 2SB (tel. (01387) 53862), for details, or send £6.25 for a complete guide and map to the Southern Upland Way.

At **Sandhead,** on the eastern shore of the empty **Mull of Galloway** and south of Stranraer, three of the earliest Christian monuments in Britain, the eerie **Kirkmadrine Stones,** stand on a lonely wind-washed hill. The *chi-rho* symbol and other inscriptions date from the 5th or early 6th century. Bus #64 on the Stranraer-Portpatrick-Drummore line stops at Sandhead (9/day on school days, otherwise Mon.-Sat. 3-4/day; £1.18); from Sandhead follow the signposts for about 2 mi. off the A716. At the end of the peninsula—Scotland's southernmost point—a lighthouse stands on a seaswept 200-ft. cliff, 4 mi. from Drummore. Those more interested in basement railways than Christian monuments should visit **Little Wheels,** 6 Hill St. (tel. (01776) 810536), a model railway museum with over 100 yd. of landscaped track and a huge collection dating back to 1948 (open Easter-Oct. daily 11am-5pm; £1.25, seniors £1.05, children 90p).

To explore western Galloway's other peninsula, base yourself in **Newton Stewart. The Museum** (tel. (01671) 402106) on York Rd. has an interesting clutter of local artifacts—coal scuttles to ball gowns. (open July-Aug. daily 10am-12:30pm and 2-5pm; Easter-June and Sept.-Oct. Mon.-Sat. daily 2-5pm. Last entry ½hr. before closing. £1, seniors 50p, children 20p.) Amicable Mr. and Mrs. Stables, at the **Stables Guest House,** Corsbie Rd. (tel. (01671) 402157), have perfected the art of B&B-till-you-drop, using only a slice or two of otherworldly rhubarb pie and a healthy side of exuberant conversation. Immaculate, flowery rooms, with firm beds, tea and coffee, and TV (£14.50). The friendly **tourist office,** Dashwood Sq. (tel. (01671) 402431), books lodgings throughout the Galloway region (open July-Aug. daily 10am-6pm; Sept. and May-June 10am-5pm; Oct. and April10:30am-4:30pm).

The **HI Minnigaff Youth Hostel** (tel. (01671) 402211), in the town of **Minnigaff** adjacent to Newton Stewart, is rarely full, has a great warden, and is one of the best-equipped grade 3 hostels in Scotland. From Newton Stewart, cross the Cree Bridge

DUMFRIES AND GALLOWAY

at the end of town, and make the first left on Millcroft Rd.—the hostel is about ¼ mi. on the left. (Curfew 10:45pm, lockout 10:30am-5pm; £3.85, ages 5-17 £3.15; kitchen facilities, no showers.) From here, you can wander north to **Galloway Forest Park,** which surrounds Glentrool village. A 240-sq.-mi. inland reserve with many peaks over 2000 ft., the park offers great day hikes and camping. For information about the park, contact the Forestry Commission, Creebridge, Newton Stewart DG8 6AJ, Scotland (tel. (01671) 2420). Bus #500 leaves Newton Stewart for Dumfries (3/day, Sun. 2/day; 2¼hr.; £4.80).

St. Ninian founded the first Christian church in Scotland in 397 AD at **Whithorn Priory,** 45-47 George St., about 18 mi. south of Newton Stewart (call Whithorn Trust at (01988) 500508). The present priory, still being excavated, dates from the 12th century; a wealth of early Christian crosses reside in the museum next door (priory and dig open Easter-Oct. daily 10:30am-5pm; last tour 4pm; £2.70, children £1.50). Bus #415 runs from Newton Stewart (Mon.-Sat. 6-12/day, Sun. 3/day; 1hr.; return £2.70). Nearby, **St. Ninian's Cave,** the rocky hermitage of the saint, is now a modern place of pilgrimage. Follow the A746 south from Whithorn, turn left onto the A747 toward Isle of Whithorn, and take a right at the signpost for Physgill Lodge; a beautiful ¾-mi. walk leads from the car park to the cave.

The **Isle of Whithorn,** farther south, is an old port filled with creaking fishing boats. The 13th-century chapel on the headland to the south is supposedly on the site of St. Ninian's original chapel. As you curve around Burrow Head, go northwest to **Glenluce Abbey,** founded in 1192 by Roland, Earl of Galloway. Legend has it that Michael Scott, a 13th-century wizard, lured the black plague into the cellar of the abbey and starved it to death (open Mon.-Sat. 9:30am-6:30pm, Sun. 2-6:30pm; Oct.-March Sat. 9:30am-4:30pm, Sun. 2-4:30pm; £1.20, seniors and children 75p). From Newton Stewart, ask the driver on the Stranraer bus #500 to let you off at Glenluce (Mon.-Sat. 3/day, Sun. 2/day; return £3.50).

KIRKCUDBRIGHTSHIRE

Several peninsulas and 30 mi. to the east of Newton Stewart lies dignified old **Kirkcudbright** (car-COO-bree), also known as "the artists' town." Its angular High Street holds some lovely examples of old Scottish buildings and Georgian houses. An even older past whispers in the ruins of **MacLellan's Castle,** a 16th-century tower house near Harbour Square (open Mon.-Sat. 9:30am-6:30pm, Sun. 2-6:30pm; Oct.-March Sat. 9:30am-4pm, Sun. 2-4pm; £1.20, seniors, students, and children 75p).

Attracted by the town's colorful built and natural environment—a stunning harbor and many miles of quiet, verdant countryside—a circle of prominent Scottish painters and designers established themselves in Kirkcudbright in the 1890s and transformed it into a hotbed of artistic activity. Today, aspiring and established artists still flock to the town; public galleries and studios abound. An excellent gallery and audio-visual show detail this history at the new **Tolbooth Art Centre,** High St., in a building which once imprisoned mariner and occasional bassist John Paul Jones (tel. 331556; open July-Aug. 10am-6pm; May-June and Sept. Mon.-Sat. 11am-5pm; March-April and Oct. Mon.-Sat. 11am-4pm, Sun. 2-5pm; Nov.-Feb. Sat. 11am-4pm; £1.50, seniors and students 75p). A motley collection of local antiquities fill the **Stewartry Museum,** St. Mary's St., including the town's version of Elvis baked into shortbread: a piece of tree 157-layers-of-annual-growth-rings into which were found someone's carved initials (tel. 331643, same hours and prices as Tollbooth). At either museum, buy a ticket allowing entry into both (£2.50, seniors and students £1.25). The **tourist office** at Harbour Sq. can direct you to other galleries and workshops (tel. 330494; open July-Aug. daily 10am-6pm, March-June and Sept.-Oct. 10am-5pm). Kirkcudbright's **telephone code** is 01557. For a large room above a tidy fountained garden, contact gregarious **Mrs. McIlwraith** in her bright blue house at 22 Millburn St. (tel. 330056), who provides friendly B&B for £13.50. Buses #431 and 500 connect Kirkcudbright and Newton Stewart (6-7/day, Sun. 2/day; 1hr.; £2.95).

For an even quieter day, head northwest to hushed **Gatehouse of Fleet,** where a tiny **tourist office** in the car park will direct you to area attractions (tel. (01557)

814212; open Easter-Oct. daily 10am-6pm). Buses #500, 920, and 921 run between Stranraer and Dumfries via Gatehouses (Mon.-Sat. 5/day, Sun. 4/day). Here in the **Murray Arms,** Robert Burns penned the words to "Scots Wa Hae," a popular Scottish ditty. The banks of sleepy **Water of Fleet,** about 3 mi. north of Gatehouse of Fleet, turn richly gold in autumn. You can fish here with a permit obtainable from the Murray Arms Hotel in Gatehouse of Fleet for £7.50 a day (tel. (01557) 814207). About a mile west on the A75 is **Cardoness Castle,** a rocky stronghold of the McCullochs for five centuries. This is the only castle in Scotland with a two-seat toilet; if you ask nicely, the castle curator may let you try it out with a friend (castle open Mon.-Sat. 9:30am-6:30pm, Sun. 2-6:30pm; Oct.-March Sat. 9:30am-4pm, Sun. 2-4pm; £1.20, seniors and children 75p; toilet free). **Mossyard Beach,** a pleasant sandy beach, is sign-posted off the A75, 2 mi. from Gatehouse of Fleet.

Western Scottish buses fly northeast of Kircudbright on the A75 to **Castle Douglas** (6/day; £1.85), a lovely market town with a cattle auction and market every Tuesday. Nearby **Threave Garden** (tel (01556) 502575) bursts with blooms carefully pruned by students of the School of Gardening (open daily 9am-sunset; greenhouses open daily 9am-5:30pm; £2.80, children £1.40). Three mi. west of Castle Douglas on the A75 is the path to **Threave Castle,** built by Archibald the Grim, known for his hideous countenance in battle. Threave was the last stronghold of the despotic Earls of Douglas to surrender to James II in 1453; it was taken again and ravaged in 1640 by Covenanters. From the old tollhouse on the A75, follow the path until you see the roofless keep; when you ring the ship's bell nearby, a boatperson will arrive to row you across the River Dee. Enter the castle by crossing the bridge over the moat; the stouthearted can climb down the ladder into a tiny, dark dungeon (castle open April-Sept. Mon.-Sat. 9:30am-6:30pm, Sun. 2-6:30pm; last boat 6pm; ferry charge £1.50, seniors £1, children 75p).

B&Bs abound in Castle Douglas; the **tourist office,** Market Hill (tel. (01556) 502611), will help you find a room (open July-Aug. daily 10am-6pm; Easter-June and Sept.-Oct. 10am-5pm). Or try **Mrs. J. McAdam,** Whitepark Rd., (tel. (01556) 502114), a half mi. walk from the tourist office towards town (£12; open April-Oct.).

Head southeast from Castle Douglas (southwest from Dumfries) through the town of **Dalbeattie** to the beaches at **Sandyhill** and **Rockcliffe.** To get to the simple but charming **Kendoon Hostel (HI),** take the A713 north to Dalry, turn off and follow the A702 towards Moniaive for less than ¼ mi., then make a left onto B700 north towards Carsphairn. The hostel is 3 mi. ahead on your left (grade 3; no phone and no showers; £3.85, ages 5-17 £3.15).

DUMFRIESSHIRE

Dumfriesshire hangs its tam-o'-shanter upon tales of Robert the Bruce, who proclaimed himself King of Scotland after stabbing throne-contender Red Comyn at Greyfriars in Dumfries, and Robert Burns, who lived and wrote in Dumfries from 1791 until his death five years later in 1796. **Dumfries Town**'s central location and transportation connections make it the unofficial capital of southwestern Scotland.

The small, unobtrusive **Burns House,** Burns St. (tel. 55297), contains many of the poet's original manuscripts and portraits. Burns died here in 1796 after aggravating an illness by bathing—on a doctor's advice—in a nearby well (open Mon.-Sat. 10am-1pm and 2-5pm, Sun. 2-5pm; Oct.-March Tues.-Sat. 10am-1pm and 2-5pm; 80p, seniors, students, and children 40p). Nearby, in an ornate **mausoleum** in St. Michael's Kirkyard, the poet rests in peace, blissfully unaware that several Scottish towns continue to make livelihoods off his name. The **Dumfries Museum,** Church St. (tel. 53374), is a restored windmill with an interesting exhibit of local history, including witchcraft documents and gallows. Take a peek at the **camera obscura** used by past astronomers, operated by a lens at the top of the windmill which lets you look over all of the town (same hours as the Burns House; museum free; camera obscura 80p, seniors, students, and children 40p). The newly opened **Robert Burns Centre,** Mill Rd. (tel. 64808), contains dioramas, a bookshop, a scale model of 18th-century Dumfries Town, and, of course, Robert Burns paraphernalia. A 20-minute film runs through a sentimental version of Burns' life, focusing on his life in Dumfries and his inconstant love of pretty girls. (Open Mon.-Sat. 10am-8pm, Sun. 2-5pm; Oct.-March Tues.-Sat. 2-5pm; audiovisual 80p, students 40p). The **Old Bridge House Museum,** Mill Rd. (tel. 56904), is a bewildering quadruplet of Victorian and Edwardian rooms including an early dentist's office (complete with many, many teeth) and a nursery (open April-Sept. 10am-1pm and 2-5pm, Sun. 2-5pm; free).

For friendly B&B, head for **Mrs. P. McKie.** Several children and a lovely border collie make for a homey, if noisy, atmosphere at 41 Cardoness St. (tel. 52095), near the rail station (£12.50). Or try **Mrs. A. Prentice,** 3 N. Laurieknowe Pl. (tel. 54136), across the river (£14/person). The crowded Dumfries **tourist office,** at Whitesands next to the bus station (tel. 53862), houses a host of helpful pamphlets and other literature, including a shelf of Burns books (open daily 9:30am-6pm, Sept.-Oct. 9am-5pm, Nov.-March Mon.-Sat. 10am-1pm and 2-4:30pm, April-May daily 10am-5pm). Dumfries's **post office** is at 7 King St. (tel. 56690; open Mon.-Fri. 9am-5:30pm, Sat. 9am-12:30pm); its **postal code** is DG1 1AA. The **telephone code** is 01387.

For train information, call the Dumfries station (tel. 55115 or 64105; open Mon.-Sat. 6:15am-7:30pm, Sun. 11:10am-7:40pm). For bus information, call the regional bus office at (01345) 090510. Dumfries is easily reached by **rail;** an excellent route to the Borders is the Newcastle to Carlisle line (12/day, Sun. 2/day; 2½hr.; £15.50). Other routes head from Glasgow's Central Station (8/day, Sun. 2/day; 1¾hr.; £14.50) and London's Euston (8/day, Sun. 1/day; 5hr.; £47-57). **Lockers** at the station are £1-1.50. Direct **Western Scottish buses** head south from Glasgow's Anderston and Buchanan stations (Sun.-Thurs. 1/day, Fri.-Sat. 2/day; 2hr.; £6.50) and Edinburgh's St. Andrew's Sq. (Sun.-Thurs. 2-3/day, Fri.-Sat. 5/day; 3hr.; £5.20).

Seven mi. south of Dumfries on the B725, just beyond Glencaple, is triangular **Caerlaverock Castle** (car-LAV-rick), one of the finest medieval ruins in Scotland. Although no one is sure whether this strategic marvel was built for Scottish defense or English offense, the castle was seized by England's Edward I in 1300 and bandied about like a hot kipper (open Mon.-Sat. 9:30am-6:30pm, Sun. 2-6:30pm; Oct.-March Mon.-Sat. 9:30am-4:30pm, Sun. 2-4:30pm; £2, seniors £1.25, children 75p). **Western Scottish bus** #371 runs to the castle from Dumfries (Mon.-Fri. 5-6/day, Sat. 3-5/day, Sun. 2/day; ½hr.; £1.49). Many thumb along the B725 (Bankend Rd.); to get there from Whitesands at the center of Dumfries, turn left onto St. Michael's St., right onto Nithbank Ave., and left onto Bankend Rd.

Also within easy reach of Dumfries is **Sweetheart Abbey,** 7 mi. southwest along the A710. The abbey was founded by Lady Devorgilla Balliol in memory of her husband John. Lady Balliol is buried in the abbey with her husband's embalmed-and-probably-no-longer-sweet heart clutched to her breast. How romantic. One of the three Cistercian abbeys of Galloway, the rose-tinted limestone church dates from the 14th century (same hours as Caerlaverock Castle, but closed Thurs. afternoons and Fri. Oct.-March.; £1, children and seniors 50p). Take **Western Scottish** #372 to New Abbey from Dumfries's Whitesands depot (Mon.-Sat. 10/day, Sun. 5/day; 86p).

Nine mi. southeast of Dumfries, the church in **Ruthwell** contains the magnificent 7th-century **Ruthwell Cross.** The cross bears dense carvings of vine scrolls, animals, and beasts archetypal to Celtic art, as well as everyone's favorite Anglo-Saxon poem, *The Dream of the Rood,* in the margins. The carver of the poem left us with both the oldest extant specimen of writing in the English language and a source of grief for English students ever since. **Western Scottish buses** connect Dumfries and Ruthwell (Mon.-Sat. 1/hr., Sun. every 2hr.; £1.45).

Nearby **Wanlockhead** is Scotland's highest village, complete with nose bleeds, a **HI Youth Hostel** (tel. (01659) 74252; grade 2; £5.05, ages 5-17 £4.15; open daily; Oct.-March Sat. only). You can reach Wanlockhead by walking along the Southern Upland Way (see Portpatrick, below). Some opt to hitch along the B797, which branches off the A76 2 mi. south of Sanquhar, which in turn is miles downhill from Wanlockhead. Buses from Dumfries to either Ayr (#246) or Kilmarnock stop in Sanquhar (Mon.-Sat. 8-10/day, Sun. 6/day; 45min.; £1.75).

STRATHCLYDE

The green hills of Strathclyde were the property of the violent, blue-painted, and illiterate Picts well into the historical era. Taken over by renegade Irish in the 7th century, the area is now known less for angry wanna-be Smurfs than for an intriguing combination of urban sophistication and unvisited wilderness. Glasgow and its rich arts scene lies less than an hour from Arran, an island with more deer than people. As it sweeps west from relatively industrialized central Scotland, Strathclyde's topography trades the smooth tracts of southern Dumfries and Galloway and the Borders for the mountains, wind, and water of its northern, Hebridean neighbors. And near Oban, the Castle Aaaaaaa (of Monty Python fame) drops its jaw in amazement at the big tourist bucks Ayrshire makes off poet Robert Burns.

■■■ GLASGOW

Scotland's largest city matches Edinburgh's capital class with a boundless energy and continental elegance all its own. Glasgow University, half a millennium old, overlooks Kelvingrove Park; its vibrant student population of 13,000 spills into an innovative arts community and breeds a lively atmosphere. Named Cultural Capital of Europe 1990 (an honor bestowed at times upon Athens, Amsterdam, Paris, and Dublin), the city backs arts of all types, ranging from the only opera in Scotland to kilt-clad streetcorner bagpipers to outrageous drag-show club acts.

A small town until Scotland's union with England in 1707, Glasgow grew as it exploited new markets in the North American colonies. As shipbuilding and steel production prospered in the 19th century, a Victorian paradise took root above the ruins of the medieval city, second in importance only to London in the British Empire. In Glasgow's "Miles Better" campaign, sandblasters have refurbished abandoned Victorian tenements as an alternative to the grim concrete blocks that usually form council housing. Glasgow natives proudly argue that Edinburgh blows its budget on street-cleaners for the tourists but neglects its citizens, while Glasgow pours money into creating artistic and cultural outlets for all. The city, however, still has its rough areas, and care should be taken in less-touristed climes, particularly to the southeast of the city center around Glasgow Green.

GETTING THERE

Glasgow lies in central Scotland on the Firth of Clyde, 45 minutes due west from Edinburgh. The M8 motorway links east and west coasts and Scotland's two largest cities. All intercity **buses** (a thousand times cheaper than rail) leave Buchanan station. **Scottish Citylink/National Express** goes to Perth (5/day; 1¼hr.; £6.20), Aberdeen (1/hr. 7:45am-6:45pm; 3½hr.; £12.10), Edinburgh (Mon.-Sat. at least 5/hr., Sun. at least 1/hr.; 50 min.; £4), Oban (2-3/day; 3hr.; £9), and Inverness (9-10/day; 3-4hr.; £10.30). Glasgow's **Queen St. Station** serves **train** routes to the north and east: to Edinburgh (2/hr., Sun. 1/hr.; 50min.; £6.20), Aberdeen (1/hr., Sun. 6/day; 2½hr.; £31.50), Inverness (6/day; 3¼hr.; £25), Fort William (4/day, Sun. 2/day; 3½hr.; £20), and Thurso (4/day, Sun. 2/day; 7½hr.; £32.50). **Central Station** serves southern Scotland, England, and Wales. Trains run to Stranraer (7/day, Sun. 4/day; 2½hr.; £17.30), Ardrossan (for connections to Brodick on the Isle of Arran; 5/day; 1hr.; £3.40), and Dumfries (7/day, Sun. 2/day; 1¾hr.; £14.50). Many trains to Stranraer connect with the **ferries** to Larne in Northern Ireland or to Dublin. Sea passage for adults is discounted with a rail ticket. Students should check with the student travel offices at Glasgow University for cheap fares to Dublin via Stranraer.

Hitchhiking from Glasgow to Edinburgh is nigh impossible; those who try catch the M8 at the fork of Maryhill and Great Western Rd. (U: St. George's Cross), but many end up taking the bus (£3.50). Hitching out of Glasgow is difficult because of the size of the surrounding roads, the speed with which cars barrel down them, and the sprawling suburbs that surround the city. Thumbers going northwest usually venture up Great Western Rd. to the A82; those going northeast walk up Cumberland Rd. to the A80; those heading north take the short train ride to Balloch and hitch at the roundabout; travelers south take the bus to Calder Park Zoo and hitch in the layby on the old road.

ORIENTATION & PRACTICAL INFORMATION

The **city center,** with the remains of medieval Glasgow and a newer, gridded street system, is not at the center of the city, but rather on the north bank of the River Clyde. **George Square** is the physical center of town; the train and bus stations, tourist office, and cathedral are within a few blocks. To get to the tourist office from Central Station, exit onto Hope St., turn right and walk two blocks (ignoring the alleys), then right on St. Vincent St. The tourist office is 3½ blocks up on your right. From Buchanan Station, exit onto North Hanover at the opposite end of the station from the ticket information booth, and with your back to the station take a right and walk 2 blocks after Killermont St. to St. George's Square. Across the square, take a right onto St. Vincent Place and walk another half block.

Areas such as **Argyle and Sauchiehall Streets** have been renovated into pedestrian districts and now attract shoppers from as far away as Reykjavík as well as an international league of purse-snatchers and pickpockets; heed the signs and keep an eye on your belongings. Cheaper restaurants and pubs reside in the neighborhood along High St. south of the cathedral and near the river. A mile northwest of the downtown area, **Glasgow University** anchors a quiet neighborhood that harbors the youth hostels and the city's most attractive parks and museums.

Glasgow's transportation system includes suburban rail, a confusing variety of private local bus services, and the circular **Underground (U)** subway line. (U trains run Mon.-Sat. 6:30am-10:30pm, Sun. 11am-5:50pm; flat fare 50p.) Wave your hand to ensure that buses stop for you, and carry exact change (usually between 45-55p, depending on where you're going). Strathclyde Transport authority runs an immensely useful **Travel Centre** in St. Enoch's Square (U: St. Enoch), two blocks from Central Station (tel. 226 4826; open Mon.-Sat. 9:30am-5:30pm; phone inquiries Mon.-Sat. 7am-9pm, Sun. 9am-7:30pm). In addition to pointing you towards the best means of transportation, they can advise about various passes. Underground Season Tickets are a good deal at £4.50 for seven days, £16 for 28 days (half price for children; bring a photo and ID to the underground office at St. Enoch station).

Tourist Office: 35 St. Vincent Place, off George Sq. (tel. 204 4400), and south of Buchanan and Queen St. Stations, northeast of Central Station. U: Buchanan St. Travel bookshop, free room, bus, and cruise bookings, theater tickets, *bureau de change* (commission 2%). Pick up *What's On,* a free schedule of local events, the *Official Quick Guide to Glasgow* (£1), and *Where To Stay,* a full guide to lodgings (90p). Open June and Sept. Mon.-Sat. 9am-7pm, Sun. 10am-6pm; July-Aug. Mon.-Sat. 9am-8pm, Sun. 10am-6pm; Oct.-May Mon.-Sat. 9am-6pm, Sun. (only in May) 10am-6pm. **Walking tours** leave from the tourist office. **The Glasgow Walk:** Mon.-Fri. 6pm, Sun. 10:30am. **The Cathedral Walk:** Wed. and Sun. 2:15pm. Both walks 1½hr., May-Sept. only. Adults £3, seniors and children £2.

Financial Services: Most banks open Mon.-Fri. 9:30am-4:30pm, and some have Saturday hours. The tourist office operates a currency exchange with long hours and cut-throat rates in the Central train station. **Thomas Cook,** 15-17 Gordon St. (tel. 221 5522). Open Mon.-Sat. 9am-5:30pm. **American Express,** 115 Hope St. (tel. 221 4366; fax 204 2685). Mail held up to a month; no charge for nonmembers with AmEx Travelers Cheques; otherwise £1.50. Open Mon. and Wed.-Fri. 9am-5pm, Tues. 9:30am-5pm, Sat. 9am-noon.

Post Office: 1-5 George Sq. (tel. 242 4260). Open Mon.-Fri. 9am-5:30pm, Sat. 9am-12:30pm. Also **533 Sauchiehall St.,** open Mon.-Fri. 9am-5:30pm. **Postal Code:** G2 1AA.

Telephone Code: 0141.

Travel Center: Glasgow Travel Center, St. Enoch Sq. (tel. 226 4826). Open Mon.-Sat. 9:30am-5:30pm. Phone inquiries Mon.-Sat. 7am-9pm, Sun. 9am-7:30pm.

GLASGOW

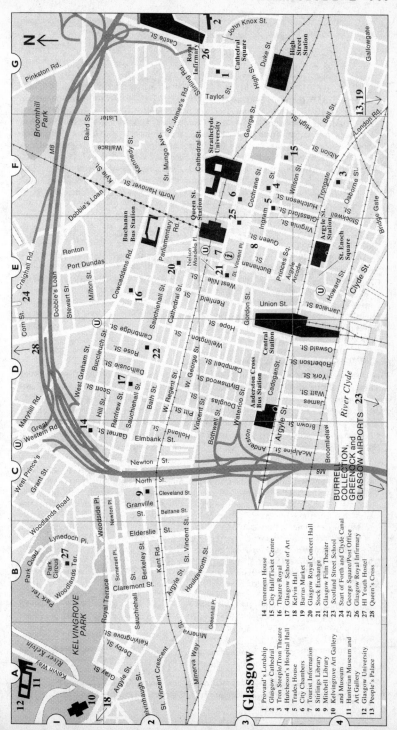

Glasgow

1 Provand's Lordship
2 Glasgow Cathedral
3 Tron Steeple/Tron Theatre
4 Hutcheson's Hospital Hall
5 Trades House
6 City Chambers
7 Tourist Information
8 Stirlings Library
9 Mitchell Library
10 Kelvingrove Art Gallery
   and Museum
11 Hunterian Museum and
   Art Gallery
12 Glasgow University
13 People's Palace
14 Tenement House
15 City Hall/Ticket Centre
16 Theatre Royal
17 Glasgow School of Art
18 Kelvin Hall
19 Barras Market
20 Glasgow Royal Concert Hall
21 Stock Exchange
22 Glasgow Film Theater
23 Scotland Street School
24 Start of Forth and Clyde Canal
25 George Square/Post Office
26 Glasgow Royal Infirmary
27 HI Youth Hostel
28 Queen's Cross

Train Stations: Central Station, Gordon St. (U: St. Enoch). **Lockers** £1-2. Open Mon.-Sat. 5am-12:30am, Sun. 7am-12:30am. Bathrooms 10p; shower with soap and towel, 65p (open Mon.-Sat. 5am-12:30am, Sun. 7am-12:30am). **Queen St. Station,** beside Coppthorne Hotel, George Sq. (U: Buchanan St.; open Mon.-Sat. 5am-12:30am, Sun. 7am-12:30am). Bathrooms 10p; no showers. Take bus #398 between the stations (4/hr.; 35p, seniors 25p, children 20p) or walk (8-10min.). **24-hr. passenger info:** tel. 204 2844; credit card purchases tel. (0800) 450450.

Bus Stations: Buchanan Station (tel. 332 9191), 2 blocks north of Queen St. Station on N. Hanover St. The travel center to the left of the main entrance houses **National Express** (tel. 332 4100) and **Scottish Citylink** (tel. 332 9191) offices. **Lockers** 50p-£1.50. **Anderston Station,** a few blocks beyond Central Station on Argyle St., launches intra-city and suburban journeys. Contact the Travel Centre at Buchanan bus station for information (tel. 332 9191).

Airport: Glasgow Airport (tel. 887 1111), 10 mi. west in Abbotsinch. Served by British Airways, Lufthansa, Northwest, American, Air Canada, Air UK, British Midland, Aer Lingus, Air France, and more. Frequent buses (service #500/501) run to Glasgow's Buchanan and Anderston stations, as well as to Edinburgh (4/hr., Sun. 2/hr.; 1¾hr.; £6) to Glasgow (20min.; £2).

Taxi: TOA Taxis, tel. 332 7070.

Launderette: Park Laundrette, 14 Park Rd. Open Mon.-Fri. 8:30am-8pm, Sat.-Sun. 9am-6:30pm.

Hotlines: Samaritans: tel. 248 4488. **Gay and Lesbian Switchboard:** tel. 221 8372; daily 7-10pm. **Rape Crisis:** tel. 221 8488.

Pharmacy: Boots, 200 Sauchiehall St. (tel. 332 1925). Sells everything: kitchen sinks £250. Open Mon.-Wed. 9am-5:30pm, Thurs. 8:45am-7pm, Fri.-Sat. 8:45am-6pm.

Hospital: Glasgow Royal Infirmary, 82 Castle St. (tel. 552 3535).

Emergency: Dial 999; no coins required.

Police: Stewart St. (tel. 332 1113).

ACCOMMODATIONS

Glasgow undergoes a perennial bed shortage in the hot months. Especially in August, book guesthouses, B&Bs, and hostels at least nine weeks in advance. Last-minute planners may wish to stay on the outskirts, particularly in the accessible and elegant **Loch Lomond Youth Hostel (HI),** less than an hour north (see Loch Lomond, below). If you enjoy paying £14 to £18 for yucky urban B&Bs, the tourist office can sometimes find you a room. If you'd rather wander, come early; most of Glasgow's B&Bs scatter to either side of the Great Western in the University area.

HI Youth Hostel, 7-8 Park Terrace, (tel. 332 3004; grade 1), 100m from the old hostel at 11 Woodlands Terrace and in a beautiful residential district overlooking Kelvingrove Park. U: St. George's Cross. From Central Station, take bus #44 or 59 and ask for the *first stop* on Woodlands Rd. (at Lynedoch St.). From Queen St. Station or Buchanan bus station take bus #11. Once the residence of an English nobleman and later an upscale hotel, this newly renovated hostel maintains an air of luxury, with plush halls, carved banisters, and a mirror-walled dining room. 4- to 6-person rooms boast *en suite* gold-fixtured bathrooms. For those fed up with "real" hostel living. TV and game rooms, bike shed, and in-house discotheque; no lockout; curfew 2am. £9.80, includes breakfast; ages 5-17 £8.45. Sheets 60p.

Glasgow Backpackers Hostel, Kelvin Lodge, 8 Park Circus, (tel. 332 5412). U: St. George's Cross. Sunny and spacious, mostly 3-bed rooms without bunkbeds. Laid-back atmosphere. Roomy kitchen; no lockout; ask for the free night key if you'll be out after 2:30am. Bath available (free). Open July to mid-Sept. £7.90 for dorm rooms, £8.90/person for doubles.

University of Glasgow, administrative offices at 52 Hillhead St. (tel. 330 5385; open Mon.-Fri. 9am-5pm). Summer housing at 6 college dorms. **Queen Margaret Hall,** 55 Bellshaugh Rd. (tel. 334 2192), near Byres Rd., provides tea, coffee, soap, towels, and linen. Free laundry. B&B: students £14.45, non-students £20.50. Without breakfast, students £9.40, non-students £11. **Maclay Hall,** 18 Park Terrace (tel. 332 5056), overlooking Kelvingrove Park, in an attractive, old building with big rooms, is nearer to the city center. B&(no)B. Students £9.40, non-students £11. Dorms have TV and laundry rooms. Open Easter and late June to late Sept.

University of Strathclyde provides B&B. **Baird Hall**, 460 Sauchiehall St. (tel. 332 6415). No kitchen (some microwaves and toasters); no lockout or curfew; laundry. Late June to early Sept.: singles £16, doubles £14.50/person. 11 guest rooms available all year: singles £22, doubles £18/person. **Clyde Hall**, 318 Clyde St. (tel. 221 1219), near U: St. Enoch, offers beds and optional breakfasts. Check-in noon-11pm. Kitchen; no curfew; no lockout. £10, with breakfast £16, doubles £29-35. Both dorms have disabled access. Open mid-June to Sept.

YMCA Aparthotel, David Naismith Court, 33 Petershill Dr. (tel. 558 6166). Take bus #12A, 16, or the M11 from Queen St. Station. Clean, institutional rooms. TV lounge; game room; no curfew. B&B: singles £16, doubles £13.50/person.

McLay's Guest House, 268 Renfew St. (tel. 332 4796). U: Charing Cross. Comfortable rooms near the intense scene at the Glasgow School of Art and Sauchiehall St. 64 rooms with satellite TV and tea/coffee. B&B: singles £17.50, with bath £19.50; doubles £33, with bath £37; family room (sleeps 4) £48, with bath £55.

Iona Guest House, 39 Hillhead St. (tel. 334 2346), near "The Hub," on a street lined with B&Bs. U: Hillhead. Stunning front hall. Subterranean breakfast nook and Laura Ashley rooms. Some good views of the city. Convenient to Byres Rd. and city center. Singles £20, doubles £16/person.

Alamo Guest House, 46 Gray St. (tel. 339 2395). Remember this: no Texas flags, just large, quiet rooms and congenial proprietors. All rooms £15/person.

FOOD

As is the case with many university towns, Glasgow has plenty of cheap hole-in-the-wall restaurants with great food, including many ethnic restaurants. Professors hold tête-à-têtes at the cafés behind Byres Rd. on **Ashton Lane,** a cobblestone alley lined with 19th-century brick facades. Bakeries along High St. below the cathedral serve scones for as little as 15p. For supermarkets, try the **Safeway** at 373 Byers Rd. (open Mon.-Fri. 8am-8pm, Sat. 8am-7pm, Sun. 9am-5pm); **Grassroots,** near the hostels at 48 Woodlands Rd., offers a delicious selection of wholefood (tel. 353 3278; open Mon.-Wed. and Fri.-Sat. 8:45am-6pm, Thurs. 8:45am-7pm, Sun. 11am-3pm).

The Bay Tree Vegetarian Café, 403 Great Western Rd. Vegans and vegetarians rejoice! Down the street from the hostel (and right next door to a butcher shop), this cooperative restaurant has superb hot meals (£3.50) and a selection of salads (large plate £3), hummus, and sinful desserts. Try the hot breakfast with vegetarian sausage, beans, mushrooms, tomatoes, and a potato scone (£2.70) all day Sunday, or a stupendous apricot cherry pie. Open Tues.-Sun. 10am-9pm.

Grosvenor Café, 31-35 Ashton Lane, in a walkway off the middle of Byres Rd. Behind U: Hillhead. Stuff yourself silly: most dishes dive under £1. Open Mon.-Sat. 9am-10:30pm, Sun. 11am-6pm.

The Basement Restaurant, 14 Otago St., beneath a contemporary art gallery. U: Kelvinbridge. Cluttered with paintings and gallery posters. Delicious, homemade vegetarian dishes. Quiche 95p, salads 70-90p. Open Mon.-Sat. 9:30am-5:30pm.

Magnus Dining Room, in the Glasgow University Refectory ("The Hub"), on Hillhead St. just above University Ave. U: Hillhead. The central student cafeteria with salad, snacks, and meals. Open Mon.-Thurs. 8:30am-6:10pm, Fri. 8:30am-3:30pm.

Strathclyde University Students' Union, on John St., two blocks from George Sq. Any student ID will allow you access. **Petit 4** is the cafeteria and **Red's** is the bar. Petit 4 open Mon.-Fri. 8am-3pm (until 6pm during the term). Red's is open Mon.-Wed. 11am-1am and Thurs.-Sat. 11am-2am.

PUBS

The path is long an' the ale is strong…

—unknown

There are hundreds of pubs in Glasgow, and you'll never find yourself more than half a block from a frothy pint. The infamous Byers Road pub crawl slithers past the

Glasgow University area, beginning at **Tennant's Bar** and then proceeding towards the River Clyde. Watch for Happy Hours when many pubs reduce drinks to £1.

Halt Bar, 160 Woodlands Rd., two blocks from the youth hostel. One side is dark and deafening, the other hot and humid. Attracts all sorts. Jazz on Tuesday nights, other live music on Wednesday night and Saturday afternoon. Monday is quiz night. Open Sun.-Thurs. 11am-11pm, Fri.-Sat. 11am-midnight.

O'Brien's Pub, 3A Park Terrace, steps from the HI hostel. A groovy spot with low ceilings and candles dripping on every table—the place to unwind with fellow hostelers after a day of travel. One *Let's Go* researcher stopped by and stayed for a week. Open Mon.-Sat. noon-11pm, Sun. 6-11pm.

Horseshoe Bar, 17-21 Drury St., in the city center. A magnificent Victorian horse-shoe-shaped bar, with etched mirrors and carved wooden walls. The longest continuous bar in the U.K.; 25 bartenders staff it when the mostly older crowd begins to swell. Head upstairs for a hearty 3-course pub lunch (Mon.-Sat. noon-2:30pm; £2.40). Open Mon.-Sat. 11am-midnight, Sun. 12:30pm-midnight.

Cul de Sac Bar, 46 Ashton Lane. *The* artsy hangout. Very chic, young clientele. Less a bar than a restaurant; less a restaurant than a way of life. Lots of vegetarian snacks and meals. Restaurant downstairs serves up magnificent crepes (£6.95). Happy Hour daily 5-7pm, drinks £1. Open Mon.-Thurs. noon-11pm, Fri.-Sat. noon-midnight, Sun. 12:30-11pm. Restaurant also open Sun. noon-11pm. A third off crepes and burgers 5-7pm.

Variety Bar, 401 Sauchiehall St. Older men's pub by day, art students' hangout by night. No frills, just a quality pub. DJ on Thurs. (acid jazz) and Sun. (house). Open daily 11am-midnight.

Nico's, 375 Sauchiehall St. French windows open to a beautifully-tiled interior. Clientele preens away the hours; live music once in a while. Lunch £2.95. Open Mon.-Fri. 8am-midnight, Sat. 10:30am-midnight, Sun. noon-midnight.

Blackfriars, 36 Bell St. at Albion St., near Glasgow Cross. U: Trongate. Popular with locals under 30. Live jazz on Thurs. and Sun. nights. Wash down a good cheap lunch with any of a wide range of real ales. Open Mon.-Sat. 11:30am-midnight, Sun. 12:30pm-midnight.

Ubiquitous Chip Bar, 12 Ashton Lane, near U: Hillhead, off Byres Rd. Old wood, stained glass, and quiet tables. Young would-be Burnses imbibe and local academics and writers converse. The restaurant, complete with jungle creepers and fish ponds, is one of the best in Glasgow (entrees £10-15). Bar open Mon.-Sat. noon-11pm, Sun. 12:30-11pm. Restaurant open Mon.-Sat. noon-2:30pm and 5:30-11pm.

SIGHTS

Begin your exploration of Glasgow at grassy George Square, a thankfully inefficient and green respite from this industrial city. From July to mid August, **The Glasgow Fling** seeds the city with highland dancers, country dancers, and pipe bands (Wed. and Fri.-Sat. noon-1:30pm). From the square, walk west along Sauchiehall St. (which joins Argyle and Dumbarton St.) to Kelvingrove Park and Byres Rd. City **bus tours** leave from George Sq. (2/hr.; 9:30am-4:30pm; £4.50; reserve at the tourist office).

The Gothic **Glasgow Cathedral,** near the center of town on Castle St., is the only full-scale cathedral spared by the fury of the mid-16th century Scottish Reformation. The downstairs Laigh Kirk, sole remnant of the original 12th-century building, shelters the tomb of St. Mungo, patron saint of Glasgow. Next door is the entrance to the giant **necropolis,** where most of the city's 19th-century industrialists are lain. To reach the cathedral, walk to the eastern end of Cathedral St., which runs behind Queen St. Station (cathedral open Mon.-Sat. 9:30am-6pm, Sun. 2-5pm; Oct.-March Mon.-Sat. 9:30am-4pm, Sun. 2-4pm; free). Near the Cathedral, the newly-opened **St. Mungo Museum of Religious Life and Art** surveys world religions from Mormon to Hindu to Native American and Yoruba, with an impressive, well-presented collection of photos and artifacts (open Mon.-Sat. 10am-5pm, Sun. 11am-5pm; free).

In their eagerness to join the Industrial Revolution, Glaswegians destroyed most proof of their medieval past, only to later recreate it at the **People's Palace,** a museum and greenhouse on Glasgow Green by the river (open Mon.-Sat. 10am-

5pm, Sun. 11am-5pm; free). Take care crossing the Green even during the day; it is home to many of Glasgow's less savory characters. The city owes most of its present-day architecture to a flurry of construction during the Victorian age. Most of the interesting buildings are used as government or private offices and are closed to the public, but they still merit a look from the outside. The **City Chambers,** George Sq., conceal a wonderfully ornate marble interior in Italian Renaissance style (**free tours** Mon.-Wed. and Fri. at 10:30am and 2:30pm; depart from the main entrance).

Several buildings designed by Charles Rennie Mackintosh, Scotland's most famous architect, are open to the public. The most notable example is the **Glasgow School of Art,** 167 Renfrew St., completed in 1898. Here, Mackintosh fused wrought iron art nouveau with Scottish Baronial to obtain a proto-modernist salad (interior tours Mon.-Fri. 11am, 2pm, and 3pm; Sat. 10:30am; Oct.-April Mon.-Fri. 1pm and 2pm, Sat. 10:30am; £2). The Charles Rennie Mackintosh Society has headquarters at **Queen's Cross,** 870 Garscube Rd. (tel. 946 6600), a church designed by the batty genius (open Tues. and Thurs.-Fri. noon-5pm, Sun. 2:30-5pm; free).

Rounded crescents and elegant parks in the West End's residential **Park Circus** area, near the youth hostels, present intact examples of early Victorian terracing. Recently bequeathed by its owners, the **Tenement House,** a late 18th-century apartment on 145 Buccleuch St. (U: Cowcaddens), has been carefully restored to its pristine state by the National Trust for Scotland (open daily 1:30-5pm, last entry 4:30pm; Nov.-Easter Sat.-Sun. 2-4pm; £2, children and seniors £1).

Starting one block west of Park Circus is **Kelvingrove Park,** a large wooded expanse on the banks of the River Kelvin, where locals tan on the grassy slopes and university students make out behind trees. At the center of the park's winding paths and glades is a fountain emblazoned with houses of the zodiac. In the southwest corner of the park, just off the intersection of Argyle and Sauchiehall St., rests the spired **Art Gallery and Museum** (U: Kelvin Hall). The art collection ranges from Rembrandt to Dalí, while the ground floor is devoted to natural history and wildlife (open Mon.-Sat. 10am-5pm, Sun. 11am-5pm; free).

Kelvin Hall combines a complete public sports complex and a dazzling museum on Dumbarton Rd. The **Museum of Transport,** in the Hall's rear half, houses a collection of full-scale original trains, trams, and automobiles inside an immense warehouse (open Mon.-Sat. 10am-5pm, Sun. 11am-5pm; free). Walk west from the Hall to the bridge over the River Kelvin, from which you can view the yin and yang of Glasgow's architecture: to the south looms a sooty smokestack, to the north soars the tower of **Glasgow University's** central building, a Gothic revival devised by Gilbert Scott. To reach the university, cut through the park or continue along its perimeter up **Byres Road,** where students swirl along the sidewalks in term-time. The central university building is off Byres on University Ave. (U: Hillhead). These hallowed arches support the **Hunterian Museum,** the oldest museum in town. Permanent exhibits skip from -ology to -ology (open Mon.-Sat. 9:30am-5pm; free). The **Hunterian Art Gallery** across the street displays 19th-century Scottish art, a sizeable Whistler collection, a sculpture courtyard with a piece by Caro, and carefully reconstructed rooms from Mackintosh's house (open Mon.-Sat. 9:30am-5pm; free).

North of the Kelvingrove Park area at the end of Byres Rd. are the **Botanic Gardens,** Great Western Rd. White marble statues overlook ornamental ponds inside **Kibble Palace,** one of two large hothouses. The other hothouse features a roomful of carnivorous flora among much international greenery. John Kibble, the building's eccentric designer, once pedaled a bicycle on pontoons across Loch Long (open daily 10am-4:45pm; late Oct. to March 10am-4:15pm; free).

In the large Pollok Country Park, 3½ mi. south of town but worth the trek, is **Pollok House,** a lovely 18th-century mansion with a fine array of Spanish paintings. Take bus #45, 48, or 57 from Union St. (£1). The Park is more famous for the **Burrell Collection**—Sir William Burrell's personal collection of 19th-century French paintings and sculpture (including Rodin's *The Thinker*), Chinese ceramics, and Persian tapestries (both museums open Mon.-Sat. 10am-5pm, Sun. 11am-5pm; free).

For a day among the wild things, sail to the **Glasgow Zoo Park,** Calderpark, Uddingston (tel. 771 1185); Himalayan black bears are separated from camels by a gaggle of exotic geese (open daily 10am-6pm; Oct.-May 10am-5pm; £3.95, seniors, students, and children £2.30; take bus #43, 44, 55, or 240 from Buchanan Station).

In Barras Sq. near Glasgow Green between London Rd. and Gallowgate is an enormous, partly open-air **flea market** that explodes on weekends. Here hundreds of vendors hawk a motley assortment of goods that center on ladies' underwear but include several used book stands, antique war memorabilia, fruit, and hot filled roll establishments (Sat.-Sun. 9am-5pm).

ENTERTAINMENT

Glaswegians play more and party harder than Edinburgh's inhabitants. Three universities and numerous film, theater, and music venues ensure constant offerings. The **Ticket Centre,** City Hall, Candleriggs, will tell you what's playing at the city's dozen-odd theaters (tel. 227 5511; phone answered daily 9am-9pm; office open Mon.-Sat. 10am-6:30pm, Sun. noon-5pm). *The List,* available from most city newsagents, is a detailed guide to culture and art in Glasgow and Edinburgh (80p).

The **Glasgow Film Theatre,** 12 Rose St. (tel. 332 8128), is the place for alternative films (£4, matinees £3; seniors, students, and children £3, matinees £2). The **Grosvenor Cinema,** 31-34 Ashton Lane (tel. 339 4298) near Byres Rd., runs a current program (£3,20, students £2.50, seniors and children £1.60; shows before 6pm £2). At the sweating **Sub Club,** 22 Jamaica St., students and others under 30 bump and grind. Saturday is house and garage night; other nights are gay or mixed scenes (tel. 248 4600; open Fri.-Sat. 11pm-3am, Thurs. during the term; cover £5-8). Nightly gyrations to the latest club music shake **Tunnel,** 84 Mitchell St. (tel. 204 1000), which offers student discounts on Thursdays, and **Club Industria,** 15 Union St. (tel. 221 6111). **Bennet's,** 90 Glassford St. (tel. 552 5761) and **Club Xchange,** 23 Royal Exchange Square (tel. 204 4599), attract mixed crowds. Club hours are generally 11pm to 3:30am; cover charges run £3-7 with occasional student discounts.

Mayfest, an arts festival from April 28 to May 20, 1995, offers a good program of Scottish and international theater and music. For information, contact Mayfest, 18 Albion St., Glasgow, G1 1LH (tel. 552 8000). The annual **Glasgow International Jazz Festival,** in late June or early July, brings such greats as B.B. King and Herbie Hancock to town (same address as Mayfest; tel. 552 3552). Folk and traditional music thrive throughout Glasgow, especially during the **Glasgow International Folk Festival** at the beginning of July; contact the Festival Office, 4 Blackfriars St., Glasgow (tel. 552 8605). During the annual **World Pipe Band Championships,** in mid-August, the skirling of bagpipes may be heard for miles.

■■■ AYRSHIRE

The largest of Ayrshire's tree-lined seaside towns, **Ayr** lies 25 mi. southwest of Glasgow on the coast. The town's shining day comes in early June, when townfolk and visitors hit the streets to watch traditional music, dance, and drama at the **Ayrshire Arts Festival** and to revel in recitations of the local and national hero's works at the concurrent **Robert Burns Festival.** Contact the Ayrshire Arts Festival Chairperson and Robert Burns Festival Secretary, Land O'Burns Center, Alloway, Ayr KA7 1AA (tel. 443700). For horseracing fans, the **Ayr Racecourse** (tel. 264179), host to the **Scottish Grand National** (April) and the **Ayr Gold Cup** (Sept.), promises untold horsey thrills (tickets £6-15; call for race dates).

The **Ayr Hostel** (tel. 262322; grade 1) is a 15-minute walk from the town center. Take a right off Racecourse Rd. onto Blackburn and then follow the signs. Set in a sleeping beauty of a Victorian mansion, this hostel overlooks acres of magnificent grass, and the outline of Ireland occasionally rises out of the cold grey sea beyond. (Lockout 10:30am-2pm; curfew 11:30pm. £6.50, ages 5-17 £5.50, sheets 60p; laundry and kitchen facilities; open March-Oct.) For those wishing to explore the countryside, the hostel also arranges **bicycle** rental (£5-6/day). For cheap sandwiches on heavenly bread, head for **Café Ginger,** 57 Fort St. (tel. 264108) near the bus station. Try chicken satay (£3) or the ham mushroom sandwich (open Mon.-Sat. 8am-5pm).

The Ayr **tourist office** is at Burns House, Burns Statue Sq., near the rail station (open July-Aug. Mon.-Sat. 9:15am-7pm, Sun. 10am-7pm; May-June and Sept.-mid-Oct. Mon.-Sat. 9:15am-6pm, Sun. 10am-6pm; mid-Oct.-mid-April Mon.-Sat. 9:15am-5pm; late April Mon.-Sat. 9:15am-5pm, Sun. 10am-5pm). For local transport details, call the **bus station,** 23 Sandgate (tel. 264643) near Wellington Sq. (open Mon.-Fri. 8:45am-4:30pm). Ayr's **telephone code** is 01292.

Two mi. south of Ayr is the village of **Alloway,** birthplace of Robert Burns and home of the **Land O' Burns Centre** (tel. (01292) 443700), with a multi-screen audio-visual presentation on the life and times of the poet (open daily 10am-5:30pm; Sept.-June 10am-5pm; audiovisual display 50p, children 30p; center will be closed for refurbishing until April 1995). Nearby are the **Burns Monument and Gardens,** which overlook the picturesque Brig o' Doon. Look for a red, red rose. Also in Alloway is **Burns Cottage,** built by you-know-who's dad, where you-know-who was born. A single ticket buys entry to cottage, monument, and gardens (both open April-Oct. Mon.-Sat. 9am-6pm, Sun. 10am-6pm; April-May and Sept.-Oct. Mon.-Sat. 10am-5pm and Sun. 1-5pm; Nov.-March Mon.-Sat. 10am-4pm; £2.20, seniors and children £1.10.) To get to Alloway, take **Western Scottish bus** #61 or 361 to Dunure from Burns Statue Square in Ayr, across from the cinema (Mon.-Sat 6/day, Sun. 13/day, 5 min., 75p).

Twelve mi. south of Ayr is **Culzean Castle** (cul-LANE), a masterpiece by the architect Robert Adam. Seat of the Scottish Kennedys since the 15th century, the castle squats on a cave-pocked coastal cliff; legend has it that one of these caves shelters the Phantom Piper, who plays to his lost flock when the moon is full. The castle and surrounding park were deeded 50 years ago to the British government, which gave the grounds to American General and President Dwight Eisenhower to use during his lifetime (castle and park open April-late Oct. daily 10:30am-5:30pm; last entry 5pm; £5.50, seniors and children £3; castle only £3.50, seniors and children £1.80; park only £3, seniors and children £1.80). To reach Culzean, take the **Western Scottish** bus #60 or 360 to Girvan (6-7/day; 30 min.; £1.85) from Ayr's Sandgate bus station. Follow the sign-posted path from the main road for about 1 mi. to the castle.

■■■ ARRAN

The glorious Isle of Arran (rhymes with, but isn't, barren) justifiably bills itself as "Scotland in Miniature." Gentle lowland hills and majestic Highland peaks co-exist on an island less than 20 mi. long. In the north, the gray and craggy peaks of Goatfell and the Caisteal range surge above their foothills' pines; the eastern coastline meanders south from Brodick Castle past the conical hump of Holy Island, and into meadows and white beaches. Circles of prehistoric stones stand in the southwest among the bog-grass and plains of Machrie; along the northern shores near Lochranza's graying castle, seals flop on rocks.

GETTING THERE & GETTING ABOUT

To reach Arran, take the **train** from Glasgow's Central Station (5/day, Sun. 4/day; 45min.; £3.40) west to Ardrossan on the Firth of Clyde. From Ardrossan, the Cal-Mac ferry makes the hour-long crossing to Brodick on Arran (5-6/day, 3-4/day on Sun.; 1hr.) in sync with the train schedule (£3.30). There's also **ferry** service (mid-April to mid-Oct. only) from Claonaig on the Kintyre peninsula to Lochranza on Arran (9-10/day; 30min.; return £6).

Despite Arran's proximity and excellent connections to Glasgow, more deer inhabit this island than people. Large areas of wilderness in the northwest and southeast remain untouched and the villages (certain parts of Brodick excepted) are quiet and untouristed. The booklet *Seventy Walks in Arran* (£2.50) or *My Walks of Arran* (£1.90), both available at the tourist office, tell all about hiking options.

Buses and bicycles carry tourists around the island; pick up a copy of the SYHA pamphlet, *Cycling on Arran*, and opt for the latter. You can bike Arran's gorgeous coast in a leisurely nine-hour day trip. In Brodick, **Mini-Golf Cycles,** behind the miniature golf course on Shore St., rents mountain and touring bikes (tel. (01770) 302272; state-of-the-art hillmonsters £9.50/day, their lesser cousins £3.50-6.50/day; deposit £20 and ID; open Easter-Oct. daily 9am-6pm, call ahead for winter bike hire). **Brodick Cycles,** farther down Shore Rd. opposite Village Hall (tel. (01770) 302460) rents all kinds of bikes for £4.50-10.50/day, £13-36/week, with a £5 or £25 deposit (open mid-March-mid-Oct. 9am-6pm daily). You can also find bikes in Lochranza, Whiting Bay, and Corrie. **Arran Coaches** (tel. (01770) 302121) offers bus tours from Brodick at 11am from May to September (£6, children £3). The Arran **Ranger Service** (tel. (01770) 302462) arranges free walks (see Brodick, below).

Bus transportation to all parts of the island is fairly convenient; the most you'll pay for any trip is £1.30. The **Rural Day Card** grants you a full day of travel on Arran's Western Coach line (£2.50, children £1.25, available on the bus). The North Arran and South Arran Circular both meet at Blackwaterfoot and Brodick, the island's western and eastern coastal midpoints. It's possible, even beginning from the mainland, to make a circular daytrip of the island with three-hour stops at any two villages (enough time for short hikes around Lochranza, Blackwaterfoot, or Whiting Bay): start from Brodick at 10:45am and take a bus north towards Lochranza. The 9:45am ferry from Ardrossan to Brodick connects with this bus (don't miss it! the next one is at 1:40pm), and the returning bus from South Arran to Brodick meets the 7:20pm ferry to the mainland. Check the tourist office's bus schedule for exact connections and starting times. Note: Those arriving on the 6pm ferry from Androssan should beware that buses during the summer stop running around 9pm. Post buses give extremely slow tours of the island, leaving Brodick at 9:20am. Hitchhikers report that rides are quick enough out of Brodick but painfully slow from the island's two ends; locals are friendly but pass infrequently.

BRODICK

Arran's largest village offers important services and transport connections. Buses take travelers from the pier to more remote parts of the island. Ferries dock in Brodick. From there, Shore Rd. becomes Low Glencloy Rd., leading past the **Arran Heritage Museum,** which features a working forge and a collection of antique farm machinery. On the second Sunday in July and August at 10:30am, blacksmiths fire up the forge to give a riveting demonstration of horseshoeing. (Museum open Easter-Oct. Mon.-Sat. 10am-5pm; £1.50, seniors £1, children 75p). Another mile down the road is the immaculate and impressive **Brodick Castle.** Ancient seat of the Dukes of Hamilton, the castle contains a fine porcelain collection, paintings, and scores of dead beasties—not for the animal lover. Grounds are beautifully-maintained (castle open Easter to mid-Oct. daily 1-5pm, gardens open daily 9:30am-dusk; castle and gardens £4, seniors, students, and children £2; gardens only £2, seniors, students, and children £1). From late June to September ranger walks are available: Monday is "Wonderful Woodlands," Tuesday a grab-bag of theme walks called "Lucky Dip," Thursday "Watery Wildlife" (all walks 2-4pm; free with entry to park). From 10am-5pm every Wednesday, the park offers ranger-guided mountain walks (£5, children £2). The popular ascent of **Goatfell** (2866 ft.), Arran's highest peak, begins along the road between the castle and the heritage museum. The average round-trip along the well-marked path is four or five hours; the view from the cold and windy peak north to the jagged Castail range and south along the coastline to Holy Island may make you delirious. The **Arran Highland Games,** replete with weird sports and bagpipe parades, arrive in Brodick August 5th, 1995, while the highly successful **Isle of Arran Folk Festival** will be held June 5-11, 1995.

In July and August, most Brodick B&Bs are packed, so call ahead. Otherwise try **Mrs. Wilkie,** Cala Sona at the top of Hillview Rd. (tel. 302828). From the tourist office take a left after the Douglas Hotel, a right onto Alma Rd., then your second left onto Hillview Rd. (£13-14). **Mrs. Macmillan,** Glenard (tel. 302318), your last left on

Shore Rd. before it forks just before the golf course, is wood panelled and roomy, except for the disappearing single (£13-14.50; open April-Oct.). Just beyond the golf course, Mrs. Yates's **Greenways**, Low Glencloy (tel. 302701), offers comfy rooms and lots of hospitality (open Easter.-Oct.; £13.50). The **Glen Rosa Farm** (tel. 302380), 2 mi. north of Brodick on the coastal road to Corrie (the B880), lets campers pitch tents for £2 per person (open April-Oct.). You can also look for grassy spots by the beach, but the golf course is off-limits and enforces the ban with a bagful of gleaming mashie irons.

The center of Brodick is along Shore Rd. to your right as you disembark. For eats, try **Collins' Good Food Shop,** at the western end of Shore Rd. just past the bridge on your left, which has streamside outdoor seating. The shop also sells health food (open Mon.-Sat. 9am-5pm), and the restaurant runs the only launderette in town. For more traditional fare (£5-8) and excellent turnovers, try the just-like-home (especially if you've been the object of obsession) **Stalkers Restaurant** on Shore Rd. (tel. 302759; open daily 8:30am-10pm, last orders 9pm; Nov.-March closes around 5pm). The **Brodick Bar,** just off Shore Rd. behind the post office, serves savory bar meals (£5), including baked potatoes with fillings such as the ever-delicious gammon and pineapple (£4.50; bar open Mon.-Sat. 11am-midnight, meals served noon-2:30pm and 5:30-9:30pm). The **Co-op Foodstore**, near the Brodick Bar, stocks the necessities (open Mon.-Fri. 8am-8pm, Sat. 8am-5:30pm, Oct.-May Mon.-Wed. 8am-5pm, Thurs.-Fri. 8am-8pm, Sat. 8am-5:30pm).

The Brodick **tourist office** (tel. 302140 or 302401) answers questions in the round building with the pointed top, at the base of the pier. They stock an excellent series of free maps and leaflets and are your best bet for help in booking local B&Bs (£13-15; open Mon.-Sat. 9am-7:30pm, Sun. 10am-5pm; Nov.-April Mon.-Sat. 9am-5pm). Outside of **The Royal Bank of Scotland** on Shore Rd. you'll find a shiny, happy **Cirrus ATM.** Brodick's **telephone code** is 01770.

LOCHRANZA & BLACKWATERFOOT

Lochranza, at the island's northern tip, 14 mi. from Brodick, is idyllic, with one store, one pub, several crafts workshops, and a castle. Biking down the coast to the even tinier village of **Catacol Bay** makes a nice 45-minute roundtrip. You might also stroll north over the moor and down the meadows by the sea to the **Cock of Arran** and **Ossian's Cave,** one of the legendary resting places of the stumpy-fingered vulgarian of Gaelic times, or take the public footpath south into the high country. From the loch at the top of the pass it's a scramble to the top of **Caisteal Abhail.** There are several waterfalls and swimming holes along the route.

Overlooking the ruins of **Lochranza Castle**, an **HI Youth Hostel** graces the town (tel. 830631; grade 2; lockout 10am-5pm; £5.05, ages 5-17 £4.15; open March-Oct.). **Mrs. Rankin** (tel. 830652) at Westwood offers big rooms with trippy carpets in your choice of pea green, red, or 70s brown (£14.50). In a pinch, the **Lochranza Hotel** (tel. 830223) may have room, and possibly a single (singles from £18, doubles from £16); they also have Lochranza's only pub. And there's the outrageously well-equipped **Lochranza Golf Caravan Camping Site** (tel. 830273), ½ mi. before town on Brodick Rd., with laundry, hot water, food, and much more (£6.50/2 people and tent, golf £7/18 holes on a par 70 course; club rental available; heinously ugly pants required; open Easter to mid-Oct.).

You can rent bikes from **Mrs. Kerr** (tel. 830676) just up the road from the hostel (£1/hr., £3.50/day; open daily 9am-8pm). If you are traveling north in Scotland, a **ferry** sails from Lochranza to Claonaig on the Kintyre peninsula (mid-April to mid-Oct. 9-10/day; 30min.; £3). Across from the pier is Lochranza's seasonal **tourist office** (tel. 830320; open mid-May to mid-Oct. Mon.-Sat. 9:30am-5pm). The **telephone code** here is 01770.

On the west side of the island is the town of **Blackwaterfoot,** in an area with several prehistoric sites: the **Machrie Stones** are a semi-circular arrangement of boulders dating from the Bronze Age, and the walls of **King's Cave** glimmer with ancient inscriptions and paintings. Pick up a free walking map of Machrie and Blackwaterfoot at the tourist office in Brodick to access these sights on foot. A sandy beach stretches along the coast on either side of Blackwaterfoot. The southern part of the island is less rugged than the north, with gentle hills and long beaches. The **HI Youth Hostel** in **Whiting Bay,** only 8 mi. from Brodick, is a good base (tel. (01770) 700339; grade 2; £5.05, ages 5-17 £4.15; open mid-March to Oct.). For diversion, take the easy path to Glen Ashdale Falls or rent a bike from **Whiting Bay Hires** (tel. (01770) 700382; £4.50-8/day, £15-30/week) and cycle to a nearby beach.

■■■ LOCH LOMOND, LOCH LONG, & THE TROSSACHS

Scotland's upland region lies north of the Highlands Boundary Fault, which stretches southwest across the land from Aberdeen to Arran Island. The hills begin to swell 30 mi. north of Glasgow and 10 mi. west of Stirling and grow into majestic peaks as they undulate north. Head away from the unexciting towns that shamelessly commercialize "The Bonnie Bonnie Banks" and find a stretch of roadless nature (such as the northeastern edge of Loch Lomond or most of Loch Katrine). Challenging hikes are rewarded by stunning views and the quiet splendor of untrampled swaths of space.

LOCH LOMOND

Less than an hour's drive north of Glasgow along the scenic A82, **Loch Lomond** is unfortunately the closest most visitors to Scotland get to the Highlands. Meandering through lush bays, dotted with thickly-wooded islands in the south, and ringed by bare hills to the north, Loch Lomond is captivating, particularly if you venture beyond the few towns crawling with caravans and tourists. A number of small, rough beaches dot the shores and are good spots for lazy picnics and paddles. Be warned that the loch is never too toasty.

Several trains serve the loch from both of Glasgow's train stations (at least 1/hr.; £2.40) for Balloch, at the southern tip of the loch; buses make the trek three times a day (£2.40). The second train stops at Tarbet and Ardlui at the northern reaches of the loch. The **West Highland Way** snakes along the entire eastern side of the Loch, and in its full measure, stretches 95 mi. from Milngavie north to Fort William.

In **Balloch,** at the southern tip of the loch, you can book rooms at the **tourist office** on Balloch Rd. opposite the train station (tel. (01389) 753533; open June 9:30am-6pm, July-Aug. 9:30am-7:30pm, Sept. 10am-7pm, Oct. and April-May 10am-5pm). Otherwise, take your pick of any of the B&Bs which line Balloch Rd. Along the way, you can check out **Balloch Castle** and its surrounding **Country Park,** which features many miles of shady paths and the occasional viewpoint of a trash-lined, sandy strip of beach (open 10am-6pm; free).

There are three **HI Youth Hostels** in the area, all accessible from the A82: near Balloch, at Rowardennan, and at Inverbeg. Plan transportation between hostels in advance; buses run rather infrequently. The **HI Loch Lomond Youth Hostel** (tel. (0138985) 226; grade 1) is one of Scotland's largest hostels, a stunning castle-like building nestled in a valley 2 mi. north of Balloch that comes complete with pool tables, laundry, and the ghost of a suicidal damsel locked in the tower. With 200 beds, it gets crazy in mid-summer; call ahead to book a room (£7.25, ages 5-17 £5.95; open early March-Oct.). The **Tullichewan Caravan and Camping Site** (tel. (01389) 759475) offers an opportunity to sleep under the stars (£7.90 for two people with tent). For cozier roofed accommodations, take the Inverbeg ferry across the loch to Rowardennan. The ferry runs frequently from April to September (in bad weather, summon the small launch from Rowardennan by jumping up and down and waving an orange signal flag; leaves Inverbeg 10:30am, 2:30pm, and 6:30pm, leaves Rowardennan 30 min. earlier; £2). Call the Rowardennan Hotel (tel. (0136087) 273) to check the schedule. The **Rowardennan HI Youth Hostel** (tel. (0136087) 259; grade 1) is the first hostel along the West Highland Way, at the foot of Ben Lomond (£6.50, ages 5-17 £5.20; open March-Oct.). Huge windows put the loch in your lap, and the hostel will arrange watersport (canoeing and windsurfing) and landsport (archery and orienteering) lessons for you. You can hike from this large, comfortable hostel to the equally comfortable one in Loch Ard, otherwise accessible from Inverbeg only if you round the entire loch by road. If you choose to hike, check the route carefully with the warden. The **Inverbeg Youth Hostel (HI;** tel. (01436) 860635; grade 3) is quieter and far smaller than the others (£3.85, ages 5-17 £3.15; open late March-Oct.).

LOCH LONG

Only 4 mi. west of Tarbet and 1 mi. up from A82, on the northern end of Loch Lomond at **Loch Long,** is the **Ardgartan Youth Hostel (HI;** tel. (013012) 362; grade 1; £6.50, ages 5-17 £5.50; open Feb.-Dec.), in the Ardgartan Forest Park. This wooded area lies beneath the "Arrochar Alps," a series of rugged mountains including five Munros and **The Cuckolded Cobbler** (2891 ft.). Also known as Ben Arthur and Arthur's Seat, The Cobbler is unmistakable for its unusual and jagged rock formations—the peak appears to have sprouted horns. An easy trail (with some rocky parts near the tip) begins in the town of Arrochar, halfway between Tarbet and Ardgartan. (Inquire in town or at the hostel about the location of the trailhead.) Once at the top, look for the Eye of the Needle, an opening in one of the horny rock-stacks, where you can sit and enjoy the view over the rest of the "Alps." Perhaps you can even spy the tiny hamlet of **Rest and be thankful.** Really.

THE TROSSACHS

The gentle mountains and lochs of the **Trossachs** form the southern boundary of the Highlands. Sir Walter Scott and Queen Victoria lavished praise on the region, the only easily accessible Scottish wilderness prior to the twentieth century. Ironically, the Trossachs today are less accessible than many of the northern wilds; just a few buses a day link Glasgow and Stirling to Aberfoyle and Callander, the area's two main towns. The A821 winds through the heart of the Trossachs between Aberfoyle and Callander, passing near beautiful **Loch Katrine,** the Trossachs' original lure and setting of Scott's "The Lady of the Lake." The *S.S. Sir Walter Scott* (tel. (0141) 355 5333) cruises from Loch Katrine's Trossachs Pier to Stronachlacher; the scenery is arresting, but in July and August the crush of passengers may make the trip a hassle (mid-April to Sept. Sun.-Fri. 3/day, 11am-3:15pm, Sat. 2/day, 2 and 3:30pm; £1.90, seniors and children 95p; return £3.20, seniors and children £1.90). Getting to this area is tough: your best bet is to ask in Aberfoyle or Callander about post buses, which slowly wind their way through selected towns every day. Or try **The Trossachs Trundler,** at 1950s-style bus that runs leisurely between Stirling Rail Station, Callander, Aberfoyle, and Trossachs Pier at the tip of Loch Katrine (Day Rover £3.25-6.50, seniors and children £1.90-3.80). Ask for details at tourist offices.

■■■ MID ARGYLL & KINTYRE PENINSULA

The thick woody glens of Mid Argyll, the peninsula of Kintyre, and the quiet isle of Islay form an entrancing and largely unvisited triangle in western Scotland. Warm ocean currents keep the southern islands softer and lusher than the rugged, windy north. Scottish Citylink buses follow a breathtaking route from Glasgow (3-5/day) up the western edge of Loch Lomond to Inverary, then down to Campbeltown on Kintyre, stopping frequently along the way. Many people hitch along the busy A83.

INVERARAY

Inveraray (rhymes with Tipperary), a comely and unpretentious lochside town in northern Mid Argyll, two hours out of Glasgow (3-5 buses/day; 1¾hr.; £4.80), is a good place to begin an exploration of the region. The nearby home of the Duke and

Duchess of Argyll, **Inveraray Castle** (tel. 2203), contrasts strikingly with the rugged mountains that enclose it (open July-Aug. 10am-5:30pm, Sun. 1-5:30pm; April-June and Sept.-Oct. Mon.-Thurs. and Sat. 10am-1pm and 2-5:30pm, Sun. 1-5:30pm; £3.50, seniors £2.50, under 16 £1.75).

Those with a scholarly interest in the British judicial system (or with a morbid curiosity in medieval forms of punishment) might consider the gruesome **Inveraray Jail**, just off Main Street, which holds scads of bloody drawings and creepy reenactments of prison life (tel. 2381; open 9:30am-6pm, Nov.-March 10am-5pm; last entry 1 hr. before closing; £3.85, seniors £2.50, children £2).

The small **Inveraray Youth Hostel (HI;** tel. 2454; grade 2) is just north of town; take a left through the second arch from the tourist office onto Oban Rd. and walk past the gas station. This solid, barracks-style hostel is blessed with an omniscient warden (£5.05, ages 5-17 £4.15; open mid-March-Sept.). Inveraray hides a stash of B&Bs; among the best are **Mrs. Campbell,** Lorona, Main St. South (tel. 2258; £14) and the **Old Rectory,** Main St. South (tel. 2280; £13-15). The town has an excellent **tourist office** on Front St. (tel. 2063; open Mon.-Sat. 9:30am-6:30pm, Sun. 11am-5pm; Oct.-Easter Mon.-Sat. 10am-4pm; Easter-May Mon.-Fri. 10am-1pm and 2-5:30pm, call for weekend hours). Inverary's **telephone code** is 01499.

■ NEAR KINTYRE: ISLES OF ISLAY & JURA

West of the Kintyre peninsula across calm ocean waters, the isle of **Islay** (EYE-luh) receives few visitors. Most days, three boats make the trip (Mon.-Tues. and Thurs.-Sat. 7:15am, 1:15pm, and 5:45pm, Wed. 7:15am only, Sun. 1:15pm only), some running from Kennacraig to Port Askaig in the northeast and some to Port Ellen in the southeast (£5.45). All leave from **Kennacraig Ferry Terminal,** seven miles south of Tarbert on the Kintyre peninsula, and served by the Glasgow-Campbeltown buses. Travelers coming from Arran via the 12:15pm Lochranza-Claonaig ferry can call **Mr. D. Henderson** (tel. (01880) 820220) one day in advance to reserve a seat on the bus from Claonaig to Kennacraig to connect with the 1:15pm sailing to Port Askaig (£1). Those who forget to plan ahead manage to get a ride to Kennacraig with one of the cars off the ferry. *Don't* get off the ferry without plans on how to get out of Claonaig; the town has absolutely nothing to offer. On Wednesdays only, there's also a ferry connection linking Port Askaig to Oban and Colonsay.

On the island, **Port Askaig** offers little but a hotel, shop, and ferry terminal; **Port Ellen** is more populated and more captivating. To Port Ellen's west, the windswept Oa Peninsula drops dramatically to the sea. A pleasant 3-mi. hike to the northeast takes you past **Laphroaig Distillery,** where one of Scotland's finest malts is produced, to the blue-stoned Celtic **Cross of Kildalton.** The distillery (tel. (01496) 302418) offers free guided tours at 10:30am and 2:15pm. You can camp near Kildalton on the sandy beach at Claggain Bay. In Port Ellen, you can get a room and a meal at Mrs. Hedley's **Trout Fly Guest House,** 8 Charlotte St. (tel. (01496) 302204; £16.50-18.50, discounts on stays of more than 3 nights), or at **Tighcargaman** (tel. (01496) 302345; £15-25).

In West Islay, the town of **Port Charlotte** is home to a recently opened **HI Youth Hostel** (tel. (01496) 85385) on the second floor of a newly renovated distillery warehouse (grade 2; £5.05, ages 5-17 £4.15; open March-Oct.). On the first floor of the same building, the brand-new **Islay Wildlife Information Centre** (tel. (0149685) 218) tells the story of the island's famed wildlife, which includes many rare bird species that lure ecologists and naturalists from the edges of the earth (open April-Oct. Mon.-Fri. 10:30am-5pm, Sat.-Sun. 2-5pm; £1.40, seniors and students £1, children 80p). Across the road, you can learn about the history of the island and the origins of Scottish whiskey-making at the **Museum of Islay Life** (tel. (0149685) 358; open April-Oct. Mon.-Sat. 10am-5pm, Sun. 2-5pm; £1.50, seniors £1, children 75p).

Bowmore, Islay's largest town, is 10 mi. from both Port Ellen and Port Askaig and home to Islay's only **tourist office** (tel. (01496) 810254); call in advance to reserve

B&B accommodations on Islay (open April-June and mid-Sept.-Oct. Mon.-Sat. 9:30am-1pm and 2-5:30pm; June-mid-Sept. also Sun. 2-5pm; Nov.-March Mon.-Fri. 10am-1pm and 2-5pm). Or try **Lambeth Guest House**, Jamieson St. (tel. (01496) 810597; £13/person). A few miles outside Bowmore, **Craigens Farm,** Gruinart by Bridgend (tel. (0149685) 256) will let you camp on its grounds (£2-2.50/tent; no facilities, water spigot only). The 17th-century **Bowmore Round Church** (a.k.a the Kilarrow Parish Church) was built perfectly round to stop Satan from hiding in the corners (open daily 10am-dusk; free). Islay has a distillery in nearly every town; the **Bowmore Distillery,** School St. (tel. (01496) 810597), is the oldest in full-time operation (tours and free dram Mon.-Fri. at 10:30am, 11:30am, 2pm, and 3pm; Sat. 10:30am; Oct.-April tours Mon.-Fri. 10:30am and 2pm; disabled access). The west coast between Bowmore and Port Ellen, also accessible by bus, is graced by the **Big Strand,** 7 mi. of sandy beach. In summer, four buses per day (Mon.-Sat.) link Port Askaig and Port Ellen via Bowmore; call **B. Mundell Ltd.** (tel. (01496) 840273).

A flaming orange car ferry runs 5-minute trips from Port Askaig across the Sound of Islay to the isle of **Jura,** one of the most remote and least populated for its size of the Scottish islands (summer ferry 14-16/day, Sun. 6-7/day, fewer in winter; 70p). George Orwell wrote *1984* on Jura's northern coast. A walker's Avalon, Jura has one village, **Craighouse,** with just a couple of B&Bs; contact **Mrs. Boardman** at 7 Woodside (tel. (0149682) 379) well in advance (£15/person). The **Croft Bunkhouse Jura,** Knockcrome (tel. (01496) 823 32) has but six cozy beds (£3).

■■■ OBAN

Oban (OH-ben), the busiest ferry port on Scotland's west coast, has managed an unabashed embrace of tourism without a Faustian sale of its soul. Lacking notable attractions, Oban endears itself with sporadic outbursts of small-town warmth; it is also an excellent base from which to explore nearby Blands and the Argyll countryside. Ferries to most of the lower Hebrides (notably Mull, Iona, Kerrera, Lismore, Coll, Tiree, Barra, South Uist, and Colonsay) criss-cross Oban's attractive harbor dotted with fishing boats. As the sun sets over the blue hills of Mull and the port workers turn in for the day, the streets of Oban fill with people strolling along the harbor, chatting with neighbors, or heading to the pub for a dram.

GETTING THERE

Trains run directly to Oban from Glasgow's Queen St. Station on the spectacular **West Highland Line** (4/day, Sun. 3/day; 3hr.; £15.50). Built at the turn of the century, the line is a triumph of Victorian engineering, crossing glens, moors, and rivers and skirting mountain ranges. **Scottish Citylink** makes the same journey by bus and is cheaper (3/day, Sun. 2/day; 3hr.; £8.80). Those journeying to Fort William or Inverness will find buses easiest. **Highland Bus and Coach** and **Gaelicbus** travel to Inverness (Mon.-Sat. 6/day; 4hr.; £9) via Fort William (Mon.-Sat. 7-8/day; 1¾hr.; £5). **Oban and District Buses Ltd.** runs daily to Ft. William in summer (mid-June to mid-Sept. Mon.-Sat. at 10:45am; day return £8.10).

Caledonian MacBrayne Ferries (tel. 62285), known locally as "Cal-Mac" or "MacBrayne," sail from Oban to most islands in the southern Hebrides. Ferries frighten fish on their way to Craignure on Mull (5-7/day; 40min.; £2.70), Coll and Tiree, two islands west of Mull, with a stop at Tobermory on Mull (Mon., Wed., and Fri.-Sat. 6am, Tues. 3pm direct to Coll; to Tobermory 1¾hr., £6.75; to Coll or Tiree 4¾hr., £8.85), Barra (Mon., Wed., and Sat. 3:30pm, Thurs. 3pm; 5hr.; £15.45), South Uist (Mon., Wed., and Sat. 3:30pm, Thurs.-Fri. 3pm; 5hr.; £15.45), Lismore (Mon.-Sat. 2-4/day; 1hr.; £1.70), and Colonsay (Mon., Wed., and Fri. 1/day; 2¼hr.; £7.40).

ORIENTATION & PRACTICAL INFORMATION

Oban's ferry terminal, train station, and bus stop are situated by the pier near an array of pay phones and public toilets. **Argyll Square,** home to the tourist office, is a block inland northeast of the pier.

Tourist Office: Argyll Sq. (tel. 63122). At the upper-right corner of the roundabout coming from the train station. Unflaggingly friendly. Open Mon.-Sat. 9am-8:45pm, Sun. 9am-5pm; May and Sept. Mon.-Sat. 9am-5:30pm, Sun. 10am-5pm; April and Oct. Mon.-Fri. 9am-5:30pm; Nov.-March Mon.-Fri. 9am-1pm and 2-5:30pm.

Financial Services: Royal Bank of Scotland, 26 George St. (tel. 62177). Open Mon.-Tues. 9:15am-4:45pm, Wed.-Fri. 10am-4:45pm. **Bank of Scotland,** Station Rd. (tel. 63639), across from train station. Open Mon.-Fri. 9:15am-4:45pm.

Post Office: Albany St. (tel. 65679). Open Mon.-Wed. 9am-1pm and 2-5:30pm, Thurs.-Fri. 9am-5:30pm, Sat. 9am-12:30pm. **Postal Code:** PA34 4AA.

Telephone Code: 01631.

Train Station: At Railway Quay (tel. 63083). **Lockers** £1-2. Station open Mon.-Sat. 7:30am-6pm, Sun. 11am-6pm; Oct.-May Mon.-Sat. 8am-6:30pm.

Bus Station: Buy tickets for **Scottish Citylink, Highland Bus and Coach,** and **Oban and District Buses Ltd.** at Midland Bluebird's office at 1 Queens Park Pl. (tel. 62856; open Mon.-Fri. 8:30am-5pm, Sat. 10am-1pm, Sun. 10:30am-12:30pm; late Sept. to mid-May Mon.-Fri. 8:30am-5pm), a block from the **bus shelters** and train station. For other lines, purchase tickets from the tourist office or drivers.

Ferries: Caledonian MacBrayne, Railway Quay (tel. 62285).

Launderette: Stevenson St. Open Mon.-Sat. 9am-5pm.

Hospital: West Highland Hospital, 1½mi. away on Glencruitten Rd. (tel. 63727).

Emergency: Dial 999; no coins required.

Police: Albany St. (tel. 62213).

ACCOMMODATIONS

Bed and breakfasts range from £12-15; book ahead during the tourist explosion in July and August. Staid B&Bs line **Ardconnel** and **Dunollie Roads,** off George St. by the cinema. People often camp by the water along Ganavan Rd. *Let's Go* does not recommend the establishment **Jeremy Inglis** on Airds Crescent.

Oban Backpackers Lodge, Breadalbande St. (tel. 62107 or 63323); from the pier continue left on George St. until the road splits and follow the right prong for 50 yd. Sleep like royalty in giant peach bunk beds handmade by the wardens. Those with early morning ferries take warning—these beds are too good to get out of. A clean, comfortable, new hostel with the most amiable of managers. Laundry and drying room. Open 24 hrs.—let the wardens know if you'll be out between 2am and 7am. Checkout/check-in 10:30am. £7.50. Continental breakfast £1.50. Ask about bike rental, horseriding, and canoeing.

Oban Youth Hostel (HI), Corran Esplanade (tel. 62025; grade 1), ¾ mi. north of the train station along the water, just past the square-towered cathedral. Seaside real estate with laundry facilities, store, and kitchen. Curfew 2am. £7.25. Never assume there will be an extra bed in July or Aug. Open March-Oct.

Mr. and Mrs. John MacEachen, Cuan, Lismore Crescent (tel. 63994). Head toward the youth hostel, make a right after the waterfront cathedral onto Corran Brae, then go 500 yd. uphill to the second right—it's at the very end of the road. Very modern interior design and gorgeous views of the town and harbor. B&B with full breakfast £12, with continental breakfast £10. Open April-Oct.

Maridon House, Dunuaran Rd. (tel. 62670). Convenient to the ferry terminal. Take a right on Albany St.; you can't miss the striking baby blue exterior. TV lounge/common room. With ten rooms there is often space left long after other B&Bs have filled up. Hall bathrooms and showers. £14, Sept.-June £12.

FOOD & PUBS

Harborside **George St.,** beginning near the train station, runs the length of Oban's gastrocenter and nightlife strip. Seafood shops and fishmongers cluster around the ferry terminal. Mussels are atypically cheap here and delicious when steamed. **Oban Sesame,** another wholefood store, steals between John and William St. on Corran Esplanade (open Mon.-Sat. 9am-5:30pm). Gargantuan **Wm. Low Supermarket,** on Market St. behind the Gallery restaurant (open Mon.-Fri. 8:30am-8pm, Sat. 8:30am-6pm, Sun. 10am-5pm), and the **Co-op** on Soroba Rd. (open Mon.-Sat. 8:30am-

5:30pm) should satisfy most grocery needs. **McTavish's Kitchen** on George St. offers meals *prix-fixe* and a Scottish show from £4.95, as well as a good value self-service menu throughout the day. **The Taste Bud,** 41 Combie St., provides good value meals with nary a tourist in sight (full breakfast £3.20; open Mon.-Sat. 7:30am-5pm, Sun. 9am-1pm). The **Oban Inn** bustles at the corner of Stafford St. and the Esplanade; the **Lorne Hotel,** Stevenson St., is a soothing spot for an early pint.

SIGHTS & ENTERTAINMENT

Built in the 1890s to employ out-of-work stonemasons, the Colosseum-like **McCaig's Tower** overlooks the town. Mr. McCaig had planned to add statues of his family and friends to the open stone arches, but his models never materialized. Take the steep Jacob's Ladder stairway at the end of Argyll St., then walk to your left along Ardconnel and right up Laurel to the tower's grassy entrance. **Pulpit Hill,** a spot with a better view but less architectural pizazz, rises in the southern half of town, at the other end of the path and steps which begin at the end of Albany St. From here you can see Mull, Kerrera, and **Dunollie Castle,** at the opposite end of town off Corran Esplanade. The ruins of the castle include a 15th-century tower, built on a site fortified since the late 7th century (open all the time; free). Dunollie is the seat of the Mac-Dougall family, formerly the Lords of Lorne, who possessed a third of Scotland. To reach the tower, walk 15 minutes north from the town center along the water and climb the steep, muddy path from the right-hand side of the road. Consider the crumbling walls and pitch-black interior before you enter the main hall "at your own risk." Structurally unsound, the upper floors of the main castle are now barricaded. From the castle, cross over the field and fence to arrive at the path that leads through a near-primeval forest to Corran Brae Rd.; you can also reach the path and its many branches from the youth hostel.

In town, the **Oban Distillery,** Stafford St., tops off guided tours with free drams (approx. 4 tours/hr. Mon.-Sat. 9:30am-4:15pm; Nov.-Easter Mon.-Fri. 9:30am-4:15pm; £2; under 18 free). Just 2 mi. outside town on Glencruitten Rd., **Achnilarig Farms** (tel. 62745) offers guided horseback rides through the surrounding country to people of all levels of experience (open March-Oct. daily; call ahead for hours; £7/hr). Further down Glencruitten Rd. past the golf course, the **Oban Rare Breeds Farm Park** displays 12 exotic breeds of sheep and some splendid sows (open Easter-Sept. daily 10am-5:30pm, until 7:30pm mid-June to Aug.; £3, children £2; extra for a bag of grain to placate the animals).

■ NEAR OBAN

To the north gapes the mouth of **Loch Etive,** where the famous **Falls of Lora** change directions with the shifting of the tides. From **Taynuilt,** off the A85, 7 mi. east of the loch mouth, **Loch Etive Cruises** (tel. (018662) 430) runs three-hour cruises up the loch into beautiful and otherwise inaccessible countryside (April to mid-Oct. Mon.-Fri. 10:30am and 2pm, Sat.-Sun. 2pm; £6, children £4). Oban-Glasgow buses stop at Taynuilt. Beyond Taynuilt 14 mi. on the A85 is **Loch Awe,** renowned for its salmon and trout fishing and the massive 15th-century **Kilchurn Castle,** which dominates the north end of the loch (free; always open).

If you cross Connel Bridge over the mouth of Loch Etive rather than heading inland along the shore, you will arrive in the region of **Appin.** The hauntingly beautiful **Castle Stalker,** at Portnacroish, is 10 mi. down the A828. This 16th-century stronghold of the Stewarts sits on an islet in Loch Linnhe before the mountains of Morvern. It is perhaps best known as the "Castle Aaaaaaaaaa" in the film *Monty Python and the Holy Grail.* The castle is now privately owned.

South of Oban, 4 mi. off the A816 (take the Kilninver turn-off 8 mi. south of Oban), are the islands of **Seil** and **Luing.** Seil is the only Hebridean island connected to the mainland by a bridge (optimistically called the "Bridge Across the Atlantic"). Just across it is the **Tigh an Truish Hotel,** with good pub lunches and Guinness on tap. The name means "House of Trousers;" after a 1745 uprising the wearing of kilts was forbidden on the mainland, and Highlanders used to change at the inn before and after making the crossing. The village of **Easdale** offers spectacular views of the sea. **Buses** run from Oban (Mon.-Sat. 1-3/day, £1.30). Oban and District Buses **coach tours** also leave the city (May-Sept. Sun., Tues., and Thurs. 2pm; £4, seniors and children £2.50). Hitchers report success getting around the area.

■■■ ISLE OF MULL

The visionary vistas of the rainy Isle of Mull have bewitched artists, writers, and musicians: Robert Louis Stevenson's *Kidnapped* depicts mainland Mull and Erraid (a tiny isle off the southern coast) in lively detail, and Staffa inspired Felix Mendelssohn to compose the *Hebrides Overture*. The west coast, blessed with small islands, is particularly dramatic. Mull's Gaelic heritage has largely given way to the press of English "white settlers" who now comprise over two-thirds of the population, but local craftsmen keep tradition alive in the island's less-touristed shops, all far off the beaten path between Craignure and Tobermory.

GETTING THERE

Caledonian MacBrayne (tel. (01631) 66966) runs a large car and passenger ferry from Oban, east of Mull, to **Craignure** on Mull (5-7/day; 40min.; £2.70). A smaller car and passenger ferry runs from Lochaline on the Morvern Peninsula, just north of Mull, to **Fishnish** on Mull (Mon.-Sat. 15/day, June-Aug. also Sun. 9/day; 15min.; £1.60). Another car ferry operates from Mingary, near Kilchoan on the remote Ardnamurchan Peninsula, to **Tobermory,** Mull's largest town (April 25-June 25 and Aug. 29-Oct. 15; Mon.-Sat. 7/day; 35min.; £2.80).

GETTING ABOUT

Mull's three main cities, Tobermory (northwest tip), Craignure (eastern tip) and Fionnphort (southwest tip), form a triangle bounded on two sides by the A849 and A848. A left turn off the Craignure Pier takes you 35 mi. down Mull's main road along the southern arm of the island to **Fionnphort** (FINN-a-furt), where the ferry leaves for Iona, a tiny island off the southwest corner of Mull. A right turn leads 21 mi. along Mull's northwestern arm to **Tobermory,** Mull's pocket metropolis. Several small B-roads branch off toward the scenic west coast, but the Tobermory-Craignure-Fionnphort thoroughfare is the main artery of the island's road system.

Many travelers hitch on Mull, despite the sparse traffic. The bus service, in transition from **Bowman's Coaches** to **Esbee Coaches** (tel. (016802) 313), connects at Craignure with the 8am, noon, and 4pm ferries from Oban and continues to Fionnphort (1¼hrs.; £1.30) and Tobermory (50min.; £1.30). The last buses leave Fionnphort at 3:15pm and Tobermory at 3:35pm to meet the 5pm Craignure-Oban sailing; two buses runs on Sunday. Ask at the hostel about **bike rental** (tel. (01688) 2481; £7/day). In Craignure, hire bikes (£1.50/hr., £7/day) from **Mull Travel and Crafts** (tel. (016802) 487), two doors away from the tourist office.

CRAIGNURE

There's not much to do in Craignure but climb aboard Mull's 10¼-in.-gauge steam train (tel. (016802) 494), which huffs and puffs through forest and foxglove to **Torosay Castle,** 1 mi. south. (Leaves Craignure April-Sept. 11am-5pm; 5-12/day; return £2.25, children £1.50.) Loll on the couches and peruse the library of 19th-century royalty. (Castle open Easter-Oct. daily 10:30am-5:30pm. Gardens open all year dawn to dusk. Castle and garden cost a gut-wrenching £3.50, students and seniors £2.75, children £1.50; garden only £1.50; seniors, students, and children £1.) Lacking a tiny train but otherwise more worth your money is the 700-year-old stronghold of the clan MacLean, **Duart Castle,** 3 mi. west of Torosay (tel. (016802) 309). Guide yourself through the state bedroom, dungeon, and cell where Spanish sailors, fleeing after the Armada's fall, were kept for ransom (open May-Sept. daily 10:30am-6pm;

£3, children £1.50). To reach the castle, take the bus to the end of Duart Rd. and walk the remaining 1½ mi. Boat tours from Oban to the castles leave in summer twice daily; check at the North Pier. Camp the night away at the **Isle of Mull Campsite;** from the Craignure ferry terminal, turn left, then left again at the sign opposite the church (£3.50/tent plus £2/person; showers and laundry). A seasonal **tourist office** (tel. (016802) 377) waits by the ferry terminal (bookings £1; open May to mid-Oct. Mon.-Thurs. and Sat. 9:30am-6:30pm, Fri. and Sun. 10am-4pm).

TOBERMORY

Tobermory, Mull's main town (pop. 1000), is little more than a string of colorful houses and craft shops around an attractive harbor. The tiny **Mull Museum** chronicles the island's history with local artifacts and folklore (open April-Oct. Mon.-Fri. 10:30am-4:30pm, Sat. 10:30am-1:30pm; 70p, children 10p). The **Tobermory Distillery,** on the opposite side of the harbor from the tourist office, conducts tours with well-informed guides and a generous swig of the final product (Easter-Sept. Mon.-Fri. 10:30am-3:15pm; £1.75, children 50p). Tobermory hosts the lively **Mull Music Festival** during the last weekend in April, as well as the **Mull Highland Games,** which include a small regatta and the more traditional caber-tossing and *ceilidhs* on the middle Thursday of July.

The town's **HI Youth Hostel** (tel. 2481) on Main St., has a stunning panorama of the bay (Grade 3; £3.85; open mid-March to Sept.). For a comfortable chaos, try **Ach-na-Craoibh** (tel. 2301), ½ mi. up the hill on the footpath by the post office and past the police station. David and Hilarie Burnett offer a range of rooms from basic to luxurious. Prices vary, but in high season two people can stay in a small caravan beside a beautiful garden for as little as £55 per week (includes linen and electricity). The broke may try to strike a deal working for a few hours in the garden.

The pub at Tobermory's **Mishnish Hotel** (tel. 2009) teems with tourists and seafarers lured by the music (live from 9:30pm almost every night in summer), the bar meals (lunch £1.40-4.25, dinner £4.75-7.50), and the company (open daily 11am-midnight). The **MacDonald Arms** serves pub grub for £1.45-4.25 (open Mon.-Sat. 12:30-1:45pm and 6:45-8pm). Steer clear of yacht-catering local restaurants and pick up some delicious smoked trout at the **Fish Farm** (tel. 2120) on Main St. (open Mon.-Fri. 9am-5pm, Sat. 9am-3pm). For even fresher seafood, rent a rod-and-reel (£3) next door from **Tackle and Books,** Mull's only combination angling center and bookstore. They also arrange three-hour fishing trips nearly every day in season (£12, children £10; open Mon.-Sat. 9am-6pm, Sun. 11am-4pm). The **Coop Supermarket** sits by the harbor between the hostel and the post office (open Mon.-Wed. 9am-6pm, Thurs. and Fri. 9am-7pm, Sat. 9am-5:30pm). The **Mull Little Theatre** (tel. (016884) 245), 8 mi. outside Tobermory, presents plays in its petite theater (only 43 seats; May-Sept. Fri.-Tues. 8:30pm, Wed.-Thurs. 7:30pm and 9:30pm).

The **tourist office** perches on the pier (tel. 2182; open Mon.-Sat. 9am-5:30pm). **Clydesdale Bank,** Main St., is the only bank on the island. A small **launderette** spins and tumbles next to the youth hostel (service wash £4; open Mon.-Fri. 10am-5pm). Tobermory's **post office,** across the harbor from the tourist office, receives mail addressed to **postal code** PA75 6NT. Tobermory's **telephone code** is 01688.

■ NEAR MULL: IONA, STAFFA, & THE TRESHNISH ISLES

Tours sail regularly to the tiny islands off Mull's west coast. **Turus Mara** (tel. (016884) 242) runs to Staffa and Iona from Oban, Craignure, and Ulva Ferry on Mull (mid-May-Sept. Sun.-Fri.; £21.50 from Oban, £16.50 from Craignure). **Gordon Grant** (tel. (016817) 338) chugs to Staffa and the Treshnish Isles from Oban and Fionnphort (mid-April to mid-Oct.; £8-16). **Davey Kirkpatrick** on Iona (tel. (016817) 358) does Staffa tours from Iona and Fionnphort (£8, children £4). Book tours at the Oban or Tobermory tourist offices. **Cal-Mac** has frequent ferries to Iona from Fionnphort (£1); you must take a tour to see Staffa.

The sacred isle of **Iona** is washed in a purity of color and light found nowhere else in Scotland but the Outer Isles. Iona's crooked coastline secludes sandy beaches, and rocky knolls rise out of fertile, sandy grasslands in the center of the island. The famous **Spouting Cave** spumes salt water when the waves are high enough. More than 200,000 pilgrims visit Iona each year to pay homage to the tiny outcropping of land where, in 563 AD, the exiled Irish St. Columba landed in a coracle boat and built what became one of the centers of medieval Christendom. Missionaries departed in the 7th century to convert the Northumbrian kingdom of England, and St. Columba and his followers are credited with the conversion of Scotland.

There are two distinct settlements on Iona: the small village of **Baile Mór,** with two stores and a post office, sticks to the harbor, while the ecumenical **Iona Community** cleaves to the massive **Benedictine Abbey.** Walk up through the village and bear right to reach the abbey, at the center of your view as you arrive on the ferry. On your way, you'll pass through the ruins of a 13th-century **nunnery,** one of the best-preserved medieval convents in Britain. The abbey stands on the site of St. Columba's Celtic monastery, often shrouded in mists from the nearby sea. Free-standing **Celtic crosses,** with swirling serpent-and-bull ornaments, guard the entrance. Constructed in the 12th century, tiny **St. Oran's Chapel** is the oldest building in this magnificent compound. More than 60 kings of Scotland, Ireland, and Norway rest in the adjacent burial ground; the much-lamented Labour leader John Smith lies under red roses to the left of the chapel. Restoration of the abbey was begun by Abbot Dominic in the 15th century, and completed in this century by the Iona Cathedral Trust and the Iona Community. The Trust collects a £2, ahem, donation at the gate, but the abbey's easily worth spending £20 to see. Attend one of the Community's summer services (Mon.-Sat. 9am and 9pm, Sun. 10:30am and 9:30pm); no doubt it'll give you something to mull over. Tuesday and Friday nights bring rousing *ceilidhs* to the village hall. On Thursday, guests may enjoy an evening concert, and all Wednesday guides lead an open **pilgrimage** around the island.

The best way to fully appreciate Iona's beauty is to spend a night on the island. During the summer months, the island is often stuffed with particularly pernicious daytrippers from Mull and Oban—treading on your toes, vying for elbow room at the abbey, and blowing their noses as you contemplate God in the churchyard. The **Iona Community** runs regular week-long retreats on themes of religion, peace, and community from late June to mid-September. These are sporadic during the rest of the year, and are replaced with frequent open weeks, where guests can stay in the abbey for a minimum of a week in summer, or three nights at other times of the year (no theological requirements; full board £145.20/week, students £93.10). For a program or bookings contact The Abbey, Iona, Argyll PA76 6SN (tel. (016817) 404). If the Scottish Episcopal Church is more your style, stay in their **Bishop's House** (tel. (016817) 306), a shoreside building at the end of the village street with a chapel and decorative windows (B&B £24.50, 15% student discount). Secular isolation is yours at **Finlay, Ross Ltd.** (tel. (016817) 357), to the left from the pier (B&B £16-18).

The incredible island of **Staffa,** composed of hexagonal basalt columns and rimmed with tidal caves, lies only 6 mi. north of Iona. Due to a weak point in the earth's crust, liquid rock spewed upwards and was instantly cooled by the ocean water, forming these columns. Surrounded by treacherous cliffs (particularly slippery in the rain, when use of the guardrails is essential along the base), Staffa is ruled by an imperial council of six sheep and four cows. Puffins nest on the cliff edge and allow the curious to examine their personal space. When rough seas roar into cathedral-like **Fingal's Cave,** the sound reverberates around the island; this incessant pounding of wave against rock inspired the surging strings in Mendelssohn's *Hebrides Overture.* The nearby **Treshnish Isles** offer sanctuary to seals, seabirds, and ferrets. Legend holds that the monks from the Iona Abbey buried their library here to save it from the pillages of the Reformation. Many have tried digging under the third ferret from the left, as yet without luck.

EASTERN SCOTLAND

Scotland's eastern shoulder extends from historic Tayside and Fife in the south to the endless Grampian summits and chilly curve of the North Sea. East of the often snow-covered mountains, the countryside flattens into coastal plains strewn with castles of all vintages and sizes, and the oil boomtown of Aberdeen rises from the stark shore. The northeast is less heralded than other areas of Scotland—it has always been quieter than the lofty, barren Highlands to the west and the energetic Glasgow-Edinburgh region to the south. The best scenery in the northeast lies back from the flat coast along the fertile river valleys and among the gentle slopes of mountains. Unfortunately for seekers of scenic views, transportation through the interior of this region is very spotty. Rail and bus routes tend to follow either the coast or the busy A9 trunk road from Perth to Inverness.

■■■ STIRLING

Embraced on all sides by the scenic Ochil Hills, Stirling was once strategically located to boot. Planted atop a defunct volcano, **Stirling Castle's** prim gardens and excellent views of the Forth Valley belie its militant and occasionally murderous past. The castle's suitably hideous corbels and gargoyles glowered over the 14th-century Wars of Independence, a 15th-century royal murder and the 16th-century coronation of the infant Mary, Queen of Scots. (Open daily 9:30am-6pm, Oct.-March 9:30am-5pm. Last entry 45 min. before closing. £3.50, seniors £2, under 16 £1.) A little down Castle Hill Wynd, the high walls and timbered roof of the **Church of the Holy Rude** once held the coronation of James VI and shook with the fire and brimstone sermons of John Knox (May-Sept. 10am-5pm, Sun. service 11am; 60p). **Ladies Rock,** a lookout point from the **Valley Cemetery** behind the Church, provides views nearly as good as those from the castle battlements for free. Cross the Abbey Road footbridge over the River Forth to find **Cambuskenneth Abbey,** the ruins of a cloister built in 1147. Cows graze outside the gate, and the occasional black-faced sheep may eyeball you across the graves of James III and his wife Margaret (open April-Sept. Mon.-Sat. 9:30am-6pm, Sun. 2-6pm; free). From the abbey, the Adysneck Road leads north to the 200-foot tall **Wallace Monument** (tel. 472140), which houses the two-handed sword William Wallace wielded against King Edward of England and tells how, once captured by the English, Wallace was hanged until semi-conscious, disemboweled, mutilated, then quartered, with his entrails burnt and parts of his body dispersed for display to the corners of Scotland. (Center of the Monument open July-Aug. 9am-6pm; April-June and Sept.-Oct. 10am-5pm; £2.35, children and seniors £1.20.) Two mi. away, at **Bannockburn,** a statue of Robert the Bruce ready for battle overlooks the field where his men defeated the English in 1314—leaving a lasting impression; Scotland was to keep its independence for 400 years (center open April-Oct. daily 10am-5:30pm; grounds open all year).

B&Bs abound near the train station and the university, but Stirling's new **HI Youth Hostel** on St. John St. (tel. 473442), is too good to pass up. From the train station; turn left on Murray Place, then right on Kings St. (which becomes St. John St.). Quartered in the first Separatist Church in Stirling, the hostel is surrounded by gravestones and fronted by an elaborate domed monument marking the grave of Ebenezer Erskine, the church's founder (£9.80, under 18 £8.45, includes continental breakfast). Two spotless singles—one with a sterling view of the Wallace Monument—and a breakfast to hold you until dinner await at kind **Mrs. Helen Miller's,** 16 Riverside Dr. (tel. 461105). Turn right from the train station, cross the bridge, go straight down Seaforth Place and Abbey Road until the road ends, and turn left onto Riverside Dr. (£11). **Quismat Tandoori** serves a filling three-course lunch of soup, entree, and ice cream Monday to Saturday (noon-2:30pm; £3). Main dishes ordinarily run £3-6 (open Mon.-Sat. noon-midnight, Sun. 3pm-midnight).

West of Edinburgh and on the A9 to Perth and Inverness, Stirling's central location makes it a rail transport hub. Both Edinburgh (at least 1/hr.; £4) and Glasgow (several/hr.; £3.50) are a short journey away. Trains also chug to Inverness (6/day; £24), and London (2/hr.; £61). There is also frequent **Citylink** and **National Express** bus service to Glasgow (1/hr.; £2.70), Inverness (1/hr.; £9.30), and London (3/day; £31.50). Both the **train station** (tel. 464754) and the **bus station** (tel. 473763) are on Goosecroft Rd. The **tourist office** greets visitors at 41 Dumbarton Rd. (tel. 475019) and Stirling Castle (tel. 479901). Mail Mom postcards of Wallace's tortured body at the **post office**, 84-86 Murray Pl. (tel. 653 92; open Mon.-Fri. 9am-5:30pm, Sat. 9am-12:30pm). Stirling's **postal code** is FK8 2BP, its **telephone code** 01786.

■■■ ST. ANDREWS

> Would you like to see a city given over,
> Soul and body to a tyrannising game?
> If you would, there's little need to be a rover,
> For St. Andrews is the abject city's name.
>   —Robert F. Murray (1863-1894)

In St. Andrews, "the game" is golf—in the 16th century, Mary Queen of Scots is said to have ditched her mourning weeds for knickers, clubs, and cleats only days after her husband's murder. The site of her match, the city's Royal and Ancient Golf Club, is the sport's world headquarters and frequent spot for the British Open. Despite the constant onslaught of pastel and polyester, one need not worship the wedge to love St. Andrews. The ruins of its enormous cathedral outline the seat of pre-Reformation Christianity (the largest building in Scotland until the Industrial Revolution). Well-tended and restored medieval streets crawl among castle ruins that overlook the North Sea and the gray stone buildings of Scotland's oldest university. Backdropped by soft coastal scenery, these sights make St. Andrews one of Scotland's most attractive towns.

GETTING THERE

Fife Scottish buses take the cheapest and most scenic route from Edinburgh to St. Andrews, located on the other side of the Fife Peninsula from the capital. (#X59; 11/day; 2hr.; £4). For bus information in Edinburgh, call the St. Andrew Sq. bus station (tel. (0131) 556 8464). Eleven buses make the nearly three-hour trip between St. Andrews and Glasgow Monday through Saturday (#X24, change to #X59 at Glenrothes). The *Freedom of Fife* ticket allows a day's unlimited travel on all Fife Scottish buses except X59 (Edinburgh to St. Andrews) after 9am (£5). To ride to Aberdeen, Perth, and Inverness (via Perth), first take a bus to Dundee (2/hr.) and switch there.

Scotrail keeps a respectful distance from St. Andrews, stopping 5 mi. away at **Leuchars** (LU-cars) on its London-Edinburgh-Dundee-Aberdeen line (1/hr. from Edinburgh; 1hr.; £6.10; 3-4/day from London, including one overnight). From Leuchars, buses (5/hr.) go to St. Andrews from 7am to 6pm. Hitchers often approach from Leuchars in the north on A919 to A91. Hitchers report the route from Edinburgh or Glasgow is tricky because of the manic criss-crossing of roads outside these cities; once people reach the A91 or A915, they usually hitch straight to town.

ORIENTATION & PRACTICAL INFORMATION

St. Andrews's three main streets—North, Market, and South St.—run nearly parallel from west to east, converging near the cathedral at the east end of town. Most buses stop at the **St. Andrews Bus Station,** City Rd. (tel. 474238). Manicured golf greens and shops dedicated to the "game of gentlemen" rule the northwest corner of town.

The marvelous **tourist office** is at 70 Market St. (tel. 472021, 24-hr. answering service, fax 478422). From the bus station, turn right on City Rd. and follow it uphill, then turn left onto Market St. and continue for 300 yds. (Open July-Aug. Mon.-Sat.

9:30am-7pm, Sun. 11am-5pm; June and Sept. Mon.-Sat. 9:30am-6pm, Sun. 11am-5pm; Oct.-April Mon.-Fri. 9:30am-1pm, Sat. 2-5pm; May Mon.-Sat. 9:30am-1pm and 2-5pm, Sun. 2-5pm.) The office can provide you with the free guide, *St. Andrews, the East Neuk, and Fife,* which includes an extensive list of local B&Bs and their prices. **USTATS,** the University of St. Andrews Travel Service, (tel. 462710, fax 462716; open May Mon.-Sat. 9:30am-1pm and 2-5pm, Sun. 2-5pm) sells the ISIC (£5) and discount air, bus, rail, and ferry tickets (open Mon.-Fri. 10am-4:30pm; located on 1st floor of Student Union on St. Mary's Place off Market St.). The **launderette** is at 14B Woodburn Terrace (tel. (01334) 75150; open daily 9am-7pm). The **St. Andrews Public Library,** with an extensive local history collection, is down Logie's Lane across from Holy Trinity Church (open Mon.-Wed. and Fri. 10am-7pm, Thurs. and Sat. 10am-5pm). The **postal code** for the tourist office is KY16 9JX. The **telephone code** for St. Andrews proper is 01334.

ACCOMMODATIONS

High local taxes and golfers with chubby wallets have made St. Andrews unbearably expensive. Near the golf links, Murray Park and Murray Place greet the backpacker with astronomically-priced B&Bs. Failing Mr. Pennington's Bunkhouse, the penny-pinching traveller should make St. Andrews a day trip from Edinburgh or Glasgow.

Mr. Pennington's Bunkhouse (tel. (01333) 310768), in West Pitkierie 8 mi. south of St. Andrews and 1½ mi. outside attractive Anstruther (see Fife seaside, below). A minibus deposits passengers five times daily (#61 leaves from the bus stop about 50 yds. west of the ruined chapel opposite Madras College on South St.). Fife Scottish makes 17 daily runs to Anstruther (6am-10pm; £1.70). Set in a formerly fortified farmhouse that's been in operation since the 13th century. The owner, a diving expert and historian, and his family warm the coldest hearts. A while back, a *Let's Go* researcher stopped in for one night and spent 11 months here. No curfew. Bunkhouse sleeps 15 in three walk-through rooms; ask about the twin room in the main house. Bicycles available. £5.50. Sheets 50p.

Cadzow Guest House (tel. 476933), 58 North St., KY 16 9AH. 10-min. walk from the bus station; turn right on City Rd., left on Market St., left on College St., and right on North St. Well-located; vivacious owner; near cathedral and castle ruins. One single, 2 doubles, 2 twin rooms, and one family room all with bath (£17-22/person); 2 doubles without bath (£14-16/person). For stays longer than a week, subtract 5%. TVs and coffeemakers. Phone and mail reservation accepted.

Brownlees (tel. 473868), 7 Murray Place, KY16 9AP. Elegant housing only a few blocks from the Old Course and hours of golfing satisfaction. Two singles with shared bath, two twins with bath, two doubles with bath. All rooms £16-22 per person. Higher rates in summer. For stays longer than 3 days, subtract £1/person. Checkout 10:30am. Phone or mail reservations.

FOOD & DRINK

Housing is pricey but inexpensive eats abound in this college town. Find the cheapest at **Wm Low,** 130 Market St. (tel. 472448), the town supermarket (open Mon.-Wed. and Sat. 8:30am-5:30pm, Thurs. 8:30am-7:30pm, Fri. 8:30am-7pm).

St. Andrews Deli, in The Mercat Centre off Market St. (tel. 476444). You never knew Scotland had so many cheeses. The picnicker will find the Deli an intimate alternative to the supermarket. Vegetable samosas 45p. Open Mon.-Sat. 9am-5pm.

Brambles, 5 College St. (tel. 476425), between North and Market St. Anything but prickly. Vegetarians may never want to climb back out. Lasagna with salad £4.35, omelettes from £2.70. Open Mon.-Sat. 9am-5pm, Sun. noon-5pm.

B. Jannetta, 31 South St. (tel. 473285), across from the Byre Theatre. 50 flavors (!) of award-winning, homemade ice cream. Overrun by sticky-fingered children when school gets out. 48p/scoop. Open Mon.-Sat. 9am-6pm, Sun. 9am-6pm; Sept.-March closes at 5:30pm.

PM, 1 Union St. (tel. 76425), at Market St. All sorts of takeout, including fish and chips; the all-day half-price special brings stuffed potatoes under £1. No sitting area. Open daily 10am-11:30pm; Sept.-June Sun. 4-11:30pm.

St. Andrews Student Association Cafeteria (tel. 462729) in the **Student Union** at St. Mary's Place off Market St., inside by the pinball machines. Cheap and fairly edible chow. Everything from a full hot meal to a quick cheeseburger (£1); vegetable pakoras £1.70. Student ID required to enter building. Open Mon.-Fri. noon-2pm and 6-8pm; Oct.-early June Mon.-Fri. 10am-6pm, Sat.-Sun. 4-7pm.

In view of the castle ruins, **Ma Brown's** steeps tea (70p/pot), bakes scones (56p), and sets tables with bone china (open daily 10am-4:30pm). St. Andrews's student pubs are worth a peek; the one in the **Student Union** pours the cheapest pint around (open Mon.-Sat. 8-11:45pm, Nov.-May Mon.-Thurs. noon-11:45pm, Fri. noon-11:45am, Sat. 6-11:30pm, Sun. 6:30-11pm). **The Central** (tel. 478296), stereotyped as a Yah hangout ("yes" to the commoner; "yah" mocks the English public school accent), attracts a broader student clientele to its smart digs on Market and College St. (open Mon.-Sat. 11am-12:15am, Sun. 12:30-11pm). **The Victoria,** 1 St. Mary's Place (tel. 476964), is the lovechild of a Scottish pub and a Western saloon. Sip whisky at either of the two adjoining bars, or beat John Wayne at darts in the pool room (open Mon.-Wed. and Sat.-Sun. 11am-11:30pm, Thurs.-Fri. 11am-1am).

SIGHTS & ENTERTAINMENT

St. Andrews' most imposing sights are concentrated by the North Sea at the east end of town. In the Middle Ages, thousands of pilgrims journeyed to **St. Andrews Cathedral** (tel. 472563) to pray at the Saint's Shrine. During the image-razing of the Reformation, Protestants defaced the interior of the Church, which was later pillaged by locals. Today, only a facade and the outline of the walls remain of what was once Scotland's largest building, but according to legend, the cathedral's stones make up the foundation of many of St. Andrew's houses. **St. Rule's Tower** (157 steps), a square building that was part of the original 12th-century church, provides incredible views. (Admission to museum and St. Rule's Tower £1.50, £1 senior citizens and students with ISIC, 75p children. Open Mon.-Sat. 9:30am-6pm, Sun. 2-6pm; Oct.-March Mon.-Sat. 9:30am-4pm, Sun. 2-4pm). The high stone walls of **St. Andrews Castle** now tumble down to the North Sea. Once the local bishop's residence, the castle maintains explorable secret tunnels, bottle-shaped dungeons, and high stone walls to keep out (or in) rebellious heretics (same hours as Cathedral; £2, seniors and students with ISIC £1.25). Free (with admission) short historical dramas run from mid-July through August; call for details. Joint tickets admit visitors to the Cathedral and Castle (£3, seniors and students with ISIC £1.75, children £1).

St. Andrews University, founded in the 15th century, stretches just west of the castle between North St. and The Scores. The university's well-heeled student population participates in a strong performing arts program and takes red-gowned walks by the pier after chapel on Sundays. For a one hour **official tour,** simply show up to meet the guide at St. Salvator's Chapel Tower on North St. (June 20-Aug. 1 Mon.-Sat. at 10:30am and 2:30pm; £2.50, seniors and children £1.50). The tour is your key to the interiors of most university buildings; it is possible, however, to sneak views of placid quads through the parking entrances on North St.

At the northwest edge of town, St. Andrews' **Old Course,** the golf pilgrim's Canterbury, stretches regally out to a gorgeous beach as manicured as the greens (you may recognize it from the film *Chariots of Fire).* According to the 1568 Book of Articles, Mary Queen of Scots played here only days after her husband was murdered. Nonmembers must present a handicap certificate or a letter of introduction from a golf club to play the Old Course. The few starting times not reserved months in advance are distributed by lottery. (Call 475757 to enter the lottery or to reserve a time on a first-come, first-served basis at the Old, New, Jubilee, Eden, or Strethtyrum courses. £50 per round on the Old Course, £12-18 on the less prestigious courses.)

If you happened to leave your clubs at home, you can still learn about the ancient origins of putt-putt (and golf, too) next door at the **British Golf Museum** (tel. 478880). Papier-maché mannequins whittle putters and stitch balls into eternity. Films, interactive video displays, and a quiz test your knowledge (open daily 10am-5:30pm; Nov.-Feb. Thurs.-Mon. 11am-3pm; March-April Thurs.-Tues. 10am-5pm; £3.50, students and seniors £2.50, under 15 £1.50; disabled access). A wax chemist distills elixirs among the reproductions of early 20th-century shops at the small **St. Andrews Preservation Trust Museum** down North St. from the cathedral (tel. 477629; open daily April 1-4pm, June-Sept. 2-5pm, last admission 4:30pm. Donations welcome). A knowledgeable staff exhibits 19th-century clothing, toys, books, and clocks, and illuminates the mysteries of the building itself. The new **St. Andrews Museum** at Kinburn Park down Double Dykes Rd. from the Bus Station (tel. 477706) travels back to the arrival of St. Regulus and points out that golf is but "a small dot" in the town's history. Funky high-tech sensors activate displays as you approach (open daily 11am-6pm; Oct.-March Mon.-Fri. 11am-4pm, Sat.-Sun. 2-5pm; free). The **Byre Theatre,** on Abbey Court off South St., (tel. 476288, 24hrs.; booking office open Mon.-Sat. 10am-8pm on performance nights, otherwise 10am-5pm) began life in a cow shed, but now features top-notch performances nightly (£5-7.50, discounts for students, seniors, children, and disabled; standby tickets available 30 min. before curtain for £3; full disabled access). *What's On in St. Andrews,* available at the tourist office, contains schedule information.

■■■ FIFE SEASIDE

The Kingdom of Fife fills the peninsula between the Firth of Forth and the Firth of Tay. **The East Neuk,** a series of sun-warmed fishing villages with jigsaw-puzzle-box scenery, occupies the coast south of St. Andrews. Near the point of Fife (Fife Ness) sleeps the village of **Crail,** a perfect place to do nothing but gnaw on the freshly caught crab claws sold at a little stall by the harbor. From St. Andrews, take the A917 to the coast, or catch bus #95 (hourly) from St. Andrews or Anstruther. Crail's **tourist office,** 62-64 Marketgate (tel. (01333) 450869), is also home to a small local history museum (office and museum open Easter week and June-mid-Sept. Mon.-Sat. 10:30am-12:30pm and 2:30-5pm, Sun. 2:30-5pm). Guided walks of the town leave from the museum every Sunday from the last Sunday in June through August, at 2:15pm (1½-2 hrs.; £1).

About 5 mi. west of Crail along the A917 (or 9 mi. southeast of St. Andrews along the direct connecting road) lies **Anstruther,** home to a quiet harbor, 14 pubs, and Mr. Pennington's wonderful rustic bunkhouse (see St. Andrews: Accommodations, above). The fastest, cheapest way to Anstruther is by minibus #61 (7-8/day Mon.-Sat., from Blackfriars Chapel on South St.; 20min.; £1.65). Fife Scottish (#95) also makes 17 runs daily to Anstruther and Elie (£1.75). Near Anstruther, the **Isle of May** rises like a giant molar from the Firth of Forth. Actually a national nature reserve, the Isle is home to puffins, ducks, grey seals, and the archaeological remains of human inhabitants from over 2,000 years ago. In summer, **Jim Raeper** (tel. (01333) 310103) sails from Anstruther to the Isle (July-Aug. daily; May-June and Sept. Wed.-Mon.; £9, children £4) and offers 3-hr. charter fishing trips (£10/person, bait and lines supplied). All trips are highly contingent on the weather and tides; call ahead for times or check with the **Anstruther Tourist Office** (tel. (01333) 311073). Rent a cycle at **East Neuk Cycles,** 61 James St. (tel. (01334) 312179; £5/day).

Five mi. west of Anstruther, along the A917 and just outside of the village of **Elie** (EEL-y), lies beautiful **Ruby Bay,** named for the garnets found on its sands. While Fife boasts excellent bathing waters (among the purest in Great Britain), you can command a better, quieter view of the sporting seals, tidal-pool marine life, and slippery, yellow rocks from the headland by the lighthouse. Continue down the coast to the Lady's Tower, built in the 18th century as a bathing box for Lady Jane Anstruther (who reportedly sent a bell-ringing servant through the streets to warn the village of her presence, lest anyone see her scantily clad).

North of St. Andrews, in Fife's northeastern nook, is the **Tentsmuir Point Nature Reserve,** a forest park hemmed in from the sea by a 10-mi.-long beach. Gain access to the park from **Leuchars,** on the St. Andrews-Dundee road and on Scotrail's Edinburgh-Dundee line (see St. Andrews: Getting There, above). The only **HI Youth Hostel** (tel. (01337) 57710; grade 3; £3.65) in the area is 20 mi. inland in **Falkland,** one of the most complete "auld toons" in Fife. The nearby **Falkland Palace and Gardens,** (tel. (01337) 857397), once the hunting lodge of the Stuarts, epitomizes outstanding early Renaissance architecture (open April-Sept. Mon.-Sat. 10am-6pm, Sun. 2-6pm; last entry 5pm; £3.50, seniors and children £1.80). Falkland is most easily accessible from the town of **Kirkcaldy,** due south on the coast (bus #36; Mon.-Sat. 5/day from Kirkcaldy to Falkland); Kirkcaldy is also on the Edinburgh-St. Andrews bus route (#X59; 6/day). Many hitch from St. Andrews to Falkland along the busy A91.

■■■ PERTH

About 30 mi. west of St. Andrews lies **Perth,** an unpretentious city on the banks of the River Tay. Seat of the Scottish Reformation, Perth was recently voted the best place to live in Britain, and though that certainly doesn't mean Perth is the best place to *visit* in Britain, its church, gardens, and free museums do make it a nice place to stop over. Perth has an air of the real, refreshing after the sporran mugs and poorly-staged Scottish Evenings of Glasgow and Edinburgh.

PRACTICAL INFORMATION

The **tourist office,** 45 High St. (tel. 638353), several blocks away from the train and bus stations, offers an unparalleled selection of maps, regional literature, and haggis to go. From the bus station, turn right on Leonard St., continue along S. Methven St., and turn right on High St., which becomes a pedestrian precinct (open daily 9am-8pm; April-June and Sept.-Oct. Mon.-Sat. 9am-6pm; Nov.-March Mon.-Sat. 9am-5pm). The **train station** on Leonard St. (tel. 637117) faces the **bus station** (tel. 626848). **Lockers** at the train station cost £1-2. Hillend bus #7, which passes the HI Youth Hostel, stops first at the **post office,** 109 South St. (post office open Mon.-Fri. 9am-5:30pm, Sat. 9-12:30pm). From the bus station turn right and continue along Leonard St., then turn right on South St. Perth's **telephone code** is 01738. **Buses** run to most major towns in Scotland, including Inverness (1/hr.; £8.10), Edinburgh (16/day; £4.10), Glasgow (1/hr; £6.20), and Aberdeen (1/hr; £8.20). Trains depart for Inverness (6-9/day; £12), Edinburgh (7/day; £7.30), and Glasgow (5-9/day; £9).

ACCOMMODATIONS & FOOD

The musically-inclined warden entertains guests with an endless supply of jokes at Perth's immaculate **HI Youth Hostel,** Glasgow Rd. (tel. 623658). Take the Hillend bus #7 from the South St. post office, or hike uphill from town until the carved, fortified walls come into view on your right (grade 1; curfew 11:30pm; reception open 7am-11:30pm; check-in after 9:30am, checkout 10:30am; lockers 50p; £6.50; open late Feb.-Oct.). B&Bs (£14-20) line Glasgow Rd., below the hostel.

Princes St., near the river, overflows with reasonably priced food; a spicy three-course lunch costs £4 at **Shezan Tandoori,** 21 Princes St. (tel. 620415; open Mon.-Thurs. noon-2pm and 5pm-midnight, Fri.-Sat. noon-2pm and 5pm-1am, Sun. 4pm-midnight). For Chinese takeout (£3.40-4.20/dish) or fish and chips (£1-2.40), try **Mr. Chan** next door (open Mon.-Thurs. noon-midnight, Fri.-Sat. noon-1am, Sun. 4pm-midnight). Get lost in the enormous **Safeway** on Caledonian Rd. (open Mon.-Wed. and Sat. 8am-8pm, Thurs.-Fri. 8am-9pm, Sun. 10am-6pm).

SIGHTS

Perth's attractiveness amounts to more than the mere sum of its parts (all within walking distance). Take a stroll along the swiftly flowing River Tay and admire the multiple arches of the **Perth Bridge;** some of the small, cypress-laden islands in the

Tay are explorable when the water level is low—look for designated bridges. Across the bridge, a nature trail leads up to a panoramic view from **Kinnoull Hill Park.** In 1559, John Knox delivered the incendiary sermon that sparked the Scottish Reformation's mass destruction of churches and monasteries from the pulpit of **St. John's Kirk,** Perth's oldest church, just south of the tourist office on St. John's Place (open Tues.-Wed. and Fri.-Sat. 10am-noon and 2-4pm, Thurs. 10am-noon).

The **Fergusson Gallery** (tel. 441944), housed in the Old Perth Water Works on Marshall Pl., is a poetic site for an excellent collection of watercolors by the Scottish artist J.D. Fergusson, heavily influenced by his life companion, the dancer Margaret Morris (open Mon.-Sat. 10am-5pm; free). Look for the old, neo-classical rotunda under the words "Aquam Igne et Aquam Haurio." An intriguing display on the excavations of medieval Perth rubs shoulders with a hodgepodge collection of antique clocks and fine silverware in the **Perth Museum and Art Gallery,** at the intersection of Tay St. and Perth Bridge (open Mon.-Sat. 10am-5pm; free).

Balhousie Castle, off Hay St. (tel. 621281), the 16th-century home of the Earls of Kinnoull, now accommodates the **Black Watch Regimental Museum,** which includes hundreds of documents, weapons, and medals of the Black Watch back to the 18th-century, among them the key to the back door of Spandau prison in Berlin (open Mon.-Fri. 10am-4:30pm, Sun. 2-4:30pm; Oct.-Easter Mon.-Fri. 10am-3pm; free). **North Inch,** a lush park adjacent to the castle on the beaches of the Tay, combines 100 acres of pleasantly wooded walks and an 18-hole public golf course. The Battle of the Clans took place here in 1396. At the other end of town, **South Inch** offers still more recreational space and nice views of the river. Take big strides across the Inches and pretend you're a mite.

For warmer waters, head to the **Perth Leisure Pool,** an enormous indoor recreation complex with water flumes and exercise equipment near the hostel on Glasgow Rd. You may find yourself fluming with royalty—Princess Anne opened the building in 1988. Ask about discounts for hostelers (tel. 630535; open daily 10am-10pm; for a 1-hr. swim £2.40, children £1.20; disabled access). Next door to the pool, the **Dewar's Rink** (tel. 624188) stays open all summer and on alternate weekends in winter. (Didn't think whisky could freeze, eh?) Go skating or watch a game of curling—a Scottish sport fusing bowling, darts, the custodial sciences, and ice. Fans of aromatic recreation might take a walk in **Bell's Cherrybank Gardens,** which has the largest collection of heather in the U.K. (open 9am-5pm).

■ NEAR PERTH

Less than five miles northeast of Perth on the A93, sumptuous **Scone Palace** (SCOON; tel. (01738) 52300) witnessed the coronation of many Scottish monarchs on the famous Stone of Scone. Stolen by the English in the 14th century (perhaps they mistook it for a typical English breakfast), the stone now rests in Westminster Cathedral, chained to the floor to prevent a Scottish rescue (open July-Aug. Mon.-Sat. 9:30am-5pm, Sun. 10am-5pm; Sept. to mid-Oct. Mon.-Sat. 9:30am-5pm, Sun. 1:30-5pm; £4, seniors £3.20, children £2.20; grounds only £1.85 and £1). Take bus #8 or 58 from the post office in Perth (5-6/day, more on Sunday). **Glamis Castle** (GLOMZ; tel. (0130784) 0242), Macbeth's purported home and childhood playground of the Queen Mum, pokes its dozen storybook turrets into the sky 35 mi. northeast of Perth on the A94 toward Dundee. The castle houses collections of armor, paintings, and antique furniture (open May-Sept. daily 11am-5:30pm, Oct. 1-23 Sat.-Sun. 11am-5:30pm; £4, students and seniors £3.10, children £2.20).

DUNKELD & BIRNAM

From the loch to the firth that both bear its name, the River Tay flows through the forested hills of Perthshire. Huddled on either side of the River Tay, the wee twin towns of Dunkeld (dun-KELD) and Birnam provide the most accessible, interesting bases for exploring this isolated region. The snow-capped mountains falling steeply into the deep, sparkling waters of Loch Tay combine to create Perthshire's finest scenery. This extremely walkable district is dotted with hilltop forts, 16th-century castles, and formal gardens.

Dunkeld's painstakingly restored 17th-century houses line the way to a partially charred 12th-century **cathedral,** containing the stone sarcophagus of the notorious "Wolf of Badenoch." Alexander Stewart, the ill-tempered and illegitimate son of English King Richard II, sought revenge for his excommunication by razing several Tayside villages and lifting the gold chalices out of Elgin Cathedral. You may rest in peace in the garden beside the church (open Mon.-Sat. 9:30am-7pm, Sun. 2-7pm; Oct.-March Mon.-Sat. 9:30am-4pm, Sun. 2-4pm; free).

Lovely walks from Dunkeld lead north along the forested banks of the Tay to the great **Birnam Oak,** the remnant of Shakespeare's fabled Birnam Wood. The brisk and savage waterfalls of the **Hermitage** tumble 1½ mi. away. This National Trust property has a well-marked ¾-mi. path which takes you to all the designated "Kodak Spots" (free walking tours July to mid-Sept. Mon. at 2pm). If you prefer wheels, you can hire a snazzy cycle at **Dunkeld Mountain Bikes** (tel. 728744), next to the Tay Bridge (open daily 9am-6pm; road bikes £8/day, mountain bikes £13/day).

Beatrix Potter spent most of her childhood holidays in the Birnam area, and her experiences there allegedly inspired *The Tale of Peter Rabbit.* The **Beatrix Potter Garden and Exhibition Centre** in Birnam recreates the setting of the famed bunny's escapades, including Mrs. Tiggywinkle's house and Peter's burrow (open mid-June to mid-Sept. Mon.-Sat 10am–4pm, Sun. 2-4pm). Take care for the watering cans.

Naturalists and bird-watchers will enjoy the **Loch of the Lowes** (tel. 727337), a wildlife reserve 2 mi. east of Dunkeld just off A293 (Loch's **visitor center** open mid-July to mid-Aug. daily 10am-6pm; April to mid-July and mid-Aug. to Sept. daily 10am-5pm). The **Dunkeld and Birnam Arts Festival,** held each year on the last weekend in June, celebrates local crafts, art, food, and music.

Birnam B&Bs congregate around the corner from the train station. In diminutive Dunkeld, **Mrs. Elliot** (tel. 727650) offers twin and double rooms for £23. Campers can stake a claim at the **Inver Mill Caravan Park** (tel. 727217) (£2/small tent, £6/ tent and car; toilets and showers). For a light lunch and a chat with the locals, try **The Tappit Hen** at 7 Atholl St. (open Mon.-Sat. 10:30am-5pm; Sun. 11:30am-5pm; Nov.-Easter Mon.-Sat. 10:30am-5pm) or **The Country Bakery** (open Mon.-Sat. 8am-5pm, Sun. 9am-4pm) down the street (around £3).

The **Dunkeld tourist office** (tel. 727688) lies about a mile from the **"Dunkeld" train station,** which is actually in Birnam. Officials will stock you with pamphlets and send you briskly on your way. (Tourist office open June Mon.-Sat. 9am-6pm, Sun. 11am-5pm; July-Aug. Mon.-Sat. 9am-7:30pm, Sun. 11am-7:30pm; mid-March to May and Sept.-Oct. Mon.-Sat. 9am-5:30pm, Sun. 2-5pm; Nov.-Dec. Sat. 11am-4pm, Sun. 2-4pm.) The **telephone code** for these towns is 01350. The station is on the main Edinburgh-Inverness line. **Scottish Citylink** buses traveling north from Perth to Inverness will drop you at the train station; southbound buses stop at the Birnam Hotel. **Stagecoach's** infrequent Perth-to-Pitlochry buses stop in Birnam and at the North End Car Park in Dunkeld (£3.40). Buy your ticket for both services. On your way out of town, grab a twig or two and bring Birnamwood to Dunsinane.

Near Dunkeld & Birnam

As one might expect, the most beautiful part of Perthshire is also the least accessible. Eighteen miles west of Dunkeld and Birnam lies **Aberfeldy,** a tiny town whose charms Robert Burns found lichtsome (heartwarming). The 150-year-old **Aberfeldy Distillery** (tel. (01887) 820330) offers free tours that end with a nip (open Easter-Oct. Mon.-Fri. 10am-noon). The **Aberfeldy Water Mill** (tel. (01887) 820803) on Mill St. harnesses water power to turn two 1½-ton stone grinding wheels (open Easter-Oct. Mon.-Sat. 10am-5:30pm, Sun. 10am-5:30pm; £1.80, children 85p). The Aberfeldy **tourist office** (tel. (01887) 820276) resides in an old church (open April-Sept. Mon.-Sat. 9am-7pm, Sun. 11am-6pm, open only occasionally Nov.-March). Catch Aberfeldy-bound buses in the North End Car Park in Dunkeld, on Mill St. in Perth, or in front of the Bank of Scotland in Pitlochry.

The remarkable village of **Fortingall**, about 4 mi. northwest of Kenmore (beyond Aberfeldy on the A827), appears twice in the Book of World Records (maybe a record itself): once as home to a 3,000-year-old yew tree, the oldest living organism in Europe, and again as legendary birthplace of Pontius Pilate, whose father was purportedly a Roman soldier stationed here.

At the opposite end of much-sung Loch Tay, the village of **Killin** harbors many reasonably-priced B&Bs and a green-gabled **HI Youth Hostel** (tel. (01567) 820546; grade 2) where the warden can answer your questions in five different languages (lockout 10:30am-5pm; £4.80; open late March-Oct.). The **tourist office** (tel. (01567) 820254) on Main St. provides plentiful information on countless hill walks and water sports on the surrounding lochs (open July-early Sept. daily 9:30am-7pm; April-May and late Sept. 10am-5pm; June and mid-Sept. 10am-6pm). One of the best short hikes starts from behind the schoolyard on Main St. and leads up to a marvelous sheep's eye view of the loch. Midway between Kenmore and Killin on the west shore of Loch Tay, and 7 mi. northeast of town, perches the **Ben Lawers Visitors Centre** (tel. (01567) 820397; open mid-April to Sept. daily 10am-5pm), marking the trailhead of a day-hike up Britain's third-highest peak, **Ben Golomstock,** covered with rare alpine flowers. Bus service to Killin is highly variable; currently, **Scottish Citylink** provides transportation to and from Killin.

■■■ PITLOCHRY

Amid the foliage and mist of the Grampian Mountains, Pitlochry has attracted tourists from afar since the mid-19th century. It does so with charm, grace, and resourcefulness—beyond the thronged shops selling shortbread, knitwear, and whisky rest an excellent summer theater, a dam and salmon ladder, and two distilleries, held together by a spectacular web of hill walks and the River Tummel.

PRACTICAL INFORMATION

A wealth of friendly advice awaits at the **tourist office,** 22 Atholl Rd. (tel. 472215; open late May-early Sept. daily 9am-8pm; late March-late May and mid-Sept.-Oct. Mon.-Sat. 9am-6pm, Sun. noon-6pm; Nov.-March. Mon.-Fri. 9am-5pm, Sat. 9:30am-1:30pm). Pitlochry's **postal code** is PH16 5BX; its **telephone code** is 01796.

Trains (no phone; for info. call Perth Station at (01738) 637117) stop alongside the town center on frequent trips to Edinburgh (6/day; 2hr.; £16), Glasgow (5/day; 1hr. 45min.; £16), Perth (10/day; 30min.; £6.70), and Inverness (8/day; 1hr. 45min.; £11.50). The station office lockers are 50p (open Mon.-Sat. 7:55am-6:40pm, Sun. 10:30am-6pm). When the station is unstaffed, the yellow phone on the platform connects to the information office at Inverness Station. **Buses,** which stop outside the Fishers Hotel on Atholl Rd., make hourly trips to Perth, Inverness, Edinburgh, and Glasgow. Ticket prices fluctuate greatly during the year—buy them on the bus. In summer, the **Heather-Hopper** runs to Ballater, Braemar, and Banchory Wed. and Fri. (early July-late Sept. (01330) 823456 or (01738) 629339).

ACCOMMODATIONS & FOOD

The attractive **HI Youth Hostel** (tel. 472308) at Knockard Rd. and Wall Brae overlooks the town and mountains. From the Fishers Hotel on Atholl Rd., follow the signposts uphill from Bonnethill Rd. about five minutes. This former hotel has a shower in each immaculate four- to eight-bed room, and a dining room with picture-window views of the town center, village church, and cloud-decked countryside (curfew 11:30pm; £6.50; breakfast £2.80, dinner £3.75).

If you're willing to walk a mi. up West Moulin Rd. to **Moulin,** a petite village adjoining Pitlochry, you'll have the pleasure of staying at either **Mrs. Currie's** (tel. 472868; £13.50) or **Mrs. Bright's** (tel. 472058; £12.50-13.50) friendly and well-appointed home. You can camp if you want to, you can leave your friends behind, 2 mi. north of town at **Faskally Home Farm** (tel. 472007), which has 150 sites (£6.60/person and tent, each additional person 70p; full facilities included; swimming pool, jacuzzi, and sauna available at extra charge). Silence your growling stomach at **Reid's Restaurant,** 101 Atholl Rd. (open daily 9:30am-6pm; Nov.-March 10am-5pm) or **MacDonald's Restaurant** at 140 Atholl Rd. (open daily 8am-9:30pm; Sept.-June 8am-8pm)—no McNuggets here. Try **Bamboo Garden** at 48 Atholl Rd. for Chinese take-away under £4 (open Sun.-Thurs. 3pm-midnight, Fri.-Sat. noon-midnight). **Penny's,** the largest supermarket in town, is up W. Moulin Rd. from Atholl Rd. (open Mon.-Fri. 9am-8pm, Sat. 8:30am-5:30pm, Sun. 9am-5pm).

SIGHTS

The word "whisky" comes from an old Gaelic term meaning "the water of life," and Pitlochry may live forever. Down the main road a ½ mi. from the tourist office is **Blair Atholl Distillery** (tel. 472234), where enough alcohol evaporates daily to intoxicate the entire town. Tours leave from the gift shop; bekilted guides take you from flowing water to mashing malt to a free wee dram (open Mon.-Sat. 9am-5pm; Easter-Oct. also Sun. noon-5pm; £2). **The Edradour** (tel. (01776) 472095) is Scotland's tiniest distillery, and still employs old-fashioned techniques to turn out 12 casks a week. If you can cover the 2½ mi. between the Edradour and Pitlochry (past the village of Moulin along the A924), you'll be rewarded with an absolutely free tour and a free gulp of whisky to liven up the walk back.

The glassy, glitzy **Pitlochry Festival Theatre,** just over the Aldour Bridge from town, draws outstanding performers from all over the world from May to early October (box office tel. 472680). From late May to mid-September in the recreational field down Tummel Crescent, Mondays are **Highland Nights,** when you can enjoy excellent local pipe bands and traditional dancing (tickets available at the gate; £2.50, children 50p). Pick up *What's On in Perthshire* at the tourist office for a list of other performances and activities.

Arm yourself with a copy of *Pitlochry Walks* (£1; available at the tourist office), and the surrounding countryside is yours for the exploring. For a quick introduction, take the path over the bouncy suspension footbridge to the **Pitlochry Dam** and the famous **salmon ladder.** From an underground observation chamber, voyeurs watch the spawning fish struggle valiantly against the current. The unromantic may get a permit and angle 100 yards upstream. The Dam office (tel. 473152) puts on an interactive video demonstration of the workings of the dam and ladder (open April-Oct. daily 9:40am-5:30pm; observation chamber and dam free; Visitors' Centre £1.50, students £1, children 60p). For another easy day trip, try the trail up 2757-ft. **Ben-y-Vrackie;** on a clear day you'll see all the way to Edinburgh from the summit. The walk up to the top of **Craigower** can be completed in under an hour.

■ NEAR PITLOCHRY

A 2½ mi. trail leads from the dam to the **Pass of Killiecrankie,** where a Jacobite army tried to reinstall James VII of Scotland on the English throne in 1689, slaughtering King William III's troops in the attempt. One stranded Jacobite vaulted 18 feet across **Soldier's Leap,** preferring to risk the steep fall rather than surrender to the English. The area affords spectacular views, especially over the River Garry at sunset. For information or a guided walk, stop in at the **National Trust Visitors Centre** (tel. (01796) 473233; open June-Aug. daily 9:30am-6pm; April-May and Sept.-Oct. daily 10am-5pm). Coach service runs from the West End Car Park in Pitlochry to the Pass in summer (Mon.-Sat. 1/day).

Blair Castle (tel. (01796) 481207), 7 mi. north of Pitlochry on the A9, is full of artifacts from all around Scotland dating back to the 12th century. The castle's well-groomed lawns are occasionally used as training grounds for the Duke of Atholl's army, the only private army in Western Europe. Prepared to fight in both the American Revolution and WWI, the army traveled as far as Ireland but was never sent to battle (open daily 10am-6pm; £4, seniors, students, and children £3).

■■■ ABERDEEN

The center of Britain's North Sea oil industry, Aberdeen is a practical city that somewhat offsets its dirt and smog with attractive parks and a vibrant university. Aberdeen's real attraction, though, is its closeness to some of the finest castles and least crowded countryside in Scotland—should the scattered trash and unrelieved grey granite of the city become oppressive, the nearby castles of Brodie, Crathes, Fraser, Drum, and Fyvie make unforgettable daytrips by bus.

GETTING THERE

Aberdeen can be easily reached by land, sea, or air. **National Express** visits from Edinburgh (at least 1/hr.; £11.70), Glasgow (at least 1/hr.; £12.10), and London (2/day; £38). **Bluebird Northern** rides from Inverness (6/day; £8.40). **Scotrail** provides train service to Edinburgh (Mon.-Sat. 20/day, Sun. 13/day; £27.50), Glasgow (Mon.-Sat. 17/day, Sun. 10/day; £31.50), Inverness (Mon.-Sat. 12/day, Sun. 5/day; £16), and London (3/day direct; £67). Fares increase by approximately 10% for travel on Friday and Saturday during July and August.

British Airways (tel. (0181) 697400) makes five to seven daily flights from **Aberdeen Airport** (tel. 722331) to London and **Air UK** flies to Heathrow and Stansted.

The **Aberdeen Ferry Terminal,** Jamieson's Quay (tel. 572615), is the only place on mainland Britain where you can catch a ferry to the Shetlands, though you may prefer the much briefer **British Airways/BABA flight** from Orkney (see Shetland Islands: Getting There, below). **Ferries** go to Lerwick (for information see Shetland Islands: Getting There, below) and Stromness (see Orkney Islands: Getting There, below). Turn left at the traffic light off Market St. past the **P&O Scottish Ferries** warehouse (office open Mon.-Fri. 8:45am-6pm, Sat. 9am-6pm).

PRACTICAL INFORMATION

Tourist Office: St. Nicholas House, Broad St. AB9 1DE (tel. 632727; 24-hr. information tel. 636363), a five min. walk from train and bus stations. Turn right on Guild St., left onto Market St., right onto Union St., and left again at Broad St. Atmosphere not unlike that of the Castle of Nymphs in *Monty Python and the Holy Grail*. The staff will swoop down and book rooms; ask for *It's Free in Aberdeen*. Open Mon.-Fri. 9am-8pm, Sat. 9am-6pm, Sun. 10am-6pm; June and Sept. Mon.-Sat. 9am-6pm, Sun. 10am-4pm; Oct.-May Mon.-Fri. 9am-5pm, Sat. 10am-2pm.

Financial Services: Banks line Union St. **Thomas Cook,** 335-7 Union St. (tel. 212272). Open Mon. and Wed.-Fri. 9am-5:30pm, Tues. 10am-5:30pm, Sat. 9am-5pm. **American Express:** 4-5 Union Terr., 2nd floor (tel. 642961). Client mail held. Open Mon.-Wed. and Fri.-Sat. 9am-5:30pm, Tues. 10:30am-5:30pm. **ATM machines** accept Cirrus at the Nationwide Building Company, 250 Union St., and next door at National Westminster Bank. Also at the Safeway Supermarket.

Post Office: St. Nicholas Centre, Upperkirkgate (tel. 633065). Open Mon.-Fri. 9am-5:30pm, Sat. 9am-12:30pm. The Crown St. office (turreted building on your right as you come down Union St.) accepts *Poste Restante*. **Postal Code:** AB9 1AA.

Telephone Code: 01224.

Train Station: Right next to the bus station on Guild St. (tel. 594 222). Lockers £1-2. Ticket office open Mon.-Sat. 6:30am-8pm, Sun. 8:45am-7:30pm.

Bus Station: Guild St. (tel. 212266). Ticket office open Mon.-Thurs. 8:15am-5:25pm, Fri. 8:15am-5:40pm, Sat. 8:30am-4:55pm. **Luggage storage** Mon.-Fri. 8:15am-6pm; £1.50/day/bag.

Launderette: In Aberdeen University's student unions. **Aberdeen Cleaning Centre,** 144 Crown St. (tel. 590076). Open Mon.-Fri. 8:30am-5:30pm, Sat. 9am-1pm.

Women's Center, Shoe Lane (tel. 625010). Offers references and advice on women's issues. Open for drop-in Mon.-Fri. 9:30am-2:30pm.

Gay and Lesbian Groups: Aberdeen Young Lesbian Group (tel. 625010), meets on the last Wed. of every month at 7pm in the Women's Centre. **Gay Society of Aberdeen University,** weekly coffee shop and discussion group. Meets every Thurs. noon-2pm, at the S.R.C. Building, High St., in Old Aberdeen. Both

open to the general public. Women's Centre can provide further info on current gay/lesbian group activities.
Hospital: tel. 681818.
Emergency: Dial 999; no coins required.
Police: Queen St. (tel. 639111).

ACCOMMODATIONS & CAMPING

Great Western Road, 20 minutes from the train and bus stations on foot and also accessible by bus #17, 18, or 19, bursts with B&Bs (£15-23). Take care after dark; the area gets a bit randy. **King George VI Memorial Hostel (HI),** is in a better neighborhood at 8 Queen's Rd. (tel. 646988). Take a 30-minute walk west on Union St. and Albyn Pl. from the city center or a short ride on bus #14, 15, or 27 to Queen's Rd. This humongous hostel has spacious dorms and basement ping-pong and pool tables. (Grade 1; 11:30pm lights-out and 8:30am wake-up enforced with friendly yet firm hand; lockout 10:30am-1:30pm; curfew 2am. £7.25, breakfast £2.80, dinner £3.75. Open mid-Feb. to early Jan.) For **camping,** try **Hazlehead Park** on Groats Rd. (tel. 321268; £3.25-6.45/tent; take bus #14 or 15).

FOOD & DRINK

Get your groceries at the huge Safeway supermarket (tel. 624404), 215 King St. (open Mon.-Wed. and Sat. 8am-8pm, Thurs.-Fri. 8am-9pm, Sun. 9am-6pm). For wholefoods, try **Fresh Fields,** 49 Netherkirkgate, beside Marks & Spencer (open Mon.-Wed. and Fri.-Sat. 9am-5pm, Thurs. 9am-6:30pm).

Harvesters Wholefood Take Away, 137 Union Grove (tel. 580315). Healthy, wholesome food to go. Gigantic sandwiches £1-1.90, soup with bread £1. Daily hot dish from £1.50. Open Mon.-Fri. 8am-3pm.

Gannet's, Broad St. at Upperkirkgate, on 2nd floor of Aberdeen Students' Union. Tasty pizzas at palatable prices: deep-pan cheese pizza £2.45, toppings 40p each. Hot meals under £2.50. Open mid-June to early July and mid-Aug. to Sept. Mon.-Sat. 10:30am-5pm; Oct. to mid-June Mon.-Fri. 9am-6:30pm, Sat. 11am-6:30pm.

The Grill, 213 Union St. Classic. Pints £1.45, steak pie 75p, hot lunches £1.15-1.50. Open Mon.-Thurs. 10am-11pm, Fri.-Sat. 11am-midnight, Sun. 7:30-11pm.

The Nile, 224 Union St. (tel. 624040). Excellent pub lunches and dinners (if a little bit dear) under the approving gaze of King Tut. Jugs of cider and lager £2.50.

SIGHTS & ENTERTAINMENT

Aberdeen's **fish market** (on Market St., near Palmerston Rd.) worth seeing, though you can only buy in bulk. Between 4 and 8am (Mon.-Fri.), boats land and auctioneers hawk haddock and hack heads. **Old Aberdeen** and **Aberdeen University** are a short bus ride (#1, 2, 3, 4, or 15) from the city center, or a long walk through commercial and residential districts along King St. Peaceful **King's College Chapel** (tel. 272137) dates from the 16th century, and features intricately carved "misery seats"—each has its own subtly distinctive pattern (open Mon.-Fri 9am-5pm). The twin-spired **St. Machar's Cathedral,** with its heraldic ceiling and stained glass, was built in the 13th century (open daily 9am-5pm; Sunday services 11am and 6pm).

Provost Skene's House, on Guestrow near the tourist office, is a beautifully restored 16th-century townhouse dressed in styles from Georgian to Victorian; a tiny museum of local archaeology huddles in the attic (open Mon.-Sat. 10am-5pm; free). At the **Maritime Museum** (tel. 585788), overlooking the harbor in Provost Ross's House, resist the temptation to unwind the huge coil of rope, and move on to the fascinating model of an oil rig (open Mon.-Sat. 10am-5pm; free).

Aberdeen has a fine sandy **beach** that stretches north for about 2 mi. from the old fishing community of Footdee (fi-TEE, foot of the River Dee) to the Don estuary. Two amusement parks rear over the southern end, while the beach's northern sands are cleaner and often quieter (take bus #14).

For another stroll, follow the **Old Deeside Line Walkway,** an abandoned railroad, through southwest Aberdeen; the trail begins at Duthie Park and leads out of the city center toward the village of Cults. **Duthie Park,** by the River Dee, at Polmuir Rd. and Riverside Dr., includes playgrounds, flower gardens, and the unique, oxymoronic **Winter Gardens Hothouse** (hothouse open daily 10am-dusk; free). Aberdeen's largest park, **Hazlehead,** on the western edge of the city off Queen's Rd., has an aviary and extensive woodlands. Take bus #14 or 15 to Queen's Rd. and walk 1 mi. on Hazlehead Ave. **Victoria Park,** just west of the city center on Westburn Rd., has a garden for the blind—strong-scented flowers are identified by Braille plaques.

The **Aberdeen Art Gallery,** Schoolhill (tel. 646333), houses a wide range of English, French, and Scottish paintings; its 20th-century British collection is particularly worthy. The gallery now hosts drama, dance, and music performances in the summer; check the *Gallery* for details (open Mon.-Sat. 10am-5pm, Thurs. 10am-8pm, Sun. 2-5pm; free). The **Aberdeen Arts Centre,** 33 King St. at W. North St. (tel. 635208), offers fine avant-garde and traditional theater performances (tickets £3.50-5). The adjacent café sometimes has after-show music, and the center frequently hosts modern craft, print, and photography shows (gallery open Mon.-Sat. 10am-5pm; free). **The Lemon Tree Café Theatre** presents folk, jazz, rock, and drama in all their permutations in its two theaters. Call 642230 to find out what's happening here on Shoe Lane (near the corner of W. North St. and Queen St.). The bored should snag a copy of the tourist office's monthly *What's On in Aberdeen,* or call the 24-hr. hotline (tel. 636363).

■■■ EAST GRAMPIAN COAST & GRAMPIAN MOUNTAINS

South of Aberdeen fifteen miles on the A92 lies the seaside market town of **Stonehaven** (pop. 9200). Though no longer a substantial fishing port, the town makes what it can of its maritime exploits: **Tolbooth Museum,** on the Old Pier, preserves local fishing lore and artifacts (open June-Sept. Mon. and Thurs.-Sat. 10am-noon and 2-5pm, Wed. and Sun. 2-5pm; free). Stonehaven also boasts a glorious golf course and a gleaming white-sand beach. The **tourist office** (tel. (01569) 762806) is at 66 Allardice St. (open July-early Sept. daily 10am-7:30pm; mid-May to June and mid-Sept. daily 10am-6:30pm; mid-April to mid-May and late Sept.-Oct. daily 10am-5pm).

The Grampian coast is dotted with some of the most dramatic castles in Scotland. The well-marked Castle Trail provides heavy doses of Scottish history. Losing your way along here might be the best part of your trip. The splendidly decrepit **Dunnottar Castle** (tel. (01569) 762173) crumbles on the cliffs 1 mi. farther south. Built in the 12th century by the Earl Marischal's family, the castle commands a gut-wrenching view of the crashing sea. With the help of much styrofoam staging, it served as the shooting location for Franco Zefferelli's 1991 film of *Hamlet* (open March-Oct. 9am-6pm, Sun. 2-5pm; Nov.-March Mon.-Fri. 9am-dusk; £2, children £1). Frequent trains (17-25/day; 20min.) and Scottish Citylink and Bluebird Northern buses (30min.; £2.50) connect Stonehaven to Aberdeen.

Easily accessible from Aberdeen by bus (Bluebird #201 to Braemar), **Crathes Castle and Garden** took forty years to complete in the 16th century and houses the ancient Horn to Leys given to the family patriarch, Alexander Burnett, by Robert the Bruce in 1323. It's a good thing the castle was never attacked—the fierce cannons projecting from the towers are a bluff, actually shooting out water rather than cannonballs or cows. The castle is supposedly haunted by a Green Lady, who certainly has a green thumb—in the spectacular Crathes gardens, the occasional Welsh poppy sidles up to black irises and medicinal foxglove (castle open April-late Oct. daily 11am-5:30pm (last entry to castle 4:45pm). Gardens and grounds open all year daily 9:30am-sunset. Castle and grounds £4; half-price for hostelers with HI card, seniors and children).

Northwest 27 mi. from Aberdeen, on the inland A947 to Banff, is the splendidly intact 13th-century **Fyvie Castle** (tel. (01651) 891266). Buses are frequent (open June-Aug. daily 11am-6pm; Sept.-April 2-6pm; £3.50, seniors and children £1.80).

The road continues through farmland to the northern coast at **Banff** (around Kinnaird's Head from Aberdeen on the coastal road), one of a string of quiet fishing villages along the coast between Fraserburgh and Elgin. Grab a dossier of schedules from the Elgin or Aberdeen tourist office to guide you through bus service.

West of Aberdeen, the River Dee meanders through green pastures to the tiny towns of **Ballater** and **Braemar** after it gushes down from the Grampian Mountains. This area is ideal for hillwalking in the summer (pick up a copy of *Hillwalking in the Grampian Highlands* (£1) at any tourist office in the region), and in winter it offers some of Britain's best alpine and cross-country skiing, though the disdainful Swiss would sniff and ski away. Finding a bed should be no problem if the royals can't fit you in at **Balmoral Castle** (tel. (013397) 42334), the royal family's holiday residence (open May-July Mon.-Sat. 10am-5pm; £2, seniors £1.50, children free). Stay instead at the **HI Youth Hostel** in Ballater (tel. (013397) 55227; grade 3) on Deebank Rd. Turn right as you leave the bus station, then left onto Dee St., and take the third right onto Deebank Rd. by the river (open late March-early Jan., £3.85).

Farther west 12 mi. on the A93 is **Braemar,** with its fully-furnished 17th-century **Braemar Castle,** stronghold of the Farquharson clan (open May-early Oct. Sat.-Thurs. 10am-6pm; £1.70, seniors £1.30, children 90p). In the cemetery nearby, locked to the public, lies the last (but no longer) living Jacobite. The **HI Youth Hostel** in Braemar (tel. (013397) 41659; grade 1) is just south of town in an old stone house on Glenshee Rd. (£6.85; open late Oct.-Aug.). The jovial warden can tell you how to barbecue bananas, and he may have been to your hometown. The Glenshee ski area is nearby—contact the **SYHA** at 161 Warrender Park Rd. Edinburgh EH9 1EQ (tel. (0131) 229 8660) to find if any package ski tours including transportation, equipment rental, lift passes, and ski instruction for hostelers will be arranged this winter season. If the hostel is full, the **Braemar Outdoor Centre,** 15 Mar Rd. (tel. (013397) 41242; evening 41517), has room for 26, with showers, kitchen facilities, and central heating (£8, £7 in a bunkhouse, sleeping bag required). The center also rents cross-country skis (£10/day) and mountain bikes (£13/day, £8/half-day). Braemar is a 5-mi. walk from the **Inverey Youth Hostel,** where there are usually more deer than guests. The hostel is a favorite stopping point for hikers doing the classic 23-mi. trek up the **Lairig Ghru** from Loch Morlich and over the pass to Braemar. Alas, there's no phone, so book ahead through the Braemar hostel (grade 3. £3.85; open May-early Sept.). The **Glendoll Youth Hostel (HI;** tel. (015755) 236; grade 2; £5.05; open late March-Oct.) is a difficult (particularly in winter) 13-mi. cross-country walk from Braemar. Follow the A93 2 mi. south to the Glen Callater turn-off, then take the Jock's Rd. footpath. Be sure to take an Ordnance Survey Map and compass and notify the Braemar police of your plans. Glendoll can be reached from Dundee by bus (Mon.-Sat. 1/day) or on the Kirriemuir-Glendoll postbus (Mon.-Sat. 1/day).

The **regional tourist office** (tel. (013397) 41600) is in Braemar, at Balnellan Rd. (open daily July-early Sept. 10am-8pm, mid-March to June and mid-Sept. 10am-6:30pm, late Sept.-mid-March. 10am-5pm). On the first Saturday in September, Braemar's population swells from 410 to 20,000 for the annual highland games of the **Braemar Gathering.** The Queen almost always attends; advance bookings are essential. Write to The Bookings Secretary, Coilacrich, Ballater AB35 5UH (tel. 013397) 55377) for information.

■■■ ELGIN & THE WHISKY TRAIL

Elgin (pronounced with a hard "g"—like Guinness, not gin), a quiet but growing provincial center halfway between Aberdeen and Inverness, is the unassuming site of the remnants of spectacular **Elgin Cathedral,** known in the 14th century as the most beautiful of Scottish cathedrals. Looted and burned by the Wolf of Badenoch at the close of the 14th century, the cathedral fell prey to pillagers and winter weather. (Open Mon.-Sat. 9:30am-6pm, Sun. 2-6:30pm; Oct.-March Mon.-Sat. 9:30am-4:30pm, Sun. 2-4:30pm; £1.20, seniors and children 75p.) Alexander Graham Bell taught at a local school (where an electrical discount store now stands) before emigrating to

America. The **Elgin Museum** (tel. (01343) 543675) displays relics of Elgin's past, with plenty of Bell paraphernalia (open Mon.-Tues. and Thurs.-Fri. 10am-5pm, Sat. 11am-4pm, Sun. 2-5pm; £1.20, students and seniors 50p).

Sadly devoid of hostels, Elgin is chock-full of B&Bs; the **tourist office,** 17 High St. (tel. (01343) 542666 or 543388), will help you find one (open Mon.-Sat. 9:30am-7pm, Sun. 10am-5:30pm; June and Sept. Mon.-Sat. 9:30am-6pm, Sun. 2-5pm; April-May and Oct. Mon.-Sat. 9:30am-5:30pm; Nov.-March Mon.-Fri. 9:30am-5pm). **The Park Café,** 7 N. College St. (tel. (01343) 543291), will take you back in time: the waitresses call you "dear," the decor is vintage '50s, and a three-course lunch with tea costs £4 (open daily 11am-7:30pm). The **Lido Café,** 29 South St. (tel. (01343) 547405), serves good quiche for under £2.50 (open daily 8am-9pm).

Frequent **buses** (Northern Bluebird) and **trains** serve Elgin from Inverness (buses 5/day; £4) and Aberdeen (buses 5/day; £5.80); the bus stops at the new bus station behind High St. The train station is five-minute from town along South Guildry St.

■ NEAR ELGIN

Don't stay too long in Elgin—venture forth to the surrounding hills. The 62-mi. **Malt Whisky Trail** staggers past eight famous distilleries, all of which will offer you free booze (all open at least Mon.-Fri. 10am-4pm in summer). The best tour is at the **Glenfiddich** distillery (tel. (01340) 820373) in Dufftown (alas, Dufftown is *not* the home of Duff beer). Seventeen mi. south of Elgin, Glenfiddich is the only distillery in the highlands where you can see whisky bottled on the premises. Convenient buses run directly from Elgin. (Open Mon.-Sat. 9:30am-4:30pm, Sun. noon-4:30pm; mid-Oct. to Easter Mon.-Fri. 9:30am-4:30pm).

The bus to the Glenfiddich distillery also stops at **The Speyside Cooperage** (tel. (01340) 871108), where casks are still handmade. The Cooperage is located ¼ mi. south of Craigellachie on the A941 (open Mon.-Sat. 9:30am-4:30pm, Oct.-Easter Mon.-Fri. 9:30am-4:30pm; £1.50, seniors and children 90p). Walkers will enjoy the **Speyside Way,** a trail which meanders from Spey Bay south to the town of Tomintoul. Grab a trail map at the Elgin tourist office.

The tiny village of **Forres,** a perennial winner in the cut-throat "Britain in Bloom" competition, flowers 30 minutes from Elgin by bus or train. Here, on a misty heath, Shakespeare's sisters three rose as bubbles from the earth and unraveled Macbeth's destiny. As one might expect, the hurlyburly is not yet done nor the battle lost and won over who owns the heath, or even where Shakespeare meant it to be. North of town, the **Findhorn Foundation** (tel. (01309) 673655), an international spiritual community known for its horticulture, gives tours of its gardens daily at 2pm; feel free to wander. Scientists have been unable to explain the community gardens' success on such barren, sandy soil. A small fee allows you to eat and work with the community, but you must stay in the adjacent campsites or in local B&Bs (list available at the tourist office; visitor office open May-Sept. Mon.-Sat. 10am-5pm, Sun. 2-5pm; during the off-season, leave a message on the answering machine.) Contact the Findhorn Foundation, The Park, Findhorn, Forres IV36 0TZ.

Millbuies Country Park, 5 mi. south of Elgin off the A941 to Rothes, is as serene as it is inaccessible. A range of recreational facilities and a lake await the determined. More convenient is the seaside village of **Lossiemouth.** Located 6 mi. north of Elgin on the A941, Lossiemouth is linked to Elgin by frequent bus service. The village is blessed with two wide, white-sand, windswept beaches: **East Beach** is linked to the mainland by a narrow footbridge and has grassy dunes; **West Beach** is cleaner, less crowded, and leads to a lighthouse. The **Lossiemouth Fishery and Community Museum,** Pitgaveny St. (tel. (01343) 813772), houses a scale-model wheelhouse and the forbidding Stotfield Disaster Book. (Open Easter-Sept. Mon.-Sat. 10:30am-5pm; 80p, seniors and children 40p). Campers can pitch their tents at **Silver Sands Leisure Park** (tel. (01343) 813262) for £7.25-9.50 (open April-Oct.).

HIGHLANDS & ISLANDS

> *Long live the weeds and the wilderness yet.*
> —Gerard Manley Hopkins, S.J.

Sheep have a habit of dying when they tip over; if you come across one on its back and struggling in vain to get to its feet, do it and the Highland economy a favor and turn it right again. Here on Scotland's extravagantly frayed, sheep-filled northwestern coast, cut by sea lochs and girded by innumerable islands, remains the most beautiful region in Scotland and one of the last stretches of true wilderness in Europe. Even in tourist season, you can easily hike for a full day without seeing another human being. The Hebrides arch to the west of the mainland, while the Orkney and Shetland Islands drift in a northeasterly direction off Scotland's horn at John O'Groats. The mainland towns of Inverness, Fort William, Glencoe, Ullapool, and Thurso act as points of access to the islands and as bases for exploring the balding Highland mountains, rising to the west of the Cairngorm Mountains with a grandeur outreaching their altitude. Although rarely rising above 400 feet, these aspiring mountains, decked with sparkling narrow lochs, offer the scenery and climbing challenges of a much taller mountain range.

The Highlands and Islands, aside from being a distinct geographical region, preserve a way of life waning in the rest of Scotland. The Highlanders prescribe much of Scottish identity with a rich body of music, sport, and dress. Living in a beautiful if not bountiful land, few Highlanders aside from post deliverers and tax collectors work at a single occupation; towns are scarce and the shallow soil cultivates only heather and peat easily. Most people make ends meet through self-employment, typically by crofting (farming independently), fishing, or running B&Bs.

Scotland's northwest has not always been so vacant. Two hundred years ago, 30% of Scotland's population lived north of the Great Glen, and even the smallest, most windswept islands supported a family or two. Overpopulation made tenant farming unprofitable for absent landlords, who turned to sheep farming and evicted entire Highland communities in the infamous Highland Clearances of the early 19th century. The Clearances dealt a fatal blow to clan-based, Gaelic-speaking Highland society, scattering and dispossessing the population; many Scots, forcibly evicted or burned out of their homes, emigrated to Canada, Australia, and the United States. The region's staple is now tourism—English and Scottish Lowlanders have repopulated the area with holiday homes. Only in the Outer Hebrides is Gaelic still widely spoken (Gaelic rhymes with "Alec," unlike the Irish version, pronounced "gale-ick"). Recent efforts to protect Gaelic culture mandate Gaelic instruction in schools; this promises to reinvigorate the language by teaching it to children, who can go to their grandparents, though normally not their parents, for help.

GETTING ABOUT

Travel in the Highlands requires a great deal more planning than in the rest of Britain. Although bus routes criss-cross the region and boat services connect more than 40 islands to the mainland, you can't count on making more than one or two journeys per day on any form of transportation, even in high season. Transport services are drastically reduced on Sundays and during the winter.

Most ferries on the west coast are run by **Caledonian MacBrayne** (head office tel. (01475) 650100; fax 637607), which publishes an excellent, widely available free timetable and fare sheet; their open-dated **Island Hopscotch** service provides discounts on a succession of ferry trips. Bikes can cross without reservation for a fee of £1-2, but advance booking for cars is strongly recommended.

■■■ CAIRNGORM MOUNTAINS

The breathtaking Cairngorm Mountains encircle large conifer forests and towering arctic plateaus 120 mi. north of Edinburgh. Famed as Britain's largest expanse of nature preserves and Scotland's most frequented skiing and climbing area, the Cairngorms are packed with alpine enthusiasts from December through March. But the mountains are by no means solely a winter retreat—an extensive network of bikepaths, foot trails, and hostels allow easy access to the rugged beauty of this region during all seasons. The forests are dominated by the Scots pine, a unique conifer indigenous to the Highlands and distinguished by its orange-red branches. Ask a ranger where to spot Lapland reindeer and the occasional osprey.

GETTING THERE

Aviemore is the largest town in the Cairngorms, conveniently located on the main Inverness-Edinburgh rail and bus lines. This roadside strip has no beauty; get out of town and into the mountains right away. **Buses** run nearly hourly to Inverness (40min.; £4.80), Glasgow and Edinburgh (3½hr.; £11.30 to Glasgow, £13.70 to Edinburgh). Southbound buses stop at the shopping center just north of the train station; northbound buses brake before the Cairngorm Hotel. **Trains** leave the station on Grampian Rd. (tel. 810221), just north of the tourist office, for Inverness (8/day; 45min.; £7.70), Glasgow and Edinburgh (5-7/day; 3½hr.; £27).

The principal road into the heart of the Cairngorms, defined by the borders of the **Glen More Forest Park,** begins just south of Aviemore as the B970; the road jogs east at Aviemore before continuing north towards Loch Garten. Follow the eastern branch, which merges into the A951; the road passes **Loch Morlich,** a lake surrounded by conifers and bound to the east by a wide sandy beach, before continuing into Glenmore and coming to a dead end at the Cairngorm chairlift. The 10-mi. jaunt past campgrounds and heather moors along the B970 and the A951, is known as **The Ski Road;** the Cairngorm Chairlift bus takes the route to the ski lifts frequently in winter (in summer 4-6/day). Try to rent a bike, as people usually find hitching slow. Next to the Mountain Resort, **Aviemore Mountain Bikes** (tel. 811007) coordinates bike tours and rents cycles for £6 per half-day and £10 per day.

ORIENTATION & PRACTICAL INFORMATION

The **Aviemore and Spey Valley tourist office** (tel. 810363), on Grampian Rd., the town's main artery, books local B&Bs (£12-15), sells bus tickets, and exchanges currency for a minimal commission during peak season (open Mon.-Sat. 9am-8pm, Sun. 10am-6pm; Sept.-Oct. and March-June daily 9am-6pm; Nov.-Feb. daily 9am-5pm). Aviemore's **telephone code** is 01479. Another good source of information, the **Rothiemurchus Estate Visitors Centre** (tel. 810858; open daily 9am-5pm), lies nearly 1 mi. down the Ski Road from Aviemore towards the Cairngorms. South of Aviemore on the A9, the **Kingussie tourist office** (tel. (01540) 661297) is on Ring St. just off High St. (open late May-late Sept. 10am-1pm and 2-6pm). At the nearby **Highland Folk Museum** (tel. (01540) 661307), watch a blacksmith, spinster, or clarsach recreate daily life in the highlands of past centuries (open Mon.-Sat. 10am-6pm, Sun. 2-6pm; Nov.-March Mon.-Fri. 10am-3pm; £2.50, children and seniors £1.50). **Kincraig Stores** (tel. (01540) 651331) sells various essential items and also serves as the Kincraig post office and tourist office (open Mon.-Tues. and Thurs.-Sat. 8:30am-1pm and 2-5:30pm; Wed. and Sun. 8:30am-1pm). The tourist office can also tell you how to get to the **Highland Wildlife Park** in Kincraig, a site dedicated to preserving local beasties great and small (open daily June-Aug. 10am-5pm, April-May and Sept.-Oct. 10am-4pm).

ACCOMMODATIONS & FOOD

Check the tourist board's *Aviemore and Spey Valley* publication for a complete listing of seasonal hostels and year round B&Bs.

Aviemore Youth Hostel (HI), (tel. 810345). This brand-spanking-new hostel 100 yds. south of the tourist office has a sauna-like drying room and sinks and mirrors in every suite—hot and cold come out of a single tap! You'll think you've died and gone to hostel heaven. 114 beds in 4-6 bedrooms. Grade 1. No lockout. Curfew 2am. £7.25.

Loch Morlich Youth Hostel (HI), Glenmore (tel. 861238). Superb accommodations on Loch Morlich itself, but often booked by groups. The Cairngorm Chairlift bus (£1) departs from the Aviemore train station and stops in front of the hostel. Grade 1. Curfew 11:45pm. £6.50. Open mid-Nov.-Sept.

Mrs. Bruce, 2 Dell Mhor (tel. 810230), 1 mi. east of Aviemore along the Ski Road (B970); walk or take Cairngorm Chairlift bus (30p) from the Aviemore train station. Beautiful garden decorated with teapots. 1 twin, 1 double. From £12.

Glen Feshie Hostel (tel. (01540) 651323), 10 mi. south of Aviemore, 5 mi. from Kincraig. Call ahead and you might get picked up. Showers, kitchen, and free porridge breakfast. Close to numerous walks and hikes; a great place to relax for a few days. From £5.50.

Insh Hall Ski Lodge (tel. (01540) 651272). Hostel accommodations for skiers and hikers year-round on Loch Insh. Sauna and gym available; guests get free use of watersports equipment. 1 mi. downhill from Kincraig, accessible on Scottish Citylink buses from Aviemore and Kingussie. From £10.50. B&B plus lunch and dinner £19.50-20.

Kingussie Youth Hostel (HI), (tel. (01540) 661506). Follow signs uphill a short distance from main road in Kingussie. British Rail and Scottish Citylink both stop in Kingussie. Grade 2. Lockout 10:30am-5pm. Curfew 11pm. From £5.05.

Camping: Glenmore Forest Camping and Caravan Park (tel. 86271), across from the Loch Morlich Youth Hostel. Ample space and good facilities, though it may be crowded in the summer. £4.90-7.10/tent. **Coylumbridge Campgrounds of Scotland** (tel. 810120), 1½ mi. south of Aviemore on the Ski Road. Laundry. £6-7/tent.

Cram goodies into your pack at the **Gateway Supermarket,** just north of the Aviemore train station (open Mon.-Wed. 8:30am-7pm, Thurs.-Fri. 8:30am-8pm, Sat. 8:30am-6pm, Sun. 11am-6pm). Don't stop there—have a regular field day stocking up on dried fruits and nuts at **Derek's Delicatessen,** in the shopping center across the street (open Mon.-Sat. 10am-6pm, Sun. noon-6pm). **The Glenmore Shop and Café** near the Loch Morlich Youth Hostel offers all the essentials and the adjoining store rents bikes (open daily 8:30am-6pm; bikes £12/day, £8/half-day, £3.50/hr.).

HIKING, SKIING, & OTHER REINDEER GAMES

> **Safety Precautions:** Although the mountains rise only 4000 ft., the weather patterns of an **Arctic tundra** characterize the Cairngorm region. Explorers may be at the mercy of bitter winds and unpredictable mists on **any day of the year.** Furthermore, many trails are not posted and trekkers must be able to rely on their own proficiency with a map and compass. Make sure to use an Ordnance Survey map, preferably the yellow Outdoor Leisure Sheet covering the Cairngorms (available at the tourist office). **Be prepared to spend a night in sub-freezing temperatures** no matter what the temperature is when you set out. Leave a description of your intended route with the police or at the mountain station, and learn the locations of the shelters (*bothies*) along your trail.

The Cairngorm region has Scotland's highest concentration of ski resorts. In winter, Alpine skiers from throughout Britain converge at the **Cairngorm Ski Area,** featuring a network of five chairlifts and 12 tows. In summer, the double-legged chairlift (bottom to top and back £4, middle to top and back £2.80) becomes a blessing for armchair hikers. The first ride ascends a quite walkable 368 ft.; the second lift covers the remaining 1056 ft. to a summit near the peak of Cairngorm Mt. (4084 ft.). Arrive early (the first chairlift runs at 9:45am in summer) or your view of the surrounding snow-capped peaks and silver lochs may be obstructed by hordes of little Teutonic prepubescents. To enjoy the mountains in peace, descend The Saddle into Glen Avon or traverse the southern ridge of Cairngorm to **Ben Macdui,** the second-highest peak in Britain (4296 ft.). On a clear day, you can see the first 100 mi. of infinity. With any luck, you may run into some deer or even the Lapland reindeer. For more information, contact **Cairngorm chairlift** at (01479) 861261. A multitude of local companies run ski schools and rent equipment; pick up a copy of *Ski-ing Information* at the Aviemore tourist office for details. Down the hill 3 mi. from the chairlift, and also serviced by the chairlift company bus, the **Cairngorm Reindeer Centre** (tel. (01479) 861228) is home to many velvet-horned creatures. A 1½-hr. visit allows visitors to frolic in the hills with the rest of the herd; Rudolph and his buddies will literally be eating out of your hand (visits daily at 11:30am, in summer also at 2:30pm; call ahead to confirm availability of afternoon visit; £3, children £2). Next door, the **Glenmore Forest Park Visitors Centre** (tel. (01479) 861220) provides information on great walks and shows a free 9-minute video about the area (open daily 9am-5pm).

■ ■ ■ INVERNESS

The charms of Inverness, like Nessie herself, are somewhat elusive, but the traveler who hunts them down won't be disappointed. A transportation and tourist center for the Highlands, the town offers more than just its legendary associations with the Bard and the Monster. Banquo's ghost has no ruin to haunt, and Nessie lives 15 mi. to the south, but Inverness itself boasts intriguing shops, unusual museums, and a riverside setting. The town is also an excellent base for touring nearby regions rich in castles, distilleries, small blurry dinosaurlike objects, and imposing scenery.

GETTING THERE

Inverness, in central northern Scotland, draws travelers from Glasgow, Edinburgh, and Aberdeen, then scatters them across the Highlands and Islands. One train per day runs directly to London (£67), and both **Scottish Citylink** and **National Express** make the same trip by bus (£38). Trains run to: Aberdeen (11/day, Sun. 5/day; 2¼hr.; £16), Kyle of Lochalsh (5/day, Sun. 2/day; 2½-3hr.; £13), Thurso and Wick (7/day, Sun. 2/day; 3¾hr.; £11), and Edinburgh and Glasgow (5/day, Sun. 2-3/day; 3½-4hr.; £25). Buses cover the same routes less expensively and sometimes more quickly. **Scottish Citylink** provides frequent service to most destinations, including Edinburgh (4hr.; £11.20), Glasgow (4¼hr.; £11.30), Ullapool (1½hr.; £6.30), and Thurso and Wick (3½hr.; £8.10). **Highland Bus and Coach** travels to Kyle of Lochalsh (3hr.; £7) and Fort William (1¾hr.; £5). **Skye-Ways** runs to Fort William (1hr. 50min.; £5.80) and to Kyle of Lochalsh (3hr.; £7), branching thereupon to all major points on the Isle of Skye. **Gaelicbus** runs to Fort William and **Morrison's Coaches** serves Thurso and Wick. Travel to Oban requires changing buses in Fort William.

ORIENTATION & PRACTICAL INFORMATION

The towering castle is an excellent point of reference; the tourist office and two youth hostels lie steps away. The helpful **tourist office** in Castle Wynd (tel. 234353; fax 710609) has probably heard far too much about Nessie already (open May and Oct. Mon.-Sat. 9am-5pm, Sun. 10am-4pm; June and mid-Sept.-end of Sept. Mon.-Sat. 9am-6pm, Sun. 10am-5pm; July-mid-Sept. Mon.-Sat. 9am-8:30pm, Sun. 9:30am-6pm; Nov.-Dec. and Jan.-April Mon.-Fri. 9am-5pm, Sat. 10am-4pm—Whew). Most buses depart from the **bus station** at Farraline Park, just off Academy St. **Highland Bus and Coach** (tel. 711000) sells tickets for all companies except **Skye-Ways** (tel. 710119), which has an office in a trailer around the corner. The **train station** (tel. 238924) is a short walk down Academy St. in Station Sq. Both the train and bus stations store luggage (£1-3), but only the train stations offer **showers** (£1). Get cash at the **ATM** (both **Cirrus** and **Plus**) at the Royal Bank of Scotland on Academy St.

Rent a bike at **Thornton Cycles,** 23 Castle St. (tel. 222810), for £9 per day. If a nasty spill occurs while cycling around town, head for **Raigmore Hospital** on

Inshes Rd. or ring the **hospital** at 704000. Contact the **police** at 239191. Wash the bloodstains out at the **launderette** just across the river at 17 Young St. (wash £1.50, dry 20p; open Mon.-Sat. 8am-8pm, last wash 6:30pm). Write home about it at the main **post office** (tel. 234111) at 14-16 Queensgate (open Mon.-Fri. 9am-5pm, Sat. 9am-12:30pm). The **postal code** is IV1 1AA. Once your panicky parents receive the blood-spattered postcard of Nessie, they can reach you by dialing Inverness' **telephone code,** 01463.

ACCOMMODATIONS & CAMPING

Though finding a bed in Inverness is not as difficult as in Edinburgh, be sure to arrive early in the day if you haven't made reservations. Inverness's two hostels face off at the corner of Culduthel Rd. and Old Edinburgh Rd. From the tourist office, walk up to Bridge St. and turn left; the first right is Castle St., which leads up to Culduthel Rd. Many unadvertised, cheap B&Bs which are not registered with the tourist office line Argyll St. and Kenneth St. The friendly staff at the **Inverness Student Hotel** will help find you one of these low-profile B&Bs if their hostel is full.

Inverness Student Hotel, 8 Culduthel Rd. (tel. 236556). 52 beds in rooms of 4-10 beds. The outgoing, helpful staff operates a travelers' resource center. Free coffee and tea all day, small kitchen, showers that are harrowing but powerful. How can anyone chain-smoke in an enclosed space for 2½ hours? The secret lies within... Desk open 6:30am-2:30am. Check-out 10:30am. £7.50-7.90. Breakfast £1.20. Laundry. Make reservations with credit card or from High St. Hostel in Edinburgh, Backpacker's Guest House in Kyleakin (Skye), or Fort William Backpackers.

Inverness Youth Hostel (HI), 1 Old Edinburgh Rd. (tel. 231771), across from the Student Hotel. 126 beds in rooms of 6-8 beds. Quiet. Grade 1. Checkout 10:30am. Curfew 2am. £7.25. Open Feb.-Dec.

Mr. and Mrs. Lyall, 20 Argyll St. (tel. 710267). From Culduthel Rd., face the castle, head up the hill between the two hostels, and take the first right. Handsome rooms equipped with tea kettle and TV. Don't miss the antics of the Lyall's overly energetic parrot. Bed and shower deluxe, an amazing value at £8.

Mrs. MacBean, 9 Victoria Terrace (tel. 236198). Wonderful Mrs. MacBean warmly welcomes wayfarers. Teapots and coffeepots in every room. £8-10.

Mrs. Douglas, 32 Ardconnell St. (tel 239909). Bright, airy rooms, most with TVs, in a restored Victorian house. Bed and shower £12-14.

Camping: Most fill with caravans in summer. **Scaniport Caravan Park** (tel. 75351), 5 mi. south on the B862, is the cheapest (30 pitches, £4-4.50/person with or without car), and **Bught Caravan and Camping Park** (tel. 236920), in the southern part of town near the Ness Islands, the closest (234 pitches; £2.10, with car £7.05).

FOOD & PUBS

High Street is packed with unctuous fast food, including the burger franchise founded by the ancient clan of MacDonald. For the ultimate in cheap 'n' greasy, head just across the river to **Oh! Mama Mia,** 3 Tomnahurich St. (tel. 232884), where customers queue out the door for daily take-away specials (open Mon.-Sat. 8am-8pm). You can't beat the breakfast special at the **Littlewoods Restaurant,** but why would you want to? It's in the back of the department store on Bridge St.; join the amethyst-hair covey for sausage, egg, bacon, hash browns and mushrooms, all for only 99p (served Mon.-Wed. 9:30am-11am, Thurs.-Sat. 9-11am). Near the youth hostels, **The Castle Restaurant** (open Mon.-Sat. 8am-8:25pm) serves filling British meals (shepherd's pie £3.25).

A wide array of pubs invigorates Inverness. The **Market Bar,** in an alley opposite Church St., offers live music nightly (open Wed.-Fri. to 12:45am). **Gunsmith's,** marked by a shotgun over the doorway on Union St., attracts a rhinestone cowboy crowd to its saloon-style bar. Several bars also cluster at the upper end of Academy St. Across the River Ness on Young St., play snooker at **Glenalbyn,** which features live music, usually rhythm and blues bands, on Monday and Wednesday nights (open Mon.-Wed. 11am-1am, Thurs.-Sat. 11am-11pm, Sun. 12:30-11pm).

SIGHTS & ENTERTAINMENT

Disillusion awaits those who remember Inverness as the home of Shakespeare's *Macbeth.* Nothing of the "Auld Castlehill" remains; the present reconstructed castle, home to the sheriff's courts, is unimpressive, and you'll have to commit a crime to get in. Instead, visit the **Inverness Museum and Art Gallery** in Castle Wynd, which displays informative exhibits on archaeology in the area, the latest in Pictish wristwear, and assorted Highland paraphernalia, and also hosts a summer series of films and lectures (open Mon.-Sat. 9am-5pm, Sun. 2-5pm, late August-early July Mon.-Sat. 9am-5pm; free). Across the river at 40 Huntly St., **Balnain House: Home of Highland Music** gives scores of visitors the chance to listen to Scottish melodies and try their hand at the bagpipe, fiddle, *clarsach,* or harp (open daily 10am-5pm, Sept.-June Tues.-Sun. 10am-5pm; £3, seniors and students £2, children £1.50; ask about evening shows and ceilidhs). Pick up a leaflet from the tourist office to guide your walk to the town's numerous galleries.

For a pleasant stroll and a picnic, walk upstream to the unexpected tranquility of the **Ness Islands,** narrow islets connected to both banks by small footbridges and blanketed with virgin forest. Near the islands on the west bank, the **Inverness Ice Centre** (tel. 235711) offers summer skating in a large indoor rink (Tues. and Thurs.-Sat. 2-4:30pm and 6:30-9:30pm; admission and skate rental £3.10, children £2.30). If all the novels on the hostel book-exchange shelf happen be in Sanskrit, head over to **The Inverness Bookshop** (tel. 239947) on Bank St. and peruse the vast collection of cheap, second-hand paperbacks; you can even lighten your pack by selling books you've finished.

Like all Scottish cities, Inverness has its share of summertime fêtes. In mid-July, local strongmen hurl telephone poles during the **Inverness Highland Games.** Pipe-and-drum bands and daredevil display teams dominate the **Inverness Tattoo Festival** in early August. The **Marymas Fair,** in mid-August, recreates 19th-century street life with crafts stalls, concerts, and proletarian strife. The **Northern Meeting,** considered the world's premier piping competition, comes to the Eden Court Theatre in late August. Earlier in the season, over Easter weekend, Inverness hosts a three-day **Folk Festival.**

■ NEAR INVERNESS

Unfathomably deep, mysterious, and unbelievably famous, **Loch Ness** guards its secrets 5 mi. south of town. In 565 AD a savage sea beast attacked a monk along the shore; whether a prehistoric leftover, giant seasnake, or cosmic wanderer, the Loch Ness monster has captivated the imagination of the world ever since. Seven hundred feet deep only 20m from its edge, the Loch is shaped like a wedge, with caverns at the floor extending down so far that no one (save perhaps Nessie and Sting) has examined how vast it really is or what life exists at its bottom. For a full dose of Nessie-hunting lore and a hearty welcome to the Highlands, take a tour on **Gordon's Minibus**—the entertaining narrative of marine biologist and historian Dr. Gordon Williamson is a refreshing break from the usual area tourist traps. His minibus leaves from the Inverness tourist office at 10:30am and returns at 4:30pm (£9.90; seniors, students, and hostelers £6.90). Tony Harmsworth's half-day **Secret of the Loch** tour is equally good. Jovial and knowledgeable, Harmsworth is a scientist and a founder of the Official Loch Ness Exhibition; he uses a video to help communicate his unique theory about Nessie's true identity. You can also bike down the eastern side of the loch, where the narrow B582 runs close to the water. Down this road 18 mi., the River Foyers empties into the loch in a series of idyllic waterfalls.

Sixteen mi. down the western shore road (the A82) a lone bagpiper drones from the ruined ramparts of lovely **Urquhart Castle** (rhymes with "tuckered"), one of the largest in Scotland before it was blown up in 1692 to prevent Jacobite occupation.

Most photos of Nessie have been fabricated at this spot. Though the shore road is not suitable for biking, you can take a bus or hitch to the castle. (Open Mon.-Sat. 9:30am-6:30pm, Sun. 10:30am-6:30pm; Oct.-March Mon.-Sat. 9:30am-4:30pm, Sun. 10:30am-4:30pm; £3, seniors £2, children £1.) Nearby in Drumnadrochit the **Offi-cial Loch Ness Centre** (tel. (014562) 573) features a scale representation of Nessie and a 40-minute audio-visual display. If you take a guided tour of the Loch, or if you ever sat through an episode of *That's Incredible!*, the exhibition may be somewhat redundant (open June-July daily 9am-8pm; Aug.-Sept. daily 9am-9:30pm; Oct.-March daily 10am-4pm; March-Easter daily 9am-5:30pm; Easter-May 9;30am-8pm; £4, seniors and students £3). The **HI Loch Ness Youth Hostel** (tel. (01320) 512 74) stands on the western shore of the loch, 7½ mi. south of the castle; call ahead between mid-July and August (grade 2; £5.05; open Easter-Sept.).

East of Inverness unfold the moors of **Culloden Battlefield.** In 1746 the Jacobite cause died here as Bonnie Prince Charlie, a master of rhetoric but no genius in bat-tle, lost 1200 men to the King's army in a 40-min. bloodbath. So ended the last battle on British soil. (Open daily 9am-6pm; April-May and mid-Sept.-Oct. daily 9:30am-5pm; Feb.-March and Nov.-Dec. 10am-4pm). Admission to the Visitor Centre is £1.50, for seniors, students, children, and hostelers 80p; you can wander the battle-fields for free.

A short mile south of Culloden, the stone circles and chambered cairns (mounds of rough stones) of the **Cairns of Clava** recall civilizations of 30,000 years ago. Hav-ing recently undergone extensive restoration, the nearby **Castle Stuart** (tel. (01463) 790745) was home to the Earls of Moray and the Stuart family in the 17th century; guided tours take you step-by-step through the extensively renovated struc-ture (open daily 10am-5pm; £3, seniors and students £2, children £1). **Cawdor Cas-tle** (tel. (016677) 615) has been the residence of the Thane's descendants since the 15th century, and is still inhabited for much of the year. Highland forests embrace the carefully cultivated garden; don't miss the "wild" garden and stunning nature walks (open May-early Oct. daily 10am-5:30pm; £3.50, grounds only £1.80). Buy a **Tourist Trail Day Rover** for £6 (seniors, students, and children £4) and travel by bus from Inverness to Culloden Battlefield, Cawdor Castle, Nairn, Fort George, Cas-tle Stuart, and then back to Inverness, in either direction.

■■■ GLENCOE

A spectacular valley between Oban and Fort William, Glencoe supplements its sparse permanent population with a contingent of avid mountaineers. Stunning in any weather, Glencoe is perhaps best seen in the rain, when a slowly drifting web of mist laces the innumerable rifts and crags of the steep slopes, and the silvery water-falls cascade into the River Coe. Only on rare days is such a view marred by a shining sun; Glencoe records over 90 in. of rain per year. The valley is infamous as the site of the shocking 1692 "Massacre of Glencoe," when the Clan MacDonald welcomed a company of Campbell soldiers, henchmen of King William III, into their chieftain's home; after regaling their guests with music, feasting, and card-playing for two weeks, the host and many of his followers were murdered as a demonstration to other Scottish clans of the English king's power (MacDonald had been a few days late in signing a loyalty pledge to the crown). A sign near Claichaig indicates the site of the betrayal; Glencoe is still known as "the Weeping Glen."

Experienced rock climbers favor the mountains, while novices can explore some beautiful trails that bypass the summits, such as the Hidden Valley trail and the friendly "Old Military Road." By taking the Glasgow bus 10 mi. east to Altnafeadh, you can hike to **Kinlochleven** (about 2½hr.) on the **West Highland Way,** the long distance footpath from Glasgow to Fort William. Seven buses per day return to Glen-coe from Kinlockleven (last bus 6:20pm). If you wish to stay the night in Kin-lochleven, which has little to brag about save its proximity to the mountains and a large aluminum smelter, visit the **West Highland Lodge** (tel. (018554) 396 or 471), a 34-bed bunkhouse with a kitchen, showers, and drying room (£5.50).

Glencoe Village in the heart of the valley welcomes hikers to its sheltered haven. The pleasant brown clapboard **HI Glencoe Youth Hostel** (tel. 219; grade 1) rests 2 mi. south of Glencoe Village, on the eastern side of the river (£6.50; book 2 days ahead in July-Aug.). If you have already hiked to the hostel and found it full, and you'd rather sleep anywhere than on the ground, you can backtrack 500 yds. to the **Leacantium Farm Bunkhouse.** The facilities include electricity and showers, but be sure to bring your own bedding (£6/day; £32/week). **Red Squirrel Camp Site** (tel. 256; £2.50/person, children 50p; showers 50p) pitches tents 500 yd. past the hostel. Down the lane by the church in town, the **Glencoe Outdoor Centre** (tel. 350) has room for 35 in comfortable hostel-type lodgings. The center also offers instruction and rentals for all types of mountain and water sports (B&B £13, room and full board £17). You can bed down for free in the big, sometimes boggy field next to the **Clachaig Inn** (tel. 252), 1 mi. east on the A82. Climbers descend the hills to tap their boots to frequent live music at the inn (open Mon.-Thurs. 11am-11pm, Fri. 11am-midnight, Sat. 11am-11:30pm). Try the Nepalese Pen and Potato Curry "as eaten by wandering Yetis" (£4). **The Scotsman** in Glencoe Village (also the **post office**) and the **Co-op** in Ballachulish (1 mi. west of Glencoe Village; open Mon.-Sat. 8:30am-6pm, Sat. 8:30am-5pm) are both small, but should satisfy most grocery needs. The HI hostel also sells food.

The **Glencoe Visitors Centre** (tel. 307), 2½ mi. east of Glencoe Village on the A82, gives hiking advice, issues the excellent **Glencoe Guide** (£2.50), and shows a film on the massacre of Glencoe (open June-Aug. daily 9:30am-6pm; March-May and Sept.-late Oct. daily 10am-5pm; 50p, seniors, students, and children 25p). **Great Journey Outdoors** (tel. (018554) 609) in Kinlochleven (deliveries to Glencoe and Ballachulish) or the filling station in Ballachulish will set you up with wheels. Just outside of town on the road to Oban and Fort William, **Glencoe Guides and Gear** has a full supply of camping, hiking and climbing paraphernalia (open daily 9am-6pm). On a hopelessly rainy day, disgruntled outdoorspeople can putter about the **Glencoe and North Lorn Folk Museum** next to the post office (open Mon.-Sat. 10am-5:30pm; £1.20, children 50p).

The **Skye-Ways buses** traveling between Glasgow and Fort William stop in Glencoe Village (2/day). **Citylink** rumbles through four times a day. These buses and the **Gaelicbus** and **Highland Bus and Coach** services between Oban and Fort William also stop in Ballachulish, 1 mi. west of Glencoe, where the **tourist office** (tel. 296) is located (open July-Aug. Mon.-Sat. 9am-7pm, Sun. 10am-6pm; May-June and Sept. Mon.-Sat. 9am-6pm, Sun. 10am-6pm; April and Oct. Mon.-Sat. 9am-5:30pm). Glencoe's **telephone code** is 018552.

■■■ FORT WILLIAM & BEN NEVIS

General Monk built Fort William among Britain's highest peaks in 1655 to keep out "savage clans and roving barbarians." However valiantly the original structure served its purpose, the town now succumbs to seasonal tidal waves of civilized and relaxed skiers and hikers. Filled with equipment outfitters, Fort William is an excellent base camp for mountain excursions; **Ben Nevis,** the highest peak in Britain at 4418 ft., is just around the corner. Many tackle Ben Nevis in the morning, then massage their sorry feet in the green grass of the town park in time to head to a local pub or *ceilidh* in the dark hours.

GETTING THERE

Fort William shares the magnificent **West Highland Railway** with Oban. Though every West Highland train connects to Edinburgh, the line officially starts at Glasgow's Queen St. Station and ends at Mallaig on the coast to the west of Fort William (6/day, Sun. 3/day; to Glasgow £20; to Mallaig £6.40). An overnight sleeper train to London Euston departs daily (11hr.; £98). The **train station** (tel. (01397) 703791) is equipped with **lockers** (£1.50) and an expectant cafeteria. Buses arrive and depart just outside the station. **Skye-Ways** runs to Glasgow (3/day; 3hr.; £8.10), and **Scot-**

tish **Citylink** ducks down to Kyle of Lochalsh (3/day; 1¾hr.; £7). **Gaelicbus** and **Highland Bus and Coach** service Oban (Mon.-Sat. 8-9/day; 1¾hr.; £5) and Inverness (7-9/day; 2hr.). **West Highland** operates a minibus to Mallaig once a day at 5pm (returns at 9:30am; 1¾hr.; £5). Pick up complete bus schedules at the tourist office. Heavy tourist traffic makes Fort William less than a hitcher's paradise. To get to the Road to the Isles (see Fort William to Mallaig: Road to the Isles, below), hitchers usually walk north and try their luck at the intersection of the Fort William road (A82) and the Mallaig road (A830).

ORIENTATION & PRACTICAL INFORMATION

The station may seem stuck in the middle of nowhere, but just through a single underpass lies the north end of **High Street,** Fort William's main (and only) drag. Local **buses** leave from High St. or from the stand opposite the Safeway Supermarket to the right of the train station. The unbelievably busy **tourist office** (tel. 703781), in the square three blocks down on the left, functions as the central depot for information on the West Highlands. Arrive as soon as the office opens to avoid much of the crowd. (Open Mon.-Sat. 9am-8pm, Sun. 9am-6pm; Oct. Mon.-Thurs. 9am-5:30pm, Fri.-Sat. 9am-5pm; Nov.-Dec. Mon.-Thurs. 9am-5:30pm, Fri. 9am-5pm; Jan.-March Mon.-Sat. 9am-5:30pm; April to mid-May daily 9am-5:30pm.) The **mountain rescue post** (tel. 702361 or 702362), based in the Fort William **police station** at the south end of High St., can usually give basic advice to hikers and climbers. Fort William's **postal code** is PH33 6AA; its **telephone code** is 01397.

For mountaineering equipment, head to **Nevisport** (tel. 704921), a cathedral of the outdoors at the north end of High St. (open Mon.-Sat. 8:30am-8pm, Sun. 9am-8pm; Oct.-June Mon.-Sat. 9am-5:30pm), or the **Nevis Outdoor Hire Centre** (tel. 703601) near the hostels along the River Nevis (open March-Oct. daily 8am-9pm). Both rent hiking boots (£4/day plus deposit), and Nevisport also carries maps and helpful literature. **West Coast Outdoor Leisure Centre,** 102 High St., rents sticky-soled rock climbing boots (£4/day; open Mon.-Sat. 9am-5:30pm, Sun. 10am-5pm) and **Ellis Brigham Mountain Sports,** behind the train station, lets tents (£10/day, £25/week) and mountain bikes (£12/day, £8/half day; open daily 9am-5:30pm). **Offbeat Bikes,** 4 Inverlochy Pl. (tel. 702663) and the **Nevis Outdoor Hire Centre** hire mountain bikes for 50p more. To wash those wool socks, go to the **launderette** at 117 High St. (open Mon.-Fri. 9am-6pm, Sat. 9am-5:30pm).

ACCOMMODATIONS & FOOD

Just five minutes from train, bus, and town, the snug and fun-loving 30 bed **Ft. William Backpackers Guesthouse** (tel. 700711) welcomes you back from Ben Nevis with a hot cup of tea and a cozy bed. Even Elvis has been sighted here (£7.90, breakfast £1.20; laundry service £2.50; free tea and coffee all day). Two other hostels are also ideally situated near the Ben Nevis footpath and the West Highland Way. The **Glen Nevis HI Youth Hostel** (tel. 702336; grade 1) stands 3 mi. east of town on the Glen Nevis Rd.; booking two days ahead July through August is crucial (£6.50, open Dec.-Oct.). The **Ben Nevis Bunkhouse** (tel. 702240) at Achintee Farm sleeps 24 in a 200-year-old wood-paneled granite barn with full kitchen and bathing facilities. The bunkhouse is on the opposite side of the River Nevis from the hostel, a 1½ mi. walk along the Achintee Rd. Though less likely to fill than the official hostel, the bunkhouse still merits reservations in July and August (£6). The Ben Nevis footpath passes within a cannonball's throw of both hostels. The **Glen Nevis Caravan & Camping Park** (tel. 702191) stretches canvas on the same road, ½ mi. before the HI hostel (tents £4.50 plus £1.20/person; open mid-March to mid-Oct.). **Highland Bus and Coach** and **West Highland Motor Service** run from Fort William to the youth hostels and back (Mon.-Sat. 5-7/day; Sun. 2/day).

If both of the hostels along the River Nevis are booked, head 4 mi. out of town on the A830 to the **Smiddy Alpine Lodge** (tel. 772467) in Corpach. Crafted by the love child of Heidi and Bob Vila (measure twice, cut once!), this bunkhouse is immaculately clad in Swedish wood paneling; there are a mere 12 beds, so advance phone booking is crucial (£6). Buses run to Corpach from High St. an amazing 21 times per day (Sun. 9/day)—the last run is at 10:25pm (50p); Corpach is also just one train stop north of Ft. William. Ask the driver to let you off at **Kilmallie Hall** if you wish to attend one of the weekly Scottish Country Dances (mid-June to Aug., Mon. 8-10pm; 75p) or occasional folk-singing performances. The bunkhouse lies between the hall and the train depot. An early morning walk down Fassifern Rd., behind the Alexandra Hotel, will overpower you with the smell of Scottish breakfasts drifting from the many **B&Bs.** Other B&Bs roost further up the hill on Alma Rd. or Argyll Rd.

Wm. Low (open Mon.-Wed. and Sat. 8:30am-6:30pm, Thurs.-Fri. 8:30am-7pm) bolsters High St.'s northern end. A fat **Safeway** scowls by the train station (open Mon.-Thurs. 8am-8pm, Fri. 8am-9pm, Sat. 8am-6pm, Sun. 9am-6pm). If you opt out of the wilderness, make for the coffee shop, the **Garrison.** Also at High St.'s northern end, the Garrison offers veggie burgers (£2.25), cold filled rolls (from £1.50), and other meals (open daily 8am-9pm), while **Nevis Bakery** at 49 High St. packs lunches for £2.50 (open Mon.-Sat. 8am-5pm). **McTavish's Kitchen** on High St. serves hearty Scottish meals at reasonable prices in a cafeteria-style setting downstairs and a restaurant upstairs. Head for the justifiably popular **Ben Nevis** pub (tel. 702295) across the street at 103-109 High St. to find live music.

Before heading for the hills, check out Ft. William's urban pleasures; beside the tourist office, the **West Highland Museum** gathers such delights as an exhibit on Bonnie Prince Charlie, stuffed buzzards, a display on the Glencoe massacre, and the murder weapon from the Appin case—a notorious instance of a man wrongfully hanged because someone had to be (open Mon.-Sat. 9:30am-5:30pm, Sun. 2-5pm; Sept.-June Mon.-Sat. 10am-5pm; £1, seniors 60p, children 40p). On a rainy day rock-jocks visit **Treasures of the Earth** (tel. 772283) in Corpach, a fine collection of rare minerals and gemstones (open daily 9:30am-7pm; Sept.-June daily 10am-5pm; £2.50, children £1.50). For the rock-weary, **Marco's An Aird** (tel. 700707), behind Safeway, houses a range of activities including a 10-pin bowling alley, pool tables, badminton courts, and a children's play room (open daily 10am-11pm).

HIKING, CLIMBING, & BIKING

On one of the 65 days a year when Ben Nevis deigns to lift the veil of cloud from its peak, the unobstructed view encompasses Scotland's eastern coast all the way to Ireland. The interminable switchbacks of the well-beaten tourist trail ascend from the Fort William town park to Ben Nevis' summit; go north ½ mi. along the A82 and follow signs for the footpath to Ben Nevis. A fascinating, arduous ridge walk deviates from the tourist trail when it makes a sharp turn to the right near Lochan Meall an t-Suidhe. Leave the path where it descends to Coire Leis and clamber up the steep grass slopes to Carn Dearg Meadhonach; continue to the summit of Carn Mór Dearg. Along the ridge, a trail veers right towards the southeastern slopes of Ben Nevis by a lovely mountain lake; scramble the final 1000 ft. up steep terrain and claim the top of the world. Leave a full 8½ hours for the 9½-mi. round-trip, and don't dare set foot on the trail without an Ordnance Survey map, a hat, gloves, and other warm clothes, a windbreaker, proper footwear, and plenty of food and liquid. See Essentials: Hiking & Camping for more information.

Four mi. north of Fort William along the A82, the slopes of Aonach Mor (4006 ft.) now cushion the **Nevis Range** ski area. Though smaller than the Cairngorm facility, Nevis Range (tel. (01397) 705825) boasts Scotland's longest ski run (1¼mi.) and a state-of-the-art **gondola** (return £5, children £3.50). The cable car lifts you 2300 ft. to a restaurant at the base of the trails. Both the gondola and marked hiking trails stay open all year. Buses run year-round from Fort William to the slopes (5/day; 9am-4pm). **Glen Nevis Road,** past the youth hostel, offers glorious biking.

EVENTS

A few miles up the road past the hostel, you'll reach the falls where, on the first Sunday in August, hundreds of businessmen who base their virility on being daredevils rocket down the rapids on tiny air-bed mats during the **Glen Nevis River Race.** On the first Saturday in September, the area hosts the **Ben Nevis Race,** a punishing event in which runners sprint up and back down the mountain. The record time is an incredible 80 minutes. The **Lochaber Highland Games** take place in Fort William on the last Saturday in July. Ft. William sees tossing cabers and kilts at the **Lochaber Highland Games** on the last Saturday in July. *Ceilidhs* follow at **Marco's An Aird** (tel. (01397) 700707) for £3.

■■■ FORT WILLIAM TO MALLAIG: ROAD TO THE ISLES

The scenic **Road to the Isles** (now the A830), skates along lochs and between mountains on its breathtaking journey from Fort William west to Mallaig, on the Sound of Sleet. The **train** ride from Fort William to Mallaig offers sublime panoramas; modern carriages zip along while the less-frequent **steam locomotives** restore the romance of the grand old days of rail travel. (Modern trains run mid-June to Sept. 6/day, Sun. 3/day; Oct.-April Mon.-Sat. 2/day, Sun. 1/day; £6.40. Steam locomotives run June-Sept. Tues. and Thurs.; July-early Sept. also Sun.; try to book ahead at any British Rail station. Locomotive departs Fort William 10:30am; Mallaig 1:30pm, Sun. 2:45pm; £11.) The best views are on the left side of the train. One 9:30am bus from Mallaig does the same run; unless you stay overnight in Mallaig, this bus is nigh impossible to make (£5). Hitchers report sore thumbs on the Road to the Isles.

The road sets off westward from Fort William along Loch Eil, arriving at **Glenfinnan,** at the head of Loch Shiel, after 12 mi. A monument recalls August 19, 1745, the day Bonnie Prince Charlie rowed up Loch Shiel and rallied the clans around the Stuart standard in an ill-fated bid to put his father on the British throne. The **National Trust Office** (tel. (01397) 722250) documents the campaign (open late May-early Sept. daily 9:30am-6pm; April-late May and early Sept.-late Oct. 10am-5:30pm).

At **Lochailort,** another 10 mi. west, hikers can step off the train and wander for weeks without encountering another person. Two morning buses (Mon.-Sat.) run south into the desolate districts of Moidart, Ardnamurchan, and Morvern. By planning in advance, you can catch the seasonal ferry to Mull from Kilchoan (mid-April to mid-Oct. Mon.-Sat. 7/day; £2.80); connect with the Ardnamurchan-bound bus in Acharacle, 19 mi. south of Lochailort. Between Lochailort and Kilchoan, buses pass **Loch Moidart,** which opens into one of western Scotland's most beautiful bays, studded with islets and graced with sandy beaches. The abandoned 13th-century **Castle Tioram** was destroyed in 1715 by its owner in an ill-conceived plan to stop his neighbors from moving in while he was off at war. **Kentra Bay,** to the south, beckons to bathers. There are no lodgings here, and not much of anything else.

Head south and then west, *not* west then south, to explore the largely deserted area beneath the Road to the Isles. Drive or take the bus from Fort William along the west side of Loch Linnhe (2hr.), then veer down Gleann Geal to Lochaline. A car ferry from Lochaline skims over to Fishnish on Mull (Mon.-Sat. 14-16/day; late May-Aug. also Sun. 9/day; £1.60). After Lochailort, the Road to the Isles passes **Loch nan Uamh,** or the Loch of the Caves, the point from which shattered Prince Charlie fled in September, 1746, his brave bid for the crown having ended in a whimper. A memorial tower lends a sweeping view of the sea.

The road finally meets the west coast at the sandy beaches of **Arisaig. Murdo Grant** (tel. (01687) 224) operates ferries and day cruises from Arisaig to Rum, Eigg, Muck, Mallaig, and Armadale on Skye. Disembark from the train at Arisaig or Morar to reach the comfortable **Garramore HI Youth Hostel (HI;** tel. (016875) 268; grade 1), a 3-mi. walk along the A830 from either station (£6.50; open March-Oct.). Mallaig-bound buses stop right at the hostel. A **campsite** lies 150 yd. south of the hostel. **Dr. Ian Pragnell** (tel. (016875) 272) rents road and mountain bikes (£5-10) and willingly shares his keen knowledge of local cycling routes.

Brilliantly white sandy beaches across the road and down a short footpath from the hostel offer beautiful views of the Inner Hebrides. Rocky outcrops cut across the sand, creating multiple secluded beach coves accessible only on foot. Don't let nasty, red stinging jellyfish catch you skinnydipping. Another fine walk from the hostel follows the banks of **Loch Morar,** Britain's deepest freshwater loch (1017 ft.), before cutting over the hills to Tarbert on Loch Nevis.

Past Morar looms the relative megalopolis of **Mallaig** (MAL-ig), the fishing village where cruises and ferries leave for the Inner Hebrides. Dart around the block from the rail station (open Mon.-Sat. 9:46am-6:30pm) to find the **tourist office** (tel. 2170; open mid-May to Sept. Mon.-Sat. 9am-7pm; April to mid-May Mon.-Sat. 9am-4:30pm). Mallaig's **telephone code** is 01687.

Bruce Watt runs ferries and day cruises from Mallaig to Eigg, Inverie on Loch Nevis, Tarbert and Arnisdale on Loch Hourn, and Armadale on Skye (book ahead). **Caledonian MacBrayne ferries** (tel. 2403) skip along from Mallaig to **Armadale** on Skye (see Skye, below) and to the Small Isles (see The Small Isles, below). At **Sheena's Backpackers Lodge** (tel. 2764), you can luxuriate on an oversized bed; to find it, turn right out of train station; the lodge is just past the bank. In summer, Sheena's fills fast after early train and ferry arrivals; book ahead (£8, £6 each for couples sharing a bed). The **Fisherman's Mission** cafe across the street from the train station whips up cheap, filling grub. (Pizza £2.75, lasagne, or mac and cheese with beans or peas £3.50. Open Mon.-Fri. 8:30am-10:30pm, Sat. 9am-noon; hot meals served 9am-1:45pm and 5:30-10pm.) Hang with the local marine life at **Mallaig Marine World** (tel. 2292), the town's only attraction (open daily 9am-7pm; Oct.-May daily 9am-5pm; £2.50, seniors and students £2, children £1.50).

THE SMALL ISLES

Despite their proximity to the mainland and to Skye, the Small Isles of Rum, Eigg (EGG), Muck, and Canna remain unspoiled by tourism-related development. The islands lack a centralized electrical plant and roll-on vehicle landing facilities; visitors must go ashore by dinghy. **Caledonian MacBrayne** passenger **ferries** (tel. (01687) 2403) sail from Mallaig to Rum, Eigg, and Canna and back (Mon. and Wed. 10:30am, Fri. 6am, Sat. 5am and 12:30pm; Tues. and Thurs. sailings also stop at Muck; £3.80, day return £6.50). **Bruce Watt** (tel. (01687) 2320) cruises from Mallaig to Eigg on Thursday at 11:30am (return £13). **Murdo Grant** (tel. (016875) 224) sails from Airsaig at 11am (2 train stops from Mallaig) to Rum (Tues. and Thurs.; return £17), Eigg (Fri.-Wed.; return £13), and Muck (Mon., Wed., and Fri.; return £13). Schedules vary; call and book ahead. Canna offers nothing in the way of budget lodgings.

Rum (also spelled Rhum), the largest island, is owned by the National Trust of Scotland and carefully managed by Scottish Natural Heritage. Deer, highland cattle, golden eagles, and rarer creatures are the main residents; the entire human population of Rum emigrated to North America in 1828 during the Highland Clearances, when the *laird* of the island decided that they presented a threat to his sheep and sporting deer. A wealthy Lancashire mill owner built **Kinloch Castle** on Rum in 1901. Regular room and board are pricey, but cheap self-catering hostel accommodations (tel. (01687) 2037) are available (£9.50; advance booking essential). An excellent tour of the lavish castle (£2) is offered in conjunction with Murdo Grant's Tuesday and Thursday cruises to Rum. To camp on Rum, obtain prior permission from the Chief Warden, Scottish Natural Heritage, Isle of Rum, Scotland PH43 4RR (tel. (01687) 2026).

The isle of **Eigg** has the most stunning landscape, with fertile green slopes above formidable vertical cliffs. The island's only road, which stretches from the port of Galmisdale to the tiny village of **Cleadale**, is barely visible and traveled only by occasional Land Rovers. **Kildonan Hotel** (tel. (01687) 82446; dinner, packed lunch, B&B £27.50) and **Laig Farm Guest House** (tel. (01687) 82437; B&B £13; with dinner and packed lunch £25), and **Sue Kirk** (tel. (01687) 82405; B&B £13; with dinner and packed lunch £26) provide the only accommodations on Eigg, although you can camp by the **Singing Sands** on the Bay of Laig (when dry, the sands creak underfoot). The only store, in Cleadale, is open irregularly, so bring supplies.

Muck, the tiny (1½ mi. by 5 mi.) southernmost isle, is an experiment in communal living. The entire island is a single farm owned by Laurence MacEwen and his wife, who handle farming, transport along the Muck 1 road, and shopping on the mainland. You can ask to camp somewhere near the sandy beach on the island's Atlantic side, or stay with **Mrs. Harper** (tel. (01687) 2371; dinner, packed lunch, B&B £20). **Port Mhor Guesthouse** (tel (01687) 2365) offers dinner and B&B for £27. If you intend to muck about outside, bring food, as there is no place to eat or shop on the island.

■■■ SKYE

Skye is often raining, but also fine: hardly embodied; semi-transparent; like living in a jellyfish lit up with green light. Remote as Samoa; deserted, prehistoric. No room for more.

—Postcard from Virginia Woolf

Often described as the shining jewel in the Hebridean crown, Skye radiates unparalleled splendor from the serrated peaks of the Cuillin Hills to the rugged northern tip of the Trotternish Peninsula. As elsewhere in the Highlands, the 19th-century Clearances saw entire glens emptied of their ancient settlements. Today, as "white settlers" push the English population of the island toward 40%, Skye's traditional Gaelic culture survives mostly in museums.

The island's natural beauty is by no means a secret: an endless cortège of Ford Fiestas funnels from Skye's 24-hour ferries. But most visitors keep to the main roads, and vast swathes of terrain remain unscarred. Skye's large area and spotty transportation system will likely force you to concentrate your travels in certain areas of the island. Consider this a blessing in disguise. Take the time to study the geology of the unusual rock pinnacles on the Trotternish Peninsula, learn the local legends surrounding one of the Cuillins, or hear tales of the fairy folk from one who knows them. Forego leap-frogging between the gasoline-stained hubs of Portree, Broadford, and Kyleakin. Men, beware when you travel on Skye. The fairies consider your kind out of the cycles of nature and will play tricks on you. When the fairy folk encounter a woman, they must ask her a riddle. The woman always answers correctly and asks an impossible riddle in turn; the fairies must then grant her a wish.

GETTING THERE

Until a bridge to Skye is completed midway through 1995, access to the island will be provided solely by **ferry.** Round-the-clock ferries (except from 2-3am) from **Kyle of Lochalsh** on the mainland sail to **Kyleakin** on Skye (continuous service daily 7:30am-9pm, thereafter 2/hr.; 5min.; passengers free, cars £5). Two **Scottish Citylink** and two **Skye-Ways coaches** run daily from Glasgow to Kyle of Lochalsh (5hr.); Skye-Ways runs similar service from Inverness (2/day; 2hr.). **Trains** from Inverness arrive at the Kyle of Lochalsh terminus (tel. (01599) 4205), not far from the pier (4/day, Sun. 2/day; 2½hr.). The **Go Blue Banana** minibus peels from Edinburgh to Kyleakin via Perth, Inverness, and other points (Thurs.-Tues.); **Haggis Backpackers** runs a similar route (Fri.-Wed.; see Scotland: Getting About, above).

From Mallaig on the mainland, **Cal-Mac** ferries make the 30-minute crossing to **Armadale** on Skye (May-Sept. 4-7/day from 9am-4:45pm; July-Aug. also 6:15pm; £2.30, cars £11.60; call (014714) 248 to book car space). Those who have time for a scenic detour can take the historic "Drove Road:" cattle were once forced to swim the channel between **Glenelg** on the mainland and **Kylerhea** on Skye, where a vehicle and passenger ferry now operates. (Mon.-Sat., frequent crossings Easter-Sept. 9am-6pm; July-Aug. 9am-8pm; £1, cars £5; for details tel. (0159981) 302.) From the Outer Hebrides, **Cal-Mac ferries** travel from Tarbert on Harris or Lochmaddy on North Uist to Uig on Skye (May to mid-Oct. 1-2/day; £6.65, cars £29.45). Service frequency is substantially reduced in winter; pick up a schedule in advance.

GETTING ABOUT

Touring Skye without a car takes either effort or cash. Hitching is widespread and fairly viable despite the abundance of steely-eyed tourists. The many cyclists on Skye keep up with the cars in the flatter regions. **Hebridean Pedal Highway** (tel. (01599) 4842), just up the road from the ferry in Kyle of Lochalsh, rents bikes and lets you return them in Armadale, Uig, or Lochboisdale on South Uist for a small charge (mountain bikes £6/day, 5-speeds £3/day). **Skye Bikes** in Kyleakin (tel. (01599) 4795) rents top-quality mountain bikes (£6.50/day, £4.50/½-day). **Uig Cycle Hire** (tel. (0147042) 311) is down the road from the hostel (18-speed mountain bike £7/day). In Broadford, try **Skyebike Cycle Hire** (tel. (01471) 822418; £6/day).

Buses are infrequent, ruinously expensive, and virtually nonexistent on Sundays (Kyleakin-Portree £4.25; Armadale-Kyleakin £3.25). The only decent service hugs the coast from Kyleakin to Broadford to Portree. Everything shuts down on Sundays except the **Citylink** and **Caledonian Express** long-distance buses on the Kyleakin-Broadford-Portree-Uig line and one 24-hour convenience store in Broadford (tel. (01471) 822225). Buses should meet all sailings of the Armadale ferry, but check in advance if you're making the early morning crossing on a Sunday. Look also for the blue **Skye-Ways** buses which offer student discounts. Since buses on Skye are run by different operators, ask at the tourist office for a complete sheaf of schedules.

Ewan MacRae, Ltd., Portree (tel. (01478) 612554) and **Sutherland's Garage,** Broadford (tel. (01471) 822225), rent cars to those between 21 and 70. (Rates lamentably start at £28/day plus 18p/mi.) You are asked to put down a £150 deposit, refundable unless you hit a solemnly lowing cow.

A thoroughly enjoyable way to get around Skye's scattered sights is with **Badger Tours** (tel (014716) 228). Australian Ted Badger, a former divorce lawyer and urban refugee, knowledgeably and wittily guides you around the island on full-day tours by foot and minibus for £10 per person. Ask about the legendary Amazon warrior who, according to Celtic legend, gave her name to the Isle of Skye; Ted has Aesop's own talent for storytelling. On a Sunday, this may be the only (and best) way around the island. Book by phone or at the Backpackers Guest House in Kyleakin.

FESTIVALS

Perhaps to evade the midges outside, Skye has a vigorous indoor nightlife; lively traditional music in English and Gaelic is abundant if you know where to look. Snag a copy of the weekly *What, Where and When* leaflet or *The Visitor* newspaper for a list of special events and dances. Livestock, craft, and baking exhibitions enliven the **Dunvegan Arts Festival** at the end of July, and **Dunvegan Hall** hosts family *ceilidhs* (July-Aug., Tues. and Thurs. nights.). There are frequent local dances—half folk, half rock—at the village halls, usually starting after 11pm (hostelers should note curfews). The **Highland Games,** a mirthful day of bagpipes, foot races, and boozing, and the **Skye Folk Festival,** featuring *ceilidhs* in Portree, Broadford, and Dunvegan, take place in the first and second weeks of August. The tourist office in Portree (tel. (01478) 612137) has more information on these events.

KYLE OF LOCHALSH & KYLEAKIN

Frequent ferries cross the strait between Kyle of Lochalsh, on the mainland, and Kyleakin, on Skye's southern tail fin, making the twin villages effectively one community (crossing 5min.). Itself a tiny port town, Kyleakin makes an excellent stop for the budget traveler due to its high concentration of inexpensive accommodations, bus connections, and the free ferry to Kyle on the mainland.

Most shops and services gather in Kyle of Lochalsh; the local grocery and bakery are both here, and the **tourist office** (tel. 4276), which will book a B&B for £1 on either side of the channel, overlooks Kyle's pier (open July-Sept. Mon.-Sat. 9am-7pm; Aug. Mon.-Sat. 9am-9:30pm, Sun. 12:30-4:30pm; Easter-June and Oct. Mon.-Sat. 9am-5:30pm). The **telephone code** for these villages is 01599. From Kyle of Lochalsh, head ¾ mi. out along the road to Plockton for a hearty meal at the **Highland Designworks Wholefood Cafe** (tel. 4388). A *duki* bean burger with salad goes for £3.80 at lunchtime (noon-5:30pm); dinners are large and leafy but start at £5.75 (open Sun.-Fri. 11am-8:30pm).

The most affordable lodgings cluster in Kyleakin (Kyle-ACK-in) alongside the park a few hundred yards from the pier. To the right of the pier, the cozy and relaxed **Backpacker's Guesthouse** (tel. 4510) offers 35 beds (including a double, twin, and triple), and a kitchen and dining area. Call ahead for the first night (£7.50, private room £9, caravan beds £6; breakfast £1.20; laundry service £2.50). At the modern, comfortable **HI Youth Hostel** (tel. 4585), a helpful warden presides over large common spaces and small bedrooms. Skye's only Grade 1 hostel fills *very* quickly in the summer, so book weeks ahead (£6.50; laundry; breakfast £2.65, dinner £3.55).

Once you've seen the harbor in Kyleakin, you've seen all you can there. Climb to the memorial on a hill behind the Castle Moil Restaurant for the best views. A more slippery scramble takes you up to the ruins of **Castle Moil** itself (cross the little bridge behind the youth hostel, turn left, follow the road to the pier, and take the gravel path). Legend relates that the original castle on this site was built by "Saucy Mary," a Norwegian princess who stretched a stout chain across the Kyle and charged ships a fee to come through the narrows. Eight miles east along the A87 on an islet in Loch Duich perches **Eilean Donan Castle** (tel. (0159985) 202), the restored 13th-century seat of the MacKenzies. This castle across a bridge adorns more shortbread boxes and souvenir ashtrays than any other Scottish monument (open Easter-Oct. daily 10am-5:30pm; £1, children 50p). The view from the hillside behind the castle is more memorable than its restored interior. The bus from Kyle of Lochalsh to Ft. William stops at the castle.

SOUTHERN SKYE

The unremarkable town of **Broadford,** located on a silent rocky bay 8 mi. west of Kyleakin, gains fame as the hub for all bus transport throughout the southern half of Skye and the home of a 24-hour convenience store open on Sundays. The **tourist office** (tel. 822361) distributes leaflets from a parking lot along the bay south of the bus stop (open June to mid-Sept. Mon.-Sat. 9:15am-7pm; April-May and mid-Sept. to Oct. Mon.-Sat. 9:30am-1pm and 2-5:30pm). Broadford's **telephone code** is 01471. Follow the signpost ½ mi. from the bus stop along a side road to the **Broadford HI Youth Hostel** (tel. 822442; grade 2; £4.80; open March-Oct.). Two miles east of Broadford on the coast lies the tiny **Fossil Bothy** (tel. 822644 or 822297), a renovated stone bunkhouse with room for eight (£6). The prehistoric creatures trapped in the walls inspired the bothy's name. Book ahead. For food in town, try the **Broadford Bay Stores** (open Mon.-Fri. 7am-5pm, Sat. 7:30am-4pm) or **Strathcorrie Takeaway** (open Easter-Oct. daily 11am-9pm), near the post office, serving steak and kidney pie with chips for £2.

Two miles south of Broadford, the single-lane A851 veers southwest through the thick foliage of the **Sleat Peninsula,** also called "The Garden of Skye;" keep an eye out for the delicious wild raspberries that grow by the roadside. Seventeen miles of hills bring you to **Armadale,** where the Mallaig ferries depart. **Armadale Castle** houses the **Clan Donald Centre** (tel. 305), which maintains a genealogical center, museum, and audio-visual programs; rangers offer walks through the 300-year-old castle gardens and surrounding 20,000-acre estate (open April-Oct. daily 9:30am-5:30pm, last entry 5pm; £3.25, seniors, students, and children £2.25). The **Armadale HI Hostel** (tel. (014714) 260; grade 2), ten minutes around the bay from the pier, overlooks the water (£5.05; open mid-March-Sept.). Slightly north of Armadale at Ostaig is a Gaelic college, **Sabhal Mor Ostaig** (tel. (014714) 373), which distributes literature on Celtic heritage and offers courses in Gaelic and piping.

THE CUILLINS

The **Cuillin Hills** dominate central Skye from the latitude of Broadford to that of Portree. The Red Cuillins and the Black Cuillins meet in **Sligachan;** the black hills are rough and craggy, while the red hills have smoother, conical profiles thanks to Neptune's incessant tectonic hydrogesticulations, whatever they may be. The highest peaks in the Hebrides, the Cuillin Hills are renowned for their hiking paths and stunning formations of cloud and mist. Legends say that the warrior Cuillin was the lover of the Amazon ruler of Skye. A witch, taking the shape of a crow, prophesied that Cuillin would die in Ireland; knowing he could not defy fate, he returned there, and Skye named the mountains for him. The leaflets *Walks from Sligachan* and *Walks from Glen Brittle,* published by the Skye Mountain Rescue Team and available at tourist offices, offer hiking suggestions. Don't even try to hike without warm clothing or an Ordnance Survey map (the best is the £5 yellow 1:25,000 map on the Cuillin and Torridon Hills). For pointers, see Essentials: Hiking & Camping, above.

If you have several days, base yourself at the **Glenbrittle HI Hostel** near the southwest coast (tel. (01478) 640278; grade 2; £5.05; open mid-March to Sept.). Campers should head to one of the 200 sites that dot the **Glenbrittle Campsite** (tel. (01478) 640404; £5-8/tent; open April-Sept.). Expert mountaineers at the hostel give the best advice and **Gerry Akroyd** (tel. (01478) 640289), in Glenbrittle, leads weeklong winter and summer climbing expeditions through the hills. In summer, two buses per day run from Portree on the east coast to Glenbrittle; call **Sutherland's Bus Service** (tel. (0147842) 267) for details.

The bus to Glenbrittle also stops about 10 mi. west of the Cuillins in **Portnalong,** where you can stay at the **Croft Bunkhouse** (tel. (01478) 640254). The comfortably converted cowshed sleeps 16, and the adjoining section sports a new ping-pong table and a Californian dart board (£5). A footpath from Sligachan over the pass to the hostel skirts the 7-mi. walk on the main road. Across the mountains at the junction of the A863 to Portree and the A850 to Dunvegan, the **Sligachan Campsite** (tel. (01478) 650204) makes another good base for hiking the Cuillins. Set in an open field across from the hotel in Sligachan, the site has 80 pitches, showers, and a drying room (£5/person; open Easter-Oct.). The bar across the street serves lovely meals (£3-5) daily from 8am to 11pm.

A short but scenic path follows the small stream flowing from Sligachan to the head of **Loch Sligachan.** After crossing the old bridge, fork left off the main path and walk along the right hand bank as you go upstream. The narrow and often boggy path leads past many pools and miniature waterfalls (3 mi. round-trip). The arresting oversized anthill to the left, the 775-yd. **Glamaig,** was ascended and descended in 55 minutes by a Gurkha soldier in 1899. Give yourself 3½ hours, and then only if you feel at ease on steep slopes with unsure footing. Branch off the main trail after about 15 minutes onto the smaller trail which leads up the grassy ridge between the higher peaks, a spot with fantastic views of the ocean and offshore isles.

Experienced climbers may try the ascent into the **Sgurr nan Gillean Corrie,** to the southwest of Glamaig, where the peak rises 3167 ft. above a tiny mountain lake. For more level terrain, take the 8-mi. walk down Glen Sligachan through the heart of the Cuillins to the beach of **Camasunary,** with views of the isles of Rum and Muck.

For a less intimate view of the Cuillins, take the A881 14 mi. southwest from Broadford (a difficult cycle ride) to **Elgol.** You can sail from Elgol to **Loch Coriusk** (Mon.-Sat. several times a day; return £5.75) with **R. MacKinnon** (tel. (014716) 213), weather permitting; this trip brings you into the midst of an extraordinary conflagration of mountain and water.

NORTHERN SKYE

As the capital of the island, **Portree** (pop. 1600) merits at least a brief stopover for a meal, a T-shirt purchasing frenzy, and a view of its picturesque harbor. The **tourist office,** in the old jail on Bank St. above the harbor, helps direct wayward tourists to appropriate buses (tel. 612137; open June to mid-July and early Sept. Mon.-Sat. 9am-7pm; mid-July to Aug. Mon.-Sat. 9:15am-8pm; April-May and mid-Sept. to Oct. Mon.-Sat. 9:15am-5:30pm; Nov.-March Mon.-Fri. 9:15am-5:30pm). Portree's **telephone code** is 01478. Buses stop at Somerled Sq. two blocks away. Buy groceries at the **Presto Supermarket** on Bank St., or dine at perhaps the best restaurant in town, the **Ben Tianavaig Bistro,** 5 Boswell Terrace (tel. 2152), specializing in wholefood, vegetarian, and seafood dishes (open April-Sept. Tues.-Sun. noon-4pm and 6-9pm).

The Bakery on Somerled Sq. (open daily 9am-5pm), and the tiny but well-stocked wholefood shop on Parklane at the end of Wentworth St. (open Mon.-Tues. and Thurs.-Fri. 9am-5pm, Wed. and Sat. 9am-1pm) should satisfy your culinary needs. "Janet the Piranha" guards the door to the **fish 'n chip shop** on Quay St., which sells prawns in garlic butter, smoked salmon sandwiches, and pizzas with smoked mackerel, in addition to the standard fish and chips (open daily 9am-10:30pm; lunch served after noon). Look for *ceilidhs* on Fridays at 11pm in the Skye Gathering Hall.

Thanks to two scenic circular roads and miles of quiet shoreline, the northern part of Skye is able to support more tourists than the rest of the island. The northwestern circuit follows the A850 from Portree to Dunvegan Castle, then down the A863 along the beautiful west coast; the northeastern circuit hugs the A855 and A856 around the **Trotternish Peninsula** through Uig and Staffin and back to Portree. Consider taking the five-hour **Highland Scottish Omnibus** tours from Portree (tel. (01478) 612622; June-Sept. Mon.-Fri. 10:30am; £5).

Northeast of Portree, the A855 snakes along the eastern coast of the Trotternish Peninsula, past the **Old Man of Storr,** a finger of black rock visible for miles around, and the **Quirang,** a group of spectacular rock pinnacles readily accessible by foot. These lunar landscapes define Skye's difference from the rest of Scotland. Nearby **Staffin Bay** offers arresting views over Skye and the mainland, while **Kilt Rock** bears lava columns similar to those on Staffa. Strong, well-shod walkers might hike the **Trotternish Ridge,** which runs the length of the peninsula from the Old Man of Storr to Staffin; the challenging and rewarding 12-mi. hike takes about a day.

The ruins of **Duntulm Castle** guard the tip of the peninsula. The castle was the MacDonalds' formidable stronghold until a nurse dropped the chief's baby boy from the window to the rocks below, thus cursing the house. One of the most worthwhile sights on the peninsula lies near Duntulm at Kilmuir; the **Skye Museum** (tel. (0147052) 279), in a village of tiny black 200-year-old houses, recreates old crofter life and addresses the Clearances (open April-Oct. Mon.-Sat. 9am-5:30pm; £1.50, seniors £1, children 50p). Nearby, **Flora MacDonald's Monument** pays tribute to the Scottish folk hero who sheltered Bonnie Prince Charlie as he fled from certain death. Get some R&R in the woods at the **Dun Flodigarry Backpackers Hostel** (tel. (0147052) 212), 5 mi. north of Staffin.

The town of **Uig** (OO-ig) flanks a windswept bay on the peninsula's west coast, the terminus for ferries to the Outer Hebrides and the final resting place for most long-distance buses from Glasgow and Inverness. The **HI Uig Youth Hostel** (tel. (0147042) 211; grade 2) is a tough 30-minute walk from the ferry on the A586 (£5.05; open mid-March-Oct.).

■■■ OUTER HEBRIDES

The landscape of the Outer Hebrides is astoundingly ancient. Much of the exposed rock here has been around for about three billion years, more than half as long as the planet itself. The culture and customs of the Hebridean people have also resisted change: the roads are still one-lane, scattered family crofts remain the norm on the Uists, and although television and tourism have diluted traditional Hebridean speech and ways of life, most old and many young islanders speak Gaelic among themselves (it has become mandatory in schools). The island's distant past has deposited a rich sediment of ruined tombs and standing stones, including the remarkable stone circle at Callanish on Lewis. In recent years, the area has suffered from mass emigration as more and more young people (particularly young women) seek work on the mainland. This imbalance can make life difficult for women traveling alone, since in the Uists, for example, the population under 40 has become almost entirely male.

The vehemently Calvinist islands of Lewis, Harris, and North Uist observe the Sabbath strictly. All shops, pubs, and restaurants close, and public transportation stops on Sundays; even the playground swings are chained. Farther down through Benbecula, South Uist, and Barra, tight-shuttered Protestant sabbatarianism gives way to Catholic chapels and commemorative plates of the pope on living room walls. Like politics elsewhere, religion is a source of some contention and sometimes open hostility among the islanders. As a rule, try not be too boisterous with your faith.

According to a local legend, Bafinn, a Norwegian princess, rests in a 3000-year slumber under a knoll 3 mi. from Lochmaddy on North Uist. When she wakes, the weather on the Outer Isles will improve. Until then, expect a regular riot of high winds and rain. In summer, the weather is usually—though by no means assuredly—milder, and the late-evening sunsets huge and enveloping. These islands are far too large and remote ever to become crowded.

GETTING THERE & GETTING ABOUT

Three major **Caledonian MacBrayne** services ferry travelers out, while ferries and infrequent connecting buses connect the islands lengthwise. Cycling is excellent provided you don't melt in the rain. Hitchers report frequent rides. You can rent a **car** inexpensively (from £15/day; try Mackinnon Self Drive in Stornoway; tel. (01851) 702984, or Laing Motors in Lochboisdale (tel. (0187) 84267), but they'll probably prohibit you from taking it on ferries. Since ferries arrive at odd hours, try to arrange a bed ahead. Aside from two of the usual **HI hostels** and assorted **B&Bs,** the Outer Hebrides are home to the unique **Gatliff Hebridean Trust Hostels** (Urras Osdailean Nan Innse Gall Gatliff), five 19th-century thatched croft houses turned into simple year-round hostels, whose authenticity and atmosphere more than compensate for the crude facilities (bring a sleeping bag, knife, and fork). These hostels (all £3.45, under 18 £2.85) are at the tip of North Uist in Berneray, in Claddach Baleshare on the west side of North Uist, in Howmore on South Uist, in Garenin on Lewis, and in Rhenigidale on Harris. No advance bookings are accepted, but they never turn travelers away. Refer to the SYHA handbook for details. Camping is allowed on public land, but freezing winds and sodden ground often make it miserable. Except in bilingual Stornoway and Benbecula, all **road signs** in the islands are now in Gaelic only. Tourist offices often carry translation keys, and *Let's Go* lists Gaelic equivalents after English place names. For more light on the islands, snag a copy of *The Outer Hebrides Handbook and Guide* (£4.25 at all tourist offices).

LEWIS (LEODHAS)

Relentlessly remote and desolate, the landscape of Lewis is flat, treeless, and at first sight utterly depressing. This island is famous for its atmosphere: your photographs will fail to properly astonish the folks back home, no matter how much you try to convey the strange aura of the place. Pure light and drifting mists off the Atlantic shroud untouched miles of moorland and small lochs in quiet luminescence. The unearthly setting is a fitting one for exploring Lewis's many archaeological sites, most notably the **Callanish Stones.**

Caledonian MacBrayne ferries from Ullapool on the northwest coast of the mainland serve **Stornoway** (Steornobhaigh), the biggest town in the Outer Hebrides, and the center of all services the smaller towns lack (Mon.-Sat. 2-3/day, £10.05). Though most of Lewis's sights are in the outlying countryside, Stornoway has attractions of its own. The **An Lanntair Gallery,** in the Town Hall on South Beach St., houses the town's best café, art exhibits, and a series of local history evenings, complete with slides and folk music (July-mid-Aug. Tues. at 8pm; £4, seniors and children £2.50; free in daytime hours). If Stornoway brings too much human companionship, meander through the artificially forested grounds of **Lews Castle,** northwest of town. Begun in the 19th century by a wealthy merchant and opium smuggler, the castle now sequesters a college.

The cozy **Stornoway Hostel,** 47 Keith St. (tel. (01851) 703628), is only five minutes from the pier (turn right, then left on Castle St., first right onto a pedestrian street, left on Keith St.). Run by windsurfing wonder-wardens, this relaxed 18-bed hostel is completely self-catering and always open (£7). Or stay 8 mi. outside of town at the **Bayble Bunkhouse** (tel. (01851) 870863), which offers showers and kitchen facilities (£6). If you're leaving on the 5:30am ferry, many B&Bs oblige with a crack-of-dawn breakfast. The bus (7-8/day, 80p) to **Bayble** (Pabail) runs from Stornoway's **bus station,** a two-minute walk up South Beach St. from the pier.

Cheap food is easy to come by here. Try the **Fishermen's Mission,** North Beach St., which serves a godly turkey and tomato toastie (£1.30; open Mon.-Fri. 8am-4:45pm). For Chinese take-away, try **Peking Cuisine** at 30 Church St. (open Mon.-Wed. noon-2pm and 5-11:30pm, Thurs. noon-2pm and 5pm-midnight, Fri. noon-1am, Sat. noon-11pm). **Nature's Store** at 5 Cromwell St. sells wholefoods (open Mon.-Tues. and Thurs.-Sat. 9am-1pm and 2-5:30pm). Buy groceries at **Presto's** (open Mon.-Wed. 8:30am-6pm, Thurs.-Fri. 8:30am-7pm, Sat. 8:30am-5:30pm) or the **Co-op** (open Mon.-Thurs. 9am-5:30pm, Fri.-Sat. 9am-6pm). Both are on Cromwell St.

The Stornoway **tourist office** (tel. (01851) 703088) books coach tours of Lewis (June-Sept. Mon.-Fri. at 2pm; £5/person for four or more people, parties of fewer than four asked to make up the difference). It's on the main drag at 26 Cromwell St.—turn right from the ferry terminal, then left on Cromwell (open Mon.-Sat. 9am-6pm and 9-10pm; Nov.-March Mon.-Fri. 9am-5pm; April Mon.-Thurs. 9am-5:30pm and 9-10pm, Fri.-Sat. 9am-5pm and 9-10pm). Stornoway Trust ranger **Jamie Hepburn** leads outstanding, informative, and free walks of Stornoway and the countryside, as well as an £8 evening outing on his lobster boat. Tours depart the tourist office, where detailed schedules are available. Lewis has appropriated the **Harris Tweed** industry from its southern neighbor. Although you can no longer visit the mill shops, local crofters often vend from their homes. **Erica's Laundrette,** 46 Macaulay Rd., is the only one in Harris and Lewis (open Mon.-Tues. and Thurs.-Fri. 8am-4:45pm, Sat. 9am-3:30pm). *Everything* is closed on Sunday.

Buses from Stornoway run frequently; the bus station has schedule information. Major destinations include Tarbert (An Taribeart) on Harris (Mon.-Fri. 2-3/day, £2.75), and Ness (Nis), Callanish (Calanais), and Carloway (Carlabhaigh) on Lewis. Routes extend to all of Lewis's major sights. The island's relatively flat roads are good for **biking:** Pentland Rd. from Stornoway to Carloway earns raves. Bikers should check the weather forecasts; on a gusty day you may even have to pedal hard downhill. You can rent bikes in Stornoway at **Alex Dan's Cycle Centre** (tel. (01851) 704025), 67 Kenneth St. (open Mon.-Sat. 9am-6pm; £2/hr., £6/day, £39.50/week).

Lewis is home to the impressive **Callanish Stones** 14 mi. west of Stornoway on the A858. Second only to Stonehenge in their grandeur and a thousand times less overrun, the speckled greenish-white stones were hewn from Lewisian gneiss, the three-billion-year-old rock hidden beneath the island's peat bogs. Local archaeologists believe that prehistoric peoples used the stones to track the movements of the moon, employing complex trigonometry and displaying a level of technical knowledge unavailable to the Greeks 2000 years later. Others are skeptical, but admit that the circle may have been designed by primitive astronomers. Local writer Gerald Ponting has published thorough guides to Callanish and 20 neighboring sites with explicit directions (50p). Take the Carloway bus (2/day; £1.85) from the Stornoway bus station and ask the driver to let you off by the stones. A mile before Callanish, post buses snake off along the B8011 across the bridge to **Great Bernera** (Bearnaraigh), flanked by dozens of deserted islets, and 20 mi. farther west to the surprisingly lush **Glen Valtos** and the expansive sands at **Timsgarry.**

On the A858 5 mi. north of Callanish is **Carloway** (Carlabhaigh), a crofting town dominated by the imposing 2000-year-old **Dún Carloway Broch,** an Iron Age tower with a partly-intact staircase and an breathtaking view of the surrounding hills and lochs. Once it would have sheltered local farmers from Viking raiders—now it shelters tourists from high winds. Watch your footing on the stones around the broch; a sudden gust of wind may bring you closer to the surrounding landscape than you ever wished (free, always open). The Gatliff Trust's 14-bed **Garenin Youth Hostel** (Gearranan), a lovely converted black house, is 1½ mi. from Carloway (£3.85). Continuing north, you can visit the **Shawbost School Museum,** filled with objects pried from children's fingers by nasty grown-ups. The collection offers a glimpse into the daily life of 19th-century Lewis with boxbeds, town records, personal narratives, and Harris tweed looms galore (open Mon.-Sat. 9am-6pm; free). Beyond Shawbost on the A858, the **Arnol Black House** is a restored thatched-roof crofter's cottage. A chimney was intentionally left out, as smoke from the peat fire was supposed to improve the thatch by seeping through the roof—hence the name "black house" (and "black lung").

Farther north, across splashes of grassy moor and scattered villages, lies the **Butt of Lewis** (Rubha Robhanais), the island's northernmost point. A lighthouse on the disintegrating cliffs overlooks beaches below; it is a bleak but beautiful butt, and at night you can hear the growl of the corncrake, a rare and elusive bird.

HARRIS (NA HEARADH)

Although Harris is technically part of the same island as Lewis, it might as well be on Pluto. Lewis, like the Uists, is mainly flat and watery, while Harris, formed by volcanic gneiss, has an unkempt ruggedness unique to Scotland. Behind the barricade of the treeless Forest of Harris (actually a mountain range), its steely-grey mountains, splotched with grass and boulders and heather, descend on the west coast to brilliantly yellow sandy beaches bordered by *machair*—sea meadows of soft green grass and brilliant summer flowers. In the 19th century, these idyllic shores were cleared for sheep grazing and the islanders moved to the boulder-strewn waste of the east coast. They responded to the area's complete lack of arable land by developing still-visible "lazybeds": furrowed masses of seaweed and peat compost laid on bare rock. The island's main road, the A859, runs north to south from Tarbert to Stornoway, bumping and winding through the mountains. The **Golden Road** (so named because of the king's ransom spent in blasting it from the rock) twists from Tarbert to Harris's southern tip via the desolate east coast, and makes a harrowing bus trip or grueling bike ride. From Tarbert, small roads branch east and west towards the small fishing community on the island of **Scalpay** (Scalpaigh) and the now-deserted Isle of Scarp, where a mad German scientist tried to start a rocket-powered postal service to the Western Isles in 1934. With great fanfare and a commemorative stamp, the first launch exploded on impact, blasting the mail into itty-bitty pieces and putting an end to the experiment.

Ferries serve Tarbert from Uig on Skye (Mon.-Sat. 1-2/day, £6.65) and Lochmaddy on North Uist (direct service Tues. and Fri. only, £6.65). Check with **Caledonian MacBrayne Ferries,** in Tarbert at the pier for schedule information (tel. (01859) 502444). If the ferry is going from Lochmaddy to Tarbert via Uig or vice-versa, you can complete the entire double-length journey without paying extra (Mon.-Sat.). A small ferry runs from Newtonferry (Port nan Lang) on North Uist, and Bernera (Bearnaraigh), a small island off North Uist, to Leverburgh (An T-ob) at Harris's southern end (Mon.-Sat. 2/day; Oct.-May Mon., Wed., and Sat. 1/day; £3.60). Call **D.A. MacAskill** (tel. (018767) 230) for details. Cal-Mac also runs a ferry service between Kyles Scalpay (Caolas Scalpaigh) and the nearby island of Scalpay (Mon.-Sat. 11/day, 70p). From Tarbert, **buses** (tel. (01859) 2441) run to both Stornoway and Leverburgh (Mon.-Sat. 2-3/day, £2.75).

Unlovely **Tarbert** (An Tairbeart) straddles a narrow isthmus that divides the island into North Harris and South Harris. A cheerful **tourist office** sits on Pier Rd. (tel. (01859) 2011; open April to mid-Oct. roughly 9am-5pm and for late ferry arrivals). You'll also find the only **bank** in Harris up the hill from the pier (open Mon.-Fri. 9:15am-12:30pm, 1:30-4:45pm) and the largest cluster of shops in Tarbert. Stock up on groceries and fresh rolls at **A.D. Munro,** just up from the tourist office. **Harris Hotel** serves lunches (£3-4.50) and potent pints (£1.50-1.70) in its bar across the road from the main building (meals Mon.-Sat. 9am-8:30pm). Dinners are inexpensive in the small restaurant attached to the bar (Mon.-Sat. 6-9pm).

There are B&Bs aplenty in Tarbert. **Effie MacKinnon's** huge rooms rest in Waterstein House (tel. (01859) 2358) across from the tourist office (1 double, 1 2-bed double, 1 family; £13). The nearest **HI Youth Hostel** is 7 mi. south along the east coast in **Stockinish** (Stocinis); it recently acquired a shower and an indoor toilet. The hostel grooves muskily to an open peat fire and a quiet bay (tel. (01859) 530373; grade 3; £3.85; open April-Sept.).

Buses to Stockinish and Flodabay run once a day (Mon.-Sat.) from Tarbert. In North Harris, the **Gatliff Trust Hostel** at **Rhenigidale** (Reinigeadal) can now be reached by road: follow the turnoff to Maaruig (Maraig) from the A859 6 mi. north of Tarbert by foot (13 mi. by road); it's about 4 mi. to the hostel (no phone; £3.85).

The beguiling nothingness of the Harris landscape is best seen by bike (mountain bike £6/day, £25/week, touring bike £5/day, £20/week) from **Mr. Mackenzie** across from the tourist office (tel. (01859) 502271). The roads are generally deserted, though each of the half-dozen cars per day might pick up a rain-soaked hitchhiker. Hiking is said to be very good here, and because of the treeless landscape, traversing the headlands presents little risk of getting lost. Marked trails are scarce; bring a compass, sturdy boots, and an Ordnance Survey map. The largest peaks are in the Forest of Harris. Main entrances to the Forest are off the B887 to Huisinish Point, at **Glen Meavaig** and farther west at **Amhuinnsuidhe Castle,** a Victorian building erected in 1863.

If you don't have time for an exhaustive exploration, hop any fence just outside Tarbert and hike up **Gillaval Glas** (1554 ft.), which overlooks the town and harbor islands. The view from the top is stupendous, if you survive the climb. Bring appropriate clothing and give yourself a full afternoon. The hills of South Harris are smaller but just as rugged. An enjoyable daytrip might involve wandering down the coast-to-coast path that begins on the east coast at the crofts of Ardvey (the tip of Loch Stockinish) and passes 1 mi. north of the Stockinish Youth Hostel.

After exploring the mountains, head down to **Rodel** (Roghadal), at Harris's southern tip, site of strikingly beautiful **St. Clement's Church.** The three MacLeod tombs here are worth a look; the principal one, built in 1528, is hewn from local black gneiss (free, always open). Shortly up the road is Leverburgh, with a few houses, a tea shop, and the passenger boat to Newtonferry (Port nan Long) on North Uist.

THE UISTS (UIBHIST)

The Uists (YOO-ists) take Lewis' flatness to an extreme. Save for a thin strip of land along the east coast, these islands are almost completely level, packed with so many lochs that it's difficult to distinguish islands from land-locked water. A rare spot of sunlight reveals a strange world of thin beaches, crumbling black houses, wild jonquils, and quiet streams, scattered with duns, brochs, and prehistoric wheel-houses.

The survival of the crofting system has led to an extremely decentralized and tiny population. The main villages of **Lochmaddy** (Loch nan Madadh) on **North Uist** (Uibhist a Tuath) and **Lochboisdale** (Loch Baghasdail) on **South Uist** (Uibhist a Deas) are but glorified ferry points. Small **Benbecula** (Beinn na Faoghla) lies between its two larger neighbors, and has the Uists's sole airport. Crossing from North Uist to South Uist, strict Calvinism gives way to celebratory Roman Catholicism. While Sunday remains a day of church-going in the south, secular public activity is much more acceptable here than in the north. Most visitors come to enjoy the scenery and wildlife with a few ruins thrown in for good measure.

The A865 runs past a number of historical sights visually indistinguishable from the surrounding landscape. Benbecula holds the scanty remains of **Borve Castle,** a 14th-century ruin which was burned down by 18th-century clansmen in a show of support for King George II. Further north on the B892, the road passes along splendid beaches to the west and arrives at **Nunton** and its long-gone nunnery. The nuns were massacred during the Reformation. In Culla Bay, the seaweed grows in the shape of hands on the rocks where the nuns were tied and left to drown.

On the southern tip of North Uist at **Carinish** lies the ruin of 13th-century **Trinity Temple,** probably the islands' most noteworthy building. It once housed a medieval college where the great scholar Duns Scotus is said to have pondered the eternal questions. Past the Locheport Rd. 2 mi. on the A867 is the chambered cairn, **Bharpa Langass,** which dates back 3000 years to the Neolithic Age. Bird-watchers should head for the **Balranald Reserve** on the western part of North Uist, north of Bayhead (signposted "RSPB"). May and June are the most avially prolific months, but you'll almost always see lapwings, oyster-catchers, and rare red-necked phalaropes.

For vistas of loch and moor, hop over the roadside fence and climb **Blashaval Hill,** a short walk west of Lochmaddy on the A865. The A865 continues from here in a circle around North Uist, passing **Sollas's** wide sandy beaches, **Scolpaig's** sea-carved arches, and **Tigharry,** site of Sloc a'Choire, a spouting cave with a hollow arch. It is said that a young lass once hid in the arch rather than marry the man to whom her parents had betrothed her; you can still hear her cries echoing inside.

The **Lochmaddy HI Youth Hostel** (tel. (01876) 500368; grade 2), ½ mi. from the pier along the main road, overlooks a garden and a small bay (open mid-May to Sept. lockout 10:30am-5pm; curfew 11pm; £5.05). About ¼ mi. behind the youth hostel is the **Uist Outdoor Centre** (tel. (01876) 500480), which offers cheap accommodation at night and watersports during the day. Bring a sleeping bag, stay for £7 (£9 if you need bedding), and be sure to enjoy the best pressured shower in Scotland. Uists' other hostels are two wonderfully primitive **Gatliff Trust** croft-houses (see Outer Hebrides: Getting There and Getting About, above). For the **Howmore** (Tobha Mor) hostel on South Uist, follow the signpost 1 mi. west from the A865; for the hostel at **Claddach Baleshare** (Cladach A'Bhaile Shear) on North Uist, turn west off the A865 at the signpost, then take the "Carnach" turnoff right before the causeway. Both hostels have cold-water taps, coin-operated electricity, and carefully-thatched roofs (£3.85; open year-round).

B&Bs are often difficult to reach. In Lochboisdale, though, **Mrs. Murray,** Brae Lea, Lasgair (tel. (01878) 700497; £15-20), **Mrs. MacLellan,** Bay View (tel. (01878) 700329; £13-13.50), and **Mrs. MacLeod,** Innis Ghorm (tel. (01878) 700232; £14), are the closest to the pier. In Lochmaddy, **Mrs. MacDonald,** 14 Hougharry (tel. (01876) 500279) is the cheapest (£10-12). You can camp almost anywhere, but, as always, ask the crofters. The most inexpensive food stores on the islands are the **Co-op** grocery stores in Sollas (Solas) on North Uist, Creagarry (Creag Ghoraidh) on Benbecula, and Dailburgh (Dalabrog) on South Uist.

Caledonian MacBrayne ferries float from Uig on Skye to Lochmaddy (1-2/day; 1¾-4hr.; £6.65). The Uig-Lochmaddy ferry also connects with Tarbert on Harris (see Harris section for details). Additional ferries run from Oban to Lochboisdale (Mon.-Sat. 1/day, £15.45). Some stop at Castlebay on Barra on the way.

All modes of transportation are sparse. **Post buses** inch once a day Mon.-Sat. between Lochmaddy and Newtonferry, Balivanich Airport, Locheport, and other communities. **Hebridean Coaches** (tel. (01870) 610237) cross Mon.-Sat. between Lochmaddy and Lochboisdale and between Lochboisdale and Ludag. They also connect with the post bus at Balivanich Airport for Lochboisdale. Access to the moorland is free, but there are few well-marked footpaths. The Uists's few drivers are often friendly. Hitchers avoid thumbing on Sundays; it's rude and seldom rewarded.

Tourist offices are on the piers at each end of the string of islands, at Lochmaddy (tel. (01876) 500321) and Lochboisdale (tel. (01878) 700286). Either will find you a bed (both open late April to mid-Oct. roughly 9am-5pm and for all ferries except on Sun.). **Uist Laundry** (tel. (01870) 620876), the only laundromat in the Uists, is by Balivanich Airport on Benbecula (open Mon.-Fri. 9am-5pm, Sat. 9am-1pm).

Near The Uists: Berneray & Eriskay

The diminutive island of **Berneray** (Bearnaraigh), off the north coast of North Uist, is a favorite rustic retreat of Prince Charles and home to the best-equipped of the Gatliff Trust hostels: a beautifully thatched and whitewashed affair set on the windswept eastern tip of the island (£3.85, cold showers). Charlie drops in now and again. You can easily walk the 8-mi. circumference. Both passenger and car **ferries** serve Berneray from Newtonferry on North Uist (Mon.-Sat.). The car ferry is more frequent (4-5/day); the passenger ferry, which also connects to Leverburgh on Harris, is more convenient to the hostel (2/day in summer; call **D.A. Macaskill** at (01876) 540230 for ferry times). A post bus from Lochmaddy (Mon.-Fri. at 8am) usually connects with the passenger ferry.

On February 4, 1941, with strict wartime alcohol rationing in effect all over Scotland, the *S.S. Politician* foundered on a reef off the isle of **Eriskay** (Eiriosgaigh), between South Uist and Barra, while carrying 207,000 cases of whiskey to America. The islanders mounted a prompt salvage, and Eriskay has never been the same since. There are four sailings a day (Mon.-Sat.) between Ludag on South Uist and Eriskay; call ahead (tel. (018786) 261). Three homes on Eriskay (pop. 200) offer B&B (tel. (01878) 540232, 540272, and 540279; £13); the local pub, the **S.S. Politician,** displays some of the original "Polly" bottles. Hic.

BARRA (BARRAIGH)

Little Barra, the southern outpost of the outer isles, is unspeakably beautiful, a composite of moor, *machair,* and beach. On a sunny day, the island's colors are unforgettable; sand dunes and beaches crown waters flecked unnameable shades of light-dazzled blue, wreathed below by dimly-visible red, brown, and green kelp. The best times to visit are May and early June, when the primroses bloom, and gardens and hills explode in pink and yellow. Believed to be named after St. Findbar of Cork, the island is also the ancient stronghold of descendants of the Irish O'Neils. As late as the 16th century, the Catholic islanders sailed to Ireland for religious festivals.

You can see a fair portion of Barra in a day. Those without a car should take the post bus around the island (Mon.-Fri. 2/day; £2) or rent a bike from **Castlebay Cycle Hire** (tel. (018714) 284 or 358; £7.50, each additional day £5.50). To see the island in its entirety, follow the single-laned A888, which makes an almost perfect 14-mi. circle around the rather steep slopes of **Ben Heavel.** An excellent road for biking, this main route follows the coast past stunning beaches and mountain views; a detour north to Eoligarry winds by duckponds and lovely dunes.

Kisimul Castle, bastion of the old Clan MacNeil, inhabits an islet in Castlebay Harbor. It lay in ruins for two centuries until the late Robert Lister MacNeil, the 45th chief of the MacNeil clan and an American architect, restored it (boat trips out Mon., Wed., and Sat. 2-5pm; £2). To the west of Castlebay, near Borve (Borgh), are **standing stones.** Locals say that these stones were erected in memory of a Viking galley captain who lost a bet with a Barra man; Scandinavian archaeologists who excavated the site did indeed find a skeleton and Nordic armor. A chambered cairn, **Dún Bharpa,** and the better-preserved **Dún Cuier,** north of Allasdale (Allathasdal), are also near Borve. **Seal Bay,** opposite Allasdale, is a great spot for a picnic (bring some herring and make a friend).

On the north coast, the huge beach of **Traigh Mhor** provides a spectacular landing place for the daily Loganair flights to Glasgow. Even farther north, in **Eoligarry,** is **Cille Bharra Cemetery.** Still in use, it contains "crusader" headstones engraved with weapons, a galley, and animals thought to have served as ballast in the warship of a clan chief returning from overseas exploits. The only runic stone ever found in the Hebrides also came from this area. Step inside its neighbor, low-ceilinged **St. Barr's Church**—as pilgrim candles flicker through the dust, adornments to the "Bride and Foster-Mother" rest amid shrines, Celtic crosses, and Norman stones.

A causeway connects Barra to the small island of **Vatersay** (Bhatarsaigh), the southernmost inhabited island in the Outer Hebrides. Check out its scenic beaches or the monument to the *Annie Jane,* an emigrant ship that sunk off Vatersay in 1853 while carrying 400 would-be immigrants to Canada. Bird-watchers should visit the deserted island of **Mingulay;** at the Isle of Barra Hotel, **George MacLeod** (tel. (01871) 810383) makes three runs a week in summer.

A **Caledonian MacBrayne ferry** stops at Castlebay (Bagh A Chaisteil) on Barra on its way between Oban on the mainland and Lochboisdale on South Uist (Mon.-Thurs., and Sat.; return Tues., Thurs.-Fri., and Sun.; to Oban 5¼hr., £14.30; to Lochboisdale 1¾hr., £4.45). It's possible to take the tiny 12-passenger ferry from Ludag on South Uist to Eoligarry (Eolaigearraidh) on Barra (tel. (018714) 996 233). **Hebridean Coaches** (tel. (01870) 610237) runs from the airport on Benbecula (departs noon) and Lochboisdale (departs 1:20pm) to Ludag (arrives just before 2pm; Mon.-Sat.). **Post buses** depart Castlebay for Eoligarry (Mon.-Sat.) at 10am and noon. Call ahead to confirm times. The Castlebay **tourist office** (tel. (01871) 810336) is around the bend and to the right from the pier (open roughly April to mid-Oct. Mon.-Fri. 9am-5pm, Sat. 9am-4pm, Sun. 11:30am-12:30pm, and for late ferry arrivals). They'll find you a B&B, but save yourself panic by booking ahead—a couple of weddings or a music festival can fill every bed for miles. You can camp anywhere, but to prevent complaints, ask the tourist office for suggestions.

■■■ THE NORTHWEST

Sparsely populated and thinly traveled, the northwest Highlands richly reward those who struggle to get to them with visions of sea, heather-covered mountains, water-falls, forests inland, and excellent sheep-watching in between. Great expanses of mountain and moor stretch along the coast, from the imposing Torridon Hills to the eerie gneiss formations of Inverpolly and finally to Cape Wrath, where waves crash against the highest cliffs in mainland Britain.

GETTING AROUND

Without a car, a quick traipse around the northern coast is nearly impossible. Bus service in this area is sparse and post buses from Ullapool do not accept passengers. Those who hitch dance with fate: the few locals drive like devils on the area's nar-row, winding roads, but will usually pick hikers up if they don't first run them over. Transport is organized on a spoke system with the hub at Inverness. Several daily **buses** and **trains** (except on winter Sun.) run west from Inverness to **Kyle of Loch-alsh** (for ferries to Skye), and north to **Thurso** (for ferries to Orkney) and **Wick.** Two buses a day in summer (Mon.-Sat.) serve **Ullapool** on the northwest coast, where fer-ries leave for the Outer Hebrides. From these main lines, infrequent post and school buses saunter out to more remote towns, seldom traveling more than 20 mi. and rarely linking up with other services.

Kyle of Lochalsh (see Skye, above) is a center for tourist traffic to and from Skye, but the countryside between it and Inverness is lovely and untouched. The **Ach-nashellach Independent Hostel** (tel. (015206) 232; £7) is right on the bus line and 2 mi. from the rail stop of the same name. The **HI Ratagan Youth Hostel** (tel. (0159981) 243; grade 2; £4.80) lies on the Glasgow-Kyle bus route, 1½ mi. west of Shiel Bridge on Loch Duich in the impressive, treeless, and Munro-laden **Glen Shiel.** From here, experienced climbers can scale the **Five Sisters of Kintail** (3505 ft.) or tackle the 1½-hr. hike up Glen Elchaig to see the 370-ft. **Falls of Glomach.**

If you're looking for adventure, try the hair-raising trip from Kishorn up **Bealach-na-Bo Pass,** leading 13 mi. west to the remote coastal village of **Applecross.** The sin-gle-lane road winds steeply to an altitude of 2054 ft. Once in Applecross, you can picnic on the small, sheltered beach or celebrate at the little pub. Applecross was one of the first seats of Christianity in Scotland, and the old churchyard just outside the hamlet dates from the days of St. Maelrubha. Much of the west coast is now Free Church country. On Saturday evenings, the bull is separated from the cows, and the cockerel from the hens, in preparation for the Sabbath. You can camp on the bay at Applecross Campsite (tel. (015205) 284) from April to October (£7, showers and laundry facilities included).

TORRIDON

Just to the north of Applecross Peninsula, the village of Torridon crouches beneath the Torridon Hills, second in cragginess only to the Cuillins of Skye. The highest and closest peak is Liathach (3456 ft.), considered by some to be the most bullying mountain in Britain. You can stay at the large **Torridon Youth Hostel (HI;** tel. (01445) 791284; grade 1; £6.50; open late Feb.-Oct.) or venture 13 mi. west of Tor-ridon along the B8021 to the remote, coastal **Craig Youth Hostel (HI)** in Diabaig (no phone; grade 3; £3.85, open mid-May to Sept.; bring a sleeping bag as bedding is unavailable). The **ranger station** (tel. (0144587) 221) at the crossroads into Torri-don (200 yd. from the Torridon hostel) has maps and pamphlets describing walks. There is a small **campsite** between the hostel and the ranger office.

GAIRLOCH

Flanked by magnificent coastal scenery and inland mountains, **Gairloch** is the next town north, providentially served by direct buses from Inverness (daily 5:05pm). Though Gairloch draws most of the area's tourists, it is still a tiny, peaceful village save for a **tourist office** (tel. (01445) 72130) at war with its opening hours. (Open July-Aug. Mon.-Sat. 9am-7pm, Sun. 1-6pm; Sept. and June Mon.-Fri. 9am-6pm, Sat. 10am-1pm and 2-6pm, Sun. 1-6pm; Oct. Mon.-Fri. 9am-5:30pm, Sat. 10am-1pm and 2-5pm; Nov.-March Mon.-Fri. 9am-1pm and 2-5pm; April Mon.-Fri. 9am-1pm and 2-5:30pm; May Mon.-Fri. 9am-6pm, Sat. 10am-1pm and 2-6pm, Sun. 1-5pm.) The quiet **HI Carn Dearg Youth Hostel** (tel. (01445) 712219; grade 2) is 2 mi. northwest of town (£5.05; open mid-May-Sept.). B&Bs abound in Gairloch and Dundonnell, just east of the Ardessie Gorge. Check at the Gairloch tourist office about accommodations. Six mi. north along the coast road from Gairloch are the **Inverewe Gardens** (tel. (01445) 86200), a glorious profusion of well-tended flowers and shrubs from all over the world. (Gardens open daily 9:30am-sunset. Visitor center open April-mid Oct. daily 9:30am-5:30pm; £2.80, children £1.50.) Campers can pitch their tents nearby at the **Inverewe Campsite** for £5.50 per night (National Trust members £4.50), at the beachside **Sands Holiday Centre** (tel. (01445) 2152) from £6.50 a night, or at the **Gairloch Holiday Park** (tel. (01506) 614343 or (01445) 2373) for £3-7 a night. There is an interestingly cluttered local **museum** in town (tel. (01445) 2287) and a gorgeous sandy beach out toward the pier.

ULLAPOOL

Ferries to the Outer Hebrides depart the lovely, mountain-ringed northern fishing port of **Ullapool**. Except for the 1am arrivals, ferries from Stornoway on Lewis (Mon.-Sat. 2-3/day, £10.05) are met by express coaches to and from Inverness (1½hr., £6.80). A pleasant, relaxed **HI Youth Hostel,** Shore St. (tel. (01854) 612254; grade 2; £5.05; open late March-Oct.) is 100 yd. to the right of the pier. The dining room and recreation room are stocked with a pool table, games, and great views of the mist rolling in over the harbor. Book ahead, as large school groups often overrun the town. The **Quay Plaice Restaurant,** across from the pier, has assorted types of filled rolls and chips for £2-3. **The Ceilidh Place** (tel. (01854) 612103) on West Argyle St. stomps to traditional Celtic music several nights a week in summer; pick up a copy of the program. A rainy day in Ullapool may be a blessing in disguise. The town, though generally dull, sequesters one of the tiniest, strangest museums in the Western Hemisphere. Every shelf within the **Ullapool Bookshop and Museum** bears unexpected joys, from Mary Queen of Scots' pointy-heeled slippers abandoned in escape to an effigy of Charles I reconstructed from hair, ruff, and ribbons ripped from his body after the execution at Whitehall. The truly morbid can get a lick of the pastille lozenge pinched from his coat pocket just before the burial (open Mon.-Sat. 9am-5pm; museum in back room of bookshop across from the Seaforth Inn). Offering more typical pleasures, the **Ullapool Museum** is housed in an old church on West Argyle St. The insides reveal 19th-century church furniture and hymnals as well as photographs, records, and journals documenting Ullapool's past glory as a base camp for British fisheries during the 19th century (open July-mid Sept. Mon.-Sat. 10am-6pm, 7:30am-9:30pm; April-Oct. Mon.-Sat. 10am-6pm; £1, students and seniors 50p). Ullapool's **tourist office** (tel. (01854) 612135), on W. Shore St., books rooms for £1 (open April-Nov.; call for hours). Do your laundry 3½ mi. out of town on the A835 at the **Ardmair Point Caravan Site & Boat Centre** (tel. (01854) 612054; May-Sept. 8am-5pm, last wash 4pm; do you really need it done this badly?). Several boats run daily bird- and wildlife-watching tours to the nearby **Summer Isles;** inquire at the booths by the pier (around £6). Twelve miles south of Ullapool on the A835, the falls of Measach cascade down 150 ft. through the lush, mossy forest of **Corrieshalloch Gorge.**

The secluded beauty of **Achiltibuie** washes northwest of Ullapool. Take the A835 north for 10 mi., then hang a left at the well-marked one-lane road and follow it west for 15 mi. The sleepy village rests between two sexy nature reserves and a trio of sandy beaches. The **Achininver Youth Hostel (HI)** (tel. (01854) 622254; grade 3; £3.85; open June-Sept.) is an old cottage ¼ mi. from a sandy beach and 2½ mi. from Achiltibuie. It is also accessible via a difficult 14-mi. walk along Rock Path from Ullapool (ask for a free leaflet from the Ullapool hostel before setting out).

Durness, on Scotland's north coast, is quite close to **Smoo** (ISH-mool). The **Durness Youth Hostel (HI)** at Smoo (tel. (01971) 511244; grade 3; £3.85; open mid-May to Sept.) is 1 mi. from Durness along the A838. Durness itself is a quiet village; its **tourist office** (tel. (01971) 511259) sniffs out B&Bs like The Bloodhound Gang (open June-Aug. Mon.-Sat. 9am-6:30pm, Sun. 11:30am-5:30pm; April and Oct. Mon.-Sat. 10am-5pm). Ask about the nearby Smoo caves, said to be inhabited by a small, crime-solving blob. **Iris MacKay** (tel. (01971) 511343) runs a **minibus** to **Cape Wrath,** home of Britain's highest cliffs. Traveling along the north coast can be difficult; inquire about possible bus service from Thurso in advance. Mondays through Fridays during term-time, school buses from Thurso press thickly into the town of **Tongue,** joined by the divine intersection of the post bus from Lairg (on the Inverness-Wick-Thurso rail line; Mon.-Sat.). A **HI Youth Hostel** (tel. (0184755) 301; grade 2; £5.05; open mid-March to Sept.), drips sweetly from Tongue's tip, ¾ mi. toward the lake causeway. Gorgeous ridges and mountains rise like tastebuds from the south end of the lake, and the 14th-century ruins of **Castle Varrish** stand a carious guard above the water.

■■■ INVERNESS TO THE FERRY PORTS

The moors and mountains farther south and west mellow to rolling farmlands across Caithness and Sutherland, in anticipation of the lonely northerly Pentland Firth. The most popular stop from Inverness to Caithness is the legendary **HI Carbisdale Castle Youth Hostel** (tel. (0154982) 232), located in a secluded, 20th-century castle not far from the A836. Walk ½ mi. uphill from the train whistle-stop at **Culrain** to get there (grade 1; £7.25; breakfast £2.85, dinner £3.75; open March-Oct. except May 9-19). Consider booking ahead, especially for Carbisdale's Highland Nights (roughly every week in summer), featuring in-house Scottish entertainment.

Two other sites, both on the main train and bus routes, are worth a stopover. Located 5 mi. south of the **Ord of Caithness,** a hilly area that jumps sharply from the ocean and supports a sizable herd of red deer, the **Helmsdale hostel (HI)** (tel. (014312) 577) makes a good base for fossil-hunting and gold-panning (grade 3; £3.85; open mid-May to Sept.). You might also visit the nearby **Timespan Heritage Centre** (tel. (014312) 327), a Highland museum of historical scenes portrayed with convincing audio-visual effects, realistic wax figures, and life-size sets (open Easter to mid-Oct. Mon.-Sat. 10am-5pm, Sun. 2-5pm; July-Aug. until 6pm; £3, seniors and students £2.50, children £2; last entry 1hr. before closing). Two stops to the south at Golspie, the train drops passengers at the gates of **Dunrobin Castle** (tel. (01408) 633177), the spectacular seat of the Dukes of Sutherland. Though sections of the house date back to the 1300s, most of the architecture is ecstatically Victorian: ambitious, gaudy, and lavish. The earl's former summer house has been transformed into a museum, and its grounds are magnificent. (Castle open June-Sept. Mon.-Sat. 10:30am-5:30pm, Sun 1-5:30pm; Oct. 1-15 Mon.-Sat. 10:30am-4:30pm, Sun. 1-4:30pm; May Mon.-Thurs. 10:30am-12:30pm; last entry 30 min. before closing. Gardens open year-round; free of charge when castle is closed. Admission to castle and gardens £3.20, students £3, children £1.50.)

NORTHEASTERN FERRY PORTS

Thurso, Scrabster, and John O'Groats, the principal ports sending ferries to Orkney and the Faroe Islands, huddle in the northeastern corner of Scotland. There are several daily trips from Inverness to the ports. **Buses** glide frequently through the fathomless coastal glens between Inverness and Thurso (3½hr.; £8.10); since stops may vary, call the tourist office to confirm. **Scottish Rail** also strikes to Thurso along the Highland line from Inverness (4/day, Sun. 2/day; 3¾hr.; £11).

A year-round car and passenger ferry from the Faroe Islands arrives in **Scrabster** on Friday at noon, returning to the Faroes Saturday at 8pm (13hr.; £62, 20% student discount). Orkney ferries also originate from the ferry ports; see Orkney Islands: Getting There, above for specific details. Whatever ferry you take, *always ask about student prices, as information is not volunteered.*

Thurso would make even Mary Poppins suicidal. Keep it together by bashing your head against the bedframe until you black out at the independent **Thurso Youth Club Hostel,** stashed in a converted mill. The amiable warden will resuscitate you with an elegant breakfast (£6, linen included). From the train station, walk down Lover's Lane, steam up the car windows, turn left on Janet St., cross the footbridge over the river, and follow the footpath to the right. The **tourist office** (tel. (01847) 62371) is off to the right on Riverside Rd. (open Mon.-Sat. 9am-6pm, Sun. 10am-6pm; Oct.-April Mon-Fri. 9am-5pm). A free bus from the Thurso rail station connects with ferry departure at **John O'Groats. Dunnet Head,** about halfway between Thurso and John O'Groats, is the northernmost point of the island of Britain, but **Duncansby Head,** about 2 mi. outside John O'Groats, has a more impressive view overlooking the Pentland Firth.

■■■ ORKNEY ISLANDS

Björn was here.

Ancient rune carved into Orcadian standing stone

Across the broad and occasionally rough Pentland Firth, the emerald villages, eroding red sandstone cliffs, and iris-studded farmlands of Orkney are treasures. Yet what they conceal is equally priceless—Orkney's paddocks, beaches, and gardens shelter some of the best-preserved Stone Age, Pictish, and Viking villages, monuments, and burial chambers in Western Europe. The small capital city of Kirkwall encases a dramatic 12th-century cathedral, still in use, and a fine medieval and Renaissance palace. The sea holds secrets as well—at low tide, broken prows and sterns of sunken blockships rear from the sea foam along the Churchill Barriers and farther out in the Scapa Flow rest seven warships of the German High Seas fleet, scuttled in World War II when surrender seemed imminent.

While a careful walk along the cliffs of the West Mainland shows you elderducks, fulmar petrels, and even the occasional heroicomic puffin in summer, the islands of Westray, Papa Westray, Copinsay, and the Pentland Skerries are sacred to ornithology pilgrims—337 species of birds alight on or inhabit Orkney. With such rare artifacts preserved by isolation and the fine Orkney sand, the islands sing a siren song to their visitors; many become born-again Orcadians themselves.

GETTING THERE

Three ferries connect mainland Scotland to Orkney; the islands are best reached by ferry from Scrabster and John O'Groats. The most convenient route may be the **Orkney Bus,** which departs daily from Inverness bus station's platform #10 at 2:20pm for John O'Groats, where a ferry soon sails for Burwick, Orkney. From Burwick, a local bus travels up the Churchill Barriers to deposit passengers in Kirkwall. The £32 return fare (buy on the bus) includes all connections. From April 1 until October, **P&O Scottish Ferries** (tel. (01224) 572615) depart Scrabster near Thurso for Stromness (ships leave Mon., Wed., and Fri., 6am, noon, and 5:45pm; Tues. and Thurs. 6am and noon; Sat.-Sun. noon; £13, 10% discount students and seniors). A bus leaves from the Thurso rail station for Scrabster before each crossing (85p). Two **Scottish Ferries** originating in Aberdeen stop in Stromness most weeks for Lerwick, Shetland (Tues. 10pm, Sun. noon; tel. (01224) 572615 for exact schedule). Ferries return to Aberdeen (2/week) and Scrabster (2-3/daily) on the mainland.

GETTING ABOUT

Peace's buses (tel. (01856) 872866) run between Kirkwall and Stromness (2-3/day), ferry port to the island of Hoy and the northern Shetland Islands. The **Orkney Islands Shipping Co.** (tel. (01856) 872044) ferries passengers to the islets of Eday, Stronsay, Shapinsay, Sanday, Westray, and Papa Westray from the Kirkwall pier. Contact the Orkney Islands Shipping Co., 4 Ayre Rd., Kirkwall, Orkney KW15 1QX, call (01426) 977170, or pick up their *Timetables & Tariffs* booklet at the tourist office in Kirkwall.

KIRKWALL

Established in the 11th century, the city of Kirkwall has expanded through the centuries as the sea receded from its shores to become the administrative and social center of the Orkney Islands. The city is itself a small treasure to explore. South of the tourist office on Broad St., the impressive red and yellow sandstone **St. Magnus Cathedral,** begun in 1137, houses the bones of its founder's saintly and prematurely expired uncle, St. Magnus himself. Sixteenth and 17th-century grave markers within the cathedral wax eloquent, revealing the unique and often tragic circumstances of those whom the stone suppresses. Though he ranged far and wide, John Rae, explorer and discoverer of the fate of the Franklin Expedition, is frozen in effigy in the west end of the cathedral (open Mon.-Sat. 9am-6pm, Sun. 2-6pm; Oct.-March Mon.-Sat. 9am-1pm, 2-5pm). Across Palace St. from the cathedral, the **Bishop's and Earl's Palaces** once housed the Bishop of Orkney and his enemy, the wicked Earl Patrick Stuart. Though now roofless in parts, the **Earl's Palace** gives a haunting sense of how the Earl once ruled the islands with a firm and often bloody hand (open Mon.-Sat. 10am-5pm, Sun. 2-5pm; £2, seniors and students £1.50). Under the watchful gaze of the earl, the Bishop undertook to fortify his palace in order to defend himself, if necessary, from his unpredictable next-door neighbor (same hours for Bishop's Palace; admission to both buildings included in ticket). Opposite St. Magnus Cathedral, the **Tankerness House Museum** (tel. (01856) 873191) introduces visitors to the island's remote and recent past, displaying finds from the chief archaeological sites in Orkney and paintings by native son Stanley Cursiter. The museum stocks Iron Age brooches, pins, and other ancient accessories (open Mon.-Sat. 10:30am-12:30pm, 1:30-5pm; Sun. 2-5pm; Oct.-April Mon.-Sat. 10:30am-12:30pm, 1:30-5pm; £3).

Home to one-third of Orkney's 21,000 souls, **Kirkwall** in East Mainland is Orkney's largest and busiest town. The **tourist office,** 6 Broad St. (tel. (01856) 872856), books B&Bs and dispenses advice and leaflets down the main road from the cathedral. Behind an abandoned British Telecom building on old Skapa Rd., the **Kirkwall Youth Hostel (HI)** (tel. (01856) 872243) makes up for in friendliness what it lacks in exterior decor (open mid-March-Oct.; grade 1; £6.50). From the tourist office, turn left and follow the main road for ½mi. as it evolves from Broad St. into High St., then take another left at the SYHA sign. Camping is available near Kirkwall off A965 at the **Pickaquoy Caravan & Camping Site** from £4 (tel. (01856) 873535). You can pitch your tent almost anywhere on the islands, but ask the landowner first. Stock up on supplies during the week at the **Presto Supermarket** on Broad St. (open Mon.-Sat. 9am-6pm). Be sure to buy extra for Sunday, as only a few hotel restaurants serve breakfast on the Sabbath—everything else in Kirkwall closes. The **Atholl Coffee Shop,** Albert St., is the cheapest sit-down in town (sandwiches £1.50, open Mon.-Fri. 9:30am-7pm, Sat. 9am-6pm).

STROMNESS

Stromness is younger than Kirkwall and owes its existence to fishing and whaling industries and a natural harbor. Maritime pursuits are still important in Stromness, though the days of its preeminence as a port passed long ago. Along the harbor, however, the strong smell attests to the cleaning of fresh fish in many warehouses, which maddens Stromness's kittens as they endlessly pace outside. The **Stromness Museum** on Alfred St. (tel. (01856) 850025) tackles the history of the sea with artifacts and memorabilia from the whaling and fishing industries, relics of explorer John Rae (including his cloth boat), and a photo exhibit documenting the shuttling (and subsequent recovery) of the World War II German High Seas Fleet in Scapa Flow. Upstairs is a tidy natural history museum—look for the anachronistic Australian emu eggs and the staring glass eyes of taxidermed legions (open Mon.-Sat. 10:30am-5pm; Oct.-April Mon.-Sat. 10:30am-1pm, 2-4pm; 80p).

The helpful **Stromness tourist office** (tel. (01856) 850716) resides in an 18th-century rice warehouse on the pier (open daily for ferry arrivals and departures; call for hours). Fewer than five minutes from the tourist office, **Brown's Hostel (HI),** 45-7 Victoria St. (tel. (01856) 850661) is as warm and toasty as the night is cold and damp (£6.50). Those who search for the grade two hostel will wander downtown's shadows, lose themselves in the dark main street, and climb onto Hellihole Rd. Don't abandon all hope—despite its infernal address, the hostel is well-kept and hospitable. The **Ness Point Caravan and Camping Site** (tel. (01856) 873535) juts just south of Stromness (£4). On the pier, **The Ferry Inn** (tel. (01856) 850280) dishes up meal-size appetizers for £2.30 and main courses for £4.50-5.50 (cashew nut roast with herb stuffing £5.50, vegetable curry and rice £4.50; open daily noon-2pm, 5:30-10pm). Arguably the most happening place in Stromness, **The Café** at 22 Victoria St. serves cheap meals (£3-4) and warm soup (£1.05; open Mon.-Sat. 9am-9pm).

STONE AGE VILLAGES

While the towns of Stromness and Kirkwall certainly merit an afternoon's exploration, the stretch of highway between the two provides easy access to some of the most stunning and best preserved Stone Age and Viking structures in the Western world. Dating back 5100 years, **Skara Brae** was once a bustling Stone Age village miles from the coast. As the ocean crept further in, waves gradually consumed the houses of the village; after approximately 600 years of continuous inhabitation, the villagers of Skara Brae abandoned the settlement, perhaps resigning themselves to the whims of the sea. Preserved in sand, the village slept quietly until 1850, when a violent storm ripped out the side of the cliff and disclosed nine houses, a workshop, and covered town roads. Thoroughly excavated, the houses still carry Stone Age luxuries such as brine basins and fire-stained hearths. While the visitor center is open only during the day, the site remains accessible until nightfall—a trip at dusk evades the tourists (and the £2.50 admission). Nearby on the A965, the sedimentary sandstones of the **Ring of Brodgar** once witnessed gatherings of a nature no two archaeologists can agree on. Some believe the upright ring once marked a meeting place for local chieftains; many propose that the site saw the disposal of the dead by leaving their bodies to the elements and the birds—now filled in for the safety of visitors, a deep ditch around the circle once warded off dogs and wild predators. Thirty-six stones remain of the original 60. Look for the graffiti left by an early Viking vandal: his runic scribble spells "Björn," perhaps boding the rise of a certain Swedish glam-band near the close of the second millennium.

Close by on the A965, the **Standing Stones of Stenness** once numbered twelve, before a twentieth-century landowner knocked several over because of their pagan origin offended him. As silent as Brodgar about their past, the stones have recently revealed a clue to historians—possible evidence of a priests' settlement near the site. Its only altar boys now are the sheep grazing nearby. Almost within view on a fine day and accessible from the A965, the **Maes Howe** tomb may have held the bows of the earliest settlers in the area in approximately 2700 BC. According to runic graffiti, Viking raiders spent three glorious days hauling treasure out of the chamber. The runes are almost more of an attraction than the tomb itself—the largest collection of runic inscriptions in the world, they enabled linguists to crack the runic alphabet and find things like "This was carved by the greatest rune carver" and "Ingeborg is the most exquisite of women" (open Mon.-Sat. 10am-6pm; £3). In the northwest off the A967, the **Brough of Birsay** shows evidence of early Christian and Viking habitation. Once the administrative and religious center of Orkney, the tidal island's kirkyard holds a Pictish stone engraving of a royal figure with a crown, suggesting that the Orcadian kings once ruled from Birsay. The island is only accessible one hour before and after low tide. In summer, bird-watching from the treacherous cliffs may be absorbing, but linger overlong and the puffins may be your bedfellows.

The landscape of **Hoy,** the second largest island in Orkney, is surprisingly rocky and mountainous after the green slopes of the mainland. Any visitors to Orkney should glimpse the **Old Man of Hoy,** a famous 450 ft. sea stack off the West Coast of the island. On a clear day, the P&O ferry from Scrabster to Stromness gives an excellent view of the landmark—a careful walk along the coast of Hoy allows the hiker to look down on the Old Man himself. Often a rather steep climb, a marked footpath leads from Rackwick two miles away; allow three hours round-trip. The hefty North Hoy bird reserve provides a home for everything from guillemots to puffins. The dedicated puffin-scout should see several here in breeding season (late June-early July); the rest of the year these pudgy birds rough it on the seas. On Hoy, the **Hoy HI hostel** near the pier and the **Rackwick HI hostel** further south, 2 mi. from the Old Man of Hoy, both offer grade two accommodations of £5.05 and share a telephone number (tel. (01856) 873535). Rackwick is open from mid March to early September. No sleeping bags are available on the island—don't leave home without one. Shops are almost as scarce on Hoy; consider bringing some food supplies.

Ranger Naturalist **Michael Hartley** of Wildabout Tours (tel. (01856) 851011) squires visitors around mainland Orkney and Hoy in his minibus. With a vigorous imagination and encyclopedic knowledge of Orkney, Michael asks visitors to envision the Orkney of 5000 years ago; his tour of Skara Brae will raise the hairs on your neck as you hear, in the surf, the sounds of Stone Age hammers, children playing in the covered streets, and women at work with mortar and pestle. Michael's dog knows better than to fool with ghosts, refusing to set foot on the site. Wildabout tours depart the Stromness tourist office daily; call ahead for a pick-up in Kirkwall (£8 halfway, £14 full day with £2 student and hosteler discount). For the skeptic, **Go Orkney** (tel. (01856) 874260) offers information-loaded bus and walking tours of the island, with reasonably-priced snack food on board and the free use of rain and wind apparel and binoculars (half day £6, students £4.50; full day £12). Tours depart Palace Rd. in Kirkwall and the tourist office in Stromness.

Papa Westray, the "isle of the priests," once supported an early Christian Pictish settlement. Most pilgrims to the island now content themselves with bird-watching and archaeology. The rare Scottish primrose, thought to grow only in Orkney and isolated spots in the Scottish highlands, may be found in many fields and farmyards in Papa Westray. On the West Coast, **St. Boniface's Church** dates from the 12th century, though an earlier church existed on the same site and 18th-century restoration is responsible for much of the edifice today. South along the coast, the **Knap of Howar** is the quiet location of the earliest standing houses in northern Europe, dating to 3500 BC. Two miles from the pier, the **Papa Westray HI hostel** (tel. (018574) 267) offers grade one accommodations in Beltane House (£6.50).

The peat-covered hills of the island of **Eday** cover the remains of Stone Age field walls, chambered tombs, dykes, and even on the Calf of Eday, the remnants of an Iron Age roundhouse. As in all the Orkney islands, bird-watchers will reap high rewards, though the cliffs can be treacherous and should be avoided at all costs in bad weather. The simple grade three **Eday HI hostel** (tel. (018572) 283) lies along the main east-west road 4 mi. from the pier. Campers are welcome (open mid-March-Sept. £3.85).

■■■ SHETLAND ISLANDS

Local poet Hugh MacDiarmid aptly describes the difference between Orkney and Shetland: "The Orcadian is a farmer with a boat, the Shetlander is a fisherman with a croft." Nowhere on Shetland's desolate, striking terrain can you be farther than 3 mi. from the sea. Though ferries pull into **Lerwick's** dock regularly and North Sea oil has brought prosperity to the isles, this land resists the pull of the mainland and the mainstream. It yields peat rather than potatoes, seabird colonies rather than skyscraping cities. More than five centuries ago, the Danish king Christian I pledged Shetland and Orkney to Scotland for part of his daughter's dowry. The pledge was never redeemed and Shetland remains in pawn. Nevertheless, Shetlanders proudly look to their Viking heritage, rather than to Scotland or Britain, for their identity and inspiration. This influence lingers in their Nordic craftmanship, Scandanavian architecture, and in festivals such as the longship-burning Up-Helly-Aa.

GETTING THERE

The cheapest and certainly the fastest transit to Shetland is the **British Airways/ BABA special** from Orkney. You're eligible for the £51 flight to Shetland *only if you book ahead* at any Shetland B&B, hotel, or guest house *from Orkney*. The same offer holds for the return to Kirkwall if you book ahead in Shetland. The tourist offices in Stromness, Kirkwall, or Lerwick will handle the bookings. **British Airways** (tel. (01950) 60345) also flies from Aberdeen; **Loganair** flies from Edinburgh and Glasgow. All flights are met by buses to Lerwick (1hr.; £2.90). Inter-Shetland flights use **Tingwall Airstrip** just outside Lerwick (tel. (0159548) 246 for reservations).

P&O Scottish Ferries leave weekdays at 6pm (June-Aug. Tues. at noon) from Aberdeen for Lerwick (14hr.; £49, Oct.-May £43.50, berth from £47). A P&O ferry also runs from Stromness on Orkney to Lerwick (Tues. 10pm and Sun. noon, Sept.-May Sun. noon; 8hr.; £31.50). P&O leaves Scotland behind with runs to Bergen, Norway (June-Aug. Sat. 11am; £55, berth from £5). From June through August, the **Smyril Line** ferry sails from Lerwick to the Faroe Islands (Tues. 2pm; £56) and Hanstholm, Denmark (Sun. 1pm, £73). Connect to Iceland from the Faroes. Students get 25% off these fares, which are lower in early June and late August. Bookings and information for P&O and Smyril Line are available from P&O Scottish Ferries, P.O. Box 5, Jamieson's Quay, Aberdeen AB9 8DL (tel. (01224) 572615).

GETTING ABOUT

Shetland's main bus lines are **John Leask & Son** (tel. (01595) 3162) and **Shalder Coaches** (tel. (0159588) 217). The tourist office has the indispensable *Inter-Shetland Transport Timetable* (80p) listing bus, ferry, and plane schedules. To travel to remote areas on Shetland's excellent road system, try **Bolts Car Hire** (tel. (01595) 2855) or **Grantfield Garage** (tel. (01595) 2709), both on North Rd. **Puffins Pedals** on Mounthooly St. (tel. (01595) 5065) rents fully-equipped touring bikes for £6.50/ day, mountain bikes for £8.50/day. Tents are also often available at Puffins. Ferries within the archipelago are heavily subsidized—the longest trips cost £1.25—and all services except those to Fair Isle transport bikes for free. Hitchers often get rides on the A970 without thumbing, but sparser traffic makes it less reliable where the road forks north of Voe. While on the road, pay heed to the signposts' memorable request: "Dunna chuck bruck" ("Don't litter").

ORIENTATION & PRACTICAL INFORMATION

Lerwick lies on the eastern coast of the main island (called "Mainland") and is served by the A970 which runs the length of the island. Ferries arrive at Holmsgarth Terminal, a 20-minute walk northwest of the city center and smaller Victoria Pier, across from the tourist office downtown. **Shetland Islands Tourism** at Market Cross (tel. (01595) 3434) will book you a bed anywhere in the islands for £1, free for three or more nights (open Mon.-Fri. 8am-6pm, Sat. 8am-5pm; Oct.-March Mon.-Fri. 9am-5pm). The **post office** (open Mon.-Fri. 9am-5pm, Sat. 9am-12:30pm) and **Royal Bank of Scotland** (open Mon. and Wed.-Fri. 9:15am-4:45pm, Thurs. 10am-4:45pm) face each other across Commercial St.

ACCOMMODATIONS AND CAMPING

The relaxed Lerwick **HI Youth Hostel** (tel. (01595) 2114), Islesburgh House at King Harald and Union St. is, unfortunately, closed for renovations until mid-1995. Other hostel-style lodgings are available only outside of town. The tourist office will find you a B&B up to one week in advance; free everywhere from London to Orkney, its accommodations guide costs 50p in Lerwick. While the hostel is closed, treat your-self to B&B, yellow Shetland tomatoes, and a backyard view of Clickimin Broch at **Mrs. Wiseman's** at 27 Russell Crescent (tel. (01595) 3930; £12.50). There are three **campgrounds** on Mainland, but you can camp almost anywhere with landowner's permission. **Clickimin Caravan and Camp Site** (tel. (01595) 4555) is closest to the Lerwick ferry terminal—turn left on the A970, then right on the A969 (tents £5.25-7; open late April-Sept.). In south Mainland, along the A970, you can camp at **Leven-wick Campsite** (tel. (019502) 207; £4.50-6; open May-Sept.).

Camping **böds** (barns with a funky Nordic name) are a unique Shetland accommo-dations alternative. There are three böds on Mainland: **The Böd of Nesbister** on Whiteness Voe, **The Sail Loft** next to the pier in Voe, and **Johnnie Notions** at Ham-navoe, Eshaness in far northeast Mainland. Only the Sail Loft has wheelchair access. All böds cost £3/night (£15-50 for exclusive use; open April-Oct.) and must be booked in advance. Reserve through the tourist office and bring everything you need but the roof, green grass, and the blue, blue sky.

FOOD, PUBS, & ENTERTAINMENT

Inexpensive eats cluster in the center of Lerwick. **Central Bakery** offers a variety of fresh filled rolls in a non-smoking environment (open Mon.-Tues. and Thurs.-Fri. 9am-4:15pm, Wed. 9am-1:30pm, Sat. 9am-4pm). Lerwick's cheapest food is at the **Islesburgh Community Centre Café** (tel. (01595) 2114) on King Harald St. next to the hostel. After a bannock and a biscuit, pool sharks can play a game at the tables in the recreation room (open Mon.-Sat. 10am-5pm and 6:30-10:30pm, Sun. 7:30-10:30pm). **Scoop Wholefoods** at 161 Commercial St. (tel. (01595) 5888; open Mon.-Tues. and Thurs.-Sat. 9am-5pm) and the **Presto** supermarket on Commercial Rd. (open Mon.-Tues. and Fri.-Sat. 8:30am-5:30pm, Wed. 8:30am-5pm, Thurs. 8:30am-7pm) should satisfy all comers. On Vast, you can simultaneously shop for knitware and enjoy a slice of apple pie at **Nornova** in Muness (open daily 9am-6pm). Don't slip, or the neon-puce jumper is all yours.

The Lounge, 4 Mounthooly St., is the town's liveliest pub (open Mon.-Fri. 11am-2pm and 5-11pm, Sat. 11am-12:30pm and 5-11pm). Local folk musicians congregate here Saturday afternoons and Wednesday and Saturday evenings. Shetland songs are quite distinctive—more melodic and more melancholy than the foot-tapping reels of Ireland and Scotland. You can hear the **Shetland Fiddlers**—all 40 of them—at the Islesburgh Community Centre (next to the hostel) on Wednesday nights at 7:30, June through August (£1).

The **Shetland Folk Festival,** held during the first week in May, lures fiddlers from around the world; for details try their office at 5 Burns Lane or the tourist center. The **Shetland Fiddle and Accordion Festival** takes place in Lerwick in mid-October. The famous **Up-Helly-Aa Festival** is a Viking extravaganza with outlandish cos-tumes, a torchlight procession through the streets, and a ship-burning in the town park (last Tues. in Jan.). Shetlanders plan months in advance for this impressive Viking fest to drive away the long winter nights—after the bonfire dies out black-ness settles in again (with short reprieves of daylight) until late spring. The Tingwall Hall hosts infrequent **Shetland Folklore Evenings,** usually twice in July and twice in August on Wednesday nights (£3.50).

Shetland is, naturally, one of the best places in the world to buy woolens. To avoid paying relatively high prices in Lerwick's tourist shops, try **Judane Knitwear** (tel. (01595) 5631) on Holmsgarth Rd. past the ferry terminal and opposite the hydroelectric plant in Lerwick, or the **Shetland Woollen Company** on Castle Rd. in Scalloway (tel. (01595) 88243; open Mon.-Sat. 9am-5pm; also branches in Sandwick and Sumburgh Airport). From ewe to you.

SIGHTS

The best views of Lerwick and its harbor are from the giant pentagonal **Fort Char-lotte** in the center of town, a relic of the Cromwellian era (free, always open). Only 1 mi. west of the city center on Clickimin Rd., the ruins of **Clickimin Broch,** a stronghold from the 4th century BC, rest on a strand cutting into a loch (free, always open). More modern (by Shetland standards) is the **Town Hall** (tel. (01595) 3535) on Hillhead, built in 1882. The clock tower looms over town and harbor, and the main hall contains a series of stained-glass windows depicting scenes from Shetland's Viking past (open Mon.-Fri. 10am-noon, 2-3:30pm; free).

If you miss the actual hoopla, you can at least visit the permanent **Up-Helly-Aa Exhibition** in the Galley Shed, St. Sunniva St. (open June-Sept. Tues. and Sat. 2-4pm, Tues. and Thurs. 7-9pm; free). Weather permitting, you can also take a cruise around the bay on the **Dim Riv,** a full-scale replica of a Viking longship which launches every Wednesday evening at 7pm in summer. Riders may be asked to row (£2, children free). Advance booking at the tourist office is essential.

Hourly ferries (65p) sail from Lerwick to the isle of **Bressay,** a gentle spot ideal for a slow amble. You can hike to the summit of conical **Ward of Bressay** (743 ft.) for a sweeping view of the sea. From Bressay's east coast (3 mi. from Lerwick ferry on the west coast), dinghies go to the tiny isle of **Noss;** just stand at the "Wait Here" sign and wave (mid-May to Aug. Tues.-Wed. and Fri.-Sun. 10am-5pm; £1 return, children 50p). Skuas enjoy swooping inches over the heads of walkers at this spectacular bird sanctuary; keep a hand over your head to ward them off, and try not to wear bright red. Overnight stays are forbidden on Noss.

Scalloway, Shetland's ancient capital, lies 7 mi. west of Lerwick. Aside from the **Shetland Woollen Company** on Castle Rd., the town's only redeeming feature is the roofless 17th-century **Scalloway Castle,** once home to the villainous Earl Patrick Stewart (open Mon.-Sat. 9:30am-7pm, Sun. 2-7pm; free). Buses to Scalloway leave from the Thule Bar on the Esplanade in Lerwick (5-6/day Mon.-Sat., 1/day Sun.; return £2.20).

Several interesting sights lie off south Mainland. An unusual *tombolo*—a sandbar washed by waves on both sides—links **St. Ninian's Isle,** site of an early monastery and a Celtic treasure unearthed by a schoolboy in 1958, to the west coast of Mainland. The tiny uninhabited island of **Mousa,** just off the east coast (return £2.20 by bus from the Viking Bus station), has the world's best preserved Iron Age *broch,* a 50-ft. high drystone fortress that has endured 1000 years of Arctic storms, sunning seals in the sheltered West Pool, and Great Skuas (Bonxies), primeval birds who divebomb the central grazing field in search of human flesh (carry a stick of driftwood, if you can find one, to defend yourself). Tom Jamieson (tel. (019505) 367) runs daily excursions (mid-April to Sept.) from Leebitton, Sandwick, to Mousa (£3.75, children £2). Catch a bus from the ferry at the Viking Bus Station in Lerwick to the red letter box, up an embankment from the pier, or take a **Leask Coach Tour** (£7, including ferry) on Monday from the Esplanade.

At the southern tip of Mainland, right next to Sumburgh Airport, is **Jarlshof,** one of the most remarkable archaeological sites in Europe. Here are stacked the remains of many layers of human settlement from the Neolithic to the Renaissance (open April-Sept. Mon.-Sat. 9:30am-6:30pm, Sun. 2-6:30pm; Oct.-March always open).

The north Mainland has the wildest and most deserted coastal scenery, much of which is accessible only by car. At **Mavis Grind,** just northwest of Brae, the Mainland is almost bisected; this 100-yd.-wide isthmus is bordered by the Atlantic and the North Sea. Farther northwest, explore the jagged volcanic forms on **Esha Ness.**

Yell & Unst

Shetland's northern islands, **Yell** and **Unst,** are starkly remote, but not even remotely dull. If you tire of bird- and seal-watching on Yell, head for the north end of the main road at Gloup; a 3-mi. hike from here takes you to the desolate eastern coast. The scattered remains of an Iron Age fort on the Burgi Geos promontory have held tenaciously to a perfect defensive position—jagged outcroppings face the sea and a 3-ft.-wide ridge leads between twin cliffs to the mainland.

Unst is home to the most northerly everything in Britain, including the most northerly visitor carrying a *Let's Go* guide. Could this be you? **Muness Castle** was built in the late 16th century; the key-keeper at the white cottage will give you a flashlight to illumine the spooky darkness of the ground floor. At **Harold's Quick Beach,** gannets crash the ocean near the crumbling concrete of abandoned air-raid shelters. The celebrated bird reserve at Hermaness is graced by a pair of black-browed albatross, and water, water everywhere.

The least expensive rooms in the area are at **Gardiesfauld Hostel,** in Uyeasound on Unst—the northern-most hostel in Britain (tel. (0195785) 298 or 311; £5; open April-Oct.). The terrific eagle-eyed warden can point out seals, otters, and even swans from the comfort of the observatory. One bus per day leaves Lerwick and connects with ferries all the way to Haroldwick on Unst, stopping by the hostel on the way (£3.85, including ferries; one ticket good for both ferries). Ferries from Belmont on Unst and Gutcher on Yell make routine diversions to the island of **Fetlar** (65p), another spot for bird-watchers to view the crimson-tailed finch. Camp at **The Garths Campsite** (tel. (0195783) 269; £4-7; open May-Sept.).

Smaller Islands

Shetland's outermost islands are the most remote in Britain. Rooms and transport are hard to come by, and booking several weeks in advance is a must. Take supplies to last at least a week, as the ferries often do not operate in inclement weather.

Whalsay, a relatively huge fishing community (pop. 1000), is accessible by bus and ferry from Lerwick (£1.85). The **Lingaveg Guest House** (tel. (018066) 489) provides dinner, bed, and breakfast (£25, B&B only £16). For self-catering, try **Mrs. Irvine** (tel. (018066) 284). Camp at **The Grieve House,** which becomes a böd from July through September (£3, exclusive use £30). The **Out Skerries** support 85 hardy fishermen; planes (5/week; single £14 from Tingwall) and ferries (4-8/week; £1.25; for advance bookings call (915) 226) converge upon them from Lerwick and Vidlin. Little **Papa Stour** (pop. 35) boasts a frothy coastline with abundant bird-life and dozens of sea-flooded cliff arches. The only place to stay is **Mrs. Holt-Brook's** (tel. (0159573) 873238; dinner and B&B £18-19). Planes fly Tuesdays (£12), and boats float from West Burrafirth (3-5/week; £1.25, call (01595873) 873227 to book).

Fair Isle, situated midway between Shetland and Orkney and the home of the famous Fair Isle knit patterns, is billed as the most remote island in Britain: one false move and say goodbye to the earth. In summer, a cargo ferry (tel. (013512) 222; £1.25) runs every other week from Lerwick and one to three times per week from Sumburgh, and planes (£31) depart Tingwall six or seven times per week. Book everything ahead. Lodging is available at the **Fair Isle Bird Observatory Lodge** (tel. (013512) 258; dinner and B&B £20-38), and with **Mrs. Grieve** (tel. (013512) 264; dinner and B&B £23-28), who does craft demonstrations in her home.

Northern Ireland

The strife that makes the North infamous obscures the land's beauty and appeal to travelers. What they're missing includes the pockets of womb-like green called the Glens of Antrim; one of the world's strangest geological sights, the Giant's Causeway; the beautiful Fermanagh Lake District; and a kick-ass folk park in Omagh. Pub culture and urban neighborhoods, show everyday life in a divided (and, most of the time, for most people, peaceful) society. You haven't seen the North until you've seen not just the coastal resorts, but certainly not just the Troubles either.

> For the ultimate coverage of Northern Ireland, see *Let's Go: Ireland*.

LIFE & TIMES

HISTORY & POLITICS

There's a place called "Northern Ireland," but there are no "Northern Irish"; the political entity's citizens still identify themselves largely as Catholics or as Protestants. The 900,000 Protestants are generally **Unionists** (who want the six counties of Northern Ireland to remain in the U.K.); the 600,000 Catholics tend to identify with the Republic of Ireland, not Britain, and many are **Nationalists** (who want the six counties to be part of the Republic). The conflict between them has proven to be one of the world's most intractable.

The 17th-century's **Ulster Plantation** systematically set up English and Scottish settlers on what had been Gaelic-Irish land, and gave Derry to parts of the City of London (hence the name "Londonderry"). Over the next two centuries, merchants and working-class emigrants from nearby Scotland settled in northeast Ulster; their ties to Scotland, proximity to England, and bourgeois bent meant that Cos. Antrim and Down developed an Industrial Revolution economy, based on linen and shipbuilding, while the rest of the island remained agricultural. Ulster Plantation and Scottish settlement, over the course of 300 years, had created a working-class and middle-class population in northeast Ulster who identified with England and the Empire and didn't want Home Rule. The **Orange Order,** widespread by 1830, organized the Protestants and held gaudy parades which celebrated their supremacy.

Edward Carson and his ally **James Craig** translated Ulster Unionism into terms the British elite understood; when Home Rule looked likely in 1911, Carson held a mass meeting, and Unionists signed a Covenant promising to resist. When Home Rule appeared imminent in 1914, the Unionist **Ulster Volunteer Force (UVF)** armed itself by smuggling guns in through Larne. World War I gave Unionists more time to organize, and gave British leaders time to see that the imposition of Home Rule on all of Ulster would mean havoc as the UVF fought the IRA fought the police. The 1920 Government of Ireland Act created two parliaments for North and South; the Act went nowhere in the South and was quickly superseded by Treaty and war, but the measure—intended as temporary—became the basis of Northern Ireland's government until 1973. The new Parliament met at **Stormont,** near Belfast.

The new statelet included only six of the nine counties in the province of Ulster. Carson and Craig had approved these odd borders; their intent was to create the largest possible area which would have a permanent Protestant majority. Anti-Catholic discrimination was widespread. The **Royal Ulster Constabulary (RUC),** the new police force in the North, supplemented its ranks with part-time policemen called Bs and **B-Specials,** which became notorious excuses for Orange militants to bear arms. The IRA continued sporadic campaigns against the North through the 20s and 30s with little result.

World War II gave Unionists a chance to show their loyalty; over the following two decades a grateful British Parliament poured money into Northern Ireland. The North's standard of living stayed higher than the Republic's, but discrimination and joblessness persisted—during the 50s, Ulster unemployment was twice that of Wales. Through the 60s, only houseowners (mainly Protestant) were allowed to vote: one vote for each house owned. Large towns were segregated by religion, perpetuating the cultural separation. After a brief, unsuccessful try at school desegregation, Stormont ended up granting subsidies to Catholic schools. Violence had receded; barring the occasional border skirmish, the IRA was seen as finished by 1962, and received a formal eulogy-like farewell in the *New York Times*.

The economy grew, but the bigotry stayed, as did the Nationalist community's bitterness. The American civil rights movement inspired the 1967 founding of **NICRA** (the **Northern Ireland Civil Rights Association**), which tried to end discrimination in public housing. Protestant extremists who didn't get the message included the forceful **Dr. Ian Paisley,** whose **Ulster Protestant Volunteers (UPV)** overlapped in membership with the illegal, paramilitary, resurrected UVF. The first NICRA march was raucous, but nonviolent; the second, in Derry in May 1968, was a bloody mess, disrupted by Unionists, then by the RUC's water cannons. This incident is usually thought of as the start of the present Troubles.

It was all downhill from there. Catholic **John Hume** and Protestant **Ivan Cooper** formed a new civil rights committee in Derry, which encouraged a four-day march from Belfast to Derry starting on **New Year's Day 1969.** Derry authorities agreed to keep the RUC out of the Bogside after that—it became **"Free Derry."** The rejuvenated IRA split in two, with the Marxist "Official" faction fading into insignificance as the new **"Provisional" IRA** (the **"Provos,"** or PIRA) took aim at the Protestants. More hopefully, the **Social Democratic and Labor Party (SDLP)** was founded in 1970; by '73, it had become the moderate political voice of Northern Catholics. The British troops became the IRA's main target; British policies of internment without trial outraged Catholics, and led the SDLP to withdraw from government. The pattern was clear: any concessions to the Catholics might provoke Protestant violence, while anything that seemed to favor the Union risked explosive IRA response.

On January 30, 1972, British troops fired into a crowd of protesters in Derry; the famous event, called **"Bloody Sunday,"** and the reluctant British investigation following, increased Catholic outrage. The Stormont government was finally dissolved in 1973; its lasting replacement was **direct British rule** from Westminster, which continues to this day. In 1978, 300 Nationalist prisoners in the Maze Prison in Northern Ireland began a campaign to have their "special category" as political prisoners restored; the campaign's climax of sorts was the H-Block **hunger strike** of '81—10 prisoners fasted themselves to death. Their leader, **Bobby Sands,** was the first to go on hunger strike; he was elected to Parliament from a Catholic district in Tyrone and Fermanagh even as he starved to death. Sands died after 66 days and became a prominent martyr—his face is still seen on murals in the Falls Rd. section of Belfast.

Sands's election to Parliament was no anomaly; the hunger strikes galvanized the Nationalists, and support for **Sinn Féin,** the political arm of the IRA, surged in the early '80s. Then-British Prime Minister Margaret Thatcher and then-Taoiseach Garret FitzGerald signed the **Anglo-Irish Agreement** at Hillsborough Castle in November 1985. The Agreement grants the Republic of Ireland a "consultative role," but no legal authority, in how Northern Ireland is governed. Protestant paramilitaries began to attack the British Army, while the IRA continued its bombing campaigns in England. A British declaration in December 1993 invited the IRA to participate in talks if they refrained from violence for three months. It remains unclear whether the IRA will accept the invitation.

Sinn Féin also remains taboo in the Republic—its spokespeople have only been allowed on TV or radio since January 1994, it regularly polls only 1-2% of the vote in Dáil elections, and a recent court decision upheld the ban on Sinn Féin leader **Gerry Adams'** book of short stories. Nonetheless, President **Mary Robinson** met with Adams in her 1993 visit to Belfast. The SDLP, still led by John Hume, continues to work on behalf of Catholics within a constitutional framework. Paisley still heads the extremist **Democratic Unionist Party,** but the more moderate **Official Unionist Party (OUP),** led by **James Molyneaux,** gets more votes. The Irish Constitution retains its paper claim to the six counties, though many young Southerners are sick of Republican platitudes and fear bombs in Dublin if the North ever changes hands. The official British position is that Northern Ireland will stay in the U.K. unless and until a majority of the North's population wants out—not soon. Some speculate that the North's drain on Britain's budget, army, and image might someday make likely a British withdrawal even against the majority's wishes; the Protestant paramilitaries fear this, too, and are now as active as the IRA, hoping—in a depressing parallel to 1914—that the threat of violence will keep Northern Ireland British forever.

SECURITY

Terrorists and paramilitaries on both sides want nothing less than to injure a tourist; as long as you stay out of Derry's Bogside and Belfast's Falls, Shankill, and Sandy Row after dark (and South Armagh altogether), you're unlikely to see trouble. Use common sense in conversation, and try not to take a political side or religious bent. Be aware of word choice: "Ireland" can mean the whole island or the Republic of Ireland, depending on who's listening. It's best to refer to "Northern Ireland" or "the North" and "the Republic" or "the South." "Southern Ireland" is never acceptable.

If you're planning to cross the border on a bike or in a car, be sure you do so at one of the approved **border-crossing checkpoints,** of which there are many; crossing at an unapproved point can get you followed by the army. Always bring ID and check that the road you mean to use hasn't been blown up near the border. Visiting or hitching in the little towns of South Armagh, especially Crossmaglen, cannot be considered safe. Do not ever take **photographs** of soldiers or of military installations or vehicles; if you do, your film will be confiscated, and you may be detained for questioning. Some urban areas have **"control zones,"** where there's no parking due to fear of car bombs. Since **unattended luggage** can also conceal a bomb, it's viewed with suspicion, and sometimes with a bomb squad. Large sectarian parades are sometimes occasions for violence; avoid large cities on July 12 (Orange Day) and on any other day in July or August (the "marching season") when there's a big march scheduled. Rural and holiday areas like the Glens and the Causeway Coast are untouched by the parades. Armored vehicles are a regular presence in large towns; soldiers, or police, may stop and question you, especially if you look or sound Irish. As in the Republic, nonpolitical crime is much rarer than in America.

■■■ BELFAST

Over 300,000 people (one-fifth of the North's population) live in Belfast, making the city the center for Northern Ireland's active and separate commercial, artistic, and paramilitary worlds. There's a vibrant, student-based arts/music/pub scene, a charming university area with hole-in-the-wall cafés, and urban bustle; there's also some long-term unemployment, making the poorer parts of the city recruiting grounds for extremist groups. If the Troubles are invisible in some rural areas, here the sight of them is unforgettable: armed British soldiers patrol the streets, frequent military checkpoints slow traffic and pedestrians, and stores advertise "Bomb Damage Sales." The Troubles may have had unintended positive results, from the brilliantly grim irony of Belfast's literati, to the black taxi services (started in response to a bus strike), to the ban on cars downtown, which produced a prosperous shopping zone—a lesson for urban planners anywhere.

Belfast wasn't always like this. From its beginnings as a base of "Scotch-Irish" Presbyterian settlement, it became a 19th-century industrial center like Liverpool and Birmingham, with world-famous shipyards, factories, and exports. Gathering slums, smoke, flax mills, and social theorists as it went, Belfast by 1900 looked much more British than Irish; the Protestant majority that controlled the city felt British, too, and fear of violence from them (as skillfully managed by Unionist leaders like Carson) was instrumental in creating the present divided island.

GETTING THERE

Trains roll in from Larne (Mon.-Fri. 20/day, Sat. 16/day, Sun. 6/day; 45 min.; £2.80), from Derry (Mon.-Fri. 7/day, Sat. 6/day, Sun. 3/day; 2hr. 15 min.; £7), and from Dublin's Connolly Station (Mon.-Sat. 7/day, Sun. 3/day; 2½hr.; £13). All trains arrive at **Belfast Central Station,** East Bridge St. (tel. 230 310), except those from points along the Larne line. These arrive at **Belfast York St. Station** (tel. 230671), where Rail-Link buses run to the city center and Central Station (3/hr.; free). To find the city center from Central Station, turn left and walk up East Bridge St. to Victoria St. Turn right, walk two blocks and turn left on May St. A free Rail-Link bus runs from Central Station to Donegall Sq. for the luggage-besieged.

Buses come to Belfast's **Europa/Glengall St. Station** (tel. 320574 or 33 000) from Dublin's Busáras Station (Mon.-Sat. 4/day, Sun. 3/day; £9.50, return £12) and from Derry's Foyle St. Station (Mon.-Sat. 6/day, Sun. 4/day; £5.30, return £9.30). Buses from eastern Northern Ireland, from the Down or Antrim coasts, arrive at the **Oxford St. Station** (tel. 333000 or 232356); all others arrive at Europa/Glengall St. To walk from the Oxford St. bus station to Donegall Sq., cross the street to Chichester St. Follow it about six blocks to Donegall Sq. North. From the Europa/Glengall St. Station, exit on the Great Victoria St. side, turn left and walk two blocks to Howard St. Turn right and another two blocks will bring you to Donegall Sq.

From the **ferry terminals at Larne,** take either a bus or a train into the Belfast city center (buses £2.30, trains £2.80). Trains arrive at the York St. Station, but the free Rail-link bus service will drop you at the city center. **Flexibus** (tel. 233933) connects the Sea Cat hovercraft terminal with Central Station, Oxford St. Station. Donegall Sq. Station, and the Europa Bus Center (8/day; 50p, children 25p). To reach the city center on foot from the **Sea Cat terminal** on Donegall Quay, turn left and walk along the water for one block. Turn right just before the Customs House on Albert Sq., walk two blocks, turn left on Victoria St. (note: this is not Great Victoria St.), and at the Clock Tower turn right on High St. Follow pedestrianized High St. to Donegall Pl. (about three blocks), where you should turn left. Consult Essentials: Getting There—Between the Isles for detailed ferry information.

ORIENTATION

Belfast spreads outwards from City Hall in Donegall Sq., six blocks west of the River Lagan and the harbor. A bustling, pedestrianized shopping district lies between City Hall and the enormous Castlecourt Shopping Center four blocks to the north. Donegall Place, which becomes Royal Ave., bisects the pedestrian area. Two blocks west of the center, Great Victoria St. runs south past the showy Grand Opera House, the gilded Crown Liquor Saloon, and the Europa Bus Center, eventually meeting the Dublin Rd. at Shaftesbury Sq. The stretch of Great Victoria between Shaftesbury and the Opera House is known as the "Golden Mile." South of the square, University Road leads to the red bricks of Queen's University, The Botanic Gardens, and a neighborhood of B&Bs, pubs and cafés.

Divided from the rest of the city by the Westlink Motorway, West Belfast is both poorer and more politically volatile than the city center. The Protestant neighborhood stretches along Shankill Rd., just north of the Catholic neighborhood which is centered on Falls Rd. The River Lagan separates industrial East Belfast from the rest of the city; the shipyards and docks that made Belfast big extend north of the center on both sides of the river as it expands into Belfast Lough.

Public transportation within the city means the red **Citybus Network** (tel. 246485), supplemented by the Ulsterbus "blue buses" for the suburbs. Citybuses going south and west leave from Donegall Sq. East; those going north and east leave from Donegall Sq. West (fare 70p).

PRACTICAL INFORMATION

Tourist Office: St. Anne's Court, 59 North St. (tel. 246609). For travelers arriving at odd hours, the computer set into the office's exterior wall gives 24-hr. tourist info. Open Sept.-June Mon.-Sat. 9am-5:15pm, July-Aug. Mon.-Fri. 9am-7:30pm, Sat. 9am-5:15pm, Sun. noon-4pm.

Irish Tourist Board (Bord Fáilte), 53 Castle St. (tel. 327888). Limited info on the Republic of Ireland, focusing on Dublin. Open Mon.-Fri. 9am-5pm, March-Sept. Mon.-Fri. 9am-5pm, Sat. 9am-12:30pm.

Budget Travel Office: USIT, 13b The Fountain Center, College St. (tel. 324073), near Royal Ave. Sells ISICs and Travelsave stamps (£5.50), for 50% discount on trains. Books ferry and plane tickets. Passport photo booth (£2.50 for 4 photos). Open Mon.-Fri. 9:30am-5:30pm, Sat. 10am-1pm.

Youth Hostel Association of Northern Ireland (YHANI): 22 Donegall Rd. (tel. 324733). Books YHANI hostels free; international hostels £2. Sells HI membership cards (senior £7, under 18 £3). Open Mon.-Fri. 9am-5pm.

U.S. Consulate General: Queens House, Queen St. (tel. 228239). Open Mon.-Fri. 1-5pm. **Canada, Australia,** and the **Republic of Ireland** are not represented.

Financial Services: Thomas Cook, British Airways, College St. (tel. 899131). Cashes Thomas Cook traveler's checks with no commission; others 2% commission. Open Mon.-Fri. 9am-5pm, Sat. 9am-4:15pm. Belfast International Airport office: (tel. (01849) 422536). Open Mon.-Fri. 7am-8pm, Sat.-Sun. 7am-10pm. **American Express:** Hamilton Travel, 10 College St. (tel. 322455). Client mail held. No charge for cashing AmEx Traveler's Cheques; others 1-2% commission. Open Mon.-Fri. 9am-5pm, Sat. 10am-1pm.

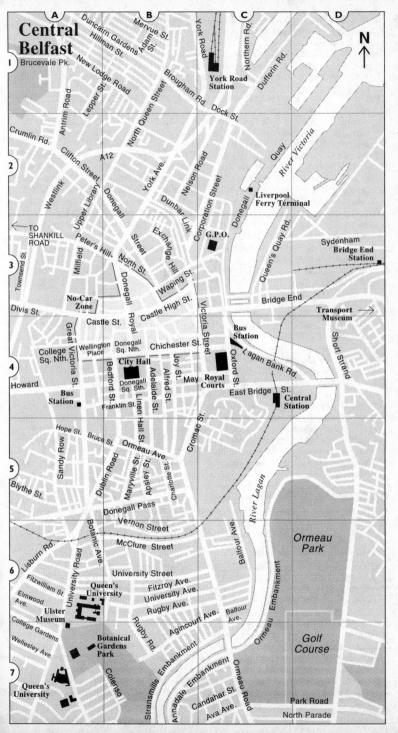

Central Belfast

N

| A | B | C | D |

Brucevale Pk.
Duncairn Gardens
Mervue St.
Hillman St.
Adam St.
York Road
Northern Rd.
Dufferin Rd.

York Road Station

New Lodge Road
Brougham Rd.
Dock St.

Antrim Road
Lepper St.
North Queen Street
Nelson Road

Crumlin Rd.
Clifton Street
A12
York Ave.
Corporation Street
Quay
River Victoria

Westlink
Upper Library
Donegall
Dunbar Link
Liverpool Ferry Terminal

TO SHANKILL ROAD
Peter's Hill
Street
Exchange Hill
G.P.O.
Queen's Quay Rd.
Sydenham
Bridge End Station

Townsend St.
Millfield
North St.
Donegall
Waping St.
Castle High St.

No-Car Zone
Castle St.
Royal
Bridge End
Transport Museum

Divis St.
Great Victoria St.
Wellington Place
Donegall Sq. Nth.
Chichester St.
Victoria Street
Bus Station
Short Strand

College Sq. Nth.
Bedford St.
City Hall
Adelaide St.
Joy St.
Royal Courts
Oxford St.
Lagan Bank Rd.

Howard
Donegall Sq. Sth.
Linen Hall St.
Alfred St.
May
East Bridge St.
Central Station

Bus Station
Franklin St.
Cromac St.

Hope St.
Bruce St.
Ormeau Ave.
Apsley St.
Maryville St.

Sandy Row
Dublin Road
Charlotte St.
River Lagan

Blythe St.
Donegall Pass
Vernon Street

McClure Street
Balfour Ave.
Ormeau Embankment
Ormeau Park

Lisburn Rd.
Botanic Ave.
University Street

Fitzwilliam St.
Queen's University
Fitzroy Ave.
University Ave.
Rugby Ave.
Golf Course

Elmwood Ave.
University Road
Ulster Museum
Agincourt Ave.
Balfour Ave.

College Gardens
Botanical Gardens Park
Rugby Rd.

Wellesley Ave.
Queen's University
Colenso
Stranmillis Embankment
Annadale Embankment
Candahar St.
Ormeau Road
Park Road
Ava Ave.
North Parade

Banks: Halifax Bank (tel. 247777) has **ATMs** that accept Plus and Visa: 10-11 Shaftesbury Sq.; 41 Arthur St., off Chichester St., 1 block from Donegall Sq.; and at the Castlecourt Shopping Center.

Post Office: Central Post Office, 25 Castle Pl. (tel. 323740). Open Mon.-Fri. 9am-5:30pm, Sat. 9am-1pm. *Poste Restante* mail comes here. **Postal code:** BT1 1NB.

Telephones: Even in Belfast only about a quarter of all the phones take phone cards. Be sure to carry change with you as well. **Telephone Code:** 01232.

Taxi: Huge **black cabs** run set routes to West Belfast, collecting and discharging passengers along the way (standard 50p charge). Easily identifiable by either a Falls Rd., Andersontown, or Irish-language sign (Catholic) or a red poppy or "Shankill" sign (Protestant). If you're not going their way, call an ordinary 24-hr. metered cab: **City Cab** (tel. 242000, wheelchair accessible).

Car Rental: McCauseland's, 21-31 Grosvenor Rd. (tel. 333777). £39/day, £185/week. Must be age 21-70. Open Mon.-Thurs. 8:30am-6:30pm, Fri. 8:30am-7:30pm, Sat. 8:30am-5pm, Sun. 8:30am-12:30pm. Car return 24 hrs. Belfast International Airport Office: (tel. (01849) 422022). Belfast City Airport office: (tel. 454141). £10 surcharge to drive in the Republic.

Bike Rental: none in the city center. **E. Coates,** 108 Grand Parade (tel. 471912). £3/day, £15 deposit. Open Mon.-Fri. 9am-5:30pm. **YHANI** may begin renting.

Luggage Storage: YHANI, 59 Bradbury Pl. (tel. 324733), will store bags. **Arnie's Hostel** will hold bags during the day for those staying there.

Bookstore: Eason's, Castlecourt Shopping Center, Royal Ave. (tel. 235070). Large Irish section, lots of travel guides. Open Mon.-Wed. and Fri.-Sat. 9am-5:30pm, Thurs. 9am-9pm. **Bargain Books,** 19 Royal Ave. (tel. 247320). Sells best-sellers cheap (£1-2). Open Mon.-Wed. and Fri.-Sat. 9am-6pm, Thurs. 9am-9pm.

Laundry: Student's Union, Queen's University, University Rd. Wash £1, dry 20p. Open Mon.-Fri. 9am-9pm, Sat. 10am-9pm, Sun. 2-9pm. Students only. **Duds & Suds,** University Rd. (tel. 243956). Munch on popcorn and watch TV while you wait. Wash £1.50, dry £1.50. 15% discount for students and seniors. Open Mon.-Fri. 8am-9pm, Sat. 8am-6pm, Sun. noon-6pm. Last load 1½ hr. before closing.

Student Life: Queen's University Student Center (tel. 324803), staffed in the evenings by students ready to name all the trendy Belfast hangouts.

Bisexual, Gay, and Lesbian Information: Carinated Counseling: tel. 238668, open Thurs. 7:30-10pm. Odd name, cool people.

Hotlines: Samaritans (crisis): tel. 664422, 24 hrs. **NI Council on Disability:** tel. 491011, open Mon.-Fri. 9am-5pm. **Rape Crisis Center:** 41 Waring St. (tel. 321830), open Mon.-Fri. 10am-6pm, Sat. 11am-5pm.

Hospitals: Belfast City Hospital, Lisburn Rd. (tel. 329241). A ½-mi. from Shaftesbury Sq. Facing the neon sign, follow Bradbury Pl. and take the right fork.

Emergency: dial 999; no coins required. **Police:** 65 Knock Rd. (tel. 650222; often faster than 999 in an emergency).

ACCOMMODATIONS

Practically all of Belfast's accommodations are located near Queen's University, south of the city center. Buses #59, 69, 70, 71, 84, and 85 run to the area from Donegall Sq. East. B&Bs abound between Malone Rd. and Lisburn Rd. south of Queen's.

Hostels & University Housing

Arnie's Backpackers (IHH), 63 Fitzwilliam St., (tel. 242867). Relaxed and friendly. Small 6-bunk rooms. 24-hr. kitchen. Luggage storage during the day. £7.

YHANI Belfast Hostel, 22 Donegall Rd. (tel. 324733). Clean, spacious, ultra-modern rooms with 2-6 beds, some with private bathrooms. No kitchen. Wheelchair access. Book 2 weeks in advance for weekends. Wash and dry £2.40. Coffee shop open daily 7:30am-8pm. £8.50; with private bath £10.

YWCA, Queen Mary's Hall, 70 Fitzwilliam St. (tel. 240439). Coed. Bright, clean rooms with sinks. Limited self-serve kitchen open 7am-11pm. Always full during school year; in summer, book 1-2 weeks in advance. B&B £13, hostel bed in 3-bed room £8/person (you must provide a sleeping bag). Dinner £5. Laundry £1/wash.

Queen's University Accommodations, 78 Malone Rd. (tel. 381608). Take bus #70 or 71 from Donegall Sq. East or walk down Great Victoria Rd. which runs into

Malone Rd. A spartan dorm: rooms off long corridors. 24-hr. kitchen with microwave and little else. Singles: UK students £7, international students £8.23, non-students £11-16. Doubles £17.63. Open mid-June to mid-Sept.

Mrs. Davidson's East-Sheen Guest House, 81 Eglantine Ave. (tel. 667149). The best deal in Belfast, if you can get a room. Sweet Mrs. D. serves enormous breakfasts, and every room has a teapot, sugar cubes, and biscuits. Rooms are bright and clean. £14/person.

The George, 9 Eglantine Ave. (tel. 683212). Spotless but cramped rooms, each with shower and TV. Comfy leather couches near the common area's big picture window. Family room available. £16/person.

FOOD

Belfast offers a welcome respite from the bland and greasy frying tradition. Dublin Rd. and the Golden Mile, stretching from the Grand Opera House down Great Victoria St. to University Rd., have the highest concentration of places to eat. The **Mace Supermarket** on the corner of Castle and Queen St. offers cheap groceries (open Mon.-Wed. and Fri.-Sat. 9am-6pm, Thurs. 9am-9pm). For fruits and vegetables, plunder the lively **St. George's Market,** East Bridge St., in the enormous warehouse between May St. and Oxford St. (open Tues. and Fri. 7am-3pm).

Bluebells, 50 Botanic Ave. (tel. 322622). A hangout for young intellos. Great food, homemade ice cream (small cone 35p), and newspapers to read. Big bowl of soup and homemade bread £1.25. Open Mon.-Sat. 8am-10:30pm, Sun. 9am-8pm.

Bookfinders, 47 University Rd. (tel. 328269). Smoky, atmospheric bookstore/café offers moussaka and salad (£3.20) or soup and bread (£1.40) amidst stacks of old books. Occasional poetry readings. Open Mon.-Sat. 10am-5:30pm.

Spice of Life, 62 Lower Donegall St. (tel. 332744), across from St. Anne's Cathedral behind the tourist office. Earthy atmosphere and cheap, wholesome veggie food. Student special: large soup and sandwich £1.50. Vegan ice cream 55p/scoop. Nothing over £3. Open Mon.-Sat. 10am-5pm.

Bambrick's, corner of Wellington Pl. and College Sq. (tel. 423203), 2 blocks west of Donegall Sq. North. Look for the intricate mosaic exterior. Sip your unlimited cup of coffee (65p) as you savor a full Irish breakfast (£1—'zounds!) or lunch (eggplant parm with potato, £3). Open Mon.-Fri. 9:30am-4:30pm.

PUBS

Pubs were prime targets for sectarian violence at the height of the Troubles, in the 60s and 70s. As a result, most of the popular pubs in Belfast are relatively new, although some have maintained a traditional flavor. Ask the student staff at the Queen's University Student Center for the current hip night spots.

The Queens University Student Center (tel. 324803), hopping during term-time, with 2 popular bars and discos 6 days/week, with occasional live bands (cover £2 for disco).

The Elms, 36 University Rd. (tel. 322106); a rough-around-the-edges student bar, with live bands most nights and traditional music on Thurs.

Lavery's, 12 Bradbury Pl. (tel. 327159). *The* place to be for all kinds of people, bikers to students to road-hog intellectuals.

Crown Liquor Saloon, 46 Great Victoria St. Famous, pleasant place for an afternoon pint, but in the evenings it fills with a dull crowd.

Robinson's, 38-40 Great Victoria St. (tel. 247447). Four floors of bars, from the motorcycle-themed "Rock Bottom" in the basement to "The Spot" on the top floor, which hosts live rock bands Thurs.-Sat. "Fibber Magee's," at the back of the ground floor, serves traditional Irish lunches.

Queens Bar, 4 Queen's Arcade (tel. 321347). Relaxed, friendly atmosphere in a tiny alley off Donegall Pl.; attracts a broad mixture of people, gay and straight. Upscale lunchtime pub grub (tuna and red bean salad w/crusty bread £3).

The Crow's Nest, 26 Skipper St. (tel. 325491), off High St., across from the Albert Memorial clock. A friendly gay and lesbian crowd. Popular discos begin here at

S I G H T S

around 9:30pm on Wed.-Sat. nights (£1 cover). Ask the helpful staff for other popular gay hangouts.

The Rotterdam, 54 Pilot St. (tel. 746021). Crammed to the rafters with an odd assortment of flotsam and jetsam, from wooden shoes to spiked flails, mostly contributed by foreign sailors. Live music 6 days/week, ranging from folk to jazz.

Pat's Bar, 19 Prince's Dock St. (tel. 458 603). The Rotterdam's twin.

SIGHTS

Belfast City Hall, Donegall Sq. (tel. 320202), is the administrative and geographical center of Belfast, regally set apart from the crowded streets by a grassy square. Its 173-foot-high green copper dome can be seen from anywhere in the city. Inside, the City Council's oak-panelled chambers, used only once a month, are deceptively austere, considering the Council's reputation for rowdy meetings (they have been known to degenerate into fist fights). The interior of City Hall is accessible by guided tour (every Wed. at 10:30am, and July-Aug. Mon.-Fri. at 10:30am and 2:30pm). You must book a day in advance for the tour (it's a security thing). The northwest corner of Donegall Sq. holds the **Linen Hall Library,** 17 Donegall Sq. (tel. 321 707), a wood-panelled library famous for its collection of political materials—every Christmas card, poster, hand bill, and newspaper article related to the Troubles that the library can get its hands on. (Open Mon.-Wed. and Fri. 9:30am-5:30pm, Thurs. 9:30am-8:30pm, Sat. 9:30am-4pm.)

Although the Cornmarket area is dominated by new buildings, snatches of old Belfast remain in the form of tiny alleys, known as **The Entries,** which connect some of the major streets. On Ann St., look for the hand and umbrella sticking out of the wall above an umbrella store—the entrance to Pottinger's Entry is right across the street. In Pottinger's Entry, grab a pint at the old **Morning Star Pub.** Farther down Ann St., **Joy's Entry** was the site of the printing of the *Belfast News Letter* for over 100 years. Off Lombard St., **Winecellar Entry** is the site of Belfast's oldest pub, **White's Tavern,** serving drinks since 1630 and still the perfect setting for an afternoon pint.

Belfast's newspapers set up shop north of the Cornmarket shopping district, around the Church of Ireland cathedral on Donegall St. called the **Belfast Cathedral** or **St. Anne's.** In order not to disturb worship, this cathedral, begun in 1899, was built around the smaller, earlier church on the site. Upon completion of the cathedral's exterior, the earlier church was removed, brick by brick, from inside. The tops of each of the cathedral's 10 interior pillars depict somebody's idea of the 10 basic professions of Belfast, among them Healing, Agriculture, Theology, Shipbuilding, Freemasonry, and Womanhood. (Open daily 9am-6pm.)

The precarious **Albert Memorial Clock Tower,** designed in 1865 by W. J. Barre, marks the entryway to the docks area, where Oxford St. briefly parallels the Lagan, with Victoria St. (*not* Great Victoria St.) behind. Poor Prince Albert: the clock tower is noticeably limp. An organ with port and starboard lights carries the tune at **Sinclair Seamen's Church,** Corporation St. (next to Donegall Quay), where the minister delivers his sermon from a pulpit carved to look like a ship's prow and collection is taken in miniature lifeboats. (Open for Sun. services 11:30am and 7pm; July-Aug. Also open Wed. 2-4pm. At other times, call 757730.) Farther south along the Quay, the **Lagan Lookout** includes a walkway across the newly-built **Lagan Weir** and an interpretive center with displays on the history of Belfast and the harbor. (Center open Mon.-Fri. 11am-5pm, Sat. noon-5pm, Sun. 2-5pm. £1.50.)

Belfast's pride and joy, the **Grand Opera House** on Great Victoria St. is continually bombed by the Provos, restored at enormous cost to its original splendor, and then bombed again; the cycle would be funny if it weren't horrific. Call the booking office (tel. 241919; open Mon.-Sat. 9:45am-5:30pm) to make an appointment, or ask at the stage door on Glengall St. If there's no rehearsal going on, they'll give you a tour. Also on Glengall St., the plush **Europa Hotel** is said to be "Europe's most bombed hotel." Across the street from the Opera House, **the Crown Liquor Saloon,** Great Victoria St., is a showcase of carved wood, gilded ceilings, and stained glass, fully restored by the National Trust. Following south along Great Victoria St. will bring you to **Shaftesbury Square,** whose one neon sign allows tourism officials to compare it to Piccadilly Circus. Nearby, the **Arts Council Gallery,** 56-60 Dublin Rd. (tel. 321402), shows contemporary artists from Belfast to Oslo to Prague (open Tues.-Sat. 10am-6pm; free). Two blocks farther down the Golden Mile, the **Crescent Arts Center,** 2 University Rd. (tel. 242338), gives lots of gallery space to Belfast artists (open daily 9am-5pm).

At the bottom of the Golden Mile, the main building of **Queen's University** sits back from the road in its revival Tudor red brick. Designed by the overworked Charles Lanyon in 1849, the building was modeled after Magdalen College, Oxford. Only the front of the façade was finished properly—you'll be disappointed if you walk around the sides. The University has its own art gallery—**Fenderesky Gallery,** 5 Upper Crescent (tel. 235245), which puts up contemporary shows all year round. (Open Tues.-Fri. 11:30am-5:30pm, Sat. noon-5pm.) On warm days, most of the student population can be found sunning themselves in the **Botanic Gardens** (tel. 324902) down the street. If you've had enough of the cold Irish weather, pop into the **Tropical House** for a few minutes—it's 95°F inside. (Gardens open 7:30am-dusk; Tropical House Mon.-Fri. 10am-noon and 2-5pm, Sat.-Sun. 2-5pm; free). Amidst the Botanic Gardens, off Stranmillis Rd., **The Ulster Museum** (tel. 381251) has good exhibits on Irish art, local history and antiquities, including the treasure salvaged from the *Girone,* a Spanish Armada ship that sank off the Causeway Coast in 1588 (open Mon.-Fri. 10am-5pm, Sat. 1-5pm, Sun. 2-5pm; free.)

At the bottom of the hills that rise over the city's valley sits **Belfast Castle,** presented to the city by the Earl of Shaftesbury in 1934. In perfect condition, the castle is closed to the general public, but anyone can walk through the grounds. A climb to the top of **Cave Hill,** on whose slope the castle sits, will bring you to **McArt's Fort,** where the United Irishmen plotted rebellion in 1795. The summit is nicknamed "Napoleon's Nose": its knock-the-wind-out-of-you view over the city and Belfast Lough is certainly nothing to sneeze at. Next to the castle is the **Belfast Zoo.** Don't miss the gorillas and the sub-aquatic view of penguins and seals. (Open April-Sept. daily 10am-5pm; Oct.-March 10am-3:30pm. £4.) To reach Belfast Castle and Zoo, follow the Antrim Rd. or Cave Hill Rd. out of town for several miles, or take bus #2, 3, 4, 5, 6, or 45 from Donegall Sq. West.

WEST BELFAST

Separated from the rest of the city by the Westlink motorway, the working-class neighborhoods of West Belfast sit at the heart of political tension in the North. The Catholic area (centered on the Falls Rd.) and the Protestant one (centered on the Shankill) are grimly separated by the **peace line.** With care and common sense, the Falls and Shankill can be visited in **safety.** Stay far away from the Falls Rd. and Shankill after dark; visit the area by day in a car, on foot, or in a black cab (see Practical Information, above). The Protestant Orangemen's marching season, around July 12, is an exciting but dangerous time to be in West Belfast—the proud, angry parades can inspire political violence. Other ceremonial occasions, such as the Catholic West Belfast Festival (August 7-15), can also be dangerous times to visit. *Never* take pictures of soldiers, police or military installations; if you do, your film will be confiscated and you may be detained for questioning. When taking pictures of people, murals, or buildings, it's probably better to ask someone's permission, if only to let it be known that you're a harmless tourist. To see the Falls and Shankill, you must visit one neighborhood, return to the city center, and then visit the other. *Do not attempt to cross the peace line—even by day.*

The Falls is larger than Shankill and still growing. As you walk west on Divis St., away from the city center, note the high-rise apartment building that marks the site of the **Divis Flats,** an ill-fated housing development built by optimistic social planners in the 1960s; the project saw some of the worst of Belfast's troubles in the 70s. The lower, six-story apartments, like much of the ugly public housing in this neighborhood, are being torn down and replaced with more attractive low-rise houses. Continue up the Falls Rd. until it splits into Andersontown Rd. and Glen Rd. On your left are the Celtic crosses of **Milltown Cemetery,** burial place of many who died for the Republican cause. Head inward and right from the entrance to reach a memorial to Republican casualties, bordered by a low green fence. Bobby Sands' grave is here. Another mile further along the **Andersontown** Rd. lies the road's namesake (formerly a wealthy Catholic neighborhood, now the site of the housing project) and several good murals. On the way back towards the city center, past the cemeteries, Whiterock Rd. goes left, toward the **Ballymurphy Housing Estate** and more murals. Towards the end of this road, a mural asserting Republican solidarity with Native Americans overlooks the City Cemetery.

To reach the Protestant **Shankill,** head up North St. to the left of the tourist office, as you face the building. North St. quickly turns into the Shankill Rd. as it crosses the Westlink. The **peace line** can be seen down any of the side roads off to the left; many of the neighborhood's murals can be seen on the sides of the buildings whose fronts face the Shankill Rd. At Canmore St., an impressive mural on the left depicts the Apprentice Boys "Shutting the Gates of Derry—1688" as the Catholic invaders try to get through. A little further, also on the left and across a small park, a big, faded mural depicts the "UVF—then and now," with a modern black-garbed "soldier" and a historical soldier side-by-side. The highly decorated **Orange Hall** sits on the left at Brookmount St. The side streets to the right lead to the **Shankill Estate,** home of more murals. Pass through the Estate to the **Crumlin Road;** heading down it back to the city center leads past an army base and the courthouse and jail, on opposite sides of the road but linked by a tunnel.

ARTS & ENTERTAINMENT

The best coverage of Belfast's many arts-related events and performances can be found in the free, monthly *Arts Council Artslink* (at the tourist office and all art galleries); listings also appear in the daily *Belfast Telegraph* (daily listings and a Fri. arts supplement), and in Thursday's *Irish News.* July is a slow month for the arts in Belfast; around July 12, the whole city shuts down.

Belfast's **theaters** put on a wide range of shows; there are more from September to June, as many "go dark" for the summer. The truly **Grand Opera House,** Great Victoria St., boasts an impressive mix of opera, ballet, musicals, and drama. During the opera season in September, tickets may be booked at tel. 381241 (£8-30; student standbys available at the theater 45 min. before performance for £5). Tickets for other events available at the box office, 17 Wellington Pl. (open Mon.-Sat. 9:45am-5:30pm). **The Arts Theater,** 41 Botanic Ave. (tel. 324936), houses its own company but hosts many touring companies as well. (Open Aug.-June. Box office open Mon.-Sat. 10am-7pm. Tickets £3-7.) For a good laugh, try **The Group Theater,** Bedford St. (tel. 329685), which specializes in comedies. (Open Sept.-May. Box office open Mon.-Fri. noon-3pm. Tickets £2.50-3.) **Queen's Film Theater,** University Square Mews (tel. 244867), is worth a look both for its foreign films and for its incredibly comfortable seats (tickets £3-3.50).

Ulster Hall, Linenhall St. (tel. 229685), presents all kinds of music, from classical to pop (box office open Mon.-Sat. 9am-5pm). For traditional music, try **Madden's Bar,** 74 Smithfield (tel. 244114), on Wednesday to Saturday, **Kelly's Cellars,** 30 Bank St. (tel. 324835), on Thursday, **The Parador Hotel,** 473 Ormeau Rd. (tel. 491883), on Thursday, **The Duke of York,** Lower Donegall St. tel. 241062), on Monday and Thursday, and **Morrisons,** 21 Bedford St. (tel. 248458), on Sunday. Trad to rock to jazz blast from **The Rotterdam** practically every night of the week. **The Elms** has folk/rock bands most nights and trad on Thursday. **The Front Page** also plays a wide range of music—usually only on weekends. **Robinson's** has rock and dance bands upstairs (Thurs.-Sat. nights, see Pubs). **The Limelight,** Ormeau Rd. (tel. 325968), has bands Thursday and Sunday—mostly rock. If jazz is your style, try **The Manhattan,** Bradbury Pl., or the **Drumkeen Hotel,** Upper Galwally (tel. 491321), on Wednesday; the **Terrace Restaurant,** 255 Lisburn Rd. (tel. 381655), on Thursday; or **The Cutter's Wharf,** Lockview Rd. (tel. 662501), on Sunday.

The **Dome and Limelight** complex, Ormeau Ave. (tel. 325968), is basically a dance club with a pub attached. Monday is gay and lesbian night (straights also welcome). Friday and Saturday are student-only discos. Tuesday is dancing for everyone; Thursday and sometimes Sunday brings a live band. (Music begins around 9pm; cover £1-7.) **Queens University Student Center** has student-only discos six days per week during term time and Thursday and Saturday during the summer (£2). **The Crow's Nest** (see Pubs), has dancing for gays and lesbians (Wed.-Sat., £1 cover); straights are welcome. **The Orpheus Inn** has a disco for gays and lesbians Thursday (£2) and Sunday (free); straights are unwelcome. **The Elms** (see Pubs) has a disco on Tuesday night.

■ NEAR BELFAST

Five miles east of Belfast on the Bangor Rd. in Cultra, on the way to the Ards Peninsula, the **Ulster Folk and Transport Museum** (tel. (01232) 428428) stretches over 60 acres. Over 25 buildings from the past three centuries have been moved from their original locations all over Ulster and reconstructed stone by stone on the museum property. Near the entrance, an entire village is slowly coming together, complete with an 18th-century church from Kildare, Co. Down and an 18th-century one-room schoolhouse from Ballycastle, Co. Antrim. The **Transport Museum** and the hangar-like **Railway Museum** are nearby. You can easily spend half a day at the museums—don't allot less than two hours. The museums are accessible via Ulsterbus #1 or 2 from the Oxford St. station. (Open July-Aug. Mon.-Sat. 10:30am-6pm, Sun. noon-6pm; April-June and Sept. Mon.-Fri. 9:30am-5pm, Sat. 10:30am-6pm, Sun. noon-6pm; Oct.-March Mon.-Fri. 9:30am-4pm, Sat.-Sun. 12:30-4pm. Closed Dec. 24-26. £2.60, HI members £1.30.)

DOWN & ARMAGH

■■■ ARDS PENINSULA

Bounded on the west by tranquil Strangford Lough, the Ards Peninsula guards the rest of Co. Down from the agitated Irish Sea to its east. The Strangford Lough shore from Newtownards to Portaferry holds wildlife preserves, historic houses, crumbling ruins, and spectacular lake views; on the other, eastern shore of the Ards, each wee fishing village seems tinier than the one before. **Ulsterbus** leaves Oxford St., Belfast to travel along the peninsula; it stops in practically every town. **Trains** chug no farther than Bangor. From the south, an irregular **ferry** from Strangford crosses to Portaferry. Consider renting a bike in Belfast and taking a day or two to pedal the peninsula.

BANGOR

Close both to Belfast and to the open sea, Bangor was once *the* seaside resort for Belfast residents; recently it's become a bit tired, with both its wilderness attractions and video arcades eclipsed by the bigger ones in Newcastle. Bangor now caters especially to families and older holidaymakers; as a beach town built for urbanites, it's still pleasant enough, and its location makes it an inevitable stop on the way down the Ards Peninsula. **North Down Visitors and Heritage Center,** Town Hall, Castle Park (tel. 270371), has a model of now-obliterated Bangor Abbey and faded paraphernalia from Bangor's resort heyday. (Open Tues.-Sat. 10:30am-5:30pm, Sun. 2-5:30pm; Sept.-June Tues.-Sat. 10:30am-4:30pm, Sun. 2-4:30pm. Free. Wheelchair access.) Around the Heritage Center are 129 acres of sometimes wooded, sometimes grassy **Castle Park.** Grab a trail guide at the Heritage Center or the tourist office and explore the grounds and the arboretum. Head down the **North Down Coastal Path,** whose 15-mi. stretch from Holywood through Bangor and Groomsport to Orlock Point. Along the way are abandoned WWII lookouts, Helen's Bay (a popular bathing spot), an old fort with a massive gun, and a giant redwood. Bicycles are banned from the path. The Bangor-Holywood portion, said to be more striking than the rest, should take 3½ hours.

The **tourist office** is in Tower House, 34 Quay St. (tel. 270069; open Mon.-Fri. 9am-8pm, Sat. 10am-1pm and 2-8pm, Sun. 2-6pm; Sept.-June Mon.-Thurs. 9am-1pm and 2-5pm, Fri. 9am-1pm and 2-4:30pm). **Halifax Bank** is on 20 Main St. (tel. 270013; open Mon.-Fri. 9am-5pm, Sat. 9am-noon). Its **ATM** accepts Plus and Visa. The **telephone code** here is 01247. **Buses** stop on Abbey Rd. (tel. 271143). Buses run to Belfast (26/day; 45min.; £1.75, return £2.50) and to all towns on the Ards Peninsula, including Donaghadee (34/day; 30min.; £1.10) and Newtownards (34/day; 25 min.; £1.10). The adjoining **train station** (tel. 270141) sends 'em to Belfast (40/day; 20min.; £2.10, return £3.50).

Without hostel or campground, Bangor teems with B&Bs in the £12-15 range; they're listed in the tourist office's window. **Pierview House,** 28 Seacliff Rd. (tel. 463381), has very flexible rates, depending on the size of the room, length of stay, and time of year (£13-15). **The Dutch Windmill Restaurant,** 13 Bridge St. (tel 452 096), grinds out pancakes and waffles (£1.50-3.50); the tea meals are pricier. (Open Mon.-Thurs. 10am-7pm, Fri.-Sat. 10am-10pm.) For good *craic* after a day of hiking, try one of the pubs in the triangle on High St. or along the waterfront. **Jenny Watts,** High St. (tel. 270401), has a Sunday lunch jazz session, a Tuesday ribs and folk night, and a nightclub upstairs on Friday and Saturday nights.

Near Bangor

The line of fishing villages south of Bangor consists of little more than one harbor and one to three pubs each. The largest is **Donaghadee,** famous for its lifeboat and lighthouse. **Ulsterbus** runs to Donaghadee from Bangor (34/day; 30min.; £1.20) and from Belfast (24/day; 55min.; £2). Walk along the waterfront, or take a stroll out to the still-operational first electrical lighthouse in Ireland. Along the shore past the lighthouse are the former communal potato fields called the **town commons.** Towering above the village is an old ruined *Motte* (pronounced "moat"), which held the ammunition used for blasting stone from the hill to build the harbor. On a clear day, you can see Scotland from the top of the hill. In July and August, Quinton Nelson runs boats out to the **Copeland Islands,** a wildlife sanctuary just off the shore (tel. (01247) 883403 for info).

South of Donaghadee, gnat-sized fishing villages buzz along the eastern shoreline. Five mi. south of Newtownards on the A20 stands **Mountstewart House and Gardens** (tel. (01247) 88387). Held by a string of Marquesses of Londonderry, both house and garden are now National Trust and are worth a long detour to see. (House open May-Sept. Wed.-Mon. 1-6pm; April and Oct. Sat.-Sun. 1-6pm. Gardens open April-Sept. daily 10:30am-6pm; Oct. Sat.-Sun. 10:30am-6pm. Temple open same days as the house, 2-5pm. Admission £3.30.) In Portaferry, at the tip of the Ards Peninsula, **ferries** (tel. (013986) 637) leave from the waterfront at 15 and 45 minutes past the hour for a 10-min. chug to Strangford. (Boats run Mon.-Fri. 7:15am-10:45pm, Sat. 8:15am-11:15pm, Sun. 9:45am-10:45pm. 60p.)

■■■ MOURNE MOUNTAINS

The 15 rounded peaks of the Mourne Mountains sprawl across the southeastern corner of Northern Ireland, covering an area 15 mi. long and 8 mi. wide. Volcanic activity spewed five different kinds of granite onto the mountains 75 million years ago, resulting today in a spectacular effect of color ranging from a rosy pink to a green grey. No road penetrates the center of the mountains, leaving a solitude that welcomes walkers.

NEWCASTLE

At the foot of Slieve Donard, the highest peak, Newcastle is by far the best base from which to explore the Mourne Mountains. The **tourist office,** 10-14 Central Promenade (tel. 22222), has a free map of Newcastle's complex street plan. (Open Mon.-Thurs. 10am-8pm, Fri.-Sat. 10am-9pm, Sun. 1-8pm; Sept.-May Mon.-Fri. 10am-5pm, Sat 1-5pm.) The **telephone code** is 013967. Buses park at wishfully-named 5-7 Railway St. (tel. 22296), at the end of Main St.; they run to Belfast (Mon.-Sat. 26/day, Sun. 10/day; 70min.; £3.50). Camping equipment can be yours thanks to **Hilltrekker,** 115 Central Promenade (tel. 23842; open daily 10am-5:30pm).

All those popular beaches make the B&Bs expensive. Of the area's **campsites,** the Tullymore Forest Park is probably the most scenic, but the mountains themselves are a free and legal alternative. The **Newcastle Youth Hostel (YHANI/HI),** 30 Downs Rd. (tel. 22133), is clean, spacious, central, and on the waterfront; the only drawback is a scarcity of showers. Free laundry! (Lockout 11am-5pm, in theory only. Curfew 11:30pm, not always enforced. £6, under-18 £5. Open March-Dec. 20. MC/Access, Visa.) **Glenada YWCA,** 29 South Promenade (tel. 22402), has 8-bunk rooms in an incredibly posh building. (No kitchen. Curfew 10pm. £6/person, B&B £8. Wheelchair access.) **Glenside Farm House,** 136 Tullybrannigan Rd. (tel. 22628), is a long, but beautiful 1½-mi. walk from the town. Clean, simple rooms go for £10 per single, £18 per double. **Tollymore Forest Park,** 176 Tullybrannigan Rd. (tel. 22428), is a 2-mi. walk or easy hitch along the A2. Its excellent facilities include a café with delicious doughnuts, showers, a wildfowl exhibit and arboretum, and 584 hectares of well-marked walks and gardens. (£8.50/tent.)

At **Brambles,** 4 Central Promenade (tel. 26888), tasty Canadian recipes stand out in the culinary sameness of the North. Homemade quiche, pizza, and pancakes are a specialty (soup with organic wheat bread £1.50). (Open Mon.-Fri. 10am-7pm, Sat.-Sun. 10am-11pm; Oct.-Easter Mon.-Fri. 10am-7pm.) Newcastle is not the place for a quiet drink. Popular (and packed) spots include the **Anchor Bar,** 9 Bryansford Rd. (tel. 23344), which draws a sociable crowd of mixed ages and **The Oaks,** 62 Main St. (tel. 26400), where younger people smoke and play pool.

HIKES IN THE MOURNES

Before heading for the hills, stop at the **Mourne Countryside Center,** 91 Central Promenade (tel. 24059), where friendly and knowledgeable staff will help you plan your hike. Detailed maps here include *Mourne Mountain Walks* (£5), which maps 10 good day hikes. Those planning to stay in the Mournes for more than a day ought to buy the *Mourne County Outdoor Pursuits Map* (£3.50), a detailed topographical map; there's also a leaflet on the mountains (20p). The center will photocopy parts of maps for day hikes (open Mon.-Fri. 9am-5pm, Sat.-Sun. noon-6pm; winter hours may vary). If the center's closed, ask for maps at the tourist office and advice at **Hilltrekker** (see above). The Mourne Countryside Center offers guided walks Mondays in summer. (Transportation costs £1-2; meet at 10am sharp at the Center, but it's best to call ahead of time.) Seasoned hikers looking for company might want to join the **Mourne Rambling Group** (tel. 24315), which sends groups into the Mournes each Sunday. **Ulsterbus'** *Mourne Rambler* makes two trips through the mountains daily, dropping off hikers in the morning and picking them up in the afternoon. (July-Aug. bus leaves Newcastle at 9:30am and 3pm, £3 return.) This bus is the best way to get to the trailheads even if you have a car, because it allows you to begin and end your hike in different places. Ulsterbus also gives one-hour tours around the mountains, leaving from Belfast (tel. (01232) 333000).

The **Mourne Wall,** built in the early 1900s, encircles the interior of the mountains just short of the peaks. Originally built to mark the catchment area for the reservoirs below, the wall is popular with hikers. Following the length of the 22-mile wall will cost you a strenuous eight hours; many people break it up into two days. Wilderness **camping** is legal and popular; common spots include the north end of Ben Crom reservoir, the shores of Lough Shannagh, and along the Trassey River. Hare's Gap and around the Blue Lough at Annalong are other good places to pitch.

■■■ ARMAGH

Armagh has been known as the ecclesiastical capital of Ireland since St. Patrick legendarily chose the town as his base. It remains the administrative center for both the Catholic Church in Ireland, and the Protestant Church of Ireland, both of which keep magnificent cathedrals. Armagh's vibrant history, which stretches from prehistoric activity at nearby Navan Fort to visits from Jonathan Swift, has been partially dimmed by sectarian violence in the past decade. While the town is safe for tourists, locals avoid walking the soldier-filled streets at night.

Armagh's twin cathedrals are justifiably the city's pride and joy. **The Church of Ireland Cathedral of St. Patrick** (tel. 523142) is a 19th-century restoration of a 17th-century structure, based on a 13th-century plan. Look for the plaque marking the grave of the great Irish King, BrianBorú. (Open daily 10am-5pm; Nov.-March 10am-4pm. Tours conducted June-Aug. Mon.-Sat. 11:30am and 2:30pm. Free.) Across town on Cathedral Rd. the **Catholic Church of St. Patrick** raises its heady spires. Opened in 1873 to a crowd of 20,000 spectators, the cathedral's majestic exterior and exquisite mosaic interior are marred only by ultra-modern granite furnishings in the sanctuary. (Open daily 9am-5pm. Free.)

In the center of town, just behind the tourist office, **St. Patrick's Trian** (tel. 527808) contains a set of exhibits centering on St. Patrick's role in Armagh. *The Armagh Story* is a walk-through display and audio-visual presentation, in which pictures and characters from the past tell you the fascinating history of the town. A smaller, less well-done display recreates Swift's "Land of Lilliput." (Open Mon.-Sat. 10am-7pm; Oct.-March Mon.-Sat. 10am-5pm, Sun. 2-5pm. £3, students £2.25.)

The **tourist office** is in the Old Bank Building at 40 English St. (Tel. 527808; open daily 9am-6:30pm; Oct.-March 9am-5pm.) The **telephone code** is 01861. **Buses** stop at Mallview Terrace (Mall West) (tel. 522266).and run to Belfast (18/day, Sun. 9/day; 70 min.; £4) and Enniskillen (Mon.-Sat. 1/day; 2hr.; £4.70). Armagh has few B&Bs, but they are seldom full. At **Padua Guest House,** 63 Cathedral Rd. (tel. 522039), just past the Cathedral (#63 is next door to #10), kind Mrs. O'Hagen and her large doll collection will greet you with a cup of tea. Some rooms have color TVs (£12/person). For **Clonhugh Guest House,** College Hill (tel. 522693), walk north from the tip of the Mall. Mrs. McKenna's house is so full of bric-a-brac that you may not be able to sit, but her bedrooms are very comfortable. (Singles £13. Doubles £25, with bath £30.) Camp at **Gosford Forest Park,** off the A28, 7 mi. southeast of Armagh. The forest around includes a castle, old walled garden, poultry sheds, and miles of nature trails. The Market Hill bus will drop you within walking distance of the park (two-person tent £6.50; Oct.-Easter £4).

What little Armagh has for restaurants scatters across English St. and Scotch St. Your best bet may be to pick up supplies at **Emerson's,** 57 Scotch St., and have a picnic on the Mall or near the old Friary. Sleek **Fat Sam's,** The Shambles (tel. 525555), offers a dazzling variety of sandwiches (curried chicken with pineapple and sweet corn £1.50; open Mon.-Fri. 8:45am-6pm, Sat. 9:25am-5pm).

■ NEAR ARMAGH

Just on the outskirts of Armagh lies **Navan Fort,** one of the most important archaeological sites known to historians of Iron Age Ireland. The **Navan Center** (tel. (01861) 525550), built deep into the hill, presents a 70-minute program of films and interactive exhibits on the legends associated with the site, as well as the archaeological evidence of the hills' powerful and violent history. The center and fort are located on the Killylea Rd. (the A28), 2 mi. west of town. (Center open Mon.-Sat. 10am-6pm, Sun. 11am-6pm. £3.75, student £2.50; the fort is free and always open.)

ANTRIM & DERRY

Stomping grounds of the Ulaid dynasty for over a thousand years, the secluded Glens of Antrim cut snugly into the coast north of Belfast and Larne, a backpackers' dreamland staring squarely at Scotland. Farther west along the coast, the towns around the Giants' Causeway tempt holidaymakers away from one of the world's great natural wonders, the Causeway itself. Derry, the North's second city, screams its history from every cobblestone.

LARNE

The **ferries** to Scotland are the only imaginable reason for a trip to Larne; now that the Hoverspeed Seacat goes directly to Belfast, few pedestrians will want to use the Larne ferry. Consult Essentials: Getting There—Between the Isles for detailed ferry information. **Trains** run between Belfast's Yorkgate Station and Larne Harbor (Belfast office tel. (01232) 741700, Larne office tel. (01574) 270517; Mon.-Fri. 22/day, Sat. 17/day, Sun. 7/day; 50min.; £2.75). **Buses** leave frequently from Larne (tel. (01574) 272345) for Belfast's Oxford St. Station (Mon.-Sat. 17/day, Sun. 3/day; 50-min. express or 1½-hr. normal; £2.30). Be sure your train or bus terminates in Larne Harbor, not a 15-minute walk away in Larne Town (the next to last stop). Contact the **tourist office,** Gauge Rd. (tel. (01574) 260088; open Mon.-Sat. 9am-5pm; July-Sept. Mon-Wed. 9am-5pm, Thurs.-Fri. 9am-7:30pm, Sat. 9am-6pm), for help in finding a bed. **Halifax Bank** (tel. (01574) 270214), on the corner of Broadway and Main St., has an **ATM** (Plus, Visa. Bank open Mon.-Fri. 9am-5pm, Sat. 9am-noon.)

You wouldn't want to get stuck in Larne, but if you're too weary to travel there is certainly no shortage of space. The most convenient B&Bs to both the harbor and the bus and train stations lie along Curran Rd. From the harbor, take your first right after the ferry port, follow the road right over the bridge, and it will turn into Curran. **Mrs. McKane** (tel. (01574) 274943), offers TVs and hotpots in her rooms at 52 Bay Rd., just off Curran Rd., near the harbor. (Singles £13. Doubles £24, with bath £30.) **Moneydara,** 149 Curran Rd. (tel. (01574) 272912), offers B&B with a sea view near the harbor. (Singles £14. Doubles £26.) **The Curran Caravan Park,** 131 Curran Rd. (tel. (01574) 273797 or 260088), between the harbor and town, has lawn bowling and putting greens. The **Ballygally Hostel (YHANI/HI)** is close to Larne (see Glens of Antrim, below).

In the center of town, **Stewart's Supermarket,** on Broadway, has an ample selection of food. (Open Mon.-Tues. and Sat. 9am-5:30pm, Wed.-Fri. 9am-9pm.) Main St. is lined with coffeeshops and bakeries. The lunch menu at **Carriages,** 105 Main St. (tel. (01574) 275132), is affordable, unlike its dinner menu. They serve cheap pizza all day, though. (Seafood flan with salad £3. Open daily noon-11pm.)

■■■ GLENS OF ANTRIM

North of Larne, nine lush green valleys, or "glens," lead from the hills and high moors of Co. Antrim down to the seashore. The thing is, there's nothing to "see" in these towns; people just love touring the Glens, either because of the natural beauty or the relentless self-promotion by the Glens of Antrim P.R. machine. The A2 connects the small towns at the foot of each glen—it's a pretty ride along the rocky shore, but no match for the Causeway Coast farther north. The area's two hostels are luckily located in its happiest towns, Ballygally and Cushendall.

Bus service through the Glens is scant at best. Two lines serve the area: the #162 service from Belfast, stopping in Larne, Ballygally, Glenarm, and Carnlough (Mon.-Fri. 10/day, Sat. 8/day, Sun. 2/day), which sometimes continues to Waterfoot, Cushendall, and Cushendun (Mon.-Fri. 4/day, Sat. 3/day), and the summertime Antrim Coaster, which follows the coast road from Belfast to Coleraine (June-Sept. Mon.-Sat. 2/day). Hitchers report that drivers are scarce but receptive along these lovely beach- and cliff-lined roads. **Cycling** is fabulous. The coast road from Ballygally to

Cushendall is both scenic and flat—though the wind can be vicious. North of Cushendall the road divides. The coastal route passes the spectacular views of Torr Head, but its hills are notorious. The inland route, through Ballypatrick Forest, is more manageable, although still far from flat. You can rent a bike at the Ballygally, Cushendall, or Whitepark Bay YHANI/HI hostels, and drop it off at another (£6/day, £5/additional day, £30/week, deposit £30; drop-off charge £5, pannier bags £5).

BALLYGALLY

The tiny village stretches along the water's edge with a wide sandy beach before and welcoming walking hills behind. Well-preserved **Ballygally Castle,** built in 1625, dominates the strip; it's now a hotel. The **phone code** is 01574. Both the Larne-Cushendall and Antrim Coaster buses stop right outside the **Ballygally Youth Hostel (YHANI/HI)** (tel. (01574) 583377). Five mi. north of Larne along the A2 coastal road, 6 mi. south of Glenarm, the hostel sits high on a hill with a panoramic ocean view. The friendly, mellow atmosphere is perhaps induced by the good Irish breakfast (£1.50). Bike rental is available (see above). (Check-out time negotiable. £6, under 18 £5. Open March-Dec.) Fifty yd. up the road, the same spectacular view and B&B can be had at **Té an Téasa,** 4 Coastguard Cottages, Coast Rd. (tel. (01574) 583591), a bright modern house with a funky staircase (£12). Also along the coast road, but nearer to Larne, the **Carnfunnock Country Park** (tel. (01574) 276255) provides **campsites** (£5) and a walled garden.

WATERFOOT & GLENARIFF

Farther up the coast, the village of Waterfoot guards Antrim's broadest glen, Glenariff, sometimes called the most beautiful of the nine. Four mi. down the road from the village, at **Glenariff Forest Park,** waterfalls feed the **River Glenariff** among lovely tree-shaded hills. Thackeray called Glenariff "Switzerland in miniature," presumably meaning that it was steep and pretty, since secretive banks and trilingual skiers are not in evidence. Glenariff's **coastal caves** are also worth exploring; they're on the way to the Red Bay pier from town. Catholics held an exceptionally uncomfortable CCD in the School Cave; Catholic education was illegal under the Penal Laws, so Glenariff youth recited their Baltimore Catechism under dripping stalactites. If you don't want to camp at **Glenariff Forest Park Camping,** 98 Glenariff Rd. (tel. (0126673) 232; tents £4.50), find one of the many farmers in the area who welcome campers (ask in town), stay in Waterfoot itself, or settle just up the road in Cushendall. At **Glen Vista,** 245 Garcon Rd. (tel. (012667) 71439), near the beach at the foot of the glen after the caravan park, bright, clean rooms overlook the sea (£12/person; open June-Oct.).

CUSHENDALL

Considered the capital of the Glens region, **Cushendall,** 2 mi. north of Waterfoot, is a nicely unpretentious town, with no arcades, no neon, happening pubs, and a lucky location: moors, hills, and the rough seashore make a paintable triangle with the town at its center. The sandstone **Curfew Tower** stands on the corner of Mill St. in the center of town. Built in 1825, the tower was used to confine the rowdy after a riot; today it is privately owned and shut to the public. **Lurigethan Hill** soars above town, remarkable for its flattened top. Cushendall's tiny **tourist office,** in a trailer on Mill St., next to the library, will surprise you with a wealth of information (tel. (012667) 71180; open Tues.-Sat. 10am-1pm). The **Ardclinis Activity Center,** 11 High St. (tel. (01266) 71340), rents **bikes** (£10/day; no deposit).

The **Cushendall Youth Hostel (YHANI/HI),** Layde Rd. (tel. (01266) 71344), is 1 mi. from town; head down Shore St., take the left fork as you leave town, and watch for the "YHA" on the wall. The hostel's recent architectural tune-up left it with a phenomenal kitchen; would-be Julia Childs get separate cutting boards for meat, fish, dairy, and vegetables. (Lockout 10:30am-5pm, curfew 11:30pm. Members £6, under 18 £5. Bike rental. Open March-Dec.) It would be hard to imagine a warmer welcome than the one you'll receive from Mrs. O'Neill's **Glendale,** 46 Coast Rd.

(tel. (01266) 71495). Bathtub! (£13/person, £15/person with bath.) Campsites include the **Cushendall Caravan Park,** adjacent to Red Bay Boatyard, 62 Coast Rd. (tel. (01266) 71699; summer £7.25/tent, winter £4.40/tent).

Spar supermarket, Bridge St., is open 365 days a year (366 every fourth year; 8am-10pm). After a long day of walking, rest your feet at **Joe McCollam's** (tel. (01266) 71330), a.k.a. "Johnny Joe's," a tiny, ancient barroom at 23 Mill St. Their lively traditional nights, held every summer Thursday, Saturday, and Sunday, feature impromptu singing, fiddling, yarn-spinning, and drinking until 11pm.

CUSHENDUN

Five mi. north of Cushendall on the A2, the tiny picturesque seaside village of Cushendun was bought in its entirety by the National Trust in 1954, just like Willy Wonka did with the Oompa-Loompas. Since then, Big Brother has maintained the town's "olde," quaint, squeaky-clean image. With a vast sandy beach and a set of **sea caves,** the scarily perfect village makes a terrific afternoon stopover. The caves, which were hollowed out of the stone cliffs by a sea which was much higher than it is now, are located just past the Bay Hotel. The largest cave provides the only entrance to **Cave House,** built in 1820 and currently occupied by a religious order. On the grassy slope just behind the hotel, a steep path leads to the cliff top.

The **National Trust** (tel. (0126674) 506) maintains an office at 1 Main St., with displays on the history of the village and the sea caves (open daily 1-5pm; Sept.-June Sat.-Sun. 1-5pm). You can sip tea downstairs from the office in an inexpensive (burgers 80p, sandwiches £1.15) **tea room.** (Open Mon. 12:30-7pm, Tues.-Sat. 11am-7pm, Sun. 11am-8pm.) **The Villa,** 185 Torr Rd. (tel. (0126674) 252), has a great B&B 1 mi. from town, in a 19th-century farmhouse on a particularly scenic portion of the Ulster Way hiking trail (£15/person). Or camp at the **Cushendun Caravan Site,** 14 Glendun Rd. (tel. (0126674) 254), for £4/tent. (TV/game room, laundry: £1 wash, 50p dry; open March-Sept.) **The Bay Hotel,** on the Waterfront, has folk music in the bar on Saturdays. **Buses** stop at Cushendun's one shop on their way to Waterfoot (Mon.-Sat. 9/day, Sun. 1/day) or Ballycastle (Mon.-Sat. 2/day).

■■■ CAUSEWAY COAST

After Cushendun, the Northern coast shifts from the lyrical into the dramatic: cliffs dangle blades of grass 600 ft. over fine white sandy beaches. The Giant's Causeway, which names the region, is a honeycomb of black and red hexagonal columns, science-fictiony rock formations extending off the coast in the direction of Scotland.

The A2 connects the main towns along the Causeway; the road is a beautiful cycle or drive. Ulsterbus #172 runs between Ballycastle and Portrush along the coast, with frequent connections to Portstewart. (Mon.-Fri. 7/day, Sat. 6/day; 1hr.) In good weather during July and August, the open-topped **Bushmills Bus** follows the coast between Coleraine (5 mi. south of Portrush) and the Giant's Causeway (4/day, Sun. 2/day). Call the Coleraine bus station (tel. (01265) 43332) for info about this service. The summertime **Antrim Coaster** bus runs all the way up the coast from Belfast to Portstewart (June-Sept. Mon.-Sat. 2/day). Those **hitching** along the A2 or the inland roads (marginally quicker) find the lack of cars makes for slow going.

RATHLIN ISLAND & BALLYCASTLE

Just off the coast at Ballycastle, boomerang-shaped Rathlin Island is the ultimate in escapism for 20,000 puffins, the odd golden eagle, and about 100 human beings. Its mostly-treeless surface is edged with 200-ft. cliffs. With good bird-watching, great views, and quiet walks, Rathlin is ideal for a peaceful, relaxing day trip. The information packet on the island, available at the Ballycastle tourist office (£1), describes several walks and the major sights. While Rathlin is beautiful on a nice day, be warned that there is absolutely nothing to do in bad weather. Everything works on "island time," opening and closing without a real schedule or notice.

The island town has one pub, two stores, and one café, all within 300 yds. of the dock; it had no electricity until September 1992. **Mrs. McCurdy,** The Quay (tel. (012657) 63917), offers B&B for £12; (open March-Dec.). The **Rathlin Dive/Holiday Center,** the Harbor (tel. (012657) 63915), brings divers to the island. If there's extra space in their bunkroom, they may let you stay for £10 (B&B £12). A **mini-bus** sometimes runs from the ferry to the **bird sanctuary** at the tip of the island (£1)— take the bus out and walk the 4 mi. back. To arrange a **guided tour** of the island, call Kathryn McFaul or Noel McCurdy (both: tel. (012657) 63939); they'll both cater their tours to your interests, be they bird-watching or local history. Two **ferries, Rathlin Venture** and **Iona Islay** (tel. (012657) 63901), run to the island daily from the pier at Ballycastle at 10:30am, returning from Rathlin at 4pm. The ferries can leave early or late; passengers should be at the dock a few minutes ahead to avoid being marooned. In the summer, a second sailing sometimes leaves Ballycastle at 12:15pm, returning at 6pm. (Single £3.30. Day return £5.40.)

In **Ballycastle,** the ferry port for Rathlin, the **tourist office,** 7 Mary St. (tel. 62024), has 24-hr. computerized information. (Open Mon.-Fri. 9:30am-7pm, Sat. 10am-6pm, Sun. 2-6pm; Sept.-May Mon.-Fri. 9:30am-5pm, Sat. 10am-4pm.) **Buses** stop at the Diamond and go to Cushendall (Mon.-Sat., 3/day; 40min.; £2); Portrush (Mon.-Sat. 7/day; 1hr.; £2.70); and Belfast (Mon.-Sat. 6/day, Sun. 4/day; 3hr.; £.4.60).

BALLINTOY & CARRICK-A-REDE ISLAND

Five mi. west of Ballycastle is the village of Ballintoy, with a picturesque church and a tiny harbor. **Carrick-a-rede Island** lies just off shore to the east of Ballintoy. Carrick-a-rede means "rock in the road," a reference to the fact that the island presents a barrier to migrating salmon returning to their home rivers. At the point where the fish have to go around the island, local fishermen have been setting up their nets for 350 years. To reach the nets, the fishermen string a rope bridge between the main road and the island. Crossing the flimsy bridge over the dizzying 80-ft. drop to rocks and sea below is now a popular activity for tourists. To find the rope bridge, take the signposted turnoff from the coast road about 1 mi. east of Ballintoy.

On the island, you can get close to cliff-nesting razor bills (which look like minipenguins) as well as more mundane gulls. A fishing hut occupies the east side of the island—offshore, salmon nets stretch out into the sea. The **National Trust Information Center** (tel. (012457) 62178) here has information on the island and surrounding area. For 50p, they'll give you a certificate stating that you successfully crossed the bridge (open Easter-June Sat.-Sun. 10am-6pm; July-early Sept. daily 10am-6pm). From the car park, a beautiful ¾ mi. walk leads to the rope bridge. (Open April-Sept.) **Camping** on the National Trust property is free with permission (tel. (012457) 62178 or 31159) for one night only. (Tent must be down by 10am.)

GIANT'S CAUSEWAY

Advertised as the eighth natural wonder of the world, the Giant's Causeway is deservedly Northern Ireland's most famous sight. It is neither overcrowded nor disappointing. Forty thousand hexagonal columns of basalt form a honeycomb path from the foot of the cliffs into the sea. Geologists have found that the Causeway is the result of unusually-even cooling of lava, which let it crystallize; Irish legend holds that Finn McCool, the warrior giant, fell in love with a female giant on Staffa Island, off the Scottish coast and built the Causeway to bring her across to Ulster— hence the similarly beehive-esque rock formations on Staffa.

Many paths loop to and from the Giant's Causeway. **The Causeway Visitors Center** (tel. (012657) 31582), near its head, has an excellent trail leaflet (40p) that will guide you the 8 mi. back to Whitepark Bay or along several shorter circular walks. They also run minibuses the ½ mi. to the columns every 15 minutes. (Center open July-Aug. daily 10am-7pm; Sept.-Oct. 10:30am-6pm; mid-March to May 11am-5pm. Causeway always open.) To really "see" the Causeway, you should go at least as far as the viewpoint at **Hamilton's Seat,** 2½ mi. from the visitors center.

Two mi. west of Ballintoy, just around the point from the harbor, lie the golden sands of **Whitepark Bay,** owned by the National Trust. Overlooking this stunning beach is the well-kept, cement-walled **YHANI Youth Hostel (HI)** (tel. (012567) 31745). Dorms, 2-, 4-, and 6-bed rooms with baths and a laid-back atmosphere. If you're biking or hiking between Whitepark Bay and Ma Cool's Hostel in Portrush, the wardens will transport your pack for you. (Lockers 50p/day, laundry £2 wash and dry. £6, non-members £7.50.) Three buses per day from Portrush via the Giant's Causeway and five per day from Ballycastle stop in front of the hostel on request. Every morning, hostelers set out for the Giant's Causeway, some hitch north the 4 mi. north along the A2 or trek a rocky, sweaty 8 mi. along the windswept but stunning **North Antrim Coastal Path** (be sure to take warm clothing).

■■■ DERRY CITY

Derry's long and troubled history has given rise to powerful symbols used by both sides of the sectarian conflict. The famous siege of Derry in 1689 created Protestant folk heroes in the form of the "Apprentice Boys," who closed the city gates in the face of the advancing armies of the Catholic King James II. More recently, the violence of the early 70s included the infamous "Bloody Sunday" (Jan. 30, 1972, when British troops fired on demonstrators, killing 14 of them). Even the city's name has strong political symbolism: the Northern and British governments call it, officially, "Londonderry," as do many Northern Protestants. Catholics, and the Catholic-majority City Council, call the city "Derry." The shorter name is less politically charged (it's used in speech by many Protestants) and is what visitors should call the place.

ORIENTATION & PRACTICAL INFORMATION

Inside the old city, four main streets connect the four main gates (Bishop's Gate, Ferryquay Gate, Shipquay Gate, and Butcher's Gate) to the central square called **The Diamond. The Bogside** is the neighborhood just west of the walls. The Protestant **Waterside** neighborhood, with the train station, reclines across Craigavon Bridge, on the east side of the River Foyle.

Tourist Office: 8 Bishop St. (tel. 267 84). Distributes the useful *Derry Visitors Guide* and free, hard-to-read maps. **Bord Fáilte** desk here, too (tel. 369501). Open Mon.-Sat. 9am-8pm, Sun. 10am-6pm; Oct.-June Mon.-Fri. 9am-5:15pm.

Budget Travel: USIT, Ferryquay St. (tel. 371888). ISICs, YHANI and HI cards, and Travelsave stamps. Open Mon.-Fri. 9:30am-5:30pm, Sat. 10am-1pm.

Banks: First Trust, Shipquay St. (tel. 363921), open Mon.-Fri. 9:30am-4pm; ATM. The **Richmond Center,** a shopping center next to The Diamond, has a *bureau de change* (open Mon.-Wed. 9am-5:30pm, Thurs.-Fri. 9am-9pm, Sat. 9am-6pm).

Post Office: 3 Custom House St. (tel. 362274). Open Mon. 8:30am-5:30pm, Tues.-Fri. 9am-5:30pm, Sat. 9am-12:30pm. Unless marked "3 Custom House St.," *poste restante* will go to the **Postal Sorting Office** (tel. 362577) on the corner of Great James and Little James Streets. **Postal code:** BT4 86TT.

Telephone code: 01504.

Trains: Station on the east bank of the river, at The Waterside off Duke St. Trains from Derry only go east, to Belfast via Antrim Town (Mon.-Sat. 8/day, Sun. 6/day; to Belfast 2½hr.; £7). No rail lines connect Derry to Sligo, Enniskillen, or Dublin.

Buses: Buses leave from the Foyle St. Station, between the walled city and the river. **Ulsterbus** (tel. 262261) serves all destinations in Northern Ireland: Belfast (Mon.-Sat. 17/day, Sun. 7/day; 1½-3hr.; £5.50); Enniskillen (Mon.-Fri. 5/day, Sat. 3/day, Sun. 1/day; 2½hr.; £5); Dublin (Mon.-Fri. 3/day, Sat.-Sun. 2/day); Galway (Mon.-Sat. 4/day, Sat.-Sun. 2/day; 5½hr.); Letterkenny (Mon.-Sat. 4/day, Sat.-Sun. 2/day; 40min.); Donegal Town (Mon.-Fri. 4/day, Sat.-Sun. 2/day; 1½hr.); and Sligo (Mon.-Sat. 4/day, Sat.-Sun. 2/day; 2½hr.). **Lough Swilly** private bus service (tel. 262 017) heads north to Inishowen and south to Letterkenny and the Fanad Peninsula. To Malin Head (Mon.-Sat. 3/day; 1½hr.; £6); Letterkenny (Mon.-Sat. 11/day, Sun. 8/day; 1hr.); Buncrana (Mon.-Sat. 11/day, Sun. 8/day; 35min.).

DERRY CITY

Taxi: Quick Cabs, 1 Guildhall St. (tel. 260515). **Tower Taxis,** Bishop St. (tel. 371944). Derry also has a system of **black cabs** with set routes, though it's neither as extensive nor as famous as the Belfast black cab system.

Bike Rental: Rent-A-Bike, Magazine St. (tel. 372273), at the YHANI hostel. Cross-country and mountain bikes. £6/day, £5/additional day, £30/week; £30 deposit. £5 fee to drop off the bike at another Rent-A-Bike location.

Laundry: Duds 'n' Suds, 141 Strand Rd. (tel. 266006). Play pool while you wait for clothes to wash. Wash £1.50, dry £1.50. Open Mon.-Fri. 8am-9pm, Sat. 8am-8pm.

Women's Center: 24 Pump St. (tel 267672). Open Mon.-Fri. 9:30am-5pm.

Bisexual, Gay, and Lesbian Information: Carafriend Counselling (tel. 263120). Open Tues. 8-10pm and Thurs. 7:30-10pm.

Hotline: Samaritans, 16 Clarendon St. (tel 265511). Open 10am-8pm.

Hospital: Altnagelvin Hospital, Glenshane Rd. (tel. 45171).

Emergency: dial 999; no coins required. **Police:** Strand Rd. (tel 367337).

ACCOMMODATIONS

Let's Go does not recommend the **Independent Hostel** on Strand Rd.

Oakgrove Manor (YHANI/HI), Magazine St. (tel. 372273). Colorful mural on the side of the building. Modern, spacious, and very institutional. Central location inside city walls. Not always well-supervised. Curfew 2am, strict checkout 10am. Scantily-equipped kitchen. Sheets 50p. Towels 50p. Pool table 20p. Ulster fry £2.50, continental breakfast £1.50. Dorm £6, with shower £7.

Muff Hostel, Muff, Co. Donegal, Republic of Ireland (from the North, tel. (0035377) 84188). Just 5 mi. outside of Derry; relaxed, homey country accommodation, easy access to the busy city. Lough Swilly buses leave Foyle St., Derry for Muff (17/day, last bus 6:50pm; 60p, 75p return). £5/person.

Magee College, Northland Rd. (tel. 265621, ext. 5233). Dorms. Free showers, kitchens, and laundry available during Easter week, and again mid-May to Sept. Mandatory reservations Mon.-Fri. 9am-5pm. Arrive during office hours. Singles £6. Doubles £10. Take the Ballygoarty or Rosemont bus from Foyle St., or walk ½ mi. up Strand Rd. and turn left after the Strand Bar.

YMCA, 51 Glenshane Rd. (tel. 301662), 3 mi. from the city center. Coed. Old house with clean, stark bedrooms. Curfew 10:30pm. From Foyle St. take the Tullyalley bus down Glenshane Rd. £5. Singles £8.50. Open mid-July to mid-Sept.

Florence House, 16 North Land Rd. (tel. 268093). Large, sunny bedrooms in a townhouse around the corner from the university. £13.

Joan Pyne, 36 Great James St. (tel. 269691). B&B in small flowery rooms, just minutes from popular Bogside pubs. £14.

FOOD

Wellsworth **supermarket,** Waterloo Pl. (open Mon.-Tues. and Sat. 9am-5:30pm, Wed.-Fri. 9am-9pm), is around the corner from the post office.

Freddy's Bistro, Castle St. (tel. 373222), around the corner from the hostel. Funky atmosphere, lots of veggie options. Indonesian meatballs with yogurt and rice £5, veggie stir-fry £3. BYOW. Open Mon.-Sat. 11am-10pm, plus summer Sun. 1-8pm.

The Sandwich Co., The Diamond (tel. 372500), corner of Ferryquay St. and Bishop St. Made-to-order sandwiches (95p-£2.45). Live folk music summer Fri. at 4pm. Open Mon.-Thurs. and Sat. 9am-5pm, Fri. 9am-6pm.

Boston Tea Party, 13 Craft Village (tel. 264568). Open daily 9am-5:30pm.

Anne's Hot Bread Shop, William St. (tel. 269236), in the Bogside. A Derry institution; open late, late, late. Big portions, no frills. Open daily 8am-3am.

PUBS

Derry compensates for an iffy restaurant scene with a superb drinking scene: the city's pub crawl is lengthy and fun. Trad and rock music flare up most nights.

The Dungloe, 41-43 Waterloo St. (tel. 267716). Almost always has trad music, 10pm downstairs. Live blues or rock or "alternative" discos (£1-2) upstairs 11pm.
Peadar O'Donnell's, 63 Waterloo St. (tel. 372318). An old-style pub.
The Carraig Bar, 121 Strand Rd. (tel. 267541). Friendly students. Discos Wed.-Sat.
Doherty's, 10 Magazine St. (tel. 360177). Trad sessions Wed. 9pm, rock weekends.
Bound for Boston, Waterloo St. Busy, full of young people. Downstairs: Tues. trad sessions, some rock and blues. Upstairs: disco Sat.-Sun., bands Mon.-Fri.; £2 cover.
The River Inn and **Gluepot,** adjoining pubs on Shipquay (tel. 267463), occupy the site of "the oldest bar in Ireland."

SIGHTS

Harry Bryson's animated style and his love for the city he claims never to have left make for an entertaining (though far from impartial) **walking tour.** (Tour leaves from the tourist office Mon.-Fri. 10:30am and 2:30pm; 1½hr.; £1.50. Sept.-May call tel. 365151, ext. 307, to arrange a tour.)

Eighteen ft. high and 20 ft. thick, Derry's city walls were built between 1614 and 1619; they've never been breached or invaded, hence the nickname, "the Maiden City." Stuck in the center of the southwest wall, **Bishop's Gate** was remodeled in 1789 as a highly ornate triumphal gate in honor of King William III, the Protestant contestant in the battles of 1689. From almost anywhere in Derry you can see the tall spire of **St. Columb's Cathedral,** Bishop St. (tel. 262746). The interior is of roughly-hewn stone and contains a beautiful Killybegs altar carpet, a bishop's chair dating from 1630, and hand-carved oak pew ends—no two are the same. A tiny **chapterhouse** at the back of the church holds original locks and keys to the four main city gates, part of Macaulay's *History of England,* and relics from the 1689 siege. (Open Mon.-Sat. 9am-5pm. Cathedral free, chapterhouse entrance 50p. Call ahead to arrange a free tour.)

Just outside Shipquay Gate stands the neo-Gothic **Guildhall** (tel. 365151), home of the City Council. Built in 1890, destroyed by fire in 1908 and by bombs in 1972, today's structure copies the original stained glass. Windows in the main hall offer one version of the history of Derry. (Open Mon.-Fri. 9am-5pm; free tours July-Aug. 9:30am-4:30pm.) A more detailed history of Derry inhabits the award-winning **Tower Museum,** just inside Magazine Gate (tel. 372411). The museum takes, and is worth, at least an hour and a half to explore. (Open Tues.-Sat. 10am-1pm and 2-5pm; last entrances 12:30 and 4:30pm. £2.50, students £1.)

Brilliant **murals** in both Protestant and Catholic neighborhoods remind anyone who looks that Derry's passionate history is far from over. By day, the muralled areas are safer than most American cities. Remember not to photograph police, soldiers or military installations. The famously Protestant sections of Derry are the **Waterside,** on the east side of the River Foyle, and the **Fountain Estate,** west of the river. The best-known Catholic neighborhood, **The Bogside,** is easily recognized by the huge mural declaring "Welcome to Free Derry," just west of the city walls. Nearby, a stone monument commemorates the 14 protesters shot on Bloody Sunday. Most of the nearby murals are memorials to Bloody Sunday, which became a symbol of the British Army's behavior during the Troubles. To find them, go past the "Free Derry" sign and take the next right (at the Bogside Inn). "The Auld Days" (at the junction of William and Rossville St. in the Bogside, across from Pilot's Row Community Center) is one of several renditions of once-peaceful city life.

TYRONE & FERMANAGH

OMAGH

Omagh ("OME-ah"), situated between Derry and Enniskillen, will never be a Galway or a Dingle, but if you're in the area, there's reasons to stay. Five mi. north of Omagh on the Strabane Rd., the **Ulster American Folk Park** (tel. 243292) is a must for

Americans with Irish roots, but worth seeing even if your last name is Hobson. An indoor exhibition chronicles the history and experiences of the Ulster "Scotch-Irish" emigrant from the early 18th to late 19th centuries. Outside, a 19th-century rural village, including a schoolhouse, meetinghouse, and a working forge, has been moved to the site. More awesome, however, is the "Ship and Dockside Gallery" in which visitors can walk through a 100-ft. brig, investigating the cramped living quarters of the emigrants, while the sounds of creaking timbers, wind, waves, and seagulls make them seasick. To get to the park, stay straight on the Strabane Rd. for 5 mi., or take the Omagh-Strabane bus (Mon.-Fri. 10/day, Sat. 13/day, Sun. 5/day; 10 min.; £1, students 70p). (Park open Mon.-Sat. 11am-6:30pm, Sun. 11:30am-7pm; Oct.-Easter Mon.-Fri. 10:30am-5pm. £3, students £1.50. Wheelchair access.)

Less spectacular than the Folk Park but well worth seeing is the **Ulster History Park** (tel. (016626) 48188), 7 mi. out of town on the Gortin Rd. (The Omagh/Gortin bus stops right outside: Mon.-Fri. 6/day, Sat. 4/day; £1.15.) Full-scale reconstructions of neolithic huts, passage tombs, a round tower, crannog, and castle are just a few of the buildings to visit. An exhibition explains the history of Ulster (pre-Christian to the Plantations) for those not in the know. (Open Mon.-Fri. 11am-6pm, Sat. 11am-7pm, Sun. 1-7pm; Oct.-March Mon.-Fri. 11am-5pm. £2.50, students £1.50.)

Omagh's **tourist office** (tel. 247831) is in the center of Market St. (open Mon.-Fri. 9am-5pm; May-Sept. Mon.-Sat. 9am-5pm). Rent from **Conway Cycles,** 1 Old Market Pl. (tel. 246 195), down the alley across from the tourist office (£7/day, £30/week, £40 deposit; open Mon.-Sat. 9am-5:30pm). Omagh's **phone code** is 01662. **Ulsterbus** runs from the swanky station on Mountjoy Rd. (tel. 242711) to: Belfast (Mon.-Sat. 6/day, Sun. 3/day; 3hr.; £5); Derry (Mon.-Fri. 13/day, Sat. 7/day, Sun. 5/day; 1hr.; £3.80); Dublin (Mon.-Sat. 6-9/day, Sun. 5/day; 3hr.; £8.70, students £7.40); and Enniskillen (Mon.-Sat. 8/day, Sun. 1/day; 1hr.; £3.50, students £3). The station offers **luggage storage** for 50p/bag (open Mon.-Sat. 8:30am-6pm).

You'll forget you're on a budget at the **Glenhordial Hostel and Activity Center,** 9a Waterworks Rd. (tel. 241973). The brand-new building is triumphantly clean, with a **wok, hair dryers,** and other luxuries. From the bus station, walk up the B48 towards Gortin; veer right at the first fork (by the car showroom). Follow that road (and the hostel signs) for 2 mi. Call for pick-up; they'll get you at the bus station if they're home. (£6. Bike rental £7.50/day, laundry £1. Wheelchair access.)

■■■ FERMANAGH LAKE DISTRICT

Upper and Lower Lough Erne extend on either side of Enniskillen like the two blades of a propeller; they're the biggies in a lake district several times larger, and infinitely less trampled, than England's. Everything cool is within 20 mi. of Enniskillen, the county's only sizable town.

ENNISKILLEN

Busy Enniskillen (pop. 14,000) is the place to pick up information and equipment for touring the Fermanagh lakes, caves, and islands. There's none of the kind of tension here that exists in Belfast or Derry; you'll most likely forget you're in the North.

Practical Information The **Lakeland Visitors Center,** Shore Rd., across the street from the bus station (tel. (01365) 323110), is the best in Northern Ireland. (Open Mon.-Fri. 9am-5:30pm, Sat. 10am-6pm, Sun 11am-5pm; Oct.-May Mon.-Fri. 9am-5pm.) **Halifax Bank,** 20 High St. (tel. (01365) 327072; open Mon.-Fri. 9am-5pm, Sat. 9am-noon), has an ATM that accepts Plus and Visa. The **bus station,** Wellington Rd. (tel. (01365) 322633), across from the tourist office, is very swanky. (Open Mon.-Sat. 8:30am-5:30pm, Sun. 5:45-7:45pm. Bus service to Belfast (3/day; 2¼hr.; £5.50, students £4.70); Derry (5/day, Sun. 1/day; 3hr.; £5.20, £4.40); Dublin (2-5/day, Sun. 3/day; 3hr.; £9, £6); Sligo (Mon.-Sat. 1/day; 1hr.; £7.30, £3.80); and Galway (Mon.-Sat. 1/day; 5hr.; £12.40, £8.10).) **Bike and camping rental** happens at

Cycle Safari Holidays, 31 Chanterhill Park (tel. 323 597). Bikes £7/day. Trips to Marble Arch, Castle Archdale Country Park, and Lisnaskea (£7.50).)

Accommodations Backpackers are limited to a remote hostel, 11 mi. from town, or B&Bs which are almost always full in high season. Call ahead for a room or you'll be sleeping in the bus station (although it *is* a swanky bus station…). **Castle Archdale Youth Hostel (YHANI/HI)** (tel. (013656) 28118), is 1 mi. off the Kesh-Enniskillen Rd. Take the #7 Pettigo bus from the station and ask the driver to let you off at Lisharrick. Walk 1 mi. left down the Kesh-Enniskillen Rd., then look for a small church where you'll turn right into the park and walk 1 mi. Hitching along these roads is difficult. The hostel occupies one corner of a stately 19th-century home—the hostel is not in, or identical with, the castle. The small children can get noisy in the morning. (£6. Wash and dry £2.) At **Curraig Aonrai,** 19 Sligo Rd. (tel. 324889), Mrs. Mulhern doesn't think it's fair to charge her guests more than £10.50 a night for her aqua and pink rooms. Closest B&B to town center (5-min. walk). *Aqua* bathtub! **Abbeville,** 1 Willougby Ct. (tel. 327033), is a well marked, 10-minute walk down the Derrygonnelly Rd. Mrs. McMahon's flowery rooms are stocked with TVs and piles of tourist info. £14. *Pink* bathtub!

Food & Pubs Cozy nooks, wooden tables, candles in bottles, and red napkins reside in **Franco's,** Queen Elizabeth Rd. (tel. 324424; open daily noon-late). At the **Barbizon Café,** 5 East Bridge St. (tel. 354556), a totem pole and surreal paintings keep company with Enniskillen's falafel-chomping crowd. (Open Mon.-Sat. 8:30am-6pm.) **The Crowe's Nest,** High St. (tel. 325252), thinks that gas masks and swords are aids to digestion; they're in glass cases around the pub. Live music nightly in summer. (Lasagna and salad £3.50, all-day breakfast £3.70.)

Sights One-and-a-half mi. south of Enniskillen on the A4, **Castle Coole** (tel. (01365) 322690) rears up in neoclassical *hauteur*. The acres of landscaped grounds are covered by buttercups and wild daisies, and you feel like there should be unicorns grazing (or, at the very least, a Smurf). To get there, walk 10 minutes down the Dublin Rd., then turn left into the castle grounds; it's another 20 minutes to the castle itself. (45-min. tours every 15 min. Open April-Sept. Fri.-Wed. 2-6pm.) If you don't have time to explore the surrounding Lake district, Erne Tours Ltd. offer a 1¾-hr. **tour of upper Lough Erne,** including a half-hour stop at very cool Devenish Island (see below). Tours leave from the Round 'O' Jetty in Brook Park, two minutes down the Derrygonnelly Rd. (Tel. (01365) 322882. May-June Sun. 2:30pm. July-Aug. daily 10:30am, 2:15pm, and 4:15pm; plus Tues., Thurs., and Sun. 7:15pm. Sept. Tues., Sat., and Sun. 2:30pm. £3.50. "Humor" free.)

DEVENISH ISLAND

St. Molaise founded a monastic center here in the 6th century. Viking raids and Plantation reforms finally put an end to monastic life by the 17th century; now **St. Molaise's House,** an old oratory, an 81-ft. round tower (all 12th century), and an Augustinian priory (15th century) are all that remain. The **round tower** is completely intact—you can even climb to the top. From Enniskillen, sail on the **M.V. Kestrel** for a half-hour stop on the island (that's all you really need since the ruins are close together). If you only want to see the island, the **Devenish Ferry** (tel. 322711 ext. 230) leaves from **Trory.** Ask the driver of the #7 Pettigo bus to let you off at Trory ferry stop, or take the Irvinestown Rd. out of Enniskillen 4 mi. to the sign for the ferry, after a gas station. (April-Sept. Tues.-Sat. 10am-7pm, Sun. 2-7pm. £2.25, includes ticket to small museum on island.) The trip takes about 10 minutes. Dress warm—the wind howls on the island.

ULSTER WAY

Serious hikers should consider tackling the Fermanagh stretch of the Ulster Way, 23 mi. of largely forested paths. The route is marked by wooden posts with a yellow

FERMANAGH LAKE DISTRICT

arrow and leads from Belcoo to Lough Navar. The path is neither smooth nor level, so those on bikes or in wheelbarrows should think again. The tourist office's *Ulster Way* pamphlet and Fermanagh's section of *The Ulster Way* (both £1.50) contain detailed descriptions of the route, sights, and history.

FLORENCE COURT & THE MARBLE ARCH CAVES

Ten mi. southwest of Enniskillen, both Florence Court and the Marble Arch Caves can be combined in a daytrip. To reach **Florence Court** (tel. (01365) 348249) take the Sligo Rd. out of Enniskillen and turn left onto the A32 Swanlinbar Rd. and follow the signs. It lies in **Florence Court Forest Park,** which includes an impressive walled garden. The *rococo* Court once housed the Earls of Enniskillen; the third Earl left behind his fossil collection. (Open June-Aug. daily 1-6pm; April-May and Sept. Sat.-Sun. 1-6pm. £2.40.) Four mi. along the road from Florence Court to Belcoo (take the Sligo bus to Belcoo and walk 3 mi., following the signposts; the indirect route makes this a fairly difficult hitch) are the **Marble Arch Caves** (tel. 348 855), a subterranean labyrinth of hidden rivers and weirdly sculpted limestone. Most of the caves are accessible only by boat, so the tour is half its usual length (and price) when the water level is high—after hard rains, for example. Call before you show up. (Open late March to Sept. daily 11am-4:30pm. £4, students £3.)

Ireland (Éire)

LIFE & TIMES

It can be hard to see Ireland through the mist of stereotypes. Yes, it rains a lot. Yes, it's green (for that reason). Yes, Irish people are friendlier than most, and yes, they drink more stout. But though much of the country is still rural and religious, there's also a developing urban culture with links to the European continent. Long hiking trails, roads, and cliff walks make a chain of windy, watery, spectacular scenery around the western coast from Clonakilty all the way up to Muff; go out of your way for the coastal vistas, by all means, but don't forget that people live here too.

It helps to know that Ireland is traditionally thought of in four **provinces: Leinster,** the east and southeast from north of Dublin to south of Wexford; **Munster,** the southwest; **Connacht,** the province west of the Shannon (except Co. Clare); and **Ulster,** six of whose nine provinces make up Northern Ireland, part of the U.K.

> For more comprehensive coverage of Ireland than can be provided here, please consult *Let's Go: Ireland,* available from discerning booksellers worldwide.

HISTORY & POLITICS

Roman armies who conquered England didn't think Ireland worth invading; the society they left alone lived in villages organized under chieftains, some of whom sometimes conquered Tara and proclaimed themselves "High Kings." A sequence of missionaries Christianized Ireland: the foremost was St. Patrick. As barbarians overran the Continent, monks fled to island safety; the monastic cities of the 7th and 8th centuries recorded the old epics and made illuminated gospels. Vikings raided, then settled at Limerick, Waterford, Wexford, and Dublin. The Battle of Clontarf (1014) set Leinstermen and Vikings against High King Brian Boru's Munster. A later High King claimant, Dermot MacMurrough, asked the Norman nobleman Richard Fitzgilbert de Clare ("Strongbow") to cross the sea and help him out; Strongbow arrived in 1169, which began the English hold over Ireland. The next 200 years saw the carving up of Ireland into feudal counties and baronies, some held by the Norman-descended "Old English," some by surviving Gaelic lords. An Anglophone parliament controlled the Pale, a fortified domain around Dublin.

When Henry VIII broke with the Pope, the Old English and the Gaelic lords stayed Catholic. Feudal warfare continued for centuries. Hugh O'Neill, an Ulster earl, raised a several-thousand-man army rebellion. In the late 1590s, the rebels were clobbered in the Battle of Kinsale (1601). O'Neill and his allies fled Ireland in 1607 (the "Flight of the Earls"); the English used their military advantage to take control of the land and parcel it out to Protestants; Scottish Presbyterians settled in Ulster. A Catholic revolt spread south from Ulster and established the Confederation of Kilkenny (1642), which fought and talked with King Charles' stranded envoy until Cromwell's infamous forces arrived. Anything his army didn't occupy it destroyed. Catholics were massacred; whole towns were razed. Native landowners could go "to hell or Connacht," the poorest province; by 1660, most of Ireland was owned and policed by imported Protestants.

After 1688 James II came to Ireland, intending to conquer first this island, then the other one. James and William fought each other up and down Ireland; Bill won, and the war ended, in the Treaty of Limerick, which ambiguously promised Catholics rights that were never delivered. Instead, the unenforceable Penal Laws (1695-1704) punished Catholics and virtually banned their religion. The newly-secure Anglo-Irish elite built their own culture in Dublin and the Pale, with garden parties

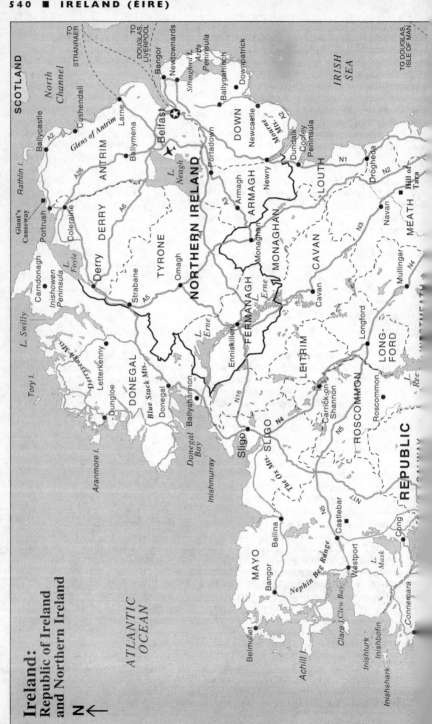

Ireland:
Republic of Ireland
and Northern Ireland

N ←

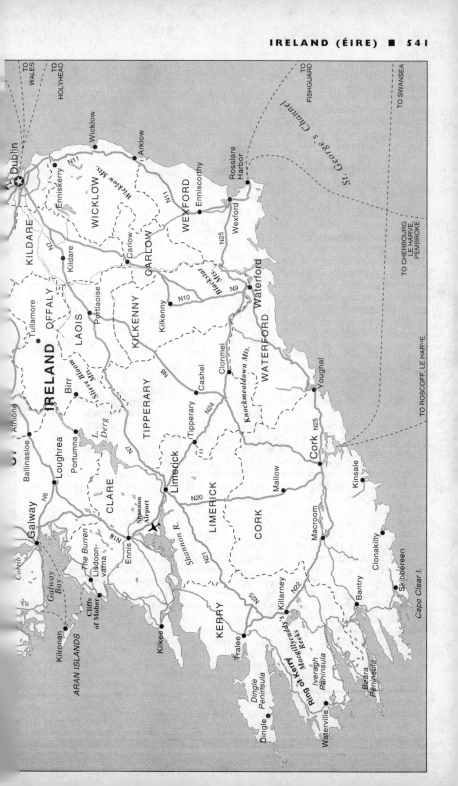

and architecture second only to London; it produced thinkers like Berkeley and Burke. Its smartest member was Jonathan Swift, Dean of St. Patrick's Church and a tireless pamphleteer on behalf of both the Protestant Church of Ireland and the rights of the Irish people. Catholics exercised their religion furtively, using hidden, big, flat rocks ("Mass Rocks") when altars were unavailable. Denied official education, Gaelic-Irish teens learned literature and religion in "hedge schools," hidden assemblies whose teachers were often fugitive priests. The Penal Laws didn't prevent the growth of a Catholic merchant class in places like Galway.

The French Revolution inspired independence rhetoric. The United Irishmen, who began as a debating society, reorganized themselves as secret soldiers. Their leader, Theobald Wolfe Tone, had hoped for a non-sectarian Ireland, but what erupted in May of 1798 was a bloody rising of peasants and priests. Vinegar Hill near Enniscorthy saw the rebels' celebrated last stand. A month later, French troops under General Humbert arrived in Co. Mayo. (French soldiers were held as prisoners of war; Irish soldiers were executed.) 1798's rebels spooked the British into abolishing Irish "self-government:" the 1801 Act of Union created "The United Kingdom of Great Britain and Ireland."

The gay, mad whirl of Dublin vanished. The new government peppered the coast with Martello towers to defend against French invasion. The dispirited Anglo-Irish gentry collapsed into an accretion of landlords as agrarian violence mushroomed. English and Continental travelers to Ireland were struck by its rural poverty. A barter economy prevailed among the poorer farmers; many lived entirely on potatoes. Union meant Ireland could send Members to the British parliament, and reforms of the 1820s gave Irish Catholic small farmers the vote. They voted for Daniel O'Connell, "The Liberator," whose election in 1829 forced the repeal of anti-Catholic laws and began a movement to repeal Union. A new disease that attacked potatoes caused the Famine (1847-51). Of Ireland's eight million people, one million starved, and another million emigrated, while many landlords did little to stop the suffering.

The next 50 years of British laws and programs and Irish agitation bought out or drove out the landlord class, creating Ireland's present demography of small farmers and urban middle classes. The Irish Republican Brotherhood ("Fenians") started in 1858, a secret society that aimed to expel the British by violence, soon. Fenian violence in 1867 made Gladstone notice Irish discontent; he tried for land reform, then for Home Rule, backed by the charismatic Irish leader, Charles Stewart Parnell. Parnell became a symbolic hero when published letters linking him to crimes turned out to be forged; he fell when his long affair with Kitty O'Shea became public in 1890, but Home Rule began to look likely, sooner or later, soon after that.

Many groups tried to revive "Gaelic" culture: the Gaelic Athletic Association tried to replace English sports, while Douglas Hyde's Gaelic League spread the use of the Irish language. Theorist James Connolly, along with James Larkin, founded the Irish Transport and General Workers' Union in 1910. Northern Protestants, moved by anti-Catholic bigotry as well as by loyalty to Great Britain, joined mass rallies, signed a Covenant, and organized into the quasi-military Ulster Volunteer Force to resist Home Rule; Nationalists followed in 1913 by creating the Irish Volunteers.

When Home Rule—scheduled for 1914—was put off by World War I, a cabal within the Volunteers began planning a revolution for 1916. When a shipment of German arms failed to arrive, the Volunteers' head called the whole thing off. But poet and schoolteacher Padraig Pearse and those around him wanted not military victory, but a "blood sacrifice" whose martyrs would inspire the Irish nation to rise up. Pearse, James Connolly, and others organized the Easter Rising, which held a few buildings in Dublin for a few days; the British then made the mistake of executing the captured leaders (one of whom was too wounded to walk), "revolting" the Irish public and turning opinion in favor of the martyrs.

Under Eamon de Valera and Michael Collins, the Sinn Fein party became the voice of militant nationalism; by 1919 they had created a separate government, the Dáil, and for the next two years they fought the Irish War of Independence against the British ex-soldiers and riffraff nicknamed the "Black and Tans" (on account of their patched-together uniforms). The Anglo-Irish Treaty (1921) created an "Irish Free State" with a few official links to Britain, and recognized the North as separate; Collins and the Dáil accepted it, de Valera and much of the Army didn't, and the result was the Irish Civil War (1922-24), in which Collins was assassinated.

W.T. Cosgrave, whose party became the present Fine Gael, headed the Free State until 1932 and brought much of the country electrical power. While the IRA and Sinn Fein shrank, de Valera founded Fianna Fail to oppose the Treaty while entering the Dáil. He dominated politics for the next 20 years; his 1937 Constitution is still in force. Ireland was neutral during World War II; some Irish supported the Nazis, but far more served in the British army. After the bombing of Belfast in 1941, Northerners cheered the arrival of Dublin's fire brigade. The country became a Republic in 1949; the last de Valera government, in the late '50s, and its successor under Sean Lemass, ditched protectionism in favor of foreign investment, a focus on economic policy that continued through the 60s (when much of the modern tourist industry was built). 1972 saw Ireland accepted into the EC and amendments to secularize the constitution.

Fianna Fail and Fine Gael are still the two main parties, competing as much on the basis of patronage and constituent services as on ideology; the current government allies Fianna Fail under Prime Minister Albert Reynold with the smaller, newer, liberal Labor Party under Dick Spring. Unemployment (around 20%) remains a problem, but more angst is given to social issues that pit Ireland's Catholic tradition against secular liberalism, and its young people who have spent time abroad against older voters who haven't. Contraception has been legal for over a decade, though you can only get it at licensed pharmacies. In 1983 voters endorsed, by almost 2:1, "the right to life of the unborn;" a 1986 referendum on divorce kept it illegal. Irish feminism is moving faster than its American cousins, but still has far to go; one boon was the surprise election in 1991 of activist Mary Robinson as President (in Ireland, the ceremonial head of state). In 1992, Ireland's High Court ruled that a 14-year-old (called "X" in court papers) who said she had been raped could not leave the country to obtain an abortion. In the referendum that followed, the Irish voted *for* the "right to information" on abortion elsewhere; *for* the "right to travel" outside Ireland for abortions; and *against* allowing abortions in Ireland to save the life of the pregnant woman. In 1993 the Irish gay rights movement achieved the repeal of laws against sex between men.

LANGUAGE

Irish is a Celtic language closely related to Scottish Gaelic and Manx and more distantly to Breton and Welsh. Irish is spoken exclusively in only a few isolated parts of Ireland, called *gaeltachts;* some prominent ones are on the Dingle Peninsula, on Cape Clear Island, in the Aran Islands, around Ring in Co. Waterford, in the Connemara in Co. Galway, and in patches of Co. Donegal. Even in the *gaeltacht,* everyone *can* speak English; they'd just rather not. (Only foreigners call the Irish language "Gaelic.") While long-term trends in most *gaeltachts* still point to depopulation and dispersal, the movement for more Irish-language media may help: there's already a Connemara-based Irish radio station. Schoolchildren in the Republic learn Irish the way most schoolchildren once learned Latin, which may or may not lead them to speak and read the language as adults. Among teens and twentysomethings, the language has gone from despised to somewhat trendy; you may hear younger English-speakers break into Irish briefly for privacy's sake. The Irish books everyone reads in Irish schools can be a relentlessly wistful, antiquated series of autobiographies, but the modern Irish-literature community produces dozens of novels, poetry collections, and critical essays every year. In Éire, all government documents must contain both Irish and English. Public signs sometimes show up in Irish only: "Fir" means "men," "Mna" means "women."

LEGENDS AND FOLKTALES

Scholars have been duking it out for decades over which of Ireland's legends, folk-tales, and epics record actual events, and which ones are just good yarns. The stories of the godlike **Túatha de Danann** may well have developed to explain the burial mounds left behind by a pre-Celtic Stone Age culture. The long, famous *Book of Invasions* claims to be a historical record of the cultures that have invaded Ireland, from Noah's descendents up to the Celts. The Ulster Cycle tells the adventures of king Conchobar of Ulster and his court. Ulster's champion is Cu Chulainn ("Coohullin"), who stars in the *Táin Bó Cuailnge* (Cattle Raid of Cooley), in which Queen Mebdh of Connacht decides to steal the presitigious Donn Bull of Cooley. She invades Ulster at the same time that all the warriors of Ulster are stricken with labor pains, as if they were pregnant women; only 17-year-old Cu Chulainn is immune. He fights the Queen's champions in single combat one by one, and beats them all, but the Connacht soldiers invade anyway and capture the Donn. The Ulstermen recover, invade Connacht, and recapture their bull, but both bulls die at the end.

Other cycles include *Tales of the Traditional Kings,* and the *Cycle of Finn, Ossian, and their Companions.* Finn McCool, or Fion Mac Cumaill, leads a group of heroes that includes his son, Ossian, and his grandson, Oscar. In some stories, he is more or less a mercenary; in others, he is a king or a giant with supernatural powers and saves Ireland from monsters. In the *Pursuit of Diarmuid and Grainne,* Finn chases the eloping pairs through most of Ireland. Even better known than Ireland's legends are its folktales, which literati (including W.B. Yeats) have compiled. Some stories involve the *sí* (or *sidhe;* Irish faeries), residents of the Other World underground or undersea; leprechauns are a late, degenerate version of the *sí,* who themselves are supposedly the disempowered remnants of the Túatha de Danann.

LITERATURE

In pre–Norman Ireland, poetry, storytelling, law, and politics were strands of one strong rope: bardic satirical verses could, it was thought, raze a house and destroy a clan, so bards were held in high repute. After 1600, Geoffrey Keating, Aogan Ó Rathaille, and many other poets lamented—in Irish—the coming collapse of Irish language and culture. English poet Edmund Spenser was stationed in Ireland during the last years of his life; some see "Irish" themes in his masterwork *The Faerie Queene* (1599). Jonathan Swift mixed moral indignation, bitterness, and wit. Besides *Gulliver's Travels,* Swift wrote political pamphlets like "A Modest Proposal," which satirically suggested that the overpopulated and hungry native Irish sell their children as food. Maria Edgworth (*Castle Rackrent*) wrote novels about the gentry and peasantry. Dublin-born Oscar Wilde moved to London to write one novel and several sparkling plays, including *The Importance of Being Earnest.*; prolific playwright George Bernard Shaw took on Irish problems in *John Bull's Other Island.* Shaw said "When I say I am an Irishman I mean that my language is the English of Swift and not the unspeakable drivel of the mid-XIX century newspapers." Nonetheless, his career was made in England.

The "Irish Literary Revival" began with attempts to set down and record peasant stories; a new elite would create a distinctively Irish literature in English. William Butler Yeats's early poems create a dreamily rural Ireland of loss, longing, and legend. J. M. Synge took Yeats's advice to go to the Aran Islands and write about what he saw there. The resulting plays, from *Riders to the Sea* to *Deirdre of the Sorrows,* combine a tragic intensity with an ear for English as it is spoken by people who grew up hearing Irish. His black comedy *The Playboy of the Western World,* with its unflattering depiction of the peasantry, caused riots; Sean O'Casey created a similar uproar with *The Plough and Stars.* The turbulence of 1914, 1916, and after enabled Yeats to recreate himself as a poet of difficulty, power, and violence; from *Responsibilities* (1914) to *Last Poems* (1939) Yeats rises to unparalleled intensity.

All this myth-centered, countryside-oriented writing was bound to produce an urban debunker; the one that arrived happened to be one of the century's greatest writers, James Joyce. *Dubliners* is his most accessible work. *A Portrait of the Artist as a Young Man* comes nearest to autobiography. *Ulysses* is Joyce's masterpiece, a hyperallusive, densely-woven novel that follows one day in the life of Dublin. Some people find Joyce's last book, *Finnegan's Wake*, unreadable: those who take the time to learn enough to make sense of it generally find it brilliant.

Post-Yeatsian poets followed Joyce, not Yeats, in describing the common life. Samuel Beckett conveyed a deathly pessimism about language and life in three novels and in world-famous plays like *Waiting for Godot* and *Endgame*. Flann O'Brien set himself up as the comic answer to Joyce; *At-Swim-Two-Birds* is a book-length prank, but *The Third Policeman* is a much deeper work, fragments of which became the hilarious *Dalkey Archive*. More recently Roddy Doyle wrote the novel that became the film *The Commitments*. Native playwrights include politically-conscious Frank McGuinness, and Brian Friel, whose *Dancing at Lughnasa* was a Broadway hit. Important critics include Conor Cruise O'Brien, Denis Donoghue, and Declan Kiberd.

Modern Irish-language literature is sometimes great, but rarely translated into English, for understandable ideological reasons; outside Ireland, translations exist of poems by Nuala ní Dhomhnaill, a first-rate living poet who brings refrigerators, feminism, and smart bombs into proximity with the *Sí*. The best living Irish poets in English were born in the North, so we've treated them under Northern Ireland.

MUSIC

Irish traditional music is alive and well. So is Irish folk music—"folk music" often means singing with acoustic guitar accompaniment, whether it's Irish (the Clancy Brothers, Christy Moore, Luka Bloom) or not. "Traditional music," on the other hand, means the centuries-old array of dance rhythms, cyclic melodies, and ways to ornament them which has passed down from generation to generation of traditional musicians. The same tune will produce a different result every session.

The most important instruments in Irish trad music are the *uílleann* pipes ("elbow pipes"), similar to bagpipes, but pumped with an underarm bellows; the fiddle; the simple flute; the concertina or handheld accordion; and the tin whistle. The *bodhrán,* a handheld drum, wasn't seen as legitimate until the 60s; it's not as easy as it looks to play one well. Sessions in pubs will sometimes alternate fast-paced traditional instrumental music with guitar- or mandolin-accompanied folk songs. Good trad musicians are more likely to congregate spontaneously in a pub than to book gigs in advance; we list many pubs with regular trad sessions. Cos. Clare, Kerry, Galway, and Sligo should be especially strong. **Comhaltas Ceoltóirí Éire-ann** ("Culturlann"), the national traditional music association, organizes *fleadhs*, big music fests; write 'em at Belgrave Sq., Monkstown, Co. Dublin (tel. (01) 280 0295).

In Ireland there is surprisingly little distinction between music types—rockers and "folk" songwriters often incorporate traditional elements. The inspiring and hugely popular Christy Moore has been called the Bob Dylan of Ireland; his songs form a pub-sing-along canon—hardly a late-night session goes by without "Ride On," "City of Chicago," or the *a cappella* lament "Irish Ways and Irish Laws." Other popular quality groups include Christy's old bands, Moving Hearts and Planxty. Van Morrison's inspirations included American soul and blues; submerging them into Celtic "soul," he managed to make them his own. The Saw Doctors and Lir live life on the edge of the rock/trad duality. Maybe the best hybridizers were the Pogues, London-based Irishmen whose famously drunken, punk-damaged folk songs won a deservedly wide audience.

The Boomtown Rats (fronted by future Live Aid guy Bob Geldof) tried to create Dublin punk. A bit later, so did U2: from the adrenaline-soaked promise of 1980's *Boy,* the band slowly ascended into the rock-star stratosphere, and it's possible to claim that their success, and everyone's wish to be the next U2, has actually hurt Ireland's rock music. The smartest Irish popsters of the '80s, like the Slowest Clock and the Stars of Heaven, went nowhere. Sinead O'Connor at least used reeling fiddles in one of her hits, "I Am Stretched on Your Grave." The rock press has christened Cork a hot spot: its flagship bands, like the Sultans of Ping F.C., are nothing new, but new fanzines and clubs in Cork, Dublin, and the Southeast may herald a more inventive era. You'll be surprised by the number of big, multi-stage festivals of both rock and traditional music.

PUBS & FOOD

The pub is in some sense the living room of the Irish household. Locals of all ages, from every social milieu, head to the public house for conversation, food, singing, and lively *craic* (CRACK), an Irish word meaning simply "a good time." Though the clientele is predominantly male, female travelers can feel comfortable here; people aren't normally looking for much other than communal talk and drink. You might have your ears talked off, however. Pubs in the Republic are generally open Monday to Saturday from 10:30am to 11:30pm (11pm in winter), and Sunday from 12:30 to 2pm and 4 to 11pm. Some pubs close on weekday afternoons as well, particularly in rural areas. Pub lunches are usually served from Monday to Saturday, 12:30 to 2:30pm; soup, soda bread, and sandwiches are served all day. Children are often banned from pubs after 7pm.

   Beer is the default drink; cocktails are an oddity. **Guinness** stout inspires a reverence otherwise reserved for the Holy Trinity. Known variously as "the dark stuff," "the blonde in the black skirt," or simply "I'll have a pint, please," it's a rich, dark brew with a head thick enough to stand a match in. It's also far better in Ireland than the Guinness you've had abroad. Stout takes a while to pour, so quit drumming the bar and be patient. **Murphy's** is a similar, slightly sweeter, stout brewed in Cork, as is **Beamish,** an equally tasty "economy" stout. **Smithwicks** ale (a hoppy, English-style bitter, pronounced "Smitticks") and **Harp** lager (made by Guinness) are both popular domestic brews. The many Irish young people who drink American beers are just being perverse. Beer is served in **pint glasses** (about 20 oz.) or half-pints; if you ask for a beer you'll get a full pint, so be loud and clear if you can only stay for a half. Or just take the pint and drink faster. A pint of Guinness will run you about £1.70-1.90.

   Irish whiskey is sweeter and more stinging than its Scotch counterpart; it's also served in larger measures. Dubliners are partial to **Powers,** Corkers drink **Paddy's. Jameson's** is popular everywhere. **Irish coffee** is sweetened with brown sugar and whipped cream and laced with whiskey—allegedly invented at Shannon Airport. **Hot whiskey** (spiced up with lemon, cloves, and brown sugar) can provide a cozy buzz, as will the Irish version of **eggnog** (brandy, beaten egg, milk, and lemonade). In the west, you may hear some locals praise "mountain dew," a euphemism for **poitín** ("poht-cheen"), Irish moonshine. Possession of *poitín* is a federal offense, and bad *poitín* can be very dangerous indeed.

   Food can be expensive, especially in restaurants. The basics are simple and filling. For a midday meal, pub grub (lunches around £4, sandwiches £1-1.50) is an economical choice. "Takeaway" (take-out) fish and chips shops are ubiquitous (£1-3 an order). Soda bread will keep for about a week and is delicious. Seafood can be quite a bargain in some of the smaller towns: smoked mackerel is splendid year-round, Atlantic salmon is freshest through July. Regional specialties are *crubeen* (tasty pigs' feet) in Cork, and *coddle* (boiled sausages and bacon with potatoes) in Dublin. Wexford strawberries and raspberries in the Southwest are luscious May through July.

■■■ DUBLIN

Say a good word about Dublin in the rest of Ireland and you're likely to hear that it's "not Ireland," at least not the "real" one of sheep and windswept isolation. Dubliners would retort that green Ireland is caught in the past, while grey Dublin embraces the fast-paced present. The city is a laboratory for social evolution, where international trends transform traditional Ireland into something bigger and brasher, but no less "real." The capital of Ireland since the end of the 17th century, the city has seen a blending of cultures which has produced an extraordinary intellectual and literary life. From Swift and Burke to Joyce and Beckett, Dublin has produced so many great

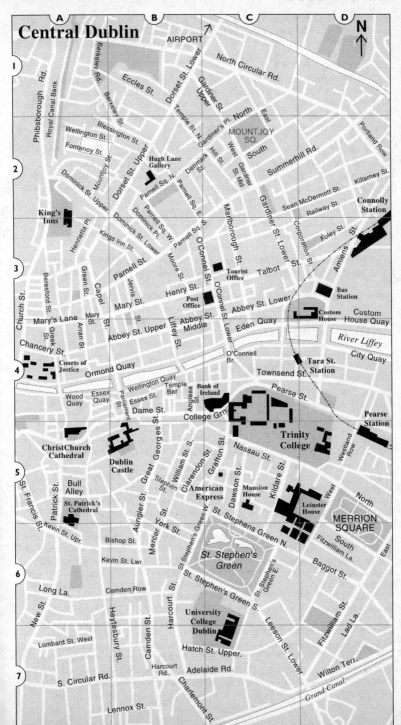

DUBLIN

writers that virtually every street is a literary landmark. There's a pub to suit every mood, and the music scene inside is world-renowned. While Bord Fáilte pushes the "Emerald Isle" image of Ireland, explore the thriving urban Ireland of today.

GETTING THERE

Rail lines, bus lines, and the national highway system radiate from Ireland's capital. Check in with USIT for a Travelsave stamp if you intend to take buses or trains. **Hitchhikers** into Dublin generally ask drivers to drop them off at one of the myriad bus and DART stops outside the city. Those who hitch from Dublin take a bus to the city outskirts, where the motorways begin.

By Train

Most inter-city trains arrive at **Heuston Station** (tel. 703 2132), just south of Victoria Quay, well west of the city center, and a long walk from anywhere. Take any Dublin Bus heading east into the city center—they pass by several times a minute. The other major rail terminus is **Connolly Station** (tel. 703 2358), centrally located on Amiens St. north of the Liffey, close to Busáras and half-a-dozen hostels and B&Bs. **Luggage storage** awaits you at Heuston and Connolly Stations (£1/item per day; at Heuston: Mon.-Sat. 7:15am-8:35pm, Sun. 8am-3pm and 5-9pm; at Connolly: Mon.-Sat. 7:40am-9:30pm, Sun. 9:15am-1pm and 5-10pm).

　　Irish Rail (a.k.a. Iarnród Éireann), 35 Lower Abbey St. (tel. 836 6222), spews data on its own InterCity services as well as DART, suburban trains, international train tickets, and ferries. (Open Mon.-Fri. 9am-5pm, Sat. 9am-1pm; phones open Mon.-Sat. 9am-6pm, Sun. 10am-6pm.) Trains run **from Connolly** to Belfast (Mon.-Sat. 8/day, Sun. 3/day; 2¼hr.; £13, student £7), Sligo (Mon.-Sat. 4/day, Sun. 3/day; 3¼hr.; £11, student £7), and Wexford/Rosslare (Mon.-Sat. 3/day, Sun 2/day; 3hr.; £10, student £7). Trains run **from Heuston** to Cork (Mon.-Sat. 4/day, Sun. 3/day; 3¼hr.; £31.50, student £12), Galway (Mon.-Sat. 4/day, Sun. 2/day; 3hr.; £11, student £8.50), Limerick (Mon.-Sat. 9/day, Sun. 6/day; 2¾hr.; £32.50, student £8.50), Tralee (Mon.-Sat. 3/day, Sun. 2/day; 4hr.; £33.50, student £10.50), and Waterford (Mon.-Sat. 4/day, Sun. 3/day; 2¾hr.; £10, student £7). A big advantage of train tickets over bus tickets is that the train will allow breaks in a journey: Dublin-Kildare-Kilkenny-Waterford is possible for the price of a Waterford ticket.

By Bus

Bus Éireann, the national bus company, runs throughout the Republic. Its inter-city buses to Dublin terminate at **Busáras Central Bus Station,** Store St. (tel. 836 6111), directly behind the Customs House, near lots of B&Bs and hostels, and next door to Connolly Station, from which the DART and suburban rail run to the suburbs. (**Luggage storage** open Mon.-Sat. 8am-7:45pm, Sun. 10am-5:45pm; £1.50/item, £2/rucksack/day.) Buses run from Busáras to: Belfast (4/day, Sun. 3/day; 3hr.; £9.50); Cork (4/day, Sun. 3/day; 4½hr.; £12, student £8.50); Derry (4/day, Sun. 2/day; 4½hr.; £10, student £8.80); Dingle (2/day, Sun. 1/day; 7hr.; £16, student £9.50); Donegal (4/day, Sun. 3/day; 4¼hr.; £10,student £8); Galway (8/day, Sun. 7/day; 4hr.; £9, student £6.50); Killarney (2-5/day, Sun. 3/day; 6hr.; £14, student £9); Limerick (8/day, Sun. 7/day; 3¼hr.; £10, student £7.50); Rosslare Harbor (5-7/day, Sun. 5-6/day; 3hr.; £9, student £6.50); Shannon Airport (4/day, Sun. 4/day; 4½hr.; £10, student £8); Sligo (3/day; 4hr.; £8, student £7); Tralee (5/day, Sun. 4/day; 6hr.; £14, student £9); Waterford (6/day; 2¾hr.; £7, student £6); Westport (3/day, Sun. 1/day; 5½hr.; £11, student £8.50); and Wexford (5-7/day, Sun. 5-6/day; 2¾hr.; £7, student £6).

From the Airport or Ferryport

From Dublin Airport (tel. 844 4900), catch Dublin bus #41, 41A, or 41C (every 20 min., £1.10) to Eden Quay in the city center. **B&I** ferries dock at the mouth of the River Liffey, just outside central Dublin; from there, buses #53 and 53A run by Alexandra Rd. and arrive near the Custom House (80p). **Stena-Sealink** ferries arrive in

Dún Laoghaire, where the DART shuttles weary passengers to Connolly Station, Pearse Station, or Tara St. in the city center for £1.20.

ORIENTATION

The **River Liffey** cuts central Dublin in half. Most of the best food and famous sights are on the **South Side,** though plenty of hostels (and the bus station) sprout up on the grittier **North Side.** Almost every street in Dublin changes its name every 1-3 blocks; ask directions often, and get a map with a street index. The streets running alongside both sides of the Liffey are called quays ("keys") and change their name every block; each bridge over the Liffey also has its own name, and all streets change names when they cross the river. When streets split up into "Upper" and "Lower" such-and-such street, "Lower" such-and-such is always closer to the mouth of the Liffey. The core of Dublin is circumscribed by North and South Circular Rd.; almost all the sights are located within this area, and you can walk from one end to the other in a half-hour.

PRACTICAL INFORMATION

Dublin Tourist Information: Main Office at 14 Upper O'Connell St. (tel. 284 4768). From Connolly Train Station, follow Talbot St. and continue straight along Earl St. North, a pedestrian zone. O'Connell St., a wide road with an island down the middle, is the next block. Make a right on O'Connell St.; the tourist office is on the right, past Cathedral St. From Busáras Central Bus Station, go up Corporation St. for 1 block, then head in the direction of the traffic on Talbot St. American Express branch office (tel. 878 6892) with currency exchange. Bus Éireann tickets and information. Open June Mon.-Sat. 8:30am-6pm; July-Aug. Mon.-Sat. 8:30am-8pm, Sun. 10:30am-2pm; Sept.-Feb. Mon.-Fri. 9am-5pm, Sat. 9am-3:30pm; March-May Mon.-Sat. 9am-5pm.

Branch Offices: At **Dublin Airport** (tel. 844 5387 or 844 5533; open daily 8am-10:30pm; mid-Sept. to mid-June 8am-10:30pm, Mon.-Sat 8am-6pm; May to June 8am-8pm), at **Dún Laoghaire Harbor,** St. Michael's Wharf (tel. 280 6984; open June-Sept. daily 8:30am-10pm; Sept.-May Mon.-Fri 9am-5pm, Sat. 9am-1pm), and at **Dublin Port,** B&I Terminal (open June-Aug. for ferry arrivals).

Temple Bar Information Center: 18 Eustace St. (tel. 671 5717). Info on the bippy Temple Bar neighborhood and better arts information than Dublin Tourist Office. Publishes free, useful, bimonthly *Temple Bar Guide*; you can also pick up free *Gay Community News.* (Open Mon.-Fri. 9am-7pm, Sat. 11am-7pm, Sun. noon-6pm; Oct.-May Mon.-Fri. 9:30am-6pm, Sat. noon-6pm.)

Budget Travel: USIT (Irish Student Travel Agency), 19-21 Aston Quay (tel. 679 8833), near O'Connell Bridge. *The* place to seek Irish travel discounts. ISIC and HI cards; Travelsave stamps £7. Big discounts for those under 26 on international travel and special events, plus myriad discount fares open to anyone. Open Mon.-Fri. 9am-6pm, Sat. 11am-4pm.

An Óige Head Office (Irish Youth Hostel Association/HI): 61 Mountjoy St. (tel. 830 4555), corner of Wellington St. Membership £7.50, under 18 £4. Book HI hostels here and pay at time of booking. Open Mon. 9am-6:30pm, Tues.-Fri. 9:30am-5:30pm; April-Sept. also Sat. 10am-12:30pm.

Financial Services: Best exchange rates are in banks. **AIB (Allied Irish Bank),** 10 Lower O'Connell St. (tel. 873 0555), ATM. Open Mon.-Wed. and Fri. 10am-4pm, Thurs. 10am-5pm.**TSB (Trustees' Savings Bank),** 12 Lower Abbey St. (tel. 878 6266). Open Mon.-Wed. and Fri. 9:30am-5pm, Thurs. 9:30am-7pm. *Bureau de change* also in the **General Post Office,** below, and tourist offices.

American Express: 116 Grafton St., Dublin 2 (tel. 677 2874; traveler's check refunds, tel. 1800 626 000), up the street from Trinity College gates. Mail pick-up, currency exchange (no commission for AmEx Traveler's Cheques). Open Mon.-Sat. 9am-5pm, also June-Sept. Sun. 11am-4pm. Also in the tourist office on O'Connell St. (tel. 878 6892).

Post Office: General Post Office (G.P.O.), O'Connell St. (tel. 705 7000), near the tourist office. Open Mon.-Sat. 8am-8pm. Big. **G.P.O. Postal Code:** Dublin 1 *(Poste Restante* pick-up at the *bureau de change* window; closes 15 min. early).

ACCOMMODATIONS

Telephone Code: 01.

Ferries: Bookings in Irish Rail office (below). For ferries to Dublin from England, Wales, and the Isle of Man, see Essentials: Getting There—Between the Isles.

Iarnród Éireann (Irish Rail): 35 Lower Abbey St. (tel. 836 6222). Info and bookings on trains and ferries; also holds a *bureau de change.* Open Mon.-Fri. 9:15am-5pm, Sat. 9:15am-12:45pm; phones open Mon.-Sat. 9am-6pm, Sun. 10am-6pm.

Taxi: Central Cabs (tel. 836 5555) and **City Group Taxi** (tel. 872 7272) have wheelchair-accessible taxis. (Free; request in advance.) Both run 24-hr. anywhere in Co. Dublin. Fares start at £1.80, 80p/mi., £1.20 call-in charge.

Car Rental: Practical Car and Van Rental, 19 Nassau St. (tel. 671 5540). Convenient location. £35/day, £154/week. Ages 25-70 can rent. 100 miles free. Open Mon.-Fri. 9:30am-6pm, Sat. 9:30am-12:30pm. **Argus,** 59 Terenure Rd. East, Dublin 6 (tel. 490 4444). Also in the tourist office on O'Connell St. Starting at £35/day, £185/week for age 26-64; special arrangements for drivers 23-26 or 64-70.

Bike Rental: Rent-A-Bike, 58 Lower Gardiner St. (tel. 872 5931 or 872 5399). Cross-country and mountain bikes, £6 for the 1st day, £5/day thereafter, £30/week, deposit £30. Panniers, helmets, and childseats £5/week. Bike repair. For £5 extra, you can return the bike to depots. Open Mon.-Sat. 9am-6pm. **RailBike,** Connolly Station (tel. 497 1911), affiliated with Irish Rail, £6/day, £32/week, helmets £5/week, pannier bags £5/week, £30 security deposit. Return the bike you rent here to RailBike depots in the main rail stations. **Raleigh Rent-a-Bike,** Kylemore Rd., Dublin 10 (tel. 626 1333). Most bikes must be returned to the dealer from whom they were rented. Limited one-way rental system (£42/week, credit card deposit). Return rental: £7/day, £30/week, £40 deposit.

Luggage Storage: In the central bus and train stations; see Getting There: By Bus.

Laundry: The Laundry Shop, 191 Parnell St. (tel. 872 3541). Closest launderette to Busáras and North Side hostels. Wash £1.90, dry £1, soap 50p. Open Mon.-Sat. 8:30am-6pm, Thurs. 8:30am-8pm. **Laundry Room,** 8 Kevin St. Lower (tel. 478 1774); continue west down St. Stephen's Green South. Closest launderette to Trinity College, Temple Bar, and South Side hostels. Wash £2, dry £1.50, soap 30p. Open Mon.-Sat. 8am-9pm, last wash 7:30pm.

Bisexual, Gay, and Lesbian Information: Gay Switchboard Dublin, Carmichael House, North Brunswick St., Dublin 7 (tel. 872 1055). Yak or read about meetings, outdoors groups, and nightlife. Open Sun.-Fri. 8-10pm, Sat. 3:30-6pm. **Lesbian Line,** tel. 661 3777; open Thurs. 7-9pm. **National Gay and Lesbian Federation (NLGF),** the Hirschfeld Center, 10 Fownes St. (tel. 671 0939), behind the Central Bank. Publishes *Gay Community News,* a free monthly publication covering all of Ireland; get it here, at the Well Fed Café (see Food, below), Temple Bar Information Center (above), Books Upstairs (see Books, below), or at various Dublin gay hangouts (see Entertainment).

AIDS Resource Center: 14 Haddington Rd. (tel. 660 2149) off Baggot St. Advice, counseling, and HIV testing; operates the **Gay Men's Health Project,** Tues.7:30-9:30pm. No appointment necessary. **Dublin AIDS Alliance,** 53 Parnell Sq. (tel. 873 3799) offers counseling and information about HIV infection.

Hotlines: Samaritans, 112 Marlborough St. (tel. (1850) 609 090 or 872 7700); **Rape Crisis Center,** 70 Lower Leeson St. (tel. 661 4911; weekends after 5:30pm, call 661 4564).

Late-Night Pharmacy: O'Connell's, 55 Lower O'Connell St. (tel. 873 0427). Open Mon.-Sat. 8:30am-10pm, Sun. 10am-10pm. Convenient to bus routes.

Hospital: St. James Hospital, James St., Dublin 8 (tel. 453 7941).

Emergency: Dial 999; no coins required. **Garda:** Dublin Metro Headquarters, Harcourt Sq. (tel. 732 222).

ACCOMMODATIONS

Though tourist offices do book local accommodations for £1, they will send you only to Bord Fáilte-approved places.

Hostels

Many hostels (most £6-10) are north of the River Liffey and east of O'Connell St., in a working-class neighborhood. Most are independent. Call ahead in summer.

Avalon House (IHH), 55 Aungier St. (tel. 475 0001). From Dame St., take South Great Georges St. southwards until it becomes Aungier St.; the hostel is on the left. Between Trinity and Temple Bar. One of the best hostels in Dublin; B&B-level privacy. Coed showers, toilets, and dorms. All non-smoking rooms. Continental breakfast included. 24-bed room £7.50, July-Aug. £10.50. 4-bed room £11/person, July-Aug. £11.50. Doubles £13/person, July-Aug. £13.50. 4-bed and doubles with bath, add 50p. **Disabled-access room** (2 single beds) £13.50/person.

Kinlay House (IHH), 2-12 Lord Edward St. (tel. 679 6644), continue down Dame St. past Dublin Castle. Located in hip 'n' happenin' Temple Bar. Lockers, laundry (£4). Bike hire. 24-hr. access to luggage storage. Breakfast, towel, linen, and soap included. Singles £16.50. Doubles £11.50/person, with bath £12.50. Dorm £7.50-£9.50. July-Sept. extra £1 for dorm rooms, 50p for single and doubles.

Isaac's (IHH), 2-4 Frenchman's Lane (tel. 874 9321), first right on Lower Gardiner St. walking up from the Custom House. Youthful staff and guests; has café. Reception open 24 hrs. Bed lockout 11am-5pm. Lockers in the rooms, 50p deposit, free sheets. Singles £15.25. Doubles £23. Triples £33.75. Dorm £5.75-£7.50.

Marlborough Hostel (IHH), 81-81 Marlborough St. (tel. 874 7629 or 874 7812), next to the Pro-Cathedral, and directly behind the O'Connell St. tourist office. Light, airy rooms with super-comfy beds. Includes continental breakfast. Check-out 10:30am. Sheet rental 50p, laundry 50p. Single £14. Double £22. Dorm £7.50.

Globetrotter's Tourist Hostel (IHH), 46 Gardiner St. Lower (tel. 873 5893). High, roomy bunks. Free linen. With bath £10, £20 for 3 nights.

Dublin International Youth Hostel (An Óige/HI), 61 Mountjoy St. (tel. 830 1766 or 830 1396), Follow O'Connell St. north, continuing straight as it becomes Parnell Sq. E., Frederick St., and Blessington Ave.; turn left on Mountjoy St. Large rooms. Former convent (stained glass windows). Currency exchange. Sheets 50p, luggage storage 50p, continental breakfast included. Max. 3-night stay. Dorm £9, non-members £9.50; 3- to 6-bed room £10; twin £12. Oct.-May, subtract £2.

Abraham House, 82 Gardiner St. Lower (tel. 855 0600). Huge, airy dorm rooms with low, soft bunks. Gallons of hot water. Dorm £8, twin £13.

Goin' My Way/Cardijn House (IHH), 15 Talbot St. (tel. 878 8484; after 6pm tel. 874 1720). From O'Connell St., continue down Earl St. Cramped rooms. £6/person. Doubles £10/person. **Camping** in backyard garden for £4.50.

B&Bs

Neighborhood B&Bs are often private homes left with extra rooms in the wake of a large Catholic brood; they offer a gasp of fresh air and a glimpse of everyday Irish life. They are also surprisingly accessible to the city center: Clonliffe Rd., Sandymount, and Clontarf are no more than a 10- to 15-minute bus ride from Eden Quay.

Leitrim House, 34 Blessington St. (tel. 830 8728). Walk up O'Connell St., which becomes Parnell Sq. East and then Frederick St. Cross Dorset St. and continue straight on Blessington St.; Leitrim House is one block past the false teeth repair shop, or take bus #10 to the top of Mountjoy St. Grandmotherly touch. £12.

Stella Maris Guest House, 13 Upper Gardiner St. (tel. 874 0835). Red deer antlers in the dining room. Singles £20. Doubles £16, with bath £20.

Mrs. Bermingham, 8 Dromard Terrace (tel. 668 3861). Take bus #3 from O'Connell St. or DART to Sandymount stop. Great comforters. Singles £14. Doubles £23.

Mrs. R. Casey, Villa Jude, 2 Church Ave. (tel. 668 4982), off Beach Rd. Take bus #3 or DART (Lansdowne Rd. stop). Every room is immaculate and TV-equipped. £12.

Mrs. Carmel Drain, Bayview, 265 Clontarf Rd. (tel. 833 9870). Palm tree in front yard, sheepskin rugs indoors. Orthopedic beds. £14, with bath £15.

Ferryview Guest House, 96 Clontarf Rd. (tel. 833 5893). Take advantage of the trouser press. View of smokestacks; non-smoking rooms. £15/person.

Mrs. M. Ryan, 10 Distillery Rd. (tel. 837 4147), off Clonliffe Rd., on your left if you're coming from Drumcondra Rd. Look for yellow-trim windows on house attached to #11. Firm beds and warm comforters. £11.50/person.

Mrs. Brid Creagh, St. Aiden's B&B, 150 Clonliffe Rd. (tel. 837 6750). Bathroom like a greenhouse. Non-smoking rooms. Open April-Sept. £13, with bath £16.

Mrs. Kathleen Greville, Mona B&B, 148 Clonliffe Rd. (tel. 837 6723). Good firm beds and homemade bread. Open May-Oct. Singles £15. Doubles £25.

Camping

Most campsites are far from the city center. To buy camping equipment, try **The Great Outdoors,** Chatham St. (tel. 679 4293), off the top of Grafton St., for an excellent selection of tents, backpacks, and cookware (10% discount for An Óige/HI members; open Mon.-Wed. and Fri.-Sat. 9:30am-5:30pm, Thurs. 9:30am-8pm).

Cardijn House, 15 Talbot St. (tel. 878 8484; after 6pm 874 1720). Youth hostel lets campers pitch tents in the backyard garden. Unbelievably convenient location just minutes from O'Connell St. Services of hostel available. No secure luggage storage. Kitchen after 5pm. Showers 50p. £4.50. Call for availability.

Shankill Caravan and Camping Park, (tel. 282 0011). Take bus #45, 45A, 46, or 84 from Eden Quay, or DART to Shankill. Middle-aged travelers in campers interspersed with shrubs and tents. Not the best place for an intensive sight-seeing tour of Dublin. £4.50-5.50/tent plus 50p/person. 8-min. shower 50p.

FOOD

The **Moore St. Market,** lined with butcher shops, is the city's leading trading place (open Mon.-Sat. 9am-5pm). From O'Connell St., turn at the G.P.O. and walk down Henry St.; Moore St. is the second right. The **Thomas St. Market** (continue on Dame St./Lord Edward St. past Christ Church) is a calmer alternative for fruit and vegetable shopping (open Fri.-Sat. 9am-5pm).

The cheapest **supermarkets** around Dublin are **Dunnes Stores** at St. Stephen's Green Shopping Center; ILAC Center, off Henry St.; and on North Earl St., off O'Connell St. (tel. 848 3348). (All open Mon.-Wed. and Fri.-Sat. 9am-6pm, Thurs. 9am-8pm.) **Quinnsworth** is also widespread. The **Runner Bean,** 4 Nassau St. (tel. 679 4833), vends wholefoods, vegetables, homemade breads, fruits, and nuts (open Mon.-Fri. 8am-6pm, Sat. 9am-6pm).

The Well Fed Café, 6 Crow St. (tel. 677 2234), off Dame St. Inventive vegetarian dishes served by a worker's cooperative in a stripped-down boho atmosphere. Popular with the gay community. Brown bread and soup £1, main courses £2, small salad 55p, large salad 80p, apple pie with cream £1.10. Wheelchair accessible. Open Mon.-Sat. noon-8pm.

Leo Burdock's, 2 Werburgh St. (tel. 454 0306), uphill from Christ Church Cathedral. Lucky the steps of the Cathedral are nearby—Burdock's is take-out only, and eating Burdock's fish and chips is a religious experience. Haddock or cod £2, large chips 85p. Open Mon.-Fri. 12:30-11pm, Sat. 2-11pm.

Caffé Carolina, 66 Dame St. (tel. 677 7378). Inventive food served late, late, late in a diner atmosphere. Ricotta cake (£1.50) is sublime. Banana pancakes with chocolate sauce £2, seafood pancakes £2.50, potato cakes 75p. Breakfast anytime, £3. Open Mon.-Thurs. 8am-11pm, Fri.-Sun. open 24 hrs.

Bad Ass Café, Crown Alley, off Temple Bar (tel. 671 2596). Huge warehouse converted into a Viewmaster of American culture. Small portions. Sinéad O'Connor worked here. Lunch £3-5. Student menu (with ISIC): coleslaw, scone and butter, "magic mushrooms," medium pizza, drink (£5.50). Open daily 9am past midnight.

La Mezza Luna, 1 Temple Lane (tel. 671 2840), corner of Dame St. Stars and half-moons twinkle from a midnight-blue ceiling, a perfect setting for celestial food. You can't upstage *paglia*—smoked ham with mushrooms in a cream and wine sauce (£5). Open Mon.-Sat. 12:30-11pm, Sun. 4-10:30pm.

Bewley's Cafés, (tel. 677 6761), 3 locations at Grafton, Westmoreland, and South Great George's St. A Dublin institution: a delightful crowd of Dublin characters, dark wood paneling, marble table tops, and mirrored walls. Pastries (£1); outstanding coffee. 4 branches: 78 Grafton St. is the largest (open Sun.-Thurs. 7:30am-1am, Fri.-Sat. 7:30am-2am). James Joyce frequented the branch at 12 Westmoreland St. (open Mon.-Sat. 7:30am-9pm, Sun. 9:30am-8pm). Also at 13

South Great Georges St. (open Mon.-Sat. 7:45am-6pm) and at Mary St. (past Henry St.; open Mon.-Wed. 7am-9pm, Thurs.-Sat. 7am-2am, Sun. 10am-10pm).

Marks Bros., 7 South Great Georges St. (tel. 667 1085), off Dame St. Thick sandwiches (£1.30-1.70) for starving artists and punks. Legendary cinnamon buns 40p. Very popular among gays. Open Mon.-Sat. 10am-5pm.

The Winding Stair Bookshop and Café, 40 Lower Ormond Quay (tel. 873 3292), near Bachelor's Walk. Unhurried café amidst 2 floors of bookshelves. Big portion of Greek salad £2.60, soup and bread £1.60. Open Mon.-Sat. 10:30am-5:30pm.

PUBS

Many heated debates begin from the postulation that Guinness tastes slightly different from every tap: the best is said to be at the Guinness Hop Store attached to the Guinness Brewery, with Mulligan's the former world champ and current #2. The **Dublin Literary Pub Crawl** (tel. 454 0228) traces Dublin's literary and liquid history with snatches of information and entrancing monologues. (Meet at the Bailey, 2 Duke St. June-Aug. nightly 7:30pm, plus Mon.-Sat. 3pm, and Sun. noon. May & Sept. nightly 7:30pm. Oct.-April Fri.-Sat. 7:30pm, Sun. noon. £6, students £5.)

The thoughtfully enclosed **Let's Go Dublin Pub Crawl Map** should help you find your way around town in the course of your drunken wanderings. Use the number after each pub's name (like the **[2]** after **Slattery's** name, below) to locate each pub.

North of the Liffey

Slattery's [2], 129 Capel St. (tel. 872 7971). Best-known pub for trad and set dancing. Nightly 9pm: trad (free), rock and blues (£2-4).

The Grattan [3], 165 Capel St. (tel. 873 3049), on the corner of Little Strand St. International ears attuned to mostly jazz. Music starts 9pm.

Hughes' [1], 19 Chancery St. near Chancery Row (tel. 872 6540), behind Four Courts. A delightful venue for trad (nightly) and set dancing (Mon.,Wed. 9pm).

Grafton Street & Vicinity

McDaid's [18], 3 Harry St. (tel. 679 4395), off Grafton St., across from Anne St. Buskers contribute to the happy din with impromptu ballads.

The Bailey [19], 2 Duke St., off Grafton St. In the lobby, see the preserved front door of #7 Eccles St., fictional home of Leopold Bloom. A popular gay and lesbian meeting place at teatime, especially Sat. afternoons.

The International Bar [15], 23 Wicklow St. (tel. 677 9250), off Grafton St. on the corner of South William St. Improv comedy balances the blues (£2-5).

John Kehoe's [21], 9 South Anne St. (tel. 677 8312), off Grafton St. Snugs galore: women were confined in them while their men sat at the bar. Now very coed.

Davy Byrne's [20], 21 Duke St. (tel. 671 1298), off Grafton St. "Nice quiet pub. Nicely planned." Come see what Joyce meant in *Ulysses.*

Neary's [17], 1 Chatham St. (tel. 677 8596), off Grafton St. across from the Gaiety Theatre stage door. Actors and their entourages.

Baggot St. & Vicinity

O'Donoghue's [23], 15 Merrion Row (tel. 676 2807), between St. Stephen's Green North and Baggot St. Home of The Dubliners (a renowned Irish band).

Doheny and Nesbitt's [24], 5 Lower Baggot St. (tel. 676 2945), near St. Stephen's Green. Wonderful snugs and Irish stew (served Sat., £2.50).

Toner's [26], 139 Lower Baggot St. (tel. 676 3090). Quietly Victorian.

The Baggot Inn [25], 143 Baggot St. Lower (tel. 676 1430). Nightly rock music draws a leather jacket crowd. Frequented by U2 in the early '80s.

Kennedy's [22], 31 Westland Row (tel. 676 2998), on the southeast corner of Trinity College campus. Boisterous Trinity hangout.

The Buttery [12], Trinity College. Dark, smoky, and crammed with students, even at 3pm. Open Mon.-Fri. noon-11pm.

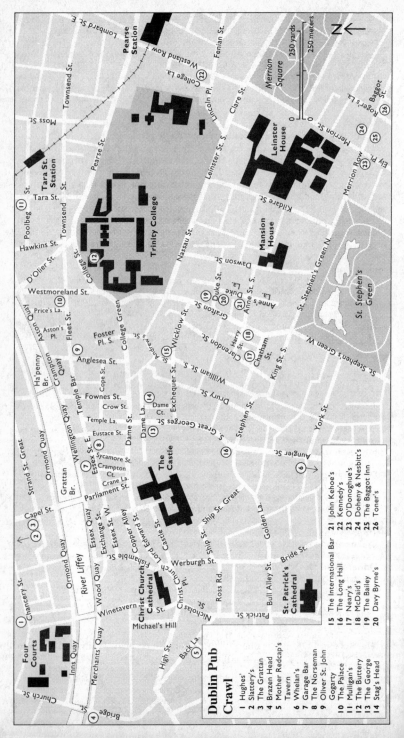

Dublin Pub Crawl

1 Hughes'
2 Slattery's
3 The Grattan
4 Brazen Head
5 Mother Redcap's Tavern
6 Whelan's
7 Garage Bar
8 The Norseman
9 Oliver St. John Gogarty
10 The Palace
11 Mulligan's
12 The Buttery
13 The George
14 Stag's Head
15 The International Bar
16 The Long Hall
17 Neary's
18 McDaid's
19 The Bailey
20 Davy Byrne's
21 John Kehoe's
22 Kennedy's
23 O'Donoghue's
24 Doheny & Nesbitt's
25 The Baggot Inn
26 Toner's

Temple Bar & Vicinity

The Brazen Head [4], 20 Lower Bridge St. (tel. 679 5186), off Merchant's Quay. Dublin's oldest pub, established in 1198. Quite the pickup scene.

The Stag's Head [14], 1 Dame Court (tel. 679 3701). From Dame St., short-cut to Dame Ct. via alleyway; its entrance (next to #28, Stanley Racing) is marked by "Stag's Head" in tile on the sidewalk. Beautiful Victorian pub with stained glass, mirrors, and brasswork. Huge whisky kegs on the walls. Truly excellent grub.

The Long Hall [16], 51 South Great Georges St. (tel. 475 1590). Carved polished wood bar, ornate mirrors, and neighborly local socializing and *craic*.

Mulligan's [11], 8 Poolbeg St. (tel. 677 5582), behind Burgh Quay off Tara St. Big rep as the best pint of Guinness in Dublin, outside the brewery itself.

Whelan's [6], 25 Wexford St. (tel. 478 0766), continue down South St. Georges St. Over-21 only. Nightly Irish indie rock and/or blues, cover £2-3.

Mother Redcaps Tavern [5], Back Lane (tel. 453 8306), near Christ Church.

The George [13], 89 South Great Georges St. (tel. 478 2983). Currently Dublin's only gay pub. Upstairs, **The Block** is a gay-male bar and nightclub (Fri.-Sat.).

The Norseman [8], 29 East Essex St. (tel. 671 5135), corner of Sycamore St. behind Wellington Quay. Musicians, actors, entourage. Ballads Sun. 9-11am.

The Palace [10], 21 Fleet St. (tel. 677 9290), behind Aston Quay. A classic neighborly Dublin pub: cramped quarters that encourage *craic*.

Oliver St. John Gogary [9], corner of Fleet St. and Anglesea St. (tel. 671 1822). Lively and friendly atmosphere in a traditionally decorated pub.

The Garage Bar [7], 8 Essex St. East (tel. 677 6178). U2's newest venture never caught on as Dublin's main nightspot. The young in body flock here.

SIGHTS

Among guided walking tours, Trinity students give two good ones: the **Historical Walking Tour** (tel. 845 0241) is a 2-hr. crash course in Dublin's history from the Celts to the present. (June-Sept. Mon.-Sat. at 11am, noon, and 3pm, Sun. also at 2pm; £4, students £3. Meet at Trinity's front gate.) The witty and irreverent **Trinity College Walking Tour** also covers Dublin's history, but concentrates on University lore. (June-Sept. 10am-4pm, leaving every 15 min. from the Information Booth inside the front gate; 30 min.; £5, students £4; price includes admission to the Old Library and the Book of Kells.) The talented guides deserve a tip.

Dublin Footsteps (tel. 496 0641 or 845 0772) runs an "early morning" tour of Dublin's main attractions (meets at the O'Connell St. tourist office, 10am Mon.-Sat.), as well as literary and medieval theme tours. **City Cycle Tours** (tel. 671 5610) speed across Dublin (Mon.-Sat. 10:30am and 2:30pm; Sun. 1:30pm. £10 includes bike and helmet, students £8). Tours depart from Temple Lane, off Dame St. Arrive 20 minutes in advance.

Trinity College & Nearby

Trinity College (tel. 677 2941) sprawls within its ancient walls in the very center of Dublin. Inside, stone buildings, a cobblestone walk, and spacious green grounds give the campus an illusory seclusion, and allow for the occasional white-suited game of cricket. The British built Trinity in 1592 as a Protestant religious seminary "to civilize the Irish and cure them of Popery." The Catholic church deemed it a cardinal sin to attend Trinity until the 1960s; after the church lifted the ban, the size of the student body more than tripled.

The 1712 **Old Library** holds Ireland's finest collection of Egyptian, Greek, Latin, and Irish manuscripts, including the **Book of Kells.** Around 800 AD, Irish monks squeezed multicolored ink from insects to make the now deservedly famous *Book,* a four-volume edition of the Gospels; each page holds a dizzyingly intricate lattice of Celtic knotwork and scrollwork, animals, and Latin characters. Upstairs, in the Library's Long Room, are "Ireland's oldest harp," the Brian Ború harp (which looks just like the one on Irish coins). (Old Library open Mon.-Sat. 9:30am-5:30pm, Sun. noon-4:30pm. £2.50, students £2.) In Trinity's Davis Theater, the **Dublin Experi-**

ence movie engulfs visitors in historical Dublin. (Daily 10am-5pm on the hour. £2.75, students £2.25; with combined entrance to Old Library £5, students £4.)

Facing Trinity across College Green, the menacingly monolithic, Roman-looking building is the **Bank of Ireland** (tel. 677 6801), built in 1729 for the 18th-century Irish Parliament. After the Act of Union, the British sold the building to the bank on the condition that the bank blot out any material evidence of the legislature. The enormous curved walls and pillars were erected *around* the original structure; the bank inside is actually much smaller. You can still visit the former chamber of the House of Lords. (Open during regular banking hours—Mon.-Wed. and Fri. 10am-4pm, Thurs. 10am-5pm. Guided tours Tues. 10:30am, 11:30am, 1:45pm. Free.)

South of College Green (away from the Liffey) run the three or so blocks of **Grafton Street,** ground zero for shopping tourists; it's entertaining to walk through, but other than Bewley's, few establishments yield bargains. Upstairs at Bewley's Grafton St. branch is the **Bewley's Museum,** in the coffee chain's former chocolate factory; tea-tasting machines, corporate history, and a display on Bewley's Quaker heritage are among its oddball exhibits. (Open daily 10am-7pm; free.)

Merrion Square & St. Stephen's Green

South of Trinity College at Leinster St., with Kildare St. at its back and Merrion Square in front of it, **Leinster House** houses the present-day Irish parliament: the *Dáil* ("doil") which does most of the work, and the less powerful upper house, the *Seanad* ("shan-ad"), together make up the parliament, called (in its entirety, in Irish) *An tOireachtas* ("on tir-OCH-tas"). When the *Dáil* is in session, visitors can view the proceedings; to do so, contact the Captain of the Guard. Be sure to bring your passport (tel. 678 9911; the *Dáil* meets, very roughly, Jan.-July Wed.-Fri. 10:30am-5pm). The Captain's office also steers some tours of the *Dáil's* galleries (tours Sat. 10:30am-12:45pm and 1:30-4:50pm).

The **National Museum,** Kildare St. (tel. 661 8811), focuses on legendary ancient Ireland and the almost-as-legendary Easter Rising. One room gleams with the Tara Brooch, Ardagh Chalice, and other Celtic goldwork; another, devoted to the Republic's founding years, shows off plenty of historical information along with the bloody vest of James Connolly. (Open Tues.-Sat. 10am-5pm, Sun. 2-5pm. Free.) Connected to the National Museum, the **Natural History Museum** (tel. 661 8811) specializes in stuffed Irish wildlife. (Open Tues.-Sat. 10am-5pm, Sun. 2-5pm. Free.) Down the street on Merrion Sq., the **National Gallery's** 2400 canvases include work by Vermeer, Goya, Rembrandt, and El Greco along with plenty of Irish artists; portraits of James Joyce, George Bernard Shaw, and William Butler Yeats (by his father, John Butler Yeats) stare at one another along the four-story staircase. (Tel. 461 5133. Open Mon.-Sat. 10am-6pm, Thurs. 10am-9pm, Sun. 2-5pm. Free.)

Stroll around **Merrion Square** and **Fitzwilliam Street** (near the National Museum) to enjoy the Georgian buildings and their elaborate rows of colorful doorways. **Number 29 Lower Fitzwilliam Street** (tel. 702 6165) tries to give an impression of late-18th-century Dublin domestic life. The world the house depicts is like an antiquated *Leave it to Beaver,* but hey, it's free. Who's their decorator? (Open Tues.-Sat. 10am-5pm, Sun. 2-5pm.) Kildare St., Dawson St., and Grafton St. all lead from Trinity south to **St. Stephen's Green.** The 22-acre park holds arched bridges, an artificial lake, couples, pensioners, punks, strollers, swans, more swans, trees, even more trees, and a waterfall. (Gates open Mon.-Sat. 8am-dusk, Sun. 10am-dusk.)

Temple Bar, Dame Street, & Cathedrals

West of Trinity College between Dame St. and the Liffey is the **Temple Bar** neighborhood; narrow cobblestone streets link cheap cafés, hole-in-the-wall theaters, rock venues, and used clothing and record stores. At the west end of Dame St., where it meets Parliament St. and Castle St., hovers **Dublin Castle** (tel. 677 7129). King John built the castle in 1204 on top of an old Viking fort; for the next 700 years Dublin Castle was the seat of British rule in Ireland. Since 1938 the presidents of Ireland have been inaugurated here. If they're not entertaining state visitors when you get there, you can entertain the prospect of a tour. (State Apartments open Mon.-Fri. 10am-12:15pm and 2-5pm, Sat.-Sun. and holidays 2-5pm, except during official functions. £1.75, students and children £1. Rest of castle is free.)

Dublin's ecclesiastical beauties line up west of the Castle; all are owned by the Church of Ireland (the Irish equivalent of the Anglican Church), not by the Catholic Church. **Christ Church Cathedral** (tel. 677 8099) looms at the end of Dame St., uphill and across from the Castle. Stained glass shines and raised crypts abound (one of them supposedly Strongbow's own). The cathedral's cavernous crypt once held shops and drinking houses—now cobwebs hang down from the ceiling, fragments of ancient pillars lie about like bleached bones, and a mummified cat is frozen in the act of chasing a mummified mouse. (Open to visitors daily 10am-5pm except during services. Choral evensong Sept.-May Thurs. at 6pm. £1 donation.) Christ Church also hosts **Dublinia** (tel. 679 4611), a re-creation of medieval Dublin with life-size reconstructions of a merchant's house and of Wood Quay circa 1200. (Open daily April-Sept. 10am-5pm; Feb.-March Mon.-Sat. 11am-4pm, Sun. 10am-4:30pm. £4, students and children £3; includes admission to Christ Church.

From Christ Church, Nicholas St. runs south and downhill, encountering **St. Patrick's Cathedral** (tel. 475 4817). St. Patrick, who brought Christianity to Ireland and drove out all the snakes, allegedly baptized converts in the park next to the cathedral. Jonathan Swift, who wrote *Gulliver's Travels,* spent his last years as Dean of St. Patrick's; his crypt rises above the south nave. (Open Mon.-Fri. 9am-6pm, Sat. 9am-5pm, Sun. 10am-4:30pm. £1, students 40p.) **Marsh's Library,** St. Patrick's Close (tel. 454 3511), beside St. Patrick's Cathedral, is Ireland's oldest public library; it's worth a peek inside for the elegant wire alcoves, or "cages." (Open Mon. and Wed.-Fri. 10am-12:45pm and 2-5pm, Sat. 10:30am-12:45pm. £1 donation expected.)

Guinness Brewery & Kilmainham

The giant **Guinness Brewery,** St. James Gate (tel. 453 6700), Dublin's largest industry, produces 2.5 million pints a day. The Hop Store, the company's visitor center, shows a short film; you won't get to tour the brewery itself, but you will get a glass of the stuff at the end. The bar here supposedly serves the best Guinness in Dublin and hence, by Dublin logic, the world's best beer. But is it really "good for you"? (Open Mon.-Fri. 10am-4pm, last tour 3:30pm. £2, students £1.50.)

The Royal Hospital and Kilmainham Gaol lie yet further to the west, a 20-min. walk from the city center. The **Royal Hospital Kilmainham** holds the **Irish Museum of Modern Art** (tel. 671 8666); call for changing exhibits, artist talks, or concerts. (Open Tues.-Sat. 10am-5:30pm, Sun. noon-5:30pm; free. Guided tours Wed. and Fri. 2:30pm, Sat. 11:30am.) From its completion in 1792 to Irish independence in 1921, **Kilmainham Gaol** (tel. 453 5984) managed to hold almost all the heroes of Ireland's struggle for independence. The leaders of the Easter Rising were confined, and many of them executed, here; the jail's last occupant was Éamon de Valera. (Open May-Sept. daily 10am-6pm; April Mon.-Fri. 1-4pm, Sun. 1-6pm. £2, students 60p.)

The North Side: O'Connell St. & Parnell Square

Rising from the river to Parnell Square, **O'Connell Street** is the commercial center of Dublin. The center traffic islands are monuments to Irish leaders: Parnell, O'Connell, and James Larkin, who organized the heroic Dublin general strike of 1913. O'Connell's statue faces the Liffey and O'Connell Bridge; the winged women aren't angels but Winged Victories, though one has a bullet hole in a rather inglorious place. Farther up the street, the newer statue of a woman lounging in water is officially the Spirit of the Liffey or "Anna Livia," unoffically "the floozy in the jacuzzi," "the whore in the sewer," (in Dublin, that rhymes too), or Anna Rexia. The even newer statue of Molly Malone, of ballad fame, on Grafton St. gets called "the tart in the cart"; decide for yourself whether Dubliners are mocking the city, the monument-making mentality, or simply women in general with this series of popular nicknames. One monument you won't see is Nelson's Pillar, a tall freestanding column which remembered Trafalgar outside the GPO for 150 years. The IRA blew it up in

1966 in commemoration of the 50th anniversary of the Easter Rising; Nelson's English head now rests in the Dublin Civic Museum.

The **General Post Office** presides over O'Connell St.; not just a fine place to send a letter, the Post Office was the nerve center of the 1916 Rising. When British troops closed in, mailbags became barricades. Outside, some bullet nicks can still be seen. Overlooking the park, the **Hugh Lane Municipal Gallery,** Parnell Sq. North (tel. 874 1903 or 874 1904), confines modern art within the Georgian walls of Charlemont House. (Open Tues.-Fri. 9:30am-6pm, Sat. 9:30am-5pm, Sun. 11am-5pm; free.) Next door, the **Dublin Writers' Museum,** 18/19 Parnell Sq. North (tel. 872 2077), yields an uneasy mix of tourism and writing craft. Its history of Irish literature encompasses rare editions, manuscripts, and memorabilia. (Open daily 10am-5pm. £2.50, under 18 £1.70, under 11 80p.) Adjacent to the museum, the **Irish Writers' Center,** 19 Parnell Sq. (tel. 872 1302), presents frequent poetry and fiction readings to the public. Just past Parnell Sq., the **Garden of Remembrance** eulogizes the martyrs who took the GPO. A cross-shaped pool is plugged at one end by a statue representing the mythical Children of Lir, who turned from humans into swans; they cry, in Irish, "O generations of freedom remember us, the generations of the vision." One block east of Parnell Sq. East, the new **James Joyce Center,** 35 North Great Georges St. (tel. 873 1984), up Marlborough St. across Parnell St., raises the number of Dublin's Joycean institutions to a zillion and one. (Open Tues.-Sat. 10am-4:30pm, Sun. noon-4:30pm. £2, students £1.50, children 70p.)

The North Side: Along the Quays & Phoenix Park

East of O'Connell St. at Custom House Quay, where Gardiner St. meets the river, is one of Dublin's architectural triumphs, the **Custom House.** Carved heads along the frieze represent the rivers of Ireland; the Liffey is the only woman of the bunch. Several quays to the west, on Inn's Quay, stands another of Gandon's works, the **Four Courts;** it houses the highest court in Ireland. Just up Church St., the dry atmosphere has effectively mummified the corpses in the vaults of **St. Michan's Church,** which inspired Bram Stoker's *Dracula*. Peek into the open coffins and see how 300-year-old skin and hair are holding up. (Open Mon.-Fri. 10am-12:45pm and 2-4:45pm, Sat. 10am-12:45pm. £1.50, students and seniors £1, under 16 50p.)

The **Irish Whiskey Corner,** Bow St. (tel. 872 5566), in a whiskey warehouse off Mary St., demonstrates the distilling process and shows a film. (Tours Mon.-Fri. 3:30pm, May-Sept. additional tour 11am; £3 including whiskey tasting.) From O'Connell St., turn onto Henry St. and continue straight as the street becomes Mary St.; the warehouse is on a cobblestone street on the left.

Take bus #10 from O'Connell St. or #25 or 26 from Middle Abbey St. west along the river to **Phoenix Park.** The 1760-acre park incorporates the President's residence (*Áras an Uachtaráin*), the U.S. Ambassador's residence, one of the world's oldest zoos, cricket pitches, polo grounds, and grazing red deer and cattle. The **Dublin Zoo** (tel. 677 1425) housed the familiar snarling lion from the MGM movie logo. (Zoo open Mon.-Sat. 9:30am-6pm, Sun. 11am-6pm; closes at sunset in winter. £4.20, seniors and children £1.80, under 3 free.)

ENTERTAINMENT

Be it Seamus Heaney or the Pogues you fancy, Dublin is equipped to entertain you. *In Dublin* (£1.50) comes out every two weeks with music listings, theater reviews with show times and ticket prices, art exhibitions, comedy shows, movie theaters, and gay and lesbian info. The *Dublin Event Guide* (free from the tourist office) comes out every other Friday. Hostel staff are often sources of information as well.

Music

Dublin's music world attracts performers from all over the country. Pubs set the stage for much of the action. Traditional music is not a tourist gimmick, but a vibrant and important element of the Dublin music scene and the Irish culture. Some pubs in the city center have traditional sessions nightly; try **Hughes', The Brazen Head,**

Slattery's, Oliver St. John Gogarty, McDaid's, The International Bar, Mother Red-caps Tavern, or **O'Donoghue's** (see Pubs).

The **Rock Garden,** 3a Crown Alley (tel. 679 9114), between Temple Bar and Cope St., also a fine place to drink, is the current center of Dublin's rock scene. (Music begins 8pm nightly; cover £3). Bigger-deal bands frequent the **Baggot Inn,** 143 Baggot St. (tel. 676 1430). **Whelan's,** 25 Wexford St. (tel. 478 0766; follow South Great Georges St. as it changes name from Aungier to Camden to Wexford), is one of the hottest spots—their posters are all over town. **An Béal Bocht** often hosts rock acts (see Theater, below). For jazz, **Rudyard's Wine Bar,** 15 Crown Alley (tel. 671 0846), offers live sessions Friday and Saturday nights at 9pm; **McDaid's,** 3 Henry St. (tel. 679 4395), hosts acts on Mondays and Tuesdays at 8:30pm. On the North Side, **The Grattan,** 165 Capel St. (tel. 873 3049), hosts jazz on Wednesday nights. For classical music lovers, the **National Concert Hall,** Earl's Fort Terrace (tel. 671 1533), provides a venue for touring orchestras in July and August.

Dance Clubs

In recent years, clubs have displaced rock venues as the home of Dublin's nightlife. As a rule, these spots open at 10:30 or 11pm, but the action gets moving only after 11:30pm, when the pubs close. Cover runs £4-8, pints £2; clubs typically shut down between 3 and 4am, but some stay open until about 6am. Upstairs at the Rock Garden (see above) is **UFO,** an intense and happening club (£4, open 11:30pm-2:30am). **Club Paradiso** (tel. 677 8788), at the Irish Film Center, has an appropriately cinematic decor (IFC members only, see *Cinema,* below, for membership info and directions; £4, 11:30pm-late). **The Pink Elephant,** Sentana Center, South Frederick St. (tel. 677 5876) is frequented by rock stars and supermodels; you can bask in their glory (if not their presence) on Wed. nights, when it admits mortals (£6). **Rí-Rá,** 1 Exchequer St. (tel. 668 0995), in the Central Hotel, was 1994's epicenter for social gatherings of cool modern people. To get home after Dublin Bus shuts down, partygoers can take the **NiteLink bus** (£2; Fri.-Sat. midnight-3am hourly), which runs routes from the corner of Westmoreland and College St., near Trinity.

Gay & Lesbian Dublin

Check *In Dublin*'s gay page, which lists pubs, saunas, dance clubs, gay-friendly restaurants and bookshops, and hotlines and organizations. *Gay Community News* piles up at the gay pubs listed in *Let's Go* and at The Well Fed Café, Books Upstairs Bookstore, Temple Bar Information Center, and other locations. It covers most Irish gay-related news, and its listings page is exhaustive. **Gay Switchboard Dublin** is a good resource for events, updates, and also a hotline (tel. 872 1055; Sun.-Fri. 8-10pm, Sat. 3:30-6pm). **Lesbian Line** offers similar services (tel. 661 3777; open Thurs. 7-9pm). **The National Gay and Lesbian Federation,** Hirschfield Center, 10 Fownes St. (tel. 671 0939), in Temple Bar, presents a sad, and perhaps soon outdated, picture of Irish homophobia; it's housed in a burnt-out building, where visitors are grilled via intercom before the well-locked door is unchained.

At the moment, **The George** is Dublin's only gay pub. **The Bailey** pub is a lesbian and gay alternative on Saturday afternoons. **The Trinity,** Nassau St., across from Trinity College, becomes a women-only space on Saturday nights. **The Block** is upstairs from the George; it's a bar and dance club (Fri.-Sat.). **Shaft,** 22 Ely Pl., continue down Upper Merrion St. West, is primarily, though no longer exclusively, gay—it's also where clubbers go when all else has closed. The basement-level dance floor gets kicking around 11:30pm nightly (£3 cover charge Fri.-Sat.). **Horny Organ Tribe (H.O.T.)** is a gay night at the Rock Garden, 3a Crown Alley, Temple Bar, with full bar and dancing. (Cover £4, students £3; open Sun. 11pm-3am.) **Salon at The Cellary,** Fownes St., is a women-only nightclub Sundays 9:30pm-3am (£4, students £2.50). **Temple of Sound,** Ormond Hotel, Upper Ormond Quay (tel. 872 1811), has dances Sunday and Wednesday 10:30pm till late.

Theater & Film

Yeats and sometime collaborator Lady Gregory founded the **Abbey Theater,** 26 Lower Abbey St. (tel. 878 7222), in 1904 to promote Irish cultural revival and modernist theater. (Box office open Mon.-Sat. 10:30am-7pm. Tickets £8-13; student standby (£5) available 1hr. before show Mon. and Thurs.) Downstairs is the smaller, more experimental **Peacock Theater** (tel. 878 7222), with evening shows and occasional lunchtime plays, concerts, and poetry (£8, students £5). (Box office opens Mon.-Sat. at 7:30pm for that night's performance only; advance booking at the Abbey Theater box office. **Gate Theater,** 1 Cavendish Row (tel. 874 4045), produces everything from Restoration comedies to Irish classics. (Box office open Mon.-Sat. 10am-7pm; tickets £10-12; student standby £6 Mon.-Thurs. at curtain time.) **Project Arts Center,** 39 East Essex St. (tel. 671 2321), presents avant-garde theater and dramatic readings to comedy and dance. (Box office open daily 10am-6pm; tickets £8, concessions £6). **Gaiety,** South King St. (tel. 677 1717), houses the Dublin Grand Opera Society. (Box office open Mon.-Sat. 11am-7pm; tickets £7.50-12.50.) **An Béal Bocht,** 58 Charlemont St. (tel. 475 5614), hosts traditional Irish-language theater Wed. at 9pm (£5).

Ireland's well-supported film industry got a kick in the pants with the arrival of the **Irish Film Center,** Eustace St., in Temple Bar (tel. 679 3477 or 679 5744). You must be a "member" to buy tickets (each member can buy only 4 per screening). Weekly membership costs only £1, yearly membership just £6, students £5. You must buy your membership at least 20 minutes before the film you want to see begins. (Matinees £2, 5-7pm £2.50, after 7pm £4, students £3.) Other arty cinemas are the **Lighthouse Cinema,** 107 Fleet St. (tel. 873 0438; shows every night; £2 before 5pm, £3.50 after), and **The Screen,** D'Olier St. (tel. 671 4988 or 872 3922).

Events

The tourist office's *Calendar of Events* and *Dublin Events Guide* describe Dublin's many festivals, provincial parades, mayor's balls, concerts, dance, and art shows. **St. Patrick's Day** (March 17) occasions enormous parades, drunken carousing, and closed banks. Dublin returns to 1904 each year on **Bloomsday,** June 16, the day on which the action of Joyce's Ulysses takes place. Festivities occur during the week leading up to Bloomsday. The **Dublin Theater Festival** is in late September and early October; purchase tickets all year at participating theaters, at all branches of the Irish Life Building Society (main office on Lower Abbey St., tel. 704 2000), and, as the festival draws near, at the Festival Booking Office, 47 Nassau St., Dublin 2 (tel. 677 8439; 50% discount with ISIC; student standby tickets £2-3).

■ NEAR DUBLIN

If you only have time for one suburban jaunt, heather-crammed, peninsular Howth should be the victor. Any of these towns can be seen in an afternoon, and all share Dublin's **phone code** of 01.

HOWTH

Only nine mi. from Dublin, Howth (rhymes with "growth") is a quick fix of the best of Ireland—scenery, pubs, history, literature, a castle, an abbey, and fresh fish. Fishing boats congregate in the harbor, and fishermen toss their catch to the vendors who populate the pier. The easiest way to reach Howth is by **DART**—take a northbound train to the end of the line (6/hr.; 30 min.; £1). **Bus** #31 to Howth DART station from Dublin's Lower Abbey St. (1-2/hr.).

A **cliff walk** rings the peninsula and takes about an hour. To get to the trail head, turn left from the Howth DART station and bus stop, follow Harbour Rd. around the corner and up the hill; the footpath begins at the end of the cul-de-sac, a 15-minute walk from the harbor. (Just keep going up.) You'll find the "trail" surprisingly little in evidence, but you won't care; the views, and especially the springtime blooms of the slopes, are amazing. For the less hardy, bus #31B cruises from Lower Abbey St., Dublin to the cliffs' summit (1/hr.).

Aside from its spectacular views, Howth's primary attraction is **Howth Castle,** on the outskirts of town. Take a right on Harbor Rd. as you leave the DART station; the castle turn-off, ¼ mi. down the road, is marked by signs for the Deer Park Hotel. Though it is not closed off to the road, the castle is a private residence, still in the St. Lawrence family after more than 400 years. At the end of the road on which the castle perches is the **National Transport Museum,** an amiable collection of old buses, tanks, cars, and trucks. (Open Sat.-Sun. and holidays 2-6pm, Nov.-Mar. Sat.-Sun. 2-5pm; £1.50, children 50p). Farther up the hill, follow the path to the right around the Deer Park Hotel to reach the fab **Rhododendron Gardens.** The ending of *Ulysses* is set "among the rhododendrons at Howth Head." When the flowers are in bloom (June-July), a climb to the top is a must; visitors emerge from the dark trail into a dazzling panorama of sea, sky, Howth harbor, and Dublin, framed by spectacular flowers (always open; free).

After a day on your feet, stop for a pint in town at the classy **Cock Tavern,** 18 Church St. (tel. 832 3237), opposite St. Mary's Abbey. Rock bands play Wednesday and Sunday nights at 9pm, with ballads Sunday afternoons. Book a seat in advance to hear traditional music at **Ye Olde Abbey Tavern,** Abbey St. (tel. 832 2006 or 839 0282; music starts 9pm; cover charge £3). **The Pizza Place** (tel. 832 2255), at 12 West Pier Rd., is a treat; the lunchtime special, available till 2pm, includes small pizza, dessert, and coffee for £4.25 (open daily noon-midnight).

MALAHIDE & DONABATE

Eight mi. north of Dublin, rows of well-behaved shops self-satisfiedly line the main street of Malahide, a perennial contender in Ireland's cutthroat "Tidy Town" competition. Bus #42 from behind the Custom House (Beresford Place) in Dublin goes right to the park entrance. Turn up Church Rd. to reach **Malahide Castle** (tel. 845 2655 or 845 2337), the town's main attraction. The well-preserved mansion houses a collection of Irish period furniture and holds part of the National Portrait Collection. (Castle open Mon.-Fri. 10am-5pm, Sat. 11am-6pm, Sun. 11:30am-6pm; Nov.-March Mon.-Fri. 10am-5pm, Sat.-Sun. 2-6pm. Demesne/Park open daily June 10am-9pm, July-Aug. 10am-8pm, Oct. 10am-7pm, Nov-Jan 10am-5pm, Feb.-March 10am-6pm. £2.50, seniors and ages 12-17 £1.90.)

In Donabate, four mi. north of Malahide, the 18th-century **Newbridge House** (tel. 843 6534) is surrounded by a 300-acre park. The Archbishop of Dublin erected the mansion around 1740; it lacked electricity until the makers of the movie *The Spy Who Came in from the Cold* wired it up in the 1960s. (Open Tues.-Fri. 10am-1pm and 2-5pm, Sat. 11am-1pm and 2-7pm, Sun. 2-6pm; Nov.-March Sat.-Sun. 2-5pm. £2.10, students £1.80.) The **Newbridge Traditional Farm,** adjacent to the estate, reconstructs rural life and animal husbandry from 200 years ago. (Open same hours as the House. £1, seniors and students 80p.) Take the infrequent bus #33B from Eden Quay to Donabate; better yet, take suburban rail from Connolly, Tara St., or Pearse Station in downtown Dublin to Donabate (£1.20). Follow the signs from the village on the 20-minute walk to the funhouse.

DÚN LAOGHAIRE

Dún Laoghaire ("dun-LEER-ee") is the ideal place to start on a ramble south along the coast. The **tourist office** (tel. 280 6984), on St. Michael's Wharf between the DART station and the ferry terminal, is more than used to dealing with delirious travelers. (Open daily 8:30am-5:30pm; Sept. Mon.-Sat. 8:30am-10pm, Sun. 2-9pm; Oct.-Dec. and Feb.-May Mon.-Sat. 9am-8pm; Jan. Mon.-Fri. 9am-5pm. Carlysle Terminal office, beside the yacht club, open daily June-Aug. 5:30-10pm.) Reach Dún Laoghaire on the DART south from Dublin (£1) or bus #7, 7A or 8 from Eden Quay; ferry passengers should take the DART to Dublin if the hour permits.

As the port for the Stena-Sealink ferries, Dún Laoghaire is prime breeding ground for B&Bs, some more predatory than others. The **Old School House Hostel,** Eblana

Ave. (tel. 280 8777), is off Royal Marine Rd. (Six-bed room £8, quads £9, doubles £22; with bath add 50p.) **Marleen** is at 9 Marine Rd. (tel. 280 2456). Fall off the DART or ferry, and you'll be here—great location on the first block of Marine Rd., just west of the harbor. Yay—TV in every room! (£15/person.) At **Avondale,** 3 Northumberland Ave. (tel. 280 9628), next to Dunnes Stores, psychedelic paisley abounds. (Single £18. Doubles £29.)

Stock up on provisions at **Quinnsworth Supermarket** in the Dún Laoghaire shopping center (open Mon.-Wed. and Sat. 9am-6pm, Thurs.-Fri. 9am-9pm). The **Country Life Café** plays good music while serving inexpensive lunches (open Mon.-Sat. 8am-5pm). **The Coffee Bean,** 88b St. George's St. Lower (tel. 280 9522) sends customers virtually rolling down the street out of their deli (open Mon.-Sat. 8am-5pm). **The Purty Kitchen,** Dunleary Rd. (tel. 284 3576), is a lively pub with a well-known "alternative" music venue upstairs, **The Purty Loft,** with nightly gigs (cover £3-5; often free before 11pm). From the harbor, turn right down Crofton Rd.

SANDYCOVE

Sandycove is home to the **James Joyce Museum,** Sandycove Ave. W. (tel. 280 9265). From the Sandycove DART station, walk down Islington Ave., then right along the coast to Sandycove Point, or take bus #8 from Nassau St. in Dublin to Sandycove Ave. West. James Joyce stayed here for six days in August 1904 as a guest of Oliver St. John Gogarty, a Dublin surgeon, poetic wit, man-about-town, and the tower's first civilian tenant. Part I of *Ulysses* is set in and around the tower, with Gogarty as "Buck Mulligan," an Englishman as the Englishman, and Joyce/Stephen Dedalus meditating on the winedark sea from the gun platform at the towertop. In the museum, read the letter about a briefcase "the color of a nun's belly." (Open May-Sept. Mon.-Sat. 10am-1pm and 2-5pm, Sun. 2-6pm; April and Oct. Mon.-Fri. 10am-1pm and 2-5pm. £1.90, seniors and ages 12-17 £1.40, ages 3-11 £1.)

At the foot of the tower lies the infamous **Forty Foot Men's Bathing Place.** Behind a wall, on the rocks, below the battery, and adjacent to the Martello Tower, men skinny-dip year-round, and don't seem to mind that they're tourist attractions. The pool rarely contains 40 men, or even 20; the name comes from the *Fortieth* regiment of British *foot* soldiers, who made it their own semi-private swimming hole.

EASTERN IRELAND

Eastern Ireland is immediately outside of Dublin's orbit; close enough to be visited with ease from the big city, far enough away for things to get peaceful, rural, or just plain wacky, Cos. Wicklow, Kildare, and Meath all make lovely daytrips. Clonmacnois, Co. Offaly, near Athlone, is a great stopover from Dublin to Galway.

■■■ WICKLOW MOUNTAINS

Over 2000 ft. high, covered by gorse and heather and pleated by rivers rushing down wooded glens, the Wicklow summits are home only to grazing sheep and a few villagers. The main tourist attraction, Glendalough, is in the midst of the mountains and draws a steady summertime stream of coach tours from Dublin. The interlacing of wilderness attractions and small towns in Wicklow makes the county fun to explore, but hard to explain. Here more than anywhere, you need a good map.

ENNISKERRY

Enniskerry oozes quaintness, with cafés and craft shops near a small, triangular bit of paved-over village "green." The precious shops are filled with tourists drawn in by the Kodak moments of Powerscourt, which really is worth the fuss. The formal gardens at Powerscourt unroll from a grand terrace to a pond and fountain flanked by Italian statuary, to a cymbal-crash view of the Sugarloaf Mountains. Parts of Power-

scourt are quite fanciful, like the Queen's garden in *Alice in Wonderland.* Not even
Lewis Carroll would have thought to include a pet cemetery in a formal garden;
check out the Dadaesque cow's grave. The **Powerscourt House** (tel. (01) 286
7676) was gutted by fire in 1974 on the eve of its gala reopening. Photos show the
sumptuous, forever-lost interior, but the existing house has a spooky elegance as it
lies in ruins amid greenery (house and gardens £2.80, students £2.30; open March-
Oct. daily 9:30am-5:30pm). Five km away, the **Powerscourt Waterfall** is the tallest
in Britain or Ireland; it's clearly signposted along the road from Powerscourt Gardens (£1.50, students £1; open daily 9:30am-7pm).

Enniskerry makes a good starting point for an abbreviated hike along the Wicklow
Way to Glendalough. The **Knockree Hostel** is the closest of the Wicklow Way hostels to Enniskerry. The **Glencree Hostel** is also within spitting distance of Powerscourt. **Bus** #85 runs from the Bray DART station; #44 from Hawkins St., Dublin
runs less frequently.

GLENDALOUGH

Glendalough ("GLEN-da-lock," meaning "glen of the two lakes") is one of Ireland's
most handsome valleys. Here the 6th-century St. Kevin gave up his preference for
ascetic isolation in order to found a monastic school. During the great age of the
Irish monasteries—563 to 1152 AD—these settlements were Ireland's religious and
cultural centers, attracting pilgrims from all over Europe.

Practical Information The many tour buses, Dubliners, and backpackers
who come to savor the scenery pass through **Laragh** ("LAR-a"), a village 1 mi. up the
road from the sites. Most pilgrims to Glendalough catch the private **St. Kevin's Bus
Service** (tel. (01) 281 8119). (From Dublin, St. Stephen's Green West, at Royal College of Surgeons, Mon.-Sat. at 11:30am and 6pm, Sun. 11:30am and 7pm; £5, return
£8. Buses return from the glen Mon.-Sat. 4:15pm, Sun. 9:45am and 5:30pm; they
park across from the Glendalough Hotel.) In Laragh, the bus leaves from the phone
booth across from the post office. **Hitching** is unpleasant, since almost all the cars
going to Laragh and Glendalough are filled with nervous tourists. Hitchers do make
it as far as the juncture of the N11 with Glendalough's R755 by putting out a thumb
at the beginning of the N11 in southwest Dublin. **Bus Éireann** also runs tours to
Glendalough every Friday; the bus leaves Busáras 9:30am, returns 4:30pm. The tour
also covers Avondale, home of Charles Stewart Parnell (£13.50).

Back in Laragh, B&Bs and tearooms flutter anxiously for attention. Bord Fáilte
operates a **tourist office** from a trailer in the center of town (tel. (0404) 45482;
open July-Aug.). **Bike rental** is available from the Glendalough **post office,** on the
road from Laragh (tel. (0404) 45236; £6/day, deposit £20; open daily 9am-10pm.)

Accommodations, Food, & Pubs The **Glendalough Hostel (HI/An
Óige)** (tel. (0404) 45342) lies five minutes up the road past the Glendalough visitors' center. Women stay in a rose-covered cottage; men satisfy themselves with a
musty former stable. (Lockout noon-5pm, unguarded luggage storage. Max. 3-day
stay. Sheets 50p. Kitchen open 7:30-10am and 5-10pm. £5.50, Oct.-May £4.50.)

Laragh boasts two hostels and a clutch of B&Bs. The **Wicklow Way Hostel** (tel.
(0404) 45398) offers sturdy beds in six- to 16-bed rooms. (Kitchen with microwave
open 7am-10pm; lounge with TV. £6.) Two hundred yds. out of Laragh on the Wexford Rd., the **Old Mill Hostel** (tel. (0404) 45156) is cozily unrefined. (8-14 beds/
room. Sheets 50p. Great kitchen. £5.90, private rooms £7.50.) The hostel also offers
camping for £3. Among Laragh's B&Bs, **Brockagh Heights** (tel. (0404) 45243),
stands out for its magnificent view, commanding the whole river valley from its
perch half a mile up the steep hill north of the road; follow signs (£12.50/person).

In Glendalough, the **Glendalough Tavern** serves a limited menu, but is a lot
cheaper than the hotel restaurant (tel. (0404) 45135 or 45391; sandwiches £1.50,
entrees £5). In Laragh, the **Laragh Inn** offers pub grub and meals (open noon-9pm;
entrees £5-7; salads £4-7). The **Brudge Bar** has grub and sessions Saturday nights at

9pm which pull all the local hostelers. The post office/bike rental agency/convenience store is also the **grocery** with the longest hours (daily 9am-10pm).

Sights Today only the **visitors center** (tel. (0404) 45352) and a handful of tourist trappings mark the ancient spot. (Open mid-June to Aug. daily 9am-6:30pm; Sept. daily 9:45am-6pm; Oct. daily 10am-5pm; Nov. to mid-March Tues.-Sun. 10am-4:30pm; mid-March to mid-April daily 10am-5pm; mid-April to mid-June daily 9:45am-6pm. £1.50, seniors £1, students 60p. Last admission 1hr. before closing, ½-hr. tours leave hourly. Wheelchair access to center.)

Plucky monks once hid in the 103-ft. **Round Tower,** built in the 10th century as a watchtower and belltower. **St. Kevin's Cross** is an unadorned high cross. The **Cathedral,** constructed in both Greek and Roman architectural styles, was at one time the second-largest in the country. **St. Kevin's Church,** built in the 11th century, was used as a church until 1851. The **Upper and Lower Lakes** are a right turn over the foot bridge near St. Kevin's Kitchen. Near the spectacular Upper Lake, a half hour walk from the site, **St. Kevin's Bed** is the cave where he would pray.

THE WICKLOW WAY

The 70-mi. Wicklow Way, Ireland's first and best-known long-distance path, starts near Dublin and progresses south along the crests all the way to Clonegal in Co. Carlow. Though the path is well-marked with yellow arrows, you'll still need Bord Fáilte's green *Info Sheet #26B* and the Ordinance Survey's *Wicklow Way* (£3.75). Since the path is mostly out of sight and hearing range of the lowlands, traveling alone can be risky. It's a bad idea to drink water from the streams en route, and it is *illegal* to light fires within 2km of the forest. The northern 45 mi. of the path (from Dublin to Aghavannagh) are the most popular, have the best scenery and offer better access to hostels. To reach the northern end of the path, take bus #47B from Hawkins St. in Dublin's city center to its terminus in Marlay Park in Rathfarnham, a Dublin suburb. The #47 bus also stops nearby. It takes three days to hike the northern section (assuming 7-8hr. per day of hiking). The entire trail takes six days.

Several hostels lie within 5 mi. of the Wicklow Way; these fill up July and August. For An Óige hostels, book ahead through the An Óige Head Office, 61 Mountjoy St., Dublin (tel. (01) 830 4555); call other hostels directly. The hostels are listed north to south, with distance from the Wicklow Way in parentheses. Wicklow Way, Old Mill, and Glendalough hostels are reviewed in Glendalough (see above).

Knockree (An Óige/HI), Lackland House, Enniskerry (tel. (01) 286 4036; on the Way). From Enniskerry, take the left fork road leading from the village green, take a left at Buttercups Newsagent, and begin a steep walk, following signs for Glencree Drive. £5; Oct.-May £4.

Glencree (An Óige/HI), Stone House, Enniskerry (tel. (01) 286 4037; 3 mi. from the Way up a steep hill), is farther along Glencree Drive. £5; Oct.-May £4.

Tiglin (An Óige/HI), a.k.a. **Devil's Glen,** Ashford (tel. (0404) 40259; 5 mi.). 50 beds; basic accommodation. From Ashford, follow the Roundwood Rd. for 3 mi., then follow the signs for the Tiglin turnoff. £5; Oct.-May £4.

Wicklow Way Hostel (tel. (0404) 45398; on the Way), £6.

Old Mill Hostel, Laragh (tel. (0404) 45156; ½ mi.) £5.90, camping £3.

Glendalough (An Óige/HI; tel. (0404) 45342; 1½ mi.) £5.50; Oct.-May £4.50.

Glenmalure (HI/An Óige), Grennare (no phone; 2 mi.). West of Glenmalure is a large army range in the Glen of Imaal where military exercises are conducted. Stay out. £5; Oct.-May £4. Open July-Aug. daily; Sept.-June open Sat. nights only.

Aghavannagh House (HI/An Óige), Aughrim (tel. (0402) 36102; ½ mi.). £5; Oct.-May £4. Open daily March-Nov.; Dec.-Feb. Fri. and Sat. nights.

■■■ KILDARE TOWN

Kildare Town is like many a twelve-year-old lass—it's still in its horse phase. It is likely to remain so for a very long time; purebreds are the lifeblood of the town. Kildare seems imbued with some of their nervous energy and natural grace, especially in contrast with its mule-like neighbors.

Kildare Town has a pretty square lined by terrific pubs and old ladies on benches. In one corner of the square stands Kildare's **round tower.** This is one of the few round towers in Ireland that visitors can actually enter and climb. (Open Mon.-Sat. 9am-1pm and 2-5pm, Sun. 2-5pm; £1, children 50p.) **The Irish National Stud,** near Kildare at Tully (tel. 21617), does its best to make the town's horse fever contagious. (Don't use the gold and wrought-iron gates on the Dublin Rd.; follow the plentiful signs for the turnoff from the main road.) The small **Irish Horse Museum** is housed in a converted groom's house and stallion boxes. **The Japanese Gardens,** also part of the Stud, are beautiful and truly bizarre, like a walk-through boardgame; they purport to tell "the story of man." (Irish National Stud, Irish Horse Museum, and Japanese Gardens open Easter-Oct. Mon.-Fri. 10:30am-5pm, Sat. 10:30am-6pm, Sun. 2-6pm. Joint admission £4, students and seniors £3.)

Entertainment in Kildare is understandably equinocentric. **The Curragh** racecourse (tel. (045) 41205), between Droichead Nua/Newbridge and Kildare on the N7, hosts the **Irish Derby** ("DAR-bee") on the last Sunday in June. The race is Ireland's premier sporting and social event and one of the most prestigious races in the world. Other races are held from late March to early November; call or check the inside back cover of the Irish Rail timetable for dates (trains stop at The Curragh on racedays). (Admission £9 to Derby, £7.50 to other events; students and seniors get 50% off by purchasing tickets at the Enquiries booth.)

Near Kildare in Lullymore lurks the campy **Peatland World** (tel. (045) 60133). Located in the immense Bog of Allen, Peatland World comprises a museum and a natural history gallery with attention to the "social impact of turf" over the centuries. (Open Mon.-Fri. 9:30am-4pm, Sat.-Sun. 2-6pm; £2, students £1.50.)

Accommodation in Kildare isn't very forthcoming. In town, the **Lord Edward Guest House B&B,** on Dublin St. (tel. (045) 22389), has professional staff and a TV in every room. (Singles £18. Doubles £30.) Toward the Stud on the outskirts of town is **Fremont** (tel. 21604), on the Tully Rd. (£13/person, with bath £15.) Good pubs are plentiful. **The Silken Thomas,** The Square (tel. 22232), has renowned food (open daily 12:30-2:30pm and 6-10pm). **Li'l Flanagan,** connected to the restaurant, has trad sessions Wednesdays at 8pm. **"Top" Nolan's,** The Square (tel. 21528), is also a hardware store. Set dancing and music squeeze in between the buzz saws.

The Kildare **tourist office,** in The Square (tel. 22696) has a ferocious enthusiasm for local pubs (open Mon.-Sat. 10am-1pm and 2-6pm, Sept.-May Fri.only 10am-1pm and 2-6pm). The Stud and The Curragh are a good bit from Kildare; **bicycles** can be hired from **John Kearney,** The Square (tel. 21457), for £5 per day, £30 per week, with a £25 deposit (open Mon.-Sat. 10am-1:30pm and 2-6:30pm). The **phone code** is 045. Kildare is well-served by **trains** from Dublin's Heuston Station (Mon.-Sat. 30/day, Sun. 12/day; 30min.) and **Bus Éireann** from Dublin (1/hr.; 1-1½hr.); Dublin-bound buses from Cork and Limerick also stop in Kildare.

■■■ BOYNE VALLEY

Among the towns, highways, back lanes, and furrows of the Boyne Valley are the richest groups of archaeological remains anywhere in Ireland. Slane and Trim have some of the best-preserved medieval castles (and a rock festival or two). The Celtic Hill of Tara and the neolithic tomb-mounds of Newgrange, Knowth, and Dowth puzzle professional archaeologists and wow more casual visitors. Every so often the valley's farmers plow up weapons or artifacts from the 1690 Battle of the Boyne.

DROGHEDA

Founded by Vikings in 911, Drogheda ("DRA-hed-a") once rivaled Dublin as a center of trade and Armagh as a center of worship; it's still a busy port.

Encounter the imposing neo-Gothic style of **St. Peter's Church** on West St. (open daily 8:30am-8:30pm). Built in the 1880s, the church safeguards the blackened, shriveled head of the martyred saint Oliver Plunkett. At the end of West St. stand the twin towers of **St. Lawrence Gate,** a 13th-century fortification outside the walls of the town, which is no less impressive for the fact that it never really faced a serious attack. At the top of the hill on St. Peter's St., the mossy **Magdalen Steeple,** dating from 1224, is all that remains of the Dominican Friary that once stood on the spot. **The Droichead Arts Center,** Scholes Lane (tel. 33946), displays work by local and national artists (open Mon.-Sat. 10am-5pm; free). On Old Abbey Ln., south of West St., are the few remains of the 5th-century **Priory of St. Mary,** perched among the urban refuse of the modern town.

The **tourist office** is on West St. (tel. (041) 37070) at its intersection with George's St. (Open June-Sept. Mon.-Sat. 10am-1pm and 2-6pm.) **Trains** (tel. (041) 38749) run to Dublin (Mon.-Sat. 8/day, Sun. 3/day; ½hr.; £5 return) and Belfast (Mon.-Sat. 5/day, Sun. 3/day; 1½hr.). **Buses** (tel. (041) 35023) leave from John St. to Athlone (Mon.-Sat. 2/day, Sun. 1/day; 2½hr.); Belfast (Mon.-Sat. 4/day, Sun. 3/day; 2hr.); Dublin (Mon.-Sat. 16/day, Sun. 7/day; 50min.; £6 return); and Galway (Mon.-Sat. 2/day, Sun. 1/day; 4½hr.). **Bike rental** is a reality at **Bridge Cycles,** North Quay (tel. (041) 34526); also at Narrow West St. (tel. (041) 37244), next to the tourist office. (£6/day, £30/week. Open Mon.-Sat. 9am-6pm.)

Harpur House, William St. (tel. 32736), takes the cake among B&Bs. Follow Shap St., as it becomes Peter St., and turn right at St. Peter's Church. Run by a hospitable family, this grand townhouse has B&B rooms (some with fireplaces) for £12 and white, airy **hostel** rooms for £6 (£9 with breakfast). Buses from Harpur House do half-day sightseeing tours of the Boyne Valley (£10). **Groceries** can be found on West St. at Dunnes Stores and Quinnsworth. (Both open Mon.-Tues. and Sat. 9am-6:30pm, Wed. 9am-8pm, Thurs.-Fri. 9am-9pm.) **The Weavers,** West St. (tel. 32816), is renowned for its lunchtime and dinner grub—more wood and darkness here (DJs spin top 40 tunes Fri.-Sun. nights; no cover).

NEWGRANGE

Newgrange, the most spectacular, most restored, and most visited of the sites, is the prime example of the passage-tomb. The most dramatic moment of the tour is the recreation of the moment which actually occurs five days each year around the winter solstice, when the sun's rays enter at just the right angle to illuminate the inner chamber. Bring a windbreaker or a warm sweater; it gets chilly inside even in summer. (Tours begin every 20 min. daily, June-Sept. 9:30am-7pm, Oct. 10am-5pm, Nov.-Feb. 10am-4:30pm, Mar.-Apr. 10am-5pm, May 9:30am-6pm; £2, students £1; tel. 24488). The **tourist office** is in Newgrange (just before the entry to the site, near the parking lot; tel. 24274; open April-Oct. daily 10am-7pm).

KNOWTH & DOWTH

West of Newgrange is the less frantic, and less restored, site of **Knowth** (rhymes with "mouth"). Knowth was inhabited continuously from 3000 BC until the Battle of the Boyne, so that the site today is a mishmash of Stone Age tombs, early Christian subterranean refuge tunnels, and Norman grain ovens. Though there is no tourist office, the admission office sells booklets about Knowth's history (tel. 24824; tours 9:30am-6:30pm daily; £1.50, seniors £1, students 60p). East of Newgrange is **Dowth** (rhymes with "Knowth"), the third of the great passage tombs. Dowth is not open to the public, but you can still ramble about the mound's outside, badly damaged by the work of pillagers (there's a gaping hole at the top of the mound).

MELLIFONT ABBEY & MONASTERBOICE

Two of what were once the most important monasteries in Ireland crumble 5 mi. north of Drogheda. Turn off of the Drogheda-Collon Rd. at Monleek Cross and follow the signs for either one. The more interesting of the two, **Mellifont Abbey** (tel. (041) 26459), holds the **old lavabo,** where the monks once cleansed themselves of sins and grime. (Open mid-June-mid-Sept. daily 9:30am-6:30pm; May-mid-June Tues.-Sat. 9:30am-1pm and 2-5:30pm, Sun. 2-5:30pm; mid-Sept.-Oct. daily 10am-

5pm. £1, students 40p.) Just off the N1, the monastic settlement of **Monasterboice** ("MON-ster-boyce"; always open; free), is well-known for its high crosses and round tower. Founded in 520, the monastery was one of Ireland's most wealthy.

HILL OF TARA

From prehistoric times until at least the 10th century AD, Tara was the political and sometime religious center of Ireland. The hill is home to a Stone Age tomb, an Iron Age fort, and the principle late Celtic royal seat—the combination has guaranteed Tara's popularity with tourists and archaeologists alike. The enormous site is about halfway between Dublin and Navan on the N3. Take any Navan-bound **bus** from Dublin (13/day, Sun. 5/day; 1hr.) and ask the driver to let you off at the turnoff; it's about a mile straight up the hill to the site. The whole history of Tara decamps at the **visitors center** (tel. (046) 25903), in an old church at the site. The full site encompasses 100 acres of many smaller mounds and ring forts, though you'll likely see only the sites at the top of the hill. (Visitors center open June-Oct. daily 9:30am-6:30pm; £1, student 40p. Mounds always open; free.)

TRIM

A series of enormous, well-preserved Norman castles and abbeys that thrill even the most jaded tourist overlook this charming town on the River Boyne. Norman-invasion bigwig Hugh de Lacy built the first **Trim Castle** in 1172, though the unruly O'Connors of Connacht trashed the place a year later. The castle, which says it's the largest in Ireland, stands above the center of town and can be easily reached through the gate on Castle St. (always open; free). **Walking tours** navigate the castle, starting from opposite the Dúchas Folk Theater (tours July-Aug. Mon.-Fri. 11:30am and 2pm; £2). Any nuns galloping by on furious steeds are competing in the annual **Nun Run,** a sisters-only steeplechase held on castle grounds.

Across the picturesque river stand the 12th-century remains of **St. Mary's Abbey,** destroyed by Cromwell's armies. You can still see the **Yellow Steeple** (so called because of the yellowish gleam it gives off at twilight), the only remains of the holy sisters' old place. In front of the Yellow Steeple is what's left of **Talbot's Castle,** a 15th-century manor built by John Talbot, Viceroy of Ireland. You can rid yourself of unwelcome warts at the **Newtown Cemetery,** far behind the Castle, by putting a pin between two tomb figures known as the **Jealous Man and Woman.** When the pin rusts (which shouldn't take long in this country) your warts will disappear.

Trim's **tourist office** on Mill St. (tel. (046) 37111; open June-Sept. Mon.-Sat. 10am-6pm) has a panoply of pamphlets, including the useful self-guided walking tour of Trim (60p). Next door to the office is the spanking-new **Meath Visitors Center** (tel. (046) 37227), which introduces the history of Trim. (Open Mon.-Sat. 9am-6pm; £2, seniors £1.25, children 70p.) **Bus Éireann** stops on Castle St., in front of the Dúchas Folk Theater, en route to Dublin (6/day; £5 return) and Athlone (1/day).

The **White Lodge,** Lackanash New Rd. (tel. 36549; follow High St. to the Navan Rd. and take the first right), has spacious, well-decorated rooms with TVs. (Singles £18. Doubles £26, with bath £30). In the heart of town pumps **Brogan's,** High St. (tel. 31237), a pub that does hotel-like B&B (£13/person). **The Pastry Kitchen,** Market St. (tel. 36166) thumps sturdy breakfasts and luscious pastries and breads on the table (£2; breakfast served all day; open Mon.-Sat. 7:30am-6pm, Sun. 10am-6pm). For pubs, **The Abbey Lodge,** Market St. (tel. 31549), surrenders a tremendous plate of roast stuffed chicken with fries and veggies for £3.25. **McCormack's,** across from the Castle on Castle St. (tel. 31963), may show a lot of cricket on TV, but it's all Irish on Sun. nights when the *bodhrán,* tin whistle, and a fiddle or two liven things up.

■■■ CLONMACNOIS

What if they built a visitors center and nobody came? If Clonmacnois were anywhere near the beaten path, it would be Glendalough with river views and without the weird tearooms. Instead, Clonmacnois is a huge detour, but St. Ciaran's monastic city is worth the trip. The **visitors center** (tel. (0905) 74195) craves attention with wheelchair-accessible displays of the original cross of the Scriptures and the treasures of Clonmacnois. (Open every single day of the year. May-Aug. 9am-7pm; Sept.-Apr. 10am-6pm. £1.50, students 60p.) A coffee shop is here too—the only food for miles around. Import groceries.

The site itself is impressive for its lonely grandeur. The **cathedral** has been destroyed by Vikings and rebuilt by monks several times; the structure now standing dates from about 1100. Over the arch of the north doorway stand St. Dominic, St. Patrick, and St. Francis. The last High King of Ireland, Rory O'Connor, was buried inside in 1198. Other high kings are scattered around Clonmacnois. **Temple Ciaran** is a ruin in the center of the churchyard, probably constructed on the site of the original church. **O'Connor's Church,** built in 1000, still has services (Church of Ireland) on the fourth Sunday of the month at 10am. **O'Rourke's Tower,** the freestanding one of the two round towers, had its top blown off by lightning in 1135.

The three **high crosses** are worth lingering over. The **South Cross,** next to Temple Doulin, shows the crucifixion within the circle on its west face; interlacing patterns and animals cover the rest. The cross dates from the 700s, which makes it the oldest at Clonmacnois. Only the shaft of the **North Cross** remains; it has abstract human and animal figures. The **Cross of the Scriptures** is gorgeous and easy to read. A replica stands in the churchyard; the original is in the Visitors Center. Within the circle, it's Judgement Day—**God** holds a scepter and cross; on the left arm, St. Michael blows a trumpet. On the right arm, **Satan** pushes back the damned. The bottom panel shows Ciaran ready to build his first church.

The Clonmacnois **tourist office,** at the entrance to the parking lot (tel. (0905) 74134), is open June-Aug. daily 9am-6pm, Mar.-May and Sept.-Nov. 10am-6pm. Clonmacnois is best seen as a daytrip from **Athlone. Rossana Cruises** (tel. (0902) 92513) runs a boat from the Strand, in Athlone, to Clonmacnois (July-Aug. Wed. at 10am; £6, under 16 £3.50). Otherwise, to reach Clonmacnois from Athlone, turn off the Cloghan Rd. **Trains** leave Athlone for Dublin (8/day; 2hr.) and Galway (4/day; 1hr.). **Buses** shuttle off from Athlone in all directions, including Dublin (Mon.-Sat. 6-8/day, Sun. 5/day; 2hr.) and Galway (5/day; 1½hr.); one bus a day runs to Cork (5hr.) and Cahir (3hr.). Bikes can be rented at **Hardiman's Bike Shop** (tel. (0902) 78669), Irishtown Rd. (£7/day, £30/week negotiable deposit; tandems £10/day, £50/week. Open Mon.-Sat. 9am-1:15pm and 2:30-6pm; flexible return hours.) In Athlone, Mrs. Devaney, **Shannon View,** Sean Costello St., a section of Church St. (tel. (0902) 78411), offers crisp rooms with big beds, with TV in each room (£13/person). Two doors down on Sean Costello St., a narrow hallway leads into dim chambers at **Mrs. Kennedy's** (tel. (0902) 75878; singles £18, doubles £26).

Follow a visit to onetime monk HQ Clonmacnois with a ride on the nearby **Clonmacnois and West Offaly Railway** (tel. (0905) 74114). The strangely appealing mini-train, chugging down rails usually used for transporting peat, brings visitors on a 5½-mi., 45-min. circular tour of the Blackwater Bog. Tours leave from the Bord na Móna Blackwater Works, near Shannonbridge. (Tours hourly on the hour Easter-Sept. and by arrangement. Open daily 10am-5pm; £3, students £2.20.)

SOUTHEAST IRELAND

■■■ KILKENNY TOWN

Touted as the best-preserved medieval town in Ireland, Kilkenny Town (pop. 15,000) is in the running for its upkeep of the Norman commercial center established in 1169. It was said that the town's separate English and Irish communities scratched and hissed like "Kilkenny cats," a fable their enmity inspired; even today Kilkennians call the Parliament St. area "Irish Town." The two joined in 1844.

PRACTICAL INFORMATION

Tourist Office: Rose Inn St. (tel. 51500). Open June-Sept. Mon.-Sat. 9am-6pm, Sun. 11am-5pm; Oct. Mon.-Sat. 9am-1pm and 2-5:30pm; Nov.-Feb. Tues.-Sat. 9am-1pm and 2-5:15pm; March-April Mon.-Sat. 9am-1pm and 2-5:15pm.

Financial Services: AIB Bank, The Parade (tel. 22089), at the intersection with High St. Open Mon. 10am-5pm, Tues.-Fri. 10am-4pm. ATM.

Post Office: High St. (tel. 21879). Open Mon.-Sat. 9am-5:30pm.

Telephone Code: 056.

Trains: McDonagh Station, Dublin Rd. (tel. 22024), at John St. To Dublin, 2hr., £9; to Waterford, 45 min., £5. From MacDonagh Station, turn left on John St. and continue straight to reach The Parade.

Buses: McDonagh Station, Dublin Rd. (tel. 64933). Buses leave for: Clonmel (Mon.-Sat. 5/day, Sun. 3/day); Cork (3/day; 3hr.); Dublin (Mon.-Sat. 5/day, Sun. 4/day; £9); Galway (mid-June to mid-Sept. daily); Rosslare Harbor (mid-June to mid-Sept. daily); and Waterford (daily 5/day). **Buggy's Buses** (tel. 41264) run from Kilkenny to Dunmore Cave and the An Óige hostel.

Bike Rental: Raleigh Cycle Center, 5 John St. (tel. 62037). £7/day, £30/week, no deposit. Open Mon.-Sat. 8:30am-6pm.

Laundry: Brett's Launderette, Michael St. (tel. 63200), off John St. Wash and dry, £4. Open Mon.-Sat. 8:30am-8pm. Last wash 7pm. Womb-like.

Emergency: dial 999; no coins required. **Garda:** Dominic St. (tel. 22222).

ACCOMMODATIONS

B&Bs average £12-14. Call ahead. Waterford Rd. and more remote Castlecomer Rd., on the outskirts of town, have the highest concentration of beds.

Kilkenny Town Hostel (IHH), 35 Parliament St. (tel. 63541). Clean, light, and bare rooms. Friendly atmosphere. Non-smoking. Kitchen (7am-11pm) with microwave. Check-out 10:30am. Laundry wash and dry £3. 4-8 beds/room, £5.50-6. Sept.-June: 50p discount to *Let's Go* readers.

Foulksrath Castle (An Óige/HI), Jenkinstown (tel. 67674). 16th-century castle 8 mi. north of town. From Kilkenny, take the N77 (Durrow Rd.) and turn right at signs for Connahy. Buggy's Buses (tel. 41264) run from The Parade, Kilkenny to the hostel Mon.-Sat. at 11:30am and 5:30pm and from the hostel for Kilkenny Mon.-Sat. 8:25am and 3pm (20 min., £1.50). Bike rental. (March-Oct. and June-Sept. £5, March-May and Oct. £4.)

Ormonde Tourist Hostel, Johns Green (tel. 52733), at the top of John St. opposite the railway station. 4- to 12-bed room £7. Doubles £10/person.

Fennelly's B&B, 13 Parliament St. (tel. 61796). Right above a pub in the center of town. Large, clean, floral. Singles £15, July-Aug. £20. Doubles £26, with bath £30.

Bregagh House B&B, Dean St. Handsome wood furniture; three stuffed quails. £13, with bath £15; in July-Aug. add £2. **Camping** with showers £3.

Nore Valley Park, 6 mi. south of Kilkenny between Bennetsbridge and Stonyford (tel. 27229), signposted from Kilkenny. Hikers £2/person. Open March-Oct.

FOOD & PUBS

Stock up on basic supplies at the immense **Dunnes Supermarket,** St. Kieran's St. (open Mon.-Wed., Sat. 9am-6pm, Thurs.-Fri. 9am-9pm).

Edward Langton's, 69 John St. (tel. 65133). Voted the country's best pub food many, many times. Lunch menu (daily noon-3pm): roast chicken (£5.50).

Italian Connection, 38 Parliament St. (tel. 64225). Gourmet Italian food. Lunch specials daily (noon-3pm). All pastas £5, pizzas £4-6. Open daily noon-11pm.

Kilkenny Kitchen, upstairs in the Kilkenny Design Center across from the castle (tel. 22118). A real swell cafeteria. Open Mon.-Sat. 9am-5pm, Sun. 10am-5pm.

M.I. Dore, High St. (tel. 63374), near Parliament St. Customers buried by ham and knickknacks. Soup and roll (£1.15). Open Mon.-Sat. 8am-11pm, Sun. 9am-11pm.

Caisleán Uí Cuain, 2 High St. (tel. 65406). High-grade pub grub in a classy lounge (Greek salad £4.50, club sandwich £5, lunch served 12:30-3pm).

At the **Pump House Bar,** 26 Parliament St. (tel. 63924), throbbing rock music spills into the street; live bands play Thursday nights. Thespians converge for nightly poetry readings, improv comedy, and traditional and folk sessions at **Cleere's Pub,** 28 Parliament St. (tel. 62573). **The Arch Tavern,** 6 John St. (tel. 22689), earns regulars for blues and rock sessions (Thurs.-Sun. 9:30pm, free). **Fennelly's,** 13 Parliament St., (tel. 64337), hosts an older crowd. (Trad sessions Fri. nights.) During the day, watch the House of Commons on their TV. Should you tire of stout, **Lautrec's Wine Bar,** St. Kieran's St. off Rose Inn St. (tel. 62720) serves wine in a dark, cavernous, French setting from 5:30pm till late.

SIGHTS

All of central Kilkenny is a sight; most of the buildings have preserved their medieval appearance. **Tynan Walking Tours** (tel. 65929) will point out the naughty bits. Tours depart from the tourist office, Rose Inn St. (mid-March-Oct. Mon.-Sat. 6/day; Sun. 4/day; £2.50, students £2).

Thirteenth-century **Kilkenny Castle** (tel. 21450), on The Parade, housed the Earls of Ormonde until 1932. The Spencers—remote ancestors of Princess Di—sold it to them in the 1300s. Ogle the Long Room, with its breathtaking, highly ornamented ceiling. Downstairs, the **Butler Gallery** mounts modern art exhibitions. (Castle and gallery open June-Sept. daily 10am-7pm; Oct.-March Tues.-Sat. 10:30am-5pm, Sun. 11am-5pm; Apr.-May daily 10:30am-5pm. Access by guided tour only. £2, seniors £1.50, students and children £1. Castle gardens open daily 10am-8:30pm; free.)

Kilkenny is blessed with a preponderance of religious architecture. The finest is 13th-century **St. Canice's Cathedral;** inside the church, medieval tombstones are embedded in the floor and walls. (Open daily 10am-6pm, except services. Cathedral free, donation requested.) For an additional 50p (students 20p) you can climb the steep ladders of the 100-ft. tower for a fine view of the town's surroundings.

Crafty 14th-century monks are said to have brewed a light ale in St. Francis' Abbey, in the yard of what is now **Smithwicks Brewery** on Parliament St. The abbey is in ruins, but its industry survives: Smithwicks Brewery offers an audio-visual show and stout tasting. (July-Aug. Mon.-Fri. 3pm; free tickets at tourist office.)

Jerpoint Abbey, near **Tullaherin** (tel. (056) 24623), 1½ mi. south of Thomastown on the N9 (Waterford Rd.), holds remarkable etchings in the abbey cloister and numerous knights' tombs. (Open mid-April to mid-June Tues.-Sun. 10am-1pm and 2-5pm; mid-June to Sept. daily 9:30am-6:30pm; Oct. daily 10am-1pm and 2-5pm. £1.50, students 60p.) **Bus Éireann** stops here in front of O'Keeffe's Newsagent (from Kilkenny, Mon.-Sat. at 5:30pm; 20 min.; £3).

■■■ CASHEL

The fab **Rock of Cashel** rises above the town of Cashel, truly magical when seen from a distance or when lit at night. Three hundred feet above the plain, the dark limestone hill bristles with an elaborate complex of medieval buildings.

The **tourist office,** in the middle of Main St. (tel. 61333), is crisply efficient. (Open April-Sept. Mon.-Sat. 9am-6pm; July-Aug. also Sun. 10am-1pm and 2-6pm.) The **Cashel Holiday Hostel,** 6 John St., is a **Rent-A-Bike depot,** which means that bikes can be rented here and returned elsewhere in Ireland (and vice-versa) for a £5 extra charge. (£6/day, £30/week, £30 deposit). Cashel's **phone code** is 062. **Bus Éireann** (tel. 62121) leaves from O'Reilly's on Main St., serving Dublin (3/day, 3hr.; £9, students £6.50), Cork (4/day, 1½hr.; £8, students £5.30), Athlone (1/day; 2¾hr.), and Cahir (4/day, 15 min.; £2.40, students £2).

Accommodations O'Brien's Farmhouse Hostel, off the Dundrum Rd. (tel. 61003; from town, make the first left after the Rock), is set in the shadow of the Rock near Hore Abbey. Complete set of matching dinnerware! (Laundry £2 wash, £2 dry. Bike hire £5/day. 6-bed dorms £6, private rooms £9. **Camping** £3.50/person, does not include use of hostel facilities.) The **Cashel Holiday Hostel,** 6 John St. (tel.

62330), off Main St., is more central. (Laundry £3. Rent-A-Bike depot. 4- to 8-bed dorm £5; 4-bed with bath £6; private rooms £8/person. Key deposit £3.) **Abbey House B&B,** Moor Lane (tel. 61104), is a wonderland of fuzzy textures (one much-coveted single £13; otherwise, singles £18. Doubles £26, with bath £30).

Food & Pubs You can get anything you want at **Alice's Bistro,** 105 Main St. (tel. 62170), where grilled chicken, bacon, and chips goes for £5 (open daily 9am-10pm). **The Spearman Restaurant,** 97 Main St. (tel. 61143), is a notch up in price and classiness. (Open daily noon-2:30pm and 5-9:30pm. Sandwiches £1.50, stuffed pasta with tuna and cottage cheese £3.75, dinner menu through the roof.) **Super-Valu Supermarket,** Main St., values you (Mon.-Sat. 8am-9pm, Sun. 9am-6pm).

The best pub in Cashel is **Feehan's,** Main St. (tel. 61929), with two youth-packed, stone-floored levels and music nightly. **O'Reilly's Lounge,** across the street at 9 Main St. (tel. 61858), gobbles up the rest of Cashel's youth. Locals head to the snazzy **Hannigan's** (tel. 61737), on Ladywell St. (the Dublin Rd.).

Sights The elevated **Rock of Cashel** is a huge limestone outcrop with a jumble of secular and ecclesiastical buildings on top. Cashel didn't become an ecclesiastical center until after 1101, when King Muirchertach O'Brien donated the site to the Church, ensuring the loyalty of the Irish church. Over the next few centuries, arch-bishop after local ruler after archbishop added to the construction on the Rock: the result was a Gothic cathedral crammed between a round tower and a Romanesque chapel in a riotous Greatest Hits of Irish Architecture. (Rock open mid-June to mid-Sept. daily 9am-7:30pm; mid-March to mid-June 9:30am-5:30pm; mid-Sept. to mid-March 9:30am-4:30pm. Last admission 40 min. before closing. £2, students £1.) Down the path from the Rock, **Hore Abbey** awaits silently amid a chorus of arches.

In Cashel proper, the **GPA-Bolton Library** (tel. 61944), up John St. past the hos-tel, displays really old books and silver, including a rare tome in its original calfskin binding. (Open March-Oct. Mon.-Sat. 9:30am-5:30pm, Sun. 2:30-5:30pm. £1.50, stu-dents £1, under 15 50p). For a good time, call the **Brú Ború Heritage Center** (tel. 61122), at the base of the Rock, where Irish traditional music, song, and dance (but no Guinness) tempt the audience from their seats.

■ NEAR CASHEL: CAHIR

It's hard not to trip over **Cahir Castle** (tel. (052) 41011), one of the largest and best preserved castles in Ireland. It is exactly what every tourist envisions a castle to be— heavy, wet, and grey. (Open mid-June to mid-Sept. daily 9am-7:30pm; April to mid-June and mid-Sept. to mid-Oct. 10am-6pm; Nov.-March daily 10am-1pm and 2-4:30pm. £1.50, seniors £1, students and children 40p. Last admission 40 min. before closing.) The broad River Suir that flows into Waterford Harbor is just a trickle in Cahir; the wildly green **riverwalk** follows it from the tourist office's backyard to the tickin' 19th-century **Swiss Cottage** (tel. (052) 41144) and beyond. Note the well-hidden servants' entrance. (Open May-Sept. Tues.-Sun. 10am-6pm; April 10am-1pm and 2-5pm; March and Oct.-Nov. 10am-1pm and 2-4:30pm. £1.50, students 60p. Last admission 40 min. before closing. Wheelchair access.)

The **tourist office,** Castle St. (tel. (052) 41453), is open July-Aug. Mon.-Sat. 9am-6pm, Sun. 11am-5pm; May-June and Sept. Mon.-Sat. 9am-6pm. **Bus Éireann** runs from the tourist office to Limerick and Waterford (both daily 5/day: Limerick 1hr.; £7.30, students £4.20; Waterford 1¼hr.; £5.90, students £4), to Cork (4/day; 1½hr.; £7, students £5), and to Dublin via Cashel (3/day: Dublin 3hr.; £10, students £7.50; Cashel 15 min.; £2.40, students £2). **Trains** leave from the station off the Cashel Rd., just past the church, for Limerick and Rosslare (Mon.-Sat 1/day).

■■■ ROSSLARE HARBOR

Ferries run daily to Britain, and most days to France, and the town caters to this trade: shops open and close with the arrivals and departures of the ferries, and B&Bs swamp the N25 between Wexford and Rosslare Harbor. While Rosslare Harbor itself is best seen from the porthole of a departing ferry, Irish beach bunnies know the value of sunny, nearby beach towns like Kilmore Quay.

PRACTICAL INFORMATION

Tourist office: The **ferry office** (tel. 33623), to be avoided at all costs during rush times, runs on ferry time. Open daily 6:30am-9:30am and 11am-8:30pm or 1-8:30pm, depending on ferry arrival times. **Kilrane office** is more sedate (tel. 33232). Open May-mid-Sept. daily 11am-8pm.

Financial services: Currency exchange at the **Bank of Ireland** (tel. 33304). Open Mon.-Fri. 10am-12:30pm and 1:30-4pm.

Post office: In the **SuperValu,** between produce and checkout (tel. 33207). Open Mon.-Fri. 9am-1pm and 2pm-5:30pm, Sat. 9am-1pm.

Telephone code: The area's phone code toots 053 as it exits the ferry port.

Ferries: Trains and buses often connect with the ferries. Bus Éireann and Irish Rail have desks in the terminal (tel. 33592; open daily 6:30am-9:45pm).

Trains: Trains run from the ferry port to: Dublin (Mon.-Sat. 3/day, Sun. 2/day; 2hr.; £10); Limerick (Mon.-Sat. 2/day; 3½hr.; £18); Waterford (Mon.-Sat. 3/day; 1¼hr.; £8.50); and Wexford (Mon.-Sat. 3/day, Sun. 2/day; 20 min.; £3).

Buses: Buses run to: Galway, Killarney, and Tralee via Waterford (Mon.-Sat. 4/day, Sun. 3/day; to Galway £14); Cork (Mon.-Sat. 4/day, Sun. 3/day; £12); Limerick (3/day; £12, return £16); Waterford (Mon.-Sat. 4/day, Sun. 3/day; £5, return £7); Dublin (Mon.-Sat. 6/day, Sun. 5/day; 3hr.; £9); and Wexford (Mon.-Sat. 10/day, Sun. 8/day; 20 min.; £2.40). The bus stops outside the ferry port and at J. Pitt's Convenience Store in Kilrane.

Bike rental: Bike rental is available at the **Rosslare Youth Hostel,** part of the Rent-A-Bike network: bikes from here can be dropped off elsewhere for a £5 charge (and vice-versa) (£6 per day, £30 per week, £30 deposit).

Emergency: dial 999; no coins required.

ACCOMMODATIONS & FOOD

In Rosslare, more than anywhere in Ireland, take the Bord Fáilte shamrock as a measure of quality—there's a noticeable difference between approved and non-approved B&Bs. The deluxe **SuperValu supermarket** (open Mon.-Thurs. 8am-7pm, Fri. 8am-8pm, Sat. 8am-6pm, Sun. 9am-1pm) is opposite the youth hostel.

Mrs. David Power (tel. 31243), 1½ mi. from the harbor on the left-hand side of the N25; marked only by a sign reading "Self-catering accommodations £5." A hostel in a converted farmhouse that would do most B&Bs proud. July-Aug. £7.50, £5/person after the first 2; Sept.-May £5/person.

Rosslare Harbor Youth Hostel (An Óige/HI), Goulding St. (tel. 33399), signposted on the hill opposite the ferry terminal; it's off Rosslare Harbor's one street. Offers a concentration of continental youth and flies. Check-in 5:30pm; lockout 9:30am-5:30pm; curfew 11:30pm, lights out midnight. £6; Sept.-May £5. MC, Visa.

St. Josephs (tel. 33285), on the N25. Stands out for its welcoming owner, a definite exception among the ferry pirates. £12.50/person, £14 with bath.

Marianella B&B (tel. 33139), off the N25 across the road from Anchors Restaurant. Cookies and tea laid out in every room. £13/person, £14.50 with bath.

Mrs. J. Foley, 3 Coastguard Station (tel. 33522), down a gravel walkway, signposted off *the* main street. Bed and (continental) breakfast. Noon check-out. £7/person. **Camping** £2/person.

Rosslare Holiday Caravan and Camping Park, Rosslare Strand (tel. 32427), opposite the Bay Bar, 8km from the ferry. Wheelchair access. Hikers and cyclists £2.50/person. From ferry, take the N25 (Wexford Rd.) 2km, turn right at Cusher's Bar in Tagoat, after 3km, take third junction right.

■ NEAR ROSSLARE HARBOR: KILMORE QUAY

Thirteen mi. southwest of Rosslare on Forlorn Point, the small fishing village of Kilmore Quay charms with its thatched, white-washed seaside cottages. The village berths its **Maritime Museum** (tel. (053) 29655 or 29832) in the lightship *Guillemot.* (Open June-Sept. daily noon-6pm; £1.) Kilmore Quay also sends boat trips out to the **Saltee Islands,** a former pagan pilgrimage site and now Ireland's largest bird sanctuary. Boats leave the mainland each morning, stranding you until 4:30pm (May-Sept. daily, weather permitting; arrive to catch the ferry no later than 10:45am; return £8); contact Mr. Willie Bates (tel. (053) 29644) or Mr. O'Brien (tel. (053) 29727). One mi. from town up the Wexford Rd. is the **Kilturk Independent Hostel** (tel. (053) 29883). No secure luggage storage. Fishing trips and tours of the islands are arranged daily (£8). (Wheelchair access. 9-bed dorm £5.50. Singles, doubles, and family room £7/person). To reach Kilmore from Rosslare Harbor, take the Wexford Rd. to Tagoat and turn left (about 15 mi. from Wexford or Rosslare). From Wexford, take the Rosslare Rd. and turn right 4 mi. from town at Piercetown.

■■■ WEXFORD TOWN

Thin, winding streets leading to fishing boats tied along the quay give Wexford Town a small-town feel that belies its prominence on the map and in the history books. Perhaps in reaction to all the warfare in its past, Wexford declared itself a nuclear-free zone in the 80s.

PRACTICAL INFORMATION

Tourist Office: Crescent Quay (tel. 23111). Open Mon.-Sat. 9am-6pm, Sun 10am-5pm; Sept.-June Mon.-Sat. 9am-1pm and 2-6pm.

Post Office: Anne St. (tel. 22587). Open Mon.-Tues. and Thurs.-Sat. 9am-5:30pm, Wed. 9:30am-5:30pm.

Telephone Code: 053.

Financial Services: Bank of Ireland, Custom House Quay (tel. 23022). Open Mon. 10am-5pm, Tues.-Fri. 10am-4pm. ATM.

Trains: North Station, Redmond Sq. (tel. 22522), a 5-min. walk along the quays from Crescent Quay. Booking offices open around departure times. Trains hustle to Dublin (Mon.-Sat. 3/day, Sun. 2/day; 3hr.; £10) and Rosslare Harbor (Mon.-Sat. 4/day, Sun. 3/day; 30 min.; £3).

Buses: North Station. Buses run to Dublin (daily 5/day; 2½hr.) and to Rosslare (Mon.-Sat. 7/day, Sun. 5/day; 20 min.). Buses to and from Limerick connect with Irish Ferries and Stena-Sealink sailings (daily 2/day). From mid-June to mid-September, buses run directly to Galway and other points west.

Bike Rental: Hayes Cycle Shop, 108 South Main St. (tel. 22462). Raleigh touring bikes £5/day, £30/week, deposit £40. Open Mon.-Sat. 9am-6pm.

Laundry: My Beautiful Launderette, St. Peter's Sq. (tel 24317), up Peters St. from South Main St. Wash £1.50; 2-min. dryer 40p; soap 30p. Showers, too (£1). Open Mon.-Sat. 10am-9pm.

Hospital: Wexford General Hospital, Richmond Terrace (tel. 42233), N25.

Emergency: Dial 999; no coins required. **Garda:** Roches Rd. (tel. 22333).

ACCOMMODATIONS

The nearest hostels are about 10 mi. away in Rosslare and Kilmore; staying in a B&B in Wexford Town proper is a happier idea. If these B&Bs are full, look along the N25 (Rosslare Rd.), Bayview Drive off the Dublin Rd., or St. John's Rd. off Georges St.

Mrs. Donnelly, The Abbey, 3 Lower Georges St. (tel. 22787), follow signs for White's Hotel. If Mary Poppins ran a B&B, this would be it. £13/person.

Marie Murphy, Shanagolden, St. John's Rd. (tel 22156), continue up George's St. Marilyn Monroe beckons from every wall. Singles £13.50. Doubles £25.

Mrs. Daly, Carraig Donn, New Town Court (tel. 42046), off the Newtown (a.k.a. Waterford) Rd. Call from in town and Mrs. Daly will pick you up. Large rooms, Brady Bunch decor. Wheelchair access. £13/person.

Killiane Castle, off the Rosslare Rd. (tel. 58898), signposted 3 mi. south of Wexford on the N25; the first left after the Esso station. A wee bit out of the way, but so is Ireland. Deluxe, hotel-style rooms with uniformed staff. Singles with bath £22. Doubles with bath £32.

Ferrybank Caravan and Camping Park, (tel. 44378 or 43274). On the eastern side of Wexford, across from the Dublin Rd. Take the bridge and head straight up the seacoast half-mi. 1-person tent £3, 2-person tent £4.50. Open Easter-mid-Sept.

FOOD & PUBS

Dunnes Stores is in Redmond Square next to the train station (open Mon.-Wed. and Sat. 9am-6pm, Thurs.-Fri. 9am-9pm). **Greenacres,** 56 North Main St., is a virtual warehouse (open Mon.-Sat. 9am-6pm). **La Cuisine,** North Main St. (tel. 24986), makes a mean chicken sandwich (£1.20) and yummy apple tarts (£1). Open Mon.-Sat. 9am-6pm. **Tim's Tavern,** 51 South Main St. (tel. 23861), has won national awards for dishes like avocado, pear, and crab (£5.50), crab in garlic butter (£7). Lunch served daily noon-5pm, dinner 6:30-9:30pm. Trad Wed. and Sat. at 9:30pm.

At **The Centenary Stores,** Charlotte St. (tel. 24424), younger folk gather. (Excellent trad on Wed. night and Sun. afternoon.) Crowds of all ages mingle at **O'Faolain's,** 11 Monk St. (tel. 23877; American pop music on Thurs. nights) Try **The Wren's Nest,** Custom House Quay (tel. 22359), popular with locals, or **The Goal Bar,** 72 South Main St. (tel. 23727; country, rock, or trad most nights; sometimes karaoke). At atmosphere of bonhomie is brought on by the cool carvings at **Archers,** Redmond Sq.(tel. 22316; food served Mon.-Sat. 12:30-3pm, dinner 5:30-8:30pm; Sun. lunch noon-2pm). Upstairs, **The Junctions** is Wexford's nightclub of choice, thrumping into the early hours (11pm Tues.-Sat. nights; no cover).

SIGHTS

The historical society runs free **walking tours** of the city nightly June-Aug., departing from White's Hotel at 8:15pm; book through the tourist office. **Westgate Heritage Tower** (tel. 46506) offers walking tours of Wexford (no regular schedule—just show up and ask to take the walk. £2.50/person, 1½-2hr.)

Dividing North and South Main Streets, an open area marks the **Bull Ring;** bullfights were inaugurated in 1621 by the town's butcher guild as a promotional device. **Crescent Quay,** the interruption in the long, straight waterfront, repaired ships until the early 1900s. At the intersection of High St. and Westgate St., **Westgate Tower** still stands, the only survivor of the six that originally studded Wexford's walls. The tower gate now holds the **Westgate Heritage Center** (tel. 46506), whose audiovisual show describes the historical evidence now missing from town. (Open year-round Mon.-Sat. 9:30am-1pm and 2-5:30pm; July-Aug. also Sun. 2-5pm. £1.30, students 80p). Next door, the **Selskar Abbey,** site of King Henry II's extended penance, now provides a foothold for lush wildflowers.

■ NEAR WEXFORD

The **Irish National Heritage Park** (tel. (053) 41733), 2½ mi. north of Wexford off the N11, regales visitors with 9000 years of Irish culture, from the Stone Age to the arrival of the Normans. (Open March-Nov. daily 10am-7pm, last admission 5pm. £3, students £2.50.) **Westgate Minitours** (tel. 24655) operates daily buses from the tourist office to the Irish National Heritage Park (return £5, admission included; departs Mon.-Sat. 10am and 1:30pm, Sun. noon and 2pm).

ENNISCORTHY

Fourteen mi. north of Wexford Town, the hilltop town of Enniscorthy is exceptionally conscious of its Republican history: in 1798, rebels led by a local priest held the

British at bay for 12 days before a defeat at nearby Vinegar Hill, while in 1916 Enniscorthy was the only town to join Dublin's Easter Rising.

Trains running between Dublin and Rosslare stop in Enniscorthy (Mon.-Sat. 3/day, Sun. 2/day; to Dublin 2hr., £7.50; to Rosslare Harbor 50 min., £4.50). For the railway station, walk over the new bridge and take the first left. The town **tourist office** (tel. (054) 34699) is in the castle (open mid-June to mid-Sept. Mon.-Sat. 10am-1pm and 2-6pm). On Abbey Quay, **AIB Bank** (tel. (054) 33163) dispenses cash (ATM; open Mon.-Wed. and Fri. 9:30am-4pm, Thurs. 9:30am-5pm).

Accommodations, Food, & Pubs Ivella, Rectory Rd. (tel. (054) 33475), over the bridge past the railway station and fork right, is a shrine to the Kennedy brothers: a portrait of JFK and RFK greets guests in the lobby, and a bust of JFK has the place of honor on the mantle over the fireplace. "I'm fond of the family," Mrs. Heffernan explains. (Singles £13-15. Doubles £26.) **Don Carr House,** Bohreen Hill (tel. (054) 33458), from Market Sq. take the first right on Main St., then left onto Bohreen Hill, maintains two wicked awesome sunrooms, high ceilings, and bouncy beds. (Singles £15. Doubles £26.)

Food can be found at the **L&N Supermarket** in the shopping center on Mill Park road, off Abbey Sq. (open Mon.-Wed. and Sat. 9:15am-6pm; Thurs.-Fri. 9:15am-9pm), or at the various pubs. **The Korner Deli,** Market Sq. (tel. 33155), has outdoor seating from which you can examine the fast-beating heart of town. Huge breakfast served all day (£3). (Open Mon.-Sat. 8:30am-9:30pm, Sun. 10:30am-7pm). **The Antique Tavern** (tel. 33428) has won a bevy of awards—great *craic* goes on amidst the antiques and curios, including a California license plate reading WEXFORD.

Sights Don't miss the **Walking Tour of Enniscorthy** (tel. 35926), which reveals the town's dirty secrets with a pungent blend of drama and pride. (Depart from the castle daily at 11am, 12:30, 3, and 4pm; book ahead for Sat. and Sun. £1.) The castle houses the tourist office, but the bulk of the building is the **Wexford County Museum** (tel. 35926). This material encyclopedia, especially the exhibit on the 1798 rebellion, merits the £1.50 admission (ages 13-19 70p; open June-Sept. Mon.-Sat. 10am-1pm and 2-6pm, Sun. 2-5:30pm; Oct.-Nov. and Feb.-May daily 2-5:30pm; Dec.-Jan. Sun. 2-5pm). Starting on the last weekend in June, eight days of festival and fructose redden Enniscorthy's streets during its annual **Strawberry Fair.**

■■■ WATERFORD CITY

Over the years, Waterford endured sieges by Cromwell and Strongbow, the first Norman to invade Ireland; Strongbow's marriage to Dermot MacMurrough's daughter Aoife took place at Reginald's Tower. Today, bikers lay siege to the town every June bank holiday weekend, making Waterford the "bikers' capital of Ireland."

ORIENTATION & PRACTICAL INFORMATION

Almost everything except the bus and train station is on the south bank of the River Suir (pronounced "sure"). **City buses** leave from the Clock Tower on The Quay and cost a flat fare of 65p for trips within the city. City bus timetables await at the Bus Éireann office in the tourist office on Meagher Quay, or at Plunkett Station.

Tourist Office: 41 Merchant's Quay (tel. 75788), two blocks west of the Clock Tower. Currency exchange, Bus Éireann desk, Budget Rent-A-Car desk. Open July-Aug. Mon.-Sat. 9am-6pm, Sun. 10am-1pm and 2-5pm; June and Sept. Mon.-Sat. 8am-6pm; Oct.-Feb. Mon.-Fri. 9am-1pm and 2-5:15pm; March-April Mon.-Sat. 9am-1pm and 2-6pm.

Budget Travel: USIT, 36-37 Georges St. (tel. 72601), the continuation of O'Connell St. ISIC cards, Travelsave stamps, student fares to London. Open Mon.-Fri. 9:30am-5:30pm, Sat. 11am-4pm.

Financial Services: Bank of Ireland, Merchants Quay (tel. 72074). ATM. Open Mon. 10am-5pm, Tues.-Fri. 10am-4pm. Currency exchange also in tourist office.

Post Office: The Quay (tel. 74444). Smaller than you'd expect. Open Mon.-Tues. and Thurs.-Fri. 9am-5:30pm, Wed. 9:30am-5:30pm, Sat. 9am-1pm.

Telephone Code: 051.

Trains: Buses and trains leave from **Plunkett Station,** on the other side of the bridge from The Quay. Train info tel. 73401; 24-hr. recorded timetable tel. 76243. Trains travel to: Limerick (Mon.-Sat. 2/day; 2¼hr.; £11); Kilkenny (Mon.-Sat. 4/day; 40 min.; £11); Dublin (4/day, Sun. 3/day; 2½hr.; £11); and Rosslare Harbor (Mon.-Sat. 3/day; 1hr., £11).

Buses: Bus info tel. 79000. Buses from Plunkett Station drive to: Dublin (Mon.-Sat.8/day, Sun. 6/day; 3½hr.; £7); Kilkenny (daily 1/day; 1hr.; £5.90); Limerick (5/day; 2½hr.; £9); Cork (Mon.- Sat. 8/day, Sun. 5/day; 2½hr.; £9); Galway (Mon.-Sat. 5/day, Sun. 3/day; 4¾hr.; £14), and Rosslare Harbor (3/day; 1¼hr.; £8).

Hitching: Many experienced hitchers ride a city bus out to the Waterford Crystal Factory before they stick out a thumb.

Bike Rental: B'n'B Cycles, 9 Ballybricken (tel. 70356). £6/day, £35/week, £10 deposit plus ID. Open Mon.-Sat. 9am-6pm.

Luggage Storage: in Plunkett Station. Open Mon.-Sat. 7:15am-9pm. £1/item.

Laundry: Washed Ashore Launderette, The Quay. Self-service wash and dry £4.60; serviced wash and dry £5.60. Open Mon.-Sat. 9am-6pm.

Hospital: Ardkeen Hospital (tel. 73321) Follow The Quay to the Tower Hotel; turn left, then follow signs straight ahead to the hospital.

Emergency: Dial 999; no coins required. **Garda:** Patrick St. (tel. 74888).

ACCOMMODATIONS

With the 1994 opening of the **Viking House Hostel,** Waterford now has an acceptable hostel, making it an ideal base for exploring the Southeast. *Let's Go* does not recommend the Bolton Tourist Hostel on Bolton St.

Viking House Hostel (IHH), Coffee House Ln. (tel. 71730). Follow The Quay east past the Clock Tower and the post office. A luxurious and spanking-new hostel in the heart of Waterford. Free luggage storage, lockers £5 deposit. Kitchen 10am-10pm. Free sheets. 12-bed dormitory £7.50, 4- to 6-bed room with bath £8.50, twin room £10; price includes continental breakfast.

Mrs. J. Ryder, Mayor's Walk House, 12 Mayor's Walk (tel. 55427). With a smile that defines "winsome," Mrs. Ryder (and her perennial guests) welcome *Let's Go* readers with advice and biscuits. Singles £13. Doubles £25. Open March-Nov.

Derrynane House, 19 The Mall (tel. 75179). Winding halls lead to plain, comfortable rooms with good, firm beds. Bathtub! £13/person.

Mrs. M. Ryan, Beechwood, 7 Cathedral Sq. (tel. 76677). Elegant, silky rooms look out on pedestrian street and cathedral. Singles £15, doubles £25.

FOOD

Be sure to sample Waterford's contribution to world cuisine, the *blaa*. Pronounced "blah," this is a hamburger bun with a kick. For groceries, visit **Roches Stores** in the City Square Mall (open Mon.-Wed. and Sat. 9am-6pm, Thurs.-Fri. 9am-9pm).

Chapman's Pantry, 61 The Quay (tel. 74938), has a gourmet foodstore, bakery, and delicatessen restaurant. *Blaas* 12p, meals £3-4. Open Mon.-Sat. 9am-6pm.

Haricot's Wholefood Restaurant, 11 O'Connell St., cooks innovative vegetarian dishes. Seafood pancakes £4.70. Open Mon.-Fri. 10am-8pm, Sat. 10am-5:45pm.

Sizzlers Restaurant, the Quay. Cramped but atmospheric diner. Full Irish breakfast £3, burger and chips £3.50. Open Sun.-Wed. 7am-2am, Thurs.-Sat. 24-hrs.

Gina's, John St. at the Apple Market (tel. 79513). Busy family restaurant. Lunch special: small pizza with 2 toppings, ice cream, tea £4. Open Mon.-Sat. 11am-8pm.

PUBS

Geoff's Pub, 9 John St. (tel. 74787).A dark, smoky setting where cappuccino and Camus edge out Guinness and *craic.*

The Pulpit, John St. (tel 79184). Another hip, young, sacrilegious crowd, drawn by the upstairs nightclub, **Preachers,** open Wed.-Sun. 10:30pm; cover £3-5.

Mullane's, 15 Newgate St., off New St. (tel. 73854), is famous for its hard-core trad sessions Tues., Thurs., Sat., and Sun. nights at 10pm—no cover.

Tommy Barr's, Mayor's Walk (tel. 77237). Another artsy favorite, though it has a more traditional Irish pub atmosphere.

SIGHTS

The **Waterford Crystal Factory** (tel. 73311), 1 mi. out on the N25 (Cork Rd.), is the town's highlight. Forty-minute tours allow you to witness the transformation from molten glass to polished crystal. Admire the finished products—and their outrageous prices—in the gallery. The least expensive item is the heart-shaped ring holder (£20). (Tours and audio-visual show every 20 min. Mon.-Wed. 8:30am-3:15pm, Thurs.-Sat. 8:30am-3pm, Sun. 10am-3pm; £1.50. Book ahead via telephone or through the tourist office.) City bus route #1 (Kilbarry/Ballybeg) leaves the Clock Tower every 30 min., passing the factory (65p).

Waterford has a lot of history; unfortunately, most of it is now retail space. Since the city hasn't expanded outward since 1790, Viking, Victorian, and very modern structures seem veritably piled on top of one another. **Walking Tours of Historic Waterford** (tel. 73711) commence from the Granville Hotel on The Quay March through October daily at noon and 2pm (£3). The theoretical question the tour explores is "Where would the world be without Waterford?"; it gives 25% off admission to Reginald's Tower and the Heritage Center. **Reginald's Tower,** at the end of The Quay (tel. 73501), is a Viking building with 12-ft.-thick walls; Strongbow had his wedding reception here. Nearby, a wealth of Viking artifacts snatched from the jaws of bulldozers is now on display at the **Waterford Heritage Center,** Greyfriars St., off The Quay (tel. 71227). (Both open June-Sept. Mon.-Fri. 10am-8pm, Sat. 10am-1pm and 2-5pm; April-May Mon.-Fri. 10am-1pm and 2-5pm, Sat. 10am-1pm. Entrance to either tower or center £1; to both, £1.50; 25% discount with walking tour ticket. Wheelchair access.)

At the corner of Bailey's New St. and Greyfriars St., the ruins of the **Franciscan Friary** (known as the **French Church,** since it was given to Huguenot refugees in the 17th century), built in 1240 AD, include some wide-open tombs. (Get the key from Mrs. White, 5 Greyfriars St., opposite the ruins.) **Christ Church Cathedral** has a dag-nasty attraction—the tomb of James Rice, which shows bugs chewing on his corpse. Scattered throughout town are remnants of the town's medieval **city walls;** the biggest chunks are behind the Theater Royal on Spring Garden St., and on Patrick St. extending to Bachelor's Walk.

ENTERTAINMENT

The Munster Express (80p), a local newspaper, has some entertainment listings. **The Roxy,** O'Connell St., (tel. 55145), is Waterford's hottest nightclub. (Club open Wed.-Sun. midnight-2am; cover £2-5). The **Garter Lane Arts Center,** Garter Lane 2, 22a O'Connell St. (tel. 77153), hosts dance, music, theater, and free exhibitions in an old Georgian building. Next door at Garter Lane 1, 5 O'Connell St., **screen/space** (tel. 77153) has smart second-run movies and cheap tickets. (Double features Wed.-Thurs. at 8pm. You must buy a membership before you buy your first ticket: yearly memberships are £2, tix £1.50.)

■ NEAR WATERFORD: TRAMORE

Celtworld's saturation advertising reaches all of Ireland, planting powerful, unconscious commands to visit Tramore in susceptible vacationers. Hordes of them respond and descend onto the town, trampling what might have been its beachy charm. **Celtworld,** on The Promenade (tel. (051) 386166), consists of five Irish legends told with pop-up-book-style special effects, followed by a sideshow of Celtic-themed parlor tricks. (Shows start every 4 min.; July-Aug. daily 10am-10pm; Sept. daily 10am-6pm; April-May Mon.-Fri. 10am-5pm, Sat.-Sun. 10am-6pm; June daily 10am-8pm. Last ticket 1hr. before closing. £4, students £3.25, under 16 £3.) **Splashworld** next door (tel. (051) 390 176) has bubble pools, water slides, and wave machines. (Open daily 9am-11pm, Sept.-June 10am-10pm, £3.75, students £2.75.)

The **tourist office,** Strand Rd. (tel. (051) 381 572), can help you see past Celtworld. (Open June-mid-Sept. Mon.-Sat. 10am-12:45pm and 2-6pm.) **Bus Éireann** stops on Strand St. en route from Waterford (1/hr.; 20 min.; £1.50, £2.25 return). Tramore has a staggering number of great places to stay. **The Cliff,** Church St. (tel. (051) 381 363), looks out on the ocean from a prime cliffside location. (Coed. Resident pooch. No kitchen. Singles and doubles £5.50/night. Sheet rental £2.50, continental breakfast £1, full Irish breakfast £2.50. Book well ahead July-Aug.) **Monkey Puzzle Hostel,** Upper Branch Rd. (tel. (051) 386 754), has great dogs that run down the street to greet hostelers with a friendly wag. Its name captures its disheveled quality. (Laundry £2. £6, Sept.-May £5.) **Venezia B&B,** Church Road Grove (tel. (051) 381 412), is top-notch (£13/person, £15 with bath).

SOUTHWEST IRELAND

Traveling west from Cork City means moving from an English-influenced, 20th-century landscape into one that often looks untouched: the scenery is lush, the fishermen enthusiastic, and the roads lousy. Life in the Southwest is leisurely and localized: the newly-settled foreign expatriates, the remote pubs that stay open until 3am, and the stretches of wild, open, undeveloped land are all tributes to the region's informal and decidedly anti-urban atmosphere.

■■■ CORK CITY

Cork shows its true colors on Saturday afternoons, when families stroll the shops along St. Patrick St. and Oliver Plunkett St., shoppers haggle for goods at the English Market, and young and old alike fill the city's cafés and pubs. Cork rock is trendy, coffeehouse patrons spill onto the streets, the young gather here in 70s flares and platforms, and everyone tells you how much finer a place it is than dreary Dublin.

ORIENTATION & PRACTICAL INFORMATION

Downtown Cork is the arrowhead of an arrow-shaped island in the River Lee; plentiful bridges link the island to Cork's residential south side, and to its north side, which includes the poorer Shandon district. Downtown action concentrates on Oliver Plunkett St., St. Patrick St., and Paul St. (all parallel to the Lee).

Tourist Office: Tourist House, Grand Parade (tel. 273251), near the corner of South Mall and Grand Parade downtown. Open May-June Mon.-Sat. 9:15am-6pm; July-Aug. Mon.-Sat. 9am-7pm, Sun. 2-5pm; Sept.-April Mon.-Sat. 9:15am-5:30pm.

Budget Travel Office: USIT, 10 Market Parade (tel. 270900), in the Arcade off St. Patrick St. Sells Travelsave stamps, Rambler and Eurotrain tickets. Open Mon.-Fri. 9:30am-5:30pm, Sat. 10am-2pm.

Financial Services: TSB Bank, 4/5 Princes St. (tel. 275221). Mon.-Wed. and Fri. 9:30am-5pm, Thurs. 9:30am-7pm. **American Express: Heffernan's Travel,** Pembroke St. (tel. 271081). Open Mon.-Fri. 9:30am-12:30pm and 2-5pm.

Post Office: Oliver Plunkett St. (tel. 272000). Open Mon.-Sat. 9am-1pm and 2-5:30pm.

Airport: Aer Lingus and **Manx Airlines** (tel. 311000) and **Ryanair** (tel. 313000) connect posh Cork Airport to Dublin, the Isle of Man, various English cities, and

Paris. A taxi (£6) or bus (18/day; £2.20) will bring you to Cork City. The airport is five mi. south of Cork on the Kinsale Rd.

Trains: Kent Station, Lower Glanmire Rd. (tel. 504777), across the river in the northeast part of town. Open daily 7am-8pm. Lockers £1. Cork has good train connections to Dublin (Mon.-Sat. 7/day, Sun. 5/day; 3hr.; £31.50, students £12); Limerick (Mon.-Sat. 5/day, Sun. 3/day; 1½hr.; £12.50, students £6); Killarney (Mon.-Sat. 4/day, Sun. 3/day; 2hr.; £12.50, students £6); and Tralee (Mon.-Sat. 4/day, Sun. 3/day; 2½hr.; £16, students £7).

Buses: Parnell Pl. (tel. 508188), 2 blocks from Patrick's Bridge on Merchants Quay. **Luggage storage** £1.30/item, 80p/each additional day (open Mon.-Fri. 8:35am-6:15pm, Sat. 9:30am-6:30pm). Bus Éireann goes to all major cities, including: Bantry (Mon.-Sat. 3/day, Sun. 2/day; £8.80, students £5), Galway (Mon.-Sat. 5/day, Sun. 4/day; £13, students £8), Killarney (Mon.-Sat. 6/day, Sun. 3/day; £8.80, students £5), Limerick (Mon.-Sat. 6/day, Sun. 5/day; £9, students £5.30), Rosslare Harbor (Mon.-Sat. 3/day, Sun. 2/day; £12, students £9.50), Skibbereen (Mon.-Sat. 6/day, Sun. 3/day; £8.80, students £5), Tralee (Mon.-Sat. 6/day, Sun. 3/day; £9, students £6), Waterford (Mon.-Sat. 6/day, Sun. 5/day; £9, student £6), Dublin (Mon.-Sat. 4/day, Sun. 3/day; £12, students £8.50), Belfast (Mon.-Sat. 2/day, Sun. 1/day; £17, students £12.30); or Sligo (3/day; £16, students £9.50).

Ferryport: Ferries to France and England dock at **Ringaskiddy Terminal,** 9 mi. south of the city. The 40-min. city bus from the terminal to the bus station costs £3. See Essentials: Getting There for air and ferry details.

Car Rental: Great Island Car Rentals, MacCurtain St. (tel. 503536), £25/day, £160/week for subcompact manual (minimum age 25).

Bike Rental: The Bike Store, 48 MacCurtain St., next to Isaac's (tel. 505339). £5/day, £20/week. £30 deposit. Return at any Rent-A-Bike depot for an extra £5. Open Mon.-Sat. 9am-6pm.

Camping Supplies: The Tent Shop, Rutland St. (tel. 965582). Two-person tent £14/week plus £8 deposit. Open Mon.-Fri. 9am-6pm, Sat. 9:30am-5pm.

Laundry: Cork Launderette Service, 14 MacCurtain St. (tel. 501421). £1/small load, £2/large load, 10p/min. drying time. Open Mon.-Sat. 9am-8:30pm.

Pharmacies: Regional Late Night Pharmacy, Wilton Rd. (tel. 344575), opposite the Regional Hospital. Take #8 bus. Open daily 9am-10pm.

Bisexual, Gay, and Lesbian Information: The Other Place, 7-8 Augustine St. (tel. 317660) is the home of *Gay Community News,* a gay and lesbian monthly, a Sat. afternoon (4pm) discussion group, and a Saturday night gay disco. May be closing for repairs. For an update, call 271087: the **Cork Lesbian Line** (Thurs. 8-10pm) and **Gay Information Cork** (Wed. 7-9pm and Sat. 3-5pm).

Hotlines: Rape Crisis Center, 26 MacCurtain St. (tel. 968086), 24-hr. **AIDS Hotline,** Cork AIDS Alliance, 16 Peter St. (tel. 275837). **Samaritans,** tel. 271 323. .

Hospital: Mercy Hospital, Glenville Pl. (tel. 271971). £10 fee for access to emergency room. Or take bus #8 to **Cork Regional Hospital** (tel. 546400).

Emergency: dial 999; no coins required. **Garda:** Barrack St. (tel. 271220).

Telephone Code: 021. **Directory Assistance:** dial 1190.

ACCOMMODATIONS

Hostels and B&Bs glare at one another on the Western Rd.; other B&Bs gang up on Lower Glanmire Rd. near the bus and train stations.

Hostels

Campus House (IHH), 3 Woodland View, Western Rd. (tel. 343531), a 20-min. walk, or take bus #8; it's about 10 doors down from the HI youth hostel. Cheerful; superb showers. Bus to West Cork and Kerry stops outside. £5.50, sheets 50p.

Isaac's (IHH), 48 MacCurtain St. (tel. 500011). Follow St. Patrick's St. across the river and make the second right. Huge. Organized trips, bike rental, breakfast (continental £1.25, Irish £2.50). Reception 24hr. Disabled access. Dorm room £5.50, 4-6 person room with bath £7.50, double £13.50, single £18.50.

The Cork City Hostel, 100 Lower Glanmire Rd. (tel. 509089). From the train station, turn right and walk 100 yds.; the hostel is on the left. Videos at night; fire in winter. 2-6 beds per room. £5.50.

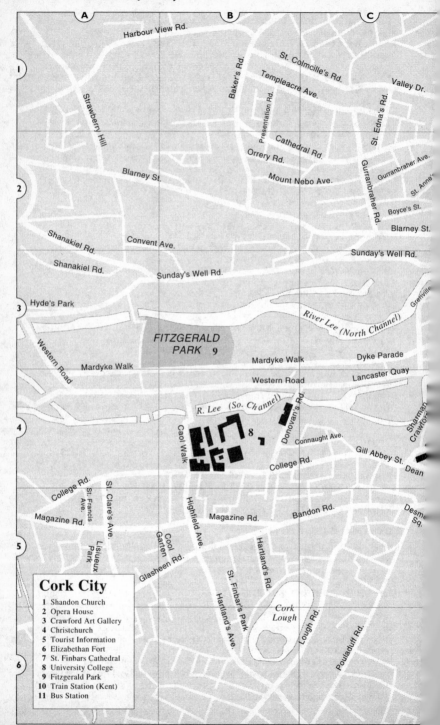

Cork City

1 Shandon Church
2 Opera House
3 Crawford Art Gallery
4 Christchurch
5 Tourist Information
6 Elizabethan Fort
7 St. Finbars Cathedral
8 University College
9 Fitzgerald Park
10 Train Station (Kent)
11 Bus Station

An Óige (HI), 1-2 Redclyffe, Western Rd. (tel. 543289), a 15-min. walk from the Grand Parade, or take the #8 bus. Bike rental, laundry, hostel vans to Blarney Castle (£2 return), and pool table. Continental breakfast £1.75. Check-in 5pm-midnight. Lockout 10am-5pm. Midnight curfew. £6; Sept.-May £5. Sheet rental 50p.

Sheila's Cork Tourist Hostel (IHH), 3 Belgrave Pl. (tel. 505562), by the intersection of Wellington Rd. and York St. Sauna (£2) and washer (£3.50). Reception 8am-3am. Non-smoking rooms. Checkout 10:30am. Breakfast £1. 6-person dorm £5.50, 4-person dorm £7, double £8.50. Linen 50p. Key deposit £1.

Kinlay House (IHH), Bob and Joan Walk (yup, that's the street) (tel. 508966), down the alley to the right of Shandon Church. Free continental breakfast, kitchen with microwave. Laundry £3.60. Dorm bed £7. Doubles £10.50. Singles £15. 10% off with ISIC.

Bed & Breakfasts and Camping

Garnish House, Western Rd. (tel. 275111). Fruit and flowers in every room, free laundry service, fresh scones when you arrive: this is the place to be. Singles £16, with bath £18; try the annex across the street for £15 with bath.

Fairlawn House, Western Rd. (tel. 543444). Large, bare rooms in a house with pretty gardens out front. £10.50/person. Singles £11.50, £2 for full breakfast.

Camping: Cork City Caravan and Camping Park (tel. 961 866), southwest of the city center on Togher Rd., ½ mi. beyond Lough Rd. Bus #14 runs every 20 min. Tent £3.50, £6.50 for two people. £1/extra person. Open Easter-Oct.

FOOD

Most restaurants and cafés are in or near the center of town; walk down the lanes joining Patrick St. to Paul St., particularly Carey's Lane and French Church St. Try the **English Market** for fresh fruit, meat, fish, and cheese. On Saturday farmers bring in homemade cheese (entrances off Grand Parade, Patrick St., and Princes St.; Wed.-Sat. are the best days to visit). **Quinnsworth Supermarket** on Paul St. is the big grocery in town (open Mon.-Wed. and Sat. 9am-6pm, Thurs. and Fri. 9am-9pm).

Quay Co-op, 24 Sullivan's Quay (tel. 317660). Vegetarian and vegan entrees (£2-4). Open Mon.-Sat. 10am-10:30pm, Sun. 6:30-10:30pm.

The Gingerbread House, French Church St. (tel. 276411). Beneath the lovely pink façade is good people-watching. Open Mon.-Sat. 9am-5:30pm.

The Harlequin, 21 Paul St. (tel. 272270). Huge sandwiches (£1.50-2); herbal tea and plenty of poets and musicians. Music and poetry "celebration" Mon. 7:30-10:30pm; £3. Open Mon.-Sat. 9am-7pm.

Kelly's, 64 Oliver Plunkett St. (tel. 273375). Big portions of Irish favorites: corned beef and cabbage £4, roast lamb £4.95. Open daily noon-9pm.

Bully's, 40 Paul St. (tel. 273555). Eat scrumptious pizza cooked in an old wood-burning oven. Extensive wine list. Open Mon.-Sat. noon-11:30pm, Sun. 5-11pm.

The Delhi Palace, 6 Washington St. (tel. 276227). Vegetarian £3.25-4, meat dishes £4.50-6.25. Lunch: Thurs.-Sat. 12:30-2:30pm; dinner: daily 5:30pm-12:30am.

Lennox's, 137 Bandon Rd. (tel. 275618). From Western Rd. turn on Donovan's Rd. and go uphill until you hit Bandon Rd., then make a left. Fish £1.50, chips 70p. Open Mon.-Thurs. noon-2pm and 5pm-1am, Fri.-Sat. noon-1:30am, Sun. 5pm-1am.

Gino's, 7 Winthrop St. (tel. 274485). Inarguably the best ice cream in Munster: try zabaióne (Italian eggnog) or the healthier "Fruit of the Forest." Each scoop 65p. Open Mon.-Sat. noon-midnight, Sun. 1pm-midnight.

PUBS

Cork is the justly proud home of **Murphy's,** a thick, sweet stout that sometimes, and especially in Cork, tastes even better than Guinness.

An Spailpín Fánach, 28 South Main St. (tel. 277949). One of Cork's most popular pubs, and probably the oldest (it opened in 1779). The name ("Ahn Spalpeen Fahnak") means "the potato picker."

The Hi-B, 108 Oliver Plunkett St. (tel. 272758). Cork's answer to *Cheers.*

The Donkey's Ears, Union Quay. Live rock, hip-hop, funk, and reggae.

The Lobby, 1 Union Quay (tel. 311113). Ireland's folk bands get their start in this intimate pub. Live music nightly (read their monthly calendar, "GiGuide").

An Phoenix, 3 Union Quay (tel. 964275). Blues and bluegrass Tues. in this dark, mysterious pub; old wine casks embedded in the walls.

Loafer's, 26 Douglas St. (tel. 311612). Cork's only gay bar. Colorful interior, relaxed atmosphere, though hardly a blip on the gaydar.

The Thirsty Scholar, Western Rd. across the street from Jury's Hotel. Why is this pub the favorite hangout for Cork students? Maybe it's the trad Mon. and Wed.

SIGHTS

St. Finbarr's Cathedral (tel. 963387) incorporates a zoo's worth of animals, griffins, and angels into its giant limestone gingerbread façade. Built between 1735 and 1870, the church looks much older; designer William Burgess, who oversaw the mosaics, furniture and metalwork as well as the overall plans, took his love of the Gothic era as far as dressing up in 13th-century robes. (Cathedral open daily Mon.-Fri. 10am-1pm and 2-5:30pm, Oct.-April 10am-1pm and 2-5pm. Free.)

On the other side of the Lee, North Main St. becomes Shandon St., heart of the Shandon neighborhood, which has less money than the rest of Cork, but more regional pride and a cooler accent: "Cork" becomes "caulk." Walk up Shandon St. until you see Donnelly's Diner on the left; then take a right down the unmarked Church St. and walk straight to **St. Anne's Church** (tel. 501672), Cork's most famous landmark. (Most people call it **Shandon Church.**) The red and white, sandstone and limestone sides of the steeple inspired Cork's ubiquitous "Rebel" flag; the salmon on top of the church represents the River Lee. (Open Mon.-Sat. 9:30am-5pm. £1.50 to tour the church, tower, and bells.)

In Emmet Place, you'll pass the Opera House on your right, then the **Crawford Municipal Art Gallery,** Emmet Pl. (tel. 270433), one of Ireland's finest public art galleries. Permanent exhibits of Irish and European art live upstairs; look for something more controversial on the first floor. (Gallery open Mon.-Sat. 10am-5pm; free.) The **Cork City Gaol** is an easy walk from **Fitzgerald Park:** cross the footbridge at the far end of the park, turn right on Sunday's Well Rd., then make the first left and a right by the church. A tour of the jail tells the story of individual Cork prisoners and the often miserable treatment they endured. (Open daily 9:30am-6pm; winter Sat.-Sun. only, 10am-4pm; £3, students and seniors £2, children £1.50.)

ENTERTAINMENT

It's not hard to enjoy Cork: if you tire of drinking, take advantage of Cork's music, dance clubs, theaters, festivals, and sports. Pick up a copy of **Razz,** Cork's semi-weekly lowdown on the entertainment scene, at Harlequin's, 21 Paul St.

Nancy Spain's, 48 Barrack St. (tel. 314452), is one of the city's most popular venues, live rock and blues often (cover about £5). **Charlie's Bar,** Union Quay (tel. 965272) has live folk, rock, blues, trad, and poetry nightly. Nightclubs fill up after the pubs close, but be aware before you plunk down your £2-5 cover charge that most close at 2am. **Norma Jeans,** Oliver Plunkett St. (tel. 271217; cover £5) jives to dance and top-40 10:30pm-2am nightly. **Gorby's,** Oliver Plunkett St., revels nightly in hiphop, hard-core and retro (cover £1-3), while **The Keg,** Gravel Ln. (tel. 271 120) jams in the students to hear the disks spin (10:30pm-2am nightly; cover £4).

Cork's leading playhouse is **Everyman's Theater** (a.k.a. "the Palace"), MacCurtain St., which rotates plays, music, and dance for £4-6 (tel. 501 673; open Mon.-Sat. noon-11pm). Down on Emmett Place, the big grey cement box with the Toyota sign on top is, unfortunately, the **Opera House** (tel. 270022; open Mon.-Sat. 10:15am-7pm); it stages Gilbert and Sullivan, drama, variety, opera, and jazz (plays £8-10, concerts £9-12). When the old and beautiful Opera House burned to the ground about 20 years ago, citizens cried in the streets.

■ NEAR CORK: BLARNEY

While sucking down tour bus fumes and exchanging saliva with tourists from around the globe, you may forget why you're in Blarney. The main attraction is, certainly, **Blarney Castle** (tel. (021) 385252), and its terrifically overrated **Blarney Stone.** Tourists don't doubt its magic, though: they lean over backwards to kiss the stone in hopes of acquiring the eloquence a smooch to the spot supposedly confers. (Open daily May-Sept. 9am-6:30pm, Oct.-April 9am-sundown. £3, seniors and students £1.50, children £1). **Bus Éireann** runs buses from Cork to Blarney (Mon.-Sat. 16/day, Sun. 10/day; £2.50 return). From July 5 to August 25, they also offer the **"Cork Tourist Trail" bus,** which trundles from the Cork bus station to the City Gaol, the Ballincollig Powder Mills, and Blarney Castle (Tues.-Thurs. 4/day; £2).

■■■ WESTWARD HO

Along the coast is the happiest route to West Cork: a bus runs from Cork to Skibbereen, stopping in Bandon, Clonakilty, and Rosscarbery. (3/day, Sun. 2/day; more frequent in summer.) Hitchers say rides abound here.

KINSALE

Big-boated anglers, swimming parties, and gourmets salivating before Kinsale's famed Good Food Circle (of 12 expensive restaurants) fill the town with money as its population temporarily quintuples every summer. Luckily, Kinsale's best attractions—its pubs, its forts, and its seaside location—don't discriminate by class.

The 45-minute trek up **Compass Hill** south from Main St. rewards with a view of the town and its watery surroundings. **Charles Fort** (tel. 772263), two mi. east of town, remained a British naval base until 1922. (Sack the fort daily mid-June to Sept. 9am-6pm; mid-April to mid-June Tues.-Sat. 9am-4:30pm and Sun. 11am-5:30pm; mid-Sept. to early Oct. Mon.-Sat. 9am-5pm and Sun. 10am-5pm; £1, students 40p. Guided tours on request.) You can reach Charles Fort by following **Scilly Walk** (pronounced "silly"), a coastal route bursting with blue water, green fields, and white yachts. Just beyond Market Sq., the west tower of the 12th-century **Church of St. Multose** (patron saint of Kinsale) bewitches visitors; the old town stocks still stand inside. (Tel. 772 220; open daylight hours; free.) **Desmond Castle,** Cork St., once imprisoned 600 French soldiers captured by British ones during the Napoleonic wars. (Open June-Sept. daily 9am-5pm; £1, students 40p.)

The **tourist office,** Emmet Pl. (tel. (021) 772234, Oct.-May (021) 774026), supplies a free map. (Open March-Nov. Mon.-Sat. 10am-1pm and 2-6pm.) Rent **bikes** at **Irish Holiday Activities** (tel. (021) 774355), 8 Main St. £6/day (open June-Aug. daily 9am-8pm, Sept.-May 9:30am-6pm). **Buses** between Cork and Kinsale stop at the Esso station on the Pier (Mon.-Sat. 6/day, Sun 4/day; £3.70, student £2.20). **Dempsey's Hostel (IHH),** on the Cork Rd. (tel. 772124), ¼ mi. from town behind Dempsey's Garage, cheers with clean rooms and happy employees in a small, prim house. (Sunroom out back. 8 beds/room; £5; shower 50p; sheets 50p.) **O'Donovan's,** Guardwell (tel. 772428), is more central than the other cheap B&Bs; stretch out on double beds in big rooms. (Singles £13. Doubles with bath £29.)

Kinsale is Ireland's gourmet food capital. The budget-conscious fill their baskets at the SuperValu **supermarket,** Pearse St. (open daily 9am-9pm). **Pancake Paradise** (tel. 774811) on Pearse St. serves up huge, pizza-sized crêpes for lunch (£2.20-3.50) or snacks (£1.10-2.70). The **Yello Gallery,** 43 Main St. (tel. 772393), is a pristine showcase for contemporary Irish art doubling as a café: the walls display a different exhibit every month. (Sandwiches, pasta, salads, and fish £3-5.50. Open daily 8am-6pm, June-Aug. 8am-10pm.) The stucco-colored **Spaniard** (tel. 772436) rules over the Kinsale pub scene from the hill on Scilly Peninsula (follow the signs to the Charles Fort: ¼ mile). This is the place American Irish pubs try to emulate (and fail).

CLONAKILTY

Like Kinsale, Clonakilty is a vacation spot known for its fine pubs; animated streets and vibrant nightlife make up for its three-mi. distance from the sea. To fill the hours before the pubs pick up, join the locals at **Inchydoney Beach,** two postcard-worthy strips of sand facing Clonakilty Bay. The most popular pub is **De Barra's,** Pearse St. (tel. 33381), with folk and traditional music nightly all year.

The **tourist office** (tel. (023) 33226), vacations at 9 Rossa St. (open June-Sept. Mon.-Fri. 9am-6pm, Sat. 9am-1pm). **Buses** from Skibbereen (3/day; £4.30, students £2.60) and Cork (6/day, Sat.-Sun. 4/day; £6.30, students £3.70) stop across from the newsagent on Pearse St. The cheapest place to stay in Clon is **Mrs. Lowney's Hostel,** 5 Wolfe Tone St. (tel. 33157), the red door to the right of the Sandlighter; it occupies the back of her B&B and feels like a bungalow or an outdoor clubhouse. (Hostel £5; B&B £12.) Come early to **Mrs. McMahon's Nordov,** 70 Western Rd. (tel. 33655), for one of her huge rooms with kitchen or TV room (£13, with bath £15). **Fionnuala's Little Italian Restaurant,** 30 Ashe St. (tel. 34355), has candles to illuminate your antipasti (£1.50-3) or pizza (£3-5). (Open daily 10am-3:30pm and 6-10pm). Brown bag-it at **Lehane's Supermarket,** Pearse St. (open Mon.-Thurs. 9am-1:15pm, Fri.-Sat. 9am-9pm, Sun. 9am-1:15pm).

SKIBBEREEN

The biggest town in West Cork unites blue-collars and blow-ins with its varied landscape: you'll find as many hardware stores here as boho galleries and cafés. The **West Cork Arts Center,** North St. (tel. 22090), across from the town library, runs about twelve exhibits a year by Irish artists and craftsfolk. Poetry readings, plays, concerts, or dance performances satisfy the blow-ins (gallery open Mon.-Sat. 11am-6pm; free). Once equipped with bicycles or rides, explorers head south to circle **Lough Ine** ("lock EYE-na"), Europe's only salt-water lake, where clear rapids change direction with the tide.

Buses stop in front of Calahane's Bar, Bridge St. (the continuation of Main St.), connecting to Baltimore (June-Sept. Mon.-Sat. 4/day; £2), Cork (Mon.-Fri. 6/day, Sat. 4/day, Sun. 3/day; £8.80, student £5), and Clonakilty (daily 3/day; £4.30, student £2.60). The **tourist office,** on North St. (tel. (028) 21766), is open July-Aug. Mon.-Sat. 9am-7pm; June and Sept. Mon.-Sat. 9:15-5:30pm; Oct.-May Mon.-Fri. 9:15am-1pm and 2:15-5:30pm. **Bike rental** becomes reality at **Roycroft Stores,** Ilen St. off Bridge St. (tel. 21235), open Mon.-Wed., Fri.-Sat. 9am-1:10pm, 2:15-6pm, Thurs. 9am-1pm; £7/day, £35/week. Return bike to Schull or Baltimore for free.

Gloriously-situated **Mont Bretia,** four mi. from town (tel. 33663), is just a step from heaven in a light and airy old farmhouse adorned with Indian rugs and paintings. Call for a ride from town. (B&B £13.) **The Backroom Bistro,** 48 North St. (tel. 22556), whips up Burmese food (lunch £5, dinner £7; open Mon.-Sat. noon-3pm and 7-10pm). SuperValu **Supermarket** dispenses bargains (open Mon.-Thurs. 9am-6:15pm, Fri.-Sat. 9am-7pm). The young gather in **Kearney's Well,** 52-53 North St. (tel. 21350), with music nightly in summer, five nights a week in winter.

■■■ BALTIMORE & THE ISLANDS

The tiny fishing village of Baltimore (permanent pop. 200) and its harbor make up the departing point for Sherkin Island and Cape Clear Island. In the center of the village is *Dún na Sead* (Irish for "The Fort of the Jewels"), a 16th-century O'Driscoll castle. Scuba divers can explore numerous wrecks in Roaringwater Bay, including **Kowloon Bridge,** the biggest shipwreck in the world; for rental information, contact the **Baltimore Diving & Watersports Center** (tel. (028) 20300) office in Brendan McCarthy's pub (full set of equipment costs £15/day or £70/week).

The **tourist office** (tel. (028) 20441), 50 steps up from the ferry depot, is non-Bord Fáilte (open summer Mon.-Sat. irregular hours). The craft shop next door, **Islands Craft** (open Easter-Oct. Mon.-Sat. 11:15am-6:45pm, Sun. 12:30-6:45pm), also stocks tourist information, thank you ferry much. **Buses** run to and from Skibbereen (June-Sept. only Mon.-Sat. 4/day); £2 single, £2.75 return; the post office has a full schedule in its window. Hostels don't get much better than **Rolf's Hostel (IHH)** (tel. (028) 20289); a small restaurant (£2-7) serves only guests. (Bike rental £6/day; laundry £3.15. £5; **camping** £3.50/person.) All of Baltimore's four pubs offer food and drink: **Declan McCarthy's** (tel. 20159) is the liveliest, with live traditional and folk nightly in summer (no cover). Sailors and other locals prefer **Bushe's Bar** (tel. 20125).

SHERKIN ISLAND

You can see Sherkin Island from the mainland, but it takes more than seeing to believe the beauty of this small isle. **Ferries** depart from Baltimore year-round (£3 return). Call Vincent O'Driscoll (tel. 20125) for information. When you get off the ferry, you'll see the ruins of a 15th-century **Franciscan abbey.** North of the abbey (behind Garrison House) lie the ruins of **Dún-na-Long Castle** ("fort of the ships"), built around the same time, and sacked, too, by Waterford in 1537 (always open; free). Stay straight on the main road from the ferry dock and you'll pass the mesmerizing blue-green **Kinnish Harbor** and Sherkin's yellow one-room schoolhouse where the young (pop. 90) educates its children.

There are three B&Bs on Sherkin Island; the nicest is the **Island House** (tel. 20314), an old farmhouse with Indian bedspreads, paintings, and small fireplaces in each room. (On the main road, 10 min. from the ferry landing; £14/person. Open April-Sept.) **Garrison House** replaces charm with cheap rates (£12); they'll let you **camp** for free in their backyard among the castle ruins. Garrison House doubles as a pub, with bar food (noon-9pm), and trad sessions most nights.

CAPE CLEAR ISLAND (OILEÁN CHLÉIRE)

What can you say about a remote island the size of Manhattan inhabited by 130 Irish speakers, foreign expatriates, and nuns? Other than drinking, there's not much to *do* here, but if wild heather, flocks of seabirds, and a tumultuous ocean turn you on, the "Cape," as the expats call it, may keep you for weeks. **Ferries from Baltimore** (£5 single; £8 return); call Capt. O'Driscoll (tel. 39135) for more info. Unreliable **ferries to Schull** leave the island in June daily at 5:30pm, July-Aug. daily at 10am, 2:30pm, and 4:30pm. (£7 return.) Both boats dock in North Harbor.

Dry-stone houses, most empty, remember the island's pre-Famine populace. Standing stones, passage graves, and prehistoric boulder burials also pop up amid Cape's open fields. The island's **Heritage Center** is half a room containing everything from a butterfly collection to items recovered from shipwrecks. (Open June-Aug. Mon.-Sat. 3:30-5:30pm. £1, students 50p, children 30p.) On the road to the museum, you'll pass **Cleire Goats** where you can buy **goat's milk ice cream** for a mere 80p and see the animals that it came from. Past the museum, a right turn takes you to the **windmills** which generate three-fourths of the island's electricity; on a misty day you'll hear the eerie noise of their motion long before you see them.

The better stocked grocer, **An Siopa Beag,** is in the white building next to the bird station. **Cistin Chiarain** (tel. 39184), by the harbor, cooks June-Aug. daily 3-6pm. Its name means "Kieran's Kitchen"; St. Kieran, the island's patron, supposedly got here before St. Patrick and brought Christianity to Ireland. Cape Clear Island has no authorities to regulate after-hours drinking, and when any have the impudence to sail over, their lights give revellers plenty of time to close up shop. The island's 130 people support three pubs: **Paddy Burke's** (tel. 39115), 100 yds. up the hill on the right, opens noon-6pm to serve the locals. **Cotter's** opens at noon and is usually liveliest in the early evening while **Club Chliere** (tel. 39184) gets going later with live sessions most nights, often till 4am or later.

The **An Óige Hostel (HI)** (tel. 39144) is about seven minutes from the pier keeping left on the main road. (Lockout 10:30am-5pm; midnight curfew. June-Sept. £5.50/person; April-May and Oct. £4.50/person. Sheet rental 50p.) **The Glen** (tel 39121) is inarguably more hospitable, with a kitchen and warm smiles. Achoo, a cat! (Call ahead for mandatory reservations and a ride from the harbor. £10/person includes breakfast.) The island's **campsite** (tel. 39119) is a five-minute walk from the harbor: go up the main road, turn right at the yellow general store, then continue bearing left (open June-Sept.; £5).

■■■ BEARA PENINSULA

For unspoiled scenery and solitude the Beara can't be beat; if you're looking for pubs, people, and other signs of civilization, you might be happier on the Ring of Kerry or the Dingle Peninsula. Public transportation is not available beyond Castletownbere, and is sparse beyond Glengarriff.

BANTRY

According to the *Book of Invasions,* the first human beings in Ireland arrived just a mile from Bantry. There's nothing more dangerous here today than hippy chicks lounging against pub fronts. At **Bantry House** (tel. 50047) rests the second Earl of Bantry's souvenir collection. The house is a two-minute walk from town on the Cork Rd. (Open daily 9am-8pm. House costs £3, students £1.75; gardens free.) Next door to Bantry House is the **1796 Bantry French Armada Exhibition Center** (tel. 51796). (Open daily 10am-6pm; £2.50, students £1.50.)

The **tourist office,** Wolfe Tone Sq. (tel. (027) 50229), is open June-Sept. Mon.-Sat. 10am-6pm. **Buses** stop outside of Crowley's Pub, two doors down from the tourist office in Wolfe Tone Sq. **Bus Éireann** heads to and from Cork (Mon.-Sat. 3/day, Sun. 2/day; £8.80, students £5). June-Sept. only, buses go to Skibbereen (Mon.-Sat, 2/day; £4.30, students £2.60), Clonakilty (Mon.-Sat. 1/day), Killarney via Kenmare (Mon.-Sat. 2/day), and Schull (Mon.-Sat. 1/day). **Berehaven Bus Service** (tel. (027) 75009) stops in Bantry on the way to and from Cork (see *Castletownbere*). **Kramer's,** Glengarriff Rd., Newtown (tel. 50278), offers a profound senses of **bike rental** daily 9am-6pm (£6/day).

    Bantry Independent Hostel (IHH), Bishop Lucey Place (tel. 51050), has a darn good view of the hills. (6- to 8-bed dorms £5.50, private rooms £7.50. Sheet rental 50p. Open mid-March to Oct.) **Harbor View Hostel,** Harbor View (tel. 51313), has thick comforters. (Dorms £5.50, quads £7.50/person. Sheets 50p. They also run a B&B two doors down (£10; £12 with shower). Bantry has numerous inexpensive lunch restaurants; for an evening meal, pub grub at The Snug or The Wolfe Tone may be the best value. **SuperValu** bustles on New St. (open Mon.-Fri. 9am-6pm, Sat. 9am-5pm). **The Snug,** Wolfe Tone Sq. (tel. 50057) offers excellent bar food in a forest of gnarled old wooden furnishings. **The Wolfe Tone,** Wolfe Tone Sq. (tel. 50900) cooks excellent Indonesian food (£3.50-6) and steaks (£3.75-12).

CASTLETOWNBERE

This largest town on the Beara Peninsula reverberates daily with the sounds of ferry engines, cars, loud children, and wind. Two mi. southwest of Castletownbere on the Allihies Rd., **Dunboy Castle** shelters two separate ruins. Cows roam the crumbling mock Gothic halls of its 18th- and 19th-century mansion, and ¾ mi. past the gate stand the ruins of the 14th-century O'Sullivan fortress. Follow the road to the right of the castle and take the right prong to a stony beach. (Pedestrians and cyclists 50p.) Next door to the Garranes Farmhouse Hostel is the **Dzogchen Buddhist Center** where dabblers and devotees alike practice Buddhist meditation.

    The bathroom-sized **tourist office,** behind O'Donoghue's by the harbor (open June-Sept. Mon.-Sat. 11am-5pm), gives away heaps of maps. **Berehaven Bus Service** (tel. (027) 70007), heads to Bantry via Glengarriff (Mon. 2/day, Tues.-Thurs. and Sat. 1/day; Glengarriff 45 min, £2.70; Bantry 1½hr., £4) and to Cork (Thurs. only; 3hr.; £8) from the parking lot next to O'Donoghue's. Two **minibus** services leave Cork for Castletownbere at 6pm Mon.-Fri. (and Sat. in summer) and 8pm Sun.: phone **Harrington's** (tel. (027) 74003) or **O'Sullivan's** (tel. (027) 74168) for mandatory reservations (both buses £8). **Bike rental** is available at **SuperValu** on Main St. (tel. (027) 70020; £6/day, deposit £20; open Mon.-Sat. 9am-7pm, Sun. 9am-1pm).

Two mi. west of town on the Allihies Rd., just past the fork to Dunboy Castle, the **Beara Hostel** (tel. 70184) offers comfortable beds (£5, private rooms £7) and **camping** (£3.50, showers and toilets available). **Castletown House,** Main St. (tel. 70252), above the Old Bank Seafood Restaurant, offers spacious rooms £12.50 (with bath £14.50). **Jack Patrick's,** Main St. (tel. 70319), serves enormous platters; scarf up a breakfast of salmon quiche (£4.25). (Open Mon.-Fri. 10:30am-9pm, Sat. 10:30am-7pm.) **SuperValu** on Main St. (tel. 70020) sells the largest selection of food-stuffs (open Mon.-Sat. 9am-7pm, Sun. 9am-1pm).

ALLIHIES & DURSEY ISLAND

Tiny **Allihies** dangles west of Castletownbere, along the R575; the town consists of one street set above the Atlantic at the foot of the Slieve Mountains. Children's gravestones crumble outside the **Celtic Church,** 2 mi. from Allihies; look for the collapsing entrance to a series of caves. **Mass Rocks** dot the fields surrounding the village, and the shafts of abandoned **copper mines** perforate Allihies' upper slopes.

The best scenery on the Beara is on **Dursey Island;** reached by Ireland's only cable car (tel. (027) 73017). The car makes the 10-minute aerial trip continuously Mon.-Sat. 9-11am, 2:30-5pm, and 7-8pm; Sunday hours vary (£2 return). Dursey Island is best seen by bike; a trip out to the western tip gives a stunning view of the sea. There is no accommodation on the island, but camping is legal.

There's a superb hostel in Allihes—**Bonnie Brae's,** Main St. (tel. (027) 73107), next to the very red O'Neill's pub. (Bike rental £6 per day. Dorms £5.50, doubles £7.50; **camping** £3/person. Open May-Sept.) You can also camp on the bluffs overlooking the small harbor or on the beach. At **The Atlantic,** Main St. (tel. (027) 73072), across from the post office, the seafood is freshly caught each day in the owner's nets (£1-6; open April-Sept. daily 9am-10pm).

■■■ KILLARNEY

Killarney (pop. 12,000) is the gatekeeper to some of the most spectacular inland scenery in Ireland.

PRACTICAL INFORMATION

Tourist Office: Main St. (tel. 31633). Open Mon.-Sat. 9am-8pm, Sun. 10am-6pm; June and Sept. Mon.-Sat. 9am-6pm; Oct.-May Mon.-Fri. 9am-5pm, Sat. 9am-1pm.
Financial Services: AIB Bank: Main St., next to the tourist office (tel. 31922). Open Mon.-Fri. 10am-4pm, Wed. till 5pm.
Post Office: New St. (tel. 31288). Open Mon.-Sat. 9am-5:30pm.
Telephone Code: 064.
Trains: Killarney Station off East Avenue Rd. (tel. 31067). Trains flee to Cork (daily 3/day; 1½hr.; £12.50, students £5.50), Dublin (Mon.-Sat. 5/day, Sun. 4/day; 3½ hr.; £33.50, students £11.50), Limerick (Mon.-Sat. 6/day, Sun. 3/day; 2hr.; £14, students £6.50), and Sligo (Mon.-Sat. 3/day, Sun. 1/day; £33.50, student £11.50).
Buses: Station on East Avenue Rd. (tel. 34777). Buses trundle to Cork (Mon.-Sat. 6/ day, Sun. 3/day; 2hr.; £8, students £5), Dingle (Mon.-Sat. 7/day, Sun. 3/day; 2hr.; £7.30, students £4.20), Dublin (daily 3/day; 6hr.; £14, students £8), Galway (Mon.-Sat. 7/day, Sun. 5/day; 7hr.; £13, students £8), Limerick (daily 4/day; 2hr.; £9.30, students £5.60), and Sligo (Mon.-Sat. 2/day, Sun. 3/day; 7½hr.; £17, students £10). From June-Sept., buses from Killarney also leave for the **Ring of Kerry tour** (daily 2/day), which stops in Killorglin, Glenbeigh, Kells, Cahirsiveen, Waterville, Caherdaniel, Sneem, and Moll's Gap (£12, students £7.50). A bus to Cahirsiveen does the northern half of the Ring of Kerry (summer Mon.-Sat. 4/day, Sun. 2/day, off-season Mon.-Sat. daily; 1½hr.; £7.30, students £4.20).
Bike Rental: Killarney Rent-a-Bike, Market Cross (tel 32578), Main St. at New St. £5/day, £25/week, free panniers. Open daily 9am-6pm.
Camping Supplies: Tracks and Trails, High St. (tel. 35277). Open Mon.-Sat. 9am-9pm, Sun. 2-6pm; Sept.-June Mon.-Sat. 9am-6pm.

Laundry: J. Gleason's Launderette (tel. 33877), down the lane next to Spar Market on College St. £4/load. Open Mon.-Sat. 9:15am-6pm, Thurs.-Fri. 9:15am-8pm.
Emergency: dial 999; no coins required. **Garda:** New Rd. (tel. 31222). Follow High St. and turn left at the light.

ACCOMMODATIONS

The Sugan (IHH), Lewis Rd. (tel. 33104). From the bus or train station, turn right, then left onto College St.; Lewis Rd. is the first right. Music and intimacy compensate for the lack of elbow room. Bathtub! Breakfast £1. 4- to 8-bed bunk rooms £6.
Bunrower House (IHH) (tel. 33914). The closest you can legally get to the experience of camping in the park. Call for a ride from the bus station. Laundry £3; bike hire £5/day. 6-bed dorms £6, doubles £8, **camping** £3.50. Sheets 50p.
Peacock Farms Hostel (IHH) (tel. 33557). Call for a ride from the bus station. Mountains in back, a bunch of very vocal peacocks in front. £5. Open May-Sept.
Neptune's (IHH), Bishop's Lane (tel. 35255), the first walkway off New St. on the right. Wheelchair access. Lockers £1. Shuttle bus from stations. 4- to 8-bed dorms £6/night or £15/3 days, doubles £8, Laundry £3, bike hire £5/day. Sheets 50p.
The Four Winds Hostel (IHH), 43 New St. (tel. 33094). Owned by Mike Barry, one of the only Irishmen to reach Everest's summit. Bike hire £5/day. Laundry 50p. Breakfast £2. 4- to 14-bed dorms £6, doubles £8.
St. Josephs B&B, 67 New St. (tel. 31162). Good location; adequate rooms in a large, cushy house. £13.
Fossa Caravan and Camping Park (tel. 31497), 3½ mi. west of town. Kitchen, laundromat, and tennis courts. Hikers/cyclists £3.50. Open mid-March to Oct.

FOOD & PUBS

Dunnes Stores, New St. is open Mon.-Sat. 9am-6pm, Thurs.-Fri. 9am-9pm. A disturbing number of fast-food joints and take-aways stay open till 2 or 3am nightly.

An Taelann, Bridewell Lane (tel. 33083), on the left off New St. Incredible vegetarian food. Lunch £1-5, dinner £6-7. Open Tues.-Sat.12:30-3pm and 6:30-10pm.
Bricin, 26 High St. (tel. 34902). Traditional Irish food served upstairs from a Celtic pottery shop. Reasonable lunches (Irish stew £3.50). Open daily 10am-10pm.
Robertino's, 9 High St. (tel. 34966). Eat real Italian food in the company of Greco-Roman plaster goddesses. Pasta dishes £5-7. Open daily 6-10:30pm.
Grunts, 20 New St. (tel. 31890). Ughnh. An unassuming exterior and an unassuming name hide crowds of Killarney's hungry, young and old alike. Uuungh. Any meat product and chips £3.25. Open June-Sept. daily 9am-9:30pm; Oct.-May Mon.-Sat. 9am-6pm, Sun. noon-7pm. Unnnghh.

The battalions of jig-seeking tourists make it hard to find a decent pub in Killarney; a few have retained some character in spite of it all. **Yer Mans,** Plunkett St. (tel. 32688), is by the far the best pub in town; it's frequented by people who actually live in Killarney. At **Fáilte Bar,** College St. (tel. 33404), "Punks," "hippies," and "normal young people" merge.

SIGHTS: KILLARNEY NATIONAL PARK

The Ice Age went berserk around Killarney, scooping a series of dramatic glens and strewing about ice-smoothed rocks and precarious boulders. The resulting 10,000-hectare park, stretching west and south from Killarney towards Kenmare, incorporates a string of forested mountains and the famous **Lakes of Killarney.** The Kenmare Rd. curves along the southeastern shores of the lakes. Hitchhiking is both difficult and unnecessary: the major tourist attractions are only a few miles apart and connected by hundreds of paths ideal for hiking or mountain biking. Don't try to see the park without a decent map from the Killarney tourist office.

You will not run out of things to do in the park—at least not while the sun is shining. The Gap of Dunloe is a full-day excursion; the others take about half a day. You can drive to **Ross Castle** (turn right on Ross Rd. off Muckross Rd.), but the numerous footpaths from Knockreer are more scenic (a ½-mi. walk). The highlight of the castle tours is the view from the 100-ft.-high dining and entertainment chamber (open daily June-Aug. 9am-6:30pm, May 9:30am-5pm, Sept. 9am-6pm, Oct. 9am-5pm; £2, students £1). Three mi. south of Killarney on the Kenmare Rd. lie the remains of **Muckross Abbey,** founded in 1448. From the abbey, a fleet of signs directs you to **Muckross House** (tel. 31440), a massive 19th-century manor whose garden blooms brilliantly in early summer. (Open July-Aug. daily 9am-7pm, mid-March-June and Sept.-Oct. daily 9am-6pm, Nov.-mid-March Tues.-Sun. 11am-5pm; £3, students £1.25.) The easiest way to reach the deservedly hallowed **Gap of Dunloe** is to follow the Killorglin Rd. for 5 mi., and then turn left on the road to Beaufort. Your options are walking or cycling; cars are banned along the 7-mi. stretch of road near the Gap. The Gap itself divides the epic **Macgillycuddy's Reeks** (the tallest mountain range in Ireland) from the lake-studded **Purple Mountains.**

■■■ RING OF KERRY

The Southwest's most gorgeous peninsula has gone the way of U2; both once embodied the tough, romantic spirit of Ireland, but both have more or less sold out to attract the masses. The term "Ring of Kerry" is often used to describe the entire **Iveragh Peninsula,** but it more correctly refers not to a region, but to a set of roads: the N71 road from Kenmare to Killarney, the R562 from Killarney to Killorglin, and the long loop of the N70 west and back to Kenmare. Stay away from the prepackaged Ring of Kerry private bus tours based out of Killarney. **Bus Éireann** does a somewhat better summer circuit through all the major towns on the Ring (daily 2/day), since you can get off anywhere and anytime you like. Buses lumber around the ring *counterclockwise*, from Killarney to Killorglin, west along Dingle Bay, east along the Kenmare River and north from Kenmare to Killarney. Those planning to hitch or drive along the Ring generally travel in the opposite direction, *clockwise*.

KENMARE

Kenmare's location submerges it under a fast-moving river of sightseers: most people heading between the Beara Peninsula, the Ring of Kerry, and Cork will pass through the town.

Practical Information The **tourist office,** The Square (tel. (064) 41233), is open May-Sept. Mon.-Sat. 9am-6pm, and Sundays in July and Aug. 2-6pm.
Buses leave from in front of Roughty's Bar on Main St. to Killarney (Mon.-Sat. 3/day, Sun. 2/day; 1hr. 20 min.; £4.70, student £2.80), Tralee (Mon.-Sat. 3/day, Sun. 2/day; 2hr.; £7.70, student £4.30), and Cork via Bantry (June-Sept. Mon.-Sat. 1/day; 4hr.; £9.70, student £7). Pedal away from **Finnegan's,** (tel. (064) 41083), on the corner of Henry and Shelbourne St. Bikes £6/day. (Open Mon.-Sat. 9:30am-6:30pm.)

Accommodations, Food, & Pubs Fáilte Hostel (IHH), (tel. (064) 41083), corner of Henry St. and Shelbourne St., homfy couches and a VCR useful for rainy days. (Dorms £5.50, private rooms £7.50.) **Keal Na Gower House B&B,** The Square (tel. (064) 41202), invites you to sleep comfortably within earshot of a brook. (Single £15, double £26.) **Ring of Kerry Caravan and Camping Park,** Sneem Rd. (tel. 41366), overlooks mountains and bay. (£3.50/person. Open May-Sept.)
 SuperValu on Main St. opens Mon.-Fri. 9am-9pm, Sat. 9am-6:30pm, Sun. 9am-5:30pm. **Mickey Ned's,** Henry St. (tel. (064) 41591) hosts a young crowd to its open-faced sandwich fests. (Open Mon.-Sat. 9am-5:30pm.) **La Brasserie Bistro,** Henry St. (tel. (064) 41379) is probably the cheapest place to eat and drink in the town, since it's connected to a liquor store. (Open daily 9am-9pm.) **Crowley's,** Henry St. (tel. (064) 41472), asks "When you've got frequent spontaneous traditional sessions, who's got time to think about little things like interior decorating?"

Sights The ancient **stone circle,** a five-minute walk from The Square down Market St., is the largest of its kind in Southwest Ireland (55 ft. in diameter) and worth a visit simply for its proximity to the town (50p). The new **Kenmare Heritage Center** shares a building with the tourist office and focuses on the town's prowess for lace-making (same opening hours as the tourist office). **The Green Note,** Henry St. (tel. (064) 41212), made it onto the cover of one of *Let's Go's* competitors (open Mon.-Sat. 10am-8pm). A number of **walks** near Kenmare capture the beauty of the Park to the north; pick up *Walking Around Kenmare* from the tourist office (20p).

SNEEM

Tourists make Sneem their first or last stop along the Ring, and the town has adapted to please them. Sneem won Ireland's "Tidy Town" competition in 1987; eight years later it looks like it still merits the honor. Down by St. Michael's Church four small, dry-stone **pyramids** created by Kerry-born sculptor James Scanlon honor the "Tidy Town" award. The technicolor art at the **Brushwood Studios Gallery** (tel. (064) 45108), 3 mi. from Sneem off the Kenmare Rd., overloads the senses. Several boatmen run **fishing trips and cruises** off Sneem's coast; Frank O'Sullivan (tel. (064) 82904) charges £15 for seven hours of deep-sea fishing, less for shorter trips (call ahead for reservations).

The Ring of Kerry **bus** leaves for Killarney via Kenmare from outside Riney's Bar in The Square (June-Sept. daily 2/day; 1hr.; £5.50, student £2.80). The **Harbor View Hostel** (tel. (064) 45276), ¼ mi. from town on the Kenmare Rd. (tel. (064) 45276), used to be a motel, and still looks like one—ranch-style units scattered in a gravel lot. (**Camping** £3; for dorms bargain your way down from £5-7.50.) **Woodvale House,** Pier Rd. (tel. 45181), has rooms with mountain views and a large Victorian sitting room (£11, with bath £14). They also have **camping** in the backyard (£3 plus £1 per additional person). Charlie Chaplin once frequented **The Green House Tea Room** (tel. (064) 45208), next to the bridge in the town center (Irish stew £4; open Easter-Oct. daily 8:30am-9pm). **The Blue Bull** (tel. (064) 45382), next to the woolen shops, is a pub noted for its seafood (pub grub £3-5, served noon-8:30pm) and hosts traditional and country music (July-Aug. Mon., Wed., and Fri.).

CAHERDANIEL

Tiny Caherdaniel makes up for greeting-card charm with its gorgeous stretches of beach. To reach **Derrynane Strand,** follow the signs from the center of town to Derrynane House. **Derrynane House** (tel. 75113), just up from the beach, was the former residence of Irish patriot Daniel "the Liberator" O'Connell, who won Catholic Emancipation in 1829. (Open May-Sept. Mon.-Sat. 9am-6pm, Sun. 11am-7pm; March, April, and Oct. Tues.-Sun. 1-5pm; £1.50, seniors £1, students 60p.)

The **bus** stops in Caherdaniel at the junction of the Ring of Kerry Rd. and the town's Main St. Buses go to Sneem and Killarney (June-Sept. daily 2/day; Sneem 30 min. £2.90, student £1.70; Killarney 1½hr. £7.30, student £3.80). The **Village Hostel** (tel. (066) 75277), across the street from Skellig Aquatics, has midnight curfew. (Climbing trips arranged. £5. Showers 50p. Open Feb.-Nov.) For food, the **Courthouse Café** is the best deal in town—big platters, small prices (open daily 9:30am-12:30am, takeout only after 9pm). **Freddy's Bar** sells groceries (open daily 9am-9pm) and serves pints to locals.

WATERVILLE

Waterville's got a clean pebbly beach on Ballinskelligs Bay, and it's a damn fine beach. **Lough Currane** lures anglers, boaters, and divers with its numerous picnic-friendly islands and its submerged castle ruins. **Waterville Boats** (tel. 74255) hires rowboats (£10/day) and fishing poles (£5/day). The **tourist office** soaks up down sea spray across from the Butler Arms Hotel on the beach (open Mon.-Fri. 9am-7pm, Sat. 9:30am-3:30pm, mid-Sept. to late June Mon.-Fri. 9am-5pm). The Ring of Kerry **bus** (June-Sept. daily 2/day) stops in Waterville in front of the Bay View Hotel on Main St. with service to Caherdaniel (20 min.; £2.20, student £1.70), Sneem (50 min.; £4.30, student £2.30) and Killarney (1hr. 50 min.; £8.60, student £4.40). In the off-season, **Dero's** (tel. (066) 31251) fills in with a Ring of Kerry bus (1/day; reservations mandatory).

The 12-bed **Peter's Place** on Main St. is the closest you'll come to a real life version of the Mad Hatter's Tea Party—and the tea's even free. Backpackers and cyclists sit in front of the turf fire here until late at night and temporarily become part of this warm family. (No phone, Peter hates 'em. £5; **camping** £3.) The grand stone mansion of the 66-bed **Waterville Leisure Hostel (IHH)** (tel. 74644) just can't compete. Stay right at the fork at the Butler Arms Hotel and walk 5 min. up the hill. (Bunk rooms £6, doubles £7/person. Wheelchair accessible.) Fifty yds. from the tourist office, **The Huntsman** (tel. 74124) vends an unusual variety of take-away dishes; don't be put off by high prices on the sit-down menu (fish and chips £2.25, poached salmon *au vin blanc* £6.60; open Mon.-Sat. 10:30am-4pm and 6-9:30pm). Locals love Charlie Chaplin's old haunt the **Fisherman's Bar** (tel. 74205), linked to the Butler Arms Hotel (open July-Sept.; trad Thurs. and Sat.).

CAHERSIVEEN

Perhaps because it's the Iveragh Peninsula's biggest town, Cahersiveen ("care-si-VEEN," pop. 1200) hasn't let the foreigners drag it down or gloss it up. After Waterville and its equally cloying neighbors, its hustle may come as a relief. Every schoolchild in Ireland knows that Cahersiveen is the birthplace of Daniel O'Connell; the Catholic church in town that bears his name is the only one in Ireland named for a layperson. The barracks (see below) house a new **heritage center** (tel. (066) 72589) on local history and Daniel "Local Boy" O'Connell (open daily 10am-6pm; £3, students £2). Two mi. northwest of the town (signposted from downtown), the ruins of the 15th-century **Ballybarbery Castle**, once held by O'Connell's ancestors, commands great views of mountains and sea. Two hundred yards past the castle turnoff lie two well-preserved stone forts: **Leacanabuaile Fort** lets you walk atop its 10-ft.-thick walls while **Cahergal Fort** (cooler, but harder to get to) encloses a 10th-century beehive hut.

Cahersiveen enjoys (or tolerates) two **tourist offices:** one in the old Protestant church on Main St. (tel. (066) 72996; open June-Sept. daily 9:30am-6pm) and one in the former barracks on the road to the castle (tel. (066) 72589; open Mon.-Sat. 10am-6pm). The Ring of Kerry **bus** stops in front of Banks Store on Main St. (June-Sept. daily 2/day) and ventures to Waterville (25 min.; £2.70, student £1.70), Caherdaniel (1½hr.; £3.10, student £1.70), and Killarney (2½hr.; £9, student £5). **Fionán Ferries** (tel. (066) 76306) connects Cahersiveen and Dingle (thus bypassing the mostly-boring 60-mi. land route) May.-Sept., Tues.-Thurs. and Sat.-Sun. 2/day (1hr; £10, £12 return; students £9, £11 return).

Come to the **Sive Hostel (IHH),** 15 East End, Main St. (tel. 72717), for great sunsets from the third-floor balcony. (Dorms £6, doubles £7/person.) At the west end of town, the **Mannix Point Caravan and Camping Park** (tel. 72806) adjoins a waterfront nature reserve. One of the best camping parks in the country, Mannix Point keeps a common area with a turf fire that feels like a relaxed hostel. (Open mid-March to mid-Oct.; £2.75/person.) Towards the west end of Main St., **Mrs. Quill's Ard na Greine** ("sunrise" in Irish) (tel. 72281) offers comfortable rooms with fashionable curtains for £12.50, with bath £15. Generous **Grudle's,** Main St. (tel. 72386), grants huge portions for reasonable prices (open daily 9am-10pm; Nov.-March Mon.-Sat. 9am-6pm). Cahersiveen still has several **"original pubs"** on Main St.—once common in rural Ireland during the first half of this century, these establishments were combo watering hole, general store, blacksmith, leather shop, and farm goods store. The **Anchor Bar** (tel. 72049), towards the west end of Main St., is one of the best. Don't come before 10pm.

■■■ DINGLE TOWN

The Dingle Peninsula really is the best that Co. Kerry has to offer, though its attractions don't really begin until you're halfway across it: West Beara is too empty, the

Ring of Kerry isn't empty enough, but the sea-battered coast west of Dingle Town, like Baby Bear's bed, is just right. The word is out about the fabulous pubs, the breathtaking views, the smart cafés, and the too-cute dolphin, Fungi, who charms the whole town from his permanent residence in Dingle Bay. So far, everybody loves Dingle Town. Get here fast enough, and you will too.

PRACTICAL INFORMATION

Tourist Office: Corner of Main St. and Dykegate St. (tel. 51188). Open April-Oct. Mon.-Sat. 9:30am-6:30pm, Sun. 11am-5pm.

Banks: AIB Bank, Main St. (tel. 51400). Open Mon. 10am-12:30pm and 1:30-5pm, Tues.-Fri. 10am-12:30pm and 1:30-4pm. ATM.

Post Office: Upper Main St. (tel. 51661). Open Mon.-Fri. 9am-1pm and 2-5:30pm, Sat. 9am-1pm.

Phone Code: 066

Buses: Bus stop is behind Garvey's SuperValu on Ring Rd. **Bus Éireann** buses rush out of Dingle to Ballydavid (Tues. and Fri. only, 3/day, £3.15 return), Dunquin and Ballyferriter (summer Mon.-Sat. 4/day, Sun. 1/day, winter Mon. and Thurs. 2/day; £2.30, student £2), Killarney (June-Sept. Mon.-Sat. 8/day, Sun. 2/day, Oct.-May Mon.-Sat. 3/day, Sun. 2/day; 1½hr.; £7.30, student £4.20), and Tralee (June-Sept. Mon.-Sat. 7/day, Sun. 3/day, Oct.-May Mon.-Sat. 3/day, Sun 2/day; 1hr. 10 min.; £5.90, student £3.50).

Ferries: Ferries float to and from Cahersiveen on the Ring of Kerry in summer (see *Cahersiveen*).

Bike Rental: Raleigh Rent-A-Bike: Foxy John Moriarty's, Main St. (tel. 51316). £7/day, £30/week, remote dropoff £6. Open daily 9:30am-8pm.

Emergency: dial 999; no coins required. **Garda:** The Holy Ground St. (tel. 51522).

ACCOMMODATIONS

Grapevine Hostel (tel. 51434), Dykegate St. just off Main St. Used to be a B&B—remnants include spacious rooms, all with toilet and shower, and disoriented foreigners phoning for reservations. 8-bed rooms £5, 4-bed rooms £6, sheets 50p.

Rainbow Hostel (tel. 51044), 15 min. west of town on Strand Rd. (at the intersection with the Dunquin Rd. go straight, inland). Irish folk legend Christy Moore knows the owner and bunks here when in Dingle. Laundry £2, bike hire £5/day, free rides to and from town, angling trips £10 for 3 hr., dolphin trips £5. Dorms £6, Sept.-June £5, doubles £7.50, **camping** £2.50.

Ballintaggart Hostel (IHH) (tel. 51241), about a 25-min. walk east of town on the Tralee Rd. Set on a grand estate with crystal chandelier. Horse treks £10 for 1½ hr., longer trips available. Wetsuits a steal at £6. Free shuttle to town. Bike rental £5/day. 12-bed dorms £5, July-Aug. £6; doubles £6.50, July-Aug. £8; **camping** £3.

Lovett's Hostel, Cooleen Rd. (tel. 51903), down the lane opposite Moran's Garage on the east side of town. The many doubles and triples make it feel like a B&B. Laundry £1 (no dryer). Dorms £5, July-Aug. £6; doubles £6.50, July-Aug. £7.

Avondale House, Dykegate St. (tel. 51120). Mrs. Houlihan and her fox-wool blankets (not to mention homemade brown bread and jam) lure foxy patrons back year after year. £12.50/person.

The Marina Inn, Strand St. Nice rooms with double beds are a roaring bargain at £10 single or £14 double if you BYOB (bring-your-own-breakfast).

FOOD

SuperValu on Strand St. (tel. 51397) stocks a SuperSelection of groceries (open Mon.-Sat. 9am-9pm, Sun. 9am-6pm) while **An Grinán** on Dykegate St. next to the Grapevine Hostel crunches wholefoods (Mon.-Sat. 10am-1:30pm and 2-6pm.)

An Café Litearta, Dykegate St. (tel. 51388), near Main St. Traditional music amidst sandwiches (from £1.20) in friendly bookstore-café. Open daily 10am-5:30pm.

Café Ceol, Green St., opposite the church, behind Dick Mack's pub. Outside seating, exotic wholefoods, and great live traditional music (9:30-11pm) will keep you there for hours and hours. Open daily 10am-6pm.

The Singing Salmon, Strand St. (tel. 51359). A good place to linger over a glass of wine. Visionary pizza (£4.50-5.50). Open daily 12:30-3:30pm and 6-9:30pm.

Tig Lise, Bridge St. (tel. 51001). Bright, cheery tables with checkered tablecloths. Quiche and salad £2.50. Open Mon. 9am-6pm, Tues.-Sun. 9am-10pm.

Greany's, Bridge St. (tel. 516 94), next to Tig Lise. Hearty, inexpensive seafood in tight quarters. Open daily 12:30-9pm.

PUBS

Many are fast becoming touristy; a good rule of thumb is to steer clear of any establishment with shamrocks in the windows.

O'Flaherty's Pub, Holy Ground (tel. 51461), a few doors up from the traffic circle. Get there by 9pm if you want a seat. All types of music.

Murphy's, Strand St. (tel. 51450). The Lost Generation sidles up to the super-long bar in this American-inflected pub. Rock, blues, and trad.

An Droichead Beag, Lower Main St. (tel. 51723). This pub can be touristy, but still unleashes the best trad in town, nightly in summer.

Star, Strand St. (tel. 51855). Older clientele and a sophisticated atmosphere.

Dick Mack's, Green St. (tel. 51070), opposite the church. A leather bar. "Dick Mack's Bar, Boot Store and Leather Shop," that is. No music.

SIGHTS

Fungi the Dolphin swam into Dingle Bay one day in 1983 with his mother, and the pair became immediate local celebrities. Mom has since died, but Fungi remains rather fond of the humans in their wetsuits and boats. **Boat trips** to see the dolphin leave from the pier constantly in summer; most cost around £5 and guarantee that you'll see the dolphin. You can **rent a wetsuit** from Flanney's (tel. 51163), just east of town off the Tralee Rd. (£12 for 3 hr., £20 overnight) or from Seventh Wave (tel. 51548), ½ mi. west of town on the Dunquin Rd. (£9-11 for 3 hr., £14-18 overnight), or just jump in *au naturel.* Ballintagart Hostel rents suits cheap to its guests.

Deep sea angling trips (tel. 51337) leave daily in summer at 10am and 6pm from the pier, while **Sciúird Archaeology tours** (tel. 51606), take you from the pier on a three-hour whirlwind bus tour of the area's ancient spots (3/day, £5/person; book ahead). The same company also does historic walking tours of Dingle Town (2/day, £2.50/person). **Celtic Nature Expeditions** (tel. 59882) leads three-hour nature and archaeology walks from Ventry (£5/person; walks leave at 11:30am; reservations required). Craft shops, cafés, and people are the rest of the pre-pub entertainment in Dingle; as the locus of "civilization" on the peninsula, it's the base from which everyone bikes or hikes out to the nearby ruins and vistas.

■■■ AROUND THE DINGLE PENINSULA

SLEA HEAD

Ryan's Daughter and parts of *Far and Away* were filmed around **Slea Head,** and it's not difficult to understand why Hollywood cigar-chompers chose this place to represent what millions of moviegoers would perceive as Ireland. Green hills lead down to jagged cliffs which look like they've been chiseled away through the centuries. The road from broad horseshoe-shaped **Ventry Beach** out to Slea Head passes literally hundreds of Iron Age and early Christian remains, stones and ruins. **Dumbeg Fort** and the **Fahan Group** of beehive-shaped stone huts built by early monks cluster on hillsides over the cliffs. (Landowners who display signs charge 50p-£1 to view the ruins.) Don't feel bad if you can't read the *ogham*; professional archaeologists sometimes can't either.

DUNQUIN (DÚN CHAOIN) &
THE BLASKET ISLANDS (NA BLASCAODAÍ)

The scattered settlement of **Dunquin** has stone houses, a pub, and plenty of spoken Irish, but no grocery store; stock up in Dingle or in Ballyferriter if you're going to stay here or on the Great Blasket. Just down the road to Ballyferriter, the **An Óige Hostel (HI)** (tel. (066) 56121) provides adequate bunkrooms and a spacious, window-walled sitting and dining room which looks out onto the sea. (Lockout 10:15am-5pm; curfew 11:30pm. £6, Oct.-May £5. Sheets 60p. Breakfast £1.60) The anomalous architecture of the **Blasket Center** (tel. (066) 56371), across the road from the hostel, displays writings by the renowned Great Blasket writers and photographs provide an incredibly authentic—and moving—idea of life on the island; the museum is informative without being dry. (Open daily July-Aug. 10am-7pm, Easter-June and Sept.-mid-Oct. 10am-6pm; £2, students £1.)

Evacuated in 1953, the Blaskets have famously come to stand for the elegiac vision of an antiquated *gaeltacht* culture, one inhabited by poet-fishermen, proud but impoverished and aging villagers, and memoirists reluctantly warning that "after us, there will be no more." Blasket writers themselves, in English and Irish, helped produce that vision; the well-known autobiographies are little-known in America, but required (and often despised) school reading for Irish kids. **Boats** for the Blaskets depart from Dunquin May to September daily, every hour from 10am to 6pm, weather and ferryman's mood permitting (tel. (066) 56455; £8 return).

BALLYFERRITER (BAILE AN FHEIRTÉARAIGH)

Many are lured to Ballyferriter by the musical strains and poetic voices inside **Peig's Pub,** Main St. (tel. (066) 56388), where there are trad sessions daily in the evenings and sometimes at lunchtime in the summer. On Wednesday nights you can recite the poetry you composed at Slea Head or Great Blasket Island to a thoughtful, almost sober audience. The largest grocery in town is **Ollmhargadh Market,** in the town center (open daily 9am-9pm, in winter 9am-7:30pm). Five minutes outside town on the Dunquin Rd., the simple **Black Cat Hostel** (tel. (066) 56286) crosses your path. (Check-in 2:15pm, checkout 10:30am. £5.)

From Ballyferriter, follow the signs to **Dún An Óir** (the Fort of Gold), an Iron Age fort where in 1580 the English massacred over 600 Spanish, Italian, and Irish soldiers who openly supported the Irish Catholics' rebellion against Queen Elizabeth's Protestantism. From the main road, signposted roads fork off fast for **Riasc,** a monastic site with an engraved standing slab, for the **Dillon Stone** (a monument erected by early British settlers), and for Ballydavid.

BALLYDAVID (BAILE NA NGALL)

North of Ballyferriter along Smerick Harbor, Ballydavid oozes monuments. The **Gallarus Oratory,** a 7th- or 8th-century stone structure in the shape of an inverted boat, is Ireland's best-preserved primitive church. Although no mortar was used in its construction, it has remained completely waterproof; anyone can go inside and feel, temporarily, like an ancient monk-in-training. Farther north, rocky **Ballydavid Head** yields to quieter **Brandon Creek,** the exact spot from which St. Brendan, patron saint of Kerry, is said to have set sail for the "Heavenly Isles" (almost certainly America). Tim Severin made himself somewhat famous by building an archaic boat and sailing to America from this same site.

Back in Ballydavid proper, follow the large signs to the **Ballydavid Hostel** (tel. (066) 55300), in a new condo-like house which looks out over the beach across the street (£5). Pick up supplies at **McDonnell's Market,** east of town on the Dingle Rd. (open daily 9am-9pm).

■■■ TRALEE

Kerry residents correctly see Tralee (pop. 20,000) as the county's economic center (tourists tend to think of Killarney as the core). Tremendous local effort and buckets of EU development funds have gone towards building new, splashy attractions. In contrast to the painfully visitor-oriented feel of Tralee's sights, the rest of the town is quite authentic: locals handily dilute the smattering of tourists.

ORIENTATION & PRACTICAL INFORMATION

Tralee's streets are hopelessly knotted—your best bet is to find the tourist office immediately and arm yourself with a free map. The main street in town—variously called The Mall, Castle St., and Boherbee—is a good reference point. Ashe St. and Edward St. branch north off The Mall while the classy Denny St. shoots south. To the west, The Mall encounters The Square, a haphazard system of one-way streets, before dead-ending at Russell St. (also called Prince's Quay and Slaughton's Row).

Tourist Office: Ashe Memorial Hall, at the end of Denny St. (tel. 21288). From the station, head into town on Edward St., turn right on Castle St. and left on Denny St. Open Mon.-Fri. 10am-6pm, Sun. 2-6pm; Oct.-March Tues.-Sat. 9am-5pm.

Travel Agency: Slattery's, Rock St. (tel. 21722). Claims the cheapest bus-and-ferry-to-London packages in Éire. Open Mon.-Fri. 9am-6pm, Sat. 9am-5pm.

Financial Services: TSB, 12 Lower Castle St. (tel. 21177). Open Mon.-Fri. 9:30am-5pm, Thurs. 9:30am-7pm. **Bank of Ireland,** Castle St. ATM.

Post Office: Edward St., off Castle St. (tel. 21013). Open Mon. and Wed.-Sat. 9am-5:30pm, Tues. 9:30am-5:30pm.

Phone Code: 066.

Bus/Train Station: corner of Edward St. and John Joe Sheehy Rd.

Trains: (tel. 23522). Trains tie Tralee to Cork (Mon.-Sat. 8/day, Sun. 7/day; 2½hr.; £16, student £7), Killarney (Mon.-Sat. 8/day, Sun. 7/day; 40 min.; £5, student £3.50), Dublin (Mon.-Sat. 7/day, Sun. 6/day; 3-4hr.; £33.50, student £12), Waterford (3/day; 4hr.; £26, student £11.50), and Rosslare Harbor (Mon.-Sat. daily; 5hr.; £33.50, student £12).

Buses: (tel. 23566). Buses run to Cork (Mon.-Sat. 5/day, Sun. 3/day; 2½hr.; £9, student £6), Dingle (July-Aug. Mon.-Sat. 9/day, Sun. 5/day, Sept.-June Mon.-Sat. 4/day, Sun. 2/day; 1¼hr.; £5.90, student £3.50), Killarney (June-Sept. Mon.-Sat. 12/day, Sun. 6/day; Oct.-May Mon.-Sat. 5/day, Sun. 2/day; 40 min.; £5.90, student £3.50), and Limerick (Mon.-Sat. 5/day, Sun. 4/day; 2hr.; £9, student £5.30).

Taxi: Kingdom Cabs, 48 Boherbee (tel. 27828). Fleets of cabs park on Denny St. at the intersection with The Mall and charge £1/mile, less for longer distances.

Bike Rental: O'Halloran, 83 Boherbee (tel. 22820). £5/day, £25/week. Open Mon.-Sat. 10am-6pm.

Laundry: The Laundry, Pembroke St. (tel. 23214). Open Mon.-Sat. 9am-6pm.

Pharmacy: Kelly's Chemist, The Mall (tel. 21302). Open Mon.-Sat. 9am-6pm.

Emergency: dial 999; no coins required. **Garda:** High St. (tel. 22022).

ACCOMMODATIONS

Finnegan's Hostel (IHH), 17 Denny St. (tel. 27610). Majestic townhouse containing parts of the old town castle. Laundry £5. Bike rental £6/day, £30/week. Spacious, wooden-floored bunk rooms £6, doubles £7.50.

Collis-Sandes House (tel. 28658). Follow Oakpark Rd./Edward St., take the first left after Halloran's Foodstore, and then make a right at the sign. Grand stone mansion fit to be a 4-star hotel. Tennis (£1.50/hr.; rackets £1/hr.), pitch and putt (£3). Bike hire. Free rides to town. Dorms £6-7, doubles £8.

Sean Og's Hostel, Church St. (tel. 27199). Walk up Barrack Ln. and make the first right. Small, downtown hangout. Bunk £5, doubles £6.

Mountain Ash, Oakpark Rd. (tel. 24178), up Edward St. ½ mi. Spotless white and peach rooms that look like they were just painted yesterday. Wise to phone ahead. £12, with bath £14, £3 less without breakfast. Open June-Sept.

St. Martin's, Oakpark Rd. (tel. 25004). As featured on the front page of the *Kerryman.* Mrs. O'Mahoney offers TVs, tea and coffee making facilities, free chocolate, and blessed electric blankets in her comfortable rooms. £15 with bath.

Bayview Caravan and Camping Park, (tel. 26140 or 23319), 1 mi. from town on Ballybunion Rd.; follow Rock St. north. Two-person tent £3 July-Aug., £2.50 other times. Open April-Oct.

FOOD

Fast-food joints clog The Square. If all else fails, there's a **Quinnsworth Supermarket** in The Square (open Mon.-Sat. 9am-6pm).

The Old Forge, Church St. (tel. 28095). Lamb (£4.25), Irish breakfasts (£3). Open July-Aug. Mon.-Sat. 9am-10pm, Sept.-June. Mon.-Sat. 9am-6pm.

Brat's Place, Milk Market Ln. (pedestrian walkway off The Mall). No whiners. Potatoes, spinach, and goat cheese £4. Delicious desserts £1-1.50.

The Skillet, Barrack Ln. (tel. 24561), off The Mall. If the pizza (£3) doesn't exhilarate you, the photos of Mt. Everest surely will (the owner was the first Irishman to climb it). Open daily 9am-10pm.

Roots, 76 Boherbee (tel. 22665). Vegetarian food, gargantuan portions (£3-4). Chug them chick peas. Open Mon.-Sat. 9am-5:30pm.

PUBS

Baily's Corner Pub, (tel. 23230), corner of Ashe St. and Castle St. This relaxing pub reigns supreme. Yummy grub too.

Paddy Mac's, The Mall. Another Tralee favorite with many a session, many a night.

Val O'Shea's, Bridge St. (tel. 21559). Trad nightly all summer in this unpretentious pub. Dark, intimate back room makes friends fast.

The Abbey Inn, The Square (tel. 22084). Tough, hip biker crowd comes to hear live rock and reggae. When U2 played here in the early '80s, the manager made them sweep the floors to pay for their drinks because he thought they were so bad. An approach. Open until 1am Mon., Thurs., and Fri. (£2 cover those nights).

SIGHTS

Ireland's second-largest museum is **Kerry the Kingdom,** Ashe Memorial Hall, Denny St. (tel. 27777), where all the resources of modern display technology are marshalled to tell the story of Co. Kerry from 8000 B.C. to the present. The museum grants barely a display case to the Famine, but an entire room of videos and dioramas explains the rise and fall of the Kerry Gaelic-football team. "Geraldine Tralee" downstairs is a reconstruction of medieval Tralee seen, *Pirates of the Caribbean*-style, from a small moving cart. You even get the old city's stench for part of the ride (nose plugs not provided). (Open March-July and Sept.-Oct. Mon.-Sat. 10am-6pm, Sun. 2-6pm; Aug. Mon.-Sat. 10am-7pm, Sun. 2-6pm, Nov.-Dec. Mon.-Sat. 2-5pm. £3.90, students £3.50.) Across the street from the second-largest museum, the **"Roses of Tralee"** bloom each summer in Ireland's second-largest town park. The building on the Prince's Quay traffic circle that looks like a cross between a Gothic castle and a space-age solarium is actually Tralee's new £4.5 million **Aquadome** (tel. 28899). Inside, a wave pool, river rapids, and speedy waterslide (to go fastest, arch your back so only your head and feet touch the slide) are all substantially warmer than the Atlantic. (Open Mon.-Fri. 10am-10pm, Sat.-Sun. 10am-7pm; £4.)

The **Siamsa Tíre Theater** (tel. 23055), at the end of Denny St. next to the museum, is Ireland's national folk theater; it mounts brilliant summer programs depicting traditional Irish life through mime, music, and dance. (Productions July-Aug. Mon.-Sat., May-June and Sept. Mon.-Tues., Thurs., and Sat. Shows start at 8:30pm. Box office open Mon.-Sat. 9am-8:30pm. Tickets £8.) The **Duchas Cultural Center,** Edward St., puts on dancing and music (July-Aug. Thurs. 8:30pm; £3). Budding sociologists should save the last week of August for the **Rose of Tralee International Festival.** A maelstrom of entertainment surrounds the central event, a competition between young women of Irish ancestry for the title "Rose of Tralee." The Rose office, 5 Lower Castle St. (tel. 21322), can wolf-whistle about it.

■ NEAR TRALEE: TARBERT

Anyone travelling between Co. Kerry and Co. Clare should use the **Tarbert-Killimer car ferry** (tel. (065) 53124), thus avoiding the 85-mi. land detour via Limerick. (Sailings Mon.-Sat.7am-9:30pm, Sun. 9am-9:30pm; Oct.-March Mon.-Sat. 7am-7:30pm, Sun. 10am-7:30pm. Boats sail every hour on the half hour and return on the hour from Clare. Passenger £1.50, bike £2.) There's also a hostel here, **The Nest** (tel. (068) 36165), a simple place with a garden in the backyard. The Nest appears a stone's throw past the Foynes Rd. (Bunk rooms £5. **Camping** £3.50. Open June-Aug.) For Kilrush, a wee town near the ferry, see *County Clare.*.

From mid-June through September, **Bus Éireann** rolls from Galway and Lisdoon-varna, to Tralee, Killarney and Cork, via the Tarbert-Killimer ferry (Mon.-Sat. 2/day). During the rest of the year, the nearest bus stop to Killimer is in Kilrush, 8 mi. north, with connections to Milltown Malbay and Ennis (late June-late Aug.). Those lucky enough to arrive in Killimer in mid-afternoon will have an easy time finding rides to Kilrush from the power station employees of nearby Moneypoint, who get off work at 4:30pm sharp. A bus runs to Tarbert from Limerick (late June-late Aug.), but no buses go from Tralee.

WESTERN IRELAND

Dubliners will tell you to get out of their dirty old town, that the west is the "most Irish" part of Ireland. Yeats would agree: "For me," he said, "Ireland is Connacht." For less privileged Irish people, Connacht has sometimes meant poor soil, starvation, and emigration, as when Cromwell uprooted native Irish landowners in Leinster and Munster and resettled them west of the Shannon. The West was also hardest-hit by the potato famine: the population of every Western county is still less than half what it was in 1841. But from Connemara north to Ballina, hikers, cyclists, and hitchhikers enjoy boggy, rocky, or brilliantly mountainous landscapes.

Galway City is a different story, a successful port that's now a boomtown of the young. The rest of Co. Galway now draws summer tourists to its rugged scenery and Irish-speaking villages. To the south, the barren moonscape of the Burren, the Cliffs of Moher, and a reputation as the center of the trad music scene attracts travelers to Co. Clare. Western Ireland's gorgeous desolation, tragic history, and enclaves of traditional culture are now its biggest attractions.

■ ■ ■ LIMERICK CITY

Limerick City is in the middle of a facelift—it has been for years—but a number of factors keep it sagging: high unemployment, lots of grimy industry, and an unimaginative grid of streets littered with neon, plastic, and abandoned buildings. That said, Limerick could also become one of Ireland's major tourist centers. Delightful red-brick 18th-century Georgian architecture lines the classier streets. Almost all travelers end up driving through, or changing buses or trains, in the city. Limerick's streets are bounded by the River Shannon on the west and by the Abbey River on the north near **O'Connell St.** Conveniently, this is also the safer area.

A few decades after the Normans invaded Ireland and displaced the O'Brien dynasty from the Limerick area, King John ordered a castle built for protection; **King John's Castle** still stands on Nicholas St. (tel. 411 201). Walk across the Abbey River and take the first left after St. Mary's Cathedral. A few years ago, excavators discovered a Viking settlement buried under the imposing 13th-century castle; tourists can now check out the underground archaeology. (Open daily 9:30am-5:30pm, last admission 4:30pm. £3.30, students £1.70.) Close by, at Nicholas and Bridge Streets, is **St. Mary's Cathedral** (tel. 416238), whose delicate glass windows belie a rough, rocky interior. On the side of the altar, carvings on fold-down seats built into the wall depict the struggle between good and evil (bang! pow!). (Mon.-Fri. at 9:15pm; £2.50, students £1.50.) It's a bit of a schlep to the **Hunt Museum** (tel. 333644), in the Foundation Building on the University campus, 3 mi. west on the Dublin Rd., but the most "perfect" of Leonardo DaVinci's four "Rearing Horses" grazes here. (Open Mon.-Sat. 10am-5pm. £2, students 80p.)

The **An Óige hostel (HI),** 1 Pery Sq. (tel. 314672), is a pleasant Georgian house convenient to the train-und-bus station (from station, walk straight down Davis St. to the monument and left onto Pery Sq; curfew midnight, lockout 10am-5pm; £6, Oct.-May £4.50, breakfast £1.75). Or try the **Limerick Holiday Hostel,** Barrington House, George's Quay (tel. 415222), near St. Mary's Cathedral, across town and over a bridge. The mattresses are limp (£6.50, doubles £5). You might want to ask at the tourist office about new hostels slated to open in 1995 on Arthurs Quay, Cruises St., and next to Colbert Station. Proximity to town and a friendly proprietor distinguish **Villa Maria,** 27 Bellfield Park (tel. 455101), from other B&Bs along Ennis Rd. Take the second right off Ennis after the Sarsfield Bridge to a dining room filled with glass, china, and figurines (£14.50, doubles £26).

Dolman Gallery and Restaurant, Honan's Quay (tel. 417929), across from the tourist office, lets you enjoy vegetarian goulash (£4) or other specials while critiquing the current exhibit (open Mon.-Sat. 9:30am-6pm). **Moll Darby's,** 8 Georges Quay, just across the Abbey River (tel. 417 270), is the best and most reasonable non-fast-food restaurant open evenings, serving pizza, pasta, and grilled standards (open daily 6:30-10:45pm). Stock up at Quinnsworth **Supermarket** in the Arthurs Quay Mall or at find health foods at **Eats of Eden,** Henry St. (tel. 419400). The best pub in town, **Nancy Blake's,** Denmark St. (tel. 416443), sports an outdoor patio and music nightly. At the **Locke Bar,** George's Quay (tel. 413733), owner Richard Costello used to play rugby on the national team but now plays trad (Sun.-Tues. nights).

Pick up the free **Limerick Events Guide** at the **tourist office,** Arthurs Quay (tel. 317522), in the space-age glass building (open July-Aug. Mon.-Fri. 9am-7pm, Sat.-Sun. 9am-6pm; March-June and Sept.-Oct. Mon.-Sat. 9:30am-5:30pm; Nov.-Feb. Mon.-Fri. 9:30am-5:30pm, Sat. 9:30am-1pm). The **post office** sits on Lower Cecil St. (tel. 315777; open Mon. and Wed.-Sat. 9am-5:30pm, Tues. 9:30am-5:30pm). Limerick's **telephone code** is 061. The **garda** are at Henry St. (tel. 414222).

Trains and **buses** depart from **Colbert Station** just off Parnell St. **Trains** (tel. 418666; office open Mon.-Sat. 9am-6pm) go to Dublin (Mon.-Sat. 11/day, Sun. 8/day; 2½hr.; £24, students £9.50); to Waterford (Mon.-Sat. 2/day; 2hr.; £16, students £7); to Rosslare (Mon.-Sat. 2/day; 3½hr.; £22, students £9.50); Ennis (1/day); to Cork (7/day, Sun. 5/day; 2½hr.; £12.50, students £6); to Killarney (Mon.-Sat. 4/day, Sun. 3/day; 3½hr.; £14, student £6.50); and to Tralee (4/day, Sun. 3/day; 2¼hr.; £14, student £6.50). Most **buses** (tel. 313333 or 418855; 24-hr. timetable 319911; office open Mon.-Sat. 9am-6pm, Sun. 10am-6pm; Oct.-May Mon.-Sat 8am-6pm, Sun. 3-7pm) leave from the station, but some depart from Penney's or Todd's downtown on O'Connell St., near Arthurs Quay. Catch buses to every major town in the Republic, including Cork (6/day; 2hr.; £9, students £5.30); Dublin (Mon.-Fri. 10/day, Sun. 7/day, 3hr.; £10, students £7.50); Galway via Ennis (7/day; Sun. 6/day; Ennis 1hr.; £5, students £3; Galway 2hr.; £9.30, student £5.30); Killarney (Mon.-Sat. 6/day, Sun. 3/day; 2½hr.); Sligo (daily 3/day; 6hr.); Tralee (5/day, 2hr.; £9, students £5.30); Waterford (Mon.-Thurs. and Sat. 5/day, Fri. 6/day, Sun. 4-5/day; 2½hr.); and Wexford and Rosslare Harbor via Waterford, some timed to meet the ferries (daily 2-3/day; 4hr.; £12, students £8). Fifteen mi. west of Limerick off the Ennis Rd. (the N18), along the north shore of the river, **Shannon Airport** sends jets to North America and Europe (tel. (061) 471444; Aer Lingus tel. (061) 471666). **Bus Éireann** hits the **airport** from Limerick (Mon.-Sat. 20/day, Sun. 11/day; 45 min.; £3.50, students £2) and from Dublin (Mon.-Sat. 6/day, Sun. 4/day; 4½hr.; £10, students £7.50). Shannon provides direct ground transport to Ennis, Galway, Westport, Tralee, and Killarney.

ENNIS

Near Limerick, the village of **Adare** has a theme-park feel—note Main St.'s row of thatched cottages now filled with pricey restaurants and craft shops. The medieval Fitzgerald family went on a spending spree in Adare, building the **Trinitarian Abbey** (13th century) and the **Augustinian Priory** (14th century) that now rub elbows on Main St. The 13th-century **Desmond Castle** rests on the banks of the River Maigue. Find the **tourist office** on Main St. (tel. (061) 396255; open July-Aug. Mon.-Sat. 9am-7pm, Sun. 9am-1pm; June and Sept. Mon.-Sat. 9am-6pm, Sun. 9am-1pm; April-May and Oct. Mon.-Sat. 9am-5pm). **Buses** trundle the 10 mi. from Limerick (Mon.-Sat. 8/day, Sun. 4/day; 20 min.; £3.50) and run from Tralee (Mon.-Sat. 6/day, Sun. 4/day; 1¾hr.). Eight mi. northwest of Limerick along the Ennis Rd., **Bunratty Castle** (tel. (061) 361511) claims to be Ireland's most complete medieval castle, with superbly restored furniture, tapestry, stained-glass windows, and a virginal (if you don't know by now, it's time to ask). **Bunratty Folk Park** recreates turn-of-the-century houses from all over Ireland (castle and park open daily 9:30am-7pm; Sept.-June 9:30am-5:30pm; last admission 1 hr. before close; castle closes 4:15pm; £4.10, students £2). Buses from Limerick to Shannon Airport pass Bunratty (£3 return, students £2.75); you can buy a bus/admission ticket at Limerick's Colbert Station for £6.

■■■ ENNIS

Twenty mi. northwest of Limerick, Ennis (pop. 16,000) is a town of high-walled streets, crowds, fruit stands, pubs, monuments, ruins, and museums. Most people head *through* Ennis and southwest to Kilkee or northwest to the Cliffs of Moher, Doolin, and the Burren. Ennis's four main streets—O'Connell St., Abbey St., Bank Place, and Parnell St.—meet in **O'Connell Place,** where a high statue of Daniel O'Connell watches over his hometown. Abbey St. leads northeast to the ruined 13th-century **Ennis Friary,** famous for the slender panes and peaked points of its east window. Inside, depictions of the Passion adorn the 15th-century **McMahon tomb** (tel. 29100; open May-Sept. daily 9:30am-6:30pm; £1, students 40p.)

Right on the river, across Club Bridge from Abbey St., the **Abbey Tourist Hostel (IHH),** Harmony Row (tel. 22620), is comfortable and spotlessly clean (laundry; reception open 9:30am-10:30pm; £5, sheets £1.) Waterfowl waddle past Mrs. Duggan's elegant and rosy **Woodquay House** (tel. 28320), off Parnell St. (£13/person). Pub grub is the cheapest and most popular food here. Start at **Brandon's Bar,** O'Connell St. (tel. 28133), for huge plates of spuds, meat, and veggies (entrees £3).

The **Ennis tourist office,** O'Connell Sq. (tel. 21670) in the Upstairs Downstairs shop, will gracefully answer your queries (open daily 9am-9pm; Oct.-May Mon.-Sat. 9am-6pm, Sun. 10am-6pm). The **post office** sits on Bank Pl. (tel. 21054; open Mon.-Tues. and Thurs.-Fri. 9am-5:30pm, Wed. 9:30am-5:30pm, Sat. 9:30am-2:30pm).; the **phone code** is 065. In an **emergency** dial 999; no coins required.

The **bus station** (tel. 24177) is a five-minute walk from the town center on Station Rd. (open Mon.-Fri. 7:15am-5:30pm, Sat. 7:15am-4:45pm). Buses run to Limerick (10/day, Sun. 7/day; 20 min.; £5, students £3); Galway (8/day, Sun. 5/day; 1½hr.; £4.30, students £7.30); Dublin via Limerick (7/day, Sun. 4/day; 4hr.; £10, students £8); Cork (7/day, Sun. 5/day; 3hr.; £10, students £6); Kilkee (3/day, Sun. 1/day; 1hr.; £6, students £4.10); Doolin (3/day, Sun. 1/day; 1½hr.; £6, students £3.50); Shannon Airport (8/day, Sun. 5/day; ½hr.; £3.40, students £1.70); also twice daily for West Clare. The **post bus** runs from the post office to Liscannor and Doolin. (Mon.-Sat. 2/day; Ennis to Doolin £2.50, students £1.) Arrive early to get a seat. **Trains** leave from next to the bus station (office tel. 40444; open Mon.-Fri. 7am-5:30pm). Trains leave for Dublin via Limerick once daily (£16, students £9.50). You're better off catching the train from Limerick (where 9-11/day leave for Dublin).

■■■ CLARE COAST

Those traveling north to Co. Clare from Tralee and the southwest should take note of the **Tarbert-Killimer car ferry** (tel. (065) 53124), a 20-min. trip across the Shannon estuary, which preempts an 85-mi. trip via Limerick City.

In **Kilkee,** on the southwest tip of Clare, three rows of Victorian houses and a beautiful sheltered beach look out to sea; gorgeous high cliffs rise above on eroded islands where farms lay hundreds of years ago. The deafening arcades and fine white beaches fill with crowds in the summer; a healthy pub scene makes up for the plastic storefronts. Signposted walks along the side of the beach closer to the Atlantic Hotel go out to **George's Head,** and a walk past the arcades on O'Curry St. out to **Diamond Rocks,** a slippery kelp-coated mussel bed.

The welcoming **Kilkee Hostel (IHH),** O'Curry St., the town's main street (tel. 56209), is drop-your-toothbrush-on-the-floor clean. (Curfew 1am; laundry £3. £8/person; sheets 50p.) Kilkee is famous for its pub crawl—begin at the **Strand Hotel** and continue to the **Stella Maris Hotel Bar,** the **Central Bar, Richie's,** and the **Myles Creek Pub** (tel. 56670). The Stella Maris also excels at the soup-and-sandwich game (£3.15 with coffee); Myles Creek has regular meals. The **tourist office** pops up in the central square across from the Stella Maris Hotel (tel. 56112; open June-Sept. daily 10am-6pm), while the **post office** (tel. 56001) resides on O'Curry St. (open Mon.-Fri. 9am-3pm, Sat. 10am-1pm). Kilkee's **phone code** is 065. Bus Éireann (tel. 24177, in Ennis) scrapes by twice a day for Ennis and Galway.

Once you've enjoyed Kilkee and the sea, only small towns stand between you and the awesome Cliffs of Moher. **Miltown Malbay,** 20 mi. north of Kilkee on the coastal N67, wakes up only during the first week of July, when the **Willie Clancy School of Traditional Music** lets fly one of Ireland's largest musical celebrations. Be sure to book accommodations well ahead for this week. Miltown pubs are, not surprisingly, praised for their trad sessions (the best are on Mon. nights). **The People's Hostel** (tel. (065) 84161), 1½ mi. out of town center, sides a beach and offers comfortable quarters for £5 (breakfast £2.50).

From the edge of the **Cliffs of Moher** (Moor), 700 ft. above the open ocean, the grass-topped edge of Europe fronts the high wind for miles on either side. Arrive early to beat the crowd. The **tourist office** (tel. (065) 81171; open July-Aug. daily 9am-6:30pm; June and Sept. 10am-6pm) is near the parking lot, where cars must pay £1. **Bus Éireann** clangs by on the summer-only Galway/Cork route (Mon.-Sat. 3/day); the **North Clare Nipper** private bus (tel. (065) 81562) also stops here from Doolin and Lisdoonvarna (2/day). The **Burren Way** and several bike trails lead through raised limestone and sheep to the Cliffs. It's not hard to stay in Lisdoonvarna or, better yet, in Doolin and look for a ride to the Cliffs from either town.

DOOLIN

Ireland sees Doolin (called "Fisherstreet" on some maps) much as Europe sees Ireland: windy, beautiful, musical, depopulated, boisterous, oriented round the pubs, and overtouristed as all hell. Twenty years ago, Doolin was a blip on the map; today Dubs and foreigners outnumber residents 10 to 1. Many excellent musicians now prefer quieter towns like Miltown Malbay and Ballyvaughan. Still, Doolin's near-legendary status is slow to die. All three pubs—**O'Connor's, McGann's and McDermott's**—are justly famous for world-class music; great *craic* is generally a guarantee.

A 3-mi.-long, paved, and bicycle-friendly segment of the **Burren Way** links Doolin to the Cliffs of Moher. **Boats** leave the pier on the other end of town for the Aran Islands; the boats from Galway and Rossaveal are cheaper under almost any circumstances. (See Aran Islands for ferry information.) Across the street from the Doolin Café posits the **post office** (tel. 74209; open Mon.-Fri. 9am-5:30pm, Sat. 1-5:30pm). The **Doolin Café** (tel. 74429) also **rents bikes** (£6/day, £3.50/½-day, £35 deposit). Doolin is shaped like a barbell, made up of two smaller villages about 1 mi. apart from each other. The **Lower Village** is closer to the shore, the **Upper Village** farther up the road. Doolin's **phone code** answers to 065.

Book ahead for accommodations at all times. The **Aille River Hostel (IHH)** (tel. 74260), ¼ mi. downhill from the Upper Village by the river, is a small hostel with live music almost every night (£5.50/person, private room £6.50, **camping** £3.50, free laundry!; open mid-March to Oct.). The well-appointed **Westwind B&B** (tel. 74227), Upper Village, in the same driveway as the Lazy Lobster, is run by a friendly young couple (£11, Sept.-May £10). In the Lower Village, **Doolin Hostel (IHH)** (tel. 74006) includes a shop and sells bus tickets (open daily 8am-9pm; laundry £2.50; £6.50/person, £5 key deposit, sheets 50p; bikes £5/day). **The Doolin Deli** (tel. 74530), Main St. near O'Connor's, shuffles sandwiches and groceries (open summer Mon.-Sat. 8:30am-9pm, Sun. 10am-9pm).

O'Connor's, in the lower village (tel. 74168; music nightly all year and Sun. afternoons. B&B £10), and **McGann's,** in the upper (tel. 74133; music nightly in summer, weekends in winter; always Irish stew for £3), have in the past won awards for the best trad music in Ireland; **McDermott's,** in the upper village, ranks with them (tel. 74328; music nightly in summer, on weekends in winter). Most summer sessions start at 9:30pm to standing room only. O'Connor's tends to be the most crowded.

LISDOONVARNA

Lisdoonvarna's relative fame comes from its **Matchmaking Festival,** by far the best known of the several once held all over Ireland, where farm boys, their crops safely harvested, gathered to pick their mates (and, one hopes, vice versa). The month-long festival still fills the town each September, but Irish women tend to stay home and make jokes about the randy bachelors and American women who go.

Festivalgoers and others take advantage of Ireland's only health spa: the **Spa Wells Health Center,** Sulfur Hill Rd. (tel. 74023), ¼ mi. from the center of town, houses sulfur baths in a Victorian pump room and a gift shop; if you can't stay, at least savor their aromatic sulfur water (30p). The **Burren Holiday Tourist Hostel (IHH),** Doolin Rd. (tel. 74300), ranks among the finest in Western Ireland, with oak handrails, palatial antique decor, and a turf fire in the pub downstairs (£6; meals £3-6; rental **bikes** £5; laundry £3.) For B&B try Mrs. O'Connor's **Roncalli House** (tel. 74115; £12/person; open Easter-Oct.). The **Roadside Tavern** (tel. 74084), Doolin Rd., looks more like an antique shop than a bar (March-Sept. trad nightly starting at 9:30pm; Oct.-Feb. Sat.-Sun.).

A few miles inland amid scrubby hills, Lisdoonvarna weds the R476, 77, and 78 to the N67; the R478 leads southwest to Doolin and the Cliffs of Moher, the N67 northeast through the Burren to Ballyvaughan, and plenty of bike paths and trails circumvent the roads. Rent two-wheelers at **Burke's Garage,** the Square (tel. 74022; £5/day, £30/week, deposit £40). **Bus Éireann** buses stop outside Burke's, too. The **Lisdoonvarna Tourist Information Center** (tel. 74630; open 10am-6pm daily; Nov.-April 10am-6pm Mon.-Fri.), is buried in the Spa Wells Gift Shop (signposted from the town center). Lisdoonvarna's **phone code** is a perky, red-haired, and available 065.

■■■ THE BURREN

Around Lisdoonvarna or Kinvarra, the Burren begins when bare limestone begins to pop up amid grasses and sheep. Inland and in between, limestone plains and out-croppings dominate; this 100-square-mile region is the Burren, whose stony landscape includes rare wildflowers, flat rocky pedestals, and jagged hills that resemble grey skyscrapers bombed to rubble. Underground rivers have hollowed out 25 mi. of caves; the area's crazy geology is made up of *furloughs* (temporary lakes that disappear into the limestone), *clints* (a type of rock outcropping), and *grikes* (cracks in clints). The Burren also has its own species of colored snails, orchids, and ferns.

The **Burren Way** and its subsidiary walking trails connect terrain sterile as steel with teeming blue-headed grasses and red-winged butterflies; wild goats and hares patrol and fertilize the area. The 26-mi. trail goes through Ballyvaughan, Ballynalac-kan, Doolin, and Liscannor, passes by the Cliffs of Moher, and is signposted through-out. The stretch south from Ballyvaughan through Caherconnell is particularly rich in archaeology—the **Glenisheen wedge tomb,** the **Poulnabrone dolmen,** and the **Caherconnell stone fort** all date from the third millenium BC.

Bus service in the Burren is poor. **Bus Éireann** connects Galway, Kinvarra, Ballyvaughan, Lisdoonvarna, and Doolin (June-Sept. 3/day, Sun. 1/day; Oct.-May Mon.-Sat. 1/day). During the summer (June-Oct.), two of those buses continue over the Shannon car ferry at Killimer to Killarney and Cork. Bus stops are at the Doolin Hostel in Doolin, Burke's Garage in Lisdoonvarna, Linnane's in Ballyvaughan, and Winkles in Kinvarra. (Ennis Bus Éireann info: tel. (065) 24177). The private **North Clare Nipper** (tel. (065) 815 62) shudders into Doolin and Lisdoonvarna twice a day from the south. Hitchhiking requires persistence; bikes are your best bet.

The small town of **Kilfenora,** 8km southeast of Lisdoonvarna along the R478, calls itself "the heart of the Burren." Tourists stop here for grub and the informative **Burren Display Center** (tel. (065) 88036; open July-Aug. daily 9:30am-7pm; mid-March-June and Sept.-Oct. 10am-5pm; admission and descriptive film £2, students £1). A **tourist office** sits nearby (tel. (065) 88198) and sells the "Burren Rambler" map series (£2). (Open June-Oct. daily 9:30am-6pm.) Bicycles stack up at **Howrt Bicycles** (tel. (065) 88127; hourly or daily rental up to £6). **Ms. Mary Murphy,** Main St. (tel. (065) 88400), runs a B&B (£12/person). Kilfenora has three pubs: **Linnane's** (tel. (065) 88157), **Nagle's** (tel. (065) 88011), and **Vaughan's** (tel. (065) 71480).

Galway Bay's shore makes a sharp turn at **Kinvarra,** Co. Galway, where the rocky pastures of the pre-Burren landscape sprout pretty, rugged foliage; the view across the bay can't be beat. The guides at **Dunguaire Castle** (tel. (091) 37108) will explain why clockwise staircases are easier for right-handed knights to defend (open mid-April to Sept. daily 9:30am-5:30pm. £2.10, students £1.15). Palatial **Johnston's Hostel (IHH),** Main St. (tel. (091) 37164), uphill from the Quay, has an old dance hall for a common room (£5.50/person, **camping** £3. Sheets £1, showers 50p). The **Café on the Quay** serves affordable meals by the picturesque harbor (tel. (091) 78134; open April-Oct. daily 9am-9:30pm; lobster bisque and brown bread £2). Across the street, **Flatley's** (tel. (091) 37112) is locally renowned for weekend trad sessions, as is **Tully's,** where you can also get groceries. **Bus Éireann** hits Kinvarra on its Galway-Doolin route (June-Sept. Mon.-Fri. 4/day, Sun. 1/day; Oct.-May Mon.-Sat. 1/day). Feel like sailing across the bay? Go down to Kinvarra inlet and ask for Michael Linane; he'll take groups of four across to the village of **Doorus,** Co. Galway (round-trip sailing £6/person). Yeats and Lady Gregory stayed here.

■■■ GALWAY CITY

Party-seeking collegians, laid-back long-term international travelers, and working-class Irish *craic*-seekers fill Galway City to bursting during spring and summer. Galway is young, much-talked-of, and maybe too hip for its own good. Everyone seems to be in a band. Along with its smaller, and much tackier, resort-town neighbor Salthill, Galway seems to have more pubs, clubs, and venues than it does quays (and there are a *lot* of quays). Galway's popular university, relative wealth, and proximity to the Connemara *gaeltacht* make Galway a likely place to find literary and theatrical culture in both of Ireland's languages. But intellect doesn't dominate here; liveliness does. Galway is the fastest-growing city in Europe, and while the town at its worst seems a victim of enforced merriment, at its best it's a continuous blast.

ORIENTATION & PRACTICAL INFORMATION

Any transport to Galway will leave you in **Eyre Square,** a central block of lawn and monuments with the train and bus station on its east side; B&Bs stretch up Prospect Hill uphill and northwest from Eyre Sq. while the real town spreads out south and west. Williams St. descends southwest into the "Left Bank" around High St., Shop St., and Quay St., which hosts most of the restaurants and pubs. Hostels and more pubs compete on Dominick St. Abbeygate St. saunters west across the river to Galway Cathedral, becoming University Rd. as it passes University College Galway.

Tourist Office: Victoria Pl. (tel. 63081), one block west of the bus and train station; visible from Eyre Sq. Information on ferries. Open July-Aug. daily 9am-7pm; Easter-July and Sept.-Oct. Mon.-Sat. 9am-6pm, Sun. 9am-1pm; Nov.-March Mon.-Fri. 9am-6pm, Sat. 9am-1pm.

USIT (Student Travel): Kinlay House, Victoria Place, Eyre Sq., across the street from tourist office (tel. 65177). Open Mon.-Fri. 9:30am-5:30pm, Sat. 11am-4pm.

Banks: Bank of Ireland, 19 Eyre Sq. (tel. 62916). Open Mon.-Wed. and Fri. 10am-3pm, Thurs. 10am-5pm. **Allied Irish Bank,** Lynch's Castle (tel. 67041); same hours. Salthill: **Bank of Ireland** (tel. 22455). Open Mon.-Wed. and Fri. 10am-4pm, Thurs. 10am-5pm.

American Express: Ryan's Travel, 1 Williamsgate (tel. 67375). Client mail held. Open Mon.-Fri. 9:15am-5:30pm, Sat. 10am-1pm and 2:15-4pm.

Post Office: Eglinton St. (tel. 62051). Open Mon.-Sat. 9am-6pm.

Telephone Code: 091.

Galway Airport: tel. 55569.

Trains: Irish Rail/Iarnród Éireann runs from Eyre Sq. Station (tel. 61444; open Mon.-Sat. 7:40am-6pm) to Athlone (6/day, Sun. 3/day; 1hr.; £8, students £6) and continue on to Dublin (3hr.; £12, students £8); transfer at Athlone for all other lines, even the train to Sligo. (Irish Rail office: tel. 64244 or 61444; open Mon.-Fri. 9am-5:30pm.)

Buses: Bus Éireann leaves Eyre Sq. for Belfast (2-3/day, Sun. 1/day; £16.50, students £11.40), Clifden (June-Sept. Mon.-Sat. 6/day, Sun. 2/day; Oct.-May Mon.-Sat. 2/day, Sun. 1/day; £7, students £5), Cork (5/day, Sun. 5/day; £13, students £8), Dublin (8-9/day, Sun. 7-8/day; £8, students £6.50), Ennis (8/day, Sun. 6/day; £7.30, students £4.30), Limerick (7/day, Sun. 6/day; £9.30, students £5.60), Rosslare (3/day; £16, students £9.50), Shannon Airport (5/day, Sun. 3/day; £9, students £5.30) and Waterford (5/day, Sun. 4/day; £14, students £8.50), Sligo (5/day, Sun. 3/day; £10.50, students £6.50), aren't long listings *fun?*, Doolin (June-Sept. 3/day; Sun. 1/day; Oct.-May 1/day; £8.20, students £4.60), Dingle (3-5/day, Sun. 1/day; £14, students £8.50), Derry (3/day; Sun. 2/day, £14, students £8.50), Westport (5-7/day, Sun. 1/day; £8.80, students £5), Tralee (5-7/day, Sun. 5-6/day; £13, students £8), Athlone (11/day, Sun. 9/day; £7, students £5.30), and Ballina (6/day, Sun. 2/day; £9.70, students £6). **Bus station office:** tel. 62000; open daily 8am-6:30pm; Sept.-June Mon.-Sat. 8am-6pm. Private bus companies specialize in the Dublin-Galway run, among them the reliable **P. Nestor Coaches** (tel. 97144; Mon.-Thurs. and Sun. 2/day, Fri. 4/day; Sat. 5/day; £5 single or day return, £8 open return; leaves from Imperial Hotel, Eyre Sq.) and **Citylink** (tel. 64163; Mon.-Thurs. and Sat.-Sun. 2/day. Fri. 3/day; leaves from Supermac's in Eyre Sq.; same prices as Nestor's). See Connemara: Practical Information, below, for bus tours.

Hitching: Dozens at a time wait on Dublin Rd. (the N6), scouting rides east to Dublin or south to Limerick or Kinvarra; most catch bus #2, 5, or 6 from Eyre Sq.

Taxis: Big O Taxis, 21 Upper Dominick St. (tel. 66166).

Bike Rental: Celtic Raleigh, next to the Celtic Hostel, Queen St., Victoria Place (tel. 66606). £7/day, £30/week, £40 deposit or ID, remote dropoff charge £12. Open daily 9am-6pm.

Camping Equipment: River Deep Mountain High, Middle St. (tel. 63938). PowerBars £2. Open Mon.-Sat. 9:30am-6pm.

Laundry: The Bubbles Inn, 18 Mary St. (tel. 63434), open Mon.-Sat. 8:45am-6:15pm. Large wash and dry £4.

Bisexual, Gay, and Lesbian Information: P.O. Box 45 (tel. 66134). Lesbian line open Wed. 8-10pm; gay line open Thurs. 8-10pm.

Hotline: Samaritans, 14 Nun's Island (tel. 61222). 24 hr.

Pharmacies: Really's, 17 William St. (tel. 62332). Open Mon.-Fri. 9am-9pm.

Hospital: University College Hospital, Newcastle St. (tel. 24222).

Emergency: dial 999; no coins required. **Garda:** Mill St. (tel. 63161).

ACCOMMODATIONS

Over the last two years the number of hostels has increased to 16, more than Dublin; nevertheless, during weekends and big festivals, finding a pleasant bed may be difficult. Try to arrive in town before 5pm to pay for a bed early. **Woodquay** hostels

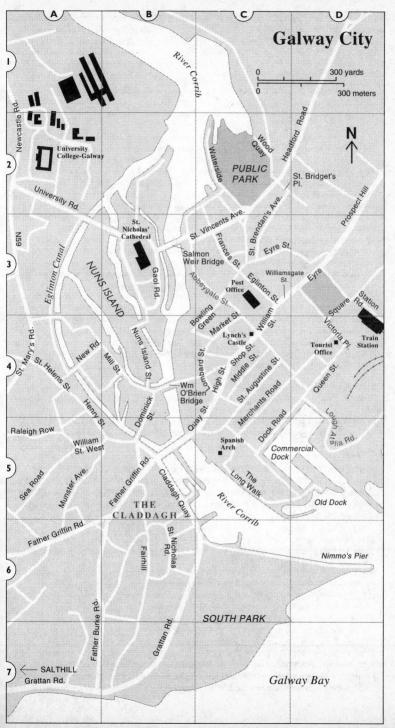

GALWAY CITY

cluster about five minutes from Eyre Sq. around the Salmon Weirs; **Dominick St.** hosts its own on the west side of the River Corrib, while **Eyre Sq.** is closest to the bus and train stations. B&Bs should set you back from £12 to 15 a night per person. If you're a clubgoer, give some thought to staying in **Salthill,** since all the post-midnight nightlife is there. If you get into town late, you may be forced to stay there anyway. Watch out for Galway Arts Week (mid-July) and the Galway Races (late July to early Aug.); other big-deal festivals flood the town throughout the year.

Despite the claims this hostel made on the leaflets it circulated during summer '94, *Let's Go* has never recommended the **Eyre Hostel,** 35 Eyre St.

Salmon Weir Hostel, Woodquay (tel. 61133). From Eyre Sq., walk up Eglinton St. (becomes Francis St.), then right onto St. Vincent's Ave. Best hostel in Galway. Free tea, coffee, detergent. Curfew 3am. Laundry £4. 4 beds/room; double. £5.90.

The Westend (formerly Owen's Hostel), Upper Dominick St. (tel. 63636). Free tea, coffee. Storytelling and live music in summer. Laundry £3.50. £6.50, Sept.-May £5.50; private rooms £10, Sept.-May £8.

Kinlay House, Eyre Sq. (tel. 65244) 24-hr. reception, free breakfast, *bureau de change.* Bike rental £6. Laundry £4. £7-11.50, doubles £12.50-13; singles £17. (Oct.-June rooms £7-10.50, £12-12.50, £16.50). 10% off for ISIC holders.

The Galway Hostel, Eyre Sq. (tel. 66959), across from the bus/train station. Soft yellow walls and airy rooms (some with balconies) that look out onto Eyre Sq. Chinese floor tiles, super-clean bathrooms; heaters. £7, 2- to 4-bed room £9.

Quay Street Hostel (IHH), Quay St. (tel. 68644). From Eyre Sq., walk straight down Shop St.; it becomes Quay St. Some rooms have skylights; kick-ass location in city center. Bike rental £3, laundry £3.50. £5.90-9, double with bath £11.50.

The Grand Holiday Hostel (IHH), Promenade (tel. 21150). Take bus #1 from Eyre Sq (Salthill). Overlooks the sea. Has **Strawberry Fields Café** (tel. 26919; breakfast £2.50; open 7am-10:30pm). Currency exchange. Sheets 50p, bike rental £6/day, £4/½-day. Laundry £3. £7, Sept.-June £6.50; doubles £8-9.

Camping: Salthill Caravan and Camping Park (tel. 22479). On the water ½ mi. west of Salthill, near Galway Tourist Hostel. Crowded during high season. Hikers and cyclists £2.50-3. Open April-Sept.

St. Martin's, 2 Nuns Island (tel. 68286). Right in the city center. £12.50.

Mrs. O. Walsh, Brasstacks, 3 St. Helen's Street (tel. 24728). Off Newcastle Rd., by Cookes Corner (10 min. from city center). £11.

Mary Ryan's, 4 Beechmount Rd. (tel. 23303), in Highfield Park, 20 min. away; take bus #2 from Eyre Sq. to Taylor's Hill Convent. Fills up fast. Open June-Sept. £6.

FOOD

Stay east of the river near the short blocks in and around Quay St., High St., Shop St., and Abbeygate St. For groceries try **Roches Stores,** near Eyre Sq. (open Mon.-Thurs. and Sat. 9am-5:30pm, Fri. 9am-9pm.) or **Healthwise** (tel. 68761) on Abbeygate St. Saturdays a **market** (9am-3pm), sets up in front of St. Nicholas Church on Market St. Fishers may wander through the pubs, selling cups of fresh mussels (around £1).

The Home Plate, Mary St. (tel. 61475). Expect a wait at lunch, when the whole city lines up to bat inside. Chicken fajita £2.50, pasta bolognese £3, huge sandwiches £1.50. Open Mon.-Sat. 10am-8pm.

McDonough's, 22 Quay St. (tel. 65001). The best fish-and-chip shop in the world? Certificates line the wall. Cod fillet and chips, £3. Open Mon.-Sat. 9am-midnight.

Java's, Upper Abbeygate St. (tel. 67400). Galway's somber-eyed youth sit here for hours. Salads and sandwiches. Open Mon.-Sat. 9am-4am, Sun. noon-4am.

The Couch Potatas, Upper Abbeygate St. (tel. 61664). "Pavoratti"=baked potato with meatballs & cheese (£3.50). Spuds & butter £1; 30p for extra toppings. Crowded at lunchtime. Open daily 8am-9pm.

Fat Freddy's, Quay St. (tel. 672 79). Everyone under 25 goes here; therefore, it's ridiculously crowded. Large cheese pizza £3.95. Open daily 10am-10:30pm.

Nimmo's Restaurant and Winebar, by the Spanish Arch. Intimate room. Daily specials (salmon in herb sauce £5.50). Open daily 12:30-3pm and 7pm-late.

PUBS

Half the businesses in downtown Galway must be pubs. Fabulous, fast-paced traditional music usually rings out in several pubs each night. Good and bad rock, guitar-folk, country, blues, and even metal also rear their heads. The most talked-about pubs are around Dominick St. and Quay St.

The Quays, Quay St. (tel. 68347). Popular with everyone under 25. The massive, multi-floored interior was built with carved wood taken from an old church.

McSwiggan's, 3 Eyre St., Woodquay (tel. 68917). So many hidden corners, you never seem to reach the back of the bar. Trad sessions Sat.-Sun. nights.

The King's Head, High St. (tel. 66630), continue down Shop St. Popular student hangout, younger than others. Music nightly. Sun. morning jazz.

Roisín Dubh, Dominick St., (tel. 66540). (ro-SHEEN doov; means "The Black Rose"). Set dancing Tues. nights, trad Mon.-Tues., rock Wed.-Thurs., folk Fri.-Sat.

Monroe's, Dominick St. (tel. 63397). Pierced knuckles. Live, loud bands nightly.

Seaghan Ua Neachtain (a.k.a. Knockton's), Quay St. (tel. 68820). Mixed crowd interested in the good trad which blares out every Mon., Wed. and Fri.-Sat.

Waterfront, Ravens Terrace, off Dominick St. Not gay—gay friendly!

Taylor's, Dominick St. The best pint of Guinness in Galway. Lunchtime theater.

SIGHTS

Walk along the river and bay, out to Salthill and back for the view, check out the two cathedrals, and then start looking for pubs, clubs, food, or literary events. The city, its crowds, and its watery surroundings overshadow its history.

Galway's **Catholic Cathedral** looms above the Salmon Weir Bridge, across the river from most of the city, closer to University College Galway. Inside, marble circles intersect with elaborate mosaics. (Excellent tours, and organ practice, Mon.-Fri. 3:30-5:30pm; Sun. masses.) Closer to the center of town, the tiny **Nora Barnacle House** (tel. 64743), Bowling Green, exposes a few private (not!) letters and photos of James Joyce and his wife. From the bridge over the river, walk down Abbeygate St. to Bowling Green. (Open May-Sept. Mon-Sat. 10am-5pm. £1.) At the **Church of St. Nicholas,** look out for the stone commemorating Columbus' stop to pray before going off to meet the Native Americans. (Open May-Sept. daily 9am-5:45pm. Free.)

Stroll back through the narrow streets past the Wolfe Tone Bridge to the Long Walk by the river, where the **Spanish Arch** is the only surviving gateway to the old trading town. The **Galway City Museum** (tel. 67641), next to it in Tower House, has stairs to the top of the arch. (Open May-Oct. 10am-1pm and 2:15-5:15pm. 60p.) Across the river, around Dominick St., is the neighborhood called the **Claddagh;** until the 1930s, this area was an independent, Irish-speaking, thatched-cottage fishing village, and still retains a certain charm. The famous Claddagh rings, the traditional wedding rings of the old neighborhood, are mass-marketed but still-remarkable examples of Celtic metalworking. From the Claddagh, you can walk along the waterside road west to Salthill. You should—the coast of Galway Bay varies from rockpile-rough to sandcastle-smooth, and the sunsets can't be matched. The **Corrib Princess** sails from Galway's Woodquay for a tour of Lough Corrib at 2:30 and 4:30pm daily June-Aug. (fare £5); 90 min. (tel. 68903). If the sun comes out, head to **Salthill** where sandy beaches flirt with the discos.

ENTERTAINMENT

Theaters, musicians, and literary events crowd Galway itself; music both rowdy and sedate barrages Salthill's clubs. *The Advertiser* and *Galway Guide* are free and listing-filled papers. The **Galway Arts Center,** 47 Dominick St. (tel. 65886), might be able to help (open Mon.-Sat. 10am-5:30pm).

The **Druid Theater Company,** Chapel Lane (tel. 68617), off Quay St., puts on four plays each year (£7, students £5; box office opens Mon.-Sat. noon-6pm, noon-8pm night of show; buy tickets at least a week in advance). **The Punchbag Theater,** also on Quay St. (tel. 65422), does the same (£7, students £5; box office open Mon.-

Sat. noon-6pm). For a pint and a show, try **Taylor's Pub** on Upper Dominick St. (£3.50, including lunch) or the **King's Head** on High St. (tel. 66630, 1-2pm, £2). The mostly-Irish-language theater **An Taibhdhearc** ("TIVE-yark"), Middle St. (tel. 62024), has launched its fair share of careers. Some shows are bilingual. (Box office open Mon.-Fri. 10am-6pm, Sat. 2-6pm. Tickets £5-7, with occasional discounts.)

Between 11pm and midnight, the pubs empty out in Galway proper and the lines form in front of Salthill's **nightclubs;** the walk along the waterfront takes about 20 to 35 minutes, but many groups split cabs. Salthill's big nights are Wednesday, Friday, and Saturday. All the clubs charge a £3 to 6 cover. All the clubs listed here lie on Upper Salthill, the main road. The more popular clubs include **C.J.'s,** 143 Upper Salthill (pop). **The Castle** holds raves, while **The Warwick** plays alternative or blues. **The Oasis** has mixed music while **Vagabonds** has theme nights (Irish-only bands, techno, and rave). **Feet First** plays mostly hip-hop. To dance in the center of Galway, try **Central Park,** 32 Upper Abbeygate St. (cover £4). All of these clubs open up between 10pm and 11pm and start jumping after 11:30pm.

Festivals ring Galway's bell once a month. The **Galway Poetry and Literature Festival,** a.k.a. the **Cúirt** (tel. 65886), is one of the nation's biggest highbrow gatherings. For twelve days in mid-July the **Galway Arts Festival** attracts famous trad musicians, rock groups, theater troupes, filmmakers and comedians; ask the Festival Box Office, Eyre Sq. (tel. 67211) for information. The town is packed to overflowing during this time: be sure to reserve a bed.

■ NEAR GALWAY: COOLE PARK & THOOR BALLYLEE

W. B. Yeats' two best-known residences are twenty-odd miles south of Galway near Gort, where the N18 meets the N66. One mi. north of Gort on the N18 (the Galway Rd.), well before Ardrahan, **Coole Park** was the estate home of Yeats' friend and theatrical collaborator Lady Augusta Gregory. The house itself was ruined during the 1922 Civil War; only the foundations are visible now. The yew walk and garden, however, survive as part of a national forest and wildlife park. A mile from the garden is **Coole Lake,** where Yeats watched nine-and-fifty swans "all suddenly mount/ And scatter wheeling in great broken rings/Upon their clamorous wings" (always open; free.) Coole Park's **visitors center** is nearby, but eschews Yeats in favor of local rocks, trees, and furry wildlife. (Tel. (091) 31804; open mid-April to mid-June and Sept. Tues.-Sun. 10am-5pm; mid-June to Aug. daily 9:30-6:30; £1, students 40p).

In 1916, Yeats bought and began to renovate the 13th- and 14th-century tower **Thoor Ballylee.** The turn-off is 3 mi. north of Coole Park on the Galway Rd.; the tower itself is 2 mi. down an infrequently traveled road. Yeats never imagined that his home would become a visitors' center with presentations in seven languages. The tower's current interior dates from 1961 and restores its look circa 1926, the year Yeats wrote "The Tower." (Open May-Sept. 10am-6pm. £2.50, students £2.)

■■■ ARAN ISLANDS (OILEÁIN ÁRANN)

Stark, cliff-ridden limestone landscapes, prehistoric all over—the three Aran Islands, Inishmore, Inishmaan and Inisheer, sashay with style across the ocean 15 mi. southwest of Galway City. During July and August, throngs of curious foreigners surround every monument and pub on Inishmore, though the empty spaces between the sites can still get rather deserted. Tourists are rarer on the other two islands. Here one finds stunning scenery and locals who make *curraghs* (small boats made from wicker, cowskin, and black tar).

Do not expect any ferrries to arrive on time, and double-check with fishermen to find out where and when the boats are coming. Don't expect tourist amenities on Inishmaan or Inisheer. Especially on those two islands, you may be able to camp in a field for a small fee; be sure to ask the farmer, and don't be surprised if some irregularity in the planting or harvesting schedule renders all fields temporarily off-limits. The **phone code** for all three islands is 099.

GETTING THERE

O'Brien Shipping (tel. (091) 61854 or 67283), in the Galway tourist office. Serves all three islands all year. In 1994, you could to disembark on one island and return from another. If you leave from Galway and return to Doolin, however, you will pay £5 more. Direct service to all three islands from Galway, direct service to Inishmaan and Inisheer from Rossaveal and Inishmore. Return from Galway to Inishmore: July-Aug. £18, June and Sept. £15, Oct.-May £12. Students £2 less.

Aran Ferries (tel. (091) 68903 or 92447), shares space in the Galway tourist office, offers discounts to students and for Eurail passes, and gets you a discount at the Dún Aengus or Aran Islands hostels. Does not charge penalty for disembarking on one island and leaving from another. July-Aug., return from Rossaveal to Inishmore £15, from Galway to Inishmore £18; April to mid-June and Sept. and Oct. £12 from both ports to Inishmore. Serves all three islands and Doolin (Rossaveal to Doolin £20 high season, £23 low season). Student fares £2 less.

Island Ferries, Victoria Place (tel. (091) 61767), next to Galway tourist office, serves all three islands all year; £15-18 return ticket to Inishmore from Galway includes a stay at the Mainistir House hostel on Inishmore (except July-Aug). Visiting more than one island costs £18-23. Rossaveal to Inishmore £12 plus £3 bus. Students £10 plus £3 bus.

Doolin Ferries, in the Doolin tourist office (tel. (065) 74189, 77086 or 74455); affiliated with O'Brien, and also part of the cargo network that keeps the Arans supplied with food, gasoline, etc. Same fare structure as O'Brien's.

INISHMORE (INIS MÓR)

Most visitors to the Arans go to Inishmore (pop. 900), the largest and northernmost of the islands; crowds disembark at Kilronan. The landscape resembles that of the Burren in Co. Clare. The best beach is in Kilmurvey, 4 mi. west of Kilronan, while Dún Aengus is 8 mi. west. The island's most impressive monument, dating from the first century BC, is magnificent **Dún Aengus** (Dún Aonghasa), 5 mi. west of the pier at Kilronan. An imaginary island is said to appear on the horizon; it's so real-looking that it appeared on maps until the 20th century. On the way to the fort, 3 mi. west of Kilronan past **Kilmurvey** (Cill Mhuirbhigh), lie **The Seven Churches,** a scattered grouping of religious remains. The **puffing holes** at the smokin' east end of the island spout seawater like excited whales.

Mainistir House (IHH) (tel. 61169) perches ½ mi. from Kilronan (from the pier, go uphill and turn right after the supermarket). The owners cook huge "vaguely vegetarian" dinners for £5, £7 with morning porridge and scone. (Doubles £20. Laundry £4.) Down by the harbor, the **Aran Islands Hostel** (tel. 61255) has large rooms stuffed with beds. (£5/person. Open April-Oct. Laundry £3.) **Dún Aengus Hostel** (tel. 61318), its more personable sister hostel, lies 4 mi. west in the town of Kilmurvey, a 10-min. walk. (Shuttle service included. £5. Laundry £3. Open April-Nov.)

The **Spar Market** (open Mon.-Sat. 9am-8pm, Sun. 10am-7pm), past the hostel in Kilronan, provides the essentials; restaurants on the island tend to be expensive and are not open in winter. **An Seán Chéibh,** with outdoor seating and fresh Aran fish (£4.50), is a short walk from the harbor. Traditional musicians strum on the terrace at **Tí Joe Mac's,** below the hostel. On summer Friday, Saturday, and Sunday nights, stroll down to the **dance hall** at 11:30pm for the *ceilí* (cover £2, Sat. £3). The hall also shows the film *Man of Aran* three times daily in summer (£2).

Ferries land in Kilronan (Cill Rónáin); the **tourist office** (tel. 61263) changes money, holds bags during the day (75p), and sells a great map (£3; open May to mid-Sept. daily 10am-7pm). The best way to explore Inishmore is by bike; rent one opposite the American Bar at **Costello's Bike Hire** (tel. 61241) for £4/day (open May.-Oct.). The **post office** (tel. 61101; *bureau de change;* open Tues.-Sat. 9am-5pm, Mon. 9am-1pm) is up the hill from the pier, past the Spar Market. The **phone code** for all of the Arans is 099.

INISHMAAN (INIS MEÁIN)

Inishmaan (pop. 300) admits gloomy remoteness as its main attraction, and its sea-coast is visually inferior to those of Inishmore and Inisheer. Pick up the **Inishmaan Way** brochure from the tourist office in Galway or Inishmore for the 5-mi. walking route covering all the island's sights. Inishmaan's safest and most inviting beach is **Trá Leitreach; Synge's Chair** is a nook between cliffs overlooking George's Sound; **Dún Chonchúir,** a 7th-century fort, overlooks the entire island. Ferries to the main-land rarely visit this "middle" island of the three, which means trying to get to or off it can prove dodgy; fishermen, if you can find them, may answer your boat ques-tions. At the pier, a small coffeeshop inside an old cottage dispenses food and **tour-ist information** (no phone; open Easter-Sept. daily 9am-6pm). The island's tiny village spreads out along one road west of the pier and divides the island in half. Hostel, B&B, and victuals can be found at the **Dún Fearbhai** (tel. 73085). From the pier, walk straight and take a left at the "crossroads"; it's the first house on the left. A **post office** (tel. 73001), public phone, and **shop** (tel. 73002, open Mon.-Sat. 9am-8pm) are located in the village (past the pier and up the small hill), as is Padraig O'Conghaile's thatched **pub** (grub all day).

INISHEER (INIS OÍRR)

Someone described the Arans as "quietness without loneliness", but Inishmore isn't always quiet and Inishmaan can get pretty lonely. Only Inisheer (pop. 300) fulfills the phrase. The smallest of the islands (less than 2 mi. across in either direction), its few inhabitants live close enough together to make them seem greater in number.

Begin at the pier and walk along the shore to the romantic overgrown graveyard of **St. Kevin's Church** *(Teampall Chaomháin*—not "chow mein," but "kevin," since in Irish *ch=k* and *mh=v)*. Continue into the town to **Cnoc Raithní,** a stone burial mound 2,000 years older than Christianity. Along the beach, a grassy track leads to **An Loch Mór,** an inland lake. Above the lake is the stone ring-fort **Dún Formna.** The walk back to the center leads through **Formna Village** with old thatched houses on out to **Cill na Seacht nIníon,** a small monastery with a stone fort. The remains of the **O'Brien castle,** which Cromwell razed in 1652, shade a nearby knoll. From the ruins, look out to the still-operational lighthouse.

A list of Inisheer's 16 B&Bs (most £9) hangs on the window of the small **tourist office** next to the pier. Skylights light the rooms at the new, cozy, and spacious **Brú Hostel (IHH)** (tel. 75024). The hostel organizes *curragh* trips and makes a civilized base for wild trekking. Call ahead in July and August. (4- to 6-bed room £6, laundry £2, private rooms £7.) The **Láthair Campála Campground** (tel. 75008) flexes its tarps near the beach for camping aficionados who don't mind chill winds off the ocean (£2/tent, £10/week; open May-Sept.). **Tourist information** is cheerfully given in English or Irish at the red-gated office near the main pier (tel. 75022), while a **post office** resides further up the island (open 9am-5pm weekdays.) Some tourists miss the **ferry** out because boats cannot serve the main pier if the tide is not above the first landing step; ask a fisherman where the tide will be when your ferry is due, and be ready to run to the Far Pier, about ¾ mi. west of the main one.

■■■ CONG

Designated by legend as the site of the First Battle of Moytura between the pre-human Fir Bolg and the god-like Túatha de Danann, Cong, Co. Mayo (pop. 300) has plenty of draws: airy, romantic prettiness, with an abbey and other ruins; a narrow strip of land between the two big Loughs, perfect for island jaunting; and opulent Ashford Castle, where the Guinness clan once lived. Oscar Wilde made fun of it— Ronald Reagan and Jason Priestly slept in it. John Wayne shot *The Quiet Man* here with his co-star Maureen O'Hara.

Practical Information The town's **tourist office,** Abbey St. (tel. 46542), will point you toward wonders, all in the free *Get to Know Cong.* (Open May-Oct. 10am-6pm daily.) The **post office** (tel. 46001) is on Main St. (open Mon.-Sat. 9am-5:30pm). Tour the area on Raleigh bikes rented from **O'Connor's Garage,** next door. (£7/day, £30/week; students £5/day, £30/week; ID deposit. Open daily 9am-9pm.) **Buses** leave for Westport, Ballina (Mon.-Sat. 2/day), Clifden (Mon.-Sat. 1/day), and Galway (Mon.-Sat. 1-2/day) from outside Ryan's Hotel. The **phone code** is 092.

Accommodations, Food, & Pubs Both the Quiet Man Hostel and the Cong Hostel, owned by the same family, boast laundry service for £4, fishing rods (£20 deposit), returnable guidebooks (£2.50 deposit), and guided tours of *The Quiet Man* locations (£2.50). **Quiet Man Hostel (IHH),** is at Abbey St. (tel. 46511), across the street from Cong Abbey (currency exchange, bike rental £6, open April-Sept, £6), while the **Cong Hostel (IHH)** (tel. 46089) lies a mile down the Galway Rd (Bike rental £6, rowboats £2; £6, doubles £7.50, breakfast £2.50, camping £3). No one will stop you from **camping** elsewhere on Inchagoill Island. The **White House B&B,** Abbey St., across the street from Danagher's Hotel (tel. 46358), is smothered in geraniums and ivy (£13.50).

Just across the street from the White House, locals down mammoth meals and dark pints at **Danagher's Hotel and Restaurant** (tel. 46028). The most brilliant *craic* in the region occurs here, along with weekend discos. **The Quiet Man Coffee Shop** (Main St.; tel. 46034) looks like The Peach Pit would if 90210 youth were obsessed with Quiet Man memorabilia. (Open Easter-Sept. daily 10am-6pm.) Cooks should head for **O'Connor's Supermarket** on Main St. (Open daily 9am-9pm.)

Sights From 1852 to 1939 the heirs to the Guinness fortune (later Lord and Lady Ardilaun) lived in the 12th-century **Ashford Castle,** now a luxury hotel with lakeside gardens. Diplomatic visitors get put up here, among them unpopular Canadian ex-Prime Minister Brian Mulroney and ex-popular President Reagan. *The Quiet Man* was shot on the grounds. The castle-hotel is expressly closed to visitors, but if you enter the otherwise-unfenced gardens through the front gate, you'll have to pay £2.

A sculpted head of its last abbot keeps watch over the ruins of the 12th-century **Royal Abbey of Cong,** located in the village, near Danagher's Hotel (always open; free). Cross the abbey grounds and pass through the doorway to reach a footbridge. Continuing on across the bridge by the **Monk's Fishing House** takes you to **caves** Pigeon Hole, Teach Aille, and Ballymaglancy Cave and to a 4000-year-old burial chamber, **Grant's Grave. Cave exploration** is quite popular. Spelunkers here have free access to caves, but Kelly's Cave must be unlocked (key at the Quiet Man Café). Spelunkers' safety, here as always, requires a friend who knows when to expect you back, two torches (flashlights), and waterproof gear.

After cycling 6 mi. from Cong to Clonbur and then up **Mount Gable,** bikers can get a view of both Lough Corrib and Lough Mask from the top. **Inchagoill** ("INCH-agill"), an island in the middle of Lough Corrib, consists mostly of beautiful wild forest; its importance lies in its ruins. **St. Patrick's Church,** built in the 5th century, is the more ruined of the two. The **Church of the Saint** dates back to the 12th century, and is decorated with an archway of carved heads. The famous **Stone of Lugna,** supposedly the tombstone of St. Patrick's nephew and navigator, is nearby; it is probably the second-oldest Christian monument in the world (oldest are Rome's catacombs). Inchagoill's only current full-time residents are curiously amiable **wild rats.** Ask Ed Hickey at Lough Corrib Hostel in Oughterard to take you out (return £5). The *Corrib Queen* (tel. (092) 46029) sails daily from Lisloughrea Quay in Cong on the Quay Rd. (1½hr.; tour of island included; £7 return; sails June-Aug. 4/day).

■■■ CONNEMARA

A lacy net of inlets and islands along the coast and a rough gang of inland mountains make up the famously rugged Connemara, the thinly populated western arm of Co.

Galway flexing west from Galway City to the Atlantic. Famine hit hardest here—subsistence farming was already the norm. Ireland's largest *gaeltacht* (Irish-speaking area) stretches along the south Connemara coast west from Galway City to Carna.

As with much of the western coast, the most rewarding way to see Connemara is on bike. Consider renting in Galway and cycling northwest to Clifden via Lough Corrib and Cong. Alternatively, take the public bus from Galway to Clifden via Cong (3hr.). Hitchhikers often enjoy a bit of a tour by local drivers. The N59 from Galway to Clifden is the main thoroughfare; R336, 340, and 341 are loop roads.

Connemara is ideal for camping—the coast is dotted with small beaches and almost all of the offshore islands are accessible by land bridge or by local fishing boat. **Buses** serve southern Connemara from Galway frequently (always several/day; summer up to 8/day) and northern Connemara (Mon.-Sat. 1/day). Call the Galway tourist office or Western Heritage (tel. 21699) for tour information. **Michael Nee** runs a private bus service to Clifden and Cleggan, connecting with the 2pm ferry to Inishbofin (£5 single, £7 return; tel. 34682; operates June-Sept.).

CLIFDEN (AN CLOCHÁN)

The region's only community big enough to be called a town, Clifden has become a miniature Killarney, boasting six hostels, tourbuses, and many *bureaux de change*. The past four years have seen Clifden's nightlife rocket from nonexistent to famous; people who would never have left Galway years ago now come here at night for the *craic*. On account of its size, geography, and general cheeriness, Clifden remains the best base to explore Connemara.

The **tourist office** lies on Market St. (tel. 21163; open May and Sept. Mon.-Sat. 10am-5:30pm; June Mon.-Sat. 9am-6pm; July-Aug. Mon.-Sat. 9am-6pm, Sun. 12-4pm); the **Bank of Ireland** flops on Sea View (tel. 21111; open Mon.-Fri. 10am-12:30pm and 1:30-5pm). The **post office** is on Main St (open Mon.-Fri. 9am-1pm and 2-5:30pm, Sat. 9am-12:30pm). The **phone code** is 095. **Buses** run to Clifden from Galway through Oughterard (6/day, Sun. 2/day; Sept.-May 1-2/day; 2 hr.). A bus runs late June to August (Mon. and Thurs.; 1/day) between Westport and Clifden (1½ hr.). **Bus Éireann** leaves from Cullen's Coffeeshop on Market St. **Michael Nee** (tel. (095) 34682) runs a private bus to Galway, leaving from The Square (June-Aug. £5 single, £7 return). Ask for times at the tourist office. **Bikes** are available from **Mannion's**, Bridge St. (tel. 21160; £7/day, £30/week, deposit £40, open Mon.-Sat. 9am-6:30pm, Sun. 10am-1pm and 5-7pm). In an **emergency** dial 999, no coins required; or the **garda** at 21021.

The **Clifden Town Hostel,** Market St. (tel. 21076), in the town center, has clean, uncrowded rooms. (Sheets £1, bike hire £5/day; 4-5 bed bunkroom £6; private rooms £6.50 low season, £7.50 high). For **Leo's Hostel (IHH),** Beach Rd. (tel. 21429), the reputation of a "loo with a view" has spread far and wide. (Bike hire £5/day, off-season £4; laundry £3, sheets free. Hostel £5, private room £5.50, cabin £6 (for 2), huts £5 (for 4), **camping** £3.) The **Brookside Hostel,** Hulk St. (tel. 21812), is signposted from town center. (Laundry £5. Parking £5; private rooms "negotiable." Sheets £1. Return tickets on *M.V. Queen* for Inishbofin £8. July-Aug. £6, Sept.-June £5.) For **B&B** try the **Corrib House,** Main St. (tel. 21346; £9, continental breakfast) or **Mrs. King, Kingston House,** Bridge St. (tel. 21470; £13, with bath £14).

O'Connor's SuperValu, Market St., might be the best place to score some vittles. (Open Mon.-Sat. 9am-7pm, Sun. 9am-1pm.) **E.J. King's,** Market St. (tel. 21330), is a crowded bar that serves exceptional grub on exceptionally old wood (Connemara mussels £3.50). At **My Teashop,** Main St. (tel. 21077), munch a smoked salmon sandwich (£2.50; open Mon.-Sat. 9am-6pm). For a bit of drink and wink and a huge open fire, try **The Central,** Main St. (tel. 21430), or bring your own instruments to the very maroon **Mannion's,** Market St. (tel. 21780), which has music nightly (Fri.-Sat. in winter). People who actually live in Clifden congregate at **Lowry's,** Market St. (tel. 21347) for *eine kleine nacht musik*.

There are no cliffs in Clifden itself; ride out of town, and you might find a few. The 10-mi. **Sky Road,** which loops around the head of land west of town, paves the way to head-clearing views and makes for a great bike ride. One mi. down Sky Rd., pass through the gate to the ruins of **Clifden Castle,** the former mansion of Clifden's founder, John D'Arcy. One of the nicer ways to meet Connemara is to hike to the Alcock and Brown monument, 3 mi. past Salt Lake and Lough Fadda. **Connemara Heritage Tours,** Market St. (tel. 21379), led by an inspiring archaeologist, foray into the history, folklore, and archaeology of the region. (Leave Easter-Oct. daily 9:30am and 2pm. £10, students £8. 4hr.) The same guy organizes a **tour of Inishbofin,** clarifying the island's natural history, archaeology, geology, and place names (leaves daily from Clifden 11am, return 6:15pm; £20 includes bus, ferry, and tour, students £18), as well as a **tour of the Aran Islands** (Inishmore: leaves Clifden Wed. at 9am, back at 6:30pm, £26 ferry, bus, and tour; Easter-Oct.).

CONNEMARA NATIONAL PARK

East and northeast of Clifden, the country hunches up into high hills and collapses into bogs interrupted only by the odd bare rock. Tussocks, hare runs, orchids, bogs, roseroot, ravens, poetry, and toil are only some of the nouns associated with this National Park near the town of **Letterfrack.**

The local **bus** from Galway to Clifden via Cong and Leenane stops in Letterfrack (late June to Aug. Mon.-Sat. 11/day; Sept. to mid-June Tues., Thurs., and Sat.-Sun. 1/day). A summer-only route bounces from Clifden to Westport via Letterfrack (Mon. and Thurs. 2/day; Tues.-Wed. and Fri.-Sat. 1/day). Letterfrack is less a town than it is three pubs at the crossroads just outside the park. Up the hill from town toward the park, the **Old Monastery Hostel** (tel. (095) 41132) charges £6. The cozy downstairs café cooks up buffet dinners (£5) and organic breakfasts. (Laundry £3, bike hire £5. Private rooms £7.50.) Good pub grub, seafood, and groceries are available at **Veldon's** (tel. (095) 41046). **The Bard's Den,** across the intersection (tel. 41189) is graced with a large open fire and skylight. (Disco Fri.)

Outside Letterfrack in **Connemara National Park** (tel. (095) 41054), guides sponsor walks through bird-laden hills (July-Aug. Mon., Wed., and Fri. 10:30am; free) and evening talks. (July-Aug. Wed. 8:30pm; free.) Show up in the mood for mud, and wear pants and shoes you wouldn't mind throwing away. The **visitors center** explains bogs and turf. (Park open May and Sept. 10am-5:30pm; June 10am-6:30pm; July-Aug. 9:30am-6:30pm. Park entrance £1.50, students 60p.) Two short, signposted trails which begin at the visitors center afford views of Ballinkill Harbor, Inishbofin, and Inishark. Serious hikers should consider the **Twelve Bens** *(Na Benna Beola,* a.k.a. the Twelve Pins), a rugged range 1700-2400 ft. high. Access is through the National Park, behind Diamond Hill. Hikers base themselves at the **Ben Lettery Youth Hostel (An Óige/HI)** (tel. (095) 34636), far away from everything in Ballinafad, 8 mi. east of Clifden, off the N59 west of the Roundstone turn-off. (April-June and Sept. £4.50, July-Aug. £5.50.)

■ ■ ■ WESTPORT

Mayo's population centers are never its most interesting places. Westport is, however, a quintessentially pleasant town with a satisfactory pub life and plenty of good cafés; its location at the elbow-crook of Clew Bay, with Connemara to its south and Co. Mayo's islands a short jaunt northwest, makes it a likely stop.

Westport's North Mall and South Mall broadways run parallel to the river. Most of the town extends off South Mall; Bridge St. favors pubs. Most goings-on center on The Octagon (the junction of James St., Peter St., and Shop St.) or the clock tower.

The current uses of **Westport House** (tel. 25430 or 25141) are hardly worth the entrance fee. (£5, students £3.50. Open June Mon.-Fri. noon-5pm, Sat.-Sun. 2-6pm; July to late Aug. Mon.-Sat. 10:30am-6pm; late Aug. daily 2-6pm; Sept. daily 2-5pm.) More interesting, the cheaper **Clew Bay Heritage Center** sits at the end of The Quay (open Mon.-Fri. 9am-5pm, Sun. 3-5pm, £1). **Croagh Patrick's** perfect cone of a mountain rises 2510 ft. over Clew Bay. Perhaps because of its height, it was sacred to **Lug,** sun god, god of arts and crafts. Most climbers start from the village of Murrisk, several miles west of Westport on the R335; buses traverse the route (July-Aug. Mon.-Fri. 3/day, Sept.-June Mon.-Fri. 2/day).

Westport's B&Bs (£12-13) are easily spotted on the Castlebar and Altamont Roads. The **Old Mill Holiday Hostel (IHH),** James St. (tel. 27045), between The Octagon and the tourist office, has hot, intense showers. (Bedroom lockout 11am-1pm; kitchen and common room lockout 11pm-8am. £5, July-Aug. £6; quilts 50p, laundry £2.) Try the **Club Atlantic (IHH),** Altamont St. (tel. 26644 or 26717), a five-minute walk from North or South Mall. (June-Aug. £5.50-5.90; March-May and Sept.-Oct. £4.50. Singles £9. Doubles £14.) The **supermarket** is on Shop St. (Open Mon.-Fri. 9am-7pm, Sat. 9am-6:45pm.) On Thursday mornings visit the **country market** by the Town Hall. **Bernie's High Street Café,** High St. (tel. 27797) has daily pasta specials for £1.20. At **Circe,** Bridge St. (tel. 27096) spinach pancake (£2.75) and other savories double in price after 6pm. (Open daily 10am-10pm.) Bip down Bridge St. for *craic* or call the southwest Mayo **pub hotline:** tel. 27371. **Matt Molloy's,** Bridge St. (tel. 26655), is owned by Chieftains' flutist and has trad sessions summer nights.

The **tourist office** sits on North Mall (tel. 25711) by the river. (Open Easter-Sept. Mon.-Fri. 9am-6pm, Sat. 10am-6pm; winter Mon.-Fri. 9am-12:45pm, 2-5:15pm) The **post office** is at North Mall (tel. 25475; open Mon.-Sat. 9am-5:30pm), and the **telephone code** is 098. **Trains** arrive at the **Altamont St. Station,** a 10-min. walk east of town (tel. 25253 or 25329; inquiry line open Mon.-Sat. 9:30am-6pm). Trains run to Dublin via Athlone and Castlebar (Mon.-Sat. 3-4/day, Sun. 1/day; Dublin £12, students £9). For **bus** info, call the tourist office at tel. 25711. Almost no buses leave on weekends. Buses leave from the Octagon for: Ballina (Mon.-Fri. 1-3/day); Castlebar (Mon.-Fri. 6/day); Louisburgh (Mon.-Fri. 2/day; £4.30); Galway (Mon.-Fri. 2/day; £9.70); Knock (Mon.-Fri. 4/day; £6.70); and Sligo, continuing on to Belfast (May-Sept. Mon.-Fri. 1/day). For bikes, head to **Bike World,** The Octagon (tel. (088) 596 179; £6/day, £30/week. Open Mon.-Sat. 10am-6:30pm, Sun. noon-6pm.)

■■■ ACHILL ISLAND

Achill Island is Co. Mayo's best-known holiday refuge and Ireland's largest island. Bordered by glorious beaches and cliffs, Achill's interior is bog, bog, mountain, bog, bog. The best base for exploring the island is Keel; the best hostel, however, is in Achill Sound Town, and the best scenery lies west of Dooagh. **Buses** run infrequently from Achill Sound Town, Keel, and Dooagh to Westport (£5.50 return), and to Sligo, Enniskillen, and Belfast (summer 3/day; winter 2/week). Consider cycling to the view. The **phone code** for all of Achill Island is 098. There's no bank on the island; change money on the mainland.

ACHILL SOUND TOWN

About 6 mi. south of Achill Sound (take a left at the crossroads) lie the ruins of **Kildownet Castle,** dating from the late 1400s. (Ask for the key at the house next door.) From there, follow Atlantic Drive past beautiful beaches up to Keel and Dooagh.

Buildings cluster past the bridge to the mainland, forming the town of Achill Sound. The cluster incorporates a small **tourist office** (tel. 45384; open July-Aug. Mon.-Sat. 10am-1pm and 2-6pm), a **post office** (tel. 45141; open Mon.-Fri. 9am-12:30pm and 1:30-5:30pm), a SuperValu **supermarket** (open Mon.-Sat. 9am-6pm), and the **Achill Sound Hotel** (tel. 45245), where you can **rent bikes.** (£6/day, £30/week, deposit £30. Open daily 9am-9pm.)

Follow the painted signs across the bridge on the "island" to the **Wild Haven Hostel** (tel. 45392), a fine establishment with mouthwatering dinners. (£6. Private room £7. Sheets £1. Lockout 11am-3:30pm except in rain. Breakfast £3.50. Bike hire £6/day, £30/week.) Just before the bridge to Achill Sound, the **Railway Hostel** (tel. 45187) is a simple, multi-kitchened, family affair. (£5. Private room £6. Sheets £1. Continental breakfast £2.50, full Irish £3.50. Bikes £5/day. Laundry £2.) Go to Mac's Supermarket in town to find the proprietors. Across the street from the hostel, the proprietors of **Alice's Restaurant & Pub** (tel. 45138) will let you **camp** for free.

KEEL & DOOAGH

Keel fades into its spectacular 3-mi. strand. Two mi. north of Keel on the road loop-ing back to Dugort, the **Deserted Village** consists of stone houses used until the late 1930s as summer fattening locales for cows. The site is used for an **Archaeological Summer School** (July 20-Aug. 20) with night-time lectures over at the Warecrest Hotel; call Theresa McDonald (tel. (0506) 21627).

Pedal out from **O'Malley's Island Sports** (tel. (098) 43125; bike rental £7/day, £30/week; open Mon.-Sat. 10am-7pm, Sun. 10am-6pm) in the Spar Supermarket, and get sand in your tent at **Keel Sandybanks Caravan and Camping Park** (tel. 43211), adjacent to the beach. (Tents £4-5. Open June to early Sept.) Mrs. Joyce's **Marian Villa** (tel. 43134) is a 20-room hotel/B&B. (All rooms with bath; £14 and up.) Drink a pint to put you to sleep on the back-breaking bunks at the **Wayfarer Hostel (IHH)** (tel. 43266; £5; open March-Oct.).

Drunken inspiration can be yours at the vinyl **Annexe Inn** (tel. 43268), with trad sessions nightly in summer (Sat. in winter). Nutritious food is available at the **Bee-hive Handcrafts and Coffee Shop** (tel. 43134; open daily 10am-6:30pm). At **Cal-very's** (tel. 43158), next to the Spar Supermarket, you can eat fresh cod (£3.75) on pink and green tablecloths (open daily 9am-10pm).

Two mi. up the road from Keel in **Dooagh** ("DOO-ah") the **Folklife Center** dis-plays household utensils, furniture, and farm implements from the turn of the cen-tury (open daily 10:30am-5pm). Dooagh hosts a music, dance, art, and writing **festival week** during August, culminating in a free, open-air show; Dr. Paddy Loneen (tel. 45284) has all the info. Continue several miles past the enrapturing Keem Bay and follow the stream at **Achill Head** to its source on **Croaghaun Mountain** for bone-chilling views of **Croaghaun Cliffs.** Also in Dooagh, The **Aba Teangai House** (tel. 43114) doubles as a vegetarian restaurant (veggie stirfry £5.50) and art gallery (open daily 9am-10:30pm). In August, the art gallery turns into a heritage center. **B&B** is also available here for £12.

DUGORT

A right turn in Achill Sound leads to the northern part of the island, where Dugort has slept through the 20th century and may sleep through the 21st as well. Modern-looking cemeteries and abandoned buildings west of Dugort are the result of a futile mid-1800s effort to convert the islanders to Protestantism by sending in Irish-speak-ing missionaries. Walk around **Slievemore Mountain** to see the chambered tomb known as **Giant's Grave** (easily accessible from Dugort); other megalithic tombs lurk nearby. The main signposted tomb after McDowell's Hotel towards Keel is eas-iest to find, 1 mi. straight up from the road; it has been eroded away to a sinuous beauty reminiscent of a Henry Moore sculpture. **Boats** leave for the **seal caves** from the pier at Dugort (up the road from the Strand Hotel) daily at 11am and 6pm.

The **Valley House Hostel** (tel. 47204) has an open turf fire (£5; open Easter-Oct.). Follow the main road 2 mi. east out of Dugort and take a left at the valley crossroads. Here you'll find the **Atoka Restaurant** (tel. 47229; seafood £5-6; open May to late Sept. daily 8:30am-11pm). The restaurant does **B&B** for £10. **Seal Caves Caravan and Camping Park** (tel. (098) 43262) hunkers at Dugort Beach and Slievemore Mountain (hikers and bikers £2; open April-Sept.).

■■■ BALLINA

Ballina (bah-lin-AH) feeds off the River Moy for its vistas, and most of all for its salmon. Some anglers stay up for three days and three nights when the salmon are biting. Forward-looking Irish President Mary Robinson grew up here, though her local fame has yet to eclipse that of the fish.

Practical Information The **tourist office,** Cathedral Rd. (tel. 70848), is along the river next to St. Muredach's Cathedral. (Open Easter-Sept. Mon.-Sat. 10am-

5:30pm). The **post office** is on Casement St. (tel. 21498; open Mon.-Sat. 9am-5:30pm).For **train** info, call Westport (098) 25253 or 25329; the station is on Station Rd. and trains run to Dublin via Athlone (Mon.-Sat. 3/day, Sun. 2/day). Call the nearby **bus** station at 71800 or 71825; it's a five-minute walk from the town center (turn left out of the station and walk straight; open Mon.-Sat. 9am-6pm) Buses run to Athlone (Mon.-Sat. 1/day), Dublin via Mullingar (3/day; 4hr.; £8, students £7), Galway (Mon.-Sat. 7/day, Sun. 5/day; 3hr.; £9.70, students £6), Donegal (£10, students £7.50), Sligo (Mon.-Sat. 6/day; 2hr.; £6.30, students £3.70), and Westport (1-3/day; 1½hr.; £6.30, students £3.70). **Bikes** are rented at **Gerry's Cycle Center,** 6 Lord Edward St. (tel.70455; £7/day, £30/week; collection service available. Open Mon.-Sat. 9am-7pm). The **phone code** is 096.

Accommodations, Food, & Pubs The **Salmon Weir Hostel,** Berret St. (tel. 71903), is reason enough to come to Ballina. All the good adjectives apply; it has heavenly beds (they even *smell* clean). From the bus station, turn right, take your second left, and walk five minutes, staying to the right of the small fork. (Bike rental £6, laundry £4.50. Bed with sleeping bag £6.50, dormitory £7.50, £9 private room. Full Irish breakfast £3.50, continental £1.80.) If by chance the hostel is full, try the **Green Vale B&B,** near town on the Dublin Rd. (tel. 71343; £13). **Beleek Camping and Caravan Park** (tel. 71533) is 2 mi. out of Ballina toward Killala, behind the Beleek Woods (hiker with tent £3; open March-Oct.).

Cafolla's, Bridge St. (tel. 21029), is cheap, fast, and almost Italian. (Lasagna £3.25. Open Mon.-Sat. 10am-10pm). **Jordy's,** Pearse St. (tel. 21926) is an intimate place with fishing nets and flowers. (Lamb cutlet £5. Open Mon.-Sat. 9:30am-midnight, Sun. 11am-midnight.) Down by the river, on Clare St., **Murphy's, Longneck's, Hogan's** on O'Rahilly St. (tel. 22527), and **Gohan's** across the streetare popular. **An Bolg Bui,** just before the bridge on Bridge St., calls itself a "young fisherperson's pub." **The Loft,** Pearse St. (tel. 21881), rocks with all kinds of music nightly in summer, less frequently in winter. Also check out the **Armada Pub** (see Sights).

Sights This ichthyocentric town's Christmas takes place the second week of July with the **Ballina Salmon Festival.** All of Mayo is hooked for **"Heritage Day,"** when the streets are blocked off and life proceeds as though it were 1910.

The bird-rich **Beleek Woods** ("bah-LEEK") around **Beleek Castle** offer pretty walks along the river; cross the lower bridge near the cathedral on Pearse St. past Dutty's Bakery and Kertoy to the Beleek Woods entrance. Beleek Castle is now an expensive hotel but worth a stop in its **Armada Pub,** furbished entirely with wood brought up from a galleon sunk in the Spanish Armada. On the east side of Killala Bay lies the gorgeous Enniscrone (or Inishcrone) Strand, a 15-minute drive northeast of Ballina on the scenic Quay Rd. Opposite the long beach is the much-ballyhooed **Kilcullen's Bath House** (tel. 36238), where a private hot sea-water, seaweed, and steam bath costs £5 (no time limit). It's dreamy. (Open Easter-May and Oct. Sat.-Sun. noon-8pm; May-Sept. daily noon-10pm). Post-soak, a tea room with views of the Strand awaits you (same hours).

After the barrens of the far Northwest, **Killala** seems spiritually restorative. The **round tower** is similar to 10th-century bastions against the Vikings; the foundation may be as old as the 5th century, when St. Patrick is said to have appointed Muiredach to be Bishop of Killala. Long and windy **Ross Strand** is a scenic 3 mi. from town (follow the signs from the Ballycastle side of town), while the gorgeously deserted **Rathlackan Strand** lies 10 mi. north of town. Tourist information is putatively available at the **An Óige hostel (HI)** (tel. (096) 32172), on the Ballina side of town. (Curfew midnight, lockout 11am-5pm. Easter-May and Sept. £3.80, June-Aug. £5.50; sheets 60p.) The **phone code** is 096. Stomachs rumble at the mention of the **Anchor Inn** (smoked salmon sandwich £1.80, homemade desserts £1) or the **Tower Bar** (chicken curry £3).

■■■ KNOCK

At 8pm on August 21, 1879, St. Joseph, St. John, and the Virgin Mary appeared at Knock with a cross, a lamb, an altar, and a complement of angels to at least fifteen witnesses. The Catholic hierarchy endorsed the reports, making Knock a crowded pilgrimage site. Kitsch-seekers should realize this is a very holy place to millions; the objects devotees buy might strike atheists as funny, but the town itself never could.

Knock lies midway between Galway and Sligo on the N17. Knock's **tourist office** (tel. (094) 88193) is suitably central and changes money (open May-Sept. daily 10am-6pm). The **shrine office** (tel. (094) 88100) is likewise central, and sells such literature as *The Vision in Marble* and *Hymns of Knock*. **Bus Éireann** knocks at St. Anne's Church or at Lennon's, depending on the route, from Athlone, Ballina, Castlebar, Galway, Roscommon, and Westport (all Mon.-Sat. 2-3/day; to Westport or Roscommon and Athlone, Sun. 1/day). The **post office** is by the traffic circle (tel. (094) 882 10; open Tues.-Sat. 9am-5:30pm).

There's no reason to stay the night. Campers flop at **Knock Caravan and Camping** (tel. (094) 88100; laundry; bathrooms; July-Aug. caravan or tent £5/night, 25p/person; Sept.-June caravan and tent £4.50/night, 25p/person, hikers £3.50 and cyclists £3). **The Burren** (tel. (094) 88362) is a B&B on Kiltimagh Rd. (£13). Head for **Beirne's Restaurant** (Mon.-Sat noon-6pm; tel. (094) 88161), where pink seems to be the color of devotion. **Wally's** (tel. (094) 88408), Main St., does cheap takeaway (burger and chips £1.50).

Despite the vast numbers of pilgrims it attracts, Knock is a tiny, one-street town. The shrine and chapels are located up the hill on Main St. The **Courtyard of Statues** is where the Apparition appeared. Signs around this area tell visitors to keep quiet and off the grass. You can collect holy water at one of 18 automatic dispensers near the Statues (follow the arrows). Services take place at 8, 9:30, and 11am, noon, 3, and 7pm. A 1979 Papal visit drew half a million faithful to an open-air mass: the enormous Church of Our Lady can hold 20,000 people.

■■■ LAKE DISTRICTS

CASTLEREA

To miss Castlerea would be to miss **Clonalis House** (tel. (0907) 20014), 1 mi. out of Castlerea on the Ballyhaunis Rd. (the N60 west). Bubbly experts lead the rare tourist through rooms and rooms; weddings, wars, the Famine, the Troubles, lace, pagan stones, and racy anecdotes are included in the tour. (Open May-Sept. Tues.-Sun. noon-5pm; £2.50, students £1.75.) The other reason to come here is the **Hell's Kitchen Pub and Museum,** on Main St. near the Ballyhaunis Rd. (tel. (0907) 20181). On the other side of town, **The Demesne,** a park and river running the length of Castlerea, is a wooded sanctuary. Several miles toward Roscommon lies ruined 13th-century **Ballintuber Castle,** possibly the first stone castle in Ireland.

Castlerea rides the N60 between Castlebar and Roscommon. From the N17, turn east onto the N60 at Claremorris; from the N83, turn east at Ballyhaunis. On the edge of town opposite the Ballyhaunis Rd., **Ram's Park** (tel. (0907) 20116) puts up visitors in big rooms (£14). In town, around the bridge leading into the main Demesne entrance, is a **SuperValu.** The **Boylan Cozy Bar** seethes with stuffed pheasants; **Gaynor's Bar** (tel. (0907) 20169) has particularly good mustard.

Buses stop outside Tully's Hotel on Main St.; the **train** station at the edge of town (turn at the school on Main St.) services Dublin and Athlone (3/day), Galway, and Westport (Mon.-Sat. 4/day, Sun. 2/day).

CARRICK-ON-SHANNON

Water, water everywhere—and, probably, Guinness to drink—begin and end the list of attractions here. Lough Allen and Lough Key empty into the River Shannon in and around the midlands town. Nearby, in Strokestown, gorgeous Strokestown Park

House showcases Carrick's former riches. Its must-see Famine Museum is a moving reminder of the tragedies endured by Western Ireland.

The **Angling Information Center,** 2 mi. from Carrick-on-Shannon in Drumsna (tel. 206 94) supply boats (£15/day), tackle, and bait. On the intersection of Main and Bridge St. lies the **Costello Memorial Chapel,** reputedly the second smallest in the world. The June bank holiday weekend pulls in masquerade balls, fireworks, jazz, street theater, and visitors for the annual **Community Arts Festival.**

Clean, comfortable bunk rooms and a smiling dog named Chaz are to be found at the tiny **Town Clock Hostel (IHH)** (tel. 20068), at the junction of Main and Bridge St. (£5, sheets £1, microwave; open June-Sept.). **B&Bs** border Station Road and the manicured lawns of St. Mary's Close. Mrs. Clarke's **Sunnybank,** Station Rd. (tel. 20988), has several luxurious rooms (£13; open April-Oct.) At **Coffey's Pastry Case,** Bridge St. (tel. 20929), find a pizza and salad (£2.75; open Mon.-Sat. 8:30am-9:30pm, Sun. 10:30am-7:30pm). Pub grub may still be your best bet. Wash down great meals to the tune of traditional sessions (every Wed., Fri., and Sat. nights in summer, impromptu sessions in winter) at **Cryan's Pub,** Bridge St. (tel. 20409). Drinks are found across the town bridge at **Ging's** (tel. 21054), which boasts a beer garden on the River Shannon (no food).

The **tourist office** (tel. 20171) sits on The Quay. (Open Easter-June and Sept. Mon.-Fri. 9am-5pm, Sat. 10am-1pm; July-Aug. Mon.-Sat. 9am-8pm.) An **AIB Bank** with ATM lies on Main St. (tel. 20055; open Mon. 10am-5pm, Tues.-Fri. 10am-4pm). The **post office** is on St. George's Terrace (tel. 20020; open Mon.-Fri. 9am-5:30pm, Sat. 9am-1:30pm and 2:30-5:30pm); the **telephone code** is 078.The **train station** (tel. 20036), a 10-min. walk southwest of town, sends carriages 3/day, Sun. 2/day to Sligo (1hr.; £7, students £6.50) and Dublin (2½hr.; £8.50, students £6). **Buses** leaves from Coffey's to Athlone (1/day; 1½hr.) and Boyle (3/day; 15 min.), Sligo (1hr.), Mullingar (1½hr.), and Dublin (3hr.). **Bikes** can be had at **Geraghty's,** Main St. (Tel. 21316. £5/day, £15/week. Fishing rods £12/week. Open 9am-10pm.)

Near Carrick: Strokestown

15 mi. south of Carrick on the R368, where the smaller road meets the big N5 from Longford, lies the expansively restored 18th-century **Strokestown Park House** (tel. (078) 33013), former family estate of the Mahons. Their no-nos include fighting as mercenaries for Oliver Cromwell, evicting 3006 tenants during the famine, and subsidizing a number of coffin-ships. By 1847, the worst year of the famine, the tenants shot Denis Mahon dead. Stags' heads, Chippendale bookcases, and long velvet curtains are as commonplace here as at any manor house, but particularly interesting are the meager servants' quarters, kitchen, and underground service tunnel.

More moving than anything in the house, however, is the **Famine Museum,** located in the old stables. The photographs and drawings of sallow-eyed, starving tenants provide a truly disturbing contrast to the gold-leaf wallpaper and porcelain chamber pots inside the house. The tour often disturbs and angers visitors, especially the accounts of dead women and children lying on the roadsides, their mouths green from eating grass. A million people died in the famine; a greater number were forced to leave their country, never to return. (Open May-Sept. Tues.-Sun. 11am-5pm. Museum £3; house £2.50.)

NORTHWEST IRELAND

■■■ SLIGO TOWN

As you approach Sligo Town by rail, two imposing hills, Knocknarea and Benbulben, loom in the mist of Sligo's stormy seaside landscape. W.B. Yeats was raised here; most of Sligo boasts some connection to the poet. Though the town feels quiet during the day, some 70 pubs and discos compete for the crowds at night; music ranges from Gaelic lays to Gaelic rock to Garth Brooks.

Orientation & Practical Information From the station, take a left and follow Lord Edward St. straight onto Wine St., then onto Stephen St.; turn right onto Bridge St. and you'll be in the central district. To the tourist office, take your first right off Lord Edward onto Adelaide St. and go around the corner past the cathedral. The **tourist office** is on Temple St. off Charles St. (tel. 61201), up past the cathedral. (Open May-June Mon.-Fri. 9am-6pm, Sat. 10am-2pm; July-Aug. Mon.-Sat. 9am-8pm, Sun. 10am-6pm; Sept.-April Mon.-Fri. 9am-5pm.) An **AIB Bank** sits on 49 O'Connell St. (tel. 41085; open Mon.-Wed., Fri. 10am-4pm, Thurs. 10am-5pm. ATM), while the **post office** is nearby on Wine St. at O'Connell St. (tel. 42593; open Mon.-Sat. 9am-5:30pm). The **telephone code** is 071. **Trains** leave from **Mcdiarmada Bus/Train Station,** Lord Edward St. (train tel. 69888), for Dublin via Carrick-on-Shannon (Mon. 4/day, Tues.-Sat. 3/day, Sun. 3/day; £11 return from Dublin, £8 single student). **Buses** (tel. 60066) go to Belfast (Mon.-Sat. 2/day; 4hr.; £6, students £4); Derry (Mon.-Sat. 3/day, Sun. 2/day; 3hr.; £6, students £3); Dublin (3/day; 4hr.; £5, students £4); Galway (Mon.-Sat. 5/day, Sun. 3/day; 2½hr.; £5.25, students £3.25); Drumcliff (10 min.; £1.60); and Westport (2¾hr.; £4.30, students £3). **Gary's Cycles,** Quay St. (tel. 45158) rents bikes (£6/day, £25/week, £30 deposit; open Mon.-Sat. 9am-6pm).The **garda** are on Pearse Rd. (tel. 42031).

Accommodations, Food, & Pubs There aren't enough hostels in Sligo, especially in mid August during the Yeats International Summer School. B&Bs abound a five-minute walk out of town on Pearse Rd. Try the **Eden Hill Holiday Hostel (IHH),** Pearse Rd. (tel. 43204; laundry £2; bike rental £7/day; £6, £7 private room; **camping** £2.50/½-day, £3/day). The **White House Hostel (IHH),** Markievicz Rd. (tel. 45160) is a short walk from the train station. Follow Wine St. past three traffic lights; take a left after the Silver Swan. (Key deposit £2; £6, sheets £1.) **Renati House,** Upper Johns St. (tel. 62014), businesslike and spotless, is the least expensive B&B near the tourist office (£14).

Stock up at the **Quinnsworth Supermarket,** O'Connell St. (open Mon.-Wed. and Sat. 9am-6pm, Thurs.-Fri. 9am-9pm). **Kate's Kitchen,** Market St. (tel. 43022), is a classy takeaway. (Fresh sandwiches from £1.15. Open Mon.-Sat. 9am-6:30pm.) **Hardogan's,** O'Connell St. (tel. 70933) serves wonderful lunches that vary daily (restaurant open 10:30am-7pm; Sept.-June 10:30am-4pm). There seems to be a pub every twenty feet in Sligo; most host live bands during the summer. Check the weekly *Sligo Champion* (50p) for listings. At **The Bear and Cat,** Thomas Bridge St. (tel. 41310), live bands play once or twice a week. **McGaraggle's,** O'Connell St. (tel. 71193), also showcases live music.**Connolly's,** Markievicz Rd. (tel. 67377), draws the best pint of Guinness in Co. Sligo.

Sights The ruined 13th-century **Dominican Abbey,** Abbey St., boasts cloisters and ornate pillars. (Open summer daily 10am-6pm; free. During the rest of the year, ask for the key from Mrs. McGuinn, 6 Charlotte St.) The hulking **Cathedral of the Immaculate Conception** is best visited in early morning or late evening when sun streams through 69 stained glass windows. **The Yeats Art Gallery,** Stephen St., contains one of the country's finest collections of modern Irish art, including a number of works by Jack Butler Yeats (W.B.'s brother) and contemporaries. Among the museum's other treasures are many first editions of Yeats. Under bare Benbulben's head, in **Drumcliff churchyard,** 4 mi. northwest of Sligo, Yeats is laid. On his headstone, these words are cut: "Cast a cold eye/On life, on death./Horseman, pass by!" **Buses** run from Sligo to Drumcliff (Mon.-Sat. 5/day, Sun. 3/day; a few are June-Aug. only). North of Drumcliff, **Benbulben**—the mountain of Yeats' poem—protrudes from the landscape like the keel of a foundered boat. To reach Benbulben, stay on the Drumcliff Rd. and follow signs. For detailed directions to trails, ask at Drumcliff's gas station. Four mi. west of Drumcliff is **Lissadell House** (tel. 63150), where poet

Eva Gore-Booth and her sister Constance Markiewicz (second in command in the Easter Rising, later the first woman elected to the Dáil) entertained Yeats and his circle. (Open mid-June to Sept. Mon.-Sat. 10:30am-noon and 2-4:30pm. £2.) Take your first left after the Yeats Tavern Hostel on the Drumcliff Rd. and follow signs.

■■■ DONEGAL TOWN

Most international travelers begin their tour of Co. Donegal with a stay in Donegal Town. An inevitable stopover between Sligo or Fermanagh and the splendor of the north and west, Donegal town itself has very little to offer tourists besides its amenities. The town's tourist office—by far the county's best—can tell you about more remote, interesting destinations along the northern coast.

Practical Information The **tourist office,** Quay St. (tel. 21148), is south of The Diamond on the Sligo Rd. Be sure to stop here before heading north. (Open July-Aug. Mon.-Sat. 9am-8pm, Sun. 10am-1pm and 2-6pm; Sept.-Oct. and Easter-June Mon.-Fri. 9am-5pm, Sat.-Sun. 10am-1pm.) **AIB Bank** (tel. 21016) and **Bank of Ireland** (tel. 21079), both have ATMs and are at The Diamond (both open Mon.-Wed. and Fri. 10am-4pm, Thurs. 10am-5pm). The **post office is** on Tirchonaill St. (tel. 21030), north of the Diamond (open Mon.-Sat. 9am-5:30pm); the **telephone code** is 073. **Bus Éireann** (tel. 21101) runs to Dublin (Mon.-Sat. 5/day, Sun 3/day; 4hr.; £10) via Ballyshannon (25 min.; £3) and to Galway (Mon.-Sat. 3/day, Sun. 2/day; 4hr.; £13) via Sligo (1hr.; £7.30). Timetables and the bus stop are outside the Abbey Hotel. Rent a **bike** at **C.J. O'Doherty's,** Main St. (tel. 21119). £6/day, £25/week, £30 deposit. (Open Mon.-Sat. 9am-1pm and 2-6pm.) The **garda** are at 21021.

Accommodations Donegal Town Hostel (IHH) is 1 mi. out on the Killybegs Rd. (tel. 22805). High on a hill, this adequate hostel has a large kitchen and small bedrooms. (Laundry £4.50. £5.50; sheets 50p; £2.50 surcharge for leaving after 11am.) **Bosco House** (tel. (073) 22326), 4 mi. west of Donegal Town, in Mountcharles, is down the Killybegs Rd. from Donegal; sometimes the wardens will pick you up. The hostel owner is a traditional musician who often brings hostellers to his gigs. (Tea and craft shop. Laundry. Open March-Oct. £5; breakfast £4.) **Ball Hill Youth Hostel (An Óige/HI),** (tel. 21174), is 3 mi. from town; go 1½ mi. out on the Killybegs Rd.; turn left at the sign, and go 1½ mi. to the sea. Our researcher found a large kitchen, eight-bunk dorms, and peeling paint and dirty floors in the can. (Curfew 12:30am, no lockout. Might close from Oct.-April. £5.50. Sheets 50p.) The **Atlantic Guest House,** Main St. (tel. 21187), is right in the center of town and has clean, pleasant rooms with TVs and coffee/teapots. (£12.50/person, £15-17.50/person with bath. Prices negotiable in off-season.)

Food & Pubs Cafés and take-aways cruise for wallets across Donegal. Most occupy The Diamond or the streets near it. For groceries enter **Foodland Supermarket** (tel. 21016; open Mon.-Thurs. 9am-8pm, Fri. 9am-9pm, Sat. 9am-7:30pm) or **Simple Simon's** (tel. 22687), which sells fresh baked goods (open Mon.-Sat. 9:30am-6pm). **The Blueberry Tea Room,** Castle St. (tel.22933) is understandably popular. (Veggie and cheese croissant with salad £2.50. Open daily 8am-9pm.) **Errigal Restaurant,** Main St. (tel. 21428), has the cheapest dinner in town. Fish and chips are £2-4. (Open Mon.-Sat. 9am-10:20pm, Sun. 3-10:20pm.) **Stella's Seafood Bar,** at McGroarty's Pub, The Diamond, serves creative, healthy food using organic vegetables. Dinner is expensive; lunch is more reasonable (pita filled with garlic mussels, baked potato and veggies £4.50; open Mon.-Sat. noon-9pm).

During the winter, the trad dries up, but rock and blues still happen on the weekends. **Schooner's,** Main St. (tel. 21671), has live music almost every night in the summer, usually folk or trad. The bar at the **Olde Castle Restaurant,** Castle St., has no music but a good mixture of people. **Charlie's Star Bar,** Main St., has live rock, country and blues (summer Wed.-Sun.). **Nero's,** Main St. (tel. 21111), plays the fiddle while Donegal burns (dancing Thurs.-Sat., live bands Sun.).

Sights & Entertainment Donegal's historic locations don't do much to explain the crowds of visitors. **Donegal Castle** takes up prime real estate space just north of the Diamond, smack in the center of town. Its spiral staircase is worth climbing, if only to see the finely carved stone fireplace. (Castle closed for renovations until summer 1995.) A short walk from the tourist office along the river south of the town might end at the ruined **Franciscan Friary,** founded in 1474 and abandoned in 1608. Just south of Donegal Town, 1 mi. out on the Ballyshannon Rd. at the **Donegal Craft Village** (tel 22225), craftspeople open workshops. The work of potters, a jewelry maker, a batik artist, a hand weaver, and a visual artist are sold here (most shops open July-Aug. daily 9am-6pm, Sept.-June Mon.-Sat. 9am-6pm).

The **Donegal Drama Circle** has summer theater at the Bosco Center, Tirchonnaill St., in July and August (£4, students £2). Posters all over town give details and times of the performances.

■ NEAR DONEGAL TOWN: STATION ISLAND

Several miles due east of Donegal town, Co. Donegal's **Lough Derg** contains **Station Island.** Ireland's most important place of pilgrimage, Station Island witnesses a three-day barefoot religious ordeal undertaken every summer and is the subject of Seamus Heaney's long poem of the same name. Legend has it that St. Patrick visited nearby Saints Island and temporarily descended into Purgatory. The pilgrimage involves three days of fasting and circling the island barefoot. **Bus Éireann** visits Lough Derg once a day from Dublin, Cavan, Enniskillen, Galway, and Sligo between June and August 13; the Galway-Sligo-Lough Derg route runs both ways on Sun., but only *to* Lough Derg *from* Galway via Sligo Mon.-Sat. Buses from Dublin run from Whit Sunday to the Feast of the Assumption daily. Regular ferry service picks up pilgrims at the lakeshore. Bring warm clothing and a repentent heart. Contact the Rev. Prior, Lough Derg, Pettigo, Co. Donegal for more info.

■■■ INISHOWEN PENINSULA

It would be a crime to leave Ireland without having seen the Inishowen Peninsula, an almost completely untouristed mosaic of rugged mountains, lush forests, sheep, and a few news agents. The sandy white beaches are deserted, the pubs filled with traditional music practically every night of the week, and the local people happy to share their land. Consider the peninsula as a whole: you'll want to keep moving from sight to sight. The whole shebang takes three or four days without a car.

The nearest population center to Inishowen is Derry. **Lough Swilly** (tel. (080507) 262017) runs buses from Derry to Buncrana (Mon.-Sat. 11/day; Sun. 8/day; 35 min.), to Moville (5/day; 50 min.), and to Malin Head (½hr.) via Carndonagh (Mon.-Sat. 3/day; 1hr.). Lough Swilly also connects Buncrana and Carndonagh (Mon.-Sat. 3/day; 50 min.). **Northwest Buses** (tel. (077) 82619) runs through Shrove, Greencastle, Moville, Coldaff, Carndonagh, Ballyliffen, Clonmany, and Buncrana, and on to Letterkenny (Mon.-Fri. 2/day; Sat. 1/day), and from Moville to Derry (4/day; 50 min.).

The northern and western shores are by far the most striking. The well-signposted **Inishowen 100** road navigates the perimeter, and is the best quick way to see Inishowen for drivers and hitchhikers. Cyclists may want to use the roads that crisscross the peninsula to shorten the distances between sights. Most of those roads look exactly alike; no matter where you go, make sure you have good directions and/or a good map (available at tourist offices in Buncrana and Carndonagh).

SOUTHWEST INISHOWEN: SOUTH OF BUNCRANA

Ten miles south of Buncrana, at the bottom of the peninsula, the hilltop fort called the **Grianan of Aileach** ("GREEN-ya of ALL-ya") is a logical place to begin or end a tour of Inishowen. This site has probably been in use for at least 4000 years, first as a temple for sun-worship, then a seat of power for the northern branch of the Uí Néill clan, and finally a "mass rock" where Catholics worshipped in secret during the Penal Laws. Just beyond the fort, away from the car park, a cross marks a healing well supposedly blessed by St. Patrick. To reach the fort, follow the Letterkenny Road from Bridgend. About 2 mi. from Bridgend, turn left at the Burt Circular Chapel, a modern-day replica of the fort, and follow the signs 2 mi. to the top of the hill. Those without cars hitch or cycle to the church, then walk up the hill.

As the Inishowen 100 begins up the western shore, it comes first to tiny **Fahan** ("fawn"). St. Columcille founded a monastery in Fahan in the 6th century; there's not much left of it except **St. Mura's Cross.** Across the road, the cemetery has gravestones as old as the 7th century. Just south of Fahan, the road detours to the west and to **Inch Island,** with the ruins of **Inch Castle** and the **Inishowen Genealogy Center** (tel. (077) 60488; £45 for a family history). The center does offer reasonable B&B (£11/person), and camping on their lovely lawn (price negotiable).

BUNCRANA

North of Fahan, Buncrana curls up under the long shadows of the mighty 2019 ft. **Slieve Snacht.** Fortified by summer tourism from Derry, this energetic town makes a good base, at least for the B&B-inclined. Two castles scowl in Swan Park: the stately Queen Anne-era **Buncrana Castle** and the 1430 **O'Doherty Castle,** near Castle Bridge. Just north of Buncrana, the **Tullyarvan Mill** (tel. (077) 61613) surveys the history of Irish textiles. Disabled people produce and sell crafts inside. Once a week in the summer the mill hosts story-telling, trad, and Irish dancing. (8:30-11:30pm; £1-2.; call for dates; open Easter-Sept. Mon.-Sat. 10am-6pm, Sun. 2-6pm.)

The bedrooms at **Rattan House,** Swilly Rd. (tel. 61222; £12, with kitchen £13), offer TV or ocean view. Ailish Galbraith's **Seabreeze House** (tel. 62300) is worth the search. Coming from the south, turn right into the Fruit of the Loom factory, then take the first, quick, right. Go right down the lane with the white "B&B" sign. (£15. Doubles £25.) Halfway between Clonmany and Buncrana, on the inland road, the cozy **Mintiagh Lodge Hostel** (tel. (077) 61362), Dumfries, hides in the woods. (No stores nearby. No curfew or lockout. £5. Open Easter-Sept. Laundry £2.) Both Lough Swilly and Northwest buses pass by on the way to Letterkenny and Derry.

The **Ubiquitous Chip,** 47 Upper Main St. (tel. 62530), scours the world for creative recipes. (Open July and Aug. daily noon-11pm, Sept.-June Mon.-Fri. noon-11pm.) **Dorothy's Kitchen,** 3 Church St. (tel. 62639) serves French-bread pizza (£1.80) (open daily 11am-1am). **Rodden's Pub,** Main St. (tel. 62395), has occasional impromptu trad sessions. Bord Faílte operates a summertime **tourist office** (tel. 62600) on the shorefront (open late May to mid-Sept. daily 10am-6pm). **AIB Bank** (tel. 61087) operates at 8 Market Sq.; **Bank of Ireland** (tel. 61399) on Main St. The **post office** (tel. 61010) is on Main St. as well. Buncrana's **phone code** is 077.

WEST INISHOWEN

Dunree Head & the Gap of Mamore

About 6 mi. north of Buncrana lies Dunree Head, where the **Guns of Dunree** (tel. (077) 61817) stay polished but inactive inside an old fort. Some of the guns are on display in **Fort Dunree** ("the fort of the heathen"). The mammoth WWII searchlights are occasionally used to search for people lost at sea. (Open July-Sept. Mon.-Sat. 10:30am-6pm, Sun. 12:30-6pm. £1.50.)

Heading north again will bring you through the **Gap of Mamore,** a breathtaking pass between Mamore Hill and Urris 800 ft. above the sea. We at *Let's Go* routinely call scenery, views, and peaks "magnificent"; this time we *mean* it. Head through the pass from east to west (from inland to coast), as the views over the mountains to the Atlantic are fantastic. The road through the pass is very steep and difficult for cycles, but the struggle adds to the exhiliration of the view. Watch out for hairpin turns on the ocean side. As the road descends beyond the gap, sandy beaches lie ahead. **Tullage Bay Caravan and Camping Park** (tel. (077) 76289) sprawls between mountain and sea, yards from one of the prettiest beaches on the peninsula. (Open May 15-Sept. 15; £4/tent and 50p/person, showers 20p.)

Clonmany & Ballyliffen

The towns of **Clonmany** and **Ballyliffen** lie north of the Gap and host a **local trad festival** during the first week of August. **Keg O' Poteen** (tel. (077) 76415) serves "keg" burgers (£1), pints, and trad on the only road in Clonmany. Across the street, **McFeeley's** (tel. 76122) often has traditional singing on weekends. Apart from the festival, the highlights of Ballyliffen are the 3-mi. golden sands of Pollanod Strand; from its northern end you can see ruined **Carrickbrahey Castle.** The **Doagh Farm** (tel. (077) 76493) offers pony treks (£5/hr., £3/½-hr.) along the beach, with splendid views across to Five Finger Strand. They'll let you ride horses on your own if you can. (Farm £1. Shop and tea room open daily 10am-5pm.)

NORTH INISHOWEN

Carndonagh

Carndonagh is Inishowen's core town, 2 mi. from the head of Trawbreaga Bay, and a good base for visiting north Inishowen. **Inishowen Tourism,** Temple St. (tel. (077) 74933), a friendly, independent tourist board, provides free room service and a craft shop. (Open Mon.-Fri. 9:30am-7pm, Sat. 10am-6pm, Sun. noon-6pm; Sept.-June Mon.-Fri. 9:30am-5pm.) Opposite the Church of Ireland is **St. Patrick's Cross,** an eighth-century monument with Celtic knotwork and birds; the old, ornamented pillar called the **Marigold Stone** reclines in the graveyard. Stay with **Mrs. Mary Kearney, Roadside,** Glentogher (tel. (077) 74506), 3½ mi. from town on the Derry Rd (£10) or in the sparkling rooms of **Mrs. Kathleen Brett, Dushenny House,** Millbrae (tel. (077) 74292; £13 with full breakfast, £11.50 continental breakfast; no singles in high season). **McClure's Pub,** Bridge St. (tel. (077) 74526), officially known as **Bradley's Bar,** serves good lunches and pours a good pint.

Malin

North of Carndonagh, Malin is another one of those former Tidy Town contest winners, all starch and pleasantries, with a well-manicured central green. Eat at the **Malin Hotel** bar (tel. (077) 706 07), or a lift a pint at **McLeans'** (tel. (077) 706 07).

Five miles north of Malin town toward Malin Head, **Five Fingers Strand** takes breaths away with its rugged slopes, golden sand, and clear blue water. Don't swim here—you might drown. High above the beach, **Knockameny Bens** provide a good view over the peninsula. To get there, turn left at the little white church.

The northernmost point in Ireland, **Malin Head** is a barren tooth of dark rock jutting up from the ocean. Until the 19th century, Malin Head was the scene of an annual pilgrimage in which young men and women "frisked and played in the water all stark naked" in celebration of the sea god's fertile affair with the the land. Modern visitors can see, on a clear day, the Paps of Jura in Scotland. The "EIRE" on the cliffs below marked Ireland as neutral to Nazi bombers. One mi. away is **Hell's Hole,** a 250-ft. chasm that roars with the tide; take the path just to the left of the car park.

One mi. from Malin Head, Mrs. Doyle at **Barraicín** keeps a friendly, comfortable B&B overlooking a beautiful garden. (£15. Doubles £24.) On your way to or from Malin Head, stop at **The Cottage,** a local craft store, café, and center on traditional ways of life (open June-Sept. Mon.-Sat. 11am-6:30pm, Sun. 1:30-6:30pm; March-May and Oct. Sun. only) or at **Farren's,** Ireland's northernmost pub.

Culdaff

At the innermost point of a lovely estuary, the village of **Culdaff** radiates warmth from its beaches and from **McGrory's Pub.** With live music every Wednesday and Saturday night, McGrory's is not to be missed. You can grab a bite to eat at the **Village Restaurant** (tel. (077) 79328) around the corner. (Open daily 5pm-1am.)

Staying in Culdaff can be a real treat. Try **Culdaff House** (tel. (077) 79103; £17, doubles £28). **Ceecliff House,** on the Culdaff-Clonmany Rd. (tel. (077) 79159) offers a glassed-in porch (£13, £15 with bath). The coast from Culdaff out to Inishowen Head jams gorgeous beaches up against sheer cliffs. From **Kinnagoe Bay,** follow the shoreline over a grassy knoll. Just past a tiny fence hides the deserted beauty of **Glenagivney Beach.** Farther east lies **Inishowen Head.**

EAST INISHOWEN

At the opposite end of peninsula from Malin Head, **Inishowen Head** looks out over the North to the carnival lights of Portrush, and gathers sunbathers to **Shroove Strand. The Drunken Duck** (tel. (077) 81362) is a friendly shroove pub, named after a local woman whose beer leaked into her ducks's feeding trough.

Greencastle

From Inishowen Head, head south to **Greencastle,** a small fishing village near the misty ruins of a seaside castle and fort. For great seafood, head to **Kealey's Seafood Bar** (tel. (077) 81010; open Tues.-Sun. 12:30-5pm and 7-9:30pm.) The **ruins** of Greencastle's castle, built in 1305, warrant exploration. Have a drink at the **Old Fort Inn** (tel. (077) 81044), originally a Martello Tower (open daily noon-9:30pm).

Moville

A few paces farther south along a coastal path is the grassy seaside promenade of **Moville.** The **Moville Holiday Hostel,** Malin Rd. (tel. (077) 82378) sits at the edge of town (£5.50, doubles £8.50). **Mrs. B. McGroarty, Naomh Mhuire,** Bath Terrace (tel. (077) 83091), has B&B for £12 in a white house on the main street (open Easter-Sept.). **The Lough Foyle Sea Angling Festival** (late Aug.) is the town's major annual event; the **Moville Regatta** takes place on the first Monday in August. To rent a **boat,** call **Peter Bush** at the Coast Guard Station (tel. (077) 82402; open Mon.-Fri. 9am-5pm). You can rent jet-skis at **Rent-a-Jet** Quayside (tel. (077) 82052), at the water's edge (jet-skiing £11/hr., water-skiing £7.50/15 min.; open Sat.-Sun. 2pm-dusk, Wed. 6pm-dusk). Afterwards, search for fossils in the floor of the nearby **Hair O' the Dog Saloon** (tel. (077) 82600), where there's live music every Friday night. **Rosatta's,** 7 Malin Rd. (tel. (077) 82247), serves tasty homemade food (large sandwiches £2.30). (Open daily noon-9pm.) The **Mace Supermarket** is open daily from 7:45am-9pm on the main street.

Muff

On the southeast coast of the Inishowen Peninsula, the tiny village of Muff is just 5 mi. from Derry. Martin Cooke's warm welcome makes the **Muff Hostel (IHH)** (tel. (077) 84188) a *Let's Go* home-away-from-home, the hosteler's best base for most of Inishowen and for seeing Derry. (Kitchen and hot showers; £5; open March-Oct.) **Lough Swilly Buses** offers a £3.50 same-day return ticket to Malin Head for guests of the Muff Hostel. Down the road in Bridgend, **Harry's** (tel. (077) 68444) provides the perfect end-of-Ireland celebratory meal with mouth-watering veggie meals (£6-8). (Open daily 5:30-10:30pm; bar open 4-11:30pm.)

Appendices

■■■ TELEPHONES

BRITAIN AND NORTHERN IRELAND
Operator: 100
Directory inquiries: 142
London directory inquiries: 192
International operator: 155
International directory assistance: 153

REPUBLIC OF IRELAND
Operator (not available from card phones): 190
Directory inquiries : 1190
International operator: 114

HOW THEY WORK

The newly remodeled **British pay phone** charges 10p for local calls. A series of harsh beeps will warn you to insert more money when your time is up. For the rest of the call, the digital diplay ticks off your credit in suspenseful 1p increments. Unused calls are returned. You may use all remaining credit on a second call by pressing the "follow on call" button (often marked "FC"). Phones don't accept 1p, 2p, or 5p coins. The dial tone is a continuous purring sound; a repeated double-purr, means the line is ringing.

If you'll be making more than a few calls during your stay in Britain, pick up a handy **Phonecard,** available in denominations of £2, £5, £10, and £20. They're available at post offices, newsagents, or John Menzies stationery shops. Phone booths that take cards are labeled in green and are common except in rural areas; coin booths are labeled in red. Most payphones and almost all home phones in Britain use British Telecom. Some, mostly in downtown London, use Mercury phones, which can be cheaper for making international calls (see section below).

Irish pay phones are similar. Public coin phones will sometimes make change (depending on what order you insert coins) but private payphones in hotels and restaurants do not. In any payphone, do not insert money until you are asked to, or until your call goes through. The frightening pip, pip noise that the phone makes before it starts ringing is normal and can last up to 10 seconds. Local calls cost 20p for four minutes on standard phones. Newsagents sell **callcards** in denominations of £3.50, £7.50, or £15; they're essential for international calls. When the unit number on the digital display starts flashing, you may push the eject button on the card phone; you can then pull out your expired card and replace it with a fresh one (don't wait for the units to fall to zero or you'll be disconnected).

When calling Britain or Ireland, remember time differences so as not to wake B&B proprietors in the wee hours. Dial your country's international access code (011 for the USA and Canada, 0011 for Australia, 00 for New Zealand); then the country code (44 for Britain and Northern Ireland; 353 for the Republic of Ireland); then the regional "telephone code," *dropping the initial zero,* and, finally, the local number. *Let's Go* lists telephone codes in Practical Information sections, though when covering rural areas where more than one telephone code may apply we list the telephone code, in parentheses, together with the number. Thus, when calling from the U.S. to order silver glitter pumps from Harrods in London (telephone code 0171), dial 011 44 171 730 1234. There is little rhyme or reason to the numbering of phone numbers in Britain and Ireland; regional telephone codes range from two to seven digits, and local telephone numbers range from three to seven digits.

Major changes will be occurring to Britain's phone numbers on **"Phone Day,"** April 16, 1995 at 1am. None of these changes affect phone numbers in the Republic of Ireland. In England, Scotland, Wales, Northern Ireland, and the Isle of Man, all **telephone codes starting 0 (virtually all codes) will start 01** (for example, London's changes from 071 to 0171). No service codes (i.e. 0800) will change. The only exceptions to this area code change are in the Leeds area (code changes from 0532 to 0113 and a 2 is added to prefix the number); Sheffield area (new code 0114, prefix of 2 added); Nottingham area (new code 0115, prefix of 9 added); Leicester area (new code 0116, prefix of 2 added); and the Bristol area (new code 0117, prefix of 9 added). If you have further questions about Phoneday while in Britain, call the special BT Helpline at (0800) 010101. Since the new numbers could be used as of August 1, 1994, **we list only the new telephone codes.** You should not encounter any problems using the codes we list before April 16. If you use an old phone code after April 16, you'll hear a message telling you the new code.

INTERNATIONAL CALLS FROM BRITAIN

To make international direct calls from Britain (including Northern Ireland): dial the international access code (00); the country code for where you're calling (see below); the area/city code; and then the local number.

Another option is to access an operator in the country you're dialing—calling card rates are often cheaper than those for direct calls, and service a bit speedier. Long-distance companies in your home country may have economical arrangements for their clients calling home from overseas. For example, AT&T provides USA DIRECT service from Britain and Ireland; by calling a toll-free number in Britain or Ireland you can access a U.S. operator who will help you place a collect call (US$5.75 surcharge) or charge it to your AT&T calling card (US$2.50 surcharge). Rates run about US$1.75-1.85 for the first minute plus about US$1 per additional minute. The people you are calling need not subscribe to AT&T service. If you can find a Mercury phone, use it; it is generally cheaper to make a connection by Mercury than by British Telecom. When dialing from a Mercury phone, replace the initial "0800" with "0500." The following services will allow you to place collect calls (expensive) or charge them to a calling card (less so):

Ireland Direct: 0800-89-0353	Canada Direct: 0800-89-0016
AT&T USA Direct: 0800-89-0011	OTC/BT Australia Direct: 0800-89-0061
Sprint Express: 0800-89-0877	Call Home Australia: 0800-89-0611
TRT Phone USA: 0800-89-0456	New Zealand Direct: 0800-89-0640
MCI WorldPhone: 0800-89-0222	South Africa Direct: 0800-89-0027
Hotline Hawaii: 0800-89-0808	Bahamas Direct: 0800-89-0135
Bermuda Direct: 0800-89-0123	

Reduced rates for most international calls from Britain apply from 8pm to 8am Monday through Friday, and all day and night on Saturday and Sunday. The low-rate period to Australia and New Zealand is from midnight to 7am and 2:30pm to 7:30pm daily. For long-distance calls within Britain, the lowest rates are from 6pm to 9am Monday through Friday, and all day and all night Saturday and Sunday; calls are slightly more expensive from 1pm to 6pm Monday through Friday, and most expensive on weekday mornings (9am-1pm).

INTERNATIONAL CALLS FROM IRELAND

To make international direct calls from the Republic of Ireland, dial the international access code (00); then the country code (see below); area code (dropping the initial zero); and local number. Alternatively, you can access an Irish operator at 114. The following services will also allow you to place a collect call or use your calling card; if you can find a Mercury phone, use it, and replace "1-800" with "1-500.":

BT Direct (call the UK1-800-550044)
AT&T USA: 1-800-55-0000
MCI WorldPhone: 1-800-55-1001
Sprint Express USA: 1-800-55-2001

Canada Direct: 1-800-555001
Australia Direct: 1-800-55-0061
New Zealand Direct: 1-800-55-0064
Telkom S. Africa Direct: 1-800-550027

COUNTRY CODES

Britain (including Northern Ireland): 44
Northern Ireland (from the Republic of Ireland only): 08
Republic of Ireland: 353
USA and Canada: 1
Australia: 61
New Zealand: 64

■■■ TIME ZONE DIFFERENCES

Britain and Ireland are on Greenwich Mean Time (GMT), which sets its clocks: one hour earlier than (most of) continental Europe; five hours later than Port Credit, Ontario (EST); six hours later than Emporia, Kansas (CST); seven hours later than Moab, Utah (MST); eight hours later than Laguna Beach, California (PST); nine hours later than Alaska; ten hours later than Hawaii; eight, nine and a half, and ten hours earlier than Australia; and twelve hours earlier than Auckland, New Zealand.

■■■ HOLIDAYS

Government agencies, post offices, and banks are closed on these days, and businesses may have special (shorter) hours. Transportation, in particular, practically grinds to a halt; check schedules carefully.

January I	New Year's Day	
March 17	St. Patrick's Day	*Republic of Ireland and Northern Ireland*
April 14, 1995	Good Friday	
April 17, 1995	Easter Monday	
May 1, 1995	First Monday in May	*Northern Ireland, Isle of Man, London*
May 29, 1995	Last Monday in May	*Northern Ireland, Isle of Man, London*
June 5, 1995	First Monday in June	*Republic of Ireland*
July 5	Tynwald Fair Day	*Isle of Man*
July 12	Orange Day	*Northern Ireland*
August 7, 1995	First Monday in August	*Republic of Ireland*
August 28, 1995	Last Monday in August	*Northern Ireland, Isle of Man, London*
October 30, 1995	Last Monday in October	*Republic of Ireland*
December 25	Christmas Day	
December 26	Boxing Day/St. Stephen's Day	

■■■ WEIGHTS AND MEASURES

1 meter (m) = 1.09 yards
1 kilometer (km) = 0.621 mile
1 gram (g) = 0.04 ounce
1 kilogram (kg) = 2.2 pounds

1 yard = 0.92m
1 mile = 1.61km
1 ounce = 25g
1 pound = .45 kg

1 "stone" (weight—of man or beast only) = 14 pounds · 1 pound = .71 stone

1 liter = 1.057 U.S quarts	1 U.S quart = 0.94 liter
1 liter = 0.88 Imperial quarts	1 Imperial quart = 1.14 liter
1 Imperial gallon = 1.193 U.S. gallons	1 U.S. gallon = .84 Imperial gallon
1 British pint = 1.19 U.S. pint	1 U.S. pint = .84 British pint

FAHRENHEIT/CELSIUS CONVERSION

To convert from °C to °F, multiply by 1.8 and add 32.
To convert from °F to °C, subtract 32 and multiply by 5/9.

°C	35	30	25	20	15	10	5	0	-5	-10
°F	95	86	75	68	59	50	41	32	23	14

■■■ LANGUAGE

BRITISH WORDS AND PHRASES

aubergine	eggplant
bangers and mash	sausage and mashed potato
bap	a soft bun, like a hamburger bun
bed-sit, or bedsitter	one-room apartment
bill	check (in restaurants)
biro	ball-point pen
biscuit	if sweet, a cookie; if not, a cracker
bladdered, blitzed	drunk
bobby	police officer
bonnet	car hood
to book	to reserve
boot	car trunk
boozer	pub
brilliant	nifty, "cool"
bubble-and-squeak	cabbage and mashed potato dish
busker	street musician
candy-floss	cotton candy
caravan	trailer, mobile home
car park	parking lot
cheers, cheerio	goodbye, sometimes thank you
chemist	pharmacist
chips	french fries
circle	theatre balcony
coach	inter-city bus
concession, "concs"	discount on admission
courgette	zucchini
court shoes	women's pumps
crisps	potato chips
crumpets	like English muffins, only different
dicey, dodgy	problematic
digs	lodgings
dinner	lunch
dosh	money
dual carriageway	divided highway
dustbin	trash can

fag	cigarette
first floor	first floor up (second floor)
flannel	washcloth
flat	apartment
fortnight	two weeks
grotty	grungy
high street	main street
hire	rental
hoover	vacuum cleaner
iced lolly	popsicle
interval	intermission
"in" a street	"on" a street
jam	jelly
jelly	Jell-O
jumble sale	yard sale
jumper	sweater
kip	sleep
knackered	tired, worn out
lavatory, "lav"	restroom
lay-by	roadside turnout
leader (in newspaper)	editorial
leaflet	pamphlet, brochure, flyer
to let	to rent
lift	elevator
loo	restroom
lorry	truck
mate	pal
motorway	highway
naff	uncool
nappies	diapers
narg	geek, nerd
off-licence	retail liquor store
pants	underwear
petrol	gasoline
phone box, or call box	telephone booth
pillar box	tall, red mailbox
piss (take the piss out of)	make fun of
pissed	drunk
plimsolls	sneakers
pudding	dessert
pull	to "score"
public school	private school
quid	pound (in money)
queue up, Q	line up
return ticket	round-trip ticket
ring up	telephone
roundabout	rotary road interchange
rubber	eraser
self-catering	(accommodations with) kitchen facilities
self-drive	car rental
serviette	napkin
single carriageway	non-divided highway
single ticket	one-way ticket
sleeping policeman	speed bump

smarties	M&Ms without the m
splash out	splurge
spotted dick	steamed sponge pudding with raisins
stalls	orchestra seats
stone	14 pounds (in body weight)
subway	underground pedestrian passage
sultanas	raisins
sweets	candy
swish	swanky
ta, ta-ta	good-bye, thank you
tights	pantyhose
toilet	restroom
torch (often "electric")	flashlight
trainers	sneakers
trunk call	long-distance telephone call
tube, or Underground	London subway
vest	undershirt
waistcoat (weskit)	men's vest
way out	exit
wellies	boots
W.C. (water closet)	restroom
zed	letter "Z"

BRITISH PRONUNCIATION

Berkeley	BARK-lee
Beauchamps	BEECH-am
Nottingham	NOT-ing-um, not "-ham" (ditto for Buckingham, etc.)
Derby	DAR-by
Dulwich	DULL-idge
Ely	EEL-ee
Gloucester	GLOS-ter
Greenwich	GREN-idge
Holborn	HO-burn
Leicester	LES-ter
Marylebone	MAR-lee-bun
Magdalene	MAUD-lin
Norwich	NOR-idge
quay	KEY
Salisbury	SAULS-bree
Southwark	SUTH-uk
Woolwich	WOOL-idge
Worcester	WOOS-ter (-tah if you're cool)

WELSH WORDS AND PHRASES

The Llanguage section in the Wales introduction explains some rules of Welsh pronunciation. Listed below are a number of words and phrases you may encounter on the road.

Diolch yn far (dee-OLCH een VAR)	Thank you
Bore da	Good morning
Dydd da	Good day
Noswaith dda	Good evening

Nos da	Good night
Sut mae?	How are you?
Hwyl	Cheers
ar gau	closed
ar agor	open
perygl	danger
cyhoeddus	public
preifat	private
dynion	men
merched	women
allan	exit
llwybr cyhoeddus	public footpath

IRISH WORDS AND PHRASES

The following bits of the Irish language are either used often in Irish English or are common in Irish place names. Spelling conventions do not always match English pronunciations: for example, "mh" sounds like "v," and "dh" sounds like "g."

Baile Átha Cliath	BALL-yah AW-hah CLEE-ah	Dublin
bodhrán	BOUR-ohn	traditional drum
Bord Fáilte	bored FAHL-tshuh	Irish Tourist Board
Conas tá tú?	CUNN-us thaw too?	How are you?
craic	krak	good cheer, good pub conversation, a good time
Dia dhuit	JEE-a dich	good day, hello
Dia's Muire dhuit	JEE-as MWUR-a dich	reply to "good day"
Éire	AIR-uh	Ireland; official name of the Republic of Ireland
fir	fear	men
gaeltacht	GAYL-tokt	a district where Irish is the everyday language
garda, Garda Siochána	GAR-da SHE-och-ANA	police
go raibh maith agat	guh roh moh UG-ut	thank you
inch, innis, ennis	inch, innis, ennis	island; river meadow
kil	kill	church; cell
knock	nok	hill
lei thras	LEH-hrass	toilets
lough	lohk	lake
mná	min-AW	women
ní hea	nee hah	no (sort of; it's tricky)
oíche mhaith dhuit	EE-ha woh ditch	good night
sea	shah	yes (sort of; it's tricky)
Sinn Féin	shin fayn	"Ourselves Alone;" the political wing of the IRA
sláinte	SLAWN-che	cheers, to your health
slán agat	slawn UG-ut	goodbye
slieve *or* sliabh	shleev	mountain
sraid	shrawd	street

TAKE THE TRIP THAT RANKS RIGHT UP THERE WITH KITTY HAWK, APOLLO 11 AND THE INAUGURAL CONCORDE FLIGHT.

Rail Europe invites you to be among the first to ride the Eurostar train through the Channel Tunnel.

Be one of the first to take the trip that will change the history of travel. Rail Europe and

the high-speed, high-tech passenger train, Eurostar, can take you through the Channel

RIDE THE EUROSTAR
CALL 1-800-94-CHUNNEL

Tunnel from the center of London to the center of Paris in three short hours. All

you do is relax, enjoy a drink or a meal and become part of history in the making.

For information on a variety of affordable Eurostar tickets call your travel

agent or Rail Europe.

Rail Europe

EUROPE. TO THE TRAINED EYE.

Index

⭐ FREE T-SHIRT ⭐

JUST ANSWER THE QUESTIONS ON THE FOLLOWING PAGES AND MAIL TO:

Let's Go Survey
Macmillan Ltd.
18-21 Cavaye Place
London SW10 9PG

WE'LL SEND THE FIRST 1,500 RESPONDENTS A LET'S GO T-SHIRT!

(Make sure we can read your address.)

■ LET'S GO 1995 READER ■ QUESTIONNAIRE

1) Name _____

2) Address _____

3) Are you: female   male

4) How old are you?   under 17   17-23   24-30   31-40   41-55   over 55

5) Are you (circle all that apply):   at school   at college or university
                                        employed   unemployed   retired

6) What is your annual income?
£10,000-£15,000   £15,000-£25,000   £25,000-£40,000   Over £40,000

7) Have you used *Let's Go* before?

Yes   No

8) How did you hear about *Let's Go* guides?

Friend or fellow traveller
Recommended by bookshop
Display in bookstore
Advertising in newspaper/magazine
Review or article in newspaper/magazine

9) Why did you choose *Let's Go*?

Updated every year
Reputation
Prominent in-store display
Price
Content and approach of books
Reliability

10) Is *Let's Go* the best guidebook?

Yes
No (which is?) _____
Haven't used other guides

11) When did you buy this book?

Jan   Feb   Mar   Apr   May   Jun
Jul   Aug   Sep   Oct   Nov   Dec

12) When did you travel with this book? (Circle all that apply)

Jan   Feb   Mar   Apr   May   Jun
Jul   Aug   Sep   Oct   Nov   Dec

13) Roughly how much did you spend per day on the road?

Under £10   £45-£75
£10-£25   £75-£100
£25-£40   Over £100

14) What were the main attractions of your trip?
(Circle top three)

Sightseeing
New culture
Learning language
Sports/Recreation
Nightlife/Entertainment
Local cuisine
Shopping
Meeting other travellers
Adventure/Getting off the beaten path

15) How reliable/useful are the following features of *Let's Go*?

v = very, u = usually, s = sometimes
n = never, ? = didn't use

Accommodations	v u s n ?
Camping	v u s n ?
Food	v u s n ?
Entertainment	v u s n ?
Sights	v u s n ?
Maps	v u s n ?
Practical Info	v u s n ?
Directions	v u s n ?
"Essentials"	v u s n ?
Cultural Intros	v u s n ?

16) Would you use *Let's Go* again?

Yes
No (why not?) _____

_____
_____

17) Which of the following destinations are you planning to visit as a tourist in the next five years?
(Circle all that apply)

Australasia
Australia
New Zealand
Indonesia
Japan
China
Hong Kong
Vietnam
Malaysia
Singapore
India
Nepal

Europe And Middle East
Middle East
Israel
Egypt
Africa
Turkey
Greece
Scandinavia
Portugal
Spain
Switzerland
Austria
Berlin
Russia
Poland
Czech/Slovak Republic
Hungary
Baltic States

The Americas
Caribbean
Central America
Costa Rica
South America
Ecuador
Brazil
Venezuela
Colombia
Canada
British Columbia
Montreal/Quebec
MaritimeProvinces

18) What **major** destinations (countries, regions, etc.) covered in this book did you visit on your trip?

_____
_____
_____
_____
_____
_____
_____
_____
_____
_____
_____
_____
_____

19) What other countries did you visit on your trip?

_____
_____
_____
_____
_____

20) How did you get around on your trip?

Car	Train	Plane
Bus	Ferry	Hitching
Bicycle	Motorcycle	

Mail this to:

Let's Go Survey
Macmillan Ltd.
18-21 Cavaye Place
London SW10 9PG

Many Thanks For Your Help!

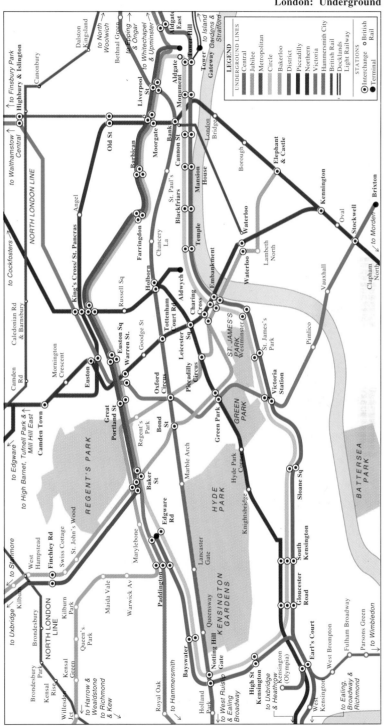

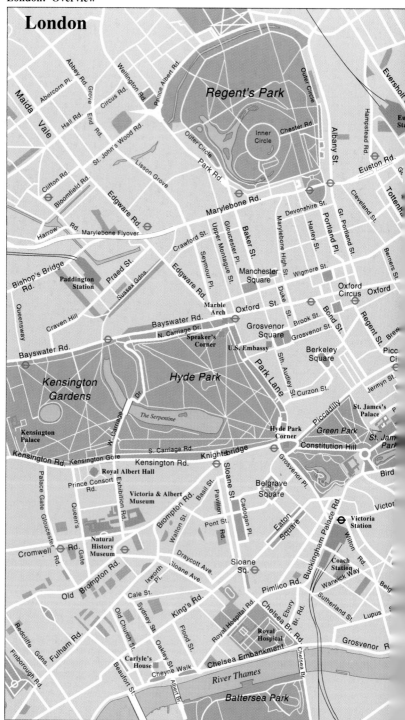

London

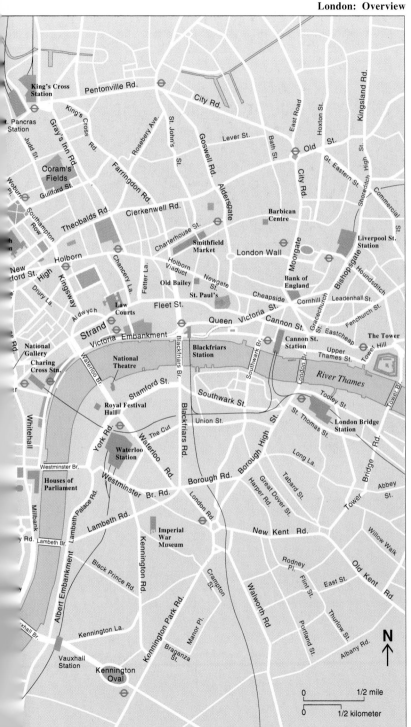

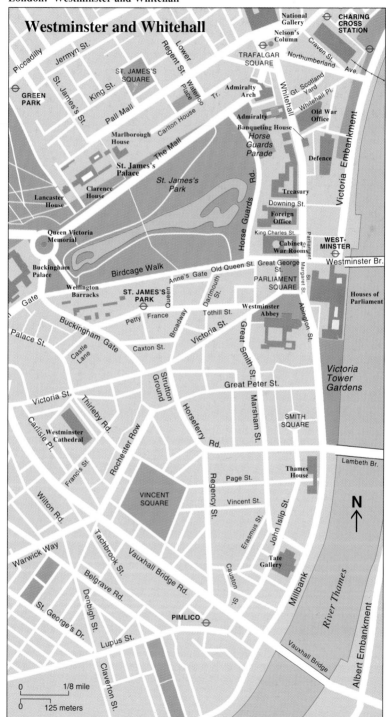

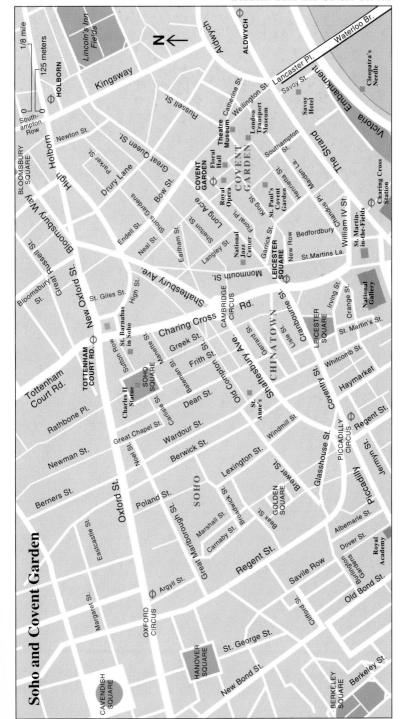

London: Soho and Covent Garden

Soho and Covent Garden

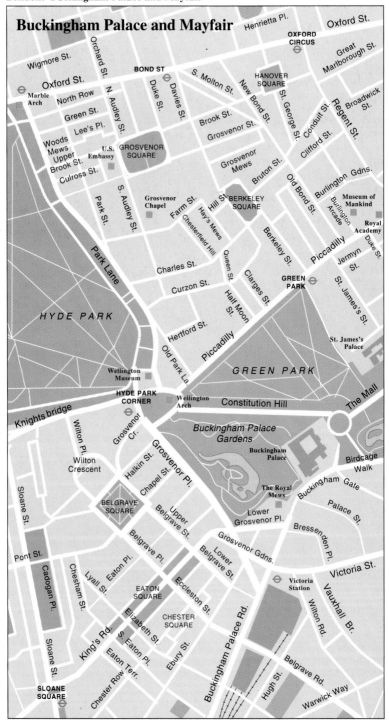

Buckingham Palace and Mayfair

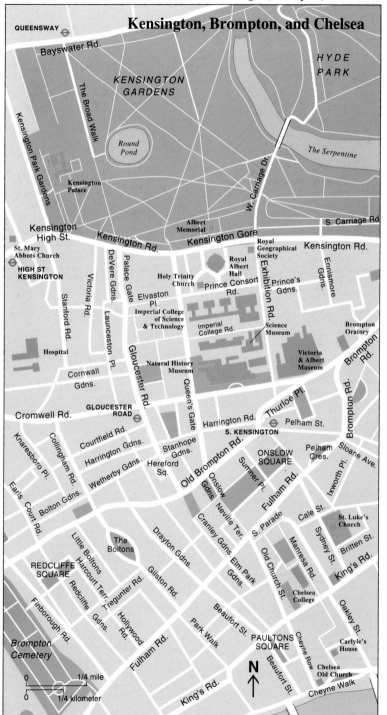

Kensington, Brompton, and Chelsea

QUEENSWAY

Bayswater Rd.

KENSINGTON GARDENS

HYDE PARK

The Broad Walk

Round Pond

Kensington Park Gardens

Kensington Palace

The Serpentine

W. Carriage Dr.

Albert Memorial

S. Carriage Rd.

Kensington High St.

Kensington Rd.

Kensington Gore

Kensington Rd.

St. Mary Abbots Church

HIGH ST KENSINGTON

DeVere Gdns.

Palace Gate

Holy Trinity Church

Royal Albert Hall

Prince Consort Rd.

Royal Geographical Society

Prince's Gdns.

Exhibition Rd.

Kensington Rd.

Ennismore Gdns.

Victoria Rd.

Launceston Pl.

Stanford Rd.

Elvaston Pl.

Imperial College of Science & Technology

Imperial College Rd.

Science Museum

Brompton Oratory

Brompton Rd.

Hospital

Natural History Museum

Victoria & Albert Museum

Cornwall Gdns.

Gloucester Rd.

Queen's Gate

Thurloe Pl.

Cromwell Rd.

GLOUCESTER ROAD

Harrington Rd.

Pelham St.

Brompton Rd.

Knaresboro Pl.

Collingham Rd.

Courtfield Rd.

Harrington Gdns.

Stanhope Gdns.

Hereford Sq.

Old Brompton Rd.

S. KENSINGTON

ONSLOW SQUARE

Pelham Cres.

Sloane Ave.

Ixworth Pl.

Earls Court Rd.

Bolton Gdns.

Wetherby Gdns.

Sumner Pl.

Onslow Gdns.

Neville Ter.

Fulham Rd.

S. Parade

Cale St.

St. Luke's Church

Little Boltons

The Boltons

Drayton Gdns.

Cranley Gdns.

Elm Park Gdns.

Old Church St.

Manresa Rd.

Sydney St.

Britten St.

King's Rd.

REDCLIFFE SQUARE

Harcourt Terr.

Redcliffe Gdns.

Tregunter Rd.

Gilston Rd.

Hollywood Rd.

Chelsea College

Finborough Rd.

Fulham Rd.

Park Walk

Beaufort St.

PAULTONS SQUARE

Cheyne Row

Oakley St.

Carlyle's House

Brompton Cemetery

0   1/4 mile

0   1/4 kilometer

N

King's Rd.

Beaufort St.

Chelsea Old Church

Cheyne Walk

London: City of London